Meditation on Emptiness

Also by Jeffrey Hopkins

Practice and Theory of Tibetan Buddhism
(with Geshe Lhundup Sopa)

The Buddhism of Tibet and the Key to the Middle Way
(with Lati Rinbochay)

The Precious Garland and the Song of the Four Mindfulnesses
(with Lati Rinbochay)

Tantra in Tibet

Death, Intermediate State and Rebirth in Tibetan Buddhism
(with Lati Rinbochay)

Compassion in Tibetan Buddhism

Yoga of Tibet

Tantric Practice in Nying-ma
(with Khetsun Sangpo Rinbochay)

Meditative States in Tibetan Buddhism
(with Lati Rinbochay, Lochö Rinbochay, and Leah Zahler)

Meditation on Emptiness

Jeffrey Hopkins

Assistant Editor:
Elizabeth Napper

Wisdom Publications · London

First published in 1983

Wisdom Publications
PO Box 4BJ
London W1
and
Conishead Priory
Ulverston, Cumbria
England

ISBN 0 86171 014 2

Illustrations by Andy Weber

Set in Plantin 11 on 13 point
by Red Lion Setters, London
and printed and bound by Biddles Ltd.,
Guildford, Surrey

Contents

List of Illustrations 7
Introduction 9
Technical Note 19
List of Abbreviations 23
Acknowledgements 25
PART ONE: MEDITATION 27
1 Purpose and Motivation 29
2 Self: The Opposite of Selflessness 35
3 Meditation: Identifying Self 43
4 Meditative Investigation 47
5 Dependent-Arising 53
6 Diamond Slivers 57
7 Realization 61
8 Calm Abiding 67
9 Special Insight 91
10 Tantra 111
11 Buddhahood 117
PART TWO: REASONING INTO REALITY 125
Introduction 127
1 The Diamond Slivers 131
2 The Four Extremes 151

3 The Four Alternatives 155
4 Dependent-Arising 161
5 Refuting a Self of Persons 175

PART THREE: THE BUDDHIST WORLD 197
Introduction 199
1 The Selfless 213
2 Dependent-Arising of Cyclic Existence 275
3 The Four Noble Truths 285

PART FOUR: SYSTEMS 305
1 Self 307
2 Non-Buddhist Systems 317
3 Hīnyāna 335
4 History of the Mahāyāna 353
5 Chittamātra 365
6 Mādhyamika 399

PART FIVE: PRĀSAṄGIKA-MĀDHYAMIKA 429
1 The Prāsaṅgika School 431
2 Debate 441
3 Bhāvaviveka's Criticism of Buddhapālita 455
4 Chandrakīrti's Defense of Buddhapālita 469
5 Chandrakīrti's Refutation of Bhāvaviveka 499
6 Prāsaṅgika in Tibet 531
7 Validation of Phenomena 539
8 Meditative Reasoning 549

PART SIX: TRANSLATION: EMPTINESS IN THE PRĀSAṄGIKA SYSTEM 561
Introduction 563
Contents 581
1 Background 583
2 Interpretation of Scripture 595
3 The Object of Negation 625
4 Refuting Inherently Existent Production 639
5 Other Types of Production 651
6 Dependent-Arising 659
7 Refuting a Self of Persons 677

APPENDICES 699
1 Types of Awareness 701
2 Other Interpretations of Dependent-Arising 707
3 Modes of Division of the Vaibhāṣhika Schools 713
4 Negatives 721
5 Proof Statements 729

Glossary 735
Bibliography 755
Notes 793
Tibetan Text 907
Emendations to the Tibetan Text 967
List of Charts 979
Index 981

List of Illustrations

Mañjushrī 8
Krakuchchhanda 28
Kanakamuni 42
Kāshyapa 60
Shākyamuni 116
Nāgārjuna 130
Āryadeva 198
Buddhapālita 284
Bhāvaviveka 316
Chandrakīrti 352
Asaṅga 398
Vasubandhu 440
Dignāga 454
Dharmakīrti 548
Shāntarakṣhita 580
Padmasaṃbhava 624
Atīsha 700
Thu-mi-sam-bho-ta 728
Mar-b̄a 794
S̄a-ḡya Paṇḍiṭa Jam-ȳang-ḡun-ga-gyel-tsen 908
D̄zong-ka-b̄a 982

Mañjushrī

Introduction

Homage to Mañjushrī.

Emptiness is the very heart of Buddhist practice in Tibet. In tantra even the visualized gods, goddesses, channels, suns, moons, and so forth are qualified by emptiness. Without an understanding of emptiness the practice of Buddhism, be it sutra or tantra, cannot be complete.

Emptiness is explained in different ways by the four Buddhist schools of tenets: Vaibhāṣhika, Sautrāntika, Chittamātra, and Mādhyamika. The Mādhyamika view and, within the division of Mādhyamika into Svātantrika and Prāsaṅgika, the Prāsaṅgika view form the basis for the transformational psychology of tantra. Thus, this book on Prāsaṅgika-Mādhyamika is written with the intent of presenting not only what emptiness is but also how emptiness is realized in meditation, so that emptiness may become more than a concept of abstract philosophy.

Phenomena are empty of a certain mode of being called 'inherent existence', 'objective existence', or 'natural existence'. This 'inherent existence' is not a concept superimposed by philosophical systems but refers to our ordinary sense of the way that things exist—as if they concretely exist in and of themselves, covering their parts. Phenomena are the things which are empty of inherent existence, and inherent existence is that of which phenomena are empty. Emptiness or, more properly, *an* emptiness is a phenomenon's lack of inherent existence; an emptiness is a negative or utter absence of this concrete mode of being with which we are so familiar.

Reasoning is the method used to establish that emptiness, or a lack of substantiality, is the mode of being of objects, and it also constitutes a yogi's approach to direct realization of emptiness. Having precisely identified this sense of the massiveness or concreteness of objects, a yogi reflects on the impossibility of such through thoroughly familiarizing himself with one of the sets of reasonings that show this lack of natural existence to be the mode of being of an object. He gains an inferential understanding of the emptiness of one object and extends this understanding to all objects. Then gradually, through the force of greater and greater familiarity, he passes to a simultaneous, direct cognition of the emptiness of all phenomena in all world systems. He thereby begins to cleanse his mind of its tendencies to misconceive the nature of phenomena; his cognition of emptiness is like medicine for eradicating his assent to the false appearance of things as inherently existent. Finally, he eradicates even the false appearance of inherent existence to his senses, thereby removing all obstacles to knowledge of everything, and becomes omniscient. He does not eradicate existence; he eradicates only the false sense of inherent existence.

Whether this book is merely abstract philosophy or whether it becomes relevant to everyday experience depends on gaining a sense of what inherent existence would be and then seeing that everything one perceives appears this way. The pivot of the practice of emptiness and of the generation of the wisdom that realizes emptiness is the identification that objects appear as if they exist in and of themselves. Then, an attempt is made to try to find these objects which so boldly appear to be self-existent; the mind becomes totally absorbed in attempting to find an object—among its parts, as the composite of its parts, as something separate from the parts, and so forth. If the search is done with keen interest, the significance of not being able to find the object will be earth-shaking. A yogi will then gain firsthand experience of the falling to extremes against which Buddha so frequently warned. Previously, the yogi took the independent existence of things as the very basis of his life; now that he cannot find anything to call an object, he falls to the opposite extreme of utter nihilism. The middle way, which is not a blending of these extremes but an utter refutation of both inherent existence and total non-existence, becomes relevant and comprehensible for the first time. The two extremes are identified in experience, and it is possible to realize a sense of valid, nominal existence through gaining the understanding that emptiness is an elimination only of inherent existence. Emptiness becomes the context within which a yogi purifies his perception, imagining the world to be the habitation of a deity and himself to be a deity—all within the continuous understanding of unfindability.

Emptiness is the same in both sutra and tantra; the difference between the two systems with regard to emptiness is in the description of the consciousness that cognizes it. In Highest Yoga Tantra there are special subtle minds, normally of no help to an individual, which become aids on the path to Buddhahood when they are generated in meditation for the purpose of realizing emptiness. An understanding of emptiness is a prerequisite for such realization, and this book attempts to present emptiness as it is taught in that system considered in Tibet to be the acme of philosophical systems, the Prāsaṅgika-Mādhyamika. The system is based on the teachings of the Indian sage, Nāgārjuna, who founded Mādhyamika through his definitive presentation of the explicit meaning of Buddha's Perfection of Wisdom Sutras (*Prajñāpāramitā*). Nāgārjuna's thought was further clarified as being Prāsaṅgika-Mādhyamika by Chandrakīrti, and in the domain of emptiness Chandrakīrti's system has held almost complete sway in the various Tibetan orders.

The sources for this e̱xplication of emptiness are almost entirely from the Ge-luk-b̄a order of Tibetan Buddhism, which stems from the teachings of D̄zong-ka-b̄a (*Tsong-kha-pa*, 1357-1419). Jam-ȳang-shay-b̄a's (*'Jam-dbyangs-bzhad-pa*, 1648-1721) *Great Exposition of Tenets*, a Ge-luk-b̄a presentation of the

Prāsaṅgika-Mādhyamika emptiness and a textbook for the Go-mang College of Dre-b̄ung Monastery in Hla-s̄a, Tibet, forms the basis for this book.

I first encountered the *Great Exposition of Tenets* in 1963 when I began studying with Geshe Wangyal, a Kalmuk-Mongolian scholar and adept from Astrakhan, who spent thirty-five years studying in Tibet in the Go-mang College of Dre-b̄ung Monastery. At that time the *Great Exposition of Tenets* seemed to be hopelessly complicated. Nevertheless, Geshe Wangyal's teaching was inspiring, and near the time of my departure from his monastery in Freewood Acres, New Jersey, in 1968, he advised me to read all of Jam-ȳang-shay-b̄a's *Great Exposition of Tenets*. I put this in mind and while acting as a resource assistant at Haverford College in 1968 began to read a little from a condensation of the *Great Exposition of Tenets* done by Jam-ȳang-shay-b̄a's next incarnation, Ḡön-chok-jik-may-w̄ang-b̄o (*dKon-mchog-'jigs-med-dbang-po*, 1728-91). Upon going to the University of Wisconsin I was able to study and translate this short text with Geshe Lhundup Sopa, a scholar of Se-ra Monastery who was first among the First Rank of the ge-shays receiving degrees in 1962 and who came to Madison from Geshe Wangyal's monastery. His excellent answers to my questions made it possible to put together an outline map of Buddhist philosophy as viewed by the Ge-luk-ba order of Tibetan Buddhism.

All this prepared me for my first encounter with a former Abbot of the Tantric College of Lower Hla-s̄a, Kensur Lekden, another Go-mang scholar who came to Geshe Wangyal's monastery in the fall of 1968 just after I left. I had returned there during a vacation and was captivated from the very start by his lucid, compact, free-flowing presentation of almost any aspect of Buddhist philosophy. I returned to the monastery in the summer of 1969 and, following Geshe Wangyal's advice, began listening to Kensur Rinbochay's (Precious Former Abbot Lekden's) commentary on the *Great Exposition of Tenets* and on the Mongolian scholar Nga-w̄ang-b̄el-den's (*Ngag-dbang-dpal-ldan*, born 1797) *Annotations*, an explanation of the difficult points of the *Great Exposition of Tenets*. I tape-recorded his teachings and translated most of Jam-ȳang-shay-b̄a's exposition of the non-Buddhist systems as described in Buddhist literature. Toward the end of the summer we skipped over the lower Buddhist systems and read the presentation of Prāsaṅgika tenets in the twelfth chapter.

Returning to Madison, I began translating the chapter on Prāsaṅgika, and in January of 1969 when Professor Richard Robinson, the co-founder of the Buddhist Studies program in Madison, and I founded Tibet House in Cambridge, Wisconsin, we invited Kensur Rinbochay to teach us. Kensur Rinbochay gave two series of fourteen lectures on the three principal aspects of the path to enlightenment and on Chandrakīrti's *Supplement to (Nāgārjuna's) 'Treatise on the Middle Way' (Madhyamakāvatāra)*, which I translated at Tibet House. (These have been published as the first part of *Compassion in Tibetan Buddhism*.) Professor Robinson also invited Kensur to give a seminar at the University of Wisconsin on Prāsaṅgika philosophy which we conducted after Professor Robinson's untimely death in the summer of 1970.

At Tibet House, Kensur Rinbochay taught me the rest of Jam-ȳang-shay-b̄a's *Great Exposition of Tenets* (approximately three hundred folios), Nga-w̄ang-b̄el-den's *Annotations* (four hundred sixteen folios), and almost all of Jam-ȳang-shay-b̄a's *Great Exposition of the Middle Way* (four hundred twenty-four out of five hundred folios), the Go-mang textbook for Mādhyamika studies. I thereby was able to cover most of the Mādhyamika reading which a monk in the Go-mang College of Dre-bung Monastery would traditionally do. Kensur Rinbochay was famous for his abilities as a lecturer, and he, indeed, could weave a fascinating and often moving story of philosophical and spiritual ideas. His kindness in explaining again and again the important points of Buddhist philosophy was a lesson in compassion and a demonstration of how Buddhist philosophy was for him a vivid, living phenomenon.

Kensur Rinbochay left Tibet House in August of 1971 by which time I had finished translating Jam-ȳang-shay-b̄a's presentation of emptiness in his *Great Exposition of Tenets*. My intention was to present a book on the meditation on emptiness, and to that end had obtained a Fulbright-Hays fellowship for a year's study in Germany and India. Four days after I left for Germany in November of 1971, Kensur Rinbochay died of congestive heart failure. In Germany at the University of Hamburg, I studied for three months with Geshe Gedün Lodrö, a Go-mang scholar of a later generation than that of Geshe Wangyal and Kensur Rinbochay. A special feature of the Go-mang scholars, probably stemming from Geshe Jinba around the turn of the century, is an unusual ability to explain philosophy, not just react to it, as sometimes happens when debate is a principal mode of instruction, and Geshe Gedün Lodrö soon showed himself to be a scholar of scholars. When he received his ge-shay degree in India in 1961, he not only was first among those of the First Rank but was also first among three who in an extraordinary year had been given the honor of being first among those of the First Rank. Geshe Gedün Lodrö's knowledge was invaluable; he knew not only how to answer questions but also how to lead to the heart of conceptual problems so that the entire context of a question would come to life. Possessing an extraordinary ability both to answer and lecture on minute questions about Buddhist philosophy, he was the ideal person to smooth out the last remaining questions on the translation.

Proceeding on to India, I went to Dharmsala in the north where the Dalai Lama has his headquarters. I arrived just in time for sixteen four-hour public lectures by His Holiness on D̄zong-ka-b̄a's *Middling Exposition of the Stages of the Path* and was fascinated to find that this reincarnated Lama was not only highly educated but also extremely practical. I had no intention of staying in Dharmsala, but the single figure of the Dalai Lama kept me there, coming back to his audience room again and again to ask my most difficult questions on the philosophy and practice of emptiness. His answers were illuminating to say the least, and after six months he had answered my questions to the point where I had no more to ask—a state which I frankly had had no hope of achieving. I had the good fortune to attend lectures by

His Holiness on Nāgārjuna's Six Collections of Reasonings during which he gave the oral transmission and explanation. His Holiness commissioned me to translate Nāgārjuna's *Precious Garland (Ratnāvalī)* along with a short poem by the Seventh Dalai Lama, *The Song of the Four Mindfulnesses*, and his own short treatise on emptiness, *Key to the Middle Way*, as well as his *The Buddhism of Tibet*. (These have been published as the first two volumes of the Wisdom of Tibet Series.) I had many interviews with the Dalai Lama about the translations, and the discovery that he was to my sight utterly worthy of being the spiritual and temporal leader of Tibet defied my cynical sense of world order.

While in Dharmsala, I also studied a N̄ying-ma-b̄a presentation of tenets as found in the first part of the *Precious Treasury of the Supreme Vehicle* (*Theg pa'i mchog rin po che mdzod*) by Long-chen-rap-jam (*kLong-chen-rab-'byams*, 1308-63) with the N̄ying-ma-b̄a lama Khetsun Sangpo. In addition, later when Khetsun Sangpo visited the University of Virginia in 1974, we read Long-chen-b̄a's presentation of the sutra schools in his *Treasury of Tenets* (*Grub pa'i mtha' rin po che'i mdzod*). Khetsun Sangpo also had acquired a photographic reprint of the S̄a-ḡya-b̄a D̄ak-tsang's (*sTag-tshang*, born 1405) *Understanding All Tenets*, which in 1972 was otherwise unavailable. A reading of it revealed how much Jam-ȳang-shay-b̄a relied on the very text that he was primarily refuting and showed the continuity of tradition between S̄a-ḡya and Ge-luk.

Contact with a Ḡa-gyu-b̄a presentation of Mādhyamika was gained through reading parts of a commentary on Chandrakīrti's *Supplement to (Nāgārjuna's 'Treatise on the Middle Way'* by Mi-ḡyö-dor-jay (*Mi-bskyod-rdo-rje*, 1507-54), the eighth Karma-b̄a. Acquaintance gained in this way with N̄ying-ma, S̄a-ḡya, and Ḡa-gyu interpretations was crucial to understanding Jam-ȳang-shay-b̄a's presentation in that it provided the historical background of many positions.

Though those texts contributed greatly to my understanding, this book primarily presents a particular interpretation within the Ge-luk-b̄a order with an aim of imparting a sense of a living system that affects the outlook, meditation, and goals of its scholar-yogi adherents. Thus, this book is not framed as an argument; still, through the stylistic choice of points of emphasis there is an implicit argument against accepting many modern views on Mādhyamika as applying to all interpretations of that system. Almost all contemporary renderings of Mādhyamika run contrary to Ge-luk-ba authors such as Jam-ȳang-shay-ba on many central points. It should be clear by the end of this book that the traditional interpretation given here does not agree with, and in fact refutes, all of the following positions with respect to Prāsaṅgika-Mādhyamika:

1 Their outlook is nihilistic, agnostic, or sceptic.
2 They are anti-reason.
3 The uncommon view of the system is that words are inadequate to evoke an experience of objects like that of direct perception.
4 They have no system, no views on cause and effect or rebirth, no positive theses, and no negative theses.
5 They are merely debaters.
6 Wisdom is emptiness.
7 Wisdom is contentless.
8 Emptiness is the Absolute.
9 The two truths are two ways of viewing the same object.
10 That objects possess a definite nature is the object of negation in the view of emptiness.
11 Their system is a turning away from philosophical analysis to the vulgar views of the world.
12 All views are bad.
13 Withdrawal from thought is the best meditation. Or, words are enemies. Or, the source of all suffering is words.
14 Reasoning is used only to refute other systems.
15 What is seen in direct sense perception is the truth; what the senses reveal cannot be denied in any way; one must appreciate the uncommon thingness of each phenomenon as its suchness.
16 Direct perception of suchness requires a leap.

17 There is no I at all.
18 The selflessness of persons denies the existence of persons.
19 Conventional truths are established only by ignorance.
20 Conceptuality is ignorance.
21 Nāgārjuna's *Treatise on the Middle Way* must be viewed in isolation.
22 Emptiness does not exist.
23 Form is one with emptiness.
24 Nāgārjuna did not set forth the path.
25 Teachings about the path are for those of low intelligence.
26 Dependent-arising and emptiness are one.
27 Emptiness and dependent-arising are a paradox.
28 None of the Hīnayāna categories are accepted.
29 Analysis is not meditation.
30 Meditation is just stabilization.
31 Phenomena are whatever one thinks they are.
32 Conventional truths are negated by ultimate truths.

The dependent-arising of this presentation of meditation on emptiness is itself a demonstration of Buddha's focal teaching, of his 'slogan', as the Dalai Lama put it, of dependent-arising. My aim is not to present original reflections on emptiness but to portray as well as I can how emptiness is a practical force within the Ge-luk-b̄a tradition of Tibetan Buddhism. The material is largely drawn from the oral explanations which I have received and from Jam-ȳang-shay-b̄a's *Great Exposition of Tenets* and *Great Exposition of the Middle Way* as well as J̄ang-ḡya's (*lCang-skya*, 1717-86) *Presentation of Tenets* (*Grub mtha'i rnam gzhag*). The flavor of the oral tradition is presented with a view to capturing how the doctrine of emptiness figures in the lives of the practitioners who embody it.

Technical Note

Renderings of the Tibetan alphabet in roman letters are almost as numerous as the scholars who have worked with Tibetan. However, Turrell Wylie, after careful analysis, has set forth in a reasoned presentation ('A Standard System of Tibetan Transcription', HJAS, Vol. 22, pp.261-7, 1959) a simple system capable of representing the letters of the Tibetan alphabet. Therefore, his system is followed here (except in that the first pronounced letter is capitalized in names).

As he says, his is only a system of transliteration, not aimed at facilitating pronunciation and, therefore, is restricted in this book to parenthetical citation, glossary, and bibliography. Tibetan names must be rendered in a pronounceable form if Tibetan Buddhist studies are to rise out of the arcane, and thus it is necessary to devise a system specifically for that purpose, not seeking a form reconstructable into Tibetan (which has many unpronounced letters). Again, practically everyone who has worked with Tibetan has attempted this, though some have either given up or not even tried, opting instead for the unpronounceable transliteration form. This writer has long thought that if Tibetan names could be written in a *simple* pronounceable form, people unfamiliar with the language could remember them, as a consequence of which Tibetan Buddhism would not seem so distant. The one obstacle has been that several names are already known in a misleading form. For instance, the capital of Tibet is Hla-s̄a, pronounced with the 'h' first, though it has almost always been spelled Lhasa. Indeed, this is like the English word 'where' in which 'h' is pronounced first, but it seems unlikely that anyone would think to do this for 'Lhasa'.

Also, due to the fact that most transliteration systems treat the first, fifth, ninth, thirteenth, and seventeenth letters of the Tibetan alphabet as *ka*, *ca*, *ta*, *pa*, and *tsa*, respectively, most writers have used these in the 'phonetic' form. Thinking that this might be due to a difference in dialect, this writer has been hesitant to interfere with this policy; however, it has been found that these letters are not pronounced this way in any Tibetan dialect. Rather, they are pronounced more like *ḡa*, *j̄a*, *d̄a*, *b̄a*, and *d̄za*, the mark above the consonant indicating that the tone is 'high', meaning that the sound is pronounced not deep in the throat but higher or more forward and tending to be sharp and short.

The third, seventh, eleventh, fifteenth, and nineteenth letters (when they are in the root position with a head or a prefix) are pronounced *ga*, *ja*, *da*, *ba*, and *dza* in a low tone (which need not be indicated by a line underneath since these letters are usually pronounced that way in English). In a simple, easily pronounceable system of 'phonetics' for use in books and essays, but not for real phonetic spelling in the sense of including all minor variations, these English letters can indicate the Tibetan despite changes due to prefixed and headed letters.

Most writers have used *kha*, *cha*, *tha*, *pha*, and *tsha* for the second, sixth, tenth, fourteenth, and eighteenth letters, the 'h' indicating that these letters are aspirated (spoken with breath such that one can even feel it on the hand close to the mouth). However, it seems to this writer that *ka*, *ta*, *pa*, and *tsa* are aspirated in English anyway, or at least semi-aspirated, whereas *kha* etc. are both unfamiliar and confusing, frequently leading to mispronunciation—*tha* and *pha* being associated with those letters in English words such as 'thin' and 'phone'. Thus, it seems appropriate to delete 'h' from these letters.

This yields a table of conversion from transliteration to 'essay phonetics' as follows: (In each pair, the transliteration form is on the left and the 'essay phonetic' form on the right.)

ka = ḡa	kha = ka	ga = ga	nga = nga
ca = j̄a	cha = cha	ja = ja	nya = nya
ta = d̄a	tha = ta	da = da	na = na
pa = b̄a	pha = pa	ba = ba	ma = ma
tsa = d̄za	tsha = tsa	dza = dza	wa = wa
zha = sha	za = sa	'a = a	ya = ya
ra = ra	la = la	sha = s̄ha	sa = s̄a
ha = ha	a = a		

In this book, the 'essay phonetic' forms are used with the following refinements to reflect actual pronunciation: *k* and *p* are substituted for *g* and *b* in suffix position; *n̄ga*, *n̄ya*, *n̄a*, *m̄a*, and *l̄a* are used when these letters appear after a prefix or under another letter, as their pronunciation becomes high at that time; also, *dbyang* is rendered as *ȳang* and *dbang* as *w̄ang* for the same reason.

For vowels, 'a' indicates the vowel sound of 'opt'; 'i', of 'it' or 'eat'; 'u', of 'soon'; 'ay', of 'bake'; 'e', of 'bet'; 'o', of 'boat'; and 'ö' indicates the vowel sound of 'er' (minus the 'r').

The names of Tibetans and Mongolians who live in or have published in the West are spelled as they spell them. Aside from these, all other Tibetan names have been rendered in the system given above in order to bring their pronunciation more in accord with actual spoken Tibetan in the central dialect; the transliterated form of each name is given in the index.

The hyphens between syllables are retained in the 'essay phonetic' form so that the beginning and end of syllables can be easily distinguished.

Throughout the book 'cognize' and 'realize' are used synonymously to translate one Tibetan word, *rtogs pa*. Similarly, 'impute' and 'designate' both translate *'dogs pa*, and thereby 'basis of imputation' and 'basis of designation' are interchangeably used for *gdags gzhi*. Also, nine Sanskrit words are treated as

English words, resulting in the dropping of their diacritics. These are Bodhisattva (hero with respect to contemplating enlightenment), Buddha (one who has awakened from the sleep of ignorance and spread his intelligence to all objects of knowledge), karma (action, and often also the predisposition established by an action), mandala (a divine circle—a deity's body or the habitat of a deity), nirvana (passage beyond sorrow), sutra (abridged expression of profound meaning—the word of Buddha except for tantra), tantra (continuum, referring here to the continuum of words that express the topics of a base, path, or fruit continuum), vajra (best of stones, diamond, symbolizing an immutability or indivisibility of method and wisdom), and yogi (a meditator who has joined or yoked mental stability and insight). A glossary of key terms giving the Sanskrit and Tibetan equivalents is given at the end of the book.

The transliteration scheme for Sanskrit names and titles is aimed at easy pronunciation, using *sh*, *ṣh*, *ch* and *chh* rather than *ś*, *ṣ*, *c* and *ch*. With the first occurrence of each Indian title, the Sanskrit is given, if available. The full Sanskrit and Tibetan titles are to be found in the bibliography which is arranged alphabetically according to the English titles of sutras and according to the authors of other works.

List of Abbreviations

(For the full entries of the Tibetan texts see the Bibliography.)

Ālaya: D̄zong-ka-b̄a's *Extensive Commentary on the Difficult Points of the 'Afflicted Mind and Basis-of-All'*

Ann: Nga-w̄ang-b̄el-den's *Annotations for (Jam-ȳang-shay-b̄a's) 'Great Exposition of Tenets'*

Concentrations: Jam-ȳang-shay-b̄a's *Great Exposition of the Concentrations and Formlessnesses*

D̄ak: D̄ak-tsang's *Revelation of All Tenets*

D̄en-dar: D̄en-dar-hla-ram-b̄a's *Presentation of the Lack of Being One or Many*

Ḡön: Ḡön-chok-jik-may-w̄ang-b̄o's *Precious Garland of Tenets*

GM: Jam-ȳang-shay-b̄a's *Great Exposition of the Middle Way*

GT: Jam-ȳang-shay-b̄a's *Great Exposition of Tenets*

J̄ang: J̄ang-ḡya's *Presentation of Tenets*

Kay-drup: Kay-drup's *General Presentation of the Tantra Sets*, as found in Lessing and Wayman's *Fundamentals of the Buddhist Tantras* (The Hague: Mouton, 1968)

Lectures: Pa-bong-ka's *Lectures on the Stages of the Path*

MHTL: Dr. Lokesh Chandra's *Materials for a History of Tibetan Literature* (New Delhi: International Academy of Indian Culture, 1963)

P: *Tibetan Tripiṭaka* (Tokyo-Kyoto: Tibetan Tripiṭaka Research Foundation, 1956)

Pā: *The Ashṭādhyāyī of Pāṇini*, ed. and trans. by Śrīṣa Chandra Vasu (Delhi: Motilal Banarsidass, 1962)

Toh: *A Complete Catalogue of the Tibetan Buddhist Canons*, ed. by Prof. Hukuji Ui, and *A Catalogue of the Tohoku University Collection of Tibetan Works on Buddhism*, ed. by Prof. Yensho Kanakura (Sendai, Japan: 1934 and 1953)

Tu-ḡen: Tu-ḡen L̄o-sang-chö-ḡyi-nyi-ma's *Mirror of the Good Explanations*

Acknowledgements

I wish to express deep gratitude to the late Professor Richard Robinson who encouraged me to write this book on how the meditation of emptiness figures in a living tradition. Also, I wish to thank Anne Klein, Joe Wilson, and John Strong for reading the text at various stages and making many helpful suggestions. A great debt of gratitude is owed to Professor Richard B. Martin, South Asian Bibliographer at Alderman Library, University of Virginia, for extensive bibliographic assistance.

I wish to acknowledge the crucial support of two Fulbright Fellowships, in 1972 and 1982, the former introducing me to the work of His Holiness the Dalai Lama and the latter, to the world of monastic debate at the School of Dialectics in Dharmsala. Also, several small grants from the University of Virginia were helpful in allaying photocopying and postage expenses.

Many thanks to Daniel Perdue and Gareth Sparham for their painstaking proofreading of the galleys. Also, the greatest gratitude is due Elizabeth Napper for countless editorial suggestions, making the index, and marking the galleys.

Part One
Meditation

Krakuchchhanda: the first Buddha of this era

1 *Purpose and Motivation*

Sources
Jang-ḡya's *Presentation of Tenets*
Kensur Lekden's oral teachings
Jam-ȳang-shay-b̄a's *Great Exposition of Tenets*

The Perfection of Wisdom Sutras set forth emptiness as the final mode of existence of all phenomena.[1] Nāgārjuna explained the approaches to that emptiness, and Buddhapālita and Chandrakīrti lucidly commented on Nāgārjuna's explanations in exact accordance with his thought. It is necessary to rely on the perfection of wisdom as these masters explain it, not only to attain omniscience, but even to attain liberation from cyclic existence. One who wishes to become a Hearer Superior, Solitary Realizer Superior, or Bodhisattva Superior must rely on this perfection of wisdom. The *Eight Thousand Stanza Perfection of Wisdom Sutra* (*Aṣhṭasāhasrikāprajñāpāramitā*)[2] says:

> Subhuti, one who wishes to realize the enlightenment of a Hearer is to learn just this perfection of wisdom. Subhuti, one who wishes to realize the enlightenment of a Solitary Realizer is to learn just this perfection of wisdom.

> The Bodhisattva, the Great Being who wishes to realize the supreme perfect complete enlightenment, is also to learn just this perfection of wisdom.

Nāgārjuna's works teach that realization of the subtle emptiness of all phenomena is a prerequisite for the path of liberation from cyclic existence. His *Precious Garland* (35ab) says:

> As long as the aggregates are [mis]conceived,
> So long is there [mis]conception of an I.

One cannot free oneself from cyclic existence merely through cognition of the coarse selflessness of the person. One must realize the final subtle suchness of the person and of the mental and physical aggregates.

One must eradicate the innate non-analytical intellect that misconceives the nature of the person and other phenomena. It is not sufficient merely to withdraw the mind from conceiving a self of persons and of phenomena, or merely to stop the mind's wandering to objects, for these do not constitute realization of emptiness. If they did, then deep sleep and fainting would absurdly involve realization of emptiness. Āryadeva says:

> When selflessness is seen in objects,
> The seeds of cyclic existence are destroyed.

Chandrakīrti says in his *Supplement to (Nāgārjuna's) 'Treatise on the Middle Way'* (VI.116):[3]

> [Extreme] conceptions arise with [the conception of inherently existent] phenomena.
> It has been thoroughly analyzed how phenomena do not [inherently] exist;
> When [the conception of an inherently existent] phenomenon does not exist,
> These [extreme conceptions] do not arise, just as there is no fire when there is no fuel.

Bhāvaviveka says:

> With the mind in meditative equipoise,

Wisdom analyzes in this way
The entities of these phenomena
Apprehended conventionally.

Shāntideva says:

When one has searched [for these] as realities,
Who desires and what is desired?

Dharmakīrti says:

Without disbelieving the object of this [misconception]
It is impossible to abandon [misconceiving it].

With one voice all the Mahāyāna masters proclaim that analysis of objects, and not mere withdrawal of the mind from them, is the path to liberation.

One must analyze well whether the inherent existence of phenomena, as it is conceived by the innate non-analytical intellect, exists or not. Through reasoning and scriptural citation one must ascertain that objects do not exist as conceived and penetratingly understand the falseness of inherent existence. It is very important to analyze again and again with discriminating wisdom. The *King of Meditative Stabilizations Sutra* (*Samādhirāja*) says:

If the selflessness of phenomena is analyzed
And if this analysis is cultivated,
It causes the effect of attaining nirvana.
Through no other cause does one come to peace.

The *Cloud of Jewels Sutra* (*Ratnamegha*) says, 'Analyzing through special insight and realizing the lack of inherent existence constitute understanding of the signless.' The *Questions of Brahmā Sutra* (*Brahmāparipṛchchhā*) says, 'The intelligent are those who correctly analyze phenomena individually.'

The great Mahāyāna masters taught many forms of reasoning, directed toward the ascertainment of suchness, in order to illuminate the path of liberation for the fortunate and not for the sake of mere disputation. D̄zong-ka-b̄a says, 'All of the analytical reasonings set forth in Nāgārjuna's *Treatise on the Middle Way* (*Madhyamakashāstra*) are only for the sake of sentient beings' attaining liberation.' The wish to attain liberation from cyclic existence is the motivation for entering into analysis of phenomena and attaining realization of emptiness.

Among Buddhist practitioners, those of lesser capacity enter into religious practice for the sake of attaining a happy migration in a future life.[4] They have seen the sufferings of bad migrations and seek to avoid pain through endeavor at virtue. One cannot make effort at religious practice merely for the sake of improving the present lifetime and be considered a practitioner of Buddhism; at least, a Buddhist's motivation is aimed at attaining a happy migration as a human or a god in a future life. Others, who have greater capacity, seek to leave cyclic existence completely. They see that the attainment of a happy migration in the next life is not sufficient because they must still grow old, become sick, die, and be reborn again in accordance with their former deeds. Their motivation for practice is the wish to attain liberation from cyclic existence for themselves. Still others, who have even higher capacity, realize the extent of their own suffering, infer the suffering of others, and practice so that they may become free from cyclic existence and attain Buddhahood in order to help all sentient beings to do the same.

Thus, it is very important that a motivation be stated verbally and explicitly before meditation:

> I am meditating on emptiness and analyzing phenomena in order to attain liberation from cyclic existence and omniscience so that I may help all sentient beings to do the same.

The other possible motivation is:

> I am meditating on emptiness and analyzing phenomena in order to attain liberation from cyclic existence.

The former is far more powerful because, through it, the meditation is related to all sentient beings. The force of the meditation increases as many times as the beings with whom it is related.

Emptiness itself is a very powerful object of meditation. Āryadeva says:[5]

> Those of little merit would not even
> Have doubts about this doctrine [of emptiness].
> Even suspicion [that objects are empty]
> Wrecks [the seeds of] cyclic existence.

Even a suspicion that emptiness—the lack of inherent existence—is the mode of being of phenomena disturbs the very causes that produce the rounds of powerless suffering. For, when one has such suspicion, the actual mode of being of objects acts for the slightest bit as an object of one's mind. Dzong-ka-ba says:

> Aspirational prayers should be made for the ability to listen to the treatises on the profound [emptiness], to memorize them, to think about their meaning, to meditate on them, and over the continuum of lives to have faith in them, all without harming ascertainment of the dependent-arising of cause and effect.

Jam-ȳang-shay-ba warns that though the transmission of the Buddhist teaching to Tibet was prophesied in sutra, it was also prophesied that there would be few who would take the perfection of wisdom all the way through to the process of meditation.[6] He says there are many who memorize the words and many who propound the Perfection of Wisdom Sutras but few who actually achieve the perfection of wisdom. He adds that there are uncountable numbers who through the force of the five ruinations do not want to meditate on emptiness but still claim to meditate on the 'natural mind' or something other than emptiness that lacks the elaborations of duality. Since 'natural mind', 'freedom from the elaborations of duality', and so forth are none other than emptiness itself, and since it is meditation on emptiness that puts an end to the elaborations of misconception, it is mistaken to think that there is another final object of meditation. The various teachings that Buddha does not even abide in the middle way, or that Buddha ultimately does not even teach emptiness must be understood as referring to his not abiding in, or his not teaching, an inherently existent middle way, or inherently existent emptiness.

Those who actually do not meditate on emptiness but claim to do so mistakenly think that merely by withdrawing the mind from objects and by ceasing thought they can realize the suchness of phenomena. Rather, analysis is the very foundation of meditation on emptiness.

2 *Self: The Opposite of Selflessness*

Sources
Kensur Lekden's oral teachings
Nga-w̄ang-b̄el-den's *Annotations*
Corresponding section of the translation pp.625-36

Emptiness in all four Buddhist schools is a 'self-emptiness', but this does not mean that objects are empty of themselves.[7] If objects were empty of themselves, then no object, not even an emptiness, would exist. Rather, 'self-emptiness' in the Prāsaṅgika system specifically refers to an object's lack of its *own* inherent existence.

The term 'self-emptiness' distinguishes the Buddhist emptiness from systems such as Sāṃkhya, which assert that the person is empty of being the various *other* objects of the world. Such an emptiness is an 'other-emptiness', and realization of it is attained through distinguishing one thing from another, as in the case of distinguishing the person (*puruṣha*) from the nature (*prakṛti*) that gives rise to all appearances according to the Sāṃkhya system. Realization of a 'self-emptiness', on the other hand, involves distinguishing the absence of a false predicate of an object, for example, the absence of its own inherent existence, and does not involve distinguishing one entity from another entity. Still, when emptiness is cognized directly, the objects that are the bases of the quality of emptiness do not appear to the mind. Based on this, some, including the Jo-nang-bas of Tibet, misinterpreted the Buddhist emptiness as an 'other-emptiness'.

That which is negated in the Prāsaṅgikas' subtle theory of selflessness is self, defined as inherent existence. The hypothetical synonyms of 'self' in the Prāsaṅgika system are:[8]

1 true establishment (*satya-siddhi/bhāva, bden par grub pa/ dngos po*)
2 true existence (*satya-sat, bden par yod pa*)
3 ultimate existence (*paramārtha-siddhi, don dam par grub pa*)
4 existence as [its own] suchness (*tattva-siddhi, de kho na nyid du grub pa*)
5 existence as [its own] reality (*samyak-siddhi, yang dag par grub pa*)
6 natural existence or existence by way of its own character (*svalakṣhaṇa-siddhi, rang gi mtshan nyid kyis grub pa*)
7 substantial existence (*dravya-sat, rdzas yod*)
8 existence able to establish itself (*tshugs thub tu grub pa*)
9 existence from the object's side [rather than being imputed from the subject's side] (*svarūpa-siddhi, rang ngos nas grub pa*)
10 objective existence (*viṣhaya-siddhi, yul gyi steng nas grub pa*)
11 existence through its own power (*svairī-siddhi, rang dbang du grub pa*)
12 existence in the object that receives designation (*prajnapti-viṣhaya-siddhi, btags yul gyi steng nas grub pa*)
13 existence right in the basis of designation (*gdags gzhi'i steng nas grub pa*)
14 inherent existence (*svabhāva-siddhi, rang bzhin gyis grub pa*)
15 existence through its own entitiness (*svabhāvatā-siddhi, ngo bo nyid gyis grub pa*)
16 existence in the manner of covering its basis of designation (*gdags gzhi'i go sa gnon pa'i tshul du yod pa*)
17 existence from the side of the basis of designation (*gdags gzhi'i ngos nas grub pa*).

The members of this list are only 'hypothetical' synonyms because in Buddhist logic 'synonym' (*ekārtha*) means 'one object', and thus all synonyms necessarily exist. Since these terms for 'self' refer to non-existents, they can only be 'hypothetical' synonyms.

The subtle self that is negated in the Prāsaṅgika view of selflessness implies an independent entity; thus, all these terms are opposites of dependent-arising. Each illuminates a little more the meaning of non-dependence.[9] For instance, 'existing from the side of the basis of designation' means that if one searched to find the object designated, one would find it either among the bases of designation, or as their composite, or as the composite of their former and later moments. 'Substantially existent' means not existing through the force of expressions but existing through the object's own power. 'Existing able to establish itself' means not established through the force of terms and expressions but existing in the object's basis of designation by way of the object's own entity. 'Existing through its own power' means existing through the object's own particular mode of being.

The Prāsaṅgikas' unique meaning of 'dependence' is 'establishment through the power of a designating consciousness'. Phenomena depend on thought in the sense that only if the thought that designates an object exists, can that object be posited as existing (conventionally), and if the thought that designates an object does not exist, the (conventional) existence of that object cannot be posited. Since this applies to all objects, nothing exists inherently.

It is similar to the imputation of a snake to a rope. If a speckled and coiled rope is not seen clearly, the thought can arise, 'This is a snake'. At that time, the composite of the parts of the rope and the parts themselves cannot at all be posited as a snake; the snake is only imputed by thought. In the same way, when in dependence upon the mental and physical aggregates the thought 'I' arises, the composite of the former and later moments of the continuum of the aggregates, or the composite of the aggregates at one time, or the individual aggregates themselves cannot in the least be posited as the I. Also, there is nothing that is a separate entity from the aggregates or their composite which can be apprehended as I. Therefore, the I is only established by thought in dependence on the aggregates and does not exist inherently, as it appears to do.

The same type of analysis can be applied to a person and his/her relationship to the six constituents that are his/her bases of imputation or designation—earth, water, fire, wind, space, and consciousness. A person is not a collection of these, nor any of them individually, nor anything separate from them. A person is thereby shown not to exist inherently.

Prāsaṅgika is the only school that accepts all the above mentioned terms as synonyms; the non-Prāsaṅgika schools do not attach the same significance to these terms and thus organize them differently (see Chart 1). For instance, the Chittamātrins certainly would not say that dependent phenomena (*paratantra*) are independent just because they inherently exist; for them 'inherent existence' merely means that objects have their own mode of being. The Prāsaṅgikas, however, answer that the very words, 'inherent existence' or 'own mode of being', imply independence.

Also, the non-Prāsaṅgikas say that if phenomena were only designated in the sense of being unfindable among their bases of designation, they would not exist at all because the unfindable could not possibly be functional. However, for the Prāsaṅgikas the other schools have missed the meaning of 'only designated' or 'only imputed' (*prajñapti-mātra, btags pa tsam*); Prāsaṅgikas say that although this term means that the object designated is not its basis of designation, it does not imply non-functionality. It is a central but difficult point of the Prāsaṅgika-Mādhyamika system that what is merely designated can be functional, just as a girl created by a magician can attract an unwitting audience.

It is said that often when a yogi thinks he is progressing in understanding the presentation of emptiness, he loses ground in understanding the presentation of conventional objects and that often when he thinks he is progressing in understanding the presentation of conventional objects, he loses ground in understanding the presentation of emptiness.[10] It must be borne in

Chart 1: *Modes of Existence*

I	II	III	IV
ultimate existence *paramārtha-siddhi* *don dam par grub pa* existence as [its own] suchness *tattva-siddhi* *de kho na nyid du grub pa* existence as [its own] reality *samyak-siddhi* *yang dag par grub pa* true existence *satya-sat* *bden par yod pa*	true establishment *satya-siddhi* *bden par grub pa*	natural existence *svalakṣhaṇa-siddhi* *rang gi mtshan nyid kyis grub pa*	inherent existence *svabhāva-siddhi* *rang bzhin gyis grub pa* existence from its own (the object's) side *svarūpa-siddhi* *rang ngos nas grub pa*

The Prāsaṅgikas view all four columns as equally non-existent, ultimately and conventionally. The Svātantrikas find columns one and two the same, denying these of all phenomena both ultimately and conventionally; they find columns three and four the same, affirming these conventionally for all phenomena, but not ultimately. The Chittamātrins affirm all four columns for emptiness and impermanent phenomena and deny the first three columns, but not the fourth, for imputed existents such as space. The Sautrāntikas Following Reasoning affirm all four columns for impermanent phenomena and deny the first three, but not the fourth, for permanent phenomena. The Vaibhāṣhikas affirm all four columns for ultimate truths, such as partless particles and partless moments of consciousness; however, they affirm only the second, third, and fourth columns for conventional truths, such as tables and houses.

mind that for one who has found the Prāsaṅgika view, progress in the presentation of emptiness aids in the presentation of conventional objects and progress in the presentation of conventional objects aids in the presentation of emptiness.

Through refuting only inherent existence and not refuting mere existence, the Prāsaṅgikas avoid the extreme of annihilation. Through affirming only nominal existence and not affirming inherent existence they avoid the extreme of permanence. In other words, they describe precisely how things do and do not exist. The lack of even nominal or designated existence would be an extreme of annihilation—an extreme of non-existence—because objects do exist imputedly. Inherent existence would be an extreme of permanence—an extreme of existence—because objects do not inherently exist.

The extremes are *no nominal existence*, which would mean no existence whatsoever, and *inherent existence*—the first being 'finer' and the second being 'coarser' than the correct presentation. The main extreme conceptions, therefore, are the conception that things do not designatedly exist and the conception that things exist inherently. The extremes do not exist, but their conceptions do and can be destroyed.

Many think that the Prāsaṅgikas have fallen to an extreme of nihilism, being no different from the Nihilists who deny the existence of rebirth, and so forth.[11] The Prāsaṅgikas themselves refuse any similarity; they say that one cannot ascertain the emptiness of former and later births through just the non-perception of former and later births. One must first identify what former and later births are and identify their existence. Then, through reasonings such as the present birth's becoming a past birth when the future birth becomes the present birth, one identifies that past, present, and future births are mutually dependent and thus do not exist inherently. Identifying that former and later births do not exist inherently, one ascertains the emptiness of births. Such identification both of the positive subject (births) and the negative predicate (non-inherent existence) is essential, for one cannot ascertain an emptiness just by seeing nothing.

The Nihilists referred to here are the Dialectician Nihilists and not the Meditating Nihilists, for some of the latter attain meditative clairvoyance and thereby realize a limited number of former and future births. The Dialectician Nihilists assert that future lives do not exist because no one is seen to come here to this life from a former life and no one is seen to go from this life to a future life. The Mādhyamikas, on the other hand, assert that future lives do not exist *inherently* because they are dependent-arisings or, in other words, because they are designated by terms and thoughts. However, they do not deny the existence of former and future lives. Both the theses and the reasons of the Nihilists and the Mādhyamikas are very different.

Kanakamuni: the second Buddha of this era

3 *Meditation: Identifying Self*

Sources
Jam-ȳang-shay-b̄a's *Great Exposition of Tenets*
Kensur Lekden's oral teachings
J̄ang-ḡya's *Presentation of Tenets*
The Fifth Dalai Lama's *Sacred Word of Mañjushrī*
Kay-drup's *Manual of Instructions on the View*
Ling Rinbochay's oral teachings
Corresponding section of the translation pp.684-5

Jam-ȳang-shay-b̄a delineates five stages in meditation on emptiness.[12] These outline the progress of one newly developing the powers of meditation:

1 how a beginner develops experience with respect to the view of emptiness
2 how to cultivate a similitude of special insight based on a similitude of calm abiding
3 how to cultivate actual special insight based on actual calm abiding
4 how to cultivate direct cognition of emptiness
5 how to meditate on emptiness during the second stage of Highest Yoga Tantra.

FIRST STAGE OF MEDITATION ON EMPTINESS
How a beginner develops experience with respect to the view of emptiness

During the first stage a yogi gains an initial familiarity with the meaning of emptiness through one of several reasonings. He proceeds through three basic essentials in meditation: identifying the object negated in the view of selflessness, ascertaining that selflessness follows from the reason, and establishing the reason's presence in the subject.

The initial object of meditation is the selflessness of the person; the reasoning used is the sevenfold reasoning as set forth by Chandrakīrti.

1 *Identifying the object negated in the theory of selflessness*

First, one concentrates and clears one's mind.[13] Sitting quietly, one waits for the I to appear. If it does not, an appearance of it is created by thinking 'I', and with a subtle type of consciousness one watches the appearance.

If the consciousness that watches the appearance is too strong, one will not see the I, or it will appear and quickly disappear. Therefore, one should allow the consciousness conceiving I to be generated continuously, and through watching this I as if from a corner, one will gain a firm sense of it.

One could also imagine that one is being accused, even falsely, and watch the sense of I. One could remember an incident of false accusation, during which one thought, 'I did not do this, I am being wrongly accused.' By watching the I who is accused, a firm sense of the way that the non-analytical intellect apprehends I can be ascertained.

If the memory of such an accusation is not strong, a yogi cultivates it until the sense of I as misconceived by the innate non-analytical intellect is obvious. This innate mind does not analyze whether the I is the same as or different from mind and body. Without any reasoning and through the force of habituation, it conceives of an I that is as if self-sufficient, able to establish itself, naturally or inherently existent from the very start and fused with the appearance of mind and body.[14]

Though such an I does not in reality exist, an image or concept of it does exist and will appear. It is initially difficult to identify the appearance of a concrete I, but in time it becomes obvious. Sometimes the I appears to be the breath, and sometimes the stomach as when one has an upset stomach and says, 'I am sick.'[15] Sometimes the I appears to be the eye, ear, nose, tongue, body, or mental consciousness. In sum, the I appears at times to be physical and at times mental. The Fifth Dalai Lama says that in the end the appearance of the I and the appearance of the mind and body are as if mixed like water and milk, undifferentiable, but so clear as to seem graspable with the hand.

D̄zong-ka-b̄a's disciple Kay-drup says in his *Manual of Instructions on the View*:[16]

> If the mind thinking 'I' is not generated, you should fabricate the thought 'I' and immediately thereafter analyze its mode of appearance. You will thereby come to know its mode of appearance without mixing it with any other object... If you look gently from a corner without losing the consciousness thinking 'I', there is a separate mode of appearance of I to the consciousness which thinks 'I', and this appearance is not any of the mental and physical aggregates. The I does not appear to be just a nominal designation, but appears as if self-established. Through holding that the I exists the way it appears, you are bound in cyclic existence.

Can the I appear to be self-established if its appearance is undifferentiatedly mixed with that of mind and body? It would seem logically impossible for it to be self-established and yet mixed, but the innate intellect apprehending I does not analyze its object logically before, during, or after its apprehension. The appearance of a self-established I is mixed with the appearance of factors of mind and body but is not exactly the same. The present Dalai Lama's Senior Tutor, Ling Rinbochay, said that if someone sticks a pin in your finger, you feel that the pin has been stuck in you and not just in your finger. You have a distinct sense of the I that is hurt.

In order to ascertain this appearance, it is extremely important to prolong subtle examination of it without letting it immediately disappear. Some teachers advise watching the I for a week or even months before proceeding to the second step.

It is interesting to note that the *jīva* or 'limited individual being' in Vedānta is often said to be the size of the thumb and located in the 'heart'. In Vedānta the *jīva* is to be merged with the infinite self, Brahman, and in Buddhism the appearance of a concrete I is analyzed, found to be non-existent, and overcome, resulting eventually in a direct realization of emptiness in which the subject, the wisdom consciousness, is merged with its object, emptiness, like fresh water poured into fresh water.

4 *Meditative Investigation*

Sources
Jam-ȳang-shay-b̄a's *Great Exposition of Tenets*
Nga-wang-b̄el-den's *Annotations*
Corresponding section of the translation pp.687-94

2 *Ascertaining that selflessness follows from the reason*

The second of the three basic steps in meditation on the personal selflessness is the ascertainment that if the I exists the way it is conceived, then it must be either the same entity as the mental and physical aggregates or a different entity from those aggregates.[17]

If the I inherently exists, it must be either inherently the same entity as the aggregates or inherently a different entity from the aggregates. Sameness and difference of entity are mutually exclusive; if two things exist, they must be either the same or different. If the I is found to be neither inherently the same entity as the mind and body nor a different entity from them, then the I does not inherently exist.

Through the seven-fold reasoning, one attempts to infer that the I does not inherently exist as it appears to do. Such an inference cannot be generated if one has not ascertained that non-inherent existence pervades, or occurs with, every instance of not being inherently the same as or different from the aggregates. In other words, a yogi must realize that whatever is inherently neither the same entity as nor a different entity from its basis of designation does not inherently exist. One must come to a firm conclusion that there is no third possibility of concrete existence. When one does, one begins to doubt the existence of the self in much the same way as one starts to doubt an old friend.[18]

3 *Establishing the presence of the reasons in the subject*

The seven-fold reasoning in brief is:

> 'I' do not inherently exist because of (i) not being the aggregates, (ii) not being an entity other than the aggregates, (iii) not being the base of the aggregates, (iv) not inherently being based on the aggregates, (v) not inherently possessing the aggregates, (vi) not being just the composite of the aggregates, and (vii) not being the shape of the aggregates.

The third step in meditation on emptiness—after identifying the inherently existent I and ascertaining that it must be either the same as or different from mind and body—is the establishment of the first reason as a quality of the I—proving that the I is not mind and body. Many reasons are suggested here, and each should be considered thoroughly until one is found which disturbs the notion that the I is mind and body.[19] (The reasonings are explained in detail in Part Two.)

i *Establishing that the I is not mind and body*

The I is not the mental and physical aggregates because then the assertion of an I would be senseless. 'I' would be just another name for the aggregates.

The I is not the aggregates because just as the aggregates are many, so the selves would be many, or just as the I is one, so the aggregates would be one.

The I is not the aggregates because the I would be produced and would disintegrate just as the aggregates are produced and disintegrate. The I is not inherently produced and does not inherently disintegrate because if it did, memory of former births would be impossible. For, the two I's of the different lifetimes would be unrelatedly different because they would be inherently other.

The I is not inherently produced and does not inherently disintegrate because then deeds done (*karma*) would be wasted as there would be no transmission of the potencies accumulated from actions since the I's of the different lifetimes would be unrelated others.

The I is not inherently produced and does not inherently disintegrate because the I would meet with the results of actions not done by itself. If, on the other hand, the potencies accumulated from actions were transmitted, an I which was totally different from the I that committed the deeds would undergo the results of those deeds.

ii *Establishing that the I is not different from mind and body*

The I is not an entity other than mind and body because if it were, the I would not have the character of the aggregates, such as production, disintegration, abiding, form, experiencing, and realizing objects.

The I is not a separate entity from the mental and physical aggregates because if it were, there would be no basis for the designation I. The I would be a non-product, and non-products are changeless whereas the I obviously changes.

The I is not a separate entity from the aggregates because if it were, there would be no object to be apprehended as I. The I would be a non-product like nirvana or a non-existent like a flower in the sky.

The I is not a separate entity from the aggregates because if it were, the I would be apprehendable apart from the aggregates just as the character of form is apprehendable separate from the character of consciousness. But it is not.

iii *Establishing that the I is not the base of mind and body*

The I is not inherently the base of the mental and physical aggregates like a bowl for yogurt or like snow that exists throughout and surrounds a forest of trees because if it were, the I and the aggregates would be different entities. This has already been refuted in the second reasoning.

iv *Establishing that mind and body are not the base of I*

The I is not inherently based on the aggregates like a person living in a tent or like a lion living in a forest because if it were, the I and the aggregates would be different entities. This has already been refuted in the second reasoning.

v *Establishing that the I does not inherently possess mind and body*

The I does not inherently possess the aggregates in the way that a person possesses a cow because if it did, the I and the aggregates would be different entities. The I does not inherently possess the aggregates in the way that a person possesses his body or a tree its core because then the I and the aggregates would inherently be the same entity. These positions have already been refuted in the second and first reasonings.

vi *Establishing that the I is not the composite of mind and body*

The I is not just the composite of the aggregates because the aggregates are the basis of the designation I and an object designated is not its basis of designation. The I is not the composite of the aggregates because the composite of the aggregates does not inherently exist; if the composite of the aggregates were inherently one with the aggregates, the composites would be many like the aggregates, or the aggregates would be one like the composite. Also, if the composite of the aggregates were a different entity from the aggregates, it would be apprehendable apart from the aggregates and would not have the character of the aggregates. But this is not so.

vii *Establishing that the I is not the shape of the body*

The I is not the shape of the body because shape is physical and if the I were merely physical, it would not be conscious. Also, the shape of the body does not inherently exist because it is a composite of the shapes of the limbs of the body.

Without any further cogitation, one realizes that the I does not inherently exist. One has already ascertained that non-inherent existence follows if a phenomenon is in none of these seven relationships with its bases of designation, and now one has seen that the I and body and mind can have none of these seven relationships. Therefore, the I does not exist as a concrete entity as it is perceived.

For beginners it is necessary to become acquainted with the reasoning over a long period of time before an understanding of emptiness can be generated. However, reasons do not require endless establishment because if every reason had to be established by another reason, one would never realize the main thesis.[20] The reasons are established to a point where experience manifestly establishes them.[21] If a person lacks this experience, it is necessary to seek other means, such as examples, to gain the necessary experience that establishes the reasons.

5 *Dependent-Arising*

Sources
Jam-ȳang-shay-b̄a's *Great Exposition of Tenets*
Nga-w̄ang-b̄el-den's *Annotations*
Corresponding sections of the translation pp.673-6

If a yogi is directed by his guru to meditate on the non-inherent existence of the I through the reasoning of dependent-arising, he would meditate on the thought:

> I do not inherently exist because of being a dependent-arising.

The meditation has three steps:

1 *Identifying the object negated in the view of selflessness*

This step is the same as that described in chapter three for the sevenfold reasoning. The yogi identifies the appearance of an I as if it covers its bases of designation and identifies how the mind assents to this appearance.

2 *Ascertaining that selflessness follows from the reason*

One ascertains that whatever is a dependent-arising does not inherently exist because inherent or independent existence is the opposite of dependent-arising.

3 *Establishing the presence of the reason in the subject*
The I is a dependent-arising because of being produced by contaminated actions and afflictions since the life of a being in cyclic existence is created by predispositions established by an action motivated by ignorance. (Even the virtuous deeds that give rise to happy migrations and the non-moving deeds that give rise to lives in the form and formless realms are motivated by ignorance with respect to the nature of the person.) The I is a dependent-arising because of achieving its entity in dependence on its parts—its former and later moments, mind and body, and so forth. The I is a dependent-arising because of being imputed in dependence on a consciousness that designates, 'I'.

Without any further cogitation one cognizes that the I does not inherently exist because one has previously ascertained that whatever is a dependent-arising does not inherently exist and has now established the presence of the reason—being a dependent-arising—in the subject I. The brevity of the reasoning of dependent-arising illustrates why yogis initially use the sevenfold reasoning, which reveals in detail how the I cannot be found under analysis. The sign of dependent-arising is sufficient to show that the subject cannot be found under analysis; however, repeated investigation of dependent-arising is required before it is seen that analytical unfindability or non-inherent existence is concomitant with being a dependent-arising.

The reasoning of dependent-arising is also used for phenomena other than persons, such as the body:

> The body does not inherently exist because of being a dependent-arising.

1 *Identifying the object negated in the view of selflessness*
One identifies an appearance of body wherein it seems as if inherently existent and self-established within the context of being undifferentiably mixed with the appearance of the five

limbs and trunk. It is an appearance of body as if it covers the five limbs and trunk.

2 *Ascertaining that selflessness follows from the reason*

Whatever is a dependent-arising does not inherently exist because inherent existence means that which exists in and of itself, independent of others.

3 *Establishing the presence of the reason in the subject*

The body is a dependent-arising because of being produced by the blood of the mother and the semen of the father. The body is a dependent-arising because of attaining its own entity in dependence on its parts—arms, legs, head, trunk, and so forth. The body is a dependent-arising because of being imputed in dependence on arms, legs, head, trunk, and so forth.

Without any further cogitation one realizes that the body does not inherently exist. Again, the brevity of the reasoning may not be sufficient for a beginner in which case one could turn to the sevenfold reasoning:

> The body does not inherently exist because of (1) not being the arms, legs, etc., (2) not being a separate entity from the arms, legs, etc., (3) not being the base of the arms, legs, etc., (4) not inherently depending on the arms, legs, etc., (5) not inherently possessing the arms, legs, etc., (6) not being the composite of the arms, legs, etc., and (7) not being the shape of the arms, legs, etc.

6 *Diamond Slivers*

Sources
Jam-ȳang-shay-b̄a's *Great Exposition of Tenets*
Nga-w̄ang-b̄el-den's *Annotations*
Corresponding section of the translation pp.639-50

If the diamond slivers are used as the mode of analysis, the meditation has six steps based on the thought:

> The body is not inherently produced because of not being produced from self, from inherently existent others, from both, or causelessly.

1 *Identifying the object negated in the view of selflessness*
This step is the same as in the last two meditations. The appearance of a body covering the limbs and trunk is mixed with the appearance of the limbs and trunk and yet appears to exist in itself, to exist concretely.

2 *Ascertaining that selflessness follows from the reason*
Whatever is not produced from self, from inherently existent others, from both, or causelessly is not inherently produced because inherent production is limited to these four possibilities.

Production is either caused or uncaused; and, if caused, the only possibilities are that the causes are the same entity as the effect, or a different entity from the effect, or both.

3 *Establishing the presence of the first reason in the subject*

The body is not produced from self (from what is the same entity as itself) (a) because, if it were, its production would be senseless and endless, (b) because what already exists in something is not produced from that something, (c) because it would contradict what the world manifestly sees, and (d) because the producer and the produced would be one.

4 *Establishing the presence of the second reason in the subject*

The body is not produced from causes which are inherently existent others because if it were, the body could be produced from anything that was other than it. For, inherently existent others are non-related others since otherness is their nature.

The body is not produced from causes which are inherently existent others because the body and its causes are not inherently existent others since the body does not exist simultaneously with its causes. For instance, the body at age ten does not exist simultaneously with the body at age five which is a cause of it. However, if cause and effect were inherently other, the body that is approaching production would have to exist at the time of the activity of its approaching production because this activity depends on it.

Also, for causes, such as the parents or the body of an earlier age, to be causes of the present body which are inherently other than it, the causes would still have to exist because it is in relation to the causes that the body is other. How can a thing be inherently other than a thing that does not exist?

5 *Establishing the presence of the third reason in the subject*

The body is not produced from both itself and others because all the fallacies of production from self and from other descend on such a theory.

6 *Establishing the presence of the fourth reason in the subject*

The body is not produced causelessly because then the copulation of the parents for the sake of conceiving a child would be senseless. The mother's care of the child in the womb and later after birth would be senseless. Taking effort to nourish the body for the sake of future health would be senseless. For, the body would arise causelessly.

The body is not produced causelessly because if it were, a body could be produced even from a chair or a door, because everything would arise from everything.

The yogi first identified the body as a product and then saw that what is inherently produced must be produced according to one of four possibilities. Thus, upon the establishment of the four reasons as qualities of the body, he realizes without further cogitation that the body is not inherently produced. He then draws out the implications of this realization to include the cognition that the body does not inherently exist. For, if the body is a product and it is not inherently produced, it does not inherently exist.

Kāshyapa: the third Buddha of this era

7 *Realization*

Sources
Jam-ȳang-shay-b̄a's *Great Exposition of Tenets*
Nga-w̄ang-b̄el-den's *Annotations*
Kensur Lekden's oral teachings
Corresponding section of the translation pp.651-8

In the Prāsaṅgika system, the sevenfold reasoning, dependent-arising, and the diamond slivers are the three main forms of reasoning for establishing selflessness. Three other forms are the refutation of the four extreme types of production, the refutation of the four alternative types of production, and the reasoning establishing the lack of being one or many.

In the refutation of the four extreme types of production a yogi would most likely take a phenomenon included within the personal continuum such as body or mind, but he might also take as his subject an external phenomenon, such as an apple:

> An apple is not inherently produced because (1) an existent is not inherently produced, (2) a non-existent is not inherently produced, (3) what is both existent and non-existent is not produced, and (4) that which is neither existent nor non-existent is not produced.

1 *Identifying the object negated in the view of selflessness*

The yogi identifies the appearance of an apple wherein the apple seems as if it exists there from its own side without being designated by the subject. The very appearance of an apple toward the subject is the appearance of an inherently existing apple.

2 *Ascertaining that selflessness follows from the reason*

Whatever product is not ultimately produced as an existent, a non-existent, what is both existent and non-existent, or what is neither is not inherently produced. For, the possibilities of the nature of an effect are limited to these four.

3 *Establishing the presence of the first reason in the subject*

An inherently existent apple is not produced because what inherently exists must always exist and thus there would be no need for it to be produced. Or, an apple which is in all ways existent at the time of its causes is not produced because causes and conditions cannot create anything that already exists.

4 *Establishing the presence of the second reason in the subject*

A non-existent apple is not produced because if it were, the horns of a rabbit or the hairs of a turtle could also be produced. Or, an apple is not newly inherently produced because of not existing at the time of its causes, as is the case with a lotus in the sky. For, whatever is inherently produced must always exist because if it did not exist at some time, it would always be inherently non-existent.

Also, an apple would have to exist at the time of its causes because the action of the apple's approaching production exists simultaneously with the action of its causes' approaching cessation. Since the apple is the base of the action of its approaching production, it must exist together with its action if the two are findable. Thus, the apple would have to exist at the time of the seed of the tree that produces it, but this is not the case.

5 *Establishing the presence of the third reason in the subject*

An apple that is both existent and non-existent is not produced because there is no such thing, since existence and non-existence are mutually exclusive.

6 *Establishing the presence of the fourth reason in the subject*
An apple that is neither existent nor non-existent is not produced because there is no such thing.

The yogi then realizes without further cogitation that an apple does not inherently exist; in other words, he knows that a concrete apple such as earlier appeared to his mind does not exist. A vacuity that is the negative of such an apple appears to his mind, and he remembers the meaning of this vacuity much as a man, who searched thoroughly for his prize bull in his four pastures and did not find it, would not forget the loss of his bull when he returned home.[22]

In the refutation of the four alternative types of production the subject meditated upon might be an eye consciousness:

> An eye consciousness is not inherently produced because of not being a case (1) of one inherently producing one, (2) of many inherently producing one, (3) of one inherently producing many, or (4) of many inherently producing many.

1 *Identifying the object negated in the view of selflessness*
The yogi identifies the appearance of an eye consciousness as if it exists in its own right without dependence on designation by thought or terms, as if it exists covering the moments of consciousness which are its basis of imputation.

2 *Ascertaining that selflessness follows from the reason*
Whatever product is not a case of one producing one, many producing one, one producing many, or many producing many is not inherently produced because the possibilities of inherently existent production are limited to these four.

3 *Establishing the presence of the first reason in the subject*
An eye consciousness is not a case of one cause inherently producing one effect because if it were, two of the three aspects of an eye consciousness (being a conscious entity, having power with

respect to colors and shapes, and being generated in the image of its object) would be uncaused.

4 *Establishing the presence of the second reason in the subject*

An eye consciousness is not a case of many causes inherently producing one effect because if it were, only one of the three aspects of an eye consciousness would be produced.

5 *Establishing the presence of the third reason in the subject*

An eye consciousness is not a case of one cause producing many effects because if it were, the three aspects of an eye consciousness would not have individual causes.

6 *Establishing the presence of the fourth reason in the subject*

An eye consciousness is not a case of many causes producing many effects because if it were, the one general eye consciousness would be uncaused and its three aspects caused.

Thereby, the yogi without further cogitation realizes that an eye consciousness is not inherently produced and thus does not inherently exist. He absorbs the import of this realization, and if it becomes weaker, he performs the analysis again until the cognition of unfindability returns in force. He tries to become accustomed to this unfindability so that he will never think the opposite again.

The reasoning establishing the lack of being one or many has already been illustrated in the sevenfold reasoning in the sense that the I does not inherently exist because of not inherently being one with or different from the aggregates. However, another form of the reasoning establishing the lack of being one or many is illustrated here in the example of a house:

> A house does not inherently exist because of not inherently being one and not inherently being many.

1 *Identifying the object negated in the view of selflessness*

The yogi calls to mind a house and identifies the appearance of the house as a whole existing in its own right. The inherently existent house is what he might point to when pointing a house out to someone else. Findability is pointability,[23] and the yogi works for a long time to catch a sense of just what is being pointed out, knowing that it is important to stay with an appearance of inherent existence both so that it becomes well known and so that the ramifications of its absence can be felt.

2 *Ascertaining that selflessness follows from the reason*

Whatever is neither inherently one nor inherently many does not inherently exist because these two positions exhaust all possibilities of inherently existent things. The yogi accustoms himself to this fact by considering hundreds of objects, such as house, boards, group, members, glass, mind, and so forth and seeing that from a specific point of view they are each either one or many. For instance, a group is definitely one from the point of view of the entity, group, and the members of a group are definitely many when considering the constituents of the group.

3 *Establishing the presence of the first reason in the subject*

A house is not inherently one because of having parts. Whatever has parts cannot have an inherent nature of oneness because then a plurality of parts would be impossible.

4 *Establishing the presence of the second reason in the subject*

A house is not inherently many because there is no inherently existent oneness. When a part of a composite is refuted, the composite which is composed of those parts is also refuted. Since the many is composed of ones, refuting inherently existent oneness refutes inherently existent manyness.

Through having ascertained the pervasion and having established the reasons as qualities of the subject, the yogi realizes without any further cogitation that a house does not inherently exist. He knows then that there is nothing he can actually point to when identifying a house. He knows that there is no house which covers its parts. He remains in the force of this realization as long as he can, not allowing the vacuity which is a negative of a pointable house to become a mere nothingness.

The main object of meditation during the first stage of meditation on emptiness is the I.[24] Through the sevenfold reasoning the yogi comes to realize that a self-established I, covering its bases of designation, does not exist at all anywhere at any time. He perceives an utter vacuity that is the absence of such an I, and he ascertains the mere elimination of the I that is negated in the view of selflessness with nothing positive in its place. He sustains this space-like realization, which is so called because just as space is the mere absence of obstructive contact, so the selflessness that he sees is the mere absence of such a self. When his certitude of the non-existence of an inherently existent I weakens, he again reflects a little on the reasoning and renews the strength of the view of the emptiness of a self-established I.

The yogi during this stage of meditation has generated an inferring consciousness that realizes the emptiness of the person, and this consciousness has no ascertainment of knower and the object known. All the elaborations of subject and object are said to disappear in the sense that a consciousness that infers emptiness does not *ascertain* subject and object; however, subject and object still *appear* at this time. Though appearing, they are not determined, for a consciousness inferring emptiness does not identify the object, emptiness, and the subject, the cognizing wisdom. The only phenomenon that is ascertained is the mere absence of a self-established I such as usually appears to the mind. It is not even thought, 'This *is* emptiness.'[25]

In an inferential realization of emptiness, an emptiness is cognized conceptually or through the medium of an image. Despite the profound nature of such inferential intuition, direct realization is yet to be attained.

8 *Calm Abiding*

Sources
Pa-bong-ka's *Lectures on the Stages of the Path*
Jam-ȳang-shay-b̄a's *Great Exposition of the Concentrations and Formlessnesses*
Jam-ȳang-shay-b̄a's *Great Exposition of Tenets*
Lati Rinbochay's oral teachings
Geshe Gedün Lodrö's oral teachings

SECOND STAGE OF MEDITATION ON EMPTINESS

How to cultivate a similitude of special insight based on a similitude of calm abiding

The second stage of meditation on emptiness is the mode of cultivating a similitude of special insight based on a similitude of calm abiding.[26] During it, the yogi achieves calm abiding, defined as a stabilization arisen from meditation and conjoined with special pliancy. Etymologically, calm abiding (*shamatha, zhi gnas*) is explained as the mind's abiding (*sthā, gnas*) on an internal object of observation upon the calming (*shama, zhi*) of distraction to the outside.

PREREQUISITES FOR ACHIEVING CALM ABIDING

The causal collections or prerequisites for achieving calm abiding are six:[27]

1 *Staying in an agreeable place*
This has five features:

a. *Good acquisitions.* One needs easily obtainable sustenance not involving wrong livelihood or offerings from sinful persons.

b. *Salutary location.* Staying in an area blessed by the presence of former holy persons affords blessings, but if such is not available, one should at least not stay where those who have lost their vows dwell, where the spiritual community has undergone disturbance, or where there are fierce animals, robbers, non-human evil spirits, and so forth.

c. *Salutary place.* The place should not generate hot or cold diseases, and the area and water should be agreeable.

d. *Salutary friends.* It is harmful for beginners to stay alone without friends, and thus one should have at least three companions whose views and behavior are concordant and whose presence promotes conscientiousness. Also, since sound is the thorn of concentration, one needs to be free of the sound of humans during the day and of dogs and water, etc., at night.

e. *Possession of the pleasant 'articles' of yoga.* Through hearing and thinking one should eliminate false ideas with respect to the object of meditation and become skilled in the essentials of practice.

2 *Few desires*
One should not have desire for food, clothing, and so forth, either of good quality or in great quantity.

3 *Knowing satisfaction*
One should be satisfied with gaining only mediocre food and clothing, for if one is not and instead is attached to them, one will be distracted to the purposes of accumulating and keeping wealth, and meditative stabilization will not be generated.

4 *Pure ethics*
The pacification of subtle internal distraction depends on

abandoning coarse external distractions; hence, ill behavior of body and speech should be restrained and pacified through proper ethics, for if one is dominated by coarse discursiveness, one's mind will not abide in a natural state.

5 *Forsaking commotion*
If commotion is not abandoned, time will be passed in senseless activities and conversation, etc. Thus, for the sake of generating concentration, one needs few purposes and few activities—this coming of its own accord if a meditator has few desires and knows satisfaction. For one-pointed practice, astrology, medical practice, prophecy, performing rites, and so forth must be forsaken. Also making effort at something of small purpose, such as a minor topic of scholarship, does not achieve the essential purpose, much like being attached to sugar-cane but not taking the sugar.

6 *Thoroughly abandoning thoughts of desire and so forth*
One must turn the mind away from these through contemplating their faults and reflecting on impermanence.

Pa-bong-ka states that if all these prerequisites are complete and one practices with effort, the achievement of calm abiding will not take more than six months.

THE OBJECT OF CALM ABIDING

Calm abiding must be achieved with respect to an internal or imagined object, and thus even when non-Buddhists use a pebble or stick as the object, these are only bases of later imagination by the mental consciousness; one cannot achieve calm abiding with the eye consciousness.[28] The Buddhist scholar-yogi Nāgabodhi, being unable to achieve progress with other objects, imagined that the horn of a buffalo had grown from his own head, since he was familiar with it; however, in general for a Buddhist not just any object is suitable. Rather, the object itself should aid in the process of eliminating the chief faults obstructing meditative stabilization, laxity and excitement. To aid in eliminating laxity, it should be easier, upon observing the object, to generate faith and enthusiasm, and to aid in eliminating excitement, it should be easier to hold the mind to that object and generate sobriety.

The object with respect to which calm abiding is achieved should possess a special purpose.[29] Observation of emptiness, as here in the second stage of meditation on emptiness, has the special feature of facilitating generation of special insight, but emptiness—due to its profundity—is a difficult object for beginners. Unless memory of the realization of emptiness during the first stage remains firm, since one must temporarily forsake analysis and remain only in stabilizing meditation in order to achieve calm abiding, the ascertainment of emptiness can weaken to the point where one is no longer meditating on emptiness but on nothingness. Such meditation would only increase ignorance, and thus many choose a different object.

It is said that the desirous should concentrate on ugliness, reflecting on (1) the ugliness of pain, (2) the relative ugliness of the beautiful in dependence on something more beautiful, (3) the ugliness of the afflictions, (4) the ugliness of rapid disintegration, or (5) the ugliness of filthy substances.[30] The hateful should concentrate on love, wishing help and happiness for friends, enemies, and neutral persons. The ignorant should concentrate on the dependent-arising of cyclic existence (see pp.275-83). The proud should concentrate on the six constituents in their own continuum—earth, water, fire, wind, space, and consciousness (see p.627)—thereby overcoming the conception of the body as an amorphous whole and attaining a discrimination of ugliness by seeing the parts, such as fat; by this means pride is deflated. Those with too much discursiveness should concentrate on the inhalation and exhalation of breath. These five types of objects are called objects of observation for purifying behavior and have the special feature of facilitating the conquest of desire and so forth and thus aid in the generation of meditative stabilization.

Those in whom either desire, hatred, obscuration, pride or discursiveness predominate should choose an object as outlined above because without overcoming the vibrancy of the afflictions by way of those objects of observation, firm meditative stabilization cannot be attained.[31] Hence, the desirous temporarily should not use joy, love, or the like as the object of observation. Similarly, the hateful should not concentrate on suffering, and those with predominate discursiveness should not use bright objects, etc. A particular object of observation, however, is not specified for those whose afflictions are small or of equal strength; they may use any of these.

It is said that observation of the body of a Buddha is better than all others because it not only has the special feature of facilitating the achievement of meditative stabilization through its blessings but also has the special feature of completing the collections of merit as well as enhancing later cultivation of deity yoga in tantra.[32] At the point when the object of observation—a Buddha body—becomes firm, ordinary appearances are replaced by pure appearances, and one sees a Buddha night and day; through this, one becomes a suitable vessel for Secret Mantra. Also, through a Buddha's always appearing to the mind, one accumulates the merit of seeing a limitless number of Buddhas, whereby innumerable benefits, such as not being overcome by pain even in dire circumstances, arise.

Thus, in order to aid in the development of calm abiding, the yogi might not take emptiness as his object of observation. However, once the object is chosen, he would not switch from it to another until a fully qualified calm abiding has been achieved, much as one would not change the place of friction when trying to ignite a fire by rubbing two sticks together.[33] During this period, continuous effort without, for instance, resting for a day or two, is required.

FAULTS AND ANTIDOTES IN DEVELOPING CALM ABIDING

In the process of developing calm abiding a yogi overcomes five faults through eight antidotes (see Chart 2).[34]

1 *Laziness*

The first fault, laziness, involves either not wishing to engage in cultivating meditative stabilization or the inability to continue

Chart 2: *Faults of Meditative Stabilization and their Antidotes*

Five Faults	*Eight Antidotes*
laziness (*kausīdya, le lo*)	faith (*shraddhā, dad pa*) aspiration (*chhanda, 'dun pa*) exertion (*vyāyāma, rtsol ba*) pliancy (*prasrabdhi, shin tu sbyangs pa*)
forgetting the advice (*avavāda-saṃmoṣha, gdams ngag brjed pa*)	mindfulness (*smṛti, dran pa*)
[non-identification of] laxity and excitement (*laya, auddhatya; bying ba, rgod pa*)	introspection (*samprajanya, shes bzhin*)
non-application (*anabhisaṃskāra, 'du mi byed pa*)	application (*abhisaṃskāra, 'du byed pa*)
[over-]application (*abhisaṃskāra, 'du byed pa*)	equanimity (*upekṣhā, btang snyoms*)

the practice once begun. Laziness is of three types: indolence through attachment to sleep and so forth; adhering to non-virtuous activities of desire and so forth; and a sense of inadequacy, thinking, 'I cannot do this'. Thus, laziness is not just sluggishness but also the factor of enthusiasm for afflictions, as well as a false sense of inadequacy. The three types of laziness cause procrastination and are overcome through faith, aspiration, exertion, and pliancy.

Faith is mainly conviction in the qualities of meditative stabilization and its fruits, but also includes both the faith of clarity, which is a captivation with those qualities, and the faith that is the wish to attain those qualities. In order to attain faith in meditative stabilization, it is necessary to contemplate the disadvantages of not having stabilization—such as losing the value of virtuous practice through distraction—and the advantages of having it—such as steadiness of mind whereby feats, clairvoyance, magical emanation, and so forth can be achieved. Also, with stabilization sleep turns into meditative stabilization, afflictions lessen, and spiritual paths are easily generated in the mental continuum. The faith that sees these qualities induces aspiration, which involves a seeking of meditative stabilization.

Aspiration, in turn, induces effort, which here is an enthusiasm for meditative stabilization, leading to exertion, which acts as the antidote to the three types of laziness. As will be explained later, exertion eventually generates a mental and physical pliancy or serviceability that is the final antidote to laziness.

2 *Forgetting the advice*

The second fault, forgetting the advice from one's lama on the object of meditation, means to lose the object of observation, the pole to which the elephant of the mind is being tied with the rope of mindfulness in order to be brought under control by the hook of introspection. Forgetfulness here is an afflicted mindfulness—taking to mind a non-virtuous object through the power of excitement, laxity, and so forth. It is overcome through mindfulness which is defined as having the function of non-forgetfulness with respect to a familiar phenomenon. This non-afflicted mindfulness has three features:

a. *Objective feature:* a familiar object. If emptiness is the object of observation, familiarity with it was gained during the first stage of meditation on emptiness; there, with realization of non-inherent existence, one 'found' the object. If, on the other hand, the body of a Buddha is the object of observation, familiarity is gained through repeated viewing of a picture or image and then causing it to appear to the mind.

b. *Subjective feature:* non-forgetfulness within observation of that object. With mindfulness, the aspects of the object appear continuously without forgetfulness, as in being mindful of food when hungry.

c. *Functional feature:* causing the mind not to scatter to other objects of observation.

One must hold to the object of observation with a tight mode of apprehension without distraction; only that object should appear to the mind.

3 *Non-identification of laxity and excitement*

Then, when mindfulness is able to hold the mind to the object of observation, the third fault, non-identification of laxity and excitement, arises. Laxity is defined as the mental factor of declination in the mind's mode of apprehension when cultivating virtue; it is an internal distraction, a depression in the intensity of the mind's clarity. In a coarse neutral form of laxity the object is not seen, as if one had entered into darkness. This is a time of suddenly losing the intensity of the factor of clarity, losing the object, and being unable to move the mind to any object; in this state, the mind abides in a subjective clarity, but without intensity, and is unable to remain on the object of observation. Another form of coarse laxity occurs when the mind has stability in the sense of abiding on its virtuous object of observation but lacks clarity; this is a virtuous form of laxity due to the mind's abiding on a virtuous object. Subtle laxity occurs when one has the stability of not losing the mode of apprehension of the object as well as clarity, but lacks an *intensity* of clarity due to having loosened the strength of the mode of apprehension.

Since both subtle laxity and actual meditative stabilization have stability and clarity, it is difficult to distinguish between the two. The factor distinguishing meditative stabilization, however, is an *intensity* of clarity. An absence of intensity refers to a looseness of mind and can occur within the stability of being able to stay on the object; firming of the factor of stability within this looseness acts as a cause of subtle laxity. Having an intensity of clarity, on the other hand, means that the mind dwells *tightly* on the object of observation. Having or not having this intensity is compared to loosely or tightly holding a bowl, or the difference between usual faith in a lama and the particularly strong faith that is occasionally generated when a tightening in the mode of apprehension occurs.

Since in a state of subtle laxity the movement of the breath in the nostrils can stop, resulting in a firm mind for even an entire day, some have mistaken this for meditative stabilization and have even advised loosening the mode of apprehension of the object. They have confused this with a similar occurrence in the stage of completion of Highest Yoga Tantra upon the entering, remaining, and dissolving of the winds in the central channel; in the latter, however, the movement of the abdomen also stops and profound states are induced. From mis-identifying subtle laxity as meditation, not only can the four concentrations and four formless absorptions not be achieved, but also in this lifetime itself forgetfulness will increase and wisdom diminish, resulting in cultivating—as if intentionally—the means of achieving rebirth as an animal.

Though lethargy and drowsiness can lead to laxity, laxity is neither of them. Lethargy is a heaviness of body and mind, included within obscuration and accompanying all root and secondary afflictions (see p.265), whereas laxity is a factor of withdrawal inside and thus cannot accompany the afflictions of desire, hatred, and so forth, which are distractions outside. Lethargy darkens and obscures the mind whereas laxity does not. However, the mention of laxity here as a fault in meditative stabilization implicitly includes lethargy, sleep, and so forth. Within laxity itself, two types are to be distinguished, one which is an over-withdrawal of the mind inside and another which is a mere diminishment of the mind's mode of apprehension.

Excitement is a disquiet of the mind and scattering to an object of desire—mindfulness of a pleasant object, such as remembering at night a dance seen during the day. Since excitement is a secondary affliction included within the factor of desire, not all scatterings are instances of excitement, as when the mind scatters to an object of anger or even to another virtuous object. Although all scattering harms meditative stabilization and is implicitly included in the mention of excitement, it is not stated explicitly because those newly cultivating meditative stabilization are of the Desire Realm. They must mainly cease attachment to pleasant forms, sounds, odors, tastes, and tangible objects whereas scattering to virtuous or hated objects is less frequent and for shorter periods. However, when cultivating calm abiding, scattering to pleasant or unpleasant objects or to virtuous ones, such as becoming mindful of making donations, interrupts the stabilizing of the mind and, therefore, must be stopped.

Coarse excitement is a case of losing the object of observation in forgetfulness, whereas in subtle excitement the object is not lost but a corner of the mind is involved in fast-moving thought such that a pleasant object is about to appear to the mind. The state of subtle excitement is compared to water moving about under ice on a frozen river.

The antidote to non-identification of laxity and excitement is introspection that quickly recognizes them. Like a spy, introspection investigates and determines whether or not laxity and excitement have arisen. Constant cultivation of introspection would prevent stability; yet, if introspection were not cultivated at all, one would not know the faults that had already occurred, like allowing a thief to enter and carry off the wealth; therefore, one must prepare mindfulness beforehand and then occasionally initiate inspection of whether laxity and excitement have arrived or not. As in the example of (1) holding a cup of tea with the hand, (2) holding it firmly, and (3) investigating with the eye to see if it is tilted, (1) mindfulness holds to the object of observation, (2) the mode of apprehension is tightened, and (3) introspection analyzes whether laxity and excitement have arisen or not.

4 *Non-application*

When either laxity or excitement have arisen, non-application of their antidotes is a fault. Application—the mental factor of intention which here is an engagement in a virtuous object—is necessary as its antidote.

Antidotes to laxity. Since subtle laxity is a case of having both the stability of being able to remain on the object and subjective clarity but of lacking intensity, it is not necessary to leave the meditative session or switch to another object when it arises. Rather, it is sufficient merely to tighten the mode of apprehension; however, if it is tightened too much, excitement will be generated, and thus a moderation of tightness and looseness is necessary, as is the case with the strings of a violin for achieving a pleasant sound. If one suspects that excitement is about to be generated, one should loosen the mode of apprehension a little, whereas if one suspects that laxity is about to be generated, one should tighten a little. The mid-point between these is known only through experience. However, just as there is greater danger from an enemy within one's own circle because of the difficulty of identification, so there is greater danger of mistaking laxity for meditative stabilization, and thus tightness should be emphasized.

If, having tried to tighten the mind, one is unable to remove the fault of subtle laxity and experiences a lack of clarity in the mode of apprehension, coarse laxity has arrived. This is the fault of over-withdrawing the mind inside; to counter it, one should 'extend' the object a little, increasing it in brilliance or noticing its details. If this still does not remove laxity, one should leave the object of observation and invigorate this depressed mind by cultivating joy—reflecting on the difficulty of finding the meaningful life of leisure and fortune as a human, on the auspicious attributes of the Three Jewels, on the advantages of relying on a spiritual guide, or on the benefits of the altruistic intention to become enlightened. One can also take to mind a luminous object or imagine great acts of charity. If the mind heightens through such techniques and awakens, one should again apprehend the original object of observation. For those who are not used to these techniques, it is difficult for them to help immediately; however, for one who is familiar with them, contemplating, for instance, the difficulty of finding this meaningful life of leisure and fortune is like throwing cold water on the face.

However, if laxity is still not removed, one can use the forceful method of imagining one's own mind as a drop of white light at the heart and with the sound '*phaṭ*' causing it to exit from the crown of the head, ascend high in the sphere of the sky, and mix undifferentiably with the sky.

If laxity is still not removed, one should leave the session and remove the causes that generate it—lethargy, sleep, darkened mind, and so forth—by staying in a cool area, going to a high place with a vast view, walking about, washing the face with cold water, and so forth. When, having done this, the mind has awakened, one should, as before, apprehend the object of observation.

Antidotes to excitement. Subtle excitement is a case of distraction within not losing the object; its arising is due to the fault of having tightened the mind too much, and thus one should loosen the mode of apprehension a little. If that does not help and one is still distracted, then coarser excitement has been generated. Since this is caused by a happy mind, one should not be too happy, for progress will be impeded, as was the case with Buddha's father who did not achieve the state of Stream Enterer due to being too happy at his son's success. At this point, it is not necessary to leave the session; rather, one should contemplate sources of sobriety, such as death, impermanence, cyclic existence, and the sufferings of bad migrations.

If excitement is still not removed, one can use a forceful method of eliminating it, such as observing the inhalation and exhalation of the breath when dominated by discursiveness; exhaling, one should think, 'Going there', and when inhaling, 'Coming here'. Or, one can mentally count the breaths, counting in rounds up to ten, back to one, up to ten, back to one, and so forth.[35] If, though this is done, excitement is not eliminated, one should temporarily leave the session.

Since beginners can only remain in contact with the object of observation for short periods, initially one should meditate in brief sessions even eighteen times a day; in due course stability will be achieved of its own accord, at which time the session can be lengthened. It is important not to try at first to meditate for long periods; otherwise, upon sight of the meditation cushion, one will feel nausea and laziness. The session should be left while it is going well, when one still feels that it would go well if continued.

5 *Over-application*

When laxity and excitement have been eliminated, application of their antidotes is a fault preventing stability of mind; as its antidote one uses equanimity, that is, one desists from applying the techniques for pacifying laxity and excitement, such as invigorating the mind, withdrawing it inside, and so forth. This is a loosening of, or leaving off, the exertion involved in those antidotes—an equanimity that causes the mind to abide naturally on the object of observation accompanied by intense clarity. This occurs on the ninth state of mind (to be explained below) when one loosens the exertion of the introspection investigating whether laxity and excitement have arisen without, however, loosening either mindfulness or the intensity of the mode of apprehension of the object.

As Pa-bong-ka concludes:[36]

> Having completed the prerequisites for calm abiding in a place having the five qualifications and so forth, one sits on a comfortable cushion [in a posture] having the seven features of Vairochana. A Shākyamuni, only a finger-length high, separates from the lama on one's head and is set in space [about six feet] in front of one's navel [or at eye level]. Initially, the object of observation will not be clear and one does not need to make it so. For if mere generalities of the parts—head, arms, legs and so forth—and a mere sense of flashing gold appear and if mindfulness keeps the mind undistractedly [on the object] without forgetfulness and with a tight mode of apprehension, this mode of sustaining [meditation] through such mindfulness alone contains all the ways of eliminating laxity and excitement. This is an unparalleled quintessential instruction to be held in the heart by great meditators, for the tight mode of apprehension eliminates laxity and non-distraction eliminates excitement.
>
> If, when meditating this way, stability arises, then because one has come closer to laxity, one should be wary of it, [increasing] clarity and tightening the mode of

apprehension. However, if clarity arises, one is closer to excitement and thus should be wary of excitement and seek stability.

One should not pretend to be achieving meditative stabilization while not knowing what is needed to possess it; rather, one should definitely achieve a meditative stabilization possessing the two features of (1) stability in general but mainly (2) clarity with a tight mode of apprehension. As explained above in detail, mindfulness holds the object of observation without losing it, and at that time whether coarse or subtle laxity or excitement are about to arise, introspection immediately recognizes them, and they are stopped through directly relying on their specific antidotes. Then, when laxity and excitement are eliminated, one should not make the exertion of the antidotes but abide one-pointedly on the object of observation, sustaining it with great clarity that possesses intensity.

NINE STATES IN DEVELOPING CALM ABIDING

There are nine states or levels in the process of developing calm abiding (see Chart 3), of which the first two occur during the first stage of meditation on emptiness; the remaining seven occur during the second. Although actual meditative stabilization (*samādhi*) is associated with calm abiding, each of the preliminary nine states is called a meditative stabilization due to being an instance of the development of the mental factor with that name (see p.247).[37]

1 *Setting the mind*

The first state is a meditative stabilization that, following the hearing of advice for meditation, withdraws the mind from all external objects of observation and aims it at an internal object. It is achieved through the power of hearing advice from a lama about an object of observation because initially one merely sets the mind on the object based on that advice, not from a natural

Chart 3: *States and Factors in Achieving Calm Abiding* (read from bottom to top)

Six Powers (*ṣhaḍbala, stobs drug*)	*Nine States of Mind* (*navākārāchittasthiti, sems gnas dgu*)	*Four Mental Engagements* (*chatvāramanaskārā, yid byed bzhi*)
familiarity (*parichaya, yongs su 'dris pa*)	9 setting in equipoise (*samādhāna, mnyam par 'jog pa*)	spontaneously engaging (*anābhogovāhana, lhun grub tu 'jug pa*)
effort (*vīrya, brtson 'grus*)	8 making one-pointed (*ekotīkaraṇa, rtse gcig tu byed pa*)	uninterruptedly engaging (*nishchhidravāhana, chad pa med par 'jug pa*)
	7 thorough pacifying (*vyupashamana, nye bar zhi bar byed pa*)	interruptedly engaging (*sachchhidravāhana, bar du chad cing 'jug pa*)
introspection (*samprajanya, shes bzhin*)	6 pacifying (*shamana, zhi bar byed pa*)	
	5 disciplining (*damana, dul bar byed pa*)	
mindfulness (*smṛti, dran pa*)	4 close setting (*upasthāpanā, nye bar 'jog pa*)	
	3 re-setting (*avasthāpanā, slan te 'jog pa*)	
thinking (*chintā, bsam pa*)	2 continuous setting (*saṃsthāpanā, rgyun du 'jog pa*)	forcibly engaging (*balavāhana, sgrim ste 'jug pa*)
hearing (*shruta, thos pa*)	1 setting the mind (*chittasthāpanā, sems 'jog pa*)	

familiarity gained by thinking on it again and again. Aside from only occasional placement on the object, the mind mostly cannot remain on it, and thus a continuum of setting cannot be established.

Through the force of engaging in investigating and analyzing what the mind is doing, one recognizes the mind's becoming lost due to scattering and excitement and consequently has the sense that thoughts are increasing. However, thought has not actually become more manifold; it is just being identified.

If the emptiness of the I is used as the object, the wrong view of the inherent existence of the person predominates due to previous familiarity such that the correct view is actually only an occasional interruption in the stream of distraction.[38]

2 *Continuous setting*

The second state is a meditative stabilization that involves an ability to lengthen a little the continuum of observing an object without distraction. It is achieved through the power of thought because, due to sustaining the continuum of tying the mind to the object of observation through repeated thought, one is for the first time able to extend that continuum a little. One can remain undistracted for the period that it would take to recite one hundred *oṃ maṇi padme hūṃ*. Still, distraction during this phase exceeds abiding on the object.

The first two states arise in the manner of forcible engagement since it is necessary to force or tighten the mind with striving. Despite this, laxity and excitement frequently and continuously arise, the one being generated after the other like a waterfall, such that the mind cannot be set in meditative stabilization.

During the second state one has the sense that thought is resting because it sometimes quiets and sometimes is generated. The difference between the first two states is that during the second the mind remains longer on the object of observation, be it the non-inherent existence of the person or the body of a Buddha, etc.

3 *Re-setting* or *withdrawal and setting*

The third state is a meditative stabilization that, due to slight familiarity with the object of observation, returns or re-ties the mind to it through mindfulness's immediate realization of distraction. Like putting a patch on cloth, the mind is returned to the continuum of observation through immediate recognition of distraction, which, therefore, is less frequent than in the previous state. This is the time when powerful mindfulness is generated, and thus the third state is said to be achieved through its power.

The difference between the second and third states is that the third involves a shorter continuum of distraction, and thus here 'meditation'—from the trilogy of hearing, thinking, and meditating—begins, although in a looser sense one was meditating earlier.[39] In the same vein, 'analytical meditation' is technically possible now even though analysis occurred earlier. However, since analysis at this point would obstruct attainment of calm abiding, the yogi does not analyze but instead attempts to remain one-pointedly on, as in the two examples, the emptiness realized analytically during the first stage of meditation or the body of a Buddha.

4 *Close setting*

The fourth state is a meditative stabilization that involves an improved stability of mind, its having been withdrawn from the vast array of objects by the power of mindfulness. During the previous state distraction was abandoned through recognizing it, and thus the mind is now, with effort, set just on its object. From having generated strong mindfulness, losing the object no longer occurs; thus, the fault of forgetting the lama's advice on the object no longer arises. This ability to remain on the object without losing it is the great difference between the third and fourth states.

The fourth state is achieved through the power of mindfulness because strong mindfulness is able to tie the mind closer and closer to its object of observation. With this state, like an adult, mindfulness has matured, or, in other words, its power has been completed. Although the object is never lost and thus coarse excitement has ceased, powerful laxity and excitement still occur; hence it is necessary to rely on their antidotes.

5 *Disciplining*

The fifth state is a meditative stabilization that involves a liking for meditative stabilization through having seen with experience its advantages. With the fulfillment of powerful mindfulness in the last state, introspection also becomes powerful, whereby it recognizes the faults of scattering to objects of discursiveness as well as secondary afflictions and does not allow such scattering. Thus, this state and the next are said to be achieved by the power of introspection.

Since during the fourth state the mind was strongly withdrawn inside, the danger of subtle laxity on the fifth is great. One must with powerful introspection distinguish subtle laxity and, through contemplating the advantages of meditative stabilization, revivify the mind. The withdrawal of the mind practiced over the first three stages culminates in the fourth with the ability to stay on the object, but this withdrawal itself proceeds too far, and now it is necessary to apply the antidotes to subtle laxity. Through contemplating the auspicious qualities of meditative stabilization, such as the resultant clairvoyances and the ability to penetrate the meaning of difficult topics such as emptiness, one takes joy in meditative stabilization. The difference between this and the former state is that now coarse laxity does not arise.

6 *Pacifying*

The sixth state is a meditative stabilization that stops distraction, knowing its faults through experience in dependence on introspection. Due to the mind's becoming overly invigorated during the fifth state, here on the sixth the danger of generating subtle excitement is great. Powerful introspection recognizes it, whereupon even subtle excitement is viewed as a fault and stopped. Thus, the difference between this and the former state is that now there is no great danger that subtle laxity will arise and the arising of subtle excitement is less frequent. During the sixth state the power of introspection becomes fully developed.

7 *Thorough pacifying*

The seventh state is a meditative stabilization that involves enthusiasm for abandoning with exertion desirous attitudes, mental discomfort, lethargy, sleep, and so forth. Since the powers of mindfulness and introspection were fulfilled on earlier levels, it is difficult for laxity and excitement to arise; however, one must generate effort, view even subtle laxity and excitement as faults, and abandon them as much as possible. The difference between this and the former state is that here one does not need great qualms about the danger of coming under the influence of subtle laxity and excitement.

Whereas during the fifth and sixth states one has qualms that laxity and excitement could damage one's concentration, during the seventh, effort is able to stop them such that they cannot greatly interrupt the process. Thus, the seventh and eighth states are achieved by the power of effort in the sense that through exertion even subtle discursiveness and secondary afflictions are abandoned, whereby laxity and excitement cannot interrupt meditative stabilization.

Although during the third through seventh states one can remain for a considerable time in a continuum of meditative stabilization without generating laxity and excitement, laxity and excitement do interrupt again and again at least in a minor way, and thus these states are characterized by interrupted engagement. During the first two states the mind is more out of meditative stabilization than in it, and thus the designation 'interrupted engagement'—meaning an interruption of meditative stabilization—is not used with respect to them. Forcible engagement is specified for the first two states even though it occurs in the first seven, because the third through seventh also involve interrupted engagement.[40]

8 *Making one-pointed*, or *making continuous*

The eighth state is a meditative stabilization that involves the ability of continuous placement in meditative stabilization for an entire session without interruption by laxity and excitement due to the exertion of applying their antidotes. At the beginning of the session one relies on a little exertion directed at maintaining mindfulness with respect to the antidotes to laxity and excitement whereby one is able to sustain the session without even subtle laxity or excitement during that period.

The eighth state is achieved through the power of this small effort, and because not even subtle laxity and excitement arise, the state is characterized by uninterrupted engagement. During the earlier states, the enemies—laxity and excitement—were powerful, then decreased in strength, and now have completely degenerated; therefore, it is no longer necessary to rely on the exertion of introspection analyzing whether laxity or excitement have or are about to arise. The difference between the seventh and eighth states is this absence of laxity and excitement.

9 *Setting in equipoise*

The ninth state is a meditative stabilization devoid of the activity of thought due to the fact that meditative stabilization shines forth of its own accord from familiarity, without depending on the striving and exertion of maintaining mindfulness of antidotes. It is achieved through the power of familiarity with one-pointedness during the eighth state such that one engages wholly in meditative stabilization spontaneously, without exertion. Thus, the ninth state is characterized by spontaneous engagement, like recitation by one trained in it.

The difference between the eighth and ninth states is that the latter does not depend on striving and exertion. A similitude of calm abiding—a one-pointed mind included within the Desire Realm—is achieved.

CALM ABIDING

Calm abiding is attained when the ninth state is conjoined with a fully qualified pliancy—a serviceability of body and mind.[41] During the ninth state one can effortlessly abide in meditative stabilization free from even subtle laxity and excitement, but this is only a similitude of calm abiding. To attain actual calm abiding, special joy and bliss of physical and mental pliancy must be developed through again and again familiarizing with meditative stabilization.

The slight form of pliancy that is generated at the beginning of the ninth state increases to the point where mental pliancy is generated. This means that winds or currents of energy involved in unsalutary physical states are first calmed and leave the body through the top of the head,[42] where a sense of bliss is generated, like the touch of a hot hand after shaving the head. Immediately thereafter, a mental pliancy, which is a pacification of the unsalutary states that make the mind heavy and prevent its usage in virtue at will, is generated, affording a serviceability of mind. Through its power, a wind of serviceability that induces physical pliancy moves throughout the body, causing separation from unsalutary physical states of roughness and heaviness and affording an ability to use the body at will in virtuous actions without any sense of hardship. In this way, a physical pliancy of smoothness and lightness in which the body is light like cotton and seems as if filled with this wind of physical pliancy is generated.

In dependence on this, a bliss of physical pliancy that has a nature of very pleasant smoothness and lightness is generated. Then, continued meditative equipoise generates a bliss of mental pliancy, in which one's body seems to dissolve into the object of observation and no other phenomena appear, whereupon the mind is so buoyantly joyous that it is as if unable to remain on its object. When this buoyant joy is purified a little and the sense of bliss diminishes slightly, one attains an immovable pliancy concordant with meditative stabilization in the sense that the mind remains stably on the object of observation. Simultaneous with this, actual calm abiding is attained.

With calm abiding, one attains a mind included within the Form Realm as well as a preparation (*sāmantaka*) for the first concentration which is called 'not unable' (*anāgamya*) because this mind can serve as the mental basis for the path consciousnesses that are the antidotes to all afflictions of the three realms —Desire, Form, and Formless. Thus, calm abiding is achieved when the mind is conjoined with physical and mental pliancy and is also in control in the sense of one's being able to direct it to whatever object of observation one wishes.

When calm abiding is achieved, there are many signs of progress:

1. the mind has the capacity to purify afflictions
2. when in meditative equipoise, pliancy is quickly generated
3. even subsequent to meditative equipoise, features of pliancy are generated
4. with pliancy and meditative stabilization mutually increasing each other, sleep and meditative stabilization become mixed, and many pure appearances are seen in dreams
5. during meditative equipoise all coarse appearances disappear, and the mind seems to have mixed with space
6. when arising from the session, one has the sense of adventitiously gaining a body
7. fewer afflictions are generated, and those that arise are weak and are immediately extinguished of their own accord
8. the five obstructions–(1) aspiration to objects of the Desire Realm, (2) harmful intent, (3) lethargy and sleep, (4) excitement and contrition, and (5) doubt—mostly do not arise
9. the mind's factor of stability is firm like a mountain and the factor of clarity is such that it seems one could count the particles in a wall.

Though such calm abiding is a prerequisite for cognizing emptiness directly, its attainment alone does not cause one to achieve any of the five Buddhist paths–accumulation, preparation, seeing, meditation, or no more learning. Non-Buddhists proceed to generate the four concentrations and four formless absorptions, but since calm abiding alone can serve as the mental basis of path consciousnesses that overcome the afflictions from the root, it is not necessary for a Buddhist to do so (though all eventually do). The Buddhist turns to the cultivation of special insight.

Identifying the second stage of meditation on emptiness

If the yogi uses emptiness as the object of observation during cultivation of calm abiding, the experience with emptiness which he gained during the first of the five stages of meditation on emptiness becomes firmer during the second stage.[43] One who is newly achieving calm abiding temporarily forsakes analysis during this second stage. Since during the first he developed a conceptual understanding of emptiness through inference by means of extensive analysis, during the second he concentrates on this image or concept of emptiness, desisting from further analysis while in the formal meditative session as it would interrupt his progress toward calm abiding. Between sessions, however, he might resort to analysis to renew his understanding of the absence of inherent existence; then, during the formal session, he merely sets his mind on emptiness with continuous mindfulness and so forth as explained above.

When he finally achieves calm abiding with respect to emptiness, he returns to analysis, but this time with a highly developed mind in that it is stable, clear, intense, and serviceable. Still, too much analysis tends to disturb the factor of stability; so, he alternates between analytical and stabilizing meditation, using the same modes of analysis as in the first stage and then setting the mind on the content understood. If analysis is not done, the ascertainment of emptiness lessens, and if after analyzing, the mind is not set on the content thus ascertained, clarity is not attained.

When an object other than emptiness—such as the body of a Buddha—is used as the object of observation in developing calm abiding, the second stage of meditation on emptiness occurs after having attained calm abiding, at which point the yogi renews analytical investigation of emptiness. In either case, he must first achieve calm abiding and then strive to conjoin this stabilized mind with analysis of emptiness. The activity of analysis causes the mind of calm abiding to become slightly nonmanifest, requiring the yogi to pass again through the nine states, but the second stage of meditation on emptiness is mainly the eighth state, making one-pointed.

In summary, whether one uses emptiness or another object as the object of observation in the development of calm abiding, one must achieve calm abiding first and then conjoin that mind with analytical investigation, cultivating a *similitude* of special insight based on a *similitude* of calm abiding. Even though one formerly attained actual calm abiding, one is not, on the second stage, able to retain a fully qualified calm abiding while analyzing. Analysis and stabilization are alternated for the sake of inducing calm abiding again, but this time with the difference of being induced by analytical meditation on emptiness, which during the second stage induces the eighth state of one-pointedness or even the ninth state of equipoise, but not actual calm abiding. When analytical meditation itself induces the eighth state, a yogi attains a similitude of calm abiding and a similitude of meditative equipoise (*samāhita, mnyam bzhag*).

9 *Special Insight*

Sources

Jam-ȳang-shay-b̄a's *Great Exposition of the Concentrations and Formlessnesses*

Jam-ȳang-shay-b̄a's *Great Exposition of Tenets*

Kensur Lekden's oral teachings

Gön-chok-jik-may-w̄ang-b̄o's *Presentation of the Grounds and Paths*

Jang-ḡya's *Presentation of Tenets*

His Holiness the Dalai Lama's oral teachings

THIRD STAGE OF MEDITATION ON EMPTINESS

How to cultivate actual special insight based on actual calm abiding

The third stage consists of the mode of cultivating actual special insight based on actual calm abiding.[44] During the initial part of this phase, stabilizing meditation and analytical meditation are harmonized by alternating from the one to the other, for too much analysis would promote excitement and reduce the factor of stability whereas too much firmness would cause one not to want to analyze.

As explained in the previous chapter, one who previously used the body of a Buddha as the object of observation in cultivating calm abiding has switched to emptiness, analyzing the final nature of the I. Since he must pass through all four mental engagements—forcibly, interruptedly, non-interruptedly, and spontaneously engaging[45]—with respect to the emptiness of the I, he must again with tight mindfulness keep on the object, investigating its nature in the manner set forth for the first stage of meditation on emptiness, without straying to other objects or modes of analysis. When, through introspection, the meditator sees that excitement is about to arise, he alternates to stabilizing meditation, concentrating just on the meaning found through analysis. At this point, calm abiding is again induced with emptiness as the object of observation;[46] however, this is still not special insight, which arises only when analytical meditation itself induces stability and thereby mental and physical pliancy.

Through this process of repeated alternation between analytical and stabilizing meditation, special insight—defined as a wisdom of thorough discrimination of phenomena conjoined with special pliancy induced by the power of analysis[47]—is generated. Its causal prerequisites are to have relied on an excellent being, to have sought much hearing of the doctrine, and to have contemplated properly the meaning heard.[48] Etymologically, special insight (*vipashyanā, lhag mthong*) means sight (*pashya, mthong*) exceeding (*vi, lhag*) that of calm abiding because a clarity is afforded through analysis, different from the non-analysis during calm abiding.[49] The arising of clarity upon repeated thought and analysis with regard to either a true or false object is a fact of dependent-arising. For, if rather than just remaining in stabilizing meditation after achieving calm abiding, one performs analytical meditation, one is able to induce a very firm meditative stabilization and powerful wisdom consciousnesses that act as powerful antidotes overcoming afflictions, and one is able easily to make previously non-manifest objects, such as emptiness, manifest.

Since both pliancy and the calm abiding of a one-pointed mind are induced by the power of analysis, the special insight which is a thorough discrimination of phenomena and the calm abiding which is a one-pointedness of mind operate in parallel at the same time and with equal power.[50] Hence this is a union of special insight and calm abiding; within stabilization one is capable of strong analysis, which in turn induces even greater stabilization. Previously, analytical meditation was cultivated so that the mind would become of the entity of special insight, but at that time one did not have actual special insight which must be conjoined with calm abiding induced by *analytical* meditation; calm abiding and analysis were like the two ends of a scale, the one becoming slightly non-manifest when the other became manifest. Now, however, one has wisdom that is arisen from meditation, as contrasted to the wisdom arisen from thinking which was the ascertainment of emptiness by inferential valid cognition attained during the first stage and the wisdom arisen from hearing which was attained when the structure of the verbal teaching was determined. For beginners, that which differentiates a state arisen from meditation is the attainment of pliancy, and thus calm abiding marks the beginning of such states; however, with the attainment of special insight one has a *wisdom* arisen from meditation, pliancy having been induced by analysis. Unlike states arisen from hearing and thinking during which the object—emptiness—and the subject—the wisdom consciousness—appear to be unrelatedly distant and cut off, one now has the experience of piercing the object of observation, without the sense of subject and object as distant and cut off. Even though some dualistic appearance remains, the very coarse dualistic appearance of subject and object at the times of hearing and thinking has disappeared. One has the sense of approaching the state in which the wisdom consciousness and emptiness are like water put in water. It is for the sake of achieving such steady meditation that desisting from applying the antidotes to laxity and excitement is cultivated during the ninth state of equipoise.

Upon the attainment of a union of calm abiding and special insight *with emptiness as the object*, the path of preparation is attained.[51] The path of preparation—which cannot be attained if one's object is something other than emptiness, such as the four noble truths or the coarse personal selflessness—is the second of the five paths, accumulation, preparation, seeing, meditation, and no more learning. The Mahāyāna path of accumulation, which is so named because it marks the beginning of amassing the collections of merit and wisdom for the sake of enlightenment, was attained earlier when, after long training, one spontaneously generated the wish to attain highest enlightenment in order to establish all sentient beings in final happiness. The path of preparation is so named because the attainment of a union of calm abiding and special insight with emptiness as the object *prepares* a yogi for his initial direct cognition of emptiness. On the path of preparation the conceptual aspect of the realization of suchness is gradually removed in four periods:[52]

1 *Heat*

The heat period of the path of preparation is a sign that the fire of the non-conceptual wisdom of the path of seeing will soon be generated. One newly attains a meditative stabilization that has clear conceptual perception of suchness.

2 *Peak*

Prior to the peak period of the path of preparation, roots of virtue could be annihilated through the force of anger and so forth, but now one has reached the peak, or end, of the instability of virtuous roots. One newly attains a 'nirvana' that is a passing beyond the sorrow of the annihilation of roots of virtue and newly attains a meditative stabilization that is a heightening of conceptual perception of suchness.

3 *Forbearance*

During the forbearance period of the path of preparation one newly attains an endurance, or lack of fear, with respect to the profound emptiness. One also attains a 'nirvana' that is a passing beyond the sorrow of bad migrations because one will no longer be born as a hell-being, hungry ghost, or animal through the force of contaminated actions and afflictions (though one might choose to be born there to be of service to such beings). One thoroughly attains conceptual, clear perception of suchness and newly attains a meditative stabilization wherein an appearance of the object meditated—emptiness—is no longer ascertained in contradistinction to the subject—the mind of special insight.

4 *Supreme mundane qualities*

This period of the path of preparation is the supreme of worldly qualities. One newly attains a meditative stabilization that immediately precedes a speedy generation of the path of seeing.

During the first two periods of the path of preparation, heat and peak, subject and object appear during meditative equipoise, and the meditator can ascertain both. A mere vacuity of the object negated, inherent existence, appears; the yogi can delineate this appearance or concept of emptiness as the object and himself as the subject. Even if the emptiness being conceptually cognized is the emptiness of oneself, one nevertheless has a sense of object and subject, emptiness on the one hand and a consciousness realizing it on the other, though not in the coarse way that these appear prior to attaining special insight. One is abiding in the space-like meditative equipoise, and the phenomenon which was investigated to determine whether it inherently exists or not and which is qualified by this emptiness no longer appears at all.

During the periods of heat and peak the capacity to forsake the conception of inherent existence with respect to objects increases, and due to this, the coarser potencies of manifest innate conceptions of inherent existence diminish. Thus, at the time of forbearance the yogi can no longer ascertain the *appearance* of the object meditated, emptiness. However, this does not mean that he ceases to ascertain emptiness; rather, the conceptual aspect of the ascertainment disappears to the point where, even though there still is an *appearance* or image of emptiness, he can no longer recognize it as such. Then, at the time of supreme mundane qualities the cognizing subject also cannot be ascertained. The sense of the object disappears first because it is more difficult to forsake adherence to the inherent existence of the subject.

FOURTH STAGE OF MEDITATION ON EMPTINESS

How to cultivate direct cognition of emptiness

The fourth stage of meditation on emptiness occurs in direct realization of emptiness. During the period of supreme mundane qualities at the end of the path of preparation, one can no longer ascertain the factors of an object meditated and a subject meditating; however, subtle forms of both still appear. Subsequently, through continuous meditation, all appearances of subject and object are extinguished in suchness—emptiness—and subject and object become like water poured into water, undifferentiable. Emptiness is then realized directly without the medium of an image, and the path of seeing, the initial direct cognition of the truth, is attained.

Through the path of seeing a yogi removes *artificial* conceptions of inherent existence, those acquired not from beginningless conditioning but from contact with false systems of teaching. False teachings fortify the *innate* misconception of the inherent existence of persons and other phenomena, which is acquired from beginningless misconception of the nature of things and is overcome on the path of meditation through continuous conditioning to the truth.

The meditative equipoise of the path of seeing is divided into two parts, an 'uninterrupted path' that abandons the artificial afflictions and a 'path of release' that is the state of having abandoned those artificial afflictions. An uninterrupted path is so named because without interruption or interval a yogi will pass on to a path of release that is a condition of having been released from these afflictions. The uninterrupted path of a path of seeing corresponds to the 'eight forbearances', and the path of release corresponds to the 'eight knowledges' (see Chart 4).[53]

During the eight forbearances the realization of the lack of inherent existence is applied to objects and subjects—to the four noble truths and the subjects that realize the absence of inherent existence with respect to them. Through direct realization of the emptinesses that qualify these objects, artificial conceptions of inherent existence with respect to the four noble truths are

Chart 4: *Path of Seeing*
(read from bottom to top)

- true paths
  - subject
    - subsequent knowledge*
    - subsequent forbearance†
  - object
    - knowledge*
    - forbearance†
- true cessations
  - subject
    - subsequent knowledge*
    - subsequent forbearance†
  - object
    - knowledge*
    - forbearance†
- true origins
  - subject
    - subsequent knowledge*
    - subsequent forbearance†
  - object
    - knowledge*
    - forbearance†
- true sufferings
  - subject
    - subsequent knowledge*
    - subsequent forbearance†
  - object
    - knowledge*
    - forbearance†

*path of release
†uninterrupted path
(The eight forbearances occur simultaneously as one uninterrupted path, and the eight knowledges occur simultaneously as one path of release).

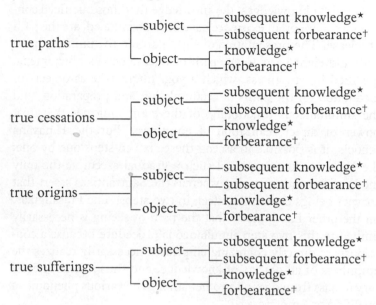

simultaneously abandoned. In other words, the initial direct realization of emptiness causes the artificial conception of inherent existence to be abandoned simultaneously with respect to true sufferings (such as an afflicted being wandering in cyclic existence), true origins (such as a conception of true existence itself), true cessations (such as the absence of an affliction brought about by cultivation of its antidote), and true paths (such as a realization of emptiness). The emptiness of the wisdom consciousness cognizing these is also realized at the same time; this realization is nevertheless called 'subsequent' because in the lower systems of tenets there is a step by step procedure, even though in this system an actual temporal sequence does not occur.

The eight knowledges, the knowledge that those artificial conceptions of inherent existence have been abandoned, are the path of release. The presentation of eight parts to the uninterrupted path and eight parts to the path of release details phenomena, qualified by emptiness, which a yogi might take as objects of meditation on the paths of accumulation and preparation, and the simultaneous functioning of the eight indicates the great power of direct realization of emptiness. For the Hīnayāna schools, it is possible to ascend these sixteen steps one by one; the Vaibhāṣhikas propound such a gradual ascent as the only mode of the path of seeing whereas the Sautrāntikas assert that sharper beings cover the sixteen in two steps. The Prāsaṅgikas, on the other hand, assert that the path of seeing is necessarily limited to this two step simultaneous procedure because a consciousness directly cognizing emptiness necessarily realizes the emptiness of all objects of knowledge, and thus it is not necessary to pass from one to the other among the various phenomena qualified by emptiness.

For a Hearer or Solitary Realizer, the uninterrupted path of a path of seeing marks the commencement of being a Superior (Āryan, 'Phags pa) and of being an Approacher to the level of a Stream Enterer. The path of release of the path of seeing marks the attainment of the level of an Abider in the fruit of a Stream Enterer. For a Bodhisattva, the uninterrupted path of the path of seeing marks the commencement of being a Superior and of attaining the first of the ten Bodhisattva grounds (*bhūmi, sa*).

In one meditative sitting a yogi passes from the fourth and last level of the path of preparation, called 'supreme mundane qualities', through the uninterrupted path and path of release of the path of seeing.[54] When he rises from meditative equipoise, he has a consciousness called 'subsequent attainment' that is influenced by the previous direct realization of emptiness. Although phenomena appear to be inherently existent, he, like a magician viewing his own creations, knows that all phenomena are empty of inherent existence. Later, when he forgets his direct realization, he has a 'distracted subsequent attainment'. His other meditative consciousnesses, such as those of compassion and of the realization of impermanence, are paths of seeing because they are in his continuum, but they are neither paths of seeing as meditative equipoise nor paths of seeing as subsequent attainment; they are a third category which is neither.

Though all artificial conceptions of inherent existence are removed on the first Bodhisattva ground and though during meditative equipoise the innate conception of inherent existence is dormant, a conception of inherent existence can arise again outside of direct contemplation of emptiness. The grosser, or artificial, stains were removed on the path of seeing, and now on the path of meditation the subtler stains, the innate sense of inherent, true, natural, or objective existence are removed, not just temporarily, but forever—never to arise again.

A path of meditation is a continuous familiarizing with the emptiness that was initially and directly cognized on the path of seeing. In meditative equipoise a Bodhisattva, Hearer, or Solitary Realizer again and again enters into direct realization of emptiness, and in subsequent attainment practices the deeds appropriate to his motivation. A Bodhisattva, ground by ground focuses on a different perfection:[55]

first ground:	giving
second ground:	ethics
third ground:	patience
fourth ground:	effort
fifth ground:	concentration
sixth ground:	wisdom
seventh ground:	method
eighth ground:	wishes
ninth ground:	power
tenth ground:	exalted wisdom.

All ten perfections are practiced on each ground, but a different one is brought to fulfilment on each. A perfection brought to fulfilment remains thus, and another is brought to its level. Finally, on the tenth ground, all ten perfections are in a state of complete development.

On the first ground, a Bodhisattva, after rising from meditative equipoise, can in one instant:[56]

1 see a hundred Buddhas
2 receive the blessings of a hundred Buddhas
3 go to a hundred Buddha Lands
4 illuminate a hundred lands
5 vibrate a hundred worldly realms
6 live for a hundred eons
7 see with true wisdom the past and future for a hundred eons
8 enter into and rise from a hundred meditative stabilizations
9 open a hundred different doors of doctrine
10 ripen a hundred sentient beings
11 emanate a hundred of his own body
12 cause each of the hundred bodies to be surrounded by a hundred Bodhisattvas.

On the second ground, these twelve qualities are a thousand; on the third, a hundred thousand; on the fourth, a hundred ten million; on the fifth, a thousand ten million; on the sixth, a hundred thousand ten million; on the seventh, a hundred thousand ten trillion; on the eighth, a number equal to the particles of a billion worlds; on the ninth, a number equal to the particles of ten million billions of worlds; on the tenth, a number equal to the particles of an inexpressible number of an inexpressible number of Buddha Lands.

As he ascends the grounds, a Bodhisattva gains the capacity to be born as a being of greater and greater influence. As his virtues increase, he is able to outshine, or suppress, greater numbers of beings and more powerful beings, not for the sake of exercising power but for the sake of helping them. As Nāgārjuna says in the fifth chapter of his *Precious Garland*:[57]

> Just as the eight levels of Hearers
> Are explained in their vehicle,
> So are the ten Bodhisattva
> Grounds in the Mahāyāna.

The first of these is the Very Joyful
Since the Bodhisattva is rejoicing.
He forsakes the three entwinements and is born
Into the lineage of the Tathāgatas.

Through the maturation of these qualities
The perfection of giving becomes supreme.
He vibrates a hundred worlds
And becomes a great lord of the world.

The second is called the Stainless
Because the ten [virtuous] actions
Of body, speech, and mind are stainless
And he naturally abides in them.

Through the maturation of these qualities
The perfection of ethics becomes supreme,
He becomes a Universal Monarch helping beings,
Master of the glorious [four continents]
And of the seven precious substances.

The third ground is called the Luminous because
The pacifying light of wisdom arises.
The concentrations and clairvoyances are generated,
While desire and hatred are extinguished completely.

Through the maturation of these qualities
He practices supremely the deeds of patience
And putting an end to desire completely
Becomes a great wise king of the gods.

The fourth is called the Radiant
Because the light of true wisdom arises
In which he cultivates supremely
The harmonies of enlightenment.

Through the maturation of these qualities he becomes
A king of the gods in [the Land] Without Combat.
He is skilled in quelling the arising of the view
That the transitory collection [is a real self].

The fifth is called the Very Difficult to Overcome
Since all demons find it extremely hard to conquer
him.
He becomes skilled in knowing the subtle
Meanings of the noble truths and so forth.

Through the maturation of these qualities he becomes
A king of the gods abiding in the Joyous Land.
He overcomes the sources of afflictions
And of the views of all Forders (*Tīrthika*).

The sixth is called the Approaching because he is
Approaching the qualities of a Buddha;
Through familiarity with calm abiding and special
insight
He attains cessation and is thus advanced [in wisdom].

Through the maturation of these qualities he becomes
A king of the gods [in the Land] of Liking Emanation.
Hearers cannot surpass him, he pacifies
Those with the pride of superiority.

The seventh is the Gone Afar because
The number [of his qualities] has increased,
Moment by moment he can enter
The equipoise of cessation.

Through the maturation of these qualities he becomes
a master
Of the gods [in the Land] of Control over Others'
Emanations.
He becomes a great leader of teachers for he knows
Direct realization of the [four] noble truths.

The eighth is the Immovable, the youthful stage.
Through non-conceptuality he is immovable
And the spheres of his body, speech, and mind's
Activities are inconceivable.

Through the maturation of these qualities
He becomes a Brahmā, master of a thousand worlds.

Foe Destroyers and Solitary Realizers and so forth
Cannot surpass him in establishing the meaning [of
the doctrines].

The ninth ground is called
Good Intelligence.
Like a regent he has attained correct individual
Realization and therefore has good intelligence.

Through the maturation of these qualities
He becomes a Brahmā who is master of a million
worlds.
Foe Destroyers and so forth cannot surpass him
In responding to questions in the thoughts of sentient
beings.

The tenth is the Cloud of Doctrine because
The rain of excellent doctrine falls.
The Bodhisattva is consecrated
With light by the Buddhas.

Through the maturation of these qualities
He becomes a master of the gods of Pure Abode.
He is a supreme great lord, master
Of the sphere of infinite wisdom.

A yogi who has attained direct realization of emptiness cannot remain in that realization while perceiving the phenomena qualified by emptiness and also cannot perceive phenomena while directly realizing emptiness.[58] He loses the direct cognition of emptiness when he rises from meditative equipoise, for the appearance of conventional phenomena rules out a direct cognition of emptiness and a direct cognition of emptiness rules out the appearance of conventional phenomena. In terms of how emptiness and other phenomena appear to him, the two truths are as if contradictory; such are the obstructions to omniscience —the simultaneous realization by one consciousness of all phenomena, both the phenomena qualified by emptiness and the emptinesses themselves. A Bodhisattva has a great wish to rid himself of this obstruction because it prevents him from knowing those things that make attempts to help other beings fruitful. Although he does not actually begin to abandon the obstructions to omniscience until the eighth Bodhisattva ground, the wish to do so is his basic motivation during the seven preceding grounds as he is ridding himself forever of the various degrees of the conception of inherent existence, the root of the obstructions to liberation.

On each ground a Bodhisattva abandons varying degrees of the innate conception of inherent existence and the poisons it induces along with their seeds.[59] These objects of abandonment are arranged in relation to the three realms and the nine levels. The three realms are the Desire, Form, and Formless Realms; of the nine levels, the first corresponds to the Desire Realm, the next four to the four divisions of the Form Realm, called the Four Concentrations, and the last four to the four divisions of the Formless Realm, called the Four Formless Absorptions. The Four Concentrations and Four Formless Absorptions are places of rebirth where beings have particularly strong concentrative powers; these powers can be achieved within a lifetime in the Desire Realm, and thus the three realms outline the possible states of consciousness in terms of concentrative ability within a human lifetime in the Desire Realm and also present in condensed form all the possible states of rebirth within cyclic existence.

The conception of inherent existence and its attendant afflictions are divided into eighty-one steps, nine each with respect to the nine levels, so that each level has a series of nine obstacles that are to be abandoned: big big, middle big, and small big; big middle, middle middle, and small middle; big small, middle small, and small small (see Chart 5). The Prāsaṅgikas assert that no one proceeds through these eighty-one steps one by one; rather, the nine big big innate afflictions are simultaneously abandoned; the nine middling big are simultaneously abandoned, and so forth through the small small. One proceeds in nine steps with each step having an uninterrupted path, which is a path of direct cognition of emptiness actively forsaking a

Chart 5: *Innate Afflictions Forsaken on the Path of Meditation in Terms of the Three Realms and Nine Levels*
(read from bottom to top)

afflictions regarding Formless Realm	Peak of Cyclic Existence (ninth level)		73-81
	Nothingness (eighth level)		64-72
	Infinite Consciousness (seventh level)		55-63
	Infinite Space (sixth level)		46-54
afflictions regarding Form Realm	Fourth Concentration (fifth level)		37-45
	Third Concentration (fourth level)		28-36
	Second Concentration (third level)		19-27
	First Concentration (second level)		10-18
afflictions regarding Desire Realm (first level)	small	small small	9
		middling small	8
		big small	7
	middling	small middling	6
		middling middling	5
		big middling	4
	big	small big	3
		middling big	2
		big big	1

corresponding affliction, and a path of release, which is a consciousness directly cognizing emptiness within the condition of having abandoned that affliction. The 'active forsaking' of an affliction does not mean that the path and the affliction combat each other; rather, simultaneously with the production of an uninterrupted path the corresponding affliction ceases.

To destroy the big big afflictions only a small small path is needed, much the same as when initially cleaning a garment the grosser stains are easily cleaned with a little washing. To destroy the small small afflictions a big big path is needed, and the same is to be respectively applied to the intermediate degrees.

On each of the second through eighth Bodhisattva grounds a portion of the innate afflictions is forsaken:

second ground:	the nine big big
third ground:	the nine middling big
fourth ground:	the nine small big
fifth ground:	the nine big middling
sixth ground:	the nine middling middling
seventh ground:	the nine small middling
eighth ground:	the nine big small, the nine middling small, and the nine small small simultaneously.

The grounds are not enumerated for Hearers and Solitary Realizers even though they abandon the same afflictions as do Bodhisattvas. As Hearers and Solitary Realizers abandon the various degrees of afflictions, they are classified into the 'eight levels of approaching and abiding' with respect to their attainment of the fruits of a Stream Enterer, Once Returner, Never Returner, or Foe Destroyer (see Chart 6).

With the attainment of the path of release of the path of seeing, a Hearer or Solitary Realizer is an Abider in the fruit of a Stream Enterer. While making effort to overcome the first six of the nine degrees of innate afflictions pertaining to the Desire Realm, he is an Approacher to the level of Once Returner, and once these six are overcome, he becomes an Abider in the fruit of Once Returner. He will return to the Desire Realm by the power of afflictions only once more, at which time he will strive to overcome the remaining three degrees of innate afflictions pertaining to the Desire Realm, becoming an Approacher to the level of a Never Returner. With success in overcoming all afflictions pertaining to the Desire Realm, he becomes an Abider in the fruit of a Never

Chart 6: *Eight Levels of Approaching and Abiding*
(read from bottom to top; afflictions refer to those in Chart 5 on p.105)

	afflictions being forsaken	*afflictions already forsaken*	*path*
Abider in the fruit of a Foe Destroyer		1-81	no more learning
Approacher to the fruit of a Foe Destroyer	10-81	1-9	meditation
Abider in the fruit of a Never Returner		1-9	meditation
Approacher to the fruit of a Never Returner	7-9	1-6	meditation
Abider in the fruit of a Once Returner		1-6	meditation
Approacher to the fruit of a Once Returner	1-6		meditation
Abider in the fruit of a Stream Enterer			seeing—path of release
Approacher to the fruit of a Stream Enterer			seeing—uninterrupted path

Returner, never again returning to the Desire Realm due to the afflictions although he might return to the Form and Formless

Realms within cyclic existence many times. When he makes effort to overcome the remaining seventy-two degrees of innate afflictions pertaining to the Form and Formless Realms, he becomes an Approacher to the level of Foe Destroyer, and when all innate afflictions have been overcome, he is an Abider in the fruit of a Foe Destroyer.

When, as in the Prāsaṅgika system, the afflictions are forsaken simultaneously rather than serially, a yogi first abandons simultaneously the first, tenth, nineteenth, twenty-eighth, thirty-seventh, forty-sixth, fifty-fifth, sixty-fourth, and seventy-third degrees of the afflictions. Thus, it is said that while abandoning this first of the nine rounds, he already is an Approacher to the fruit of a Foe Destroyer.

When a Hearer or a Solitary Realizer has abandoned all nine rounds of the innate afflictions, he is a Foe Destroyer and has attained the path of no more learning *of his vehicle*. However, he has not ceased learning in general; he is urged by Buddhas to enter the Mahāyāna both in order to help other beings and to perfect his own aims. Though he has eliminated the innate afflictions and thereby removed the obstructions to liberation from cyclic existence, he has not even begun to remove the non-afflicted ignorance that constitutes the obstructions to omniscience—the appearance of inherent existence and the stains of viewing the two truths as separate entities.

Upon their generation of a spontaneous, strong wish to attain highest enlightenment for the sake of all sentient beings, Hearer and Solitary Realizer Foe Destroyers enter the Mahāyāna path of accumulation. They proceed through the paths of accumulation, preparation, seeing, and meditation and ascend the Bodhisattva grounds, eliminating not the innate afflictions, because these have already been destroyed through the Hīnayāna path, but the obstructions to attainment of the many special qualities of Bodhisattvas. They must spend one period of countless eons on the paths of accumulation and preparation and another period of countless eons on the first eight grounds doing this.

On the eighth ground all Bodhisattvas—those who proceed only on the Mahāyāna path and those who first completed the

Hīnayāna path—finally begin to eliminate what they have sought to overcome since their entry into the Mahāyāna, the obstructions to omniscience. They spend one period of countless eons proceeding from the second part of the eighth ground to Buddhahood, forsaking by degrees the stains that prevent them from full effectiveness in their efforts to help other beings. The obstructions to omniscience (literally, obstructions to objects of knowledge: *jñeyāvaraṇa*) plague all sentient beings, not just eighth ground Bodhisattvas, for the appearance of inherently existent objects to the sense and mental consciousnesses lends a false support to the innate conception of inherent existence, the assent to this false appearance. However, only eighth ground Bodhisattvas have the capacity to begin to counteract the appearance of inherent existence. The long endeavor in amassing the collections of merit and wisdom has been for the purpose of so empowering the mind that it is possible to counteract these most subtle obstructions.

The obstructions to omniscience are divided into four degrees that are to be eliminated on the last three grounds, called 'pure' because eighth through tenth ground Bodhisattvas are purified of the innate afflictions:

second part of eighth ground:	big obstructions to omniscience
ninth ground:	middling obstructions to omniscience
first part of tenth ground:	coarse small obstructions to omniscience
last part of tenth ground:	subtle small obstructions to omniscience.

The final uninterrupted path in the continuum of a sentient being eliminates the subtlest obstructions to Buddhahood, and the corresponding path of release is Buddhahood itself. In order to generate this final uninterrupted path, however, it is necessary to enter the path of tantra. Even though the Buddhahoods described in sutra and in tantra are the same, the paths of sutra alone can carry a yogi only to the tenth Bodhisattva ground. To achieve Buddhahood, it is necessary to supplement these paths with the paths of Secret Mantra.

10 *Tantra*

Sources
His Holiness the Dalai Lama's oral teachings
J̄ang-ḡya's *Presentation of Tenets*
Nga-w̄ang-b̄el-den's *Illumination of the Tantric Texts*

A Bodhisattva spends at least three countless eons on the paths of accumulation, preparation, seeing, and meditation and reaches the last part of the tenth ground, but in order to remove the subtle small obstructions to omniscience he still must enter the Secret Mantra Vehicle.[60] His path has been very long; if he were fully qualified and had entered the tantric vehicle from the beginning, he would have been able to attain Buddhahood in just one lifetime. Tantra is the quick path for those who are fit receptacles, but not for those who cannot bear the difficulties of the long path.[61] To practice tantra requires even greater compassion and greater intelligence than are required on the sutra path; thus, though many persons in the degenerate era are interested in tantra, tantra is not for degenerate persons.

Tantra is limited to persons whose compassion is so great that they cannot bear to spend unnecessary time in attaining Buddhahood, as they want to be a supreme source of help and happiness for others quickly.[62] The most qualified of tantric practitioners complete the path in one lifetime, and it is said that those who are less qualified but maintain their vows will attain the supreme achievement in either seven or sixteen lifetimes.

In order to enter the tantric path it is necessary to have good understanding of the three principal aspects of the path to full enlightenment: the thought to leave cyclic existence, the aspiration to highest enlightenment for the sake of all sentient beings, and the correct view of emptiness.[63] Therefore, it is impossible to enter the Mantra Vehicle before the first of the five stages of meditation on emptiness; however, it could be entered anytime after the yogi had gained an acquaintance with emptiness, the first of these five stages, provided he had the other qualifications of compassion and so forth.

There is an exoteric explanation that once a Bodhisattva has attained a non-tantric path of seeing he must wait until he reaches the tenth ground to enter the tantric path.[64] However, according to an oral transmission, a Bodhisattva can enter the Mantra Vehicle at any time; his great compassion and sharpness of mind as well as his ability to create manifestations which visit Buddhas in different lands insures that he would know of the tantric path and seek it. Thus, the second, third, and fourth of the five stages of meditation on emptiness could be replaced by similar stages within the practice of tantra, beginning at any point within these three. It is not obligatory to pass through the ten Bodhisattva grounds to enter the practice of tantra, nor is it obligatory to pass through the three lower tantras to enter Highest Yoga Tantra.

CALM ABIDING AND SPECIAL INSIGHT IN TANTRA

Tantra in general is divided into four types which in ascending order are: Action (*Kriyā*), Performance (*Charyā*), Yoga (*Yoga*), and Highest Yoga (*Anuttarayoga*). The mode of developing a union of calm abiding and special insight with emptiness as the object is similar in the first three tantra sets to that in the sutra teachings in the sense that, after attaining calm abiding, analytical meditation and stabilizing meditation are alternated in order to prevent respectively laxity and excitement, or lack of penetrating ascertainment and lack of stability.[65] However, unlike the sutra system, all four tantras emphasize a union of manifestation and emptiness—the vivid appearance of oneself as a deity in conjunction with conceptual cognition of emptiness.

In other words, it is accepted in the tantric systems that a phenomenon which is qualified by emptiness can continue to appear to an inferential consciousness that realizes its emptiness. Both the vivid appearance of a deity and realization of the deity's non-inherent existence are practiced by one consciousness. In most interpretations of the sutra systems, however, a phenomenon qualified by emptiness does not appear to an inferential consciousness cognizing its emptiness; just its emptiness appears. Thus, in the sutra systems the union of wisdom and method refers merely to cognition of emptiness as supplementing the Bodhisattva deeds, or the Bodhisattva deeds as supplementing cognition of emptiness. In tantra, on the other hand, one consciousness is sufficient to contain the practice of the profound—the wisdom realizing non-inherent existence—and the practice of the vast—the appearance of oneself as a deity. Furthermore, because from the beginning a yogi imagines himself as having the body, enjoyments, abode, and activities of a Buddha, he amasses far more quickly the merit necessary to produce a Buddha's Form Body, and in this sense tantra is the quick path.

In the yoga of union of the profound and the manifest, a meditator reflects on emptiness through any of the reasonings outlined in the first stage of meditation on emptiness. According to the three lower tantras, he achieves calm abiding and then alternates between analytical meditation and stabilizing meditation, within continuous realization of emptiness and within vivid appearance of himself as a deity. However, in Highest Yoga Tantra it is not necessary either to achieve calm abiding first or to perform such alternation.[66] Highest Yoga Tantra is divided into stages of generation and completion, during both of which the yoga of the union of manifestation and emptiness is performed, but with a difference. In the stage of generation, due to the force of holding the mind fully to a subtle object in a special place within the body, such as a tiny drop or letter at the heart, and due to the type of object being meditated, the winds gradually abide inside, whereby excitement can be quickly stopped. Thus, the yogi can perform strong analytical meditation without concern that he will lose the factor of stability. When the eighth state preliminary to calm abiding is achieved, a type of analytical meditation involving the emanation and withdrawal of, for instance, vajras, easily stops coarse conceptuality and induces the simultaneous achievement of calm abiding and special insight. Attainment of the union of calm abiding and special insight is thus very fast in Highest Yoga Tantra—provided that the meditator is qualified.

FIFTH STAGE OF MEDITATION ON EMPTINESS

How to meditate on emptiness during the second stage of Highest Yoga Tantra

In the second and final stage of Highest Yoga Tantra, that of completion, there are a series of techniques, suited to the meditator's physical constitution and mental temperament, that cause the winds (*prāṇa*) to enter, remain, and dissolve in the central channel.[67] The purpose is to manifest a series of four subtle minds and, in turn, to use the subtlest, the mind of clear light, to cognize emptiness. When the winds have fully entered, remained, and dissolved in the indestructible drop in the center of the heart, emptiness is directly cognized by the very subtle mind of clear light. At this point in just one period of the path of seeing, the yogi forsakes not only the artificial but also the innate afflictions. The emptiness that is cognized is exactly the same emptiness that is taught in sutra; however, the bliss consciousness that cognizes emptiness is far subtler than the corresponding consciousness presented in the sutra systems.

Since even some Hearers are said to forsake the innate afflictions in as little as three lives, the extraordinary speed of Highest Yoga Tantra is not just the instantaneous abandoning of the artificial and innate afflictions on the path of seeing; it also refers to the swift abandonment of the obstructions to omniscience. Rising from the path of seeing, a yogi's very subtle mind and the very subtle wind that is its mount serve as the causes of an illusory body which is pure in the sense that the afflictions have been abandoned and is actual in the sense that it is not just imagined. With this special mind and body, the obstructions to omniscience are quickly eliminated, and Buddhahood is realized.

During the stage of completion in Highest Yoga Tantra the emphasis is not on meditation analyzing emptiness by way of reasoning but on stabilizing meditation for the sake of gathering the winds in order to manifest a subtle consciousness cognizing emptiness. However, these stabilizing concentrations cannot be effective unless they are built on firm ascertainment of emptiness attained through analytical reasoning, undertaken during the stage of generation and before.[68] It is within the context of an ascertainment of emptiness that a yogi concentrates on the physical and psychic centers although during the actual session itself he desists from applying his mind to analytical reasoning. Still, analytical meditation of a different type is required in order to generate a sharpness and brightness of concentration,[69] in dependence on which the winds are gathered, thereby generating through meditation the same subtle minds that are actualized powerlessly and without benefit at death. The deepest and subtlest of these minds and the wind that is its mount are the actual substances that develop into a Buddha's mind and body.[70] Though it may be possible without the view of emptiness to actualize some of these subtle consciousnesses, it is impossible without the view of emptiness to actualize the most subtle.[71] As the tutor of the Eighth Dalai Lama, Ye-s̄hay-gyel-tsen (*Ye-shes-rgyal-mtshan*) reports:[72]

> It is said that this profound view of the middle way is the life of both the sutra and tantra paths. Also, it is said that particularly with respect to Highest Secret Mantra there is no chance of having an actual path of Mantra without this view.

Shākyamuni: the fourth Buddha of this era

11 *Buddhahood*

Sources
Jang-gya's *Presentation of Tenets*
Jam-yang-shay-ba's *Great Exposition of Tenets*
Kensur Lekden's oral teachings

On the path Bodhisattvas familiarize themselves in innumerable ways with the six perfections.[73] They develop limitless wishes and dedications, and they experience in myriad forms the joys of the wisdom that cognizes the profound suchness of all phenomena in the manner of a fusion of subject and object. Whether following the sutra or tantra path, the Bodhisattva's base is the same: the aspiration to highest enlightenment for the sake of all sentient beings. The deeds are, in general, also the same: the six perfections. In the sutra systems a limitless variety of these deeds is prescribed whereas in tantra an additional method, yoga of the union of the profound and the manifest, is used to empower the mind to combat the obstructions to omniscience. The effect of these paths is the attainment of a Buddha's Form Body and Truth Body which are the fulfilment of the aims of both oneself and others.

The uninterrupted path at the end of the tenth ground is called the end of the continuum as a sentient being because although a Buddha is sentient, he does not have a mind that has obstructions yet to be eliminated. The uninterrupted path at the end of the continuum of a sentient being is the antidote to the very subtle obstructions to omniscience; it cognizes the suchness of all phenomena in the manner of being of one taste with suchness. Like fresh water poured into fresh water, there is no distinction experienced between the wisdom consciousness and emptiness. Still, it has the potentialities that will make possible, immediately afterwards, the instantaneous appearance of the inconceivable qualities of a Buddha.

While the yogi is in deep contemplation on emptiness only, he passes into a condition wherein, simultaneous with continuous direct cognition of emptiness, all the phenomena that are qualified by emptiness appear to him. He passes to the final path of release, and while in a meditative equipoise in which there is not the slightest interference of duality, this same consciousness directly cognizes all the many varieties of objects of knowledge as clearly as one sees an olive in the palm of one's hand. Since the potencies of mistaken dualistic appearance have been eradicated, the yogi attains the divine eye that has no impediments with respect to objects of knowledge and is not impeded from seeing one object by seeing another. He has exhaustively eliminated the obstructions to omniscience, has actualized the limit of reality, has actualized the Truth Body, and has become thoroughly and completely enlightened with respect to all phenomena.

The bodies of a Buddha are variously enumerated as one, two, three, four, or five.[74] These are more extensive or condensed forms of each other and thus to not indicate a difference of meaning.

One:	Truth Body
Two:	Truth Body and Form Body
Three:	Truth Body, Enjoyment Body, and Emanation Body (the last two being included within Form Body above)
Four:	Nature Body, Wisdom Body, Enjoyment Body, and Emanation Body (the first two being included within Truth Body above)

Five: Nature Body, Wisdom Body, Actual Enjoyment Body, Imputed Enjoyment Body (such as the body of a tenth ground Bodhisattva), and Emanation Body (the middle two being included within Enjoyment Body above).

When the wisdom of meditative equipoise at the end of a yogi's continuum as a sentient being (that is, his uninterrupted path consciousness directly cognizing emptiness) becomes the final path of release, this wisdom of meditative equipoise itself becomes the Wisdom Body, a composite in one entity of both meditative equipoise and subsequent attainment. This means that all phenomena, emptinesses and conventionalities, are directly cognized all of the time. The emptiness of this final uninterrupted path becomes the Nature Body, the absence of all obstructions in the continuum of a Buddha.

The Truth Body is so called because its two parts, the Nature Body and the Wisdom Body, are respectively the ultimate true cessation and the ultimate true path.[75] A Nature Body is of two types, a naturally pure Nature Body which is the absence from beginningless time of inherent existence in the pure sphere of Buddhahood, and an adventitiously pure Nature Body which is the absence in the pure sphere of Buddhahood of the adventitious stains—the afflictive obstructions and the obstructions to omniscience—through the application of their antidotes. Both are non-products and mere absences, but only the first is called a non-product because it lacks production, duration, and disintegration and lacks a beginning, middle, and end. The second type of Nature Body is called 'spontaneous' because the aspect of having utterly eliminated the subtle motivational effort that initiates deeds of body and speech allows for the spontaneity of the Enjoyment and Emanation Bodies.

Both aspects of the Nature Body are emptinesses which are the absence of inherent existence of a Buddha's omniscient mind; the naturally pure Nature Body is an emptiness from the point of view that the mind is always naturally free of inherent existence. The adventitiously pure Nature Body is this emptiness from the viewpoint of its being a quality of a mind that has been cleansed of all contaminations. Thus, both Nature Bodies are emptinesses and ultimate truths.

The Nature Body is said to have five qualities:

1 non-production, because of having no production, duration, or disintegration and no beginning, middle, or end
2 non-difference, because of being undifferentiable from the final nature of phenomena in terms of not being a different entity from phenomena
3 non-perversity, because it has not fallen to the two extremes of reification of what does not exist and denial of what does exist
4 purity, because of being free of the afflictive obstructions, the obstructions to omniscience, and the obstructions to meditative absorption
5 clear light, because the stains do not inherently exist, because it is not fully cognizable by the intellect, and because it is an object of perception by yogis in individual meditative equipoise.

The Nature Body is *vast* because it is not knowable as being limited to any measure. It is *innumerable* because it surpasses the number of sands of the Ganges. It is *unthinkable* because it cannot be conceived as any of the four alternatives. It is *unequal* because one who has actualized it is unequal with all who have not. It is *completely pure* because the defects of the afflictions and their predispositions have been completely abandoned.

The Wisdom Body is the final, perfect wisdom. It is called the wisdom cognizing the mode of existence of phenomena in the sense that it perceives all emptinesses. It is called the wisdom cognizing the varieties of phenomena in the sense that it also perceives all conventionalities. In brief, the Wisdom Body is a Buddha's omniscient consciousness; his eye, ear, nose, tongue, body, and mental consciousnesses are each omniscient. Thus, a single moment of any consciousness cognizes all phenomena; his eye consciousness perceives not just colors and shapes, but also sounds, odors, and so forth, including the emptiness of each phenomenon perceived. A Wisdom Body is everywhere because a

Buddha's wisdom consciousness cognizes the emptiness of everything non-dualistically.

When a Bodhisattva arrives at the end of the continuum of being a sentient being, his body ornamented with a similitude of the major and minor marks of a Buddha becomes a Buddha's Enjoyment Body. Through the power of former wishes and without any intellection, various Emanation Bodies are issued from the Enjoyment Body, appearing simultaneously in countless lands throughout the ten directions and aiding sentient beings in accordance with their interests, dispositions, and beliefs. One does not first become a Buddha and then think about what needs to be done; one responds immediately and without thought or effort to the needs of all sentient beings. The Enjoyment Body and Emanation Bodies are achieved simultaneously because (1) both are fruits of training in the equality of cyclic existence and peace; (2) both are fruits of training to produce pure lands for Enjoyment and Emanation Bodies in order to provide bases for sentient beings to gain enlightenment; and (3) both are fruits of training in wisdom and method such that at the time of highest enlightenment there are no obstructions with respect to the perfection of all qualities.

An Enjoyment Body abides in a Highest Pure Land (*Akaniṣhṭa*). Highest Pure Lands are above the seventeen types of lands in the Form Realm and thus are called 'Highest' (literally, 'not below'). Each Buddha has his own Highest Pure Land produced by his limitless collections of merit and wisdom and as vast as space; it is achieved from a portion of his wisdom and is not composed of particles of matter.

An Enjoyment Body is said to have five qualities:

1 An Enjoyment Body is impermanent, but it continuously displays the same type of body ornamented with the major and minor marks of a Buddha; therefore, it is immortal.
2 An Enjoyment Body continuously speaks the same type of doctrine, the Mahāyāna, and thus is a Body that enjoys or uses the Mahāyāna doctrine as opposed to the Emanation Bodies which abide in Pure Lands and preach both Hīnayāna and Mahāyāna.

3 An Enjoyment Body continuously displays the activities that arise from wisdom and compassion.
4 These activities of body, speech, and mind are performed without effort.
5 Though an Enjoyment Body does not exist as many different personal continuums, it displays many Emanation Bodies.

It is said that even though the displayer of Emanation Bodies is an Enjoyment Body, Emanation Bodies are not Enjoyment Bodies but are of the same continuum as an Enjoyment Body.

Through the force of compassion and wishes over countless eons the ultimate wisdom itself appears in the aspect of a body. Each of the parts of the body directly cognizes all phenomena and proclaims inconceivable intonations of doctrine; mind and body are no longer separate phenomena. Not only is the Enjoyment Body an appearance of the wisdom consciousness itself, but also the pure numberless phenomena that a Buddha cognizes from his own point of view are the entity of this wisdom itself. In dependence on others, a Buddha also perceives impure phenomena which have as their final cause afflicted ignorance (the conception that phenomena inherently exist) and non-afflicted ignorance (the appearance of these phenomena as if inherently existent).

Based on the accumulation of inconceivable merit for untellable eons and based on repeated, inconceivable, powerful wishes while a Bodhisattva, an Enjoyment Body continuously displays countless Emanation Bodies that appear in accordance with the dispositions of beings and act for the sake of furthering their aims of attaining high status as humans and as gods and attaining the definite goodness of liberation and omniscience. Spontaneously and without thought a Buddha, like a wish-granting jewel, achieves the aims of beings but does not stir for an instant from the sphere of the final nature of phenomena.

There are three main types of Emanation Bodies:

1 artisans, such as a guitarist, goldsmith, or scribe
2 constructions, such as a tree or a deer
3 supreme beings, who display the twelve activities of a Bodhisattva who becomes a Buddha.

Responding to sentient beings' needs throughout time and space, Emanation Bodies appear, perform their task without effort, and are withdrawn. A sentient being's noticing or not noticing them as such depends on his fortune which is formed through the potencies established on the mind by his virtuous and non-virtuous deeds. As long as space exists, the various activities of a Buddha, arising from great compassion, come into existence spontaneously and continuously.

Part Two
Reasoning into Reality

Introduction

Sources
Jang-gya's *Presentation of Tenets*
Jam-yang-shay-ba's *Great Exposition of the Middle Way*
Geshe Gedün Lodrö's oral teachings
Corresponding section of the translation pp.636-8

Phenomena are divided into persons and phenomena, with the latter 'phenomena' meaning 'phenomena other than persons'.[76] Objects are so divided because adherence to the inherent existence of persons and adherence to the inherent existence of other internal phenomena, such as the body, are the two principal binders of beings in cyclic existence. Persons are enjoyers or users, and other phenomena are the enjoyed or the used.

The non-inherent existence of persons is the personal selflessness (*pudgalanairātmya*), and the non-inherent existence of other phenomena, such as mind, body, hand, house, and mountain, is the selflessness of other phenomena (*dharmanairātmya*). The two selflessnesses—of persons and of other phenomena—are not divided by way of different objects of negation—different interpretations of 'self'—but by way of classes of objects that are the bases of the quality of non-inherent existence.

The Mahāyāna schools other than Prāsaṅgika do not divide the two selflessnesses this way. For the Chittamātrins and Svātantrikas, the selflessness of phenomena (non-difference of entity of object and subject for the Chittamātrins and non-true existence for the Svātantrikas) applies to all phenomena including persons. For them, the selflessness of phenomena is subtler than the selflessness of persons, and thus the personal selflessness can be realized without realizing the subtler selflessness of phenomena. They assert a difference of intelligence between Hearers, who meditate mainly on the personal selflessness, and Bodhisattvas, who meditate on the subtler selflessness of phenomena.

For the Prāsaṅgikas, the two selflessnesses are equally subtle and an inferential realization of one yields an ability to realize the other. Furthermore, when emptiness is directly cognized, all emptinesses are directly cognized, and, therefore, even Hearers and Solitary Realizers on the path of seeing cognize the subtle emptiness of all phenomena directly.[77] Still, Bodhisattvas are said to be more intelligent than Hearers in the sense that they approach emptiness from many and various points of view, as in the twenty-seven chapters of Nāgārjuna's *Treatise on the Middle Way*, instead of through only one or two.[78]

There is a question as to whether the selflessness of persons in the Chittamātra and Svātantrika systems applies only to persons or to all phenomena.[79] This selflessness is the non-existence of a self-sufficient person, and some say that to speak of a 'person' with respect to a phenomenon such as a house is absurd. They say that the personal selflessness of phenomena other than persons refers to their not being objects of use of a self-sufficient person. Others say that phenomena other than persons do not have a self-sufficient entity separate from their parts and that this is their personal selflessness. Still others say that a meditator realizes the non-existence of a self-sufficient person with respect to the mental and physical aggregates, and then by extension realizes that other external phenomena are not a self-sufficient person. In any case, for the Chittamātrins and Svātantrikas, meditation on the personal selflessness is mainly based on the person but can be extended to a person's relationship with external phenomena. Meditation on external objects as not being objects of use of a self-sufficient person is said to be very helpful in breaking the web of relationships that support and nourish the conception of a self-sufficient person.

In the Chittamātra and Svātantrika systems the two selflessnesses differ in degree of subtlety; therefore, these systems have separate sets of reasonings to prove the different types of selflessness. The two selflessnesses in the Prāsaṅgika system do not differ in subtlety, but the Prāsaṅgikas still use separate sets of reasonings. The self of phenomena is refuted by the diamond slivers, refutation of production of the four extremes, and refutation of production of the four alternatives. The reasoning of dependent-arising refutes the self of both persons and other phenomena. The self of persons is refuted by the five-cornered and seven-cornered sets of reasonings.

The two sets of reasonings are divided not because they *exclusively* prove either persons or other phenomena to be selfless but because the various Mādhyamika masters have *mainly* used them this way.[80] A student is advised to apply the five-cornered and seven-cornered reasonings to all phenomena, and the three sets of reasonings that examine production can also be applied to persons.

Nāgārjuna

1 *The Diamond Slivers*

Sources
J̄ang-ḡya's *Presentation of Tenets*
Jam-ȳang-shay-b̄a's *Great Exposition of the Middle Way*
Nga-w̄ang-b̄el-den's *Annotations*
Geshe Gedün Lodrö's oral teachings
D̄zong-ka-b̄a's *Essence of the Good Explanations* and
Illumination of the Thought
Corresponding section of the translation pp.639-50

Nāgārjuna's *Treatise on the Middle Way* begins with an analysis of production that mainly refutes the inherent existence of products other than persons.[81] In the *Treatise* and in Chandrakīrti's *Supplement to (Nāgārjuna's) 'Treatise on the Middle Way'* the diamond slivers are the main means for approaching the absence of true production.

It is said that through understanding this absence of true production it is easy to understand the other nine of the ten samenesses of phenomena. Realization of the ten samenesses is explained in the *Sutra on the Ten Grounds* (*Dashabhūmika*) as the means by which a fifth ground Bodhisattva proceeds to the sixth ground. The ten samenesses are:

1 sameness of all phenomena as signless, or the sameness of all phenomena in the absence of signs such as white, red, and so on for a consciousness in meditative equipoise on the nature of phenomena
2 sameness of all phenomena as natureless, or as free from being established by way of their own nature
3 sameness of all phenomena as productionless, or as free from naturally existent production in the future
4 sameness of all phenomena as non-produced, or the sameness of all past and present phenomena as free from naturally existent production and cessation
5 sameness of all phenomena as vacuous, or the sameness of things yet to be produced and things already produced as void or empty of natural existence
6 sameness of all phenomena as pure from the start, or as purified of natural existence, not through scripture and reasoning, but from the start
7 sameness of all phenomena as free from the elaborations of thought, or as free from the elaborations of dualistic perception for a consciousness in meditative equipoise on the nature of phenomena
8 sameness of all phenomena in being ultimately non-adopted and non-discarded (as in the case of adopting virtues and discarding non-virtues)
9 sameness of all phenomena in being like a magician's illusions, dreams, shadows, echoes, moons in the water, reflections, and emanations, or in being empty of inherent existence as illustrated by these seven examples
10 sameness of all phenomena in not having the duality of things (*bhāva*) and non-things (*abhāva*), or the sameness of products in not inherently being things and of non-products in not inherently being non-things.

The seventh is an attribute of the first; the third, fourth, and fifth are attributes of the second; and the rest are attributes of both the first and the second.

Nāgārjuna chose to explain the sameness of non-production because through it the other samenesses are easily understood.

The main means that he chose to establish non-true production is the diamond slivers.

STATEMENT OF THE REASONS

The diamond slivers are so called because each is a powerful means of destroying the conception of inherent existence.[82] The reasoning is composed of a thesis:

> The subjects, things, are not inherently produced.

And a four-cornered proof:

> Because of not being produced from themselves, from naturally existent others, from both, or causelessly.

These four reasons are themselves each theses which are non-affirming negatives. They do not imply anything positive in their place, such as the *existence* of no production from self. Still, they do imply another non-affirming negative—that things are not inherently produced—because although non-affirming negatives lack positive implications, they can imply other non-affirming negatives of the same type. The reasoning which proves that things are not inherently produced does not establish that things are nominally or conventionally produced. The diamond slivers are non-affirming negatives, and just the *absence* of inherently existent production, not the *presence* of nominal production, is realized when inferring or directly cognizing the emptiness of production. The four negative theses do serve as proofs of another thesis—that things are not inherently produced—and thus their import can be stated syllogistically, as above.

The reason why no more than four negative theses are needed to prove that things are not inherently produced is that the four are refutations of all possibilities of true production. Production is either caused or uncaused. If caused, the cause and the effect are either the same entity, different entities, or both the same and different. Thus, the possibilities for inherently existent production, or production that can be found under analysis, are only four: production of an effect that is of the same entity as the cause, production of an effect that is a different entity from the cause, production of an effect that is both the same entity and a different entity from the cause, and causeless production. Because the possibilities of inherently existent production can be limited, when all possibilities have been refuted, inherently existent production has been perforce refuted, and the thesis of no inherently existent production can be realized. If the possibilities could not be limited, one would be forever waiting in a state of doubt for new possibilities, and the thesis could never be realized. Therefore, it is an important step in meditation to investigate and decide firmly, based on the above reasoning, that the possibilities have been limited to those stated and that if those can be refuted, the thesis will be proved.

Since production from imputedly existent others is the only existent type of production, when production from other is refuted under analysis, this alone establishes that things lack inherent existence. Still, it is necessary to examine the problem of production from the viewpoints of other philosophical systems, all of which can be included into these four modes. If three of these modes of production do not stand a chance conventionally, they could not possibly withstand ultimate analysis; however, persons and systems must be approached on their own grounds, and, therefore, all four positions are attacked.

A meditator seeks to generate a consciousness realizing that there is no inherently existent production, and, thus, refutations are not stated aimlessly. The generation of an inferential cognizer (*anumāṇapramāṇa, rjes dpag tshad ma*) depends on the establishment of the reasons and the fact that the predicate of the thesis, the absence of inherently existent production, follows from these reasons.

Still, the presence of the reasons (non-production from self and so forth) in the subject (things), the pervasion of the reasons by the predicate of the thesis (not being inherently produced), and the counter-pervasion do not have to be proved in the manner of the logicians through syllogisms. The Prāsaṅgikas' main means for generating an inferential consciousness is to state unwanted consequences of the four possibilities and thereby generate in an intelligent person a consciousness inferring the thesis that there is no inherently existent production. The Sautrāntikas, Chittamātrins, and Svātantrikas say that one must first state unwanted consequences in order to break the pointedness or vibrance of the opponent's adherence to his own view but that the consequences must be followed by a syllogistic statement. (The Vaibhāṣhikas are omitted here because of lack of information regarding their positions.)

Although the Prāsaṅgikas do not accept the need for this, Jam-ȳang-shay-b̄a does use the syllogistic mode to present the thesis and the four reasons for the sake of ease in explanation (see p.640). He takes as his subject 'things which have production', a seemingly redundant phrase because, in the strict use of the word, 'things' (*bhāva*) mean products.[83] The reason he qualifies 'things' with 'which have production' is that the Vaibhāṣhikas say that permanent phenomena are 'things'. As his annotator, Nga-w̄ang-b̄el-den, says, he wants to make sure that when he proves that things are not naturally produced, the Vaibhāṣhikas will not say, 'You are proving the already proved because we agree that permanent things are not produced.' The Prāsaṅgikas are proving to the non-Buddhist schools and the other Buddhist schools that impermanent things are not inherently produced. Since the Svātantrikas assert that conventionally things are inherently produced, they are included in the opposition.

The thesis of no production from other is qualified as no production from *naturally existent* others because conventionally things are produced from causes that are other than themselves but do not naturally exist. (The remaining three possibilities do not require qualification because, unlike production from what is merely other, they do not exist even conventionally.) If the qualification were not given for production from other, then there would be no production at all, and this would deny the cause and effect of actions and result in an utter nihilism. Still, some non-Ge-luk-b̄a interpreters say that the qualification is unnecessary either because phenomena are unpredicable dependent-ariṣings or because there is no need to present production in Mādhyamika itself because the Mādhyamikas have no system. D̄zong-ka-b̄a's position[84] is that the Mādhyamikas obviously have a system; he explains that when Chandrakīrti says that production from other does not exist either ultimately or conventionally, he means that production *which can be found under analysis* does not exist even conventionally. The meaning of 'naturally existent production' implies 'production which can be found under analysis', and thus the qualification is necessary in order to eliminate the mistake that mere production from causes that are other is being refuted. Chandrakīrti in his *Clear Words* (*Prasannapadā*) often predicates his refutations with 'under such analysis' lending credence to D̄zong-ka-b̄a's view.[85]

At issue is the best means of leading students—whom all accept as not knowing the difference between naturally existent production and production—to the Mādhyamika realization of no production without utterly destroying the possibility of illusory-like production. The criticism of D̄zong-ka-b̄a seems mainly based on the feeling that the qualification of production from other with 'naturally existent' would keep students from realizing the startling import of the Mādhyamika sense of no production. Many non-Ge-luk-b̄as seem to feel that the brilliant philosophical subtlety of D̄zong-ka-b̄a's view is beyond comprehension and thus obscures the path. However, D̄zong-ka-b̄a himself says[86] that beings who have not entered the Mādhyamika view cannot discriminate between conventional existence and inherent existence; thus, his affirmation of the valid establishment of conventional existence should not be taken as confirming the common ignorant misconceptions of the nature of existence. The meaning of conventional or imputed existence must be sought as something new; otherwise, the very reason for D̄zong-ka-ba's subtle presentation of cause and effect and so forth in the Mādhyamika system will be lost. He calls his followers to realize that even conventionally the validly established phenomena of the world are not their bases of designation.

NON-PRODUCTION FROM SELF

The refutation of production of something from self, or from its own entity, is done through demonstrating the consequent absurdity of senseless production:[87]

> The production again of a sprout is senseless because of having already achieved its own entity. Since the production of a thing means the attainment of its own entity, then if once having achieved its own entity, it is produced again, its re-production is purposeless.

The opponent answers:

> Having already attained its own entity and needing production are not contradictory.

His thought is that a sprout, for instance, has attained its own entity in its unmanifest state (in its causes) but still requires production in the sense of manifestation.

This is refuted by the absurdity of endless production:

> If so, then sprouts, and so forth would be produced again and again because though they have achieved their own entity, they must be produced.

The opponent might answer:

> That which exists non-manifestly as a potential entity must be produced manifestly, but once it has been manifested, it need not be produced. Therefore, both the former and latter consequences do not follow from the reasons given.

The Sāṃkhyas cannot extricate themselves from error this way, for if a manifestation exists from the start, it need not be produced. Also, if a manifestation were reproduced, then its production would be endless. Thus, the fallacies remain. If a manifestation did not exist from the start, one has let fall the position that only what exists formerly in the cause is produced.

Since the already produced—that which has already achieved its own entity—must be produced again, there would be no opportunity for the production of effects, such as sprouts, because the causes, seeds, would be produced endlessly. There is no point in something's being produced from itself.

A Sāṃkhya might respond:

> The natures of both the seed and the sprout are a partless one, but the transformations as seed and sprout are different. Therefore, from the viewpoint of the transformations, the seed disintegrates and the sprout is produced. It is not asserted that a sprout is produced from a sprout. So, there is no fallacy.

A Mādhyamika answers:

> It follows that a sprout would not cause its seed to disintegrate because the natures of the seed and the sprout are one. For example, a sprout cannot cause a sprout to disintegrate.

Though the Sāṃkhya himself does not assert that a sprout is produced from a sprout, his position that the natures of both the seed and the sprout are a partless one forces him to accept the absurdity that the appearance of a sprout could not cause the disintegration of its seed because they are a partless one.

Furthermore, there is a refutation of the oneness of the natures of the seed and the sprout:

> It follows that a seed and its sprout would not have different shape, color, taste, powers, and fruition because the natures of the seed and its sprout are one in all respects.

A Sāṃkhya might respond:

> The natures of the seed and its sprout are one, but their states are different; therefore, the state of the seed is abandoned when the state of the sprout is assumed.

Answer:

> It follows that the nature of a seed is not the nature of its sprout because when the phenomenon of the state of the seed is done away with, there is the phenomenon of the state of a sprout. It so follows because the phenomenon of the state of the seed is the phenomenon of the seed and there is no phenomenon of the seed other than the entity of the seed.

Further, there is an unwanted consequence of the mutuality of apprehension of both seed and sprout in each state:

> Just as during the state of the sprout the seed is not apprehendable by a sense consciousness, so it follows that the sprout would be non-apprehendable.

Further:

> Just as during the state of the sprout the sprout is apprehendable by a sense consciousness, so it follows that the seed would also be apprehendable. For, the entity of the seed and the entity of the sprout are one in all respects.

Because these consequences cannot be accepted, one should not assert that the natures of the seed and the sprout are one.

All Buddhist schools except Vaibhāṣhika accept that in general an existent is produced and that what is non-existent prior to its production is produced or attains an existent entity.[88] Vaibhāṣhika is omitted because this school asserts that at the time of the seed the future of the sprout exists and that at the time of the sprout the past of the seed exists and, for them, the future of the sprout is a sprout and the past of the seed is a seed. Their view is that things cannot be produced from what does not exist earlier because of the unwanted consequence that production would be adventitious and causeless. Therefore, they assert that an effect exists at the time of its future, which occurs previous to the aggregation of its causes and conditions. The aggregation of its causes and conditions produces the sprout at the time of its present. Thereby, the entity abides before and after its production.

All other Buddhist schools—Sautrāntika, Chittamātra, and Mādhyamika—consider Vaibhāṣhika to be almost like Sāṃkhya on this point. All Buddhist schools except Vaibhāṣhika say that at the time of the seed the sprout is the seed; at that time, the sprout is not a sprout; the sprout does not then exist.[89] The horns of a rabbit[90] (an example of an utter non-existent) also do not exist at that time, but the difference between the horns of a rabbit and a sprout is that at the time of its seed a sprout abides as the entity of a seed even though it is non-existent. If the sprout were existent, it could not abide as the entity of its seed because it would be a sprout. The Sāṃkhya view is that only the existent can be produced; thus, the Buddhist sense that effects abide as the entity of causes but are non-existent at the time of their causes differs greatly. Just as the yogurt in a bowl is not produced from the bowl, so that which already exists in something is not produced from that something.

NON-PRODUCTION FROM OTHER

There are three ways of refuting production of effects from causes that are inherently other than those effects:[91]

1 refuting both inherently existent otherness and inherently existent production
2 refuting inherently existent production
3 refuting inherently existent otherness.

Refuting both inherently existent otherness and inherently existent production

> It follows that thick darkness arises from a tongue of flame and that any effect arises from what are commonly considered to be its causes or non-causes because inherently other effects arise in dependence on inherently other causes.

If causes and effects were inherently existent others, then they would not be dependently existent others but would be non-related others. If an effect were produced from a cause that is an unrelated other, it is the same as allowing that it could be produced from everything that is conventionally considered not to be its causes because they are equally other than the effect. In the same way, if a cause produced an effect that is an unrelated other, it is the same as allowing that a cause could also produce any entity, such as darkness being produced from a lamp.

A proponent of production from other might object:

This consequence does not apply; though cause and effect are inherently other, an effect which a cause is able to produce is the effect of that cause, and a cause which is able to produce that effect is the cause of that effect. A sprout of rice is not produced from a barley seed and is not produced from its non-producers, such as the future moments of its own continuum. A sprout of rice is produced from that which is included in its same continuum and from producers that are prior to it. Therefore, everything is not produced from everything.

Answer:

This is not correct; once cause and effect are inherently other, this otherness must be their mode of being. Once otherness is their mode of being, they must be utterly non-related. Thus, it is not possible for a rice seed and a barley seed to be different with respect to whether they can produce a shoot of rice or not because they both are inherently other than a rice shoot.

Further:

A seed is not inherently other than a sprout because a seed has no inherently existent otherness. It so follows because if a seed were inherently other than its sprout, then it could not be a dependent existent or nominal other. It would necessarily have a separate entity of otherness such as is mistakenly propounded by the Vaisheṣhikas.

Further:

A seed and its sprout are not inherently other because a sprout does not exist simultaneously with its seed. It so follows because if they existed inherently, they would neither depend on nor be affected by anything. They would never disappear, and thus the sprout would have to exist even at the time of the seed. However, they do not exist simultaneously because without a transformation

> of the seed there is no production of a sprout. Thus, a seed and its sprout are not inherently other, and production of a sprout from a seed does not exist inherently. For this reason, one should forsake the thesis that things are produced from inherently existent others.

Refuting inherently existent production

> If the entities of the phenomena that are effects, such as sprouts, do not exist in their causes either collectively or individually or as things other than their causes, then the entities of the effects to be produced do not exist prior to their production. If so, how could production from other exist?

An effect would have to exist prior to its production if production existed inherently. Once production is accepted, the cause's approaching cessation and the effect's approaching production are simultaneous, as it is even in the Prāsaṅgika's own presentation of conventionally existent production.[92] The activity of approaching production depends on the effect because it is the effect that is approaching production. If production were findable under analysis, then, whenever the activity of approaching production existed, the base of this activity, the sprout, would have to exist. For, the two are in a relation of supported and supporter, and since this is their nature, it cannot change.

The activity of approaching production exists at the time of the cause's approaching cessation, and since the effect must exist along with its activity, the seed and the sprout would have to exist simultaneously. This is impossible because simultaneity would rule out that the one produced the other. If the sprout were already existent, what could a seed do to produce it?

Still, if a seed produces something, this something that is growing forth must exist, but if it already exists, how can it be said that the seed produces it?

If they do not exist simultaneously, how can it be said that production exists inherently? For, the activity of approaching production and that thing which is approaching production would have to exist simultaneously if production were findable. How could there be growing without the thing that is growing?

Someone might object:

> It is seen that one end of a scale moves downward at the same time that the other end moves upward. Just as these activities exist simultaneously, the activities of approaching cessation and of approaching production exist simultaneously. Thereby, it is shown that seed and sprout exist simultaneously.

Answer:

> Even if the activities of the rising and lowering of the two ends of a scale exist simultaneously, a seed and a sprout are not similar because they do not exist simultaneously, and, thus, their activities do not exist simultaneously. A sprout's state of presently being produced is its approaching production; therefore, it does not exist at that time. A seed's present ceasing is its approaching cessation; even though the seed is existent, in the next moment it will not exist. Therefore, a sprout and its seed do not exist simultaneously and are not similar to the two ends of a scale.

Buddha used the example of the scale in the *Rice Seedling Sutra* (*Shālistamba*) to show that these two actions exist simultaneously as dependent-arisings, when there is no analysis, like a magician's illusions.

Refuting inherently existent otherness

> If the effect's own entity does not exist at the time of the cause, then there is no referent in relation to which the causes could become 'other'. Thus, there is no phenomenon of otherness in seeds and so forth, and so no production from other.

Someone might try to avoid this fallacy by stating:

> Though there is no inherently existent otherness in what

> does not exist simultaneously, since cause and effect exist simultaneously and are other, there is production from other.

Answer:

> What already exists has no need for production.

Errors concerning the refutation of production from other

Many interpreters of Mādhyamika think that since two things that are other must exist simultaneously in order to be other and since cause and effect necessarily exist at different times, the production of an effect from a cause other than it is impossible.[93] D̄zong-ka-b̄a rejects this interpretation of the Prāsaṅgika refutation of production from other because the very faults that are ascribed to others by the Prāsaṅgikas would apply to themselves. In other words, since the Prāsaṅgikas assert cause and effect conventionally, they must also assert that conventionally cause and effect exist at different times and that cause and effect are other. If the Prāsaṅgikas refuted all otherness in what do not exist simultaneously, it would be impossible for them to present cause and effect.

Therefore, the refutation of production from other refers not to other in general but to 'inherently existent other'. When this is refuted, mere analytically unfindable, conventional otherness of cause and effect is not refuted, and cause and effect can be presented without fault.

If *analytically findable* production from other existed, then an effect would have to exist at the time of its causes in order for its causes to be other than it, and since cause and effect are necessarily serial, analytically findable otherness cannot obtain between them. Thus, D̄zong-ka-b̄a objects to other interpreters' failure to delineate inherently existent otherness as the object of refutation.

It is necessary to present the reasoning that refutes inherently existent production in such a way that it does not harm one's own presentation of conventional phenomena. For instance, it is said that the action of approaching production can exist *conventionally* without the existence of the sprout that is approaching production, much the same as a seed and a sprout do not exist simultaneously even though they are related.[94] Conventionally, a seed is the source or object related to and its sprout is the relater; however, both do not have to exist simultaneously within the context of analytically unfindable nominalities. It is necessary to distinguish between what constitutes ultimate analysis and what constitutes conventional analysis. Making complicated distinctions does not necessarily constitute ultimate analysis. Here, ultimate analysis is a searching for an otherness that can bear analysis, such as investigating whether the something in relation to which a thing is called 'other' is present or not.

Seeing all analysis as ultimate analysis, many interpreters of Prāsaṅgika say that the Mādhyamikas themselves have no presentation of cause and effect; thus, they think that it is not necessary to qualify production from other with 'inherently existent'. For D̄zong-ka-b̄a, production exists conventionally and validly, and production from the merely other must be accepted because the remaining three possibilities—self, both, and causelessly—are absurd. Therefore, the refutation of production from other must be qualified as 'production from inherently existent other'. From his viewpoint many Mādhyamika interpreters have overextended the scope of Nāgārjuna's refutations.

It is a cardinal point in the systems of interpreters of Prāsaṅgika who do not accept valid establishment that Prāsaṅgikas assert nothing themselves but use only the inner contradictions of others' assertions to refute them. Thus, some Tibetan scholars say that Prāsaṅgikas hold that a reason is not validly established for both parties in a debate because the stater would not know what was validly established for his opponent since he would not know the other's mind either through direct perception or inference. They add that he himself would not know what was validly established because even when one has 'decided' that something is validly established, error is possible.

D̄zong-ka-b̄a answers that if such an interpretation of Prāsaṅgika were true, then Prāsaṅgikas could not refute others from the point of view of others' own assertions because they would not know what the others actually asserted since they would not know others' minds. They could not state refutations of others because even though they had 'decided' that something is a refutation, it is possible to be mistaken.

These same interpreters of Prāsaṅgika say that pervasion of a reason by a predicate cannot be validly established because through direct perception one only realizes, for instance, that the existence of fire pervades the existence of smoke in a specific place, such as a kitchen. One does not realize that the existence of fire pervades the instances of smoke in all places and at all times. They say that an inferring consciousness cannot realize the pervasion because it would have to cognize all phenomena in order to certify that all instances of smoke in all places and all times are pervaded by the existence of fire. Therefore, they say that there is no valid establishment of the pervasion of a reason (presence of smoke) by a predicate (presence of fire); they say that there is only pervasion that accords with the conventions of the world.

D̄zong-ka-b̄a answers that this is extremely wrong. When one inferentially realizes that on a mountain pass there is fire because of the presence of smoke, as in a kitchen, the pervasion is not of a particular instance of smoke by a particular instance of fire. Rather, the generality 'fire' is realized as pervading the generality 'smoke'. If it were taken that the pervasion referred to fire on a pass pervading smoke on a pass, then, when this pervasion is realized, the thesis would already be realized. In other words, when it is determined that fire on a pass pervades smoke on a pass, one would already have realized the thesis—'On the pass there is fire.'

Furthermore, examples are given in order to facilitate realization of the same predicate, and, therefore, the predicate of the thesis which is implied in the example ('as in a kitchen') must be the same as in the main thesis, 'there is fire'. If the predicate of the example were specified as kitchen-fire, then the main thesis would absurdly have to read, 'on the pass there is kitchen-fire'. Rather, D̄zong-ka-b̄a says that the subject ('on the pass') is the base with respect to which one realizes the presence of fire because of the presence of smoke and that this base should not be confused with the predicate of the thesis ('there is fire') through making it into 'there is pass-fire'.

According to D̄zong-ka-b̄a, scholars who reject valid inference on the basis of the requirement of having to realize the pervasion of a specific reason by a specific predicate do not understand the Buddhist position on the subject. Rather than using good reasoning, they use a mass of coercives that are exactly alike in their lack of force. He says that they are similar to those who have fallen into a river and are trying to save themselves by grasping at floating grass. Though a specific smoke is seen on the pass, the pervasion based on which one realizes the specific thesis is a general pervasion.

The S̄a-ḡya scholar D̄ak-tsang (*sTag-tshang*) refuted D̄zong-ka-b̄a saying that it is contradictory to accept that seed and sprout are different substantial entities (*dravya*) and then not accept 'production from other'.[95] Jam-ȳang-shay-b̄a turns the same reasoning back on D̄ak-tsang, saying that D̄ak-tsang then must accept production from other because the latter implies that he accepts that the 'other' of 'production from other' means just an otherness of entity and not 'inherently existent others'.

D̄zong-ka-b̄a's assertion is that seed and sprout are other entities and that a sprout is produced from its seed. However, this does not constitute an assertion of 'production from other' because the 'other' of 'production from other' means 'inherently existent other'. D̄ak-tsang himself does not accept that seed and sprout are even 'other', but Jam-ȳang-shay-b̄a thinks that D̄ak-tsang is 'forced' to assert this because the term 'substantial entity' is a part of common analysis. Since cause and effect must be accepted conventionally and since they must be accepted as other substantial entities, D̄ak-tsang must accept production from other if he says that 'other' means just 'other substantial entities' rather than 'inherently existent others'.

D̄ak-tsang then would contradict the many dictums of the Prāsaṅgika system which say that both ultimately and conventionally production from other is not asserted. D̄ak-tsang, however, is quite aware that production from other cannot be accepted even conventionally. For him, it is Ḏzong-ka-ḇa who breaks the dictum by applying analysis and then accepting that cause and effect are different entities.

Ḏzong-ka-ḇa's answer probably is that once dependently arisen production is accepted, it must be asked whether cause and effect are the same entity or different entities. If it is unsuitable to ask about sameness of entity or difference of entity, or mere self and other, it would be tantamount to saying that any analysis of the terms 'self' and 'other' would immediately involve ultimate analysis, even in cases of looking into whether something done several years ago was done by oneself or another.

Once valid establishment of conventional production is accepted, production must be explained as involving causes and effects which are either the same or different. If it cannot be said that cause and effect are merely other, the whole presentation of reasoning and valid establishment falls to the ground. Ḏzong-ka-ḇa's followers cogently say that analysis into whether an apple seed and the tree that will grow from it are merely different is just conventional analysis.[96] Any further investigation into whether they are totally unrelated and so forth would constitute ultimate analysis and would exceed the sphere of the conventional. Thus, the 'other' of 'production from other' refers to others that can be found under analysis. Conventionally existent inherent otherness is also refuted, but mere conventionally existent otherness is not.

Still, when a mother says, 'I gave birth to a boy,' this is not accepted as a case of production from self. Although from the mother's viewpoint her son is produced from herself, conventionally she and her son are other. The world's merely saying something does not make it conventionally existent; reasoned, systematic analysis is not forbidden.

NON-PRODUCTION FROM BOTH SELF AND OTHER

The theistic Sāṃkhyas assert that all transformations are produced from the nature (*prākṛti*) which is the same entity as its transformations, as well as from the god Īshvara, who is other than the transformations.[97] Therefore, all transformations are produced from both self and other.

The Jainas assert that, for example, a man named Maitreya who already existed as a living being (*jīva*) in a former life took re-birth, and thus, Maitreya is produced from himself since Maitreya and his living being are not other.[98] Also, Maitreya is produced from that which is other than himself—parents, virtue, non-virtue, contaminations, and so forth—therefore, he is also produced from the other. In the same way, a pot is the same entity as the clay but a different entity from the potter's activities.

These assertions might seem to combine the advantages of production from self and production from other; however, they also accrue the fallacies of both. Each part of the dual assertion is refuted by the respective refutations of production from self and production from other already given.

NON-PRODUCTION CAUSELESSLY

The Nihilists do not assert that there is utterly no caused production because causation that can be observed, such as the making of a pot, does exist. However, the sharpness of thorns, the plunging downward of water-falls, the colors of flowers, and so forth are said to be causeless, arising just by the nature of the entity.[99] They draw the conclusion that making effort at ethics is a waste of precious time because no moral carry-over from one lifetime to another is seen. Not being seen, such causation does not exist.

The Buddhists say that the sharpness of thorns is produced from the same seeds that produce the thorns.[100] The ascertainment that the sharpness of thorns arises sometimes in some places is a proof that they are produced in dependence on other entities, and these entities upon which they depend are called causes.

If things were uncaused, the planting of fields and the like would be senseless because things would arise themselves.

Anything could arise from anything. If the production of things were adventitious, then just as a bread-fruit tree, for instance, would not be the cause of its own fruit, so because all things, such as lemon and mango trees, are also not causes of bread-fruit, bread-fruit would be produced from them because they are equally non-causes in relation to bread-fruit.[101]

CONCLUSION

The four possibilities of inherently existent production are thereby proved to be non-existent.[102] It is thus established that things are not inherently produced. This, in turn, establishes that products do not exist inherently because for products to exist inherently they would have to be inherently produced. Realization of the absence of inherently existent production of a product is a realization of its emptiness.

Refutations of the views of philosophical systems on the four possibilities of inherently existent production are not just refutations of rival systems but should be taken as a branch of the process of overcoming one's own innate sense that things are inherently produced.[103] The innate non-analytical intellect does not conceive cause and effect to be either the same, or inherently different, or both, or neither; however, if the objects that the intellect misconceives as inherently existent did in fact inherently exist, they would necessarily exist in one of these four ways. Thus, through eliminating these four possibilities, the inherently existent products that are the objects of this innate ignorance are shown to be non-existent. By attacking in this way the falsely conceived object, the falsely conceiving subject is gradually overcome. The false subject is removed by overcoming belief in the false object.

Actual realization of an emptiness of inherent production transforms a person's view of the world and frees him or her from the chains of attachment toward products. Ultimately, direct cognition of emptiness in a totally non-dual manner elevates one to the level of a Superior, and through continuous cultivation of this cognition cyclic existence—the beginningless round of birth, aging, sickness, and death—is terminated.

2 *The Four Extremes*

Sources
Nga-w̄ang-b̄el-den's *Annotations*
Chandrakīrti's *Commentary on the 'Supplement'*
Corresponding sections of the translation pp.651-3

Does a cause produce an effect which is existent, non-existent, both, or neither?[104] This analysis is a refutation of the four extremes but can also be called a refutation of the four alternatives. (The diamond slivers can also be called a refutation of the four extremes and a refutation of the four alternatives simply because there are four extremes or four alternatives considered.)[105] As above, the possibilities for inherently existent production are limited to four, and when these four are eliminated, the absence of inherently existent production is established.

The reasoning in brief is:[106]

> An existent effect is not ultimately produced because whatever exists ultimately must always exist, and thus there would be no need for producers, that is, causes.
>
> A non-existent effect is not ultimately produced because if a non-existent effect were produced, the horns of a rabbit could also be produced.

> An effect which is both existent and non-existent is not produced because there is no such thing as an existent and non-existent effect; no one thing possesses contradictory natures.
>
> An effect which is neither existent nor non-existent is not produced because there is no such thing.

Or, in another way:

> A sprout which is in all ways existent at the time of its causes is not produced by causes and conditions because causes and conditions cannot create anything that already exists.
>
> A sprout is not ultimately produced newly because of not existing at the time of its causes, just as a lotus in the sky, which is utterly non-existent, does not exist at the time of its causes and is not newly produced.

An effect, if ultimately existent, must exist at the time of its causes because whatever is ultimately produced must always exist since if at any time it did not exist, it would ultimately be non-existent forever. The ultimately existent is not fit to depend on causes and conditions; hence, there could be no difference between production when the causes and conditions are complete and non-production when the causes and conditions are non-complete.

Also, an effect would have to exist at the time of its causes because the action of the growing forth of an effect such as a sprout must depend on the sprout. Thus, at the time when the sprout is approaching production (which is the same time that its seed is approaching cessation), the sprout which is the base of the activity of growing forth must exist. Since the cause has not yet ceased at that time, both would exist at the same time.

Chandrakīrti says in his *Commentary on the 'Supplement'*:[107]

> Now, there is no time when a cause, from among cause and effect, depends on an effect [and thus could achieve otherness with respect to an effect]. In order to show this,

it is said [in the *Supplement*, VI.21], 'If producers are causes producing products other [than themselves], it is to be considered whether they produce an existent, non-existent, that which is both, or that which is neither. If it exists, of what use are producers? What could these producers do for the non-existent? What could they do for that which is neither?'

Causes, that is, producers, are not producers of an existent product because of the fallacies already set forth, such as, 'It is just not reasonable that what has already been produced be produced again.'[108] Thus, there is no need at all of causes [for what already exists].

Also, what could these producers do for a non-existent product?[109] It would be non-existent like the horns of an ass.

It is said, 'For whoever asserts that the effect is existent and for whoever asserts that the effect is non-existent, it would be senseless to set pillars and so forth for a house.'

Nāgārjuna's *Treatise on the Middle Way* [XX.21-22] also says:

If the entity of the effect exists,
What will a cause produce?
If the entity of the effect does not exist,
What will a cause produce?

If it is not producing,
A cause is not possible.
If causes are not existent,
Of what would there be an effect?

Even if an effect were both existent and non-existent, what could causes do for it? For, the fallacies previously set forth would follow. 'Bothness' [here] is a thing that is both, or that which exists as both [existent and non-existent]. Possession of the entities of existence and non-existence does not occur in one thing at one time. Therefore, a thing that has such a nature does not exist. Because it is just not existent, what could causes which are producers do for it?

The *Treatise* [XXV.14] says:

How could nirvana
Be both a thing and a non-thing?
These two do not exist in one,
Like light and darkness.

Just so [VIII.7]:

An existent and non-existent doer
Does not do an existent and non-existent [doing].
How could one [entity] have existence and non-existence
Which are mutually exclusive?

Also, what could causes do for an effect which is neither existent nor non-existent? For, an effect that has forsaken the entities of existence and non-existence does not exist. If the existent and non-existent do not occur, that which is both not existent and not non-existent, being the negative of these, would not be any different. When these two are not established, that which is both not existent and not non-existent just does not occur.

The *Treatise* [XXV.15] says:

The teaching of nirvana
As [both] not a thing and not a non-thing
Would be established
If things and non-things were established.

Chandrakīrti applies this refutation of the four extremes to various types of production from other, and Nāgārjuna and Atīsha extend its import to include a refutation of inherently existent abiding and ceasing. For, once there is no inherently existent production, how could there be inherently existent abiding or ceasing?

3 *The Four Alternatives*

Sources
Nga-w̄ang-b̄el-den's *Annotations*
Geshe Gedün Lodrö's oral teachings
Corresponding section of the translation pp.653-8

The principal Indian source for the refutation of the four alternatives is the Svātantrika Jñānagarbha's *Discrimination of the Two Truths* (*Satyadvayavibhaṅga*) and his own commentary.[110] Not finding any Prāsaṅgika sources, many scholars, including J̄ang-ḡya, do not accept this reasoning as Prāsaṅgika.[111] It is not that the import of the refutation of the four alternatives cannot be considered Prāsaṅgika but a question of whether this reasoning is emphasized sufficiently among Indian Prāsaṅgikas to be considered an integral part of their system.

Jam-ȳang-shay-b̄a, however, lists it as one of the Prāsaṅgikas' means of refuting the inherent existence of phenomena, saying that the reasoning refuting the four alternatives is so attractive that it literally captivates the mind of the intelligent (see p.654). It is:[112]

A product such as an eye consciousness is not ultimately

> produced because ultimately only one effect is not produced from only one cause, ultimately many effects are not produced from only one cause, ultimately only one effect is not produced from many causes, and ultimately many effects are not produced from many causes.

The very meaning of production mitigates against ultimate existence because 'ultimately existing' means 'existing through its own power'. If an entity's existence depends on production, the entity does not exist through its own power. Still, one's mind will not be captivated by this interesting reasoning unless one probes the refutation further. The establishment of the four-cornered reason must be investigated thoroughly in order to gain its import.

An eye consciousness is chosen as the example because the three causes of the production of an eye consciousness are well known in Buddhist literature. An eye consciousness is caused by three factors: a visible form, an eye sense power, and a former moment of consciousness. A visible object—color and shape—causes an eye consciousness to be produced in the image of that object. An eye sense power causes an eye consciousness to have the ability to apprehend colors and shapes and not sounds, odors, and so forth. A former moment of consciousness causes an eye consciousness to be a conscious entity. In other words, the ability of an eye consciousness to apprehend visible objects is derived from its respective sense; its being generated in the image of a particular object is caused by a particular visible form; its being conscious is caused by a previous moment of consciousness.

The refutation of the first alternative, that ultimately only one effect is produced from only one cause, is based on the fact that an eye sense power not only produces an eye consciousness but also produces its own next moment.

> If it were said that the single effect produced by an eye sense power is only its own second moment, it would absurdly follow that all beings would be blind because the production of an eye consciousness from an eye sense power would not occur.

> If it were said that an eye sense power produces only an eye consciousness, it would absurdly follow that all beings would be blind because there would be no continuous production of two moments of an eye sense.

The first moment of the eye sense would generate an eye consciousness, but because there would be no second moment of the eye sense, a second moment of eye consciousness would be non-existent, and an ordinary being cannot realize anything in just one moment.

The refutation of the second alternative, that ultimately many effects are produced from only one cause, is accomplished through three absurd consequences:

> It would absurdly follow that:
> 1 the experiential aspect of an eye consciousness would not be the imprint or effect of an immediately preceding moment of consciousness
> 2 the aspect which is the image's generation in the consciousness would not be the effect of the visible form
> 3 the aspect of an eyc consciousness which is its ability to apprehend a particular type of object would not be the effect of an eye sense power, its special empowering cause.

The reason is that ultimately only one cause would produce many effects, and only one cause would be assigned for these three effects.

The refutation of the third alternative, that ultimately only one effect is produced from many causes, is:

> It absurdly follows that only one of the three attributes of an eye consciousness is produced by the three causes of an eye consciousness. Therefore, it absurdly follows that the other two attributes either do not exist or are produced causelessly.

The fourth alternative, that ultimately many effects are produced from many causes, is the most likely alternative, and its refutation is many-sided:

> It might be said that a composite of the three causes ultimately produces the three attributes and that the three attributes are not ultimately different but only appear to the mind to be different. Then, because they would actually exist one way but appear another way, they would be false and thus could not be truly existent. Further, if the three attributes are not different and do not appear to be different to any mind, the three attributes would be one, and it could not be said that many causes produce many effects.
>
> If the three attributes are ultimately different, it would follow that an eye consciousness and the three attributes of an eye consciousness would be ultimately different. Then, since the composite of the three causes produces the three attributes, one would have to find a cause for the consciousness which is different from them. Furthermore, an eye consciousness and its three attributes are not ultimately different because if they were, the wisdom realizing suchness would have to perceive them as different since difference would be their mode of being, but it does not.
>
> Moreover, an eye consciousness would be produced by a visible form because its being generated in the image of the object is produced by the form. Also, an eye consciousness would not be produced by a visible form because its being a conscious entity is not produced from a visible form. An eye consciousness is not a different entity from its attribute of being produced in the image of its object and also it is not a different entity from its attribute of being a conscious entity. Therefore, it would be both produced from a visible form and not produced from a visible form.

The pivot around which these consequences turn is that if an eye consciousness were ultimately the same entity as its attributes, it would be one with its attributes in all respects. Such are the conditions that an object findable under analysis must fulfill; if the sameness of an eye consciousness with its attributes is its inherent nature, how could it also be different from these attributes?

In the same vein:

> A visible form absurdly would be both a producer and a non-producer of an eye consciousness. It would produce an eye consciousness because it generates the consciousness in its image, and it would not produce an eye consciousness because it does not generate its quality of being conscious.
>
> If the three attributes are produced from the composite of the three causes, then the causes individually would not be producers. If the three causes are individually the producers, then the effect, the eye consciousness, would be uncaused because only the three attributes of an eye consciousness would be caused. If it is asserted that the three causal factors produce an eye consciousness, then the eye consciousness which is not different from its three different attributes would be uncaused. For, the three attributes would be uncaused, and the eye consciousness is not different from them.

It is said that not finding things such as cause and effect under analysis is somewhat like searching a room from top to bottom for a big, obvious thing such as a good-sized box.[113] One is not able to find it, and the search generates utter conviction that it cannot be found. This analytical consciousness which does not find objects is a wisdom consciousness. Through cultivating it, realization dawns, revealing how objects are utterly unfindable when analyzed in such a manner but are imputedly existent, effective, and validly established.

ELIMINATION OF ERROR

Because these four types of production do exist conventionally, it is necessary that the qualification 'ultimately', 'inherently', or 'naturally' be affixed to the refutations. Otherwise, the scope of the refutation would be over-extended. In the Prāsaṅgika system there is nominal production of one from one, many from one, one from many, and many from many.

The best source for showing that one producing one and so forth exist conventionally is in sutra where it is taught that (1) one action can produce one life, (2) one action can produce many lives, (3) many actions can produce one life, and (4) many actions can produce many lives (see p.657). It could be asked whether a single life is only one effect, but such investigations into whether a series can rightly be considered a unit or not is a mode of ultimate analysis. When the continuum of a lifetime is sought in the individual moments of the continuum, it cannot be found. The continuum is not the individual moments nor their composite; if a continuum were a composite of the moments, either each moment would be a continuum or there would be no separate moments.

Conventionally, or nominally, cause and effect are preserved. It is said that just as external cause and effect can differ greatly in size, as in the case of an apple seed's producing an apple tree, even more so does the force and endurance differ between cause and effect in the internal sphere.[114] The mind's power is such that a little non-virtue can cause tremendous havoc and a little virtue can cause tremendous advancement. Just so, one complete action with strong motivation to attain Buddhahood for the sake of living beings can act as the basis not just for one lifetime but for many. The marvels of cause and effect are not lost in the devastating import of no inherent existence. An understanding of emptiness enhances an understanding of cause and effect.

4 *Dependent-Arising*

Sources
J̄ang-ḡya's *Presentation of Tenets*
Corresponding section of the translation pp.659-76

In the Mādhyamika system all phenomena, both impermanent and permanent, are dependent-arisings (*pratītyasamutpāda*). Through the reason of their being dependent-arisings, their emptiness is established.[115] The *Questions of Sāgaramati Sutra* (*Sāgaramatiparipṛchchhā*) says:

> Those which arise dependently
> Are free of inherent existence.

The *Questions of the King of Nāgas, Anavatapta, Sutra* (*Anavataptanāgarājaparipṛchchhā*) says:

> Those which are produced from causes are not
> produced.
> They do not have an inherent nature of production.
> Those which depend on causes are said to be
> Empty; he who knows emptiness is aware.

In this quote, the reason which establishes an emptiness of

products is indicated by 'produced from causes'. The meaning of not being produced is clarified by the next line, 'They do not have an inherent nature of production'; it is not mere production but inherently existent production that is eliminated. Also, Buddha himself clarified his teaching of no production in the *Descent into Laṅkā Sutra* (*Laṅkāvatāra*), 'O Mahāmati, thinking of no *inherently existent* production, I said that all phenomena are not produced.'

In the quote from the *Questions of Anavatapta Sutra* the words 'those which' indicate the phenomena that are subjects being shown to lack inherently existent production; they are outer phenomena, such as sprouts, and inner phenomena, such as actions. The third line, 'Those which depend on causes are said to be empty', indicates that reliance and dependence on causes is the meaning of being empty of inherent existence. An emptiness of inherent existence is the meaning of dependent-arising; emptiness does not mean the negation of mere production or an absence in phenomena of an ability to perform a function.

The reasoning is:

> Sprouts and so forth are not inherently produced because of being dependent-arisings.

The predicate of the thesis ('are not inherently produced') eliminates the extreme of permanence; the reason ('being dependent-arisings') eliminates the extreme of annihilation. Seeing that the reasoning of dependent-arising refutes all extremes and that this teaching is a quality elevating Buddha above all other teachers, Nāgārjuna praised Buddha in the opening verses of his *Treatise on the Middle Way*:

> I bow down to the perfect Buddha,
> The best of teachers, who propounded
> That what dependently arises
> Has no cessation, no production,
> No annihilation, no permanence, no coming,
> No going, no difference, no sameness,
> Is free of the elaborations [of inherent
> Existence and of duality] and is at peace.

The word 'dependent-arising' in Sanskrit is *pratītyasamutpāda*. It has two parts: *pratītya*, a continuative meaning 'having depended', and *samutpāda*, an action noun meaning 'arising'. The formation of *pratītya* is:

> iṇ − ṇ + prati + su − su + ktvā which changes to lyap − l − p + tuk (between i and ya) − k − u + su − su = pratītya.

In other words, the verbal root *iṇ*, meaning 'going', loses its indicatory letter *ṇ*, leaving *i*. To this, *prati* is affixed, and the nominative case ending *su* is affixed to *prati* but immediately erased because *prati* is an indeclinable. The continuative ending *ktvā* is added to *i* in the form of *lyap*, of which the accent letter *l* and the *p* that indicates the addition of the augment *tuk* are dropped. This leaves *prati i ya*. *Tuk* is added between *i* and *ya*, and the indicatory *k* and pronunciation letter *u* are dropped. The *i* of *prati* and the *i* of the verbal root are combined, making *pratītya*. The nominative case ending *su* is added but is immediately dropped because the continuative *pratītya* is an indeclinable.

The formation of *samutpāda* is:

> pada + ut (before pada) + sam (before utpada) + su (after ut) + su (after sam) − su − su + ghañ (which is a *vṛddhi*-ing of a) + su − u (with the s changing to) ru − u (with the r changing to) ḥ = samutpādaḥ.

In other words, the prefixes *ut* and *sam* are added to *pada* which means 'going'. The nominative case ending is added to these two and then is immediately dropped because they are indeclinables, making *samutpada*. The vowel of *pad* is strengthened for the sake of denoting an action noun, making *samutpāda*. The nominative case ending *su* is added; the *u* is erased; the *s* changes into *ru*; the *u* is erased, and the *r* changes into visarga, making *samutpādaḥ*.

Pratītya is thus shown to be a continuative meaning 'having depended' and not a secondary derivative noun as many Mādhyamikas and non-Mādhyamikas wrongly claim. For them, the *t* of *itya* is added because the root *i* is being used to form an action noun. *Ya* is then an affix used to form a secondary derivative noun.

Thus, for them *itya* means 'that which goes', and '*prati*' means 'multiple', or 'diverse', or 'this and that'. In this mistaken interpretation *pratītya* means 'that which goes or disintegrates diversely'. *Pratītya* being viewed not as a continuative but as a noun, it is wrongly asserted that in the compound *pratītya-samutpāda* a genitive plural case ending has been erased and should be added when taken out of compound, making *pratītyānāṃ* which means 'of those which go, depart, or disintegrate diversely'. The etymological meaning of *pratītyasamutpāda* is thereby wrongly taken to mean 'the composition and arising of effects which disintegrate in each diverse moment and which have definite, diverse causes and conditions'.

Chandrakīrti does not say that this meaning is wholly wrong, but that it is a bad etymology because though it would apply to a use of *pratītyasamutpāda* in a general sense, it would not apply when *pratītyasamutpāda* refers to a specific arising of a single effect from a single cause. However, taken as 'having depended, arising' or 'dependent-arising', it applies to both general and specific references.

The Prāsaṅgikas say that *samutpāda* does not just mean 'arising' (lit., 'going out'), in the sense of arising from causes and conditions in the way that a sprout arises from a seed. It also means 'establishment' (*siddha, grub pa*) and 'existence' (*sat, yod pa*), (two words that are often used interchangeably in Buddhist terminology). The term *pratītyasamutpāda* thereby refers not just to products, or things which arise from causes, but also to non-products since their existence is relative. All phenomena are dependent-arisings.

The term 'dependent-arising' not only refers to a *process* of production and of coming into existence but also to these *things* which are produced and come into existence.[116] Phenomena themselves are dependent-arisings; a pot is a dependent-arising; a consciousness is a dependent-arising; an emptiness is a dependent-arising, and so forth.

The non-Buddhist Grammarians object to the term and its meaning, saying that since *pratītya* is a continuative, the act of depending must precede the act of arising. If that which depends or meets its causes exists before its arising, then it would contradict the Buddhists' own dictum that an effect does not exist at the time of the cause. Therefore, the Grammarians reject both the grammatical correctness of the term and the philosophical correctness of its meaning. However, according to Buddhists an effect does not have to exist at the time of its causes for it to depend on those causes; the mere production of an effect by causes is the meaning of 'dependence'.

Bhāvaviveka, in effect, refuses to etymologize the term in detail, thereby suggesting that *pratītyasamutpāda* attains its meaning through conventional usage and is not bound to an etymological meaning. Chandrakīrti speculates that Bhāvaviveka compares it to the compound *araṇyetilaka* which literally means 'sesame in the forest' but is used to indicate anything that does not answer to one's expectations. Just as wild sesame yields no oil, so events that do not yield one's expectations are called 'sesame in the forest'. The etymology, though connected to the meaning, is much narrower than the meaning which is gained through common convention. Chandrakīrti speculates that for Bhāvaviveka the etymology of the term *pratītyasamutpāda* likewise does not bear close scrutiny; by common convention, however, it just means 'conditionality', that is, 'when this is, that arises'.

Chandrakīrti disagrees, making reference to a verse in Nāgārjuna's own *Sixty Stanzas of Reasoning* (*Yuktiṣhaṣhṭikā*) where the master himself obviously etymologizes *pratītyasamutpāda*:

> *Tat tat prāpya yadutpannaṃ notpannaṃ tat svabhāvataḥ*
> 'That which is produced having met this and that [collection of causes and conditions] is not inherently produced.'

The word substituted for *pratītya* is another continuative, *prāpya*,[117] which means 'having attained' (or 'having met' according to the Tibetan translation in this context for *prāpya*, *phrad nas*). The stanza thereby refutes Bhāvaviveka's contention that Buddhapālita erred in taking *prāpya* as the meaning of *pratītya*. Bhāvaviveka's contention, as is made clear by his commentator Avalokitavrata,[118] is like that of the Grammarians. His point is that if an eye consciousness, for example, were existent, it could meet with the eye sense and form which are its causes. However, if it were existent at the time of its causes, it would be senseless for the causes to produce it. According to Avalokitavrata, Bhāvaviveka's objection is based on the principle that phenomena which meet must be simultaneously existent, but Bhāvaviveka himself does not make clear the reasons for his objection. Chandrakīrti surmises that perhaps Bhāvaviveka means that only physical things can meet; Avalokitavrata's interpretation is broader, but the requirement of simultaneous existence is present for a physical meeting also.

Chandrakīrti's answer to Bhāvaviveka's objection is two-fold:

> First, Buddha made statements such as, 'This monk has met with (that is, attained) the fruit'. Second, Nāgārjuna himself used the word *prāpya* as a substitute for *pratītya*.

His answer is indeed to the point because Bhāvaviveka would not want to quarrel with Nāgārjuna.

Interestingly, in Nāgārjuna's verse etymology, *prati* seems to be etymologized as 'this and that' (*tat tat*); this would affirm the view that *prati* is to be taken as meaning 'multiplicity', or 'diverse', or 'this and that', contradicting Chandrakīrti's contention on this point. Chandrakīrti might answer, however, that Nāgārjuna is giving an example of things relied upon, not an etymology of *prati*. For, *prati* itself means *prāpti*, 'meeting' or 'attainment', and it modifies *i*, which usually means 'go', to cause it to mean *prāpti*.[119] *Prāpti* means *apekṣha*, 'reliance', and thus the compound *pratītyasamutpāda* means 'arising in reliance' and 'arising in dependence', or, more cogently, 'dependent-arising'. It means the arising of things in dependence on causes and conditions, a very sign of their non-inherent existence.

Prāpyasamutpāda, *apekṣhyasamuṭpāda*, and *pratītyasamutpāda* are synonyms; however, they are sometimes explained with individual meanings. *Prāpyasamutpāda*, 'arising through meeting', is taken as referring to the dependent-arising which is the production of things by their causes. This is the meaning that the Vaibhāṣhikas, Sautrāntikas, and Chittamātrins give to 'dependent-arising'; for them, however, dependent-arising is a sign of things' true existence, not a sign of their non-true existence. 'Meeting' can even be taken literally in the sense of indicating that a cause's approaching cessation and its effect's approaching production are simultaneous.

Apekṣhyasamutpāda, 'existing in reliance' or 'relative existence', is taken as referring to the dependent-arising which is the attainment by products and non-products of their own entities in reliance on their parts. This meaning of dependent-arising is a distinguishing feature of the Mādhyamika system and is said to be the Svātantrika-Mādhyamikas' favored means of proving no true existence, but it is also shared with such Prāsaṅgika masters as Āryadeva.[120] Things undeniably appear to the mind to be separate from their parts as when it is thought, 'This house has ten rooms'. The house appears to be one thing and the ten rooms appear to be another.

Pratītyasamutpāda, 'dependent-existence', is taken as referring to the dependent-arising which is the designation of all phenomena in dependence on the thought that designates them. Without thought to designate the existence of phenomena, the arising of phenomena does not occur. However, phenomena undeniably appear to common beings as if they exist in and of themselves, appearing from the object's side toward the subject rather than appearing to be imputed by the subject toward the object. 'Existing in dependence on a designating consciousness' is the special meaning of dependent-arising in the Prāsaṅgika system. The other two meanings are also wholeheartedly accepted by the Prāsaṅgikas, but their own special interpretation is to take *pratītyasamutpāda* as referring to the designation of phenomena dependent not just on their parts or bases of designation but also on the thought that designates them.

When Chandrakīrti says that dependent-arising is the arising of things dependent on causes and conditions, the words 'causes and conditions' do not refer just to usual causes and conditions such as seeds or ignorance. 'Causes and conditions' also refer to the parts of an object—an object's basis of designation—and to the thought that designates the existence of an object. The word 'arising' means not just 'production' but also 'existence' and 'establishment'; all phenomena are dependent existents or relative existents. Nāgārjuna's *Treatise on the Middle Way* (VIII.12) says:

> A doer arises dependent on a doing,
> And a doing exists dependent on a doer.
> Except for that, we do not see
> Another cause for their establishment.

It is clear that Nāgārjuna does not mean that these two cause each other with each one arising after the other one; such would be impossible. Doer and doing are mutually dependent in terms of the attainment of their entities through designation by thought.

Dependent-arising is the king of reasonings because it can, without residue, overcome both extremes. The reasoning is:

> All phenomena do not inherently exist because of being dependent-arisings.

Or, in its most powerful form:

> All phenomena do not inherently exist because of being dependently imputed.

Here, 'all phenomena' means 'each and every phenomenon'. Through ascertaining the reason—that all phenomena are dependent-arisings—the extreme of annihilation is avoided, and realization of the dependent-arising of causes and effects is gained. Through ascertaining the thesis—that all phenomena do not inherently exist—the extreme of permanence is avoided, and realization of the emptiness of all phenomena is gained.

Furthermore, through ascertaining the reason—that all phenomena are dependent-arisings—the extreme of permanence is also avoided because it is realized that phenomena are just interdependently existent, not inherently existent. Through ascertaining the thesis—that all phenomena do not inherently exist—the extreme of annihilation is also avoided because it is realized that only inherent existence is negated, not existence in general. As a yogi progresses in understanding dependent-arising, realization of how the reason and the thesis each avoid the two extremes becomes subtler and subtler.

All other reasonings that prove no inherent existence derive from this king of reasons, dependent-arising. In the Prāsaṅgika system the main reasonings proving no inherent existence are the refutation of the four extreme types of production, called the diamond slivers, and the sevenfold analysis of the relationship of the person and the mind-body complex, to be explained in the next chapter. Ultimately, the diamond slivers meets back to dependent-arising as Chandrakīrti says in his *Supplement* (VI.114):

> Because things are not produced causelessly,
> Or from Īshvara and so forth,
> Or from other, from self, or both,
> They are dependently produced.

The very fact that external phenomena, such as sprouts, and internal phenomena, such as actions, arise dependent on their causes (seeds and ignorance) establishes that their production is empty of natural existence and eliminates that they are produced from self, other, both, or causelessly. This is mainly based on the reasoning of dependent-production, and in this sense the diamond slivers derives from dependent-arising.

The diamond slivers also derives from dependent-designation, which is more difficult to realize than dependent-production. When a yogi searches to find the object that is being imputed in the expression, 'A sprout is growing,' he gains ascertainment that it does not grow from self, other, both, or causelessly. Through the force of this realization he develops ascertainment that the production of sprouts and so forth is just a conventional designation and through this develops ascertainment that if the object imputed in the expression 'production' is sought, it cannot be found. This is how the reasoning which refutes production of the four extreme types derives from dependent-arising, or dependent-designation.

Ultimately, the sevenfold reasoning refuting an inherently existent person also derives from dependent-arising. As Chandrakīrti says (*Supplement* VI.158):

> [The person] is not established in fact
> Or in the world in the seven ways,
> But without analysis, here in the world
> Is imputed in dependence on its parts.

The non-finding of a person as either the same as mind and body, or as different from them, or as their base, or as based on them, or as possessing them, or as their shape, or as their composite induces the ascertainment that a person is just imputed to the mental and physical aggregates. Similarly, a realization that a person is just imputed to the aggregates induces the ascertainment that a person is not findable in these seven ways. Thus, the sevenfold analysis can be seen as contained in an investigation of dependent-designation, the subtlest meaning of dependent-arising.

It is even said that emptiness and dependent-arising are synonyms, but this is not in the sense that 'pot' and its definition 'that which is bulbous and able to hold water' are synonyms. Also, the synonymity of emptiness and dependent-arising does not mean that a consciousness which ascertains that effects arise dependent on causes and conditions also ascertains the meaning of their being empty of inherently existent production. Furthermore, the meaning of the term 'dependent-arising' is not asserted to be the meaning of emptiness. An explicit ascertainment of a dependent-arising does not even carry with it an implicit ascertainment of emptiness. Rather, emptiness is synonymous with dependent-arising for Mādhyamikas who through valid cognition have refuted inherent existence.

Not just anyone who realizes dependent-arising can realize its synonymity with emptiness since many even see dependent-arising as a reason for asserting inherent existence. However, when a Mādhyamika ascertains that external and internal things are dependent-arisings, he realizes, based on the force of this very understanding, that being empty of inherent existence is the meaning of being a dependent-arising. For, he has realized that what inherently exists does not rely on anything, and he has realized that inherent existence and dependent-arising are contradictory.

Since through dependent-arising itself he has found realization of the emptiness that negates inherent existence, when he sees, hears, or is mindful that sprouts and so forth depend on causes and conditions, he is drawn to thinking of the manner in which these sprouts do not inherently exist. His mind has been thoroughly trained to consider the unfindability of phenomena through merely perceiving that they arise dependent on causes and conditions. He is so conditioned to think of emptiness as soon as he notices causal conditionality that in a future life, even though emptiness is not taught to him, the mere hearing of the doctrine of cause and effect revivifies his former understanding. His probing of the unfindability of phenomena is renewed, and his progress on the path toward direct cognition of emptiness is enhanced. He overcomes the bonds of forgetfulness that accompany the passage from one lifetime to another due to the difficulties of birth and the accustoming to a new body. Since cause and effect are taught practically everywhere, the yogi can 'outwit' the contrary forces that would take him away from continuing penetration of emptiness by taking the doctrine of cause and effect and using it as his means to penetrate emptiness.

Through realizing how the other types of reasoning meet back to dependent-arising, it is seen how working properly on any one of them could involve understanding the meaning of all the others. Through seeing dependent-arising, it is said that a yogi sees Buddha in the sense that Buddha as a Truth Body is not different from the nature of dependent-arisings.[121]

ELIMINATION OF ERROR

Because all phenomena, including emptinesses, are dependent-arisings and thus do not truly exist, Jam-ȳang-shay-b̄a (see p.676) criticizes Ḍak-tsang for claiming that 'ultimate' (*paramārtha, don dam*), 'validly established' (*pramāṇasiddha, tshad mas grub pa*), and 'able to set itself up' (Tib: *tshugs thub tu grub pa*) are synonyms. Ḍak-tsang refuses to accept that conventional phenomena are validly established because for him 'validly established' means that an object is able to establish itself independently.[122] Jam-ȳang-shay-ḃa points out that there is no system of tenets, even within Hīnayāna, which asserts that what is validly established must also be 'able to set itself up'. For, in the Sautrāntika system 'generally characterized phenomena' (*sāmānyalakṣhaṇa, spyi mtshan*) or permanent phenomena are validly established but are not able to establish themselves because they depend on thought.

Still, it does seem that the Vaibhāṣhikas assert that all phenomena are self-established because they assert that every phenomenon has its own self-sufficient entity.[123] The Vaibhāṣhikas maintain that all existents are 'substantially established' (*dravyasiddha, rdzas grub*) though they reserve 'substantially existent' (*dravyasat, rdzas yod*) merely for those phenomena that can bear analysis. For the Vaibhāṣhikas, ultimate truths are not emptinesses, as the Mādhyamikas and Chittamātrins assert, but objects such as forms and consciousnesses which, even if analyzed down to their smallest particles or moments, are still instances of form or consciousness. Objects such as tables and chairs, however, disappear from the mind if one considers their individual particles and asks if those are tables; thus, they are conventional truths. However, each particle is still an instance of form; therefore, the Vaibhāṣhikas assert that partless particles, partless moments of consciousness, and permanent phenomena can bear ultimate analysis. For them forms, consciousnesses, spaces, and so forth are ultimate truths. All composite objects, such as chairs and pots, are conventional truths, and Jam-ȳang-shay-ḃa seems to be implying that though conventional truths are for them 'substantially established', they are not 'able to set themselves up'.

In any case, the Sautrāntikas, Chittamātrins, and Mādhyamikas agree that what is validly established need not be self-established. Jam-ȳang-shay-ḃa says that if one insists that in the Prāsaṅgika system an ultimate, that is, an emptiness, must be both validly established and able to set itself up, one misses the distinctive feature of Mādhyamika and the Perfection of Wisdom Sūtras, this being the dependent existence of everything. However, Dak-tsang does not accept the valid establishment *of anything* and says further that whatever is 'validly established' must be also 'self-established'. He, therefore, does not himself accept that emptinesses are 'self-established', but Jam-ȳang-shay-b̄a forces on him the conclusion that emptinesses are 'self-established' or truly existent because for Jam-ȳang-shay-b̄a an emptiness must be validly established just because it exists.

Since an analytical consciousness *discovers* or *finds* the unfindability of an object, this unfindability (emptiness) might seem to be inherently existent.[124] It is true that when an analytical consciousness searches to find whether an object inherently exists or not, it does find an emptiness of the object; however, when this very analytical consciousness searches to find the emptiness of the object, it 'finds' or cognizes an emptiness of the emptiness of the object. Thus, though an emptiness is an ultimate truth, it does not ultimately exist. This does not diminish the fact that when conjoined with practice of the Bodhisattva deeds, cognition of and thorough acquaintance with emptiness grant the highest of boons, liberation from cyclic existence and, finally, omniscience.

5 *Refuting a Self of Persons*

Sources
Jam-ȳang-shay-b̄a's *Great Exposition of the Middle Way*
J̄ang-ḡya's *Presentation of Tenets*
Nga-w̄ang-b̄el-den's *Annotations*
Geshe Gedün Lodrö's oral teachings
Kensur Lekden's oral teachings
Corresponding section of the translation pp.677-97

In general 'self' (*ātman, bdag*), 'person' (*pudgala, gang zag*) and 'I' (*ahaṃ, nga*) are synonyms along with 'creature' or 'being' (*purușha, skyes bu*), which has also been translated here as 'person'.[125] However, when Prāsaṅgikas speak specifically of a self of persons (*pudgalātman, gang zag gi bdag*), this 'self' does not refer to the conventionally existent person which is imputed in dependence on the aggregates of mind and body. In the term 'self of persons', 'self' means 'inherent existence', and the word 'persons' means 'nominally exist persons'. Hence, the term 'selflessness of persons' means the non-inherent existence of nominally existent persons. 'Inherent existence' means 'independent existence', 'objective existence', 'natural existence', or 'existence under its own power', etc. The meaning of inherent existence is best seen when one progresses toward realizing the imputed nature of the person.[126]

Yogis who long to be freed from the round of birth, aging, sickness, and death do not initially meditate on the emptiness of pillars, pots and sprouts but on the emptiness, or selflessness, of persons.[127] Having gained an understanding of the emptiness of persons, a yogi turns to meditation on the emptiness of the other phenomena which are included within the continuum of a person, such as body and mind, and finally to meditation on the emptiness of phenomena not included within the personal continuum, such as pillars and houses. He might use the king of reasons, dependent-arising, in his meditation on the emptiness of the person, but the fivefold and sevenfold reasonings are renowned among the Prāsaṅgikas as the easiest means for gaining a quick and penetrating understanding of emptiness.

The fivefold reasoning is based on a description in sutra of twenty false views of a real self:[128]

1 viewing forms, i.e., body, as a self
2 viewing the self as inherently possessing forms
3 viewing the self as inherently existing in forms
4 viewing forms as inherently existing in the self

5 viewing feelings as a self
6 viewing the self as inherently possessing feelings
7 viewing the self as inherently existing in feelings
8 viewing feelings as inherently existing in the self

9 viewing discriminations as a self
10 viewing the self as inherently possessing discriminations
11 viewing the self as inherently existing in discriminations
12 viewing discriminations as inherently existing in the self

13 viewing compositional factors as a self
14 viewing the self as inherently possessing compositional factors
15 viewing the self as inherently existing in compositional factors
16 viewing compositional factors as inherently existing in the self

17 viewing consciousness as a self
18 viewing the self as inherently possessing consciousness
19 viewing the self as inherently existing in consciousness
20 viewing consciousness as inherently existing in the self.

These are five sets of four positions; Nāgārjuna's fivefold analysis is based on these four positions with the addition of a fifth: viewing the self as a different entity from forms and so forth. Five modes are not mentioned in sutra because Buddha had already taught that without apprehending the aggregates, it is impossible for the innate false view of a self to conceive of a real self. For this reason, a false view of the self as a totally different entity from the aggregates is not innate but artificial, learned through the mistaken teachings of the non-Buddhist Forders. Also, because the innate false view of a real self does not conceive the person and the aggregates to be either one or different, all twenty false views of a self are only artificial. However, if the self existed as conceived by the innate view of a real self, it would be either one with the aggregates or a different entity from the aggregates. Therefore, the self as conceived by the innate misconception of inherent existence is analyzed in the same way as the self that is misconceived through artificial teachings.

The object of observation of an innate false view of an inherently existent person is the nominally existent self or person and not the mental and physical aggregates. However, among the twenty false views of a self the object of observation is often the aggregates. Still, the aggregates are phenomena related to the self which is the object observed by a false view of a self, and, therefore, even these are named 'false views of a real self'. For instance, if forms are viewed as an inherently existent self, the base of the view or the object of observation is a form, and, therefore, such a misconception is a conception of a self of phenomena and not of a self of persons. When, on the other hand, the person is viewed as inherently possessing form, the object of observation is the person, and, therefore, such a misconception is a conception of a self of persons. If the person is viewed as inherently existing in forms, the base of the view or the object of observation is a form, and, therefore, such a misconception is a conception of a self of phenomena and not of a self of persons. If it is viewed that forms inherently exist in the person, the person is the base of the view or the object of observation, and such a misconception is a conception of a self of persons.

The same distinctions can be extended to the other sixteen views. Thus, some of the so-called 'false views of a real self' are actually misconceptions of a self of phenomena other than persons. Since Nāgārjuna's fivefold reasoning is based on the modes of the false view of a real self, both the fivefold and the sevenfold reasonings can be said to involve refutation of a self of phenomena other than persons in order to establish the selflessness of the person. Due to the fact that the base or object of observation of the false view of a real self must be the person and not the aggregates, it might be necessary to say that not all twenty false views of a real self are *actual* false views of a real self but are only named so. The fivefold reasoning as stated in Nāgārjuna's *Treatise on the Middle Way* is:

> The self does not inherently exist because of (1) not being the aggregates, (2) not being other than the aggregates, (3) not being the base of the aggregates, (4) not depending on the aggregates, and (5) not possessing the aggregates. An example is a chariot.

The reason is fivefold, and thus it is called the fivefold reasoning. Chandrakīrti added two more 'corners' to the reason:

> (6) not being the shape of the aggregates, and (7) not being the composite of the aggregates.

In a slightly longer form the sevenfold reasoning is:[129]

> Except for only being imputed to the aggregates which are its basis of imputation, there is no self-subsistent self, for:
>
> 1 the aggregates which are the basis of the imputation are not the person

2 the person is not an entity other than the aggregates which are the basis of its imputation
3 the person is not the support of the aggregates which are its basis of imputation
4 the person ultimately does not depend on the aggregates which are its basis of imputation
5 the person ultimately does not possess the aggregates
6 the person is not the shape of the aggregates which are its basis of imputation
7 the person is not the composite of the aggregates which are the basis of its imputation.

For example, if a chariot is sought analytically, there is no self-subsistent chariot to be found.

In the sevenfold reasoning, in order to realize the thesis that the I does not inherently exist, it is necessary first to realize the pervasion of the sevenfold reason by the predicate of the thesis. In other words, one must first realize that whatever does not exist in these seven ways does not inherently exist. After that, one establishes the presence of the seven reasons in the subject, I. By the force of realizing the pervasion of these seven reasons by the predicate of non-inherent existence and by the force of establishing the presence of these seven reasons in the subject, I, the I can be realized as not inherently existent.

First, the predicate of the thesis ('does not inherently exist') is to be applied to an example ('chariot') which is familiar in the world, since an example is easier to understand than the actual thesis. It is not that the emptiness of a chariot is to be realized before realizing the emptiness of a person, but it is important first to see how the mode of analysis works through an example which is easier than the actual subject. Applied to a chariot the reasoning is:[130]

A chariot does not inherently exist because of not being its parts, not being other than its parts, not being in its parts, not being that in which its parts exist, not possessing its parts, not being the composite of its parts, and not being the shape of its parts.

These seven reasons must be established as qualities of the subject, a chariot.

A chariot is not inherently the same entity as its own parts (axles, wheels, etc.) because if it were one with them, just as its parts are many, so the chariot would also be many. Or, just as the chariot is one, its parts also would be one. Furthermore, the agent—the chariot as the whole which conveys its parts when it moves—and the object—the conveyed parts—would absurdly be one.

A chariot is not inherently other than its own parts because if it were other, it would be a different entity from its parts. Things which are different entities and which exist at the same time must be unrelatedly other; therefore, just as a horse and a cow are unrelatedly other and apprehendable separately, so a chariot would have to be apprehendable separately from its own parts. However, it is not so apprehended. Therefore, a chariot is not inherently other than its parts.

A chariot's parts do not inherently depend on the chariot because if they did, the parts and the chariot would have to be inherently other. The impossibility of this has already been explained.

Also, a chariot does not inherently depend on its parts because if it did, the chariot and its parts would have to be inherently other. The impossibility of this has already been explained.

A chariot does not inherently possess its parts either in the manner that a man possesses a cow or in the manner that a man possesses his body. For, the former mode of possession is that of different entities, and the latter mode of possession is that of the same entity. Thus, the chariot and its parts would have to be either different entities or the same entity. Both of these have already been refuted.

A chariot is also not just the composite of its parts because the shapes of the individual parts cannot be a chariot nor can the shape of the composite of the parts be a chariot since it is impossible for the shapes before or after arrangement to be a chariot. If it were said that the shapes of the parts which are not different from their shapes before arrangement are a chariot, then since there is no difference in shape before and after arrangement, just as the shapes are not a chariot before arrangement, so they would not be a chariot after arrangement. If it were said that the shapes of the parts which are different from the shape that they had before arrangement are the chariot, then since there would be different shapes to the axles, wheels, and so forth, after arrangement, these different shapes would have to be apprehendable. However, they are not.

Also, the shape of the composite of the parts is not a chariot because the composite of the parts does not inherently exist. There is no composite of the parts of a chariot separate from the parts of a chariot because if there were, the composite could be apprehended without apprehending the parts. Nor is the composite of the parts one with the parts themselves because if it were, either the composite would be many like the many parts or the parts would be one like the one composite.[131] Therefore, the shape of the composite of the parts only imputedly exists and is not suitable to be a substantially existent chariot. For the Prāsaṅgikas, the shape of the composite of the parts is a basis of the imputation of a chariot, but not even conventionally can it be considered a chariot.

When a chariot is sought in these seven ways, it is not found, but a chariot does not thereby become non-existent. Still, the non-finding of a chariot in these seven ways is true both ultimately and conventionally. Even as a conventional truth a chariot is unfindable in these seven ways; however, a chariot conventionally exists because the assertion of a chariot is not made from the point of view of its being established by the reasoning that analyzes whether it inherently exists or not. A chariot is established as existing when there is no analysis to find the object imputed; it is established only by a non-defective, conventional, worldly consciousness. Thus, a chariot is presented as only imputedly existent in the sense that it is imputed in dependence on its parts (the axles, wheels, etc.) and is not any of them.

The Svātantrikas, Chittamātrins, Sautrāntikas, and Vaibhāṣhikas all say that if the composite of the parts, or the shape, etc., could not be assigned as the whole, the chariot (or whole) would be non-existent. For there is no whole which is a separate entity from its parts. Therefore, in all these schools chariots and so forth are assigned as some phenomenon from among their bases of designation: either their composite, their shape, or one of the bases of imputation. These schools do not accept that chariots and so forth are just nominally imputed in the sense of being unfindable among their bases of designation. For them, things have their own natural existence. In these schools, to be merely nominally imputed only means that a phenomenon is not something separate from its bases of designation. For instance, though a person appears to be the boss of his aggregates of mind and body, he is shown to be one of the aggregates—either the mental consciousness, or a mind-basis-of-all (*ālayavijñāna, kun gzhi rnam shes*), or the continuum of the aggregates, or the continuum of the mental consciousness, and so forth.

In the extraordinary Prāsaṅgika system, neither the composite of the parts nor the individual parts are taken to be the whole. Still, the Prāsaṅgikas are able to present well all the objects and agents of cyclic existence and of nirvana within the context of just nominally imputed wholes, parts, qualities, qualificands, and so forth. Dzong-ka-ba urgently advises that this method of analysis be studied and practiced because it is a profound means of quickly finding the view of emptiness. As Chandrakīrti says in the *Commentary to the 'Supplement'*, 'These worldly conventionalities do not exist when analyzed in this way, but exist through non-analytical renown. Therefore, when yogis analyze these through this series [of reasons], they penetrate very quickly to the depth of suchness.'

Through the example of a chariot one gains familiarity with the modes of the sevenfold reasoning.[132] However, unlike the other Buddhist schools, the Prāsaṅgikas do not say that for the example of the chariot to be correct the meditator must first realize the predicate of the thesis, 'does not inherently exist', as a quality of the chariot and then proceed to the subject of the original syllogism, the person. If one first had to realize the emptiness of a chariot before realizing the emptiness of a person, then the emptiness of a person would not be the initial object of meditation for those who seek liberation. Furthermore, it would be pointless to state many reasons to prove the selflessness of a person because one would realize the emptiness of a person through merely turning one's mind to this subject. For, the emptiness of a chariot would already have been validly cognized, and a realization of the emptiness of one thing is sufficient preparation for the realization of the emptiness of anything else that the mind turns to while still remembering the first realization. In the Prāsaṅgika system, examples which are merely more familiar in the world than the subject of the main thesis are often given. This is why mirror images and magician's illusions are so often used as examples; just as a mirror image of a face is empty of being a face, so objects are empty of being inherently existent. However, realization that a mirror image of a face is not a face is not a cognition of the emptiness of a mirror image. It is a conventional analog of the extraordinary and unfamiliar cognition of emptiness.

Thus, a yogi's aim in analyzing a chariot is not to gain a thorough realization of a chariot's emptiness but to gain familiarity with the mode of reasoning so that he can apply it to the person, for it is misconception of the nature of the person that causes transmigration and the repeated rounds of the suffering of birth, aging, sickness, and death. The seven-cornered reason must be established as a quality of the person:[133]

1 The self and the aggregates are not inherently one because the assertion of a self would then be senseless. For, 'self' would only be a synonym of the aggregates, just as 'rabbit-bearer' (that which has the figure of a rabbit in it) is a synonym of 'moon'. Also, just as the aggregates are many, so the selves would be many. Or, just as the self is one, so the aggregates would only be one. Also, because the aggregates are entities which are produced and which disintegrate, the self also would be produced and would disintegrate.

If it is accepted that the self is nominally produced and nominally disintegrates, there is no fault. However, if

> the production and disintegration of the self naturally existed, then there would be three faults: memory of former births would be impossible, deeds done would be wasted, and one would meet with the results of actions not done by oneself. These three faults arise because the selves of former and later births would be naturally individual and thus would be unrelatedly other. Moreover, it is impossible for those which are naturally other to belong to one continuum, just as the being named Maitreya and the being named Upagupta who are other and are contemporaries are not one continuum. For, Chandrakīrti says (*Supplement* VI.61):
>
> > The phenomena which are based on Maitreya and Upagupta
> > Are different and thus not included within one continuum.
> > Whatever are naturally separate are not
> > Fit to be included within one continuum.
>
> If two lives were naturally or inherently other, this otherness would be their nature; a sameness of continuum could not obtain between them.

If the self were inherently produced and inherently disintegrated, Buddha could not have remembered that in the past he was such and such a person because the two persons would be naturally separate. For instance, when someone named Devadatta remembers his past lives, he does not remember that he was Yajña who is his own contemporary. The fallacy of there being no memory of former lives is similar to the consequence that if cause and effect were naturally existent others, then darkness would arise from a tongue of flame. In other words, once the elements of a continuum are naturally existent or analytically findable as others, then a continuity cannot obtain between them, and there can be no continuum.

Deeds done would be wasted because the self which performed the deeds would have utterly ceased by the time the effects are experienced in another lifetime. For, the aggregates would inherently disintegrate at the end of a lifetime, and the self would be one with them. If the person did experience the results of former deeds, since those deeds would not have been done by him, he would be undergoing the effects of deeds done by another since each lifetime would be inherently separate from all other lifetimes.

The same faults do not accrue to the Prāsaṅgikas' own presentation of the self and of the relationship between deeds done in one lifetime and the effects that are experienced in another lifetime. For the Prāsaṅgikas, the 'mere I' gives rise to the thought 'I', and the various selves in the different lifetimes are instances of the 'mere I'.[134] The 'mere I' exists from one lifetime to another just because the expression 'I' is common to former and later lifetimes. Conventionally or nominally, the generality I exists from one lifetime to another, even though the particular beings which are its instances do not live from one lifetime to another. It is said to be much the same as the fact that a gold pot and a bronze pot are pots but a gold pot is not a bronze pot and a bronze pot is not a gold pot. Just so, the particular I of one lifetime is not the particular I of another lifetime, but they are both I. Still, this does not mean that there is a generality which is a separate entity from its individual instances. Just the reasoning that the particular I of each lifetime is an I is sufficient to establish that the 'mere I' exists nominally from one lifetime to another. Any further analysis into the nature of the general and particular I would constitute ultimate analysis in the face of which nothing is found.

> 2 The self and the mental and physical aggregates are not different entities because if they were, the self would not have the character of the aggregates such as production, disintegration, abiding, form, experiencing objects, and so forth.[135] In that case, there would be no basis for the designation 'self', and there would be no object to apprehend as a self because the person would be a non-product.

All products are included within the five aggregates; thus, if the person did not have the character of the aggregates, it could not be a product. If the person were a non-product, it would have to be either a permanent existent, like nirvana, or a non-existent, like a flower in the sky. Such a phenomenon could not be a basis of the designation 'self' and could not serve as an object to be apprehended as a self. For, the self would then be changeless, and a changeless self could not take rebirth, die, cognize objects, and so forth.

> Also, if the self were a different entity from the aggregates, then just as the character of consciousness can be apprehended separately from the character of form, so a self without the character of mind and body would have to be apprehendable. However, since the self is not apprehendable separately from the aggregates of mind and body, the self is not a separate entity from the aggregates.

The non-Buddhist Forders assert that the self has a different character from the aggregates when they say that it is beyond mind and body. However, D̄zong-ka-ba says that the Forders fail to realize that the self is only a name, that the self only nominally exists. Since the Forders see that it is impossible for the self to be the aggregates of mind and body, they fabricate a view of a permanent self, separate from mind and body.[136] Chandrakīrti says that the Forders fall from conventional truths through not realizing the character of the self as a designation dependent on the aggregates and fall from ultimate truths through not realizing the lack of inherent existence of the self.[137]

One of the most incisive reasonings refuting a self separate from the aggregates is that it would be useless to call such an unchangeable phenomenon 'self'. Without the experiencing of objects or the taking of rebirth the word 'self' loses any meaning.

The Vedāntins use the term 'self', however, to refer to the non-dual and final nature of the universe. They refer to cognition of the all pervasive Brahman which is the self of the universe as well as one's own actual self. The finitude and diseased nature of the ordinary self is cancelled in its identification with Brahman, and the distance of Brahman as the ultimate reality is cancelled in its identification with the self. The immediacy of the self remains and is extended through identification to Brahman, and the ultimacy or absolute nature of Brahman remains and is extended through identification to the self. The finite living being (*jīva*) becomes the infinite Brahman in vivid realization. The transmutation of the living being into Brahman requires a complete destruction of egocentricity. Still, the essence of reality is called 'self'.

In Buddhism, also, when emptiness is directly cognized, the object—emptiness—and the subject—a wisdom consciousness—become like water poured into water, totally undifferentiable. However, the Prāsaṅgikas seem to be questioning the value of calling the highest reality 'self' just because such a designation would increase egocentricity. The usage of the word 'self' is not required to preserve a sense of immediacy, for immediacy is the very mode of direct perception as is witnessed every day, and when it is said that reality is perceived directly, a sense of the immediacy of reality is conveyed without reliance on the word 'self'. Also, the teaching of one all-pervasive entity would only block the way to destroying the sense that each individual thing is a truly existent one. The very chains of cyclic existence are forged with the conception of true existence that does not analyze oneness and manyness. Beings are bound in cyclic existence by their failure to investigate whether phenomena, which they habitually conceive to exist inherently, are truly one or truly many. To conceive reality as a truly existent one pervading the many might further the habitual non-analytical intellect that causes the powerless wandering in cyclic existence. If the manifold universe could be subsumed under a truly existent Brahman, it might seem that the many parts of a table, for instance, could be subsumed under a truly existent table.

Still, it is not to be thought that meditations on the all-pervasive are absent in Buddhism. The formless meditative absorptions in which space, consciousness, nothingness, or something subtler than even nothingness are seen as all-pervasive are common to both Hīnyāna and Mahāyāna and the non-Buddhist systems as well. In tantric practice a meditator often views himself and his environment as one entity; the world is visualized as a mandala and is reduced to the size of a drop. Also, the metaphor of water poured into water as a description of the mode of the direct cognition of emptiness intentionally indicates a fusion of subject and object. Technically, everything true of the subject is not true of the object and vice versa, but the experience must be something like that. No ordinary being has ever experienced such a complete oneness, for a oneness is always a composite of parts, and each part is not one with every other part in terms of function, position, and so forth. It is questionable whether the word 'one' can convey any of the sense of such a state. Still, some Tibetan orders do refer to the one mind, or the one sphere of the nature of phenomena, whereas the Ge-luk-b̄as restrict themselves to a metaphor, the undifferentiability of fresh water poured into fresh water.

The question here is not whether there are practices common to Hinduism and Buddhism that are aimed at developing a sense of pervasion but whether these practices are the primary means of cognizing reality. For the Buddhists such practices are means to enhance the concentrative power of the mind in order to further analytical penetration into the nature of things. This analysis revolves around developing an understanding that oneness and manyness do not naturally inhere in objects. An unsuccessful attempt to find the self under specific types of analysis is seen as a prerequisite for progress toward liberation from cyclic existence. In both sutra and tantra teachings such analysis is a necessity because it is this which breaks the bonds of misconception, and misconception of the nature of things is the ignorance that causes the powerless rounds of birth, aging, sickness, and death. For instance, Buddhists accept that non-Buddhist yogis have attained the marvelous experience of the entry, abiding, and dissolving of the winds into the central channel. However, the Buddhist form of the practice is still considered to be basically different because the non-Buddhists' practice is not preceeded by this type of analysis of phenomena.[138] Thus, it is said that without the view of emptiness a yogi cannot cause the winds to dissolve into the indestructible mid-point of the heart center.

What the Prāsaṅgika analysis is refuting in the sevenfold reasoning must be clearly defined; the self is not being reduced to miniscule size nor is it being expanded to pervade the universe. The self is realized as an imputation dependent on the mental and physical aggregates. The meditator is told again and again that when he realizes the unfindability of the self, what appears is an utter vacuity which is the mere absence of an inherently existent self.[139] He is told again and again that at the time of direct cognition subject and object become like fresh water poured into fresh water and that the emptinesses of all phenomena are directly cognized without the slightest appearance of those phenomena themselves.

Conventionally, the self and the aggregates are the same entity and different opposites of negatives because even conventionally the self is not the aggregates nor is it a separate entity from the aggregates. A person (or self) is none of the aggregates which are its basis of designation but is an instance of the fourth aggregate, *saṃskāraskandha*, or pile of compositional factors. Being impermanent, the self must be an aggregate, and the self is designated as a member of the fourth aggregate because it has the character of all the aggregates. Since the self has the character of all the aggregates, it cannot be designated as a form aggregate, feeling aggregate, discrimination aggregate, or consciousness aggregate. It is, therefore, called a 'compositional factor' aggregate because this aggregate is the repository for all impermanent things which are not included among the other aggregates.

It has been established in the first two 'corners' of the sevenfold reasoning that the self is neither inherently the same as nor different from the aggregates. The remaining five reasons are included in these two positions because sameness and difference of entity are a dichotomy. If the self and the aggregates inherently exist, they must be either one entity or different entities. When these two positions are refuted, the inherent existence of the self is refuted. Thus, even though all possible positions have already been refuted, the other five positions are refuted for the sake of attacking the various modes of the habitual misconception of a self.

> 3 The self does not act as the base of the aggregates like a bowl for yogurt or like snow that exists throughout and surrounds a forest of trees.[140] For, in that case the self and the aggregates would be different, and this position has already been refuted.

The examples provide clues for glimpsing and eventually identifying ways in which the non-analytical intellect tends to conceive the self.

> 4 The self does not inherently exist in or depend on the aggregates like Devadatta living in a tent or a lion living in a forest. For, in that case the self and the aggregates would be different, and this position has already been refuted.

> 5 The self does not possess the mental and physical aggregates either as a different entity, as in the case of a man possessing a cow, or as the same entity, as in the case of a man possessing his body or a tree possessing its core. For, in the first case the self and the aggregates would be different entities, and in the second case they would be the same entity. Refutations of these positions have already been stated.

The meaning of the word 'have' or 'possess' is being analyzed here. It seems most likely that a self would possess its aggregates in the manner of sameness of entity, but once a sameness of entity is asserted to be findable under analysis, then the possessor and the possessed become one. The concept of 'my body' or 'my mind' cannot bear such analysis.

> 6 The self is not just the composite of the aggregates of mind and body because the composite is the basis of the designation 'self' and, therefore, cannot be the self.

It is said[141] that a Buddha does not confuse or mix the basis of the designation of a phenomenon with the phenomenon that is designated. Jang-ḡya says that this difficult point is based on a sutra that teaches that just as 'chariot' is imputed to the parts of a chariot, so the person is imputed conventionally in dependence on the aggregates.[142] The Prāsaṅgikas view this as meaning that the person is not the aggregates and that this non-identity is clearly perceived by a Buddha.

> Furthermore, the composite of the mental and physical aggregates does not inherently exist because the composite is unfindable as either inherently one with or different from the aggregates.

If the composite of the aggregates were one with the aggregates, the composite would be as many as the aggregates, or the aggregates would be one just as the composite is only one. If the composite were inherently different from the aggregates, then it would be apprehended separately from the aggregates and would not have the character of the aggregates, but this is not so.[143]

> The reasoning that the object imputed cannot be the basis of the imputation also refutes the view that the self is the continuum of the aggregates because then object imputed and basis of imputation would be one. Also, if the self were the composite of the aggregates, then the self as the agent of the appropriation, or assumption, of the aggregates would be one with the aggregates which are its appropriation.

The five aggregates are accepted as that which is appropriated by a self as when it is said that such and such a person takes rebirth or assumes a new body and mind. The *composite* of the five aggregates is thus also accepted as the appropriation. If the self were the composite, the appropriator and the appropriated would be one.

> If the composite of a person's various consciousnesses—eye, ear, nose, tongue, body, and mental consciousnesses

—is asserted to be the person, then the absurdity of the plurality of the composites and the persons would follow. Similarly, if it is said that only the mental consciousness is the person, each moment of the mental consciousness would absurdly be a different person because each moment of the mental consciousness is different.

7 The self is not the shape of the aggregates because shape is physical, and if a self were merely shape, then the mind, etc., would not be posited as the self. If it were said that both the physical shape and the mind are the self, then either the self would be two, or shape and consciousness would be one.

In most cases, beings are identified by their shape; the difference between a cow and a human is commonly determined by their different shapes.[144] It is being taught here that common beings confuse the basis of the designation, which is not the person, with the person that is designated. (All animals—cows, horses, and so forth—are accepted as persons.) It is commonly said, for instance, that a dog is black whereas it is meant that the color of its hair is black. The color of a dog is a basis of the designation 'dog', but it itself is not a dog.

The non-finding of the person in any of these seven modes is the meaning of the non-inherent existence of the person. Since even as a conventional truth a person is not findable in these seven ways, even conventionally a person does not naturally exist. However, when there is no analysis to find the object imputed, a person undeniably is validly established as able to perform functions; therefore, the self does nominally exist. Furthermore, when a consciousness thinking, 'I', is generated, it is generated based on the five aggregates. Hence, it is said that a person is only imputed or designated in dependence on the five aggregates.

As Chandrakīrti's *Commentary on (Āryadeva's) 'Four Hundred' (Bodhisattvayogachāryachatuḥshatakaṭīkā)* says,[145] 'Therefore, when analyzed in this manner, an inherent existence of things is not established. Thus, [only] an illusory nature remains individually for things.' Chandrakīrti thereby indicates that an illusory object does remain.

The Mādhyamika view is the complete negation without residue of inherent existence, which is refuted through analytical reasoning. After the negation, there must also remain a flawless presentation of all the objects and agents of the dependent-arising of cause and effect which are like the creations of a magician, appearing to be inherently existent but actually not inherently existent. Thus, the Mādhyamika view is a composite of (1) a non-affirming negative of inherent existence and (2) a presentation of agents and objects which are like illusions. Jang-gya says there are practically none who understand the Mādhyamika view, emphasizing that it is extremely difficult to find the correct view. One is exhorted to make great effort to understand this view without allowing the pure teaching to be distorted by one's own tendencies toward nihilism or eternalism.

The mine

When reasoning investigates whether the self inherently exists, it does not find the self in any of the seven ways.[146] This having been done, an inherent existence of the mine is easily refuted. It is not that the very same consciousness that realizes the non-inherent existence of the I realizes that the mine does not inherently exist. Rather, if the yogi merely turns his attention to the mine, its emptiness is easily realized in dependence only on the consciousness that realized the emptiness of the I. Since further reasoning is not required, Mādhyamika treatises do not offer a separate reasoning to aid in realizing the non-inherent existence of the mine.

When an emptiness has been realized indirectly and inferentially through the medium of a concept, this realization is sufficient to clear the way for the immediate but subsequent realization of the emptinesses of other phenomena.[147] Separate reasoning is not required even though the realization of one emptiness is not itself a realization of all emptinesses. However, when the emptiness of one thing is cognized *directly*, the emptiness of all phenomena is cognized directly. It is not that the emptiness of one thing *is* the emptiness of everything; rather, the extraordinary mode of the direct cognition of emptiness—in which the object, emptiness, and the subject, the wisdom consciousness, are undifferentiable like fresh water poured into fresh water—allows for cognition of the emptiness of all objects.

Having inferentially realized the emptiness of the I, one can readily realize the non-inherent existence of the mine both as the possessor of mind, body, and so forth and as the phenomena included within the continuum and possessed by the person. Then, passing outside of the sphere of the false view of a transitory collection as a real I and mine, one meditates on the emptiness of phenomena which are mine but not included within the continuum, such as a house, and then meditates on other phenomena which are not mine, such as a city. The same sevenfold reasoning is used to analyze the relationship between the phenomena designated and the bases of designation, as in the example of a chariot. These phenomena cannot be found under analysis and thus do not inherently exist; however, they are still accepted as validly established conventionally when there is no analysis. This acceptance is congruous with Buddha's statement that he does not debate with the world about the existence or non-existence of objects.[148] The sevenfold reasoning does not refute nominal existence, only objectively established existence.

The mere apprehension of I and mine are not erroneous; the error is the further misconception of the nominally existent I and mine as objectively existent. Even Buddhas have valid cognizers that perceive I and mine, but they do not confuse the basis of designation with the phenomenon designated. Some say that this teaching is so subtle and difficult to penetrate that it is not only useless but also injurious.[149] They say that those who cannot discriminate between nominal existence and objective existence would be led into affirming their misconceptions of I and mine as real because Dzong-ka-ba asserts that the mere apprehension of I and mine is valid. Still, this most unusual and penetrating of Dzong-ka-ba's teachings is a call to eradicating misconceptions and should not be taken as affirming one's accustomed conception of oneself. It is undeniable that ordinary beings see the bases of designations as the phenomena designated, and Ḏzong-ka-ḇa's teaching is clear that *even conventionally* nothing is its basis of designation. Ḏzong-ka-ḇa is able, through the subtlety of affirming the apprehension of I and mine as valid, to present all the objects and agents of cyclic existence and of nirvana under the rubric of valid establishment and thereby block one gate of the road to nihilism. This subtlety does not in any way affirm an ordinary being's consent to the appearance of objects as objectively existent; eternalism, or the reification of what exists, is not a concomitant of affirming valid existence. As Jam-ȳang-shay-ḇa says, to think that the valid establishment of objects implies their objective existence does not pass beyond the thought of non-Mādhyamikas.

The cardinal difference between the Prāsaṅgikas and the non-Prāsaṅgikas, as defined by Ḏzong-ka-ḇa, Jam-ȳang-shay-ḇa, and so forth, is the Prāsaṅgikas' uncommon notion that the *existent* person is not any or all of the mental and physical aggregates. The other Buddhist schools accept either the composite of the aggregates, or the continuum of the aggregates, or the mental consciousness, or the continuum of the mental consciousness as the self. For them, actions could have no cause or effect if the self were merely imputed in the sense of being totally unfindable among the bases of designation of the self. The Prāsaṅgikas answer that if objects were analytically findable as the concrete entities they seem to be, cause and effect would be impossible.

According to the Prāsaṅgikas, even Hearers and Solitary Realizers cognize the same emptiness as Bodhisattvas; all Superiors realize that persons and other phenomena do not inherently exist.[150] It is necessary to be freed from the afflictions to achieve nirvana, which is the passage beyond the afflictions, and the chief of afflictions is the conception that persons and other phenomena inherently exist. Thus, without destroying this conception, liberation from cyclic existence is impossible. Chandrakīrti clearly states that the emptiness of both the person and other phenomena must be cognized in order to achieve liberation.[151] The reason is that the conception of a self of phenomena causes the conception of a self of persons. For Chandrakīrti, to be liberated from cyclic existence means to have destroyed the conception that persons and other phenomena inherently exist.

When a yogi has penetrated the selflessness of the person, he applies the same reasoning to the mind and body and all other phenomena since the principle of a lack of sameness or difference of a phenomenon designated and its basis of designation can be applied to all phenomena. In other words, the emptiness understood with respect to the person is easily applied to each and every phenomenon. If one gains a penetrating understanding of the imputed nature of the person, it is impossible still to hold the view that the aggregates of mind and body are not merely imputedly existent.

The power of inferential realization of the emptiness of one phenomenon is such that a yogi is caused thereby to drop any tenets asserting the inherent existence of any phenomenon whatsoever. This conveys some sense of the esteem in which an inference of emptiness is held and of how difficult it is to develop. A yogi must proceed through the stage of correct doubt during which he suspects that phenomena are not inherently existent. In time, through long meditation, he develops a reasoned assumption that phenomena do not inherently exist. Eventually, an inference of such is generated, and through becoming familiar with this inference, he directly perceives emptiness in an utterly non-dual cognition.

Part Three
The Buddhist World

Āryadeva

Introduction

Sources
Jam-ȳang-shay-b̄a's *Great Exposition of Tenets*
L̄ong-döl's *One Hundred and Eight Bases of Explanation*
Nga-w̄ang-b̄el-den's *Annotations*
Gyel-tsap's *Commentary on (Maitreya's) 'Sublime Continuum'*
Corresponding section of the translation pp.625-6

Before meditating on emptiness it is necessary to know what exists; otherwise, a yogi will not know what is to be meditated upon as empty of inherent existence.[152] Without identifying what exists, one would think that an emptiness means an utter non-existence and not just an absence of inherent existence as a predicate of a conventionally existent object. All the excellent masters asserted that it is incorrect to teach emptiness from the very beginning because, as Jam-ȳang-shay-b̄a says, 'If emptiness were taught to the stupid from the beginning, their ignorance would increase, and they would be harmed.'

Nāgārjuna's *Sixty Stanzas of Reasoning* says:

> Initially for one seeking suchness
> It is taught that everything exists.

Chandrakīrti echoes this in his commentary, saying:

> If emptiness were taught in the very beginning to those who have not developed their intellect, very great ignorance would be produced; therefore, the Superiors do not teach emptiness in the very beginning.

Also, a great many tantric texts make it clear that no matter how gifted a student is he must practice tantra in stages.

Some commentators, however, have mistakenly taken advanced teachings on the final stage of tantra, such as not being allowed to touch images and books made from clay, stone, or wood, and have applied them to sharp beginners. Particularly, many have misapplied the teaching in the Highest Yoga Tantras that analysis is not suitable in the meditative equipoise of the stage of completion, mistakenly claiming that sharp beginners should not analyze but set their minds in utter vacuity. Their view is based on the misconception that all conventional objects are like the horns of a rabbit and the falling hairs seen by a person with cataracts, that is, non-existent. They proclaim that all conventional objects do not exist and that the meaning of conventional existence is 'what exists for a mistaken mind'. They declare that the 'gradual' teachings are for the dull, misapplying teachings pertaining to the final stages of tantra to sharp beginners. They are wrong because even the intelligent must analyze to discover suchness, be it through sutra or tantra practice. A non-conceptual and totally non-dualistic cognition of emptiness must be preceded by an inference of emptiness.[153] Inference, in general, is the cognition of a hidden meaning through having perceived a sign (reason) and having realized the concomitance of a predicate with this sign. Emptiness is cognized in dependence on a realization of, for instance, dependent-arising. Proper thought is indispensible.

If the emptiness of something is to be realized, this 'something' must be identified; an emptiness is not a vacuity which is merely the non-perception of an object. If the aggregates (*skandha, phung po*), constituents (*dhātu, khams*), sources (*āyatana, skye mched*), and so forth do not appear to the mind, an explanation of emptiness will be applied 'as if to a midnight sky', and a vacuousness of ignorance will only be increased. Therefore, one must comprehend the Prāsaṅgikas' presentation of phenomena.

Jam-ȳang-shay-b̄a (see p.626) refers to (in paraphrase) 'the phenomena that are renowned and well known in the world' which are so called because they are established as existing by an innate non-analytical awareness. This is not the mistaken innate intellect that apprehends phenomena as inherently existent, but the valid innate mind. A consciousness that analyzes whether an object can be found among or separate from its bases of imputation does not find objects; therefore, it is not in the face of an analytical consciousness that objects are said to exist. They exist in the face of a valid, innate, non-analytical awareness which every being has, from a hell-being to a Buddha. The objects that are established as existing conventionally by such a consciousness are never refuted; an analytical consciousness refutes merely their ultimate or objective existence.

Phenomena are divided into two classes: an afflicted class consisting of fifty-three phenomena and a pure class consisting of fifty-five phenomena.[154] These one hundred and eight phenomena are the bases of the explanations of emptiness in the Perfection of Wisdom Sutras and are called 'the one hundred and eight bases of commentary'. The classification into afflicted and pure classes does not imply that all members of each class are afflictions or pure phenomena; the groupings are merely rough divisions.

The fifty-three phenomena of the afflicted class

The five aggregates which are the bases for the further division of most of the other phenomena:

1 forms
2 feelings
3 discriminations
4 compositional factors
5 consciousnesses

The six senses which are the supports of their respective consciousnesses:

6 eye sense powers
7 ear sense powers
8 nose sense powers
9 tongue sense powers
10 body sense powers
11 mental sense powers

The six consciousnesses which depend on these senses:

12 eye consciousnesses
13 ear consciousnesses
14 nose consciousnesses
15 tongue consciousnesses
16 body consciousnesses
17 mental consciousnesses

The objects of those consciousnesses:

18 visible forms
19 sounds
20 odors
21 tastes
22 tangible objects
23 phenomena

The six contacts (distinguishing objects as pleasant, unpleasant, or neutral) which arise upon the aggregations of a sense, an object, and a consciousness:

24 contacts upon the aggregation of an eye sense, a visible form, and an eye consciousness
25 contacts upon the aggregation of an ear sense, a sound, and an ear consciousness
26 contacts upon the aggregation of a nose sense, an odor, and a nose consciousness
27 contacts upon the aggregation of a tongue sense, a taste, and a tongue consciousness
28 contacts upon the aggregation of a body sense, a tangible object, and a body consciousness

29 contacts upon the aggregation of a mental sense, a phenomenon, and a mental consciousness

The six feelings which are the experiences arising from contacts:

30 feelings arising from contact upon the aggregation of an eye sense, a visible form, and an eye consciousness
31 feelings arising from contact upon the aggregation of an ear sense, a sound, and an ear consciousness
32 feelings arising from contact upon the aggregation of a nose sense, an odor, and a nose consciousness
33 feelings arising from contact upon the aggregation of a tongue sense, a taste, and a tongue consciousness
34 feelings arising from contact upon the aggregation of a body sense, a tangible object, and a body consciousness
35 feelings arising from contact upon the aggregation of a mental sense, a phenomenon, and a mental consciousness

The six elements which are the bases of production:

36 earth
37 water
38 fire
39 wind
40 space
41 consciousness

The twelve branches of dependent-arising, which are to be seen as disadvantageous:

42 ignorance
43 action
44 consciousness
45 name and form
46 six sources
47 contact
48 feeling
49 attachment
50 grasping
51 existence
52 birth
53 aging and death

The fifty-five phenomena of the pure class

The six perfections which are the paths of practice:

1 giving
2 ethics
3 patience
4 effort
5 concentration
6 wisdom

The eighteen emptinesses which are the paths of the view:

7 emptiness of the internal, that is, of the five senses (*adhyātmashūnyatā*)[155]
8 emptiness of the external, that is, of the six types of objects which are the objects of the five senses and of the mental consciousness (*bahirdhāshūnyatā*)
9 emptiness of the internal and external, that is, of the loci of the senses, the gross orbs of the eyes, etc. (*adhyātmabahirdhāshūnyatā*)
10 emptiness of emptiness, that is, of the emptiness that is the nature of phenomena (this eliminates the qualms of those who might think that emptiness truly exists because it is established by a consciousness which analyzes suchness) (*shūnyatāshūnyatā*)
11 emptiness of the great, that is, of the ten directions (*mahāshūnyatā*)
12 emptiness of the ultimate, that is, of nirvana (*paramārthashūnyatā*)
13 emptiness of products (*saṃskṛtashūnyatā*)
14 emptiness of non-products (*asaṃskṛtashūnyatā*)
15 emptiness of what has passed beyond the extremes, that is, of what is free of the extremes of permanence and annihilation (*atyantashūnyatā*)
16 emptiness of what is beginningless and endless, that is, of cyclic existence (*anavarāgrashūnyatā*)
17 emptiness of the indestructible, that is, of the indestructible Mahāyāna (*anavakārashūnyatā*)
18 emptiness of nature, that is, of the emptinesses which are the

nature of phenomena (this eliminates the qualms of those who might think that an emptiness truly exists because a final nature exists without being produced by anyone) (*prakṛtishūnyatā*)

19 emptiness of all phenomena, that is, of the eighteen constituents, etc. (*sarvadharmashūnyatā*)

20 emptiness of definitions, that is, of the definitions of all phenomena from forms through to omniscient consciousnesses (*lakṣhaṇashūnyatā*)

21 emptiness of the unapprehendable, that is, of the past, present, and future which are unapprehendable as the cessation of phenomena, their presence, and their non-production (*anupalambhashūnyatā*)

22 emptiness of the inherent existence of non-things, that is, of inherently existent non-products (*abhāvasvabhāvashūnyatā*)

23 emptiness of things, that is, of the five aggregates (*bhāvashūnyatā*)

24 emptiness of non-things, that is, of non-products (*abhāvashūnyatā*)

The thirty-seven harmonies with enlightenment which are the yogic paths, divided into seven sections:[156]

25 four establishments in mindfulness—of body, feelings, thoughts, and phenomena—attained with the lesser path of accumulation. These are meditations on the impermanence, misery, emptiness, and selflessness of one's own body, feelings, thoughts, and other internal phenomena. Bodhisattvas would extend the field of meditation to include all sentient beings' bodies, feelings, and so forth.

26 four thorough abandonings—the abandoning of afflictions already generated, the non-generation of afflictions not yet generated, the increasing of pure phenomena already generated, and the generation of pure phenomena not yet generated—attained with the middling path of accumulation. These are called 'thorough' abandonings because the mode of practice is suitable, when supplemented by the aspiration

to highest enlightenment for the sake of all sentient beings, to lead one to Buddhahood. Without changing the type of object or mode of cognition, these paths lead to final enlightenment whereas the non-Buddhist 'abandonings' have to be altered in form to lead to the final aim. Even the accomplishments of virtues are 'abandonings' because their respective opposites must be forsaken.

27 four legs of manifestation – aspiration, effort, thought, and analysis. These are called 'legs' because they are prerequisites for magical manifestation. The four exist simultaneously when a manifestation is actually being made, and they are serial when one is practicing magical manifestation, first generating an aspiration to create a manifestation, and so forth. They are attained on the great path of accumulation

28 five powers—faith, effort, mindfulness, meditative stabilization, and wisdom—attained on the levels of heat and peak of the path of preparation

29 five forces—faith, effort, mindfulness, meditative stabilization, and wisdom—attained on the levels of forbearance and supreme mundane qualities of the path of preparation

30 seven branches of enlightenment—mindfulness, discrimination of phenomena, effort, joy, pliancy, meditative stabilization, and equanimity—attained with the path of seeing

31 eight-fold path—correct views, correct realization, correct speech, correct aims of actions, correct livelihood, correct effort, correct mindfulness, and correct meditative stabilization—attained with the path of meditation. When the state of Foe Destroyer is actualized, all thirty-seven harmonies of enlightenment have been attained.

The paths of calming:

32 four noble truths—true sufferings, true origins of suffering, true cessations of suffering, and true paths out of suffering

33 four concentrations—first, second, third, and fourth concentrations

34 four immeasurables—equanimity, love, compassion, and joy

35 four formless absorptions—infinite space, infinite consciousness, nothingness, and peak of cyclic existence

36 eight liberations: these eight are called 'liberations' not because they liberate beings from cyclic existence but because they free beings from the manifest activity of specific afflictions. They are to be distinguished from complete cessations of afflictions which involve the conquest of both the manifest appearance and the potencies of the afflictions.

1 the embodied looking at a form: a yogi considers himself to be a being with a body and cultivates any of the four concentrations which are included in the Form Realm

2 the formless looking at a form: a yogi considers himself to be a being without a body and cultivates any of the four concentrations which are included in the Form Realm

3 beautiful form: a yogi considers himself to have an attractive body and cultivates any of the four concentrations which are included in the Form Realm. (The above three are considered prerequisites for making physical manifestations and are called the three paths of manifestation.)

4 infinite space: a yogi concentrates on space and imagines it is infinite with just space as his object of observation

5 infinite consciousness: a yogi concentrates on consciousness and imagines it is infinite with just consciousness as his object of observation

6 nothingness: a yogi imagines that there is nothing to be apprehended and no apprehender

7 peak of cyclic existence: a yogi imagines that there are no coarse objects to be apprehended but that there are subtle objects of apprehension

8 equipoise of cessation: a yogi enters a state of meditative equipoise which is the absence of the manifest activity of the six consciousnesses

37 nine serial absorptions—first concentration, second concentration, third concentration, fourth concentration, infinite space, infinite consciousness, nothingness, peak of cyclic existence, and absorption of cessation

38 paths of insight—meditative stabilization on the three doors

of liberation: wishlessness, signlessness, and emptiness. Wishlessness is the emptiness of a phenomenon from the point of view of its not inherently producing effects.[157] Signlessness is the emptiness of a phenomenon from the point of view of its not having been inherently produced from causes. Emptiness is the emptiness of the entity of a phenomenon itself.

The paths of special qualities:

39 five clairvoyances–divine eye, divine ear, knowledge of others' minds, memory of former lives, and knowledge of the extinction of contaminations

40 four meditative stabilizations–'going as a hero', 'sky treasury', 'stainless', and 'loftily looking lion'

41 four doors of retention–the retention of patience (for the sake of fearlessness with respect to emptiness), the retention of secret speech (for the ability to make spells to pacify the injurious), the retention of words (for not forgetting names, thoughts, and meanings), the retention of meaning (for not forgetting the individual and general characteristics of phenomena)

The paths of effect:

42 ten powers:[158]

1 knowledge of sources and non-sources. This is direct knowledge of cause and effect within cyclic existence, such as the arising of pleasure from virtues and of pain from non-virtues, and direct knowledge of causes and effects included within the class of pure phenomena, such as the paths and their fruits. This first power is achieved through steadiness with respect to ascertaining the relation of cause and effect and with respect to the two forms of the mind of enlightenment–the aspiration to highest enlightenment for the sake of all beings as well as its consequent practices and the wisdom directly cognizing emptiness.

2 knowledge of the fruition of actions. This is direct knowledge of the definiteness of actions (such as the fact that non-virtues never cause pleasure and virtues never cause

pain), the increase of the potencies established by actions, the non-wasting of deeds done, and the non-meeting with the effects of actions not done by oneself. It is achieved through conviction in the relationship of actions and their effects.

3 knowledge of those who are superior and those who are inferior, or those who have faith and those having heavy afflictions and so forth. It is achieved through teaching doctrines in accordance with the faculties of trainees.

4 knowledge of the varieties of dispositions. This is the knowledge of the many different lineages in the mental continuums of trainees. It is achieved through teaching doctrines in accordance with the dispositions of trainees.

5 knowledge of the varieties of trainees' interests in the various great and small vehicles. It is achieved through teaching doctrines in accordance with the interests of trainees.

6 knowledge of the paths proceeding to cyclic existences and of the paths to the three enlightenments of Hearers, Solitary Realizers, and Bodhisattvas. It is achieved through practicing the various vehicles and paths.

7 knowledge of the concentrations (*dhyāna*), liberations (*vimokṣha*), meditative stabilizations (*samādhi*), and meditative absorptions (*samāpatti*), and knowledge of others' afflictions and others' non-contamination. It is achieved through completing the practice of meditative stabilization.

8 knowledge mindful of former states. This is direct knowledge of all former lives of oneself and others. It is achieved through not having spoiled the roots of virtue during the paths of learning.

9 knowledge of one's own and others' deaths and births. This is included within the clairvoyance of the divine eye and is achieved through formerly giving lamps and supramundane paths to sentient beings.

10 knowledge of the extinction of all contaminations. This is achieved through formerly teaching doctrines for the

sake of extinguishing contaminations and through one's own actualization of such meaning.

The six knowledges of (1) sources and non-sources, (2) fruition of actions, (3) the superior and inferior, (4) varieties of dispositions, (5) varieties of interests, and (6) paths are similar to a diamond instrument piercing the armor of the obstructions to omniscience. The three knowledges of (7) the concentrations and so forth, (8) former states, and (9) death and birth are similar to a diamond instrument destroying the wall of the obstructions to meditative absorption. The knowledge of (10) extinction of all contaminations is similar to a diamond instrument cutting the trees of the afflictive obstructions.

43 four fearlessnesses:[159]

1 fearlessness with respect to the assertion, 'I am completely and perfectly enlightened with respect to all phenomena.' For, one will not encounter even the name of an opponent who could correctly say that one does not know such and such a phenomenon. It is achieved through lacking any stinginess with respect to the doctrine.

2 fearlessness with respect to teaching that the afflictive obstructions are obstacles to liberation and that the obstructions to omniscience are obstacles to simultaneous cognition of all phenomena, and that, therefore, these are to be ceased. For, one will not encounter even the name of an opponent who could correctly say that reliance on desire and so forth would not obstruct a being from liberation. It is achieved through not falling under the influence of an obstructive doctrine.

3 fearlessness with respect to teaching the paths of deliverance. For, there is no opponent who could say correctly that these paths are not paths leading to liberation. It is achieved through practicing the paths to liberation.

4 fearlessness with respect to asserting that the

contaminations have been extinguished. For, one will not see even the name of an opponent who could correctly dispute the assertion that one has attained the cessation of all afflictions and their potencies. It is achieved through formerly abandoning pride.

44 four sciences—knowledge of doctrines, of the general and specific characters of phenomena, of the many languages so that appropriate definitions can be given, and of the varieties of entities, aspects, relationships, and differences of phenomena in the sense of having the bravery to make these distinctions

45 great love

46 great compassion

47 eighteen unshared attributes of Buddhas:[160]

1 being non-mistaken physically, such as not going on the wrong road

2 being non-mistaken verbally

3 not decreasing in mindfulness

4 not ever not being in meditative equipoise

5 not having the various discriminations of one-pointedly apprehending cyclic existence as to be forsaken and nirvana as to be attained, or, in other words, not discriminating cyclic existence and nirvana, or phenomena and their emptiness, as different entities

6 not being disinterested

7 aspiration

8 effort

9 mindfulness

10 wisdom

11 non-degeneration of liberation, that is, non-degeneration from the abandonment of obstructions

12 non-degeneration of the wisdom realizing liberation

13, 14, 15 governing by wisdom the activities of body, speech, and mind

16, 17, 18 non-obstructed wisdom with respect to all objects of knowledge in the past, present, and future due to the absence of any impeding obstructions

The five beings who actualize the paths:

48 Stream Enterers
49 Once Returners
50 Never Returners
51 Foe Destroyers
52 Solitary Realizers

The three final fruits:

53 knowers of the bases, or Hearers' cognizers of emptiness
54 knowers of the paths, or Bodhisattvas' cognizers of emptiness
55 omniscient consciousnesses, or Buddhas' cognizers of all phenomena simultaneously.

1 *The Selfless*

Sources
Kensur Lekden's oral teachings
J̄ang-ḡya's *Presentation of Tenets*

Traditionally, a master begins a student's instruction with a presentation of the Buddhist world.[161] He starts with the selfless as a basis and divides the selfless into the existent and the non-existent:

Chart 7: *Divisions of the Selfless*

selfless *nairātmya* *bdag med*
- non-existent *asat* *med pa*
- existent *sat* *yod pa*

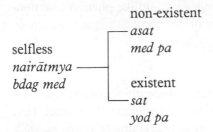

In the Prāsaṅgika system 'the selfless' means that which does not inherently exist. The first category of the Buddhist world is the non-inherently existent because both existents and non-existents do not inherently exist. Since nothing inherently exists, this is the broadest possible category.

Non-existents

Some of the more famous examples of non-existents are the horns of a rabbit, the hairs of a turtle, a garment made of turtle hairs, the diadem of a frog, a blue snow mountain (a snowy mountain appearing to be blue), a double moon, a self-sufficient person, and inherently existent phenomena. The horns of a rabbit do not inherently exist because they do not exist at all. The mere realization of their non-existence reveals that the horns of a rabbit do not inherently exist; therefore, the non-inherent existence of the horns of a rabbit is not an emptiness. An emptiness is not understood through realizing the mere non-existence of an object; it is known through comprehending in an existent object the absence of the quality of inherent or objective existence.

It is said that the horns of a rabbit do not inherently exist, are not inherently existent, and are non-inherently existent. In Buddhist logic none of these statements is necessarily an affirming negation; the fact that the horns of a rabbit are non-inherently existent does not imply that they have some other type of existence. The statement indicates a non-affirming negation.

A synonym of 'non-existent' is 'non-phenomenal non-product'. Non-existents are non-products because they are not produced from an aggregation of causes and conditions; they are also non-phenomena because they do not exist, unlike phenomenal non-products, such as the permanent phenomenon space, which do exist.

Existents

An existent is selfless, or non-inherently existent; its non-inherent existence is an emptiness. Synonyms of 'existent' (*sat, yod pa*) are 'phenomenon' (*dharma, chos*), 'object' (*viṣhaya, yul*), 'object of knowledge' (*jñeya, shes bya*), and 'established base' (*vastu, gzhi grub*). Thus, everything that exists is a phenomenon (*dharma*), so translated because all *dharmas* are objects of knowledge and can *appear* to the mind, even permanent phenomena such as emptiness and space. All existents are phenomena, and there is no noumenon which is a separate entity from the category of phenomena because nothing independently exists. The word 'noumenon' is not used in this translation scheme though it might be used for words indicating the nature of phenomena, such as *dharmatā*, as long as it is understood that all noumena are phenomena.

All existents are *objects* because whether they are subjects or objects they can be objects of a consciousness. All existents are objects of knowledge, or more literally objects of knowing, because all objects are continually known by some consciousness. Without even considering the penetrating clairvoyances of Buddhas and yogis, the various hungry ghosts and unusual types of beings which exist everywhere insure that even particles in the centers of huge rocks are cognized by some being.

All existents are *existent bases* or *established bases* because they are established as existing by valid cognizers. Valid cognizers are consciousnesses that are either direct perceivers, which cognize their objects without the medium of images and concepts, or inferring consciousnesses, which cognize their referent objects through images and concepts (see pp.346-7).

Existents are divided into two types:

Chart 8: *Divisions of Existents*

existent
- permanent phenomenon / *nitya* / *rtag pa*
- thing / *bhāva* / *dngos po*

PERMANENT PHENOMENA

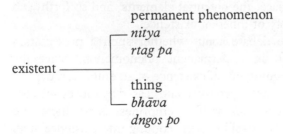

Permanent phenomena are defined as phenomena that do not disintegrate, disintegrating phenomena being those which cease every instant due to causes and conditions. The permanent are specified as non-disintegrating *phenomena* because the non-existent or non-phenomenal are also non-disintegrating. Because of the inclusion of the word 'phenomena' in the definition of the permanent, non-existents are not permanent, even though they do not disintegrate. A synonym of permanent phenomenon is 'uncompounded phenomenon' (*asaṃskṛtadharma, 'dus ma byas kyi chos*).

There are two types of permanent phenomena: the occasional permanent and the non-occasional permanent. Though in common parlance 'permanent' means 'always existent', the philosophers of the Sautrāntika school and above have limited its meaning to 'non-disintegrating existent'. Therefore, phenomena that come into existence and go out of existence but do not disintegrate momentarily due to causes and conditions are 'occasional permanents'. For instance, the emptiness of a cup comes into existence when the cup is made and goes out of existence when the cup is destroyed; however, because the emptiness of a cup does not disintegrate moment by moment and does not change momentarily from one thing into another through the action of causes and conditions, it is non-disintegrating. Thus, because the emptiness of a cup is both a phenomenon and non-disintegrating but does not exist forever, it is an 'occasional permanent'. However, emptiness in general, though not existing as a separate entity from its specific instances, is always existent because there never is a moment when there is no instance of emptiness. There are always minds, space, the potential elements, and so forth, and these are all empty of inherent existence.

There is some debate about whether such a presentation makes emptiness an impermanent phenomenon. Since the coming into and going out of existence of an emptiness depend on a phenomenon that is produced and ceased by causes and conditions, it begins to look as if an emptiness is produced and ceased. However, it is said that the coming into existence of an emptiness, which is merely the non-inherent existence of an object, is unlike the production of an object by causes and conditions, and thus no one speaks of the production and disintegration of emptinesses.

Permanent phenomena are divided, but not exclusively (there are other phenomena which are technically permanent, such as the double reverse of pot which only appears to thought through the mental exclusion of non-pot or, more accurately, non-one with pot) into four types:

Chart 9: *Divisions of Permanent Phenomena*

- permanent phenomenon
  - space
ākāsha
nam mkha'
  - analytical cessation
pratisaṃkhyānirodha
so sor brtags 'gog
  - non-analytical cessation
apratisaṃkhyānirodha
so sor brtags min gyi 'gog pa
  - suchness
tathatā
de bzhin nyid

Space

A space is a mere absence of obstructive contact. Space is all pervading because there is an absence of obstructive contact everywhere, even where solid objects exist, for without an absence of obstructive contact an obstructive object could not be there in the first place.

Because a space is a mere absence of obstructive contact, it is a non-affirming negative—there is no positive thing implied in its place—and it is in this sense that an emptiness, which is a non-affirming negative of inherent existence, is said to be similar to a space. Also, space, like emptiness, has parts because each physical object has a lack of obstructive contact, just as each object has a lack of inherent existence. The space of an object refers not to the area of the object but to the absence of obstructive contact associated with it.

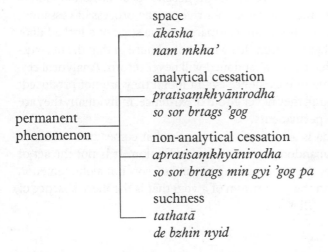

Analytical cessations

Analytical cessations are final states of cessation of obstructions upon analysis of the nature of phenomena, which are such that those obstructions will never return. They are enumerated as true cessations, the third of the four noble truths, in terms of the individual obstructions being abandoned on the levels of the paths. 'Cessation' here means the absence of an affliction following abandonment and does not refer to the process of cessation. Analytical cessations are compared to the state of a locked door after a robber has been thrown out of a house in that the obstructions that have been abandoned will never return. Analytical cessations come into existence even though they are not produced; thus, although they never go out of existence, individually they are occasional permanents.

A nirvana is an analytical cessation that comes into existence upon the abandonment of the last affliction. It is not the act of cessation or the act of passing beyond sorrow but a phenomenon possessed in the continuum of a yogi that is the mere absence of the ceased afflictions.

Non-analytical cessations

Non-analytical cessations are compared to the state of having thrown out a robber but having failed to lock the door. They are temporary absences of afflictions and so forth due to the incompleteness of necessary conditions, upon the aggregation of which the afflictions will return. For instance, when a person pays intense attention to what he is seeing, he does not desire food. The desire for food has not disappeared from his mental continuum forever, but has temporarily disappeared. Non-analytical cessations come into existence and go out of existence and so are, in terms of specific instances, occasional permanents.

Suchness

'Suchness' refers to 'emptiness' because whether Buddhas appear or not the nature of phenomena remains as such.[162] A suchness is also a 'natural nirvana' (*prakṛtiparinirvāṇa, rang bzhin myang 'das*) which does not refer to an actual passage beyond sorrow, that is, an overcoming of the afflictions, but to an emptiness itself that naturally is passed beyond inherent existence. The teaching that cyclic existence and nirvana are not different means that the phenomena of cyclic existence are the same entities as their natural nirvanas, or emptinesses, and not separate entities. It does not mean there is no difference between being afflicted with the conception of inherent existence and not being so afflicted.

THINGS

The other division of existents is comprised of things or actualities. The definition of thing is: that which is able to perform a function (particularly the function of producing an effect). Therefore, according to all schools except Vaibhāṣhika, permanent phenomena are not things. The Vaibhāṣhikas say that permanent phenomena are things because, for instance, a space performs the function of allowing an object to be moved. The other systems of tenets, including Prāsaṅgika, say that the presence or absence of another obstructive object is what allows or does not allow an object to be moved, not space itself which is just a non-affirming negative of obstructive contact. Still, even the Prāsaṅgikas call emptiness—a non-affirming negative of inherent existence—a 'cause' of Buddhahood because without it the transformation of the mind into wisdom would not be possible. However, it is not said that space causes the possibility of movement, just as emptiness does not actually cause Buddhahood.

Things are impermanent (*anitya, mi rtag pa*) because of being phenomena that disintegrate moment by moment. Though impermanent things are momentary, they are not just one moment; if they were, it could not be said that beings without yogic direct perception ever perceive things because they are not capable of realizing a single isolated instant. The impermanent things that these beings cognize are series of moments; the phenomena are imputed to a series of moments and are unfindable among the various moments or as the series itself. Still, the imputed nature of things does not prevent their performing functions; rather, being merely imputed is a prerequisite for the performance of a function. If things were frozen in a world of inherent existence, unaffected by causes and conditions and unable to affect anything else, there could not be any cause and effect. Non-inherent existence is the very basis of cause and effect, and the presence of cause and effect is a sign of non-inherent existence.

Things are also products, or caused phenomena, or compounded phenomena (*saṃskṛta, dus byas*) because they are made (*kṛta, byas*) in dependence on the aggregation (*saṃ, 'dus*) of causes and conditions. The term 'thing' (*bhāva, dngos po*), when used strictly as it is here in the table of phenomena, applies only to products; however when it is used loosely as it often is in the Perfection of Wisdom Sutras, it refers to both products and non-products as when Buddha says that all things do not ultimately exist.

Things, or products, are divided into three:

Chart 10: *Divisions of Things*

thing
- form / *rūpa* / *gzugs*
- consciousness / *jñāna* / *shes pa*
- non-associated compositional factor / *viprayukta-saṃskāra* / *ldan min 'du byed*

Forms
Source:
Cha-har Ge-shay's *Identification of Elements, Elemental Evolutes, And So Forth*

Etymologically, a form is so called because it is suitable to become an object of a sense consciousness upon the aggregation of other causes, such as the presence of an eye sense.[163] However, because there are forms that are perceived only by the mental consciousness, this explanation is merely an etymology and not a definition.

Forms are divided into eleven types—the five physical sense

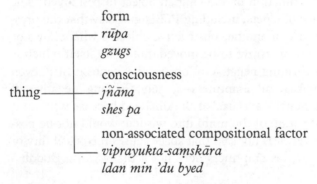

powers, the five objects of the senses, and forms which are objects only of the mental consciousness:

Chart 11: *Divisions of Forms*

form
- eye sense
  chakṣhurindriya, mig gi dbang po
- ear sense
  shrotrendriya, rna ba'i dbang po
- nose sense
  ghrāṇendriya, sna'i dbang po
- tongue sense
  jihvendriya, lce'i dbang po
- body sense
  kāyendriya, lus kyi dbang po
- visible form
  rūpa, gzugs
- sound
  shabda, sgra
- odor
  gandha, dri
- taste
  rasa, ro
- tangible object
  sprashṭavya, reg bya
- form for the mental consciousness
  dharmāyatanarūpa
  chos kyi skye mched pa'i gzugs

Sense powers

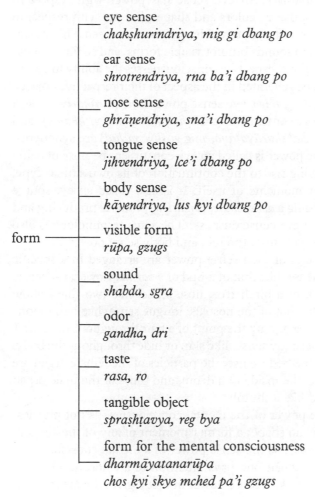

The five sense powers are neither the coarse organs, which are the eyes, ears, nose, tongue, and body, nor are they consciousness. They are clear matter located in the coarse organs which cannot be seen with the eye but can be seen by certain clairvoyants. They give their respective consciousnesses dominance or power with respect to certain objects and are thus called 'powers' (*indriya, dbang po*). An eye sense has power with respect to visible forms, that is, colors and shapes, but not with respect to sounds, odors, tastes, or tangible objects. An ear sense has power with respect to sounds but not visible forms, and so forth. Sense powers give their respective consciousnesses the ability to apprehend and to be generated in the aspect of their respective objects.

Eye (*chakṣhuḥ, mig*), eye sense power (*chakṣhurindriya, mig gi dbang po*), eye-constituent (*chakṣhurdhātu, mig gi khams*), and eye-source (*chakṣhurāyatana, mig gi skye mched*) are synonyms. An eye sense power is called an eye-constituent because of being the *cause* giving rise to the continuation of its own similar type, that is, later moments of itself. It is also called an eye-source because of being a *door, cause, condition,* or *source* producing and increasing an eye consciousness. The same terminology is also used for the ear, nose, tongue, and body sense powers.

The particles of each sense power are arranged in a specific shape: eye sense, like that of a bud of a *zar-ma* flower; ear sense, like the knot of a birch tree; nose sense, like two fine hollow needles at the root of the nostrils; tongue sense, like half moons having the area of only the point of a hair throughout the center of the tongue; body sense, like skin or hide throughout the body. As types of the body sense, the particles of the female organ are arranged like the inside of a drum, and those of the male organ are arranged like a thumb.

The sense power of the mental consciousness is not physical and thus has no shape; a former moment of any of the six consciousnesses acts as the sense power of a mental consciousness. For instance, when one pays attention to a color, an eye consciousness acts like a sense power in that it gives the mental consciousness the ability to perceive a visible object.

A sense power is an uncommon empowering condition (*asādhārana-adhipatipratyaya, thun mong ma yin pa'i bdag rkyen*) of a consciousness because it gives it power with respect to its own special type of object. Also, a former moment of consciousness causes it to be an entity capable of *experiencing* objects. Thus, a mental consciousness has two consciousnesses as its causes: any of the six consciousnesses which is its empowering condition and a former moment of consciousness which is its 'immediately preceding condition' (*samanantarapratyaya, de ma dag rkyen*).

A consciousness is also caused, or affected, by an object in the sense that an object causes a consciousness to be generated in its image, much as objects cause a mirror to reflect their image. These objects are called 'observed-object-conditions' (*ālambana-pratyaya, dmigs rkyen*). However, the world which is being seen is not just a mental image; the co-ordination of an image in consciousness with an object certifies that the object is being perceived properly, but the object seen is an external object, not an internal image. The Buddhist theory is not that everything being perceived exists inside either the eye or the brain.

Visible forms

Visible forms (*rūpa, gzugs*) are defined as objects of apprehension by an eye consciousness and are to be distinguished from the general term 'form' which is the basis of the division into eleven types of forms. A visible form is called a form-constituent (*rūpadhātu*) because of being a *cause* giving rise to the continuation of its own similar type, that is, later moments of visible form, and is called a form-source (*rūpa-āyatana*) because of being a form that is a *door, cause, condition,* or *source* of an eye consciousness. Visible forms are of two types:

Chart 12: *Divisions of Visible Forms*

- visible form
  - color / *varṇa* / *kha dog*
  - shape / *saṃsthāna* / *dbyibs*

Colors. There are twelve colors, four primary and eight secondary (see Chart 13). The four primary colors are the colors of the four elements. Wind is blue; earth, yellow; water, white; and fire, red.

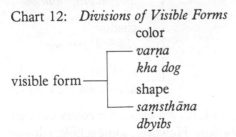

Chart 13: *Divisions of Colors*

- color
  - primary color
    - blue — *nīla, sngon po*
    - yellow — *pīta, ser po*
    - white — *avadāta, dkar po*
    - red — *lohita, dmar po*
  - secondary color
    - cloud — *abhra, sprin*
    - smoke — *dhūma, du ba*
    - dust — *rajaḥ, brdul*
    - mist — *mahikā, khug sna*
    - illumination — *āloka, snang ba*
    - darkness — *andhakāra, mun pa*
    - shadow — *chhāyā, grib ma*
    - sunlight — *ātapa, nyi ma'i 'od ser*

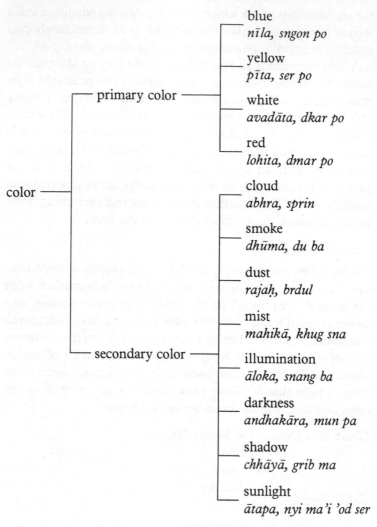

It is not that clouds and so forth are secondary colors but that their colors are secondary colors. However, some scholars do say that illumination, darkness, sunlight, and shadow themselves are secondary colors. Illumination refers to the light of the moon, stars, fire, medicine, and jewels. Darkness refers to a form that obscures other forms and causes one to see gloom and blackness. Darkness obscures other forms such that they cannot be seen, whereas shadow makes other forms a little unclear but still perceivable; thus, darkness and shadow have a difference of density. Sunlight refers to the illumination of other forms when the sun appears.

The eight secondary colors do not include the secondary colors that are mixes of primary colors, such as green which is a mix of blue and yellow, and thus the category is not all-inclusive.

An eye consciousness actually apprehends only colors and shapes. Although pots, pillars, and so forth appear to an eye consciousness and although it is said that an eye consciousness sees them, pots, pillars, and so forth are not objects of apprehension by an eye consciousness. Rather, the color and shape of pots, pillars, and so forth—that is, their visible form—are objects of apprehension by an eye consciousness and thus are also form-constituents and form-sources. Although pots and pillars are matter and are forms, they are not visible forms, form-constituents or form-sources, but tangible objects, tangible-object-constituents, and tangible-object-sources. Similarly, when one sees the visible form of a human or horse, one sees their shape and color but does not, in a sense, see a human or horse. Also, seeing earth and water is a case of seeing their color, for earth and water are tangible objects, and, therefore, the eye does not see the capacity of hardness or of moistening. Furthermore, when the visible form of a pot is seen, an eye consciousness does not conceive, 'This is a pot'; a mental consciousness is the identifier and designator of names.

Shapes. Shapes are of eight types only (see Chart 14). Long refers to the form of a long board, a long rope, a long (deep) spring, and so forth. Short arises in relation to those. High and low refer to, for instance, a high mountain and a low valley. A square, or perhaps polygon, is technically a shape of equal sides, such as dice, or a pentagon, hexagon, and so forth; however, the shapes of a rectangular box or a board are also included. Round refers to

Chart 14: *Divisions of Shapes*

shape
- long — *dīrgha, ring ba*
- short — *hrasva, thung ba*
- high — *unnata, mtho ba*
- low — *avanata, dma' ba*
- square — *vṛtta, lham pa*
- round — *parimaṇḍala, zlum po*
- level — *shāta, phya le ba*
- non-level — *vishāta, phya le ba ma yin pa*

either the globular, like an egg, or the flat, like a mandala. Level refers to any shape having an even surface, whereas non-level refers to a shape with, for instance, bumps and depressions.

Sounds

Sounds, which are defined as objects of hearing by an ear consciousness, are of only eight types (see Chart 15). Sound, sound-constituent, and sound-source are synonyms. Although sounds are entities constructed from particles, they are not form-sources, that is to say, visible forms.

Odors

Odors, which are defined as objects of smelling by a nose consciousness, are of only four types (see Chart 16). An equal odor, such as the odor of sesame, does not infuse other objects, whereas the opposite is true of an unequal odor such as the odor of garlic. Odor, odor-constituent, and odor-source are synonyms.

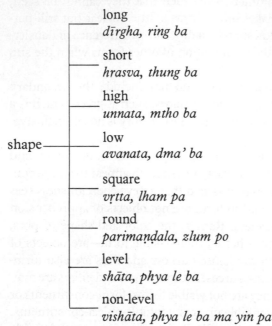

Chart 15: *Divisions of Sounds*

- sound
  - sound caused by elements conjoined with consciousness *upāttamahābhūtahetuka, zin pa'i 'byung ba chen po rgyur byas pa*
    - articulate sound *sattvākhya, sems can du ston pa*
      - pleasant sound, e.g., words of doctrine *yasha, snyan pa*
      - unpleasant sound, e.g., harsh words *ayasha, mi snyan pa*
    - inarticulate sound *asattvākhya, sems can du mi ston pa*
      - pleasant sound, e.g., sound of fingers snapping *yasha, snyan pa*
      - unpleasant sound, e.g., sound of a fist on impact *ayasha, mi snyan pa*
  - sound caused by elements not conjoined with consciousness *anupāttamahābhūtahetuka, ma zin pa'i 'byung ba chen po rgyur byas pa*
    - articulate sound *sattvākhya, sems can du ston pa*
      - pleasant sound, e.g., words of doctrine taught by trees rustled by a Buddha's extraordinary powers *yasha, snyan pa*
      - unpleasant sound, e.g., words of scolding from a tree rustled by a Buddha's extraordinary powers *ayasha, mi snyan pa*
    - inarticulate sound *asattvākhya, sems can du mi ston pa*
      - pleasant sound, e.g., sound of a drum *yasha, snyan pa*
      - unpleasant sound, e.g., sound of crashing stones *ayasha, mi snyan pa*

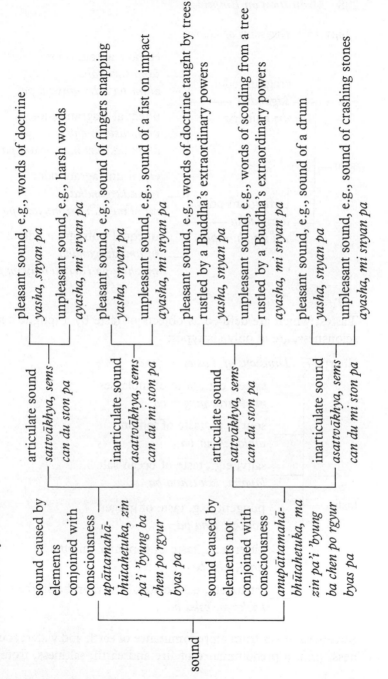

Chart 16: *Divisions of Odors*

- odor
  - fragrant odor / *sugandha* / *dri zhim pa*
    - equal fragrant odor / *samasugandha* / *zhim pa'i dri mnyam pa*
    - unequal fragrant odor / *visamasugandha* / *zhim pa'i dri mi mnyam pa*
  - unfragrant odor / *durgandha* / *dri mi zhim pa*
    - equal unfragrant odor / *samadurgandha* / *mi zhim pa'i dri mnyam pa*
    - unequal unfragrant odor / *visamadurgandha* / *mi zhim pa'i dri mi mnyam pa*

Tastes.

Tastes, which are defined as objects of taste by a tongue consciousness, are of only six types:

Chart 17: *Divisions of Tastes*

- taste
  - sweet, e.g., taste of molasses / *madhura, mngar ba*
  - sour, e.g., taste of lemon / *āmla, skyur ba*
  - salty, e.g., taste of ocean salt / *lavaṇa, lan tshva ba*
  - pungent, e.g. taste of ginger / *kaṭuka, tsha ba*
  - bitter, e.g., taste of gentiana chiretta / *tikta, kha ba*
  - astringent, e.g., taste of the myrobalan fruit / *kaṣhāya, bska ba*

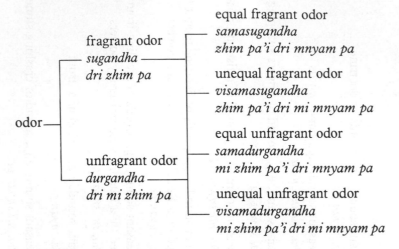

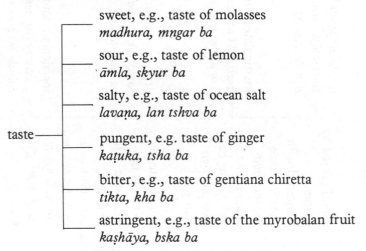

Sweetness arises from a predominance of earth and water; sourness, from a predominance of fire and earth; saltiness, from a predominance of water and fire; pungency, from a predominance of fire and wind; bitterness, from a predominance of water and wind; and astringency, from a predominance of earth and wind.

Tangible objects.

Tangible objects, which are defined as objects of touch by a body consciousness, are of only eleven types—the four elements and seven tangible objects that are arisen from the elements:

Chart 18: *Divisions of Tangible Objects*

- tangible object
  - element — *bhūta, 'byung ba*
    - earth — *pṛthivī, sa*
    - water — *ap, chu*
    - fire — *tejas, me*
    - wind — *vāyu, rlung*
  - tangible object arisen from elements — *bhautika, 'byung 'gyur*
    - smoothness — *shlakṣhṇatva, 'jam pa*
    - roughness — *karkashatva, rtsub pa*
    - heaviness — *gurutva, lci ba*
    - lightness — *laghutva, yang ba*
    - cold — *shīta, grang ba*
    - hunger — *bubhūkṣhā, bkres pa*
    - thirst — *pipāsā, skom pa*

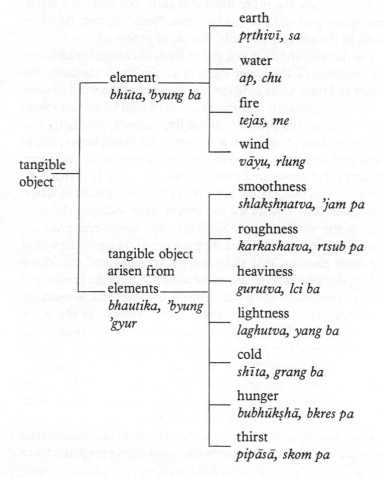

The definition of earth is the hard and obstructive; its entity is hardness, and its function is the obstruction of other physical objects. The definition of water is the damp and moistening. The definition of fire is the hot and burning. The definition of wind is the light and moving.

The particles that serve as the bases for the construction of physical objects are aggregates of the eight substances: earth, water, fire, wind, visible form, odor, taste, and tangible object arisen from elements. (Sound is not included because it does not have a continuum of similar type.) Thus, wherever one of the elements exists, the other three also exist, but there is a difference of strength and, thus, dominance. (Some say that the others dwell in the manner of seeds, that is, in potency.)

The fact that stone, wood, and so forth hold together indicates the presence of the water element in the earth element; that stones and trees move indicates the presence of the wind element in the earth element; that sparks are produced when two stones meet indicates the presence of the fire element. Similarly, that the water element can serve as a support for boats, leaves, and so forth indicates that the earth element is present in the water element; that leaves and roots rot in water and that there are warm springs indicate the presence of the fire element in water; that water flows downward and moves about indicates the presence of the wind element. Similarly, that leaves and grass are held up in the wind indicates the presence of the earth element in the wind element; that there are warm winds and that damp objects dry when spread out to the wind indicates the presence of the fire element in the wind element; that currents of wind are held together in a twister indicates the presence of the water element. Similarly, that one tongue of fire grasps another and that a tongue of fire can support leaves, grass, and so forth indicates the presence of the earth element in the fire element; that tongues of fire do not split apart but burn together indicates the presence of the water element; that tongues of flame move about indicates the presence of the wind element.

The seven tangible objects that are evolutes of the elements arise from the four elements. Smoothness arises from a preponderance of water and fire. Roughness arises from a preponderance of earth and wind. Heaviness arises from a preponderance of earth and water. Lightness arises from a preponderance of fire and wind. Cold arises from a preponderance of water and wind. Hunger arises from a preponderance of wind. Thirst arises from a preponderance of fire.

The colors of particles depend upon the element that is predominant. If the earth element is predominant, the color is yellow; if water, white; if fire, red; and if wind, blue. The shapes of particle clusters are determined by the arrangement of color particles and are not separate particles themselves. The particles of color/shape are different from the particles of odor, shape, or touch and thus are classed separately from the four elements as visible objects.

Visible forms, sounds, odors, tastes, and tangible objects are all 'atomic' in that they are masses of particles, but these are not necessarily single particles.[164] Otherwise, the only sense objects would be single particles, and there would be no gross objects. Though visible forms, sounds, odors, tastes, and tangible objects are 'atomic', many say that these are not 'established atomically' (*rdul du grub pa*) because the word 'established' carries with it the force of 'truly established' (*satyasiddha, bden grub*) or its synonym 'truly existent' (*satyasat, bden par yod pa*). Since 'established atomically' is the definition of matter (*kanthā, bem po*), it can be said that the Prāsaṅgikas do not accept 'matter'. This, however, does not mean that particles or gross objects constructed from particles are not accepted in the Prāsaṅgika system. Indeed, the word 'matter' seems to refer to the atomically constructed and nothing more; however, the difficulty is not merely in translation. For, in a similar way the Chittamātrins accept forms and particles which are of the same entity as a perceiving consciousness, but they do not accept 'matter' because for them the term itself implies an external object. To say in Tibetan that there are particles and objects constructed from particles but no *bem po* is as forceful as saying in English that there are particles and objects constructed from particles but no matter. The word 'matter' carries with it a connotation of findability under analysis, or true existence. That there are particles and masses of particles is accepted conventionally, but matter, because of the implications of the word, is not accepted even conventionally (according to Jam-ȳang-shay-b̄a).

Since visible forms and so forth are atomically constructed, it may be wondered why the four elements which are necessarily present in every particle are classified under tangible objects. The reason is that without touch, the function of earth, hardness and obstructiveness, cannot be experienced. Similarly, without touch, the function of water, dampness and moistening, cannot be experienced; without touch, the function of fire, heat and burning, cannot be experienced; without touch, the function of wind, lightness and moving, cannot be experienced. Therefore, the four elements are classed as tangible objects. Visible forms, odors, tastes, and the other tangible objects are evolutes of the elements.

The five sense powers and the five objects are called the ten obstructive physical objects. Among these, colors and shapes that can be shown to an eye consciousness are called demonstrable obstructive forms; thus, demonstrable form and object of apprehension by an eye consciousness are synonyms. The five sense powers and the four remaining objects—sounds, odors, tastes, and tangible objects—are undemonstrable obstructive forms.

Forms for the mental consciousness

The final category of forms is comprised of forms for the mental consciousness, which are undemonstrable and non-obstructive. They are defined as form aggregates which are objects only of the mental consciousness and thus are classed not as form-sources (*rūpāyatana, gzugs kyi skye mched*) but as phenomena-sources (*dharmāyatana, chos kyi skye mched*)[165] (see Chart 19)

Forms arising from aggregation. A single particle does not appear to an ordinary being's sense consciousness, but when the mental consciousness analyzes a gross form into parts, a single particle does appear, and thus it is classed as a form for a mental consciousness.

Chart 19: *Divisions of Form for the Mental Consciousness*

form for the mental consciousness

- form arising from aggregation (of the eight substances), e.g., a single particle
  abhisaṃkṣhepika
  bsdu ba las gyur ba
- space-form, e.g., appearance of clear space only to a mental consciousness
  abhyavakāshika
  mngon par skabs yod pa
- form arising from promises, e.g., a vow or an absence of a vow
  samādānika
  yang dag par blangs pa las gyur ba
- imaginary form, e.g., a horse, elephant, or house in a dream, or a non-actual meditative object such as an area filled with corpses
  parikalpita
  kun btags pa
- form for one with meditative power, e.g., earth or water appearing to one in isolated meditative stabilization on earth or water
  vaibhūtvika
  dbang 'byor ba

The shape of a single particle is necessarily round, but its colors are various as described above for the four elements. Since single particles appear only to the mental consciousness, all shapes and colors are not included in the category of visible forms seen by an eye consciousness.

Space-forms. Space appears both to an eye consciousness and a mental consciousness and thus the bluish space that appears to an eye consciousness is a visible form whereas the space that appears to a mental consciousness is a form for a mental consciousness.

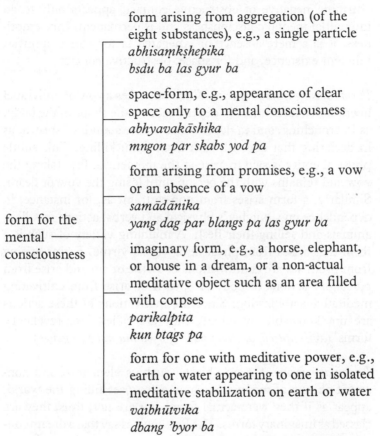

Both are impermanent whereas uncaused space, which is a non-affirming negative of obstructive contact, appears only to an inferential mental consciousness and is permanent. Like emptiness, it is a mere absence of a negated factor—for emptiness, inherent existence, and for space, obstructive contact.

Forms arising from promises. When one takes a vow of individual liberation, a form arises in dependence on the shape of the body, as in crouching, and in dependence on the sounds of speech, as in declaring that one will turn away from killing. This subtle physical entity is said to arise at the moment of first taking the vow and remains with the person until losing the vow or death. Similarly, a form arises from non-restraint as, for instance, in dependence on a butcher's physical and verbal actions in killing animals and selling their flesh. A middling variety of such is a form that arises from physical or verbal virtue. Forms arising from promises are continuations of virtue or sin and arise from revelatory actions of body or speech or arise from cultivating meditative stabilization. Since the motivations of these actions are not knowable by others, they are called 'non-revelatory forms' (*avijñaptirūpa, rnam par rig byed ma yin pa'i gzugs*).

Imaginary forms. Dream objects, such as elephants, and non-actual objects of meditation, such as corpses filling the world, appear as if they were actual forms but are not; thus, they are classed as imaginary forms. The Prāsaṅgikas say that a dream consciousness is solely a mental consciousness appearing in the aspects of the five sense consciousnesses. A dream object is an external object affecting a mental consciousness just as a reflection in a mirror is an external object affecting an eye consciousness. The non-Buddhist Mīmāṃsakas say that the light of the eye hits the mirror, and through returning to the eye an image is seen. The Buddhist Vaibhāṣhikas say that a clear type of form arises in the mirror. The Sautrāntikas, Chittamātrins and Yogāchāra-Svātantrikas say that a mirror image is a false appearance to the mind and is not a different entity from the mind. The Prāsaṅgikas, however, say that reflections, the falling hairs seen by one with cataracts, and mirages are visible forms just as echoes are sounds. A consciousness perceiving these is nevertheless mistaken because, for example, a mirror image of a face appears to be a face and not just a mirror image.

Forms for one with meditative power. Forms that appear to one who has attained mastery in meditation are objects of meditation that exist in fact. Mere earth or mere water as a meditative manifestation of one who has attained mastery in meditation is actual and is not an imaginary form. Included in this category are objects of meditative manifestation that can be shown to another being's eye consciousness, but this does not make the object as it appears to the master a visible form; for him it still is a form for the mental consciousness. This is compared to the varieties of externally existent objects seen by different types of beings, as in the case of a god's seeing a bowl of fluid as ambrosia and a hungry ghost's seeing pus and blood in the same place.

Consciousness

Sources:

Ye-s̄hay-gyel-tsen's *Clear Exposition of the Modes of Minds and Mental Factors*

Lati Rinbochay's oral teachings

The second division of things, or impermanent phenomena, is consciousness, defined as the clear and knowing.[166] Consciousness is of two types:

Chart 20: *Divisions of Consciousness*

consciousness
- mind *chitta* *sems*
- mental factor *chaitta* *sems byung*

Minds

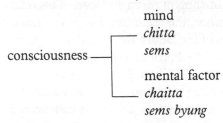

A mind is a knower of the mere entity of an object, whereas a mental factor is a knower which, on the basis of observing that object, engages in the object from the point of view of other features, such as function and so forth. Minds and mental factors are different within being the same entity; they possess five similarities which, as described in Vasubandhu's *Treasury of Knowledge* (*Abhidharmakosha*) are:

1 *Sameness of base.* A mind and its accompanying mental factors depend on the same sense power, as in the case of an eye consciousness and its mental factors which both depend on the physical eye sense power.
2 *Sameness of object of observation.* A mind and its mental factors observe the same object. For instance, when the main eye consciousness apprehends blue, so does the mental factor of feeling that accompanies it.
3 *Sameness of aspect.* For instance, if the main eye consciousness is generated in the aspect (or image) of blue, so is the mental factor of discrimination that accompanies it.
4 *Sameness of time.* A mind and its mental factors are produced, abide, and cease simultaneously.
5 *Sameness of substantial entity.* Just as at any one time the substantial entity of a particular mind is single and there are not many minds of the same type, such as several eye consciousnesses, so the substantial entity of, for instance, the mental factor of intention that accompanies the eye consciousness is also single.

Asanga's *Compendium of Knowledge* (*Abhidharmasamuchchaya*) combines the sameness of object of observation and sameness of aspect and adds another, sameness of realm and level. This refers to the fact that if, for instance, the main mind is of the Desire Realm, only mental factors of the Desire Realm will accompany it, and not mental factors of the Form or Formless Realms.

Minds are of only six types (see Chart 21). An eye consciousness is an individual knower depending on the eye and observing visible form. An ear consciousness is an individual knower depending on the ear and observing sound. A nose consciousness is an individual knower depending on the nose and observing odor. A tongue consciousness is an individual knower

Chart 21: *Divisions of Minds*

- mind
  - eye consciousness
chakṣhurvijñāna
mig gi rnam par shes pa
  - ear consciousness
shrotravijñāna
rna ba'i rnam par shes pa
  - nose consciousness
ghrāṇavijñāna
sna'i rnam par shes pa
  - tongue consciousness
jihvāvijñāna
lce'i rnam par shes pa
  - body consciousness
kāyavijñāna
lus kyi rnam par shes pa
  - mental consciousness
manovijñāna
yid kyi rnam par shes pa

depending on the tongue and observing taste. A body consciousness is an individual knower depending on the body and observing tangible objects. A mental consciousness is an individual knower depending on the mind sense (which is a former moment of consciousness and thus non-physical) and observing phenomena.

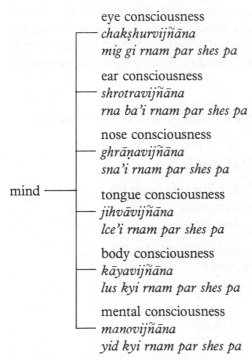

The mind cognizing emptiness, either inferentially or directly, is a mental consciousness, not an eye, ear, nose, tongue, or body consciousness, except in the case of a Buddha whose consciousnesses are cross-functional. The mental consciousness has the capacity to penetrate, first conceptually and then non-conceptually, the nature of phenomena, which not only is beyond the realm of a non-Buddha's sense perception but also is obscured by a false overlay that until Buddhahood accompanies sense perception. In dependence on reasoning, the mental consciousness first realizes an emptiness of a particular object conceptually—by way of the image of a vacuity which is a negative of inherent existence; then through familiarity with that knowledge, the imagistic element is removed, whereupon the mental consciousness becomes a Superior's wisdom directly cognizing emptiness.

Mental factors

There are fifty-one mental factors which are classed in six groups:

Chart 22: *Divisions of Mental Factors*

- mental factor
  - omnipresent factor (5) *sarvatraga* *kun 'gro*
  - determining factor (5) *viniyata* *yul nges*
  - virtuous factor (11) *kushula* *dge ba*
  - root affliction (6) *mūlaklesha* *rtsa nyon*
  - secondary affliction (20) *upaklesha* *nye nyon*
  - changeable factor (4) *aniyata* *gzhan 'gyur*

Omnipresent mental factors. The omnipresent mental factors are so named because they necessarily accompany all minds, even the wisdom cognizing emptiness. The five omnipresent mental factors are:

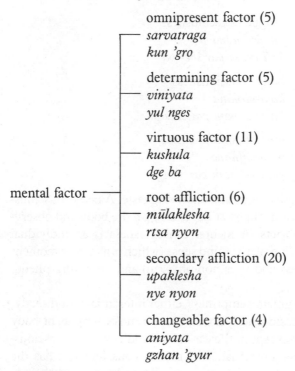

Chart 23: *Divisions of Omnipresent Mental Factors*

omnipresent mental factor
- feeling / *vedanā* / *tshor ba*
- discrimination / *saṃjñā* / *'du shes*
- intention / *chetanā* / *sems pa*
- contact / *sparsha* / *reg pa*
- mental engagement / *manaskāra* / *yid la byed pa*

Feeling. Feeling is an entity of experience individually experiencing the fruitions of virtuous and non-virtuous actions. Its objects are pleasure, pain, and neutrality. Pleasure is that with which, when it ceases, one wants to meet again; pain is that from which, when it arises, one wants to separate; and neutrality, being neither pleasure nor pain, is that with respect to which, when it arises, neither the wish to meet nor the wish to separate occurs. Pleasure, pain, and neutrality are called 'fruitions' in order to emphasize that all generations of pleasure, pain, and neutral feeling are results of former actions.

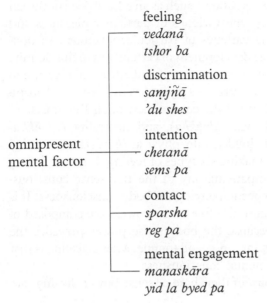

All pleasures, even that arising from a cool breeze in a hell, arise from virtuous actions (*karma, las*) accumulated in the past. Similarly, all pains, even a headache in the continuum of a Foe Destroyer, arise from non-virtuous actions accumulated in the past. In other words, pleasure and pain do not arise causelessly, or from a discordant cause, such as the nature (*prakṛti, rang bzhin*) asserted by the Sāṃkhyas or the lord Īshvara as asserted by the Aishvaras. Rather, general pleasure and pain, such as being born as a human or as a hell-being, arise from general virtuous and non-virtuous actions, such as an ethical deed or the sin of murder. Similarly, the varieties of particular pleasures and pains arise from the varieties of particular virtuous and non-virtuous actions. The development of certainty as to this definite and undeceived relationship of action and effect—of pleasure to virtue and pain to non-virtue—is praised as the basis of all auspicious doctrines and called the correct view of all Buddhists.

Pleasure (*sukha*), pain (*duḥkha*), and neutrality (*aduḥkhāsukha*) can each be divided into physical (*kāyikī*) and mental (*chaitasikī*) feeling, making six types of feeling. Physical feeling refers to that accompanying any of the five sense consciousnesses, not just that accompanying the body consciousness. It is called physical because the five sense powers are composed of clear matter and because the body sense power pervades the sense powers of eye, ear, nose, and tongue. Mental feeling is that accompanying the mental consciousness.

From the viewpoint of their base or sense power, feelings are of six types:

1 feeling arising from contact upon the aggregation of a visible object, eye sense, and eye consciousness (*chakṣhuḥsaṃsparshajā vedanā*)
2 feeling arising from contact upon the aggregation of a sound, ear sense, and ear consciousness (*shrotrasaṃsparshajā vedanā*)
3 feeling arising from contact upon the aggregation of an odor, nose sense, and nose consciousness (*ghrāṇasaṃsparshajā vedanā*)
4 feeling arising from contact upon the aggregation of a taste, tongue sense, and tongue consciousness (*jihvāsaṃsparshajā vedanā*)
5 feeling arising from contact upon the aggregation of a tangible object, body sense, and body consciousness (*kāyasaṃsparshajā vedanā*)
6 feeling arising from contact upon the aggregation of a phenomenon, mental sense, and mental consciousness (*manaḥsaṃsparshajā vedanā*).

Taking into account pleasure, pain, and neutrality, these six are further divided into eighteen types of feeling.

When divided from the viewpoint of object of abandonment and antidote, there are two types:

1 feeling as the base of attachment (*gredhāshritavedanā*), which is feeling accompanying attachment to attributes of the Desire Realm
2 feeling as the base of deliverance (*naiṣhkamyāshritavedanā*), which is feeling accompanying a mental consciousness that has turned away from desire for attributes of the Desire Realm and is included within an actual concentration.

This division into two is made in order to make known how attachment is induced by the power of feeling and how one separates from attachment to feeling in dependence on the concentrations.

There is also a division of feeling into materialistic (*sāmiṣha-vedanā*) and non-materialistic (*nirāmiṣhavedanā*). The former is feeling accompanying attachment to contaminated mental and physical aggregates, whereas the latter is feeling accompanying a wisdom consciousness directly cognizing selflessness.

Discrimination. Discrimination apprehends, upon the aggregation of an object, sense power, and a consciousness, the uncommon signs of an object. There are two types:

1 non-conceptual apprehension of signs: apprehension of the uncommon signs of an object appearing to a non-conceptual mind
2 conceptual apprehension of signs: apprehension of the uncommon signs of an object appearing to thought.

These two types of discrimination operate on (1) *perceptions*, involving the designation of expressions to objects manifestly perceived, (2) *hearing*, involving the designation of expressions in dependence on hearing believable words, (3) *differentiations*, involving the designation of expressions to objects ascertained in dependence on signs (such as in determining that an article is good due to possessing the signs of superior quality), and (4) *knowledge*, involving the designation of expressions to objects ascertained directly.

There is also a division of discrimination into two types:

1 discrimination apprehending signs in objects: apprehension individually differentiating the features of an object, such as blue, yellow, and so forth
2 discrimination apprehending signs in expressions: apprehension individually differentiating the features of expressions, such as in, 'This is a man; that is a woman.'

From the viewpoint of its base, discrimination is of six types:

1 discrimination arising from contact upon the aggregation of a visible object, eye sense, and eye consciousness (*chakṣhuḥsaṃsparshajā saṃjñā*)
2 discrimination arising from contact upon the aggregation of a sound, ear sense, and ear consciousness (*shrotrasaṃsparshajā saṃjñā*)
3 discrimination arising from contact upon the aggregation of an odor, nose sense, and nose consciousness (*ghrāṇasaṃsparshajā saṃjñā*)
4 discrimination arising from contact upon the aggregation of taste, tongue sense, and tongue consciousness (*jihvāsaṃsparshajā saṃjñā*)
5 discrimination arising from contact upon the aggregation of a tangible object, body sense, and body consciousness (*kāyasaṃsparshajā saṃjñā*)
6 discrimination arising from contact upon the aggregation of a phenomenon, mental sense, and mental consciousness (*manaḥsaṃsparshajā saṃjñā*).

From the viewpoint of object of observation, it is also of six types:

1 reasoned discrimination (*sanimittasaṃjñā*): (a) discrimination skilled in the relationship of names and meanings, (b) discrimination observing products as impermanent and so forth, and (c) discrimination having a clear subjective aspect and object of observation

2 unreasoned discrimination (*animittasaṃjñā*): (a) discrimination unskilled in the relationship of names and meanings, (b) discrimination observing products as permanent and so forth, and (c) discrimination lacking clear subjective aspect and object of observation
3 discrimination of the small (*parīttā saṃjñā*): (a) discriminations in the continuum of an ordinary being in the Desire Realm who has not attained an actual concentration and (b) discriminations observing attributes of the Desire Realm
4 discrimination of the vast (*mahadgatā saṃjñā*): (a) discriminations observing the Form Realm and (b) discriminations in the continuums of beings of the Form Realm
5 discrimination of the limitless (*apramāṇasaṃjñā*): (a) discriminations observing limitless space or limitless consciousness
6 discrimination of nothingness (*akiñchinsaṃjñā*): discriminations observing nothingness (a state beyond coarse feeling and discrimination).

In general, discrimination involves the differentiation and identification of objects; as a mental factor accompanying a non-conceptual mind such as an eye consciousness, it implies a non-confusion of the details of the object without which a later identification could not be made.[167] Discrimination is the heart of identifying the object of negation in the view of selflessness and then reflecting on a reasoning proving non-inherent existence; thus, far from being a hindrance to the path, correct discrimination is to be enhanced.

Intention. Intention (or attention) is the mental factor that moves and directs the mind that accompanies it to its object; it has the function of engaging the mind in the virtuous (*kushala, dge ba*), non-virtuous (*akushala, mi dge ba*), and neutral (*avyākṛta, lung du ma bstan pa*). Intention is the most important of all mental factors because through its power minds and mental factors engage in objects, like pieces of iron powerlessly moved by a magnet.

From the viewpoint of its base, intention is of six types:

1 intention arising from contact upon the aggregation of a

visible object, eye sense, and eye consciousness (*chakṣhuḥ-saṃsparshajā chetanā*)
2 intention arising from contact upon the aggregation of a sound, ear sense, and ear consciousness (*shrotrasaṃsparshajā chetanā*)
3 intention arising from contact upon the aggregation of an odor, nose sense, and nose consciousness (*ghrāṇasaṃsparshajā chetanā*)
4 intention arising from contact upon the aggregation of a taste, tongue sense, and tongue consciousness (*jihvāsaṃsparshajā chetanā*)
5 intention arising from contact upon the aggregation of a tangible object, body sense, and body consciousness (*kāyasaṃsparshajā chetanā*)
6 intention arising from contact upon the aggregation of a phenomenon, mental sense, and mental consciousness (*manaḥsaṃsparshajā chetanā*).

Intention is mental action (*manaskarma, yid kyi las*) from among the two types of action (*karma, las*), actions of intention (mental actions) and intended actions (physical and verbal actions).

Contact. Contact distinguishes its object—upon the aggregation of object, sense power, and mind—as pleasant, unpleasant, or neutral in accordance with subsequent feelings of pleasure, pain, or neutrality; thus, it has the function of serving as a basis for feeling. Since contact distinguishes its object as pleasant, unpleasant, or neutral, it serves as a cause for the feelings of pleasure, pain, or neutrality which in turn serve as causes for desire, hatred, and ignorance.

From the viewpoint of its base, contact is of six types:

1 contact upon the aggregation of a visible object, eye sense, and eye consciousness
2 contact upon the aggregation of a sound, ear sense, and ear consciousness
3 contact upon the aggregation of an odor, nose sense, and nose consciousness
4 contact upon the aggregation of a taste, tongue sense, and tongue consciousness

5 contact upon the aggregation of a tangible object, body sense, and body consciousness
6 contact upon the aggregation of a phenomenon, mental sense, and mental consciousness.

Mental engagement. Mental engagement directs the mind accompanying it to a specific object of observation (*ālambana, dmigs pa*). The difference between intention and mental engagement is that intention moves the mind to objects in general whereas mental engagement directs the mind to a specific object.

Without the five omnipresent factors, the experience of an object would not be complete. Without feeling, there would be no experience of pleasure, pain, or neutrality. Without discrimination, the uncommon signs of the object would not be apprehended. Without intention, the mind would not approach its object. Without contact, there would be no basis for feeling. Without mental engagement, the mind would not be directed to a specific object of observation. Thus, all five are needed to experience an object.

Determining mental factors. The five determining mental factors are shown in Chart 24.

Aspiration. Aspiration observes a contemplated phenomenon and seeks it. Aspiration serves as a base for the initiation of effort in the sense that, for instance, through perceiving the advantages of meditative stabilization, a captivating faith in meditative stabilization is produced, and in dependence on this, a strong continuous aspiration seeking meditative stabilization is generated such that one is able to generate continuous effort. Effort in meditative stabilization, in turn, generates a pliancy of mind and body that bestows an ability to remain in the practice of virtue night and day, thereby overcoming the laziness which is a non-delight in cultivating meditative stabilization and liking for what is discordant with meditative stabilization. Thus, faith, aspiration, effort, and pliancy are the antidotes to laziness.

Chart 24: *Divisions of Determining Mental Factors*

determining mental factor
- aspiration / *chhanda* / *'dun pa*
- belief / *adhimokṣha* / *mos pa*
- mindfulness / *smṛti* / *dran pa*
- stabilization / *samādhi* / *ting nge 'dzin*
- knowledge / *prajñā* / *shes rab*

Aspiration is divided into three types: aspiration wishing to meet, aspiration wishing not to separate, and aspiration that seeks. The last is again divided into aspiration seeking desires, aspiration seeking views, and so forth.

Belief. Belief holds an ascertained object to be just as it was ascertained; it has the function of keeping the mind from being captivated by another view. For instance, when one considers Buddha and other teachers and analyzes to discover which is an undeceiving refuge, one ascertains that only Buddha is the teacher of an undeceiving refuge. Then, when the doctrine taught by him and the spiritual community properly achieving his doctrine are ascertained by valid cognition as undeceiving, a firm belief in them as final refuges is gained. Thereupon, Forders and so forth cannot lead one away from this position. One has then entered among the number of Buddhists, and based on this, all auspicious qualities increase.

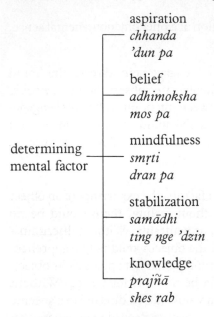

Mindfulness. Mindfulness is non-forgetfulness with respect to a familiar phenomenon; it has the function of causing non-distraction. Mindfulness has three features:

1 objective feature: a familiar object. Mindfulness cannot be generated toward an unfamiliar object.
2 subjective feature: non-forgetfulness within observation of that object. Even though one might have become familiar with an object previously, if it does not presently appear as an object of mind, mindfulness cannot occur.
3 functional feature: causing non-distraction. Since the stability of the mind increases in dependence on mindfulness, non-distraction is specified as the function of mindfulness.

Mindfulness that possesses these three features is extremely important for both sutra and tantra practice, as all auspicious qualities of the grounds and paths increase in dependence on mindfulness and introspection. In particular, all achievements of meditative stabilization in sutra and tantra are attained through the power of mindfulness.

Stabilization. Stabilization is a one-pointedness of mind with respect to an imputed object; it has the function of serving as the base of knowledge, that is, special insight. The object of stabilization is specified as 'imputed' because when meditative stabilization is cultivated, the mind is held to a mentally imputed or imagined object of observation. This indicates that meditative stabilization is not generated by a sense consciousness, such as by an eye consciousness staring at an object, but by the mental consciousness observing an internal object. Through continuous cultivation of meditative stabilization, the object of observation —whether true or untrue—will be perceived clearly and non-conceptually.

In dependence on the meditative stabilization of calm abiding, which is a setting of the mind internally in equipoise, special insight is achieved through the force of analytical wisdom. Therefore, the function of stabilization is specified as serving as the base of knowledge. Stabilization, in turn, depends on ethics.

Knowledge. Knowledge (or wisdom) individually differentiates the faults and virtues of objects of analysis; it has the function of overcoming doubt. When one analyzes with reasoning and gains ascertainment, doubt is overcome; thus, the function of knowledge is specified as overcoming doubt.

Virtuous mental factors. The eleven virtuous mental factors are:

Chart 25: *Divisions of Virtuous Mental Factors*

- virtuous mental factor
  - faith
    shraddhā, dad pa
  - shame
    hrī, ngo tsha shes pa
  - embarrassment
    apatrāpya, khrel yod pa
  - non-attachment
    alobha, ma chags pa
  - non-hatred
    adveṣha, zhe sdang med pa
  - non-ignorance
    amoha, gti mug med pa
  - effort
    vīrya, brtson 'grus
  - pliancy
    prasrabdhi, shin tu sbyangs pa
  - conscientiousness
    apramāda, bag yod pa
  - equanimity
    upekṣhā, btang snyoms
  - non-harmfulness
    avihiṃsā, rnam par mi 'tshe ba

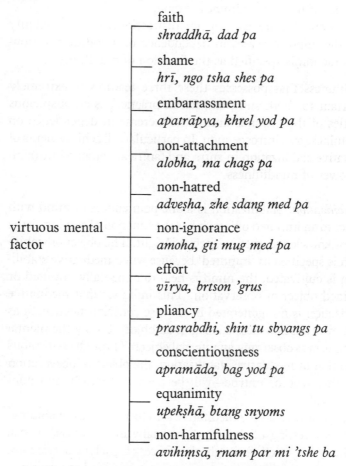

Faith. Faith has the aspect of clarity (*prasāda, dang ba*), conviction (*abhisampratyaya, yid ches*), or a wish to attain (*abhilāṣha, 'thob 'dod*) with respect to the existent (such as actions and their effects), the possession of qualities (such as by the Three Jewels), or powers (such as the powers of the path to actualize cessation). It has the function of serving as a basis for aspiration. The faith of clarity, or clarifying faith, is, for instance, the clarity of mind that comes through perceiving the qualities of the Three Jewels; it is called 'clarifying' because just as when a water-clarifying jewel is put in water, the dirtiness in the water is immediately cleansed, so when this type of faith is generated in the continuum, mental troubles are cleared away, whereupon the qualities of realization are suitable to be generated.

The faith of conviction is, for instance, the gaining of conviction in dependent-arising or in actions and their effects through contemplating these doctrines as set forth by the Conqueror. The faith which is a wish to attain is, for instance, the faith thinking, 'I will definitely attain the cessation of suffering', upon contemplating the four noble truths, ascertaining true sufferings and true sources as objects of abandonment and true cessations and true paths as objects of attainment, and realizing that through striving in the proper way these can be attained.

Although the world equates faith (*dad pa*) and liking (*dga' ba*), they are not the same. Liking one's child or spouse and liking beer are cases of liking but not of faith. Also, the faith which is a concern and conviction from one's depths with respect to the faults of cyclic existence is faith but not liking. The faith which is a conviction and liking from the depths through contemplating the qualities of a spiritual guide or the benefits of wholesome actions and their effects is both faith and liking.

Furthermore, faith and respect (*gus pa*) are not the same though they are considered to be so in the world. For instance, liking a spiritual guide is faith, but respecting a spiritual guide involves contemplating his kindness, knowing shame, and valuing him highly; thus, faith and respect are different mental factors.

As explained earlier, effort is the cause of all auspicious qualities, and in order to generate effort, aspiration seeking those qualities is necessary. In order to generate aspiration, one must perceive those qualities and have the faith of conviction in them. Thus, faith is frequently praised in the scriptures and their commentaries as the basis of all auspicious attainments.

Shame and embarrassment. Shame is an avoidance of misconduct due to one's own disapproval whereas embarrassment is an avoidance of misconduct due to others' disapproval. These mental factors both have the function of serving as a basis for restraining misconduct. In the case of shame, when one is about to engage in misconduct, one avoids it by thinking, 'This is not something I should do,' whereas in the case of embarrassment, one avoids it by thinking, 'Since others will despise me, this is not suitable.' This latter involves concern for the displeasure of a lama, teacher, or the like.

Shame and embarrassment serve as a basis for restraining misconduct in the sense that to restrain physical, verbal, and mental misconduct, one must definitely have shame and embarrassment; for if one does not have either concern from one's own point of view over the fruition of an action or concern for the discomfort of a lama or teacher, there is no way to cease misconduct.

Non-attachment, non-hatred, and non-ignorance. Non-attachment is an emergence from and non-desire for cyclic existence and the articles of cyclic existence. Non-hatred is a factor that, in observing either harmful sentient beings, sufferings, or sources of suffering, conquers the generation of hatred; it is an absence of the intent to harm. Non-ignorance is a knowledge of individual analysis that can serve as an antidote to ignorance; it is either attained from birth through the fruition of actions in an earlier lifetime without depending on contributing causes in this lifetime or arises through application by way of hearing, thinking, or meditating.

Non-attachment, non-hatred, and non-ignorance have the function of serving as bases for non-engagement in misconduct, being *roots* of all virtuous practices, *methods* for ceasing all misconduct, and the *essence* of all paths. Since all grounds and paths are for the sake of abandoning the three poisons of desire, hatred, and ignorance and since these three mental factors cause one to emerge from the three poisons that cause all misconduct, their function is specified as serving as bases for restraining misconduct.

A being of small capacity generates non-attachment to this life and, turning away from this life, seeks his own welfare in future lives. A being of middling capacity generates non-attachment toward all the marvels of cyclic existence and, having reversed his grasping from the depths, seeks release from all cyclic existence. A being of great capacity generates non-attachment to both cyclic existence and a state of solitary peace and seeks the non-abiding nirvana of a Buddha wherein he can remain in meditative equipoise on emptiness while at the same time manifesting countless forms in order to help migrators in cyclic existence. In this way, all paths can be related to non-attachment as well as to non-hatred and non-ignorance.

Effort. Effort is a mental delight in virtue; it has the function of fulfilling and accomplishing virtues. Although in the world everything that involves striving is called effort, toil only for the sake of the affairs of this lifetime is not effort but is laziness that is an attachment to bad activities; it is discordant with effort.

There are five types of effort:

1 effort of armoring—this is the thought prior to engaging in virtue that is the mind's taking delight in that activity. It is like putting on great armor in that it affords a willingness to engage in extended activity.
2 effort of application—a mental delight while engaging in practice
3 effort of non-inferiority—a delight generated such that one will not be discouraged, thinking, 'How could one such as I do this?'
4 effort of irreversibility—a fullness of mental delight such that circumstances cannot divert one from engaging in virtuous activity

5 effort of non-satisfaction—a striving for higher qualities without being satisfied with achieving small virtues.

All auspicious qualities depend on effort.

Pliancy. Pliancy is a serviceability of mind and body such that the mind can be set on a virtuous object of observation as long as one likes; it has the function of removing all obstructions. It is of two types:

1 physical pliancy—through the power of meditative stabilization physical unserviceability is purified, whereupon the body is light like a ball of cotton and capable of being used in virtuous activity according to one's wish
2 mental pliancy—through the power of meditative stabilization the mind becomes free of unserviceability, whereupon it has the facility to engage in a virtuous aim without impediment.

The function of pliancy is specified as removing all obstructions because through its power all unfavorable conditions of mind and body are purified. Once pliancy is attained, meditative stabilization is increased from within; through this the bliss of pliancy increases, whereupon meditative stabilization again increases. Through this, in turn, the mind becomes empowered, when conjoined with special insight, to overcome obstructions.

Conscientiousness. Conscientiousness keeps the mind from contaminations and causes the achievement of virtue while abiding in effort. It keeps the mind from coming under the influence of the afflictions and has the function of serving as a basis for the achievement of all mundane and supramundane marvels. Conscientiousness is of five types:

1 conscientiousness with respect to the former—a remedying of past faults in accordance with the doctrine
2 conscientiousness with respect to the later—an earnest intention to remedy future faults
3 conscientiousness with respect to the middle—remedying faults without forgetfulness in the present

4 conscientiousness prior to activity—a tightening of the mind, thinking, 'How nice it would be if I could behave and abide in such a way that faults do not arise!'
5 conscientiousness of concordant behavior—abiding and behaving in such a way that faults do not arise.

Conscientiousness is very important as a root of all grounds and paths.

Equanimity. Equanimity is an evenness of mind, a dwelling in a natural state, and a spontaneous abiding discordant with the afflictions. It is associated with non-attachment, non-hatred, and non-ignorance and has the function of not allowing an opportunity for the afflictions.

In dependence on techniques for setting the mind one-pointedly, the nine states of mind (see pp.80-86) are gradually achieved. When the ninth is attained, the exertion of using the antidotes to laxity and excitement is no longer needed. At that point one attains a spontaneous abiding of the mind on its object, and with this state an equanimity that involves non-application of the antidotes to laxity and excitement is attained. Thus, equanimity here is an equanimity of application, not an equanimity of feeling nor the immeasurable equanimity of wishing that all sentient beings abide in an equanimity free of desire and hatred, intimacy and alienness.

The function of equanimity is specified as not allowing an opportunity for the afflictions because when the ninth state of mind is attained, it is easy to overcome the afflictions of the Desire Realm and also at the time of meditative equipoise laxity and excitement do not arise.

Non-harmfulness. Non-harmfulness is a compassionate attitude, included as part of non-hatred, which is patience devoid of intention to injure. It observes suffering sentient beings and thinks, 'May they be free of such suffering!' The function of non-harmfulness, not injuring sentient beings, is said to be the essence of Buddha's teachings.

These eleven virtuous mental factors are called 'natural virtues' because they are virtuous entities in themselves, without depending on consideration of other factors such as motivation and so forth. Though these eleven are the principal virtues, there are four other types:

1 virtue through relation—the minds and mental factors that accompany any of the eleven virtues
2 virtue through subsequent relation—virtuous predispositions established by virtuous minds and mental factors
3 virtue through motivation—physical and verbal actions motivated by faith and so forth
4 virtue through ultimacy—suchness, or emptiness, is designated a virtue because when one observes and meditates on it, all obstructions are purified; however, it is not an actual virtue.

From the viewpoint of state or situation, virtues are divided into eight types:

1 virtue by way of attainment at birth—such as faith that arises through the force of predispositions established in former lifetimes without depending on familiarization in this lifetime
2 virtue by way of application—such as the faith of wishing to attain Buddhahood that arises in dependence on relying on a virtuous spiritual guide, listening to the excellent doctrine, properly taking such to mind, and achieving doctrines that are conducive to attaining nirvana
3 virtue by way of an activity in front—imagining, for instance, a field of assembly of Buddhas, Bodhisattvas, and so forth in front of oneself, and then bowing down and making offerings
4 virtue by way of helping—actions such as ripening sentient beings by way of the four means of gathering students (giving articles, teaching the means for attaining high status in cyclic existence and definite goodness, causing others to practice what is beneficial, and behaving that way oneself)
5 virtue by way of bearing—such as wholesome actions that serve as the means for attaining high status and definite goodness

6 virtue by way of acting as an antidote—such as actions that possess the special power of directly overcoming objects of abandonment and the unfavorable
7 virtue by way of pacification—such as true cessations
8 virtue by way of concordant cause—such as the five clairvoyances and ten powers that arise through the force of attaining true cessations.

A similar presentation of seven types is made with respect to non-virtues:

1 non-virtue by way of attainment at birth—such as spontaneously engaging in murder due to predispositions from a former lifetime
2 non-virtue by way of application—such as misconduct of body, speech, and mind that arises in dependence on relying on a non-virtuous friend, listening to specious doctrine, improperly taking such to mind, and so forth
3 non-virtue by way of an activity in front—such as offering a blood sacrifice to an image
4 non-virtue by way of harming—such as actions of body, speech, and mind that injure sentient beings
5 non-virtue by way of bearing—such as actions impelling future lifetimes and actions completing the character of a future lifetime that yield only suffering as their fruit
6 non-virtue by way of non-conduciveness—such as bad views that prevent generation of non-contaminated paths
7 non-virtue by way of interruption—such as bad views that interfere with virtuous activity.

Root afflictions. Afflictions, in general, are defined as knowers that, when generated, cause the mental continuum to be very unpeaceful. The six root afflictions, which are so called because they are the sources of all other afflictions, are shown in Chart 26.

Desire. Desire perceives an internal or external contaminated phenomenon to be pleasant from the point of view of its own

Chart 26: *Divisions of Root Afflictions*

root affliction
- desire / *rāga* / *'dod chags*
- anger / *pratigha* / *khong khro*
- pride / *māna* / *nga rgyal*
- ignorance / *avidyā* / *ma rig pa*
- doubt / *vichikitsā* / *the tshom*
- afflicted view / *dṛṣhṭi* / *lta ba nyon mongs can*

entity and thereupon seeks it. It has the function of generating suffering. Like oil that has set in cloth, desire adheres to its object of observation and thus is difficult to separate from it.

Desire is divided into three types: desire of the Desire Realm, desire of the Form Realm, and desire of the Formless Realm. The reason for stating that the function of desire is the generation of suffering is that the root of all suffering is birth, and the main cause of birth in cyclic existence is desire, or attachment.

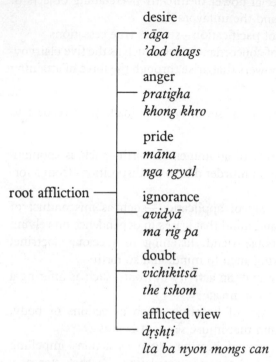

Anger. Anger is an intention to harm sentient beings, to harm sufferings in one's own continuum, or to harm phenomena that are sources of suffering (such as thorns). It has the function of causing oneself not to remain in contact with happiness and serves as a basis for misconduct. Through anger, one does not abide in happiness in this lifetime, and immeasurable suffering is induced in the future.

Pride. Pride depends on the view of the transitory collection as a real I and has the aspect of a puffing up of the mind upon observing one's own wealth, qualities, youth, and so forth. It has the function of serving as a basis for the arising of disrespect and suffering. There are seven types of pride:

1 pride—a puffing up of the mind, thinking that one is superior to lower persons
2 excessive pride—a puffing up of the mind, thinking that one is superior to equal persons
3 pride beyond pride—a puffing up of the mind, thinking that one is greatly superior even to persons who are superior to others
4 pride of thinking I—a puffing up of the mind, observing the appropriated aggregates of mind and body and thinking, 'I'
5 pride of conceit—a puffing up of the mind, thinking that one has attained what has not been attained, such as clairvoyance or meditative stabilization
6 pride of slight inferiority—a puffing up of the mind, thinking that one is just a little lower than others who are actually greatly superior
7 wrongful pride—a puffing up the mind, thinking that one has attained auspicious qualities when one has actually deviated from the path, such as claiming high attainments when one has actually been carried away by a spirit.

Because pride causes disrespect for high qualities and for those who possess high qualities, it serves to obstruct the new attainment of doctrines of verbalization and realization, to cause rebirth in bad migrations, and, even when reborn as a human, to cause birth in a low class, such as a servant. Thus, it produces the unwanted in both this and later lives.

Ignorance. Ignorance is an absence of knowledge that involves obscuration with respect to the status of phenomena. It has the function of serving as a basis for the arising of false ascertainment, doubt, and afflictions. Its principal antidote is the wisdom cognizing selflessness.

Ignorance is of two types: obscuration with respect to actions and their effects and obscuration with respect to suchness. The latter serves as the causal motivation for all rebirth in cyclic existence, but in terms of operational motivation at the time of actions, obscuration with respect to actions and their effects is specified as the cause of accumulating actions that result in birth in bad migrations whereas obscuration with respect to suchness is specified as the cause of accumulating actions that result in birth in happy migrations.

In dependence on ignorance, the other afflictions arise, and in dependence on them contaminated actions are accumulated. From those, all sufferings in cyclic existence are produced. Therefore, all afflictions and faults arise in dependence on ignorance.

Doubt. Doubt is a two-pointedness of mind with respect to the four noble truths, actions and their effects, and so forth. It has the function of serving as a basis for non-engagement in virtues. Doubt obstructs all virtuous activities and especially interferes with seeing the truth.

Afflicted views. There are five afflicted views: (see Chart 27).

View of the transitory collection. A view of the transitory collection observes the appropriated mental and physical aggregates and conceives them to be a real I and mine. It is an *endurance* in the sense of not fearing the mistakenness of inherently existent I and mine; a *desire* in the sense of seeking a mistaken object; an *intelligence* in the sense of thoroughly discriminating its object; a *conception* in the sense of adhering strongly to its object; and a *view* in the sense of observing its object. A view of the transitory has the function of serving as a basis for all bad views.

It is called the view of the transitory collection because the mental and physical aggregates, which are the base of the view,

Chart 27: *Divisions of Afflicted Views*

- afflicted view
  - view of the transitory collection (as real I and mine)
satkāyadṛṣhṭi
'jig tshogs la lta ba
  - view holding to an extreme
antagrāhadṛṣhṭi
mthar 'dzin pa'i lta ba
  - conception of a (bad) view as supreme
dṛṣhṭiparāmarsha
lta ba mchog 'dzin
  - conception of (bad) ethics and modes of conduct as supreme
shīlavrataparāmarsha
tshul khrims dang brtul zhugs mchog 'dzin
  - perverse view
mithyādṛṣhṭi
log lta

are impermanent, and thus transitory, and are a composite of the plural, and thus a collection. The name itself indicates that there is no permanent and partless person. (See p.176 for its divisions.)

A view of the transitory collection conceives of an inherently existent I and exaggerates the distinction between self and other. Thereupon, desire for one's own side and hatred for others arises.[168] Through viewing the self, pride is generated, a view of the self as eternal or as annihilated at death arises, and the conception of one's own bad behavior as superior is generated. Similarly, teachers of selflessness and their teachings of cause and effect, the four noble truths, the Three Jewels, and so forth are conceived to be non-existent or become objects of doubt. In this way, the view of the transitory collection acts as the basis of all afflictions. Although usually identified as ignorance, in this context its relation to ignorance is like the relation of a mind conceiving the presence of a snake to the dimness surrounding a rope in a dark area.

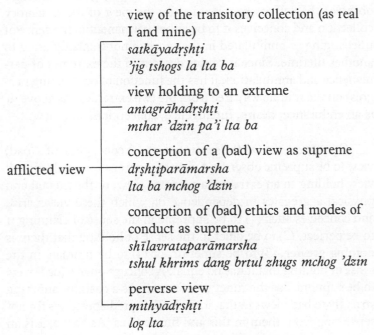

View holding to an extreme. A view holding to an extreme observes the self as apprehended by the view of the transitory collection and conceives it to be either permanent in the sense of unchanging or annihilated in the sense of not transmigrating to another lifetime. Since it causes descent to the extremes of permanence and annihilation, it has the function of obstructing progress on the middle way free from the two extremes. As above, it is an endurance, desire, intelligence, conception, and view.

Conception of a (bad) view as supreme. A conception of a (bad) view to be supreme observes a view of the transitory collection, a view holding to an extreme, a perverse view, or the mental and physical aggregates in dependence on which these views arise and conceives such (1) to be supreme in the sense of claiming it to be perfect, (2) to be chief in the sense of holding that there is nothing greater, (3) to be superior, or (4) to be ultimate in the sense of holding that it has no equal. A conception of a (bad) view to be supreme has the function of serving as a basis for adhering strongly to bad views in that it establishes predispositions for not separating from them in this and future lives. As above, it is an endurance, desire, intelligence, conception, and view.

Conception of (bad) ethics and modes of conduct as supreme. A conception of (bad) ethics and modes of conduct to be supreme takes as its object (1) a faulty system of ethics that is intended to abandon faulty ethics, (2) a faulty mode of conduct that prescribes dress, behavior and physical and verbal activities, or (3) the mental and physical aggregates in dependence on which these are performed. It considers these to purify sins, liberate from afflictions, and release from cyclic existence. It has the function of serving as a basis for fruitless fatigue. As above, it is an endurance, desire, intelligence, conception, and view.

Perverse view. A perverse view is a denial of cause, effect, functionality, and existent phenomena and can involve holding that Īshvara and so forth are the cause of beings migrating in cyclic existence. Denial of cause is a view that good and bad behavior and so forth do not exist. Denial of effect is a view that fruitions of virtuous and sinful actions do not exist. Denial of functionality is a view that former and later lives and so forth do not exist. Denial of existent phenomena is a view that, for example, attainment of the state of a Foe Destroyer does not exist.

Perverse views have the function of severing virtuous roots, causing tight adherence to non-virtuous roots, serving as a basis for engaging in non-virtue, and causing non-engagement in virtue. Since denial of cause, effect, and rebirth sever all virtuous roots, these are the worst among all perverse views.

Secondary afflictions. The twenty secondary afflictions, which are so called because they are close to or portions of the root afflictions, are shown in Chart 28.

Belligerence. Belligerence is an intention to harm another through striking and so forth when one is in any of the nine situations of harmful intent, thinking:

1 'This person has harmed me.'
2 'This person is harming me.'
3 'This person will harm me.'
4 'This person has harmed my friend.'
5 'This person is harming my friend.'
6 'This person will harm my friend.'
7 'This person has helped my enemy.'
8 'This person is helping my enemy.'
9 'This person will help my enemy.'

Belligerence has the function of serving as a basis for bearing weapons, punishing, and preparing to injure others. It differs from the root affliction anger in that anger is an impatience and intent to harm that arises when a harmful sentient being, or one's own suffering, or sources of suffering appear to the mind. Belligerence is an extremely disturbed state of mind which, upon a great increase of anger, is a wish to inflict harm on another such as by physically striking that person when he is in one's presence.

Chart 28: *Divisions of Secondary Afflictions*

- secondary affliction
  - belligerence, *krodha, khro ba*
  - resentment, *upanāha, 'khon 'dzin*
  - concealment, *mrakṣha, 'chab pa*
  - spite, *pradāsha, 'tshig pa*
  - jealousy, *irṣhyā, phrag dog*
  - miserliness, *mātsarya, ser sna*
  - deceit, *māyā, sgyu*
  - dissimulation, *shāṭhya, g.yo*
  - haughtiness, *mada, rgyags pa*
  - harmfulness, *vihiṃsā, rnam par 'tshe ba*
  - non-shame, *āhrīkya, ngo tsha med pa*
  - non-embarrassment, *anapatrāpya, khrel med pa*
  - lethargy, *styāna, rmugs pa*
  - excitement, *auddhatya, rgod pa*
  - non-faith, *āshraddhya, ma dad pa*
  - laziness, *kausīdya, le lo*
  - non-conscientiousness, *pramāda, bag med pa*
  - forgetfulness, *muṣhitasmṛtitā, brjed nges pa*
  - non-introspection, *asaṃprajanya, shes bzhin ma yin pa*
  - distraction, *vikṣhepa, rnam par g.yeng ba*

Resentment. Resentment is a wish to harm or to answer harm, involving non-release of a continuum of anger. It has the function of serving as a basis for impatience.

Concealment. Concealment is a wish, through the force of ignorance, to hide a fault when another person, such as a spiritual guide, points out that fault. It has the function of increasing faults, of serving as a basis for contrition and not abiding in contact with happiness, and of impelling rebirth in bad migrations.

Spite. Spite is a wish, through the force of belligerence and resentment, to speak harsh words out of ill-will to another who has pointed out a fault. It has the function of causing one not to abide in happiness in this lifetime by causing engagement in many faulty actions, such as speaking harsh words, and by generating many non-meritorious actions. Spite also generates unpleasant fruitions in future lives.

Jealousy. Jealousy is a disturbance of the mind from the depths that involves an inability to bear another's fortune due to being attached to goods and services. It involves hatred and has the function of causing discomfort of mind and not abiding in contact with happiness.

Miserliness. Miserliness is a tight holding onto articles without letting them go through the power of attachment to goods and services. It has the function of serving as a basis for the non-diminishment of possessions, and it generates the unwanted in this and later lives.

Deceit. Deceit is a pretension of having good qualities, whereas one does not, through the force of strong attachment to goods and services. As in the case of the hypocrisy of pretending to have a disciplined mind in order to deceive others, deceit can involve ignorance and desire and has the function of serving as a basis for wrong livelihood. 'Wrong livelihood' refers to deceitfully gaining goods

(1) through hypocrisy, (2) through speaking soft words in accordance with another's thought, (3) through praising others' possessions, (4) through speaking on the faults of miserliness and so forth, and (5) through praising another's act of giving and so forth.

Dissimulation. Dissimulation is a wish to hide one's faults from others through the force of desire for goods and services. Both dissimulation and deceit have the function of preventing the attainment of true preceptual instruction and cause one in this and future lifetimes not to meet with a Mahāyāna spiritual guide.

Haughtiness. Haughtiness is a puffing up of the mind through taking joy and comfort in observing one's own good health, youth, beauty, power, signs of long life, prosperity, and so forth. It has the function of serving as a basis for all afflictions and secondary afflictions and acts as a root of non-conscientiousness.

Harmfulness. Harmfulness is an unmerciful wish to harm other sentient beings. Involving anger, it is a lack of compassion as in wanting to harm or to cause others to harm, or in taking delight when seeing or hearing of harm to sentient beings. It has the function of injuring others.

Non-shame. Non-shame is a non-avoidance of faults from the viewpoint of one's own disapproval or of religious prohibition. It can involve desire, hatred, and ignorance and has the function of assisting all root afflictions and secondary afflictions. For example, if a monk, when encountering an intoxicant, did not avoid drinking it, thinking, 'This is something I should not do,' he would have the mental factor of non-shame.

Non-embarrassment. Non-embarrassment is non-avoidance of faults from the viewpoint of another's disapproval. It can involve desire, hatred, and ignorance and has the function of assisting all root afflictions and secondary afflictions. If one does not avoid faults thinking that the Teacher Buddha and clairvoyant gods would be disturbed and others would criticize oneself, one would have non-embarrassment. It and non-shame assist all afflictions and act as causes of all faults, for without a wish to avoid faults, one cannot keep from them. Thus, these two mental factors are said to accompany all non-virtuous minds.

Lethargy. Lethargy is a heaviness and unserviceability of body and mind. It involves ignorance and has the function of assisting all root and secondary afflictions, for in dependence on lethargy these increase.

Excitement. Excitement is a scattering of the mind to attributes of the Desire Realm experienced previously and an engagement in them with attachment. Excitement is a non-peacefulness of mind that involves desirous engagement in the pleasant; it has the function of preventing calm abiding. Thus, all scatterings of the mind are not instances of excitement since excitement is a portion of desire whereas the mind is frequently distracted to objects by way of afflictions other than desire and even scatters to virtuous objects of observation. Scattering involving desire is both scattering and excitement whereas other instances are just scattering.

Non-faith. Non-faith is non-conviction, non-delight, and non-wishing with respect to virtuous phenomena. It involves ignorance and has the function of serving as a basis for laziness. Non-faith is the opposite of the three types of faith; it is non-conviction in actions and their effects, etc., non-delight and dislike of the possessors of auspicious qualities such as the Three Jewels, and non-wishing or non-seeking of liberation and so forth.

Laziness. Laziness is a non-delight in virtue due to attachment to lying down and so forth. It involves ignorance and has the function of preventing application in virtue. (See p.71.)

Non-conscientiousness. Non-conscientiousness causes a looseness of mind, not keeping it from afflictions and faults and resulting in non-cultivation of virtuous phenomena. It can involve an abiding in desire, hatred, and ignorance as well as laziness and has the function of serving as a basis for the increase of non-virtues and decrease of virtues.

Forgetfulness. Forgetfulness is an unclarity of mind and a forgetting of virtuous objects through mindfulness of objects of the afflictions. It has the function of serving as a basis for distraction in that, based on afflicted mindfulness, the mind is distracted to the objects of observation of the afflictions.

Non-introspection. Non-introspection is an unknowing engagement in physical, verbal, and mental deeds. It has the function of serving as a basis for the infractions of codes of ethics.

Distraction. Distraction is a scattering of the mind from its object of observation. It can involve desire, hatred, and ignorance and has the function of preventing separation from desire. Excitement is a scattering of the mind to pleasant objects whereas distraction is a scattering to any object.

Changeable mental factors. The four changeable mental factors are so called because they become virtuous, non-virtuous, or neutral by the power of the motivation and the minds accompanying them. They are shown in Chart 29.

Sleep. Sleep is a powerless withdrawal inside of the engagement by sense consciousnesses in objects. It depends on causes such as heaviness of body, weakness, fatigue, taking the figure of darkness to mind, and so forth. Sleep involves ignorance and has the function of serving as a basis for losing virtuous activities. The proper time for sleep is the middle watch of the night, not the first or last watches nor during the day. During the middle watch of the night one should sleep with a wish to practice virtue, and not motivated by afflictions. Thus, there are two types of sleep, virtuous and non-virtuous, the latter having the function of degenerating virtuous activities.

Chart 29: *Divisions of Changeable Mental Factors*

changeable mental factor
- sleep / *middha* / *gnyid*
- contrition / *kaukṛtya* / *'gyod pa*
- investigation / *vitarka* / *rtog pa*
- analysis / *vichāra* / *dpyod pa*

Contrition. Contrition is remorse or regret for a deed done by oneself in accordance with one's own thought or upon pressure by someone else which one subsequently comes to dislike. It involves ignorance and has the function of interrupting the stability of the mind. Contrition is of three types:

1 virtuous—remorse for sins done previously
2 non-virtuous—remorse for meritorious actions done previously, such as making donations and then feeling sorry for having depleted one's wealth
3 neutral—remorse for activities that neither helped nor harmed others, such as making a mistake sewing.

Contrition for sins is suitable when their fruition has not yet occurred and they can still be affected by confession and so forth. When the fruition of a sin has already occurred, such as in having been born blind, contrition can no longer overcome the effect of the deed.

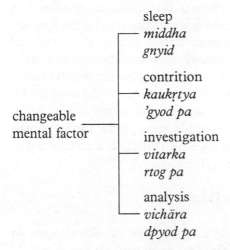

Investigation and analysis. Investigation is an inquiry into the rough entities of objects as well as their names whereas analysis is a fine discrimination of these. In dependence on their objects, investigation and analysis are of three types, virtuous, non-virtuous, and neutral. The virtuous, such as analyzing selflessness with an intention to emerge from cyclic existence, has the function of serving as a basis for abiding in contact with happiness in that it generates pleasant effects. Non-virtuous investigation and analysis, such as inquiring into pleasant and unpleasant objects motivated by desire and hatred, has the function of serving as a basis for not abiding in happiness in that it generates unpleasant effects. Investigation and analysis into crafts, styles, and so forth without a virtuous or non-virtuous attitude are neutral. (For another way of presenting consciousness see Appendix 1.)

Non-associated compositional factors
Source
Ḡön-chok-d̄en-b̄ay-drön-may's *Beginnings of Annotations on (D̄zong-ka-b̄a's) 'Essence of the Good Explanations'*

The final division of impermanent phenomena is comprised of compositional factors which are neither form nor consciousness.[169] They are called compositional factors because of being factors that allow for the aggregation of causes and conditions and for the production, abiding, and cessation of products. They are called 'non-associated' because, unlike minds, they are not associated with minds or mental factors. Non-associated compositional factors are divided into two types:

Chart 30: *Divisions of Non-Associated Compositional Factors*

non-associated compositional factor
- person
  pudgala, gang zag
- non-person compositional factor
  apudgalaviprayuktasaṃskāra
  gang zag ma yin pa'i ldan min 'du byed

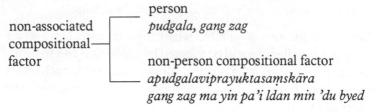

A person is a non-associated compositional factor because of being designated in dependence upon a collection of form and consciousness. Since a person is neither form nor consciousness but impermanent, it can be only an instance of the remaining category of impermanent phenomena, a non-associated compositional factor.

Non-person non-associated compositional factors are of twenty-three types (see Chart 31). These twenty-three are called 'designations to states'. 'Acquisition' is designated to a state of the increase and decrease of virtues and so forth, of which there are two types: 'finding acquisition' which is a new attainment of such increase or decrease and 'possessive acquisition' which is the retention of it.

'Absorption without discrimination' is designated to a state involving a lack of the coarse feelings and discriminations associated with the third concentration and below. It is produced in dependence on the fourth concentration by common beings only. 'Absorption of cessation' is designated to a state achieved only by Superiors in which there is a lack of the coarse feelings and discriminations associated with the peak of cyclic existence (the highest formless level) and below. 'One having no discrimination' is designated to the state of a person born among the gods in the condition of being without coarse feelings and discriminations.

'Life faculty' or 'life' is designated to the state of living; it is the base of consciousness and warmth. 'Similarity of type' is designated to the state or condition of likeness. 'Birth' (or 'production'), 'aging', 'duration', and 'impermanence' are designated to states of the characteristics of things. 'Group of stems', 'group of words', and 'group of letters' are designated to various states of verbal conventions. Stems are bare names without case endings, etc., whereas words are stems with case endings, etc.

'State of an ordinary being' is designated to one who has not attained the qualities of Superiors. (The Vaibhāṣhikas substitute non-acquisition for this category and do not assert the remaining nine, limiting their presentation of non-associated compositional factors to fourteen.) 'Continuity' is designated to the non-interrupted state of a continuum of causes and effects. 'Distinction' is of three types: distinction of the particular and the general, distinction of virtues and sins and pleasures and pains, and distinction of causes and effects. 'Relatedness' is of three

Chart 31: *Divisions of Non-Person Non-Associated Compositional Factors*

non-person non-associated compositional factor

- acquisition; *prāpti, 'thob pa*
- absorption without discrimination; *asaṃjñisamāpatti, 'du shes med pa'i snyoms 'jug*
- absorption of cessation; *nirodhasamāpatti, 'gog pa'i snyoms 'jug*
- one having no discrimination; *āsaṃjñika, 'du shes med pa pa*
- life faculty; *jīvitendriya, srog gi dbang po*
- similarity of type; *nikāyasabhāgata, rigs 'thun pa*
- birth; *jāti, skye ba*
- aging; *jarā, rga ba*
- duration; *sthiti, gnas pa*
- impermanence; *anityatā, mi rtag pa*
- group of stems; *nāmakāya, ming gi tshogs*
- group of words; *padakāya, tshig gi tshogs*
- group of letters; *vyañjanakāya, yi ge'i tshogs*
- state of an ordinary being; *pṛthagjanatva, so so skye bo nyid*
- continuity; *pravṛtti, 'jug pa*
- distinction; *pratiniyama, so sor nges pa*
- relatedness; *yoga, 'byor 'grel*
- rapidity; *jāva, 'gyogs pa*
- order; *anukrama, go rim*
- time; *kāla, dus*
- area; *desha, yul*
- number; *saṃkhyā, grangs*
- collection; *sāmagrī, tshogs pa*

types: 'means' which is the collection of, for instance, an artisan's tools, 'aggregation' which is a collection of causes but specifically their reliance on each other within the collection, and 'suitability' which is each thing's having its own function.

'Rapidity' is designated to a condition of the arising of effects immediately after their causes and to the speed caused by persons, magical emanations, and so forth. 'Order' is designated to a serial state of former and later, high and low, and so forth. 'Time' is designated to states of the past, present, and future. 'Area' is designated to the composite of a place and the persons therein. 'Number' is designated to a condition of measure. 'Collection' is designated to the state of a complete collection of causes, and specifically to that completeness.

AGGREGATES, CONSTITUENTS, AND SOURCES

Sources
Kensur Lekden's oral teachings
Jam-ȳang-shay-b̄a's *Great Exposition of Tenets*

Another way of dividing all impermanent things is into the five aggregates, or, more literally, 'heaps' or 'piles' (*skandha, phung po*).[170] These five are:

Chart 32: *The Five Aggregates*

thing
- forms (*rūpa, gzugs*)
- feelings (*vedanā, tshor ba*)
- discriminations (*saṃjñā, 'du shes*)
- compositional factors (*saṃskāra, 'du byed*)
- consciousnesses (*vijñāna, rnam shes*)

The heaps are so called because when Buddha taught them he heaped up various grains—rice and so forth—into five piles, to represent the categories of impermanent phenomena. These heaps are defined as aggregates of phenomena, and, therefore, 'aggregate' is often used here as the translation equivalent.

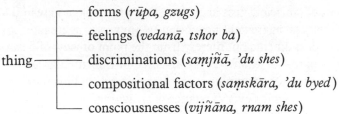

The eleven types of forms and all their instances constitute the first aggregate, 'forms'. The three types of the mental factor 'feeling'—pleasure, pain, and neutrality—and all their instances constitute the second aggregate, 'feelings'. The mental factor of discrimination and all its instances constitute the third heap, 'discriminations'. Non-associated compositional factors and the remaining forty-nine mental factors as well as all their instances constitute the fourth aggregate, 'compositional factors'. The six main minds and all their instances constitute the fifth aggregate, 'consciousnesses'. The person is imputed to these aggregates of impermanent phenomena and is unfindable either separate from or among them.

All *impermanent* phenomena not only of the personal continuum but also of the external world are included in these five. However, the emptiness of the mind, a permanent phenomenon included within the personal continuum, is not counted among the five aggregates because the five aggregates are exclusively impermanent. Thus, all phenomena of the personal continuum are not included in the five aggregates, only the impermanent.

The last four aggregates are mental phenomena and the first is physical; thus, the five are the 'mental and physical aggregates'. Each instance of the five is also called an 'aggregate' because, for instance, a table itself is an aggregate of particles and a consciousness is a continuum of moments. A single particle and a single moment of consciousness are also called a form aggregate and a consciousness aggregate not because they are aggregates of particles or moments but merely from the point of view of designating a part—for example, an instance of a form aggregate—with the name of the whole—'form aggregate'.[171] This mode of appellation in which every instance of an aggregate is itself called an aggregate accords with the relationship between a generality and its instances. If the generality is 'form aggregate', each of its instances must be a form aggregate. To be an instance of a generality (such as pot), a phenomenon (such as a gold pot) must be the same entity as the generality, the phenomenon must be it (a pot), and there must be other instances.

All phenomena, both permanent and impermanent, can be divided into the eighteen constituents (*dhātu, khams*), which are so called because they give rise to phenomena of similar type.[172] These are the six objects, the six sense powers, and the six consciousnesses, every instance of which is called a constituent:

Chart 33: *The Eighteen Constituents*

object	*sense power*	*consciousness*
form	eye sense power	eye consciousness
sound	ear sense power	ear consciousness
odor	nose sense power	nose consciousness
taste	tongue sense power	tongue consciousness
tangible object	body sense power	body consciousness
phenomenon	mind sense power	mental consciousness

'Phenomenon', the sixth category of objects, refers to *other* phenomena, those that are not sense objects but are objects only of the mental consciousness, such as impermanence and emptiness. Since sense objects are also objects of a mental consciousness, the category 'phenomena' does not include all objects of a mental consciousness—just its exclusive objects among which mental factors and permanent phenomena, such as space, are included.

Since each of a Buddha's six consciousnesses cognizes all phenomena, this list does not apply to Buddhas. However, the ability of a Buddha to cognize all objects with any consciousness does not imply that there is only one mind which is merely designated with the names of the six consciousnesses when it arrives at the various organs and experiences their respective objects. The cross-functionality of a Buddha's consciousnesses is an extraordinary quality and does not affect the presentation of the consciousnesses and objects of non-Buddhas.

The eighteen constituents include all phenomena, both permanent and impermanent, due to the inclusion of all permanent phenomena in the category 'phenomenon'. These eighteen can be reduced to the twelve sources (*āyatana, skye mched*) through eliminating the six consciousnesses, yet still contain all phenomena because the six consciousnesses are still included in the category 'mind sense power'. The mind sense power is a previous moment of any of the six consciousnesses which acts as the base of a mental consciousness much as a physical sense power acts as the base of a sense consciousness.

The twelve sources are so called because they open the way for the production of the six consciousnesses.[173] They are the six objects and the six sense powers:

Chart 34: *The Twelve Sources*

object	*sense power*
form	eye sense power
sound	ear sense power
odor	nose sense power
taste	tongue sense power
tangible object	body sense power
phenomenon	mind sense power

Teachers repeatedly enumerate the twelve sources or the eighteen constituents in order to emphasize a sense of the multiplicity of phenomena that are the bases of imputing or designating a person. The tables are memorized, with students not only repeating the names but causing the phenomena to appear to their minds. This practice helps greatly to crowd out the sense of self and prepare the way for a recognition of the imputed nature of the person. Then, one can proceed to investigate the imputed nature of these phenomena themselves.

2 *Dependent-Arising of Cyclic Existence*

Sources
D̄zong-ka-b̄a's *Great Exposition of the Stages of the Path*
Geshe Lhundup Sopa's oral teachings
Pan-chen S̄ö-nam-drak-b̄a's *General Meaning of (Maitreya's) 'Ornament for Clear Realization'*
D̄en-b̄a-dar-gyay's *Analysis of Dependent-Arising*

The last twelve of the fifty-three phenomena of the afflicted class are the twelve members of the dependent-arising of cyclic existence.[174] These twelve are to be viewed as faulty because they obstruct the path to liberation. They are:

1 ignorance (*avidyā, ma rig pa*)
2 action (*saṃskārakarma, 'du byed kyi las*)
3 consciousness (*vijñāna, rnam shes*)
   a. cause consciousness
   b. effect consciousness
4 name and form (*nāmarūpa, ming gzugs*)
5 six sources (*ṣhadāyatana, skye mched drug*)
6 contact (*sparsha, reg pa*)

7 feeling (*vedanā, tshor ba*)
8 attachment (*tṛṣhṇa, sred pa*)
9 grasping (*upādāna, len pa*)
10 existence (*bhava, srid pa*)
11 birth (*jāti, skye ba*)
12 aging and death (*jarāmaraṇa, rga shi*).

Ignorance does not just mean non-knowledge; it is also a consciousness that conceives the opposite of correct knowledge. Ignorance here is a misconception of oneself as inherently existent and of phenomena included in one's own continuum as being objects controlled by an inherently existent I. Ignorance views the nominally existent I, which is merely designated to the mental and physical aggregates, as an inherently existent self and views the aggregates themselves as under the control of this self. Thus, its principal antidote is knowledge of the true nature of the I as empty of inherent existence. Ignorance can also refer to obscuration with respect to the coarse relationships of actions and their effects, as in the case of ignorantly making sacrifices in order to gain liberation, but as the first of the twelve members of dependent-arising, it is necessarily a conception of a self of persons that gives rise to the later members.

In a particular round of dependent-arising, the first member applies only to the period of obscuration or misconception which in a previous life served as the motivator of one particular action. This single complete action, the second member of the twelve, is called a *path* of action because it serves as a path to rebirth in a bad migration (hell-being, hungry ghost, or animal) or a happy migration (human, demi-god, or god). For an action to be a complete path of action it must have its necessary members: an intention (such as the wish to kill someone), thought which identifies the object properly, preparation for the accomplishment of the action, successful conclusion, and non-reversal of intention before the action is completed.[175] This complete action establishes a potency on the 'cause consciousness' or the consciousness at the time of the action, the first half of the third member.

Action as the second member usually refers only to one meritorious or non-meritorious contaminated action in a former life, either in the life immediately preceding this life or in any other former life. Based on ignorance with respect to the nature of the person, a path of action leading to a happy migration is accumulated. Based also on ignorance with respect to actions and their effects, a path of action leading to a bad migration is accumulated. The former is a meritorious action projecting or impelling rebirth as a human or god of the Desire Realm, and the latter is a non-meritorious action projecting rebirth in a bad migration as an animal, hungry ghost, or hell-being. Based on ignorance with respect to the nature of the person, an action of meditative stabilization projects, or provides the power for, a happy migration in a Form or Formless Realm; it is a meritorious action which is called 'unmoving' because its effect can reach fruition only in the type of life and level for which it was projected, this corresponding to the type of meditative stabilization. An example of an unmoving action is a deed of meditative absorption in the first concentration that projects an effect included within the first level of the Form Realm and which will only ripen in the first level of the Form Realm. An example of a moving action is a deed such as murder that projects an effect included within a bad migration but which might not actually ripen in a bad migration, reaching fruition in a human life as a form of human suffering. Thus, meritorious and non-meritorious actions are 'moving' actions because their projected effects and actualized effects are not necessarily of the same type of life and level even though they may be the same.

Dependent on the motivational ignorance that precedes and gives rise to them, virtuous actions and actions of meditative absorption lead to rebirth in cyclic existence, albeit in a favorable situation. Pa-bong-ka's commentary on Dzong-ka-ba's *Great Exposition of the Stages of the Path* says,[176] 'The second member, action, is the performance of an activity, motivated by ignorance, which produces the mental and physical aggregates of a rebirth. It is like doing work.' The first half of the third member, 'cause consciousness', refers only to the moment when the potency of the action 'stains' the consciousness which exists at the time the action is completed.

The first two and a half members, ignorance, action, and cause consciousness, are causes projecting a future birth (see Chart 35); they are, therefore, called a 'future dependent-arising'. What they project are the next four and a half members, effect consciousness, name and form, sources, contact, and feeling. The first of these, 'effect consciousness', refers only to the moment of the mental consciousness just after bridging the gap from the previous life to the new life, which in womb-birth is the first moment in the womb. Then, with the next moment, name and form apply. 'Name' refers to the four non-form aggregates—feelings, discriminations, compositional factors, and consciousnesses—and 'form' refers to the aggregate of forms.

A being in the intermediate state between lives has all six consciousnesses as well as at least the five omnipresent mental factors, including feeling and discrimination. Together with the mind are potencies, established by countless actions, in a dormant state; these are instances of compositional factors, and thus all four non-form aggregates are present during the intermediate state. Also, a being in the intermediate state has a subtle physical body which is called an 'unobstructed body' because it can pass through walls, mountains, and so forth; thus, the form aggregate is also present during transmigration.

Name and form, as the fourth member of dependent-arising, refer to the five aggregates of the new life immediately after conception. At that point there are mental and body consciousnesses. 'Form' refers to the roundish shape (embryo), oblong shape (the lengthening embryo), and so forth. (In the Formless Realm 'form' refers only to the dormant seeds of form, which are neither form nor consciousness.)

The six sources are the eye, ear, nose, tongue, body, and mental sense powers. Through the development of the form aggregate which at that time is the embryo (the semen of the father and the blood of the mother penetrated by the consciousness) and the four 'name' aggregates (feelings, discriminations, compositional factors, and consciousnesses) the remaining four of

Chart 35: *Buddha's Explicit Teaching in the 'Rice Seedling Sutra' of One Round of a Twelve-Membered Dependent-Arising*

life A	1 ignorance 2 action 3 consciousness a. cause consciousness	projecting causes
life B	b. effect consciousness 4 name and form 5 sources 6 contact 7 feeling	projected effects
	8 attachment 9 grasping 10 existence	actualizing causes
life C	11 birth 12 aging and death	actualized effects

Life A precedes life B at any time, and life B precedes life C with no interval.

the six sources—eye, ear, nose, and tongue sense powers—come into being. (The body and mental sense powers exist from the first moment of the embryo.) If the birth is spontaneous as in a hell or heaven, the sense powers all come into being with the inception of the new life, unlike the serial development as in birth from a womb, from an egg, or from heat and moisture.

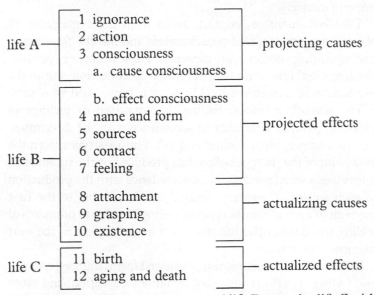

The term 'sources' as the fifth member of dependent-arising refers to a specific five moments in the development of a life in cyclic existence; the first is the achievement of the sense powers of mind and body, and the second through fifth occur at the production of the other four sense powers which depend on the gradual development of name and form. Therefore, 'sources' are identified as only the six sense powers, excluding the six objects (see p.274). The six objects or external sources are ever present and need not be produced in dependence on name and form because the embryo has color and shape, sound (for example, if hit), odor, taste, softness and so forth as tangible objects, and impermanence.

The sixth member, contact, arises from the aggregation of object, sense power, and consciousness and has the function of distinguishing objects as pleasant, unpleasant, or neutral. 'Aggregation' refers not to a simultaneous collection, but to the production of a consciousness by a sense power and an object.

The seventh member, feeling, is comprised of feelings of pleasure, pain, or neutrality in accordance with the discrimination by contact. Since feeling is divided into six types from the viewpoint of the six types of contact produced by the six sources, it involves a serial production in accordance with the production of each source. However, 'feeling' refers not just to the first moment of each of the six types of feeling but also to moments of feeling throughout the life that serve as the objects of the next member, attachment.

In sum, effect consciousness, name and form, sources, contact, and feeling are effects projected by ignorance, action, and cause consciousness in the sense that the latter make them suitable for actualization. An action that depends on ignorance projects these through staining a potency on the cause consciousness. This potency of a particular type of life is similar to the outline of a picture, the details of which are provided by other deeds, called completing actions.

The potency is actualized by attachment, grasping, and existence. The eighth member, attachment, is desire not to separate from a feeling of pleasure, to separate from a feeling of pain, and for a non-diminishment of neutral feeling. The ninth member, grasping, an increase of attachment, is of four types:

1 desirous grasping—desire involving strong attachment to the Desire Realm attributes of pleasant forms, sounds, odors, tastes, and tangible objects
2 grasping for views—desire involving aspiration to bad views, not including the view of the transitory collection of mind and body as real I and mine
3 grasping for ethics and modes of conduct—desire involving

strong attachment to bad ethics and bad modes of conduct which are associated with bad views

4 grasping for a self—desire involving strong attachment to the pride of selfhood and the view of the mental and physical aggregates which have the nature of transitoriness and of an aggregation as real I and mine.

Attachment and grasping nourish or actualize the particular potency that is the projecting cause of the next life and thus can occur at any time during the life. However, since such moments of attachment and grasping are most efficacious near the time of death, attachment and grasping here for the most part refer to instances near the time of death.

The tenth member, existence, is a case of giving the name of the effect to the cause. For it is the potency established by the second member, action, when it has been thoroughly nourished by attachment and grasping and has become empowered to develop into the next life. Since 'existence' occurs at the moment just preceding the new existence or life which is its effect, calling the tenth member 'existence' is a designation of it with the name of its effect.

Attachment, grasping, and existence are causes that actualize the potency projected by ignorance, action, and cause consciousness. The actualizer is grasping, which is caused by attachment, and birth and aging and death are what are actualized. Through grasping, the potency previously established in the consciousness by an action is fully empowered, this state being called 'existence'.

Among the twelve members, ignorance, action, and cause consciousness take place in a former life. Effect consciousness, name and form, sources, contact, feeling, attachment, grasping, and existence occur in the present life. Birth and aging and death occur in the future life. For the production of this life only ignorance, action and cause consciousness are explicitly presented; for the production of the future life only attachment, grasping, and existence are explicitly presented. However, each birth has both the three projecting causes and the three actualizing causes. Particular causes are emphasized for each of the two births for the sake of pointing out the existence of all of them for all births.

The actualized effects are birth, that is, the five mental and physical aggregates just after transmigrating to the new life, and aging and death. Aging refers to the process of change beginning from the second moment of the new life and applying through to death. Death is the cessation of the continuum of a similar type of mental and physical aggregates. Aging and death are put as one member because there are cases of death immediately after rebirth, without aging.

In this way one round of the twelve members of dependent-arising is completed in three lifetimes. The effect consciousness, name and form, sources, contact, feeling, attachment, grasping, and existence of this lifetime are not in the same round of dependent-arising as the birth and aging and death of this lifetime. The birth and aging and death of this lifetime are the result of the actualizing members of the last lifetime. In this way, two rounds of dependent-arising are occurring simultaneously. Similarly, actions motivated by ignorance in this lifetime are each beginning other new rounds of dependent-arising. (For other presentations, see Appendix 2.)

A benefit of contemplating dependent-arising is the creation of a sense of distress. Through understanding that a life is created by nourishment—through attachment and grasping—of a potency established by an action that is motivated by ignorance, one can thereby infer the existence of past and future lives. Through this, one sees that innumerable potencies have been established in the mind and are ready for actualization. The impermanence and precariousness of this life is obvious, and the conditions for empowering another potency to create a new life that might be very miserable are ever-present. Similar to a person who knows that calamity is about to befall him, one will, upon understanding one's position, seek with great effort to extricate oneself from such a situation. The afflictions that give rise to the rounds of dependent-arising will be identified as enemies, and one will seek the means of overcoming them.

After a practitioner identifies the misery in his own continuum, he knows through inferential extension that other sentient beings are suffering the same miseries. Just as he wishes to free himself from misery, so he develops the wish to free all sentient beings due to their closeness over the continuum of lives. In this way compassion is generated, and with it as a motivation, one will seek with great vigor to vanquish ignorance, attachment, and grasping which are now identified as the enemies of all sentient beings. The benefit of the study and realization of dependent-arising is eventually the attainment of Buddhahood.

Buddhapālita

3 *The Four Noble Truths*

Sources
Jang-gya's *Presentation of Tenets*
Geshe Gedün Lodrö's oral teachings
Gön-chok-den-bay-drön-may's *Presentation of the Four Truths*
Pan-chen-Sö-nam-drak-ba's *General Meaning of (Maitreya's) 'Ornament for Clear Realization'*
Jam-yang-shay-ba's *Great Exposition of the Middle Way*

Like the two truths, the four noble truths—true sufferings, origins of suffering, cessations, and paths—are objects and not concepts of truth, beauty, and so forth.[177] Unlike the two truths, however, the four noble truths do not include all objects; absent are permanent phenomena, such as spaces and non-analytical cessations, as well as impermanent phenomena such as a Buddha's Enjoyment and Form Bodies or an ordinary being's body in a pure land.

The first truth is *true sufferings*, which are the mental and physical aggregates produced by contaminated actions and afflictions. They include all instances of mind and body of ordinary beings except those generated by pure wishes, meditation, and so forth. Even the environments shared by beings in the various cyclic existences are true sufferings because they are created from potencies established by contaminated actions and afflictions. However, the body of an ordinary being born in a pure land is not a true suffering because it is not created by contaminated actions and afflictions but by pure wishes for rebirth in a pure land. A common being's consciousness inferentially realizing impermanence or emptiness is also not a true suffering because it arises from cultivation of the path and is born from meditation, not from the afflictions. Still, a common being's inferential cognizer of emptiness is said to be 'contaminated' (*sāsrava, zag bcas*) because it is polluted with dualistic perception in the sense that its object, emptiness, *appears* to be inherently existent though it is not being *conceived* as inherently existent.

Of the two types of true sufferings, internal and external, internal true sufferings are 'cyclic existences' (*saṃsāra, 'khor ba*) and are included within the three types of suffering. The first is the suffering of misery, or all feelings of physical and mental pain. The second is the suffering of change, or all feelings of pleasure which are contaminated with the misconception of inherent existence. For example, just as the warmth of the sun is pleasant on a cool day but is a source of pain if one stays too long in it, all the pleasures of cyclic existence, if over-extended, become sources of suffering. Furthermore, even if one enjoys the pleasures of cyclic existence in measure, these still are sufferings of change because they are suitable to create suffering if overused. If such were inherently pleasurable, long-term usage would increase the pleasure; however, suffering is eventually induced. Thus, the need for moderation is a sign of their not naturally being pleasurable.

Discouragement with the suffering of misery and of change is not sufficient to induce a fully qualified aspiration for liberation. The third type of suffering, that of composition, is the root and pervader of the other two, and discouragement with it must be sought with particular emphasis. The suffering of composition means simply to be under the outside influence of contaminated actions and afflictions such that one is ready to suffer pain upon the aggregation of minor causes. The main conditions are always present—when one is in cyclic existence—to undergo considerable suffering upon the sudden aggregation of the remaining causes, such as a change in the environment. Thus, even though one might not have manifest feelings of pain, one is still subject to suffering upon meeting with minor causes. This type of suffering is called 'pervasive' because no matter how one searches among the ordinary body and mind, every instance of it is miserable, either manifestly painful or capable of inducing suffering. It is called 'compositional' because it induces suffering in the future. As Gön-chok-den-bay-drön-may says:[178]

> Though a prisoner certain to be executed is not punished physically, there is no opportunity for pleasure in his inner mind which realizes the daily approach of death. Similarly, a person carrying a burden, even when resting, does not take much pleasure until reaching the destination.

In this way, a yogi develops discrimination of the phenomena of cyclic existence as unfavorable, like executioners raising swords, and the wish to leave cyclic existence arises. Thereupon, by inferring the plight of others based on one's own, compassion wishing to protect others arises without difficulty. This is the special purpose of Buddha's setting forth true sufferings first.

The second of the four truths is *true origins*, the sources of suffering—the afflictions and actions contaminated with the afflictions. Here 'afflictions' specifically are the first member of dependent-arising—ignorance—and the other afflictions that are produced based on ignorance, the remaining five root afflictions and the twenty secondary afflictions (see p.255-66). Actions, as the other source of suffering, refer to the second member of dependent-arising—the meritorious, non-meritorious, and non-moving actions motivated by ignorance that impel rebirth respectively in happy migrations as humans or gods, in bad migrations as hell-beings, hungry ghosts, or animals, or in the Form and Formless Realms. Afflictions and actions are the *causes* of suffering even though in general they themselves are true sufferings because they are what give rise to true sufferings. Like illnesses, true sufferings are to be identified, and like the causes of illness, true origins are to be abandoned.

The third of the four truths is *true cessations*, the extinguishment of true sufferings and origins. These are the individually enumerated cessations that are states of having abandoned obstructions and correspond to the uninterrupted paths causing their attainment. By stages one attains complete deliverance from the various levels of afflictions such that they will never return, culminating in the attainment of nirvana, the emptiness of the mind in the continuum of one who has abandoned all afflictions whatsoever.

The chief affliction is ignorance, and its chief type is the conception of inherent existence. Therefore, anyone who has attained nirvana, even if he has not attained Buddhahood, has completely destroyed the conception of inherent existence. Foe Destroyers (*Arhan, dGra bcom pa*) are those who have destroyed (*han, bcom*) their enemy (*ari, dgra*), the afflictions. All Foe Destroyers—whether Hearers, Solitary Realizers, or Buddhas—have attained a nirvana that is an utter cessation of the afflictions.

Even though true cessations, the ultimate of which are nirvanas, are attained in dependence on a path that eradicates the afflictions, they are said to be permanent phenomena in the sense that since they do not change moment by moment, they are non-disintegrating. However, the true cessations in the continuum of a yogi come into being upon his attainment of the various levels of the paths; thus, there are debates about whether or not true cessations and nirvanas are impermanent phenomena. The answer given is that a true cessation is not an act of cessation but an emptiness of the mind in the continuum of one who has utterly and forever removed at least some portion of the afflictions. All true cessations are emptinesses and thus permanent, but all emptinesses are not true cessations as is the case with the emptiness of inherent existence of the body. Emptinesses, except for those of the mind in the continuum of persons *who have overcome afflictions*, are not any of the four noble truths.

The fourth noble truth is *true paths*, which are the means of attaining true cessations. Just as a state of health is to be attained by the sick and the medicines to attain that state are to be relied upon, so true cessations are to be realized and true paths are to be relied upon. Except for vows which are non-revelatory forms, all true paths are consciousnesses, called paths because they are factors which, through being generated in the mental continuum, take one to liberation from cyclic existence. Here, there are eight paths:[179]

1 correct view—the opposite of the view of the transitory collection of mind and body as real I and mine, the opposite of the permanent and annihilistic views of the self and the aggregates, the opposite of perverse views such as asserting the absence of cause and effect, the opposite of views conceiving bad ethics and bad disciplines to be superior, and so forth. Thus, a correct view is not necessarily just a consciousness cognizing emptiness though such is included in the term.
2 correct realization—especially the consciousnesses which subtly analyze emptiness
3 correct speech—the vows and so forth which are the contraries of wrong livelihood and so forth
4 correct aims of actions—the actions of body and speech in dependence on vows
5 correct livelihood—the abandonment of wrong modes of livelihood, such as butchering animals
6 correct effort—the mental factor of effort that causes gradual progress on the path
7 correct mindfulness—constant attentiveness to objects of awareness and to modes of perception of those objects necessary for ascending the paths
8 correct meditative stabilization—the meditative ability to remain one-pointedly on the objects of the paths.

The four noble truths are called 'noble' (*ārya*) because they are taught by Nobles or Superiors (*Āryan, 'Phags pa*) or because they are ennobling.[180] They are called truths (*satya, bden pa*) because through meditation on them one unmistakenly enters into the paths of liberation and omniscience. Because the teachings that sufferings and their origins are to be abandoned and that cessations and the paths that actualize them are to be adopted are true and thus do not deceive disciples into cultivating false paths, they are truths. However, unlike ultimate truths they do not necessarily exist the way they appear, because except for true cessations, they are falsities in the sense that true sufferings, for instance, appear in direct perception to exist inherently but do not. Therefore, the four noble truths are not just truths for Nobles or Superiors because, if they were, they would have to be truths for the special cognizers of Superiors—their direct perceivers of suchness—whereas when emptiness is directly perceived, conventional truths such as true sufferings do not in any way appear to the mind. Thus, the Prāsaṅgikas say that the four noble truths are truths for conventional valid cognizers. For the Vaibhāṣhikas, however, they are truths just for Nobles (Superiors) because they are perceived directly by a Superior's wisdom of meditative equipoise.

Buddha set forth the four noble truths—true sufferings, origins, cessations, and paths—in the order not of their causation but of their realization. In causal order, true origins—afflictions and actions contaminated with the afflictions—give rise to true sufferings—the phenomena included within the scope of the contaminated mental and physical aggregates—while true paths, such as the realization of emptiness, cause the attainment of true cessations—the state of being freed forever from a certain portion of the afflictions and their consequent sufferings. However, in his presentation of the four noble truths Buddha put the effects before the causes to indicate their application in practical realization.

When one recognizes sufferings as like an illness, one understands that one must become free from them. Then, seeing that abandoning sufferings depends on overcoming their origins, one generates a wish to abandon these. Having identified the origins of suffering as the afflictions, the chief of which is the ignorance conceiving inherent existence, one realizes that since the conception of inherent existence is baseless, the causes of suffering can be abandoned whereby a wish to actualize cessation is generated. Having seen that sufferings and their origins must and can be abandoned, one engages in the means for abandoning them, true paths. This is said to be the general procedure of intelligent persons and an unparalleled quintessential instruction not just for initial realization but also for initially training the mind. As Gön-chok-den-bay-drön-may says:[181]

> When we analyze our own mental continuum carefully, we see that beyond a mere verbal image of it, it is extremely difficult to develop an aspiration to liberation from the depths of the heart; rather, we are naturally involved in the causes of suffering—contaminated actions and afflictions. This is because beginninglessly we have mistaken a mind which is under the influence of the afflictions, and thus actually a suffering, to be happiness. For example, when certain types of hidden heat disorders are mistaken to be cold disorders, the antidotes to heat disorders are not taken and one intentionally seeks the diet, behavior, and so forth increasing the heat disorder. Just as to overcome the heat disorder, it is absolutely essential to identify it, so if one does not recognize that which has a nature of suffering as suffering and turn away from it from the depths, there is no way to be led upward through annihilating the root of suffering. In this condition, though one pretended to seek liberation, one would proceed only to error, conceiving some low contaminated state to be it; thus, an actual wish for liberation would not occur. As Āryadeva's *Four Hundred* says:
>
> > How could one who is not discouraged
> > About this aspire to its pacification?

MEDITATION ON THE FOUR NOBLE TRUTHS

The four noble truths are objects of extensive meditation, with each truth having four attributes, making a total of sixteen attributes.

1 *True sufferings*

i *Impermanence.* The meditation centers on the thought:

> The contaminated mental and physical aggregates are impermanent because of being produced occasionally (not existing forever).

The impermanence of true sufferings is their momentary disintegration, which is a fault arising from the afflictions and actions contaminated with the afflictions. However, the impermanence of a Buddha's omniscient consciousness is an advantage of this consciousness and arises from the force of the completion of the accumulations of wisdom and merit. Unlike a Buddha's omniscient consciousness which, though impermanent, continuously remains of the same type, true sufferings change in the process of disintegration, gradually leading one to lower rebirths. Meditation on the impermanence of true sufferings overcomes viewing them as permanent.

ii *Misery.* The meditation centers on the thought:

> The contaminated mental and physical aggregates are miserable because of being under the outside influence of contaminated actions and afflictions.

True sufferings are miserable because they are not independent phenomena but under the outside influence of former afflictions and actions contaminated with the afflictions. The experience of ordinary beings confirms the misery of birth, aging, sickness, and death whereas realization of the suffering of being under an outside influence requires long analysis. Meditation on the misery of true sufferings counters viewing them as pure and pleasurable.

iii *Emptiness.* The meditation centers on the thought:

> The contaminated mental and physical aggregates are empty because of being devoid of a supervisory self that is a different entity from them.

True sufferings are empty of being a permanent, single, independent self. The permanent is the non-disintegrating; the single is the partless; and the independent is what does not depend on others for its existence. That true sufferings are empty of being a permanent, single, independent self or of being objects of use of such a self is their emptiness. Meditation on the emptiness of true sufferings overcomes viewing them as a self.

iv *Selflessness.* The meditation centers on the thought:

> The contaminated mental and physical aggregates are selfless because of not existing as an independent self, but being under the influence of many other impermanent factors.

True sufferings are empty of being a self-sufficient person. A self-sufficient person would be a controller of the mental and physical aggregates, like a master over his servants. That true sufferings are empty of being such a self-sufficient person or objects of its use is their selflessness. Meditation on this counters the view of true sufferings as a self-sufficient person or as the objects of use of such a person.

2 *True origins*

i *Cause.* The meditation centers on the thought:

> Contaminated actions and attachment are causes because of being the roots of suffering.

Meditation on these as causes counters the notion that suffering is causeless, as is asserted by the Hedonists (*Chārvāka, Tshu rol mdzes pa*).

ii *Origin.* The meditation centers on the thought:

> Contaminated actions and attachment are origins because they again and again produce suffering in all its forms.

Meditation on these as origins counters the notion that suffering is caused by just one cause, such as permanent time as is asserted by the Dīpakas.

iii *Strong production.* The meditation centers on the thought:

> Contaminated actions and attachment are strong producers because they produce suffering with great force.

Meditation on true origins as strong producers counters the notion that the nature of things is permanent but their states changeable, as is asserted by the Vaidakas and the Sāṃkhyas.

iv *Condition.* The meditation centers on the thought:

> Contaminated actions and attachment are conditions because attachment to cyclic existence acts as a cooperative condition for suffering.

Meditation on true origins as conditions counters the notion that suffering is created under the supervision of a deity, as is asserted by the Naiyāyikas and Vaisheṣhikas.

3 *True cessations*

i *Cessation.* The meditation centers on the thought:

> A separation which is a total extinguishment of a suffering by its antidote is a cessation because of being a state of having abandoned that suffering.

Meditation on true cessations as cessations counters the view that there is no liberation from cyclic existence, as is asserted by the Hedonists.

ii *Pacification.* The meditation centers on the thought:

> A separation which is a total extinguishment of a suffering by its antidote is a pacification because of being a state of having abandoned an affliction.

Meditation on true cessations as pacifications of contaminations counters notions conceiving contaminated states to be liberation as is the case with the Jaina assertion of a place of liberation on top of the worlds that is like an upside-down white umbrella.

iii *Auspicious highness.* The meditation centers on the thought:

> A separation which is a total extinguishment of a suffering by its antidote is auspiciously high because of being a liberation other than which there is no superior source of help and happiness.

Meditation on true cessations as auspiciously high counters the notion that there is a liberation superior to the cessation of suffering, as is the case with the Sāṃkhya assertion of the liberated self as high liberation.

iv *Definite emergence.* The meditation centers on the thought:

> A separation which is a total extinguishment of a suffering by its antidote is a definite emergence because of being a liberation from that suffering such that it will never return.

Meditation on true cessations as definite emergences from suffering counters the notion that liberation, once attained, is reversible.

4 *True paths*

i *Path.* The meditation centers on the thought:

> The wisdom directly cognizing selflessness is a path because it causes one to proceed to liberation.

Meditation on this as a path counters the notion that there are no paths of liberation from cyclic existence.

ii *Suitability.* The meditation centers on the thought:

> The wisdom directly cognizing selflessness is suitable because of being the antidote to ignorance.

Meditation on the wisdom realizing selflessness as suitable counters the notion that it is not a path of liberation.

iii *Achievement.* The meditation centers on the thought:

> The wisdom directly cognizing selflessness is an achiever because it realizes the nature of the mind unmistakenly.

Meditation on this wisdom as an achiever counters the notion that such paths as worldly concentrations, receiving initiation in a mandala of Īshvara, or undergoing the asceticism of the five fires (one each on the four sides and the sun above as in Jainism) are paths of liberation.

iv *Deliverance.* The meditation centers on the thought:

> The wisdom directly cognizing selflessness is a deliverer because it unquestionably causes one to pass to a state of irreversible liberation, extinguishing sufferings and afflictions completely.

Meditation on wisdom as a deliverer counters the notion that there is no total eradicator of suffering.

COARSE AND SUBTLE SELFLESSNESS

The Vaibhāṣhika sub-schools, except for the five schools advocating a self, say that through direct cognition of the four noble truths and their sixteen attributes Hearers, Solitary Realizers, and Bodhisattvas reach their respective paths of seeing. Through continuously meditating on them during the path of meditation, they also reach their goals, the states of Hearer, Solitary Realizer, and Buddha Foe Destroyers. Dharmakīrti says that the purpose of the first two attributes of true sufferings is to help in the realization of the last two attributes, emptiness and selflessness.[182] Thus, the Sautrāntikas Following Reasoning say that paths of seeing and the state of Foe Destroyer are attained through direct cognition of the mental and physical aggregates that lack being a self-sufficient person or lack being the objects of use of self-sufficient persons.

Among the Mahāyāna schools, the Chittamātrins and Sautrāntika-Svātantrika-Mādhyamikas say that Hearers and Solitary Realizers take the emptiness that is a person's lack of being self-sufficient as their main object of meditation (see Chart 36).[183] The Yogāchāra-Svātantrika-Mādhyamikas say that only Hearers take the emptiness of a self-sufficient person as their main object of meditation; Solitary Realizers take the emptiness that is the non-existence of subject and object as different entities as their main object of meditation.

The non-Prāsaṅgika schools agree that the conception of the person as a self-sufficient entity and the poisons that arise from it are the afflictive obstructions. They are the afflictions obstructing one from liberation from cyclic existence (*kleshāvaraṇa, nyon sgrib*). All these schools agree that through eradication of the afflictive obstructions, Hearers attain the state of Foe Destroyer. Vaibhāṣhika, Sautrāntika, Chittamātra, and Sautrāntika-Svātantrika add that Solitary Realizers have the same principal object of meditation, with Vaibhāṣhika and Sautrāntika also saying that it is the same for Bodhisattvas.

The Chittamātrins say that Bodhisattvas principally meditate on a non-difference in entity of subject and object, whereas the Svātantrikas say that Bodhisattvas principally meditate on an absence of true existence. These two schools thereby propound that Bodhisattvas rid themselves of subtler obstructions than do Hearers and Solitary Realizers. They remove the obstructions to simultaneous cognition of all phenomena (*jñeyāvaraṇa, shes bya'i sgrib pa*). For Chittamātrins and Svātantrikas, though Hearers and Solitary Realizers do not meditate on the final nature of things, their meditation, despite its coarseness, is still capable of destroying the bonds to cyclic existence.

The Prāsaṅgikas disagree; they say that the conception of a self-sufficient person is only a *coarse* afflictive obstruction and that no one can attain liberation from cyclic existence through eradicating it. However, meditation on the emptiness of a self-sufficient person is indeed helpful for eventual abandonment of the subtle afflictive obstruction, the conception that phenomena truly exist (see Charts 37, 38, and 39). The Prāsaṅgikas do not separate out one type from among the coarse and subtle emptinesses as the main object of meditation for Hearers and Solitary Realizers and another for Bodhisattvas. For Prāsaṅgika, beings

Chart 36: *Principal Objects of Meditation*

	Hearers	*Solitary Realizers*	*Bodhisattvas*
Vaibhāṣhika and Sautrāntika	non-existence of a self-sufficient person	non-existence of a self-sufficient person	non-existence of a self-sufficient person
Chittamātra	non-existence of a self-sufficient person	non-existence of a self-sufficient person	non-existence of subjects and objects as different entities
Yogāchāra-Svātantrika	non-existence of a self-sufficient person	non-existence of subjects and objects as different entities	non-existence of truly existent phenomena
Sautrāntika-Svātantrika	non-existence of a self-sufficient person	non-existence of a self-sufficient person	non-existence of truly existent phenomena
Prāsaṅgika	non-existence of inherently existent phenomena	non-existence of inherently existent phenomena	non-existence of inherently existent phenomena

Chart 37: *Self*

	coarse self of persons	*subtle self of persons*	*coarse self of phenomena*	*subtle self of phenomena*
Vaibhāṣhika and Sautrāntika	a permanent, single, independent person	a self-sufficient person	none	none
Chittamātra	a permanent, single, independent person	a self-sufficient person	none	phenomena as naturally bases of names; object and subject as different entities
Yogāchāra-Svātantrika	a permanent, single, independent person	a self-sufficient person	object and subject as different entities	truly existent phenomena
Sautrāntika-Svātantrika	a permanent, single, independent person	a self-sufficient person	none	truly existent phenomena
Prāsaṅgika	a self-sufficient person	an inherently existent person	none	inherently existent phenomena other than persons

Chart 38: *Obstructions*

	coarse afflictive obstructions	*subtle afflictive obstructions*	*coarse obstructions to omniscience*	*subtle obstructions to to omniscience*
Vaibhāṣhika and Sautrāntika	conception of a permanent, single, independent person	conception of a self-sufficient person	none	none
Chittamātra	conception of a permanent, single, independent person	conception of a self-sufficient person	none	conception of phenomena as naturally bases of names; conception of object and subject as different entities
Yogāchāra-Svātantrika	conception of a permanent, single, independent person	conception of a self-sufficient person	conception of object and subject as different entities	conception of phenomena as truly existent
Sautrāntika-Svātantrika	conception of a permanent, single, independent person	conception of a self-sufficient person	none	conception of phenomena as truly existent
Prāsaṅgika	conception of a self-sufficient person	conception of persons and other phenomena as inherently existent	none	appearance of inherent existence; stains of conceiving the two truths as different entities

Chart 39: *Selflessness*

	coarse selflessness of persons	*subtle selflessness of persons*	*coarse selflessness of of phenomena*	*subtle selflessness of phenomena*
Vaibhāṣhika and Sautrāntika	non-existence of a permanent, single, independent person	non-existence of a self-sufficient person	none	none
Chittamātra	non-existence of a permanent, single, independent person	non-existence of a self-sufficient person	none	non-existence of phenomena as naturally bases of names; non-existence of object and subject as different entities
Yogāchāra-Svātantrika	non-existence of a permanent, single, independent person	non-existence of a self-sufficient person	non-existence of subject and object as different entities	non-existence of truly existent phenomena
Sautrāntika-Svātantrika	non-existence of a permanent, single, independent person	non-existence of a self-sufficient person	none	non-existence of truly existent phenomena
Prāsaṅgika	non-existence of a self-sufficient person	non-existence of an inherently existent person	none	non-existence of inherently existent phenomena other than persons

on all three types of paths realize the same emptiness, the lack of inherent existence of all phenomena. The conception that phenomena inherently exist obstructs beings from liberation from cyclic existence; without realizing that all phenomena—both persons and other phenomena—do not inherently, truly, or objectively exist, conquest of cyclic existence is impossible.

The destruction of the afflictive obstructions is simultaneous with the attainment of the state of Foe Destroyer for both Hearers and Solitary Realizers and is simultaneous with the attainment of the eighth ground for Bodhisattvas. On the eighth, ninth, and tenth grounds Bodhisattvas proceed to destroy the obstructions that prevent simultaneous cognition of all phenomena. Being eighth-grounders or above, they have destroyed the conception that phenomena inherently exist, but due to previous conditioning phenomena still *appear* as if inherently existent; nevertheless, they know that these appearances are false just as a magician knows that his creations are false, no matter how vividly the illusion may appear. Finally, through the eradication of the appearance of inherent existence, an omniscient consciousness of Buddhahood is attained, and one is able for the first time to perceive objects through the senses with no trace of false appearance. One is then able to cognize simultaneously and directly the emptinesses of all phenomena and all phenomena themselves.

A selflessness is an emptiness, to be viewed as a predicate or quality of existent persons and phenomena. These predicates vary from the coarse—or easier to realize—to the subtle—or more difficult to realize. It is said that the non-existence of a permanent, single, independent person is easy to realize through such reasons as the impossibility of a permanent being's taking rebirth since the permanent can never change.

In the Prāsaṅgika system the emptiness of a self-sufficient person is not the final mode of existence of the person, and thus one cannot be liberated from cyclic existence through realization of and meditation on it. Cognition of the person as empty of such a self will not even cause one to ascend to the path of preparation of a Hearer. For, Hearers, Solitary Realizers, and Bodhisattvas all attain special insight into the emptiness of inherent existence simultaneously with their attainment of the path of preparation. Still, the realization of the emptiness of a self-sufficient person is a stepping-stone to realization of the emptiness of inherent existence. If one is incapable of understanding the coarse emptiness, one will certainly not be capable of cognizing the subtle; therefore, it is important that the coarse selflessness be identified as well.

A 'self-sufficient' (Tib. *rang rkya ba*) person is a 'substantially existent' (*dravyasat, rdzas yod*) person.[184] In general, both terms refer to an object than can appear to the mind without depending on the appearance of other objects; thus, the opposite of 'substantially existent' is 'imputedly existent' (*prajñaptisat, btags yod*). Here in the coarse selflessness, 'imputedly existent' is identified as eliminating the possibility that the person is an entity independent of the aggregates of mind and body. All Buddhist schools, except Prāsaṅgika and the Vaibhāṣhika sub-schools that advocate a self, say that a person is 'imputedly existent' in the sense of not being a separate entity from the mental and physical aggregates. However, these schools propound that the person is either the composite of these aggregates, or one of them, or their continuum, or the continuum of one of them. For Prāsaṅgika, however, this is incorrect; a person is neither separate from the mental and physical aggregates, nor the mental and physical aggregates themselves; rather, a person is merely imputed to the aggregates. The imputedly existent person of the other schools is considered by the Prāsaṅgikas to be substantially existent because the latter say that the meaning of 'substantially existent' is to be findable separate from or *among* the bases of imputation of the object.

Here in the four noble truths in the realization that a person is not self-sufficient, the meaning of 'only imputed' is not so subtle; the term merely indicates that a person depends on his mental and physical aggregates. Opposite to this, many mistaken systems teach that a person has a character separate from that of his aggregates; they view a person as like a herder or a lord and the mental and physical aggregates as his herd or subjects.[185] For the non-Prāsaṅgika schools of Buddhist tenets, this view of a self-sufficient person exists innately in ordinary beings, but for Prāsaṅgika it is only a product of false teachings. The Prāsaṅgikas say that the innate sense of a self-sufficient person is the person's appearing to be like a head salesman and his aggregates appearing to be like salesmen. The head salesman, unlike the relationship between a shepherd and his flock, is not separate from the category 'salesman', but he is the boss of the other salesmen. Similarly, though a person is of the nature of the aggregates, he appears to be the controller of them; the aggregates, like salesmen, appear to depend on the person who, like a head salesman, appears not to depend on the aggregates. In fact, the person depends on the aggregates; however, when one thinks, 'My body', it seems that first there must be an I and then a body which is owned or controlled. This is the way that a self-sufficient person appears.

When the dependent nature of the person is reflected upon in meditation and when it is seen that the person is nothing separate from the aggregates, one can withdraw from desires and so forth that are entered into for the sake of such a person. One can then reflect on phenomena other than persons, such as mind and body or external possessions, as not being objects of use and enjoyment by a self-sufficient person. Such meditation is powerful and serves to advance one to the point of being a fit vessel for the doctrine that persons and other phenomena do not inherently exist. Through being taught non-self-sufficiency, a meditator is led into seeing the dependent nature of the person and is thereby drawn into probing the significance of dependence, the very sign of non-inherent existence.

Part Four
Systems

1 *Self*

Source
Nga-w̄ang-b̄el-den's *Annotations*

THE ASSERTION OF SELF

The non-Buddhist systems assert the existence of a substantially existent self based on scripture and counterfeit reasoning.[186] The scriptures are those transmitted from one to another, setting forth the existence of a personal self. The reasonings are:

> A self exists because without prior consideration, when phenomena such as the shape of a face are seen, the thought of the presence of a person is generated, not just the thought of the presence of a shape.
>
> A self exists because without prior consideration, when enjoyment preponderantly of pleasurable feelings is perceived, the thought of the presence of a high person is generated, not just of feeling. When enjoyment preponderantly of painful feelings is perceived, the thought of the presence of a low person is generated, not just of feeling.

> When the name 'Devadatta' is designated, one thinks of a person, not just of a discrimination of the name.
>
> When engagement in afflictions—such as desire—or virtues—such as faith—are perceived, the thought of the presence of a childish person or a wise person is generated, not just of engagement.
>
> When the mind understands its objects through the eyes and so forth, one does not just think that the mind sees but that 'I see.' This shows that there is a sentient being, or I separate from the mind.
>
> If there were no self separate from the mental and physical aggregates, one would not think, 'I have seen a form,' or 'I will see a form,' but would only think of the aggregates as engaging in activities. However, this is not the case; one must definitely think of the self prior to engagement in activities.

BUDDHIST REFUTATION OF SELF

Since those seeking liberation must completely refute the referent object of the view of the transitory collection as a real I and must assert a mere I or mere person, they must become skilled in the ways of refutation and proof through reasoning. Otherwise, falling to the extreme either of asserting no I at all or of affirming a substantially existent I, all their efforts will be senseless. Since the mere person is not to be refuted, a person as qualified by a certain attribute is. This is called a true (**satyaka, bden pa*), ultimate (*paramārtha, don dam*), or substantially existent (*dravyasat, rdzas yod*) person.

In short, the person is conceived to exist substantially whereas it only exists imputedly (*prajñaptisat, btags yod*). Here, an imputedly existent object is a phenomenon, such as a forest or army, which when it appears as an object of the mind must depend on the appearance of some other basis which has a character different from it, such as trees or soldiers. However, the substantially existent appears under its own power without depending on such—for instance, a tree or soldier. This explanation of 'substantial existence' comes from the lower systems because in the Prāsaṅgika system nothing substantially exists since the appearance of any phenomenon must depend on the appearance of its basis of imputation, which is not itself.

1 *Refuting the reasoning that the person substantially exists because it is observed that when phenomena such as the shape of a face are seen, the thought of the presence of a person is generated without prior consideration*

Are phenomena, such as the shape of a face and so forth, perceived and the thought of a sentient being generated with respect to them, or is something else perceived and the thought of a sentient being generated with respect to it? If the former, then that thought is erroneous because it conceives such to be a sentient being whereas a sentient being is other than the shape of a face and so forth. If the latter, one has let fall the position that the thought of a sentient being is generated only from perceiving such phenomena.

Does that base which, when perceived, generates the thought of a sentient being have the nature of a sentient being or not? If the former, then that thought is erroneous because the sentient being appears to be self-sufficient in the sense of having a character different from that of the mind and body. If the latter, then one would have to assert that even a pot could serve as a cause generating the thought of woolen cloth.

Do you accept that the thought of a sentient being can be generated with respect to what is not a sentient being or not? If not, it is manifestly contradicted by the experience of generating the thought of a human to a pile of stones seen in the distance. If, however, the thought of a sentient being can be generated with respect to what is not a sentient being, then the basic assertion that the thought of a sentient being understands its object just as it is is indefinite.

Do you accept that the thought of non-sentient being can be generated with respect to a sentient being? Do you accept that the thought of a certain sentient being can be generated with respect to another sentient being?

When the aggregates are perceived, is the base that generates the thought of a sentient being manifest or hidden? If manifest, then the aggregates would be the sentient being because another phenomenon not included among them is not manifestly perceived. If hidden or obscure, then a small untrained child would not generate a thought of a sentient being.

2 *Refuting that the person substantially exists just because it is observed that one engages in activities having first thought, 'I will murder,' or 'I will forsake murder'*

Do these activities arise from mental causes or from the cause of the self? If the former, then one has let fall the position that these are activities of a substantially existent person. If the latter, then it contradicts the position that these activities are preceded by thought.

Is the cause of the activities permanent or impermanent? If permanent, then it could not act. If impermanent, then these could not be the activities of a permanent self.

Does the sentient being who is the agent have a nature of exertion or non-exertion? If the former, then the self could not be permanent. If the latter, it would be contradictory to say that the non-exerting exerts.

Do the activities of a sentient being have causes or not? If not, then the activities would always be performed. If caused, then since they would be preceded by other causes, they would not be the independent activities of a self.

Are activities performed under one's own power or under the influence of the other? If the former, then the sufferings of birth, aging, sickness, death, and so forth would never be experienced because what one experienced would be in one's own power. If the latter, then it would not be suitable for these to be the activities of the self because the self is asserted to be under its own power.

3 *Imputation of the self to the aggregates*

If the person is imputed to the mental and physical aggregates, then it could not be a self-sufficient entity different from the aggregates.

If the person abides in the aggregates like a pile of grain in a mandala, is the person permanent or impermanent? If permanent, then it could not be helped or harmed by pleasure and pain; hence, it would not accumulate virtuous and non-virtuous actions (*karma las*) and thus would not assume a body, in which case there would be no sense in asserting it as a person. If impermanent, then something that is other than the aggregates and is produced and disintegrates would have to be observed, but it is not.

If the person is other than the aggregates (which include all products) like sticks set side by side, then since the person would be a non-product, it would be senseless to assert it.

If the aggregates do not exist at all, then since there could be no relation with fetters, one would be liberated effortlessly.

4 *Positing the character of the person*

If a person separate from the aggregates exists, does it have the nature of being the viewer of forms and so forth or not? If it does, is it imputed to the eye consciousness and so forth or is it another object altogether? If the former, then it could not be substantially existent.

If the self is the viewer of forms and so forth but is other than the eye consciousness, then it would be either the object or the instrument of viewing. If it is the object, then it would be the basis of the activity of viewing. This could be in the sense of, like a seed, newly producing its own similar type in the next moment, but then the viewer would be impermanent, not permanent as is asserted. Or, this could be in the sense of transformation, like a potter or a human with magical powers, but then it would be impermanent and conventional. If just as a magician emanates illusions under his own power, so the self is under its own power, then the viewer would not undergo any suffering. The self might be conceived as the basis of the activity of viewing in the same way as the earth serves as the basis of and destroys the moving (sentient beings) and non-moving (the environment), but this is not observed in the self. Or, the self could be the basis of activity, like space, in the sense that one can stretch out and contract one's limbs in space which is non-obstructive, but this also is not observed in the self. Furthermore, if just as space is posited to a mere elimination of obstructive contact, so the viewer is posited to a mere elimination of its object of negation, then the self could not appear to the mind under its own power because it would be a mere absence.

If the viewer is the instrument of viewing, then like a sickle, its engaging in activity would definitely depend on an agent in which case it would be dual-natured, being both that which engages the object (as the instrument) and that which is engaged in the object (as the object upon which the agent acts). If, like a fire, it sometimes engages its objects under its own power without an agent (as in spontaneous combustion), then it would be senseless to assert the existence of the person in fear of the lack of an agent.

If the person does not have the nature of being the viewer of forms and so forth, then it is senseless to assert a person that does not have any valid cognition.

5 *Positing the self as afflicted and purified*

Does the self have the character of being afflicted and purified, or is it other than these? If it does, then it would be unreasonable to assert a person separate from the aggregates because food, clothing, and so forth help the self, imbalance of the elements and so forth harm it, and afflictions are perceived only in the aggregates, not in anything else. If the self does not have the character of the afflicted and the purified, then it could not be afflicted and purified.

6 *Positing the self as engaging and disengaging*

Does a person who has the character of engagement and disengagement engage and disengage or does a person who does not have the character of engagement and disengagement do such? If the former, then a person separate from the aggregates could not exist because the activity of engagement is observed only in the phenomena of the aggregates. There is (1) engagement by way of having causes, like the body from its causes of semen, blood, and so forth, (2) engagement by way of having a nature of production, like a sprout, (3) engagement by way of having a nature of disintegration, like the gradual descent of a waterfall, (4) engagement from the one to the other like the connection of a flame to its next moment of similar type, and (5) engagement of transformation—having done one activity, engaging in another—like mounting a mount and thereby changing one's situation. All of these are observed only in the aggregates.

If a person who does not have the character of engagement and disengagement engages and disengages, then the self would not become engaged, because of not having the character of engagement. Since disengagement depends on a previous engagement, it is impossible when engagement is impossible.

7 *Positing the self as the experiencer, agent, and liberator*

Is something that is affected by pleasure and pain which are generated by objects asserted as the experiencer or is one who is not? One who is not affected by pleasure and pain could not be the experiencer since something that is helped or harmed from enjoying objects of experience is the meaning of an experiencer. If something that is affected by pleasure and pain generated by objects is the experiencer, then it is senseless to say that the self substantially exists because the state of being affected is perceived only in impermanent products.

Is something that is affected by the mind asserted as the agent, or is something that is not? As above, being affected is perceived only in impermanent products. Something that is not affected by the mind is not an agent because 'agent' means something that is affected by the mind.

Is something that is affected by the root and secondary afflictions asserted as the self that is liberated or is something that is not? As above, being affected is observed only in impermanent products. Something that is not affected by the afflictions could not be liberated because of not having been formerly bound.

8 *Positing the self as the instrument*

Is agentship posited only to the self or can it also be posited to others? If only the self, then it would not be suitable to say 'The light of burning fire illuminates the area,' indicating an agent other than the self. If others can be posited as agents, then it would be allowable to *designate* the self as the agent in seeing, hearing, and so forth, but there would be no point in asserting a substantially existent self.

9 *Positing the self as what is expressed by 'person'*

Is the verbal convention 'person' used only for the self or also for others? If only the self, then it would be wrong for one, having observed only the body of a being, to use the verbal convention of his name with respect to it. If 'person' can be used for other things than the self, it could also be used for the viewer of forms and so forth. Though such would be allowable, it would be pointless to assert a further self.

10 *Positing the view of self*

It is not feasible for the view of self to be virtuous because it is especially produced in the obscured, is generated without application of effort, generates fear with respect to liberation, and is seen to nourish faults such as desire. Being non-virtuous, the view of a self is erroneous and mistaken with respect to its referent object, in which case one cannot prove the existence of self through citing the existence of the view of self. Furthermore, it is not feasible for the view of selflessness to be non-virtuous because the Omniscient Buddha spoke highly of it and because it must be achieved with great effort, does not generate fear with respect to liberation, causes the speedy attainment of auspicious fruits, and acts as the antidote of faults.

Is it that a substantially existent self abides as an objective reality and thus through its power the view of self is generated, or is it that whereas the person lacks substantial existence, the existence of a substantially existent self is superimposed through the power of conditioning to improper thought? If the former, then it would follow that Buddhists could not generate ascertainment of selflessness because this view of self, which would be produced by the power of the thing itself, would prevent it. If the latter, then it cannot be proved that a substantially existent self exists by way of citing the existence of the view of self.

In brief, a person which is not imputed in dependence upon the collection, continuum, and so forth of the mental and physical aggregates does not inherently exist because of not being established as one nature with or a different nature from the aggregates. However, the opposite, the substantial existence of the self, is believed due to the assumption that the self exists validly as it appears to the innate false view of the transitory collection as a real I. To such an innate false view the self only appears to be a different object from the aggregates, for one seeks to leave these aggregates and gain others that are better than these but does not wish to leave the self.

When the substantial existence of the person is refuted, one understands implicitly that the person only imputedly exists. A mere person must be asserted on the positive side, and mere imputation is to be realized through the implicit force of refuting substantial existence. Thus, although self (*ātman, bdag*) and person (*pudgala, gang zag*) are *in general* synonyms, they are not synonyms in the expression 'selflessness of the person'; in this context, the term 'self' refers to substantial existence (*dravyasat, rdzas yod*), whereas the term 'person' refers to the nominally existent sentient being imputed to the mental and physical aggregates. Though some Buddhist Vaibhāṣhika systems (exemplified by some modern-day T̄heravādins) assert that there is no agent, only action, D̄zong-ka-b̄a says[187] that they are mistakenly opposing worldly conventionalities. The fact that a substantially existent agent cannot be found does not mean that person or agent do not exist at all; they exist imputedly and effectively.

Bhāvaviveka

2 *Non-Buddhist Systems*

Sources
Jam-ȳang-shay-b̄a's *Great Exposition of Tenets*
Nga-w̄ang-b̄el-den's *Annotations*
J̄ang-ḡya's *Presentation of Tenets*

The Buddhist tenet systems are differentiated from the non-Buddhist in that their teacher—Buddha—has extinguished all faults, attained all auspicious attributes, and taught from his own insight the profound doctrine of dependent-arising.[188] Their teaching harms neither themselves nor others, and their view is the assertion of the non-existence of a permanent, single, independent self.

Non-Buddhist teachers, teachings, and views are just the opposite; their teachers have not extinguished all faults, their teachings harm some sentient beings, and their view is of a permanent, single, independent self. This is not to say that their teachers do not have some auspicious attributes, or that all of their teachings harm, or that all of their views are wrong. Rather, their teachers do not have the perfection of a Buddha; within their teachings there is at least one that harms a sentient being, and they have a wrong view on the status of the self. Even the

Jainas, who cultivate not harming others, harm themselves in extreme asceticism and thereby also harm the organisms that live in their bodies. Also, even the Nihilists claim that the self is permanent or unchanging during its existence, however short.

It is necessary to take into account the meaning and not just terminology in dividing the Indian systems into Buddhist and non-Buddhist, for Buddhists are not the only ones to use the terms 'emptiness' and 'selflessness'. The Vaiṣhṇavas and Aishvaras assert an emptiness which for them is merely the vacuity resulting from destruction at the end of a great eon. Also, the native Tibetan Bön religion asserts a selflessness which for them is a permanent truly existent essence.

Non-Buddhist Indian systems of tenets are almost innumerable; however, twenty-five are mentioned by Avalokitavrata, D̄zong-ka-b̄a, and D̄zong-ka-b̄a's disciple K̲ay-drup as having split off from Sāṃkhya.[189] Jam-ȳang-shay-b̄a selects twelve for his discussion of non-Buddhist systems due to their being explained clearly in texts surviving in Tibet. From the Buddhist point of view, eleven of these are assertions of an extreme of permanence, that is, they assert as existent what is non-existent. The remaining one is an assertion of an extreme of annihilation, that is, they assert as non-existent what is existent.

The eleven schools adhering to a view of permanence are:

1 Sāṃkhyas and Kāpilas (Enumerators and Followers of Kapila)
2 Brāhmaṇas (Followers of Brahmā)
3 Vyākaraṇas (Grammarians)
4 Vedāntins (Adherents to the Finality of the Vedas)
5 Guhyakas (Secretists)
6 Vaiṣhṇavas (Followers of Viṣhṇu)
7 Mīmāṃsakas (Performers, or Analyzers)
8 Shaivas (Followers of Shiva)
9 Vaisheṣhikas (Differentiators)
10 Naiyāyikas (Logicians)
11 Nirgranthas or Jainas (The Naked or Followers of the Jinas).

The school adhering to a view of annihilation is that of the Chārvākas (Hedonists). Unlike the Buddhist schools of tenets which are all included in four types (with tantrists included among the Chittamātrins and Mādhyamikas), all the non-Buddhist schools cannot be included in these twelve, or even in the twenty-five alluded to above.

The way to determine whether a system is inner—Buddhist—or outer—non-Buddhist—is to investigate whether or not the teacher has extinguished all faults and has attained all auspicious attributes, whether or not the teaching abandons harming sentient beings, and whether the view is of selflessness or self. Or in another way, the Buddhist teaching can also be established through four means: view, meditation, behavior, and fruit. The view, avoiding the extremes of asserting that a person is a separate substantial entity from the mental and physical aggregates or that a person designated in dependence upon these does not exist, is that of the four seals (see p.336). The meditation, avoiding the extremes of being too tight or too loose, eradicates all transmigration, including the Peak of Cyclic Existence which is the highest Formless Realm. The behavior avoids the extremes of both sensuous indulgence and fatiguing asceticism with regard to clothing, food, abode, and medicine.[190] The fruit is the non-return of obstructions that have been abandoned through individual analytical cessation.[191]

The non-Buddhist view is of a permanent, partless, independent self. Their meditation leads only to rebirth in higher realms within cyclic existence. Their behavior has fallen to extremes of severe asceticism or indulgence. Their fruit is the return of obstructions which only seem to have been abandoned.

To distinguish an insider from an outsider without identifying him or her as a proponent of specific tenets is merely to examine where refuge is taken. One who takes refuge in Buddha, his Doctrine, and the Supreme Community from the depths of his heart is a Buddhist. Therefore, it is said to be mistaken to assert that the teacher of non-Buddhists and of Buddhists is the same, for Buddha is the only perfect teacher, and his teaching is unique.

Proponents of outer tenets affirm that the self apprehended by a consciousness viewing a permanent, partless, independent self is real. Proponents of inner tenets refute such. Those outsiders who accept only objects of direct perception, refusing to accept inference as valid, are proponents of annihilation (*uchchhedavādin, chad smra*). Outsiders who also accept hidden objects which are revealed by inference and/or scripture are proponents of permanence (*shashvatavādin, rtag smra*).

According to Prajñāvarman's *Commentary on (Udbhaṭasiddhasvāmin's) 'Exalted Praise' (Visheṣhastavaṭīkā)* and according to Chandrakīrti's *Supplement to (Nāgārjuna's) 'Treatise on the Middle Way'*, all non-Buddhist systems are traced to the founder of the Sāṃkhya system, Kapila.[192] The Brahmin Kapila appeared in the world during the first of the twenty intermediate eons of abiding of this world system, when a life-span was immeasurable, and in retreat attained a solitary liberation through asceticism. In order to teach his path to others, he composed the Sāṃkhya texts that mainly set forth the twenty-five categories of realities. The many and various systems of Forders (*Tīrthika, Mu stegs pa*) split off from the root Sāṃkhya as a result of disagreement over minute differences of opinion concerning the self as it was explained by Kapila.

However, some scholars, in accordance with the thought of Bhāvaviveka's *Blaze of Reasoning (Tarkajvālā)*, say that all the Forder systems arose individually, having their own fundamental teachers and different books, without relying on the Sāṃkhya treatises.

According to the Jainas, however, the fundamental teacher of all Forders is the sage Arhat, who gave all the many and various systems of tenets to his companions. Afterwards, when Brahmā came, Arhat said, 'Great Brahmā, you have come leisurely; you have come very late. Because I have given away all the treatises, use these Vedas.'

Jam-ȳang-shay-b̄a says that these various accounts show how very difficult it is to come to any conclusion about the origins of the Forders.[193] J̄ang-ḡya, who in his presentation of tenets relied heavily on Jam-ȳang-shay-b̄a, says that the story of the twenty-five Forder schools splitting off from the Sāṃkhyas is meant to refer to their basic similarity of view of a permanent, partless, independent self, and not to an actual historical origin.[194]

Bhāvaviveka's *Blaze of Reasoning*[195] reports that the pure offerings set forth in the Vedas initially spread widely. However, at a time when the morality of beings had diminished, sages debated about the Vedic injunction, 'Various things are good [for offering].' Some said that the offering of animals was not suitable, whereas some said it was. Those who wished to eat meat performed impure offerings and even altered the Vedas. Thus, the two types of offerings arose in stages, the initial pure offerings without animal sacrifice and later impure offerings that include blood sacrifice.

In general, non-Buddhists are called 'other sectarians' because they are followers of sects other than those of the Buddhists. They are called 'outsiders' because they are outside of the correct view of emptiness. Their treatises teaching paths to high status within cyclic existence and to liberation from cyclic existence are called 'Fords to the End'. The authors of such treatises are called 'Makers of the Ford to the End' (*Tīrthāṅkara, Mu stegs byed*).

SĀṂKHYAS

According to Bodhibhadra, Sāṃkhyas (Enumerators) are so called because they advocate a definite enumeration of the causes that produce existents.[196] Or, according to Bhāvaviveka's *Blaze of Reasoning*, they are called Sāṃkhyas because they assert that one is liberated through understanding the enumeration of the twenty-five categories of realities. They propound that all products are produced from their own nature and thus are called Proponents of the Nature as Cause. Because they follow the sage Kapila, they are called Kāpilas. Because they accept that the non-manifest principal (*pradhāna, gtso bo*) is the cause of all products, they are called Proponents of the Principal.

The school is divided into the non-theistic and the theistic. The non-theistic Sāṃkhyas are followers only of Kapila and do not take the lord Īshvara to be the motivating cause of the manifestation of the world. They assert that all products exist at the time of their causes and are made manifest by conditions. The theistic Sāṃkhyas, following Patañjali, take the lord Īshvara to be their teacher and assert that the transformations or manifestations of phenomena depend on his supervision. They say that though all causes and effects are the same in nature, they differ as transformations.

The twenty-five categories of realities that both Sāṃkhya schools accept

1 person (*puruṣha, skyes bu*) [or self, consciousness, conscious self, mind, sentience, knower of the field]
2 fundamental nature (*prakṛti, rang bzhin*) [or nature, principal, universality, general principal]
3 intellect (*buddhi, blo*), or great one (*mahat, chen po*)
4 I-principle (*ahaṃkāra, nga rgyal*)
  a. I-principle dominated by motility (*rajas, rdul*)
  b. I-principle dominated by darkness (*tamas, mun pa*)
  c. I-principle dominated by lightness (*sattva, snying stobs*)

Five subtle objects or potencies of objects which evolve from the I-principle dominated by motility:
5 visible forms (*rūpa, gzugs*)
6 sounds (*shabda, sgra*)
7 odors (*gandha, dri*)
8 tastes (*rasa, ro*)
9 tangible objects (*sprașhṭavya, reg bya*)

Eleven faculties which evolve from the I-principle dominated by lightness:

Five mental faculties:
10 eye (*chakṣhus, mig*)
11 ear (*shrota, rna ba*)
12 nose (*ghrāṇa, sna*)

13 tongue (*rasana, lce*)
14 body or skin (*sparshana, pags pa*)

Five physical faculties or action faculties:
15 speech (*vāch, ngag*)
16 arms (*pāṇi, lag pa*)
17 legs (*pāda, rkang pa*)
18 anus (*pāyu, rkub*)
19 genitalia (*upastha, 'doms*)

20 Intellectual faculty (*manas, yid*) the nature of which is both mental and physical

Five elements:
21 earth (*pṛthivī, sa*) which evolves from the odor potency
22 water (*āp, chu*) which evolves from the taste potency
23 fire (*tejas, me*) which evolves from the visible form potency
24 wind (*vāyu, rlung*) which evolves from the tangible object potency
25 space (*ākāsha, nam mkha'*) which evolves from the sound potency.

The person lacks the qualities of motility, darkness, and lightness. Inactive because of pervading all migrators, it is neither an agent of virtue or non-virtue nor the creator of manifest phenomena. The person is a permanent existent because of not changing and is consciousness because of not being an aggregate of particles. It is the experiencer because of experiencing pleasure and pain. The person 'dwells beside' the nature until liberation in the sense that the manifestations which evolve from the nature are confused with the person until yogic discrimination separates the two and all manifestations disappear.

The other twenty-four categories—the nature and so forth—are aggregates of particles and, therefore, are matter. The nature is a permanent and partless entity that pervades all its transformations and is the agent of virtue and non-virtue, etc. The nature and its transformations are the objects enjoyed by the person, but it itself is always non-manifest; even the sage Kapila did not directly see it. The nature is the three qualities of motility, darkness, and lightness in equilibrium. These three qualities (*guṇa, yon tan*) are:

1 lightness (both in light/heavy and light/dark), desire, and pleasure: *sattva, snying stobs*
2 motility, hatred, and pain: *rajas, rdul*
3 darkness, obscuration, and gloom: *tamas, mun pa*.

The nature is also called the final mode of existence of phenomena and the ultimate. However, the person also is an ultimate, and the intellect, I-principle, and the five subtle elements are also natures in that they are sources of transformations. The nature is the original source of all the transformations.

From the nature the great one or intellect is produced. It is like a two-sided mirror, in which the images of objects from the outside and of the person from the inside meet or mix. The intellect 'empowers' the senses and apprehends the objects that the senses apprehend which in turn are then known by the person. This is the way that the person knows objects.

From the intellect three I-principles are produced. From the dark I-principle the subtle elements of odors, tastes, visible forms, tangible objects, and sounds are produced. These five respectively produce the five elements: earth, water, fire, wind, and space. From the lightness I-principle the eleven faculties are produced. The motile I-principle is the motivator of the former two. This is how Avalokitavrata presents the functions of the three I-principles; however, D̄zong-ka-b̄a, in his commentary on Chandrakīrti's *Supplement*, and Gyel-tsap, in his commentary on Dharmakīrti's *Ascertainment of Valid Cognition* (*Pramāṇavinishchaya*), say that the dark I-principle is the motivator and the motile I-principle is the source of the five subtle elements.

The twenty-five categories are divided into four types: natures (causes), transformations (effects), both natures and transformations, and neither natures nor transformations. The nature is only a nature since it is the cause of all the transformations and is not itself caused. The intellect, I-principle, and the five subtle elements are both natures and transformations in that they both cause transformations and are themselves caused by something else. The eleven faculties and the five elements are only transformations because, though they are caused, they do not produce anything else. The person is neither a nature nor a transformation because it neither creates nor is created.

The nature and the person are truly existent phenomena because they are non-manifest. The other twenty-three are manifest and are, therefore, only conventionally existent; they are falsities.

The Sāṃkhyas explain production as the manifestation through minor causes of what is already existent. Disintegration is an effect's dissolution into its own nature. The theistic Sāṃkhyas add that the varieties of environments and animate beings are not produced from just the nature because it is mindless. That which is mindless is not capable of being a supervisor, and without a supervisor the creation of effects is not possible. The person is not suitable to be the supervisor because when the person is alone, before the appearance of the transformations, there is no knowledge; the intellect has not yet been produced, and without ascertainment by the intellect there is no realization of objects. Therefore, the varieties of effects are produced through the mutual dependence of the great lord Īshvara and the nature. An increase in strength of motility—among the three qualities that abide in the entity of the nature—causes Īshvara to issue forth all beings. An increase of lightness causes duration. An increase of darkness causes disintegration.

Though Īshvara and the nature, which are the causes producing all environments and animate beings, always exist, the serial production, duration, and disintegration of effects is said to be admissible. For, the three qualities—motility, darkness, and lightness—increase and diminish serially.

When the person wishes to enjoy objects, the nature realizes its desires, unites with the person, and creates the varieties of transformations. Eventually, through a lessening of desire, the person comes to view objects as faulty and parts from desire. By cultivating the concentrations and formless absorptions the divine eye is obtained. When this eye looks at the nature, the latter is ashamed just as a mistress is when she is discovered by a wife. Having been discovered, the nature parts from the person, and, opposite to the stages of production, all the transformations dissolve into the nature. When these have become non-manifest and the person remains alone, liberation is attained.

Since discrimination is the means to liberation, a yogi meditates in general on the twenty-five categories and in particular on the person as empty of the nature and on the nature as empty of the person. This type of emptiness is called 'emptiness of the other'—the person is empty of being the nature, and the nature is empty of being the person. When the two are no longer confused, the root of cyclic existence is cut, and liberation is attained.

BUDDHIST REFUTATION OF SĀṂKHYA

If, as the Sāṃkhyas claim, that which existed at the time of its causes were nevertheless produced again, it would be a senseless production, and there would be no end to the re-production. For, the already existent would require production.

If their causes are permanent and thus do not diminish, the disappearance of the twenty-three effects is contradictory.

Because the intellect is matter, it cannot experience pleasure and pain.

Because the nature and the person pervade all, it is contradictory for them to be partless. Does all or only a part of the principal pervade every individual thing?[197] If the former, the principal would be separate from itself just as a bull and a pot, which the principal and the person pervade, are separate entities. If only a part of the principal pervades individual manifestations, then it is admitted to have parts.

Is Īshvara a person? If he were, he would not be suitable to be the supervisor because persons are not agents in the Sāṃkhya system and persons alone, without the nature, have no knowledge. If Īshvara is not a person, then there is a twenty-sixth category. Also, if nothing appears to a liberated person due to the parting of the principal and all its transformations, is Īshvara, the supervisor of all appearances, non-liberated?

If the person is a partless entity, it cannot be consciousness. If the person is permanent, how could it be bound and freed?

It follows that one cannot be freed from cyclic existence merely through cognizing that the person and happiness, pain, and so forth are different. For, even untrained children realize a separation of themselves from their faculties and from happiness, pain, and so forth. Conceiving themselves as the seeker, they seek happiness and faculties which are superior to those of the present. Furthermore, they conceive of themselves in former and later moments as one but realize that happiness and pain arise and cease.

It is not possible to be liberated from cyclic existence through meditating on one's faculties as suffering and through seeking to become separate from them. For, such a mind of disgust for suffering is accompanied by hatred. Also, at that time one still has desire, even if suppressed. To achieve liberation from cyclic existence it is necessary to destroy the misconception of objective existence that gives rise to desire, hatred, and suffering.

CHĀRVĀKAS

The Chārvākas (Hedonists) are so called because they advocate satisfaction with only what is pleasant (*charu, mdzes pa*) here in this life.[198] They are called Proponents of Annihilation because they propound that at death, or after a number of lives, the continuum of the self ceases. They are called Nihilists because they propound that rebirth does not exist and that moral cause and effect do not exist. They are called Barhaspatyas because they follow the god Bṛhaspati. They are called the Gone-Afar (*Ayata, rbyang phan pa*) because they have gone apart from the right view. They are called Daivagurus after their teacher Devaguru, that is, Bṛhaspati, and Juk-dop-jen-bas (*'Juk-stobs-can-pa*) after their teacher Juk-dop, a student of the renowned sage Lokachakṣhu and a contemporary of the logician Dharmakīrti.[199] They are called Proponents of Inherence and Proponents of Nature because they consider that many things, such as the sharpness of thorns and the descent of a waterfall, appear naturally, without depending on causes.

They are nihilists not because of believing in nothing or that life is totally worthless, but because they believe only in what they can perceive directly, discarding inference as a means of valid knowledge. Seeing that charity does not necessarily bring wealth as the clergy claim, they propound that this life and its attributes of life-span, wealth, and so forth are not results of merits and demerits in former lives. They are moral nihilists. Since they rely on direct perception as their sole source of knowledge, they deny causation where it cannot be seen, such as even in the coloring of flowers and the roundness of peas. However, they affirm causation that can be seen, such as the molding of a vase from clay.

The Nihilists are divided into Meditators and Dialecticians. The Meditators attain clairvoyance through which they perceive former and future births for thirty, sixty, or ninety eons according to their mental level.[200] Unlike Buddhists, they assume that the cycle of rebirth has a beginning because their clairvoyance is limited and they do not perceive a beginningless cycle of births. With their clairvoyance they follow themselves and others from lifetime to lifetime noticing no immediate relationship of cause and effect with respect to the experience of pleasure and pain.

The Dialecticians see the same lack of causal relationship in the stages of a single human's life and thus deny moral law along with rebirth. Wishing to save the world from uselessly wasting its riches on clergy and uselessly participating in efforts aimed at improving a future life, they advocate no cause and effect in the moral sense. It is also said that the sage Lokachakṣhu desired to lie with his daughter and so explained to her the absence of moral law.

For a Nihilist, consciousness is a fermentation of the elements, much like inebriation produced from alcohol. Mind is not considered to be a phenomenon of a different nature from matter. Matter in all systems is composed of particles, but mind in most systems is not. The Buddhists, based on a view of an essential difference between mind and matter, expound a theory that mind and body have their own separate substantial causes—the mind's main cause being a former mind. Thereby, a beginningless cycle of existence is established because a mind must always have a mind preceding it as its substantial cause. The Nihilists reject this notion saying that mind has a physical nature just as the capacity to cause inebriation is of the same nature as beer. The mind is an effect of the body just as light is an effect of a lamp. The mind is a quality of the body just as a mural is a quality of a wall.

Nihilists say that the scope of the person is limited to the scope of the senses. This counters the Buddhist notion of a subtle type of impermanent self that transmigrates and the non-Buddhist notion of a permanent self beyond sense perception. Nirvana is then the annihilation of mind and body with the return of the body to the four elements and the dispersion of the senses into space. 'Live happily until death. After death you have no location or place. When the body has become ashes, how can it live again? Therefore, former and later [lives] do not exist.'

A Dialectician Nihilist asserts that a mind on the point of death has no conjunction with a later mind just because it is a mind on the point of death. Even though he does not believe that there are Foe Destroyers, he cites the example of the final moment of the mind of a Foe Destroyer which, according to the Buddhist Vaibhāṣhikas, ceases upon death. For a Vaibhāṣhika, the continuum of mind and body of a Foe Destroyer ceases when he dies whereas the Mahāyāna schools say that this is impossible, declaring that in this respect the Vaibhāṣhikas are like Nihilists.

Nihilists assert that because the mind is produced from the elements, there are no Foe Destroyers who have eradicated the afflictions of desire, hatred, and ignorance. Therefore, they do not accept an omniscient Buddha or Supreme Community.

Similarly, there is no excellent Doctrine because there is no abandonment of afflictions and no path that abandons them.

The Dialecticians add that there are no Foe Destroyers because beings are permanent, stable, perpetual, and unchanging as long as they exist and thus do not become good or bad through the power of causes. The Meditators, when they attain any of the equipoises of the four concentrations or of the four formless absorptions, think that they are Foe Destroyers. Near the time of their death, they fall from their meditative stabilization, see their rebirth in a lower condition, and conclude, 'There is no Foe Destroyer, and there is no path of a Foe Destroyer.'

BUDDHIST REFUTATION OF NIHILISM

The mind right after conception has a preceding mind just because it is a mind. For, cause and effect must be of a harmonious nature. Even one whose mental powers are not clear and whose senses are torpid immediately after birth searches to eat food and searches to drink the milk of the breast without being taught. This is by the force of previous conditioning in other lives.

Consciousness is not produced from inanimate causes because the substantial causes of the inanimate and of consciousness are definitely separate. The natures of the two are different; the one is an aggregation of particles and the other is not.

Nihilists say that the mind is produced from the mindless elements because the mind is a product, just as inebriation is produced from beer and fire is produced from a magnifying glass and those two are products. However, because inebriation is an attribute of a mind and not a mind, the example is not proper. Because causes must accord in type with their effects, the reason cited is in fact contradictory; it proves that the mind is not produced from the mindless elements.

The Nihilists say that a mind at the point of death has no conjunction to another life because it is a mind at the point of death, like the final mind of a Foe Destroyer. The reason is inconclusive because there are cases of memory of former lives and because babies have different styles of behavior. Furthermore, that the Vaibhāṣhikas claim that the mind of a Foe Destroyer ceases at death does not make it so. The continuum of the mind never ceases, and the Vaibhāṣhikas merely fall to the depth of the Nihilists in claiming so, as do some wrong interpreters of Prāsaṇgika who say that in meditative equipoise on emptiness there is no mind (confusing the fusion of subject and object at the time of direct cognition of emptiness with disappearance of the mind).

Body is not the main cause of mind because if it were, a dead body would absurdly be conscious. Also, the mind does not depend on the body in the sense of being its substantial effect because the increase and diminishment of wisdom and so forth do not depend on the increase and diminishment of the body. This is not to deny that mind and body affect each other; rather, *all* states and changes of mind do not depend on the body. Also, mind does not depend on body in the sense of its having a physical nature because if it did, a person's mental qualities would be perceived by a sense consciousness that perceives the body. Because the Nihilists say that the body is permanent as long as it lasts, the mind also would always have to have the same disposition.

The Nihilists are wrong in claiming that there is no omniscient consciousness. The development of clear and direct perception by a conditioned mind is the proof through which omniscience is established. Much as an object of desire repeatedly taken to mind can appear vividly before a lustful person, emptiness can be seen directly and not just through the medium of images or concepts. Once this is shown, then the gradations of the path and final omniscience are easily established.

The limitless development of love and wisdom is established by proving the existence of former and future lives. For, since love and wisdom are qualities of mind, they develop naturally together with a consciousness that becomes conditioned to the ways of love and wisdom. A feature of consciousness is that the same effort required to begin a continuum of love or wisdom is not required for each of the successive moments, much like the natural continuance of fire once it has been started. Since there are future lives, there is sufficient time for the full development of wisdom and love.

Because thorns and so forth are produced from their own seeds and because the sharpness of thorns and so forth are produced from those same seeds, the sharpness of thorns is not a suitable example of the causeless production of suffering. The ascertainment that thorns arise sometimes in some places proves that they are produced in dependence on their own objects of dependence, and these objects of dependence are accepted as their causes. A cause is that which aids its own effect; that which does not aid is not an object depended upon for production. If things were causelessly produced without depending on others, things would either always exist, or never exist, or everything would be produced from everything.

The Nihilists say that there are no former and later births, no omniscience, and no effects of charity, etc., because they have not seen them directly. Does this mean that all persons have not seen them directly or that just the Nihilists have not seen them directly? Also, do they directly see them to be non-existent or do they realize them to be non-existent through inference? That all persons have not seen them is doubtful; how, without omniscience, can anyone know what all have and have not seen? If only the Nihilists have not seen them, it is answered that it is mistaken that the non-existent is co-extensive with what the Nihilists have not seen.

If the Nihilists say that a direct perceiver sees former and later births, omniscience, and so forth as non-existent, the answer is that non-existence of other lives and so forth could not be an object of direct perception because, according to the Nihilists, other lives are non-existent entities. How can the non-existent be seen directly? If their non-existence is established by way of inference, then by accepting such an inference the fault is entailed of first denying the validity of inference and then of using inference to establish a point. For, the proponents of Nihilism say that only direct perception is valid. The non-existence of former and later births and so forth not only cannot be established by valid inference, but also an attempt to do such would demolish their own position that inference is not valid.

3 *Hīnayāna*

Sources
Kensur Lekden's oral teachings
J̄ang-ḡya's *Presentation of Tenets*
Jam-ȳang-shay-b̄a's *Great Exposition of Tenets*
Nga-w̄ang-bel-den's *Annotations*
Ḡön-chok-jik-may-w̄ang-b̄o's *Precious Garland of Tenets*

A Buddhist is one who accepts the Three Jewels—Buddha, his Doctrine, and the Supreme Community—as the final refuge, whereas a non-Buddhist is one who does not.[201] Buddha is the teacher of refuge; the Doctrine—especially the true cessation of obstructions—is the actual refuge, and the Supreme Community are the friends helping persons toward refuge.

Refuge may be taken with any of three motivations:

1 Some persons have concern and fear for the sufferings of bad migrations as animals, hungry ghosts, and hell-beings. (Lives within cyclic existence are called 'migrations' [*gati, 'gro ba*] because beings move from one to another within the round.) Due to their belief that the Three Jewels have the power of protecting from bad migrations, they take refuge in them from the depths of their hearts.

2 Others, realizing the impermanence and changeability of even happy migrations, have concern and fear for the sufferings of all cyclic existences including those of happy migrations as humans, demi-gods, and gods. Due to their belief that the Three Jewels have the power of protecting from all these sufferings, they take refuge in them from the depths of their hearts.

3 Still others, having realized their own miserable condition, infer that all are suffering and generate fear for all sentient beings' cyclic existence. They fear that even if beings turn toward a religion, they will seek one that leads only to a solitary peace, thereby neither perfecting themselves nor devoting themselves to the welfare of others. They also have concern and fear for others' afflictions preventing liberation from cyclic existence, and their obstructions preventing omniscience. Due to their belief that the Three Jewels have the power of protecting all beings from these four faults, they take refuge in them from the depths of their hearts.

This last is the motivation of a Mahāyānist, a being of greatest capacity.

Vaibhāṣhikas, Sautrāntikas, Chittamātrins, and Mādhyamikas are Buddhists and also proponents of particular systems of tenets. 'Tenet' is a translation of *siddhānta* or *siddhyanta (grub mtha')*, which literally means 'established conclusion' or 'that which is an establishment and a conclusion'.[202] An established conclusion is so called because a meaning has been established for the holder's mind through reasoning, scriptural citation, or both, and he will not pass beyond this conclusion. A Buddhist proponent of tenets is one who not only accepts the Three Jewels as the highest refuge but also propounds the tenets of the four seals which testify to the fact that a doctrine is Buddha's.

Thus, all Buddhist systems—Vaibhāṣhika, Sautrāntika, Chittamātra, and Mādhyamika—propound the four seals:[203]

1 all products are impermanent
2 all contaminated objects are miserable
3 all phenomena are selfless
4 nirvana is peace.

For the highest system, the Prāsaṅgika division of Mādhyamika, products are conventionally but not inherently existent phenomena produced from the aggregation of causes and conditions. Products are impermanent even to the point that other than their own production they require no cause, major or minor, for their disintegration. Contaminated objects are mainly consciousnesses that conceive things to exist inherently but are also the environments and other phenomena that are created from the merit and demerit accumulated by sentient beings when they engage in actions motivated by the ignorant misconception of inherent existence. All phenomena are selfless in the sense that both persons and all other phenomena such as body, mind, house, and fence do not inherently exist. The passage beyond ignorance and its consequent miseries is nirvana, which is explained as meaning 'passed beyond sorrow'. 'Sorrow' is here identified as the afflictions, the principal of which is the conception that things inherently or naturally exist. Peace is not bestowed by a deity or obtained otherwise than through nirvana.

VAIBHĀṢHIKA

'Vaibhāṣhika' means a follower mainly of the *Great Detailed Exposition (Mahāvibhāṣha)* which is a compendium on knowledge (*abhidharma, chos mngon pa*), a study of phenomena.[204] This text distills the meaning of the Seven Treatises of Knowledge which only the Vaibhāṣhikas accept as spoken by Buddha. 'Vaibhāṣhika' (*Bye brag smra ba*) also means one who asserts that past, present, and future objects are all instances (*visheṣha, bye brag*) of 'substantial entities' (*dravya, rdzas*). It is further said that Vaibhāṣhikas are so called because, like the non-Buddhist Vaisheṣhikas, they propound many 'substantially established phenomena' (*dravyasiddhadharma, rdzas grub kyi chos*) such as uncaused space which the other Buddhist systems say are existent but only designated by thought.

Vaibhāṣhikas assert partless particles that aggregate into gross objects. According to the Kashmiri sub-school, the particles do not touch each other but are held together by space. Others say that the particles surround each other without interstice, while others say that they touch each other. In any case, gross objects are formed through the aggregation of partless particles, and thus external objects—objects which are entities external to a perceiving consciousness—are said to exist truly.

The Vaibhāṣhikas also assert partless moments of consciousness. An aggregation of these is a continuum of consciousness that perceives its object 'nakedly', that is, without itself being generated in the image of its object.

For Vaibhāṣhika, ultimate truths (*paramārthasatya, don dam bden pa*) are objects that can bear analysis. This means that even when reduced, either physically or through the process of analysis, they still generate in a perceiver an apprehension of themselves. For instance, a clay pot, if broken with a hammer or analyzed into its parts, no longer generates a consciousness that perceives a pot or thinks 'pot.' Therefore, a pot is not an ultimate truth. However, the matter of the pot is still matter even down to the finest unbreakable particle. Therefore, objects such as partless particles, partless moments of consciousness, and permanent phenomena are ultimate truths—true for the ultimate analytical supramundane consciousness. They are also called ultimate truths because they definitely have ultimate existence.

All objects that require an aggregation of particles or of moments are conventional truths (*saṃvṛtisatya, kun rdzob bden pa*)—conventional because they are designated in accordance with worldly conventions and truths because such designations are true.

Both ultimate and conventional truths are substantially established (*dravyasiddha, rdzas grub*), though only ultimate ones are substantially existent (*dravyasat, rdzas yod*). Vaibhāṣhika is the only school to differentiate 'substantially established' and 'substantially existent', the intention being to provide a status of 'substantiality' for conventional truths. Though conventional truths are imputedly existent (*prajñaptisat, btags yod*) they are substantially established because in this system these imputations are true; when the objects designated are sought, an autonomous entity is found.

The non-Buddhist Vaisheṣhikas and Naiyāyikas carry the doctrine of substantially existent entities to the point where whole and part are separate entities, as are quality and qualificand, doer and doing, and definition and definiendum.[205] For the Naiyāyikas, within the realm of the existent, whatever appear to the mind to be different are different substantial entities.

The Vaibhāṣhikas are said to have been highly influenced by non-Buddhist thought even to the point where they are a mixture of Buddhist and non-Buddhist. Their name is, therefore, sometimes traced to the name 'Vaisheṣhika'.[206]

Furthermore, like the Sāṃkhyas, the Vaibhāṣhikas accept that a sprout, for instance, exists as a sprout at the time of its future, that is, when the sprout is yet to be produced. They say that if a product did not exist before its actualized state in present time, its production would be adventitious. If non-existents were produced, even non-existent things like the horns of a rabbit could be produced. For the other Buddhist schools, however, a sprout at the time of its future exists as the entity of its seed, but the sprout does not exist as a sprout and, therefore, does not exist.[207]

The Vaibhāṣhikas are also the only Buddhist school to accept simultaneous cause and effect as, for example, in the case of a consciousness and its accompanying mental factors, such as intention and feeling, which support each other like the poles of a tripod. No other Buddhist school accepts simultaneous cause and effect, citing as their reason that one thing cannot affect another that already exists; it can only affect later moments of the other.

'Vaibhāṣhika' is a general name referring to eighteen sub-schools that, according to differing explanations, split off from one, two, three, or four basic orders after Buddha's death. According to an explanation by Bhāvaviveka of a division from two basic orders, they are as shown in Chart 40.[208] Bhāvaviveka says that there are six Mahāsaṃghika, seven Sarvāstivādin, and four Vātsīputrīya sects and that this is a list of eighteen; thus the eighteenth would have to be the Haimavatas. (For other renditions of the split into eighteen sub-schools, see Appendix 3.)

Not all eighteen sub-schools actually accept the 'Vaibhāṣhika'

Chart 40: *Division of Vaibhāṣhika into Eighteen Schools*
(The dates are based on Buddha's death, After the Nirvana.)

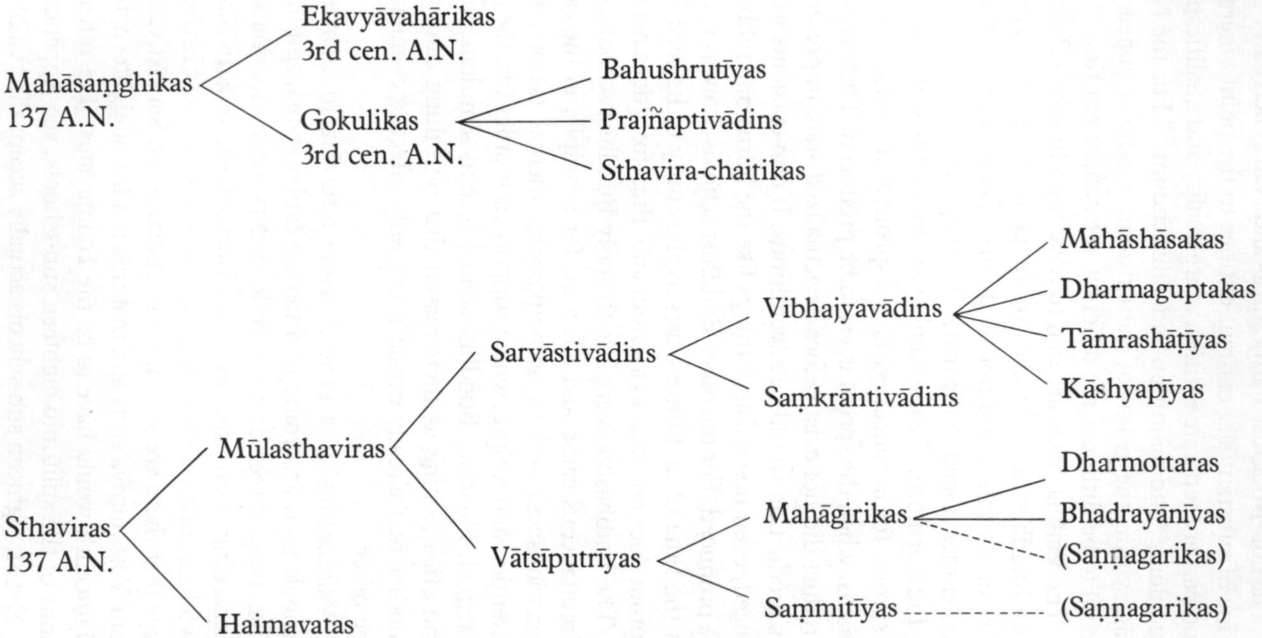

notion that past, present, and future objects are substantial entities. The Mahāshāsakas, for instance, say that past objects and future objects do not substantially exist; only present objects do.[209] Furthermore, not all accept that there is no simultaneous cognition of all phenomena because the 'one expression' of the Ekavyāvahārika (literally, those who have one expression) school is the assertion of a Buddha's simultaneous cognition of all phenomena.[210]

Some of the eighteen sub-schools arose from the simple fact that their teachers were different or that their monasteries were located in different areas. Difference of language also contributed to the divisions, but according to Kensur Lekden, the chief cause was the Hīnayāna notion that all Buddha's sūtras are literal. (The evidence does not show this to be the case as interpretation of scripture was important in many Hīnayāna schools.)[211]

The five Saṃmitīya sub-schools (see Padmasambhava's rendition in Appendix 3) assert the existence of a person that is neither the same as nor different from the mental and physical aggregates. However, they and the other thirteen Vaibhāṣhika schools all assert the non-existence of a permanent, partless, independent self. The thirteen non-Saṃmitīya schools also assert the non-existence of a substantially existent or self-sufficient person. Their assertion of selflessness does not mean that there is utterly no self or person but refutes the existence of a certain type of self. For these thirteen Vaibhāṣhika schools, a person is not independent of the mind and body but is a phenomenon within the mind-body complex. Some say that a person is the *continuum* of the five aggregates of forms, feelings, discriminations, compositional factors, and consciousnesses. Others say that a person is the mental consciousness; still others say that a person is all five aggregates.

For these thirteen Vaibhāṣhika schools, the non-existence of a self-sufficient person is known as the subtle selflessness of persons. The coarse selflessness is a person's non-existence as a permanent, partless, independent entity. Through cognizing and becoming accustomed to the subtle personal selflessness, the knot of cyclic existence is cut, and the state of Foe Destroyer is attained. One has destroyed the foe which is the conception of the person as a substantial or self-sufficient entity.

Simultaneously with becoming a Foe Destroyer, one attains a nirvana with remainder—the state of having passed beyond the afflictions (the chief of which is the conception of a self-sufficient person) while still possessing a physical support that receives its impetus from former contaminated actions and afflictions. Then, at death the continuum of mind and body is severed in a nirvana without remainder. The attainer of the nirvana without remainder is thus said to be the Foe Destroyer who is about to die because once dead, his continuum of mind and body has utterly ceased, and there is then no one who could possess a nirvana without remainder.[212]

For the Vaibhāṣhikas, five of the six types of Foe Destroyers can fall from their attainment even as far back as the path of seeing. According to the other schools, however, such degeneration makes a mockery of the conception of the total abandonments of afflictions which are called true cessations, the third of the four noble truths.[213]

The Vaibhāṣhikas, despite being Hīnayāna in terms of their tenets, accept a Bodhisattva path that is trod by very rare beings —the one in our age being Shākyamuni Buddha.[214] That they accept such is clear from their literal acceptance of Buddha's *Life Stories (Jātaka)* which recount his generation of the aspiration to enlightenment and his practice of the six perfections. They also accept as literal the *Discipline (Vinaya)* which recounts Buddha's performance of the twelve deeds of a fully enlightened being.

The Bodhisattva path requires an accumulation of the collections of merit and wisdom for three periods of countless eons whereas the path of a Solitary Realizer requires only one hundred eons. A Buddha completely removes both the afflictive and non-afflictive obstructions whereas the Hearers and Solitary Realizers, though they utterly abandon the afflictive obstructions, only 'abandon' the non-afflictive obstructions through non-attachment. In the Vaibhāṣhika system the afflictive obstructions are the conception of a self-sufficient person and the poisons of desire, hatred, and ignorance that result from it.

The non-afflictive obstructions are ignorance of the distant in time, the distant in place, the profound and subtle qualities of a Buddha, and subtle objects such as the subtle details of cause and effect relationships. These are eradicated through a Bodhisattva's great accumulation of merit.

With respect to how practitioners ascend the paths, the Vaibhāṣhikas say that a rhinoceros-like Solitary Realizer and a Bodhisattva pass in one meditative sitting from the beginning of the path of preparation through the paths of seeing, meditation, and no more learning. Thus, a Buddha's body is an ordinary human body of matter and is a true suffering even though it no longer can generate suffering for him. It is a true suffering because his body receives its impetus from former contaminated actions and afflictions. Therefore, the Buddha Jewel that is the object of refuge only refers to the phenomena of no more learning in his continuum.

Famous Vaibhāṣhika masters are Vasumitra, Dharmapāla, Buddhadeva, Saṃghabhadra and so forth.

SAUTRĀNTIKA

The other Hīnayāna school of tenets is Sautrāntika.[215] Jam-ȳang-shay-b̄a distinguishes it from the Sautrāntika that is a sub-school of Vaibhāṣhika, but the scholar D̄ak-tsang (b.1405) of the S̄a-ḡya (*Sa-skya*) order, whom Jam-ȳang-shay-b̄a frequently refutes in his *Great Exposition of Tenets*, disagrees. He says that there are eighteen Hīnayāna sub-schools, seventeen Vaibhāṣhika and one Sautrāntika.[216]

Etymologically, the Sautrāntikas are so called because they rely mainly on sutras in propounding tenets. However, since all Buddhist systems cite scripture and reasoning to support their tenets, the name Sautrāntika is not a definition but an indication of emphasis. Etymologies are traditionally examined to discover whether they apply to a wider or narrower range than the precise meaning of the word, or whether the etymology can also serve as a definition. Here, the etymology of Sautrāntika covers a wider set than those actually indicated by the term.

The Sautrāntikas are of two types: Followers of Scripture—mainly of Vasubandhu's *Treasury of Knowledge*—and Followers of Reasoning—mainly of Dignāga's *Compendium of Valid Cognition (Pramāṇasamuchchaya)* and Dharmakīrti's Seven Treatises on Valid Cognition (see Bibliography). The latter are considered to be the higher of the two because of their resemblance to Mahāyāna counterparts, the Chittamātrins Following Reasoning, and because their assertions on the processes of reasoning are more developed. The Ge-luk-b̄a order of Tibetan Buddhism, of which Jam-ȳang-shay-b̄a is a member, is fond of Dharmakīrti's logic, especially as described by his Sautrāntika followers. They see the Sautrāntika system of Dharmottara and so forth as a stepping-stone to an understanding of Mahāyāna tenets—their fondness refuting any suggestion that the Hīnayāna schools are despised in Tibet.

The Followers of Reasoning are more famous than the Followers of Scripture for their works on logic, but it cannot be said that the Followers of Scripture are not advocates of reasoning. Dignāga himself was a student of Vasubandhu, who was a Sautrāntika Following Scripture before becoming a Chittamātrin, though Dignāga is said to have surpassed his teacher in the field of logic.[217]

The tenets of the Sautrāntikas Following Scripture are similar to those of the Vaibhāṣhikas; however, they, along with the Followers of Reasoning, do not accept that past and future objects are instances of substantial entities. They also do not accept that a Foe Destroyer can fall from his attainment. All Sautrāntikas agree that the Seven Treatises of Higher Knowledge were not uttered by Buddha, and most add that they were not even uttered by Foe Destroyers because the latter would not set forth mistaken teachings, such as that of the substantial existence of space. Sautrāntikas say that space, analytical cessations, and non-analytical cessations are mere negatives or absences of tangibility, afflictions, and so forth and thus are only imputedly existent, though permanent in the sense of being non-disintegrating. All Sautrāntikas also assert that cause and effect cannot be simultaneous and that a consciousness does not perceive its object nakedly but is generated in its image. On these points the Sautrāntikas disagree with the Vaibhāṣhikas and agree with the Mahāyāna schools of tenets.

The differentiation between Sautrāntika and the Mahāyāna schools is the former's agreement with Vaibhāṣhika that objects, which are entities external to the consciousness perceiving them, truly exist. The Hīnayāna schools also do not assert that phenomena other than persons are selfless except in the sense that they do not exist as objects of use of a self-sufficient person. They consequently do not assert that there are obstructions to omniscience—obstructions to simultaneous cognition of all phenomena (*jñeyāvaraṇa, shes bya'i sgrib pa*). As a result, they also do not accept the ten Bodhisattva grounds.

The Hīnayāna schools do not accept the existence of a Buddha's Enjoyment Body (*Saṃbhogakāya, Longs sku*) which immortally preaches doctrine to Bodhisattva Superiors. Therefore, it is very difficult for one who is a Hīnayānist by tenet to become a Mahāyānist by path as defined by the Mahāyāna schools.[218] In order to do so, he would have to generate an altruistic aspiration to enlightenment, as a Mahāyānist by path does when he takes upon himself the burden of freeing all sentient beings from cyclic existence and establishing them in the happiness of Buddhahood. Without the possibility of omniscience and an immortal Enjoyment Body, the generation of such an unusual compassionate attitude would be next to impossible.

Many of the Hīnayāna schools do not even accept the Mahāyāna sutras as being Buddha's word, thinking that many Mahāyāna teachings contradict the four seals.[219] For instance, the teaching that a Buddha's Enjoyment Body abides forever without disintegrating contradicts the first seal that all products are impermanent. (The Mahāyānists answer that though an Enjoyment Body disintegrates moment by moment, its continuum remains of the same type, unlike an ordinary body which becomes sick, old, and so forth; thus, it is immortal but still impermanent.) The Hīnayānists say that the Mahāyāna teaching that a Bodhisattva proceeds from joy to joy contradicts the second seal that all contaminated objects are miserable. They say that the Mahāyāna teaching that through cultivating the path one attains a superior self contradicts the third seal that all phenomena are selfless. Also, they say that the teaching that a Hearer or Solitary Realizer Foe Destroyer, after attaining a nirvana without remainder, enters into cultivation of the Mahāyāna path contradicts the fourth seal that nirvana is peace.

With such an aversion to the special Mahāyāna teachings that make an aspiration to help all sentient beings realistic, it would be almost impossible for a practitioner's sense of compassion to counter the influence of such tenets. However, it is said that a few Hīnayānists by tenet have generated the full aspiration to altruistic enlightenment as described in the Mahāyāna scriptures. They thus become Mahāyānists in terms of their path and not just in the way that the Bodhisattva path is described by the Hīnayāna schools. For the Hīnayāna schools of tenets, the Bodhisattva path merely entails a much longer period of the collection of merit; it does not involve such unusual aspirations.

The most marked difference between the Sautrāntikas Following Reasoning and those Following Scripture lies in their assertions on the two truths. The Followers of Scripture agree with the Vaibhāṣhikas that ultimate truths are objects such as partless particles and partless moments of consciousness which can withstand breakage and analysis, still generating a consciousness that apprehends them. For the Followers of Reasoning, however, ultimate truths are objects ultimately able to perform a function, especially the function of creating an effect. For them, all impermanent objects are ultimate truths—truths for an ultimate consciousness which is not mistaken with respect to its appearing object .

Valid sense consciousnesses that correctly perceive visible forms, sounds, odors, tastes, and tangible objects and mental consciousnesses that directly perceive such objects as the four noble truths are non-mistaken. However, an inferring consciousness, though non-mistaken with respect to its referent object, is mistaken with respect to its appearing object. The reason is that it perceives an image of an object, and the image appears to be that object.[220] For instance, when an inferential consciousness realizes the impermanence of an ox based on the sign that an ox is born and the pervasion of whatever is born by impermanence, the impermanence of an ox is its referent object. Its appearing object is a generic image or concept of the impermanence of an ox that seems to be the real thing; thus, it is said that a correct inferential consciousness is mistaken in terms of its appearing object.

Images or concepts, not being objects of a totally non-mistaken consciousness, are not ultimate truths. They also are not impermanent but permanent, not in the Vaibhāṣhika and non-Buddhist sense of the continual existence of a thing from one moment to the next, but in the sense of not undergoing momentary disintegration.

Each person's images or concepts do indeed come into existence in dependence on the person's having formed an image of such an object, but from the viewpoint of their representing the exclusion of everything which is not that object, they are said to be permanent. For the non-Buddhist Forder systems, a generality (*sāmānya, spyi*) is permanent and partless. Through identifying it in one object, a person thereafter notices it in its other instances and thereby knows its manifestations. Thus, for the non-Buddhist Forders, the naming and noticing of objects is positive; terms and thoughts are affixed to objects through the power of the objects themselves. In short, for the Forders, one initially learns of the presence of a universal in an instance, and through that process of naming, one is able to know all instances of the universal when they appear in one's ken.

For the Sautrāntikas Following Reasoning and for the Mahāyāna schools of tenets, the process of naming and noticing is negative or exclusionary. Ox appears as an exclusion (*apoha, gzhan sel*) of non-ox to a consciousness that thinks, 'Ox.' In other words, the process of naming relies on the elimination of non-ox. Without the appearance to the mind of something as the negative of non-ox, thought cannot identify 'ox'. Non-non-ox does indeed mean ox, but it must appear to the mind through the negative route of eliminating non-ox.

Though non-non-ox means ox, it is a negative implying a

positive object whereas ox is just a positive phenomenon. It is not that ox does not exclude or negate non-ox, but ox is positive rather than negative because ox does not appear to thought through an *explicit* exclusion of non-ox. A further complexity is that though ox is impermanent, the isolate of ox, which means ox in isolation, is permanent because of appearing only to thought, for ox devoid of all of its instances is something that can appear only to thought. Thus, though ox is the isolate of ox, the isolate of ox is not ox.

Furthermore, an appearance as non-non-ox (which here means a conceptual appearance of ox to a mental consciousness) is permanent, that is, non-disintegrating. Some contemporary Tibetan scholars identify this appearance (or as it has been translated here, generic image or meaning-generality) as the thing that appears to the mind when we think about 'ox'. They agree that it seems to move and change, sometimes being one color, sometimes another, etc., but they still say it is permanent because it does not disintegrate moment by moment as do external objects such as stones. The appearance of change is due to the mind. Others say that the appearance of this white-haired thing that appears to the inner mind is not the meaning-generality (*arthasāmānya*, *don spyi*) of ox, but they have no identification of 'appearance' in this context. One scholar says that the meaning-generality of ox is impermanent, an internally created picture, and added that when he says this in the debating courtyards, the heads of the other scholars split wide open.

In any case, the Sautrāntikas Following Reasoning, as well as the Mahāyānists, present an essentially negative or exclusionary process of naming. One takes as one's basis the white-haired thing and takes as one's reason the presence of certain characteristics such as a dew-lap and a hump and then applies the name 'ox' to a generic image or meaning-generality that is actually an appearance as non-non-ox. A consciousness which has such a generic image as its appearing object is mistaken in that it understands its referent objects, such as the actual many and various oxen, through the medium of an image which is not manifold and various—thereby confusing place, time, and nature. Thus, an inferring consciousness realizing the impermanence of an ox, though valid with respect to its main object, impermanence, is mistaken in terms of its appearing object, an image of the impermanence of an ox which appears to be actual impermanence. A definite preference for direct cognition is implied, with inferential realization valued as a means to it.

A generic image or meaning-generality appears to the mind through dependence on thought, not through its own entity; therefore, it is said to be permanent. Such phenomena are conventional or obscured truths (*saṃvṛtisatya, kun rdzob bden pa*) because they are truths, or existents, for thought. Thought—the intellect—is obscured because it cannot act directly on impermanent objects; it must work through the medium of images and concepts. The intellect, as has been seen, is mistaken; however, the intellect, when correct, does not *conceive* or *hold* the internal appearance as non-non-ox to be non-non-ox, that is, ox; such only *appears* to it, much as a reflection of a face in a mirror appears to be a face but is not usually *conceived* to be so. Thus, a correct intellectual consciousness is mistaken with regard to its appearing object but not with regard to its referent object.

The Sautrāntikas Following Reasoning hold that the explicit objects of direct perception are impermanent objects. The Mahāyānists, on the other hand, assert that the permanent phenomenon, emptiness, can be directly perceived. The Sautrāntikas Following Reasoning explain that a yogi, in direct perception, explicitly realizes the impermanent mental and physical aggregates and implicitly realizes the permanent phenomenon of emptiness which in their system is the non-existence of the person as a self-sufficient entity. An emptiness is thus not an ultimate truth but an obscured truth because it is a truth for thought, appearing to the mind through the route of the negation of a self-sufficient person. A selflessness, or an emptiness, is a non-affirming negative (*prasajyapratiṣhedha, med dgag*), not implying anything in its place, and thus is permanent and cannot be seen directly.

The Sautrāntika emphasis on impermanent things is obvious: impermanent objects are called ultimate truths, and yogis, in the most exalted of cognitions, explicitly realize not emptiness but the impermanent aggregates. If an object can perform the function of creating an effect, it is determined as ultimately existing; a pot, which for Vaibhāṣhikas and for Sautrāntikas Following Scripture is a conventional truth, is an ultimate truth for the Sautrāntikas following Dharmakīrti.

On the subject of impermanence itself the Sautrāntikas offer a presentation that differs significantly from Vaibhāṣhika and agrees with Mahāyāna.[221] The Vaibhāṣhikas say that production, abiding, aging, and disintegration are not four activities but four agents: (1) that which causes production, (2) that which causes aging, (3) that which causes abiding, and (4) that which causes disintegration. These four characteristics of impermanent phenomena are substantial entities separate from the phenomena themselves. They are said to exist simultaneously as characteristics of one phenomenon, but to perform their functions serially. According to the Vaibhāṣhikas, the momentariness of impermanent things actually refers to the period of these four instants.

Both types of Sautrāntikas, however, hold that (1) production is the new arising of what did not exist before, (2) abiding is the remaining of a type similar to what preceded it, (3) aging is the non-similarity in entity of a later moment and a former moment, and (4) disintegration is a product's not remaining a second moment after its present. All four characteristics exist simultaneously because what is newly produced is just what does not remain for a second moment. What is newly produced is also just what abides as a type similar to its preceding cause and is just what is a different entity from its former cause. Therefore, all products last only the instant of their production; they require no further cause for their disintegration than their own production. Products have a *nature* of momentary disintegration; it is not something else that makes them so.

The Sautrāntikas Following Reasoning also differ from the Vaibhāṣhikas in that they assert self-consciousness. Self-consciousness is here not introspection or self-awareness, but a consciousness's cognizance of itself non-dualistically much as the sun illumines itself while it illumines others. In this context, self-consciousness has little function in the spiritual path, and despite its somewhat impressive name does not occupy even a degree of importance that elicits a clear position from each school. Still, self-consciousness figures into the definitions of the proponents of Hīnayāna tenets. The definition of a Vaibhāṣhika is:

> a Hīnayāna proponent of tenets who does not assert self-consciousness and who asserts the true existence of external objects—with qualification.[220]

(The qualification excludes the Sautrāntikas Following Scripture who *seem* also not to accept self-consciousness, but this is a matter of controversy.) The definition of a Sautrāntika is:

> a Hīnayāna proponent of tenets who asserts the true existence of self-consciousness and of external objects—with qualification.

Chandrakīrti

4 *History of the Mahāyāna*

Sources
Kensur Lekden's oral teachings
Jam-ȳang-shay-b̄a's *Great Exposition of Tenets*

This great eon is called the Fortunate Eon because during it one thousand Buddhas will appear in this world.[223] A great eon is composed of eighty intermediate eons, divided into four periods of twenty each for formation, abiding, destruction, and vacuity of the world system. The last great eon ended in a destruction by fire, in which the whole of the Desire Realm and the first of the four areas of the Form Realm, called the First Concentration, were destroyed.

The Four Concentrations are situated, one on top of the other, above the Desire Realm, which is our habitation. After seven great eons end with destructions by fire, the next one ends with destruction by water, during which the Second Concentration is also destroyed. After seven cycles ending in destruction by water, the Third Concentration is also destroyed by wind. The Fourth Concentration is never destroyed by fire, water, or wind because it is free from the eight faults of inhalation, exhalation, investigation, analysis, pleasure, pain, mental pleasure, and mental displeasure.[224] The individual environments of the Fourth cease with the death of the being on which their existence depends.

When the twenty intermediate eons of formation in this eon began, the area of the First Concentration was formed, and sentient beings were born there once again. Thereafter, the four abodes of the Desire Realm gods who inhabit the sky were formed. Our own world, in a system of one billion worlds, was formed when a great and powerful blue wind began blowing and circulating in the shape of a half moon.[225] Great rains of seven types of precious substances fell and formed a vast white round ocean, supported by the dense winds. From the turbulence of the ocean were formed a yellow square of gold and then earth. From the dependent-arising of the combination of these three, a red triangle of fire formed, at which time the basis of the great Mount Meru and its surrounding mountains, four continents, and eight sub-continents was complete.

At first the land surface was a marvelous substance that someone, through previous conditioning, was led into eating. Until that time, their spontaneously produced bodies had no anus or genitals; for the sake of excretion these now appeared. Gradually, the marvelous radiance of the beings degenerated, and the earth became hard with a corn-like plant growing in abundance. Some, however, were not satisfied with merely taking their portion day by day and began hoarding. Some began stealing; some killed; houses were built to hide the sexual act. Gradually the sins were committed, and the causes of birth in the bad migrations were made. The twenty eons of formation were finished with the formation of the birth-places for animals, hungry ghosts and hell-beings.

The pattern was produced a billion times simultaneously, providing lands for gods, demi-gods, humans, animals, hungry ghosts, and hell-beings in accordance with their nature as determined by previous deeds. The life-span for humans, which at that time was extremely long, gradually began to shorten, and when it was forty thousand years, the first of the thousand Buddhas of this great eon, Krakuchchhanda, appeared.[226] When the average life-span was thirty thousand years, the second Buddha, Kanakamuni, appeared. At twenty thousand years, the third, Kāshyapa (who is to be distinguished from the Hearer Kāshyapa who was Shākyamuni Buddha's senior disciple) appeared. When the average life-span was only one hundred years, the very length of which reflects the poor state of the world, the heroic Shākyamuni, already a Buddha, appeared simultaneously in all one billion worlds of this world system to show the way to enlightenment. His teaching will remain for five thousand years. Eventually, the human life-span will degenerate to an average of ten years, accompanied by a destruction of the beings—but not the environment—by either weapons, sickness, or starvation, the current intermediate eon ending with a destruction by weapons. The remaining beings will experience renunciation whereupon emanations of Buddhas will appear to lead them on the path of virtue due to which the life-span will again begin to lengthen. During the period of lengthening, no Buddhas will appear as such, with the next openly declared Buddha—Maitreya—appearing four billion nine hundred million human years from now after the next decrease has begun.

The current era is that of Shākyamuni Buddha, whose lineage is traced back to a child born from an egg.[227] The egg formed from semen that dripped onto a sugar cane leaf from a man wrongly accused as a killer. He was strung up for punishment, and having proved his innocence through causing his teacher's very black face to turn golden, his semen dripped down onto a sugar cane leaf. It formed an egg which his teacher nurtured, and a child hatched. Thus, the child, the lineage, and eventually Shākyamuni himself came to be known as Sugar-Cane-One (*Ikṣhvāku, Bu ram shing pa*).

His clan was called Shākya or 'the able' because of the clan-king's amazement at his banished sons' and daughters *ability* to inter-breed in exile. They had been banished to satisfy a second wife's wish for her son to become king, and later when the king's attitude changed, his family was sought in exile with resultant amazement at their prolific inter-breeding.

Shākyamuni Buddha lived for eighty-one years, during which

the highest of his philosophical teachings were the Perfection of Wisdom Sutras. They present the most profound of all views, the absence of inherent existence in all phenomena. Offering the essence of Buddha's thought, they contain not only the doctrine of emptiness but also in hidden form, the modes of the paths to supreme enlightenment.

Four hundred years after Buddha's death, Nāgārjuna, the prophesied upholder of Buddha's deepest teaching, was born.[228] He systematically explained the meaning of the Perfection of Wisdom Sutras in his *Treatise on the Middle Way* which is called 'fundamental' (*mūla*) because it is the basic text of the Mādhyamika system he founded. Living for six hundred years, his teachings are divided into three proclamations of doctrine which he performed based on former prayer-aspirations made in the presence of the Tathāgata L̄u-rik-gyel-b̄o (*kLu-rigs-rgyal-po*). Nāgārjuna's first proclamation of doctrine began with his becoming a monk under the abbot of Nālanda, Rāhulabhadra, that is, Saraha,[229] at which time he was called Shrīmān (*dPal-ldan*). While prefect of Nālanda, Nāgārjuna protected the monks from famine through alchemy, exhorted the indolent, and expelled the wayward.

His second proclamation commenced before one hundred years had passed in his lifetime. He went to Nāga-land, taught doctrine to the Nāgas, and brought back to this 'continent' the *One Hundred Thousand Stanza Perfection of Wisdom Sutra*, etc., along with a great quantity of clay from which he made almost ten million reliquaries (*stūpa*) and many images. He composed the Five Collections of Reasonings that establish emptiness as the mode of existence of all phenomena and thus founded the Mādhyamika system which avoids all extremes. At that time he was called Nāgārjuna. Nāgas, or dragons, have their abode in the ocean, have treasures such as wish-granting jewels, and spew forth fire from their mouths, burning fuel and overcoming others. Just so, Nāgārjuna possessed the profound understanding that eradicates the two extremes, possessed the treasure of profound good doctrine, and burned the fuel of bad views, thus clearing away mental darkness. Also, just as Arjuna protected the kingdom and tamed his enemies, so Nāgārjuna protected the kingdom of doctrine and conquered the foe, cyclic existence, itself. Therefore, he was called Nāga-Arjuna, Nāgārjuna.

His third proclamation of doctrine commenced with a visit to the northern continent three hundred years into his lifetime. On the way he met the king Shātavāhana, then in his youth, and prophesied his ascension to the throne.[230] From the northern continent, where he stayed for two hundred years in altruistic activity, he wrote the king a letter called the *Precious Garland of Advice for the King*. When the average life-span was eighty years —nine hundred years after the death of Buddha and five hundred years into his lifetime—Nāgārjuna came for the third time to South India, the first time being his birth and the second his return from Nāga-land. He brought with him the *Great Drum Sutra (Mahābherīhārakaparivarta)*, the *Lion's Roar of Shrīmālādevī Sutra (Shrīmālādevīsiṃhanāda)*, the *Tathāgata Essence Sutra (Tathāgatagarbha)*, and the *Ornament of the Wisdom Engaging the Sphere of All Buddhas Sutra (Sarvabuddhaviṣhayāvatārajñānālaṃkāra)*.[231] These four sutras became the basis of extensive explanation in Maitreya's *Sublime Continuum of the Great Vehicle (Uttaratantra)* which clarifies the meaning of the Tathāgata essence, or emptiness of the mind, that permits development into Buddhahood.

During the third proclamation, Nāgārjuna wrote praises of the Tathāgata essence and lectured on the *Great Drum Sutra* etc., living another one hundred years. Upon his death he himself went to the Blissful Pure Land (*Sukhāvati, bDe ba can*) and sent a manifestation to the Joyous Pure Land (*Tuṣhiṭa, dGa' ldan*) to question Maitreya about the *Great Drum Sutra*. In the future he is to become a Buddha. After the passage of the thousand Buddhas of this eon, there will be sixty-two eons without the appearance of any; then, after one hundred thousand ten million Solitary Realizers have appeared, seven Buddhas will appear. Nāgārjuna will appear as the eighth, living for fifteen intermediate eons in extremely favorable conditions, with his teaching remaining for ten billion years.

Since he was away from South India for such long periods,

many have thought that there were two or three Nāgārjunas, but it is clearly indicated in the *Great Cloud Sutra (Mahāmegha)* and the *Great Drum Sutra* that there was only one. With respect to his level of attainment, Bhāvaviveka's disciple Avalokitavrata wrote, in accordance with the way things seemed to the world, that Nāgārjuna was a first ground Bodhisattva; however, he actually was a seventh grounder who attained the eighth in that lifetime. Thus, the prophesies of Nāgārjuna in the *Descent into Laṅkā Sutra* and the *Fundamental Tantra of Mañjushrī (Mañjushrīmūlatantra)* as a first ground Bodhisattva should be taken to mean that although he was a seventh ground Bodhisattva, he manifested the ways of a first grounder for the sake of leading sentient beings. Still, the tantra system—which is accepted as having the final say—views Nāgārjuna as having attained Buddhahood during that lifetime.

He did not newly invent the teachings of the Mādhyamika system; Hīnayāna and Mahāyāna arose simultaneously during Shākyamuni's lifetime.[232] After his death, the Mahāyāna sutras remained in the lands of humans for forty years, but then with tumultuous times they disappeared. This is why the Mahāyāna had to be brought back, making it necessary for many authors to prove that it was the word of the Buddha—Maitreya in his *Ornament for the Mahāyāna Sutras (Mahāyānasūtrālaṃkāra)*, Shāntideva in his *Engaging in the Bodhisattva Deeds (Bodhisattvacharyāvatāra)*, Bhāvaviveka in his *Heart of the Middle Way (Madhyamakahṛdaya)*, etc.[233] Though one hundred and twenty years after Buddha's death the great religious king Ashoka respected and spread the teaching, it is clear that the Mahāyāna was then practically non-existent among humans; however, it had spread widely in the lands of gods and dragons and even in other areas.[234] On this 'continent' it was limited to Bodhisattvas abiding on the earth and to tantric yogis who were secretly practicing it themselves and teaching it to the fortunate.

Because of the wide dissemination of the Hīnayāna Hearer orders, the Mahāyāna scriptures were as if non-existent. Though the great Brahmin Saraha appeared and spread mainly the Mahāyāna tantric teaching, it was the prophesied Nāgārjuna who restored the teaching of the Mahāyāna to the world and, through the help of his students, spread it widely. The chief of his students was Āryadeva who also attained the eighth Bodhisattva ground during that life. Nāgārjuna and Āryadeva are called the Model Mādhyamikas because the founders of the two branches of Mādhyamika—Svātantrika and Prāsaṅgika—quote them as equally reliable sources.

Nine hundred years after Buddha's death and five hundred years into Nāgārjuna's six hundred year life, the teacher Asaṅga was born.[235] He attained the third Bodhisattva ground during that life and, roughly during the time of Nāgārjuna's third proclamation of doctrine, founded the Chittamātra (Mind-Only) system. The timing had to have been like that, for Nāgārjuna refuted mind-only in his *Essay on the Mind of Enlightenment (Bodhichittavivaraṇa)*, and this shows that he was still alive when the Chittamātra system was formed. In accordance with the doctrine of mind-only, Asaṅga commented on the meaning of the *Sutra Unravelling the Thought (Saṃdhinirmochana)* in his Five Treatises on the Levels and Two Compendiums, etc. (see Bibliography). However, in his commentary on Maitreya's *Sublime Continuum of the Great Vehicle*, Asaṅga explained the thought of the *Questions of King Dhāraṇīshvara Sutra (Dhāraṇīshvararāja-paripṛchchā)* and the *Tathāgata Essence Sutra* in accordance with Prāsaṅgika, which was actually his own final system.

He showed that the mind-basis-of-all (*ālayavijñāna, kun gzhi rnam shes*) is taught in Hīnayāna scriptures just as Nāgārjuna had showed that the Mādhyamika selflessness is taught in them and that the Hīnayāna teaching of complete forsaking of the mental and physical aggregates in the final nirvana refers to the mode of appearance in meditative equipoise on emptiness.

Living for one hundred and fifty years, Asaṅga was mainly intent on founding the Chittamātra system. It is said[236] that he did so in order to convert to the Mahāyāna his brother Vasubandhu who first was a Vaibhāṣhika, then a Sautrāntika, and finally a Chittamātrin due to Asaṅga's persistent efforts.[237]

Just after Asaṅga's founding of the Chittamātra system, Buddhapālita laid the foundation for the Prāsaṅgika system with the writing of his commentary on Nāgārjuna's *Treatise on the Middle Way*. Even though Chandrakīrti, through his defense of Buddhapālita, opened the way for Prāsaṅgika, Jam-ȳang-shay-b̄a considers Buddhapālita to be the founder. For, Buddhapālita in his commentary on the *Treatise on the Middle Way* used many consequences (*prasaṅga, thal 'gyur*) rather than syllogisms to establish emptiness. The commentaries by Devasharma, Guṇashrī, Guṇamati, and Sthiramati were not translated into Tibetan,[238] but those authors as well as Bhāvaviveka and his commentator, Avalokitavrata, mainly used syllogisms (*prayoga, sbyor ba*). The other commentaries on the *Treatise*, the *Akutobhayā*—accepted as being falsely attributed to Nāgārjuna[239]—and Chandrakīrti's *Clear Words* do not mainly use syllogisms; however, Buddhapālita's commentary predates Chandrakīrti's. Also, the authorship of the short *Akutobhayā* is doubtful, though it certainly is not by Nāgārjuna because his chief disciples did not quote it whereas they did liberally quote Nāgārjuna's commentary on his *Refutation of Objections (Vigrahavyāvartanī)*. Also, chapter twenty-seven of the *Akutobhayā* quotes Āryadeva, and Nāgārjuna would not have quoted his own student.[240] Thus, because Buddhapālita was the first main commentator on the *Treatise* to use consequences instead of syllogisms, Jam-ȳang-shay-b̄a considers him to be the founder of the Prāsaṅgika system. Still, not even Jam-ȳang-shay-b̄a says that Buddhapālita specifically rejected the usage of syllogisms as the best means of generating in an opponent the view that all phenomena are empty of inherent existence.[241]

Buddhapālita is said to have written many books, but only his commentary on Nāgārjuna's *Treatise* survives in Tibetan or any other language. He achieved a meeting with Mañjushrī and attained tantric realization.

The great teacher Bhāvaviveka (or Bhavyakāra, Bhavaviveka, Bhavya, Bhavyaka, Bhavyakara, Bhavyaviveka, Bhāvivikta, Bhāviveka, or Bhagavadviveka)[242] author of many books and source for much of what is known about Buddhist and non-Buddhist tenets, objected to Buddhapālita's consequences used in refuting the four extreme types of production—from self, other, both, or neither. Bhāvaviveka also heartily refuted the Chittamātra position of no external objects and its notion that imaginary phenomena (*parikalpitadharma, kun btags pa'i chos*), such as analytical cessations, do not inherently exist. He asserted that all phenomena do not exist ultimately but do conventionally exist inherently or naturally; he thereby founded the great system of Svātantrika-Mādhyamika.

Bhāvaviveka is considered to be the founder of Svātantrika even though his commentator, Avalokitavrata, says that Bhāvaviveka was following Devasharma's commentary on Nāgārjuna's *Treatise*, for he was the first to set forth extensively the incorrectness of Chittamātra (which he considered to be just Asaṅga's fabrication and not taught by Buddha at all) and the correctness of Mādhyamika within the context of asserting that conventionally all phenomena exist inherently. Similarly, Nāgārjuna was preceded in his views by the king Indrabhuti and the great Brahmin Saraha, but they are not assigned as the founders of Mādhyamika because they did not set off Mādhyamika in contradistinction to the other Buddhist systems.[243]

Bhāvaviveka founded the Svātantrika system when Asaṅga's Chittamātra system had been widely disseminated. He vowed to attain Buddhahood during his life, but attained it in the next as Vajraghaṇṭapāda. Both he and Chandrakīrti were students of Nāgārjuna toward the end of his six hundred year life.

After Bhāvaviveka's founding of the Svātantrika system, Chandrakīrti rejected the usage of autonomous syllogisms (*svatantraprayoga, rang rgyud kyi sbyor ba*) and established the Prāsaṅgika system as different from Svātantrika and the other Buddhist schools of tenets. He refuted inherent existence (*svabhāvasiddhi, rang bzhin gyis grub pa*) both ultimately and conventionally, establishing that even conventionally phenomena are only designated by thought.

Mañjushrī told D̄zong-ka-b̄a, founder of the Ge-luk-b̄a order in Tibet, that the tenth ground Bodhisattva Chandrakīrti had descended from a realm very high in the world system to spread Nāgārjuna's system and that his explanations were in all ways reliable. Though Chandrakīrti openly refuted Bhāvaviveka,

Vasubandhu, Dharmapāla, Dignāga, and so forth,[244] no one openly refuted him. To some this shows that Chandrakīrti lived much later than them; however, Jam-ȳang-shay-b̄a is of the opinion that Chandrakīrti was an actual student of Nāgārjuna. D̄zong-ka-b̄a's disciple Kay-drup says that this view is supported by the masters of the *Guhyasamāja Tantra (Guhyasamāja)*, scriptural citation, and reasoning.[245] Thus, through living for three hundred years, Chandrakīrti was roughly contemporaneous with those scholars whom he refuted.

In order to overcome others' sense that things exist the way they appear, Chandrakīrti once milked a picture of a cow. Living for three hundred years in the usual gross physical body, he is said still to be alive in a rainbow body. As evidence of this, he met with a Tibetan translator of his *Supplement to (Nāgārjuna's) 'Treatise on the Middle Way'*; due to his speaking quickly some errors appeared in the translation.[246]

Just after Chandrakīrti's three hundred years, Shāntarakṣhita founded the Yogāchāra-Svātantrika-Mādhyamika system. He is similar to a Yogāchārin, or Chittamātrin, in that he shows that external objects do not exist either conventionally or ultimately and that objects conventionally are of the same entity as the perceiving consciousness.[247] He is a Svātantrika because he holds that phenomena only conventionally exist inherently and a Mādhyamika because he accepts that all phenomena do not exist ultimately. Similarly, Bhāvaviveka's Svātantrika-Mādhyamika system is called Sautrāntika-Svātantrika-Mādhyamika because, like a Sautrāntika, he asserts the existence of objects external to a perceiving consciousness—that is, gross objects which are aggregates of particles. (Prāsaṅgikas assert conventionally existent objects that are external to a perceiving consciousness but are not aggregates of particles, only imputed to them.)

Just as Nāgārjuna and Bhāvaviveka were anticipated in their teachings by other scholars who, however, did not open a broad path for the chariots of their systems to travel, so Shāntarakṣhita was anticipated by others. Vimuktisena's view is clearly that of a Yogāchāra-Svātantrika-Mādhyamika, and Maitreya's *Ornament for Clear Realization (Abhisamayālaṃkāra)*, which was brought to this world by Asaṅga on his return from the Joyous Pure Land, manifests the same view. Also, it is clear that the Yogāchāra-Svātantrika-Mādhyamika system was present during the time of Bhāvaviveka who was a definite predecessor of Shāntarakṣhita. For he refuted it, saying that to accept mind-only first and then to pass on to the view of no ultimate existence is like spreading mud on the body and then washing. Avalokitavrata interprets Bhāvaviveka's referent as Chittamātra, but the only system that passes through the gradation of realizing first mind-only and then no ultimate existence is Yogāchāra-Svātantrika. Also, Yogāchāra-Svātantrika was present later when Shāntarakṣhita was examining to discover which type of Mādhyamika was the best. He made this choice and through his extensive works founded the system that was the final major development in the Mādhyamika system, the Yogāchāra-Svātantrika-Mādhyamika. Chandrakīrti's Prāsaṅgika-Mādhyamika, however, held sway, ultimately becoming the dominant system throughout Tibet and Mongolia.[248]

Chart 41: *Mahāyāna Chronology in India*

0 A.N. (After the Nirvana)	Buddha died, having lived eighty-one years and two months.[249]
400 A.N.-1000 A.N.	Nāgārjuna, the founder of the Mahāyāna system in general and the Mādhyamika system in particular.
900 A.N.-1050 A.N.	Asaṅga, the founder of the Chittamātra system.
Approx. 975 A.N.-1275 A.N.	Chandrakīrti, the disseminator of Prāsaṅgika.

Bhāvaviveka, the founder of Svātantrika-Mādhyamika in general and Sautrāntika-Svātantrika-Mādhyamika in particular, preceded Chandrakīrti by a little, and Buddhapālita, the founder of Prāsaṅgika-Mādhyamika, preceded Bhāvaviveka by a little. Shākyamitra, Nāgabodhi, and Ashvaghoṣha were students of Nāgārjuna near the end of his life.

Padmasambhava died in 864 A.D. after living one thousand seven hundred and seventy-three years, and Shāntarakṣhita died in 845 A.D. after living nine hundred and ninety-nine years.[250]

5 *Chittamātra*

Sources
Kensur Lekden's oral teachings
Jam-ȳang-shay-b̄a's *Great Exposition of Tenets*
J̄ang-ḡya's *Presentation of Tenets*
Nga-w̄ang-b̄el-den's *Annotations*
Corresponding section of the translation pp.602-20

The Chittamātrins (Mind-Only-ists) are so called because they assert that all phenomena are of the nature or entity of the mind.[251] (They are also called Vijñānavādins and Vijñaptivādins for the same reason.) This is not the same as asserting that all phenomena are mind because minds are observers of objects, and if all phenomena were minds, stones and so forth would absurdly have objects of observation.[252] Rather, just as dream objects are not the mind that perceives them but also not separate entities from the mind, so the objects of the world are not the consciousnesses that perceive them but also not separate entities from those consciousnesses.

Another name for Chittamātrins is Yogāchārins, (Practitioners of Yoga), because they arrange the practices of the path from the viewpoint of yoga. This, however, is just an etymology and not a definition because all Buddhist tenets are presented for the sake of yogic practice.[253]

The Chittamātrins are divided, like the Sautrāntikas, into Followers of Scripture and Reasoning. The former are followers mainly of Asaṅga's Five Treatises on the Levels, and the latter of Dignāga's *Compendium of Valid Cognition* and Dharmakīrti's Seven Treatises on Valid Cognition. Though, in general, the term 'Chittamātrin' refers to the Followers of Scripture, that is, of Asaṅga, the Followers of Reasoning are said to be the more advanced of the two groups.[254] This is because Asaṅga teaches that there are three final vehicles, meaning that some sentient beings never achieve Buddhahood because their vehicle is completed at a lower stage on which they remain forever. According to him, some Hearers only realize that a person is not a self-sufficient entity and never realize that objects and subjects are empty of being separate entities. These Hearers aim only toward a solitary peace. The Chittamātrin followers of Dharmakīrti, however, point to the impermanence of fetters and to the skill of the Buddha in teaching and thereby show that all eventually cognize both selflessnesses and attain the highest enlightenment. Thus for them there is only one final vehicle and all sentient beings eventually attain Buddhahood.

The Sautrāntikas Following Reasoning interpret Dharmakīrti's teachings otherwise and accept three final vehicles but with only one type of realization of selflessness. This selflessness is the emptiness, or absence, of a self-sufficient person. In both Chittamātra schools, however, there are different types of selflessness which vary in difficulty of realization, it being more difficult to realize that objects and subjects are empty of being separate entities than to realize that a person is not a self-sufficient entity. Thus, there are two types of selflessness: one of phenomena in general and one only of persons.

The Chittamātra Followers of Scripture are the only Buddhist school to accept eight consciousnesses: the five sense consciousnesses, a mental consciousness, a mind afflicted with egoism (*klishṭamanas, nyon yid*) and a mind-basis-of-all (*ālayavijñāna, kun gzhi rnam shes*). The Followers of Reasoning and all other

Buddhist schools assert only six consciousnesses with some of the functions of the seventh and eighth being performed by the mental consciousness. There are sub-schools of Chittamātra which assert one, two, seven, and nine consciousnesses, but they are considered to have strayed from the positions of the four Buddhist schools of tenets.

The definition of a Chittamātrin is:

> a person propounding Buddhist tenets who uses reasoning to refute external objects and who asserts that dependent phenomena, such as consciousnesses, truly exist.

MIND-ONLY

Mind-only is the very core of the Chittamātrin teachings; for them it means that there are no objects which are entities external to a perceiving consciousness. They and the Yogāchāra-Svātantrikas, who assert mind-only conventionally, are the only Buddhist schools which assert that there are no external objects. All the other schools—Vaibhāṣhika, Sautrāntika, Sautrāntika-Svātantrika, and Prāsaṅgika—assert that an object of a sense consciousness is an entity external to the perceiving consciousness. For them, objects are a cause of a consciousness in that they cause it to be produced in their image. Causes must exist before their effects, not simultaneously or afterward because nothing can affect an already existent entity in that very moment.[255] Thus, because of the cause and effect relationship of object and sense consciousness, and because causally related things must be different entities, the non-mind-only oriented schools assert that object and subject are different entities.

The Chittamātrins disagree, saying that Buddha taught that a sense consciousness perceives a present object, whereas if object and subject were cause and effect, then, since a cause has ceased when its effect exists, a sense consciousness would be perceiving a past object. The non-mind-only schools must accept that an object of a sense consciousness exists one instant prior to its apprehender, but they say that the object is *present* in that there is no moment intervening between the object moment and the perceiver moment. The Chittamātrins, however, are able to uphold Buddha's teaching on this point without any qualifications; for them, object and subject exist simultaneously. A seed (*bīja, sa bon*) or predisposition (*vāsanā, bag chags*) is activated and simultaneously produces both an object and a cognizing subject, much as in a dream. (A Buddha has no seeds or latencies but perceives objects through the complete awakening or actualization of his collections of merit and wisdom.)

For the Chittamātrins, an object is of the same nature or entity as its perceiving subject, although an object is not a mind, not a cognizing agent, illuminating and realizing objects. If an object were a mind, it would have to be shown that it apprehends objects, and such cannot be shown. In this way, with object and subject the same entity and different isolates, not synonyms but mutually exclusive with one never the other, the Chittamātrins are able to uphold mind-only and still present the five aggregates, including forms. There are no forms that are separate entities from a perceiving consciousness, but there are forms that are the same entity as a perceiving consciousness. Again, as with the Prāsaṅgikas' assertion of nominally existent objects, the view is extremely subtle, and it should not be thought that because the system says there are objects, it is referring to objects as one knows them. For, a sense consciousness of a sentient being perceives objects as if they were distant and cut off, whereas the objects declared to be existent in the Chittamātra system are not cut off from the subject.

According to the Chittamātrins, the final root of cyclic existence is the conception that object and subject are different entities; this is the subtlest and strongest of all misconceptions, and when it is destroyed, all misconceptions are destroyed. Thus, the subtle selflessness of all phenomena is a non-difference in entity between subject and object. Bodhisattvas mainly meditate on this and thereby overcome the obstructions to simultaneous and direct cognition of all phenomena.

Included in the obstructions to simultaneous and direct

cognition of all objects of knowledge, together with the conception of object and subject as different entities, is the conception that phenomena naturally exist as the grounds or bases of engagement of names.[256] The non-existence of objects as natural bases of engagement of names is a selflessness of phenomena that is as subtle as the non-existence of subject and object as different entities, but is easier to realize. An understanding of it serves as a means of entering into an understanding of non-duality.

In refuting that phenomena naturally exist as grounds or bases of names, the Chittamātrins are not merely saying that the appearing objects of thought, meaning-generalities, do not naturally exist because of depending on thought. For the Sautrāntikas propound such, and here a subtle selflessness of phenomena must be more subtle than anything found in the lower systems of tenets. Nor are they saying that forms and so forth do not naturally exist because for them forms naturally exist as unpredicable phenomena. Forms do naturally, truly, inherently, and ultimately exist because if they did not, they would not exist at all. For the Chittamātrins, the Prāsaṅgika view that objects do not naturally, truly, inherently, and ultimately exist is a denial of phenomena; if impermanent things did not naturally exist, they would be totally non-existent.

When the Chittamātrins speak of objects as not being naturally bases of names, they base this on the adventitious relationship between objects and names and between names and objects. For instance, when an ordinary being's eye consciousness perceives a pot, the pot not only appears to be a bulbous thing able to hold fluid, but also the bulbous thing *appears* to be the basis of the designation 'pot'. The bulbous thing seems to be the basis of the designation 'pot' by way of its own being and not just established so by verbal convention. After an eye consciousness perceives the object, thought imputes, 'This is a pot,' without the intervention of any other thought. The sense consciousness alone is able to draw thought into imputing, 'This is a pot,' without the aid of intervening reflection. Therefore, when another asks what the expression 'pot' means, people do not say 'It is the "pot" that is only nominally imputed to a bulbous thing capable of holding water.' They say, 'It *is* a bulbous thing capable of holding water.'

Due to previous conditioning, objects falsely appear to sense consciousnesses as if naturally bases of names, and then thought, assenting to this appearance, falsely conceives them likewise. This is the Chittamātrin assertion. The Sautrāntikas say that both the appearance of objects as naturally bases of names and the conception of them as so are correct because sense objects are truly existent external objects, and when they appear to a faultless sense consciousness, their very mode of being must appear just as it is. Still, they say that mental images which appear to internal thought do not naturally exist and are only a reification of what depends on thought for its existence.

In the Chittamātra system, forms and so forth are not external objects; they appear to be external objects through the force of predispositions accumulated through beginningless conditioning to the naming of objects. Forms are only of the nature of inner consciousness, but appear to be natural bases of names through the force of predispositions for expression. Therefore, the appearance of forms as naturally existent bases of names is not suitable to arise from the way things are, without dependence on establishment by names and thoughts. Otherwise, the fact that forms are the bases of names would not depend on a consciousness, in which case forms would be different entities from a perceiving consciousness, and this is refuted by many reasonings. The assertion that things are not by way of their own character grounds of the designation of names meets back to the assertion that subject and object are not different entities.

If the opposite were true—if things were naturally bases of names—then the establishment of a bulbous thing as the basis of the name 'pot' would not depend on thought because it would exist as the basis of the name 'pot' through its own mode of being. If this were accepted, then the generation of a consciousness that thinks, 'Pot,' would not depend on thought. If this were accepted, then it would follow that before one learned the name 'pot' a consciousness thinking, 'This is a pot,' would be generated through only looking at a bulbous thing.

Furthermore, since one being who has many names would inherently be the bases of these names, this one being would have to be that many beings. Just as the names appear to be different to thought, their objects would have to be different in reality because objects would naturally generate a naming consciousness.

Also, two beings who have the same name would be one being, similar to their one name which appears the same to thought.

Therefore, phenomena do not naturally exist as bases of the affixing of names, and thought which apprehends them so is mistaken. It is undeniable that beings perceive objects as if they were of their own nature the bases of the affixing of names; this false perception must be destroyed.

One is exhorted to engage in the four investigations and the four cognitions:

1 investigation into whether names are merely adventitious, mere imputation, or whether they are designated through the force of the object's own mode of being
2 investigation into whether objects naturally or adventitiously exist as bases of names
3 investigation into whether in the designation of entities the relationship between the word and the object exists substantially
4 investigation into whether objects exist naturally as bases of the designation of qualities, such as their production, destruction, color, impermanence, and use.

1 realization that names do not exist inherently in the objects they denote
2 realization that objects do not exist inherently as the bases of the designation of names
3 realization that the designation of entities based on the relationship of names and objects does not exist inherently
4 realization that the designation of qualities does not exist inherently.

The latter four are realized conceptually on a Bodhisattva's paths of accumulation and preparation and directly or non-conceptually on the paths of seeing, meditation, and no more learning. They act as a means of entering into a realization of mind-only.

Through establishing that a mental consciousness is mistaken when it apprehends objects as naturally existent bases of names, it is also established that such an appearance to a sense consciousness is mistaken. It is thereby negated that objects are external entities, unrelated to consciousness, and thus it is established that objects are only appearances to the consciousness that apprehends them. Thereby, it is refuted that a spot of blue, for instance, is a different entity from its perceiving consciousness.

Asaṅga collected many examples from sutras to show that cognition is possible without external objects. For instance, no one considers it to be contradictory for a yogi who is meditating on ugliness to have a consciousness of an image of foulness without this foulness existing in reality. Just so, it is not contradictory to have a consciousness of external objects due to the predispositions of ignorance even though there are no external objects.

Similarly, hell-beings see a bowl of fluid as molten bronze. Hungry ghosts see it as pus and blood; animals such as fish, as an abode; humans, as water for drinking; gods, as ambrosia. If these existed as external objects, there would be the contradiction of one thing having many contrary natures. Therefore, everything is just consciousness, that is, of the nature of mind.

Furthermore, if there were external objects, the externality of objects would be their mode of being, and thus the uncontaminated wisdom that cognizes the mode of being would be conceptual. Ordinary beings would absurdly be directly perceiving the mode of being and so would lack ignorance. There also would be no liberation from ignorance and thus no means of developing an omniscient consciousness. Therefore, external objects are only fabrications of thought.

The example of a magician's illusions is given to overcome doubt that without external objects one could not apprehend objects. The example of a mirage is given to overcome doubt about how minds and mental factors could be produced without external objects. The example of a dream is given to overcome doubt about how one could find things attractive and unattractive without external objects. The example of a hallucination is given to overcome doubt about how the varieties of consciousness could be produced without external objects. The example of an echo is given to overcome doubt about how the various expressions could arise without external objects. The example of a moon reflected in water is given to overcome doubt about how an image that is an object of meditative stabilization could arise without external objects. The example of magical manifestation is given to overcome doubt about how Bodhisattvas are born in accordance with the thoughts of beings.

From these examples of the production of a consciousness without the presence of an external object one can realize that it is possible for external objects to be non-existent.

The Chittamātrins refute the view that material objects are constructed from the amassing of partless particles through pointing out that if a partless particle is surrounded by other particles, the place where one of the surrounders touches the one in the center would not be the place where the others do and thus there would be touched and untouched *parts*. Or, if the supposed six particles surrounding the center one all touch the same place on the center particle, then nothing could be larger than the one partless particle. Some respond saying that the surrounding particles do not touch the center particles, but it is answered that nevertheless one of the surrounders would be closer to one side of the center particle than the others, and so the center particle would have to have sides and thus parts.

Furthermore, a spot of blue and an eye consciousness that apprehends it are not different entities because the observation of one by a valid cognizer is co-extensive with the observation of the other by a valid cognizer. In other words, whenever an eye consciousness observes an object, a self-consciousness observes the eye consciousness. (For Chittamātrins and some Sautrāntikas every consciousness is self-conscious because later when an object seen is remembered, one also remembers the subject. This shows that the subject must have perceived itself at the same time as it was perceiving its object; otherwise, the subjective element would not be remembered.)[257] Dharmakīrti states the reasoning of necessary simultaneity of observation of the subject and the object to prove that a sense consciousness and its objects are not different entities. This is based on the concomitance of whatever are necessarily simultaneously observed with absence of difference of entity.

J̄ang-ḡya[258] explains that the above reasoning does not just prove a non-affirming negative which is a non-difference of entity of subject and object; it also implicitly proves that a sense object and a sense consciousness which apprehends this object are one entity. For if two things that exist are not different entities, they must be one entity. Also, this reasoning is used as a means to realize mind-only; therefore, how could it merely be establishing a non-affirming negative—a non-difference of entity of subject and object? To cognize the thesis would imply a cognition of sameness of entity of subject and object. Thus, J̄ang-ḡya, unlike Jam-ȳang-shay-b̄a, finds it difficult to say that for Chittamātrins what is being proved here is just a non-affirming negative. However, on other occasions, he seems to agree with Jam-ȳang-shay-b̄a that a subtle selflessness of all phenomena is a non-affirming negative—a mere non-difference in entity between subject and object. This non-affirming negative is a quality of each and every phenomenon because an object is empty of, or lacks, a difference in entity from a subject, and a subject is empty of a difference in entity from its object.[259] Each phenomenon from a form through to an omniscient consciousness possesses such a quality, which is an ultimate truth because of being a final object of observation of a path of purification. Blind to this excellent quality, sentient beings wander in cyclic existence, assenting habitually to the false appearance to their senses of a difference in entity between subject and object.

PRĀSAṄGIKA CRITIQUE OF MIND-ONLY

The Prāsaṅgikas say that Buddha set forth a non-literal teaching of mind-only in order to overcome certain trainees' attachment to forms; the basis in his own thought was the fact that the mind is the principal creator of everything.[260] The explicit teaching that objects are of the same entity as the mind is refuted by the reasoning that subject and (external) object are mutually existent; if one exists, the other must exist, and if one does not exist, the other must not exist. Therefore, mind-only in the sense of no external objects is not taken literally. Both object and subject are conventionally existent, and conventionally there are objects external to a perceiving consciousness.

According to Prāsaṅgika, the mind is the principal creator of everything because sentient beings accumulate predisposing potencies through their actions, and these actions are directed by mental motivation. These potencies are what create not only their own lives but also the physical world about them. All environments are formed by *karma*, that is, actions and the potencies they establish. The wind, sun, earth, trees, what is enjoyed, used, and suffered—all are produced from actions. Potencies on the mind of each person in combination with those of similar beings create the very substance of their world system. The Prāsaṅgika assertion is not like the Chittamātrin one that a potency or seed simultaneously creates a cognizing subject and a cognized object. Rather, the physical world is constructed through the former actions of beings of similar type, and that world is conventionally an entity external to a consciousness which perceives it. For, the world of objects acts as a cause of consciousness, affecting it in various ways.

Still, the mind, the motivator of actions, is the principal creator. The Prāsaṅgika view, like that of Chittamātra, is of a world inextricably involved with the person. Mahāyānists practice the Bodhisattva deeds of compassion with a view toward the creation of pure lands for temporary Emanations (*Nirmāṇakāya, sPrul sku*), who are surrounded by both common beings and Superiors, and a Highest Pure Land (*Akaniṣhṭa, 'Og min*) for their immortal Enjoyment Body (*Saṃbhogakāya, Longs sku*) which is surrounded only by Bodhisattva Superiors. In these lands one provides the conditions for others to advance on the path, including the land on which they stand. Perhaps it could be said that development of the ability to produce pure lands is a conscious sublimation of the uncontrolled process of the creation of less suitable worlds by contaminated actions.

Both Chittamātrins and Prāsaṅgikas accept roughly the same presentation of phenomena; they disagree on their nature. For instance, both schools accept that when different types of beings look at a bowl of fluid, the fluid actually becomes different things. For a human it is cool water; for a god, ambrosia; for a hungry ghost, pus and blood etc. To a Chittamātrin this in itself proves that there are no external objects; the very world of objects is under the influence of the mind, changing in entity due to the presence of different types of beings. To a Prāsaṅgika, however, such changes in the external world show that objects do not inherently exist and show how powerful the mind and the potencies of actions are. Such changes are a sign of the lack of inherent existence in that objects depend on their perceivers and are not existent just in and of themselves under their own power.[261] Even when a human and a hungry ghost perceive a bowl full of fluid simultaneously, a Prāsaṅgika is ready to say that there are two parts to the fluid, one water and one pus and blood, existing simultaneously as external objects. It is even said that a hungry ghost, who possesses a coarse body, can stand in the same spot as a human, who also possesses a coarse body.

For a Prāsaṅgika, the examples of dreams and so forth show that objects can appear to be inherently existent but not be so; they can be unfindable among their bases of imputation and still be effective. That objects are not naturally bases of names proves, for a Prāsaṅgika, that phenomena do not inherently exist; the Chittamātrins misunderstand the import when they add that sense objects are inexpressible truly existent phenomena. From their examination of names and the naming process the Chittamātrins make the unwarranted conclusion that objects are of the nature of the mind. They mistakenly think that by knowing that a sense consciousness misperceives its objects as naturally bases of names one will somehow be caused to realize that the perception of objects as external entities is mistaken. For the Prāsaṅgikas the reasoning which proves that objects are not naturally bases of the designation of names proves that all phenomena do not inherently exist. All phenomena depend on the mind which imputes them; this very dependence is a sign of their non-inherent existence. Still, the Chittamātrin analysis of names and objects is a stepping-stone to the Prāsaṅgikas' more subtle teaching.

According to Prāsaṅgika it is simply wrong to say that a spot of blue and an eye consciousness that apprehends it are necessarily simultaneously observed by valid cognizers and, therefore, are not different entities. For there is no self-consciousness. If there were self-consciousness, then agent and object would be one; a knife could cut itself; a finger could touch itself, with toucher and touched exactly identical. A lamp does not illumine both itself and the other because a flame itself has no darkness to clear away; it is bright by nature. If light illumined light, then darkness would obscure darkness in which case darkness would not be seen.

Here 'self-consciousness' (*svasaṃvedanā, rang rig*) refers specifically to a consciousness's cognition of itself simultaneous with cognizing its object and does not refer to introspection or watching oneself. All systems advocate reliance on introspection and self-awareness which are essentials for effective meditation; in these cases the mind is perceiving a previous moment of the mind or a part of the mind is perceiving the general mind. Even in systems that assert self-consciousness, it is not an aid to self-awareness. 'Self' in 'self-consciousness' means the consciousness itself and not the person. Self-consciousness is a consciousness's perceiving itself in a non-dualistic manner; it does not involve analysis such as whether the mind is wandering or remaining with its object.[262]

Without self-consciousness, it cannot be shown that an eye consciousness apprehending a spot of blue is observed by a self-consciousness at the same time that the spot of blue is observed by the eye consciousness. Thus, another supposed proof of the non-existence of external objects falls, the conclusion for Prāsaṅgika being that a difference in entity between subject and object exists conventionally though certainly not in the manner in which common beings perceive it.

Still, for Chandrakīrti not all teachings of mind-only even

literally mean that there are no external objects; sometimes this teaching literally and without interpretation indicates that the mind is the principal creator of all the varieties of objects. Thus, there are two types of mind-only doctrines: non-literal and literal. Both need finally to be interpreted to discover the final mode of existence of the mind and its objects as lacking inherent existence, but when the teaching of mind-only only indicates that the mind is the principal creator as in the *Sūtra on the Ten Grounds*, it is validly established and literal. This is Chandrakīrti's Prāsaṅgika interpretation of the literal and non-literal teachings of mind-only.

The Sautrāntika-Svātantrika Bhāvaviveka is far more severe.[263] He says that Buddha never taught a mind-only which means no external objects; even the teachings that Chandrakīrti accepts as superficially teaching no external objects Bhāvaviveka says do not. They are all literal, teaching that the mind is the principal creator. Bhāvaviveka accuses Asaṅga of fabricating a teaching of no external objects and polluting Buddha's teaching out of pride in his abilities as a scholar. Bhāvaviveka takes the Yogāchāra-Svātantrika teaching that first one realizes mind-only and afterwards realizes the lack of true existence of the mind and compares it to first smearing mud on the body and then bathing. He questions why one should not from the beginning attempt the best teaching which is the lack of true existence of all objects. For him the Chittamātra emptiness is not a step on the ladder toward the Mādhyamika emptiness whereas for the Ge-luk-b̄as it is.

Still, according to the Ge-luk-b̄a interpretation of Prāsaṅgika one cannot be liberated from cyclic existence through cognizing a lack of difference in entity between subject and object and cannot attain omniscience through the Chittamātra system. For the Prāsaṅgikas, to be a Superior (*Āryan, 'Phags pa*)—one who has attained a direct cognition of emptiness either as a Hearer, Solitary Realizer, or Bodhisattva and thereby risen above common beings—means that one has cognized the absence of inherent existence of all phenomena. Unlike the other Mahāyāna schools, the Prāsaṅgikas assert that all Superiors, whether Hīnayāna or Mahāyāna, cognize the same emptiness;[264] Mahāyānists are more intelligent and their mode of cognition is more forceful, but the emptiness cognized is the same for all. Without cognizing the lack of inherent existence of the person, one cannot be liberated from cyclic existence, and the very cognition of the absence of inherent existence in the person implies the ability to cognize its absence in other phenomena, such as mind, body, possessions, and so forth, because the mode of emptiness is similar. It is only the base of the predicate emptiness that is different.

Despite the Prāsaṅgikas' view on the profound attainment of all Superiors, Hīnayāna and Mahāyāna, they do not accept that one can be liberated through cognizing emptiness as set forth by the other Buddhist tenet systems, Hīnayāna or Mahāyāna. One is thus to distinguish between Hīnayāna and Mahāyāna as modes of the practice of paths and as systems of tenets that describe the paths followed by Hīnayānists and Mahāyānists.

Consequently, there are Prāsaṅgikas who attempt to cognize the emptiness of inherent existence as Hīnayānists, that is to say, with the motivation of liberating only themselves from cyclic existence. They are Mahāyānists by tenet but Hīnayānists by path. A Prāsaṅgika can be a Mahāyānist by path only through generating in his or her mental continuum the non-artificial determination to attain Buddhahood in order to liberate all sentient beings from misery and join all with happiness. He must generate an attitude of compassion which exceeds the usual by taking upon himself alone the burden of liberating all beings from suffering. Through much artificial practice he must bring this wish to the point of spontaneity. Finally, whether walking, eating, standing, or lying down he is able to generate a sense of dedication toward altruistic enlightenment through just turning his mind to the topic. When he is able to do this out of meditative session just as strongly as he can at the time of meditation, this is the sign that he has attained the spontaneous aspiration to enlightenment for the sake of all sentient beings. Thereby, he becomes a Bodhisattva and attains the path of accumulation, which is this spontaneous wish itself as well as his other practices. He then becomes a Mahāyānist by both path and tenet.

Buddha Superiors as well as Bodhisattva, Solitary Realizer,

and Hearer Superiors are all Prāsaṅgikas by tenet because they have cognized emptiness directly. The attainment of special insight into emptiness is simultaneous with the attainment of the path of preparation, and thus even persons on any of the three paths of preparation (Hearer, Solitary Realizer, and Bodhisattva) must also be Prāsaṅgikas.[265]

Cognition of a non-difference in entity between object and subject is mistaken because it contradicts what exists, since a difference does exist conventionally. It must be remembered that for something to be conventionally or nominally existent the object cannot be found separate from or among the bases of its designation. Also, it must be remembered that the mode of direct cognition of emptiness is such that subject and object are undifferentiated like fresh water poured into fresh water and that a Buddha continually abides in this state even when he is perceiving conventional objects. Perhaps, the Chittamātrins are attempting to describe this aspect of the final state and extend its significance to every mental state.

The Prāsaṅgikas are describing another aspect, the continual perception of the unfindability of the imputed object in its bases of imputation, relegating the unusual mode of direct cognition of this unfindability to the analogy of water poured into water. Also, when Prāsaṅgikas practice the stage of generation in Highest Yoga Tantra, they visualize themselves as deities and their surroundings as the habitation of a deity, with the persons and objects forming their environment as the same entity as themselves. It is specifically said that one is not to view the surrounding sentient beings as having minds that are entities separate from one's own mind. The sameness of entity of subject and object is brought into practice as an aid to realizing the more subtle presentation of emptiness as the lack of inherent existence.

The Prāsaṅgikas do not say that the Chittamātrin teachings are not appropriate for certain trainees; at issue is which teaching is the higher, which can liberate sentient beings from cyclic existence, and which can establish sentient beings in omniscience. Their exclusivity comes in declaring their own teaching to be the only final teaching. For either school to declare that the other is its equal would be to deny their own emphasis on reasoning as a means of bridging the gap between misconception and insight.

BUDDHA NATURE

In the *Tathāgata Essence Sutra*, the *Nirvana Sutra*, and so forth,[266] Buddha speaks of a permanent, fully developed Buddha possessing the ten powers and existing in the continuum of each sentient being. The Prāsaṅgikas say that this teaching is an example of giving to the 'cause' the name of the effect, for the emptiness of the mind of each sentient being is what allows for change of that person's mind, and this emptiness is being called a fully developed Buddha. The emptiness of the mind, its lack of existence by way of its own being or its dependence on causes and conditions, is that most marvelous quality of the mind allowing it to be transformed into the wisdom of a Buddha. This emptiness is not a fully developed Buddha but is like a 'cause' of Buddhahood in that if the mind did not lack inherent existence, it would be utterly static, unable to be affected by practice of the paths.

Buddha praised this essential and marvelous 'cause' calling it a fully developed Buddha. In order to lead beings who were incapable of understanding emptiness correctly, he taught a Tathāgata essence which is a fully developed Buddha obscured in the sheaths of misconception. The basis in his thought was the existence of the Tathāgata essence or Buddha nature which is the emptiness of the mind—not a fully developed Buddha, which could never be obscured, dulled, or hidden by anything. Buddhahood is not a temporary but an immortal state in which body and mind, though impermanent, are similarly and endlessly produced.

Buddha set forth the non-literal teaching of a Tathāgata essence for Mahāyāna trainees who are not yet able to cognize the profound emptiness; he taught it in order to allay their fears of emptiness. The refutation of the explicit teaching is that all sentient beings would be Buddhas, and practice of the path would be senseless.

The Buddha nature, that is, emptiness of the mind, of each sentient being is his natural lineage, that quality which naturally abides in the mental continuums of all sentient beings allowing them to attain Buddhahood and thus giving them the Buddha lineage (*gotra, rigs*) or Buddha constituent (*dhātu, khams*). It is called a 'cause' of development into Buddhahood even though, being permanent, it is not actually so. The emptiness of the mind is permanent, or non-disintegrating, because although it is a predicate of the mind, it is not produced and destroyed each moment as the mind is. Emptiness is the mere negative or absence of objective existence. 'Permanent' for all Buddhist schools except Vaibhāṣhika means 'non-disintegrating', without necessarily indicating perpetual existence. However, the emptiness of the mind is both non-disintegrating and always existent because from beginningless cyclic existence each sentient being's mind has existed and will continue to exist uninterruptedly right through Buddhahood when it is the Wisdom Body (*Jñānakāya, Ye shes kyi sku*). The emptiness of the mind, because it is the precondition of change and transformation, is called a 'cause' of Buddhahood and according to a practitioner's position on the path is temporarily called a Hearer, Solitary Realizer, or Bodhisattva lineage. At Buddhahood, the Bodhisattva lineage becomes the Nature Body (*Svabhāvikakāya, Ngo bo nyid sku*) of a Buddha. Though the emptiness of the mind is permanent and non-changing, it is said to improve when the mind of which it is a predicate improves. Finally, the mind itself reaches consummation as the Wisdom Body, and the emptiness of the mind becomes the Nature Body—these being the two aspects of a Buddha's Truth Body (*Dharmakāya, Chos sku*), so called because the Wisdom Body is the ultimate true path and the Nature Body is the ultimate true cessation.[267]

For the Chittamātrins also, the teaching of a Tathāgata essence as a fully developed Buddha in the continuums of all sentient beings is non-literal. For them, the basis in Buddha's thought was the mind-basis-of-all (*ālayavijñāna, kun gzhi rnam shes*), the impermanent basis of all attainments. A seed naturally abiding in the mind-basis-of-all is the natural lineage, an impermanent phenomenon which is the potential for spiritual attainment.[268] Here, it is not emptiness that is called the Buddha nature but a potency predisposing the individual to certain paths and allowing the attainment of states that never existed before in the mental continuum. This seed, therefore, is not planted or established newly 'on' the mind-basis-of-all but abides there naturally, without beginning.

In sum, neither Chittamātrins nor Prāsaṅgikas accept as literal the teaching of a permanent body of Buddha obscured in the continuums of all sentient beings. According to the Ge-luk-b̄as an assertion of this teaching as literal is beyond the pale of the four schools of tenets of this Buddha's teachings. The Prāsaṅgikas, taking the *Descent into Laṅkā Sutra* as their source, show that the teaching of a permanent essence points to the lack of independent existence of the mind, that quality which when cognized can lead to Buddhahood. Emptiness in general is the element of (superior) qualities (*dharmadhātu, chos dbyings*) because meditation on it acts as a cause generating the qualities of Superiors.[269] The emptiness *of the mind* is singled out as the Buddha nature because it specifically allows for mental improvement and the cognition of what previously was not cognized.

MIND-BASIS-OF-ALL

According to the Chittamātra system as explained by Asaṅga, each sentient being has a mind-basis-of-all.[270] It is a repository of seeds or predispositions, including those that simultaneously produce an apprehending subject and an apprehended object. It is a non-defiled, neutral consciousness and thus capable of being 'infused', or 'stained', or 'perfumed' with virtuous, non-virtuous, and neutral potencies. It is a steady consciousness capable of existing through states which are otherwise mindless, such as deep sleep, the meditative equipoise of cessation, and fainting. It derives its potency from one complete action done in the past and lasts as long as the potency established by that action lasts.

It pervades the entire body, and when a person is about to die, his mind-basis-of-all withdraws from the limits of the body, slowly making those parts cold. Finally, it leaves the body and takes rebirth through the force of another of its seeds, carrying with it the seeds already accumulated but not yet activated. It is a continuum of seeds, similar to a stream, existing for Hearers and Solitary Realizers until they become Foe Destroyers and for Bodhisattvas until the eighth ground. Beyond these levels it is called a fruition consciousness (*vipakavijñāna, rnam smin rnam shes*) until Buddhahood when it is transformed into a mirror-like wisdom.

The principal function of the mind-basis-of-all is contained in its seed aspect. However, the senses themselves and all the objects that appear to them also appear to the mind-basis-of-all, but it does not notice or identify them, nor is it capable of either remembering or inducing another consciousness to take notice of them. A sense consciousness directly perceives its objects and is capable of drawing the mental consciousness into noticing or identifying them; however, although objects appear to a mind-basis-of-all, it is incapable of drawing the mental consciousness into noticing those objects.

The Chittamātrins who follow Asaṅga are the only school to assert the existence of a mind-basis-of-all. Along with it, an afflicted mind (*klişhṭamanas, nyon yid*) is asserted, together with the other six consciousnesses that are commonly accepted: eye, ear, nose, tongue, body, and mental consciousnesses. A mental consciousness ascribes names to objects, perceives slightly hidden objects such as impermanence and emptiness, misconceives a difference of entity of subject and object, and so forth. A mind-basis-of-all does not cognize emptiness even though it has seeds with it that ripen and cause a mental consciousness to do so.

The afflicted mind, or the seventh from among the eight consciousnesses, mistakenly conceives the mind-basis-of-all to be a self-sufficient person. Even though the mind-basis-of-all, because it is the transmigrating entity, is indeed found to be the actual person when one searches to find it, it is not a self-sufficient person. Thus, the seventh mind is described as afflicted by four mental factors: view of a self, obscuration with respect to a self, pride in a self, and attachment to a self. When these mental factors are overcome through their antidote—realization of selflessness—the untainted entity of the seventh mind remains. Then, when the conception of subject and object as different entities is destroyed totally and forever at Buddhahood, the seventh mind is transformed into the wisdom of sameness cognizing all phenomena as equally free from a difference in entity between subject and object.

All Buddhist schools refute a certain type of self and accept another.[271] All deny that there is a permanent, single, independent self. All except the Pudgalavādins (Proponents of a Person) deny that there is a substantially existent or self-sufficient person; they present the person as something other than these two. The Pudgalavādins assert a self which is neither the same as nor different from the mental and physical aggregates. The Kashmiri Vaibhāṣhikas and the Sautrāntikas Following Scripture assert that the *continuum* of the mental and physical aggregates is the self. The Sautrāntikas Following Reasoning, the Chittamātrins Following Reasoning, and the Sautrāntika-Svātantrika-Mādhyamikas assert that a subtle form of mental consciousness is the self. The Chittamātrins Following Scripture assert that the mind-basis-of-all is the self. The Yogāchāra-Svātantrika-Mādhyamikas assert that the continuum of the mental consciousness is the self. For Prāsaṅgika, none of these is the self, which is the I *imputed* in dependence upon the mental and physical aggregates.

Those who accept a consciousness as the actual self are specifically referring to the transmigrator, a neutral, subtle entity. They also accept that there is a self imputed to the aggregates, but in all systems except Prāsaṅgika 'only imputed' (*prajñapti-mātra, btags pa tsam*) eliminates only that something *separate* from its bases of imputation is the self, not that the composite of the bases of imputation or any one of them is it. Therefore, Tu-gen (*Thu'u-bkvan*, 1737-1802) says that only in the Prāsaṅgika system does the word 'only imputed' have its full meaning.[272] In all the other systems something must *be* the self; otherwise, for them there could be no transmigration, activity, and so forth. They identify the mental consciousness or the continuum of the aggregates as the self. Their meaning of 'only imputed' carries the sense of identification with one or more of the bases of imputation. In the Prāsaṅgika system 'only imputed' means that also not any of its bases of imputation is the self; nonetheless, the imputed self or person can function. The mere-I is the transmigrator and the carrier of the seeds or potencies from one life to another. It is the object that gives rise to the thought 'I' in lifetime after lifetime. It is the I that is imputed or designated in dependence upon the mental and physical aggregates in the Desire and Form Realms and upon only the mental aggregates in the Formless Realm. The Chittamātrins, however, assert that the mind-basis-of-all is the actual I since it is the transmigrator and carrier of seeds.

Thus, it should not be thought that because the Buddhist systems deny self, there is no transmigrator. The non-Buddhist systems could not posit transmigration without a permanent self; the Buddhist schools of tenets, on the other hand, posit many different modes of transmigration without a permanent self.

The Chittamātrins following Asaṅga feel that because Buddha said that the six consciousnesses of a person do not function in deep sleep and in the meditative equipoise of cessation, etc., there must be another very subtle consciousness, the continuity of which keeps the person alive.[273] Also, since the six consciousnesses have periods of non-existence, the seeds or predispositions, if stored there, would be destroyed, and the continuity of lives would be severed. Therefore, they posit the existence of a mind-basis-of-all. The schools that accept the mental consciousness or its continuum as the self answer that Buddha was referring to the coarse states of the mental consciousness and that there is a subtle, neutral, stable mental consciousness that passes from one lifetime to another and exists through the equipoises of cessation, bearing the continuity of the seeds.[274]

The Chittamātrins following Asaṅga accept that a mind-basis-of-all is accompanied by the five mental factors that accompany any consciousness—feeling, discrimination, intention, contact, and mental engagement. The equipoise of cessation is nevertheless without coarse feeling and discrimination even though the mind-basis-of-all and its five factors are present because the feeling and discrimination that accompany the mind-basis-of-all are subtle and non-manifest. This same reasoning allows the other schools to posit a subtle mental consciousness that is accompanied by such subtle, non-manifest factors and thus to say that there is no need to assert a separate mind-basis-of-all as an eighth consciousness.[275]

PRĀSAṄGIKA POSITION ON THE MIND-BASIS-OF-ALL

In the Prāsaṅgika system, external objects, and not seeds, are what provide sense objects although the overlay of false appearance is produced from seeds. A mental consciousness, and not an afflicted mind, misconceives the nature of the person. A subtle mental consciousness, and not a mind-basis-of-all, abides throughout the 'mindless' states. The mere-I, not a mind-basis-of-all, transmigrates. The six consciousnesses are temporary bases of seeds; the mere-I, not the mind-basis-of-all, is the constant basis of the seeds.

The basis in Buddha's own thought when he taught a mind-basis-of-all was emptiness, the basis of all phenomena which is to be minded well (*ālayavijñāna*). Taking *vijñāna* not as referring to the agent or action of knowing but as the object, the Prāsaṅgikas see the mind-basis-of-all as referring to the 'basis of all to be known well or in detail', emptiness. Emptiness is the basis of all in that it makes possible all the various types of beings, nirvana, cyclic existence, and so forth.

Buddha's purpose in teaching a mind-basis-of-all was to provide a base for the transmission of cause and effect through a continuum of lives for those disciples who could not understand the mere-I as the bearer of predisposing tendencies. The refutation of the explicit teaching is that, although a mind-basis-of-all is said to be impermanent, it is like the Sāṃkhyas' nature (*prakṛti, rang bzhin*) which contains all causes.[276] Because the causes already exist, everything would necessarily be produced all of the time, or once and never again.

The Yogāchāra-Svātantrikas, who do not assert an external world, do not even conventionally assert a mind-basis-of-all; for them, a mental consciousness bears the seeds that create the appearance of an external world. Thus, it is said that no Mādhyamika school asserts the existence of a mind-basis-of-all even though one Indian Mādhyamika, Abhayākara, early in his life is said to have asserted a mind-basis-of-all.[277] There are also a few passages in Nāgārjuna's writings that refer to a basis-of-all, but these are said to refer to the mental consciousness that takes rebirth.[278]

Although Nāgārjuna does say once in his *Precious Garland* and once in his *Sixty Stanzas of Reasoning* that everything is included in the mind, the Ge-luk-bas point to his *Essay on the Mind of Enlightenment* for his position:[279]

> A knower realizes an object known.
> Without an object known, there is no knower.

Also, many yogic treatises make reference to a basis-of-all (*ālaya, kun gzhi*), but there the term means the nature of phenomena (*dharmatā, chos nyid*), or emptiness.[280] Thus, not even conventionally do the Prāsaṅgikas accept a mind-basis-of-all; they say that this teaching points to emptiness, the basis of all change.

THREE NATURES

Buddha said that every phenomenon has three natures (*trisvabhāva, rang bzhin gsum*): imaginary or imputed (*parikalpita, kun btags*), other-powered (*paratantra, gzhan dbang*), and thoroughly established (*parinişhpanna, yongs grub*).[281] There are an endless number of non-existent imaginaries, such as the horns of a rabbit or the hairs of a turtle, but according to the Chittamātra system the most significant imaginary nature of every phenomenon is its being a different entity from an apprehending subject. Buddha called attention to an illusory element in ordinary perception, the bifurcation of object and subject into separate entities, calling it 'imaginary' to show that it is utterly unfounded and should be eradicated.

Subject and object as different entities are non-existent imaginaries, as are objects that are established by way of their own character as bases of names and self-sufficient persons. Ordinary beings experience objects in an unfounded way, as if they were entities separate from themselves and as if they were naturally bases of the affixing of names, and conceive themselves to be the lord or controller of mind and body. Buddha called these elements imaginaries because they are mere reifications through names and thoughts and do not actually exist.

The objects that serve as the bases for misconceiving imaginaries are other-powered natures. These are impermanent phenomena produced not by their own power but in dependence on specific aggregations of causes and conditions which are other than themselves. These phenomena lack independence, unable to remain any longer than their own one moment. By calling impermanent products 'other-powered natures', Buddha draws attention to the dependent nature of products, countering the usual tendency to see objects as if they exist in themselves. These phenomena are falsities because they appear to be natural bases of names and to be entities separate from a perceiving subject but are not. They are said to deceive because they appear one way and exist another. However, products, though falsities, do not falsely exist; rather, they truly exist since they are produced from causes and conditions.

The non-existence of such an imaginary nature in a dependent nature is a thoroughly established nature. This is immutable and the final object of observation by a path of purification. An object which is a different entity from a subject does not exist; a subject which is a different entity from its object does not exist; these non-existences are emptinesses in the Chittamātra system. The emptiness of subject and object as different entities is named 'thoroughly established' in direct contrast to 'imaginary' in order to show that this is the highest quality of an object and should be sought. The thoroughly established nature includes the emptiness not only of subject and object as different entities but also of objects which are naturally existent as bases of names and of a self-sufficient person. 'Emptiness' in the Chittamātra system refers to these three.

All phenomena, from forms through to omniscient consciousnesses, have the three natures—even permanent phenomena such as space and emptiness, though for these the term 'dependent nature' does not mean 'that which is dependent on causes and conditions for its production' but just identifies the entity of permanent phenomena as a base of an imaginary nature and a thoroughly established nature. Or, according to another interpretation, the dependent nature of a permanent phenomenon refers to a consciousness which cognizes it and is an impermanent phenomenon dependent on causes and conditions.[282]

Products, or impermanent phenomena, themselves are dependent natures, and thus it should not be thought that a product is one thing and its dependent nature another. Among permanent phenomena, emptinesses are thoroughly established natures, and space, analytical cessations, and non-analytical cessations are a special category of *existent* imaginaries, being imaginary in the sense that they appear to exist by way of their own character but do not, since they are posited in dependence on terms and thoughts. Space, for instance, is the mere absence of obstructive contact and is cognized by non-Buddhas only through inference—appearing to the mind through the elimination of obstructive contact.

A phenomenon's thoroughly estab̤lished nature (ultimate truth) is not a different entity from its dependent nature (conventional truth). The relationship of the two is a sameness of entity within a difference of isolates. An emptiness is a dependent nature's own non-difference in entity between subject and object.

Emptinesses—that is, thoroughly established natures—truly, ultimately and naturally exist as do dependent natures, because the Chittamātrins consider that for an emptiness or a product to exist at all, it must ultimately exist.

PRĀSAṄGIKA VIEW ON THE THREE NATURES

The Prāsaṅgikas say that Buddha taught that thoroughly established and dependent natures truly exist in order to overcome the fright of those who could not understand how an emptiness or an impermanent phenomenon could not truly exist but still exist. According to the Prāsaṅgikas, the basis in Buddha's thought was the conventional existence of all phenomena, since objects are imputed by terms and thoughts, unfindable among their bases of imputation, but conventionally existent.

The Prāsaṅgikas also substitute inherent existence as the chief non-existent imaginary in place of non-difference in entity between subject and object. In their interpretation the non-existence of dependent phenomena as this imaginary is a thoroughly established nature because no phenomenon ultimately exists and all phenomena exist only conventionally. Beings are called to identify a mistaken aspect in all ordinary perceptions, the appearance of objects as if they exist right there in their bases of imputation; such objects are called 'imaginaries' in order to show their unfounded character and the necessity of ridding oneself of the misperceptions and misconceptions of inherent existence. In the Prāsaṅgika system, the absence of inherent existence as a predicate of dependent phenomena is their thoroughly established nature, appearing in direct perception to exist the way it actually does. Emptiness is not a realm separate from the world of objects but their highest quality. Buddha implicitly exhorts yogis to discover and cognize it through giving it the name 'thoroughly established nature'.

An emptiness no more truly exists than any other phenomenon, but just as products can be cognized directly despite their lack of true existence, so an emptiness can be cognized directly despite its lack of true existence. Through accustoming oneself to its import, the cyclic existence which is generated through the conception of imaginaries can be stopped, and dependent natures can be seen as they are.

Since in Prāsaṅgika emptiness—the absence of inherent existence (*svabhāvasiddhi, rang bzhin gyis grub pa*)—is the nature (*svabhāva, rang bzhin*) of all phenomena, it should not be thought that *svabhāva* is refuted in all its meanings. *Svabhāva* meaning *svabhāvasiddhi* or 'inherent existence' is refuted, but *svabhāva* as 'final nature' or just 'character' (such as heat and burning as the character of fire) is not refuted.

The final nature that ordinary beings imagine in dependent phenomena is an imaginary, but for a Buddha the actual final nature is a thoroughly established nature. However, this does not mean that there are two ways of looking at dependent phenomena, one in which a dependent phenomenon itself becomes an imaginary and another in which it becomes a thoroughly established nature. Rather, the 'final nature' in reference to an untutored being is an imaginary because he or she conceives the inherent existence of dependent phenomena to be real, and the final nature in reference to a Buddha is a thoroughly established nature because a Buddha continually perceives the absence of inherent existence as the reality of objects. The attempt here is to avoid making products into emptinesses, to preserve thoroughly established natures as the nature of phenomena and not make them the phenomena themselves even in the eyes of a Buddha. Still, Buddhas simultaneously and directly cognize all phenomena and their emptiness with the same consciousness.

THREE FINAL VEHICLES

All Buddhist systems of tenets, Hīnayāna and Mahāyāna, accept three vehicles: Hearer, Solitary Realizer, and Great Vehicles.[283] These are three different modes of practice for three different types of individuals. The Vaibhāṣhikas, Sautrāntikas, and Chittamātrins who follow Asaṅga accept that there are three final vehicles or, in other words, that there are some beings who never attain the highest achievement because, after completing their lower vehicle, they do not pass on to the higher. Specifically, it means that there are some sentient beings who never attain Buddhahood.

For the Vaibhāṣhikas, Shākyamuni Buddha is the only being of this period to attain Buddhahood; a Buddha is a being who accumulated the collections of wisdom and merit for three countless eons whereas the most that any other being is capable of achieving is in the neighborhood of one hundred eons, as in the case of a rhinoceros-like Solitary Realizer.[284] Also, Buddha eradicated both obscurations, the afflictions of desire, hatred, and ignorance and the non-afflictive ignorance. The first prevents the attainment of liberation from cyclic existence, and the second prevents the attainment of an all-knowingness which in their system is not the simultaneous cognition of all phenomena but the knowledge of everything one by one. Hearer and Solitary Realizer Foe Destroyers have eradicated the afflictions, but they have merely abandoned the non-afflictive ignorance through non-attachment.[285] Thus, for the Vaibhāṣhikas, Hearer and Solitary Realizer Foe Destroyers are inferior to a Buddha and never attain Buddhahood; they finish their paths, and upon death the continuum of mind and body ceases in a remainderless nirvana. 'Remainderless' means that there no longer is any mind-body complex that derives its impetus from contaminated actions and afflictions; a remainderless nirvana is a substantiality (*dravya, rdzas*) and a functioning thing (*bhāva, dngos po*) which is the cessation of the obstructions to liberation from cyclic existence, its function being the prevention of obstructions.[286] Since Vaibhāṣhikas do not accept that a Foe Destroyer after death forms a new physical support through pure wishes and meditative powers, the attainer of a remainderless nirvana is said to be a person about to pass into extinction but not one who has passed into extinction, for there is no mind, body, or person after a remainderless nirvana.

The Sautrāntikas' assertion of three final vehicles is roughly similar; however, they assert that a remainderless nirvana is a phenomenon (*dharma, chos*), not a functioning thing (*bhāva, dngos po*) but rather a non-affirming negative which is a nothingness. For the Hīnayāna schools, manifestation after the death of an enlightened being is impossible, whereas the Mahāyānists disagree, comparing Hīnayānists to Nihilists on this point.

The Chittamātrins who follow Asaṅga also propound three final vehicles, saying that because sentient beings have different types of minds and different styles of behavior, their vehicles must also be different.[287] Some beings want only their own happiness; some want others to suffer; some want happiness for themselves and desist from harming others; some want only the happiness of cyclic existence; some want only to liberate themselves from cyclic existence; and some want only to free others from cyclic existence. These differences of attitude and style of behavior arise from differences in faith and interest which in turn are due to the presence of different lineages. Since it is thus unquestionable that the various lineages are different in the causal state, in the effect state they would not all pass into only one vehicle.

These Chittamātrins, therefore, assert three final vehicles as well as five lineages. The five are:[288]

1 those who from the point of attaining the path of accumulation right through to attaining the path of no more learning are Hearers, not changing or abandoning paths in mid-stream
2 those who from beginning to end are Solitary Realizers
3 those who from beginning to end are Bodhisattvas
4 those who are indefinite, first in one vehicle and then another, either advancing upward as from a Hearer path to a Bodhisattva one, or falling downward as from a Bodhisattva path to a Hearer one
5 those who have no lineage for liberation from cyclic existence, will never free themselves from misery, and will never attain omniscience.

Hearers are so called because they hear the doctrine from others and when they attain the fruit of practice, cause others to hear that they have attained the goal, 'I have done what was to be done; other than this I will not know another existence.'[289] Or in another etymology, Hearers are so called because they hear about the superior fruit of Buddhahood or its path from a Buddha and, without practicing it, proclaim it to others. According to the Chittamātrins following Asaṅga, the Hearers 'who travel only to peace', upon attaining the state of Foe Destroyer, do not pass on to the Mahāyāna but at death enter into a remainderless nirvana.

However, those Hearers do not become extinct but possess a wisdom of perpetual meditative absorption in the sphere of peace. They have eradicated the obstructions to liberation from cyclic existence and through their meditation do not possess the obstructions to omniscience, but the latter have not been abandoned through their antidote, and, therefore, they are not Buddhas.[290] Thus, Chittamātra, unlike the Hīnayāna schools of tenets, does not propound that the continuum of mind and body ceases in a remainderless nirvana because a Hearer Foe Destroyer is reborn in a pure land in meditative absorption inside a great lotus.[291] A distinctive feature of the Mahāyāna teaching is the assertion that pure wishes and meditative powers can cause one to be reborn in a pure land, whereas for the Hīnayānists it is as if cleansing the process of rebirth involves destroying the ability to manifest. For the Mahāyānists, the process of purification reveals increasing control over mind and matter to the point where Buddhas and Bodhisattvas even after their 'deaths' can appear simultaneously in many places in order to aid beings. That each Buddha has an immortal Enjoyment Body abiding in his Highest Pure Land is a Mahāyāna tenet not shared with Hīnayāna.

The Chittamātrins following Asaṅga say that there are other Hearers who complete their vehicle, attain the state of Foe Destroyer, and through the urgings of a Buddha, pass on to the Mahāyāna, eventually attaining Buddhahood.[292] They enter the Mahāyāna after attaining a nirvana with remainder. They have been liberated from cyclic existence but still possess a body—remainder—that derives its impetus from contaminated actions and afflictions. However, they have attained nirvana because they have passed beyond sorrow, which is identified as the afflictive obstructions, the chief of which in the Chittamātra system is the conception that a person is a self-sufficient entity separate from the mental and physical aggregates. They enter the Mahāyāna and are empowered by the Buddhas and Bodhisattvas so that although they appear to pass into a remainderless nirvaṇa, they do not, remaining alive in a magical manifestation which not even the gods can see. They complete the collections of wisdom and merit, meditating on the non-difference in entity between subject and object, thereby destroying the obstructions to simultaneous cognition of all phenomena. Becoming Buddhas, they complete the Mahāyāna path.

The Chittamātrins following Asaṅga say that Buddha sometimes taught one vehicle rather than three in order to draw those of indefinite lineage into the Mahāyāna and to keep those Bodhisattvas who might fall to a lower path within the Mahāyāna. However, the Chittamātrins Following Reasoning—the Mahāyāna followers of Dharmakīrti—answer that there is only one final vehicle,[293] for contaminations are caused and, therefore, impermanent. Also, it is not that there is no means of eradicating the afflictions because through cultivating the antidotes to their causes all contaminations are eradicated. Also, it is not that there is a means but no one knows it because one who knows the nature of the causes knows their antidotes. Also, it is not that there are none who seek it because the compassionate seek to overcome suffering. Also, it is not that there is no teacher of the means because a protector Buddha teaches a path he manifestly sees, knowing the effects of his teaching and thereby not erring.

ONE FINAL VEHICLE IN PRĀSANGIKA

The Prāsaṅgikas agree that there is only one final vehicle, saying that when Buddha taught three final vehicles the basis in his own thought was that *temporarily* there are three different vehicles. His purpose in teaching three final vehicles was to overcome the fright of those who could not imagine completing the immeasurable collections of merit and wisdom of the Mahāyāna. The explicit teaching of three final vehicles is contradicted by the presence of a Buddha nature in every sentient being.

Just as the proponents of mind-only assert that a basis-of-all acts as the basis of the phenomena of cyclic existence and of nirvana, so the Mādhyamikas assert that a natural lineage, or the mind's lack of inherent existence, acts as the base and support of all phenomena of cyclic existence and of nirvana.[294] Emptiness should not, however, be confused with a physically pervasive entity that produces all phenomena. Emptiness is the base of all phenomena because due to the lack of inherent existence all the actions and agents of cyclic existence and of nirvana are possible. For if phenomena existed inherently, they would be independent and thus incapable of change through being acted upon by causes. Emptiness does pervade all phenomena in the sense that wherever there is a phenomenon there is an emptiness, but it is not a material substance that produces phenomena. Still, without it change would be impossible, and in this light emptiness can be viewed even as the 'substance' of phenomena.

Emptiness is not only the object of the highest wisdom and of the path of deliverance; it is the very justification of change, allowing beings of different types to reach the same high achievement. The mind's character of dependence on causes— its non-inherent existence—is the Buddha nature that makes Buddhahood possible for all.

Asaṅga

6 *Mādhyamika*

BACKGROUND

Sources
Jam-ȳang-shay-b̄a's *Great Exposition of the Middle Way*
D̄zong-ka-b̄a's *Ocean of Reasoning*

In the Ge-luk-b̄a monasteries of Tibet the Mādhyamika system was studied through textbooks written as commentaries on Chandrakīrti's *Supplement to (Nāgārjuna's) 'Treatise on the Middle Way' (Madhyamakāvatāra)*.[295] *Madhyamaka*, in the title, refers to Nāgārjuna's *Madhyamakashāstra* and not to his other works because when Chandrakīrti quotes the *Madhyamakashāstra*, he merely says, 'From *Madhyamaka*,' whereas when he quotes Nāgārjuna's other works, he refers to them by their own names.

The word *madhyamaka* itself is formed from the stem *madhya* meaning 'middle', with the affix *ma* yielding a derivative noun that has the same meaning as its base. *Madhyama* means 'the very middle' or 'the middlemost'. Bhāvaviveka derives the affix *ka* from the verbal root for 'proclaiming', *kai*, thus taking *madhyamaka* as meaning 'that which proclaims the middle', that is, either a person, a system of tenets, or treatise that propounds the middle. In the case of Nāgārjuna's title, it refers to a treatise setting forth the middle, or middle way not in the sense of the middle path but the middle way things are; therefore, the word *Madhyamaka* when used in this sense is translated as *Treatise on the Middle Way* even when it is not accompanied by the explicit word for 'treatise', *shāstra*.

Nāgārjuna's *Treatise on the Middle Way* extensively teaches both the profound emptiness and the extensive varieties of spiritual paths, etc. His text delineates reasonings that establish an emptiness of inherent existence as the final mode of existence of all phenomena, not with one or a few but many examples and through many approaches in twenty-seven chapters. The four noble truths, the two truths, nirvana, production, perception, etc. are analyzed with respect to activity, agent, and object, appropriator and appropriated, substance and attribute, and so forth. In his treatise, Nāgārjuna treats the two truths even more extensively than Chandrakīrti does in his *Supplement*. The *Treatise* teaches:[296]

1 the nature of the two truths
2 that if one does not know the two truths, one does not know the essence of Buddha's scriptures
3 the purpose of teaching the two truths
4 the faults of misconceiving the two truths
5 that because the two truths are difficult to realize, Buddha did not teach them in the beginning.

Nāgārjuna says:

> 1 (XXIV. 8)
> Doctrines taught by the Buddhas
> Rely wholly on the two truths,
> Worldly conventional truths
> And ultimate truths.

Truths are objects that exist the way they appear. Thus, conventional objects are truths only in the sense that they seem to exist the way they appear for an ignorant consciousness, a concealer (*saṃvṛti*) of suchness through conceiving phenomena to exist inherently. Hence, all objects except emptinesses are conventional truths or truths-for-a-concealer. An emptiness, however, is a truth because it exists the way it appears to direct perception, this is, as empty of inherent existence. It is an ultimate truth, because among phenomena it is supreme since through meditating on it obstructions are removed and since it is the object of the highest wisdom.

2 (XXIV. 9)
Those who do not comprehend
The difference between these two truths
Do not know the nature
Of the profound doctrine of Buddha.

Those who do not know the difference between conventional and ultimate truths do not know the essence of Buddha's teaching, the principle of the profound dependent-arising. Therefore, one who wants to know the actuality of the Conqueror's teaching should comprehend the suitability of all actions, objects, and agents in dependently produced and dependently designated conventionalities that appear like a moon in water. Also, one must comprehend by that very reason the mode of the ultimate that abandons the two extremes of inherent existence and total non-existence.

3 (XXIV. 10)
Without relying on conventions
The ultimate cannot be taught.
Without realizing the ultimate
Nirvana is not attained.

Someone says, 'If the ultimate is a nature free of [dualistic] elaborations, then it needs to be taught, but what is the point of teaching conventionalities such as the aggregates, constituents, and sources? If the unreal is to be abandoned, there is no point in teaching what is to be abandoned.'

Answer: Although it is true that the erroneous—conventionalities that appear to be real but are not—are to be abandoned, the ultimate cannot be taught without depending on worldly ultimates such as object of expression, expresser, knowing, object known, and so forth—the conventions related with Superiors that are asserted to be conventional truths. Also, without teaching the ultimate, it cannot be realized, and without that, nirvana cannot be attained. Therefore, because of being the means of attaining liberation, just as one who wants water has need of a vessel, so initially one definitely should assert conventionalities just as they are.

4 (XXIV. 11)
If emptiness is viewed wrongly,
Those of small intellect are hurt,
Like wrongly holding a snake
Or wrongly using a spell.

A yogi who realizes that conventional truths produced merely through ignorance do not inherently exist and realizes their ultimate emptiness will not fall to the two extremes. For he does not conceive that an objectively existent nature, which formerly existed, now does not exist. Also, because he has not damaged (or refuted) worldly conventionalities that are like reflections, he has not damaged actions and their fruits (and thus does not fall to an extreme of nihilism). Such a yogi also does not falsely superimpose ultimate existence on phenomena because he has seen that actions and their fruits can occur in only non-inherently existent things; he knows that things do not inherently exist, and that all actions, their fruits, and so forth would not be possible if they inherently existed. Those, however, who see that phenomena do not inherently exist without perceiving such a difference between the two truths either think that things do not exist or impute true existence to emptiness and thereby think that things inherently exist as bases of emptiness. These are both wrong ways of viewing emptiness, and in this way those with little intellect are hurt.

When they see that things do not inherently exist, it seems to them that there is no way of positing actions, agents, and objects, whereby they conclude that all does not exist—falling to a view of deprecation. Or, if they do not deprecate everything, they question how these things, while they are being apprehended, could be empty of inherent existence—concluding that the meaning of non-inherent existence is not the meaning of emptiness and thereby abandoning emptiness. Through this they accumulate an action (*karma, las*) resulting in being bereft of the doctrine and are born in a bad migration.

5 (XXIV. 12)
Therefore, realizing that the dull-witted
Would have trouble understanding this doctrine,
The mind of the Subduer
Turned away from teaching doctrine.

Since one who views emptiness wrongly is harmed and since those of little intelligence cannot apprehend the meaning of suchness correctly, after enlightenment Shākyamuni—when he saw the dispositions of sentient beings and the great profundity of the doctrine—knew that those of little intellect could not realize the depths of the profound doctrine of dependent-arising. Therefore, his mind turned away from teaching. (This, however, is accepted as being his first teaching, for his pretended retreat from teaching indicated the profundity of his doctrine and thereby generated interest.)[297]

Chandrakīrti did not treat all these topics in his *Supplement*, which is, therefore, less extensive than the *Treatise* though of greater length. A work is extensive not because of a great number of words, but because of covering many topics; for instance, Maitreya's *Ornament for Clear Realization* is short but its meanings are indeed vast. Therefore, Nāgārjuna's *Treatise* is more extensive than Chandrakīrti's longer *Supplement*.

Furthermore, the *Treatise* is not limited to an extensive explanation of emptiness; it also extensively sets forth the suitability of conventional phenomena within an emptiness of inherent existence as well as the four truths, actions and their effects, the Three Jewels, the eight levels of approaching and abiding in the fruits of Stream Enterer, Once Returner, Never Returner, and Foe Destroyer, and so forth. Jam-ȳang-shay-b̄a[298] says that if, as some scholars say, Nāgārjuna's *Treatise* does not set forth the varieties of phenomena, paths, and so forth, then to do so, it would be necessary to give a tally of the bugs in the world. Still, Jam-ȳang-shay-b̄a agrees that these varieties are not the principal object of discourse in the *Treatise*; the profound emptiness is. When Nāgārjuna identifies particular phenomena which are the bases of their own emptiness, he explicitly but secondarily indicates the paths, grounds, fruits, and so forth. As Nāgārjuna says (XXIV.14ab):

> For whom emptiness is possible
> For him all is possible.

The establishment of the phenomena of cyclic existence and nirvana is possible when emptiness is possible. If things inherently or naturally existed, they would be independent and could not be affected by causes and conditions. Emptiness, or the lack of inherent existence, makes possible production, abiding, and disintegration.

Chandrakīrti's *Supplement* reveals emptiness through far less forms than the *Treatise*; it is a supplement in that it fills certain holes in the *Treatise* that became apparent with the founding of the Chittamātra and Svātantrika systems. Nāgārjuna wrote the *Treatise* during his second proclamation of doctrine which preceded the founding of those two systems. Therefore, the *Treatise* required clarification to show that it was not suitable to interpret its meaning according to those systems.

Chandrakīrti also provides an extensive discussion of the three types of compassion (compassion observing sentient beings, observing sentient beings as qualified by momentary impermanence, and observing sentient beings as qualified by non-inherent existence), the ten Bodhisattva grounds, Buddhahood, and the cultivation of calm abiding on the fifth ground and special insight on the sixth. Jam-ȳang-shay-b̄a explains that Chandrakīrti was not filling holes in the *Treatise* in the sense of providing what was incomplete or making extensive what was not already extensive, but rather in the sense of making the extensive more so and of taking secondary subjects as principal. He explains that Chandrakīrti makes clear that students of the *Treatise* should practice the Bodhisattva paths and ascend the grounds.[299]

Chandrakīrti wrote a commentary to his own *Supplement*; the founder of the Ge-luk-b̄a order, D̄zong-ka-b̄a (1357-1419) wrote a commentary called *Illumination of the Thought, Extensive Explanation of (Chandrakīrti's) 'Supplement to (Nāgārjuna's) "Treatise on the Middle Way"'*, and the major Ge-luk-b̄a monastic colleges have their own commentaries on both Chandrakīrti's and D̄zong-ka-b̄a's works, usually in the form of general explanations accompanied by debates. These works are the basis for the study of Mādhyamika and more particularly of Prāsaṅgika, centering on the topic of the two truths.

TWO TRUTHS

Sources
Jam-ȳang-shay-b̄a's *Great Exposition of Tenets*
Nga-w̄ang-bel-den's *Annotations*
Kensur Lekden's oral teachings

The two truths are objects, not vague concepts of truth, beauty, and so forth.[300] They are phenomena (*dharma, chos*), objects (*viṣhaya, yul*), existents (*sat, yod pa*), and objects of knowledge (*jñeya, shes bya*).

Truths are those things that exist the way they appear, and thus only ultimate truths (*paramārthasatya, don dam bden pa*) or emptinesses qualify as truths. The other various and sundry objects do not exist the way they appear, except to Buddhas. These objects are truths only for a concealer of suchness, an ignorant consciousness; therefore, they are called truths-for-a-concealer (*saṃvṛtisatya, kun rdzob bden pa*).

Truths-for-a-concealer are falsities, appearing one way and existing another. Thus, since only an ultimate truth can actually sustain the meaning of truth, it is not truths that are divided into the two truths. Objects of knowledge, or phenomena, are the basis of division of the two truths. The *Meeting of Father and Son Sutra (Pitāputrasamāgama)* says, 'Objects of knowledge are exhausted in the two truths.'

Since those which are divided into the two truths are phenomena (and the synonyms of 'phenomena'), each member of either division is a phenomenon, an object, an existent, and an object of knowledge. This means that an emptiness is a phenomenon, object, existent, and object of knowledge as are all other various and sundry objects.

Among six positions on the topic of what is divided into the two truths which are refuted by Jam-ȳang-shay-b̄a is that of the translator Ngok, (*Ngog-lo-tstsha-ba bLo-ldan-shes-rab*) and his followers, who do not accept that an emptiness is an object of knowledge because the mere non-finding of an object under analysis is just *called* an emptiness, and, thus, there is no phenomenon 'emptiness' existent there. Ngok's idea is that if an analytical consciousness cognized an emptiness, then that emptiness would necessarily inherently exist. For, an analytical consciousness is searching to find whether an object inherently exists or not, and if it 'finds' or cognizes an emptiness of inherent existence of that object, then it would seem that the emptiness must inherently exist since, according to him, it would be able to bear ultimate analysis. Therefore, according to him mere appearances are the basis of the division into the two truths and not objects of knowledge because an ultimate truth, that is, an emptiness, is not an object of knowledge.

The Ge-luk-b̄a answer[301] to this is: An analytical consciousness investigating whether a table, for instance, is separate from its basis of designation, or is the composite of its bases of designation, or is some one of its bases of designation does not find a table. This very non-finding is an emptiness, and this non-finding is 'found' or cognized by an analytical consciousness. However, because an analytical consciousness is not investigating whether the emptiness of the table can be found, its 'finding' or cognizing the emptiness of the table, i.e., its lack of inherent existence, does not necessitate that the emptiness be inherently existent. This is because the analytical consciousness was not searching for the emptiness of the table but for the table. When, in turn, an analytical consciousness searches for the emptiness of the table, it also cannot be found; an emptiness of the emptiness of the table is 'found'. This type of finding does not mean that the object can bear ultimate analysis; nothing can bear ultimate analysis; even an emptiness cannot.

Every emptiness is, in turn, qualified by an emptiness, necessitating an infinite regress, but this does not entail a fallacy just as there is no fallacy in the fact that there are an infinite number of causes that eventually lead to the production of a sprout. Infinite regresses are damaging only when they necessitate an impossibility; since the causal sequence that leads to the production of a sprout can stretch back through measureless time, there is no fallacy such as the impossibility of millions of causes having to occur in a tiniest moment.

Still, the situation with an infinite number of emptinesses is different from that of an infinite chain of causes over time. Since each emptiness of the emptiness of the emptiness of the emptiness, etc., of a table is a phenomenon, they must all be cognized by a Buddha if he is to be omniscient. Also, if first one emptiness is understood and then the mind turns to the next, and the next, and the next, there would be no time in which all the emptinesses related with just one object could be known. However, this is true only for the mode of cognition of emptiness by inference. An inferring consciousness first realizes the emptiness of a thing through the medium of a concept; then, through merely turning the mind to another object, its emptiness is immediately known. However, when emptiness is directly cognized—that is to say, without the medium of concepts and images—all emptinesses throughout all world systems are simultaneously known. The mind and its objects—all emptinesses—are totally undifferentiated like fresh water poured into fresh water; a transformation has been effected that allows simultaneous cognition of the emptiness of everything.

Direct cognition of all emptinesses does not mean that all phenomena are directly known; rather, the mode of existence of all phenomena is realized. When a yogi has become familiar with direct cognition of emptiness on the Bodhisattva's path of meditation and has completed the necessary stock of merit, he becomes a Buddha, able to know directly and simultaneously both the emptinesses of all phenomena and the phenomena themselves. An analytical consciousness does not create an emptiness; it discovers the nature of a phenomenon; thus, an emptiness of an emptiness does not come into being when the first emptiness is understood. An emptiness, like any other phenomenon, is itself empty of inherent existence, just as hotness is the nature of red pepper even when it is not being tasted.[302]

The emptiness of one thing, though no different in color, shape, and so forth from another emptiness, is not the emptiness of another thing. However, because of their similarity of type, meditation on the emptiness of one thing functions as meditation on the emptiness of all things. For, having inferentially realized the emptiness of one thing, merely turning the mind to another subject yields cognition of its emptiness without having to rely again on the process of reasoning.

If the emptiness of one thing were the emptiness of another, one would be forced to accept that the lack of inherent existence of a pot is the lack of inherent existence of a person and that the apprehension of the inherent existence of a pot is the apprehension of the inherent existence of a person, but this is clearly not the case. One must understand that emptinesses are divided by way of their bases, that is, the things that are empty. Therefore, ultimate truth is not partless; otherwise, it would contradict the various scriptures that speak of two, four, sixteen, eighteen, etc., divisions of emptinesses. The *King of Meditative Stabilizations Sutra* says, 'Just as you have understood the discrimination of a self, so apply [this understanding of the lack of inherent existence] to all.'[303] Having learned about the emptiness of the person, a yogi is to apply this understanding to all phenomena; therefore, knowing one emptiness inferentially does not mean that all emptinesses are already known. Otherwise, why, after knowing the emptiness of the person, would one have to apply it to other phenomena?

The presentation of emptinesses as different emphasizes the stage of the path concerned with developing an inferential understanding of emptiness. However, there is the powerful experience of utter undifferentiability of subject and object in a direct cognition of emptiness in which it seems that subject and object become more 'one' than the word 'one' could ever convey. For 'one' is always a composite of different things; there is no 'one' that can appear to thought which is not a composite. The Ge-luk-b̄as must resort to the realm of exceptions and analogies at the time of presenting the *mode* of direct cognition of emptiness; all emptinesses in all world systems are realized, subject and object are like water in water, but for an outside 'observer' subject and object are different and each emptiness is different from every other emptiness. Sometimes, it seems as if the Ge-luk-b̄as deliberately disregard the more fantastic, relegating it to the realm of exceptions rather than attempting to blend the outlooks of higher experiences with their presentation. It seems as if they occasionally lose sight of the goal during their highly intricate philosophical maneuverings whereas other interpreters seem more content to keep the goal in mind and risk some apparent difficulties in presenting conventional objects.

This indeed is the way the difference between the Ge-luk-b̄as and the non-Ge-luk-b̄as often appears, if only because the Ge-luk-b̄as, having accepted the task of laying out all phenomena under the umbrella of valid establishment, must spend so much time in formulating conventionalities. However, there is a deeper point; in his tantra teaching D̄zong-ka-b̄a objects to those who do not thoroughly practice the stage of generation—roughly speaking, imagination of oneself as a deity and one's surroundings as the environment of a deity. He objects to those who immediately, without ripening their mental continuum, rush to clear away all forms and abide in some sort of vacuity, which is not the vacuity that is a negative of inherent existence but nothingness.[304] Similarly, Jam-ȳang-shay-b̄a says that in Tibet few have wished to meditate on emptiness and have called meditation on a vacuity of nothingness meditation on emptiness.[305] For him and for D̄zong-ka-b̄a, analytical meditation on emptiness involves reflection on the reasons why things do not inherently exist. The meditator should state to himself a subject, such as 'I', a predicate, such as 'do not inherently exist', and a reason, such as 'because of not being the same as or different from the mental and physical aggregates, mind and body'. Then, he should continue to prove the reason, reflecting on the meaning until conviction and the resultant intuition are generated. This type of meditation acts as an *antidote* to the misconception of inherent existence whereas mere withdrawal of the mind from the object I, though often felicitous, will not counteract the misconception of an inherently existent I.

In Ge-luk-b̄a teachings, analysis is stressed, and emptiness is presented as the highest predicate, quality, or nature of each object—its lack of inherent existence. Non-perception of it is like not perceiving the best quality of everything one sees—their thoroughly established nature. The attempt to keep emptinesses individual is in order to emphasize that each and every one of these various and sundry objects lacks inherent existence; emptiness is not a vague negative, but a specific negative of inherent existence in each and every object. The content of wisdom is the incontrovertible cognition of this.

Other than saying that the experience of a direct cognition of emptiness is like fresh water poured in fresh water, of what benefit are words like 'one' in leading a yogi to the experience? The experience is entered through analysis, through gaining an inferential intuition into emptiness and directly attacking the very cause of cyclic existence, not through superimposing a vague concept on experience. Though most Tibetan orders, after the defeat of the Chinese Ho-shang Mahāyāna, accept analysis, its use is often more limited for non-Ge-luk-b̄as than for Ge-luk-b̄as.

For D̄zong-ka-b̄a an emptiness is an imputedly existent phenomenon like any other object, but for Ngok it is only a designation pointing to this non-finding of objects by an analytical consciousness. Jam-ȳang-shay-b̄a says that in that case an emptiness would not exist, and there would be no ultimate truths. These differing systems serve to highlight the fact that nothing can bear analysis. That the Ge-luk-b̄as are able to view this non-finding as an object, an ultimate object, and as validly established allows them to take literally passages in sutras that others find require interpretation, such as the presentation of suchness as a phenomenon in the *Meeting of the Father and Son Sūtra* above when it presents objects of knowledge—existents—as the basis of the division into the two truths. Still, suchness is a mere non-affirming negative of inherent existence, not a positive phenomenon, and when it is realized, one is not thinking, 'This *is* emptiness.'

The next position that Jam-ȳang-shay-b̄a refutes is that of Tang-s̄ak-b̄a (*Thang-sags-pa*) who says that the entities of all phenomena beginning with forms, feelings, discriminations, compositional factors, and consciousnesses and extending through to and including omniscient consciousnesses are the bases of division into the two truths. The problem with this position is that since, for instance, a form would be a basis of division into a truth-for-a-concealer and an ultimate truth, the ultimate truth which is a division of the form would have to be a form in which case it would be composed of material particles. This, of course, is not Tang-s̄ak-b̄a's intention; he means that every phenomenon, from a form through to an omniscient consciousness, *has* two entities, one a truth-for-a-concealer and the other an ultimate truth. However, Jam-ȳang-shay-b̄a would perhaps say that when searching for proper terminology, even unintended absurdities must be considered.

Some say that non-reified objects are the basis of the division into the two truths. Just objects which exist, not those falsely reified into existence, are divided into the two truths. To this Jam-ȳang-shay-b̄a makes the trifling objection that then reified systems, such as Sāṃkhya which falsely reifies many objects, would not be truths-for-a-concealer whereas they are. Wrong systems, even if they involve reifications, do exist as systems.

D̄ak-tsang, in turn, is criticized for his assertion that non-investigated and non-analyzed objects of knowledge are the basis of the division into two truths. D̄ak-tsang's reason is that under investigation and analysis nothing is found; thus, the two truths are only non-analytical. Jam-ȳang-shay-b̄a rejects this view because the two truths themselves are objects of intensive analysis. One would have to contradict Chandrakīrti's statement that Mādhyamikas are skilled in presenting what conventionally exists.[306] Also, since an emptiness is found by an analytical consciousness, how can it be said that ultimate truths are non-analyzed objects of knowledge?[307] Jam-ȳang-shay-b̄a thereby also rejects Ḏak-tsang's view that objects of knowledge are established as existing by an ignorant consciousness, refusing a role for valid establishment in a presentation of what exists.

A fifth position that truths are the basis of division is refuted by the fact that then truths-for-a-concealer would exist the way they appear, since they would be truths. The sixth is actually not a position but a lack of interest in what is divided into the two truths despite extensive discussion on the two divisions; Jam-ȳang-shay-b̄a refutes this by saying that then the truths would be attributes without a substratum.

Thus, the basis of division into the two truths is only objects of knowledge, and since all existents are divided without residue into the two truths, there is no third or fourth truth. The four noble truths are included in the two truths, with true sufferings, origins, and paths being truths-for-a-concealer and true cessations being ultimate truths, that is, emptinesses within the continuum of those who have abandoned totally and forever any portion of the obstructions.

Also, the two truths are mutually exclusive and a dichotomy; in other words, if something exists, it must be either a truth-for-a-concealer, or an ultimate truth. Thus, if something is a truth-for-a-concealer, it is not an ultimate truth, and if something is an ultimate truth, it is not a truth-for-a-concealer. Jam-ȳang-shay-b̄a quotes the *Meeting of Father and Son Sūtra* to prove through scriptural citation that there is no third truth:[308]

> Without depending on others the Knower
> Of the World taught these two truths,
> Conventional and likewise ultimate—
> A third truth does not exist.

He quotes Kamalashīla's *Illumination of the Middle Way* to show that the two truths are mutually exclusive contradictories:[309] 'With respect to phenomena that have the character of mutual abandonment [i.e., a dichotomy], when having refuted [that something under consideration] is the one, if it is [also] not established as the other, then it does not exist. Therefore, a position that is neither is not feasible.'

The two truths are not different entities but one entity within nominal difference.[310] If conventional and ultimate truths were different entities, the lack of inherent existence of a form would not be the final mode of existence of the form because it would be completely separate from the form. Just so, realization of the non-inherent existence of a form would not overcome the conception of the form as inherently existent. Also, a yogi's cultivation of high paths would be senseless because understanding emptiness would not be related with destroying misconception of the objects themselves. Similarly, a Buddha would not have forsaken the apprehension of inherent existence because he would have only a powerless apprehension of an emptiness which was entirely separate from objects.

On the other hand, if the two truths were utterly the same, everything true of the one would be true of the other. In that case, for every truth-for-a-concealer such as desire and hatred which was overcome on the path, an ultimate truth also would be overcome. Just as truths-for-a-concealer have many dissimilar and different aspects such as color, shape, odor, and taste, so ultimate truths would be dissimilar and different. Just as many truths-for-a-concealer are afflictions, so many ultimate truths would also be afflictions. Just as common individuals directly cognize truths-for-a-concealer such as forms, sounds, odors, and tastes, so they would absurdly directly cognize the emptiness of forms and so forth.

Therefore, the two truths are not different entities; they are the same entity. This is what the *Heart of Wisdom* (the *Heart Sutra*) means when it says that emptiness is form and form is emptiness.[311] The two truths are not one, but are nominally different, for they appear differently to thought. The relationship is called a oneness of entity but a difference of isolates or opposites of the negatives. The negative of truth-for-a-concealer is non-truth-for-a-concealer, and its opposite is non-non-truth-for-a-concealer, which indeed is truth-for-a-concealer but as known through a negative route. Similarly, the negative of ultimate truth is non-ultimate truth, and its opposite is non-non-ultimate truth. Because non-truth-for-a-concealer is different from non-ultimate truth, the opposites of the negatives are also said to be different.

The meaning can be more easily seen with an example. Take table and product. If the mind turns to deciding whether the two are different, it determines whether there are any non-tables which are products and any non-products which are tables. When it is said, pointing at the basis of the imputation 'table', 'This is a table,' and 'This is a product,' it is not obvious just from the statement whether only tables are products. It then must be seen that there are non-tables, such as cups, which are products and that there are no non-products which are tables because non-products are either permanent phenomena or non-existents. From this approach, non-table and non-product are different, and thus it is said that the opposites of those negatives, non-non-table and non-non-product, are different. However, table and product are the same entity just because a table is a product. Though there are products which are not tables, product is the same entity as table because there is no generality product which is a separate entity from its specific instances, such as tables, houses, fences, mountains, and so forth.

A truth-for-a-concealer and an ultimate truth are a case of two phenomena which are the same entity and different opposites of the negatives with the two terms being mutually exclusive; nothing can be both. Product and table are the same entity and different opposites of the negatives within the relationship of a generality and its particular instance. Impermanent thing and product are the same entity and different opposites of the negatives wherein the two terms are not mutually exclusive but synonymous because all instances of either are instances of the other. They are nevertheless one entity but different opposites of the negatives and not utterly one because the mention of the one does not necessarily entail the appearance to the mind of the other. Still, product and impermanent thing are synonyms, the first being a thing from the viewpoint of its being made by causes and conditions and the second from the viewpoint of its disintegrating moment by moment. In the same way, *khyi* (which means 'dog' in Tibetan) and dog are the same entity and different opposites of the negatives because when '*khyi*' is said, 'dog' does not necessarily appear to the mind. Only *khyi* and *khyi* are the same entity and the same opposite of the negative, or more strictly, the same isolate.

These distinctions yield a sense of the impact for this writer when, after a discussion of the fresh water poured into fresh water metaphor for the direct cognition of emptiness, the late Ge-luk-b̄a scholar and tantric abbot, Kensur Lekden, leaned toward me and said that it almost seems as if the cognizer and cognitum are one opposite of the negative.

Nāgārjuna says in his *Essay on the Mind of Enlightenment*[312] that the two truths are like product and impermanent thing; however, his example is said[313] not to show that the two are synonyms but that they are the same entity, with the existence of one being impossible without the existence of the other. That the two truths are not synonyms is determined through the *Sutra Unravelling the Thought*,[314] which nevertheless does not explicitly state that they are the same entity and different opposites of the negatives. In a similar vein, D̄zong-ka-b̄a reports that some have said that the two truths, though not different entities, have a difference which is a mere negation of their being one.[315]

The Jo-nang-b̄as hold that the two truths are different entities.[316] Theirs is a view of 'emptiness of other'—an ultimate truth is empty of being a truth-for-a-concealer and a truth-for-a-concealer is empty of being an ultimate truth. This is said to be similar to the Sāṃkhya teaching that the root of cyclic existence is the confusion of the person and the nature and that liberation is gained by realizing that the person is not the manifesting nature and that the manifesting nature is not the person. Through differentiating the two, a yogi is released from cyclic existence.

For a Ge-luk-b̄a, it is true that an ultimate truth is not a truth-for-a-concealer and vice versa, but this distinction does not constitute emptiness. An emptiness is a phenomenon's *own* lack of inherent existence; thus, this doctrine is called 'emptiness of self' which does not mean that a table is empty of being a table but that a table is empty of its own inherent existence. Otherwise, if a table were empty of itself, there would be no tables and, by extension, no phenomena; an emptiness would also be impossible because an emptiness would be empty of being an emptiness.

The Jo-nang-b̄a assertion of a difference of entity between the two truths contradicts the *Sutra Unravelling the Thought*, but it does reflect the Ge-luk-b̄a acceptance that at the time of direct cognition of emptiness (by anyone except a Buddha) none of the conventional phenomena which are the bases of the quality emptiness appear to the mind. A direct cognition of emptiness is non-dual in four ways:[317] (1) all appearances of inherent existence have ceased, (2) all appearances of conventionalities have ceased, (3) all appearances of subject and object have ceased, and (4) all appearances of generic images (or conceptual meaning-generalities) have ceased.

The disappearance of conventional phenomena is said to be due to the mind's concentration solely on emptiness and due to the cessation of the five sense consciousnesses. Until Buddhahood a direct cognition of suchness precludes cognition of other phenomena just as cognition of other phenomena precludes direct cognition of emptiness; the stains of the mind are such that the one blocks the other.[318] When anyone except a Buddha directly realizes emptiness, merely the quality emptiness appears without the appearance of the qualificands—the phenomena which are empty.

Thus, though the two truths are inextricably related, it is possible to perceive one and not the other; common beings perceive truths-for-a-concealer without perceiving ultimate truths, and sentient beings in meditative equipoise on emptiness perceive ultimate truths without perceiving truths-for-a-concealer. However, if it is wrongly viewed that an ultimate truth is a different entity from a truth-for-a-concealer, an emptiness could not be the final mode of existence of phenomena and meditation on it would not serve to dissolve misconceptions about the nature of objects.

An ultimate truth, or more literally, a highest object truth (*paramārthasatya, don dam bden pa*) is so called because an emptiness is the most exalted of all phenomena and is the object of the wisdom that realizes suchness.[319] It is a truth because it exists the way it appears in direct cognition. Truths-for-a-concealer (*saṃvṛtisatya, kun rdzob bden pa*) are so called because all other objects are assumed by ignorance to exist the way they appear. An ignorant consciousness is not just a consciousness which does not know suchness but a concealer of suchness through actively assenting to the false appearance of objective existence. Even in direct sense perception, forms, sounds, odors, tastes, and tangible objects appear to exist inherently, as if they existed in their own right. *All* phenomena except emptinesses appear to the cognizers that certify them as existing as if they exist inherently. Since the ignorance that assents to this appearance is the root of cyclic existence, its role in everyday perceptions is emphasized through naming all phenomena except emptinesses 'truths-for-a-concealer', truths for ignorance.

Even for Foe Destroyers and eighth ground Bodhisattvas, who have totally and forever overcome the conception that phenomena inherently exist, phenomena still appear to exist inherently, to *be* their bases of imputation, but these liberated beings know that they are not. Like magicians who see their own creations but, unlike the deceived audience, know them to be illusions, Foe Destroyers and eighth ground Bodhisattvas have destroyed ignorance and know that phenomena do not inherently exist. Therefore, it is only through their knowledge of how other beings conceive conventionalities that these conventionalities are still for them truths-for-a-concealer. Though they have destroyed the concealer of suchness in their own continuums, they realize how others misconceive phenomena.

To a Buddha, conventionalities appear the way they exist, for a Buddha has eradicated not only the afflictions, the chief of which is the ignorance that misconceives the nature of phenomena, but also the *appearance* of inherent existence caused by beginningless conditioning to ignorance. Therefore, the explanation that conventionalities do not exist the way they appear does not hold true for a Buddha. Still, even for a Buddha conventionalities—all phenomena except emptinesses—are truths-for-a-concealer because he knows how things are perceived and conceived by others.

Chandrakīrti etymologizes the word *saṃvṛti* of *saṃvṛtisatya* as 'concealer' (*samantādvaraṇa, sgrib byed*), 'conventionality' (*vyāvahāra, tha snyad*), and '*interdependence*' (*parasparasaṃbhavana, phan tshun rten pa*).[320] All existents except emptinesses are conventional truths and interdependent existents. They are conventional in the sense that they are conventions as consciousnesses or expressions or as objects of consciousnesses or expressions. They are interdependent in the sense that doer depends on doing and doing depends on doer, etc. However, the latter is only an etymology and not a definition, for an emptiness is also interdependent in that it depends on the phenomenon of which it is the final mode of being.[321] Just as the nature of a phenomenon depends on that phenomenon, so the phenomenon also depends on its nature. Furthermore, an emptiness depends on the meditative equipoise that certifies it, and it also depends on its basis of imputation, the non-inherent existence of an object. Thus, though all phenomena are interdependent, conventionalities are called interdependent existents in order to stress their false appearance as if they exist in and of themselves.

Since neither ultimate truths nor truths for a concealer inherently exist, the division of the two truths is not an ontological division. Both exist only conventionally (*saṃvṛtisat, kun rdzob tu yod pa*) with *saṃvṛti* here referring to a valid dualistic cognizer; both truths exist for valid dualistic cognizers and not in ultimate analysis. The division of the two truths emphasizes two types of objects of consciousness, truths and falsities. Both, however, are falsely existent or falsely established because neither is independent; each depends on its imputing consciousness and on the other.

Whether understood by a particular being or not, emptiness is forever established as the nature of objects, which do not gain non-inherent existence through being cognized as lacking inherent existence. They never did, never do, and never will inherently exist. Emptiness is validated by a consciousness of meditative equipoise, and there has always been someone cognizing emptiness.[322] Though each person needs to validate it for himself, this does mean that because it is not validated for someone, it is not validated in general. If this were the case, it would be difficult to establish the existence of anything.

For Prāsaṅgika nothing exists objectively, that is to say, as if of its own will right with its basis of imputation. Prāsaṅgika philosophy, though emphasizing the subjective element, is still not a turn to utter subjectivity in which what exists for the individual is what exists. There are standards and criteria for valid establishment, and in this sense both suchness and the phenomena qualified by it are objective.[323] The division into two truths on epistemological grounds is a call to eradicate ignorance and to attain the highest wisdom. It is a call to recognition that a conventional cognizer, even if valid with respect to the existence or non-existence of objects, is not valid with respect to their suchness. It is a call to a new mode of perception, to a cognition of a reality that has been ever-present.

The two truths are not vague realms of misty truth as suggested by translations which use the singular, such as 'Absolute Truth' and 'Conventional Truth'. In Sanskrit and Tibetan the singular is used for a class name whereas in common English usage a general term is most often either in the plural, or in the singular with the indefinite article 'a'. It would be correct to refer to conventional truths as 'Conventional Truth' only if it were suitable to refer to tables as table, e.g., 'Table is object,' rather than 'Tables are objects.'

However, translating *paramārthasatya* in the singular as 'ultimate truth' even without an article can be considered a matter of choice depending on the context, because though there are many types of emptinesses, they are only enumerated as such in accordance with the various types of phenomena that are bases of the quality emptiness. Still, at least in the Ge-luk-b̄a interpretation the emptiness of one thing is not the emptiness of another in the sense of exact identity, and from this viewpoint the term has often been translated here either in the singular with the article 'an' as 'an ultimate truth' or in the plural as 'ultimate truths'. Despite this, when referring to a direct cognition in which all emptinesses are simultaneously realized, it seems cumbersome to say, 'A yogi directly cognizes ultimate truths', because it seems to imply that only some ultimate truths are being cognized. Rather, usage of the singular as in, 'A yogi directly cognizes ultimate truth in a totally non-dualistic manner,' or 'A yogi directly cognizes emptiness after having become accustomed to an inferential realization,' at least suggests that there is no ultimate truth which at that point is not being cognized. The meaning, nevertheless, is not amorphous, but specific; an emptiness is a phenomenon's lack of inherent existence. Thus, one 'reflects on *an* emptiness' or 'generates an inferential cognition of *an* emptiness' because it is the emptiness of a specific phenomenon that is being reflected upon and realized.

Also, for *paramārtha*, 'ultimate' is a better translation than 'Absolute' because 'Absolute' suggests something that exists in and of itself, independently, whereas nothing is independent in the Mādhyamika system, even an emptiness.

As was said earlier, a truth-for-a-concealer is not established as existing by a concealer—an ignorant consciousness. Its erroneous inherent existence is 'established' by ignorance. Since the mere existence of truths-for-a-concealer is not refuted by emptiness, the division into the two truths is not of mental objects into those of the stupid and those of the wise. The conventional existence of objects is certified by valid cognizers and never eradicated by ultimate analysis, which refutes only the inherent existence of objects, both conventionally and ultimately. Once ultimate analysis establishes that the inherent existence of an object cannot be found, it cannot be found ultimately or conventionally; hence, the doctrine of the two truths is not a concession to the ways of ignorance. Chandrakīrti establishes that even conventionally objects are not their bases of imputation; even conventionally objects are merely interdependent.

This does not mean that when a truth-for-a-concealer, such as a chair, is perceived, a common being perceives it *as* a truth-for-a-concealer.[324] Though one must depend on truths-for-a-concealer, such as words, definitions, examples, and so forth, in order to realize an ultimate truth, one must gain an understanding of an ultimate truth—an emptiness—in order to realize that a truth-for-a-concealer is just a truth-for-a-concealer. Beings whose minds have not turned toward emptiness do not actually know truths-for-a-concealer as such, though indeed they perceive and use them every day. Thus, the name 'truth-for-a-concealer', itself is a call toward an understanding of emptiness. The same impact is present when *saṃvṛtisatya* is taken as 'conventional truth', for it implies that there is a non-conventional analytical consciousness for which these objects do not exist the way they appear. Also, *saṃvṛtisatya* as 'interdependent existent' calls for a recognition of the lack of independent or inherent existence. However, the most forceful meaning of *saṃvṛtisatya* is 'truth-for-a-concealer' which is used so predominantly that Jam-ȳang-shay-b̄a points out that it is not the only etymology of the term.[325]

In the Prāsaṅgika system there is no division of truths-for-a-concealer into the real and the unreal from the point of view of a reasoning consciousness because all are unreal in the sense of being falsities that do not exist the way they appear.[326] However, based on the world's discrimination of what is true or untrue, real or unreal, through determining whether, with respect to impermanent objects, they can perform functions in accordance with their appearance, the Prāsaṅgikas accept a division of truths-for-a-concealer into the real and unreal. The unreal are objects such as a mirror image which appears to be a face but cannot perform the functions of a face. A mirror image exists, however, and, therefore, can be classed among the two truths. An example of a real conventional truth is a face.

Even though an ignorant consciousness accepts an inherently existent person to be true, an inherently existent person is not a truth-for-a-concealer, real or unreal, because such does not exist. Therefore, the etymology of *saṃvṛtisatya* as an object which the concealer, ignorance, takes to exist the way it appears is wider than the actual meaning of the term. Things that ignorance assumes to be true but do not at all exist cannot be classed among the two truths, which are only existents. Thus, the name 'truth-for-a-concealer' is not a definition. Just as Buddha said that all products are deceptive, so his choice of a name for conventional objects, 'truths-for-a-concealer', points to an error in the perception of them: they seem to exist in and of themselves, but do not.

INTERPRETATION OF SCRIPTURE AND PHENOMENA

Sources
Geshe Gedün Lodrö's oral teachings
Corresponding section of the translation pp.595-623

Sutras that mainly and explicitly teach ultimate truths are definitive (*nītārtha, nges don*) because the mode of existence of the phenomena discussed in such passages is *definite* as just what is said.[327] No further interpretation is necessary to discover the way things are.

Though a direct cognition of ultimate truth cannot be described exactly as it is, the cognition and its object can be taught.[328] For example, as Chandrakīrti says, if one without cataracts tells another who has and sees hairs falling before him, 'There are no hairs here,' the person with cataracts will not realize the lack of hairs the way the person without the disease does; however, it cannot be said that he does not realize the non-existence of the hairs. In the same way, when someone who lacks the contaminations of the darkness of ignorance teaches about suchness, a listener cannot realize it the way the speaker does, but it is accepted that in general it is not that he does not realize suchness.

When Shāntideva says that 'the ultimate is not an object of the mind', he means that it is not an object of direct perception by a dualistic mind.[329] A non-dualistic wisdom consciousness, which in relation to its cognitum emptiness is like water poured into water, is needed in order to know an emptiness just as it is experienced by a Superior. Kensur Lekden said that after direct cognition a yogi intensely wishes to tell others how it is, but no words succeed.

Sutras that mainly and explicitly teach truths-for-a-concealer require interpretation (*neyārtha, drang don*). Because the mode of being of the phenomena discussed in such passages is not explicitly presented, it is necessary to search out a mode of being other than what is explicitly said. In other words, sutras that do not explicitly teach emptiness must be interpreted in order to understand it. Their subjects may be validly established, but the final mode of being of these subjects is not explicitly mentioned.

Also, sutras that teach non-existent objects, such as a permanent self, must be interpreted to discover Buddha's intention in preaching such a doctrine to a particular type of trainee. The teaching of a permanent self has as its basis Buddha's thought that there is continuous rebirth. The purpose is to influence listeners, who for the time being cannot posit an impermanent self without becoming morally nihilistic, to accept cause and effect and thereby generate devotion to virtue which yields rebirths of high status. The teaching of a permanent self is refuted by the reasoning that a permanent self cannot be reborn since what is permanent cannot change.

Other sutras must be interpreted just to discover what is being said. For instance, a passage that says, 'Father and mother are to be killed,' does not even say that father and mother are to be killed. Rather, it says that 'existence'—the fully potentialized latency that in the next moment will become a new life—and 'attachment', which nourishes this latency (see pp.280-1), must be destroyed. Such passages must be interpreted first to determine what is being said and then to determine the mode of existence—emptiness—of the phenomena discussed.

In definitive sutras the mode of being is *definite* right there in the texts, but this does not mean that literal passages requiring interpretation are indefinite in the sense of not being validly established.[330] 'Definitive' here connotes not only validity but also ultimacy.

'Sutras' are passages spoken by Buddha and not necessarily whole texts; even a few words or a phrase can be a sutra. Thus, because all actual Perfection of Wisdom Sutras are definitive, some phrases in books called Perfection of Wisdom Sutras which set forth conventionalities, such as the location of the discourse, are not actual Perfection of Wisdom Sutras. For they require interpretation to determine the final mode of being of the phenomena discussed, such as the location's emptiness of objectively established existence. Also, because actual Perfection of Wisdom Sutras are literal, though the phrase, 'There are no forms', is accepted as spoken by Buddha, Buddha did not speak a phrase *teaching* that there are no forms. He taught that forms are not *inherently* existent as is clearly specified in various Perfection of Wisdom Sutras, such as the *Heart of Wisdom*; this qualification is extended to all similar instances in the text. Buddha never taught that there are no forms because teaching or not teaching a doctrine is determined on the basis of whether there is or is not a student for it. There must be a special or specific type of trainee for a teaching, and there are no special students for a teaching that there are no forms. Buddha taught that forms do not inherently exist, that forms are impermanent, that forms are not different entities from perceiving consciousnesses, and so forth.

The Chittamātrins, unlike the Prāsaṅgikas, do not make a division of definitive and requiring interpretation on the basis of whether ultimate or conventional truths are taught but on the basis of whether the teaching in the sutra is literally acceptable. This means that for the Chittamātrins all sutras of which the teaching is validly established, such as of the five aggregates, are definitive; those which are not validly established, such as of a self-sufficient person, require interpretation.

For the Chittamātrins, the Perfection of Wisdom Sutras are nevertheless the supreme of all Buddha's sutras, but their speaking of an absence of natural existence is not said to be literal. For them, Perfection of Wisdom Sutras are not definitive and require interpretation, not because their subject matter is secondary but merely because they are not literal. The special students of the Perfection of Wisdom Sutras must be of sharper faculties than those of the *Sutra Unravelling the Thought*, a definitive sutra, because from the Perfection of Wisdom Sutras themselves they must be able to determine the Chittamātrin presentation of the three natures and so forth without relying on a text, such as the *Sutra Unravelling the Thought*, which clearly differentiates what does and does not truly exist.

The Svātantrikas agree with the Prāsaṅgikas that definitive sutras mainly and explicitly teach emptiness. However, the Svātantrikas hold that a definitive sutra must be literal. For instance, the *Heart of Wisdom Sutra* where it says that phenomena do not inherently exist is non-literal because it requires qualification to indicate that *ultimately* (*paramārthatas, don dam par*) phenomena do not exist inherently, since for Svātantrikas phenomena inherently exist *conventionally*. In the Svātantrika school, to be literal a sutra that teaches ultimate truths must specify 'ultimately' in its refutation of inherent existence, though it need not be specified explicitly in every instance.

That scriptural passages are to be divided into definitive and requiring interpretation is taught in sutra itself through the four reliances:[331] (1) rely on doctrine, not on persons; (2) rely on meaning, not on words; (3) rely on definitive sutras, not on those requiring interpretation; and (4) rely on wisdom, not on knowledge.

Initially, at the time of hearing the teaching, one should not rely on the person of the teacher, looking to his fame, wealth, and so forth. Rather, one should listen to anyone's teaching that explains the path out of suffering. One should not take the words as most important but mainly pay attention to the meaning. Again, when thinking about the teaching, one should take definitive sutras as most important and should recognize that those requiring interpretation are a means of realizing the definitive—emptiness. When practicing, one should not feel satisfied with just the knowledge arising from hearing and thinking but should devote oneself to generating the non-conceptual wisdom arising from meditation.

The two types of scriptures are also differentiated in sutras teaching that all products are falsities, thus establishing that passages propounding the non-true existence of products are definitive. (Sutras often take products as their examples of falsities, but this does not mean that non-products, such as space, are not falsities. Rather, products are the chief of objects encountered by common beings and, therefore, are singled out as falsities, appearing one way and existing another.)[332]

Nāgārjuna's refutation of production, establishing that production does not inherently exist, indicates through reasoning that sutras which speak of inherently existent production or do not mention the actual empty status of production require interpretation. Consequently, sutras that specify production as lacking inherent existence are definitive.

Nāgārjuna himself did not explicitly state in any of his works on which sutra he was relying for his differentiation of sutras into two types.[333] However, one can infer from his mode of procedure that he was relying on the *Teaching of Akṣhayamati Sutra* which is quoted as a source for the differentiation by Chandrakīrti in his

Clear Words, by Avalokitavrata in his commentary on Bhāvaviveka's *Lamp for (Nāgārjuna's) 'Wisdom' (Prajñāpradīpa)*, and by Kamalashīla in his *Illumination of the Middle Way*.

It is said that the Prāsaṅgika system presents Buddha's own final differentiation of the two types of scriptures even though it contradicts the thought of the *Sutra Unravelling the Thought*, which the Chittamātrins use as their basis for the division. However, it does not contradict *Buddha's* thought when he taught the *Sutra Unravelling the Thought*, in that the latter merely accords with the mentality of certain Mahāyāna disciples who were incapable of comprehending the final teaching. It is similar to the non-contradiction in terms of Buddha's own thought when he taught Hīnayānists that killing was totally forbidden but taught Mahāyānists that killing is permitted in certain circumstances. (Bodhisattvas—some say eighth grounders and above and some say first grounders and above—may, in order to help others, commit seven of the ten non-virtues: killing, stealing, sexual misconduct, lying, speaking harshly, speaking divisively, and chattering senselessly.[334] However, they are never allowed to commit the three mental non-virtues—covetousness, harmfulness, and wrong views. In general, these seven non-virtues are permitted when they are the only possible way to stop someone from bringing great harm on himself or others; thus, they are performed altruistically, not with an intent to harm.)

The *Sutra Unravelling the Thought* sets forth three turnings of the wheel of doctrine by Buddha. The division into three is made according to subject matter, specifically the manner in which selflessness is presented.[335] The first turning is comprised of sutras that set forth the selflessness of persons but do not refute that phenomena are established by way of their own character as bases of names and conceptions. The second is comprised of those that on the literal level set forth the non-true existence of all phenomena, without distinguishing that some do and others do not truly exist. The third is comprised of those that clearly discriminate the true existence of emptinesses and impermanent phenomena and the non-true existence of imaginary phenomena. Since the Chittamātrins follow the *Sutra Unravelling the Thought*, they assert that all sutras of the first and second wheels require interpretation whereas all those of the third wheel are definitive. The Prāsaṅgikas, on the other hand, assert that the first and third wheels as explained in the *Sutra Unravelling the Thought* require interpretation and that the middle wheel is definitive.

The three wheels of doctrine can also be arranged in a different manner. In this system the first wheel is comprised of sutras mainly spoken for Hīnayāna disciples, teaching the four noble truths and concordant topics. 'Hīnayāna disciples' are Hearers and Solitary Realizers, who do not have separate wheels of the teaching because Solitary Realizers can attain their paths in reliance on the Hearers' division of the teaching. The second wheel is comprised of sutras mainly spoken for Mahāyānists, those of the wheel of signlessness, such as the Perfection of Wisdom Sutras and so forth, as well as those teaching concordant topics. The third wheel is comprised of sutras mainly spoken for Mahāyānists, those of the wheel of good discrimination, such as the *Sutra Unravelling the Thought* and so forth as well as those teaching concordant topics.

According to the Prāsaṅgikas, a sutra of the first wheel, which is meant for Hīnayānists, is not necessarily a first wheel sutra *as set forth* in the *Sutra Unravelling the Thought*, for according to the Prāsaṅgika system, Hīnayānists cognize the same selflessness as Mahāyānists, and therefore, many first wheel passages do not require interpretation. Without realizing the emptiness of inherent existence through understanding that analytically findable existence does not occur, liberation is impossible. Thus, a central Prāsaṅgika tenet is that some Hīnayāna scriptures also teach the final mode of being of objects.[336]

Without understanding the mode of being of objects—without understanding that objects are not their own final mode of being—no one, Hīnayānist or Mahāyānist, can uproot the basis for the afflictions that bind beings in cyclic existence, the mistaken notion that objects exist from their own side right with their bases of designation. Thus, both Hīnayānists and Mahāyānists—those motivated primarily to get out of cyclic existence for themselves and those mainly seeking others' welfare—must cognize the middle way between the extremes of over-concretized existence and no existence at all, seeing the compatibility between emptiness and dependent-arising.

To accomplish this, a practitioner must distinguish between what teachings are definitive in that they present the final mode of subsistence of objects and what teachings require interpretation to arrive at that final mode of being. This differentiation, moreover, is not limited to scriptures, but must be carried over to objects as well—emptinesses being definitive and all other objects requiring interpretation to arrive at their final mode of subsistence. The basis of this is a division of hermeneutics in Mādhyamika into two categories—of the objects of expressions (*brjod bya'i drang nges*) such as chairs, tables, bodies, and emptinesses; and of means of expression (*rjod byed drang nges*) such as sutras. A practitioner is called to interpret all ordinary objects of experience to discover their inner nature.

Part Five
Prāsaṅgika-Mādhyamika

1 *The Prāsaṅgika School*

Sources
Nga-w̄ang-b̄el-den's *Annotations*
Kensur Lekden's oral teachings
Corresponding section of the translation pp.586-8

The works of both Nāgārjuna and Āryadeva are considered by both Svātantrikas and Prāsaṅgikas to be reliable sources.[337] From the Prāsaṅgika point of view Nāgārjuna and Āryadeva are Prāsaṅgikas though neither specified themselves as such nor openly presented the special features of that system. They are called Model Mādhyamikas.[338]

Buddhapālita did not clearly specify that consequences are to be used in place of autonomous syllogisms;[339] however, his extensive use of consequences qualifies him, according to Jam-ȳang-shay-b̄a, to be the founder of the Prāsaṅgika school. It is with Bhāvaviveka's refutation of Buddhapālita and insistence on autonomous syllogisms that the necessity for a clear statement of Prāsaṅgika method arose. At that point, Chandrakīrti defined the system in relation to the other schools, clearly explicating the incorrectness of using autonomous syllogisms and the correctness of consequences for generating in another the view of the middle way, and it is for this reason that most Tibetan monastic colleges consider Chandrakīrti to be the founder of Prāsaṅgika.

Thus, the Partisan Prāsaṅgikas are those who explicitly differentiate themselves as Prāsaṅgikas through extensive use of consequences and/or through specific challenges of the Svātantrika viewpoint from a Prāsaṅgika standpoint. Among them are Buddhapālita, Chandrakīrti, Shāntideva, and Atīsha.

There are other Prāsaṅgikas who are neither Models because they were not used as valid sources by all Prāsaṅgikas and Svātantrikas nor Partisans because they did not explicitly reject the Svātantrika viewpoint. However, it can be seen from their works that their view accords with Prāsaṅgika; they are the Non-Partisan Prāsaṅgikas: Shākyamitra, Nāgabodhi, Rik-b̄ay-ku-juk (*Rigs-pa'i-khu-byug*, a student of Chandrakīrti), Shūra (Ashvaghoṣha), etc.

SYNONYMS

Prāsaṅgikas are called Only Appearance Mādhyamikas, for as Chandrakīrti says (see p.586), they assert the existence of conventional phenomena—those phenomena which appear to the conventional mind—by way of their conditionality, not through asserting any of the four extremes: that phenomena inherently exist, utterly do not exist, both inherently exist and utterly do not exist, or are another inherently existent alternative.

'Conditionality' (*idaṃpratyayatā, rkyen nyid 'di pa tsam*), or 'having this particular condition, is a synonym for the dependent-arising of compounded phenomena.[340] Not covered by the term 'conditionality' is the dependent-arising of uncompounded phenomena, such as space, analytical cessations, non-analytical cessations, and emptinesses. Non-products—or permanent phenomena—are dependent-arisings in two ways: (1) they arise, or exist, in dependence on their parts or bases of imputation, and (2) they arise, or exist, in dependence on a conceptual consciousness that imputes them. For example, the space of a room is imputed or designated to an absence of obstructive contact and to the space of the various parts of the room; thus, it depends both on its bases of designation and on the mind that designates it.

Here, with regard to permanent phenomena, 'arising' in the term 'dependent-arising' does not mean 'being produced' but 'existing' (*sat, yod pa*) or 'established' (*siddha, grub pa*). Permanent phenomena are dependent-arisings in that they are 'dependently existent' or 'dependently established'.

The dependent-arising of impermanent phenomena is itself a sign that products are not produced from themselves, naturally existent others, both, or causelessly. The first alternative and the last two alternatives require no qualification; however, the second, production from other, does require the qualification 'naturally existent'. For products are indeed conventionally produced from causes that are conventionally existent others. There is no production, even conventionally, which can bear analysis, but there is conventionally existent self and other and conventionally existent production from what is other. Self and other are mutually dependent as are cause and effect. Because of being interdependent, they cannot be naturally existent, that is to say, established by way of their own character.

It is by way of this conditionality that a Prāsaṅgika accepts phenomena. The Sanskrit word translated by 'phenomena' is *dharma*. Because all *dharma* are objects of knowledge (*jñeya, shes bya*), they can appear to the mind, and thus the word 'phenomena' from the Greek *phainómenon* meaning 'appearance' is used as a translation equivalent. There are impermanent and permanent phenomena, and in this system of translation there is no noumenon which is not a phenomenon. For even emptiness is a phenomenon in that it appears to the mind and is an object (*viṣhaya, yul*); in the Prāsaṅgika system nothing exists independently, in and of itself, as 'noumenon' suggests. Even an emptiness is a dependent-arising because it is imputed to a lack of inherent existence which is its basis of imputation and, like all other phenomena, cannot be found when sought among its bases of imputation.[341] Just as much as a chair is not its legs, arms, back, or seat, or even their composite, so the emptiness of a chair is not the lack of inherent existence of the legs, arms, back, or seat, or even their composite.

'Conditionality' refers to the dependent-arising of products, and indeed all Buddhist schools of tenets accept that products are dependent-arisings inasmuch as all effects depend on causes. However, the Prāsaṇgika sense of 'conditionality' is brought into focus when it is seen that they accept the dependence not only of effects on causes but also of causes on effects. For a seed is a cause only in relation to its effect, a sprout. (For convenience, a sprout can be considered to be a shoot of some height when the two bulbous halves of the seed are no longer present and a root system has developed.) Its ability to produce an effect, given the proper conditions, makes it a cause. Except in relation to the sprout, how can it be said that a seed is a cause? This is obvious and requires no special analysis, for in the Prāsaṅgika system, if anything could bear ultimate analysis, it would inherently exist whereas nothing inherently exists. That a cause is dependent on an effect is obvious to the ordinary non-analytical intellect.

However, no other Buddhist system of tenets—Vaibhāṣhika, Sautrāntika, Chittamātra, or even Svātantrika—accepts that causes are dependent on effects. They reason that causes do not rely on effects for their production whereas effects do rely on causes for their production. However, the Prāsaṅgikas' approach is from the viewpoint of the designation of the ultimately unfindable nominality 'cause' and not from the viewpoint of its production, for they agree that a cause does not depend on its effect for its production. The Prāsaṅgika assertion of the interdependence of cause and effect highlights their emphasis on the interrelated nature of names and the naming process, the dependence of all phenomena on thought.

All phenomena are interdependent though each and every phenomenon is not interdependent with each and every other phenomenon. A calf depends on its causes, cow and bull, etc., and the cow and bull as parents depend on their calf though they were not born from the calf. Still, a calf and a pony are not dependent on each other.

It is by way of this conditionality that the one hundred and eight afflicted and purified phenomena are asserted to exist, but the name 'Only Appearance Mādhyamika' does not imply that

Prāsaṅgikas assert that phenomena merely appear to the mind whereas in fact they do not exist. Though analysis shows that phenomena ultimately do not exist, ultimate analysis does not deny that objects exist conventionally. Truly existent or inherently existent objects are rejected through Mādhyamika analysis but not the mere objects themselves. However, it is to be remembered that the status of conventionalities is such that they are not separate from their parts; they are neither their parts individually nor the composite of their parts. They are not their bases of imputation even conventionally. A chair is only the 'chair' imputed in dependence on legs, arms, back, seat, and so forth arranged in a certain shape. The conventions of the world are exactly the opposite of the Prāsaṅgika view on this point; the world, through beginningless ignorance, confuses the object imputed with the basis of imputation. All of the conventions of the world are not, then, accepted in the Prāsaṅgika system. The Prāsaṅgikas mostly accept those phenomena which the world says exist, but not the way the world feels those phenomena exist. Phenomena appear to the world to exist naturally, and the world assents to this appearance; such appearances are false, and such assent is mistaken.

In the same vein, Bu-dön (*Bu-ston*)[342] says that Prāsaṅgikas are called 'Mādhyamikas using what is renowned in the world' (*Loka-prasiddha-varga-chāri-mādhyamika*). The name is perhaps a deliberate contrast with the Hindu emphasis on scriptural wisdom over ignorant worldly conventions. However, even in the Prāsaṅgika system the world's ignorance is still the first link of the dependent-arising of the misery of cyclic existence. Therefore, the Prāsaṅgikas, though mostly accepting the world's opinion on what exists, do not enshrine every aspect of the worldly non-analytical intellect. For it is analysis itself that will break the knot of cyclic existence through rescuing beings from the tangles of misconception.

Prāsaṅgikas are also called Non-Abiding Mādhyamikas, or Thoroughly Non-Abiding Mādhyamikas, because through refuting inherent existence they avoid the extreme of permanence and through asserting conventional existence they avoid the extreme of annihilation. They do not abide in any way, coarse or subtle, in either, but in the middle or center which denotes neither a mixture of existence and non-existence nor a gray area of agnostic doubt. The middle way philosophically is the way things are—not mistaking what exists for what does not exist and not mistaking what does not exist for what exists.

All systems claim to occupy the center.[343] For example, the Dialectician Nihilists say that they avoid the extreme of permanence through not asserting phenomena which are beyond sense perception and avoid the extreme of annihilation through asserting those that are manifest to the senses. The Sāṃkhyas say that they avoid the extreme of permanence through asserting the transformation of states and avoid the extreme of annihilation through asserting the unchangeability of the nature. The Vaibhāṣhikas, the lowest Buddhist school of tenets, say that they avoid the extreme of permanence through asserting that all products are impermanent and avoid the extreme of annihilation through asserting that past and future objects are substantialities. The Sautrāntikas say that they avoid the extreme of permanence through not asserting that permanent phenomena, such as space, are substantial entities and avoid the extreme of annihilation through asserting that forms and so forth are naturally bases of names. The Chittamātrins say that they avoid the extreme of permanence through asserting that forms and so forth are not naturally bases of the affixing of names and avoid the extreme of annihilation through asserting that products and emptinesses truly exist.

The Svātantrika-Mādhyamikas say that they avoid the extreme of permanence through asserting that objects do not exist from the viewpoint of an objective mode of subsistence which is not established through the object's appearing to a non-defective consciousness. For all objects attain their inherent existence through appearing to a non-defective consciousness. The Svātantrikas do not find it contradictory to assert that objects have no objective, inherent existence which is not established by the mind and to assert that objects do exist inherently.[344] A beautiful woman created by a magician has no mode of being that is not posited by the mistaken minds of the audience who have come under the spell of the magician. However, this does not mean that the beautiful woman has no mode of being; she has one posited by a mistaken consciousness. Just so, though phenomena seem to have their own mode of being or own mode of subsistence free from any positing consciousness, they do not; however, they do have their own mode of subsistence within the scope of its being posited to them through their appearing to consciousness. In the case of the illusory woman, the positing consciousness is mistaken whereas in the case of phenomena the positing consciousness is correct or non-defective—free from error due to spells, moving objects, disease, and so on. The Svātantrikas, therefore, say that they avoid the extreme of annihilation through asserting that conventionally objects exist inherently or exist in their own right.

The Prāsaṅgikas find such to be contradictory, and thus they say that they avoid the extreme of permanence through asserting that objects do not exist inherently. For them, existing ultimately (*paramārthasiddha, don dam par grub pa*) and existing inherently (*svabhāvasiddha, rang bzhin gyis grub pa*) are synonymous whereas for the Svātantrikas they are not. The Prāsaṅgikas say that they avoid the extreme of annihilation through asserting that conventionally all phenomena are only nominal and exist only imputedly. They do not find it contradictory for phenomena to exist only designatedly and yet be able to perform functions. They do not find it contradictory for things to be unfindable among their bases of designation either singly or as a composite and yet exist. In fact, the only way that things can perform functions is to exist merely imputedly, for if objects did inherently exist, they could not be affected by causes nor could they affect anything. Existence would be impossible in a world of frozen substantialities; things would be static, for they would not depend on causes.

Objects are imputed in the way that a snake is imputed to a rope.[345] Just as much as a snake cannot be found among the parts of the rope either individually or collectively, so phenomena, even when correctly imputed, cannot be found among their bases of imputation, individually or collectively, and, of course, not separately. Nevertheless, there is a difference between a snake wrongly imputed to a rope and a snake rightly imputed to a proper basis of designation because the latter can perform the functions of a snake.

Therefore, when Prāsaṅgikas cite the example of a rope-snake, it illustrates only the mode of imputation; the purport of the example is not that the *existence* of phenomena is the same as the existence of a rope-snake. A rope-snake does not exist and cannot perform the functions of a snake whereas things do exist and create effects within the context of being ultimately unfindable nominalities.

The most difficult point in the Prāsaṅgika system is this: the utter unfindability of phenomena in their bases of designation and yet their ability to perform functions. Prāsaṅgikas do not deny the *bhāva* (*dngos po*) which is defined as 'that which is able to perform a function', particularly the function of creating an effect. They deny the *bhāva* which means inherent existence (*svabhāva, rang bzhin* in the sense of *rang bzhin gyis grub pa*), the non-dependence of things on their parts, their bases of designation, or the consciousness that designates them. Thus, when an emptiness of inherent existence is rightly seen in an object, understanding of imputed existence is furthered. When imputed existence is rightly seen, understanding of the emptiness of inherent existence is furthered. As long as these two are seen to be contradictory, that is, as long as a refutation of inherent existence seems to refute the effective existence of phenomena, one has not passed beyond the views of non-Mādhyamikas. Nāgārjuna's *Treatise on the Middle Way* (XXIV.14ab) says:

> For whom emptiness is possible
> For him all is possible.

This eliminates the view that Mādhyamikas themselves accept emptiness but accept conventional phenomena only in dependence on others' misconceptions. Nāgārjuna said that 'for him', that is, for the Mādhyamika who accepts emptiness, everything —all the objects, agents, and actions of cyclic existence and of nirvana—is suitable. The key to the Prāsaṅgika assertion of conventional phenomena is that though they assert the existence of what the world says exists, they do not assert that phenomena exist the way that the world sees them.

Not only are the world's habitual conceptions wrong but also other philosophies, far from actually abiding in the middle way, have fallen to extremes. They tie even tighter the knot of cyclic existence. All of these extremes are forsaken by the Prāsaṅgikas who detail with exactitude the way that phenomena exist. When emptiness of inherent existence is seen to be harmonious with imputed existence, then the middle way in which the Prāsaṅgikas abide can be cognized.

Vasubandhu

2 *Debate*

Sources
Jam-ȳang-shay-b̄a's *Great Exposition of the Middle Way*
Kensur Lekden's oral teachings
Geshe Gedün Lodrö's oral teachings

Buddhapālita's refutation—in commentary on the first chapter of Nāgārjuna's *Treatise on the Middle Way*—of the Sāṃkhya position that an effect is produced from a cause which is of the same nature as itself drew heavy criticism from Bhāvaviveka.[346] An examination of Buddhapālita's refutation, Bhāvaviveka's criticism, and Chandrakīrti's defense of Buddhapālita reveals central differences between the two divisions of Mādhyamika: Prāsaṅgika, founded by Buddhapālita/Chandrakīrti, and Svātantrika, founded by Bhāvaviveka.

The Sāṃkhya position is:

> The cause of a barley shoot is a barley seed, and its minor causes are water, manure, and so forth. The nature of the cause and of the minor causes is partless, and thus the nature of the seed is the nature of the water and of the manure, and the nature of the water is the nature of the

> seed and of the manure, and so on. For these causes have a common effect.
>
> The barley shoot exists at the time of the barley seed because the barley shoot abides in the nature of its causes at the time when they are still causes and when the effect or manifestation has not yet been produced. For example, a pot exists in the nature of the clay. Therefore, the nature of the causes and the nature of the effect are one and thus are each other.

Though some Sāṃkhyas speak not of production but of manifestation, the relationship of oneness of the nature and the manifestation is the same as with producer and produced, or cause and effect.

Buddhapālita flings consequences at the Sāṃkhyas' assertion. First he sets his thesis:

> Things are not produced from their own entities.

Then in answer to anyone's wondering what fallacies there are in asserting production of something from that which is of the same nature, he gives a brief refutation in the form of two consequences:

> There are the fallacies that their re-production would be senseless and, not only that, would also be endless.

Buddhapālita's actual words are: 'Things are not produced from their own entities because their production [again] would be just senseless and because production would be endless.'

The way he flings the consequence that re-production would be senseless is:

> It follows with respect to the subject, a sprout, that its production again is senseless because of already existing in its own entity.[347]

The Sāṃkhya, however, holds that what is existent but unmanifest must be made manifest. Therefore, he might answer that it is not entailed by something's already existing in its own entity that its production again is senseless. In that case, the second consequence of the endlessness of its production is flung:

> It follows with respect to the subject, a sprout, that its production is endless because, though it already exists in its own entity, there is sense in (or a need for) its re-production.

If the existent requires re-production, then even when the effect is manifest, it would still require re-production because it exists. Buddhapālita says, 'The production again of things already existent in their own entities is purposeless. If though existent they are produced, they would never not be produced.'

The Sāṃkhya holds that what has already been *manifested* need not be produced; therefore, he might again answer that there is no entailment. However, his answer does not hit the mark, for by switching from the vocabulary of production to that of manifestation he cannot escape inquiry about whether the manifestation exists at the time of its unmanifest state. If he says that the manifestation does not exist at the time of its unmanifest state, he would fall from his view that all products, *though formerly existent*, are manifested by causes because the manifestation would not exist at the time of its unmanifest state. Therefore, he might accept that the manifestation existed from the time of its unmanifest state. He would be saying that it is not entailed by a manifestation's existing at the time of its unmanifest state that it would not be produced again. Then the consequence of endlessness is flung:

> It follows about the subject, a manifestation, that its production is endless because, though it exists from the time of its unmanifest state, it has a need for production again.

CONSEQUENCES AND SYLLOGISMS

Consequences (*prasaṅga*) are used to generate in an opponent a consciousness that infers a thesis.[348] Unwanted consequences that contradict an opponent's position and arise from his position are frequently used. Employing a reason and a pervasion approved by the opponent, a consequence of his views which contradicts another of his views is presented to him.

For instance, if among the various tenets of a school there were the assertions that a sound is permanent, that a sound is a product, and that all products are impermanent, the following consequence would be stated:

> It follows that the subject, a sound, is not a product because of being a permanent phenomenon.

The opponent himself has accepted the reason, that a sound is a permanent phenomenon. He has accepted the pervasion, that whatever is a permanent phenomenon is not a product. Thus, he is forced to accept the unwanted thesis that a sound is not a product, and this contradicts his own view that a sound is a product. The stater of the consequence would say, 'The three spheres have been accepted!' This means that the reason, the pervasion of the reason by the predicate of the consequence, and the opposite of the consequence have been accepted.[349]

The sample consequence above also implies its opposite meaning:

> The subject, a sound, is an impermanent phenomenon because of being a product.

The opposite of the original reason is put as the predicate of the implied thesis, that is, 'permanent phenomenon' becomes 'impermanent phenomenon'. The opposite of the predicate of the original thesis is put as the reason of the implied syllogism, that is, 'not a product' becomes 'a product'.

To repeat, the consequence,

> It follows that the subject, a sound, is not a product because of being a permanent phenomenon,

implies the syllogism,

> The subject, a sound, is an impermanent phenomenon because of being a product.

Through the statement of the consequence, a consciousness that infers the implied opposite meaning is generated in the opponent.

Non-Prāsaṅgikas also use consequences to break down the vibrance or pointedness of the opponent's adherence to his own view. However, they do not accept that a consequence *alone* can generate in the opponent a consciousness inferring the implied thesis. Prāsaṅgikas assert that the statement of a consequence alone is sufficient, provided the opponent is intelligent and ready. To such an opponent, a further explicit statement of a syllogism is purposeless.

The intent is to generate in the opponent an inferring consciousness, though not necessarily through the route of implying the opposite meaning as just explained. For instance, Buddhapālita's consequences above are intended to generate in the Sāṃkhya a consciousness which infers that there is no production from self and not that there is production from other.

Jam-ȳang-shay-b̄a's *Great Exposition of the Middle Way*[350] lists five types of consequences.

1 *Consequence generating an other-approved inference, i.e., generating an inference in another using a subject, reason, and pervasion approved in the opponent's system*

> *Example:* It follows that the subject [of this consequence], a sprout, is not a dependent-arising because of being objectively existent.

This type is also called 'a consequence implying its opposite meaning'. It both contradicts the opponent's assertion that a sprout is a dependent-arising and implicitly establishes that a sprout does not objectively exist. The other-approved syllogism which is implied by the consequence is:

> The subject [of this syllogism], a sprout, is not objectively existent because of being a dependent-arising.

The above consequence would be flung at a Buddhist proponent of objectively existent things. Svātantrika and the other lower

Buddhist systems accept that all impermanent things are dependent-arisings at least in the sense that they arise dependent on an aggregation of causes and conditions, and they also accept that the very sign of their dependent-arising proves their objective existence. For them, if things did not objectively exist, they would not exist at all.

If, after the statement of the consequence, the opponent were still recalcitrant, his answer would be, 'The opposite is entailed', meaning that whatever is a dependent-arising is objectively existent. However, his answer would not hit the mark because the meaning of 'objectively existent' is 'independently existent', thereby contradicting dependent-arising. The opponent might require more consequences to reveal to him his self-contradiction. However, for one who is ready to realize his self-contradiction, the above consequence is sufficient to generate in him a consciousness inferring that a sprout does not objectively exist and, by extension, that all phenomena do not objectively exist.

2 *Consequence through similarity of reason*

> *Example:* It follows that a sound apprehending ear consciousness sees colors and shapes because a color and shape apprehending eye consciousness *ultimately* sees colors and shapes.

If an eye consciousness ultimately saw colors and shapes, then it would be independent, that is, would not depend on the eye sense that endows it with the ability to perceive colors and shapes but not sounds. Since consciousnesses would apprehend their objects without dependence on their respective senses, an ear consciousness would also absurdly apprehend colors and shapes. The thesis being implied is that an eye consciousness and, in general, sense consciousnesses do not ultimately perceive their objects. The implied thesis here, however, is not, as in the previous example, the subject plus the opposite of the reason.

3 *Contradictory consequence*

> *Example:* It follows that the subject, the ox-generality

which is a permanent thing, does not pervade its many particular instances because of being a partless unity.

This consequence merely demonstrates a contradiction in the opponent's view and neither implies the opposite meaning, like the first type of consequence, nor uses a similarity of reason, like the second. The opposite meaning would be:

The subject, the ox-generality which is a permanent thing, is not a partless unity because of its pervading its many instances.

It is true that the ox-generality is not a partless one because it has as many parts as the number of oxen it 'pervades' or encompasses. However, the ox-generality is impermanent because all instances of ox are impermanent. Thus, the subject of the thesis, the permanent ox-generality, does not exist and, therefore, could not be proved to possess the quality of the reason, that is, it could not be shown that the permanent ox-generality has as many parts as the number of oxen it pervades.

The implied thesis of this consequence is not its opposite meaning but that an ox-generality which is a permanent thing does not exist. Another implied is:

The ox-generality has parts because of pervading its many particular instances.

The opponent here is a non-Buddhist Vaisheṣhika.

The other types of consequences are contradictory, but this type is *merely* contradictory in that it does not share the special qualities of the other four types.

4 *Consequence expressing contradiction and proving one's own assertion*

Example: It follows that the subject, a sprout, is senselessly re-produced because of already having attained its own entity.

A Sāṃkhya accepts that re-production is sensible in the sense that what has already attained existence in its non-manifest state still requires production to become manifest. Therefore, the consequence of senseless re-production expresses an inner contradiction of this position. Furthermore, since the view being proved by this consequence is that there is no production from self, the Prāsaṅgika's own assertion is being proved. Again, the issue is not that only some consequences prove something, either positive or negative, for all correct consequences prove something. Rather, this type of consequence is distinguished by its particular force, as in the example where no production from self is proved but the opposite of the reason is not implied.

5 *Consequence established through similarity of reason and thesis*

If someone said that it followed that the form aggregate exists inherently because the feeling aggregate exists inherently, this consequence would be stated:

> It follows that the reason 'the feeling aggregate inherently exists' cannot prove that the form aggregate inherently exists because the reason and thesis are equally difficult to prove.

Even if there were inherent existence, there is no difference in difficulty of realization in establishing that the feeling aggregate inherently exists and that the form aggregate inherently exists. To fulfill the purpose of generating the inference of a thesis in another, the establishment of the sign (reason) as present in the subject must be easier than the realization of the thesis. For instance, a sound is proven to be an impermanent thing through the sign of its being a product. Though 'impermanent thing' and 'product' are synonyms because all instances of the one are instances of the other, being a product can serve as a correct sign of being an impermanent thing, for being a product is easier to understand than being an impermanent thing. To be a product means to be made, and a mere snapping of the fingers can demonstrate that a sound is made or created by causes and conditions. That products are impermanent, i.e., that they necessarily disintegrate moment by moment, is harder to realize. Therefore, when the reason is as hard to establish as the thesis, the reason is not suitable.

Much like a consequence, a syllogism (*prayoga, sbyor ba*) consists of a thesis and reason; however, in the logic school of Dignāga and Dharmakīrti the stater of a syllogism must himself accept the reason's presence in the subject, the pervasion of the reason by the predicate of the thesis, and the pervasion of the negative of the predicate by the negative of the reason. For instance:

> The subject, a pot, is an impermanent thing because of being arisen from exertion—just as, for example, speech [is arisen from exertion and is impermanent].

The stater of the syllogism must accept the reason's presence in the subject—that a pot is arisen from exertion. He must accept the pervasion—that all things arisen from exertion are impermanent—and the counter-pervasion—that all permanent things are not arisen from exertion. However, in the case of a consequence neither subject, predicate, nor reason need be accepted by the stater. It is only necessary that the opponent accept, or be forced from his own position to accept, these three. Consequences are means of dealing with opponents on their own grounds, and Chandrakīrti declares that, if the opponent will not accept consequences stemming from his own views, there is no point in proceeding to state syllogisms to him.[351]

Thus, first of all, the difference between the Svātantrika Bhāvaviveka on the one side and the Prāsaṅgika Buddhapālita on the other is Bhāvaviveka's insistence on the eventual statement of syllogisms. It is not that Prāsaṅgikas do not use syllogisms amongst themselves when there is agreement on the status of the subject, etc.; rather, the point at issue is what constitutes the necessary and best means of generating in an opponent the view that phenomena do not truly exist.

This controversy stems from different opinions on whether phenomena appear correctly to a non-defective sense consciousness. The Prāsaṅgika position is that not only do ordinary beings misconceive the nature of phenomena but also phenomena *appear* to them in a mistaken aspect. In other words, an assenting to an *incorrect appearance* of phenomena as inherently existent is what constitutes the misconception that phenomena inherently exist. Even for eighth ground Bodhisattvas and Foe Destroyers (both of whom have totally overcome the conception that things inherently exist) phenomena still *appear* as if inherently existent. It is only for a Buddha that phenomena appear just as they are.

Thus the Prāsaṅgikas say that although a sense consciousness can be valid with respect to the existence of its object, it is never, except in the case of a Buddha, correct about the mode of existence of the object. For, due to the force of previous conditioning, objects appear to a sense consciousness as if existing objectively whereas they do not. They cannot be found among their bases of designation when sought, but appear as if existent in their own right.

However, Bhāvaviveka's school, Sautrāntika-Svātantrika, asserts that phenomena appear correctly in terms of their inherent existence to a non-defective sense consciousness. Bhāvaviveka agrees that phenomena appear to sense consciousnesses to exist by way of their own character and asserts that they exist so. From this basis, he says that it is possible to state a syllogism in which subject and reason appear similarly to both parties in the debate. Bhāvaviveka asserts that being arisen from exertion conventionally exists *inherently* in a pot, as do the natures of pervasion and counter-pervasion whereas a Prāsaṅgika sees the presence of the reason in the subject, the pervasion, and the counter-pervasion as existing imputedly or nominally, without inherent existence.

Both systems accept that an inferring consciousness is a valid cognizer (*pramāṇa, tshad ma*). The statement of a valid reason that the subject possesses and which itself possesses the proper pervasion and counter-pervasion is not just verbal manipulation but a revelation of the nature of things which is hidden to the direct perception of ordinary beings. Prāsaṅgika, as well as Svātantrika, relies on inference to gain an understanding of emptiness. A meditator's statement to himself and intense reflection on consequences and syllogisms in meditation are presented in both sutra and tantra systems as the means of gaining a familiarity with emptiness. Thus, in both sutra and tantra, cognition of emptiness through inference is a prerequisite for direct cognition.

According to Prāsaṅgika, once the view of emptiness is about to be entered, syllogisms about the final nature of phenomena are appropriate; however, when debating with those who are not yet about to generate the view in their continuum, consequences mainly are used. The case is the same in meditation; consequences are stated in order to break down one's own adherence to the wrong view; then, syllogisms may be stated, if necessary.

Without considering the difference between Prāsaṅgika and Svātantrika, the definition of a Mādhyamika in general is:[352]

> A proponent of Buddhist tenets who totally refutes all extremes of permanence, i.e., that any phenomenon ultimately exists, and refutes all extremes of annihilation, i.e., that phenomena do not exist conventionally.

Therefore, all Mādhyamikas—Prāsaṅgikas and Svātantrikas—avoid the extreme of permanence or existence through refuting that phenomena ultimately exist, truly exist, or exist as their own reality. They avoid the extreme of annihilation or non-existence through asserting that all phenomena exist conventionally, or nominally.

The word *madhyama* itself refers to the middle way that things are, the profound meaning of dependent-arising free from the two extremes, permanence and annihilation. The extremes here are misrepresentations of existence and non-existence. Because phenomena do not exist ultimately, the ultimate existence of phenomena is an extreme of existence. Because phenomena do exist conventionally, the non-existence of phenomena conventionally is an extreme of non-existence. Avoiding the extremes of existence and non-existence, however, does not mean that Mādhyamikas refrain from making assertions about existence and non-existence because they do assert that phenomena exist conventionally but not ultimately, even if these assertions exist only nominally.

A Svātantrika is a Mādhyamika who asserts that a non-defective consciousness which perceives an object as existing inherently in its basis of imputation is valid and thus accepts that an object so cognized appears similarly to both parties in a debate.[353] Based on the common appearance of a subject, the Svātantrika states a reason to prove a predicate about this subject. Thus, the definition of a Svātantrika-Mādhyamika is:

> A proponent of no true existence who asserts that conventionally all phenomena exist by way of their own character.

Truly existent phenomena are refuted by Svātantrikas through relying on a logical mark, a reason, that has the inherently existent threefold aspects: presence in the subject, pervasion, and counter-pervasion. This usage of autonomous inferences (*svatantra-anumāna, rang rgyud kyi rjes dpag*) to generate in an opponent a cognition of emptiness is the source of their name.

The definition of a Prāsaṅgika is:

> A Mādhyamika who does not assert that phenomena exist by way of their own character even conventionally.

Etymologically, a Prāsaṅgika is so called because of asserting that an inferential consciousness realizing a thesis of no inherent existence can be generated in the mental continuum of a disputant through only the demonstration of consequences (*prasaṅga, thal 'gyur*).[354]

According to Prāsaṅgika all sense information is characterized by misinformation about the status of objects, for things undeniably appear to common beings to exist inherently in their bases of designation. Therefore, consequences that operate within the sphere of a non-Mādhyamika's own views are relied upon to convince him that nothing can bear analysis, thereby causing him to realize the absence of objectively established existence.

Thus, Svātantrikas and Prāsaṅgikas are named on the basis of the means by which they generate in others the view that phenomena do not truly exist.

Dignāga

3 *Bhāvaviveka's Criticism of Buddhapālita*

Sources
Bhāvaviveka's *Lamp for (Nāgārjuna's) 'Wisdom'*
Avalokitavrata's *Commentary on (Bhāvaviveka's) 'Lamp for (Nāgārjuna's) "Wisdom"'*
Jam-ȳang-shay-b̄a's *Great Exposition of the Middle Way*
Kensur Lekden's oral teachings

The split between Svātantrika and Prāsaṅgika grew out of Bhāvaviveka's criticism of Buddhapālita's refutation of the Sāṃkhya view that an effect is produced from a cause which is the same entity as the effect.[355] Their commentaries on the first chapter of Nāgārjuna's *Treatise on the Middle Way* reveal their differences. Buddhapālita said:

> Things are not produced from their own entities because their production [again] would be just senseless and because production would be endless. It is thus: the production again of things already existing in their own entities is purposeless. If though existent they are produced, they would never not be produced.

Bhāvaviveka took the first sentence not merely as a brief display of a thesis and consequences but as indicating an autonomous syllogism (*svatantra-anumāna, rang rgyud kyi rjes dpag*). (*Svatantra* is usually translated as 'independent' rather than 'autonomous'; however, the very motto of Buddha's teaching is dependent-arising, and thus 'independent' for *svatantra* seems a too obvious self-contradiction. Also, here 'inference' does not refer to a consciousness, but to a syllogistic statement. Therefore, *svatantra-anumāna* is translated often as 'autonomous syllogism'.)

According to Bhāvaviveka, Buddhapālita's autonomous syllogism, if taken at face value, is:

> The subjects, things, are not produced from their own entities because production is senseless and endless.

Bhāvaviveka thought that the reason as stated would obviously not be Buddhapālita's intended reason, for Buddhapālita himself would not assert that production is senseless and endless. He thought that Buddhapālita's intended meaning would have to be:

> The subjects, things, are not produced from their own entities because production is sensible and has an end.

According to Bhāvaviveka, this autonomous syllogism sets forth a thesis of non-production from self but cannot prove it because it offers neither a reason nor an example which have the capacity of refuting production from self. This is Bhāvaviveka's first objection to Buddhapālita's mode of reasoning.

Bhāvaviveka states his own syllogism refuting production from self as an example of a correct autonomous syllogism:

> The subjects, the inner sources (see p.273) such as an eye sense, are not ultimately produced from self because of existing—like, for example, existent consciousness [which exists and is not produced from itself].

For a Sāṃkhya, the person or consciousness is eternal and thus not a product; therefore, just as a person or consciousness requires no production, so an eye sense requires no production because it exists (even in its unmanifest state).

Bhāvaviveka's second objection to Buddhapālita's supposedly intended syllogism is this: A Sāṃkhya would question what 'production from self' or 'production from their own entities' means. Does it mean production of effects from already manifest entities? If it does, Buddhapālita's syllogism is proving what is already established for Sāṃkhyas since Sāṃkhyas themselves accept that the manifest is produced from the non-manifest and, once manifest, requires no further manifestation. Because Sāṃkhyas do not accept that effects are produced from entities which are already manifest, Buddhapālita would be laboring to prove what they already accept.

Or, the Sāṃkhya's question would be: Does the reference to production from self apply to production of an effect from the entity of the non-manifest nature (*prakṛti, rang bzhin*)? If so, the syllogism would prove just the opposite of what Buddhapālita intended. It could not prove that there is no production from self because all products are produced from the nature. The Sāṃkhya would say:

> The subjects, things, are produced from themselves, that is, from the nature which is the same entity as themselves, because production is sensible and has an end.

Therefore, Bhāvaviveka concludes that Buddhapālita's intended syllogism does not avoid the fallacies that a Sāṃkhya, having analyzed the thesis, would be expected to adduce.

Also, as a third fault, because Buddhapālita stated something that is not established as his reason—that production would be senseless and endless—it must be reversed into: production is sensible and has an end. This being so, the predicate of the thesis also must be reversed; it must be changed from 'Things are not produced from themselves' to 'Things are produced from others'.

To restate this step, the reason as stated ('production is senseless and endless') is unacceptable because it must be a property of the subject ('things'), and it is not established that things have senseless and endless production. Therefore, the reason must be changed to 'production is sensible and has an end' in consideration of Buddhapālita's 'actual' meaning, for it is established that things have sensible and finite production.

Furthermore, Bhāvaviveka would claim that Buddhapālita could not have intended his reason to mean:

> If produced from themselves, it would be senseless and endless.

For syllogistically this would be:

> The subjects, things, are not produced from self because, if produced from self, their production would be senseless and endless.

The reason why Buddhapālita supposedly could not have meant this is that when the reason is established, the thesis would already be established. Contrary to this, it is always necessary to establish that the reason is a property of the subject, then establish that the predicate of the thesis follows from the reason, and then, for the first time, realize the predicate of the thesis as a quality of the subject. In other words, when it is established that if things are produced from self, their production is senseless and endless, it is already established that things are not produced from self. There would be no point in further establishing the concomitance of the predicate of the thesis, 'no production from self' with the reason, 'if produced from self, their production would be senseless and endless'. Therefore, Bhāvaviveka concludes that since it is 'clear' that Buddhapālita himself did not accept what he explicitly stated, he must have meant:

> The subjects, things, are produced from others because production is sensible and has an end.

Bhāvaviveka says that Buddhapālita thereby contradicts the Mādhyamika tenet that the refutation of the four extreme types of production is a non-affirming negation (*prasajya-pratiṣhedha, med dgag*). In other words, when production from self is refuted, production from other should not be implied in its place. Even though Buddhapālita did not state as an explicit thesis that things are produced from others, Bhāvaviveka decided that this was his implicit thesis, and, therefore, his explicit thesis becomes an affirming negation (*paryudāsa-pratiṣhedha, ma yin dgag*)—an explicit negation of production from self which implies an affirmation of production from other in its place. According to Bhāvaviveka, Buddhapālita's explicit thesis actually is:

> About the subjects, things, their production from themselves is not just eliminated.

In the Mādhyamika system a thesis of any of the four extreme types of production is just to be eliminated; nothing is to be implied in its place, not even conventionally existent production, even though such is validly established as existing. If an affirming negation were set forth, it would contradict the intention of Nāgārjuna's *Treatise* to eliminate all elaborations (*prapañcha, spros pa*) of true existence for which only non-affirming negations are appropriate. If an affirming negation were used, one would then be seeking to affirm that things are conventionally produced, rather than merely eliminating that phenomena are produced from self, other, both, and neither and seeking to take this mere absence as one's object in meditative equipoise. Thus, if Bhāvaviveka's description of Buddhapālita's intention is correct, the latter would indeed have erred.

Bhāvaviveka would add that although it is not the case in general that when a reason is reversed the thesis also has to be reversed, Buddhapālita's intention was clearly not just to prove no true existence but also to prove that production exists nominally or conventionally.[356] For in his introductory remarks to his commentary on the first chapter of the *Treatise*, Buddhapālita indicates that the first chapter is in answer to an objector who says,[357] 'Show how this which is called production is only a convention.' Also, concluding a brief refutation of production from self, other, both, and neither, Buddhapālita says, 'Since the production of things is thus in all ways inadmissible, there is no production; therefore, this called production is only a convention.'[358]

Let us cite the entire passage in question from Buddhapālita's commentary:[359]

> Here [an objector] says, 'Show how this which is called production is only a convention.'
>
> Answer: That is shown first [in the first stanza of the first chapter of Nāgārjuna's *Treatise on the Middle Way*]:
>
> There is never production
> Anywhere, of any thing
> From itself, from others,
> From both, or without cause.
>
> Concerning this, if some things are produced, consider whether the production of those things is from self, from other, from both self and other, or causelessly. Upon examination it is not feasible in all ways.
>
> 'From self' is synonymous with 'from [its own] entity'. About that, respectively, things are not produced from their own entities because their production [again] would be just senseless and because production would be endless.[360] It is thus: the production again of things already existing in their own entities is purposeless. [Also] if though existent they are produced, they would never not be produced. Hence, that also is not asserted. Therefore, respectively, things are not produced from self.
>
> They also are not produced from other. Why? For it would [absurdly] follow that everything would be produced from everything.
>
> They also are not produced from both self and other because [such] would [absurdly] entail the fallacies of both [production from self and from other].
>
> They also are not produced causelessly because it would [absurdly] follow that everything always would be produced from everything and because there would be the fallacy that all endeavor would be just senseless. Since the production of things is thus in all ways inadmissible,

> there is no [inherently existent] production; therefore, this called production is only a convention.

According to Jam-ȳang-shay-b̄a, these statements led Bhāvaviveka to believe that Buddhapālita was taking it that since production is delimited to either production from self or production from other, the refutation of the former implies the affirmation of the latter. Thus, the root of Bhāvaviveka's criticism of Buddhapālita is the latter's own introductory remarks to the refutation of production which seem to indicate that his intention is to show through the refutation that production exists conventionally. Because of this, Bhāvaviveka viewed Buddhapālita's consequences as implying a proof of a positive phenomenon, that is, conventionally existent production from other.

In a brilliant display of intellectual ingenuity that exists to this day among the Ge-luk-b̄a colleges, Jam-ȳang-shay-b̄a traces Bhāvaviveka's objection back to Buddhapālita's somewhat questionable introductory remarks. Bhāvaviveka himself only says:[361]

> About this, one [that is, Buddhapālita] who is other [than Bhāvaviveka himself] makes the explanation, 'Things are not produced from their own entities because their production would be just senseless and because production would be endless.'
>
> That is not suitable (1) because [Buddhapālita] does not express a reason [capable of proving that there is no production from self] as well as an example; (2) because [the reasoning as Buddhapālita states it] does not avoid the fallacies adduced by another [that is, the fallacies that a Sāṃkhya would be expected to adduce]; and (3) because [Buddhapālita's] words afford an opportunity [to an opponent to expose contradiction within his own system.[362] His explanation affords such an opportunity] because since [the thesis and the reason must] be reversed from what is explicitly stated, what emerges is the opposite of the thesis and the reason—that things are produced from other because production is fruitful and because production has an end—due to which [he] would contradict [Mādhyamika] tenets.[363]

Bhāvaviveka's commentator, Avalokitavrata, elaborates on the criticism, clarifying points largely through making sure that the grammar is understood and the moves are properly identified. His commentary is painstakingly slow and repetitive but is worth citing because it clearly reveals the broad outlines of Bhāvaviveka's argument:[364]

> [Bhāvaviveka's *Lamp for (Nāgārjuna's) 'Wisdom'*] says:
>
> > About this,[365] one [that is, Buddhapālita] who is other [than Bhāvaviveka himself] makes the explanation, 'Things are not produced from their own entities because their production would be just senseless and because production would be endless.'
>
> This indicates that also on this occasion of proving that things are not produced from self the commentator, the master Buddhapālita, makes such and such an explanation. In that, 'About this' means 'on this occasion of proving that things are not produced from self'. 'Other' refers to the Elder (*Sthavīra, gNas rtan*) Buddhapālita who is other than most of the many commentators on this *Treatise* [on the Middle Way]—ranging from the honorable master [Nāgārjuna] himself,[366] the Elder Buddhapālita, Chandrakīrti, Devasharma, Guṇashrī, Guṇamati, and Sthiramati through to the master Bhāvaviveka.
>
> The master Buddhapālita makes this explanation: 'Things are not produced from their own entities because their production would be just senseless and because production would be endless.' In that, 'Things' (*bhāvāḥ, dngos po rnams*)[367] are the external and internal sources (*āyatana, skye mched*). 'From themselves' (*svata, bdag gi bdag nyid las*) [which is rendered into English above as 'from their own entities' following the Tibetan which is following this very gloss by Avalokitavrata] means 'from [their] entities' (*bdag nyid las*).

[Buddhapālita is referring to production] from that. 'Are not produced' means '[are not produced] ultimately'.

Why are things not produced from their own entities? 'Because their production would be just senseless' [or, more literally, 'because of the senselessness of their production']. 'Their production' (*tadutpāda, de dag gi skye ba*) means the production of those things. 'Senseless' (*vaiyarthya, don med pa*) means 'devoid of sense', 'purposeless', 'fruitless'. 'Ness' (*ya*[?], *nyid*) is the fact of their production being without sense, the senselessness of their production.

By saying 'because their production would be just senseless' [Buddhapālita] is indicating: If things are produced from an existent [state], their production would be just senseless because there would be nothing different from what had already been produced, nothing which had not arisen earlier.

Also, 'because their production would be endless' [indicates]: If, though existent, something were produced, then through being produced it would be produced in that aspect without cessation; therefore, [its repeated] production would just not finish. 'Makes the explanation' means that the Elder Buddhapālita makes that explanation on this occasion of proving that things are not produced from self.

[Bhāvaviveka's *Lamp for (Nāgārjuna's) 'Wisdom'*] says:

> That is not suitable (1) because [Buddhapālita] does not express a reason [capable of proving that there is no production from self] as well as an example; (2) because [the reasoning as Buddhapālita states it] does not avoid the fallacies adduced by another [that is, the fallacies that a Sāṃkhya would be expected to adduce]; and (3) because [Buddhapālita's] words afford an opportunity [to an opponent to expose contradiction within his own system. His explanation

affords such an opportunity] because since [the thesis and the reason must] be reversed from what is explicitly stated, what emerges is the opposite of the thesis and the reason—that things are produced from other because production is fruitful and because production has an end—due to which [he] contradicts [Mādhyamika] tenets.

In this passage the commentator [Bhāvaviveka] himself proves that the explanation by the Elder Buddhapālita is not suitable. In that, 'is not suitable' is [Bhāvaviveka's] thesis that the explanation by the Elder Buddhapālita is not suitable. Why is it not suitable? 'Because [Buddhapālita] does not express a reason [capable of proving that there is no production from self] as well as an example.' This indicates that in his explanation he has only proclaimed a mere thesis, 'Things are not produced from self,' and has not expressed a reason why they are not produced from self such as [Bhāvaviveka did in his syllogism when he gave as the reason] 'because of existing' and has not expressed an example of the non-production of the existent from self such as [Bhāvaviveka did when he said] 'like, for example, an existent consciousness,' and therefore [his explanation] is not suitable.

Furthermore, [it is not suitable] 'because [the reasoning as Buddhapālita states it] does not avoid the fallacies adduced by another [that is, the fallacies that a Sāṃkhya would be expected to adduce'. This indicates that] even if he had fully expressed and established a reason and an example, it would, without question, have the fallacies adduced by another who propounds [ultimately existent] production, but you [Buddhapālita] did not avoid them; therefore, because of not avoiding the fallacies adduced by another, [the explanation] is not suitable.

For what further reason is it not suitable? 'And because [Buddhapālita's] words afford an opportunity [to an opponent to expose contradiction within his own system].' [This indicates that] the explanation by the Elder Buddhapālita is also unsuitable because of being a passage that affords an opportunity for censure by another party. 'And' (*cha, yang*) is to be taken as [indicating] that not only is [his explanation] unsuitable because of not expressing a reason and an example and because of not avoiding the fallacies adduced by another but also it is unsuitable because of affording an opportunity [for censure].

To indicate just that [third fault, Bhāvaviveka] says, '...[the thesis and the reason must] be reversed from what is explicitly stated'. What is explicitly stated? It is just Buddhapālita's explanation, 'Things are not produced from their own entities because their production would be just senseless and because production would be endless.' [368] To be reversed from that is to be reversed from that which is explicitly stated. The opposite of 'Things are not produced from their own entities' is 'things are produced from other'; the opposite of 'because their production would be just senseless' is 'because their production is fruitful', and the opposite of 'because production would be endless' is 'because production is finite'. Hence, because of affording an opportunity [for censure] it is also unsuitable.

How [does Buddhapālita's explanation] come to be a passage affording an opportunity [for censure] through reversing what is explicitly stated? Therefore, [Bhāvaviveka] says, '...what emerges is the opposite of the thesis and the reason [or, more literally, the property of that].' The 'thesis' (*sādhya, bsgrub par bya ba*) is the thesis, 'Things are not produced from their own entities.' 'What emerges is opposite of that' means that what emerges is the opposite of 'Things are not produced from their own entities,' i.e., things are produced from other.

The 'property of that' (*taddharma, de'i chos*) is the property of that thesis, that is to say, [the reason which is] the property of the subject of that thesis: namely, 'because their production would be just senseless and because production would be endless.' 'What emerges is the opposite of those': what emerges is the opposite of 'because their production would be just senseless'—namely, because production is fruitful—and the opposite of 'because production would be endless'—namely, because production is finite.

How does [Buddhapālita's explanation] come to afford an opportunity [for censure] due to the emergence of the opposite of those? Therefore, [Bhāvaviveka] says, 'things are produced from other because production is fruitful and because production has an end'. [This means that Buddhapālita gives someone an opportunity for censure through opening up] the opportunity of [someone's saying that he is holding] (1) that things are produced from other, which emerges as the opposite of the thesis 'Things are not produced from their own entities'; (2) production is fruitful, which emerges as the opposite of the property [proving the thesis] 'because their production would be just senseless'; and (3) production is finite, which emerges as the opposite of the property [proving the thesis] 'because production would be endless'.

What fault is there in such? As a possible response by his opponent, [it would show that Buddhapālita] 'contradicts [Mādhyamika] tenets'. For it would contradict the tenets in the master [Nāgārjuna's] scriptures that he does not assert that things are [ultimately] produced from other, that he does not assert that production[369] is [ultimately] fruitful, and that he does not assert that production is [ultimately] finite.

Therefore, this explanation by the Elder Buddhapālita is not suitable since it contradicts reasoning and scripture.

D̄zong-ka-b̄a, in commenting on these points in his *Ocean of*

Reasoning,[370] disagrees with Avalokitavrata about what tenet is contradicted. He says that it is the tenet that the statement in Nāgārjuna's *Treatise* 'there is no production from self' is a mere elimination of production from self. As Jam-ȳang-shay-b̄a[371] points out, the three points show that a tenet is contradicted—they are not the tenet that is contradicted.

There is no question that Bhāvaviveka is indeed right in saying that the refutation of the four extreme types of production is just a non-affirming negation and that it would contradict Mādhyamika tenets if Buddhapālita indulged in an affirming negation on this occasion of ultimate analysis. However, a defender of Buddhapālita would answer that his refutation of the four extreme types of production is indeed a non-affirming negation. For his emphasizing that production exists conventionally does not mean that he considers that the refutation of production *establishes* conventionally existent production. Buddhapālita is briefly setting out the general thrust of Nāgārjuna's *Treatise* that nothing exists ultimately and that everything is feasible within the context of mere nominalism; he means:

> Though non-production from the four extremes is here a non-affirming negation, production does exist nominally.

Furthermore, even if Buddhapālita's words do seem to suggest an affirming negation, since he did not wish to suggest such, he cannot be called to task for it. Even sutra says, 'That which is produced from causes is not produced,' and Bhāvaviveka himself says, 'The subject, a form, does not exist ultimately because of existing—like, for example, a magician's illusion [which exists and does not exist ultimately].' No one asserts that these statements imply conventional production or conventional existence even though they might seem to.

Based on Buddhapālita's somewhat misleading words, Bhāvaviveka took his consequences as implying a proof of conventionally existent production from other. Then, he proceeded to extract Buddhapālita's supposed actual meaning according to this notion. He then showed that this would contradict the

Mādhyamika tenet that the refutation of production is a non-affirming negation.

This does not mean, however, that non-affirming negations have no implications.[372] A non-affirming negation cannot imply a positive phenomenon or even an affirming negation but can imply another non-affirming negation of the same type. For instance, the non-affirming negation (or negative phenomenon), the non-existence of a son of a barren woman, implies the non-affirming negation, the non-existence of the beauty or ugliness of the son of a barren woman. Also, meditation on emptiness, a non-affirming negation of inherent existence, with respect to one phenomenon functions as meditation on the emptiness of everything. In the same vein, it is said that until one has eradicated adherence to the inherent existence of the mental and physical aggregates, one has not cognized the absence of inherent existence of the person. Similarly, the thesis that things are not inherently produced from self, other, both, and neither implies that production does not exist inherently, thereby implying that things lack inherent existence.[373] These are all non-affirming negations that imply other non-affirming negations.

Therefore, non-affirming negations (or negative phenomena) may have implications, but those implications are all other non-affirming negations of the same type. An affirming negation, on the other hand, implies something positive in its place. For instance, the fat Devadatta's not eating during the day implies his eating at night. (For a discussion of negatives see Appendix 4.)

In conclusion, Bhāvaviveka's criticism of Buddhapālita's consequences revolves around his interpretation of the latter's prefatory and concluding remarks to the refutation of production. He interpreted them as showing that Buddhapālita saw conventionally existent production as being proved by the refutation of true production, thereby contradicting the basic Mādhyamika tenet that the object realized through a refutation by ultimate analysis is a mere negation or elimination of true existence.

4 *Chandrakīrti's Defense of Buddhapālita*

Sources
Chandrakīrti's *Clear Words*
Jam-ȳang-shay-b̄a's *Great Exposition of the Middle Way*
Gom-day Nam-ka-gyel-tsen's *Settling Difficult Points in the Opposite of the Consequences*
Kensur Lekden's oral teachings
Corresponding section of the translation pp.584-6

For Chandrakīrti, all of the fallacies that Bhāvaviveka found in Buddhapālita's refutation of production from self are inadmissible.[374] Chandrakīrti's *Clear Words* (14.1-15.3, 10.11-11.2) says:

> The master Buddhapālita says, 'Things are not produced from their own entities because their production [again] would be just senseless and because production would be endless. There is no need for production again (*punarutpāda, yang skye ba*) of things which already exist in their own entities. If though existent they are produced, they would never not be produced.'
>
> About this, some [namely, Bhāvaviveka] express faults,

'That is not suitable (1) because [Buddhapālita] does not express a reason [capable of proving that there is no production from self] as well as an example; (2) because [the reasoning as Buddhapālita states it] does not avoid the fallacies adduced by another [that is, the fallacies that a Sāṃkhya would be expected to adduce]; and (3) because [Buddhapālita's] words afford an opportunity [to an opponent to expose contradiction within his own system.[375] His explanation affords such an opportunity] because since [the thesis and the reason must] be reversed from what is explicitly stated, what emerges is the opposite of the thesis and the reason—that things are produced from other because production is fruitful and because production has an end—due to which [he] would contradict [Mādhyamika] tenets.'

We [that is, Chandrakīrti] view all of these fallacies as not being reasonable.

CHANDRAKĪRTI'S DEFENSE AGAINST THE FIRST FALLACY

The first fallacy was that Buddhapālita could not refute production from self because he did not state a reason and an example of an autonomous syllogism. Chandrakīrti's answer is that through disputation with contradictory consequences an opponent can indeed come to accept that there is no production from self. Buddhapālita demonstrated the inner contradictions in production from self with two consequences:

It follows about the subject, a sprout, that its production again is senseless because of already existing in its own entity.[376]

If it is answered that the consequence is not entailed by the reason, the second consequence is:

It follows about the subject, a sprout, that its production is endless because though it already exists in its own entity, there is need for its re-production.

The opponent can perceive that these consequences contradict his tenets because a Sāṃkhya asserts that production again (into a manifest state) is sensible (even though he does not assert that the production again of the already manifest is sensible) and does not assert that products are produced endlessly. Thereby, Buddhapālita shows that the proofs for the existence of production from self are unreasonable, for a Sāṃkhya can find no example of re-production of that which has already been produced. Since senseless re-production and endless production of that which has already been produced contradict his own tenets about production, the Sāṃkhya is caused to fall away from his assertion of production from self.

Furthermore, if one is able to show such inner contradictions and the opponent perceives them yet persists in his error, there is no point in further stating reasons and examples of autonomous syllogisms. Bhāvaviveka's rushing to state autonomous syllogisms just shows his liking for logic.

Also, if one is a Mādhyamika who refutes all extremes as in the *King of Meditative Stabilizations Sutra*, one should not use autonomous syllogisms, in which the reason has inherently existent presence in the subject, pervasion, and counter-pervasion. This is because a Mādhyamika has no assertion of other positions among the four extremes and so forth, such as that things inherently exist, utterly do not exist, both inherently exist and inherently disintegrate, or that there is an inherently existent middle way that forsakes the two extremes of existence and non-existence. A Mādhyamika has no thesis which contradicts the Mādhyamika system.

Nāgārjuna's *Refutation of Objections* says:[377]

> If I had any [inherently existent] thesis,
> Then I would have that fault [of contradicting my own
> thesis that there is no inherent existence].
> Because I have no [inherently existent] thesis,
> I am only faultless.

It is not being said that a Mādhyamika has no theses; he merely has no theses that inherently exist. He has no theses upholding the existence of phenomena which can be found under analysis. However, Mādhyamikas do have both negative and positive theses.[378] That they have negative theses is clear in the refutations of going and coming and of production, for instance. Nāgārjuna's *Treatise on the Middle Way* says (II.8):

Respectively, a goer is not going,
A non-goer also is not going,
Indeed what third other than
A goer and a non-goer is going?

Also, (I.1):

There is never production
Anywhere of any phenomenon
From itself, from others,
From both, or causelessly.

Mādhyamikas also have positive theses as in Nāgārjuna's *Essay on the Mind of Enlightenment*, 'I assert dependently arisen activities to be like dreams and magicians' illusions.' His *Refutation of Objections*[379] says, 'We do not set forth a non-assertion of conventionalities.' His *Sixty Stanzas of Reasoning* says:

Those who assert dependent phenomena
As like moons in water,
As not real and not unreal,
Are not tricked by views.

His *Praise of the Supramundane (Lokātītastava)* says, 'You [Buddha] have taught agent and object as conventionalities. Your assertion is that they are established as mutually dependent.'

Also, Chandrakīrti says in his own commentary on his *Supplement*, 'The wise should think that this position is faultless and beneficial and should definitely assert it.' Also, 'Therefore, because dependent imputation is asserted in the same way as the assertion of dependent-arising as just conditional, it does not follow for our position that all conventionalities are annihilated; it is suitable also for the opponent to assert just this.' Throughout his commentary to his own *Supplement to (Nāgārjuna's) 'Treatise on the Middle Way'* and in his *Clear Words* Chandrakīrti refers to theses stated in the basic text and the reasonings or consequences which prove these theses.[380] Thus, Mādhyamikas have both negative and positive theses.

Since Nāgārjuna does seem to say in his *Refutation of Objections* that he does not have any theses, the background of that statement needs to be known.[381] A Mādhyamika has said, 'Phenomena do not inherently exist,' to which a proponent of inherently existent phenomena has answered, 'If the words of this thesis inherently exist, then it would not be correct that all phenomena do not inherently exist. If the words of this thesis do not inherently exist, they are nothing and cannot refute the inherent existence of phenomena.' The idea of the opponent is that if things exist, they must exist by way of their own being. If things do not, then they do not exist at all and, like the hairs of a turtle, cannot effect anything.

Thus, the debate in the *Refutation of Objections* is not about having or not having a thesis in general. It is about whether the words of the thesis, 'Phenomena do not exist inherently,' exist inherently. The meaning of Nāgārjuna's answer is:

> If I asserted that the words of such a thesis existed inherently, I would have the fault of contradicting my own thesis that all phenomena do not exist inherently. However, because I do not assert that the words of my thesis exist inherently, I do not have this fault.

Thus, this passage which is often quoted to show that Mādhyamikas have no theses does not do so. Mādhyamikas have nominally existent positive and negative theses; they do not have any theses which are analytically findable or any theses which affirm the existence of analytically findable phenomena.

It is not fitting for a Mādhyamika to assert the existence of autonomous syllogisms because, even conventionally, nothing exists autonomously or inherently. However, D̄zong-ka-b̄a adds that it does not necessarily follow that if one accepts autonomous syllogisms, one is not a Mādhyamika, for Svātantrikas do so but are still Mādhyamikas.[382] Since they are higher than Chittamātrins because they prove with limitless forms of reasoning that all phenomena do not truly exist, they are not suitable to be other than Mādhyamikas. The non-contradiction of being a Mādhyamika and yet accepting what is not fit for a Mādhyamika is similar to the non-contradiction of being a monk and yet having minor infractions of the monk's code.[383]

In defense of Buddhapālita against Bhāvaviveka's attribution of the first 'fallacy', Chandrakīrti's *Clear Words* (15.3-16.10, 11.1-12.4) says:[384]

> I view all of these fallacies as not being reasonable. How? His saying 'because [Buddhapālita] did not express a reason [capable of proving that there is no production from self] as well as an example' is not reasonable.
>
> Why? [Buddhapālita] is inquiring in the following way of an opponent who asserts production from self:[385]
>
> > You [Sāṃkhyas] propound that 'from self' [means] that the existence [of things that involve production acts] as a cause and that just it [i.e., the existent] is produced.[386] However, we do not see that there is purpose in the production again of the existent, and we also see that [such production] would be endless. However, you [Sāṃkhyas] do not assert that the already produced [that is, the already manifest] is produced again and also do not assert that [the production of a thing] is endless. Therefore, your debate [that is to say, your position of production from self] is devoid of correctness and contradicts your own assertion.
>
> When [Buddhapālita] debates through just these [consequences] which have the effects [derived] from stating a reason and example, would the opponent not accept it? However, if the opponent is not overcome even through debate by way of contradicting his own assertions, then due to [his] shamelessness he also just would not be

overcome by [stating] reasons and examples. We [Prāsaṅgikas] do not debate with the crazily stubborn. Therefore, when the master [Bhāvaviveka] sets out inferences at inappropriate times, he is manifesting just his own liking for inference.

Also, it is not suitable for one who is a Mādhyamika to make autonomous inferences because of not asserting other positions [among the four extremes]. Moreover, Āryadeva [XVI.25] explains:[387]

> Even over a long period of time
> Censure cannot be expressed
> For one who has no position of [inherent] existence,
> Non-existence, or existence and non-existence.

Also, [Nāgārjuna's] *Refutation of Objections* [stanzas 29 and 30] says:

> If I had any [inherently existent] thesis,
> Then I would have that fault [of contradicting my own thesis that there is no inherent cxistence].
> Because I have no [inherently existent] thesis,
> I am only faultless.
>
> If [in accordance with your thought][388] the factualities
> Of direct perception and so forth did observe some [inherently established objects of comprehension],
> Then [it would be suitable] to prove those [in your own system] and refute [others], but since [valid cognizers observing
> Such objects of comprehension] do not exist [even conventionally], there is no [chance for you] to censure me.

CHANDRAKĪRTI'S DEFENSE AGAINST THE SECOND FALLACY

Chandrakīrti next declares inadmissible the second fallacy adduced by Bhāvaviveka in what the latter considered to be

Buddhapālita's intended syllogism refuting the Sāṃkhya position.[389] Bhāvaviveka's criticism was that Buddhapālita did not avoid the fallacies which a Sāṃkhya would be expected to adduce upon analyzing his thesis and reason. Chandrakīrti's answer is that Buddhapālita did not state an autonomous syllogism like Bhāvaviveka's:

> The subjects, the inner sources such as an eye sense, are not produced from self because of existing—like, for example, an existent consciousness.

Chandrakīrti objects to Bhāvaviveka's syllogism, saying that he has not avoided the fallacy of proving what is already established for Sāṃkhyas if non-production from self refers to non-production from an entity of an effect. For, Sāṃkhyas hold that manifestations are not produced from the manifest, that is, from effects, but from the non-manifest. On the other hand, if non-production from self refers to non-production from the entity of a cause, one would have the fallacy of the reason's proving exactly the opposite for a Sāṃkhya.

Similarly, if the reason of Bhāvaviveka's autonomous syllogism ('because of existing') is analyzed, the same faults need to be eradicated. If 'existing' means that an eye sense exists from the time of its causes, then the reason, for a Sāṃkhya, only goes to prove that things are produced from self. If 'existing' means that an eye sense exists at the time of its manifestation, then one would be proving what is already established for the Sāṃkhyas since they themselves assert that it has already been produced into its manifest or effect state and thus does not require production.

Chandrakīrti says that though Bhāvaviveka himself incurs these fallacies, Buddhapālita did not state such a thesis or reason. Rather, the thesis of Buddhapālita's consequence is:

> It follows about the subjects, things, that their production again is senseless.

The reason is:

> Because of already existing in their own entities.

(It should be remembered that Buddhapālita only said, 'Things are not produced from their own entities because their production would be just senseless and because production would be endless.')

According to Jam-ȳang-shay-b̄a, Chandrakīrti saw in Buddhapālita's refutation the positing of a thesis:

> Things are not produced from their own entities.

Then, he saw two consequences demonstrating damage to the view that things are produced from their own entities:

1 It follows about the subjects, things, that their production again is senseless because of already existing in their own entities.
2 It follows about the subjects, things, that their production is endless because, although already existent in their own entities, there is need for their production.

In other words, Chandrakīrti is saying that Bhāvaviveka misread Buddhapālita's text, for aside from positing a general thesis that things are not produced from self (that is, from their own entities), Buddhapālita did not express a syllogism (see p.456) such as 'The subjects, things, are not produced from their own entities because production is senseless and endless' (or in its altered form 'because production is sensible and has an end').

The fallacies which Bhāvaviveka imputed to Buddhapālita are flung back at him by Chandrakīrti. It is Bhāvaviveka and not Buddhapālita who has the questionable autonomous syllogism with a vague predicate of the thesis ('are not produced from self' or 'are not produced from their own entities') and a vague reason ('because of existing'). In this vein, Chandrakīrti's *Clear Words* (16.11-18.4, 12.4-12.18) says:

> When in that way a Mādhyamika just does not express autonomous inferences, how could [Buddhapālita] have an autonomous thesis [such as Bhāvaviveka stated]—'The inner sources are not produced from self'—which the Sāṃkhyas would cause to be overturned as follows:

> What is the meaning of this thesis? Does 'from self' mean from the entity of the effect or from the entity of the cause? Which is it? If it is from the entity of the effect, then [you have the fault of] proving what is already established [for us]. If it is from the entity of the cause, then it has the sense of [proving] the opposite because [according to us Sāṃkhyas] all that have production are produced only within the context of existing in the entities of [their] causes.

> Also, how could we [Buddhapālita and Chandrakīrti] have a reason [such as that stated by Bhāvaviveka]—'because of existing'—which would be either [a case of] proving what is already established [for a Sāṃkhya] or of having the opposite meaning [for a Sāṃkhya] and with respect to which we would have to toil to get rid [of the fault that we would be] proving what is already established or [the fault of] having the opposite meaning!
>
> Therefore, just due to not being susceptible to the consequence of those faults, answers to them did not [need] to be expressed by the master Buddhapālita.

An hypothetical extension of Bhāvaviveka's argument

Chandrakīrti goes on to say that hypothetically Bhāvaviveka might accept that the reasons, etc., which prove non-true existence do not appear similarly to Mādhyamikas and non-Mādhyamikas, making an autonomous syllogism impossible, in which case Buddhapālita should have stated a correct other-approved inference (*parasiddha-anumāna, gzhan grags kyi rjes dpag*). (Even though an actual *anumāna* refers to an inferring consciousness, here in *parasiddha-anumāna*, literally 'other-approved inference', it refers to the application of a reason approved by the other party in the debate, an 'other-approved syllogism'. Synonymous with *parasiddha-anumāna* is *parasiddha-liṅga* (*gzhan grags kyi rtags*), 'other-approved reason'. *Svasiddha-anumāna* (*rang grags kyi rjes dpag*), 'self-approved inference', and *svasiddha-liṅga* (*rang grags kyi rtags*), 'self-approved reason', are also synonymous with *parasiddha-anumāna*, 'other-approved inference', because 'self' and 'other' here both refer to the opponent from different points of view.)[390] Thus, according to Chandrakīrti, Bhāvaviveka may mean that Buddhapālita did not state a correct other-approved inference because the latter did not give a proper reason and example.

In answer to this, Chandrakīrti states that there is no need for an other-approved syllogism because the inner contradictions and unreasonableness of the opponent's view can be shown by consequences and by showing him that his proofs of production from self are unreasonable, and thus there is no further purpose in stating an other-approved syllogism. That the Sāṃkhya's 'proofs' of production from self have no capacity to do so is the clearest sign of the eradication of the Sāṃkhya's own view. For, if upon statement of contradictory consequences, he wants to hold to his position, he must proceed to prove that there is production from self, for it is the way of logicians to state reasons in order to generate in another an ascertainment of a thesis just as one oneself has ascertained it. The Sāṃkhya's syllogism would, for instance, be:

> The subject, a sprout unmanifest at the time of its causes, is produced from its own entity because the non-existent is not produced and because the causes of one thing are distinct from the causes of another.

The Sāṃkhya's idea is that if the non-existent were produced or made manifest, then the horns of a rabbit could be produced. Also, things have their own distinct causes, and this indicates that they exist non-manifestly in their causes.

However, a Buddhist would not accept the reason as correct. For a Buddhist (that is to say, for a Sautrāntika on up), even though what is non-existent *at the time of its causes* is produced, what is non-existent in general is not produced, and also the causes of one thing are indeed distinct from the causes of another thing, but these two facts do not entail that things are produced from their own entities. The reason, therefore, does nothing to advance why things are produced from their own entities; the syllogism is only a repetition of the basic thesis itself. Technically speaking, there is no concordant example to be found which can serve as a basis for ascertaining the entailment.[391] The Sāṃkhya's proofs are no proofs at all in that they are just outflows of his own assertions, incapable of establishing them. In this vein, Chandrakīrti's *Clear Words* (18.5-19.7, 12.18-13.18) says:

> [Bhāvaviveka] might think, '[I might allow that] since according to Mādhyamikas the position [or thesis], reason, and example [of an *autonomous* syllogism] are not established, autonomous inferences are not to be expressed, and, therefore, one would not prove the meaning of a thesis refuting production from self and would not clear away the other's thesis through an inference established for both [parties]. Still, one must express contradiction of the other's thesis through one's own [other-approved] inference. Hence, one must have a position [that is, a thesis] and so forth that are devoid of the faults of position, reason, and example. Thus, since [Buddhapālita] did not express such and did not avoid the fallacies of those [which a Sāṃkhya would be expected to draw, Buddhapālita] just has those faults [of not stating a reason and example capable of proving no production from self and of not avoiding the fallacies which a Sāṃkhya would cite upon examining what no production from self means].'
>
> *Answer:* That is not so. Why? One [such as a Sāṃkhya] who [upon being pressed by the consequences set forth by Buddhapālita] wishes to generate ascertainment of something which he holds as a thesis in others in just the way that he has ascertained it, should demonstrate to others [that is, Mādhyamikas] just that logical proof through which that meaning is understood. Therefore, it is respectively the custom for just the other party [here, the Sāṃkhya] to state a proof of the meaning of a thesis which he himself asserts [in response to the contradictions shown by Buddhapālita's consequences rather than for Buddhapālita to proceed to set forth an other-approved inference]. However, this [reasoning which a

> Sāṃkhya states to a Mādhyamika to try to prove production from self] is not a [valid] reasoning for the other [party, the Mādhyamika]. Because the reason and example [which a Sāṃkhya cites] are not [valid], the proof of the meaning of his thesis is just a statement of outflows of [his own] assertions. Therefore, since he has asserted a position that is devoid of logical correctness, it deceives just himself, due to which it cannot generate ascertainment in another. In this way, just this inability of his attempt to prove the meaning of his thesis [due to being faulty] is the clearest eradication of his [position]. What need is there here to express damage [to his position] by way of inference! [For, the contradiction of his view that something exists and yet needs to be reproduced has been shown, and upon the Sāṃkhya's presentation of his own view in syllogistic inference, the Mādhyamika has given answers showing its illogicality.]

Buddhapālita's indication of an other-approved inference

Still, hypothetically, Bhāvaviveka might insist on the statement of a self-approved or, as it is also called, an other-approved syllogism, because there are many other-approved syllogisms in Nāgārjuna's writings and in many sutras. Chandrakīrti answers that even if an other-approved syllogism needed to be stated, Buddhapālita did state one when he said, 'Things are not produced from their own entities because their production [again] would be just senseless.' This indicates a correct other-approved syllogism:

> With respect to the subjects, things such as a non-manifest pot and so forth abiding in the potential entities of their causes, their production again is senseless because of already existing in their own entities—like, for example, a manifest pot [which already exists in its own entity and the re-production of which would be senseless].

This other-approved syllogism is similar to the consequence which Jam-ȳang-shay-ba first interpreted in Buddhapālita's statement as:

> It follows about the subject, a sprout, that its production again is senseless because of already existing in its own entity.

Except for slight differences in format, there is no substantial difference in this case between the consequence and other-approved syllogism. In general, however, consequences have greater usage than other-approved syllogisms because they must be stated in all instances of generating an inference in another in order, at least, to break the pointedness or the vibrance of the other party's adherence to a wrong view.[392] An other-approved syllogism need not be stated for intelligent opponents, when a consequence alone is sufficient to generate a consciousness inferring the intended thesis.

The question between Chandrakīrti and Bhāvaviveka is whether Buddhapālita's statement indicates such a correct other-approved syllogism. To quote Buddhapālita again:

> Things are not produced from their own entities because their production [again] would be just senseless.

Chandrakīrti sees the word 'their' in the reason clause as indicating the subject and the example. His source is Buddhapālita's more extensive rendition:

> The production again of things already existing in their own entities is purposeless.

This more extensive statement of 'their' as 'of things already existing in their own entities' implicitly contains within it an example—like a manifest pot—which possesses both the reason—already existing in its own entity—and the predicate—senseless production again. A valid example must possess both the reason and the predicate and be approved by the Sāṃkhya, who agrees that a manifest pot already exists in its own entity and does not require further production. Since this more extensive statement is Buddhapālita's own commentary on the brief statement, it must be applied to the condensed version.

Similarly, the phrase, 'existing in their own entities', in the longer statement bears the reason of the syllogism. The predicate of the thesis is indicated in the shorter version itself, 'production would be senseless', though the word 'again' (*punar, yang*) does need to be added from the longer statement, making 'production again would be senseless'.

Therefore, even if Buddhapālita's words are taken from the viewpoint of presenting an other-approved inference, the faults imputed by Bhāvaviveka do not apply. This is because Buddhapālita's words contain a five-membered statement of proof:

1 *Thesis:* With regard to things such as a non-manifest pot and so forth, their production again is senseless.
2 *Pervasion:* That production again is senseless pervades, or applies to all cases of, things already existing in their own entities.
3 *Example:* Like an already manifest pot.
4 *Exemplification:* Just as an already manifest pot already exists in its own entity, so things such as a non-manifest pot already exist in their own entities.
5 *Summary:* Therefore, because things already exist in their own entities, the production again of things is senseless.[393]

(See Appendix 5 for a discussion of other proof statements.) About this, Chandrakīrti's *Clear Words* (19.8-21.7, 13.18-15.4) says:

> [Bhāvaviveka] might say, 'Nevertheless, the fault of contradiction with one's own inference [that is to say, with an inference acceptable to a Sāṃkhya] must, without question, be expressed.'
>
> [*Answer:*] The master Buddhapālita also just expressed such. How? For he said, 'Things are not produced from their own entities because their production [again] would be just senseless.' In that, the [word] 'their' (*tad, de dag*) [in the reason clause] holds [or indicates] 'those which already exist in their own entities'. Why? This is because [Buddhapālita's subsequent statement] 'The production again of things already existing in their own

entities is purposeless,' is [his] commentary on that abbreviated statement [and we must, therefore, carry it over to the shorter statement]. Also, this [longer] statement ['those which already exist in their own entities'] bears a concordant example ['a manifest pot'] renowned to the other [party, the Sāṃkhya] which possesses the qualities of [the predicate of] the probandum ['senseless production again'] and the proof ['already existing in its own entity'].

In [Buddhapālita's longer statement], 'already existing in their own entities' bears the reason. [In the shorter statement itself] 'because production would be just senseless' holds the predicate of the probandum [once it is changed to 'production again (*punarutpāda, yang skye ba*) is senseless' in accordance with the longer statement].

In:

> A sound is an impermanent thing because products are [necessarily] impermanent things. It is seen that products are impermanent things, as in the case, for example, of a pot. Likewise, a sound is also a product. Therefore, because of being a product, [a sound] is an impermanent thing.

product which is manifested [or used] due to its connection [with the predicate of the probandum] is the reason. Just so, here also [the syllogism is]:

> Things [such as a non-manifest pot and so forth] are not produced from self because the production again of what already exist in their own entities is just senseless. Just as it is seen that pots and so forth which already abide in front [of oneself] and which already exist in their own manifest entities do not rely on being produced again, so if you think that there are pots and so forth which already exist in their own entities at the time of the lump of clay and so forth,

then production even at that time of what already exist in their own entities does not exist.

In that [syllogism], the reason—'already existing in their own entities'—which is manifested [or used] due to its connection [with the predicate of the probandum, 'senseless production again'] and which is unmistaken with respect to refuting re-production expresses contradiction through the Sāṃkhya's own inference [that is, an inference acceptable to a Sāṃkhya].

Therefore, how is it that [Bhāvaviveka] says, 'That is not suitable because [Buddhapālita] does not express a reason as well as an example'?

The unassailability of Buddhapālita's other-approved inference

Chandrakīrti found in Buddhapālita's commentary a syllogism that is unassailable. For a Sāṃkhya would have no qualms about the thesis since the subject is clearly stated as a non-manifest pot and so forth, and a non-manifest pot does not require production. Also, the thesis—that a non-manifest pot and so forth have no need of production again—is new to a Sāṃkhya and cannot be said to be a case of trying to prove what is already established for him since he accepts that the first production of a thing is its attainment of an existent entity in its causes and that it requires further production into a manifest state. He would also have no qualms that the reason was proving exactly the opposite because the thesis is that the production *again* of a non-manifest pot is purposeless. About this, the *Clear Words* (21.8-.14, 15.4-.15) says:

Not only is it just not that a reason and example were not expressed, but also it is not that the fallacies adduced by the other [party, the Sāṃkhya] were not avoided. How? For, the Sāṃkhyas do not assert that a pot dwelling in front [of oneself] which has a manifest form (*abhivyakta-rūpa, mngon par gsal ba'i rang bzhin*) manifests again, and [thus] here it is an entity established as an example [of something which already exists in its own entity and is not produced again].[394] Since the probandum is:

> those which are potential entities and do not have a manifested nature, predicated with a negation of production,

how could [the Sāṃkhyas] have the qualm that [Buddhapālita's syllogism has] the fault of a position [thesis] that is proving what is already established [for them] or has the sense of a contradictory reason [proving for them not that things are not produced from self but that they are].

Therefore, even if [Buddhapālita] did express contradiction[395] [of the Sāṃkhya view] through self[-renowned] inference [that is, a syllogistic statement approved by the Sāṃkhyas], they would not set forth the fallacies which [Bhāvaviveka] mentioned. Hence, it is just not that [Buddhapālita] did not avoid fallacies adduced by the other [party since they would not adduce them]. For these reasons, it should be known that these [two] objections [to Buddhapālita's remarks by Bhāvaviveka] are just senseless.

Chandrakīrti says that, furthermore, Buddhapālita's syllogistic statement does not have the fault of not applying to all products, since by using 'a pot *and so forth*' as the subject all things that have production are included in the subject and not just some specific products, such as pots. Thus, a Sāṃkhya would not have any qualms that the reasoning did not apply to all products. The *Clear Words* (22.1-.2, 15.15-.18) says:

> Because the phrase 'and so forth' in 'a pot (*ghaṭa, bum pa*) and so forth' was expressed with the intention of including all things asserted as being produced, [Buddhapālita's syllogistic statement] also does not become indefinite by way of [not including] cloth (*paṭa, snam bu*) and so forth.[396]

A second other-approved inference contained in Buddhapālita's commentary

In the above syllogism which Chandrakīrti found in Buddhapālita's commentary, the thesis is that things such as non-manifest pots *have no need of being produced again*, not that they are not produced from self (or from their own entities), the latter being considered, in the context, to be vague and thus subject to questioning by a Sāṃkhya. In this interpretation of Buddhapālita's remarks, his opening statement that things are not produced from their own entities is, according to Jam-ȳang-shay-b̄a, just a general thesis applying to the section, not the specific thesis of either the consequences or the other-approved syllogism just explained. Nevertheless, Chandrakīrti finds a second other-approved syllogism in the same passage that has the absence of production from self as the predicate of the thesis:

> The subjects, objects other than the person which are asserted by the Sāṃkhyas to be produced, are not produced from self because of existing in their own entities, as is the case, for example, with the person (*puruṣha, skyes bu*).

According to Jam-ȳang-shay-b̄a,[397] Chandrakīrti's point is that even if Buddhapālita is proving for a Sāṃkhya that objects other than the person *are not produced from self*, there is no fault of the Sāṃkhya's having qualms that Buddhapālita is trying to prove what is already established for them, or that it proves just the opposite, or that it is indefinite due to not being all-inclusive. In other words, the argument is so well framed that none of these faults can be adduced.

Jam-ȳang-shay-b̄a does not explain how this syllogism is faultless; he merely says that it is easy to realize that it is. Clearly, it is all-inclusive in that 'objects other than the person which are asserted by the Sāṃkhyas to be produced' includes all phenomena that are subject to production, since it excludes even the fundamental nature (*prakṛti, rang bzhin*), which is other than the person but is not produced, and yet includes all evolutes of the fundamental nature. Also, it is clear that the example is established for the Sāṃkhya, who holds that the person exists in its own entity and is not produced from self since it is not produced at all. Perhaps, the specification of the subject as all phenomena *that are subject to production* rules out any question about the predicate of the thesis—'are not produced from self'—such as whether it means that these are not produced from their manifest form since manifest objects are not subject to production, and thus 'are not produced from self' must mean that 'not produced from their unmanifest causal form in which they pre-exist.' Chandrakīrti's *Clear Words* (22.3-.5, 15.18-16.1) only says:

> Or, [the brief statement by Buddhapālita indicates] this other syllogism:
>
> > Objects other than the person which [the Sāṃkhyas] propound as being produced from self are not produced from self because of existing in their own entities, as is the case, for example, with the person.
>
> [In that] this example [of the person] is expressed.[398]

Refuting production from self also refutes manifestation from self

Buddhapālita's refutation of production from self also applies to those Sāṃkhyas who assert not production but manifestation. For production and manifestation are similar in the non-appearance first of what is later apparent. Thus, any objection by a Sāṃkhya that Buddhapālita's refutation does not hit its mark would be unfounded. Chandrakīrti's *Clear Words* (22.6-.8, 16.1-.5) says:

> Even if [a Sāṃkhya objected that] a refutation of production does not harm a proponent of manifestation, manifestation is designated with the term 'production', and due to qualitative similarity [of production and manifestation] with respect to earlier non-apprehendability and later apprehendability, the term 'production' just expresses manifestation. Thereby, it is not that refuting it [i.e., production] does not damage [the assertion of the manifestation of what already exists in an unmanifest state].

But did Buddhapālita really say all that?

Chandrakīrti, who has been conducting this debate based on

what Bhāvaviveka actually said and extending it into the hypothetical, now indicates that Bhāvạviveka's only possible answer at this point would be that one cannot actually find these meanings in Buddhapālita's remarks. Chandrakīrti's answer is that although Buddhapālita did not extensively state these exact words, his statements are laden with meaning and that he, Chandrakīrti, has said nothing not indicated by Buddhapālita. The *Clear Words* (22.9-23.2, 16.5-.9) says:

> [Bhāvaviveka might object:] Without [Buddhapālita's] having anything that expresses the meanings which you have set out, how was such analysis found?
>
> *Answer:* These statements of meaning[399] [by Buddhapālita], due to having great import, contain the above-mentioned meanings. Being explained, they issue forth this having the nature of the meanings given. Hence, there is nothing [in what I have said] that is not indicated in them.

In summary, the purpose of Chandrakīrti's defense of Buddhapālita is to show:[400] (1) that consequences are sufficient to generate in an opponent an inference of the desired thesis, (2) that autonomous syllogisms are utterly out of place in the Mādhyamika system, and (3) that if it is insisted that other-approved syllogisms are required, Buddhapālita's more extensive statement together with the initial brief one contain a correct five-membered syllogism.

His defense is reminiscent of the style of Nāgārjuna's *Treatise* in that he gives a complete presentation and then, taking another tack, sets forth a new one. In the same way, in the second chapter of the *Treatise* Nāgārjuna refutes inherently existing going through analyzing the area gone over, then begins again and refutes it through analyzing the goer, then through analyzing the beginning of going, and finally through analyzing its opposite, rest. Each is sufficient to refute naturally existent going completely, and yet he resorts to other methods for the sake of attacking the diverse ways in which the misapprehension of one topic is supported. When many angles are analyzed, it is more likely that the proper inferring consciousness will be generated in the other party. Also, it is necessary to refute the different philosophical systems directly through their own approaches and tenets.

The root of Bhāvaviveka's objection is that he did not think that Buddhapālita's brief demonstration meant what it is found to mean by the more sympathetic. As Jam-ȳang-shay-b̄a so clearly spells out, the reason behind Bhāvaviveka's disagreement is found in Buddhapālita's prefatory remarks where he seems to indicate that something positive, the conventional existence of production, is being proved on this occasion of refuting the four extreme types of production. Jam-ȳang-shay-b̄a agrees with Bhāvaviveka that Buddhapālita's remark is questionable, but says that Buddhapālita was summarizing not what is specifically proven by the refutation of the four extreme types of production but the general meaning of the chapter taken in the light of the whole text: inherently existent production is refuted but production does exist nominally.

CHANDRAKĪRTI'S DEFENSE AGAINST THE THIRD FALLACY

This brings us to the third and final fallacy adduced by Bhāvaviveka—that since it is necessary for Buddhapālita to assert the opposite of his thesis and reason, he contradicts the Mādhyamika tenet that the refutation of the four extreme types of production is a non-affirming negation.[401] According to Bhāvaviveka, Buddhapālita's intended meaning is that production from self is not just eliminated but is replaced by production from other because production is purposeful and has an end.

To repeat, Buddhapālita said, 'Things are not produced from their own entities because their production [again] would be senseless and because production would be endless.' Bhāvaviveka saw the statement as indicating two consequences:

1 It follows that the subjects, things, are produced senselessly because of being produced from self.

2 It follows that the subjects, things, are produced endlessly because of being produced from self.

When a consequence implies its opposite meaning, the negative of the reason in the consequence is put as the predicate in a syllogism, and the negative of the predicate in the consequence is put as the reason in the syllogism. Bhāvaviveka saw these consequences as implying their opposite meaning:

1 The subjects, things, are not produced from self because their production is not senseless.

2 The subjects, things, are not produced from self because their production is not endless.

Chandrakīrti answers that Buddhapālita did not state such consequences at all, never mind intending to imply their opposite meaning. Instead, the two consequences should read:

1 It follows the subjects, things, are *produced again* senselessly because of being produced from self (or because of already existing in their own entities).

2 It follows that the subjects, things, are produced endlessly because of being produced from self (or because, although existing in their own entities, there is sense in their being produced again).

The idea is that for the Sāṃkhyas the first production of things is their attainment of existence in the nature or entity of their causes; then, they are produced again when made manifest. The reason why the first consequence should read 'produced again', rather than 'produced', is that although Buddhapālita's brief statement says only 'produced' (*utpāda, skye ba*), the more extensive statement following it (see p.460) says 'produced again' (*punarutpāda, yang skye ba*).

Bhāvaviveka thought that Buddhapālita was flinging the absurd consequence that, in general, production is senseless and endless, and thus he thought that the opposite—sensible and limited production—was being asserted. However, once it is understood that the consequences are that things are produced *again* senselessly and endlessly, it can be seen that the opposite meaning—that things are produced again sensibly and not endlessly—is accepted only by a Sāṃkhya. For, a Prāsaṅgika has no such thesis of the sensible and limited re-production of things.

Understanding what Buddhapālita's consequences actually are and that their opposite meaning is asserted only by a Sāṃkhya is so central to the controversy between Buddhapālita and Bhāvaviveka that the Ge-luk-b̄a colleges call this phase of their Middle Way studies 'The Opposite of the Consequences' (*thal bzlog*). Chandrakīrti's *Clear Words* (23.3-24.2, 16.10-.17) says:

> The opposite meaning of the consequences [—that things are produced again sensibly and not endlessly—] is related only with the other [party, the Sāṃkhya], not with us because we do not have [such] a thesis. Therefore, how could we be contradicting [the Mādhyamika tenet that the refutation of production is a non-affirming negation]?[402] Through proving that the opposite of the consequences [is related with, or held by, the other party] we only wish to adduce as many fallacies as possible to the other party [so that he will give up his assertion of production from self].[403] Therefore, how could the master Buddhapālita—following the unerring system of the master Nāgārjuna [in which production from other, as well as sensible and finite re-production are not asserted][404]—have said any words that would make him susceptible in the sense of affording an opportunity for another [to show contradiction with the Mādhyamika system]!

Some Tibetans (and indeed many Western scholars) have explained that this passage indicates that Mādhyamikas (or Prāsaṅgikas) do not have any theses in general. Jam-ȳang-shay-b̄a[405] says that it is easy to realize that this is wrong. Since the referent of Chandrakīrti's remark that Mādhyamikas have no thesis is specific—meaning specifically that Mādhyamikas do not hold the thesis that production again is sensible and limited —the passage cannot serve as a source showing that Mādhyamikas have no theses in general.

Consequences do not have to imply their opposite meaning

The mere fact that these statements are properly constructed unwanted consequences does not mean that Buddhapālita must assert their opposite. As Chandrakīrti has just indicated, through showing a Sāṃkhya that he is logically subject to consequences that are opposite to his own views he can see the internal contradictions of asserting production from self and thereby will drop it, provided he does not shamelessly persist in his error.

Thus, on this occasion when a proponent of no inherent existence, a Prāsaṅgika, is adducing for a proponent of inherent existence, a Sāṃkhya, the consequences that re-production is senseless and endless, these are not consequences implying their opposite meaning from among the five types of consequences (see pp.445-9), but merely unwanted consequences stated for the sake of refuting the opponent's thesis of production from self. For, Buddhapālita did not state them intending to imply their opposite, and words accord with the intention of the speaker—they do not coerce the speaker powerlessly but accord with the speaker's motivation. For instance, when a Buddhist says 'consciousness' and a Sāṃkhya says 'consciousness', the two have radically different meanings. In this vein Chandrakīrti's *Clear Words* (24.2-.6, 16.17-17.3) says:

> When a proponent of no inherent existence adduces a consequence for a proponent of inherent existence, how could it follow that he is subject to the opposite meaning of the consequence? Words do not make the speaker powerless like [an executioner][406] with a club or noose [forcing a victim to say all sorts of things]. Then, how [do words indicate what they express]? If they have the capacity [to indicate their respective meaning], they accord with the speaker's intention in speaking. Therefore, [Buddhapālita's] adducing consequences [here] has the

effect only of refuting the other party's thesis [that reproduction is sensible and finite];[407] hence he does not come to have the opposite meaning of the consequences.

As Jam-ȳang-shay-b̄a notes,[408] Chandrakīrti is saying that Buddhapālita's consequences here at the point of refuting production from self do not imply their opposite meaning; he is not saying that no consequences imply their opposite meaning.

This is frequently Nāgārjuna's procedure

It is clearly Nāgārjuna's method in the *Treatise* frequently to use consequences, rather than syllogisms, to refute others' positions. For example, in refuting through an absurd consequence that a definition inherently subsists in what is defined,[409] he says (V.1cd):

> If space existed before its definition,
> It would follow that it was without definition [at that time, due to which it would not exist].

He states an unwanted consequence in order to refute another's position and to cause him to cognize that a definition does not inherently subsist in what is defined and, therefore, that the existence of a definition does not serve to show that the defined inherently exists. The consequence implies its opposite meaning: Space does not exist before its definition because of having a definition. However, it does not imply that space exists after its definition.

Also, in refuting through an absurd consequence that dependent establishment exists inherently in conventionalities, Nāgārjuna says (IV.2abc):[410]

> If a form [such as a sense power] existed [inherently]
> Separate from the form's cause [the elements],
> It would follow that a form is causeless [because depending on causes would be contradictory with its inherent existence].

Nāgārjuna here is implying the opposite meaning, i.e., that a form is not inherently separate from its causes because a form is caused. An unwanted consequence is being stated to refute a position, and the opposite is also being implied.

Similarly, in refuting that nirvana is a functioning thing (*bhāva, dngos po*), Nāgārjuna says (XXV.4ab):

> Nirvana is not a [functioning] thing.
> [For] it would follow that it would have the characteristics of aging and death.

Since the consequence is:

> It absurdly follows that nirvana has the characteristics of aging (changeability) and death (disintegration)[411] because of being a functioning thing,

the opposite is something that a Prāsaṅgika in the Ge-luk-b̄a school, which indeed asserts that nirvana is not a functioning things since it is unchanging, could assert:

> Nirvana is not a functioning thing because of not having the characteristics of aging and disintegration.

Though consequences sometimes imply their opposite meaning as in these cases, Bhāvaviveka cannot insist that Buddhapālita's consequences do so just because they are consequences, for there are many types, including those that do and do not imply their opposite. D̄zong-ka-b̄a[412] gives an illustration of one that implies its opposite: If it is asserted that a sprout exists by way of its own entity, then the consequence is flung:

> It follows that a sprout would not arise in dependence upon a seed because of existing by way of its own entity.

This implies the opposite:

> A sprout does not exist by way of its own entity because of arising in dependence upon a seed.

As D̄zong-ka-b̄a says, there are a great many instances of consequences' proving a thesis which is the opposite of the reason in the consequence by way of a reason which is the opposite of the predicate of the consequence. However, even in these cases, all that is being established is a mere elimination of the inherent existence which is asserted by the other party. A positive phenomenon is not being implied, and thus the Mādhyamika tenet that the reasonings proving emptiness establish only a non-affirming negation of inherent existence is not contravened even when the opposite is implied. Still, the question why Chandrakīrti cites as his three examples consequences that do imply their opposite remains; one could only say that he is giving examples of Nāgārjuna's procedure of using consequences, not of consequences that do not imply their opposite meaning.

Chandrakīrti's *Clear Words* (24.7-25.2, 17.3-.10) says:

> In this way, the master [Nāgārjuna] mostly eradicates others' positions by way of merely adducing consequences as through (V.1):
>
> Space does not at all exist
> Before its definition.
> If space existed before its definition,
> It would follow that it was without definition [at that time, due to which it would not exist].
>
> And (IV.2):
>
> If a form [such as a sense power] existed [inherently]
> Separate from the form's cause [the elements],
> It would follow that a form is causeless [because depending on causes would be contradictory with its inherent existence].
> Nowhere is there any [functioning] object that is causeless.
>
> Likewise (XXV.4):
>
> Nirvana is not a [functioning] thing (*bhāva, dngos po*).
> [For] it would follow that it would have the characteristics of aging and death.
> There are no [functioning] things
> Without aging and death.
>
> Etc.

Chandrakīrti's pointing out here that Nāgārjuna's procedure frequently is to adduce consequences (*prasaṅga, thal 'gyur*) appears to be a central reason why, in Tibet, Chandrakīrti's school came to be called Prāsaṅgika.

Why does Bhāvaviveka not find Buddhapālita's words to be rich with syllogisms like Nāgārjuna's?

Bhāvaviveka would find syllogisms implied in Nāgārjuna's consequences; so, Chandrakīrti asks him why he does not find them in Buddhapālita's statements. The hypothetical Bhāvaviveka answers that it is the job of a commentator in the process of expanding on the meaning of a root text to present syllogisms with proper reasons and examples. To this, Chandrakīrti cites the devastating fact that Nāgārjuna, in commenting on his own *Refutation of Objections*, did not extensively use syllogisms. The *Clear Words* (25.3-.7, 17.11-.16) says:[413]

> If the master [Nāgārjuna's] statements are considered to be causes of many syllogisms due to being meaningful statements and thus of great import, why are the master Buddhapālita's statements also not considered that way?
>
> *Objection* [by the hypothetical Bhāvaviveka]: It is the custom of commentators to set forth syllogisms at length.
>
> [*Answer:*] That also is not so because when even the master [Nāgārjuna] commented on [his] *Refutation of Objections*, he did not set out syllogistic statements.[414]

Thus, Mādhyamika custom or tradition does not call for the usage of syllogisms. Bhāvaviveka's insistence on syllogistic reasoning goes against Mādhyamika procedure.

Chandrakīrti next probes more deeply into the reasons behind Bhāvaviveka's insistence on syllogistic statements, concluding that it stems from a basic misconception about the nature of reasoning, which in turn stems from a misapprehension of emptiness. In this way, in the next and final phase of this controversy Chandrakīrti goes on the offensive—having defended Buddhapāliṭa by (1) first showing that consequences are sufficient,

(2) inbetween showing that even if one insists on a syllogistic statement, it is there in Buddhapālita's remarks, and (3) finally showing again that consequences are sufficient. By rimming his argument with demonstration of the sufficiency of consequences, Chandrakīrti causes us to wonder what is behind Bhāvaviveka's view. He is now ready to set out his view of emptiness, more profound than Bhāvaviveka's. It is a dramatic moment.

5 *Chandrakīrti's Refutation of Bhāvaviveka*

Sources
Chandrakīrti's *Clear Words*
Jam-ȳang-shay-b̄a's *Great Exposition of the Middle Way*
Gom-day Nam-ka-gyel-tsen's *Settling Difficult Points in the Opposite of the Consequences*
Kensur Lekden's oral teachings
Corresponding section of the translation pp.696-7

THE GENERAL INDICTMENT

To start, Chandrakīrti turns to analyzing Bhāvaviveka's refutation of the Sāṃkhya position of production from self.[415] The general indictment of Bhāvaviveka is that even though he asserts the Mādhyamika view, he states many faulty autonomous syllogisms —despite a wish to show great skill in logic. For instance, he states the following syllogism to refute production from self:

> Ultimately the internal sources (eye sense, ear sense, etc.) are not produced from self because of existing, like, for example, an existent consciousness. (Hereafter, 'eye sense' will be substituted for 'inner sources' for the sake of brevity.)

Many fallacies, such as the non-establishment of the presence of the reason ('existing') in the subject ('the inner sources'), are seen. Chandrakīrti's *Clear Words* (25.7-26.2, 17.16-18.2) says:

> Furthermore, this logician [Bhāvaviveka], while wishing merely to demonstrate that he has great skill in treatises of logic, expresses autonomous syllogisms which are realized to be the locus of collections of a great many fallacies, despite his asserting the Mādhyamika view. How? Respectively, here he states this syllogism, 'Ultimately the internal sources are not produced from self[416] because of existing, like existent consciousness.[417]

Since, in the Sāṃkhya system the person, or consciousness, is permanent, it is not produced and thus obviously not produced from self; so, a Sāṃkhya can easily agree with the suitability of the example, i.e., that consciousness is existent and not produced from self. In this type of reasoning, the reason is not a non-observation of a related object but an observation of something contradictory (existence) with the predicate of what is being negated (being produced from self). Bhāvaviveka's penchant for this style of reasoning is said to be based on the easy availability of cogent examples[418] approved by the other party.

According to Jam-ȳang-shay-b̄a, Bhāvaviveka's intention in this syllogism is to convey that just as the non-apprehension of production and cessation mentioned by Nāgārjuna in the expression of worship at the beginning of his *Treatise on the Middle Way* is taken in reference to a mind of meditative equipoise on emptiness, so the four extreme types of production should be explained as not existing in the face of meditative equipoise on emptiness. Considering 'ultimate' as referring to a mind of meditative equipoise on emptiness, Bhāvaviveka is actually wishing to say, 'For an ultimate consciousness, an eye sense is not produced from self because of existing, like, for example, an existent consciousness.'

DOES 'ULTIMATELY' GO WITH THE PREDICATE?

Chandrakīrti says that Bhāvaviveka's syllogism is not correct because—within its being unclear why the qualification 'ultimately' is affixed and to what it should be affixed—it is fallacious no matter how it is taken. He questions where 'ultimately' should be affixed in the syllogism. Does it go with the predicate? If so, it would mean:

> An eye sense is not ultimately produced from self because of existing, as in the case of, for example, an existent consciousness.

Bhāvaviveka might want to affix it to the predicate because to refute production conventionally would contradict the Mādhyamika's own tenets; therefore, it should be refuted only ultimately.

However, Chandrakīrti answers:

> 1 There is no need from the Mādhyamika's point of view to affix 'ultimately' to the predicate because, though a Mādhyamika asserts production conventionally, he does not assert production from self even conventionally. Therefore, production from self is to be refuted in general without affixing the qualification 'ultimately'. For this reason both Buddha in the *Rice Seedling Sutra*, etc., and Nāgārjuna in his *Treatise* refute production from self in general and do not affix 'ultimately' to the refutation.
>
> 2 There is no need from a Sāṃkhya's point of view to affix 'ultimately' to the predicate because there is value in refuting the Sāṃkhya, who has fallen from both ultimate truths and conventional truths, both ultimately and conventionally. Not recognizing emptiness, he falls from ultimate truths; falsely ascribing existence to a permanent person and so forth, he falls from conventional truths.
>
> 3 There is no need from the ordinary worldly person's point of view to affix 'ultimately' to the predicate in order to preserve worldly production from self because the world also does not assert production from self. Without considering whether things are produced from any of the four alternatives—self, other, both, or neither—the world

just accepts that a sprout, an effect, arises from a seed, a cause. Buddha said that he accepts what the world accepts, and this also is the way that Nāgārjuna accepts production conventionally—without analysis, such as investigating whether an effect is produced from itself, others, both, or causelessly.

About this, Chandrakīrti's *Clear Words* (26.2-27.6, 18.2-19.6) says:

> Why is the qualification 'ultimately' put in this [syllogism]?
>
> [Hypothetical answer by Bhāvaviveka: It is affixed to the predicate] because production which is asserted in accordance with worldly conventions is not to be refuted and because if it were refuted [conventionally], it would follow that one would be damaged by [one's own] assertion [of conventionally existent production].
>
> [*Response:*] This is not suitable because [a Mādhyamika] does not assert production from self even conventionally. [The *Rice Seedling*] *Sutra*[419] says:
>
>> Also, when a sprout is produced, arising from its cause—a seed—it is not created by self, not created by [naturally existent others], not created by both, not produced causelessly, not created by Īshvara, and not metamorphosed by time. It does not arise from particles, does not arise from the nature (*prakṛti, rang bzhin*), and does not arise from its own entity.
>
> Similarly [the *Extensive Sport Sutra (Lalitavistara)*][420] says:
>
>> If a seed exists, the sprout does also.
>> The sprout is not what the seed is.
>> It is not [inherently established as] other than it or just it.
>> Hence the nature of phenomena (*dharmatā, chos nyid*) is not permanent and not annihilatory.[421]
>
> Also, this very [text, Nāgārjuna's *Treatise on the Middle Way*, XVIII.10] says:

Whatever arises dependently is respectively
Not just that [i.e., its causes] and is not
Also other than that. Hence [causes]
Are not annihilatory nor permanent.

[Hypothetical response by Bhāvaviveka:] The qualification is made relative to the other's [that is, the Sāṃkhya's] system.

[*Answer:*] That also is not suitable because their presentations are not asserted [by Mādhyamikas] even conventionally. It is to be realized that it is advantageous to refute in both ways [that is, conventionally and ultimately] the Forders (*Tīrthika, Mu stegs pa*) who have fallen from non-erroneous perception of the two truths. Thus, to express the qualification relative to the other's system (*mata, gzhung*) is also not suitable.

Furthermore, the world—in relation to which the qualification would be meaningful [if it asserted production from self]—does not construe production from self. The world does not employ analysis such as 'from self' or 'from other' and so forth. The world understands only this, 'An ef- fect arises from a cause.' The master [Nāgārjuna] presented [cause and effect] this way too.

Therefore, the qualification ['ultimately'] is ascertained as meaningless in all respects.

DOES 'ULTIMATELY' GO WITH THE SUBJECT?

Bhāvaviveka might, however, say that 'ultimate' should be affixed to the subject because the production of an eye sense, which Sāṃkhyas accept as ultimate, is refuted even conventionally:

> An ultimate eye sense is not produced from self because of existing, as in the case, for example, of an existent consciousness.

Chandrakīrti answers that since Bhāvaviveka himself does not accept an ultimate eye sense, the subject and thus the reason are not established for him. (In an autonomous syllogism the subject and reason must be mutually and similarly established for both parties in a debate; in addition, an ultimate eye sense is not a fit subject for any type of syllogism with a positive reason such as 'existing', since it simply is not established.) The *Clear Words* (27.7-.9, 19.6-.9) says:

> [Hypothetical response by Bhāvaviveka:] This qualification was made wishing to refute the conventional production [of subjects which are asserted to exist ultimately].
>
> [*Answer:*] Then, you would have a fallacious position [thesis] in which the base [subject] is not established (*asiddhādhāra, gzhi ma grub pa*) and a fallacious reason in which the base [subject] is not established (*āshrayāsiddha, gzhi ma grub pa*) since you do not assert sources—eyes and so forth—ultimately.[421a]

It might be said that there is no fault because Bhāvaviveka accepts conventionally existent production, and a conventionally produced eye sense is taken as the subject of the syllogism. However, there then would be no place to which 'ultimately' could be affixed, for it would be affixed neither to the subject nor to the predicate.

Again, it might be said that 'a conventional eye sense' is the subject and 'is not ultimately produced' is the predicate. However, this also is incorrect because Bhāvaviveka did not say it, and even if he had, the subject would not exist for a Sāṃkhya. The Sāṃkhyas do not accept that an eye sense exists conventionally the way Mādhyamikas use 'conventionally'. In Mādhyamika terms, the Sāṃkhyas accept an eye sense as substantially existent (*dravyasat, rdzas yod*) and not as imputedly existent (*prajñaptisat, btags yod*) or conventional as the Mādhyamikas do. Though the Sāṃkhyas assert that the principal (*pradhāna, gtso bo*) and person (*puruṣha, skyes bu*) are ultimate truths and that the rest of the twenty-five categories are conventional truths, since they ascribe a different meaning to 'conventional', it would be necessary to explain which meaning of 'conventional' was being used. Using the Mādhyamikas' meaning would be unacceptable to the Sāṃkhyas; using the Sāṃkhyas' meaning would make the subject non-existent for the Mādhyamikas. Even on this level Bhāvaviveka's argument is ill-framed. Chandrakīrti's *Clear Words* (27.9-28.3, 19.9-.17) says:

> [Hypothetical response by Bhāvaviveka:] Since eyes and so forth exist conventionally, there is no fault.
>
> [*Answer:*] Then what does 'ultimately' qualify?
>
> ['Bhāvaviveka':] Since the ultimate production of conventionalities such as eyes is being refuted, 'ultimately' qualifies the refutation of production.
>
> [*Answer:*] In that case, [you] should have said, 'Ultimately there is no production of conventionalities such as eyes,' but such was not said. Even if you had, because the other party [the Sāṃkhya] asserts eyes and so forth just as substantially existent (*dravyasat, rdzas su yod pa*)[422] and does not assert them as imputedly existent (*prajñaptisat, btags par yod pa*), the position [thesis] would be fallacious in that the base [subject] would not be established. Hence, that is not suitable.

COMMONLY APPEARING SUBJECTS

Bhāvaviveka might answer that one should not qualify either the subject or the predicate with 'ultimate' or 'conventional' but take as the subject just a general eye sense which is common to both disputants. He might assert that when various schools of tenets debate, it is necessary to take just general terms for the subject and the predicate, for if each school affixed its own particulars, there would be no such thing as inference. (I feel that with this final major move in the now entirely hypothetical argument Chandrakīrti has gotten down to his basic point: Bhāvaviveka's insistence on the statement of syllogisms indicates that for him the elements of a syllogistic argument—subject, predicate, reason, and example—appear commonly to both parties of a debate, Mādhyamika and non-Mādhyamika, that is to say, are asserted as certified by valid consciousnesses in a similar way in their respective systems, whereas if Bhāvaviveka knew Mādhyamika well, he would know that such is impossible. The defense of Buddhapālita has prepared the ground by revealing the intensity of Bhāvaviveka's insistence on syllogistic reasoning, and the examination of the qualification 'ultimately' has removed a possible objection—Chandrakīrti is suggesting that Bhāvaviveka really did not mean anything by it anyway. In other words, we are not dealing in the merely hypothetical but in what Chandrakīrti feels is actually at the core of Bhāvaviveka's thought.)

Bhāvaviveka might cite some examples. For instance, if, when a Buddhist proved to a Vaisheṣhika that a sound is an impermanent thing, he specified the subject as a sound which is derived from the great elements, the subject would not exist for the Vaisheṣhika. If, in accordance with Vaisheṣhika tenets, 'a sound which is a quality of space' were specified, it would not exist for the Buddhist. Similarly, if, when a Vaisheṣhika debated with a Jaina, he specified 'a sound which is a product' as the subject, it would not exist for the Jaina. If he specified in accordance with Jaina tenets 'a sound which existed formerly and is manifested by conditions', the subject would not exist for the Vaisheṣhika himself.

Similarly, Bhāvaviveka might add that the predicate of a thesis also cannot possibly be qualified with the particular tenets of each school but must be only the general term. For instance, if when proving that a sound is an impermanent thing, a Buddhist specified the predicate as 'an impermanent thing the disintegration of which is [externally] caused', the predicate would not exist for the Buddhist himself because things require no further cause for their disintegration other than their own production. Still, if he took as the predicate 'an impermanent thing the disintegration of which is uncaused', the predicate would not exist for the Vaisheṣhika.

Bhāvaviveka might add that the reason why even the predicate must be just the generality which appears similarly to both parties in the debate is that before proving a thesis, one must give a concordant example which possesses both the predicate (impermanent thing) and the sign (product). Since the predicate is, therefore, a quality of the example, it is clear that the predicate must appear similarly to both parties and, if so, must be just a generality not qualified by any school's particular tenets. In this vein, Chandrakīrti's *Clear Words* (28.4-29.7, 19.17-20.8) says:[423]

> [Hypothetical response by Bhāvaviveka: For example,] in [the proof] that sound is an impermanent thing just generalities are to be taken as the subject and the predicate, not specified [with the particular tenets of the debaters]. If specifics were used, the conventions of inference [that is, inferring consciousness] and object inferred would be non-existent. For, if [as the subject] one used 'sound which is derived from the elements', it would not be established for the other party [the Vaisheṣhika]. However, if one used 'sound which is a quality of space (*ākāsha, nam mkha'*)', it would not be established for oneself, the Buddhist.
>
> Similarly, even when a Vaisheṣhika posits the thesis that sound is an impermanent thing, if [as the subject] he used 'sound which is a product', it would not be established for the other [party, the Jaina]. However, if [the subject were specified as 'sound] manifested [by conditions]', it would not be established for himself.
>
> Similarly, [with respect to the predicate] if [impermanence were specified as] that of which the disintegration is caused, it would not be established for the Buddhist himself. However, if [it were specified as] causeless, it would not be established for the other party [a Vaisheṣhika]. Therefore, just as here [in these examples] mere generalities are to be used as the subject and the predicate, so here also [in the refutation of production from self] a mere subject devoid of qualification is to be used.

There are no commonly appearing subjects

Chandrakīrti's answer is that all of this is inadmissible. A valid cognizer must certify the subject of a syllogism as existing, and in systems such as Bhāvaviveka's and a Sāṃkhya's which assert (either explicitly or implicitly) that all objects exist by way of their own character this valid cognizer must be non-mistaken in terms of the object's establishment by way of its own character. Thus, in Bhāvaviveka's system, a mistaken sense consciousness is not accepted as finding or certifying its object of comprehension; rather, the subject about which the two parties are debating whether it is ultimately produced or not must be certified as existing by such a non-mistaken consciousness. Because of this, Bhāvaviveka cannot assert that eyes and so forth are falsities, appearing one way and yet existing another—that is to say, appearing to be established by way of their own character but not—since he asserts that the consciousness certifying the subject is non-mistaken. However, eyes and so forth which are found by a non-mistaken valid cognizer just plain do not exist. Thus, although Bhāvaviveka and a Sāṃkhya agree on the status of the subject with respect to its being established by way of its own character, such a subject simply does not exist. In this way, the meaning of there being no commonly appearing subjects is that the subject in a syllogism such as Bhāvavivek's simply does not exist. Chandrakīrti's *Clear Words* (29.7-30.3, 20.8-.12) says:

> That is not so, because at this time [of proving that eyes and so forth are without truly established production][424] when it is just the case that a negation of production is asserted as the predicate of the probandum, this one [Bhāvaviveka] himself just asserts the degeneration [or non-establishment][425] of the entity of subjects [eyes and so forth]—the basis of that [predicate, non-production from self]—which are found by a mere erroneous [consciousness. Bhāvaviveka instead holds that the subjects of his syllogism, eyes and so forth, are found by a non-erroneous or non-mistaken consciousness in which case they would not be falsities; however, they *are* falsities

since they appear to exist inherently but do not, and thus the subject is not established.] The erroneous and the non-erroneous are different [that is, a dichotomy].

To repeat, at this time when Bhāvaviveka is attempting to prove that for an ultimate or reasoning consciousness an eye sense is not produced, he might not qualify the subject with tenets peculiar to any system, but the subject must still be validly cognized by both parties. However, in Bhāvaviveka's system if a consciousness is mistaken with respect to the inherent existence of an object, it is not valid. For him, to be valid with respect to an object a consciousness must also be valid with respect to the object's being established by way of its own character. Thus, once a sense consciousness apprehending blue, for instance, is valid, it must be non-mistaken with respect to its appearing object (the blue), and once a conceptual consciousness, such as an inferential consciousness realizing the impermanence of the body, is valid, it must be non-mistaken with respect to its referent object (the impermanence of the body).[426] Since the consciousnesses that realize these are non-mistaken, these objects cannot be falsities, appearing to exist one way but actually existing in another way; otherwise, the consciousnesses would be mistaken with respect to that seeming mode of being.

However, they *are* falsities, and falsities simply cannot be among objects found by a non-mistaken consciousness. The reason for this is that false objects and true objects—that is to say, erroneous objects found by a mistaken consciousness and non-erroneous objects found by a non-mistaken consciousness—are mutually exclusive, even a dichotomy; whatever exists must be either one or the other. In this context, a mistaken consciousness is one to which eyes and so forth, for instance, appear to be established by way of their own character because objects which are so established do not exist, just as the falling hairs which appear to someone with cataracts do not exist in the least. Chandrakīrti's *Clear Words* (30.3-.4, 20.12-.15) says:

Therefore, like the falling hairs [seen by] one with cataracts and so forth, when what does not exist [by way of

> its own character] is apprehended by [i.e., appears to] an erroneous [consciousness] as just existing [that way], how could even a portion of an object existent [by way of its own character] be observed?

Similarly, in this context a non-mistaken consciousness is one which directly perceives only the nature of phenomena, emptiness, since it does not involve the appearance of false objects that even in direct perception seem to exist one way but do not. A consciousness in meditative equipoise perceives only emptiness in a totally non-dualistic way, without the slightest appearance of conventional objects which appear to sentient beings as if they are established by way of their own character but do not. To a consciousness of meditative equipoise on emptiness, there is not the slightest appearance of something that does not exist the way it appears; this is like the fact that the consciousness of one without cataracts does not see falling hairs and so forth and thus it does not certify those falling hairs as existing. In this vein, Chandrakīrti's *Clear Words* (30.5-.8, 20.15-.20) says:

> Like the falling hairs and so forth of one without cataracts, when a non-erroneous [consciousness of meditative equipoise on emptiness] does not superimpose the unreal [i.e., objects established by way of their own character], how could it observe the merest portion of a conventionality that does not exist [by way of its own character]? Therefore, the honorable master [Nāgārjuna] says [in his *Refutation of Objections*]:[427]
>
> > If [in accordance with your thought] the factualities
> > Of direct perception and so forth did observe some
> > [inherently established objects of comprehension],
> > Then [it would be suitable] to prove those [in one's own system] and refute [others], but since [valid cognizers observing
> > Such objects of comprehension] do not exist [even conventionally], there is no [chance for you] to censure me.

According to Chandrakīrti, all consciousnesses of sentient beings except a direct cognizer of emptiness are mistaken, and thus there can be no valid cognizer of the subject in a syllogism which is not mistaken with regard to the mode of being of that subject. However, a non-deceived consciousness, which nevertheless is mistaken about the inherent existence of its object in the sense not that it *conceives* the object to exist inherently but that the object merely *appears* to exist that way, can establish the existence of objects that are falsities—objects which appear to exist by way of their own character or inherently but do not. A distinction is made between the appearing object (*snang yul*) of a consciousness and its object of engagement (*'jug yul*); a valid cognizer (*pramāṇa, tshad ma*) can be mistaken with respect to its appearing object but not with respect to its object of engagement.

Thus, it is not that Prāsaṅgikas hold that the subject in a debate is not certified by the valid cognizers of both parties, for they hold that each party—whether they recognize it or not—has valid cognizers of mere objects, such as eyes, which are valid with respect to neither the inherent existence nor the non-inherent existence of the object.[428] However, only a Prāsaṅgika recognizes valid cognizers to be such; a non-Prāsaṅgika holds that the very valid cognizer which certifies the existence of the subject of the syllogism certifies its being established by way of its own character. Thus, in one way it is said that there are no commonly appearing subjects in the sense that *in the systems* of the two, the Prāsaṅgika and the non-Prāsaṅgika, the establishment of the subject by valid cognition is not *asserted* similarly.

In another way, even though the two parties, such as Bhāvaviveka and a Sāṃkhya, might agree that the subject of a syllogism is certified by a consciousness that is non-mistaken with respect to its being established by way of its own character, the subject, when qualified this way, does not exist, and thus from this point of view it can be said that a commonly appearing subject does not exist.

Again, in another way, if in a debate in which one was seeking to prove non-ultimate production, the other party understood the subject as being certified by a consciousness that is valid with respect to neither its inherent existence nor its non-inherent existence, that person would already have understood the Prāsaṅgika view of the emptiness of inherent existence. The person would have come to be able to differentiate between inherent existence and mere existence—making it possible to identify that there are consciousnesses which neither certify inherent existence nor realize non-inherent existence but only realize their object. Thus, there would be no need to establish non-ultimate production for such a person. In this case, there is also no commonly appearing subject—even though both parties recognize the 'subject' as being certified by a similar type of valid cognizer—simply because there is no subject which needs to be proven as lacking ultimately existent production.

Thus, when there is no non-erroneous consciousness to certify the existence of the subjects of syllogisms such as eyes (the subject of Bhāvaviveka's syllogism proving that eyes are not produced from self) which for Bhāvaviveka are qualified by being found by a non-erroneous consciousness, the subjects just plain do not exist. Since such a subject cannot be established, the two parties—even if they, like Bhāvaviveka and a Sāṃkhya, both hold the view that the consciousness certifying the subject certifies its inherent existence—do not have a common mode of establishing the subject with valid cognition. For a non-erroneous consciousness in this context just perceives emptiness, resulting in there being no valid cognizer non-erroneously knowing subjects such as eyes.

In this way, the subject is shown not to be established in common for the two proponents. This makes the thesis, the combination of subject and predicate, non-established simply because the subject is not established. For the same reason, the sign's being a property of the subject (*pakṣhadharmatā, phyogs chos*) also is not established. Chandrakīrti's *Clear Words* (30.9-.11, 20.20-21.5) says:[428a]

> Because in that way the erroneous and the non-erroneous are different, on an occasion when the non-erroneous [is realized by the wisdom of meditative equipoise] the

erroneous does not exist [in its perspective]. Hence, how could a conventionality [that is to say, falsity such as] an eye which is the subject [in this syllogism] be [in its perspective]? Therefore, due to the irreversibility of having a fallacious position [thesis] in which the base [subject] is not established (*asiddhādhāra, gzhi ma grub pa*) and a fallacious reason in which the base [subject] is not established (*āshrayāsiddha, gzhi ma grub pa*), this [attempt at an answer—that commonly appearing generalities are to be used—] is just not an answer [since there is no valid cognizer, mistaken or non-mistaken, to certify the existence of such subjects].

Are there ever commonly appearing subjects?

Chandrakīrti is saying that there is a difference between proving impermanence and proving emptiness with respect to whether or not there can be commonly appearing subjects. Thus, it might seem that we are to conclude that even in the Prāsaṅgika system there are occasions when commonly appearing subjects are possible.[429] However, Gom-day Nam-ka-gyel-tsen[430] specifies that the Buddhist here is of the lower schools, thereby suggesting that even when debating on impermanence there is no commonly appearing subject in the Prāsaṅgika system. This is cogent because the non-Prāsaṅgika would still hold that the valid cognizer which certifies the subject certifies its inherent existence, but no such subject exists.

However, if one held that even in the Prāsaṅgika system there are commonly appearing subjects on occasions such as in debating about impermanence, one could say that the question of inherent existence is here of no consequence and that this is why both Chandrakīrti and D̄zong-ka-b̄a center their discussion of no commonly appearing subjects around the proof of no ultimately existent production or no production from self, in which the question of inherent existence is intimately involved. In this way, some Tibetan scholars say that the Prāsaṅgika tenet that a subject does not appear similarly to both parties in a debate applies only to occasions when proving emptiness.[431] Chandrakīrti's *Clear Words* (30.12-.14, 21.5-.9) says:

> There also is no similarity with the example. Even if there [in the example] a generality of sound and a generality of impermanence which are not asserted as qualified [with particular tenets] do exist for both [the Buddhist and the Vaisheṣhika], nevertheless proponents of emptiness and proponents of non-emptiness do not [agree on] asserting a generality of eyes as conventionally [existent in the sense of not being established by way of its own character] or as ultimately [existent]. Hence, there also is no similarity with the example.

Bhāvaviveka has to admit his own reason is not established

Chandrakīrti indicts Bhāvaviveka further, saying that he must accept the consequence that his reason refuting production from self is not established. For when another Buddhist school stated the syllogism:

> The subjects, the inner sources, are only caused because the Tathāgata said so,

Bhāvaviveka said that the reason was not established. His thought was that if it were said that the Tathāgata meant ultimately existent causation, the reason would be non-existent for a Mādhyamika whereas if the Tathāgata meant only conventionally existent causation, the reason would be non-existent for a Proponent of True Existence. Since besides these two there is no third category, Bhāvaviveka himself objected that the reason had the fallacy of not being established for both disputants.

Here in the case of Bhāvaviveka's attempt to refute production from self, there is also no third category other than (1) objects found by mistaken consciousnesses and (2) objects found by non-mistaken consciousnesses. If the subject, the sign, and so forth are claimed to be cognized by a non-mistaken consciousness, then they would not be established for Mādhyamikas. For Mādhyamikas (actually Prāsaṅgikas) say that except for the wisdom of meditative equipoise on emptiness any consciousness of a sentient being is mistaken. If it is claimed that the subject, the sign, and so forth are cognized by a mistaken consciousness, then they would not be established for non-Mādhyamikas. For the Proponents of True Existence assert that a valid consciousness is non-mistaken with respect to the inherent nature of its object. It is self-contradictory for Bhāvaviveka to assert something parallel to what he finds to be a fallacy in others.

This is a convincing argument, but the debate does stem from a difference of tenet in the Prāsaṅgika and Svātantrika systems.[432] Chandrakīrti does not accept that consciousnesses of sentient beings are non-mistaken valid cognizers with respect to the inherent existence of their objects, whereas Bhāvaviveka does. The latter finds that it is not contradictory for a consciousness to perceive things as inherently existent and to be non-mistaken because things do conventionally exist inherently. Chandrakīrti finds the two to be contradictory because both true existence and inherent existence are equally to be refuted, both ultimately and conventionally.

This means that for Bhāvaviveka when an object is sought among its bases of imputation, it can be found. For instance, a table is the composite of its parts, and the actual person is a subtle form of the mental consciousness. For Chandrakīrti, an object cannot be found among its bases of imputation; a table is not the composite of its parts, and a person is not a consciousness. In the Prāsaṅgika system, even conventionally objects are only imputedly existent; they are designations. Furthermore, it is undeniable that sentient beings perceive objects just the opposite way; the basis of imputation appears to be the thing itself. Thus, a Prāsaṅgika asserts that all sentient beings' sense and mental consciousnesses, except direct cognizers of emptiness, are mistaken. Hence, it is not that Bhāvaviveka has a manifest contradiction[433] but that he does not assert something which a Mādhyamika, as interpreted by Chandrakīrti, should—that conventional objects are certified only by mistaken consciousnesses. If he did assert this, he would be subject to the same kind of analysis that he makes with respect to the Hearer school's syllogism. In other words, in proving to a Sāṃkhya that eyes and so forth are not produced from self, he would be holding that such conventionalities are certified by mistaken consciousnesses, whereas for the Sāṃkhya the consciousness certifying the subject—eyes—would also certify its inherent existence; in that case the subject would not be established in common for the two of them.

The claim of self-contradiction is Chandrakīrti's way of highlighting the fact that Bhāvaviveka, in asserting that a valid cognizer of a conventionality is unmistaken, is going against what should be a basic Mādhyamika tenet—that except for a consciousness directly realizing emptiness all consciousnesses of sentient beings are mistaken in that their objects appear to exist inherently but do not.

Chandrakīrti offers no explicit evidence that Bhāvaviveka asserts that such consciousnesses of conventionalities are non-mistaken; there is merely his earlier statement (p.508) that Bhāvaviveka himself accepts that objects found by a mistaken consciousness are not established:

> . . . at this time [of proving that eyes and so forth are without truly established production] when it is just the case that a negation of production is asserted as the predicate of the probandum, this one [Bhāvaviveka] himself just asserts the degeneration [or non-establishment] of the entity of subjects [eyes and so forth], the basis of that [predicate, non-production from self], which are found by a mere erroneous [consciousness].

If Bhāvaviveka asserts that objects found by an erroneous or mistaken consciousness are not established, then since he obviously holds that the subjects of his syllogisms are established, he must hold that they are certified or realized by non-mistaken consciousnesses. From this, many Tibetan scholars have drawn the conclusion that for Bhāvaviveka the object of negation in the view of emptiness does not appear to sense consciousnesses.

In Tibet, these points have been formalized into a Svātantrika system by scholars using as their basis brilliant exploration of the implications of brief statements such as this. By presenting a system in structured form, what is gained is clarity and sharpness in differentiating positions, resulting in ease in applying such tenets in meditation. Still, in the debating courtyards of the monastic universities, the sources for these now seemingly hardened positions are examined in detail with the result that those who pursue the topics in depth realize the almost fluid nature of the sources while reconstructing and examining the patterns of Dzong-ka-ba's thought as he formalized these systems. The challenge is first to come to know Dzong-ka-ba's interpretation so well that one can read it into his sources and then to examine the sources to determine if the interpretation is justified—both of these phases being required in the debating courtyard. A basic requirement is to go beyond the texts to construct what Bhāvaviveka, for instance, was getting at. Thus, dynamic ingenuity is not limited to the past; it is ever-presently required. Our examination of the texts here is, therefore, only the tip of the iceberg.

About Bhāvaviveka's being forced to accept that his own reason is faulty, Chandrakīrti's *Clear Words* (30.15-31.10, 21.9-2.6) says:

> Just this mode of expressing the fallaciousness of the position [or thesis] which is that the basis [the subject] is not established is to be applied also in expressing the fault of non-establishment with respect to this reason—'because of existing'.[434] For, this logician [Bhāvaviveka] himself [comes to] assert the points explained above. How? Another stated this proof:
>
> > Causes and so forth producing the internal sources just exist because the Tathāgata said so. Whatever the Tathāgata said is that way, as, for example, is the case with [his] saying that nirvana is peace.
>
> At that time [Bhāvaviveka] expressed the following fault:
>
> > What are you asserting is the meaning of the reason? [Are you saying] 'because the Tathāgata said such [in terms of] conventional [existence]'[435] or 'because the Tathāgata said such [in terms of] ultimate [existence]'? If conventionally, the meaning of the reason is not established for yourself, but if ultimately, [then as

Nāgārjuna, I.7ab, says,] 'When [one analyzes whether][436] the phenomena [of effects] exist, do not exist, or [both] exist and do not exist [at the time of their causes], they are [understood as] not established [by causes].' At that time, conditions [producing] effects which have a nature of existence, non-existence, or both [at the time of their causes] are refuted. Therefore (I.7cd) 'How could [an ultimately established definition, that is,] establisher (*nirvartaka, sgrub byed*) [or producer] be [the definition of] causal [condition (*hetupratyaya, rgyu'i rkyen*)]? In that case, it is not feasible [to say that because the definition of causal condition ultimately exists, causal conditions ultimately exist].' The meaning of [Nāgārjuna's] statement is that those [ultimately existent things] are just not causes producing [effects]. Therefore, because [we Mādhyamikas assert that][437] what is established [that is, effects] and establishers [that is, causes] do not exist ultimately, [for a Mādhyamika] that reason is just non-established [if the referent is to ultimate existence]. Or it is just contradictory [if the referent is to ultimate existence due to being very contradictory with a predicate of the probandum which should be a conventionality].

Bhāvaviveka's other autonomous reasons are not established

Chandrakīrti adds that Bhāvaviveka's other autonomous syllogisms similarly incur the fallacy of the non-establishment of the subject, reason, and example since in the latter's system these must be certified by a valid cognizer which is non-mistaken with respect to the mode of being of the object. For a Prāsaṅgika a valid cognizer can be mistaken with regard to the object's inherent existence but still be able to certify the existence of the object as a falsity; however, this does not mean that ignorance establishes the existence of objects.[438] Ignorance wrongly imputes the inherent existence of objects; valid dualistic cognizers establish the existence of objects.

About these other autonomous syllogisms, Chandrakīrti's *Clear Words* (31.11-33.3, 22.6-3.12) says:

> Because this one [Bhāvaviveka] himself [comes] in this way to assert the non-establishment of reasons, in all inferences in which [he] states inherently existent phenomena (*vastudharma, dngos po'i chos*)[439] as reasons, the reason and so forth are not established for him. Hence, all [his] proofs are destroyed. For, in:
>
> > Ultimately the internal sources are not produced from their conditions which are other [than them] because of being other, as, for example, is the case with a pot,[440]
>
> or:
>
> > The producers of the internal sources such as eyes, which others[441] want to say [exist] ultimately, are not ascertained as conditions [producing the internal sources] because of being other, as, for example, is the case with threads and so forth,
>
> 'other' and so forth are not established for oneself [i.e., Bhāvaviveka].
>
> On an occasion when another expressed the following reason:
>
> > The internal sources are only produced because of making the special designations of those which possess their objects [that is to say, because of being the reasons why their respective consciousnesses are called 'eye consciousnesses' and so forth],[442]
>
> this one [Bhāvaviveka], wanting to speak of the non-establishment of that reason, says that if production, going, and so forth were established as existing ultimately by the eye of[443] wisdom of a yogi in meditative equipoise seeing the reality of things just as it is, then that reason—'because of making the special designations

of those which possess their objects'—would just have the sense of being established [but it is not established] because [ultimately existent] going is also refuted just through the refutation of [ultimately existent] production.

This [sort of reasoning that Bhāvaviveka used against his opponent] likewise is to be applied also[444] to a reason which he formulates:

> Ultimately the not-yet-gone-over is not being gone over because of being a path, like the path already gone over.

In that, the reason—path—is not established for him [due to not being established by the meditative equipoise of a yogi seeing suchness, this being the only unmistaken consciousness that a non-Buddha has].

Also, in:

> An eye that serves as a basis [of an eye consciousness], does not ultimately see forms because of being an eye sense power, as, for example, is the case with [an eye sense power] that is similar [to one that serves as the basis of an eye consciousness but does not actually serve as a basis of an eye consciousness such as during sleep],

and likewise:

> An eye does not [ultimately] see forms because of having arisen from the elements, as, for example, is the case with form,[445]

and:

> Earth is not [ultimately] an entity of hardness because of being an element, as, for example, is the case with wind,[446]

and so forth it is to be applied that the reasons and so forth are not established for yourself [Bhāvaviveka].

Bhāvaviveka's reason is inconclusive

Furthermore, the reason of Bhāvaviveka's autonomous syllogism would be inconclusive for a Sāṃkhya:

> The subject, an eye sense, is not ultimately produced from self because of existing, as, for example, is the case with an existent consciousness.

A Sāṃkhya might think that an eye sense, because it exists, is not produced from self as in the case of consciousness but is produced from self as in the case of a pot. For him, a consciousness or person is not a product and thus, of course, is not produced from self; therefore, an eye sense is not produced from self in the sense that a consciousness is not produced from self, but it is produced from self in the way that a pot is. Bhāvaviveka might object that pots are equally proven not to be produced from self, but that is not what he said since his subject was limited to the internal sources unlike Buddhapālita's broad subject that includes all things involving production. Chandrakīrti's *Clear Words* (33.4-.6, 23.12-18) says:

> Also,[447] this reason—'because of existing'—is indefinite in that the other party [would wonder], 'Is it that the internal sources because of existing are not produced from self in accordance with how consciousness exists or is it that, like pots and so forth, they are produced from self?'
>
> ['Bhāvaviveka' objects:] It is not indefinite because pots and so forth are equally proven [not to be produced from self because of existing].
>
> [*Answer:*] That is not so because such was not expressed.

Our other-approved syllogisms do not incur those faults

Chandrakīrti says that all of these fallacies accrue to Bhāvaviveka because of his using autonomous syllogisms in which the subject and so forth must appear similarly to both parties in the sense that they must be established similarly in the systems of both. It is not sufficient in an autonomous syllogism that the subject be just validly established by one party and just validly established by the other party. Rather, the subject must be established or certified similarly in the *systems* of both disputants. Just so, the presence of the sign in the subject, the pervasion, counter-pervasion, and example must be validly established in the systems of both parties in a similar manner. This is the meaning of there being no similarly appearing subject, etc.

These fallacies do not accrue when one uses other-approved syllogisms. For instance, Nāgārjuna says (III.2cd):

> How can that which does not
> See itself see another?

This is an other-approved syllogism:

> The subject, an eye, does not inherently see another, a form, because of not seeing itself, like, for example, a pot.

It is not necessary to establish the reason, the example, and the subject (even though they are established for a Mādhyamika)[448] because the opponent himself accepts them. In order to ascertain the pervasion, i.e., that non-inherently existent perception of others pervades that which does not perceive itself, first a general pervasion is to be ascertained. This is done through a general counter-pervasion:

> If things have an inherently existent nature, first that nature is to be apprehended in a thing, and then this nature can be apprehended in another which possesses that thing. For instance, because water has moisture, moisture is apprehended in earth which possesses water. Also, because a pleasant odor is apprehended in a certain flower, the pleasant odor is apprehended in a cloth which possesses, or is infused with, the odor of this flower.

Then, a general pervasion is stated:

> If there is non-apprehension of a nature in a thing, then it follows that there is non-possession of this nature in another phenomenon which possesses this thing. For example, since jasmine flowers do not possess a foul odor, a foul odor is not apprehended in clothing that possesses, or is infused with, them.

Having demonstrated the general pervasion, it is applied to the present context:

> It is admissible that if an eye has perception of itself, then it inherently sees another form when together with it. However, since an eye does not see itself, it does not inherently see another form.

When the opponent ascertains such a refutation *as* a refutation through realizing that not seeing oneself and inherently seeing another are contradictory, he ascertains the Mādhyamika view of no inherent existence. At this time, he forsakes the theses and tenets of a Proponent of True Existence and simultaneously realizes that though things do not have inherent existence, conventionally existent activity and agency are possible. He then comes to distinguish non-existence and non-inherent existence for the first time, understanding that non-inherent existence does not contradict functionality. Chandrakīrti's *Clear Words* (34.1-.12, 23.18-4.16) says:

> [Hypothetical objection by Bhāvaviveka:] Is it not that just those faults which you ascribe to another's [that is, my, Bhāvaviveka's, own] syllogisms accrue to your inferences, due to which they would just have the fallacies of non-establishment of the subject, reason, and so forth? Therefore, do not object to one [of us] with the faults that are incurred by both. Therefore, all these faults are not suitable.
>
> *Answer:* Proponents of autonomous inferences (*svatantra-anumāna, rang rgyud kyi rjes su dpag pa*) come to have these faults but we do not use autonomous

inferences because our[449] inferences have the fruit of only refuting others' theses.

It is as follows. [For example] another[450] who thinks that the eye [inherently] sees is refuted by inference renowned to himself:

> You assert that an eye [has] the attribute of not seeing its own entity and also[451] assert that if it does not have the attribute of [inherently] seeing other [forms such as blue, then that an eye sees] just does not occur. Therefore, whatever [substratum] does not possess [the attribute of] seeing its own entity also does not possess [the attribute of] seeing others [such as blue and so forth], as, for example, is the case with a pot [which does not inherently see others because of not seeing its own entity]. Also, an eye does not possess [the attribute of][452] seeing its own entity; therefore, it also does not possess [the attribute of inherently] seeing others [such as forms]. Therefore, seeing others—blue and so forth—which is contradictory with not seeing its own entity is contradicted just by inference renowned to yourself.

Since only such is expressed by our[453] inferences, how could our position be subject to those faults as mentioned and due to which[454] fallacy would be equally incurred?

The syllogism is valid because the subject and so forth are validly established for the opponent. It is not necessary that the subject and so forth be validly established in the same manner for the stater of the refutation. However, this does not mean that they are not established for the Mādhyamika; they are, and they *must* be. What is not required is that the subject and so forth be validly established in a similar manner in the systems of both disputants. Therefore, the term 'other-renowned syllogism' eliminates that the subject and so forth are established *in a similar manner* for the Mādhyamika; it does not suggest either that these are not established for the Mādhyamika or are a matter of doubt. Thus, something's being 'other-renowned' or 'other-approved' comes down to *how* it is renowned or established for the other party, not to whether it is accepted as validly existing. As Dzong-ka-ba says:[455]

> Therefore, the subject, predicate, and reason of an other-renowned syllogism must exist conventionally; it is not sufficient that they merely be asserted as existing by him [the other party].

The conventions of the world alone are appropriate for logical treatises, and in the world disputes are settled either by a third party accepted by both disputants or by one's own word, but not by the opponent's word. Just so, people are convinced by reasons established for them and not merely by the fact that reasons are established for others. Chandrakīrti's *Clear Words* (34.13-35.4, 24.16-5.5) says:

> [Hypothetical rejoinder by Bhāvaviveka:] Is there damage by inference even from an inference established for either [of the parties]?
>
> *Answer:* There is. It is just by a reason established for oneself, not by one established for the other [disputant], since such is seen in the world. In the world, sometimes [one party] prevails and [the other] is defeated by the word of a judge which both take to be valid, and sometimes, by just one's own word, but victory or defeat is not by the other's word. Just as it is in the world, so it is also in logic because only the conventions of the world are appropriate in treatises of logic.

Vasubandhu and Dignāga assert that in both affirmations and negations the subject and so forth must be established for both parties, but according to Chandrakīrti they actually should accept the usage of other-approved or other-renowned syllogisms. For in a refutation by scriptural citation the scripture need not be accepted as a valid teaching by both in the debate, just by the defending party. Also, in inferences for oneself (as in meditative reflection) it is sufficient that the subject and so forth be established for oneself and need not be established for both because in an inference for oneself there is no second party. Thus, it is senseless for them to insist on common establishment of the subject and to say that consequences alone cannot generate an inferring consciousness. Buddhas aid those worldly beings who do not know suchness with just what is renowned among them. Chandrakīrti's *Clear Words* (35.4-36.2, 25.5-.16) says:

> Therefore, some say, 'There is no harm by inference that is through the force of being renowned to the other [party] because [we] wish to refute mere renown to others.' Also, there is someone who thinks, 'That [reason][456] which expresses ascertainment [established] for both is [capable of] proof and refutation; that which is either established for just one or about which there is doubt [by either party as to whether it is established] is not capable of such.' In dependence upon the world's presentation of conventions they also should assert just this mode, as described above, with respect to inference. For, damage through scripture is not only by way of scripture established for both [parties]. Then how? It is [also] by way of [scripture] established for [the other party] himself. [Furthermore] in inference for oneself just what is established for oneself is weightier at all [times], not what is established for both.
>
> Therefore, expression of the definitions of logic [as they are renowned in the systems of the Svātantrikas and below][457] is not needed because the Buddhas help beings who are trainees and who do not know suchness with reasoning as it is renowned to them. Enough extensive elaboration.

REMARKS

There is great emphasis in the Prāsaṅgika system on the conventions of the world, which provide a common ground and insure that the Prāsaṅgika will not be trying to help the world with a language it does not understand.[458] Yet, it should not be thought that a Prāsaṅgika seeks to defeat all logicians through contradictory consequences in order to return to the vulgar views of the world. The refutations of other doctrinal systems are to be applied to the eradication of one's own innate ways of misconceiving the person and other phenomena. Though Prāsaṅgikas mostly assert the existence of the phenomena which the world says exist, they do not accept what the world conceives about how these phenomena exist. No phenomenon exists by way of its own character; all phenomena exist imputedly, including emptiness. No phenomenon is its basis of imputation; all phenomena lack inherent existence. It is undeniable that the opposite appears to worldly beings and that, in turn, the world adheres to this appearance.

The insistence on referring to what is renowned in the world is not anti-philosophical; it is a call to see what appears without philosophical fabrication to the ordinary mind. This ordinary mind is possessed by one and all, philosopher and non-philosopher. The innate intellect is of two kinds: one the referent objects of which are non-existent and the other the referent objects of which are existent. The first is the habitual untutored intellect which without analysis conceives phenomena to exist inherently. Because an inherently existent object is utterly non-existent, the referent object of a consciousness conceiving inherent existence is non-existent. However, the image or concept of inherent existence which it perceives does exist. This mind is to be extirpated through hearing, thinking, and meditating on the non-existence of that referent object.

The second type of habitual non-analytical intellect is just the usual mind of everyday affairs that enters into thoughts and activities without analyzing whether the object exists ultimately as it appears or not. The Prāsaṅgikas are emphasizing attention to this mind, for it is this in its conceptual and non-conceptual forms which certifies the existence of all phenomena, establishing even the *existence* of emptiness although it is a mind of meditative equipoise that certifies emptiness itself. Through attending to this mind one can determine what exists, and through determining what exists one learns what the bases of emptiness are. Since emptiness is a quality of objects—their lack of inherent existence—one must first identify what exists and then, using these existents as bases, meditate on their lack of inherent existence. Prāsaṅgikas assert what the world asserts not only because these phenomena do indeed exist but also because just these same phenomena are to be seen as lacking inherent existence. The concern is with the mind and its objects, as they are, without the fabrications of mistaken philosophical systems.

It is clear from Chandrakīrti's lengthy defense of Buddhapālita and from his attack on Bhāvaviveka that he was versed in both their systems. His refutations of Sāṃkhya, Nihilism, and so forth indicate a thorough study of non-Buddhist and Buddhist schools of tenets, comparative logic, and so on. Chandrakīrti's reliance on the world's renown or what is established in the world is not a turning away from philosophy, study, or analysis but a refined view of an analytical philosophy.

Though phenomena such as the ten Bodhisattva grounds which form the structural basis of Chandrakīrti's *Supplement to (Nāgārjuna's) 'Treatise on the Middle Way'* are also said to exist conventionally, it is undeniable that they are not well known to ordinary beings. However, Ḏzong-ka-ḇa says[459] that when the ten grounds become objects of the mind through hearing and experience, they appear to a non-analytical ordinary awareness; therefore, they are said to exist conventionally. Through this maneuver he shows that there is no need to abandon the extraordinary features of the spiritual path for the sake of according with the world.

Similarly, Chandrakīrti lays out in great detail and with abundant definitions the standard phenomena of the world and those fabricated by other philosophical systems. He thereby stresses a study of definitions and an identification of the bases of emptiness before entering into the reasoning that refutes inherent existence.

Also, Chandrakīrti accepts what the world accepts *for the most part*—that is, except in cases such as the world's assumption that the body is clean (if it is washed), pleasant, unchanging, and under the control of a self.[460] Furthermore, he refuses to allow that there can be a subject of a syllogism which is validly established in a similar manner for a Mādhyamika and a non-Mādhyamika; this is because all consciousnesses of a sentient being, except for a direct cognizer of emptiness, are mistaken with regard to the mode of existence of objects. Only a Buddha has both sense and mental consciousnesses which perceive objects exactly as they are, imputedly existent; only he does not, in sense perception, confuse the object imputed with its basis of imputation. (A Buddha is not a sentient being, *sattva* (*sems can*), because, though he is conscious and has mind—sense and mental consciousnesses—he does not have a consciousness which still has obstructions yet to be abandoned, and this is the definition of a sentient being.[461] All beings except for Buddhas have obstructions yet to be abandoned—even the highest of Bodhisattvas as well as Hearer and Solitary Realizer Foe Destroyers.)

Since beginningless cyclic existence all sentient beings have been chained to the false conception that phenomena exist inherently in their bases of imputation such that even a sense consciousness, though free from thought construction, perceives its objects as if they inherently exist. This appearance of inherent existence is assented to, and cyclic existence continues its unbroken round. All beings, non-Buddhist and Buddhist, Hīnayānist and Mahāyānist, must overcome the conception of inherent existence to break the round of powerless birth, aging, sickness, and death. As a technique to do so, a Prāsaṅgika removes the very basis of usual syllogistic debate by denying the existence of unmistaken valid cognizers of conventional objects in all who are not Buddhas. He uses consequences that call for analysis of everyday objects to discover the nature of objects. Analysis, the very opposite of ordinary intellect, which is defined as unanalytical, is demanded. Even syllogistic statements about this final nature cannot be used until one is about to realize the view of non-inherent existence and of the conventional valid existence of nominalities.

Uneducated beings would have difficulty understanding the format of a consequence, never mind its import. Therefore, the Prāsaṅgika's reliance on consequences and on what is renowned in the world does not reflect a vulgarization of Buddhism for the masses. Rather, it is an acknowledgement that people are convinced on their own grounds—an emphasis on watching one's own mind to discover or reveal what exists for oneself so that these existents may serve as bases for meditation on emptiness. In paying such close attention to the ordinary workings of the mind, the other type of ordinary mind—the non-analytical consciousness which assents to the false appearance of things as truly existent—can be seen more easily.

Prāsaṅgikas and Svātantrikas were named in Tibet from the point of view of the way in which they seek to generate in others a consciousness that infers the non-true existence of things, but it does not follow that all Prāsaṅgikas and Svātantrikas are debaters. They are seeking to accustom themselves to the view of emptiness through the statement of consequences and syllogisms to themselves in meditation and do not necessarily go about debating. Even a follower of Prāsaṅgika tenets may temporarily follow the Hīnayāna path, taking for the motivation of meditation on emptiness the wish to liberate himself or herself from cyclic existence and leaving for later the full development of the wish to free all beings from cyclic existence. Even those with the motivation of a Mahāyānist would not necessarily debate or even teach during that particular lifetime, for it is necessary first to educate oneself before educating others.

Still, even a person who is a Mahāyānist by tenet and Hīnayānist by path or motivation reveres and will eventually generate the great compassion of the Mahāyāna which requires taking upon oneself the burden of liberating all sentient beings. Eventually he will teach to others the view of the middle way through consequences.

6 *Prāsaṅgika in Tibet*

Sources
Jang-gya's *Presentation of Tenets*
Khetsun Sangpo's oral teachings

Buddhism first came to Tibet when books rained from the sky on the palace of King Hla-to-to-ri-ñyan-dzen (*Lha-tho-tho-ri-gnyan-btsan*, 374-494*) in 433 A.D.[462] The King was sixty at the time, and through paying respect to the books he assumed the appearance of a twenty year old, living for sixty more years to the age of one hundred twenty. Five generations later, during the reign of King Song-dzen-gam-bo (*Srong-btsan-sgam-po*, 617-698*), Buddhism was established in the snowy land through the efforts of his minister Thu-mi-sam-bho-ta who travelled to India, learned Sanskrit, created a Tibetan alphabet, and translated many books including sutras brought from Nāga-land by Nāgārjuna.

The first of the two disseminations of Buddhism into Tibet extends to the time of the translator Rin-chen-sang-bo (*Rin-chen-bzang-po*, 954-1055) whose translations form the boundary line beginning the new translations of tantra. The thorough transmission of the explanation and achievement in practice of the

Buddha's complete system occurred in the first dissemination during the reign of Tri-s̄ong-day-d̄zen (*Khri-srong-lde-btsan*, 790-848*) beginning in 803. During that period many Indian panditas visited Tibet; the Prāsaṅgika master Padmasaṃbhava (877 B.C.-A.D. 864*) who was the founder of the N̄ying-ma order, Dharmakīrti (not the famous logician), Vimalamitra, and Buddhaguhya who are all included within the N̄ying-ma order, all came at this time. The N̄ying-ma-b̄as, or followers of the old translations, are so named because they use translations, especially of Highest Yoga Tantras, made prior to the time of Rin-chen-sang-b̄o.

These panditas, along with the Yogāchāra-Svātantrika-Mādhyamika Shāntarakṣhita (ca. 165 B.C.-A.D. 844*) bore the burden of explaining everything from the discipline (*vinaya, 'dul ba*) to Mādhyamika philosophy as well as tantra.[463] Padmasaṃbhava tamed the spirits of Tibet and initiated the king, princes, and others into tantra. Together with Shāntarakṣhita and the king, Padmasaṃbhava established doctrinal colleges at S̄am-yay (*bSam-yas*), Hla-s̄a, and Yar-l̄ung-drang-druk (*Yar-klung-grang-'brug*) and established meditation centers at S̄am-yay-chen-b̄o (*bSam-yas-chen-po*), S̄hel-drak (*Shal-brag*), Chu-wo-ri (*Chu-bo-ri*), and Drak-yer-b̄a (*Brag-yer-pa*). Students in turn founded many doctrinal colleges and meditation centers, and thus though Padmasaṃbhava mainly taught tantra, he spread all forms of the teaching. Similarly, Dharmakīrti performed the mandala initiations of the Yoga Tantras, and so forth, but his teaching was not confined to tantra. The rules of tantra at that time were very strict, and it was not until later when the Tibetans were more educated in Buddhism that these and other masters spread tantra widely.

The Svātantrika-Mādhyamika master Shāntarakṣhita bore the Hīnayāna Sarvāstivāda lineage of discipline which is traced back to Rāhula, Buddha's own son. Thus, the Sarvāstivāda discipline was favored over the other lineages. Later the king decreed that all were to follow the Bodhisattva abbot Shāntarakṣhita in behavior, with the result that the texts of the other lineages of discipline were not even translated into Tibetan.

Shāntarakṣhita warned that though no non-Buddhist could harm the continuation and development of Buddhism in Tibet, a dangerous internal schism would arise. Leaving his advice in bronze in the king's treasury, he counselled the king to call his student Kamalashīla when the prophecy came to pass. After Shāntarakṣhita's departure from Tibet, the Chinese abbot Ho-shang Mahāyāna (*Hva-shang*) composed many texts primarily setting forth his view of non-application of the mind to anything. His system spread widely in Tibet, even being accepted by the queen. King Tri-sōng-day-dzen saw that this system, which deprecated the many techniques of skillful means, did not accord with Nāgārjuna's teaching. Being reminded of Shāntarakṣhita's words, he invited Kamalashīla to come to Tibet to debate with Ho-shang Mahāyāna at Sām-yay (ca. A.D. 846*).[464] Through citation of scripture and reasoning Kamalashīla defeated the Chinese abbot, spread again the complete teaching, and praised analytical wisdom in his three books on the *Stages of Meditation* (*Bhāvanākrama*). The king decreed that all were to follow Nāgārjuna's Mādhyamika view, but unlike the translation into Tibetan of only the Sarvāstivāda discipline, this did not prevent the views of other schools of tenets from being translated—the reason being that the great Indian teachers considered a study of various views valuable in ascertaining the features of the final view. It is said that Kamalashīla was killed by a Chinese spy shortly before the king's own death in A.D. 848.

Even though some Indian scholars who upheld Chittamātra did visit Tibet during the first dissemination, since Padmasaṃbhava, Dharmakīrti, and so forth were Prāsaṅgikas in view and Shāntarakṣhita was a Svātantrika, there is no question that the view of Tibet at that time was Mādhyamika. Jang-gya reports that Ye-shay-day (*Ye-shes-sde*), who was a student of both Padmasaṃbhava and Shāntarakṣhita, accorded with the latter's Yogāchāra-Svātantrika-Mādhyamika, but some say that his view was mainly Prāsaṅgika in accordance with the view of Padmasaṃbhava.[465] Ye-shay-day was a great translator who used the name Vairochana for his tantra translations, Indrabodhi for his translations of medical treatises, Gen-jak-tang-da (*Gan-jag-thang-ta*) for his Bön translations from Shang-shung (*Zhang-zhung*) language into Tibetan, and Ye-s̄hay-day for his sutra translations. Ye-s̄hay-day's breadth is typical of many scholars of the period.

During the second dissemination, a while after the persecution of Buddhism during the last six years of the reign of King L̄ang-dar-ma (*gLang-dar-ma*, 877-906*), the great translator Rin-cheng-sang-b̄o (954-1055) relied on many Indian teachers, learned a great deal of philosophy and tantra, and translated many, many texts. His view was said to be that of a Thoroughly Non-Abiding Mādhyamika, that is, Prāsaṅgika; overcoming many mistaken tantric practices, he spread the teaching widely throughout Tibet. Thus, when Buddhism returned to prominence in Tibet, it was still the Mādhyamika view and especially Prāsaṅgika that dominated philosophy.

The principal agents of the second dissemination were Rin-chen-sang-b̄o and his teacher Atīsha (982-1054*).[466] Atīsha re-established the system of studying all aspects of Buddhism—the various sutra and tantra systems in terms of the practice of one individual—and this method persists through to the present. His student Drom-d̄ön (*'Brom-ston*) was able to penetrate Chandrakīrti's system, and Atīsha declared with pleasure that only the Prāsaṅgika view was to be upheld in Tibet. Atīsha wrote that one could cognize suchness through the precepts transmitted from Chandrakīrti, and the Ḡa-dam-b̄a (*bKa'-gdams-pa*) lineage stemming from Atīsha contains many texts that accord with the thought of Chandrakīrti's Prāsaṅgika-Mādhyamika.

Relying heavily on Atīsha's works, the Ge-luk-b̄a order, originally a branch of Ḡa-dam-b̄a, took Prāsaṅgika as their own final system. The famous *Great Exposition of the Stages of the Path* by D̄zong-ka-b̄a (1357-1419), the founder of Ge-luk-b̄a, is a commentary on Atīsha's *Lamp for the Path to Enlightenment* (*Bodhipathapradīpa*); in it D̄zong-ka-b̄a presents, among other things, the particular features of special insight (*vipashyanā, lhag mthong*) in the Prāsaṅgika system. Not just the Ge-luk-b̄as, but also the N̄ying-ma-b̄as, Ḡa-gyu-b̄as (*bKa'-brgyud-pa*), and S̄a-ḡya-b̄as pay great respect to Atīsha and study his works thoroughly.[467]

The great Ḡa-dam-b̄a Ngok-lo-d̄za-wa L̄o-den-s̄hay-rap (*Ngog-lo-tstsha-ba bLo-ldan-shes-rab*), a student of Atīsha, quotes Bhāvaviveka and Chandrakīrti as sources but, along with his students, appears to agree mainly with Shāntirakṣhita's Yogāchāra-Svātantrika. Also, there were some Chittamātrin followers of the teacher Suvarṇadvīpa (*gSer-gling-pa*), who, though a Chittamātrin, was Atīsha's principal guru for the generation of the altruistic aspiration to enlightenment.

The view of the Jo-nang-b̄a or Jo-mo-nang-b̄a school, a division of the S̄a-ḡya order, is said by some to be a fabrication that is beyond the pale of the Indian schools of tenets. Their interpretation of the Mādhyamika emptiness is that the permanent, unchanging realm or constituent (*dhātu, khams*) of the Tathāgata which exists in all sentient beings is empty of all impermanent phenomena. Emptiness here is an emptiness of the other: the Tathāgata realm, or Buddha nature, is empty of being impermanent phenomena and impermanent phenomena are empty of being the Tathāgata realm. The other orders say that though emptiness is not impermanent phenomena and vice versa, this does not constitute emptiness; emptiness is a negation of self in the sense that phenomena are empty of, or lack, their own inherent existence. The Jo-nang-b̄as were refuted by many, but despite being considered as similar to the Vedāntins in view, their founder Yu-mo-b̄a is renowned among scholars of all orders for his literature on the *Kālachakra Tantra*.

The great S̄a-ḡya-b̄a scholar, Bu-d̄ön (*Bu-ston*, 1290-1364), originally a N̄ying-ma-b̄a and later a scholar of literally all orders and systems of tenets, accords greatly with the Prāsaṅgika Ḡa-dam-b̄as in view. It is said that he held Chandrakīrti's works to be the best of all.

The great Ḡa-dam-b̄a translator B̄a-tsap-nyi-ma-drak-b̄a (*Pa-tshab-nyi-ma-grags-pa*) spent twenty-three years in Kashmir, invited the pandita Kanakavarman (*gSer-gyi-go-cha*) to Tibet, and translated and taught many Mādhyamika treatises. His four famous students, as well as many of his other students, spread Chandrakīrti's system even more widely than he did.

There are some Mādhyamika followers in Tibet about whom

it is difficult to say whether they are Svātantrika or Prāsaṅgika. Gö-rin-b̄o-chay Kuk-b̄a-hlay-d̄zay (*'Gos-rin-po-che Khug-pa-lhas-btsas*) travelled to India twelve times, met with seventy-two scholars, and made many explanations of tantras. He was most likely a member of both the Ḡa-dam and S̄a-ḡya orders, and though he was a Mādhyamika, it is not clear which branch he asserted as his final system. Similarly, the translators Ba-kay-gay (*Ba-khe-gad, Khe-gad-'khor-lo-grags*), Ra (*Rva, Rva rDo-rje-grags*), Dro (*'Bro, 'Bro Shes-rab-grags*), and N̄yen (*gNyan, gNyan Dar-ma-grags*) and so forth either because of their teachers or because of their own assertions are seen to be Mādhyamikas, but no clear delineation of Svātantrika or Prāsaṅgika can be made.

The S̄a-ḡya order stems from Drok-mi Shākya-ye-s̄hay (*'Brok-mi Shākya-ye-shes*, 933 to either 1047 or 1050*) who spent twelve years in India studying especially with tantric teachers, then returned to Tibet, and spread tantra. He became Mar-b̄a's first Sanskrit teacher when Mar-b̄a was still a child. Drok-mi practices the mother tantras under the Indian pandita Gayadhara whose coming to Tibet greatly furthered the S̄a-ḡya order and who ultimately died there in order to be near his place of rebirth. Drok-mi is said to have been a Mādhyamika; also, since he sought to explicate the thought of the great Indian yogi Virūpa, his view is Prāsaṅgika. The final view of the S̄a-ḡya order is that of the Great Mādhyamika, that is, Prāsaṅgika, their identification of the view being mixed with tantric precepts and known as the union of manifestation and emptiness. The great S̄a-ḡya pandita Jam-ȳang-ḡun-ga-gyel-tsen (*'Jam-dbyangs-kun-dga'-rgyal-mtshan*) was a Prāsaṅgika in view in both his tantra and sutra teachings. The later S̄a-ḡya scholar Ren-da-wa (*Red-mda'-ba*), a teacher of D̄zong-ka-b̄a, wrote a commentary on Chandrakīrti's *Supplement* as well as instruction manuals for meditation on the Prāsaṅgika view. A Prāsaṅgika himself, his writings on the view agree greatly with D̄zong-ka-b̄a's.

The founder of the Shi-jay (*Zhi-byed*) order was Pa-dam-b̄a-sang-gyay (*Pha-dam-pa-sangs-rgyas*), who many say was Bodhidharma, also known as Kamalashīla (but not Shāntarakṣhita's student Kamalashīla). He was a student of eighty gurus, including Nāgārjuna, Maitripāda, and Nāropa, lived for over five hundred years, visited Tibet five times, spread Buddhism widely in both China and Tibet, and is said to have visited Mi-la-re-b̄a near the end of his life. Based on the Perfection of Wisdom Sutras, he divided his teaching into three systems—sutra, tantra, and union of sutra and tantra—spreading a doctrine much like that of sudden enlightenment. It is said that he pretended to die a few times in China.[468]

The writings of the famous clairvoyant Ma-j̄i-lap-drön (*Ma-cig-lab-sgron*) who is the founder of the J̄ö (*gCod*) branch of the Shi-jay order accord significantly with the Prāsaṅgika system. After she defeated Indian yogis through debate and feats of yoga, her system of exorcism, or elimination of suffering (*gCod*), originally brought to Tibet by Bodhidharma who received it from Āryadeva, spread back to India where it remained for a short while.[469]

The renowned founder of the Ḡa-ḡyu order, Mar-b̄a (*Lho-brag Mar-pa-chos-kyi-blo-gros*, 1012-1096) visited India three times and Nepal four, meeting with one hundred and eight gurus, including Nāropa, Maitripāda, Jñānagarbha (not the Svātantrika Jñānagarbha), Shāntibhadra, and so forth. He practiced in detail the yoga of the *Guhyasamāja Tantra* and most of the father and mother tantras. Returning to Tibet, Mar-b̄a had many students who upheld his lineage, and because his tantric activities were vast, his lineage spread widely. It is obvious that he relied on many teachers of both Chittamātra and Mādhyamika views, but in his own words he relied mainly on Nāropa and Maitripāda in all aspects—whether view, meditation, practice, or tantra. That both Nāropa and Maitripāda were Prāsaṅgikas can be seen from their own words; thus, it is clear that the instructions on the view in the Mar-b̄a lineage are the great Mādhyamika-Prāsaṅgika. Still, it is not necessary that every instruction in his lineage be Prāsaṅgika, for it is a sign of a great master that he does not teach the same to everyone or immediately attempt to explain his own view. Thus, some precepts in his lineage accord with Chittamātra.

Many of the songs of Mar-b̄a's famous student Mi-la-re-b̄a (*Mi-la-ras-pa*, 1040-1123) accord with Prāsaṅgika. Even those that speak of the four yogas, which is also a topic of the Chittamātrin Ratnākarashānti, can be explained as either Chittamātrin or Mādhyamika. Since his teachings are not general presentations of tenets but answers to questions put by disciples, they accord with the disposition of the questioner. Mi-la-re-b̄a's student Gam-b̄o-b̄a (*sGam-po-pa*, 1079-1153) made popular usage of the term '*mahāmūdra*' as a name for Ḡa-gyu-b̄a instructions on suchness in both sutra and tantra teachings. Gam-b̄o-b̄a's student Pak-mo-drup-dor-jay-gyel-b̄o (*Phag-mo-grub-rdo-rje-gyal-po*) had many students who formed branches of the Ḡa-gyu order.

In sum, the eight principal Tibetan orders—N̄ying-ma, S̄a-ḡya, Ḡa-dam (which includes Ge-luk), Ḡa-gyu, S̄hang-b̄a Ḡa-gyu (*Shang-pa bKa'-rgyud*, which was founded earlier than Mar-ba's Ḡa-gyu), Shi-jay (which includes J̄ö-yul), Jor-druk (*sByor-drug*, a tantric order based on the *Kālachakra Tantra*), and Dor-jay-day-b̄a (*rDo-rje-bzlas-pa*, a tantric order based on the tantras of the deity Bhairava)—mostly base their study of Mādhyamika on Chandrakīrti's *Supplement*.[470] Students would memorize and debate Chandrakīrti's *Supplement*, and only some would memorize Nāgārjuna's *Treatise on the Middle Way*.

In terms of the view of emptiness, all the major Tibetan orders are Mādhyamika, and almost all who differentiate between Prāsaṅgika and Svātantrika are Prāsaṅgika. Prāsaṅgika was and still is seen as the acme of philosophical systems and the basis for the special techniques of deity yoga in tantra.

7 Validation of Phenomena

Sources
D̄en-dar-hla-ram-b̄a's *Presentation of the Lack of Being One or Many*
Kensur Lekden's oral teachings
Geshe Gedün Lodrö's oral teachings
Geshe Lhundup Sopa's oral teachings
Corresponding section of the translation pp.632-6

Even from the Prāsaṅgika standpoint it is not sufficient merely to tear down other philosophies.[471] Not only must external debate be used as a branch of the attempt to overcome one's own misconceptions but also one must in one's own system of conventional existence present with valid confirmation all the actions, objects, and agents of cyclic existence and nirvana.

This very assertion of the valid establishment of all phenomena is what the S̄a-ḡya-b̄a scholar D̄ak-tsang and others find so objectionable in D̄zong-ka-b̄a. D̄ak-tsang cites as the cause for D̄zong-ka-b̄a's 'error' the latter's addiction to logic.[472]

> The cause for such a burden of contradictions [in D̄zong-ka-b̄a's writings] is that, despite [Chandrakīrti's

> and others'] statements again and again [that phenomena exist] only for the world without analysis, [Dzong-ka-ba] applied reasoning and proved [their valid conventional existence] due to the force of his habituation to logic.

Dak-tsang found eighteen 'contradictions' in Dzong-ka-ba's writings, the foremost of which is his assertion that there is a valid establishment of all phenomena in the Prāsangika system:[473]

> Those [pretending] to follow Chandrakīrti who assert through analysis with many reasons that impure mistaken appearances are validly established have a great burden of contradictions.

The basic problem is that in the Prāsangika system when objects are sought among or separate from their bases of imputation, they cannot be found and, thus, how can it be said that phenomena are validly established? How can valid cognition, either direct perception or inference, affirm an unfindable phenomenon as existing?

According to Dzong-ka-ba, every phenomena has its establisher, that is, a consciousness that certifies it as existing.[474] A correct sense consciousness which directly perceives its object—or in other words apprehends its object without the medium of images and concepts—certifies the existence of visual objects, sounds, odors, tastes, and tangible objects. The mere realization of their objects by those consciousnesses in turn certifies their own existence.[475] There is no further certifier of the certifier, and this is the reason why a valid cognizer exists in dependence on its own realization and does not inherently exist.

Similarly, an inferring consciousness which realizes uncaused space—a mere negative of obstructive contact—is the certifier of space. Just so, the wisdom of meditative equipoise certifies emptiness, although before directly cognizing emptiness, its *existence* can be certified by a valid dualistic mental consciousness that arises in dependence on reasoning and scripture. Emptiness is more difficult to realize than its existence, just as liberation from cyclic existence is more difficult to realize than the mere existence of liberation. However, sense consciousnesses certify both their objects and the existence of their objects because the one is no more difficult to realize than the other and because it is impossible to identify another consciousness which, after a sense consciousness has certified its object, certifies the existence of that object.

Since it is obvious that double moons, blue snow mountains, a permanent self, and so forth are seen but do not exist at all, it cannot be said that everything which is perceived by the six consciousnesses is certified as existing. Some distinction of error has to be made; otherwise, there would be no way to determine which conventional phenomena exist and which do not. How else could Chandrakīrti say:[476]

> From fear, not realizing that the self is just nominal, not knowing dependent imputation as it is, fallen away even from conventional truths, fooled by sheer wrong imagination through counterfeit inferences, [the non-Buddhist Forders] imagine a self and propound its character due to ignorance. A refutation of them even conventionally was given [in chapter eight where] the mutual establishment of a self and its appropriation [the mental and physical aggregates] was set forth.

How could Chandrakīrti say that the Forders fall away even from conventional truths if there were not a valid means to determine what does and does not exist conventionally? How could Chandrakīrti assert that the self is just nominal, a dependent imputation? It could not be done merely through polling the populace because, though the populace might not say that the self is permanent, they certainly would not even get a hint of what dependent imputation means.

By what means is it that Shāntideva determines what is and what is not the path in his *Engaging in the Bodhisattva Deeds*? By what means is it that Nāgārjuna determines the modes of the ethics he advises for the king in his *Precious Garland of Advice for the King*? If it were said that these are determined by the valid establishment which is just popular in the world, then Chandrakīrti's nominalism would also have to be an object of popular valid establishment.

Ḏzong-ka-ḇa's answer is that these correct direct and indirect cognizers are valid within their sphere, in the sense that they determine whether, with respect to impermanent phenomena, the object imputed can perform the functions of the object or not.[477] For instance, there is no difference with respect to the non-findability of a man imputed to a conscious human body and a man imputed to a pile of stones. However, the common intellect can determine without any special analysis which of the two is imputedly existent and which is just an imputation. The one can perform the functions of a man whereas the other cannot. Approaching and taking a good look is sufficient as a valid check of the coordination of basis of imputation and object imputed. Though an object imputed is not its basis of imputation and cannot be found among the bases of imputation or separately, it can be determined through simple checks whether the imputation is correct or not. To exist does not mean just to exist for thought; coordination of basis of imputation and object imputed is required.[478]

The difference between a picture of a cow and a cow is that the former cannot perform the functions of a cow but the latter can. However, Chandrakīrti is renowned for having milked a picture of a cow in order to overcome others' sense of inherent existence. Might it not be that the ability to perform a function is linked inextricably with thought and thus the great yogis can do anything with anything? The Ge-luk-ḇas answer that, of course, they too accept the special powers of yogis but add that the yogis' and the world's presentations of phenomena should not be mixed. For the yogis' presentation would utterly eradicate the world's conventions;[479] some yogis' eye consciousness can cognize odors, and their ear consciousness can cognize colors and shapes. A Buddha's hair cognizes all phenomena simultaneously; moments are stretched to eons; eons are reduced to moments. A Buddha can fit the world into a hair pore without changing the size of the hair pore or of the world. Thus, the sphere of valid establishment is the coarse conventions of the world; within that context what is validly established holds true, and even Buddhas and yogis need not contradict these truths just because their sphere is subtler.[480]

Still, does this mean that we poor worldlings are to have our dull presentation of phenomena and the yogis their subtle presentation? Even if it is granted that it is not ignorance that validly certifies these phenomena, but correct cognizers within a certain sphere, are we to hallow the admitted dullness of our sphere? What is the purpose of adhering to the world's limited knowledge? Why consecrate it with 'valid establishment' (*pramāṇasiddhi, tshad mas grub pa*)?

The Ge-luk-b̄as answer that it is necessary first to realize the existence of phenomena before meditating on their emptiness.[481] Otherwise, the Nihilists who cognize an absence of former and future lives and the Mādhyamikas who cognize an absence of inherent existence of former and future lives would be the same (see p.632-3). Furthermore, the cause and effect of actions are very subtle, and beings are bound in cyclic existence by the laws of cause and effect until they cognize emptiness directly and then become familiar with it over a long time. If a practitioner does not correctly outline the laws of cause and effect, he will be caught by his mispractices, whereby his very opportunity to meditate on emptiness will be lost. Furthermore, Buddhahood is not a mere state of total non-duality; rather, it is the perfection of mind and body, and dualistic perception in the sense of subject, object, and so forth continue though without the dualism of misperceived or misconceived inherent existence. A Buddha's wisdom and body are continuing effects of profound and vast practice. The cognition of emptiness is not the eradication of phenomena but a thorough understanding of their mode of existence. One learns how to perceive phenomena without confusing the basis of imputation with the object imputed.

Because ordinary beings cannot distinguish between inherent existence and conventional existence, as soon as it is said that objects are validly established, they tend to believe that objects as they perceive them are affirmed. Therefore, some non-Ge-luk-b̄a masters have taught that nothing except emptiness validly exists; they feel that since a student is unable to distinguish between inherent existence and conventional existence, he can destroy his conception of inherent existence through destroying his sense of existence and then afterwards determine what remains. Agreeing with them, the twentieth century renegade Ge-luk-b̄a monk Gen-dun-chö-pel (*dGe-'dun-chos-'phel*) says that no teacher need fear that his students would fall to a view of utter annihilation or nihilism because no one can escape the data of his senses.[482] He agrees that there is something left over after the fabrications of inherent existence are destroyed, but in the meantime students do not require fortification from nihilism through a teaching of valid establishment.

Gen-dun-chö-pel is said to have led an exciting life, and this may be the cause for his conviction that students would not fall into nihilistic views. He wrote a commentary on the *Aphorisms on Desire* (*Kāmasūtra*) from his own experience; he visited India and was arrested upon his return to Tibet as a Russian spy. He is said to have been quite a drunk, but also it is reported that upon retiring from the street with a friend in a drunken stupor he explained Nāgārjuna's teaching with a very clear head.[483] The vibrance of his life may have prevented him from falling into nihilism despite his obvious devotion to the doctrine of the unfindability of objects. However, that sense data are enough to keep all students from nihilism does not stand in the face of some current 'Buddhist' literature; the shadow of nothingness is often dark; the lack of discrimination between non-inherent existence and non-existence is obvious.

Still, Gen-dun-chö-pel's point is significant; he often refers to scholars who pressed him with their debates, and it appears that his objections are not to a philosophical incorrectness in D̄zong-ka-b̄a's teaching but to a pedagogical fault. Since even D̄zong-ka-b̄a says that no beginner can discriminate between existence and inherent existence, an emphasis on the valid establishment of conventionalities might merely fortify the habitual sense that things exist the way they appear. Gen-dun-chö-pel essentially is accusing the Ge-luk-bas of being too subtle for their own good.

The highly respected Mongolian scholar and Ge-luk-b̄a ge-s̄hay D̄en-dar-hla-ram-b̄a (*bsTan-dar-lha-ram-pa*) in his *Presentation of the Lack of Being One or Many* says in the same vein:[484]

> Except for refuting just these mountains, fences, houses, and so forth which so forcefully appear to exist concretely, we are very wrong if we search for some other horn-like thing to refute. ['Horn-like' means something sticking out above everything else, obvious or prominent, something separate from the object itself.] For Jang-ḡya-röl-way-dor-jay's (*lCang-skya-rol-ba'i-rdo-rje*) *Song on the Practice of the View* says, 'It seems that having fully accepted these concrete appearances as givens, they are searching for some horn-like thing to refute.'
>
> Still, some say [in answer] to this, 'This is wrong because the mountains, fences, houses, and so forth as they appear to common beings are the objects of direct apprehension by sense consciousnesses. Therefore, it is unsuitable to refute them in any way because [D̄zong-ka-b̄a's] "Great Exposition of Special Insight" [in his *Great Exposition of the Stages of the Path*] says, "None of the objects of non-conceptual sense consciousnesses are ever refuted through reasoning."'
>
> That indeed is true; however, an object which appears to a non-conceptual [sense] consciousness is the object which is conceived to exist inherently by a conceptual consciousness [in the sense that a conceptual consciousness assents to the object's appearance of inherent existence]. Therefore, related with this object are the appearance of objective existence which is to be refuted and the mere appearance [of the object] which is not to be refuted. [However] before attaining the view [of non-inherent existence but conventional, valid, effective existence] these two appear confused as one. When the view is found, these two [the appearance of objective existence and the mere appearance] are discriminated, and it is well renowned in the words of the wise that

there is this essential that the mere appearance is not refuted. When mountains, fences, houses, and so forth appear to ordinary beings, they appear in all respects to exist objectively. Therefore, one should meditate until, destroying this mode of appearance, it is cancelled in all respects for one's mind, and the fear, 'Now there is nothing left over,' is generated.

The generation of such fear is extremely rare. Kay-drup's *Opening the Eyes of the Fortunate* says, 'If even arrival at the point of actual generation of fear and fright of the profound emptiness is extremely rare, what need is there to say that arrival at an actual ascertainment, which is an understanding of an emptiness through experience, is almost non-existent.'

Therefore, greatly superior to the present-day philosophers to whom not even an image of the mode of objective existence has appeared are those in former times who overextended what is refuted [in the view of selflessness and held that the objects themselves are refuted].

There are reasons for not being frightened about emptiness. On the one hand, the stupid who do not know either the term or meaning of emptiness are not frightened because they do not know any of its disadvantages or advantages. For example, the stupid who do not know about how one can fall from a horse are brave to mount a wild horse. On the other hand, those who perceive emptiness directly do not fear it because they lack the cause of fear, that is, the conception of inherent existence which is abandoned through seeing [the truth], like a being who has learned well the ways of controlling a wild horse.

Then, who fears [emptiness]? It is suitable for fear to be generated in one who has understood emptiness a little and is investigating whether such and such a phenomenon exists or not. For suddenly the phenomenon appears to his mind to be totally non-existent. An

> example is a person who has understood a little but not completely how to mount a wild horse.

Even though the 'mere appearance' of an object is not negated in the view of selflessness, one has to bring oneself in analysis to the point where the object is utterly unfindable and totally disappears. One can at that time come up with nothing that is the object; this is a time of fright. It is said that eventually one will be able to comprehend what the 'mere appearance' that is not refuted is.

The Ge-luk-ba view is indeed subtle. It attempts to describe what nominal existence is: the non-identification of the imputed object as its basis of imputation and yet the coordination of these two as determined by whether the object so designated can perform its functions. Ge-luk-bas do sometimes seem to proceed to disregard emptiness and enter into long discussions about this or that conventional phenomenon. However, it rests on the oral teaching to emphasize attention to what objective existence and nominal existence mean and not just to enumerate and justify what conventionally exists.

Gen-dun-chö-pel's revolt from Ge-luk-ba teachings suggests that in the eyes of one intelligent being, not too many scholars and yogis were able to follow such a difficult middle path.

Dharmakīrti

8 *Meditative Reasoning*

Sources
D̄zong-ka-b̄a's *Great Exposition of the Stages of the Path*
Nga-w̄ang-b̄el-den's *Explanation of the Conventional and the Ultimate in the Four Systems of Tenets*
Jam-ȳang-shay-b̄a's *Great Exposition of the Concentrations and Formless Absorptions*
J̄ang-ḡya's *Presentation of Tenets*

Many, both in the East and in the West, have interpreted Prāsaṅgika-Mādhyamika to be a systemless system that, based on the realization that words are incapable of generating an experience of objects like that of direct perception, uses reasoning merely to refute other views while propounding a meditation that is solely a withdrawal from conceptuality. This view contrasts sharply with the Ge-luk-b̄a interpretation. That Prāsaṅgikas have no system is refuted by D̄zong-ka-b̄a in his *Great Exposition of the Stages of the Path*:[485]

> Nowadays some who wish to be Prāsaṅgika-Mādhyamikas [say]: 'Our own system even conventionally does not have any assertions based on the ultimate or the

conventional. For, if we had such theses, then we would have to assert examples and reasons that prove them, in which case we would become Svātantrikas. Therefore, there is no such thing as an 'own system' for Prāsaṅgikas since [Nāgārjuna, Āryadeva, and Chandrakīrti] say that Mādhyamikas have no position and no thesis. As Nāgārjuna's *Refutation of Objections* says:

> If I had any thesis,
> Then I would have that fault.
> Because I have no thesis,
> I am only faultless....'

Answer: If this which you propound is not the Mādhyamika system, then it is contradictory to establish it through citing passages from the Superior [Nāgārjuna] and his spiritual sons. Also, since [according to you] it cannot be posited as Chandrakīrti's or any other Buddhist system, it would be outside this religion. [However] if you say that it is Mādhyamika and, from within that, the system of Chandrakīrti, then it would contradict [your assertion] that Mādhyamikas [in general] and Chandrakīrti [in particular] do not have their own system.

Likewise, it is not feasible to propound—in hopes of being freed from assertions—that all presentations are solely from others' point of view. For, in saying, 'The existence of forms and so forth should be asserted solely from the viewpoint of other,' though you do not assert the existence of forms and so forth, you certainly must assert a positing from others' viewpoint, in which case you are not freed from assertions. Since at that time you must assert the others from whose viewpoint [these presentations] are posited, as well as the positer, and so forth, to propound that assertions are made solely from the viewpoint of others not only does not help but harms your [position of] not having your own system.

Ḏzong-ka-ḇa rejects the interpretation that Prāsaṅgikas in particular or Mādhyamikas in general have no system. Those who propound such have misunderstood the various passages in Mādhyamika texts that seem to indicate this. (Ḏzong-ka-ḇa's interpretation of the passage from Nāgārjuna's *Refutation of Objections* is given on pp.471-3.)

Nor is it the uncommon Prāsaṅgika-Mādhyamika view that words are inadequate to convey experience just as it is. For according to Nga-w̄ang-ḇel-den, Jam-ȳang-shay-ḇa's annotator, this is the view of the Hīnayāna Sautrāntikas. In his *Explanation of the Conventional and the Ultimate in the Four Systems of Tenets*[486] he explains in detail that in the system of the Sautrāntikas Following Reasoning—that is, those following Dignāga and Dharmakīrti—impermanent phenomena such as pots, pillars, bodies, minds, and so forth are:

> ... specifically characterized phenomena (*svalakṣhaṇa, rang mtshan*) because of being phenomena that must be realized by a mind that takes them as its appearing object through the appearance of their own uncommon characteristics [in direct perception]. Due to this, they are not objects of terms since their entities cannot fully appear to a terminologically arisen [conceptual] consciousness. Also, a mind realizing them is not generated through the mere existence of terminology, mental application, and so forth that are other than them.

Thus, to say that the uncommon Mādhyamika view is that words cannot generate perception of an object as direct sense perception can is to say that there is no difference in view between Sautrāntika and Mādhyamika. It is not the latter but the former who explicitly point out that the appearing object of a thought or conceptual consciousness is a meaning-generality (*arthasāmānya, don spyi*) which is necessarily simple, being merely an appearance as the opposite of everything that is not that particular object.

Rather than trying to prove that reasoning and words are

inadequate, the Prāsaṅgika-Mādhyamikas base themselves on the adequacy of these to show that the appearance of objects as if concretely or solidly existent is false. Far from deciding that reasoning is mistaken because it does not agree with appearance, reasoning is used to show that the appearance of objects is false—that their nature is other than what appears, that the sense consciousnesses of sentient beings are mistaken with respect to their appearing objects, that, as Kensur Lekden so often said, there is a conflict between what appears and what is. The point at issue is not whether words can generate an experience like that of direct perception. That they cannot is accepted and held in common with lower systems of tenets. Investigation into emptiness means examining whether phenomena actually have the concrete existence that even in non-conceptual direct sense perception they appear to have. It is from this point of view that Ḡön-chok-jik-may-w̄ang-b̄o says,[487] 'All sense consciousnesses in the mental continuum of a sentient being [a non-Buddha] are necessarily mistaken.'

The process of reasoning itself, used by a competent yogi, is viewed as the means of gaining access to emptiness—a slightly hidden phenomenon that is not accessible to initial understanding through direct perception.[488] Far from being counter-productive to realizing emptiness, reasonings such as dependent-arising, the lack of being one or many, and so forth reveal emptiness in an incontrovertible cognition of the nature of phenomena, albeit through the medium of an image. Inferential cognition is thus not a mulling over of concepts but a conclusion reached through perceiving a sign in a subject, realizing its concomitance with a predicate, and then realizing that the subject has that predicate. The conceptual or imagistic element of this realization is removed through repeated cultivation, resulting in direct cognition. Thus, conceptual and direct realization are in a harmonious relationship of cause and effect.[489] To discard reason would be to forsake the sole access to this which is hidden to the direct perception of an ordinary being.

Hence, meditation on emptiness is not the same as withdrawing from conceptuality. Jam-ȳang-shay-b̄a makes this point clearly and at length in his *Great Exposition of the Concentrations and Formless Absorptions*:[490]

> Someone says: 'Since the mode of subsistence, emptiness, is not anything, the mind of its meditation should not apply itself to anything. [Such non-application] is how to meditate on emptiness—selflessness—and its achievement is the measure of having achieved special insight realizing selflessness.'
>
> *Answer:* Then it would [absurdly] follow that the son of a barren woman and his mind would be meditating on emptiness—selflessness—because both do not apply the mind to anything. The three circles [of self-contradiction]! [You have accepted the reason, the predicate's following from the reason, and the opposite of the consequence.] The reason is so because [both the son of a barren woman and his mind] do not exist.
>
> Someone [refining the above position] says: 'Within the scope of minds and persons, any conception such as, "It is this or that," is a case of conceiving true existence. Therefore, not conceiving such and not applying the mind to anything [constitute meditation on emptiness].'
>
> *Answer:* It [absurdly] follows that, within the scope of minds, if one remains without conceiving, 'It is this or that,' one is meditating on emptiness because [for you] that is the meaning of meditation on emptiness. If you accept this, then it [absurdly] follows that the five sense consciousnesses of an ordinary fool individually realize emptiness and meditate on it because they remain without conceiving, 'It is this or that.' You have accepted the entailment. The reason is so because [those five] are sense consciousnesses. You cannot accept [that the sense consciousnesses of such a person realize emptiness and meditate on it] because these are of an ordinary being. [The reason] entails such because it is explained that the sense consciousnesses of a sentient being [that is, anyone but a Buddha] are not valid with respect to suchness. For,

Chandrakīrti's *Supplement to (Nāgārjuna's) 'Treatise on the Middle Way'* says, 'It is not feasible that the dumb be valid,' and the *King of Meditative Stabilizations Sutra* says, 'Eye, ear, and nose are not valid'.

Even if [this position] is put in the framework of the mental consciousness, then it [absurdly] follows that every case of thick sleep would be a meditation on emptiness because even the stupid know that at that time the mind cannot be applied to anything. If you accept that such is meditation on emptiness, then it [absurdly] follows that even though one meditates on emptiness, it is not possible to be liberated because even though there has been limitless meditation on such emptiness since beginningless time, there are still a limitless number of animals and so forth who are not liberated. You accept the reason. If you accept [the consequence], then it [absurdly] follows that there does not at all exist a path that liberates from cyclic existence because through meditation on emptiness one cannot be liberated. You accept the reason. The three circles [of self-contradiction]!

Someone says: 'At that time [during thick sleep] one does indeed experience emptiness and the Truth Body, but since it is not with mindfulness, one is not liberated'.

Answer: Then, it follows from your assertion that there is something to be mindful about with respect to emptiness. If you accept this, then it follows that it is not correct that emptiness is not an object of any mind because it is an object of mindfulness. You have accepted the reason. The three circles [of self-contradiction]!

Furthermore, [one can through using this reasoning] examine fainting and so forth as well as the existence and non-existence of meditator and means of meditation and so forth and refute [wrong positions]. Such [positions] are opposed and extensively refuted in the *Kālachakra Tantra*. For an extensive [rendition] see Dzong-ka-ba's *Great Exposition of the Stages of the Path*.

Also, it follows that the views of your system and of

[the Chinese Abbot] Ho-shang (*Hva-shang*) are similar because he asserted that not applying the mind to anything is meditation on emptiness and you also assert the same.

To this someone says: It follows that the views of Ho-Shang's and our systems are not the same because Ho-shang refuted giving and so forth whereas we do not.

Answer: Then it follows that with respect to the view you two do not differ because you speak of a difference of deeds and implicitly accept that there is no difference in view.

Someone who follows such [a system] says: To refute the conception of self through analysis is to adjust conceptual elaborations like a dog chasing after a stone [that has been thrown at it. However] from the start to hold the mind without scattering to anything is like a dog's seizing the hand that threw the stone, and thus this alone is profound. When the view is settled through scripture and reasoning, one is sunk in verbal conventions.

Answer: It follows that this is not correct because without analyzing and refuting the referent object of the conception of self [that is, inherent existence] it cannot be abandoned. For, this is the thought of the Conqueror [Buddha] and the supreme ornaments of the world. Sutra says:

> 'How is it that a Bodhisattva conquers over strife?'
> 'Mañjushrī, [by] analyzing and abiding in the
> unapprehendable nature of phenomena.'

The *King of Meditative Stabilizations Sutra* says:

> If the selflessness of phenomena is analyzed
> And if this analysis is cultivated,
> It causes the effect of attaining nirvana.
> Through no other cause does one come to peace.

Āryadeva's *Four Hundred* says:

> When selflessness is seen in objects,
> The seeds of cyclic existence are destroyed.

Chandrakīrti's *Supplement to (Nāgārjuna's) 'Treatise on the Middle Way'* says:

> The wise say that the reversal of conceptions
> Is the fruit of analysis.

Dharmakīrti says:

> Without disbelieving the object of this [misconception]
> It is impossible to abandon [misconceiving it].

Furthermore, [one can through using this reasoning] examine whether the mind meditating [on emptiness] is [necessarily] conceptual or free from conceptuality and refute [wrong positions that it is necessarily one or the other as it can be either].

Also, someone says: When one has not yet found the view of selflessness, mere setting [of the mind] without thinking of anything is not meditation on emptiness, but once the view has been found, all such setting without thought is meditation on emptiness.

Answer: It [absurdly] follows that once the view has been found, even [thick] sleep would be meditation on emptiness because all settings [of the mind] without thought once the view has been found are meditation on emptiness. You accept the reason. If you accept the consequence, then it [absurdly] follows that such sleep is cultivation of the wisdom realizing emptiness because it is cultivation of the view realizing emptiness. You accept the reason. [The reason] entails such because the view is necessarily of the substantial entity (*dravya, rdzas*) of wisdom. The reason is easy to establish. If you accept the consequence, then it [absurdly] follows that such sleep is cultivation of the discrimination of phenomena which is an investigation of emptiness.

Someone says: Although all setting [of the mind] in non-conceptuality once the view has been found is not meditation on emptiness, prior to each [session of] sustaining non-conceptuality one should analyze with the wisdom of individual investigation and then, after that, all setting in non-conceptuality is meditation on emptiness.

Answer: It [absurdly] follows that once the view has been found and analysis is done for each [session], falling into [thick] sleep is meditation on emptiness because it is a setting in non-conceptuality by one who has found the view and performed a stint of analysis. You have accepted that such follows. The reason is established because the subject is what it is. You cannot accept the consequence.

Someone says: When meditating on emptiness, ascertainment of it is induced [by reasoning]. Then within non-degeneration of the mode of apprehension of emptiness, setting [the mind] in non-conceptuality is the mode of sustaining the full form of the view or special insight into emptiness.

Answer: Then it [absurdly] follows that such meditation is the mode of cultivating wisdom and special insight realizing emptiness because [according to you] it is the mode of cultivating the view and special insight realizing emptiness. You have accepted the reason. You cannot accept the consequence because that is the mode of cultivating the calm abiding and meditative stabilization realizing emptiness. For, that is stabilizing meditation realizing emptiness. That the reason is so follows because stabilizing meditation realizing emptiness is the cultivation of meditative stabilization and calm abiding realizing emptiness, whereas analytical meditation realizing emptiness is the cultivation of wisdom and special insight realizing emptiness. This is so because individual modes of cultivating calm abiding and special insight realizing emptiness exist and because in general

> analytical meditation is cultivation of special insight and stabilizing meditation is cultivation of calm abiding. [See Part One, chapters eight and nine for a discussion of calm abiding and special insight.]

Meditation on emptiness is not a matter of withdrawing from conceptuality but of creating through reasoned analysis a mind that is capable of acting as an antidote or counter-agent to the conception of inherent existence. In dependence on this investigation the view is found, whereupon it is possible to use emptiness as the object in the process of developing calm abiding. Once that is achieved, stabilizing and analytical meditation are alternated until analysis itself induces greater stabilization and special insight is attained. This special insight—with analysis and stabilization in union—is cultivated through continued reliance on reasoning to the point where it becomes direct perception, when emptiness is no longer known through the medium of a meaning-generality but nakedly in non-dual cognition.

As J̄ang-ḡya says:[491]

> In particular, the many forms of reasoning for ascertaining suchness that were set forth [by the Mahāyānists] are only for the sake of clarifying the path of liberation for the fortunate, not for the sake of becoming intent on debate. Buddhapālita says, 'What is the purpose in teaching dependent-arising? The master [Nāgārjuna] whose very nature is compassion saw that sentient beings are beset by various sufferings and assumed the task of teaching the reality of things just as it is so that they might be liberated. Therefore, he began teaching dependent-arising.' Also, Chandrakīrti's *Supplement to (Nāgārjuna's) 'Treatise on the Middle Way'* says, 'The analyses in the *Treatise* were not done for the sake of attachment to debate; suchness was taught for the sake of liberation.' Also, D̄zong-ka-b̄a says, 'All the reasoned analyses set forth in the *Treatise on the Middle Way* are only so that sentient beings might attain liberation.'

Thus, the main purpose of the twenty-seven chapters of Nāgārjuna's *Treatise on the Middle Way* with its many forms of reasoning is taken to be the refutation not of other systems but of one's own innate conception of inherent existence. Though beings do not innately conceive that products, for instance, are produced from themselves, others, both, or neither, refutation of these four refutes the innate conception of the inherent existence of products because if products did exist in accordance with their concrete mode of appearance, they would have to exist in one of these four ways. Also, since other systems variously hold these views, they are refuted secondarily in the process of developing a meditative consciousness that understands the impossibility of such concrete or inherent existence and becomes accustomed to that emptiness. The primary aim is to become a source of help and happiness through penetrating the empty nature of phenomena that serves as the foundation of transformation into Buddhahood.

Part Six
Translation
Emptiness in the Prāsaṅgika System

From the twelfth chapter
of Jam-ȳang-shay-b̄a's
Explanation of 'Tenets',
Sun of the Land of Samantabhadra
Brilliantly Illuminating
All of Our Own and Others' Tenets
And the Meaning of the Profound [Emptiness],
Ocean of Scripture and Reasoning
Fulfilling All Hopes of All Beings

Introduction

Jam-ȳang-shay-b̄a's *Great Exposition of Tenets*, published in 1699, is one of only several books of its kind, two of the others being J̄ang-ḡya's *Presentation of Tenets* (*Grub mtha'i rnam bzhag*), which is based on Jam-ȳang-shay-b̄a's text, and D̄ak-tsang's *Understanding All Tenets* (*Grub mtha' kun shes*) which Jam-ȳang-shay-b̄a takes as his main object of refutation. There are many other short books which present the basic tenets of the various non-Buddhist and Buddhist systems; however, there is none of the length and breadth of the *Great Exposition of Tenets*. Replete with quotations from Indian sources, it presents the tenets of the philosophical culture of India in three hundred and ten folios (Dalama edition). A translation into English in the manner of the section done here, with all quotes restored to full length, would take 2500 pages.

According to Kensur Lekden, a master of the *Great Exposition of Tenets* would have the many sources for the work around his room and refer to them as quoted. Daily the students in Go-mang (*sGo-mang*, meaning 'many doors' because Buddha's teaching has many doors or approaches and because those who have realized emptiness can walk through walls), the college of Dre-b̄ung (*'Bras-spung*) monastery that uses Jam-ȳang-shay-b̄a's textbooks, would have to present back to the teacher from memory the teacher's previous commentary on the *Great Exposition of Tenets*. The students would take sides and debate the many points, becoming clever at upholding and demolishing various positions and developing their intelligence and memory. The basic text would be memorized; the master would teach the whole work twice, and at the conclusion the students would have a map of the whole field of Buddhist philosophical literature. They would then be able to differentiate the systems and avoid confusing the works of authors of conflicting systems. They would be ready for the specialized texts on the path structure, Prāsaṅgika-Mādhyamika, logic and epistemology, phenomenology, and discipline.

Jam-ȳang-shay-b̄a also wrote a textbook just on Prāsaṅgika-Mādhyamika, a commentary to Chandrakīrti's *Supplement*, which is in some ways far more extensive than his chapter on Prāsaṅgika in the *Great Exposition of Tenets*, such as in the discussion of autonomous syllogisms. Still, in other respects, the *Great Exposition of Tenets* is more extensive than the former, as in presenting the Prāsaṅgika theory of interpretation and formation of the Sanskrit of 'dependent-arising', *pratītyasamutpāda*. Thus, each is studied for a fuller appreciation of the other. These two form the basis of the knowledge of Mādhyamika in the Go-mang College of Dre-b̄ung which, within the sphere of the dominant Ge-luk order, was also influential—along with other colleges—in the Am-do province of Tibet as well as in Inner Mongolia, Outer Mongolia, the Buryat area of Siberia, and the Kalmuk areas of Russia.

Jam-ȳang-shay-ba's *Great Exposition of Tenets* has thirteen chapters:

1 Discussion of tenets in general
2 Refutation of the extreme of nihilism: Chārvāka
3 Refutation of an extreme of permanence: Sāṃkhya and Kāpila
4 Refutation of an extreme of permanence: Brāhmaṇa, Vyākaraṇa, Vedānta, and Guhyaka
5 Refutation of an extreme of permanence: Vaiṣhṇava and Mīmāṃsaka

6 Refutation of an extreme of permanence: Shaiva, Naiyāyika, and Vaisheṣhika
7 Refutation of an extreme of permanence: Nirgrantha (Jaina)
8 Introduction to Buddhist tenets in general and presentation of Vaibhāṣhika
9 Sautrāntika
10 Introduction to the Mahāyāna and presentation of Chittamātra
11 Introduction to Mādhyamika, its history, refutation of wrong views about Mādhyamika, and presentation of Svātantrika
12 Prāsaṅgika
13 Elimination of doubts about the Vajrayāna.

Jam-ȳang-shay-b̄a's root text, written in verse mainly with nine syllables per line, consists of sixteen folios; his commentary is three hundred and ten folios (Dalama edition). The basic text is called (see bibliography for Tibetan titles): *Presentation of Tenets, Roar of the Five-Faced [Lion] Eradicating Error, Precious Lamp Illuminating the Good Path to Omniscience.* His commentary is called: *Explanation of 'Tenets', Sun of the Land of Samantabhadra Brilliantly Illuminating All of Our Own and Others' Tenets and the Meaning of the Profound [Emptiness], Ocean of Scripture and Reasoning Fulfilling All Hopes of All Beings.*

The word 'tenets' in the title of the commentary refers to the root text; his commentary on it is like the light of the land of Samantabhadra, which is not lit by a sun that rises and sets but shines continuously through the power of meditative stabilization. This book of tenets fulfils the hopes of all beings seeking the ability to gain the wanted and avoid the unwanted since it explains what the wanted and unwanted are and how to achieve and avoid them. Through delineating the profound meaning of emptiness, it shows the path to liberation from cyclic existence and the eventual attainment of omniscience.

The great Outer Mongolian scholar, Nga-w̄ang-b̄el-den (*Ngag-dbang-dpal-ldan*, born 1779), known more commonly as B̄el-den-chö-jay (*dPal-ldan-chos-rje*), wrote an extensive commentary of annotations (four hundred and sixteen folios, Sarnath edition) on Jam-ȳang-shay-b̄a's autocommentary (three hundred and ten folios, Dalama edition). It is called: *Annotations for (Jam-ȳang-shay-b̄a's) 'Great Exposition of Tenets', Freeing the Knots of the Difficult Points, Precious Jewel of Clear Thought.* Nga-w̄ang-bel-den's annotations do indeed untie the knots of many difficult points in Jam-ȳang-shay-b̄a's text especially by elaborating the meaning of quotations, and thus it has been used extensively in the translation for both interpretation and addition of bracketed material.

Jam-ȳang-shay-b̄a is famous for his lengthy works replete with citations of Indian sources. Whereas his followers often point to his frequent citation of sources as a great advantage, the followers of the textbook literature by Paṇ-chen Sö-nam-drak-b̄a (1478-1554), used in the L̄o-s̄el-l̄ing College of Dre-b̄ung and the S̄har-d̄zay College of Gan-den, conversely point to their writer's ability to condense important topics into easily readable prose, highly accessible to beginners. In the middle is Jay-d̄zun Chö-ḡyi-gyel-tsen (1469-1546), whose textbooks, used by the S̄e-ra Jay and Gan-den Jang-d̄zay Colleges, tend to fall between those two in terms of length.

Here in the *Great Exposition of Tenets* Jam-ȳang-shay-b̄a's devotion to the source literature is particularly helpful as it makes his presentation of Prāsaṅgika an anthology of the basic literature both in sutra and the commentarial treatises. In order to reduce the bulk of the text, Jam-ȳang-shay-b̄a condensed many quotations. However, since, as Kensur Lekden reported, a master of the *Great Exposition of Tenets* would have the cited texts available and make use of them during instruction, this translator has sought out those texts and filled in the ellipses, with the result that thirty percent of the translation is comprised of these reconstructions. The full, edited Tibetan text, with the reconstructions clearly marked, is given at the end of this book; the page numbers in parentheses throughout the translation refer to it.

About the author

According to Lokesh Chandra's account given in his *Materials for a History of Tibetan Literature,*[492] Jam-ȳang-shay-b̄a Nga-w̄ang-d̄zön-drü was born in the Am-do province of Tibet in 1648. Having studied the alphabet at age seven with his uncle, who was a monk, he mastered reading and writing and six years later became a novice monk. He went to Hla-s̄a at age twenty-one to pursue his studies at the Go-mang College of Dre-b̄ung Monastic University; six years later he received full ordination and at age twenty-nine entered the Tantric College of Lower Hla-s̄a. He spent two years in meditative retreat in a cave near Dre-b̄ung from age thirty-three. (Perhaps it was at this time that Mañjushrī, also called Mañjughoṣha, appeared to him and smiled, due to which, according to Kensur Lekden, he came to be called 'One On Whom Mañjughoṣha Smiled', Jam-ȳang-shay-b̄a.)

At age fifty-three he became abbot of Go-mang and at sixty-two returned to Am-do province where he founded a monastery at D̄ra-s̄hi-kyil (*bKra-shis-'khyil*), this being 1710. Seven years later he founded a tantric college at the same place. He wrote prolifically on the full range of topics of a typical Tibetan polymath and, having received honors from the central Tibetan government and the Chinese Emperor, died at the age of seventy-three or four in 1721/2.

Partly because of the close connection between Go-mang College and the Mongolian peoples stretching from the Caspian Sea through Siberia, who were predominantly Ge-luk-b̄a by this time, Jam-ȳang-shay-b̄a's influence on the Ge-luk-b̄a order has been considerable. Like the other textbook authors, he was seeking to explicate the thought of the founder of the Ge-luk-b̄a order, D̄zong-ka-b̄a (1357-1419), and perhaps it was because he was the last of the great textbook authors and thus had the others' works before him and could speak from a fully developed tradition of such study that he could put such great emphasis on the Indian sources of D̄zong-ka-b̄a's thought.

About the editions of the text used

Five editions of Jam-ȳang-shay-b̄a's *Great Exposition of Tenets* were gathered over several years. Four of them turned out to have the same basis:

1 the Dalama edition published in Musoorie in 1962
2 photographs (of the part translated here) of the text in the possession of His Holiness the Dalai Lama. The photography was kindly done by Sherpa Tulku and Khamlung Tulku. Unfortunately, the final pages were not included, and thus publishing data is not available. The margin of every page reads '*grub 'grel*', as do the other three in this class.
3 a hand-written copy (of the part translated here) of the edition held in the library of Go-mang College in Mundgod, Karnataka State. This was graciously provided through the efforts of Kensur Lekden, by way of the then abbot of Go-mang D̄en-b̄a-d̄en-dzin. Again, the pages with publication data were not copied.
4 a hand-written copy (of the twelfth and thirteenth chapters) of an edition, surreptitiously procured—from a library in a country that shall remain unnamed—by Mr. Gyatso Tsering, Director of the Library of Tibetan Works and Archives in Dharmsala. The colophon states that it was commissioned by '*gam bcar mkhan po chos 'byor rgya mtsho*'.

The first, third, and fourth contain variations due to scribes' and print-setters' inaccuracies, but they share basic inaccuracies with the second; thus we can posit that they stem from a common edition. These basic inaccuracies do not appear in the other edition obtained:

5 a photographic reprint of the D̄ra-s̄hi-kyil edition published in 1972 in New Delhi by Ngawang Gelek Demo in Volume 14 of the Collected Works of 'Jam-dbyaṅs-bźad-pa'i-rdo-rje.

The last is by far the best edition due to not having some major errors, which all the other four have, and due to using the virāma extensively in the section on forming the Sanskrit term *pratītya-samutpāda* under renderings of Sanskrit groups of letters in Tibetan. (A copy of this edition has recently been made by Go-mang College; it contains no publication information above and beyond what is in the D̄ra-s̄hi-kyil edition.)

According to Kensur Lekden, Jam-ȳang-shay-b̄a's works

have suffered from poor printing from the start due to the fact that the author wrote quickly in his old age, with little attention to the details of publication. The annotator, Nga-w̄ang-b̄el-den, frequently points out printing errors, which appear in the edition represented by one through four in the list above. It can be deduced from his commentary (dbu 67b.8 note *ca*, for instance) that he did not have the D̄ra-s̄hi-kyil edition at his disposal since he challenges readings that are clearly not in the D̄ra-s̄hi-kyil edition but are in the other.

Both editions are replete with error; nevertheless, due to Jam-ȳang-shay-b̄a's proclivity for quotation, it was possible to compare a great portion of the text with the Peking edition as found in the *Tibetan Tripiṭaka* published under the auspices of the Tibetan Tripiṭaka Foundation (Tokyo-Kyoto, 1956). Thus, in counsel with the Go-mang scholars mentioned below, it was possible to edit the text; a list of a hundred and ninety-one emendations of the Go-mang hand-copy is given after the reconstructed text.

Jam-ȳang-shay-b̄a's sources

The portion of the *Great Exposition of Tenets* translated here has two hundred and nine quotations, counting a few quotes within quotes. The sources in order of frequency of quotation are:

1 Chandrakīrti's *Supplement to (Nāgārjuna's) 'Treatise on the Middle Way' (Madhyamakāvatāra)* and his own commentary, thirty-eight quotations
2 Chandrakīrti's *Clear Words, a Commentary on (Nāgārjuna's) 'Treatise on the Middle Way' (Madhyamakavṛtti-prasannapadā)*, twenty-eight quotations
3 *Chandragomin's [Sanskrit] Grammar (Chāndravyākaraṇa)*, eleven quotations
4 Nāgārjuna's *Treatise on the Middle Way (Madhyamakashāstra)*, eight quotations
5 Nāgārjuna's *Compendium of Sutra (Sūtrasamuchchaya)*, seven quotations
5 Nāgārjuna's *Precious Garland of Advice for the King (Ratnāvalī)*, seven quotations

5 *Buddhapālita's Commentary on (Nāgārjuna's) 'Treatise on the Middle Way' (Buddhapālitamūlamadhyamakavṛtti)*, seven quotations

6 *Perfection of Wisdom Sutra (Prajñāpāramitā*, in twenty-five thousand or eighteen thousand stanzas), five quotations

6 *Descent into Laṅkā Sutra (Laṅkāvatāra)*, five quotations

6 Āryadeva's *Four Hundred (Chatuḥshataka)*, five quotations

6 Chandrakīrti's *Commentary on (Āryadeva's) 'Four Hundred' (Chatuḥshatakaṭīkā)*, five quotations

6 Jñānagarbha's *Discrimination of the Two Truths (Satyadvayavibhaṅga)*, five quotations

7 Shāntideva's *Engaging in the Bodhisattva Deeds (Bodhisattvacharyāvatāra)*, four quotations

7 D̄zong-ka-b̄a's *Essence of the Good Explanations (Legs bshad snying po)*, four quotations

7 D̄zong-ka-b̄a's *Explanation of (Nāgārjuna's) 'Treatise on the Middle Way' (rTsa shes ṭik chen)*, four quotations

7 *Kalāpa's Aphorisms* (*Kalāpasūtra*), four quotations

8 *Sutra Unravelling the Thought (Saṃdhinirmochana)*, three quotations

8 *Sutra on the Ten Grounds (Dashabhūmika)*, three quotations

8 *Rice Seedling Sutra (Shālistamba)*, three quotations

8 Nāgārjuna's *Sixty Stanzas of Reasoning (Yuktiṣhaṣhtikā)*, three quotations

8 Bhāvaviveka's *Lamp for (Nāgārjuna's) 'Wisdom' (Prajñāpradīpa)*, three quotations

9 Ashvaghoṣha's *Cultivation of the Ultimate Mind of Enlightenment (Paramārthabodhichittabhāvanākramavarṇasaṃgraha)*, two quotations

9 *Teaching of Akṣhayamati Sutra (Akṣhayamatinirdesha)*, two quotations

9 *King of Meditative Stabilizations Sutra (Samādhirāja)*, two quotations

9 Nāgārjuna's *Seventy Stanzas on Emptiness (Shūnyatāsaptati)* and his own commentary, two quotations

9 Mahāmati's *Commentary on (Nāgārjuna's) 'Friendly Letter' (Suhṛllekhaṭīkā)*, two quotations

9 Kamalashīla's *Illumination of the Middle Way (Madhyamakāloka)*, two quotations
9 Bhāvaviveka's *Blaze of Reasoning (Tarkajvālā)*, two quotations
9 Fifth Dalai Lama's *Sacred Word of Manjushrī*, two quotations
9 Atīsha's *Lamp for the Path to Enlightenment (Bodhipathapradīpa)*, two quotations
9 Dzong-ka-ba's *Praise of Dependent-Arising*, two quotations
9 Kay-drup's *Opening the Eyes of the Fortunate*, two quotations
10 one quotation each:
Nāgārjuna's *Refutation of Objections (Vigrahavyāvartanī)*
Nāgārjuna's *Essay on the Mind of Enlightenment (Bodhichittavivaraṇa)*
Nāgārjuna's *Friendly Letter (Suhṛllekha)*
Chandrakīrti's *Commentary on (Nāgārjuna's) 'Sixty Stanzas of Reasoning' (Yuktiṣaṣṭikāvṛtti)*
Avalokitavrata's *Commentary on (Bhāvaviveka's) 'Lamp for (Nāgārjuna's) "Wisdom"' (Prajnāpradīpavṛtti)*
Dharmakīrti's *Commentary on (Dignāga's) 'Compendium of Valid Cognition' (Pramāṇavārttika)*
Dzong-ka-ba's *Explanation of (Chandrakīrti's) 'Supplement'*
Extensive Sport Sutra (Lalitavistara)
Heart of Wisdom Sutra (Prajñāhṛdaya)
White Lotus of the Excellent Doctrine Sutra (Saddharmapuṇḍarīka)
Chapter of the True One Sutra (Satyakaparivarta)
Questions of King Dhāraṇīshvara Sutra (Dhāraṇīshvararājaparipṛcchā)
Irreversible Wheel Sutra (Avaivartachakra)
Lion's Roar of Shrīmālādevī Sutra (Shrīmālādevīsiṃhanāda)
Sutra on the Heavily Adorned (Ghanavyūha)
Questions of the King of Nāgas, Sāgara, Sutra (Sāgaranāgarājaparipṛchchhā)
Kāshyapa Chapter Sutra (Kāsyapaparivarta)
Meeting of Father and Son Sutra (Pitāputrasamāgamana)

Compendium of Doctrine Sutra (Dharmasaṃgīti)
Six unidentified sutra quotations.

The authors in order of frequency of quotation are:

1 Chandrakīrti, seventy-three quotations
2 Buddha (sutra), forty quotations
3 Nāgārjuna, thirty quotations
4 Dzong-ka-ba, eleven quotations
4 Chandragomin, eleven quotations
5 Buddhapālita, seven quotations
6 Āryadeva, five quotations
6 Bhāvaviveka, five quotations
6 Jñānagarbha, five quotations
7 Kalāpa, four quotations
8 Ashvaghoṣha, Mahāmati, Kamalashīla, Atīsha, Kay-drup, and the Fifth Dalai Lama, two quotations each
9 Avalokitavrata and Dharmakīrti, one quotation each.

The above tally is just for the parts of Jam-ȳang-shay-ba's chapter on Prāsaṅgika translated here on the definition, synonyms, divisions, literature, and emptiness of the Prāsaṅgika system. It is obvious from the two lists that at least for Jam-ȳang-shay-ba Chandrakīrti is by far the principal source for the Prāsaṅgika position on emptiness and its relation to the other schools. (The last part of Jam-ȳang-shay-ba's presentation of the Prāsaṅgika system deals with the attributes of a Buddha and relies heavily on Maitreya's *Sublime Continuum of the Great Vehicle [Uttaratantra]*. Thus, the tally should be taken as applying not to Jam-ȳang-shay-ba's entire presentation of the Prāsaṅgika system but mainly to his presentation of emptiness.)

When Mādhyamika is studied in the Ge-luk-ba monastic colleges, it is Chandrakīrti's *Supplement* that is memorized and that serves as the basis for the entire study of Mādhyamika. Dzong-ka-ba's commentary and the individual monastic textbooks are used as aids for illuminating the meaning of Chandrakīrti's text.

These books by Chandrakīrti which are so often quoted are all explanations, directly or indirectly, of Nāgārjuna's philosophy. Even the sutras quoted by Jam-ȳang-shay-ba are mostly those which Nāgārjuna quoted in his *Compendium of Sutra* or made reference to in his *Treatise* or Chandrakīrti quoted in his books. It is, of course, not surprising, since Nāgārjuna was the founder of Mādhyamika, to find that almost all of the philosophical quotes for Mādhyamika derive from him either directly or through his chief commentator, Chandrakīrti. What is noteworthy is that Chandrakīrti's works of clarification are heavily relied upon to determine Nāgārjuna's meaning.

As Jam-ȳang-shay-b̄a says at the end of his section on Prāsaṅgika literature, the main source for the content of his presentation is Ḏzong-ka-b̄a. It seems that almost all of Jam-ȳang-shay-b̄a's quotes from Indian philosophical commentaries—Nāgārjuna through Atīsha—are cited by Ḏzong-ka-b̄a; Jam-ȳang-shay-b̄a is not giving a new presentation but arranging Ḏzong-ka-b̄a's presentation in a more convenient form for comparative study.

That most of the forty sutra quotations are also to be found in Ḏzong-ka-b̄a is not coincidence; Jam-ȳang-shay-b̄a was seeking to clarify Ḏzong-ka-b̄a's teaching especially in contradistinction to Ḏak-tsang (born 1405), a scholar of the S̄a-ḡya (*Sa-skya*) order who indicted Ḏzong-ka-b̄a for self-contradiction. Jam-ȳang-shay-b̄a defended the founder of his order and indicted Ḏak-tsang for self-contradiction in return. Jam-ȳang-shay-b̄a's genius and importance lies not in innovation in Mādhyamika philosophy but in his defense of Ḏzong-ka-b̄a's interpretation and in his thorough presentation of the non-Buddhist and Buddhist philosophical systems. Jam-ȳang-shay-b̄a's work came almost three hundred years after both Ḏzong-ka-b̄a and Ḏak-tsang and at a time when Ge-luk-b̄a influence was on the rise under the leadership of the Fifth Dalai Lama; thus, he by no means saved Ḏzong-ka-b̄a's teaching. It is more that his particular style of vast and thorough presentation, coupled with what at times is partisan fire, was suitable for developing the kind of sharp intellect that the monastic colleges of Tibet value.

Nāgārjuna was clarifying the thought of Buddha; Chandrakīrti was clarifying the thought of Nāgārjuna; Ḏzong-ka-b̄a was clarifying the thought of Chandrakīrti; and Jam-ȳang-shay-ba was clarifying the thought of Ḏzong-ka-b̄a. A measure of how important each clarification was is how often the clarifier is subsequently quoted as opposed to how often what is clarified is cited; still, though Chandrakīrti is quoted most frequently and though his works finally drew more study and attention in Tibet than Nāgārjuna's, Chandrakīrti is definitely secondary to Nāgārjuna. Nāgārjuna was the master and Chandrakīrti the commentator; Chandrakīrti did not write a book like the *Treatise on the Middle Way* which set a whole new trend in Buddhist philosophy and practice. A study of Chandrakīrti is viewed as a study of Nāgārjuna.

Though it could also be said that a study of Nāgārjuna is a study of Buddha, the sutras are far too vast and varied to lend the sense that a study of Nāgārjuna is a study of Buddha in general. Nāgārjuna's *Treatise* is an epitome of the Perfection of Wisdom Sutras, and without the *Treatise*, as Chandrakīrti says (commenting on VI.3 of his *Supplement*), it would be extremely difficult to understand what these sutras mean. The difference between Nāgārjuna's and Chandrakīrti's clarifications is that Nāgārjuna's is far more basic. It sets an order where order seemed not to exist. Chandrakīrti shed additional light on the order revealed by Nāgārjuna.

According to all the various Ge-luk-b̄a interpretations, Chandrakīrti showed that phenomena do not exist by way of their own character even conventionally whereas Bhāvaviveka at least implies that phenomena conventionally exist by way of their own character. This means that for Chandrakīrti even conventionally phenomena are not the composite of their parts or their bases of imputation. In relation to the other commentaries this was his 'innovation'.

D̄zong-ka-b̄a's 'innovation' was to present the conventional *valid* existence of all phenomena, detailing the acceptability of the certification of the conventional existence of all phenomena by valid cognizers. D̄zong-ka-b̄a showed that Mādhyamikas do have a system of their own and that it is supported by valid cognition despite the utter unfindability of phenomena among their bases of imputation. D̄zong-ka-b̄a thus distinguished his teaching from most of the other Tibetan commentators, preserving in a very subtle way the validity of the classic Buddhist phenomenology through delimiting the scope of the Mādhyamika reasoning.

According to Ḏzong-ka-ḇa, Nāgārjuna's analysis refutes the inherent existence of conventionally existent phenomena; it does not refute their conventional existence which is validly established. Emptiness and dependent-arising are compatible within valid establishment.

Jam-ȳang-shay-ḇa had no such central 'innovation' for Prāsaṅgika philosophy. His commentary on Chandrakīrti's *Supplement* provides a work in a different genre: scholastic debates which provide final conclusions about Prāsaṅgika. Despite Jam-ȳang-shay-ḇa's many differences with the other Ge-luk-ḇa monastic textbook lineages, no difference was nearly as important as Ḏzong-ka-ḇa's astoundingly different and cogent definition of emptiness, delimiting the scope of what is negated in the theory of selflessness to inherent existence and preserving valid, conventional, effective existence.

Thus, Jam-ȳang-shay-ḇa's 'innovation' was to give a presentation of Buddhist and non-Buddhist systems of tenets in far greater detail than any previous Tibetan scholar had given. He thereby furthered in Tibet and Mongolia the study of comparative philosophy. His principal sources are Bhāvaviveka's presentation of the Indian systems in his *Heart of the Middle Way (Madhyamakahṛdaya)* and commentary, the *Blaze of Reasoning*, Shāntarakṣhita's *Compendium on Reality (Tattvasaṃgraha)*—though of course Bhāvaviveka and Shāntarakṣhita, being Svātantrikas, are not his source for the Prāsaṅgika system—and Chandrakīrti's commentaries.

In the *Great Exposition of Tenets*, the Buddhist systems are presented in ascending order of importance, but the presentations are remarkably unbiased. The cause for this is probably the Tibetan insistence on debate as a teaching method. Since the aim of each debate is to defend one's position, whatever position one is assigned is defended at all costs in the sense that unfair presumptions by any opponent are unhesitatingly refuted. Each monastic college has its favored and peculiar assertions which are indeed often defended with partisan vigor; however, this very partisan vigor is also invested in their opponents' positions within the debating courtyards of each college when their own members take the opposite viewpoint.

The philosophical disagreements are many, and it is therefore quite often impossible to speak of a Tibetan position on a subject. Often it is impossible to speak of a particular sect position because of differences within the sect. Sometimes, also, it is impossible to speak of a monastery position because of differences between the colleges which are the basic divisions of the monastery. There are even different lineages of assertions within monastic colleges; according to Geshe Gedün Lodrö, Go-mang, for instance, had four. However, the principal units are the monastic colleges, with far more happening between the various monastic colleges of the Ge-luk-b̄a order than between Ge-luk-b̄a and non-Ge-luk-b̄a.

Not to discriminate differences in tenet as a pretension of non-bias is considered to be a sign of great ignorance and of dislike of religion, and indeed the devotion to debate cultivates both an excellent memory and a quick sense of discrimination, necessary for penetrating reality. Bias and partisanship are rejected, but discrimination is hallowed, though, of course, this is not easily accomplished. Jam-ȳang-shay-b̄a openly attacks the S̄a-ḡya-b̄a scholar D̄ak-tsang, often in an inflammatory way, in his *Great Exposition of Tenets* which was written for the dual purpose of refuting D̄ak-tsang and of establishing the 'correct' view of emptiness. Jam-ȳang-shay-b̄a cites scripture and reasoning in his unceasing indictment of D̄ak-tsang; he not only devotes forty folios solely to refuting D̄ak-tsang but also spices many sections with brief refutations and even name-calling. D̄ak-tsang is a 'spouter of disconnected discourse through possession by the madness causing one to mouth ignorance' (*GT*, ca 19a.5), 'one who wishes to do a dance having cut off the head of a crazy, dancing peacock and hung it on his behind' (see p.648), and so on endlessly.

The nasty comments provide occasional comic relief in this heavy book, but there is no denying that the insults are inflammatory and counter-productive. It often seems as if Jam-ȳang-shay-b̄a's head was about to be rent asunder in amazement at quite common positions. In the debating courtyards scholars sometimes resort to ridiculous laughter and absurd comparisons in order to heap upon the opponent the full devastating force of embarrassment and thereby cause him to lose footing even if he has not lost it logically. Still, each scholar must in turn take D̄ak-tsang's side in debate and win using his tenets. The aim in the debating courtyard is not to heap more abuse on D̄ak-tsang; rather, it is an enactment of a hypothetical encounter between D̄ak-tsang (born 1405) and Jam-ȳang-shay-b̄a (1648-1721/2) for the sake of exploring the principles of interpretive systems.

Most scholars in the Go-mang College of Dre-b̄ung College have won debates as a hypothetical D̄ak-tsang against a hypothetical Jam-ȳang-shay-b̄a. Indeed, even when teaching, they do not automatically leap into the stream of abuse but analyze to determine whether D̄ak-tsang's supposed contradictions are explicitly so or ones he would be 'forced' to accept from another viewpoint. The designations of insanity and so forth quickly lose their shock value due to over-use and the shared knowledge that it is a game, but the technique also sometimes engages fierce aspects of the personality and lays at one's intellectual disposal energy that would otherwise be cut off. There is also, no doubt, a fascination with the tremendous importance that the utterly fabricated situation of re-enacting debates from the past assumes as a participant watches his attempts at waylaying the opponent and then revels in ridicule when the opponent is trapped or undergoes the opposite when he himself is trapped. Debate, above all, is used for group stimulated learning, the members increasing each other's knowledge through bringing special knowledge gained from their own research to the courtyard and then creatively exploring issues. The process of forcing each participant to identify with what are supposedly ridiculous positions causes one to become self-scrutinizing through seeing that other positions have their own logic, thereby challenging one's uncritical acquiescence to abusive caricature. The group dynamic (at least at the School of Dialectics in Dharmsala) is such that the participants keep a check on each other to prevent the type of over-kill that occasionally leaps into Jam-ȳang-shay-b̄a's style.

Kensur Lekden reported that Jam-ȳang-shay-b̄a's own devotion to citing sources came from embarrassment in debate when attempting to defend a Buddha's more fantastic qualities, such as the cognition of all phenomena by his hair. The requirement of accommodation to scripture balances the strong emphasis on reasoning. In even the most reasonable of books on Buddhist tenets, the fantastic is by no means obscured.

Collaborators for the translation

As mentioned at the beginning of this work, I studied almost all of Jam-ȳang-shay-b̄a's *Great Exposition of Tenets* and Nga-w̄ang-b̄el-den's *Annotations* under the guidance of Kensur Lekden (1900-71), a Go-mang scholar and former abbot of the Tantric College of Lower Hla-s̄a while still in Tibet. Without his help—his openness, willingness, and skill in introducing and expanding on topics—the task would have been impossible. Also, the clarification of fine points gained from three months work with Professor Geshe Gedün Lodrö (1924-79) at the University of Hamburg, a Go-mang scholar who was a student of Kensur Lekden, was essential. They were both excellent scholars with hearts of compassion ever eager to help.

Emptiness in the Prāsaṅgika System
by Jam-ȳang-shay-ḇa

Translated in collaboration
with Kensur Lekden
and Geshe Gedün Lodrö

The text has been divided
into seven chapters
to facilitate understanding

Shāntarakṣhita

Contents

BACKGROUND 583

Definition and Etymology of Prāsaṅgika 584

Synonyms of 'Prāsaṅgika' 586

Divisions of Prāsaṅgika 587

Literature on Which the Prāsaṅgikas Rely 588

2 INTERPRETATION OF SCRIPTURE 595

3 THE OBJECT OF NEGATION 625

The Object of Negation in the View of Selflessness 625

Measure of What is Negated 625

Correctness of that Measure 632

Reasonings Refuting Inherent Existence 636

Brief Indication 636

4 REFUTING INHERENTLY EXISTENT PRODUCTION 639

Diamond Slivers 639

Statement of the Reasons 639

Proofs for the Modes of the Reasons 640

Non-Production from Self 640

Non-Production from Other 643

Non-Production from Both Self and Other 649
Non-Production Without Causes 649

5 OTHER TYPES OF PRODUCTION 651
Simultaneous Refutation of Production of the Four Extremes and of the Existent, Non-Existent, Both, and Neither 651
Refutation of Production of the Four Alternatives 653
Actual Exposition 653
Elimination of Error 655

6 DEPENDENT-ARISING 659
Actual Exposition 659
Correct Way of Interpreting Dependent-Arising 662
Formation of *Pratītyasamutpāda* 662
Explanation of the Meaning of Dependent-Arising 664
Refutation of Errors 665
Refutation of Other Commentators 665
Refutation of Bhāvaviveka's Interpretation 668
Elimination of Error Concerning Dependent-Arising 676

7 REFUTING A SELF OF PERSONS 677
Actual Exposition 677
Elimination of Error 696

1 *Background*

Namas Svarasvatyai cha gurumañjughoṣhāya cha.[493] Homage to both Svarasvatī and Guru Mañjughoṣha.

With respect to this Prāsaṅgika system the foremost lama, the great D̄zong-ka-b̄a, says [at the end of his *Essence of the Good Explanations*]:[494]

> One respects from the heart all the good explanations
> Of those like adornments among the wise of the world.
> Still, the eye of intelligence, a garden of jasmine, is opened fully
> By the white rays of good explanations come from the moon [Chandrakīrti],
> Overcoming all extreme conceptions though the reasoning that cyclic existence
> And nirvana are inevitable dependent-arisings.
> Having seen the path revealed by Buddhapālita,
> Who would not take Nāgārjuna's good system as chief?

Thus, the Prāsaṅgika-Mādhyamika system is the very acme of the best among all systems and schools of tenets. It is the great path of perfection travelled, being travelled, and to be travelled by all the Conquerors of the three times [past, present, and future], the incomparable unparalleled mother that gives birth to the four types[495] of Superiors, [2] and the sole, excellent path of passage. Without considering body, enjoyments, and so forth, all the Buddhas, Bodhisattvas, and Superiors made effort toward it, sought it, concentrated on it, and meditated on it. It is the unsurpassed ambrosia delighting others, the profound middle path clearing away all coarse and subtle extremes and extreme conceptions, the final thought of Nāgārjuna which Buddhapālita established as the Prāsaṅgika system. For its chariot a great way was made by the honorable Chandrakīrti.

The explanation of the Prāsaṅgika system has six parts:

1 the definition [of a Prāsaṅgika] along with an etymological explanation
2 synonyms
3 divisions
4 the texts on which they rely
5 scriptural passages of definitive meaning and those requiring interpretation
6 tenets.

DEFINITION AND ETYMOLOGY OF 'PRĀSAṄGIKA'

(See pp.441-530.) The root text says:

Because they do not accept autonomous inferences
But mainly state consequences
That contradict the assertions of their opponents,
They are called Prāsaṅgikas.

Chandrakīrti's *Clear Words* [3] says,[496] 'It is not admissible for one who is a Mādhyamika to use an autonomous inference because another position [among the four extremes] is not asserted.'

'Existing under its own power' (*rang dbang du grub pa*),[497] 'existing inherently' (*svabhāvasiddha, rang bzhin gyis grub pa*), and 'autonomous' (*svatantra, rang rgyud*) are synonyms. Thus, the application of a reason [that is, a syllogism] the three aspects of which exist inherently is an autonomous inference (*svatantra-anumāna, rang rgyud kyi rjes dpag*).

If such autonomous inferences are asserted, then [other phenomena such as] production would perforce [be asserted to exist inherently].[498] Thus, when analyzing, there would necessarily be a position which would be one of the four extremes [and which could withstand ultimate analysis]. In that case, a thesis which is a position of one of the four extremes[499] would have to be asserted. However, the assertion of any of the four extremes is not suitable [for Mādhyamikas] because they must uphold the meaning of the middle way which avoids those extremes. Āryadeva's *Four Hundred* says:[500]

> Even over a long period of time
> Censure cannot be expressed
> For one who has no position
> Of [inherent] existence, non-existence,
> Or existence and non-existence.

Nāgārjuna's *Refutation of Objections* says:[501]

> If I had any [inherently existent] thesis, [4]
> Then I would have that fault [of contradicting my own thesis that there is no inherent existence].
> Because I have no [inherently existent] thesis,
> I am only faultless.

Therefore, [a Prāsaṅgika] does not assert autonomous [inferences or any other autonomous phenomena even] conventionally.

Even so, Prāsaṅgikas have a great many means of generating in opponents the view realizing that phenomena do not truly exist. For the definition of a Prāsaṅgika-Mādhyamika is:

> a Mādhyamika who mainly states refutations of an opponent's assertion of any of the four extremes through the expression of a correct contradictory consequence—a consequence which either implies or does not imply the opposite meaning, and so forth, as will be explained below.

This is also an etymological explanation of 'Prāsaṅgika-Mādhyamika' (Middle Way Consequentialist).

In this Prāsaṅgika system, the statements of consequences and other-approved syllogisms have respectively greater and lesser usage,[502] but they are not entirely mutually exclusive. For, the usage of an other-approved syllogism is mostly similar to that of a consequence. An example of an other-approved syllogism is:

> There is no sense in the production again of a thing which [already] exists in its own entity, [5] as in the case of a manifest pot.

SYNONYMS OF 'PRĀSAṄGIKA'

(See pp.432-9.) The root text says:

> *They are known as Prāsaṅgikas,*
> *Only-Appearance Mādhyamikas,*
> *And Non-Abiding Mādhyamikas.*

They mainly use contradictory consequences to generate in others the view [that no phenomenon inherently exists]; therefore they are called Prāsaṅgikas (Consequentialists).

Chandrakīrti's *Clear Words* says,[503] 'The establishment of conventional phenomena is asserted by way of mere conditionality (*idaṃ pratyayatāmātra, rkyen nyid 'di pa tsam*), not by way of asserting [any of] the four positions . . . ' Also, 'When mere conditionality is asserted, both cause and effect are mutually dependent; hence, their establishment does not inherently exist . . . ' Therefore, Prāsaṅgikas are also called Only-Appearance Mādhyamikas. They are Mādhyamikas who assert the existence of just these appearances from the viewpoint of conditionality when there is no analysis and no investigation [to find an object designated].

Shūra's [Ashvagoṣha's] *Cultivation of the Ultimate Mind of Enlightenment (Paramārthabodhichittabhāvanā)* says:[504]

> [Buddha] proclaimed selflessness with the great roar of a lion.

Through synonyms such as emptiness, [suchness, final
reality,] and so forth,
Limitless examples such as likeness with a magician's
illusions, [dreams, mirages] and so forth [6]
And the skillful means of a variety of vehicles,
[Buddha] made known the meaning of the middle way
not abiding [in any gross or subtle extremes].

Thus, because [Prāsaṅgikas] do not abide in even any of the extremes of permanence or annihilation, they are called Non-Abiding Mādhyamikas and Thoroughly Non-Abiding Mādhyamikas.

DIVISIONS OF PRĀSAṄGIKA

(See pp.431-2.) The root text says:

Their divisions are Models,
Partisans, and Non-Partisans.

With respect to the divisions of Prāsaṅgika, earlier Tibetans rightly called the 'father' Nāgārjuna and his 'son' Āryadeva the Mādhyamikas of the model texts. This is because all—the two founders of the chariot-ways of Prāsaṅgika and Svātantrika [Buddhapālita or Chandrakīrti, and Bhāvaviveka] etc.—without difference treated Nāgārjuna and Āryadeva as totally reliable sources.[505]

The partisan Prāsaṅgikas are Buddhapālita, the honorable Chandrakīrti, Shāntideva [and so forth]. Those who are non-partisan but maintain the Prāsaṅgika view are Shākyamitra, Nāgabodhi, Rik-bay-ku-juk (*Rigs-pa'i-khu-byug*)[506] and so on. Dzong-ka-ba's *Essence of the Good Explanations* says,[507] 'Also, there are many eminent scholars, the masters Shūra [Ashvaghoṣha], Nāgabodhi, and so forth; however, [7] there are no translations of their treatises on Mādhyamika [here in Tibet].' The latter part of the second chapter of *The Five Stages (Pañchakrama)* by Shākyamitra[508] clearly manifests [the Prāsaṅgika view]. Also, upon consideration, Nāgabodhi's *Classification of the Ends of Actions (Karmāntavibhaṅga)* and so forth [clearly manifest the view of a non-partisan Prāsaṅgika].

Though Ashvaghoṣha's view is very clearly that [of a non-partisan Prāsaṅgika], D̄ak-tsang asserts that Ashvaghoṣha is a model [Mādhyamika] and then that he explicitly refutes Svātantrika. However, Buddhapālita, Nāgabodhi, and so forth are not seen to have quoted Ashvaghoṣha as a source [and they would have if he were a model]. Though the two, Bhāvaviveka [and his chief student Jñānagarbha],[509] as well as those coming after them quoted Ashvaghoṣha, this does not of itself make Ashvaghoṣha a model. Also, [D̄ak-tsang claims that] Shūra's statement [in his *Cultivation of the Ultimate Mind of Enlightenment*],[510] 'Also, illusions are not just illusions', refutes Svātantrika. If [D̄ak-tsang were right], then it is clear that Ashvaghoṣha would be a partisan Prāsaṅgika-Mādhyamika [and not, as D̄ak-tsang claims, a model].[511]

Objection: D̄zong-ka-b̄a's *Essence of the Good Explanations* says,[512] 'Also, there are many eminent scholars, the masters Shūra [Ashvaghoṣha], Nāgabodhi, and so forth; [8] however, there are no translations of their treatises on Mādhyamika [here in Tibet].' Thus, if this Prāsaṅgika text [*Cultivation of the Ultimate Mind of Enlightenment*] is Ashvaghoṣha's, then does it not contradict D̄zong-ka-b̄a?

Answer: Ashvaghoṣha's *Cultivation of the Ultimate Mind of Enlightenment* is a meditation manual; therefore, even though it does teach Mādhyamika, D̄zong-ka-b̄a's remark was made [with reference to treatises on the Mādhyamika view and not its meditation], as in the case of the separate treatment of Nāgārjuna's Collections of Praises and his Collections of Reasonings.[513]

LITERATURE ON WHICH THE PRĀSAṄGIKAS RELY

The root text says:

> *Their books are the profound sutras,*
> *The Collections of Reasonings, the* Four Hundred,

Engaging in the Deeds, *the* Compendium of Sutra,
The Compendium of Learnings, *the* Lamp for the Path,
and so forth.

The sutras quoted by the Superior [Nāgārjuna] and his spiritual son [Āryadeva] as sources for the definitive meaning [emptiness] are taken as sutras teaching the profound meaning. These are the following sutras from the turning of the wheel of the doctrine of signlessness:

1 the seventeen mother and son sutras of the Perfection of Wisdom class[514]
2 *Teaching of Akṣhayamati Sutra (Akṣhayamatinirdesha)*
3 *King of Meditative Stabilizations Sutra (Samādhirāja)*
4 *Compendium of Doctrine Sutra (Dharmasamgīti)*
5 *Questions of the King of Nāgas, Anavatapta, Sutra (Anavataptanāgarājaparipṛchchhā)*
6 *Questions of the King of Nāgas, Sāgara, Sutra (Sāgaranāgarājaparipṛchchhā)*
7 *Jewel Mine Sutra (Ratnākara)*
8 *Sport of Mañjushrī Sutra (Mañjushrīvikrīḍita)*
9 The first chapter of the *Heap of Jewels Sutra (Ratnakūṭa)*, called *Chapter Showing the Three Vows Sutra (Trisambaranirdeshaparivarta)*
10 And further from the *Heap of Jewels Sutra:*

Kāshyapa Chapter Sutra (Kāshyapaparivarta)
Bodhisattva Section Sutra (Bodhisattvapiṭaka) [9]
Sutra Showing the Inconceivable Secrets of the Tathāgatas (Tathāgatāchintyaguhyanirdesha)

etc.

The following are sutras teaching both the profound [emptiness] and the extensive [deeds of compassion]:

1 *Sutra on the Ten Grounds (Dashabhūmika)*
2 *Sutra Showing the Realm of the Inconceivable Qualities and Wisdom of the Tathāgatas (Tathāgataguṇajñānāchintyaviṣhayāvatāranirdesha)*

3 *Questions of Sāgaramati Sutra (Sāgaramatipariprṛchchā)*
4 The four sutras on the four meditative stabilizations[515]
5 *Buddhāvataṃsaka Sutra (Buddhāvataṃsakanāmamahā-vaipulya)*
6 *Questions of King Dhāraṇīshvara Sutra (Dhāraṇīshvararāja-pariprṛchchhā)*
7 *Sutra on the Heavily Adorned (Ghanavyūha)*
Etc.

Though the sutras of the last wheel require interpretation, [the Prāsaṅgikas] rely on the six perfections and so forth in them. They are:

1 *Great Drum Sutra (Mahābherīhārakaparivarta)*
2 *Tathāgata Essence Sutra (Tathāgatagarbha)*
3 *Sutra Unravelling the Thought (Saṃdhinirmochana).*

If one wonders on what commentarial treatises [the Prāsaṅgikas] rely, the texts considered to be completely valid are those [Chandrakīrti mentions] in his *Clear Words*,[516] 'Having seen the *Compendium of Sutra*, the *Precious Garland of Advice [for the King]*, the Praises, and . . .' Thus, again and again [these works of Nāgārjuna] are quoted in the *Clear Words*:

1 *Compendium of Sutra (Sūtrasamuchchaya)*
2 *Precious Garland of Advice for the King (Rājaparikathāratnāvalī)* [10]
3 And among Nāgārjuna's Praises of Reality directed toward the ultimate [emptiness]:
Praise of the Element of Qualities (Dharmadhātustotra)
Praise of the Supramundane (Lokātītastava).

Moreover, he speaks of:
Praise of the Three Bodies (Kāyatrayastotra)
Peerless Praise (Nirupamastava)
Praise of What Surpasses Praise (Stutyatītastava)
Praise of the Inconceivable (Achintyastava)
Praise of the Mind Vajra (Chittavajrastava)
Etc.

Also, the *Clear Words* says,[517] '...with effort over a very long time the stanzas propounded in the *Treatise*, the *Sixty Stanzas of Reasoning*, the *Finely Woven*, the *Seventy Stanzas on Emptiness*, and the *Refutation of Objections*,...' Thus, there are Nāgārjuna's Five Collections of Reasonings [that establish emptiness]:

1 *Fundamental Treatise on the Middle Way Called 'Wisdom' (Prajñānāmamūlamadhyamakakārikā)*
2 *Sixty Stanzas of Reasoning (Yuktiṣhaṣhṭikākārikā)*
3 *Treatise Called 'The Finely Woven' (Vaidalyasūtranāma)*
4 *Seventy Stanzas on Emptiness (Shūnyatāsaptatikārikā)* [11]
5 *Refutation of Objections (Vigrahavyāvartanīkārikā).*

Furthermore, the *Clear Words*[518] says, 'And having seen the [*Four*] *Hundred* and so forth [by Āryadeva, etc.] and likewise many profound sutras...' Thus, there are Āryadeva's texts: the *Treatise of Four Hundred Stanzas (Chatuḥshatakashāstrakārikā)* as well as those included in 'and so forth', the *Length of a Forearm*[519] *(Hastavālaprakaraṇakārikā)* and the *Establishment of the Reasoning and Logic Refuting Error (Skhalitapramathanayuktihetusiddhi).* Also, the several texts about the accumulations for enlightenment, etc., and the profound sutras are those quoted as sources in Nāgārjuna's *Compendium of Sutra* and by this master [Chandrakīrti] mentioned earlier.

Buddhapālita's Commentary on (Nāgārjuna's) 'Treatise on the Middle Way' (Buddhapālitamūlamadhyamakavṛtti) and above [that is, the texts of the early Prāsaṅgikas such as Nāgārjuna and Āryadeva] are taken as completely reliable [by Chandrakīrti and later Prāsaṅgikas].

Also, the *Clear Words* says:[520]

> ...as well as the commentary done by Buddhapālita, I have gathered together the good explanations of Bhāvaviveka [and those of these masters] which were transmitted from one to another [and the texts of Shūra, Jñānagarbha, etc.] as well as what I received from [Nāgārjuna's own] analysis [of the meaning of his words] and have

> expounded this in order to please those of great intelligence. [12]

Thus, one must rely on the correct explanations by Bhāvaviveka and so forth which were transmitted from one to another. One should not scar the teaching of the Conqueror with fabrications not in the sutras and commentaries. [For instance, D̄ak-tsang without foundation speaks] of the nine spheres of objects in the mental continuum of a Buddha Superior which are to be abandoned through meditation.[521] The precious Elder [Atīsha] and the precious Teacher [Drom-d̄ön (*'Brom-ston*)] said, 'It is not suitable for a follower of the Elder to be brash [and not cite scripture and reason]; be wary of the effects of actions.' Considering that statement as well as how the Teacher [Buddha] earnestly transmitted the teaching to Ānanda, please press your palms together [in respect] toward all, not allowing yourself and others to be ruined.[522]

The *Clear Words*[523] also says:

> Nāgārjuna, with the honorable Rāhulabhadra [Saraha], clearly taught the system of this [*Treatise on the Middle Way*] for a long time, [their] word being followed by [Ārya]deva. His students, with decisive minds [gained] through analyzing the *Treatise*, defeated all the Forders and set forth the supreme Subduer's teaching for a long time. [13]

Thus, [Chandrakīrti] speaks of the master, the Superior [Nāgārjuna's], long period of teaching, also his students' composition of many commentaries on the master's texts, and their eradication of the Forders. Therefore, it is clear that this master [Chandrakīrti] also relied on the oral transmission of their teachings, but [Chandrakīrti goes on to] explain that most of those texts had already disappeared.[524]

The master Chandrakīrti stated the names of Vasubandhu, Dignāga, and so forth [in commentary on his *Supplement*][525] and refuted them, but there is no one who stated Chandrakīrti's name and refuted him. The four great commentaries and so forth of this master [Chandrakīrti] who was renowned as a tenth ground Bodhisattva [are:

1 *Clear Words, Commentary on (Nāgārjuna's) 'Treatise on the Middle Way' (Mūlamadhyamakavṛttiprasannapadā)*
2 *Commentary on (Nāgārjuna's) 'Sixty Stanzas of Reasoning' (Yuktiṣhaṣhṭikāvṛtti)*
3 *Commentary on (Nāgārjuna's) 'Seventy Stanzas on Emptiness' (Shūnyatāsaptativṛtti)*
4 *Commentary on (Āryadeva's) 'Four Hundred Stanzas on the Yogic Deeds of Bodhisattvas' (Bodhisattvayogacharyāchatuḥshatakaṭīkā)*
And so forth]. [14]

Also, in general, stabilizing and analytical meditation, the three vows of Bodhisattvas,[526] the ways of meditating on the profound [emptiness], etc., as well as hearing and explaining, etc. —all beginning from reliance on a spiritual guide—are extensively set forth in the Bodhisattva Shāntideva's texts:

1 *Engaging in the Bodhisattva Deeds (Bodhisattvacharyāvatāra)*
2 *Compendium of Learnings (Shikṣhāsamuchchayakārikā).*

Therefore, these two [Chandrakīrti and Shāntideva] are completely reliable.

One can take as reliable Atīsha's *Lamp for the Path to Enlightenment (Bodhipathapradīpa)* and those works of Atīsha included within the term 'and so forth' in the basic text, *Quintessential Instructions on the Middle Way (Madhyamakopadesha)* and *Introduction to the Two Truths (Satyadvayāvatāra)*, as well as Prajñāmokṣha's *Commentary on (Atīsha's) 'Quintessential Instructions on the Middle Way' (Madhyamakopadeshavṛtti).*

One should take the good parts of Atīsha's[527] *Explanation of (Shāntideva's) 'Engaging in the Bodhisattva Deeds' (Bodhisattvacharyāvatārabhāṣhya)* and *Commentary on the Difficult Points of 'Lamp for the Path to Enlightenment' (Bodhimārgapradīpapañjikā).*

One can rely on Maitreya's *Treatise on the Sublime Continuum of the Great Vehicle (Mahāyānottaratantrashāstra)* and Asaṅga's

Explanation of (Maitreya's) 'Treatise on the Sublime Continuum of the Great Vehicle' (Mahāyānottaratantrashāstravyākhyā).

One should take whatever is common to Prāsaṅgika and Svātantrika in Maitreya's *Ornament for Clear Realization (Abhisamayālaṃkāra)* and in Āryavimuktisena's and Haribhadra's discussions on the path, etc.

For an unconfused account with respect to what is uncommon [to Prāsaṅgika I, Jam-ȳang-shay-b̄a,] having taken as valid the good explanations of the three—the great being, the foremost [D̄zong-ka-b̄a who is the] father and his two spiritual sons [Gyel-tsap and Kay-drup], will explain the Prāsaṅgika system just according to them even though I might not cite them in quotation. For, free from error, they expounded clearly through millions of reasons.

2 *Interpretation of Scripture*

About definitive sutras and those requiring interpretation (see pp. 422-8, 365-97) the root text says: [15]

Sutras teaching the two truths
Are respectively those to be interpreted,
Because they must be interpreted otherwise,
And the definitive, because the mode
Of existence is definite there.
There are two ways of interpretation:
When even the literal meaning is not suitable
And when the literal meaning, though established,
Is not the final mode of existence.
The first and last wheels require interpretation.
The middle are definitive sutras.
Five sutra sections of the Descent into Laṅkā,
The Unravelling the Thought, *and* The Heavily Adorned,
Thinking that there is no other creator
And thinking of emptiness
Teach mind-only [meaning] no external objects,
A permanent essence, the existence of the basis-of-all,
The true existence of other-powered phenomena

And of thoroughly established phenomena,
And three final vehicles. These five
Teachings are proved to require interpretation.

There are many purposes for the master, the Superior [Nāgārjuna's], composing the *Treatise on the Middle Way* and differentiating what requires interpretation and what is definitive. For, the *Treatise* was written for the sake of non-obscuration with regard to the two truths, for the sake of making known the purpose of the two truths, for the sake of eliminating doubt in those who wonder just what requires interpretation and what is definitive, [16] and for the sake of dispelling the wrong understanding that conceives what requires interpretation to be definitive, that is, to be the way things are. Chandrakīrti's *Clear Words* says:[528]

> This *Treatise on the Middle Way* was composed by the master [Nāgārjuna] for the sake of showing the difference between that requiring interpretation and the definitive. With respect to this, those scriptural passages speaking of production and so forth of dependent-arisings were not spoken from the viewpoint of the nature of objects [as known by] the non-contaminated wisdom of those free from the dimness of ignorance. Rather, they were spoken from the viewpoint of the objects of mind of those whose eye of intelligence is obscured by the dimness of ignorance.
>
> From the viewpoint of perceiving suchness, the Supramundane Victor[529] said, 'O monks, this which is nirvana, having the attribute of non-deceptiveness, is the ultimate truth. All conditioned things are false, having the attribute of deceptiveness [appearing to exist in their own right when in fact they do not].' Etc.
>
> Similarly, 'There is here no suchness and no non-erroneous suchness. [17] These have the attribute of deception. These also have the attribute of destructive allurement.[530] These also are falsities; these are illusions, delusions of children.'
>
> Similarly:

Forms are like balls of foam.
Feelings are like bubbles.
Discriminations resemble mirages.
Compositional factors are like banana tree trunks.[531]
Consciousnesses resemble magical illusions.
Thus the Sun Friend Buddha said.

Similarly, 'If a monk, mindful and attentive, exerting effort, analyzes phenomena day and night, he should realize peace, the auspicious abode of the extinction of conditioned things, the selflessness of phenomena.'[532] Etc.

Due to not understanding the thought of [Buddha's] teaching set forth in this way, some would have doubt: 'Here, what is the teaching having the meaning of suchness? [18] What indeed is that having [some other] thought [as its basis]?' Also, due to having a weak intellect some think teachings which in fact require interpretation are definitive. In order to dispel with reasoning and scripture the doubt and wrong understanding of these two types of beings, the master [Nāgārjuna] composed this *Treatise*.

There are differentiators of scriptures requiring interpretation and those of definitive meaning, because they are done so (1) by the four reliances [the third being, 'Rely on sutras of definitive meaning, not on those requiring interpretation,'], (2) by reasoning as in Nāgārjuna's *Treatise on the Middle Way*:[533]

Things are never produced
At all anywhere
From themselves, other,
Both, or causelessly.

etc., and (3) also through many scriptural citations such as in Nāgārjuna's *Treatise*:[534]

The Supramundane Victor said that fraudulent
Phenomena are falsities.

All conditioned things have the attribute of deception, [19]
Therefore, they are falsities.

When asked 'Is a former limit [of cyclic existence][535] discerned?'
The Great Subduer said, 'No.'
Cyclic existence is without beginning or end.
[Ultimately] it has no former and later parts [and thus does not inherently exist].

In the 'Advice to Kātyāyana'
'Exists', 'does not exist', and 'both'
Are rejected by the Supramundane Victor, knower of
[The nature of][536] things and non-things.

The differentiation of what requires interpretation and what is definitive is devised from the viewpoint of the subject matter [in the passage]. A sutra mainly teaching the ultimate [emptiness] is said to be definitive whereas one mainly teaching conventionalities [phenomena other than emptinesses] is said to require interpretation. The *Teaching of Akṣhayamati Sutra* says,[537] 'What are definitive sutras? What require interpretation? Sutras setting forth the establishment of conventionalities [20] are called "requiring interpretation". Sutras setting forth the establishment of the ultimate are called "definitive".'

Question: How are conventionalities and the ultimate established?

Answer: There are ways of establishing them. Respectively, the setting forth of any of the varieties of actions and agents through various words and letters is the way that conventionalities are established. The setting forth of the doctrine of [emptiness which] is unapprehendable [as inherently existent], is beyond the [dual] intellect, difficult to view, and difficult to realize is the way that the ultimate is established. The *Teaching of Akṣhayamati Sutra* says:[538]

Those sutras teaching [about various objects] by way of various words and letters are said to require interpretation.

> Those teaching the profound, difficult to view, and difficult to realize are called definitive. Those teaching, for instance, [the inherent existence of] an owner when there is no [inherently existent] owner and teaching those objects indicated by various words [such as] self, sentient being, life, nourisher, being, person, progeny of Manu, son of Manu, agent, and experiencer are said to require interpretation. [21] Those sutras teaching the doors of liberation, the emptiness of phenomena, no [inherently existent] signs, no [inherently existent] wishes, no [inherently existent] products, no [inherently existent] production, no [inherently existent] sentient being, no [inherently existent] living being, no [inherently existent] person, and no [inherently existent] controller are called the definitive. This is called reliance on definitive sutras and non-reliance on those requiring interpretation.

The teachings of conventional phenomena in the first wheel of the teaching and in the *Sutra Unravelling the Thought* require interpretation. For it is necessary to search out the mode of existence [of the phenomena mentioned in these texts] apart from what was explicitly taught there. The *King of Meditative Stabilizations Sutra*, the *One Hundred Thousand Stanza Perfection of Wisdom Sutra*, and so forth are definitive because the mode of existence of the phenomena [discussed in those texts] is definite as just the meaning of their explicit teaching.

With respect to interpreting the mode of existence [of the conventional phenomena mentioned in the first and third wheels] there are examples [such as a magician's illusions that contradict them] but the interpretation is from the viewpoint of [there being a pedagogic] need [which gave rise to the teaching]. Most passages requiring interpretation should have [both examples contradicting them and pedagogic need]. With respect to interpretation of the subject matter, reasonings such as not being able [in analysis] to find [the object designated] damage [the teaching of conventionalities if one takes merely that to be the final mode of subsistence]. [22] Also, scriptures saying in one voice that all products are false and so forth damage [such].[539]

Also, [with respect to definitive sutras] many examples such as illusions, many reasons such as, 'If [the object designated] is sought, it is not found,' and many scriptures teaching the profound non-production determine that the final mode of existence is just this [that is set forth explicitly in the text].

Here [in the Prāsaṅgika system] the way that texts requiring interpretation are to be interpreted [or literally, 'led'] does not refer to *leading* trainees—as by the indirect teachings [of a real self for the sake of] introducing them [to virtuous endeavor] but to *interpreting* the subject being discussed. In brief, there are two ways of interpretation: one when the literal meaning of the passage is not even suitable to be what is expressed by the sutra as in, 'Father and mother are to be killed,' [which actually teaches that 'existence' and 'attachment' are to be abandoned [540] and the other when the literal meaning of the passage is suitable to be what the sutra expresses but interpretation is required to determine the mode of existence of the phenomena discussed in the text]. For instance, though the teaching that pleasures are produced from wholesome actions and sufferings from unwholesome actions is literal, it would not be suitable to assert these facts as the mode of existence of the two. One must interpret their mode of existence otherwise, as lacking self [objective existence]. Thus, there are, in brief, two modes of interpretation: of that which is not literally acceptable in order to discover the subject matter and of the literally acceptable to discover the nature of the phenomena discussed. The *King of Meditative Stabilizations Sutra* [23] says:[541]

> One knows the features of definitive sutras
> In accordance with the Sugata's teaching of emptiness.
> All doctrines of a sentient being, a person, a being,
> Are to be known as requiring interpretation.

Therefore, [the Prāsaṅgikas'] differentiation of the three wheels of the teaching [as to whether they require interpretation] does not accord with the system set forth in the *Sutra Unravelling the Thought*. The *Extensive Sport Sutra* says:[542]

I have found a truth, profound, peaceful, lacking
The elaborations [of thought], radiant, non-conditioned,
 the ambrosia.
Though I taught it, no one would understand.
I should stay without speaking in the forest.

[Hīnayāna passages] such as this and the Hīnayāna scriptures quoted in Nāgārjuna's *Treatise on the Middle Way* that explicitly teach the ultimate are sutras of the first wheel; yet, [the Prāsaṅgikas] say that these do not require interpretation. Therefore, there is no necessity that the individual three wheels [as taught by the Prāsaṅgikas] be the first, second, and third wheels as identified in the *Sutra Unravelling the Thought* [which states that every scripture of the first wheel requires interpretation].

Of the three wheels [identified] in the *Sutra Unravelling the Thought*, the first wheel explains that the four truths and so forth exist by way of their own character (*svalakṣhaṇasat, rang gi mtshan nyid kyis yod pa*).[543] [24] The last wheel explains that imaginaries do not exist inherently and that other-powered phenomena and thoroughly established phenomena exist ultimately and inherently. [According to the Prāsaṅgika system] these two types of sutras require interpretation.

Also, the *Heart of Wisdom Sutra*[544] of the middle [wheel of the teaching], for instance, says, '[Avalokiteshvara] was viewing [the five aggregates] as empty of inherent existence.' Therefore, such [sutras] are definitive.

This way [that the Prāsaṅgikas divide scriptures into those requiring interpretation and the definitive] does not accord with the *Sutra Unravelling the Thought* [which states that the first and second wheels require interpretation and that the third wheel is definitive. However, the Prāsaṅgikas' disagreement with this sutra] does not mean that it contradicts the thought [of Buddha], for such [a system as is set forth in that sutra] is suitable for certain types of trainees, and [no matter how much it differs from the final system] it does not contradict Buddha's thought. For example, Hearers are never permitted to kill, but certain Mahāyānists are, according to the purpose. Though these two are systems of one speaker, they are not contradictory [in that the difference is explained through taking into account the level of the listener].

[All non-literal passages requiring interpretation such as, 'Father and mother should be killed,' or, 'A mind-basis-of-all exists,' must have another basis in Buddha's thought, a purpose, and refutations of their explicit meaning.]

Question: With respect to passages that are to be interpreted [and are non-literal], what are here [in the Prāsaṅgika system] the basis in Buddha's thought, the purpose, and the refutation of the explicit meaning?

Answer: [In general, there are numerous types of passages requiring interpretation. However, Chandrakīrti cites the *Descent into Laṅkā Sutra* as proof that four types of teachings require interpretation.]

Some persons [cite Chandrakīrti's *Supplement*]:[545]

> This passage [in the *Descent into Laṅkā Sutra*] shows
> That other such sutras require interpretation. [25]

These [interpreters wrongly] say that from among the Chittamātrin teachings just four passages require interpretation [whereas they should say four *types* do]:

1 the *Sutra Unravelling the Thought* where it teaches the three natures of Chittamātra [the sixth through ninth chapters]
2 the two chapters of the *Sutra Unravelling the Thought* teaching a basis-of-all (*ālaya, kun gzhi*)[546]
3 [the eighth chapter of the *Sutra Unravelling the Thought* called] 'Questions of Maitreya' where it teaches that there are no objects external [to a perceiving consciousness]
4 [the seventh chapter of] the *Sutra Unravelling the Thought* where it teaches three final vehicles.

The third is indicated by the term 'and so forth' in Chandrakīrti's own commentary to his *Supplement*.

[It is correct that these are four *types* of passages which Chandrakīrti says require interpretation. However,] it is incorrect [that there are only four passages from Chittamātra teachings referred to here and requiring interpretation]. For D̄zong-ka-b̄a's *Illumination of the Thought, Explanation of (Chandrakīrti's) 'Supplement'* says,[547] 'This [Prāsaṅgika] system considers all of the aforementioned four categories to require interpretation.' This statement explains that by way of topical abridgement and unification under subjects there are mainly four.

There are the three explicitly mentioned in Chandrakīrti's own commentary on his *Supplement* and the teaching of three final vehicles discussed in Nāgārjuna's *Compendium of Sutra*. However, if passages requiring interpretation are differentiated by way of various modes of expression and inner divisions, there are a great many. For example, there are the ways that three final vehicles are taught, such as in the *Sutra on the Myrabolan Fruit* (*Myrabola*) [which says that, if a person removed one by one myrabolan fruits from a pile as large as Mount Sumeru, he would finish quickly whereas, if he attempted to name individually all the types or lineages (*gotra, rigs*) of sentient beings, he would never finish].[548] The *Sutra Unravelling the Thought* says:[549]

> Thinking that [the purification and the path of purification of the three vehicles are the same in the sense that all three deliver beings from cyclic existence and are the same in the sense that the path is the meditation of selflessness] I teach one vehicle. However, it is not that there are no varieties of sentient beings—[26] the naturally dull, middling, and sharp—among the types of sentient beings.

Also, [there is the teaching that there are three final vehicles because three] truly existing lineages are apprehended individually.[550] Furthermore, [there is the teaching that] Foe Destroyers are not reborn through transmigration as found, for instance, in the *[Twenty-Five Thousand Stanza] Perfection of Wisdom Sutra* [which is taken by the Chittamātrins who follow Asaṅga as indicating that some sentient beings never reach Buddhahood]:[551]

> Those [Hearers] who strictly abide in the right [in a nirvana without remainder] do not have the power to

> generate the aspiration to unsurpassed, complete, perfect enlightenment. Why? Because they have severed the continuum of cyclic existence [through not being born by the power of either afflictions or compassion].

Also, the *Sutra Unravelling the Thought* says:[552]

> He who has the lineage of a Hearer, proceeding solely to peacefulness, is set in the essence of enlightenment. Though all the Buddhas exert themselves, he does not have the power to generate an intention toward the highest, complete, perfect enlightenment.

Also, there is, for example, the explanation [in the *Sutra Unravelling the Thought*][553] that through fear [of the suffering of cyclic existence Foe Destroyers have forsaken helping others, and thus] their Buddha lineage has been severed. There are many passages and many ways of indicating that no matter how much Foe Destroyers meditate, [27] they cannot generate compassion and the unusual attitude [of taking upon oneself the burden of helping all sentient beings].

The individual scriptures showing that each of these [ways of teaching three final vehicles] requires interpretation were quoted in Nāgārjuna's *Compendium of Sutra* and were just not quoted here [in Chandrakīrti's commentary to his *Supplement*]. Thus, [it is wrong to say that Chandrakīrti is referring to just four passages requiring interpretation]. Nāgārjuna's *Compendium of Sutra* quotes the explanations that all the Buddhas of the three times and all the present Buddhas of the ten directions teach one vehicle:[554]

> It is extremely difficult to find sentient beings who have faith in one vehicle [due to the difficulties of the required accumulations of merit and wisdom in the Mahāyāna]. However, [all vehicles] are exhausted in one because such was taught in many sutras. The *White Lotus of the Excellent Doctrine Sutra* says, 'Also, based on one vehicle, I teach doctrine to sentient beings in this way. Buddha's vehicles arrive at their conclusion in omniscience. There

> is no ascription of two or three vehicles. This is the nature [of the teaching] even in all the transient worlds of the ten directions.
>
> 'Why? All those Tathāgatas who appeared in the past in all the transient worlds of the ten directions [28] taught doctrine to sentient beings based on one vehicle. This is the vehicle to Buddhahood. Also, all those Tathāgatas who will appear in the future will teach doctrine to sentient beings based on one vehicle. Also, all those Tathāgatas who are presently appearing in all the transient worlds of the ten directions are teaching doctrine to sentient beings based on one vehicle.
>
> 'Through that format this is to be understood: If there is even no ascribing of two vehicles in any of the transient worlds of the ten directions, what need is there to mention three?'

In this sutra[555] [Hearers such as] Shāriputra [29] are prophesied to attain the unsurpassed enlightenment; [this implies that there is only one final vehicle since even Hearers finally attain the highest enlightenment].

Also, Nāgārjuna's *Compendium of Sutra* quotes[556] the explanation that, if different vehicles had been taught, Buddha would have had different discriminations [in the sense of desire for some students and hatred for others]. He would have had the fault of miserliness [because he would have withheld the best teaching from some. Thus, it is shown that all the vehicles] only flow into the Mahāyāna. The *Compendium of Sutra* says:

> The *Chapter of the True One Sutra* says, 'Mañjushrī, because [trainees] emerge [from all obstructions] through one vehicle, the field of Buddha has the essence of the Mahāyāna. I do not ascribe vehicles of Hearers and Solitary Realizers. Why? Because the Tathāgata does not have various discriminations. Mañjushrī, if the Tathāgata taught the Mahāyāna to some, the vehicle of the Solitary Realizers to some, and the vehicle of the Hearers to some, the Tathāgata's mind would be very

impure, would have the fault of attraction and also little compassion, and would be secretive with regard to the doctrine.

'Mañjushrī, all the doctrines that I teach to sentient beings are for the sake of attaining omniscient wisdom. Flowing to enlightenment [30] and descending into the Mahāyāna, they are the means of achieving omniscience; they lead completely to one place [omniscience]. Therefore, I have no establishment of vehicles.

'Mañjushrī, an establishment of vehicles is done to set persons in Tathāgatahood. It is done to set them in a small collection [of merit and wisdom] and in a limitless collection. However, because the element of qualities (*dharmadhātu*)[537] [emptiness] is not diverse, they do not have different vehicles. These teachings of conventionalities are uttered only as means of entering [the path to omniscience]. Ultimately there is one vehicle, not two.'

Also, [Nāgārjuna's *Compendium of Sutra* quotes] a Perfection of Wisdom Sutra [translated here in accordance with the Prāsaṅgika interpretation]:[558]

Those devaputras who have not generated the aspiration to unsurpassed, complete, perfect enlightenment [31] will generate that aspiration. Those [Hearers] who abide strictly in the right [a nirvana without remainder] do not have the power [that is, are far from having the power] to generate the aspiration to unsurpassed, complete, perfect enlightenment. Why? Because they have [temporarily] severed the continuum of cyclic existence [their Buddha lineage]. When they generate the aspiration to unsurpassed, complete, perfect enlightenment, even I will be pleased, and I will not upset their roots of virtue. They will take great cognizance of the doctrine that far exceeds even the superior.

This passage shows that if Foe Destroyers generate the attitude [of aspiration to enlightenment for the sake of all sentient beings,

Buddha] will be pleased and will not upset [their roots of virtue, that is, will not propound to them a teaching of five lineages or three vehicles].[559] They will become cognizant of the very superior doctrine [that is, will generate the aspiration to enlightenment relying on extraordinary births].

Thus, it is explicitly taught that even Foe Destroyers generate the aspiration to perfect enlightenment for the sake of all beings. Therefore, the three scriptures [the *Sutra on the Myrabolan Fruit*, the *Sutra Unravelling the Thought*, and the *Perfection of Wisdom Sutra* mentioned above] are said to require interpretation.

Also, [Nāgārjuna's *Compendium of Sutra* quotes] the *Questions of King Dhāraṇīshvara Sutra*:[560]

> The Buddhas, the Supramundane Victors, [32] do not appear for the sake of a variety of discourses [diverse vehicles]. They appear in order to cause sentient beings to be fully enlightened and realize the element of qualities, which is of one taste, without obstruction, the boon of all sentient beings. Thus, they turn the irreversible wheel [of doctrine causing continual progression toward Buddhahood].
>
> O child of good lineage, a jeweler, for instance, takes an unpolished jewel from a jewel-mine. He washes it with a strong solution of soda and wipes it with a black haircloth. However, he does not cease his efforts with just this; he washes it with a strong solution of quicksilver and rubs it with wood and wool. However, he does not cease his efforts with just this; he washes it with the juice of a great herb and wipes it with a fine cloth. Having polished it, the jewel is free of the types of fetters and is called *vaidurya* (cat's-eye gem).
>
> Just so, a Tathāgata ascertains the impure [Buddha] nature of all sentient beings. [33] He causes sentient beings who greatly enjoy cyclic existence to be disquieted through disquieting discourse on impermanence, suffering, selflessness, and unpleasantness. He introduces them to the disciplinary practice of Superiors.

> A Tathāgata does not cease his efforts with just this; he causes them to understand the Tathāgata's own mode of discourse through discourse on emptiness, signlessness, and wishlessness. However, a Tathāgata does not cease his efforts with just this; he leads those sentient beings to the Tathāgata's land through discourse on the irreversible wheel [cultivation of the union of method and wisdom][561] and discourse on the complete purification of the three spheres [of agent, action, and object].
>
> Those sentient beings of various lineages and natures —having become equal—realize the nature of Tathāgatahood. Thus, they realize [the six perfections and so forth], the highest boon [bestowing omniscience]. [34]

This passage explains through the example of the three stages of cleansing a gem that [a Buddha] cleans away the stains of even Foe Destroyers' obstructions and establishes them in Buddhahood. Therefore, the teachings that Foe Destroyers do not have the capacity for Buddhahood are explained as requiring interpretation.

Also, [Nāgārjuna's *Compendium of Sutra* quotes] the *Irreversible Wheel Sutra* (*Avaivartachakra*):[562]

> The youthful Mañjushrī asked, 'What is the teaching of doctrine by the Buddhas, the Supramundane Victors, like?' Buddha said, 'The teaching of doctrine by the Buddhas, the Supramundane Victors, is like an irreversible wheel of doctrine.' Mañjushrī asked, 'Supramundane Victor, how is it that the Supramundane Victor, based on three vehicles, teaches doctrine?'
>
> Buddha said, 'Son of good lineage, those sentient beings [to whom I teach three vehicles] admire low [vehicles]; they do not understand the one vehicle. The skillful in means lead them thus. Son of good lineage, the Buddhas, the Supramundane Victors, possess great skill in means. [35] The Supramundane Victor has appeared at the time of the five ruinations;[563] these are non-admirers of the one vehicle.'

This explains that the teaching of three vehicles is for the sake of leading those who do not understand the one vehicle.

Also, [Nāgārjuna's *Compendium of Sutra*] quotes the *Lion's Roar of Shrīmālādevī Sutra*:[564]

> The so-called utter passing away (*parinirvāṇa, yongs su mya ngan las 'das pa*) is a skillful means of the Tathāgatas. All three vehicles are aspects of the one vehicle; he who understands the one vehicle understands the unsurpassed, complete, perfect enlightenment.

The foregoing sutras were quoted together [in one section of Nāgārjuna's *Compendium of Sutra*]. Also, here in the *Lion's Roar of Shrīmālādevī Sutra*,[565] as before, the non-birth of Foe Destroyers is shown to require interpretation. [The *Compendium of Sutra* quotes the *Descent into Laṅkā Sutra*:[566]

> Their faults due to predispositions and their madness due to meditative stabilization having ceased, Hearers and Solitary Realizers [36] rise again from the uncontaminated realm. Through fulfilling the collections included within the worldly realm (the collection of merit) and the non-worldly uncontaminated realm (the superior collection of the wisdom of emptiness), they attain the capacity for the extraordinary body of wisdom and emptiness.]

The *Descent into Laṅkā Sutra* says:[567]

> Even Hearers who have attained an abiding in the bliss of meditative stabilization will attain the body of bodies of the Conqueror.

And:

> Having attained the body
> Of meditative stabilization,
> They do not rise for eons.
> Just as drunken persons
> Forsake beer and become sober,
> So even they will attain
> My body of wisdom and emptiness. [37]

Though there are many scriptural passages teaching the rebirth of Foe Destroyers and their attainment of the Mahāyāna path through the Buddhas' prodding, these were counted as one in Chandrakīrti's *Supplement*: the teaching of one final vehicle.

Not only that, but also the *King of Meditative Stabilizations Sutra* shows that [the teaching of] a true existence of individual lineages requires interpretation. It says:[568]

> The essence of the Tathāgata exists in all migrators,
> And thus there are no unfortunate sentient beings.

Also, there are the explanations in the *Tathāgata Essence Sutra* and in Maitreya's *Sublime Continuum of the Great Vehicle* that the Buddha lineage exists in all sentient beings. Even these teachings are just included in [the one topic of] the teaching of one vehicle. Thus, Chandrakīrti's *Supplement* says:[569]

> This passage [in the *Descent into Laṅkā Sutra*] shows
> That other such sutras require interpretation.

His own commentary on this [38] says:[570]

> What are the 'other such passages [that require interpretation'? The teaching of] the non-existence of imaginaries and the [inherent] existence of other-powered phenomena that occurs in the *Sutra Unravelling the Thought* when explaining the three natures: imaginaries, other-powered phenomena, and thoroughly established phenomena. Similarly, [the *Sutra Unravelling the Thought* teaches]:[571]
>
> > There is a deep and subtle consciousness, the taker [of rebirth],
> > Having all the seeds and flowing like the continuum of a river.
> > If it were understood as a self, it would not be proper,
> > Thus I do not teach it to children.
>
> And so forth. [The *Descent into Laṅkā Sutra*] says:[572]
>
> > Just as a doctor distributes
> > Medicines to the ill,

> So Buddha teaches
> Mind-only to sentient beings.
>
> This passage [from the *Descent into Laṅkā*] shows that [those types of passages] require interpretation.

Thus, it is said that just as a doctor distributes individual medicines in accordance with illnesses, so Buddha [39] teaches trainees mind-only and so forth.

Also, all passages taught merely in conformity with the thoughts of sentient beings require interpretation. Since it is mistaken to take these teachings literally, like apprehending water in a mirage, it is said that one should not be enamoured of the words but seek the definitive meaning [emptiness]. The *Descent into Laṅkā* says:[573]

> Sutras teaching in conformity with the thoughts of sentient beings have meaning that is mistaken; they are not discourse on suchness. Just as a deer is deceived by a waterless mirage into apprehending water, so doctrine which is taught [in conformity with the thoughts of sentient beings] pleases children but is not discourse causing the wisdom of Superiors. Therefore, you should follow the meaning and not be enamoured of the expression.

This indeed describes all [non-literal passages requiring] interpretation. However, if they are described individually, on this occasion five types of sutras are mentioned:

1 mind-only and no external objects
2 the teaching in the *Tathāgata Essence Sutra* of a permanent, stable essence in the continuums of all sentient beings which has the [major and minor] marks of a Buddha [40]
3 the description of a basis-of-all
4 the description of the true existence of other-powered phenomena and thoroughly established phenomena
5 the teaching of three final vehicles.

[The first, third, fourth, and fifth are accepted by the Chittamātrins Following Scripture as definitive or literal; they assert the second, the teaching of a permanent Tathāgata essence, to be non-literal and actually to be referring to the impermanent mind-basis-of-all.]

In the *Descent into Laṅkā Sutra* the teaching of mind-only is explained through the example of [the distribution of medicine to] the sick. This shows that the teaching of mind-only in the 'Questions of Maitreya' chapter of the *Sutra Unravelling the Thought* requires interpretation.

[Still, according to Prāsaṅgika 'mind-only' is not always a non-literal teaching requiring interpretation, since it is often taught for the sake of emphasizing that the principal creator of pleasure, pain, activities, and so on is the mind and not a deity or anything else. Thus, when the teaching of mind-only does not reject external objects, it is a valid literal teaching even for Prāsaṅgika. It requires interpretation only to determine the final mode of existence of the phenomena discussed.] The statement in the *Sutra on the Ten Grounds*,[574] 'These three realms are mind-only,' is said by Bhāvaviveka to mean that the creator propounded by the Forders does not exist and that only the mind is the principal creator. Chandrakīrti's *Supplement* [similarly] explains [the meaning of 'mind-only' based] on the *Sutra on the Ten Grounds* itself:[575]

> The Bodhisattva of the Manifest [sixth ground],
> Who is nearing [the element of qualities]
> And understands that the three realms are only mind
> Realizes that the creator [of the world] is only mind,
> Thus he knows there is no permanent self as the creator.

Not only that, but also the *Descent into Laṅkā Sutra* says:[576] [41]

> I explain as mind-only
> [What is said to be] the creator—
> Person, continuum, aggregates, causes,
> Particles, principal, and Īshvara.

Thus, there are those who, though they are Buddhists, advocate as the creator a substantially existent person or a continuum or aggregates which are asserted to be the person. Also, some Buddhists advocate substantially existent causes as the creator.

The Vaisheṣhikas advocate particles as the creator of the world; the Sāṃkhyas, the principal; and the Aishvaras, Īshvara. Refuting them, Buddha said that only the mind is the creator.

[Some say that this passage from the *Sutra on the Ten Grounds* refutes forms which are entities external to a perceiving consciousness and that this is done through understanding that the three realms are only the truly existent mind. However, it would be inadmissible for Buddha to say in the same sutra that the mind exists inherently and that the mind is produced from causes. For inherent existence and dependent-arising are mutually exclusive.][577] If [this passage from the *Sutra on the Ten Grounds* means that] there are no forms separate from a [truly existent] mind, [why did Buddha in the same sutra] say,[578] 'The mind [is produced] by the cause of actions'? Also, he would not have spoken [of the production] of name and form [by consciousness if there were no form]. Thus, because [the *Sutra on the Ten Grounds*] explains that the mind creates the varieties of the world, one should understand [that here the word 'only' of mind-only] refutes a creator which is not mainly the mind [and thus in this context does not refute external objects].

Question: The *Descent into Laṅka Sutra* says:[579]

> [Objects] do not exist as external objects as perceived. [42]
> The mind appears as various [objects through the power of predispositions].
> [Because the mind is generated] in the likeness of bodies [senses], enjoyments [objects of senses], and abodes [physical sense organs and environments],
> I have explained [that all phenomena are] mind-only.

Is this to be explained [as referring to the mind as the main creator and not refuting external objects]?

Answer: No. Here a doctrine of mind-only which refers to the non-existence of external objects is presented, and it is said that what is perceived as bodies, enjoyments, and abodes is the entity of the mind [perceiving them]. The teaching of such in the *Sutra Unravelling the Thought* and so forth is for the sake of overcoming trainees' attachment to forms and so forth. With respect to the basis of Buddha's thought [when he taught this non-literal teaching of mind-only meaning no external objects], it is clear that he was thinking that all phenomena are posited through their mental images as [is taught in] Nāgārjuna's *Sixty Stanzas of Reasoning.*[580] In this context he set forth mind-only.

The refutation of this type of mind-only by both Bhāvaviveka and this master [Chandrakīrti] is the thought of the Superior [Nāgārjuna] himself. Nāgārjuna's *Essay on the Mind of Enlightenment* says:[581]

> The Subduer's teaching
> That all these are mind-only
> Was so that children would forsake [43]
> Their fears. It is not suchness.

Also, Nāgārjuna's *Precious Garland* says:[582]

> Just as a grammarian [first] has [his students] read a model of the alphabet, so Buddha taught his trainees the doctrines they were able to bear. To some he taught doctrines in order to turn them away from sins. This was so that some [beings of small capacity] would achieve [the fruits of] merit [in rebirths as gods and humans]. He taught some [beings of middling capacity] doctrines based on the dualism [of object and subject as different entities]. To some he taught doctrines not based on dualism [that object and subject are empty of being separate entities and that consciousness ultimately exists]. He taught some [beings of heightened faculties] doctrines profound and frightening to the fearful, having an essence of emptiness and compassion, the means of achieving [highest] enlightenment. [44]

Therefore, Chandrakīrti's *Supplement* says:[583]

> These sutras teaching no external objects of perception,
> Teaching that the mind appears as the varieties of objects,
> Turn away from forms those extremely attracted to forms.
> These also just require interpretation.

[A teaching that requires interpretation according to both Chittamātra and Prāsaṅgika is that of a permanent, fully developed Tathāgata essence.] Similarly, the *Descent into Laṅkā Sutra* says:[584]

> Mahāmati said, 'The Tathāgata essence taught in the Supramundane Victor's sutras is said by the Supramundane Victor to be naturally radiant [lacking the elaborations of thought], pure [free of adventitious contaminations], and thus from the beginning just pure. The Tathāgata essence is said to possess the thirty-two characteristics [of a fully developed Buddha] and to exist in the bodies of all sentient beings.
>
> 'The Supramundane Victor says that like a precious gem wrapped in a dirty cloth, the Tathāgata essence is wrapped in the cloth of the aggregates, constituents, and sources, overwhelmed by the force of desire, hatred, and ignorance, [45] and dirtied with the defilements of thought.
>
> 'If so, Supramundane Victor, how is this propounding of a Tathāgata essence not like the Forders' propounding of a self? Supramundane Victor, the Forders teach and propound a self which is permanent, a non-agent, without the qualities [of form and pleasure, etc.], pervasive, and non-perishing.'
>
> The Supramundane Victor said, 'Mahāmati, this teaching of a Tathāgata essence is not like the Forders' propounding of a self. O Mahāmati, the completely perfect Buddhas, Tathāgata Foe Destroyers, teach a Tathāgata essence meaning emptiness, the final reality, nirvana, no [inherently existent] production, signlessness, wishlessness, and so forth. [46] So that children might avoid the fear of selflessness, they teach through the means of a Tathāgata essence the state of no thought, the object [of the wisdom] free from appearances.
>
> 'Mahāmati, future and present Bodhisattvas—the great beings—should not adhere to this as a self.

> Mahāmati, for example, a potter makes a variety of vessels out of one mass of clay particles with his hands, manual skill, a rod, water, thread, and mental dexterity. Mahāmati, the Tathāgatas teach the selflessness of phenomena which overcomes all imagined signs. Through [their techniques] having wisdom and skill in means—whether they teach it as the Tathāgata essence or as selflessness—they, like a potter, teach with various formats of words and letters.' [47]

Thus, there is the teaching in the *Tathāgata Essence Sutra* of a permanent body adorned with the major and minor marks of a Buddha, possessing the powers and so forth, and existing in the continuums of all sentient beings. This is explained, as before [in the case of the teaching of mind-only that means no external objects] to require interpretation from the viewpoint of another basis in [Buddha's] thought, his purpose, and the fact that there are refutations of the explicit teaching. Both this [teaching of a permanent Buddha Body in all sentient beings] and the teaching of the existence of a basis-of-all have emptiness as the basis in his thought. The refutation of the explicit teaching is that if it were taken literally, such a teaching would be like that of the Forders [who absurdly ascribe change to the permanent]. Thus, the teaching of a permanent Buddha Body in all sentient beings is proved by reasoning to require interpretation. Chandrakīrti's *Supplement* says:[585]

> The teachings that a basis-of-all exists, that the person [inherently] exists,
> And that only the aggregates [inherently] exist
> Should be taken as teachings for those who would not understand
> The very profound meaning [of emptiness].

[For the Prāsaṅgikas, the teaching of an impermanent mind-basis-of-all actually is based on a permanent Tathāgata essence—the emptiness of the mind.] The *Sutra on the Heavily Adorned* says:[586]

[Just as] lands [are the basis of] the varieties [of all things grown],
So the basis-of-all [is the basis for cyclic existence and nirvana].
The virtuous Tathāgata essence is also this [basis-of-all], [48]
Tathāgatas teach the essence with the term 'basis-of-all'.
Though the essence is proclaimed as the basis-of-all,
Those of weak intellect do not understand.

Thus, a natural lineage which is the emptiness of true existence of the mind in each sentient being—the Sugata essence or Buddha lineage—is called a basis-of-all. For it abides as the nature of all the phenomena [which make full enlightenment possible, these terms all referring to the emptiness of the mind].

[The natural lineage or Buddha lineage—the emptiness of inherent existence of the mind—is called *ālayavijñāna* which here means 'basis-of-all which is to be known well'.] *Vijñāna* is so called because of being that which knows [that is, the knower] or because of being this which is to be known well or in detail [that is, the known]. Taking [the term *vijñāna* of *ālayavijñāna*] according to the latter etymology [as 'that which is to be minded or known in detail'], the Tathāgata essence is proclaimed as *vijñāna*, that which is to be known in detail. Chandrakīrti's *Commentary on the 'Supplement'* says,[587] 'It should be known that because it abides as the nature of all the phenomena [which make full enlightenment possible], only emptiness is indicated by the term "mind-basis-of-all" (*ālayavijñāna, kun gzhi rnam shes*).'

[The three natures as taught by Chittamātra also require interpretation.] Chandrakīrti's *Supplement* says:[588]

Thus, one has understood the arrangement of scriptures [of definitive meaning and requiring interpretation]. Any sutra setting forth non-suchness, [49] teaching that which requires interpretation, is to be interpreted. Through realizing [this, these provisional teachings become a cause of entering into the realization that phenomena do not exist inherently]. Also, know that [any

> sutra] which bears the meaning of emptiness is definitive.

Through such passages it is explained that the *Sutra Unravelling the Thought* requires interpretation where it shows the differentiation of the [true] existence and non [-true] existence of the first two of the three natures of the Chittamātra system [other-powered phenomena and imaginaries. The explanation in the *Sutra Unravelling the Thought* that impermanent phenomena truly exist needs to be interpreted as having as its basis in Buddha's thought their conventional existence.] For the *Teaching of Akṣhayamati Sutra* and so forth explain that the teachings of truly existent phenomena require interpretation.

Also, [another reason why the explanation that other-powered and thoroughly established phenomena truly exist requires interpretation is that Prāsaṅgikas] distinguish the existence and non-existence of the three natures [in another way]. According to the 'Questions of Maitreya' [chapter] of the *Twenty-Five Thousand Stanza Perfection of Wisdom Sutra*, all phenomena from forms through to omniscient consciousnesses do not ultimately exist but exist only in the terminology and conventions of the world. There it is said in answer to a question about the way that forms and so forth exist,[589] 'They exist according to the terminology and conventions of the world but not ultimately.' Thus, it is said that all phenomena from forms through to omniscient consciousnesses [only nominally exist].

Therefore, Chandrakīrti's commentary on his *Supplement* says:[590]

> I will say a little bit [about our own system's presentation of the three natures]. For instance, a snake is [only] imagined in a coiled rope which is a dependent-arising, [50] for there is no snake in the rope. However, a snake is thoroughly established in an actual snake because it is not imagined. Similarly, that the final nature of things is in other-powered phenomena which are products is imagined [because] the final nature is not a product, for [Nāgārjuna] said:[591]

The nature is not fabricated
And is not dependent on another.

This final nature that is imagined in presently apprehended products which are dependent-arisings and like reflections [in that the way they appear and the way they exist do not agree] is the actual final nature as the object of a Buddha. For [as the object of a Buddha's cognition] it is not imagined. Not contacting [or being obstructed by] things that are products, [his wisdom knowing the mode of existence] actualizes only the final nature. Thus, since he understands suchness, he is called 'Buddha'.

One has thus understood the presentation of the three natures: imaginaries, other-powered phenomena, and the thoroughly established. [51] [In this way] the thought of the *Sutra [Unravelling the Thought]* is to be explained [as requiring interpretation and the thought of the 'Questions of Maitreya' (see p.620) on the three natures is to be understood].

[The Chittamātrins treat the imputation of a difference of entity of] the two, apprehending subjects and apprehended objects [imputed in dependence on other-powered phenomena] as an imaginary. This should be considered [or analyzed], because apprehending subjects and apprehended objects [are other-powered phenomena and] other-powered phenomena [which are not subjects or objects] do not exist as things.

Let us illumine a little the meaning of his words. The way of [wrong] imagination is that whereas the final mode of existence does not exist as perceived in an other-powered phenomenon, it is perceived there through superimposition. For, the perception [that other-powered phenomena exist in their own right] despite their not actually so existing is an imaginary superimposition, like the superimposition by a consciousness apprehending a rope as a snake despite the snake's not existing in the rope. For, other-powered phenomena do not fulfill the sense of a non-fabricated nature, etc.

Other-powered phenomena presently being seen or apprehended are like mirror reflections in that there is no agreement between the way they appear and the way they are. Their nature or mode of being is an actual thoroughly established phenomenon [an emptiness] according to the sight of a Buddha [52] because he perceives without superimposing [true] existence when there is no [true] existence. It is like a snake's not being superimposed on an actual snake, and thus the object apprehended is thoroughly established. This sets out the definition and etymology of 'thoroughly established' (*pariniṣhpanna, yongs grub*) and also explains that other-powered phenomena are the bases of the superimposition of imaginaries as well as the bases of emptinesses—thoroughly established phenomena.

Question: [It has been shown that the 'Questions of Maitreya' chapter of the *Twenty-Five Thousand Stanza Perfection of Wisdom Sutra* teaches that all phenomena do not exist ultimately but exist only nominally; however, the same chapter seems to show just the opposite.] The 'Questions of Maitreya' says,[592] 'Maitreya, these imagined forms [the ultimate existence imagined of forms] should be viewed as not existing substantially. These imputed forms [forms themselves] should be viewed as existing substantially because thought substantially exists and not because [the forms] exist under their own power.' [Here it says that thought 'substantially exists'; 'substantially existent' (*dravyasat, rdzas yod*) means 'ultimately existent' (*paramārthasat, don dam par yod pa*) in the Prāsaṅgika system, and since the Prāsaṅgikas say nothing ultimately exists] how is [one to understand this quote]?

Answer: Here 'substantially existent' means just 'existent' (*sat, yod pa*) because one can understand from the context that [substantially existent] here does not refer to anything other than [just 'existent']. It does not refer to the 'substantiality' meaning 'inherently existent' or 'truly existent'. The *Twenty-Five Thousand Stanza Perfection of Wisdom Sutra* says:[593] [53]

> 'In dependence on the name, discrimination, and convention of the term "form" to these and those things which have the character of compositional phenomena,

an intrinsic existence of forms is imagined. These are imagined forms.

'Maitreya, in dependence on the name, discrimination, designation, and convention of the terms "feelings", "discriminations", "compositional factors", "consciousnesses",—through to—"qualities of a Buddha" to these and those things which have the character of compositional phenomena, there is imagined an intrinsic existence of feelings, discriminations, compositional factors, consciousnesses—through to—the intrinsic existence of the qualities of a Buddha. These are imagined feelings, discriminations, compositional factors, consciousnesses—through to—imagined qualities of a Buddha. [54]

'[Then with respect to other-powered phenomena] there are the nominal, discriminated, imputed, and conventional "forms", "feelings", "discriminations", "compositional factors", "consciousnesses"—through to—"qualities of a Buddha" that are designated to these and those things which have the character of compositional phenomena, in dependence on thought abiding in just the nature of thought. These are imputed forms, imputed feelings, imputed discriminations, imputed compositional factors, imputed consciousnesses—through to—imputed qualities of a Buddha.

'Whether the Tathāgatas appear or not, reality and the sphere of the actual status of phenomena just abide. Reality's forms are imputed forms' permanent, permanent, stable, stable non-intrinsic existence and non-self of phenomena as imagined forms—suchness, final reality. [55] These are reality's feelings, discriminations, consciousnesses—through to—reality's qualities of a Buddha.' Thus Buddha said.

The Bodhisattva Maitreya asked, 'From among these three types of forms [imagined forms, imputed forms, and reality's forms], which forms are to be viewed as not substantially existing? Which as substantially existing?

Which as neither not substantially existing nor substantially existing but as distinguished by being ultimate objects? From among the three types of feelings, the three types of compositional factors, the three types of consciousnesses—through to—the three types of qualities of a Buddha, which are to be viewed as not substantially existing? Which as substantially existing? [56] Which as neither not substantially existing nor substantially existing but distinguished by being ultimate objects?' Thus [Maitreya] asked.

The Supramundane Victor said to the Bodhisattva Maitreya, 'O Maitreya, these imagined forms [the ultimate existence imagined in forms] should be viewed as not substantially existing [because of not existing at all]. These imputed forms [forms themselves] should be viewed as substantially existing [that is, conventionally existing] because thought substantially exists and not because forms exist under their own power. Reality's forms [emptinesses] should be viewed as neither not substantially existing [because of existing as the nature of phenomena] nor as substantially existing [because of not existing by way of their own character] but as distinguished by being ultimate objects.'

D̄zong-ka-b̄a's *Essence of the Good Explanations* says:[594]

Therefore, the 'substantiality' of the 'substantially existing' and 'not substantially existing' mentioned in the 'Questions of Maitreya' is not the 'substantiality' set forth in other texts as the pair, 'substantiality and imputation' (*dravya* and *prajñapti, rdzas btags*). They also are not the 'establishment by way of [the object's] own character' (*svalakṣhaṇa-siddhi, rang gi mtshan nyid kyis grub pa*) set forth by the Mādhyamikas as 'substantiality' (*dravya, rdzas*).

[It has been shown that many teachings, accepted literally by the followers of Chittamātra, are interpreted otherwise by the

Prāsaṅgikas. However] the Prāsaṅgika system does not assert that whatever the Chittamātrins accept as literal or as being definitive is necessarily actually non-literal [since both systems assert that the teachings of the six perfections and so forth are literal].[595] Also, the Prāsaṅgikas do not assert that the opposite follows [either; they do not assert that whatever the Prāsaṅgika system says is literal the proponents of Chittamātra necessarily say is non-literal]. For the *Sutra on the Ten Grounds* says,[596] [57] 'These three realms are mind-only,' and [the *Mahāyāna Sutra of Knowledge (Mahāyānābhidharma)* says]:[597]

> The beginningless realm
> Is the source of all phenomena.
> Because it exists, all migrations
> And even nirvanas are attained.

The Prāsaṅgikas accept these passages literally, [the first as negating a main agent other than the mind and the second as setting forth a Tathāgata essence which is the emptiness of the mind.[598] The Chittamātrins also accept these passages literally but with a different interpretation of their literal meaning; for them the first refutes forms which are entities external to a perceiving consciousness, and the second sets forth the mind-basis-of-all.]

Padmasaṃbhava

3 *The Object of Negation*

The explanation of Prāsaṅgika tenets has three parts: their presentation of (1) the base, (2) paths, and (3) fruits of these paths. [The first of these is translated here.]

The Prāsaṅgika presentation of the base has five parts: (1) the object of negation in the view of selflessness, (2) the reasonings refuting the object of negation, (3) the basic objects of the two truths, (4) the uncommon features [of the Prāsaṅgika system], and (5) the valid cognizers certifying the above as well as an elimination of error. [The first two are translated here.]

THE OBJECT OF NEGATION IN THE VIEW OF SELFLESSNESS

This section has two parts: the measure of what is negated [58] and the correctness of this measure.

Measure of what is negated in the view of selflessness

(See pp.35-41.) The root text says:

> *All of cyclic existence and nirvana*
> *Appearing and renowned [to the mind]—*

The varieties [of phenomena] and their mode [emptiness]—
Are posited by the inborn non-analytical [awareness]
As existing according to the conventions of the world.
Therefore, 'existing objectively [without just being an imputation] there by thought',
'Substantially existing', 'existing by way of its own character',
'Existing from its own [the object's] side',
'Truly existing', 'existing in its own right', and so forth
Are synonymously what is negated.

Forms and so forth are the phenomena of cyclic existence—the afflicted class—and [the phenomena of nirvana]—the pure class (see pp.201-12). These phenomena are all included within 'the varieties and their mode which appear to and are renowned to the mind'. All these phenomena must be posited [as existing] for the inborn worldly [mind] which does not analyze [to try to find] the object designated and does not superimpose [falsity] through the conception [of phenomena] as truly existent.

Therefore, all the varieties and their mode [their emptiness] are only imputed [from the subject's side to] there [the object's side] by terms and thoughts. This is because these phenomena, except for being just nominally imputed [from the subject's side] to there, are not their individual parts, nor the mere composite of their parts, nor the continuum [of their moments], etc. [59] For example, in darkness a coiled speckled rope is imputed by thought to be a snake, and from a distance a cairn [a pile of stones] is merely imagined to be a human. Nāgārjuna's *Precious Garland* says:[599]

Because the phenomena of forms [which have the obstructiveness of which space is the absence] are only names, space also is just a name [and does not exist inherently. If someone said that forms exist inherently, then] when the elements do not exist [inherently], how could forms exist [inherently]? Therefore, even name-onlyness does not exist [inherently because that which possesses a name does not exist inherently].

Āryadeva's *Four Hundred* says:[600]

> Without [imputation by] thought [like the imputation of a snake to a rope] there is no [finding of] the existence of desire and so forth. If so, who with intelligence would maintain that a real object is [produced dependent on] thought? [For, being imputed by thought and existing as its own reality are contradictory.]

Chandrakīrti's *Commentary on (Āryadeva's) 'Four Hundred'* says:[601]

> Undoubtedly, those which exist only through the existence of thought and those which do not exist when there is no thought are to be ascertained as not existing by way of their own entities, like a snake imputed to a coiled rope. [60]

Also, the *Meeting of Father and Son Sutra* says:[602]

> O Great King, a person, a being, has the six constituents, the six bases of contact, and the eighteen activities of mind.
>
> Based on what is it said that the person has the six constituents? Great King, the six constituents are these: the constituent of earth, the constituent of water, the constituent of fire, the constituent of wind, the constituent of space, and the constituent of consciousness. Great King, these are the six constituents. My saying that a person has the six constituents is based on this.
>
> Based on what is it said that a person has the six bases of contact? Great King, the six bases of contact are these: the base of contact which is the eye for seeing forms, the base of contact which is the ear for hearing sounds, [61] the base of contact which is the nose for smelling odors, the base of contact which is the tongue for sensing tastes, the base of contact which is the body for feeling the tangible, and the base of contact which is the mind for knowing phenomena. Great King, these are the six bases

of contact. My saying that the person has the six bases of contact is based on this.

Great King, based on what is it said that the person has the eighteen activities of mind? Great King, the eighteen activities of mind are these. When a human sees a form with his eyes, he experiences the form as pleasurable, painful, or neutral. When he hears a sound with his ears, he experiences the sound as pleasurable, painful, or neutral. When he smells an odor with his nose, he experiences the odor as pleasurable, painful, or neutral. [62] When he senses a taste with his tongue, he experiences the taste as pleasurable, painful, or neutral. When he feels the tangible with his body, he experiences the tangible as pleasurable, painful, or neutral. When he realizes a phenomenon with his mind, he experiences it as pleasurable, painful, or neutral. Great King, these six experiences of pleasure, these six experiences of displeasure, and these six experiences of neutrality are in brief the eighteen activities of mind. Great King, these eighteen are activities of mind. Great King, my saying that these activities are the eighteen activities of mind is based on this.

Great King, [63] the constituent of earth is of two types: internal and external. Great King, what is the internal constituent? It is, inside the body, any of the hard and solid aspects, the close, conjoined with consciousness. Also, what are they? The internal earth constituent is to be known as hair, mustache, nails,[603] teeth, impurities, excrement, skin, flesh, veins, sinews, bones, marrow, heart, liver, lungs, kidneys, spleen, diaphragm, large intestine, small intestine, bladder, urinary canal, anal canal, anus, brain, veins of the brain—also, any type of hardness, solidity, and the close, conjoined with consciousness inside the body.

Great King, what is the external earth constituent? Any type of hardness, solidity, the non-close, [64] not conjoined with consciousness is to be known as the external earth constituent.

Great King, when the internal earth constituent arises, it does not come from anywhere. When it ceases, it does not go anywhere.

Great King, a woman thinks of the internal, 'I am a woman.' Having imputed, 'I am a woman,' internally, she thinks of the external with respect to a man, 'A man.' Having imputed 'man' to the man externally, she becomes desirous and wishes to join with the external man.

The man also thinks of the internal, 'I am a man.' Having imputed, 'I am a man,' internally, he thinks of the external with respect to a woman, 'A woman.' Having imputed 'woman' to the woman externally, he becomes desirous and wishes to join with the external woman. Through desiring to join, they join together. Through the cause of joining there is the state of the fluid embryo.

Great King, both the imputed and the imputer do not [inherently] exist. [65] There is no woman in the woman [that is, in the basis of the imputation 'woman']. There is no man in the man [that is, in the basis of the imputation 'man']. Though they are thus non-existent, wrong thought is generated, but even this thought does not exist inherently.

Even the joining and the fluid embryo do not exist inherently as is imagined. How can that which does not exist inherently become hard?

Great King, having understood thought thus, you should understand hardness. It is to be understood that whenever hardness is produced, it does not come from anywhere. Great King, this body has a time in the end of going to the cemetery. When its hardness disintegrates and ceases, it does not go east, south, west, north, up, down, or to the intermediate directions. Great King, view thus the internal earth constituent.

Great King, there are occasions when the world abides in the sky as a heavenly mansion of Brahmā, [66] consisting of the seven types of precious substances. O King, when its hardness arises, it does not come from anywhere. Though it abides as the massive [mountains], hard and firm, established through the cause of the diamonds of the Chakravāḍa and Mahāchakravāḍa mountains, when its hardness arises, it does not come from anywhere. Though it abides as Meru—the King of Mountains—Yugaṃdhara, Nimiṃdhara, Īṣhādhara, Vajradhara, Khadiraka, Vinataka, Ashvakarṇa, Sudarshana, Mahāsudarshana, Bare [Mountains],[604] Gandhamādana, or the Kīṭādri which are other than those, [67] or though it abide as the billion world systems including everything, or though it abide as an earth eighty thousand yojanas in height and sixty thousand yojanas in width, O King, when its hardness arises, it does not come from anywhere.

Great King, when this world is destroyed, there is a time when this great earth is burnt by fire, or destroyed by water, or wrecked by wind. When it is burned by fire, there will be no smoke, and there will be no remains of ashes. For instance, when the flame of a butter or oil lamp burns space, there is no smoke and no remains of ashes. Just so, when this world system of one billion worlds is burned by fire, there will be no smoke, and there will be no remains of ashes.

Also, when it is destroyed by water, there is no remainder. For instance, [68] when salt dissolves in water, there is no remainder. Just so, when this world system of one billion worlds is destroyed by water, there will be no remains.

When it is wrecked by wind, there will be no remainder. For instance, when a scattering wind drives about, no little birds are seen remaining. Just so, when this world system of one billion worlds is wrecked by wind, there will not be even a little remainder.

Great King, the arising of the earth constituent is thus empty. The destruction and arising of the earth

> constituent are also empty of inherent existence. Great King, the earth constituent, except for only being a designation, should not be viewed as an earth constituent. That which has the designation [the basis of the designations 'woman' or 'man'] is not the woman and is not the man. Thus, O King, with wisdom realize these as they are in reality. [69]

The meaning of this sutra is that [the constituents and so forth] do not exist, except as only nominal imputations. This is indicated by the quote from the beginning through to 'The earth constituent, except for only being a designation should not be viewed as an earth constituent.' Then the passage, 'That which has the designation is not the woman and is not the man,' explains that the basis of the imputation—that which has the name—is not the phenomenon which is imputed, a woman or a man.

Nāgārjuna's *Precious Garland*, condensing the meaning of that, says:[605]

> If a person is not earth, not water,
> Not fire, not wind, not space,
> Not consciousness, and not all of them,
> What person is there other than these?

The passage 'a person is not earth, not water, not fire, not wind, not space, not consciousness' explains that a person is not each of the bases of the imputation 'person'. The statement 'not all' explains that a person is not even the composite of the bases of imputation 'person' [that is, not even the composite of the six constituents]. The statement 'What person is there other than these?' explains that there is no person which does not depend on [the six constituents that are] the bases of the imputation 'person'.

Thus, [70] the Perfection of Wisdom Sutras say that even [the highest of phenomena,] nirvanas and emptinesses, are only established [from the subject's side to] there [the object's side] through names and thoughts. Similarly, [the Prāsaṅgika system,] unlike Svātantrika and so forth, asserts that the members of the following list, except for being different names, are [hypothetical][606] synonyms. [The Prāsaṅgika system] treats these terms as [hypothetical] synonyms in that they are what is negated by the reasonings [proving emptiness. The terms that mean 'self' in the view of selflessness are:]

1 existing 'on' [that is, as a natural predicate of] the object [which gets] the imputation
2 substantially existing
3 existing able to establish itself—[this term and the preceding term] are opposites of dependent-arising [as are all the others in the list]
4 existing by way of its own character
5 existing from [the object's] own side [rather than being imputed from the subject's side]
6 existing through its own power
7 truly existing
8 existing inherently.

Āryadeva's *Four Hundred* says:[607]

> All these [phenomena] are not self-powered;
> Thus, there is no self [inherent existence].

Chandrakīrti's commentary says,[608] 'Here, that which has its own intrinsic existence, has inherent existence, has its own power, or has no dependence on another would exist by itself; therefore, it would not be a dependent-arising.'

Correctness of the measure of what is negated

(See pp.539-47.) The root text says: [71]

> *The Mādhyamikas, those free from the extremes,*
> *Posit all actions and agents*
> *In this [system] of no 'existence from [the object's] own side'*
> *And of 'imputation by name and thought there [to the object]'.*
> *Anything coarser or finer than this*
> *Is an extreme of permanence or annihilation.*

Thus, that which is to be refuted [by reasoning] must be identified from its subtlest level. For, if it is not, one cannot ascertain the actual non-existent which is the negative [of self]. For, Shāntideva's *Engaging in the Bodhisattva Deeds* says:[609]

> Without contacting the superimposed existent
> One cannot apprehend its non-existence.

Also, one cannot ascertain the emptiness of formeer and later births, for example, without ascertaining that aspect which is their non-existence by way of their own being. Thus, the emptiness of births is not ascertained through only perceiving an utter vacuity that is merely the non-perception of former and later births. Buddhapālita, the honorable Chandrakīrti, and many others assert this; Buddhapālita says [in his commentary on Nāgārjuna's *Treatise on the Middle Way*]:[610]

> [The Nihilists say,] 'This world [or life] does not exist [as an effect of past lives]. A future world does not exist. [Also] spontaneously born sentient beings [such as hell-beings] do not exist,' and so forth. [72] What is the difference between their view and the [Mādhyamikas'] view that all things are not produced and do not cease?
>
> *[Answer:]* There is a great difference between these two. Not knowing the meaning of emptiness, you think that these two are similar. Acting with equanimity [that is, indifference] when one has not analyzed [to find that all sentient beings should be valued equally] and acting with equanimity when one has so analyzed are similar only in that both can be characterized as acting with equanimity. However, acting with equanimity but without analysis is involved in the entwinements of ignorance. Acting with equanimity when one has analyzed [is the result of knowledge and] is used by the Supramundane Victors.
>
> Just as these two differ very greatly, so here also the perceptions [found in the texts of the Nihilists] such as, 'This world does not exist,' [meaning that this life is not

> the effect of other lives] are thoughts beclouded with ignorance. However, the other one [the Mādhyamika] who sees that all phenomena are not [inherently] produced and do not [inherently] cease because they are empty of existing by way of their own being has preceded his conclusion with the mind of analysis. [73] Therefore, these two [Nihilist and Mādhyamika] are very different.

Also, [Chandrakīrti's] *Clear Words* says:[611]

> Here some say, 'The Mādhyamikas are indistinguishable from Nihilists because they propound that virtuous and non-virtuous actions, agents, fruits, and all worlds [lives] are empty of inherent existence. Also, the Nihilists say that these are non-existent. Therefore, Mādhyamikas are indistinguishable from Nihilists.'
>
> It is not so.
>
> How?
>
> Mādhyamikas are proponents of dependent-arising; they say that due to arising dependent on, or reliant on, causes and conditions[612] all—this world, the next, and so forth—lack inherent existence. The Nihilists do not ascertain that future worlds [future lives] and so forth do not truly exist (*abhāva, dngos po med pa*) because of being empty of inherent existence due to being dependent-arisings.

Therefore, [the Prāsaṅgikas] refute the subtle object of negation—that is, refute that even particles exist from their own side—[74] but know how to posit all actions and agents of cyclic existence and nirvana within [asserting] that all phenomena are only nominalities and only imputations by thought. [A person who maintains such a system] is a Mādhyamika—one who does not abide in the extreme of existence or permanence [such as asserting that phenomena] exist inherently, etc., and who, [through propounding] the suitability of the existence of all phenomena conventionally as only nominalities, does not abide in the extreme of non-existence or annihilation. As [Buddha] says in the *Kāshyapa Chapter*:[613]

> [Inherent] existence is the one extreme. No [conventional] existence is the second extreme. That which is the center between these two is unanalyzable [because it cannot be analyzed just as it is by thinking about it], is undemonstrable [because it cannot be explained to another just as it is], is not a support [because it is not an object of the senses], is unperceivable [because from the viewpoint of the mind directly realizing it duality has disappeared], is unknowable [because it cannot be ascertained just as it is by a dualistic mind], and is placeless [because it is not a place or source of the afflictions]. Kāshyapa, this is called the middle path, individual analysis of phenomena.

Also, such is said in Nāgārjuna's *Treatise on the Middle Way*:[614]

> '[Inherent] existence' is a holding to permanence.
> 'No [conventional] existence' is a view of nihilism.
> Therefore, the wise do not abide in either
> [Inherent] existence or no [conventional] existence.

Also, through affixing 'inherent existence' (*svabhāva, rang bzhin*) [to the refutation of existence] the extreme of non-existence is avoided. [75] [This is because that which is negated as a predicate of phenomena is only inherent existence and not existence in general; a negation of existence in general would be an extreme of non-existence because phenomena do exist conventionally.] The extreme of [inherent] existence is avoided by [affirming that phenomena are] only imputations [and thus not inherently existent]. Therefore, the Svātantrikas' estimation of what is to be negated [merely true existence and not inherent existence] is coarser than that [of the Prāsaṅgikas who refute that phenomena inherently exist even conventionally].

Also, with respect to this assertion of phenomena as only imputations, some Tibetans [wrongly] do not accept even worldly trueness and falseness. [It is true that there is no difference between] an illusory horse created by a magician and an actual horse with respect to their existing or not in accordance with how they appear. [Both an illusory hòrse and an actual horse appear as if they inherently exist, but in fact do not; therefore, they equally do not exist even conventionally in accordance with how they appear.] However, if one does not accept a [worldly][615] trueness and falseness with respect to whether something does or does not exist, then one contradicts Chandrakīrti:[616]

> If the world does not harm you, based on the world itself
> Refute these [conventionalities].
> You and the world debate about these,
> And afterwards I will rely on the stronger.

And, 'Do not lose the conventionalities renowned in the world.' And, 'Perceivers of falsities are asserted as two types [those perceiving the real and unreal relative to a worldly consciousness].'

One should understand that [not accepting any worldly trueness and falseness] does not pass beyond adhering to extremes. [Asserting a coarser object of negation] also does not pass beyond adhering to extremes. Thus, one should cast aside [such assertions].

REASONINGS REFUTING INHERENT EXISTENCE

This section has two parts [76]: brief indication and extensive explanation.

Brief indication of the reasonings refuting inherent existence

(See pp.127-9.)

Question: [The two selflessnesses, i.e., the lack of inherent existence in persons and in other phenomena] are realized by way of separate reasonings. Is this similar to the opinion of Svātantrikas and below [i.e., Chittamātrins] and some Tibetan 'Prāsaṅgikas' that the objects negated in the two selflessnesses differ in that the selflessness of persons is coarser and the selflessness of other phenomena is subtler?

Answer: [No, the two selflessnesses are realized by way of separate reasonings, but the object of negation, inherent existence, is the same in each case; thus, one is not coarser or subtler than the other.] Though the two selflessnesses do not differ in subtlety, the reasonings used for their realization are separate. In order to indicate this the root text says:

> *There are the two selves*
> *Of persons and [other] phenomena.*
> *The non-existence of these there*
> *Is asserted as the two selflessnesses.*
> *A self of [other] phenomena*
> *Is refuted by the four:*
> *The diamond slivers and so forth.*
> *A self of persons is refuted*
> *By the fivefold and sevenfold [reasons].*
> *Both also [are refuted] by dependent-arising.*

Chandrakīrti's *Commentary on (Āryadeva's) 'Four Hundred'* says,[617]

> Here 'self' is an inherent existence (*svabhāva*) of phenomena, that is, non-dependence on another. The non-existence of this is selflessness. This [selflessness] is realized as twofold through a division into persons and [other] phenomena—a selflessness of persons and a selflessness of [other] phenomena. [77]

Thus, the self to be negated is non-dependence or non-reliance on another, the 'other' being terms, thoughts, and so forth. Absences of this self on its bases—persons and [other] phenomena—are respectively posited as the selflessness of persons and of phenomena. This is the thought of the master Buddhapālita.

Four types of reasonings refute a self of phenomena [other than persons], whereas a self of persons is refuted by the reasoning in sutra and in Nāgārjuna's *Treatise*[618] that is a searching for it in five ways. A self of persons is also refuted in Chandrakīrti's *Supplement* by the reasoning that is a searching for [but not finding the self] in seven ways. [Chandrakīrti added to the fivefold reasoning] two more refutations based on the teaching that the mere composite of the five aggregates is the basis of the imputation [and not the I]; these refute the assertions that the mere composite of the aggregates is the self and that the shape [of the body] is the self.

Both selves [of persons and of phenomena] are refuted by the reasoning that they lack being one and many and by the reasoning that they are dependent-arisings. These will now be explained.

4 *Refuting Inherently Existent Production*

The extensive explanation of the reasonings refuting inherent existence has two parts: reasoning refuting a self of phenomena [other than persons] and reasoning refuting a self of persons together with an elimination of error.

The reasoning refuting a self of phenomena [other than persons] has four parts: (1) the diamond slivers, [78] (2) the [simultaneous] refutation of production of the four extremes and production of the existent, the non-existent, [both, and neither], (3) the refutation of production of the four alternative types, and (4) along with an elimination of error, the reasoning of dependent-arising making known [the absence of true existence in] all phenomena.

DIAMOND SLIVERS

(See pp.57-9, 131-50.) This section has two parts: statement of the reasons and of the proofs for the modes of the reasons.

Statement of the reasons

(See pp.137-42.) Sautrāntikas, Chittamātrins, and Mādhyamikas agree that when stating reasons to prove a thesis there should be no statement of proof without first overcoming the pointedness of the wrong view adhered to by the opponent with a demonstration of a [contradictory] consequence. However, here for the sake of easy exposition [a syllogism is put forth] in the root text:

Because production from self,
Other, both, or causelessly
Does not exist, inherently
Existent production does not exist.

The subjects, things which have production, have no inherently existent production because there is no production of them from themselves, from [inherently existent] others, from both, or causelessly—as in the case of a mirror image. Chandrakīrti's *Supplement* says:[619] [79]

Because there is no production from self, or other, or both,
Or without relying on causes, things lack inherent
existence.

Atīsha's *Lamp for the Path to Enlightenment* says:[620]

Things are not produced from
Themselves, others, both, or
Causelessly; thus there is no
Inherent existence.

Truly established production would have to accord with one of these four extremes. Furthermore, if something is not produced from any of these four, it follows that it is not truly produced. Not only is this proved by reasoning, but also those who assert truly established production assert such. Therefore, it is not necessary to state a proof here [that not being produced from any of the four extremes entails an absence of truly existent production].

Proofs for the modes of the reasons

Non-production from self

(See pp.136-40.) The root text says:

If [things] were produced from themselves,
[Their re-production] would be senseless and endless.

That which [already exists in something] is not [produced from] it,
Causes and effects would always be seen,
It would contradict worldly perception,
All objects and agents [of production] would be one. [80]

Some Sāṃkhyas say, 'A sprout exists at the time of its seed or of its [causal] entity. Since the natures of both the seed and the sprout are a partless unit—being mutually each other—there is no confusion of effects with wrong causes, and production is possible. However, if at the time of the cause [the effect] were totally non-existent, a non-existent [effect] could not be produced. If [that which is non-existent at the time of its causes] were produced, then even the horns of a rabbit could be produced.'

The Sautrāntikas and above [Chittamātrins and Mādhyamikas] agree that *in general* a non-existent is not produced, and, therefore, an existent is produced. Furthermore, they agree that 'production' is so called because it is the attainment of an existent entity by what is non-existent previous to its production. No one [among the Sautrāntikas, Chittamātrins, and Mādhyamikas] asserts, like the Sāṃkhyas, that [a thing] is produced from its own entity or that it is produced again.

Hence, it follows about the subjects, things which have production, that their production again would be senseless because they would have previously attained their entity.

Objection: There is no necessity [that if things had previously attained their entity, their production again would be senseless].

Answer: It follows about the subjects, these [things], that their production would be endless because [for you] production again of what is already existent is meaningful.

Here also, the Sāṃkhya might say, 'There is no necessity [that, if production again of what is already existent is purposeful,[621] the production of things would be endless. For we Sāṃkhyas say that what already exists in a non-manifest state must be produced or made manifest.]'

However, his answer does not hit the mark because he does

not assert that what was previously non-existent [a non-existent manifestation] is newly produced. [Thus, he cannot say that a manifestation of the sprout which was previously non-existent is produced since he would fall away from his own theory of the production of the existent.]

Also, [81] it follows that there would be no point in production of something from itself because it would have already achieved its own entity.

Moreover, it follows either that a white seed only continues endlessly or that the production of only a green sprout continues endlessly because that which has already been produced would be produced again.

Furthermore, though a cause such as a white seed has disintegrated and is non-existent, its effect—a sprout—is seen. Thus, even the world does not accept the simultaneity of seed and sprout. [Therefore, the Sāṃkhya's view] also contradicts what is seen.

It follows that the agent and the object of cause and effect [producer and produced] would be one because a thing would produce itself.

Buddhapālita [says in his commentary on Nāgārjuna's *Treatise*]:[622]

> Things are not produced from their own entities because [if they were] their production [again] would be just senseless and because production would be endless. The production again of things already existing in their own entities is purposeless. If though existent, they are produced, they would never not be produced.

Chandrakīrti's *Supplement to (Nāgārjuna's) 'Treatise on the Middle Way'* says:[623]

> There is no point in the production of something from itself [that is, from a cause that is the same entity as itself because it would have already attained existence]. [82]
>
> Also, it is just not reasonable that what already has been produced be produced again.

If it is thought that the already produced is produced again, the growing of a sprout, etc., would not be found here [in the world]; the seed would be produced endlessly.

How could that [seed] be destroyed by that [sprout? For, according to you, seed and sprout are not other.]

For you, the sprout's shape, color, taste, capacity, and maturation would not be different from those of its creator cause, the seed.

If, having forsaken the entity [of the state] of the seed, it becomes an entity [of a state] different from it, then how could it have the nature of that [seed]?

If for you the seed is not other than the sprout here [in the world], just as the seed [is unapprehendable at the time of the sprout], the sprout would not be apprehendable. Or, because they are one, just as the sprout [is apprehendable], so the seed would be apprehendable [at the time of the sprout]. Therefore, this [non-otherness of seed and sprout] is not to be asserted.

Though the cause is destroyed, the effect is seen; [83] thus, even the world does not assert that they are one. Therefore, this ascription of things arising from self is not admissible in reality or even in the world.

If production from self were asserted, the produced and the producer—object and agent—would be one. Since they are not one, production from self is not to be asserted because of the fallacies extensively explained [here and in Nāgārjuna's *Treatise*].

Non-production from other

This section has two parts: the actual exposition of the proofs of non-production from other and an elimination of error.

Actual exposition of non-production from other. (See pp.140-44.) The root text says:

If things were produced from [what is inherently] other,
Then darkness would arise from a flame,

And all would arise from all,
Both causes and non-causes.
Because [cause and effect would be] other,
They could not be one continuum, like wheat and barley.
Cause and effect would have to be simultaneous,
But because it is not so, what production
Is there of another from another?

If [it is claimed that there is inherently existent and thus analytically findable] production from what is other, then it contradicts many scriptures and reasons. The reasons are as follows.

It [absurdly] follows that thick darkness arises from a flame [84] because another arises from what is other by way of its own character. Also, the Superior [Nāgārjuna] says:[624]

A [naturally existent] otherness
Of cause and effect is never admissible.
If there were an otherness of cause and effect,
A cause would be the same as a non-cause.

Thus, it [absurdly] follows that all would arise from what are its causes and from what are not its causes because cause and effect would be naturally existent others. Chandrakīrti's *Supplement* says:[625]

If depending on others another arises, then from a tongue of fire even thick darkness would arise. All would also be produced from all because non-producers [non-causes] would have otherness the same [as producers or causes].

Objection: The fallacies of these consequences do not apply. [Though a cause and its effect are naturally existent others][626] an effect which is helped [by a cause] is the effect of that [cause]. [85] A substantial cause and its effect are included in the one continuum of [for instance] a seed; they must be one continuum. That which is of a continuum different [from the effect] is not suitable to be [its] substantial cause, etc. For example, a barley seed is the cause of a barley sprout which is in its same continuum but is not a cause of a *kiṃshuka* flower.[627]

[In answer to this, there are these contradictory consequences:]

It [absurdly] follows that the subjects, a barley seed—a substantial cause—and a barley sprout—its effect—are not one continuum because [according to you] they mutually are naturally existent others, as in the case of Maitreya and Upagupta or as in the case of wheat and barley.

It follows that a seed and its sprout are not naturally existent others because they do not exist simultaneously and also because, when cause and effect are naturally existent others, the actions of production and cessation, etc., are impossible. The Superior [Nāgārjuna says in his *Treatise on the Middle Way*]:[628]

> The entities of the things [which are effects such as sprouts] do not exist in their causes [either collectively or individually or in something other than their causes]. If [the effect's] own entity does not exist [at the time of its causes], then how could there be an entity of otherness [in the causes without the existence of the effect in relation to which they are called other]? [86]

Chandrakīrti's *Supplement* says:[629]

> *Objection:* Just this is called something's effect because that something is able to create it. That which is able to produce it, even though [a naturally existent] other, is the cause. [Therefore, because of being special others, two things are cause and effect but not because of just being others in general.] Because there is production from what is included in the same continuum and from what is a producer, a sprout of rice is not [produced] from a barley [seed], etc.
>
> *Answer:* Barley, the *kesara* lotus,[630] the *kiṃshuka* flower, and so forth [because of being other than a rice shoot] are not asserted to be producers of a rice shoot, do not have the capacity [of producing a rice shoot], are not included in the same continuum [as a rice shoot], and are not [what precedes a rice shoot and is][631] homogeneous

[with a rice shoot]. Just so, a rice seed also does not have these [four qualities] because it is just [a naturally existent] other.

Sprout and seed do not exist simultaneously. [The sprout in relation to which a seed is called 'other' does not exist at the same time as the seed, and thus there is no otherness.] Without otherness how could the seed be other [than the sprout]? Thus, it is not established that a sprout is produced from a seed. Cast aside this position that there is production from the [naturally existent] other.

Objection: Just as the ascending and descending of the two ends of a scale are not seen to be non-simultaneous, [87] so the production of what is to be produced and the cessation of the producer are [simultaneous. Therefore, cause and effect exist simultaneously and thus can be other in relation to each other.]

Answer: [Even] if [the two activities of the ascending and descending of the two ends of a scale] are simultaneous, here [in what is exemplified] there is no [simultaneity]; it is non-existent. Because that which is presently being produced [for example, a sprout] is approaching production, it is non-existent. That which is presently ceasing [for example, a seed], though existent, is asserted to be approaching disintegration. Thus, how is this similar to a scale [the activities of the two ends of which exist simultaneously]? When [the sprout which acts as the base of the action of growing and thus is] the agent is non-existent, [the existence of the activity of the sprout's] growing is also not an admissible entity.

Here, some Svātantrika-Mādhyamikas say:

It is true that there is no truly existent otherness and no simultaneity of [truly existent] actions of production and cessation. However, is it not the thought of the *Rice Seedling Sutra* [when it gives the example of the two ends of a scale] [632] that without analysis the actions of the seed's

> cessation and of the sprout's production simultaneously exist from their own side?

However, damage accrues to this view the same as before. The thought of the sutra is that these activities exist conventionally, not from their own side.

Objection: [According to you Prāsaṅgikas, production is not admissible because of the non-existence of otherness which in turn is due to the non-simultaneity of seed and sprout. If so, then production would exist because of the existence of otherness in whatever exists simultaneously. For example][633] an eye consciousness is produced through depending on an eye sense, a visible form, and feeling which just are simultaneous [with the eye consciousness]. Therefore, production from other is just established.

Answer: It follows that the subject, an eye consciousness, [88] is not produced from others which exist simultaneously with it and which are its producers—that is, a visible form, an eye sense, feeling, and so forth—because of already existing simultaneously with these as another. Chandrakīrti's *Supplement* says:[634]

> *Objection:* An eye consciousness has otherness in relation to its producers, an eye sense and so forth which exist simultaneously [with the eye consciousness] and the discrimination and so forth which arise together [with an eye consciousness].
>
> *Answer:* Of what use is production [to what already exists]?
>
> *Objection:* [An eye consciousness] does not exist [at the time of its causes].
>
> *Answer:* For this the fallacy [that the eye sense etc. would not be other than a not yet existent eye consciousness] has already been explained.

Elimination of error concerning the refutation of production from other

(See pp.144-8.) The root text says:

> *That others temporally different are refuted is mistaken.*

[Using] a mass exactly the same and so forth are also mistaken.
Because the four extremes are not asserted
And because production from other is said
To be non-existent even in the world,
Its assertion here is a dance of the insane.

As Dzong-ka-ba's *Illumination of the Thought, Explanation of (Chandrakīrti's) 'Supplement'* says,[635] some Tibetans assert that this refutation of production from other is a refutation of others that are temporally different [without the qualification of being naturally existent]. Also, some Tibetans use 'logical' coercives which are exactly the same [instead of good logic. These assertions] etc. are easily understood to be erroneous.

Dak-tsang, as was explained before [in chapter eleven which is not translated here][636] here again [89] asserts production from other. This assertion shows the nature of one who wishes to do a dance having cut off the head of a crazy, dancing peacock and hung it on his behind. For, you [Dak-tsang] quoted the *Rice Seedling Sutra*:[637]

> Also, when a sprout is produced, arising from its cause—a seed—it is not created by itself, not created by [naturally existent] others, not created by both, not created by Ishvara, and not metamorphosed by time. It does not arise from particles, does not arise from its own nature, and is not produced causelessly.

Also, you are seeking to explicate the system of this passage from Chandrakīrti's *Clear Words*:[638]

> The world does not employ analysis such as 'from self' or 'from [naturally existent] others' and so forth. The world understands only this, 'An effect arises from a cause.' The master [Nāgārjuna] presented [cause and effect] this way too.

Also, Chandrakīrti's *Supplement* says,[639] 'Production from other is non-existent even in the world.' [90]

Non-production from both self and other

(See p.148-9.) The root text says:

> *Because there is no [production]*
> *From self and other separately,*
> *Production from both is refuted.*

Both the [theistic] Sāṃkhyas who propound Īshvara as the cause [of all phenomena together with the nature] and the Nirgranthas [Jainas] assert, as was explained before [in chapters three and seven which are not translated here], that pots and so on are produced both from themselves and from others.

These assertions are inadmissible because that part of the assertion which is the production of something from self is damaged by the earlier refutations of production from self and that part which is production from other is damaged by the earlier reasonings refuting production from other. Chandrakīrti's *Supplement* says:[640]

> Also, production from both is not an admissible entity because those fallacies already set forth accrue [to the assertion of production of something from both self and others].

Non-production without causes

(See p.149-50.) The root text says:

> *If things were produced causelessly,*
> *Exertion would be senseless.*
> *It would contradict perception.*
> *All would be produced from all.*

It [absurdly] follows that planting seeds, cooking food, and engaging in commerce for the sake of the arising of temporary and final effects are senseless [91] because, though there are no causes, effects arise. Also, it [absurdly] follows that crows would have the decorations of peacock feathers and that horses would have horns. Also, it [absurdly] follows that, just as a bread-fruit tree would not be a cause of that tree's fruit, so trees bearing *nimba* [a bitter fruit], mango, and so forth also would not be the causes of their own fruit.[641] Also, it [absurdly] follows that the ripening of mangos, *lakucha* [a type of bread fruit],[642] and so forth would not depend on the seasons because they would be produced causelessly.

Even if these consequences are accepted, it is not admissible because there is much damage [to asserting such]. For instance, not only does causeless production contradict what is seen by the world, it *strongly* contradicts what is seen by the world. Chandrakīrti's *Supplement* says:[642a]

> If it is viewed that [things] are produced only causelessly, then everything would always be produced from everything, and for the sake of the arising of certain effects the world would not gather seeds and so forth, doing many hundreds of things [for the sake of those effects].

These positions were refuted formerly [in chapter two on the Nihilists which is not translated here]. [92]

5 *Other Types of Production*

SIMULTANEOUS REFUTATION OF PRODUCTION OF THE FOUR EXTREMES AND OF THE EXISTENT, NON-EXISTENT, BOTH, AND NEITHER

(See pp.61-3, 151-4.) The root text says:

If [things] are produced from others,
Consider [whether the effects are]
Existent, non-existent, both, or neither.
Of what use [are causes] for the existent?
The non-existent lacks object and agent.
These [reasonings] refute their being both.
What would causes do for what lacks both?

No things have any of the three—inherently existent production, abiding, or ceasing—or production from [inherently existent] others. For the existent, non-existent, both, and neither are not produced. As before, [reasoning and others' systems establish that if things have inherently existent production, abiding, and ceasing or production from inherently existent others], it is necessary [that the effect must be either existent, non-existent, both, or neither].

Furthermore, among the four modes of the reason, [first] that which has already attained an existent entity is not produced again because the damages to production from self are incurred. The totally non-existent is not produced because of having no activity. That which is both existent and non-existent is not produced because, since the two—existence and non-existence—are mutually exclusive, they do not subsist in one entity. That which is neither existent nor non-existent is not produced because such does not exist. Nāgārjuna's *Seventy Stanzas on Emptiness* says:[643]

> Because the existent exists, it is not produced. [93]
> Because the non-existent does not exist, it is not
> [produced].
> Because the qualities are incompatible,
> The existent and non-existent is not [produced].
> Because there is no production,
> There is no abiding and no ceasing.

Nāgārjuna's own commentary on this says:[644]

> Because a thing (*bhāva, dngos po*) exists, it could not be produced from causes. For the existent is explained as 'the presently existent'. Because the non-existent does not exist, it could not be produced from causes. Because the existent and non-existent are not concordant, such is not produced, for they are mutually exclusive. The existent and the non-existent possess mutually exclusive qualities; hence, due to their incompatibility how could that which is both existent and non-existent be produced? Because there is no [inherently existent] production, there also is no [inherently existent] abiding and no [inherently existent] ceasing.

Chandrakīrti's *Supplement* says:[645]

> If producers are causes producing products that are other [than themselves], it is to be considered whether they produce an existent, non-existent, that which is both, or that which lacks both. If it exists, of what use are producers? What could these producers do for the

non-existent? What could they do for that which is both?
What could they do for that which lacks both? [94]

In Chandrakīrti's own commentary the reasons are individually established.[646]

Atīsha's *Lamp for the Path to Enlightenment* says:[647]

> The production of the existent is not admissible.
> The non-existent also is like a flower of the sky.
> Because both fallacies are entailed,
> That which is both is not produced.

Chandrakīrti's *Supplement* applies [this refutation of production of the four extremes] to production from other, whereas the Superior [Nāgārjuna] and the Elder Atīsha give general explanations [of it without specifying production from other]. They refute not only production but also abiding and ceasing.[648]

Moreover, because there are four alternatives to be considered —only existent, only non-existent, both, and neither—this reasoning can be called a refutation of four alternatives [and not just four extremes]. Therefore, do not think that a refutation of the four alternatives (*mu bzhi*) precludes a refutation of the four extremes (*mtha' bzhi*).

REFUTATION OF PRODUCTION OF THE FOUR ALTERNATIVES

This section has two parts: the actual exposition of the reasoning and an elimination of error.

Actual exposition of the reasoning refuting production of the four alternatives

(See pp.63-4, 155-9.) As is stated in Kamalashīla's *Illumination of the Middle Way*,[649] our own Buddhist schools which propound [truly existent] things say:

> It is not admissible that there is no true production, for it is said and seen that there is production of many effects and of one effect from one cause—[for example] a seed—

and that many causes and conditions also [95] produce many effects and one effect.

In order to refute the systems that assert such, the root text says:

Things are not truly produced by causes.
One does not produce one, nor many one,
Nor one many, nor many many.

The subjects, things, are not ultimately produced by causes because ultimately one cause does not produce one effect, ultimately many causes do not produce many effects, ultimately one cause does not produce many effects, and ultimately many causes do not produce one effect. For there are reasons captivating to the intelligent. For example, if one eye consciousness has the imprints of many causes, then it would not ultimately be produced by one cause. Also, it would [absurdly] follow that just as the causes are many, the effect which is their imprint would be many consciousnesses. [96] Jñānagarbha's *Discrimination of the Two Truths* says:[650]

Many do not create one thing,
Many do not create many,
One does not create many,
One does not create many things,
One also does not create one.

Also:

You [Proponents of Truly Existent Things] assert that [an eye consciousness which is] the effect [of three causes —object, eye sense, and former moment of consciousness—] is not plural but that its qualities [that is, the qualities of its being produced in the image of the object, of its ability to apprehend a particular type of object such as visible forms rather than sounds, and of its being an experiencer], are different. Thus, alas, why not [assert] that Īshvara creates [everything]?

Also:

> Just as [it would be contradictory for an eye consciousness to be] simultaneously produced [from a form] and not produced [from a form], so say why it would not be contradictory [for the form to be] ultimately (*yang dag par*) a producer [of the eye consciousness] and not a producer [of the eye consciousness]? [97]

Also:

> If it is asserted that the [three imprints or] qualities are produced from [the composite of the three] causes, the individual [causes] would not be the producers. Also, if [the three causes] are [individually the producers, the eye consciousness which is] the effect would be causeless.

Also:

> If you assert that [the eye consciousness which is] the effect is produced from [the three] causes, then it [absurdly] follows that the [three imprints or qualities which are] plural and the [eye consciousness which is] non-plural would, as before, be causeless.

Elimination of error concerning the refutation of the four alternatives

(See pp.159-60.) The root text says:

> *Because one produces one and*
> *Because the others are suitable,*
> *Not affixing here a qualification*
> *Of what is negated is mistaken.*

Here also Ḏak-tsang says that because the four alternatives—one cause producing one effect, etc.—are non-existent, [98] a qualification such as 'ultimately' or 'naturally' should not be affixed to what is negated [in the four reasons].[651] This is not correct because it is asserted that [conventionally] a cause, such as one instant of the eye sense, produces one effect, one instant of an eye consciousness. Also, Chandrakīrti's *Clear Words*, when [giving an etymology of] dependent-arising (*pratītyasamutpāda*), says:[652]

> In a passage such as, 'Dependent on an eye sense and forms an eye consciousness arises,' a particular object [of dependence] has been openly accepted [—'dependent on an eye sense']. When the production of one consciousness, which has as its cause one eye sense, has been asserted, how could the term *pratītya* have the meaning of multiplicity?

Also, the same text at the point of giving the meaning of the term 'direct perceiver' (*pratyakṣha*)[653] says:

> Because there is no sense of [an eye consciousness's depending on] a multiplicity [of sense powers], one eye consciousness which has as its base one moment of an [eye] sense could not be a *pratyakṣha* [according to the wrong etymology as 'depending on a multiplicity of sense powers'].

Also, Chandrakīrti's commentary on Āryadeva's *Four Hundred* says:[654]

> How could one moment of a consciousness be a *pratyakṣha* [i.e., that which depends on a multiplicity of sense powers, according to the wrong etymology]? For [one moment of consciousness] does not engage [its object] through depending on a multiplicity of sense powers. [One moment of an eye consciousness does not depend on a multiplicity of sense powers of dissimilar type, such as also depending on an ear sense] because they are non-compatible. [Also, one moment of an eye consciousness does not directly depend on a multiplicity of former and later moments of a sense power of similar type, i.e., eye senses] because the moments of the sense power and of the consciousness [99] disintegrate right after they are produced.

Asaṅga's *Compendium of Knowledge*, for instance, contains collections of individual sutra teachings explaining that one action [in one lifetime] empowers many bodies [in other lifetimes], that many actions empower one body, that many actions empower many bodies, and that one action empowers one body. Such is asserted also here in Prāsaṅgika texts. Shāntideva's *Engaging in the Bodhisattva Deeds* says:[655]

> The effects [produced] by one clear consciousness [which is enthusiastic in cultivating the first concentration, etc.] are [births in the rank of] a Brahmā, etc. [However, if the mind is not powerful] the effect [of the consciousness]as well as of body and speech is not such because the activity is weak.

Also, as quoted earlier, the fruits of one moment of faith in Buddhas and Bodhisattvas are immeasurable. Also, there is the explanation that if one even makes a ritual object called *sachcha*[656] the essence of which is a relic, one will be born as a universal emperor as many times as there are particles in it.

However, if one's base or mind is weak, though one performs virtues and so on for a long time, [100] the effects are small. Shāntideva's *Engaging in the Bodhisattva Deeds* says:[657]

> [Buddha] the Knower of Suchness said
> That though one performs for a long time
> All the repetitions and asceticisms,
> Doing them with a mind distracted is useless.

Also, sutra says, 'O monks, asceticisms, recitations, and so forth when the mind is distracted to desire are fruitless.' Also, Shāntideva's *Engaging in the Bodhisattva Deeds* says:[658]

> Due to a sin done even for a single moment
> One dwells in the Most Tortuous Hell for an eon.

Similarly, one should realize [that production of one effect from one cause, and so forth, exist conventionally] through many biographies and [Buddha's] life stories. One should look in Nāgārjuna's *Compendium of Sutra*, Shāntideva's *Compendium of Learnings*, and so forth [for further confirmation].

In brief, Kamalashīla's *Illumination of the Middle Way* says:[659]

> *Question:* Is it not seen that many are produced from one and that one is produced from many? [101] Therefore, how can these [views] be forsaken?
>
> *Answer:* These are not [ultimately] admissible, but even we are not proving that these are not seen.

Thus, he explains that [the four alternative types of production] are not admissible ultimately but are not not manifestly perceived. Also, Kamalashīla's *Illumination of the Middle Way* says:[660]

> The master [Nāgārjuna] also saw that cause and effect exist conventionally and that conventionally there is, as reputed, production of many from one and of one from many. Also, he realized that the attributes of an eye consciousness and so forth exist through the operation or non-operation of an eye sense and so forth. Thus, in order to take care of childish beings, when demonstrating the usage of effect-signs (*phalaliṅga, 'bras rtags*)[661] he said that if the causes were plural, [the effects] would be plural. However, it is to be known that it is not so *ultimately.*

6 *Dependent-Arising*

The presentation of the reasoning of dependent-arising, making known the absence of true existence in all phenomena, has two parts: the actual exposition of dependent-arising and a refutation of errors.

ACTUAL EXPOSITION OF DEPENDENT-ARISING

(See pp.53-5, 161-71.) The root text says:

> *Because here there are no phenomena*
> *That are not dependent-arisings [102]*
> *And because dependent-arising [means]*
> *Only 'existing upon meeting',*
> *'Existing in reliance', and 'existing dependently',*
> *All phenomena are not able to set themselves up*
> *And do not exist from their own side.*
> *Profound and extensive, eradicating the two extremes,*
> *This is the king of reasonings.*

Unlike the Proponents of [Truly Existent] Things, here [in the Prāsaṅgika system] phenomena which are not dependent-arisings are not asserted. For whatever exists must both be relatively existent and lack inherent existence. Nāgārjuna's *Treatise on the Middle Way* says:[662]

> Because there are no phenomena
> That are not dependent-arisings,
> There are no phenomena that are not
> Empty [of inherent existence].

Also, Āryadeva's *Four Hundred* says:[663]

> There is not ever anywhere
> Anything's existence without dependence.
> Thus there is also not ever anywhere
> Any permanent [self]. [103]
>
> Common beings think
> Space and so forth are permanent [realities].
> The wise do not see these as realities
> Even with worldly [understanding].

Also, [the *Questions of the King of Nāgas, Sāgara*,] *Sutra* says:[664]

> The wise realize phenomena as dependent-
> Arisings, they also rely not on extreme views.
> They know phenomena as having causes and conditions.
> There are no phenomena without causes and conditions.

Also, Chandrakīrti's *Clear Words* says:[665]

> Thus, 'There are no phenomena that are not dependent-arisings,' and dependent-arisings are also empty. Hence, 'There are no phenomena that are not empty.'

Also, Nāgārjuna's *Treatise* says:[666]

> We explain 'arising dependent [on causes and conditions]' [104]
> As [the meaning of] the emptiness [of inherently existent production].
> That [emptiness of inherently existent production] is dependent imputation.
> Just this [emptiness of inherently existent production] is the middle path.

Also, Chandrakīrti's *Clear Words* says:[667]

> Due to lacking the two extremes of [inherent] existence and non-existence, just this emptiness which is characterized as no inherently existent production is called the middle path, the middle passage. Therefore, emptiness, dependent imputation, and middle path are synonyms of dependent-arising [for one who has generated the Mādhyamika view in his continuum].

With respect to the term 'dependent-arising' (*pratītyasamutpāda*) and its meaning, the Grammarians say that if what depend and meet are cause and effect, then because effect would exist at the time of cause, 'arising' would be impossible. Also, it would contradict the non-assertion of the existence of the effect at the time of its causes. Thus, they do not accept either the term *pratītyasamutpāda* or its meaning.

Also, the [Buddhist] [668] Proponents of [Truly Existent] Things assert that all dependent-arisings are truly existent and are products. [105] Therefore, the attempt to prove a selflessness [which means no true existence] through the reason of dependent-arising proves just the opposite for them. [In syllogistic form, this is: the subject, a sprout, is not inherently produced because of being a dependent-arising. About this] [669] Dzong-ka-ba's *Praise of Dependent-Arising* says:[670]

> How can those who see the opposite [proved] and those who see [the reason] as non-established understand your [i.e., Buddha's] system [of emptiness as no inherent existence]?'

In [Chandrakīrti's commentary on] Nāgārjuna's *Sixty Stanzas of Reasoning* [a qualm is raised by an objector about whether dependent-arising can serve as a sign of no inherently existent production]:[671]

> Here some say, 'Your way of speaking is one that never existed before. It is not reasonable that the term "dependent-arising" indicates no production and no cessation.

> Just as your saying, "A child was born," would not mean you were saying, "A child was not born," this [usage of dependent-arising to prove no production and no cessation] is just inadmissible.'

For extensive [discussion on the Grammarians' non-acceptance and others' misinterpretations of dependent-arising] see Vasubandhu's own explanation of his *Treasury of Knowledge (Abhidharmakoshabhāṣhya)* and its *Commentary (Abhidharmakoshaṭīkā)* by Rājaputra Yashomitra[672] and also Vasubandhu's *Commentary on the 'Sutra on Dependent-Arising' (Pratītyasamutpādādivibhaṅganirdesha)* and its *Explanation* by Guṇamati.

Because there are also different ways of forming the term *pratītyasamutpāda*, I have arranged the interpretations of the former great translators and [grammatical references] to *Kalāpa's Aphorisms (Kalāpasūtra)* and *Chandragomin's Grammar (Chāndravyākaraṇasūtra)* [106] and will explain a little the thought of Chandrakīrti's *Clear Words* on the topic.

Correct way of interpreting dependent-arising

This section has two parts: formation of the term *pratītyasamutpāda* and explanation [of its meaning].

Formation of pratītyasamutpāda

(See pp.163.) To form *pratītyasamutpādaḥ* put down the root for going, *iṇ*. Erase the *ṇ* since it is an indicatory letter. Put down *i*; before it put *prati*. [The nominative ending] *su* is added to this. Due to its being an indeclinable,[673] *su* disappears.

Chandragomin's Grammar (I.iii.129) says,[674] '*Ktvā* is suitable when *alaṃ* and *khalu* have a prohibitive [sense]. After *meṅ*. [Affix it] to the former in time of two [actions with] the same agent.' Also, in *Kalāpa's Aphorisms* the sixth section on verbal affixes says,[675] 'Also, *ktvā* [is affixed] when *alaṃ* and *khalu* have a prohibitive sense. After *meṅ*. [Affix it] to the anterior of [actions with] the same agent.' Therefore, [the continuative] *ktvā* is added.

Chandragomin's Grammar (V.iv.6) says,[676] 'In a compound which does not have the negative particle, *lyap* [is substituted] for *ktvā*.' Therefore, *ktvā* changes to *lyap*. According to the sixth section on verbal affixes in *Kalāpa's Aphorisms*,[677] *ktvā* becomes *yap*, but Chandrakīrti's *Clear Words* accords with *Chandragomin's Grammar*. [107]

Because the *l* of *lyap* is for the sake of accent and the letter *p* is indicatory of the addition of the augment *tuk*, they are erased. Put down *ya*.

Chandragomin's Grammar (V.i.69) says,[678] '[Affix] *tuk* to a [root ending in] a short [vowel] which has no personal ending when [a verbal affix] having an indicatory *p* follows.' Therefore, *tuk* is added between *i* and *ya*.

Because the *k* is indicatory and the *u* is for the sake of pronunciation, the two are erased. Put down *t*.

In *Kalāpa's Aphorisms* the first section on verbal affixes says,[679] '[Affix] *t* to the end of a root which has an indicatory *p*.' [Because] the consonant has no vowel, it is drawn to the latter letter. Thus, *tya* is achieved.

Chandragomin's Grammar (V.i.106) says,[680] 'When a simple vowel [is followed by] a simple vowel, the long [corresponding vowel is the single substitute for both vowels].' Thus, joining *prati* and *i*, make [the vowel long]. *Pratītya* is achieved; it is a stem.

Chandragomin's Grammar (II.i.93) says,[681] 'When the meaning only [of the noun is denoted], the first [case is employed].' Thus, the singular of the first case, *su* is added. According to *Kalāpa's Aphorisms* it is *si*.

Chandragomin's Grammar (II.i.38) says,[682] 'The case affix is erased after an indeclinable.' *Kalāpa's Aphorisms* says, 'After an indeclinable also [the case affix is erased].' Thus, the *si* [or *su*] is erased; thereby, *pratītya* is achieved. It is used for three [meanings]: 'having met', 'having relied', and 'having depended'. [108] Here in the Prāsaṅgika system, it is explained [that *pratītya* refers to any of these three meanings] according to the context and that it does not necessarily mean just one of them.

Also, *pad* has the sense of 'going'. Put down *pad*. Before it, put down the prefix *ut*, and before it put down *sam*. *Su* is added to these two and is erased as before [due to their being indeclinables].

Chandragomin's Grammar (I.iii.7) says,[683] '*Ghañ*, [the verbal affix *a* causing the substitution of *vṛddhi* for the preceding vowel, comes] also when an action [is denoted].' [In *Kalāpa's Aphorisms*] the fifth section on verbal affixes says,[684] '[The affix] *ghañ* [comes] after [the roots] *pad*, *ruj*, *vish*, *spṛsh*, and *uch*.' Therefore, at the end of the root *pad*, *ghañ* is added. The significatory *gh* and the *ñ* which signifies *vṛddhi* are erased. Put down the *a* which is the life of *gha*. The initial of the root is augmented. Putting [these parts] together in stages, one achieves *samutpāda*.

Chandragomin's Grammar (II.i.93) says,[685] 'When the meaning only [of the noun is denoted] the first [case is employed].' Thus, to this add *su*; erase *u*. Also, (VI.iii.98),[686] 'For the [final] *s* and the *ṣh* of *sajuṣh*, *ru* [is substituted at the end of a word].' *S* becomes *ru*.

Chandragomin's Grammar (V.i.119) says,[687] '[The *u* is the substitute] of *ru* when [it is followed by] a soft consonant and [preceded] by a non-protracted *a*.' Thus, the *u*, being indicatory, is erased.

Chandragomin's Grammar (VI.iv.20?) says,[688] 'When there is a pause, *visarga* [is substituted for *r*].' Thus, *r* is made into *visarga*; *samutpādaḥ* is achieved. It is explained at this point as meaning 'arising', 'established', and 'existing'. [109]

Explanation of the meaning of dependent-arising (see pp.164.)
Thus, the meaning of *pratītyasamutpāda* is the arising of things dependent on causes. For *prati* is a prefix meaning 'meeting', and *i* is the root for going, *iṇ*, but—with the continuative ending and modified by the prefix *prati*—*pratītya* is used for 'meeting' and 'relying'. Also, *pāda* with *samut* before it is used for 'arising' and at other times is also explained as 'existing' (*sat*) and 'established' (*siddha*). Chandrakīrti's *Clear Words* says:[689]

> *Prati* has the meaning of meeting (*prāpti*, *phrad pa*). [The verbal root] *i* has the meaning of going. Here the term *pratītya*, a continuative, is used for 'meeting' or 'relying' because of the modification of the meaning of the verbal root by the modifier [prefix]. It is explained, 'The meaning of the verbal root is led forcefully

> elsewhere by a modifier [prefix], like the sweetness of the waters of the Ganges [110] [being changed] by ocean water.' [The root] *pad* preceded by *samut* means 'arise' (*prādurbhāva, 'byung ba*); therefore, the term *samutpāda* is used for 'arising'. Hence, the meaning of *pratītya-samutpāda* is 'the arising of things in reliance on causes and conditions'.

Many commentators who have written about this explanation think that *lyap* is the [Sanskrit] equivalent of [the genitive particle] *kyi* [in Tibetan]. They are also seen to make coarse errors about *prati* and *iti*. Also, though the great translator Sthiramati forms the term *pratītyasamutpāda*, it is not clear.[690] Having seen that without understanding these [explanations of the formation of *pratītyasamutpāda*] one does not understand the early part of Chandrakīrti's *Clear Words*, I have clearly expounded a little, free from error.

Refutation of error concerning the etymology of pratītyasamutpāda

This section has two parts: refutation of other commentators' formation and of Bhāvaviveka's.

Refutation of the formation of pratītyasamutpāda by other commentators

This section has two parts: statement of their assertion and refutation of it.

Statement of other commentators' assertion on the formation of pratītyasamutpāda (See p.163-4.) Some former commentators on Nāgārjuna's *Treatise*, other than Buddhapālita and Bhāvaviveka, say:

> The term *prati* has a distributive meaning like 'diversely' or 'this and that'. [111] [The verbal root] *i* or *iṇ* has the meaning of 'going', or 'departing and disintegrating'. *Itya*, which is the affix *ya* added to the verbal root, means 'that which goes'. Taking *itya* as a secondary

> derivative noun, [*pratītyasamutpāda* means] the arising of what possesses departing or disintegrating diversely, diversely.

Chandrakīrti's *Clear Words* says:[691]

> Others say that [the noun] *iti* means going, disintegrating. *Itya* means that which is conducive to going.[692] *Prati* has the sense of multiplicity. Having explained that the term *itya* has an ending for a secondary derivative noun, they say [*pratītyasamutpāda* means] the arising of those which go or disintegrate, diversely, diversely (*prati prati ityānāṃ vināshināṃ samutpāda*).

Bhāvaviveka's *Lamp for (Nāgārjuna's) 'Wisdom'* says,[693] 'Some others say that the arising of those which disintegrate diversely is *pratītyasamutpāda*.' Avalokitavrata's *Commentary (Prajñāpradīpaṭīkā)* on this says:[694]

> The 'some others' are some other proponents of Mādhyamika tenets.[695] [112] 'The arising of those which disintegrate diversely' means the composition and arising of effects that disintegrate in each diverse moment and have definite, diverse causes and conditions; it is synonymous with 'arising upon meeting'.
>
> [In Bhāvaviveka's text] 'is *pratītyasamutpāda*' indicates the conclusion of the meaning of the preceding words. It indicates that the composition and arising of effects that disintegrate in each diverse moment and have definite, diverse causes and conditions is *pratītyasamutpāda*. Proponents of Mādhyamika tenets other than the commentator [Bhāvaviveka] himself say this.

When they form the term *pratītyasamutpāda*, the *ṇ* of the verbal root for going, *iṇ*, is erased. [The zero affix] *kvip* is added and entirely erased. '*T* is suitable [to be affixed] at the end of a root which has an indicatory *p*.'[696] Because of the sense of 'going' [an action noun], *t* is added. Since it was said, '*Ya* [is affixed] also as an affix for derivative nouns [meaning] "good in that",' *ya* which is an affix for derivative nouns is added. [The case ending] *si* is added. [113] When this is joined with *prati*, there is [the noun] *pratītyaḥ*. The rest [of their formation of *pratītyasamutpādaḥ*] is similar to that given above. Chandrakīrti, Bhāvaviveka, and Avalokitavrata refute this assertion that there is a case ending [that is, a genitive ending making *pratītyānāṃ*] which has been deleted [in the compound].

Refutation of these other commentators' way of forming pratītya-samutpāda (see pp.163-4.) Their explanation of *prati* as meaning multiplicity and *itya* as being a derivative noun is not correct. For, the explanation of *prati* as meaning multiplicity, though suitable for just general [applications of the term], does not cover specific applications. A term for 'many' or multiplicity is [hypothetically][697] suitable when a general [reference for the term is given as in], 'He who sees *pratītyasamutpāda*, that is, the arising of those which depart or disintegrate diversely, [sees suchness].'[698] In *yaḥ pratītyasamutpādaṃ pashyati* the term *pratītyasamutpādaṃ* is a compound; therefore, it is [hypothetically] correct that a case-ending inside the compound could have been deleted. However, when a particular referent is given as in, 'An eye consciousness is produced depending on an eye sense and a form' *chakṣhuḥ pratītya rūpaṃ cha utpadyate chakṣhurvijñānaṃ*,[699] multiplicity is not suitable in one particular. Here *pratītya* is not compounded with anything. It is not suitable [to say that] there is a compound here because the Sanskrit original for 'and' (*cha*) in 'an eye sense and a form' was not deleted and [the accusative ending] *aṃ* of 'on a form' (*rupaṃ*) was not deleted. Also, there is no case ending to be seen from the end of *pratītya* until *chakṣhuḥ*. This is because [*pratītya* is here just] fit to be an indeclinable, a continuative. Chandrakīrti's *Clear Words* says:[700] [114]

> Their etymology would be excellent in a passage such as, 'O monks, I will teach you *pratītyasamutpāda*,' or 'He who sees *pratītyasamutpāda* sees suchness.' For the meaning of multiplicity occurs, and there is a compound [thus allowing for the possibility that *pratītya* means *pratītyānāṃ*].

However, here in a passage such as, 'Dependent on an eye sense and forms an eye consciousness is produced,' a particular object [of dependence] has been openly accepted—'dependent on an eye sense'. When the production of one consciousness, which has as its cause one eye sense, has been asserted, how could the term *pratītya* have the meaning of multiplicity?

However, the meaning of 'meeting' occurs in the term *pratītya* even when a specific object is not asserted; arising having met [causes and conditions] is dependent-arising. Also, [the meaning of 'meeting'] occurs when a specific object is asserted, [115] for it is said that dependent on an eye and forms—that is, meeting an eye and forms or in reliance on an eye and forms—[an eye consciousness arises].[701]

If the term *itya* were a derivative noun, then here in 'Dependent on an eye sense and forms an eye consciousness is produced' (*chakṣhuḥ pratītya rūpāṇi cha utpadyate chakṣhurvijñānaṃ*) the term *pratītya* would [absurdly] not be an indeclinable. Also, since there would not be a compound, a case termination would be present [at the end of *pratītya*]. The reading would [absurdly] be: *chakṣhuḥ pratītyaṃ vijñānaṃ rūpāṇi cha*, 'That which departs to an eye sense and to forms, a consciousness, [arises].' And [since such is total nonsense] it is not so. Therefore, its etymology as just an indeclinable, a continuative, is to be accepted.

The meaning [is that *pratītya* must be accepted as a continuative] because *chakṣhushcha*[702] *rūpaṃ pratītya chakṣhu[rvijñānaṃ]* appears [in the sutra and no case-ending is given for *pratītya*].

Refutation of Bhāvaviveka's way of interpreting pratītyasamutpāda (see pp.165-6.)

Incorrectness of Bhāvaviveka's refutation of another

Bhāvaviveka's *Lamp for (Nāgārjuna's) 'Wisdom'* states Buddhapālita's way [of interpreting *pratītyasamutpāda*]:[703]

> With respect to *pratītyasamutpāda*, [116] one [Buddhapālita] says that due to the sense of multiplicity in the prefix *prati* (*rten cing*), due to the sense of 'meeting' (*'brel ba*) in *i*, and due to the sense of 'arising' (*'byung ba*) in the term *samutpāda*, *pratītyasamutpāda* means 'arising dependent on these and those [causes and conditions]' or 'arising upon meeting these and those [causes and conditions]'.

Bhāvaviveka also states [the other way of interpreting the term cited] previously [on p.666].

Chandrakīrti, thinking that such an explanation shows Bhāvaviveka's lack of skill in stating an opponent's position, asserts that Buddhapālita's thought is not as Bhāvaviveka stated it. For Buddhapālita says that *pratītya* means 'meeting' (*prāpti*, *phrad pa*); and thus *prati* (*rten cing*) does not have a sense of multiplicity, and *itya* (*'brel ba*) does not mean 'meeting'. Chandrakīrti's *Clear Words* says:[704]

> Thus, he [Bhāvaviveka] states others' positions and refutes them. It is regarded that there is a lack of skill in his stating of others' positions. [117] Why? He [Buddhapālita] who explains the term *pratītya*[705] as meaning 'meeting' does not explain *prati* as having a sense of multiplicity or that *i* means 'meeting'.

Then, what [does Buddhapālita say]? Buddhapālita says that *prati* (*rten cing*) means 'meeting' and *itya* (*'brel bar*) means 'going'. Though individually they have different meanings, when these two are combined, the prefix [*prati*] changes the meaning of the latter word [*itya*]. It is like the sweet water of the Ganges becoming salty when it meets the salt water [of the ocean]. Thus, the two words indicate just one meaning, 'meeting'. Hence, the meaning of *pratītyasamutpāda* is 'arising upon meeting [causes and conditions]'.

When the term *pratītyasamutpāda* is applied to all things in the sense of 'arising upon meeting this and that collection of causes and conditions' and one says, '*Hetupratītyasamutpāda*,' it is taken as being related with multiplicity. However, [118] Buddhapālita did not assert [that there is any sense of] multiplicity in a specific [application of the term] as in 'Dependent on an eye sense and a form [an eye consciousness is produced].' Chandrakīrti's *Clear Words* says:[706]

> Then what [does Buddhapālita say]? He says that *prati* (*rten cing*) means 'meeting'. *I* (*'brel bar*) means 'going'. The combination *pratītya* means just 'meeting'.[707]
>
> Now when a consideration of all possible entities is asserted as being expressed by the term *pratītyasamutpāda*—etymologized as 'arising upon meeting' or dependent-arising—then a relation with multiplicity is being stated: 'Arising upon meeting this and that collection of causes and conditions' is [the meaning of] dependent-arising. [However,] when a consideration of a particular instance is asserted, there is no relation with multiplicity, [as in] 'Having met an eye sense and forms [an eye consciousness arises].'
>
> Such is the unskillfulness of the master [Bhāvaviveka] in citing [another's position].

Not only that, but also [Bhāvaviveka's] way of refuting the others' system is not correct [119] because [his statement] is reduced to being just the thesis, '[Buddhapālita's explanation] is not correct,' without any reason.

However, Bhāvaviveka's thought may have been that because a consciousness has no form, it could not meet an eye sense and a form because meeting exists only between the physical. However, even if that were his thought, it would be incorrect because it is asserted that monks meet [that is, attain] the four fruits [Stream Enterer, Once Returner, Never Returner, and Foe Destroyer, which are not physical]. Sutra says, 'This monk is one who has met [attained] the fruit.'

Also, *prāpya* ('having met' or 'upon meeting', *phrad nas*) is a synonym of *apekṣhya* ('having relied' or 'in reliance upon', *ltos nas*). Also, the Superior Nāgārjuna [in his *Sixty Stanzas of Reasoning*] asserts that the term *pratītya* (*rten cing 'brel ba*) means *prāpya* ('having met', *phrad pa*):[708]

That which is produced having met this and that
[collection of causes and conditions]
Is not inherently produced.
(*Tat tat prāpya yad utpannaṃ notpannaṃ tat svabhāvataḥ.*)

Chandrakīrti's *Clear Words* says:[709]

[Bhāvaviveka says,] 'That is not admissible because of the non-existence of the meaning of these two [wrong interpretations of *pratītyasamutpāda*][710] in 'An eye consciousness is produced depending on an eye and forms.'

This refutation is not correct. [120] Why? He does not state a reason why there is no occurrence [of a meeting], and, therefore, he has only a thesis.

Then, this might be [Bhāvaviveka's] thought: 'A consciousness has no form; therefore, it has no meeting with an eye sense. For it is seen that there is a meeting just of those which have form.'

This is also not admissible because of the assertion of 'meeting' here in, 'This monk is one who has met the fruit.' Also, the term 'having met' (*prāpya, phrad nas*) is a synonym of the term 'having relied' (*apekṣhya, bltos nas*). Also, the master Nāgārjuna accepts the term *pratītya* as meaning just *prāpti* 'meeting', [or 'having met' when used as a continuative. Nāgārjuna's *Sixty Stanzas of Reasoning* says:][711]

That which is produced having met this and that
[collection of causes and conditions]
Is not inherently produced.
(*Tat tat prāpya yad utpannaṃ notpannaṃ tat svabhāvataḥ.*)

Therefore, others [Chandrakīrti himself] say that even [Bhāvaviveka's] refutation is not admissible.

Incompleteness of Bhāvaviveka's own etymology and meaning of pratītyasamutpāda

(See pp.165-6.) Even Bhāvaviveka's own way of explanation is incorrect [121] because though he asserts that he will [etymologize *pratītyasamutpāda*] explaining [the parts] individually, he does not state individual meanings for *pratītya* and *samutpāda*. Also, [in his *Lamp for (Nāgārjuna's) 'Wisdom'*] Bhāvaviveka says no more than,[712] 'the meaning of "conditionality" is the meaning of *pratītyasamutpāda*—"When this is, that arises; due to the production of this, that is produced"'.[713] Chandrakīrti's *Clear Words* says:[714]

> What then is [the meaning of *pratītyasamutpāda* according to Bhāvaviveka? He] presents his own system as, 'The meaning of conditionality is the meaning of *pratītyasamutpāda*—when this is, that arises; due to the production of this, that is produced.' This also is incorrect because he did not state a particular meaning for each of the two terms, *pratītya* and *samutpāda*, and because he asserted that he would give an etymology.

Objection: Bhāvaviveka says such asserting that *pratītyasamutpāda* is a term the meaning of which is determined by conventional usage and does not have the character set forth in its etymological explanation. It is like *araṇyetilaka* [which literally means 'sesame in the forest'[715] but is conventionally used to mean anything not answering to one's expectations]. The word 'et cetera' [in Chandrakīrti's text, which is soon to be quoted, refers to other such non-literal terms derived] from the transmission of earlier forms of speech, such as 'lakeborn' (*saraja*) for a lotus grown on dry earth [122] and 'lying on the earth' (*mahiṣha*) for a buffalo that is standing.

Answer: This also is not correct because the master, the Superior Nāgārjuna, individually differentiated *pratītya* and *samutpāda* as components of the term: *tat tat prāpya* 'having met this and that' [collection of causes and conditions] and *utpannaṃ* 'arisen'. [Nāgārjuna's *Sixty Stanzas of Reasoning* says,][716] '*Tat tat prāpya yad utpannaṃ notpannaṃ tat svabhāvataḥ* : That which is produced having met this and that [collection of causes and conditions] is not inherently produced.'

Also, you [Bhāvaviveka] wish, for instance, to explain [the term] in accordance with Nāgārjuna's *Precious Garland*:[717]

> When this is, that arises,
> Like long when there is short.

However, even you must explain this as [having the meaning of 'depending' or 'relying' or][718] 'meeting'. Therefore, that which you have refuted becomes [that which you yourself must assert]. [123] Chandrakīrti's *Clear Words* says:[719]

> *Objection:* Such is said [by Bhāvaviveka] having asserted *pratītyasamutpāda* to be a conventional term [not necessarily following its etymological meaning] like *araṇyetilaka* [meaning anything which does not answer to one's expectations].
>
> *Answer:* This also is not correct because the master [Nāgārjuna] asserts *pratītyasamutpāda* just in relation to its members: '*Tat tat prāpya yad utpannaṃ notpannaṃ tat svabhāvataḥ*. That which is produced having met this and that [collection of causes and conditions] is not inherently produced.'
>
> [Bhāvaviveka] explains *pratītyasamutpāda* with:
>
> > When this is, that arises,
> > Like long when there is short.
>
> Then, does he not assert just that depending (*pratītya, rten te*) on short, meeting (*prāpya, phrad cing*) to short, relying (*apekṣhya, bltos nas*) on short, long comes to be? Therefore, it is not fitting that he assert just what he refutes.

Thus, *pratītyasamutpāda* means the dependent-arising of products—their arising in reliance on their own causes and conditions. [124] It also means the dependent-arising [of all phenomena, products and non-products]—their existence meeting to or in reliance on their own parts, their own bases of imputation, or their own members. For with regard to the Sanskrit original of 'arising' (*samutpāda*), Vasubandhu's *Commentary on the 'Sutra on Dependent-Arising'* explains *sam* as 'coming together', 'aggregating', etc. Also, Rājaputra Yashomitra[720] explains *pada* as 'existing' etc.

Because all phenomena are just existent in dependence upon, in reliance upon, or meeting to [causes and conditions, their parts, and their basis of imputation], they are not able to set themselves up and do not exist through their own power. Āryadeva's *Four Hundred* says:[721]

> That which has a dependent arising
> Cannot be self-powered; since all these
> Lack being under their own power,
> There is no self [inherent existence].

Also, the Superior Nāgārjuna says [in his *Sixty Stanzas of Reasoning*]:[722]

> That which is produced having met this and that
> [collection of causes and conditions]
> Is not inherently produced. [125]

Also, it is as Chandrakīrti's *Commentary on (Āryadeva's) 'Four Hundred'* says:[723]

> I am not a proponent of no phenomena (**abhāvavādin, dngos po med par smra ba*) because I propound dependent-arising.
>
> *Question:* Are you a proponent of [inherently existent] phenomena (**bhāvavādin, dngos por smra ba*)?
>
> *Answer:* No, [I am not a proponent of inherently existing phenomena] because I am a proponent of dependent-arising.
>
> *Question:* What do you propound?
>
> *Answer:* I propound dependent-arising.
>
> *Question:* Then, what is the meaning of dependent-arising?
>
> *Answer:* It means no inherent existence. It means no inherently existent production. It means the arising of

> effects which have a nature like that of magical illusions, mirages, reflections, magical cities of Smell-Eaters, emanations, and dreams. It means emptiness and selflessness.

Also, here [in the syllogism, 'The subject, such and such, does not inherently exist because of being a dependent-arising'] the profound is the predicate—'does not inherently exist'—and the vast is the reason—'being a dependent-arising'. The way that the profound is fully present in the predicate and the vast is fully present in the reason should be sought in detail in Nāgārjuna's *Sixty Stanzas of Reasoning*, Chandrakīrti's commentary on it, Nāgārjuna's own commentry on his *Seventy Stanzas on Emptiness*, and his *Precious Garland* as well as in Gyel-tsap's commentary, etc. Nāgārjuna's *Friendly Letter (Suhṛllekha)* says:[724] [126]

> This dependent-arising is the profound preciousness
> Of the treasury of the Conqueror's speech.
> Who sees this correctly sees the highest aspect
> [Of the teaching] of Buddha, the Knower of Suchness.

Also, Mahāmati's commentary on this says:[725]

> This dependent-arising is the preciousness of the Tathāgata's speech because one who knows this well realizes correctly the teaching of the Tathāgata. 'Profound' means 'solely profound'.

Also:

> Or, 'He who sees this correctly ...' means seeing just the preciousness of the treasury which is the Conqueror's speech. The profundity is non-creation by self, non-creation by other ...

Thus, this dependent-arising overcoming all conceptions of both extremes is the king of reasonings. The foremost lama [D̄zong-ka-b̄a in his *Praise of Dependent-Arising*] says:[726] [127]

> Among teachers the teacher of dependent-arising
> And among types of knowledge the knowledge of
> dependent-arising

Are like the Conqueror King [Buddha] among worldly beings.

ELIMINATION OF ERROR CONCERNING DEPENDENT-ARISING

(See pp.171-3.) The root text says:

Therefore, [asserting] that the ultimate
Is able to set itself up is [like wanting]
To eat space; no one takes 'validly established'
And 'able to set itself up' as synonyms.

Dak-tsang, as was explained before [in the eleventh chapter which is not translated here],[727] asserts that 'ultimate object' (*paramārtha, don dam*), 'able to set itself up' (*tshugs thub*), and 'validly established' (*pramāṇasiddha, tshad grub*) are synonyms. However, the three—the father, the Superior [Nāgārjuna], and his spiritual sons [Āryadeva and Buddhapālita]—explain that dependent-arisings are not autonomous. Therefore, this assertion that an ultimate [an emptiness] is able to set itself up is like asserting that space can be eaten.

Also, Dharmakīrti's *Commentary on (Dignāga's) 'Compendium of Valid Cognition' (Pramāṇavārttika)* says,[728] 'Because there are two types of objects of comprehension, there are two types of valid cognizers.' Thus, Vaibhāṣhikas, Sautrāntikas, and so forth assert that even generally characterized phenomena (*sāmānya-lakṣhaṇa, spyi mtshan*) [permanent phenomena] are validly established [but, of course, do not accept that they are able to set themselves up]. Thus, there is not even one [school of tenets] asserting that 'able to set itself up' is necessarily present in the meaning of 'validly established'. Therefore, do not scar Buddha's teaching [with such absurdity]! [128]

7 *Refuting a Self of Persons*

The presentation of the reasoning refuting a self of persons has two parts: actual exposition and elimination of error.

ACTUAL EXPOSITION OF THE REASONING REFUTING A SELF OF PERSONS

(See pp.31-51, 175-95.) The root text says:[729]

> *A self under its own power is non-existent*
> *Because the aggregates are not the person,*
> *The person is not [an entity] other [than the aggregates],*
> *The person is not the base of the aggregates,*
> *The person also does not [ultimately] depend on the*
> *aggregates,*
> *The person does not [ultimately] possess the aggregates,*
> *The shape [of the aggregates] is not the person,*
> *Like a chariot. Apply [this analysis] to all phenomena.*

With respect to this, I have extensively refuted elsewhere[730] many wrong notions about these sets of twos:

1. I and my
2. the view of the transitory collection as a real I and the view of the transitory collection as real my

3 the conventional, mental valid cognizer apprehending I and the conventional, mental valid cognizer apprehending my
4 basis of imputation and phenomenon imputed, etc.

Therefore, here I will just illustrate the difficult points.

Sutra says,[731] 'O monks, any devotee or Brahmin who views a self is viewing only these five appropriated aggregates.' Also, the root text [Chandrakīrti's *Supplement*] says,[732] [129] 'There is no [innate] apprehension [of a self] separate from the aggregates.' Also, '[The teaching by Buddha that the self is the aggregates] is [just] a refutation of a self different from the aggregates because other sutras say that forms and so forth are not the self.' Chandrakīrti's own *Commentary on the 'Supplement'* says:[733]

> The object of observation of [a consciousness viewing the transitory collection as an inherently existent self] is the [nominally existent] self. For, that which conceives an [inherently existent] I has its object [an inherently existent] self.

Thus, the appearance of a [nominally existent] I, or self, sentient being, god, etc., *in dependence on* the transitory aggregates which are composites of plural [factors] is the [nominally existent] I, or self, sentient being, god, etc.

Furthermore, Buddhapālita says [in his commentary on Nāgārjuna's *Treatise*],[734] 'That which the self possesses is called mine.' Thus, the maker into own of eyes and so forth—which are the things owned and are qualified as being 'own'—is assigned as own, mine, a sentient being's mine, a god's mine, etc.

A viewing consciousness which, having apprehended a [nominally existent] I, conceives that I to exist truly [130] is both a consciousness viewing the transitory collection as a real I and an ignorance. A viewing consciousness which, having apprehended [nominally existent] mine, conceives that mine to exist truly is both a consciousness viewing the transitory collection as real mine and an ignorance. These are explicitly said to be consciousnesses viewing the transitory collection [as real I and mine] in Chandrakīrti's own *Commentary on the 'Supplement'*:[735]

> There [in VI.120] a 'consciousness viewing the transitory collection' is an afflicted knowledge dwelling in thoughts of such [inherently existent] I and mine.

Also, Chandrakīrti's *Supplement* says:[736]

> Initially adhering to a self, I,
> And then generating attachment for things, 'This is mine.'

His *Commentary on the 'Supplement'* says:[737]

> These worldly beings, before adhering to mine, imagine through the conception of an [inherently existent] I that a non-[inherently] existent self does exist [inherently], and they adhere to just this as true. Then thinking 'mine', they adhere also to all things other than the object of the conception of I [as truly established].

Also, D̄zong-ka-b̄a's *Ocean of Reasoning, Explanation of (Nāgārjuna's) 'Treatise on the Middle Way'* says in detail:[738]

> The [conventionally existent] I is the base generating the thought 'I'. There is a consciousness observing it which as its mode conceives [the I] to exist by way of its own character. [131] This is both an innate consciousness viewing the transitory collection which [falsely] conceives I and an obscuration with respect to a self of persons. There is a consciousness observing the [conventionally existent] mine which as its mode conceives [the mine] to exist by way of its own character. This is both an innate consciousness viewing the transitory collection which [falsely] conceives mine and an obscuration with respect to the mine of a person.

[Thus, 'mine' refers not to things which are considered as belongings but to the *maker* of things into one's belongings; hence, mine is a type of person.][739] Nevertheless, the person does not become many continuums [I being one and mine being another] due to the fact that I and mine are one entity, differentiated only in thought through their isolates. For example, in the Superior Ānanda's continuum the I, monk, human, Stream Enterer, Shākya clan member, and royal caste member have different meanings but are one continuum. Therefore, it should be understood that the types of consciousnesses conceiving I in his continuum are manifold.

The appearance as I with respect to the aggregates and the appearance as I in dependence on the aggregates are I. However, not only are the aggregates not I, but also the aggregates appearing as I are not I. For, the appearance as an I established from its own side is not the object I.

Also, eyes, ears, and so forth are bases of the imputation 'mine' (*nga yi ba*) and [132] illustrations [not of the mine but] of what is owned (*nga yi yin rgyu*), but they are not mine. For they are not that which possesses mine (*nga yi can*) nor the maker of mine (*nga yir byed pa po*). Also, the conception of eyes, ears, and so forth as existing by way of their own character is a conception of a self of phenomena; what conceives the mine which appears in dependence on them to be inherently existent is the [false] conception of mine. D̄zong-ka-b̄a's *Ocean of Reasoning* says:[740]

> A consciousness observing a base [such as an eye generating the thought] 'mine' and conceiving it to exist in that way [by way of its own character] is a conceiver of a self of phenomena. Therefore, 'observing the mine' does not refer to observing those [eyes, ears, and so forth which are the bases giving rise to the thought 'mine'].

Also, Kay-drup's *Opening the Eyes of the Fortunate* [seems to speak of eyes and so forth as illustrations of mine but actually] is explaining that they are illustrations of things owned (*bdag gi yin rgyu*):[741]

> The eyes, ears, and so forth included within one's own continuum are illustrations of both mine and phenomena in the division [of all phenomena] into persons and phenomena.

Chandrakīrti's *Clear Words* says:[742]

> That which pertains to the self is the mine; it means one's own five aggregates.

Still, he is referring to the base₃ [generating the thought] 'mine' (*bdag gi ba'i gzhi*) [and not mine itself]. Kay-drup's *Opening the Eyes of the Fortunate* says:[743] [133]

> The eyes, ears, and so forth included within one's own continuum are illustrations of both mine and phenomena in the division [of all phenomena] into persons and phenomena. They appear to innate [non-analytical] awarenesses as mine which is established from the object's own side or they appear to innate awarenesses as mine, and then observing such mine, one conceives that it exists by way of its own character. This is the innate [mis]conception of mine.

Therefore, on the basis that [the eyes, ears, and so forth in one's own continuum] are the objects generating the view of the transitory collection that [falsely] conceives of mine, you should know that when mine appears to a Buddha, he perceives it as only imputed to its basis of imputation and does not perceive the basis of the imputation as the phenomenon imputed. Also, you should know that a composite of the two [mistaken appearance of the mine as inherently existent and the emptiness of such] appears to lesser Superiors.

Furthermore, Ḍak-tsang and so forth say:[744]

> It is wrong that when the conception of self is analyzed, one refutes the identification of a self separate from the aggregates and afterwards refutes the true existence of the aggregates. This is because the self and the aggregates appear as one to the innate [non-analytical intellect], for the root text [Chandrakīrti's *Supplement*] says,[745] [134] 'There is no [innate] conception [of a self] separate from the aggregates.'

Ridiculing the instruction manuals on the view [of emptiness], even one of our own logicians propounds [that there is no innate conception of the self and aggregates as different].[746] These assertions are the bad talk of those with partial vision much like the way a one-eyed yak eats grass.

[Contradictory consequences are now stated to refute the view that innate, non-analytical awarenesses perceive the self as one with the aggregates and that, therefore, analysis of the self means analysis of the aggregates.] It [absurdly] follows that an innate [non-analytical] awareness would not conceive [the self and the aggregates] as different as in 'my body' and 'my mind'.

It [absurdly] follows that there would be no innate [non-analytical awareness mis]conceiving the self and the aggregates as like a master and his subjects.

If it is accepted [that there is no innate non-analytical awareness misconceiving the self and the aggregates as like a master and his subjects], then it [absurdly] follows that Chandrakīrti would be wrong to say,[747] 'What is related to [or preceded by] the view of self [that is, of inherent existence] is extinguished.'

It [absurdly] follows that the *Sutra on the Ten Grounds* concerning the fourth ground [and quoted by Chandrakīrti][748] at this point [in the fourth chapter of his *Commentary on the 'Supplement'*] would be wrong. There are many [such contradictory consequences].

You seem to be basing your opinion on [Chandrakīrti's statement in his *Supplement*],[749] 'There is no [innate] conception [of a self] separate from the aggregates.' [However,] this refutes [the theory that there is an innate conception of][750] a self that has a character discordant with the aggregates and that there is an innate conception of a permanent self independent of the aggregates; it does not refute that the self and the aggregates are just different. [For you] it [absurdly] follows that this distinction would be incorrect because of your thesis [that the self and the aggregates appear as one to an innate non-analytical awareness]. The three circles of self-contradiction! [You have accepted (1) the reason, (2) that the predicate of the consequence is entailed by the reason, and (3) the opposite of the consequence.]

If it is accepted [that the self and the aggregates are not merely different], then since the self and the aggregates exist and a difference between them has been rejected, it [absurdly] follows that the self and the aggregates would be one.

Also, [if it is accepted that the self and the aggregates are not merely different], then it [absurdly] follows that Chandrakīrti would be wrong when he clearly states in his root text [that the self and the aggregates are not different entities but are just different]:[751] [135]

> Those who have fallen down senseless into [lives as] animals for many eons also do not perceive this unborn permanent [self]. Having seen that the conception of [an inherently existent] I operates even in them, [what intelligent being would think that such an unborn permanent self is the base of the innate conception of an inherently existent self?] Thus, there is no self other than the aggregates.

Furthermore, while saying such, [we][752] say that the way that the I in a human continuum appears is that it appears undifferentiable from the aggregates and as if standing on its own (*hrang hrang ba*) and concrete (*phob phob pa*). About this also, some [D̄ak-tsang and so forth][753] say, 'Such an appearance of the I is totally incorrect because the I is a non-associated compositional factor [that is, a product which is neither form nor consciousness] and because non-associated compositional factors do not appear this way.'

[Contradictory consequences are stated in response.] It [absurdly] follows that there would be no appearance of I [to the mind] because [according to you] the appearance of the aggregates which are the bases of the imputation 'I' is not the appearance of the I.[754] The three circles of self-contradiction!

It [absurdly] follows that when the I appears, an independent I would appear because the I would have to appear without depending on the appearance of the aggregates. The three circles of self-contradiction!

It [absurdly] follows that when the I appears to an innate [non-analytical awareness], without the appearance of the aggregates —the basis of the imputation—the appearance of an I, the phenomenon imputed which is merely neither form nor consciousness, would occur. For, your thesis is correct [according to you]! [136]

If that were accepted, it would contradict Chandrakīrti's statement,[755] 'There is no [innate] conception [of a self] separate from the aggregates.'

Not only that but also the way that the I appears to an innate [non-analytical awareness] is that it seems to exist from the side of the aggregates [and not just as an imputation from the subject's side] within the context that the basis of the imputation 'I' and the phenomenon imputed are inseparably mixed like milk and water. For at that time, it must appear by way of a mixture of the appearance of the aggregates, which are the basis of the imputation, and the appearance of the I, which is the phenomenon imputed [in dependence upon them]. If the I appeared separately from the aggregates, then the self would not appear to have the character of the aggregates—production, disintegration, shape, etc., being the feeler, discriminator, accumulator of actions, actor, knower, and so forth. Nāgārjuna's *Treatise on the Middle Way* says:[756]

> If [the self] were other than the aggregates,
> It would not have the character of the aggregates.

Also, Chandrakīrti's *Clear Words* says:[757]

> If the self were separate from the aggregates, it would have the character of non-aggregates. [137] The five aggregates have the character of suitability as form,[758] experiencing, apprehending signs, composition, and realizing objects individually. Also, just as consciousness [is different] from form, so the self which is being asserted to be different from the aggregates would be established as having a character different [from the aggregates]. Also, its different character would be apprehended just as [the character of] mind [is apprehended separate] from form, but it is not apprehended so. Therefore, the self is not separate from the aggregates.

Buddhapālita also says such. [If the person and the aggregates appeared totally separately] then a white horse, a speckled bull, and so forth would be impossible.

Also, the *Sacred Word of Mañjushrī* by [the fifth Dalai Lama,] the great master and foremost of Conquerors, says:[759]

> Sometimes the I will seem to exist in the context of the body. Sometimes it will seem to exist in the context of the mind. Sometimes it will seem to exist in the context of the other individual aggregates [feelings, discriminations, and compositional factors]. At the end of the arising of such a variety of modes of appearance, [138] you will come to identify an I that exists in its own right, that exists inherently, that from the start is self-established, existing undifferentiatedly with the mind and body which are [also] mixed like milk and water.
>
> This is the first essential [in meditation on the selflessness of I], the ascertainment of the object to be negated [in the view of selflessness]. You should analyze until deep experience of it arises. Having generated such in your mental continuum, you thereby crystallize an identification of the I conceived by the innate consciousness conceiving I as able to set itself up within the context that it and your own aggregates are like water put in water. [139]

This appears to be an unprecedented good explanation, based on experiencing the meaning of the texts by the father Nāgārjuna and his spiritual sons.

The objects generating the thought 'I' in the mind of a person such as Devadatta are not of different continuums, but there is a plurality of gods, humans, animals, and so forth [because he was, is, and will be these at various times over his continuum of lives]. The finer points should be known, such as that the I and the mind of his continuum have operated beginninglessly and that though [the I and the mind] have been produced and have ceased [moment by moment], they have never been destroyed. However, the states of being a god or animal, etc., are established through assuming such a body, and the states are destroyed through casting off such a body.

Also, since gods, humans, and so forth are differentiated by way of their physical supports [that is to say, their bodies], the I sometimes seems to exist in the context of the body. On the other hand, since the passage of the mere I through to Buddhahood depends on the mind [which leaves one body and assumes another], the I sometimes seems to exist in the context of the mind. If one [wishes to] penetrate the depths of the view, one should analyze these points well in accordance with Nāgārjuna's *Treatise on the Middle Way* and Ḏzong-ka-ba̱'s *Great Commentary* on it. Ḏzong-ka-ba̱'s *Ocean of Reasoning* says:[760]

> Therefore, do not hold that the two, the human who is the imputer of the designation 'I' and the [conventionally existent] self which is the basis that is being imputed with the designation, are co-extensive. Know that the human is one part of the self. [140]

Also:

> When Devadatta's selves of former and later lives are not individually differentiated, the self that serves as the basis of the [valid] conception of I is the mere I which has existed beginninglessly. Therefore, the selves of the individual migrators when they appropriate the bodies of gods and so forth are instances of the former[ly mentioned mere I].

Also, it is said in the word of the foremost Conqueror [the Fifth Dalai Lama's *Sacred Word of Mañjushrī*],[761] 'Sometimes the I will seem to exist in the context of the body. Sometimes it will seem to exist in the context of the mind.'

Also, Chandrakīrti's own *Commentary on the 'Supplement'* says:[762]

> There is no [innate] adherence to a self anywhere except with respect to the aggregates. Hence, there is no fifth form of the [false] view of the transitory collection [as real I and mine].

Thus, there are twenty artificial views of the transitory collection, like twenty mountain peaks,[763] and as antidotes to destroy them Chandrakīrti states as signs or reasons the meaning of a statement in sutra that he quotes:[764]

> Form is not the self; also the self does not possess form. The self is not in form; form is not in the self. . . . Just so, the self is not consciousness; [141] the self does not possess consciousness. The self is not in consciousness; consciousness is not in the self.

[Chandrakīrti] establishes [through those reasons] the subtle selflessness, that is, the lack of inherent existence in all phenomena, mentioned in a sutra which says,[765] 'All phenomena are selfless.' Therefore, it is with such in mind that the foremost precious [D̄zong-ka-b̄a] says[766] that the refutation of artificial [misconceptions] is a branch of refuting innate [misconceptions of persons and phenomena]. Also, refutations of extremes with respect to the selflessness of phenomena [other than persons] are used as reasons [in the sevenfold reasoning refuting a self of persons].[767]

Let us summarize the meaning of these sutras. The subjects, a Tathāgata or a person,[768] do not exist autonomously or inherently because:

1 they are not the mental and physical aggregates which are the basis of their imputation, that is, they are not one with the aggregates which are the basis of their imputation
2 they are not others separate from the aggregates which are the basis of their imputation, that is, they do not exist as entities separate from these aggregates which are the basis of their imputation
3 inherently they are not like a tub, the support of the mental and physical aggregates which would then be like a juniper[769] [142]
4 they do not inherently depend on the mental and physical aggregates
5 they do not inherently possess the mental and physical aggregates in the manner of a sameness of entity, as in the

case of Devadatta's possessing an ear, and they do not possess the aggregates in the manner of a difference of entity, as in the case of Devadatta's possessing wealth.

In Nāgārjuna's *Treatise* the reason is given with:[770]

> [The Tathāgata] is not [inherently one with his own five] aggregates; [the Tathāgata] is not [inherently] other than [his own five] aggregates; the aggregates are not [inherently dependent] on him; he is not [inherently dependent] on those [aggregates]; the Tathāgata does not [inherently] possess the aggregates.

Then, the thesis is given as:

> What [inherently existent] Tathāgata is there? [That is, there is no inherently existent Tathāgata.]

Also, Nāgārjuna's *Precious Garland* gives the reason with:[771]

> The aggregates are not [inherently one with] the self; those [aggregates] are not [inherently dependent] on that [self]; that [self] is not [inherently dependent] on those [aggregates]; without those [aggregates] that [self] is not [apprehendable separately; the self] is not mingled with the aggregates like fire and fuel.[772]

The 'mingling' [of the self and the aggregates] refers to possession [in which possessor and possessed] are one entity as explained previously [on page 687] when indicating what is negated [in the view of selflessness]. [143] The thesis is given with:

> Therefore, how could a self exist?

Furthermore, the reasons are to be established individually:

> If those two [a Tathāgata or a person] are one with [their respective] mental and physical aggregates, it [absurdly] follows that they are impermanent. It [absurdly] follows that they are [each] multiple. It [absurdly] follows that a self is not asserted. It [absurdly] follows that remembering other births is impossible.

Buddhapālita's Commentary on (Nāgārjuna's) Treatise says:[773]

> Respectively, the aggregates are not the Tathāgata. Why? The aggregates possess the qualities of arising and disintegration; therefore, it would follow that the Tathāgata was just impermanent. Also, the appropriator [the self] is not suitable to be just one with the appropriated [aggregates].

Also, Chandrakīrti's *Clear Words* says:[774]

> With respect to this [first stanza of the eighteenth chapter in Nāgārjuna's *Treatise*], if the self were thought to be the aggregates, then the self would have production and disintegration because of depending on the production and disintegration of the aggregates. Also, the self is not asserted thus [144] because of the consequence of many faults.[775] As [Nāgārjuna] will explain (XXVII.12):
>
> Also it does not arise [newly]
> Not having existed [in a former life]
> For fallacy follows there,
> The self would be a product
> And its arising would be causeless.
>
> And similarly (XXVII.6):
>
> The appropriated [aggregates] are not the self,
> [For] the aggregates arise and disintegrate.
> How indeed could the appropriated
> Be the appropriator?
>
> Furthermore, this position is to be understood from the extensive analysis in the *Supplement*:[776]
>
> If the aggregates were the self,
> Then because of the plurality of those aggregates, the selves would also just be many.
> Also the self would be a substantiality and viewing it as such
> Would not be erroneous if it is acting on a substantiality. [145]

In nirvana annihilation of the self would definitely occur.
There would be destruction and production of the self in the moments prior to nirvana.
Due to the destruction of the agent, effects of those [actions] would be non-existent.
Also another would experience [the effects of actions] accumulated by another....

Here I will not extensively elaborate on it. Thus, respectively the aggregates are not the self.

If these two [a Tathāgata or a person] were entities different from their mental and physical aggregates [which are their bases of imputation], then it would [absurdly] follow that they are not aggregates. It would [absurdly] follow that they would not be feelers and so forth. It would [absurdly] follow that they would be permanent. It would [absurdly] follow that they would be apprehended apart from the mental and physical aggregates. It would [absurdly] follow that they would not be existent selves. It would [absurdly] follow that they would be without activity and would not be agents. *Buddhapālita's Commentary on (Nāgārjuna's) Treatise* says:[777]

> A Tathāgata also is not other than his aggregates; he does not exist as a separate phenomenon which is not the aggregates. Why? He would not accord with the impermanent aggregates; therefore, he would just be permanent. If [a Tathāgata and his aggregates] were other, it would follow that he would be apprehended [separate from the aggregates which are his basis of imputation]. Because he is not apprehended [separate from his aggregates], [146] a Tathāgata is not other than his aggregates.

Also, Chandrakīrti's *Clear Words* says:[778]

> If the self were separate from the aggregates, it would have the character of non-aggregates. The five aggregates have the character of suitability as form, experiencing,

apprehending signs, composition, and realizing objects individually. Also, if the self is asserted to be different from the aggregates, just as consciousness is different from form, the self would be established as having a character different from the aggregates. Also, its different character would be apprehended just as [the character of] mind [is apprehended separate] from form, but such is not apprehended. Therefore, the self also is not separate from the aggregates.

Even if a self or a Tathāgata inherently acted as the base of the mental and physical aggregates [which are in their continuum] or even if these two inherently depended over there on the aggregates, the fallacies of a self different from the aggregates would ensue. *Buddhapālita's Commentary on (Nāgārjuna's) Treatise* says:[779] [147]

> Aggregates do not exist in a Tathāgata like a forest of trees in snow. Why? Those which are supported [aggregates] and their base [a Tathāgata] would be other; therefore, it would follow that a Tathāgata was permanent. Also, a Tathāgata does not exist in aggregates like a lion in a forest of trees. Why? There would be the fallacy just indicated.

Also, Chandrakīrti's own *Commentary on the 'Supplement'* says:[780]

> If [the self and the aggregates] were [inherently] other, they would be fit to be the [intrinsically existent] entities of that which is supported and its support like yogurt in a metal bowl, for example. Since the two, yogurt and bowl, are just other in worldly conventions, they are seen to be the entities of that which is supported and its support. However, the aggregates are not thus different [entities] from the self, and the self also is not a different [entity] from the aggregates. Therefore, these two are not the entities of support and supported.

A Tathāgata and a person do not possess the mental and physical aggregates in the mode of being inherently different or non-different entities. [148] If they possessed the mental and physical aggregates in the mode of inherent non-difference as if mingled or like a core, the fallacies of their being one with the aggregates would ensue. It would [absurdly] follow that a Tathāgata and a person were impermanent, etc. If they possessed the mental and physical aggregates in the mode of inherent difference, the fallacies resulting from a difference of the self and the aggregates would ensue. *Buddhapālita's Commentary on (Nāgārjuna's) Treatise* says:[781]

> A Tathāgata does not possess [his] aggregates in the way that a tree possesses [its] core. Why? He would not be other than the aggregates; therefore, there would be the fallacy of his being impermanent.

Also, Chandrakīrti's *Supplement* says:[782]

> It is not accepted that the self [inherently] possesses the body. For the self [has already been refuted as inherently one with or different from the aggregates and thus] is not [inherently existent]. Therefore, the relationship of the self's possessing the aggregates does not exist [inherently]. If it is said that they are other [entities, like Devadatta's] possessing a cow or that they are not other [entities like Devadatta's] possessing his body, [the answer is that] the self is not one with or other than the body. [Therefore, the self's possessing form does not inherently exist.]

Furthermore, Chandrakīrti's own *Commentary on the 'Supplement'* says:[783]

> Also, the suffix indicating possession [*mat-* or *vat-pratyaya*] is employed for the non-different in *rūpavān devadattaḥ*, 'Devadatta is a possessor of a form [a body].' It is employed for the different in *gomān*, 'Devadatta is a possessor of a cow.' [149] Since form and the self do not

have [naturally existent] sameness or otherness, there is
no saying that the self [inherently] possesses form.

Hence, when these are condensed, they are included within [the reasoning that the self and the aggregates] lack [true] oneness and difference. However, Chandrakīrti's *Clear Words*[784] explains that [five positions instead of just two] are refuted in relation to the modes of operation of the consciousnesses viewing the transitory collection [as real I and mine].

This reasoning is able to prove selflessness with respect to all phenomena since when any of the aggregates, constituents, or sources are analyzed into their basis of imputation and phenomenon imputed, they do not exist in any of those five ways. Therefore, one takes as one's reason that which refutes the object adhered to by artificial conceptions and refutes the innate conception that the phenomenon imputed exists from the side of its basis of imputation. Nāgārjuna's *Precious Garland* says:[785]

> Just as the person is not [established as its own] reality
> Because of being [only designated in dependence upon]
> a composite of the six constituents,
> So each of the constituents also
> Is not [established as its own] reality because of being
> [designated in dependence upon] a composite.

Also: [150]

> The three elements are not [one with] earth.
> The three elements are not [dependent] on this [earth].
> This [earth] is not [dependent] on those [three elements].
> Without those [three elements] there is no earth.
> Like [earth] each [of the other three elements]
> Is not [findable when analyzed in those four ways],
> Therefore the elements also are false like the self.

Also, some Svātantrikas and some of our own schools which propound [inherently existent] things explicitly posit the mind as the self that takes rebirth.[786] Some propound as the self the special configuration [or shape] of the aggregates because gods and humans are posited by way of special configurations of the aggregates due to former actions (*karma, las*). In order to refute these [Chandrakīrti] adds two facets of reasons:

> The mere composite [of the five aggregates or of the consciousness aggregate] is not the self, and the physical shape is not the self.

Chandrakīrti's *Supplement* says:[787]

> A chariot is not accepted as other than its members [or parts]. That it is not other [but is one with its members] is not [established. Inherently] it does not possess its members. It is not [inherently dependent] on its members. Its members are not [inherently dependent] on it. It is not the composite [of its members]. It is not the shape [of its members. The self and the aggregates] are similar. [151]

This sevenfold analysis is also a supreme of reasonings for settling everything—forms and so forth—as selfless. Chandrakīrti's *Supplement* says:[788]

> All things whatsoever—pots, cloths, tents, armies, forests, rosaries, trees, houses, carts, hotels, etc., and likewise [other things] designated by beings from whatsoever point of view—are to be known [as existing only according to unanalytical renown]. For the King of Subduers did not dispute with the world. Quality, part, passion, definition, fuel, and so forth as well as qualificand, whole, the impassioned,[789] illustration,[790] fire, and so forth—these [objects] do not exist in the seven ways when subjected to the analysis of the chariot. They exist through [non-analytical] worldly renown which is other than that.

Also, about this, D̄ak-tsang says [in paraphrase]:[791]

> The Saṃmitīyas and so forth assert that the five aggregates are the basis of the imputation 'self'. Also, Bhāvaviveka and so forth assert that only the mind is the basis

> of the imputation 'self'. However, none of our own schools asserts that the mind *is* the self. [152]

Without even reading any of Bhāvaviveka's and Chandrakīrti's books, Ḍak-tsang has the courage to make distinctions, thereby making an external display of his own ignorant innards. [Contradictory consequences are offered in response.] Then it [absurdly] follows that when another [non-Buddhist] school proves that the mental consciousness is the self, it would not [for Bhāvaviveka] prove what is already established [for him]. Also, it [absurdly] follows that Bhāvaviveka would not assert that the collection of the body and the senses are a basis of the imputation 'self'. For [according to you] (1) Bhāvaviveka does not assert that the mental consciousness is the self and (2) from among the five aggregates, he takes only the mental consciousness as the basis of the imputation 'self'. The three circles of self-contradiction!

If both consequences are accepted, then it [absurdly] follows that it is wrong for [Bhāvaviveka] to explain in his *Blaze of Reasoning* [when another school tries to prove that the mental consciousness is the self] that they are proving what is already established [for him]:[792]

> This is a proof of what is already established [for me] since we also actually impute the term 'self' to [the mental] consciousness conventionally. Because [the mental] consciousness takes rebirth, it is called the self.

It [absurdly] follows that it is wrong [for him] to say, '[we also] actually impute the term "self" to [the mental] consciousness', that is, that the term 'self' is used as an actual name for [the mental] consciousness [because, according to you, he does not assert such]. [153] Also, it [absurdly] follows that it is wrong [for Bhāvaviveka] to prove that [the mental] consciousness is the self through the reason of its being the taker of rebirth [because, according to you, he does not assert such].

Furthermore, it [absurdly] follows that it is wrong [for Bhāvaviveka] in his *Blaze of Reasoning* to explain that the collection of the body and the senses is a basis of the designation 'self' [and thus is the self]:[793]

> Because [the mental] consciousness takes rebirth, it is called the self. It is imputed to the collection of the body and the senses.

Also, it [absurdly] follows that it is wrong [for Bhāvaviveka] to cite as a source for this [a sutra] teaching that the collection of the aggregates is the basis of designation [of the self and thus is the self]:[794]

> It is said, 'Just as one thinks "chariot", for example, with respect to a collection of parts, so in dependence on the aggregates "sentient being" is designated conventionally.'

Also, it [absurdly] follows that, when Chandrakīrti quotes this sutra, he would be refuting that the aggregates are the basis of the imputation 'self' [instead of that the collection of the aggregates is the self since it is clear that he is refuting Bhāvaviveka's interpretation and you claim that Bhāvaviveka interprets the passage as showing that the collection of the aggregates is not the person but is the basis of imputation of the person in which case Chandrakīrti must be refuting this]. Also, [for the same reason] it [absurdly] follows that Chandrakīrti would not assert that the mind and the aggregates are bases of the imputation 'self' [whereas he obviously does]. Also, it [absurdly] follows that the two—Bhāvaviveka and Chandrakīrti—do not differ with respect to asserting or not asserting establishment by way of [the object's] own character (*svalakṣhaṇasiddhi, rang gi mtshan nyid kyis grub pa*) [154] because [according to you] they are the same in not positing the phenomenon imputed as its basis of imputation. Etc. You have a mass of the three circles of self-contradiction!

ELIMINATION OF ERROR CONCERNING THE REFUTATION OF A SELF OF PERSONS

(See pp.449-51, 505-30.) The root text says:[795]

They assert that on some occasions there is valid establishment
With the three modes appearing similarly
And that there are just [similarly appearing] reasons.
However, they do not assert self-powered valid establishment,
Therefore, they do not assert autonomous [syllogisms].
That autonomous [syllogisms are asserted] in this system is mistaken.

Ḏak-tsang's saying that the Prāsaṅgikas assert autonomous syllogisms conventionally is, as was explained before [in chapter eleven which is not translated here],[796] the tremendous mistake of confusing an other-renowned reason and an autonomous reason as the same.[797] For on some occasions when Prāsaṅgikas critically investigate the meaning of the profound [emptiness] among themselves, there is valid establishment, like a magical illusion, with the three modes [of the reason] appearing similarly to both parties in the debate.[798] Also, though the three modes, subject, and reason are established as like illusions and as appearing similarly to both parties in the debate, there is no valid establishment in which the three modes [of the reason] exist under their own power. Also, [Prāsaṅgikas] do not assert that [autonomous syllogisms] exist even conventionally because they assert that inherent establishment does not exist even conventionally.

Appendices

Atīsha

1 *Types of Awareness*

(See Chart 41; the numbers indicate the progression toward a direct non-conceptual cognition of emptiness.)

A cognizing consciousness or valid cognizer not only is correct with respect to its main object but also is an incontrovertible knower.[799] Therefore, a mind such as correct assumption, since it is not incontrovertible, is not a valid cognizer. Because the Prāsaṅgikas do not etymologize the syllable *pra* in *pramāṇa* as meaning 'new', but as either 'main' (*gtso bo*) or 'correct' *yang dag pa*), *pramāṇa* does not refer to a 'prime valid cognizer' in the sense of being new but to a consciousness which is non-deceived with respect to its prime or main object. 'Non-deceived' means that the mind is incontrovertible, and 'main object' refers to the object of the mode of apprehension (*'dzin stangs kyi yul*) of the consciousness. A conceptual consciousness such as when thinking about one's house is mistaken with regard to its appearing object (*snang yul*) in the sense that an image of an object *appears* to be that object, but a correct conceptual consciousness is not mistaken with regard to the main object to which the image refers. Therefore, a conceptual consciousness can be valid, as in the case of an inferential consciousness, which is incontrovertible with respect to its main referent object (*zhen yul*).

Chart 41: *Types of Awareness*

- *awareness*
  - *cognizing consciousness (or valid cognizer)*
    - *direct valid cognizer*
      - sense direct valid cognizer
      - *mental direct valid cognizer*[7]
      - yogic direct valid cognizer[8]
    - *inferential valid cognizer*
      - *inference through the power of the fact*[6]
      - *inference through renown*
      - *inference through example*
      - *inference through scripture*
  - *non-cognizing consciousness (or non-valid consciousness)*
    - *correct assumption*[5]
    - *doubt*
      - *doubt tending toward the fact*[4]
      - *equal doubt*[3]
      - *doubt not tending toward the fact*[2]
    - *wrong consciousness*[1]
    - appearing but not ascertained

Key

Underline indicates that there are non-conceptual consciousnesses of this type.

Italic indicates that there are conceptual consciousnesses of this type.

Numbers indicate the progression toward a direct non-conceptual cognition of emptiness.

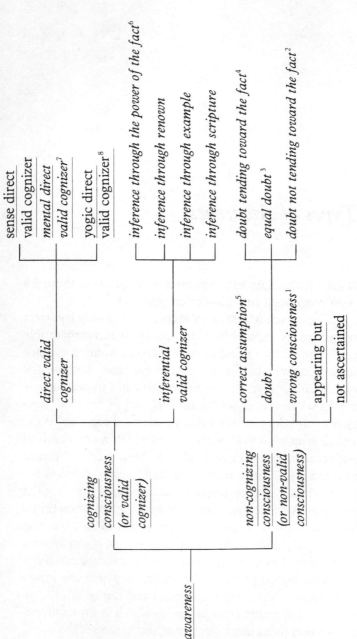

English and Tibetan

awareness—*blo*
cognizing consciousness—*rtogs pa'i blo*
valid cognizer—*tshad ma*
non-cognizing consciousness—*ma rtogs pa'i blo*
non-valid consciousness—*tshad min gyi blo*
direct valid cognizer—*mngon sum gyi tshad ma*
inferential valid cognizer—*rjes dpag gi tshad ma*
wrong consciousness—*log shes*
doubt—*the tshom*
correct assumption—*yid dpyod*
appearing but not ascertained—*snang la ma nges*

sense direct valid cognizer—*dbang po mngon sum gyi tshad ma*
mental direct valid cognizer—*yid kyi mngon sum gyi tshad ma*
yogic direct valid cognizer—*rnal 'byor mngon sum gyi tshad ma*
inference through the power of the fact—*dngos stobs rjes dpag*
inference through renown—*grags pa'i rjes dpag*
inference through example—*dpe nyer 'jal gyi rjes dpag*
inference through scripture—*lung gi rjes dpag*
doubt not tending toward the fact—*don mi gyur gyi the tshom*
equal doubt—*cha mnyam pa'i the tshom*
doubt tending toward the fact—*don gyur gyi the tshom*

A direct valid cognizer (*pratyakṣha-pramāṇa*) is not, for the Prāsaṅgikas, necessarily a non-conceptual consciousness; the word 'direct' merely eliminates dependence on a sign or reason. Therefore, the second moment of an inferential consciousness (*anumāna*) is no longer inferential but direct (*pratyakṣha*) in that it perceives its object (emptiness, for instance) without relying on a sign, such as dependent-arising, but through the force of the previous cognition.

In his progress toward a non-conceptual direct cognition of emptiness a yogi's consciousness of the nature of objects changes radically (see the numbers on Chart 41). First he has a strong sense that objects inherently exist; this is a wrong consciousness. Then, through hearing about emptiness and/or reflecting on its meaning, his conception of inherent existence weakens a little, and he merely suspects that objects inherently exist; this consciousness is doubt not tending toward the fact—he suspects that objects inherently exist. Then, he has doubt not tending and tending toward the fact equally, thinking that objects probably do and do not inherently exist. Then, through study and extended meditation he develops doubt tending toward the fact, thinking that objects probably do not inherently exist, but still he only suspects so. Further hearing, study, and extended meditation on the profound brings him to the point of correct assumption—a conceptual understanding of emptiness which can be generated through the *processes* of inference but is not yet inference because it is not incontrovertible.

Penetrating more and more the reasons for non-inherent existence, he gains a conceptual cognition of emptiness—an inference. An image or concept of the vacuity which is an object's lack of inherent existence appears to him; thus, 'conceptual' does not mean that he is sunk in discursiveness. He has already cognized, for instance, the concomitance of non-inherent existence with whatever cannot be found in the seven ways outlined by Chandrakīrti; he has already cognized the presence of the sign (non-findability in the seven ways) in the subject (I). Therefore, at the moment of inference he no longer is considering the preliminary factors of inference but is realizing emptiness. He attempts to remain in this conceptual cognition as long as possible, developing special insight based on calm abiding, so that he can progress toward his first non-conceptual direct cognition of emptiness in which even the image of the vacuity of concrete findable existence has disappeared, and the subject—the wisdom consciousness—and the object—the emptiness of inherent existence—are like water put in water, undifferentiable.

2 *Other Interpretations of Dependent-Arising*

Asaṅga sets forth Buddha's implicit teaching of the twelve members of a dependent-arising of cyclic existence (see Charts 42 and 43).[800] In the implicit teaching there is only one round of dependent-arising, but this is similar only in name to the one round of the explicit teaching which refers to one turning of the wheel of the twelve. In the implicit teaching, a round or unit does not refer to one cycle of the twelve but to one round of cause and effect. This one round is determined by the time of the effect.

Thus, if all of the effect members—'effect consciousness' through 'existence', as well as 'birth' and 'aging and death'—occur in one lifetime, the set of twelve would involve only one round of cause and effect. However, with this interpretation of the meaning of 'round', the explicit teaching which shows the completion of the members in three lifetimes would indicate two rounds of cause and effect because the projected effects, 'effect consciousness' through 'existence', take place in this life, and the actualized effects, 'birth' and 'aging and death', take place in the next life. Since 'rounds' are not determined by the time of cause, the time of the causes does not affect the computation.

Chart 42: *A Version of Buddha's Implicit Teaching According to Asaṅga* (the completion of the twelve members at the least in two lives with one unit or round of cause and effect)

1		ignorance	
2		action	
3		consciousness	projecting causes: life A
	a.	cause consciousness	
	b.	effect consciousness	
4		name and form	
5		sources	projected effects: life B
6		contact	
7		feeling	
8		attachment	
9		grasping	actualizing causes: life A
10		existence	
11		birth	actualized effects: life B
12		aging and death	

Lives A and B are successive.

Asaṅga's system is a one round system because all of the effect members occur in the present life. It is a two or three life system because the projecting causes and the actualizing causes might occur in the same life, that is, the immediately preceding life, in which case it would take two lives, or the projecting causes might take place before the immediately preceding life in which case it would take three lives.

Even when Asaṅga lays out a two-round system (see Charts 44 and 45, he does not consider a future life as in the explicit teaching. The twelve members are divided into two rounds by considering effect consciousness, name and form, sources, contact, and feeling as seeds in the sense that the projecting causes make them ready for actualization. Therefore, the time of the effect—the formation of the seeds—occurs in the same lifetime as the projecting causes—ignorance, action, and cause consciousness.

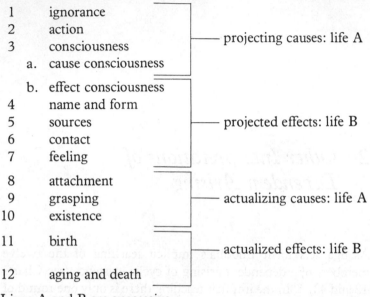

Chart 43: *A Version of Buddha's Implicit Teaching According to Asaṅga* (the completion of the twelve members at the most in three lives with one unit or round of cause and effect)

1	ignorance	projecting causes: life A
2	action	
3	consciousness	
a.	cause consciousness	
b.	effect consciousness	projected effects: life C
4	name and form	
5	sources	
6	contact	
7	feeling	
8	attachment	actualizing causes: life B
9	grasping	
10	existence	
11	birth	actualized effects: life C
12	aging and death	

Life A precedes life B at any time, and life B and life C are successive.

Their actualization by the actualizing causes—attachment, grasping, and existence—is birth and aging and death. Since the time of the actualized effects and the time of the projected effects are not the same when considered this way, the set of twelve here consists of two rounds of cause and effect.

By considering 'effect consciousness' through 'feeling' as seeds ready to be actualized, the two sets of causes for the production of a life—the projecting causes and the actualizing causes—are manifestly seen to apply to one lifetime, without relying on inference as in the explicit teaching. Also, the point is emphasized that there is potential suffering in the form of 'effect consciousness' through 'feeling' as seeds, and actual suffering in the form of 'birth' and 'aging and death'.

There also is a teaching, emphasized by the Sautrāntikas,

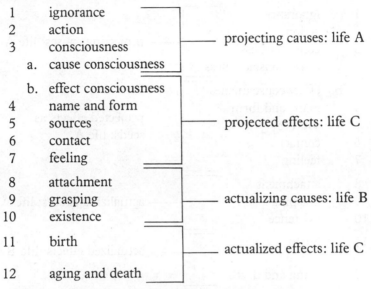

Chart 44: *A Version of Buddha's Implicit Teaching According to Asaṅga* (the completion of the twelve members in at least two lives with two units or rounds of cause and effect)

1	ignorance	projecting causes: life A
2	action	
3	consciousness	
a.	cause consciousness	
b.	effect consciousness	projected effects as seeds: life A
4	name and form	
5	sources	
6	contact	
7	feeling	
8	attachment	actualizing causes: life A
9	grasping	
10	existence	
11	birth	actualized effects: life B
12	aging and death	

Lives A and B are successive.

that the twelve members occur simultaneously. This does not mean that all members occur in the same instant, but in the period of one action. Here, ignorance forms the motivation of the action with the aid of grasping, attachment, and existence. Action is the actual production of the activity with 'effect consciousness' through 'feeling' as well as 'birth' and 'aging and death' being further delineations of this action. In this interpretation the order of the twelve does not have reference to temporal sequence.

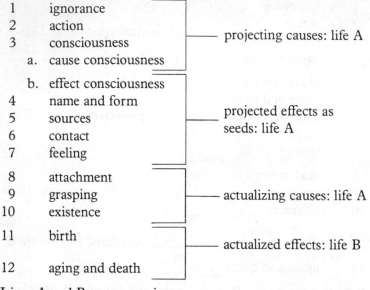

Chart 45: *A Version of Buddha's Implicit Teaching According to Asaṅga* (the completion of the twelve members at the most in three lives with two units or rounds of cause and effect)

1	ignorance	projecting causes: life A
2	action	
3	consciousness	
	a. cause consciousness	
	b. effect consciousness	projected effects as seeds: life A
4	name and form	
5	sources	
6	contact	
7	feeling	
8	attachment	actualizing causes: life B
9	grasping	
10	existence	
11	birth	actualized effects: life C
12	aging and death	

Life A precedes life B at any time, and life B and life C are successive.

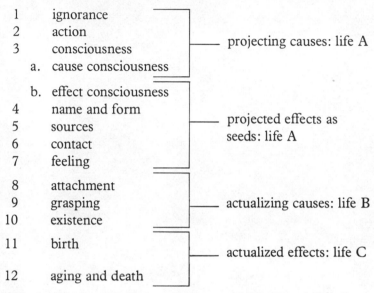

3 *Modes of Division of the Vaibhāṣhika Schools*

Bhāvaviveka's three versions of the division of the spiritual community into eighteen schools are preserved in the Tibetan translation of his *Blaze of Reasoning* (P5256, Vol. 96 66.4.4-68.4.4). Exactly the same material is also preserved in the Tibetan translation of his *Nikāyabhedavibhaṅgavyākhyāna* (P5640, Vol. 127).

Bhāvaviveka's first rendition

(See Chart 46.) The first schism is variously reported to have taken place in 600 A.N. (After the Nirvana), 160 A.N., and 116 A.N.[801] The last accords with Paramārtha's description of the schism,[802] and Jam-ȳang-shay-b̄a says that 116 A.N. is correct.[803] Paramārtha adds the information that at the Council of Rājagṛha, held two months after the death of the Buddha, the Saṃgha was nominally split into Sthaviras and Mahāsaṃghikas, the former being the five hundred Foe Destroyers and the latter being ordinary monks. Later at the second Council in 116 A.N. the division became doctrinal. Both Tāranātha[804] and Jam-ȳang-shay-b̄a indicate that Bhāvaviveka's first list is the assertion of the Sthaviras with regard to the way the Saṃgha divided.

Chart 46: *Bhāvaviveka's First Rendition of the Eighteen Vaibhāṣhika Schools* (as found in his *Blaze of Reasoning,* Vol. 96 66.4.4ff)

Mahāsaṃghikas	1	Mahāsaṃghikas (*dGe 'dun phal chen pa*)
	2	Ekavyavahārikas (*Tha snyad gcig pa*)
	3	Lokottaravādins (*'Jig rten 'das par smra ba*)
	4	Bahushrutīyas (*Mang thos pa*)
	5	Prajñaptivādins (*bTags par smra ba*)
	6	Chaitikas (*mChod rten pa*)
	7	Pūrvashailas (*Shar gyi ri bo pa*)
	8	Aparashailas (*Nub kyi ri bo pa*)
Sthaviras	9	Sthaviras (*gNas brtan pa*) = Haimavatas
	10	Sarvāstivādins (*Thams cad yod par smra ba*) = Vibhajyavādins = Hetuvādins = Muruntakas
	11	Vatsīputrīyas (*gNas ma'i bu pa*)
	12	Dharmottaras (*Chos mchog pa*)
	13	Bhadrayānīyas (*bZang lam pa*)
	14	Saṃmitīyas (*Mang bkur ba*) = Avantakas = Kurukullas
	15	Mahāshāsakas (*Mang ston pa*)
	16	Dharmaguptakas (*Chos sbas pa*)
	17	Suvarṣhakas (*Char bzang 'bebs pa*) = Kāshyapīyas
	18	Uttarīyas (*bLa ma pa*) = Saṃkrāntivādins

It should be noted that the synonyms which Bhāvaviveka gives are synonyms only with respect to this table. For instance, in his first list the Sthaviras and Haimavatas are synonyms, but in his second the Haimavatas are a sect which split off from the Mahāsaṃghikas who are neither synonymous with, nor a division of, nor the parent of the Sthaviras.

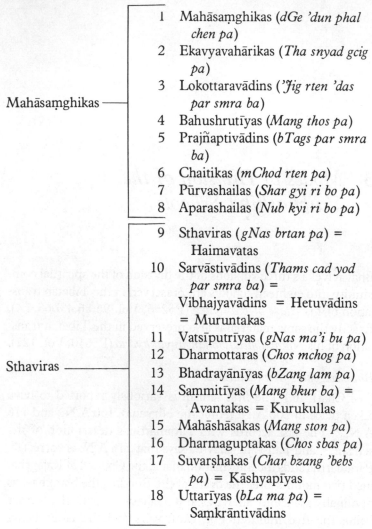

Chart 47: *Bhāvaviveka's Second Rendition of the Eighteen Vaibhāṣhika Schools* (as found in his *Blaze of Reasoning*, Vol. 96 67.2.1ff)

- Sthaviras
  - Sarvāstivādins
    - 1 Sarvāstivādins
    - 2 Sūtravādins (*mDo sde smra ba*)
  - Vatsīputrīyas
    - 3 Saṃmitīyas
    - 4 Dharmottaras
    - 5 Bhadrayānīyas
    - 6 Saṇṇagarikas (*Grong khyer drug pa*)
- Mahāsaṃghikas
  - 7 Mahāsaṃghikas
  - 8 Pūrvashailas
  - 9 Aparashailas
  - 10 Rājagirikas (*rGyal po'i ri*)
  - 11 Haimavatas (*Gangs ri pa*)
  - 12 Chaitikas
  - 13 Siddhārthikas (*Don grub pa*)
  - 14 Gokulikas (*Ba lang gnas pa*)
- Vibhajyavādins
  - 15 Mahīshāsakas (*Sa ston pa*)
  - 16 Kāshyapīyas (*'Od srungs pa*)
  - 17 Dharmaguptakas
  - 18 Tāmrashāṭīyas (*Gos dmar ba*)

Bhāvaviveka's second rendition

Bhāvaviveka says that the second list (see Chart 47) has the same 'foundation' as the first list. Jam-ȳang-shay-b̄a[805] explains that this means that the time and place of the original schism are the

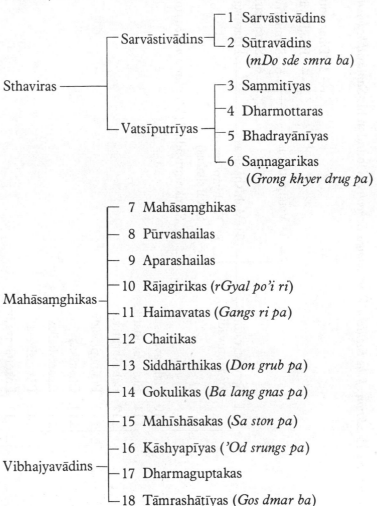

Chart 48: *Vasumitra's Rendition of the Eighteen Vaibhāṣhika Schools* (as found in his *Samayabhedoparachanachakra*, P5639, Vol. 127)

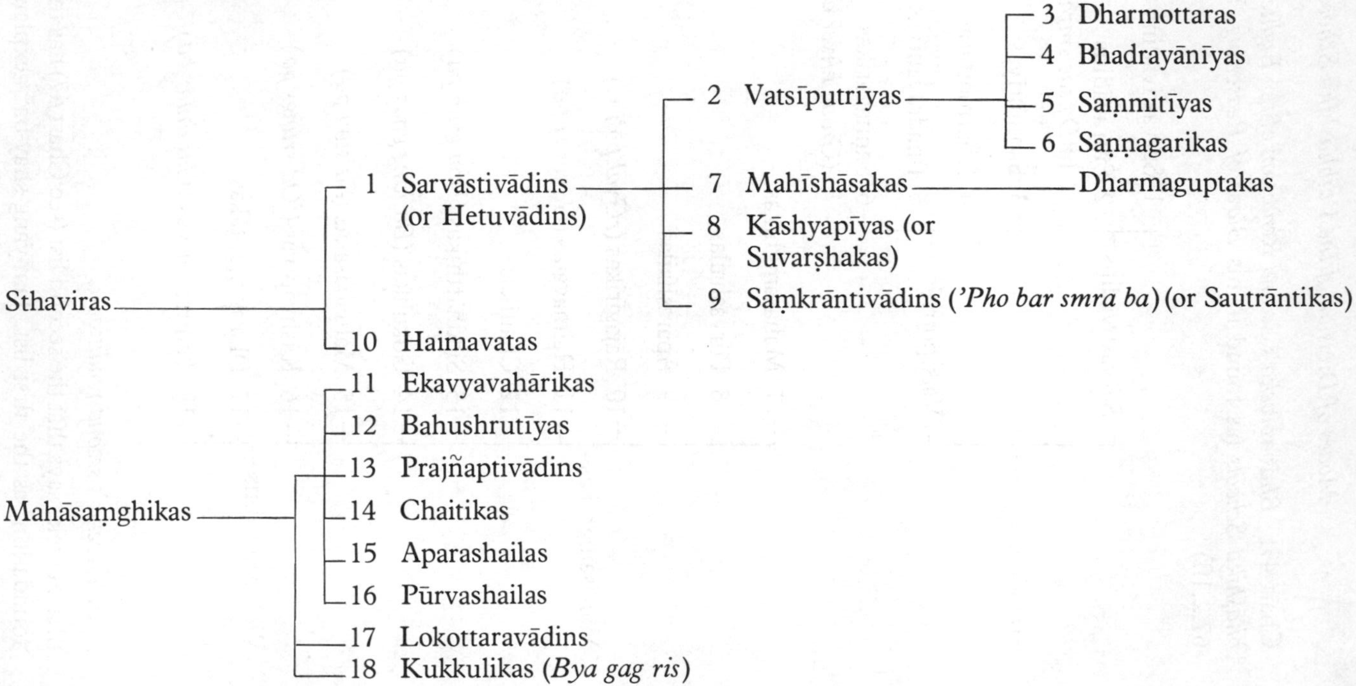

Chart 49: *Vinītadeva's Rendition of the Eighteen Vaibhāṣhika Schools* (as found in his *Samayabhedoparachanachakre nikāya-bhedopadeshanasaṃgraha*, P5641, Vol. 127)

Mahāsaṃghikas	*Sarvāstivādins*
1 Pūrvashailas	6 Sarvāstivādins
2 Aparashailas	7 Kāshyapīyas
3 Haimavatas	8 Mahīshāsakas
4 Lokottaravādins	9 Dharmaguptakas
5 Prajñaptivādins	10 Bahushrutīyas
	11 Tāmrashāṭīyas
	12 Vibhajyavādins (*rNam par phye ste smra ba*)

Sthaviras	*Saṃmitīyas*
13 Jetavanīyas (*rGyal byed tshal gnas*)	16 Kurukullas (*Sa sgrogs ris*)
14 Abhayagirikas (*'Jigs med gnas*)	17 Avantakas (*Srung ba pa*)
15 Mahāvihārins (*gTsug lag khang chen*)	18 Vatsīputrīyas

same as in the first list. This is significant in that it indicates that the schism which took place at the second Council in 116 A.N. was a schism into three schools. Both Tāranātha[806] and Jam-ȳang-shay-b̄a say that this second list is the assertion of the Mahāsaṃghikas with regard to the way the Saṃgha divided.

Bhāvaviveka's third rendition

Jam-ȳang-shay-b̄a identifies Bhāvaviveka's third list (see Chart 40, p.340) as the assertion of the Saṃmitīyas. Bhāvaviveka reports that some say that the Saṇṇagarikas are a division of the Mahāgirikas and that others assert that they are a division of the Saṃmitīyas.[807]

Chart 50: *Padmasaṃbhava's Rendition of the Eighteen Vaibhāṣhika Schools* (as reported by Jam-yang-shay-ba, *GT*, kha 6a.7)

Sarvāstivādins	*Mahāsaṃghikas*
1 Kāshyapīyas	5 Pūrvashailas
2 Mahīshāsakas	6 Aparashailas
3 Dharmaguptakas	7 Haimavatas
4 Mūlasarvāstivādins	8 Vibhajyavādins
	9 Prajñaptivādins
	10 Lokottaravādins

Saṃmitīyas	*Sthaviras*
11 Tāmrāshaṭīyas	16 Jetavanīyas
12 Avantakas	17 Abhayagirikas
13 Kurukullas	18 Mahāvihārins
14 Bahushrutīyas	
15 Vatsīputrīyas	

Shākyaprabha's rendition

Jam-yang-shay-ba reports that Shākyaprabha conceived all of the sub-schools to be derived from the Sarvāstivādins.[808]

Vasumitra's and Vinītadeva's renditions

Vinītadeva says that he based his list on Vasumitra's rendition (see Charts 48 and 49) and that it represents the Sarvāstivādins' assertion. The evident disagreement between the two lists suggests that Vasumitra had another rendition which has not survived.

Padmasaṃbhava's rendition

Padmasaṃbhava's version (see Chart 50) is based on the *Bhikṣhuvarṣhāgrapṛchchhāsūtra* (P5649, Vol. 127).

The Ceylonese Chronicles

The renditions of the Ceylonese Chronicles (see Chart 51) have been Sanskritized for the sake of consistency.[809]

Chart 51: *The Rendition of the Eighteen Vaibhāṣhika Schools according to the 'Dīpavaṃsa' and 'Mahāvaṃsa'*

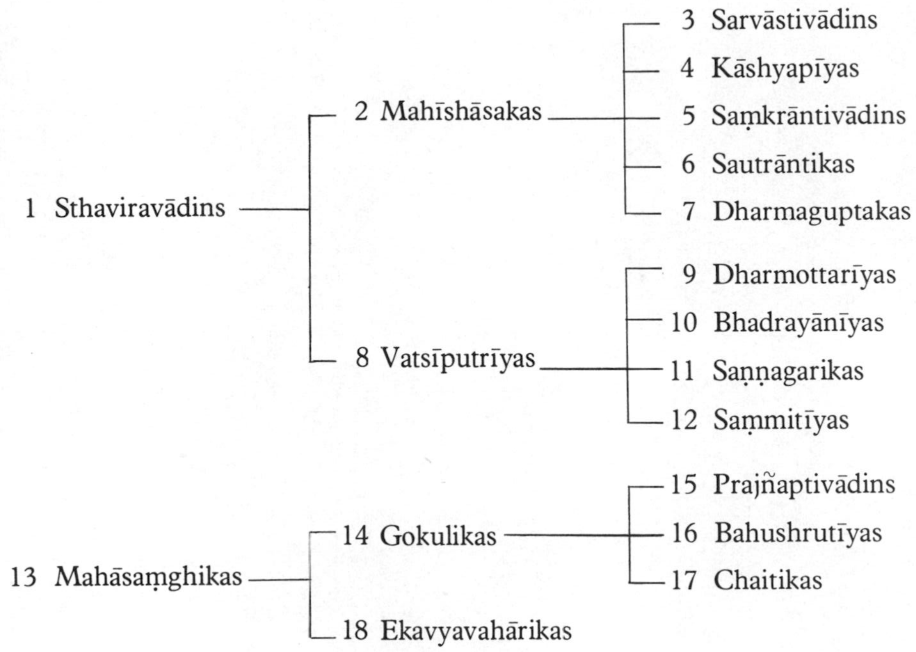

4 *Negatives*

Phenomena (*dharma, chos*) are divided into positive phenomena (*vidhi, sgrub pa*) and negative phenomena (*pratiṣhedha, dgag pa*).[810] It is important to note that the basis of division is phenomena and not statements, propositions, and acts of logic, and thus this is not a division of propositions and so forth into positive and negative statements, or logical affirmations and negations. Rather, this is a division of objects, or existents, into those that are positive and those that are negative. Since the divisions are exhaustive, anything that exists is either a positive or a negative phenomenon; there is no third category. Also, every instance of a positive or negative phenomenon is an existent.

Following is a table of synonyms of 'existent' with their respective definitions:

1 existent: something observed by valid cognition
2 established base: something established by valid cognition
3 object of knowledge: something fit to be taken as an object of an awareness
4 phenomenon: something holding its own entity
5 object of comprehension: something realized by valid cognition

6 object: something known by an awareness
7 object of comprehension by an omniscient consciousness: something realized by an omniscient consciousness.

That the above are synonyms means that whatever is a negative or a positive phenomenon is necessarily an existent, an established base, an object of knowledge, a phenomenon, an object of comprehension, an object, and an object of comprehension by an omniscient consciousness as well as something observed by valid cognition, etc. Hence, the mere fact that an emptiness is a negative means that it is an existent, an object, and so forth.

A positive phenomenon is defined as:

> a phenomenon which is not an object realized by the thought consciousness apprehending it in the manner of an explicit elimination of its object of negation.

First of all, a positive thing (*vidhi*) is a phenomenon, an existent; a non-existent such as the horns of a rabbit could never be a positive phenomenon. Second, the division into positive and negative phenomena is made by way of how objects appear to thought or conceptual consciousnesses; if a conceptual consciousness must realize the object by way of openly and explicitly eliminating an object of negation, the object is not positive but negative. For instance, to realize non-cow, cow must be openly eliminated, but to realize cow, non-cow does not have to be *explicitly* eliminated though indeed it is *implicitly* eliminated. Thus, non-cow is a negative phenomenon, and cow is a positive phenomenon.

The definition of a negative phenomenon is:

> an object realized by the thought consciousness apprehending it in the manner of an explicit elimination of its object of negation.

Again, a negative must be an object, an existent, a phenomenon. It is also something that must be conceptually realized through the open or explicit negation of an object of negation. Examples of negative phenomena are non-pot, (*bum pa ma yin pa*), non-non-pot (*bum pa ma yin pa ma yin pa*), opposite from non-pot (*bum pa ma yin pa las log pa*), and non-existence of pot (*bum pa med pa*). Although non-non-pot means just pot, it must be realized by way of explicitly eliminating non-pot, and thus it is a negative phenomenon. Although it does not exist as a different entity from pot, which is a positive phenomenon, it is merely different from pot and is a negative.

Negatives are divided into two types—affirming negatives (*paryudāsapratiṣhedha, ma yin dgag*) and non-affirming negatives (*prasajyapratiṣhedha, med dgag*). In brief, the difference between the two is that the term which expresses an affirming negative suggests something else in place of its negation, whereas the term that expresses a non-affirming negative does not. For instance, the sentence, 'The fat Devadatta does not eat during the day,' expresses a phenomenon, namely, fat Devadatta's not eating during the day, but it does not merely eliminate eating during the day since the mention of 'fat' implies or suggests that he eats at night. Thus, fat Devadatta's not eating during the day is an affirming negative; it is an object, an existent, a phenomenon, and an object of knowledge that is negative, but the expression of it implies something in place of what it negates. Though the determination that it is a negative depends on how it is expressed, it is the phenomenon itself that is thereby determined to be a negative. For, the sentence, 'The fat Devadatta does not eat during the day,' is itself, as a sentence or group of sounds, a positive phenomenon. Thus, it is not the proposition, but the object of reference of the proposition that is the negative.

The formal definition of an affirming negative is:

> a negative which is such that the term expressing it suggests in place of the negation of its own object of negation another, positive phenomenon which is its own object of suggestion.

In the example of fat Devadatta's not eating during the day, eating at night, a positive phenomenon, is suggested. Another example of an affirming negative is non-non-pot, which suggests pot. Another is non-pot, which suggests things that are not pots.

Affirming negatives are further divided into four types depending on how the terms that express them suggest positive phenomena in place of their negations—either explicitly, implicitly, both, or by context. These four are:

1 *Affirming negative which is such that the term expressing it explicitly suggests another, positive phenomenon which is its own object of suggestion*

For example, a mountainless plain is expressed by the term 'mountainless plain'. The term eliminates mountains but openly speaks of a plain; thus, a mountainless plain is an affirming negative which explicitly suggests or reveals a positive phenomenon. The same is true of the existence of the absence of inherent existence, for the term expressing it, 'The absence of inherent existence exists', or 'existence of the absence of inherent existence' eliminates inherent existence but openly speaks of the *existence* of its absence, a positive phenomenon. Thus, though the absence of inherent existence is a non-affirming negative, its *existence* is an affirming negative of the explicitly suggestive variety. Since meditation on an emptiness means to meditate on a specific non-affirming negative, the object of meditation is not the *existence* of an emptiness (although it does exist) but an emptiness itself.

2 *Affirming negative which is such that the term expressing it implicitly suggests another, positive phenomenon which is its own object of suggestion*

For example, fat Devadatta's not eating during the day. Also, since non-non-pot eliminates non-pot but does not *explicitly* suggest pot, it is an affirming negative of the implicitly suggestive type.

3 *Affirming negative which is such that the term expressing it both explicitly and implicitly suggests another, positive phenomenon which is its own object of suggestion*

For example, the phrase, 'The existence of the non-emaciated body of the fat Devadatta who does not eat during the day,' eliminates eating during the day, implicitly suggests eating during the night, and explicitly speaks of the existence of his body. Thus, the phenomenon which it expresses is an affirming negative the suggestiveness of which is both implicit and explicit.

4 *Affirming negative which is such that the term expressing it suggests by context another, positive phenomenon which is its own object of suggestion*

For example, in the context of knowing that King Siddhārtha is either of the royal or brahmin class, his not being of the brahmin class eliminates that he is of the brahmin class and, through the context of one's having determined that his lineage is either the royal or brahmin class, suggests that he is of the royal class.

In all four of these cases, something is suggested in place of the negation of the object of negation. However, with a non-affirming negative nothing positive is suggested—only an object of negation is negated. Nevertheless, a non-affirming negative is an object, an existent, a phenomenon, and so on.

Thus the definition of a non-affirming negative is:

> a negative which is such that the term expressing it does not suggest in place of the negation of its own object of negation another, positive phenomenon which is its own object of suggestion.

For example, the non-existence of the horns of a rabbit is expressed by the sentence, 'The horns of a rabbit do not exist,' and this does not suggest anything positive in place of the horns of a rabbit. Though it can suggest another non-affirming negative such as the non-existence of the beauty of the horns of a rabbit, it does not suggest any positive phenomenon in place of its object of negation.

In this same vein, an emptiness merely eliminates inherent existence; it does not imply anything positive in its place. Though emptiness is compatible with conventional existence, it does not suggest conventional existence in place of its object of negation; still, it is stressed that a proper *understanding* of emptiness acts to assist an understanding of conventional existence. An emptiness is the mere elimination of inherent or objective existence and thus is a mere negative, a non-affirming negative, a mere absence of its object of negation.

Even the emptiness of inherent existence of a table does not suggest a positive phenomenon even though the phrase 'the emptiness of inherent existence of a table', or the sentence, 'A table is empty of inherent existence,' openly and explicitly speaks of table. For, table is not suggested in place of the negated object of negation, inherent existence; it merely is the base of the negation.

Non-affirming negatives are divided into two classes—those whose object of negation does occur among objects of knowledge and those whose object of negation does not occur among objects of knowledge. For example, the non-existence of the horns of a rabbit negates the horns of a rabbit which do not exist anywhere, and similarly the absence of inherent existence eliminates inherent existence which never has nor will occur anywhere. Thus, these two are non-affirming negatives whose object of negation does not occur among objects of knowledge, that is to say, among existents. On the other hand, the non-existence of a pot, such as on a certain table, eliminates the existence of a pot there, but pot does occur among existents at some other place, and thus non-existence of a pot is a non-affirming negative whose object of negation does occur among objects of knowledge.

Through making this division in terms of whether the object negated is, in general, an existent or not, it is being stressed that an emptiness is a lack of something—inherent existence—that never did nor will exist. Though an emptiness exists, its object of negation never does. Realization of an emptiness, therefore, is not a case of destroying something that once existed or of realizing the passing away of something that did exist; rather, it means to realize a quality of objects, a negative attribute, that is the mere absence of something that never existed but nevertheless was imagined to occur.

The existence of an object right in its own basis of designation never did or could occur, but beings conceive the opposite and thus have been drawn beginninglessly into cyclic existence. Extrication from that misconception can happen only through realizing the absence of such reified existence, becoming accustomed to it in intense meditation, realizing it directly in meditative equipoise in which nothing but emptiness appears and the mind is merged with it like fresh water poured into fresh water, and over and over again re-entering that direct cognition. Meditation on emptiness is the medicine that, when accompanied by compassionate method, can clear away all obstructions such that unimpeded altruistic activity is manifested. Thus, though emptiness is a mere negative, it is a doctrine neither of nihilism nor of agnosticism, but a confident affirmation of a basic nature, the realization of which yields powerful, beneficial results.

Thu-mi-sam-bho-ta

5 *Proof Statements*

Chandrakīrti gives an example of a five-membered proof which Jam-ȳang-shay-b̄a says can be interpreted correctly in two ways:[811]

1 *Thesis:* A sound is an impermanent thing.
2 *Pervasion:* Being an impermanent thing pervades being a product.
3 *Example:* Being an impermanent thing pervades being a product, as in the case, for example, of a pot.
4 *Exemplification:* Just as a pot is a product, so a sound is a product.
5 *Summary:* Therefore, because a sound is a product, it is an impermanent thing.

Or,

1 *Thesis:* A sound is an impermanent thing.
2 *Sign:* Because products are impermanent things.
3 *Demonstration of the pervasion in an example:* It is seen that being an impermanent thing pervades being a product as in the case, for example, of a pot.
4 *Applying the example to the meaning:* Like a pot, a sound is also a product.

5 *Summary:* Therefore, because of being a product, a sound is an impermanent thing.

The Buddhist logicians of the Dignāga-Dharmakīrti school consider such a five-membered statement of proof to be redundant. In their school a correct statement of proof has two members:

1 *Expression of pervasion:* Being an impermanent thing pervades whatever is a product, as in the case, for example, of a pot.
2 *Expression of the presence of the sign in the subject:* A sound is also a product.

The example has been affixed to the expression of pervasion; the thesis, exemplification, and summary are not stated because they are considered to be implicit. The five-membered statement is, therefore, redundant.

However, in the Dignāga-Dharmakīrti school the actual, full process of debate is as follows for proving that a sound is impermanent to an opponent who asserts that a sound is permanent.

1 *Statement of a consequence implying a proof of the opposite*

It follows that the subject, a sound, is not a product because of being a permanent thing.

The consequence is stated for the sake of 'breaking down the pointedness or vibrance' of the opponent's adherence to the wrong view. Through the demonstration of inner contradictions in his own system (that a sound is permanent, that a sound is a product, and that whatever is a product is impermanent) he becomes doubtful about his own view. This prepares him for the statement of the reasoning which proves that sounds are impermanent; he becomes a suitable vessel for the second step.

2 *Statement of the reasonings that establish the presence of the sign in the subject, the pervasion, and the counter-pervasion*

a. *Statement of the reasoning that establishes the presence of the sign in the subject*

The subject, a sound, is a product because of being produced from causes and conditions.

The reason of this syllogism need not be established because it is obvious from, for instance, a snapping of the fingers that sounds are produced from causes and conditions. If it were necessary to establish every reason—if there were not an appeal to obvious experience—the number of reasons required to establish the presence of the original sign in the subject would be limitless, and there would be no opportunity to realize the basic thesis. Still, if the opponent is not yet satisfied, it is not the proper occasion for establishing the three modes of the sign, i.e., for proving to him that sounds are impermanent. Other indirect means are required to bring him to the point of recognizing the obvious dependence of sounds on causes and conditions.

b. *Statement of the reasoning that establishes the pervasion*

> The subject, a product, is an impermanent thing because of being a momentary thing.

The mind that explicitly realizes the pervasion also implicitly realizes the counter-pervasion and vice versa; therefore, only either the pervasion or the counter-pervasion needs to be established. This is because explicitly realizing that the sign exists in only similar cases implies cognition that the sign is only non-existent in dissimilar cases. Just so, if the sign is explicitly cognized as only non-existent in dissimilar cases, it is implicitly cognized as existent only in similar cases.

If it is necessary to establish that products are momentary things, one can state:

> The subject, a product, is a momentary thing because without its disintegration depending on any other cause, it—from its inception—has a nature of disintegration, just as in the case of lightning.

If this is not obvious, further proof is not warranted, and it will be necessary to approach the opponent in a roundabout manner to prepare him for another try at the basic thesis.

c. *Statement of the reasoning that establishes the counter-pervasion*

> The subject, space, is not a product because of being a permanent phenomenon.

This reason could, in turn, be established with:

> The subject, space, is a permanent phenomenon because of being existent and not being produced from causes and conditions.

No further proof is warranted.

3 *Correct statement of proof for similar instances*

> Whatever is a product is pervaded by being an impermanent thing, as in the case, for example, of a pot; a sound is also a product.

(This is exactly the same as the two-membered statement of proof.) A person of very sharp intellect would also grasp the opposite, and, therefore, for him the next step would not have to be stated. Or, the fourth step might be stated and not the third. The choice of whether to state a proof for similar or dissimilar instances is determined by the type of opponent. If he is dominated by indecision, not being able to decide whether products are permanent or impermanent, a proof for similar instances is stated. If the opponent is dominated by the opposite view that products are permanent, a proof for dissimilar instances is stated. However, to all except the very sharp, both must be proved. The stater bases his decision of what is necessary on the opponent's responses during step two and to questions asked him.

4 *Correct statement of proof for dissimilar instances*

> Whatever is a permanent thing is pervaded by being a non-product, as in the case, for example, of space; a sound, however, is a product.

5 *Restatement of the correct statement of proof for either similar or dissimilar instances*

This is done for the sake of generating in the opponent a simultaneous awareness of the three modes of the reason, i.e., its presence in the subject, the pervasion, and the counter-pervasion. This awareness is also called 'a mind apprehending the sign (or reason)' and is the direct cause of the inferring consciousness realizing that a sound is impermanent. At this moment the opponent becomes a correct, or full-fledged, second party of a debate in that he is prepared for the basic reasoning that a sound is an impermanent thing because of being a product. (The first party is the stater.)

6 *The statement of the basic syllogism*

> The subject, a sound, is an impermanent thing because of being a product.

The then full-fledged second party realizes that a sound is impermanent, after which he ceases to be a second party because he has finished realizing the thesis.

Thus, though a statement of proof in the Dignāga-Dharmakīrti school has only two members, the actual prescribed mode of debate entails many more. What a Prāsaṅgika is saying is that all these steps are not necessary for sharp opponents. The mere statement of a consequence, 'It follows that the subject, a sound, is not a product because of being a permanent phenomenon,' can generate in a proper second party a consciousness inferring the thesis that a sound is an impermanent thing. It is not the usage of consequences that singles out the Prāsaṅgika but his assertion that the statement of a consequence alone is sufficient to generate in another a consciousness realizing a thesis.

Glossary

An asterisk beside an entry indicates a reconstruction of the Sanskrit

Glossary

English	*Sanskrit*	*Tibetan*
able to set itself up	—	tshugs thub tu grub pa
absorption	samāpatti	snyoms 'jug
action	karma	las
Action Tantra	kriyātantra	bya rgyud
affirming negation/ affirming negative	paryudāsaprati-ṣhedha	ma yin dgag
afflicted mind	kliṣhṭamanas	nyon yid
affliction	klesha	nyon mongs
afflictive obstruction	kleshāvaraṇa	nyon sgrib
aggregate	skandha	phung po
analysis	vichāra	dpyod pa
analytical cessation	pratisaṃkhyāni-rodha	so sor brtags 'gog
analytical meditation	—	dpyad sgom
anger	pratigha	khong khro
application	abhisaṃskāra	'du byed pa
artificial	parikalpita	kun btags
aspiration	chhanda	'dun pa

English	*Sanskrit*	*Tibetan*
autonomous inference	svatantrānumāna	rang rgyud kyi rjes dpag
autonomous syllogism	svatantraprayoga	rang rgyud kyi sbyor ba
basis-of-all	ālaya	kun gzhi
basis of designation	—	gdags gzhi
belief	adhimokṣha	mos pa
belligerence	krodha	khro ba
bliss	sukha	bde ba
Blissful Pure Land	sukhāvatī	dbe ba can
Bodhisattva	bodhisattva	byang chub sems dpa'
body consciousness	kāyavijñāna	lus kyi rnam par shes pa
body sense	kāyendriya	lus kyi dbang po
calm abiding	shamatha	zhi gnas
cause	hetu	rgyu
changeable factor	aniyata	gzhan 'gyur
Chittamātra	chittamātra	sems tsam
clairvoyance	abhijñā	mngon par shes pa
close setting	upasthāpanā	nye bar 'jog pa
coarse selflessness	—	bdag med rags pa
color	varṇa	kha dog
common being	pṛthagjana	so so skye bo
compassion	karuṇā	snying rje
Complete Enjoyment Body	saṃbhogakāya	longs spyod rdzogs pa'i sku
compositional factor	saṃskāra	'du byed
concealment	mrakṣha	'chab pa
concentration	dhyāna	bsam gtan
conception of self	ātmagrāha	bdag tu 'dzin pa

English	*Sanskrit*	*Tibetan*
condition	pratyaya	rkyen
conditionality	idaṃpratyayatā	rkyen 'di pa tsam nyid
Conqueror	jina	rgyal ba
conscientiousness	apramāda	bag yod pa
consciousness	jñā/vijñāna	shes pa/rnam shes
consequence	prasaṅga	thal 'gyur
constituent	dhātu	khams
contact	sparsha	reg pa
contaminated	sāsrava	zag bcas
contaminated action	sāsravakarma	zag bcas kyi las
contamination	āsrava	zag pa
continuous setting	saṃstāpanā	rgyun du 'jog pa
continuum	saṃtāna	rgyun/gyud
contradictory consequence	—	'gal brjod thal 'gyur
contrition	kaukṛtya	'gyod pa
conventional existence	saṃvṛtisat	kun rdzob tu yod pa
conventional truth/ truth-for-a-concealer/ obscured truth	saṃvṛtisatya	kun rdzob bden pa
cooperative condition	sahakāripratyaya	lhan cig byed rkyen
correct view	samyakdṛṣhṭi	yang dag pa'i lta ba
counter-pervasion	vyatirekavyāpti	ldog khyab
creature/being/ person	puruṣha	skyes bu
cyclic existence	saṃsāra	'khor ba
deceit	māyā	sgyu
deed	karma	las
definitive	nītārtha	nges don

English	*Sanskrit*	*Tibetan*
deity yoga	*devayoga	lha'i rnal 'byor
dependent-arising	pratītyasamutpāda	rten 'byung
dependent phenomenon	paratantra	gzhan dbang
desire	rāga	'dod chags
desire realm	kāmadhātu	'dod khams
determining factor	viniyata	yul nges
direct cognition	—	mngon sum du rtogs pa
direct perception/ direct perceiver	pratyakṣha	mngon sum
discipline	vinaya	'dul ba
disciplining	damana	dul ba byed pa
discrimination	saṃjñā	'du shes
dissimulation	shāṭhya	g.yo
distraction	vikṣhepa	rnam par g.yeng ba
doubt	vichikitsā	the tshom
ear consciousness	shrotravijñāna	rna ba'i rnam par shes pa
ear sense	shrotrendriya	rna ba'i dbang po
effort	vīrya	brtson 'grus
elaborations	prapañcha	spros pa
element of [superior] qualities	dharmadhātu	chos dbyings
Emanation Body	nirmāṇakāya	sprul sku
embarrassment	apatrāpya	khrel yod pa
emptiness	shūnyatā	stong pa nyid
Enjoyment Body	saṃbhogakāya	longs sku
enlightenment	bodhi	byang chub
equanimity	upekṣhā	btang snyoms
established atomically	—	rdul tu grub pa
excitement	auddhatya	rgod pa

English	*Sanskrit*	*Tibetan*
exertion	vyāyāma	rtsol ba
existence able to set itself up	—	tshugs thub tu grub pa
existence as [its own] reality	*samyaksiddhi	yang dag par grub pa
existence as [its own] suchness	*tattvasiddhi	de kho na nyid du grub pa
existence by way of its own character	svalakṣhaṇasiddhi	rang gi mtshan nyid kyis grub pa
existence from the object's side	*svarūpasiddhi	rang ngos nas grub pa
existence from the side of the basis of designation	—	gdags gzhi'i ngos nas grub pa
existence in the manner of covering its basis of designation	—	gdags gzhi'i go sa gnon pa'i tshul du yod pa
existence in the object designated	—	btags yul gyi steng nas grub pa
existence right in the basis of designation	—	gdags gzhi'i steng nas grub pa
existence through its own entityness/ inherent existence	*svabhāvatāsiddhi	ngo bo nyid kyis grub pa
existence through its own power	*svairīsiddhi	rang dbang du grub pa
existent	sat	yod pa
existent base	*vastu	gzhi grub
existing in reliance/ relative existence	apekṣhyasamutpāda	ltos nas grub pa
extreme	anta	mtha'
extreme of annihilation	uchchhedānta	chad mtha'

English	*Sanskrit*	*Tibetan*
extreme of permanence	shashvatānta	rtag mtha'
eye consciousness	chakṣhurvijñāna	mig gi rnam shes
eye-constituent	chakṣhurdhātu	mig gi khams
eye-source	chakṣhurāyatana	mig gi skye mched
faith	shraddhā	dad pa
familiarity	parichaya	yongs su 'dris pa
feeling	vedanā	tshor ba
Foe Destroyer	arhan	dgra bcom pa
forbearance	kṣhānti	bzod pa
forcibly engaging	balavāhana	sgrim ste 'jug pa
Forder	tīrthika	mu stegs pa
forgetfulness	muṣhitasmṛtitā	brjed nges pa
forgetting the advice	avavādasammoṣha	gdams ngag brjed pa
form	rūpa	gzugs
Form Body	rūpakāya	gzugs sku
form-constituent	rūpadhātu	gzugs kyi khams
form for the mental consciousness	dharmāyatanarūpa	chos kyi skye mched pa'i gzugs
Form Realm	rūpadhātu	gzugs khams
form source	rūpāyatana	gzugs kyi skye mched
Formless Realm	ārūpyadhātu	gzugs med khams
fruit	phala	'bras bu
fruition consciousness	vipakavijñāna	rnam smin rnam shes
generally characterized phenomenon	sāmānyalakṣhaṇa	spyi mtshan

English	*Sanskrit*	*Tibetan*
generic object/ generic image/ meaning-generality	arthasāmānya	don spyi
giving	dāna	sbyin pa
great compassion	mahākaruṇā	snying rje chen po
ground	bhūmi	sa
harmfulness	vihiṃsā	rnam par 'tshe ba
haughtiness	mada	rgyags pa
Hearer	shrāvaka	nyan thos
hearing	shruta	thos pa
heat	uṣhmagata	drod
Hedonist	chārvāka	tshu rol mdzes pa
Highest Pure Land	akaniṣhṭa	'og min
Highest Yoga Tantra	anuttarayogatantra	bla med kyi rgyud
I	ahaṃ	nga
ignorance	avidyā	ma rig pa
imaginary	parikalpita	kun btags
imaginary phenomenon	parikalpitadharma	kun btags pa'i chos
impermanent	anitya	mi rtag pa
imputedly existent	prajñaptisat	btags yod
inference	anumāna	rjes dpag
inferential valid cognizer	anumānapramāṇa	rjes dpag tshad ma
inherent existence	svabhāvasiddhi	rang bzhin gyis grub pa
innate	sahaja	lhan skyes
innate affliction	sahajaklesha	nyon mongṣ lhan skyes
intention	chetanā	sems pa

English	*Sanskrit*	*Tibetan*
interruptedly engaging	sachchhidravāhana	bar du chad cing 'jug pa
introspection	samprajanya	shes bzhin
investigation	vitarka	rtog pa
jealousy	īrṣhyā	phrag dog
Joyous Land	tuṣhiṭa	dga' ldan
Knowledge	abhidharma	chos mngon pa
knowledge/wisdom	prajñā	shes rab
laziness	kausīdya	le lo
lethargy	styāna	rmugs pa
liberation	vimokṣha/mokṣha	thar pa
lineage	gotra	rigs
love	maitri	byams pa
Mādhyamika	mādhyamika	dbu ma pa
making one-pointed	ekotīkaraṇa	rtse gcig tu byed pa
matter	kanthā	bem po
meditative absorption	samāpatti	snyoms 'jug
meditative equipoise	samāhita	mnyam bzhag
meditative stabilization	samādhi	ting nge 'dzin
mental and physical aggregates	skandha	phung po
mental consciousness	manovijñāna	yid kyi rnam shes
mental engagement	manaskāra	yid la byed pa
mental factor	chaitta	sems byung

English	*Sanskrit*	*Tibetan*
merit	puṇya	bsod nams
method	upāya	thabs
migrator	gati	'gro ba
mind	chitta	sems
mind-basis-of-all	ālayavijñāna	kun gzhi rnam shes
mind of enlightenment	bodhichitta	byang chub kyi sems
mindfulness	smṛti	dran pa
miserliness	mātsarya	ser sna
natural existence/existence by way of [the object's] own character	svalakṣhaṇasiddhi	rang gi mtshan nyid kyis grub pa
natural nirvana	*prakṛtiparinirvāṇa	rang bzhin myang 'das
nature	prakṛti	rang bzhin
Nature Body	svabhāvikakāya	ngo bo nyid sku
negation/negative phenomenon	pratiṣhedha	dgag pa
neutral	avyākṛta	lung du ma bstan pa
Never Returner	anāgāmin	phyir mi 'ong
Noble/Superior	ārya	'phags pa
nominal existence	—	ming tsam du yod pa
non-affirming negation/non-affirming negative	prasajyapratiṣhedha	med dgag
non-analytical cessation	apratisaṃkhyāni-rodha	so sor brtags min gyi 'gog pa
non-application	anabhisaṃskāra	'du mi byed pa
non-associated compositional factor	viprayuktasaṃskāra	ldan min 'du byed

English	*Sanskrit*	*Tibetan*
non-attachment	alobha	ma chags pa
non-conceptual wisdom	nirvikalpajñāna	rnam par mi rtog pa'i ye shes
non-conscientiousness	pramāda	bag med pa
non-embarrassment	anapatrāpya	khrel med pa
non-existent	asat	med pa
non-faith	āshraddhya	ma dad pa
non-harmfulness	avihiṃsā	rnam par mi 'tshe ba
non-hatred	adveṣha	zhe sdang med pa
non-ignorance	amoha	gti mug med pa
non-introspection	asaṃprajanya	shes bzhin ma yin pa
non-person compositional factor	*apudgalavipra-yuktasaṃskāra	gang zag ma yin pa'i ldan min 'du byed
non-produced phenomenon/ uncompounded phenomenon	asaṃskṛtadharma	'dus ma byas kyi chos
non-revelatory form	avijñāptirūpa	rnam par rig byed ma yin pa'i gzugs
non-shame	āhrīkya	ngo tsha med pa
non-thing	abhāva	dngos med
non-virtuous	akushala	mi dge ba
nose consciousness	ghrāṇavijñāna	sna'i rnam shes
nose sense	ghrāṇendriya	sna'i dbang po
not unable	anāgamya	mi lcogs med
object	viṣhaya	yul
object of knowledge	jñeya	shes bya
object of negation	pratiṣhedhya	dgag bya
object of observation	ālambana	dmigs yul/dmigs pa

English	*Sanskrit*	*Tibetan*
objective existence	—	yul gyi steng nas grub pa
observed-object-condition	ālambanapratyaya	dmigs rkyen
obstructions to liberation/afflictive obstructions	kleshāvaraṇa	nyon mong pa'i sgrib pa
obstructions to omniscience/obstructions to objects of knowledge	jñeyāvaraṇa	shes bya'i sgrib pa
odor	gandha	dri
omnipresent factor	sarvatraga	kun 'gro
omniscience/exalted knower of all aspects	sarvākārajñāna	rnam pa thams cad mkhyen pa
Once Returner	āgāmin	phyir 'ong
only imputed	prajñaptimātra	btags tsam
other-approved inference/other-renowned inference	parasiddhānumāna	gzhan grags kyi rjes dpag
other-approved reason/other-renowned reason	parasiddhaliṅga	gzhan grags kyi rtags
other-approved syllogism/other-renowned syllogism	parasiddhaprayoga	gzhan grags kyi sbyor ba
other-powered	paratantra	gzhan dbang
pacifying	shamana	zhi bar byed pa
pain/suffering	duḥkha	sdug bsṅgal
path	mārga	lam

English	*Sanskrit*	*Tibetan*
path of accumulation	saṃbhāramārga	tshogs lam
path of meditation	bhāvanāmārga	sgom lam
path of no more learning	ashaikṣhamārga	mi slob lam
path of preparation	prayogamārga	sbyor lam
path of release	vimuktimārga	rnam grol lam
path of seeing	darshanamārga	mthong lam
patience	kṣhānti	bzod pa
peak	mūrdhan	rtse mo
perfection	pāramitā	phar phyin
Perfection Vehicle	pāramitāyāna	phar phyin kyi theg pa
Performance Tantra	charyātantra	spyod rgyud
permanent phenomenon	nitya	rtag pa
person	pudgala/puruṣha	gang zag
personal selflessness	pudgalanairātmya	gang zag gi bdag med
pervasion	vyāpti	khyab pa
phenomenon	dharma	chos
phenomenon-source	dharmāyatana	chos kyi skye mched
pleasure/bliss	sukhā	bde ba
pliancy	prasrabdhi	shin sbyangs
position	pakṣha	phyogs
potency	vāsanā/bāla	bags chags/nus pa
Prāsaṅgika	prāsaṅgika	thal 'gyur pa
predisposition	vāsanā	bags chags
preparation	sāmantaka	nyer bsdogs
pride	māna	nga rgyal
principal	pradhāna	gtso bo
product	saṃskṛta	'dus byas
Proponent of Annihilation	uchchhedavādin	chad par smra ba

English	*Sanskrit*	*Tibetan*
Proponent of Permanence	shashvatavādin	rtag par smra ba
reason	hetu	gtan tshigs
reasoning	yukti	rigs pa
referent object/ determined object	—	zhen yul
reliquary	stūpa	mchod rten
requiring interpretation	neyārtha	drang don
re-setting	avasthāpanā	slan te 'jog pa
resentment	upanāha	'khon 'dzin
root affliction	mūlaklesha	rtsa nyon
Sautrāntika	sautrāntika	mdo sde pa
Sautrāntika-Svātantrika-Mādhyamika	sautrāntikasvātan-trikamādhyamika	mdo sde spyod pa'i dbu ma rang rgyud pa
secondary affliction	upaklesha	nye nyon
seed	bīja	sa bon
self	ātman	bdag
self-approved inference/self-renowned inference	svasiddhānumāna	rang grags rjes dpag
self-approved reason/self-renowned reason	svasiddhaliṅga	rang grags kyi rtags
self-consciousness/ self-knower	svasaṃvedanā	rang rig
self of persons	pudgalātman	gang zag gi bdag
self of phenomena	dharmātman	chos kyi bdag
self-sufficient	—	rang rkya ba
selflessness	nairātmya	bdag med

English	*Sanskrit*	*Tibetan*
selflessness of persons	pudgalanairātmya	gang zag gi bdag med
selflessness of phenomena	dharmanairātmya	chos kyi bdag med
sentient being	sattva	sems can
setting in equipoise	samādhāna	mnyam par 'jog pa
setting the mind	chittastāpanā	sems 'jog pa
shame	hrī	ngo tsha shes pa
shape	saṃstāna	dbyibs
similar immediately preceding condition	samanantaraprat-yaya	mtshungs pa de ma thag rkyen
sleep	middha	gnyid
Solitary Realizer	pratyekabuddha	rang sangs rgyas
sound	shabda	sgra
source	āyatana	skye mched
space	ākāsha	nam mkha'
special insight	vipashyanā	lhag mthong
spite	pradāsha	'tshig pa
spontaneously engaging	anābhogovāhana	lhun grub tu 'jug pa
stabilization	samādhi	ting nge 'dzin
stabilizing meditation	—	'jog sgom
stage of completion	niṣhpannakrama	rdzogs rim
stage of generation	utpattikrama	bskyed rim
Stream Enterer	shrotāpanna	rgyun zhugs
substantial cause	upādāna	nyer len
substantial entity	dravya	rdzas
substantial existence	dravyasat	rdzas su yod pa
substantially established	dravyasiddha	rdzas su grub pa
substantially existent	dravyasat	rdzas su yod pa

English	*Sanskrit*	*Tibetan*
suchness	tathatā	de bzhin nyid/de kho na nyid
Sugar-Cane-One	ikṣhvāku	bu ram shing pa
Superior	āryan	'phags pa
suppleness/pliancy	prasrabdhi	shin tu sbyangs pa
supramundane	lokottara	'jig rten las 'das pa
supreme mundane qualities	laukikāgryadharma	'jig rten pa'i chos kyi mchog
Svātantrika	svātantrika	rang rgyud pa
syllogism	prayoga	sbyor ba
synonym	ekārtha	don gcig
tangible object	spraṣhṭavya	reg bya
taste	rasa	ro
Tathāgata essence	tathāgatagarbha	de bzhin gshegs pa'i snying po
ten grounds	dashabhūmi	sa bcu
1 very joyful	pramuditā	rab tu dga' ba
2 stainless	vimalā	dri ma med pa
3 luminous	prabhākarī	'od byed pa
4 radiant	archiṣhmatī	'od 'phro ba
5 difficult to overcome	sudurjayā	sbyang dka' ba
6 manifest	abhimukhī	mngon du gyur pa
7 gone afar	dūraṃgama	ring du song ba
8 immovable	achalā	mi g.yo ba
9 good intelligence	sādhumatī	legs pa'i blo gros
10 cloud of doctrine	dharmameghā	chos kyi sprin
tenet/system of tenets	siddhānta/ siddhyanta	grub mtha'
thesis	pratijñā	dam bca'
thing/actuality	bhāva	dngos po

English	*Sanskrit*	*Tibetan*
thinking	chintā	bsam pa
thorough pacifying	vyupashama	nye bar zhi bar byed pa
thoroughly established	pariniṣhpanna	yongs grub
Three Refuges	trisharaṇa	skyabs gsum
tongue consciousness	jihvāvijñāna	lce'i rnam par shes pa
tongue sense	jihvendriya	lce'i dbang po
true establishment	satyasiddhi/bhāva	bden par grub pa/ dngos po
true existence	satyasat	bden par yod pa
truly established	satyasiddha	bden par grub pa
truly existent	satyasat	bden par yod pa
truth	satya	bden pa
Truth Body	dharmakāya	chos sku
ultimate	paramārtha	don dam pa
ultimate existence	paramārthasiddhi	don dam par grub pa
ultimate truth	paramārthasatya	don dam bden pa
uninterrupted path	ānantaryamārga	bar chad med lam
uninterruptedly engaging	nishchhidravāhana	chad pa med par 'jug pa
Vaibhāṣhika	vaibhāṣhika	bye brag smra ba
valid cognition/ valid cognizer	pramāṇa	tshad ma
valid establishment	*pramāṇasiddhi	tshad mas grub pa
validly established	*pramāṇasiddha	tshad mas grub pa
vehicle	yāna	theg pa
view	dṛṣhṭi	lta ba
view of the transitory collection	satkāyadṛṣhṭi	'jig tshogs la lta ba

English	*Sanskrit*	*Tibetan*
virtuous/virtuous factor	kushala	dge ba
visible form	rūpa	gzugs
wind/current of energy	prāṇa	rlung
wisdom	prajñā/jñāna	shes rab/ye shes
Wisdom Body	jñānakāya	ye shes chos sku
wrong view	mithyādṛṣhṭi	log lta
Yoga Tantra	yogatantra	rnal 'byor rgyud
Yogāchāra-Svātantrika-Mādhyamika	yogāchārasvātantrikamādhyamika	rnal 'byor spyod pa'i dbu ma rang rgyud pa

Bibliography

of works cited

Note

Sutras and tantras are listed alphabetically by English title in the first section (p.757); Indian and Tibetan treatises are listed alphabetically by author in the second (p.766); other works are listed alphabetically by author in the third (p.788).

The words *ārya* and *mahāyāna* have been deleted from the Sanskrit and Tibetan titles, and many of the English titles are abbreviated.

For modern editions of texts of the Mādhyamika school and their Tibetan versions as well as a more complete list of translations, see David S. Ruegg's *The Literature of the Madhyamaka School of Philosophy in India* (Wiesbaden: Otto Harrasowitz, 1981).

1 *Sutras and Tantras*

Bodhisattva Section Sutra
Bodhisattvapiṭakasūtra
Byang chub sems dpa'i sde snod kyi mdo
P760.12, Vol. 22-3

Buddhāvataṃsaka Sutra
Buddhāvataṃsakanāmamahāvaipulyasūtra
Sangs rgyas phal po che zhes bya ba shin tu rgyas pa chen po'i mdo
P761, Vol. 25-6

Chapter of the True One Sutra
Satyakaparivartasūtra
bDen pa po'i le'u'i mdo
[?]

Chapter Showing the Three Vows Sutra
Trisambaranirdeshaparivartasūtra
sDom pa gsum bstan pa'i le'u'i mdo
P760.1, Vol. 22

Cloud of Jewels Sutra
Ratnameghasūtra
dKon mchog sprin gyi mdo
P879, Vol. 35

Compendium of Doctrine Sutra
Dharmasaṃgītisūtra
Chos yang dag par sdud pa'i mdo
P904, Vol. 36

Condensed Perfection of Wisdom Sutra
Sañchayagāthāprajñāpāramitāsūtra
Shes rab kyi pha rol tu phyin pa sdud pa tshigs su bcad pa
P735, Vol. 21

Descent into Laṅkā Sutra
Laṅkāvatārasūtra
Lang kar gshegs pa'i mdo
P775, Vol. 29
Trans. by D.T. Suzuki, *The Lankavatara Sutra* (London: Routledge, 1932)

Eight Thousand Stanza Perfection of Wisdom Sutra
Aṣhṭasāhasrikāprajñāpāramitāsūtra
Shes rab kyi pha rol tu phyin pa brgyad stong pa'i mdo
P734, Vol. 21
Translated by E. Conze, *Aṣṭasāhasrikā Prajñāpāramitā* (Calcutta: Asiatic Society Bibliotheca Indica no. 284, 1958; reprinted by Four Seasons Foundation, Bolinas, Cal., 1962)

Eighteen Thousand Stanza Perfection of Wisdom Sutra
Aṣhṭadashasāhasrikāprajñāpāramitāsūtra
Shes rab kyi pha rol tu phyin pa khri brgyad stong pa'i mdo
P732, Vol. 19-20
See E. Conze's *The Large Sūtra on Perfect Wisdom* (Berkeley: U. Cal., 1975).

Extensive Sport Sutra
Lalitavistarasūtra
rGya cher rol pa'i mdo
P763, Vol. 27

Fifty Stanza Perfection of Wisdom Sutra
Bhagavatīprajñāpāramitāpañchāshatikāsūtra
bCom ldan 'das ma shes rab kyi pha rol tu phyin pa lnga bcu pa'i mdo
P740, Vol. 21
Translated by E. Conze in *The Short Prajñāpāramitā Texts* (London: Luzac, 1973), pp.154-6

Five Hundred Stanza Perfection of Wisdom Sutra
Pañchashatikāprajñāpāramitāsūtra
Shes rab kyi pha rol tu phyin pa lnga brgya pa'i mdo
P738, Vol. 21
Translated by E. Conze in *The Short Prajñāpāramitā Texts*, pp.108-21
Fundamental Tantra of Mañjushrī
Mañjushrīmūlatantra
'Jam dpal gyi rtsa ba'i rgyud
P162, Vol. 6
Great Cloud Sutra
Mahāmeghasūtra
sPrin chen po'i mdo
P898, Vol. 35
Great Drum Sutra
Mahābherīhārakaparivartasūtra
rNga bo che chen po'i le'u'i mdo
P888, Vol. 35
Guhyasamāja Tantra
Sarvatathāgatakāyavākchittarahasyaguhyasamājanāmamahākalparāja
De bzhin gshegs pa thams cad kyi sku gsung thugs kyi gsang chen gsang ba 'dus pa zhes bya ba brtag pa'i rgyal po chen po
P81, Vol. 3
Partial translation in A. Wayman's *The Yoga of the Guhyasamājatantra* (Delhi: Motilal, 1977)
Heap of Jewels Sutra
Mahāratnakūṭadharmaparyāyashatasāhasrikagranthasūtra
dKon mchog brtsegs pa chen po'i chos kyi rnam grangs le'u stong phrag brgya pa'i mdo
P760, Vol. 22-4
Heart of Wisdom Sutra
Prajñāhṛdaya/Bhagavatīprajñāpāramitāhṛdayasūtra
Shes rab snying po/bCom ldan 'das ma shes rab kyi pha rol tu phyin pa'i snying po'i mdo
P160, Vol. 6
Translated by E. Conze in *Buddhist Texts Through the Ages* (Oxford: Cassirer, 1954), pp.152-3

Hevajra Tantra
Hevajratantrarāja
Kye'i rdo rje zhes bya ba rgyud kyi rgyal po
P10, Vol. 1
Translated by D.L. Snellgrove, *Hevajra Tantra* (London: Oxford, 1959)
Irreversible Wheel Sutra
Avaivartachakrasūtra
Phyir mi ldog pa'i 'khor lo'i mdo
P906, Vol. 36
Jewel Mine Sutra
Ratnākarasūtra
dKon mchog 'byung gnas kyi mdo
P792, Vol. 31
Kālachakra, King of Tantras, Issued from the Supreme Original Buddha
Paramādibuddhoddhṛtashrīkālachakranāmatantrarāja
mChog gi dang po'i sangs rgyas las phyung ba rgyud kyi rgyal po dpal dus kyi 'khor lo
P4, Vol. 1
Kāshyapa Chapter Sutra
Kāshyapaparivartasūtra
'Od srung gi le'u'i mdo
P760.43, Vol. 24
King of Meditative Stabilizations Sutra
Samādhirājasūtra/Sarvadharmasvabhāvasamatāvipañchita-samādhirājasūtra
Ting nge 'dzin rgyal po'i mdo/Chos thams cad kyi rang bzhin mnyam pa nyid rnam par spros pa ting nge 'dzin gyi rgyal po'i mdo
P795, Vol. 31-2
Partial translation by K. Regamey, *Three Chapters from the Samādhirājasūtra* (Warsaw: 1938)
Life Stories
Jātakanidāna
sKyes pa rabs kyi gleng gzhi
P748, Vol. 21

Lion's Roar of Shrīmālādevī Sutra
Shrīmālādevīsiṃhanādasūtra
Lha mo dpal 'phreng gi seng ge'i sgra'i mdo
P760.48, Vol. 24
Translated by A. and H. Wayman, *The Lion's Roar of Queen Śrīmālā* (New York: 1974)
Mahāyāna Sutra of Knowledge
Mahāyānābhidharmasūtra
Theg pa chen po'i mngon pa'i chos kyi mdo
[?]
Meeting of Father and Son Sutra
Pitāputrasamāgamasūtra
Yab dang sras mjal ba'i mdo
P760.16, Vol. 23
Nirvana Sutra
Mahāparinirvāṇasūtra
Yongs su mya ngan las 'das pa chen po'i mdo
P787-9, Vol. 30-1
Translated by K. Yamamoto, *The Mahāyāna Mahāparinirvāṇa-Sutra* (Ube City; Karinbunko, 1974), 3v.
One Hundred and Fifty Means Perfection of Wisdom Sutra
Prajñāpāramitānayashatapañchāshatikāsūtra
Shes rab kyi pha rol tu phyin pa'i tshul brgya lnga bcu pa'i mdo
P121, Vol. 5
Translated by E. Conze in *The Short Prajñāpāramitā Texts*, pp.184-95
One Hundred Thousand Stanza Perfection of Wisdom Sutra
Shatasāhasrikāprajñāpāramitāsūtra
Shes rab kyi pha rol tu phyin pa stong phrag brgya pa'i mdo
P730, Vol. 12-18
See E. Conze's *The Large Sūtra on Perfect Wisdom* (Berkeley: U. Cal., 1975)
One Letter Perfection of Wisdom Sutra
Ekākṣharīmātānāmasarvatathāgataprajñāpāramitāsūtra
De bzhin gshegs pa thams cad kyi yum shes rab kyi pha rol tu phyin pa yi ge gcig ma'i mdo
P741, Vol. 21

Translated in E. Conze's *The Short Prajñāpāramitā Texts*, p.201

Ornament of the Wisdom Engaging the Sphere of All Buddhas Sutra
Sarvabuddhaviṣhayāvatārajñānālokālaṃkārasūtra
Sangs rgyas thams cad kyi yul la 'jug pa'i ye shes snang ba'i rgyan gyi mdo
P768, Vol. 28

Perfection of Wisdom in Several Words Sutra
Svalpākṣharaprajñāpāramitāsūtra
Shes rab kyi pha rol tu phyin pa yi ge nyung ngu
P159, Vol. 6
Translated by E. Conze in *The Short Prajñāpāramitā Texts*, pp.144-7

Questions of Brahmā Sutra
Brahmāparipṛchchhāsūtra
Tshangs pas zhus pa'i mdo
P825, Vol. 33

Questions of King Dhāraṇīshvara Sutra
Dhāraṇīshvararājaparipṛchchhāsūtra/ Tathāgatamahākaruṇānirdeshasūtra
gZungs kyi dbang phyug rgyal pos zhus pa'i mdo/De bzhin gshegs pa'i snying rje chen po bstan pa'i mdo
P814, Vol. 32

Questions of Sāgaramati Sutra
Sāgaramatiparipṛchchhāsūtra
bLo gros rgya mtshos zhus pa'i mdo
P819, Vol. 33

Questions of Suvikrāntavikrami Perfection of Wisdom Sutra
Suvikrāntavikramiparipṛchchhāprajñāpāramitāsūtra
Rab kyi tshal gyis rnam par gnon pas zhus pa'i shes rab kyi pha rol tu phyin pa'i mdo
P736, Vol. 21
Translated by E. Conze in *The Short Prajñāpāramitā Texts*, pp.1-78

Questions of the King of Nāgas, Anavatapta, Sutra
Anavataptanāgarājaparipṛchchhāsūtra

kLu'i rgyal po ma dros pas zhus pa'i mdo
P823, Vol. 33
Questions of the King of Nāgas, Sāgara, Sutra
Sāgaranāgarājaparipṛchchhāsūtra
kLu'i rgyal po rgya mtshos zhus pa'i mdo
P820, Vol. 33
Rice Seedling Sutra
Shālistambasūtra
Sā lu'i ljang pa'i mdo
P876, Vol. 34
Seven Hundred Stanza Perfection of Wisdom Sutra
Saptashatikāprajñāpāramitāsūtra
Shes rab kyi pha rol tu phyin pa bdun brgya pa'i mdo
P737, Vol. 21
Translated by E. Conze in *The Short Prajñāpāramitā Texts*, pp.79-107
Sport of Mañjushrī Sutra
Mañjushrīvikrīḍitasūtra
'Jam dpal rnam par rol pa'i mdo
P764, Vol. 27
Sutra on the Heavily Adorned
Ghanavyūhasūtra
rGyan stug po bkod pa'i mdo
P778, Vol. 29
Sutra on the Myrabolan Fruit
Myrabolasūtra
Ba ru ra'i mdo
[?]
Sutra on the Ten Grounds
Dashabhūmikasūtra
mDo sde sa bcu pa
P761.31, Vol. 25
Translated by M. Honda in 'An Annotated Translation of the "Daśabhūmika"' in *Studies in Southeast and Central Asia*, ed. D. Sinor; Śatapiṭaka Series 74. (New Delhi: 1968), pp.115-276
Sutra Showing the Inconceivable Secrets of the Tathāgatas
Tathāgatāchintyaguhyanirdeshasūtra

De bzhin gshegs pa'i gsang ba bsam gyis mi khyab pa bstan pa'i mdo
P760.3, Vol. 22

Sutra Showing the Realm of the Inconceivable Qualities and Wisdom of the Tathāgatas
Tathāgataguṇajñānāchintyaviṣhayāvatāranirdeshasūtra
De bzhin gshegs pa'i yon tan dang ye shes bsam gyis mi khyab pa'i yul la 'jug pa bstan pa'i mdo
P852, Vol. 34

Sutra Unravelling the Thought
Saṃdhinirmochanasūtra
dGongs pa nges par 'grel pa'i mdo
P774, Vol. 29
Translated by É. Lamotte, *Saṃdhinirmocana-sūtra* (Paris: Louvain, 1935)

Tathāgata Essence Sutra
Tathāgatagarbhasūtra
De bzhin gshegs pa'i snying po'i mdo
P924, Vol. 36

Teaching of Akṣhayamati Sutra
Akṣhayamatinirdeshasūtra
bLo gros mi zad pas bstan pa'i mdo
P842, Vol. 34

Ten Thousand Stanza Perfection of Wisdom Sutra
Aṣhṭadashasāhasrikāprajñāpāramitāsūtra
Shes rab kyi pha rol tu phyin pa khri pa'i mdo
P733, Vol. 20-1
See E. Conze's *The Large Sūtra on Perfect Wisdom* (Berkeley: U. Cal., 1975)

Three Hundred Stanza Perfection of Wisdom Sutra/The Diamond Sutra
Trishatikāprajñāpāramitāsūtra/Vajrachchedikā
Shes rab kyi pha rol tu phyin pa'i sum brgya pa'i mdo/rDo rje gcod pa
P739, Vol. 21
Translated by E. Conze in *The Short Prajñāpāramitā Texts*, pp.122-39

Twenty-Five Doors Perfection of Wisdom Sutra
Pañchaviṃshatikaprajñāpāramitāmukhasūtra
Shes rab kyi pha rol tu phyin pa'i sgo nyi shu rtsa lnga pa'i mdo
P124, Vol. 5
Translated by E. Conze in *The Short Prajñāpāramitā Texts*, pp.199-200

Twenty-Five Thousand Stanza Perfection of Wisdom Sutra
Pañchaviṃshatisāhasrikāprajñāpāramitāsūtra
Shes rab kyi pha rol tu phyin pa stong phrag nyi shu lnga pa
P731, Vol. 18-19
Translated by E. Conze, *The Large Sūtra on Perfect Wisdom* (Berkeley: U. Cal., 1975)

White Lotus of the Excellent Doctrine Sutra
Saddharmapuṇḍarīkasūtra
Dam pa'i chos pad ma dkar po'i mdo
P781, Vol. 30
Translated by L. Hurvitz, *Scripture of the Lotus Blossom of Fine Dharma* (New York: Columbia, 1976)

2 *Sanskrit and Tibetan Treatises*

Akutobhayā (Ga-las-'jigs-med)*

Akutobhayā's Commentary on (Nāgārjuna's) 'Treatise on the Middle Way'

Mūlamadhyamakavṛtti-akutobhayā

dbU ma rtsa ba'i 'grel pa ga las 'jigs med

P5229, Vol. 95

Āryadeva ('Phags-pa-lha)

Establishment of the Reasoning and Logic Refuting Error

Skhalitapramathanayuktihetusiddhi

'Khrul pa bzlog pa'i rigs pa gtan tshigs grub pa

P5247, Vol. 95

Four Hundred/Treatise of Four Hundred Stanzas

Chatuḥshatakashāstrakārikā

bsTan bcos bzhi brgya pa zhes bya ba'i tshig le'ur byas pa

P5246, Vol. 95

Length of a Forearm

Hastavālaprakaraṇakārikā

* Geshe Gedün Lodrö suggested that this text had been given the name of its author, as is the case with Buddhapālita's commentary on the same. The text is falsely attributed to Nāgārjuna (see p.360).

Rab tu byed pa lag pa'i tshad kyi tshig le'ur byas pa
P5248, Vol. 95; P5244, Vol. 95

Asaṅga (Thogs-med)

Explanation of (Maitreya's) 'Sublime Continuum of the Great Vehicle'
Mahāyānottaratantrashāstravyākhyā
Theg pa chen po'i rgyud bla ma'i bstan bcos kyi rnam par bshad pa
P5526, Vol. 108

Five Treatises on the Levels

Actuality of the Levels/Levels of Yogic Practice
Bhūmivastu/Yogacharyābhūmi
Sa'i dngos gzhi/rNal 'byor spyod pa'i sa
P5536-8, Vol. 109-10

Compendium of Ascertainments
Nirṇayasaṃgraha
gTan la dbab pa bsdu ba
P5539, Vol. 110-11

Compendium of Bases
Vastusaṃgraha
gZhi bsdu ba
P5540, Vol. 111

Compendium of Enumerations
Paryāyasaṃgraha
rNam grang bsdu ba
P5542, Vol. 111

Compendium of Explanations
Vivaraṇasaṃgraha
rNam par bshad pa bsdu ba
P5543, Vol. 111

Śrāvakabhūmi
Tibetan Sanskrit Works Series, Vol. XIV. Ed. Dr. Karunesha Shukla
Patna: K.P. Jayaswal Research Institute, 1973

Two Compendiums

Compendium of Knowledge
Abhidharmasamuchchaya

mNgon pa kun btus
P5550, Vol. 112
Sanskrit text: *Abhidharma Samuccaya*, ed. Pralhad Pradhan Santiniketan: Visva-Bharati, 1950
Translated by W. Rahula, *Le Compendium de la Super-Doctrine Philosophie* (Paris: École Française d'Extrême Orient, 1971)

Compendium on the Mahāyāna
Mahāyānasaṃgraha
Theg pa chen po bsdus pa
P5549, Vol. 112
Translated by Étienne Lamotte, *La Somme du Grand Véhicule d'Asaṅga*, Vol. II. (Louvain: 1939)

Ashvaghoṣha (rTa-dbyangs)

Cultivation of the Ultimate Mind of Enlightenment/Essay on the Stages of Cultivating the Ultimate Mind of Enlightenment
Paramārthabodhichittabhāvanākramavarṇasaṃgraha
Don dam pa byang chub kyi sems bsgom pa'i rim pa yi ger bris pa
P5431, Vol. 103

Atīsha, 982-1054

Commentary on the Difficult Points of 'Lamp for the Path to Enlightenment'
Bodhimārgapradīpapañjikā
Byang chub lam gyi sgron ma'i dka' 'grel
P5344, Vol. 103

Explanation of (Shāntideva's) 'Engaging in the Bodhisattva Deeds'
Bodhisattvacharyāvatārabhāṣhya
Byang chub sems dpa'i spyod pa la 'jug pa'i bshad pa
P5872, Vol. 146

Introduction to the Two Truths
Satyadvayāvatāra
bDen pa gnyis la 'jug pa
P5298, Vol. 101; P5380, Vol. 103

Lamp for the Path to Enlightenment
Bodhipathapradīpa

Byang chub lam gyi sgron ma
P5343, Vol. 103
Quintessential Instructions on the Middle Way
Madhyamakopadesha
dbU ma'i man ngag
P5324, Vol. 102; P5326, Vol. 102; P5381, Vol. 103
Avalokitavrata (sPyan-ras-gzigs-brtul-zhugs)
Commentary on (Bhāvaviveka's) 'Lamp for (Nāgārjuna's) "Wisdom"'
Prajñāpradīpaṭīkā
Shes rab sgron ma'i rgya cher 'grel pa
P5259, Vol. 96-7
Bhāvaviveka (Legs-ldan-'byed)
Blaze of Reasoning, Commentary on the 'Heart of the Middle Way'
Madhyamakahṛdayavṛttitarkajvālā
dbU ma'i snying po'i 'grel pa rtog ge 'bar ba
P5256, Vol. 96
Partial translation by S. Iida in *Reason and Emptiness* (Tokyo: Hokuseido, 1980), chap. III. 1-136, pp.52-242
Heart of the Middle Way
Madhyamakahṛdayakārikā
dbU ma'i snying po'i tshig le'ur byas pa
P5255, Vol. 96
See directly above for partial translation
Lamp for (Nāgārjuna's) 'Wisdom', Commentary on the 'Treatise on the Middle Way'
Prajñāpradīpamūlamadhyamakavṛtti
dbU ma rtsa ba'i 'grel pa shes rab sgron ma
P5253, Vol. 95
Bhāvaviveka the Lesser (Legs-ldan-chung-ba)
Precious Lamp for the Middle Way
Madhyamakaratnapradīpa
dbU ma rin po che'i sgron ma
P5254, Vol. 95
Buddhapālita (Sangs-rgyas-bskyangs)

Buddhapālita's Commentary on (Nāgārjuna's) 'Treatise on the Middle Way'
Buddhapālitamūlamadhyamakavṛtti
dbU ma rtsa ba'i 'grel pa buddha pā li ta
P5254, Vol. 95

Char-har Ge-shay (Char-har dGe-bshes), 18th century
Identification of Elements, Elemental Evolutes, And So Forth
'Byung ba dang 'byung gyur sogs kyi ngos 'dzin
The Collected Works of Cha-har dge-bshes blo-bzang-tshul-khrims, Vol. 10
New Delhi: Chatring Jansar Tenzin, 1973

Chandragomin
Chandragomin's Grammar
Chāndravyākaraṇasūtra
Lung du ston pa cāndra pa'i mdo
P5767, Vol. 140
Sanskrit edition: *Cāndravyākaraṇaṃ*. Jodhapura, 1967

Chandrakīrti (Zla-ba-grags-pa)
Clear Words, Commentary on (Nāgārjuna's) 'Treatise on the Middle Way'
Mūlamadhyamakavṛttiprasannapadā
dbU ma rtsa ba'i 'grel pa tshig gsal ba
P5260, Vol. 98; also: Tibetan Publishing House, 1968
Partial translation by J. May, *Candrakīrti Prasannapadā Madhyamakavṛtti* (Paris: Adrien-Maisonneuve, 1959); also J.W. De Jong, *Cinq Chapitres de la Prasannapadā* (Paris: Paul Geuthner, 1949); also M. Sprung, *Lucid Exposition of the Middle Way* (London: Routledge, 1979)

Commentary on (Āryadeva's) 'Four Hundred Stanzas on the Yogic Deeds of Bodhisattvas'
Bodhisattvayogacharyāchatuḥshatakaṭīkā
Byang chub sems dpa'i rnal 'byor spyod pa bzhi brgya pa'i rgya cher 'grel pa
P5266, Vol. 98

Commentary on (Nāgārjuna's) 'Seventy Stanzas on Emptiness'
Shūnyatāsaptativṛtti

sTong pa nyid bdun cu pa'i 'grel pa
P5268, Vol. 99

Commentary on (Nāgārjuna's) 'Sixty Stanzas of Reasoning'
Yuktiṣhaṣhṭikāvṛtti
Rigs pa drug cu pa'i 'grel pa
P5265, Vol. 98

Commentary on the 'Supplement to (Nāgārjuna's) "Treatise on the Middle Way"'
Madhyamakāvatārabhāṣhya
dbU ma la 'jug pa'i bshad pa
P5263, Vol. 98
Partial translation by L. de La Vallée Poussin, Muséon 8 (1907), pp.249-317; 11 (1910), pp.271-358; and 12 (1911), pp.235-328

Supplement to (Nāgārjuna's) 'Treatise on the Middle Way'
Madhyamakāvatāra
dbU ma la 'jug pa
P5261, Vol. 98; P5262, Vol. 98

D̄ak-tsang (sTag-tshang-lo-tsā-ba Shes-rab-rin-chen), 1405-?
Ocean of Good Explanations, Explanation of 'Freedom From Extremes Through Understanding All Tenets'
Grub mtha' kun shes nas mtha' bral grub pa zhes bya ba'i bstan bcos rnam par bshad pa legs bshad kyi rgya mtsho
Photographic reprint in the possession of Khetsun Sangpo; no other data
Also: Thim-phu: Kun-bzang-stobs rgyal, 1976

D̄en-b̄a-dar-gyay (bsTan-pa-dar-rgyas), 1493-1568
Analysis of Dependent-Arising
rTen 'brel gyi mtha' bcod
Mey College of Sera Monastery, 1969

D̄en-dar-hla-ram-b̄a (bsTan-dar-lha-ram-pa), 1759-?
Presentation of the Lack of Being One or Many
gCig du bral gyi rnam gzhag legs bshad rgya mtsho las btus pa'i 'khrul spong bdud rtsi'i gzegs ma
Lhasa: Great Press at the base of the Potala, Fire Dog Male year of the sixteenth cycle
Also: Collected gsung 'bum of Bstan-dar Lha-ram of A-lag-sha. Vol. 1 New Delhi: Lama Guru Deva, 1971

Dharmakīrti (Chos-kyi-grags-pa)
Seven Treatises on Valid Cognition
Analysis of Relations
Saṃbandhaparīkṣhāvṛtti
'Brel pa brtag pa'i rab tu byed pa
P5731, Vol. 130
Ascertainment of Valid Cognition
Pramāṇavinishchaya
Tshad ma rnam par nges pa
P5710, Vol. 130
Commentary on (Dignāga's) 'Compendium of Valid Cognition'
Pramāṇavarttikakārikā
Tshad ma rnam 'grel gyi tshig le'ur byas pa
P5709, Vol. 130
Drop of Reasoning
Nyāyabinduprakaraṇa
Rigs pa'i thigs pa zhes bya ba'i rab tu byed pa
P5711, Vol. 130
Translation by T. Stcherbatsky, *Buddhist Logic* (New York: Dover, 1962)
Drop of Reasons
Hetubindunāmaprakaraṇa
gTan tshigs kyi thigs pa zhes bya ba rab tu byed pa
P5712, Vol. 130
Proof of Other Continuums
Saṃtānāntarasiddhināmaprakaraṇa
rGyud gzhan grub pa zhes bya ba'i rab tu byed pa
P5716, Vol. 130
Reasoning for Debate
Vādanyāyanāmaprakaraṇa
rTsod pa'i rigs pa zhes bya ba'i rab tu byed pa
P5715, Vol. 130
Dignāga (Phyogs-glang)
Compendium of Valid Cognition
Pramāṇasamuchchaya
Tshad ma kun las btus pa
P5700, Vol. 130

Partial translation by M. Hattori, *Dignāga, On Perception* (Cambridge: Harvard, 1968)

D̄zong-ka-b̄a (Tsong-kha-pa), 1357-1419

Essence of the Good Explanations, Treatise Discriminating What is to be Interpreted and the Definitive

Drang ba dang nges pa'i don rnam par phye ba'i bstan bcos legs bshad snying po

P6142, Vol. 153

Translation by R.A.F. Thurman (Princeton: forthcoming)

Extensive Commentary on the Difficult Points of the 'Afflicted Mind and Basis-of-All', Ocean of Eloquence

Yid dang kun gzhi'i dka' ba'i gnas rgya cher 'grel pa legs par bshad pa'i rgya mtsho

Delhi: Lhalungpa, no date

Four Interwoven Commentaries on (D̄zong-ka-b̄a's) 'Great Exposition of the Stages of the Path'

The Lam rim chen mo of the incomparable Tsong-kha-pa, with the interlineal notes of Ba-so Chos-kyi-rgyal-mtshan, Sde-drug Mkhan-chen Ngag-dbang-rab-rtan, 'Jam-dbyangs-bshad-pa'i-rdo-rje, and Bra-sti Dge-bshes Rin-chen-don-grub

New Delhi: Chos-'phel-legs-ldan, 1972

Golden Rosary of Eloquence/Extensive Explanation of (Maitreya's) 'Treatise of Quintessential Instructions on the Perfection of Wisdom, Ornament for Clear Realization', As Well As Its Commentaries

Legs bshad gser gyi phreng ba/Shes rab kyi pha rol tu phyin pa'i man ngag gi bstan bcos mngon par rtogs pa'i rgyan 'grel pa dang bcas pa'i rgya cher bshad pa

P6150, Vol. 154

Great Exposition of the Stages of the Path

Lam rim chen mo

P6001, Vol. 152

Also: Dharmsala: Shes rig par khang, 1964

Partial translation by A. Wayman, *Calming the Mind and Discerning the Real* (New York: Columbia, 1978)

Illumination of the Thought, Extensive Explanation of (Chandrakīrti's) 'Supplement to (Nāgārjuna's) "Treatise on the Middle Way"'
dbU ma la 'jug pa'i rgya cher bshad pa dgongs pa rab gsal
P6143, Vol. 154
Partial translation by J. Hopkins in *Compassion in Tibetan Buddhism* (London: Rider, 1980)

Middling Exposition of the Stages of the Path
Lam rim 'bring
P6002, Vol. 152
Also: Dharmsala: Shes rig par khang, 1968
Partial translation by R.A.F. Thurman in *The Life and Teachings of Tsong Khapa* (Dharmsala: LTWA, 1982)

Ocean of Reasoning, Explanation of (Nāgārjuna's) 'Treatise on the Middle Way'
dbU ma rtsa ba'i tshig le'ur byas pa shes rab ces bya ba'i rnam bshad rigs pa'i rgya mtsho
P6153, Vol. 156
Also: Varanasi: Pleasure of Elegant Sayings Printing Press, no date.
Translation of chapter two by J. Hopkins, 'Ocean of Reasoning' (Dharmsala: LTWA, 1977)

Praise of Dependent-Arising/Praise of the Supramundane Victor Buddha from the Approach of His Teaching the Profound Dependent-Arising, Essence of the Good Explanations
Sangs rgyas bcom ldan 'das la zab mo rten cing 'grel bar 'byung ba gsung ba'i sgo nas bstod pa legs par bshad pa'i snying po
P6016, Vol. 153
Translation by Geshe Wangyal in *The Door of Liberation* (New York: Girodias, 1973)

Quintessential Instructions on the King of Tantras, the Glorious Guhyasamāja, Lamp Thoroughly Illuminating the Five Stages
rGyud kyi rgyal po dpal gsang ba 'dus pa'i man ngag rim pa lnga rab tu gsal ba'i sgron ma
P6167, Vol. 158

Stages of Instruction from the Approach of the Profound Path of Nāropa's Six Practices
Zab lam nā ro'i chos drug gi sgo nas 'khrid pa'i rim pa
P6201, Vol. 160
Translated by C.C. Chang, *Esoteric Teachings of the Tibetan Tantra* (Lausanne: Aurora, 1961)

Fifth Dalai Lama (Ngag-dbang-blo-bzang-rgya-mtsho), 1617-82
Sacred Word of Mañjushrī, Instructions on the Stages of the Path to Enlightenment
Byang chub lam gyi rim pa'i 'khrid yig 'jam pa'i dbyangs kyi zhal lung
Blockprint in the possession of Trijang Labrang, Dharmsala; no other information
Also: Thim-phu: Kun-bzang stobs-rgyal, 1976
Partial translation by J. Hopkins, 'Practice of Emptiness' (Dharmsala: LTWA, 1974)

Gen-dün-chö-pel (dGe-'dun-chos-'phel), 1905?-1951?
Ornament to Nāgārjuna's Thought, Eloquence Containing the Essence of the Profundities of the Middle Way
dbU ma'i zab gnad snying por dril ba'i legs bshad klu sgrub dgongs rgyan
Kalimpong: Mani Printing Works, no date

Gom-day Nam-ka-gyel-tsen (*sGom-sde Nam-mkha' rgyal mtshan*), 1532-92
Settling Difficult Points in the Opposite of the Consequences, Key to (Chandrakīrti's) 'Clear Words', Written by Jam-bay-yang Gom-day Nam-ka-gyel-tsen
Thal bzlog gi dka' ba'i gnas gtan la 'bebs pa 'jam pa'i dbyang sgom sde nam mkha' rgyal mtshan gyis mdzad pa'i tshig gsal gyi lde mig in *The Obligatory Texts (Yig-cha) for the Study of Madhyamika of Byes Grwa-tshaṅ of Se-ra Monastery*, Madhyamika Text Series Vol. 4
New Delhi: Lha-mkhar yons-'dzin bstan-pa-rgyal-mtshan, 1973

Gön-chok-den-bay-drön-may (dKon-mchog-bstan-pa'i-sgron-me), 1762-1823
Beginnings of Annotations on (Dzong-ka-ba's) 'Essence of the

Good Explanations' on the Topic of Mind-Only, Illumination of a Hundred Mind-Only Texts
bsTan bcos legs par bshad pa'i snying po las sems tsam skor gyi mchan 'grel rtsom 'phro rnam rig gzhung brgya'i snang ba
Tibetan blockprint in the possession of HH the Dalai Lama; no other data

Explanation of the Difficult Points of (D̄zong-ka-b̄a's) 'Afflicted Mind and Basis-of-All', Entrance for the Wise
Yid dang kun gzhi'i dka' gnad rnam par bshad pa mkhas pa'i 'jug ngogs
Musoorie: Gomang College, no other data

Presentation of the Four Truths, Port of Those Wishing Liberation, Festival for the Wise
bDen bzhi'i rnam gzhag thar 'dod 'jug ngogs mkhas pa'i dga' ston
Collected Works of Gun-thaṅ dkon-mchog bstan-pa'i sgron-me, Vol. 2
New Delhi: Ngawang Gelek Demo, 1972

Ḡön-chok-jik-may-w̄ang-b̄o (dKon-mchog-'jigs-med-dbang-po), 1728-91

Precious Garland of Tenets/Presentation of Tenets, A Precious Garland
Grub pa'i mtha'i rnam par bzhag pa rin po che'i phreng ba
Dharmsala: Shes rig par khang, 1969
Translated by Sopa and Hopkins in *Practice and Theory of Tibetan Buddhism* (London: Rider, 1976) and by H.V. Guenther in *Buddhist Philosophy in Theory and Practice* (Baltimore: Penguin, 1972)

Presentation of the Grounds and Paths, Beautiful Ornament of the Three Vehicles
Sa lam gyi rnam bzhag theg gsum mdzes rgyan
Buxaduor: Gomang College, 1965
Also: The Collected Works of dkon-mchog-'jigs-med-dbang-po, Vol. 7. New Delhi: Ngawang Gelek Demo, 1972

Guṇamati (Yon-tan-blo-gros)
Explanation of (Vasubandhu's) 'Commentary on the "Sutra on Dependent-Arising"'
Pratītyasamutpādādivibhaṅganirdeshaṭīkā
rTen cing 'brel bar 'byung ba dang po dang rnam par 'byed pa bstan pa'i rgya cher bshad pa
P5497, Vol. 104-5

Gyel-tsap (rGyal-tshab), 1364-1432
Commentary on (Maitreya's) 'Sublime Continuum of the Great Vehicle'
Theg pa chen po rgyud bla ma'i ṭīkka
Blockprint in the possession of HH the Dalai Lama; no other information.

Jam-ȳang-shay-b̄a ('Jam-dbyangs-bzhad-pa), 1648-1721
Great Exposition of Tenets/Explanation of 'Tenets', Sun of the Land of Samantabhadra Brilliantly Illuminating All of Our Own and Others' Tenets and the Meaning of the Profound [Emptiness], Ocean of Scripture and Reasoning Fulfilling All Hopes of All Beings
Grub mtha'i rnam bshad rang gzhan grub mtha' kun dang zab don mchog tu gsal ba kun bzang zhing gi nyi ma lung rigs rgya mtsho skye dgu'i re ba kun skong
Musoorie: Dalama, 1962

Great Exposition of the Concentrations and Formless Absorptions/Treatise on the Presentations of the Concentrative and Formless Absorptions, Adornment Beautifying the Subduer's Teaching, Ocean of Scripture and Reasoning, Delighting the Fortunate
bSam gzugs kyi snyoms 'jug rnams kyi rnam par bzhag pa'i bstan bcos thub bstan mdzes rgyan lung dang rigs pa'i rgya mtsho skal bzang dga' byed
Folio printing in India; no publication data

Great Exposition of the Middle Way/Analysis of (Chandrakīrti's) 'Supplement to (Nāgārjuna's) "Treatise on the Middle Way"', Treasury of Scripture and Reasoning, Thoroughly Illuminating the Profound Meaning [of Emptiness], Entrance for the Fortunate

dbU ma 'jug pa'i mtha' dpyod lung rigs gter mdzod zab don kun gsal skal bzang 'jug ngogs
Buxaduor: Gomang, 1967

Presentation of Tenets, Roar of the Five-Faced [Lion] Eradicating Error, Precious Lamp Illuminating the Good Path to Omniscience
Grub mtha'i rnam par bzhag pa 'khrul spong gdong lnga'i sgra dbyangs kun mkhyen lam bzang gsal ba'i rin chen sgron me
Folio printing in India; no publication data.

Jang-ḡya (lCang-skya), 1717-86
Presentation of Tenets/Clear Exposition of the Presentations of Tenets, Beautiful Ornament for the Meru of the Subduer's Teaching
Grub pa'i mtha'i rnam par bzhag pa gsal bar bshad pa thub bstan lhun po'i mdzes rgyan
Varanasi: Pleasure of Elegant Sayings Printing Press, 1970

Song on the Practice of the View
dbU ma'i lta ba nyams su len tshul de kho na nyid snang bar byed pa'i sgron me
MHTL: 3915

Jñānagarbha (Ye-shes-snying-po)
Discrimination of the Two Truths
Satyadvayavibhaṅga
bDen gnyis rnam 'byed
[Not in P] Toh.3881

Jñānashrībhadra (Ye-shes-dpal-bzang-po)
Commentary on the 'Descent into Laṅkā'
Laṅkāvatāravṛtti
Langkar gshegs pa'i 'grel pa
P5519, Vol. 107

Jñānavajra (Ye-shes-rdo-rje)
Commentary on the 'Descent into Laṅkā Sutra', Ornament of the Heart of the Tathāgata
Laṅkāvatāranāmamahāyānasūtravṛttitathāgatahṛdayālaṃkāra

Langkar gshegs pa zhes bya ba theg pa chen po'i mdo'i 'grel pa de bzhin gshegs pa'i snying po'i rgyan
P5520, Vol. 107

Kalāpa
Kalāpa's Aphorisms
Kalāpasūtra
Ka lā pa'i mdo
P5775, Vol. 140

Kamalashīla
Commentary on the Difficult Points of (Shāntarakṣhita's) 'Compendium on Suchness'
Tattvasaṃgrahapañjikā
De kho na nyid bsdus pa'i dka' 'grel
P5765, Vol. 138
Translated by G. Jha, *The Tattvasaṅgraha of Śāntarakṣita with the commentary of Kamalaśīla*, Gaekwad's Oriental Series Vol. lxxx and lxxxiii (Baroda: 1937-9)
Illumination of the Middle Way
Madhyamakāloka
dbU ma snang ba
P5287, Vol. 101
Stages of Meditation
Bhāvanākrama
sGom pa'i rim pa
P5310-12, Vol. 102

Kay-drup (mKhas-grub), 1385-1438
Manual of Instructions on the View
lTa khrid mun sel sgron me
Toh.5499
Opening the Eyes of the Fortunate, Treatise Brilliantly Clarifying the Profound Emptiness
Zab mo stong pa nyid rab tu gsal bar byed pa'i bstan bcos skal bzang mig 'byed
Tibetan blockprint edition in the possession of Geshe Wangyal; no other information. [Toh.5459]

Long-dröl (kLong-drol), 1719-94
Tibetan Buddhist Studies of Kloṅ-drol bla-ma Ṅag-dbaṅ-blo-bzaṅ

Mussoorie: Lokesh Chandra, 1963
Also: New Delhi: International Academy of Indian Culture, 1973

Mahāmati (bLo-gros-chen-po)
Clear Words, Extensive Explanation of (Nāgārjuna's) 'Friendly Letter'/Commentary on (Nāgārjuna's) 'Friendly Letter'
Vyaktapadāsuhṛllekhaṭīkā
bShes pa'i spring yig gi rgya cher bshad pa tshig gsal ba
P5690, Vol. 129

Maitreya (Byams-pa)
Five Treatises of Maitreya's Doctrine
Discrimination of Phenomena and the Nature of Phenomena
Dharmadharmatāvibhaṅga
Chos dang chos nyid rnam par 'byed pa
P5523, Vol. 108
Discrimination of the Middle Way and the Extremes
Madhyāntavibhaṅga
dbUs dang mtha' rnam par 'byed pa
P5522, Vol. 108
Translated in part by T. Stcherbatsky, *Madhyānta-Vibhanga* (Calcutta: Indian Studies Past and Present, 1971)
Sanskrit text: *Madhyānta-Vibhāga-Śāstra*, ed. Ramchandra Pandeya, Delhi: Motilal Banarsidass, 1971
Ornament for the Mahāyāna Sutras
Mahāyānasūtralaṃkārakārikā
Theg pa chen po'i mdo sde'i rgyan gyi tshig le'ur byas pa
P5521, Vol. 108
Ornament for Clear Realization
Abhisamayālaṃkāra
mNgon par rtogs pa'i rgyan
P5184, Vol. 88
Translated by E. Conze, *Abhisamayālaṅkāra*, Serie Orientale Roma VI (Rome: IS.M.E.O., July 1954)
Sublime Continuum of the Great Vehicle
Mahāyānottaratantrashāstra
Theg pa chen po rgyud bla ma'i bstan bcos

P5525, Vol. 108
Translated by E. Obermiller, *Sublime Science of the Great Vehicle to Salvation* (Acta Orientalia, XI, ii, iii, and iv); and by J. Takasaki, *A Study on the Ratnagotra-vibhāga* (Rome: IS. M.E.O., 1966)

Nāgabodhi (kLu-byang)
Classification of the Ends of Actions
Karmāntavibhaṅga
Las kyi mtha' rnam par 'byed pa
P2676, Vol. 62

Nāgārjuna (kLu-sgrub)
Commentary on 'Seventy Stanzas on Emptiness'
Shūnyatāsaptativṛtti
sTong pa nyid bdun cu pa'i 'grel pa
P5231, Vol. 95

Compendium of Sutra
Sūtrasamuchchaya
mDo kun las btus pa
P5330, Vol. 102

Essay on the Mind of Enlightenment
Bodhichittavivaraṇa
Byang chub sems kyi 'grel pa
P2665, Vol. 61; P2666, Vol. 61

Five Collections of Reasonings (see Six Collections and delete the *Precious Garland*)

Friendly Letter
Suhṛllekha
bShes pa'i spring yig
P5682, Vol. 129
Translation by Geshe L. Tharchin and A.B. Engle, *Nāgārjuna's Letter* (Dharmsala: LTWA, 1979)

Peerless Praise
Nirupamastava
dPe med par bstod pa
P2011, Vol. 46

Praise of the Element of Qualities
Dharmadhātustotra

Chos kyi dbyings su bstod pa
P2010, Vol. 46
Praise of the Inconceivable
Achintyastava
bSam gyis mi khyab par bstod pa
P2019, Vol. 46
Praise of the Mind Vajra
Chittavajrastava
Sems kyi rdo rje la bstod pa
P2013, Vol. 46
Praise of the Supramundane
Lokātītastava
'Jig rten las 'das par bstod pa
P2012, Vol. 46
Praise of the Three Bodies
Kāyatrayastotra
sKu gsum la bstod pa
P2015, Vol. 46
Praise of What Surpasses Praise
Stutyatītastava
bsTod pa las 'das par bstod pa
P2020, Vol. 46
Six Collections of Reasonings
Precious Garland of Advice for the King
Rājaparikathāratnāvalī
rGyal po la gtam bya ba rin po che'i phreng ba
P5658, Vol. 129
Translated by J. Hopkins and Lati Rimpoche in *The Precious Garland and The Song of the Four Mindfulnesses*. (London: George Allen and Unwin, 1975); partial translation by G. Tucci, JRAS 1934, pp.307-25; 1936, pp.237-52, 423-35
Refutation of Objections
Vigrahavyāvartanīkārikā
rTsod pa bzlog pa'i tshig le'ur byas pa
P5228, Vol. 95
Translated by K. Bhattacharya, *The Dialectical Method of Nāgārjuna* (Delhi: Motilal, 1978)

Seventy Stanzas on Emptiness
Shūnyatāsaptatikārikā
sTong pa nyid bdun cu pa'i tshig le'ur byas pa
P5227, Vol. 95
Sixty Stanzas of Reasoning
Yuktiṣhaṣhṭikākārikā
Rigs pa drug cu pa'i tshig le'ur byas pa
P5225, Vol. 95
Treatise Called 'The Finely Woven'
Vaidalyasūtranāma
Zhib mo rnam par 'thag pa zhes bya ba'i mdo
P5226, Vol. 95
Treatise on the Middle Way/Fundamental Treatise on the Middle Way, Called 'Wisdom'
Prajñānāmamūlamadhyamakakārikā/Madhyamakashāstra
dbU ma rtsa ba'i tshig le'ur byas pa shes rab ces bya ba
P5224, Vol. 95
Translated by F.J. Streng, *Emptiness* (Nashville and New York: Abingdon, 1967); etc.
Stanzas on the Essence of Dependent-Arising
Pratītyasamutpādahṛdayakārikā
rTen cing 'grel par 'byung ba'i snying po'i tshig le'ur byas pa
P5236, Vol. 95
The Five Stages
Pañchakrama
Rim pa lnga pa
P2667, Vol. 61
Nga-wang-bel-den (Ngag-dbang-dpal-ldan), 1797-?
Annotations for (Jam-yang-shay-ba's) 'Great Exposition of Tenets', Freeing the Knots of the Difficult Points, Precious Jewel of Clear Thought
Grub mtha' chen mo'i mchan 'grel dka' gnad mdud grol blo gsal gces nor
Sarnath: Pleasure of Elegant Sayings Printing Press, 1964
Explanation of the Conventional and the Ultimate in the Four Systems of Tenets

Grub mtha' bzhi'i lugs kyi kun rdzob dang don dam pa'i don rnam par bshad pa legs bshad dpyid kyi dpal mo'i glu dbyangs
New Delhi: Guru Deva, 1972
Illumination of the Texts of Tantra, Presentation of the Grounds and Paths of the Four Great Secret Tantra Sets
gSang chen rgyud sde bzhi'i sa lam gyi rnam bzhag rgyud gzhung gsal byed
rGyud smad par khang edition; no other data
Pa-bong-ka (Pha-bong-kha), 1878-1941
Lectures on the Stages of the Path, compiled by Trijang Rinpochay
Lam rim zin bris/rNam grol lag bcangs su gtod pa'i man ngag zab mo tshang la ma nor ba mtshungs med chos kyi rgyal po'i thugs bcud byang chub lam gyi rim pa'i nyams khrid kyi zin bris gsung rab kun gyi bcud bsdus gdams ngag bdud rtsi'i snying po
Sarnath: Pleasure of Elegant Sayings Printing Press, 1965
Pan-chen Sö-nam-drak-ba (Paṇ-chen bSod-nams-grags-pa), 1478-1554
General Meaning of (Maitreya's) 'Ornament for Clear Realization'
Phar phyin spyi don/Shes rab kyi pha rol tu phyin pa'i man ngag gi bstan bcos mngon par rtogs pa'i rgyan 'grel pa dang bcas pa'i rnam bshad snying po rgyan gyi don legs par bshad pa yum don gsal ba'i sgron me
Buxaduor: Nang bstan shes rig 'dzin skyong slob gnyer khang, 1963
Prajñāmokṣha (Shes-rab-thar-pa)
Commentary on (Atīsha's) 'Quintessential Instructions on the Middle Way'
Madhyamakopadeshavṛtti
dbU ma'i man ngag ces bya ba'i 'grel pa
P5327, Vol. 102
Explanation of (Shāntideva's) 'Engaging in the Bodhisattva Deeds'
Bodhisattvacharyāvatārabhāṣhya

Byang chub sems dpa'i spyod pa la 'jug pa'i bshad pa
P5872, Vol. 146

Prajñāvarman (Shes-rab-go-cha)
Commentary on (Udbhaṭasiddhasvāmin's) 'Exalted Praise'
Visheṣhastavanāmaṭīkā
Khyad par du 'phags pa'i bstod pa'i rgya cher bshad pa
P2002, Vol. 46

Pṛthivibandhu (Sa'i-rtsa-lag)
Commentary on the 'White Lotus of the Excellent Doctrine Sutra'
Saddharmapuṇḍarīkavṛtti
Dam pa'i chos puṇḍarīka'i 'grel pa
P5518, Vol. 107; Dharma 4017

Rājaputra Yashomitra (rGyal-po'i-sras Grags-pa'i-bshes-gnyen)
Commentary on (Vasubandhu's) 'Treasury of Knowledge'
Abhidharmakoshaṭīkā
Chos mngon pa'i mdzod 'grel bshad
P5593, Vol. 116

Ratnākarashānti (Shānti-pa/Rin-chen-'byung-gnas-zhi-ba)
Commentary on (Nāgārjuna's) 'Compendium of Sutra', Ornament Sparkling with Jewels
Sūtrasamuchchayabhāṣhyaratnālokālaṃkāra
mDo kun las btus pa'i bshad pa rin po che'i snang ba'i rgyan
P5331, Vol. 102

Ren-da-wa (Red-mda'-ba), 1349-1412
Commentary on (Nāgārjuna's) 'Friendly Letter'
bShes pa'i spring yig gi 'grel pa
Tibetan blockprint in the possession of Geshe Wangyal; no publication data
Translated by Geshe L. Tharchin and A.B. Engle, *Nāgārjuna's Letter* (Dharmsala: LTWA, 1979)

Sha-mar Gen-dun-den-dzin-gya-tso (Zhwa-dmar dGe-bdun-bstan-'dzin-rgya-mtsho), 1852-1910
Lamp Illuminating the Profound Thought, Set Forth to Purify Forgetfulness of the Difficult Points of (Ḏzong-ka-ḇa's) 'Great Exposition of Special Insight'

lHag mthong chen mo'i dka' gnad rnams brjed byang du bkod pa dgongs zab snang ba'i sgron me
Delhi: Mongolian Lama Guru Deva, 1972

Shāntideva (Zhi-ba-lha)

Compendium of Learnings
Shikṣhāsamuchchayakārikā
bsLab pa kun las btus pa'i tshig le'ur byas pa
P5336, Vol. 102
Translated by C. Bendall and W.H.D. Rouse, *Śikṣā Samuccaya* (Delhi: Motilal, 1971)

Engaging in the Bodhisattva Deeds
Bodhisattvacharyāvatāra
Byang chub sems dpa'i spyod pa la 'jug pa
P5272, Vol. 99
Translated by Stephen Batchelor, *A Guide to the Bodhisattva's Way of Life* (Dharmsala: LTWA, 1979); contemporary commentary by Geshe Kelsang Gyatso, *Meaningful To Behold* (London: Wisdom Publications, 1980)

Tu-ḡen L̄o-sang-chö-ḡyi-nyi-ma (Thu'u-bkvan bLo-bzang-chos-kyi-nyi-ma) 1737-1802

Mirror of the Good Explanations Showing the Sources and Assertions of All Systems of Tenets
Grub mtha' thams cad kyi khungs dang 'dod tshul ston pa legs bshad shel gyi me long
Sarnath: Chhos Je Lama, 1963

Udbhaṭasiddhasvāmin (mTho-btsun-grub-rje)

Exalted Praise
Visheṣhastava
Khyad par du 'phags pa'i bstod pa
P2001, Vol. 46

Vasubandhu (dbYig-gnyen)

Commentary on the 'Sutra on Dependent-Arising'
Pratītyasamutpādadivibhaṅganirdesha
rTen cing 'brel bar 'byung ba dang po dang rnam par dbye ba bshad pa
P5496, Vol. 104

Explanation of the 'Treasury of Knowledge'

Abhidharmakoshabhāṣhya
Chos mngon pa'i mdzod kyi bshad pa
P5591, Vol. 115
Translation by Louis de La Vallée Poussin, *L'Abhidharmakośa de Vasubandhu* (Paris: Geuthner, 1923-31)

Treasury of Knowledge
Abhidharmakoshakārikā
Chos mngon pa'i mdzod kyi tshig le'ur byas pa
P5590, Vol. 115
For translation, see previous entry

Ye-s̄hay-gyel-tsen (Ye-shes-rgyal-mtshan), 1713-93

Clear Exposition of the Modes of Minds and Mental Factors, Necklace for Those of Clear Mind
Sems dang sems byung gi tshul gsal bar ston pa blo gsal mgul rgyan
The Collected Works of Tshe-mchog-gliṅ yoṅs-'dzin ye-śes-rgyal-mtshan, Vol. 16
New Delhi: Tibet House, 1974
Translation by H.V. Guenther and L.S. Kawamura, *Mind in Buddhist Psychology* (Emeryville: Dharma, 1975)

Special Instructions on the View of the Middle Way, the Sacred Word of L̄o-sang
Zab mo dbu ma'i lta khrid thun mong min pa blo bzang zhal lung
Appendix to Guenther's *Tibetan Buddhism Without Mystification*, Leiden: Brill, 1966; translated therein

3 *Other Works*

Bareau, André. *Les sectes bouddhiques du Petit Véhicule*. Saigon, 1955.

Batchelor, Stephen. *A Guide to the Bodhisattva's Way of Life*. Dharmsala: LTWA, 1979.

Bendall, C., and Rouse, W.H.D. *Śikṣā Samuccaya*. rpt. Delhi: Motilal, 1971.

Bhattacharya, K. *The Dialectical Method of Nāgārjuna*. Delhi: Motilal, 1978.

Chang, C.C. *Esoteric Teachings of the Tibetan Tantra*. Lausanne: Aurora, 1961.

Conze, Edward. *Abhisamayālaṅkāra*. Serie Orientale Roma VI. Rome: Is.M.E.O., July 1954.

______. *Aṣṭasāhasrikā Prajñāpāramitā*. Bibliotheca Buddhica n. 284. Calcutta: Asiatic Society, 1958. Reprint: Bolinas: Four Seasons, 1962.

______. *Buddhist Texts Through the Ages*. Oxford: Cassirer, 1954.

______. *The Large Sūtra on Perfect Wisdom*. Berkeley: U. Cal., 1975.

______. *The Short Prajñāpāramitā Texts*. London: Luzac, 1973.

De Jong, Jan W. *Cinq chapitres de la Prasannapadā*. Paris: Geuthner, 1949.

______. 'La Madhyamakaśāstrastuti de Candrakīrti' in *J. W. De Jong Buddhist Studies*, pp.541-50. Rep. of China: Asian Humanities Press, 1979.

______. 'Textcritical Notes on the Prasannapadā'. *Indo-Iranian Journal* 20 (1978), pp.25-59.

Demieville, Paul. 'L'origine des sectes bouddhiques d'apres Paramārtha'. *Melanges Chinois et Bouddhiques*, Vol. 1 (1931-2), pp.14-64.

Geiger, Wilhelm. Trans. *The Mahāvaṃsa, or the Great Chronicle of Ceylon*. London: Pāli Text Society, 1934.

Gokhale, V.V. 'The Vedānta-Philosophy Described by Bhavya in his *Madhyamakahṛdaya*'. *Indo-Iranian Journal*, 2 (1958), no. 3, pp.165-80.

Guenther, Herbert V. *Tibetan Buddhism Without Mystification*. Leiden: Brill, 1966.

Guenther, Herbert V., and Kawamura, Leslie S. *Mind in Buddhist Psychology*. Emeryville: Dharma, 1975.

Gyatso, Kelsang. *Meaningful to Behold*. London: Wisdom Publications, 1980.

Gyatso, Tenzin (bsTan-'dzin-rgya-mtsho), Dalai Lama XIV. *The Buddhism of Tibet and The Key to the Middle Way*. Trans. by J. Hopkins and Lati Rimpoche. London: George Allen and Unwin, 1975.

Hattori, Masaaki. *Dignāga, On Perception*. Cambridge: Harvard, 1968.

Honda, M. 'An Annotated Translation of the "Daśabhūmika"'. *Studies in Southeast and Central Asia*, ed. by D. Sinor. Śatapiṭaka Series 74. New Delhi: 1968, pp.115-276.

Hopkins, Jeffrey. Trans. *Compassion in Tibetan Buddhism*. London: Rider, 1980.

Iida, Shotaro. *Reason and Emptiness*. Tokyo: Hokuseido, 1980.

Jha, G. *The Tattvasaṅgraha of Śāntirakṣita with the Commentary of Kamalaśīla*, Gaekwad's Oriental Series Vol. lxxx and lxxxiii. Baroda: 1937-9.

Lamotte, Etienne. *Saṃdhinirmocana-sūtra*. Paris: Louvain, 1935.

La Vallée Poussin, Louis de. *L'Abhidharmakośa de Vasubandhu*. Paris: Geuthner, 1923-31.

______. Madhyamakāvatāra. *Muséon* 8 (1907), pp.249-317; 11 (1910), pp.271-358; and 12 (1911), pp.235-328.

______. *Mūlamadhyamakakārikās de Nāgārjuna avec la Prasannapadā de Candrakīrti* (Bibliotheca Buddhica, Vol. IV). St. Petersberg: Imperial Academy of Sciences, 1913.

Law, Bimala. Trans. 'The Chronicle of the Island of Ceylon, or the Dīpavaṃsa'. *The Ceylon Historical Journal*, Vol. VII (1957-8).

Lessing, Ferdinand, and Wayman, Alex. *Fundamentals of the Buddhist Tantras*. The Hague: Mouton, 1968.

May, Jacques. *Prasannapadā Madhyamakavṛtti, douze chapitres traduits du sanscrit et du tibètain*. Paris: Adrien-Maisonneuve, 1959.

Murti, T.R.V. *The Central Philosophy of Buddhism*. London: George Allen and Unwin, 1955.

Obermiller, E. *History of Buddhism by Bu-ston*. Rpt. Suzuki Reprint Series, 1931.

______. 'Sublime Science of the Great Vehicle to Salvation'. *Acta Orientalia*, XI, ii, iii, and iv.

______. 'The Doctrine of the Prajñā-pāramitā as exposed in the Abhisamayālaṃkāra of Maitreya'. *Acta Orientalia*. Lugduni Batavorum: E.J. Brill, 1932.

Rahula, Walpola. *Le Compendium de la Super-Doctrine Philosophie*. Paris: École française d'Extrême-Orient, 1971.

Regamey, K. *Three Chapters from the Samādhirājasūtra*. Warsaw: 1938.

Ruegg, David S. *The Literature of the Madhyamaka School of Philosophy in India*. Wiesbaden: Otto Harrasowitz, 1981.

Schiefner, Anton. *Geschichte Des Buddhismus in Indien*. St. Petersburg, 1869.

Smith, E. Gene. *Tibetan Catalogue*. Seattle: U. of Washington, 1969.

Snellgrove, David L. *Hevajra Tantra*. London: Oxford, 1959.

Snellgrove, David L., and Richardson, Hugh. *A Cultural History of Tibet*. New York: Praeger, 1968.

Sopa, Geshe Lhundup, and Hopkins, Jeffrey. *Practice and Theory of Tibetan Buddhism*. London: Rider, 1976.
Sprung, Mervyn. *Lucid Exposition of the Middle Way*. London: Routledge, 1979.
Stcherbatsky, Theodore. *Buddhist Logic*. New York: Dover, 1962.
______. *Madhyānta-Vibhanga*. Calcutta: Indian Studies Past and Present, 1971.
______. *The Conception of Buddhist Nirvāṇa*. Leningrad: Office of the Academy of Sciences of the USSR, 1927; rev. rpt. Delhi: Motilal, 1977.
Streng, Frederick J. *Emptiness*. Nashville and New York: Abingdon, 1967.
Suzuki, Daisetz T. *The Lankavatara Sutra*. London: Routledge, 1932.
Takasaki, J. *A Study on the Ratnagotravibhāga*. Rome: Is.M.E.O., 1966.
Tāranātha. *History of Buddhism in India*. Trans. by Lama Chimpa and Alaka Chattopadhyaya. Calcutta: Bagchi, 1980.
Tharchin, Geshe Lobsang, and Engle, Artemus B. *Nāgārjuna's Letter*. Dharmsala: LTWA, 1979.
Thurman, Robert A.F., ed. *The Life and Teachings of Tsong Khapa*. Dharmsala: LTWA, 1982.
Vasu, Śrīśa Chandra. Ed. and trans. *The Aṣhtādhyāyī of Pāṇini*. Delhi: Motilal, 1962.
Wangyal, Geshe. *The Door of Liberation*. New York: Girodias, 1973.
Wayman, Alex. *Calming the Mind and Discerning the Real*. New York: Columbia, 1978.
______. *The Yoga of the Guhyasamājatantra*. Delhi: Motilal, 1977.
Wayman, A., and Wayman, H. *The Lion's Roar of Queen Śrīmālā*. New York: Columbia, 1974.

Notes

Mar-ba̅

Notes

Since this book is for the most part interwoven with paraphrase of the texts mentioned in the introduction and paraphrase of explanation gleaned from the oral tradition, the main function of the notes, except in the translation sections, is to provide the reader with a key to this weaving through identifying the particular sources. The most commonly cited texts are abbreviated, a list of which is given on pp.23-4 Entries in the Tibetan Tripiṭaka Research Foundation publication of the *Tibetan Tripiṭaka* (Tokyo-Kyoto, 1956) are indicated by the letter 'P', standing for 'Peking edition', followed by the entry number. See the Bibliography for the full Sanskrit and Tibetan titles.

1 Part One, chapter one is mainly a paraphrase of *J̄ang*, 416.20-421.17.
2 Quoted by Chandrakīrti in his *Clear Words*, P5260, Vol. 98 54.4.7.
3 Brackets are from D̄zong-ka-b̄a's *Illumination of the Thought, Extensive Explanation of (Chandrakīrti's) 'Supplement to the Middle Way'*, P6143, Vol. 154 81.1.5-7.
4 The source for this and the next paragraph is Kensur Lekden, whose teaching is based on Atīsha's *Lamp for the Path to Enlightenment* and D̄zong-ka-b̄a's elaboration of it in his *Great Exposition of the Stages of the Path*.
5 The brackets and the succeeding two sentences are taken from *Ann*, dbu 104a.5ff.

6 The remainder of the chapter is based on *GT*, cha 32a.4-32b.7.
7 Part One, chapter two is mainly taken from Kensur Lekden's teachings, which are based on common Ge-luk-b̄a literature.
8 The Sanskrit is, for the most part, felicitously reconstructed from the Tibetan. For *svairī*, see *GT*, ca 61a.1.
9 Source for this and the next three paragraphs is *Ann*, dbu 68a.1ff and 67a.1ff.
10 Oral teachings of His Holiness the Dalai Lama and Geshe Lhundup Sopa.
11 Source for this paragraph and the last three sentences of the next is *Ann*, dbu 68b.2ff, following Buddhapālita (see p.633-4).
12 Part One, chapter three follows the pattern set by Jam-ȳang-shay-b̄a in *GT*, cha 32b.7ff, with other writings as cited below.
13 Until the next note, the source is Kensur Lekden.
14 *J̄ang*, 416.5.
15 Source until the next note is the Fifth Dalai Lama's *Sacred Word of Mañjushrī* (blockprint in the possession of Trijang Labrang, Dharmsala; no other information), 89a.ff. See also pp.685 of this text.
16 *Ann*, dbu 83b.5.
17 Part One, chapters four through seven are condensations of Part Two, chapters one through five for the sake of meditation; therefore, see the corresponding chapters in Part Two for the specific sources.
18 Geshe Rapden.
19 Geshe Rapden.
20 Geshe Gedün Lodrö.
21 See Tenzin Gyatso's *The Buddhism of Tibet and The Key to the Middle Way* (New York: Harper and Row, 1975), p.56.
22 Geshe Gedün Lodrö.
23 His Holiness the Dalai Lama, when bestowing the oral transmission and explanation of Nāgārjuna's Six Collections of Reasonings in Dharmsala, 1972.
24 Sources until the next note are Kensur Lekden and *GT*, 33a.2ff.
25 Tenzin Gyatso, *The Buddhism of Tibet and The Key to the Middle Way*, p.77.
26 Part One, chapter eight is mainly drawn from Pa-bong-ka's *Lectures on the Stages of the Path*, compiled by Trijang Rinbochay (Sarnath: Pleasure of the Elegant Sayings Printing Press, 1965), 302b.3-315b.6, and Jam-ȳang-shay-b̄a's *Great Exposition of the*

Concentrations and Formlessnesses (modern folio printing in India, no place or date of publication), 22b.3-81b.1. The next two sentences are from the latter, 55b.5-56a.4.

27 The section on prerequisites is taken from *Lectures*, 312b.3-314a.7.

28 *Lectures*, 315b.4, and *Concentrations*, 45a.4. The remainder of the paragraph is from *Concentrations*, 47a.2-47b.1.

29 This sentence is from *Concentrations*, 45a.6. The rest of the paragraph is taken from the oral teachings of Lati Rinbochay.

30 This paragraph paraphrases *Concentrations*, 57a.5-58a.2.

31 This and the last sentence of this paragraph are drawn from *Concentrations*, 68a.2-4. The middle two sentences are from the same, 48b.5-6.

32 *Concentrations*, 45b.3. The next two sentences are from the same, 68a.4-69b.3.

33 This and the next sentence are drawn from *Lectures*, 306a.8-306b.2.

34 The section on faults and antidotes is drawn from *Concentrations*, 69b.4-75b.5, and *Lectures*, 304a.7-311a.2. The Sanskrit for Chart 2 is taken from Maitreya's *Madhyānta-Vibhāga-Śāstra*, ed. Ramchandra Pandeya (Delhi: Motilal Banarsidass, 1971), pp.130-1.

35 *Concentrations*, 59b.2.

36 *Lectures*, 311a.3-311b.1. The brackets are from Lati Rinbochay's teachings.

37 The section on the nine states is drawn from *Lectures*, 311b.5-313b.3, and *Concentrations*, 76b.3-77b.3. The Sanskrit for Chart 3 is taken from Asaṅga's *Śrāvakabhūmi*, Tibetan Sanskrit Works Series, Volume XIV, ed. Dr. Karunesha Shukla (Patna: K.P. Jayaswal Research Institute, 1973), pp.363-6; and Asaṅga's *Abhidharma Samuccaya*, ed. Pralhad Pradhan (Santiniketan: Visva-Bharati, 1950), p.75. This sentence is taken from the oral teachings of Lati Rinbochay.

38 Geshe Gedün Lodrö.

39 This and the next sentence are drawn from *GT*, 33a.3.

40 These last two sentences are from D̄zong-ka-b̄a, *Great Exposition of the Stages of the Path* (Dharmsala: Shes rig par khang, 1964), 347b.1-4.

41 The section on actual calm abiding is drawn from *Lectures*, 314a.5-315a.5; and *Concentrations*, 78a.2-81b.1.

42 Lati Rinbochay.

43 This final section of the chapter is based on Geshe Gedün Lodrö's commentary on *GT*, cha 33a.3-7, and *Ann*, dbu 105a.4ff.

44 Part One chapter nine is drawn from many sources as cited in the following notes. The next sentence is from *Concentrations*,49b.3.

45 *Concentrations*, 84a.5.

46 *Concentrations*, 39a.6.

47 *Concentrations*, 81b.3.

48 *Concentrations*, 83b.2.

49 This sentence and the remainder of the paragraph are taken from *Concentrations*, 83b.7-84a.2.

50 This paragraph is drawn from *Concentrations*, 86b.4-7 and 54b.1-55b.4.

51 Until n.52 the text follows *GT*, cha 33a.7ff.

52 Ḡön-chok-jik-may-w̄ang-b̄o, *Presentation of the Grounds and Paths, Beautiful Ornament of the Three Vehicles* (Buxaduor: Gomang College, 1965), 13b.5-14a.6.

53 *J̄ang*, 500.9-501.1. The Hīnayāna presentation substitutes the Desire Realm and the upper two realms for 'object' and 'subject', according to Geshe Lhundup Sopa.

54 See n.52 for source.

55 *J̄ang*, 498.17-506.7.

56 Ḡön-chok-jik-may-w̄ang-b̄o, *Presentation of the Grounds and Paths, Beautiful Ornament of the Three Vehicles*, Collected Works, Vol. 7 (New Delhi: Ngawang Gelek Demo, 1971), 458ff.

57 Nāgārjuna and the Seventh Dalai Lama, *The Precious Garland and The Song of the Four Mindfulnesses* (London: George Allen and Unwin, 1975), pp.84-7, stanzas 440-60.

58 Source for this paragraph is the oral teachings of His Holiness the Dalai Lama.

59 The rest of the chapter is based on *J̄ang*, 500.9-501.1, as well as the oral teachings of Kensur Lekden, recounting standard *abhidharma* teachings as modified by the Mahāyāna tenet systems.

60 Part One, chapter ten is based for the most part on the oral teachings of His Holiness the Dalai Lama which this author translated and edited as the first part of *Tantra in Tibet* (London: George Allen and Unwin, 1977). The other sources are *J̄ang*, 525.15-531.3, and Nga-w̄ang-b̄el-den, *Illumination of the Texts of Tantra, Presentation of the Grounds and Paths of the Four*

Great Secret Tantra Sets (rGyud smad par khang, no date), entire.
61 Source for this and the next sentence is *J̄ang*, 529.18.
62 This sentence is from the oral teachings of His Holiness the Dalai Lama. The next is from Nga-w̄ang-b̄el-den's *Illumination of the Texts of Tantra*, 12a.2.
63 Kensur Lekden.
64 This and the next sentence are taken from the oral teachings of His Holiness the Dalai Lama.
65 For amplification on this and the next paragraph see *Tantra in Tibet* (London: George Allen and Unwin, 1977). Also see Nga-w̄ang-b̄el-den's *Illumination of the Texts of Tantra*, 13b.2-14b.2.
66 The remainder of this paragraph is taken from *Concentrations*, 53b.3, and Nga-w̄ang-b̄el-den's *Illumination of the Texts of Tantra*, 13b.1-4.
67 General source for the rest of the chapter is Nga-w̄ang-b̄el-den's *Illumination of the Texts of Tantra*, 14b.7ff (see 31b.7 and 33a.6 for the reference to abandoning the innate afflictions).
68 This and the next sentence are taken from *Ann*, dbu 105b.6-106a.1, and Geshe Gedün Lodrö's oral teachings.
69 Ling Rinbochay.
70 His Holiness the Dalai Lama.
71 Geshe Gedün Lodrö.
72 *Special Instructions on the View of the Middle Way, the Sacred Word of L̄o-sang*, 13b.4-5. This is number 48 in Herbert V. Guenther's *Tibetan Buddhism Without Mystification* (Leiden: Brill, 1966).
73 Part One, chapter eleven mainly paraphrases *J̄ang*, 506.7-525.15, with amplification from Kensur Lekden.
74 *GT*, cha 49a.8-51a.5.
75 His Holiness the Dalai Lama gave this as an etymology that was meaningful to him though not based on any text.
76 Part Two, introduction is drawn mainly from *J̄ang*, the first two paragraphs being from 421.20 and 410.3. The last sentence of the first paragraph is taken from the oral teachings of His Holiness the Dalai Lama, lecturing in 1972 on D̄zong-ka-b̄a's *Middling Exposition of the Stages of the Path*.
77 *GM*, 106b.3ff.
78 *GM*, 142b.5.
79 The main source for this paragraph is Geshe Gedün Lodrö. Also see *J̄ang*, 183.7-14.

80 This paragraph is taken from the oral teachings of Kensur Lekden.

81 Part Two, chapter one mainly follows Jam-ȳang-shay-b̄a's presentation of the diamond slivers, which is translated in Part Six, relying heavily on *Ann*, as cited below. The first two paragraphs are drawn from *J̄ang*, 422.7, and *GM*, 223b.1 and 197a.3ff.

82 See pp.639ff. The commentary relies heavily on the oral teachings of Geshe Gedün Lodrö and Kensur Lekden.

83 *Ann*, dbu 70 gong a.2ff. See p.640.

84 *Great Exposition of the Stages of the Path* (Dharmsala: Shes rig par khang, no date), 387a.6ff.

85 In Sanskrit, *evaṃ vichāryamāṇa*. See, for instance, *Clear Words*, (Poussin, 107.13; P5260, Vol. 98 19.1.8: *yatashchaivaṃ gantṛ-gantavya gamanāni vichāryamāṇāni na santi*).

86 Quoted by Gen-dün-chö-pel in his *Ornament to Nāgārjuna's Thought* (Kalimpong: Mani Printing Works, no date), 13a.2. See also *GM*, 139b.6 and 256a.4.

87 The section on non-production from self paraphrases *Ann*, dbu 70 'og a.6ff.

88 This paragraph is drawn from *Ann*, dbu 70a.3ff.

89 This paragraph is taken from the oral teachings of Geshe Gedün Lodrö.

90 Kensur Lekden reported that this animal has a split lip, and thus is actually a hare. In this case, 'rabbit' would actually be *g.yos* in Tibetan.

91 The section on non-production from other, until the refutation of error, paraphrases *Ann*, dbu 71a.5ff.

92 *J̄ang*, 427.10.

93 Sources for the discussion of error, until the next note, are D̄zong-ka-b̄a's *Essence of the Good Explanations, Treatise Discriminating What is to be Interpreted and the Definitive*, P6142, Vol. 153 197.5.5-198.2.2, and D̄zong-ka-b̄a's *Illumination*, P6143, Vol. 154 37.4.2-37.5.3.

94 *Ann*, dbu 52a.1.

95 *GM*, 281b.3ff; *GT*, ca 37b.4.

96 This and the next paragraph are taken from the oral teachings of Kensur Lekden.

97 *Ann*, dbu 52a.1.

98 This paragraph paraphrases Chandrakīrti's *Commentary on the 'Supplement'*, P5263, Vol. 98 136.8.7.

99 *Ḡön*, 13.7. See Sopa's and Hopkins' *Practice and Theory of Tibetan Buddhism* (New York: Grove, 1976), p.64.
100 Source for this and the next sentence is *GT*, ka 27a.6.
101 This sentence paraphrases Chandrakīrti's *Commentary on the 'Supplement'*, P5263, Vol. 98 137.3.6. This is more cogent than Jam-ȳang-shay-b̄a's corresponding passage (p.649-50); perhaps the latter version is corrupt.
102 This paragraph is taken, with amplification from Geshe Gedün Lodrö, from *J̄ang*, 424.11ff.
103 See *J̄ang*, 419.16-421.2 and 411.6.
104 Part Two, chapter two is drawn from *Ann* and Chandrakīrti as cited in n.106 and n.107.
105 *J̄ang*, 424.6 and 429.7.
106 Source until the quote from Chandrakīrti is *Ann*, dbu 52a.2ff.
107 P5263, Vol. 98 122.5.2ff.
108 *Supplement*, P5262, Vol. 98 101.3.4, Chap. VI.8c-13. See pp.642-3.
109 *Bskyed par byed pa* should read *bskyed par bya ba*.
110 Part Two, chapter three is mainly a paraphrase of *Ann*; see n.112.
111 *J̄ang*, 429.4.
112 The remainder of this section until the last paragraph paraphrases *Ann*, dbu 52b.2ff and 73a.2ff.
113 Geshe Gedün Lodrö.
114 Lati Rinbochay.
115 Part Two, chapter four, until the elimination of error, is mainly drawn from *J̄ang*, 443.5-458.9.
116 This paragraph is based on the common usage of 'dependent-arising' among Tibetan scholars.
117 The significance of Nāgārjuna's use of *prāpya* is lost in the Tibetan translation which substitutes *brten*, i.e., *pratītya*, for *prāp̄ya*. This and the next two paragraphs leave off paraphrasing *J̄ang*, offering other opinions and the author's reflections.
118 Avalokitavrata, *Commentary on (Bhāvaviveka's) 'Lamp for (Nāgārjuna's) "Wisdom"'*, P5259, Vol. 96 170.2.1.
119 The text returns to paraphrasing *J̄ang*; see n.115.
120 See his *Length of a Forearm*, P5248 (which some Western scholars attribute to Dignāga).
121 Ren-da-wa, *Commentary on (Nāgārjuna's) 'Friendly Letter'*, 51b.6: *sangs rgyas ni chos kyi skus rab tu phye bas rten 'brel gyi gnas lugs las tha mi dad pa'i phyir ro.*

122 *Ḏak*, 71b.5.
123 This paragraph is taken from the oral teachings of Geshe Gedün Lodrö.
124 This paragraph is taken from the oral teachings of Kensur Lekden.
125 Part Two, chapter five is drawn from many sources, but primarily from *J̄ang* as indicated below. The first sentence is from *GM*, 485b.1, with commentary by Kensur Lekden.
126 D̄zong-ka-b̄a, *Illumination*, P6143, Vol. 154, chap. VI, beginning.
127 *J̄ang*, 435.15.
128 Source for this and the next two paragraphs is *Ann*, dbu 84a.2ff.
129 *Ann*, dbu 129a.2ff.
130 Except where noted, the commentary paraphrases *J̄ang*, 431.18ff.
131 *Ann*, dbu 27a.5.
132 This and the next paragraph are drawn from the oral teachings of Geshe Gedün Lodrö.
133 The commentary returns to paraphrasing *J̄ang*, 437.7ff, and *Ann*, dbu 85a.5ff.
134 *Ann*, dbu 81b.8. Source for the remainder of the paragraph is *Ann*, dbu 82a.8ff.
135 Commentary returns to paraphrasing *J̄ang*, 437.7ff, and *Ann*, dbu 86a.8ff.
136 *Ann*, dbu 86b.6.
137 *Clear Words*, P5260, Vol. 98 53.3.7. The paraphrase of *J̄ang* and *Ann* leaves off; the commentary is now basically the author's.
138 This and the next sentence come from the oral teachings of Geshe Gedün Lodrö.
139 Kensur Lekden emphasized this point many times. The next paragraph is also taken from his teaching.
140 The commentary returns to paraphrasing *J̄ang*, 438.1ff, and *Ann*, dbu 87a.1ff. For the examples, see p.691.
141 See p.681.
142 *J̄ang*, 438.10.
143 *Ann*, dbu 27a.5.
144 Source for the rest of the paragraph is Kensur Lekden.
145 This and the next paragraph are from *J̄ang*, 439.8ff.
146 This paragraph paraphrases *J̄ang*, 441.20ff.

147 The remainder of the chapter is mainly based on the teaching of Kensur Lekden.

148 *J̄ang*, 443.2.

149 See Gen-dün-chö-pel's *Ornament to Nāgārjuna's Thought*.

150 See *Tantra in Tibet* (London: George Allen and Unwin, 1977) for D̄zong-ka-b̄a's presentation of Hīnayānists' cognition of emptiness, pp.93-9. Also, see *Compassion*, pp.150-71.

151 *Commentary on the 'Supplement'*, P5263, Vol. 98 111.1.8ff.

152 Part Three in general is a reflection of Kensur Lekden's embodiment of an approach to Mādhyamika that does not eliminate the rich Buddhist presentations of phenomena but incorporates them under the umbrella of dependent-arising and emptiness of inherent existence. The beginning of the Introduction, until the next note, is drawn from *GT*, ca 12a.6ff.

153 Geshe Gedün Lodrö. The 'midnight sky' reference is from *GT*, ca 12b.6.

154 The remainder of the Introduction is mainly taken from *Tibetan Buddhist Studies of Kloṅ-drol bla-ma Ṅag-dbaṅ-blo-bzaṅ* (Mussoorie: Lokesh Chandra, 1963), Vol. I, 247-8.

155 Source for the interpretations is *Ann*, dbu 93a.8ff. The Sanskrit is from T.R.V. Murti's *The Central Philosophy of Buddhism* (London: Allen and Unwin, 1960), pp.351-2.

156 *Ann*, dngos 55a.8ff. Source for the point of attainment is *Ann*, dbu 121a.4 and dngos 23b.4.

157 Geshe Gedün Lodrö.

158 Gyel-tsap, *Commentary on (Maitreya's) 'Treatise on the Sublime Continuum of the Great Vehicle*, 182a.6-183a.6, chap. III.

159 IBID, 183a.6-183b.6.

160 IBID, 184b.1-184b.5.

161 Part Three, chapter one is based in general on the oral teachings of Kensur Lekden; using 'the selfless' as the source of the chart, rather than 'existent', is his own uncommon quintessential instruction. For the general list see *J̄ang*, 87.16-92.7. For discussion of many of the terms see Sopa's and Hopkins' *Practice and Theory of Tibetan Buddhism* (London: Rider and Co., 1976). The material, for the most part, is usually taught with the *Collected Topics of Valid Cognition (bsDus grva)*, the process of which relies to a great degree on the oral tradition, which Lati Rinbochay imparted at the University of Virginia in the spring and summer of 1976. Geshe Gedün Lodrö's and Geshe

Lhundup Sopa's elaborations on specific terms were particularly illuminating.

162 *GT*, nga 43b.1. For a fuller discussion see the second part of the Supplement in *Tantra in Tibet* (London: George Allen and Unwin, 1977), pp.193-4.

163 The main source for the section on forms is Cha-har Ge-s̄hay's *Identification of Elements, Elemental Evolutes, And So Forth*, The Collected Works of Cha-har dge-bshes blo-bzang-tshul-khrims (New Delhi: Chatring Jansar Tenzin, 1973), Vol. 10, 389-427. This section deviates at several points from Asaṅga's *Compendium of Knowledge* as found in *Abhidharma Samuccaya of Asanga*, ed. by Pralhad Pradhan (Santiniketan: Visva-Bharati, 1950), pp.3-4. The Sanskrit terms were mainly taken from Vasubandhu's *Treasury of Knowledge*. The etymology of 'form' is from Geshe Gedün Lodrö.

164 This paragraph is based on teachings from Geshe Gedün Lodrö.

165 This section on forms for the mental consciousness also relies on *GM*, 352a.3ff.

166 The main source for the section on consciousness is Ye-s̄hay-gyel-tsen's *Clear Exposition of the Modes of Minds and Mental Factors, Necklace for Those of Clear Mind*, The Collected Works of Tshe-mchog-gliṅ yoṅs-'dzin ye-śes-rgyal-mtshan (New Delhi: Tibet House, 1974), Vol. 16, 1-101. See H.V. Guenther's and L.S. Kawamura's translation of this in *Mind in Buddhist Psychology* (Emeryville: Dharma, 1975). Ye-s̄hay-gyel-tsen's Indian source is Asaṅga's *Compendium of Knowledge*; see pp.4-10 of the edition given in n.163.

167 Geshe Gedün Lodrö.

168 With the exception of the last sentence, which is drawn from the oral teachings of Lati Rinbochay, the paragraph paraphrases D̄zong-ka-b̄a's *Middling Exposition of the Stages of the Path* (Dharmsala: Shes rig par khang, 1968), 87a.2-5.

169 The main source for the section on non-associated compositional factors is Ḡön-chok-d̄en-b̄ay-drön-may's *Beginnings of Annotations on (D̄zong-ka-b̄a's) 'Essence of the Good Explanations' on the Topic of Mind-Only, Illumination of a Hundred Mind-Only Texts* (blockprint in the possession of HH the Dalai Lama, place and date of publication unknown), 60a.2-61a.6. His Indian Source is Asaṅga's *Compendium of Knowledge*; see

pp.10-11 of the edition given in n.163. The etymology given in this paragraph is from the oral teachings of Geshe Gedün Lodrö.

170 This section is drawn, for the most part, from Kensur Lekden's teachings. This first sentence, however, is from *GT*, kha 10b.6.

171 Geshe Lhundup Sopa.

172 *GT*, kha 10b.6.

173 IBID.

174 Part Three, chapter two is largely based on D̄zong-ka-b̄a's *Great Exposition of the Stages of the Path*, P6001, Vol. 152 54.2.5ff. Geshe Lhundup Sopa's explanation of this text was invaluable. The section is also supplemented with points from monastic texts, namely, Paṇ-chen S̄ö-nam-drak-b̄a's *General Meaning of (Maitreya's) 'Ornament for Clear Realization'* (Buxaduor: Nang bstan shes rig 'dzin skyong slob gnyer khang, 1963), 314b.3-332a.1, and D̄en-b̄a-dar-gyay's *Analysis of Dependent-Arising* (Mey College of Sera Monastery, 1969), entire.

175 Geshe Lhundup Sopa.

176 Pa-bong-ka, *Lectures on the Stages of the Path*, compiled by Trijang Rinbochay (Sarnath: Pleasure of Elegant Sayings Printing Press, 1965), 279a.

177 Part Three, chapter three is drawn from *J̄ang*, 126.10-128.4, Geshe Gedün Lodrö's oral teachings, Ḡön-chok-d̄en-b̄ay-drön-may's *Presentation of the Four Truths, Port of Those Wishing Liberation, Festival for the Wise*, Collected Works, Vol. 2 (New Delhi: Ngawang Gelek Demo, 1972), 877-914, and Paṇ-chan S̄ö-nam-drak-b̄a's *General Meaning of (Maitreya's) 'Ornament for Clear Realization'* (Buxaduor: Nang bstan shes rig 'dzin skyong slob gnyer khang, 1963), 69a.6-74a.1.

178 *Presentation of the Four Truths*, 887.3.

179 The descriptions are condensed from explanations by Geshe Gedün Lodrö.

180 *GM*, 184b.3-4. The source for the next sentence is Geshe Gedün Lodrö.

181 *Presentation of the Four Truths*, 885.3.

182 *Presentation of the Four Truths*, 908.3, and *GT*, ca 55a.7.

183 Charts 36-9 are tabular forms of teachings emphasized by Kensur Lekden and common to Ge-luk-b̄a teaching.

184 *J̄ang*, 179.18ff.

185 This paragraph follows *GM*, 179b.5ff. The last paragraph is a summation by the author.
186 Part Four, chapter one is drawn from *Ann*, stod 20b.3-23b.7.
187 *Ann*, dngos 25b.6.
188 Part Four, chapter two is taken mainly from *GT* and *Ann*. The first section until the separate discussion of Sāṃkhya is drawn from *GT*, ka 9b.8-15b.1, and *Ann*, stod 19b.7-20a.6.
189 Source for this and the next paragraph is *Ann*, 33a.6-33b.2.
190 *D̄ak*, 4b.4.
191 With respect to the term 'individual analytical cessation', Geshe Gedün Lodrö reported that the word 'individual' is usually treated as referring to the individual four truths and their sixteen attributes.
192 The text until the next note is drawn from *Ann*, stod 32b.5ff.
193 Kensur Lekden.
194 *J̄ang*, 18.13ff.
195 Source for this and the next paragraph is *Ann*, stod 33a.2-5.
196 The section on Sāṃkhya is drawn from *GT*, ka 29a.2-35b.8, *Ann*, stod 63b.3-65b.7, and *J̄ang*, 29.8-37.4.
197 The rest of the paragraph and the next are drawn from the oral teachings of Kensur Lekden.
198 The section on Chārvāka is drawn from *GT*, ka 21a.6-28a.2, *Ann*, stod 43b.7-44b.7, and *J̄ang*, 29.8-37.4.
199 *D̄ak*, 9a.5.
200 *D̄ak*, 9a.5.
201 Part Four, chapter three is drawn from several sources, as listed below. For the topic of refuge see *J̄ang*, 13.2ff. The next two paragraphs are taken from the oral teachings of Kensur Lekden.
202 *GT*, ka 9a.8ff. The source for the next sentence is *Ḡön*, 4.1-4.
203 Though this teaching is common to *GT*, *J̄ang*, *Ḡön*, *D̄ak*, and so forth, this explanation mainly follows the oral teachings of Kensur Lekden. See *GT*, ka 13b.6ff.
204 The sources for the section on Vaibhāṣhika are *GT*, kha 1-18, *Ann*, dngos 34b.3-36a.2, *J̄ang*, 84.13-97.7, Tu-ḡen, 25.3-27.1, and *Ḡön*, 17.12-30.3.
205 *Ann*, stod 11b.8. The source for the next sentence is *Ann*, stod 106b.4.
206 Kensur Lekden.
207 Geshe Gedün Lodrö.
208 *Blaze of Reasoning*, P5256, Vol. 96 67.2.6ff.

209 *GT*, kha 17a.5.
210 *GT*, kha 7b.2.
211 Kensur Lekden. The counter-evidence is from John Buescher.
212 Kensur Lekden.
213 Kensur Lekden.
214 *D̄ak*, 28a.5.
215 The sources for the section on Sautrāntika are *GT*, ga 1-18, *Ann*, dngos 55a.3-56a.6, and *J̄ang*, 97.8-131.4.
216 *D̄ak*, 28a.4.
217 Kensur Lekden.
218 Jam-ȳang-shay-b̄a emphasizes that such does occur whereas D̄ak-tsang emphasizes the extreme difficulty of it.
219 The source for the contradictions is *D̄ak*, 28b.4-29a.2. The Mahāyāna answer to the first qualm is from Kensur Lekden.
220 This section on generic images or, more literally, meaning-generalities (*arthasāmānya, don spyi*) is drawn from conversations with Tibetan scholars over a long period of time—Geshe Sopa, Geshe Gedün Lodrö, Kensur Lekden, Geshe Rapden, Ling Rinbochay, and Lati Rinbochay.
221 This section on impermanence is drawn from *Ann*, dngos 27b.6-31a.7.
222 The source for this and the next definition is *Ḡön*, 17.16 and 30.10.
223 Part Four, chapter four is mostly drawn from the oral teachings of Kensur Lekden. The first part until the discussion of Nāgārjuna's history reflects a story that he particularly liked to tell. The intention of the chapter is to give an example of a brief traditional history, not a definitive history, in order to give a broader picture of the culture. For a history of Mādhyamika, see D.S. Ruegg's *The Literature of the Madhyamaka School of Philosophy In India* (Wiesbaden; Harrassowitz, 1981).
224 The source here is Lati Rinbochay, citing the eighth chapter of Vasubandhu's *Treasury of Knowledge*.
225 The colors and shapes are taken from Cha-har Ge-s̄hay, *Identification of Elements, Elemental Evolutes, And So Forth*, The Collected Works of Cha-har dge-bshes blo-bzang-tshul-khrims, Vol. 10 (New Delhi: Chatring Jansar Tenzin, 1973), 414.
226 See E. Obermiller's *History of Buddhism by Bu-ston* (Heidelberg: Heft, 1932), Part One, p.98.

227 Geshe Gedün Lodrö said that these stories, which were related by Kensur Lekden, can be found in *Lho brag chung chung*.
228 The general source for Nāgārjuna's history is *GT*, ca 4a.2ff.
229 See *Tāranātha's History of Buddhism*, translated by Lama Chimpa and Alaka Chattopadhyaya (Varanasi, 1964), p.67.
230 The source for this and the next sentence is Geshe Gedün Lodrö; then the text returns to a paraphrase of *GT*, as cited in n.228.
231 The source for this and the next sentence is Geshe Gedün Lodrö; then the text returns to paraphrasing *GT*, as cited in n.228.
232 *GT* (ca 3b.4) cites Maitreya, 'Not formerly prophesied [as arising later], they arose simultaneously.'
233 *Ālaya*, 6a.
234 The source for the remainder of this paragraph and the first sentence of the next is *Tu-g̅en*, 13.15ff; then the text returns to paraphrasing *GT*.
235 The text paraphrases *GT* (ca 6b.7ff), except where noted, until the last sentence of this chapter.
236 *Tu-g̅en*, 18.15ff.
237 Kensur Lekden.
238 *J̄ang*, 282.9.
239 Avalokitavrata (see p.462) accepts the book as Nāgārjuna's own work (P5259, Vol. 96 190.2.8).
240 *Kay-drup*, 88.6. Also, see n.414.
241 The text returns to paraphrasing *GT*, ca 9a.6ff.
242 V.V. Gokhale, 'The Vedānta-Philosophy Described by Bhavya in his Madhyamakahṛdaya', *Indo-Iranian Journal*, 2, (1958), no. 3, p.166, n.1.
243 *J̄ang*, 288.13ff.
244 Chandrakīrti openly refutes Bhāvaviveka in the first, ninth, and eighteenth chapters of his *Clear Words* and criticizes Vasubandhu, Dharmapāla, and Dignāga in his commentary to the third stanza of the colophon to his *Supplement to (Nāgārjuna's) 'Treatise on the Middle Way'*.
245 *Kay-drup*, 90.1.
246 Kensur Lekden.
247 The remainder of this paragraph is drawn from the teachings of Kensur Lekden, who was relating a commonly held Ge-luk-b̄a interpretation.

248 See Part Five, chapter one.

249 The Southern Buddhist tradition and Western scholarship generally put Buddha's death date at 483B.C. The contemporary N̄ying-ma scholar Khetsun Sangpo, in accordance with an interpretation of the *Kālachakra Tantra* by Puk-b̄a Hlun-drup-gya-tso (Phuk-pa Lhun-grub-rgya-mtsho), places it at 881 B.C.

250 The source here is the oral teaching of Khetsun Sangpo.

251 Part Four, chapter five is mostly drawn from *GT*, nga 1-66, *Ann*, dngos 112b.7-116a.6, *J̄ang*, 157.4-275.10, and *Ḡön*, 40.7-55.3.

252 This and the next sentence are from the oral teachings of Kensur Lekden.

253 Kensur Lekden.

254 Kensur Lekden.

255 The rest of this paragraph and the next two are elaborations from Kensur Lekden.

256 The source for the rest of this section through to the Prāsaṅgikas' refutation is *J̄ang*, 234.18ff.

257 Kensur Lekden.

258 *J̄ang*, 251.12ff. The section begins at 250.1.

259 This and the next two sentences are drawn from the oral teachings of Kensur Lekden.

260 This critique mainly follows the corresponding section in Part Six, chapter two, with considerable commentary from Kensur Lekden.

261 *D̄en-dar*, 3b.4. For the rest of the paragraph see *GM*, 374.6ff.

262 *GM*, 398b.1.

263 *GT*, ca 63a.3ff.

264 See *Tantra in Tibet* (London: George Allen and Unwin, 1977), Part Two, chapter two. D̄zong-ka-b̄a's most extensive exposition of this point is found in his commentary to the first chapter of Chandrakīrti's *Supplement to (Nāgārjuna's) 'Treatise on the Middle Way'*, translated by J. Hopkins in *Compassion in Tibetan Buddhism*, (London: Rider and Company, 1980), pp.150-81.

265 *GT*, cha 37b.2.

266 Jñānavajra (P5520, Vol. 107 246.4.4) identifies these as the sutras teaching a Tathāgata essence. This section on the Buddha nature is mainly explication of the corresponding section in Part Six, chapter two, drawn from the oral teachings of Kensur Lekden.

267 HH the Dalai Lama gave this etymology, relating that though he has not seen it in the literature, he has found it helpful.
268 *Ālaya*, 17a.1.
269 *Ann*, dbu 8b.6.
270 The presentation of the Chittamātra assertion on the mind-basis-of-all is taken from D̄zong-ka-b̄a's *Ālaya*, as well as from Geshe Lhundup Sopa's oral teachings.
271 This and the next two paragraphs are drawn from the oral teachings of Kensur Lekden, as well as from *Ann*, dbu 25b.ff, and *Tu-ḡen*, 20.3ff.
272 *Tu-ḡen*, 22.20.
273 The discussion returns to being based on *Ālaya*, 30a.9ff.
274 Kensur Lekden.
275 Kensur Lekden.
276 Geshe Gedün Lodrö.
277 Ḡön-chok-d̄en-b̄ay-drön-may, *Explanation of the Difficult Points of (D̄zong-ka-b̄a's) 'Afflicted Mind and Basis of All', Entrance for the Wise* (Musoorie: [Gomang College], no date), 5b.7.
278 *GT*, ca 48b.3 and 48b.6.
279 P2665, Vol. 61 286.1.6; see *GT*, ca 48b.5.
280 See n.277.
281 The main sources for this section are *GT*, nga 25b.7-27b.1, and *J̄ang*, 175.8-178.14. The oral teachings of Kensur Lekden are particularly important throughout this section.
282 Kensur Lekden identified this as the position of the L̄o-s̄el-l̄ing College of Dre-b̄ung Monastery.
283 The over-riding source for this section on the three vehicles is Kensur Lekden. Individual texts are cited in further notes.
284 *Ḡön*, 26-7.
285 *J̄ang*, 95.2.
286 *GT*, kha 12b.4.
287 The source for this paragraph is *J̄ang*, 269.7ff.
288 *GT*, nga 14b.6ff.
289 The two etymologies are from *GM*, 16a.3ff. See n.495.
290 Geshe Gedün Lodrö.
291 Kensur Lekden mentioned this teaching several times.
292 This paragraph is drawn from *J̄ang*, 270.8ff.
293 The remainder of the paragraph is taken from *Ann*, stod 89a.4ff.

294 *Ann*, dbu 66a.5ff.

295 The background section of Part Four, chapter six is drawn, except for the first sentence and last paragraph, from *GM*, 3b.3-13a.2.

296 Jam-ȳang-shay-b̄a is drawing here from D̄zong-ka-b̄a's *Ocean of Reasoning, Explanation of (Nāgārjuna's) 'Treatise on the Middle Way'* (Varanasi: Pleasure of Elegant Sayings Printing Press, 1973), 401.15-426.7. The commentary on the stanzas is taken from D̄zong-ka-b̄a's explanation.

297 Kensur Lekden.

298 *GM*, 8a.4. When Jam-ȳang-shay-b̄a (*GM*, 8a.6) says that conventional phenomena which are the bases of emptiness are 'suitable to be explicitly indicated [by Nāgārjuna's *Treatise*] in a secondary manner' (*stong gzhi phal pa'i tshul du dngos bstan la rung ba*), he seems to suggest that a Perfection of Wisdom Sutra would also explicitly indicate conventional phenomena such as the paths when it indicates these as bases of emptiness. However, it is said that the Perfection of Wisdom Sutras indicate the path structure and so forth neither explicitly nor implicitly but in a hidden way. The reason for this is that the reasonings proving emptiness only establish a non-affirming negation, not something positive, with the result that a consciousness realizing emptiness realizes only emptiness. Jam-ȳang-shay-b̄a would not go against this point; thus, there is a question how he could uphold it. Still, his other point—namely, that the *Treatise* extensively indicates the suitability of conventional phenomena within the rubric of an emptiness of inherent existence—is very well taken, even though whether this shows that it explicitly indicates the path structure and so forth is questionable. Paṇ-chen Sö-nam-drak-ba and Jay-d̄zun-b̄a hold that the *Treatise* does not explicitly indicate the path structure, etc.

299 See n.295. For more discussion of the title, see n.545.

300 This section on the two truths is taken mainly from *GT*, cha 19b.2-36a.2, *Ann*, dbu 89a.3-108a.4, and Kensur Lekden's oral commentary.

301 Kensur Lekden.

302 Trijang Rinbochay.

303 *GT*, cha 21b.1.

304 D̄zong-ka-b̄a, *Stages of Instruction From the Approach of the Profound Path of Nāropa's Six Practices*, P6201, Vol. 160 211.4.2.

305 *GT*, cha 32b.5.
306 *GT*, ca 42b.1.
307 *GT*, ca 32b.2.
308 *GT*, cha 20a.5.
309 *GT*, cha 20a.8.
310 The following reasonings are based on the *Sutra Unravelling the Thought*; see *GT*, cha 21b.4 and 21b.8.
311 This and the next three paragraphs are drawn from the oral teachings of Kensur Lekden.
312 P2665 (also P2666), Vol. 61 286.4.1, and *GT*, 22a.3.
313 Kensur Lekden.
314 *GT*, cha 21b.4.
315 *Ann*, dbu 98a.7.
316 The main source for the discussion surrounding the Jo-nang-b̄as is Kensur Lekden.
317 See *J̄ang*, 356.9, for a listing of these three.
318 Oral teachings of HH the Dalai Lama.
319 *GT*, cha 23b.5. The surrounding commentary is drawn from Kensur Lekden's answers to questions.
320 P5260, Vol. 98 76.2.5. This is in commentary on XXIV.8.
321 *Ann*, dbu 92b.4.
322 Geshe Gedün Lodrö.
323 See Tenzin Gyatso's *The Buddhism of Tibet and the Key to the Middle Way*, trans. by Hopkins and Lati Rimpoche (New York: Harper and Row, 1975), p.74.
324 See D̄zong-ka-b̄a's *Ocean of Reasoning* (Varanasi: Pleasure of Elegant Sayings Printing Press, 1973), 406.17.
325 *GT*, cha 25a.6.
326 See Sopa's and Hopkins' *Practice and Theory of Tibetan Buddhism* (London: Rider and Co., 1976), p.135-6.
327 This section on the two types of scriptures mainly follows the corresponding section of Jam-ȳang-shay-b̄a's *Great Exposition of Tenets* in Part Six, chapter two, embellished with the oral teachings of Geshe Gedün Lodrö.
328 This paragraph is taken from *Ann*, dbu 91a.8ff.
329 *Ann*, dbu 90b.5.
330 This and the next four paragraphs are taken from Geshe Gedün Lodrö's oral teachings.
331 See *J̄ang*, 144.16ff. The commentary is a paraphrase of *J̄ang*, 162.6.

332 Geshe Gedün Lodrö.
333 Paragraph paraphrases *J̄ang*, 313.9ff.
334 The parenthetical addition is taken from the oral teachings of Kensur Lekden.
335 This and the next paragraph are mainly taken from *J̄ang*, 162-6-163.11.
336 See D̄zong-ka-b̄a's *Tantra in Tibet*, ed. and trans. by Hopkins (London: George Allen and Unwin, 1977), Part Two, chapter two, for an extensive discussion of this. D̄zong-ka-b̄a's commentary on the first chapter of Chandrakīrti's *Supplement* is even more extensive; see J. Hopkins' *Compassion in Tibetan Buddhism*, pp.150-81.
337 Part Five, chapter one mainly follows the corresponding section in the translation pp.586-8, with commentary from Kensur Lekden's oral teachings.
338 *Tu-ḡen*, 15.20.
339 D̄zong-ka-b̄a, *Great Exposition of the Stages of the Path*, P6001. Vol. 152 151.513.
340 *Ann*, dbu 59b.3. The commentary is from Kensur Lekden.
341 This and the next sentence come from a conversation with the junior tutor of His Holiness the Dalai Lama, Trijang Rinbochay.
342 Obermiller, *History of Buddhism by Bu-ston*, Vol. II, p.135.
343 *GT*, ka 16a.2 and *Ann*, stod 25a.4ff.
344 This sentence and the rest of the paragraph are drawn from *Ann*, dbu 69a.8-70b.2.
345 This sentence and the next are taken from *Ann*, dbu 67a.3-67b.1. The rest of the section is drawn from the teachings of Kensur Lekden.
346 Part Five, chapters two through five are drawn almost entirely from *GM*, 224b.5-83a.1. This is Jam-ȳang-shay-b̄a's explanation of the controversy between Buddhapālita, Bhāvaviveka, and Chandrakīrti in their respective commentaries on Nāgārjuna's *Treatise on the Middle Way* and especially as recounted by Chandrakīrti in his *Clear Words*. Throughout this explanation, my work at the Buddhist School of Dialectics in Dharmsala during April, May, and June of 1982 figures prominently. During that period I attended daily lectures by the Principal, Lobsang Gyatso of L̄o-s̄el-l̄ing-College, and debated with the class on an almost daily basis. The experience lifted this

important topic out of the textbooks into a living dilemma of interpretation, requiring a far greater grasp of the movement of the controversy than I had previously.

Throughout the explanation, the teachings of Kensur Lekden from Go-mang College who first introduced me to the topic are important. I have also made extensive use of a textbook on the topic from the Jay College of S̄e-ra Monastery by Gom-day Nam-ka-gyel-tsen: his *Settling Difficult Points in the Opposite of the Consequences, Key to (Chandrakīrti's) 'Clear Words', Written by Jam-bay-yang Gom-day Nam-ka-gyel-tsen (Thal bzlog gi dka' ba'i gnas gtan la 'bebs pa 'jam pa'i dbyang sgom sde nam mkha' rgyal mtshan gyis mdzad pa'i tshig gsal gyi lde mig)* in *The Obligatory Texts (Yig-cha) for the Study of Madhyamika of Byes Grwa-tshaṅ of Se-ra Monastery*, Madhyamika Text Series, Vol. 4 (New Delhi: Lha-mkhar yoṅs-'dzin bstan-pa-rgyal-mtshan, 1973), entire.

In the syllabus of the Gel-luk-b̄a monastic universities, this topic surfaces in the Middle Way class during discussion of the refutation of production from self in Chandrakīrti's *Supplement to (Nāgārjuna's) 'Treatise on the Middle Way'*, D̄zong-ka-b̄a's *Illumination of the Thought* which is his commentary on the former text, and the respective monastic textbook such as Jam-ȳang-shay-b̄a's *Great Exposition of the Middle Way* (referred to here as *GM*). Since Chandrakīrti treats the topic in his *Clear Words*, the material from that text is brought over to this class which revolves around his *Supplement to (Nāgārjuna's) 'Treatise on the Middle Way'*.

The first phase is called Opposite of the Consequences (*thal bzlog*); this leads into the second phase called Commonly Appearing Subjects (*chos can mthun snang ba*). Then, the texts return to the refutation of production from other which leads to a third phase called Two Truths (*bden pa gnyis*). Pertinent here are the first two phases—centrally important in the Ge-luk-b̄a educational system for Prāsaṅgika-Mādhyamika as they are used for acquiring a working knowledge of the differences between Svātantrika and Prāsaṅgika. This is our great fortune, for their training program provides highly developed commentaries on this very difficult controversy.

Jam-ȳang-shay-b̄a, Gom-day Nam-ka-gyel-tsen, and so forth base their expositions on those of D̄zong-ka-b̄a in three of his works on Mādhyamika which in chronological order are as follows.

1 D̄zong-ka-b̄a's fullest treatment of Commonly Appearing Subjects is in the 'Great Exposition of Special Insight' in his *Great Exposition of the Stages of the Path.* This is pages 525.1-93.2 in the *Four Interwoven Commentaries on (D̄zong-ka-b̄a's) 'Great Exposition of the Stages of the Path' (The Lam rim chen mo of the incomparable Tsong-kha-pa, with the interlineal notes of Ba-so Chos-kyi-rgyal-mtshan, Sde-drug Mkhan-chen Ngag-dbang-rab-rtan, 'Jam-dbyangs-bshad-pa'i-rdo-rje, and Bra-sti Dge-bshes Rin-chen-don-grub*, New Delhi: Chos-'phel-legs-ldan, 1972). Dzong-ka-ba's text is translated by Alex Wayman in *Calming the Mind and Discerning the Real* (New York: Columbia, 1978), pp. 309-36.
2 Not as full a treatment of Commonly Appearing Subjects as the former but presenting a slightly different interpretation later in his life is found in D̄zong-ka-b̄a's *Essence of the Good Explanations* (189.10-201.10 of the Varanasi 1973 edition).
3 Opposite of the Consequences is treated at some length in D̄zong-ka-b̄a's *Ocean of Reasoning, Explanation of (Nāgārjuna's) 'Treatise on the Middle Way'* (52.2-7.13) after which he refers his readers to the discussion in his '*Essence of the Good Explanations* and so forth' for the topic of Commonly Appearing Subjects, suggesting perhaps a preference for the interpretation there over that in the 'Great Exposition of Special Insight' (see n.424).

As both aspects of the controversy had been explained in these works, the topics are mentioned only in passing in D̄zong-ka-b̄a's *Illumination of the Thought* (80.16-1.1 in the Tibetan Cultural Printing Press edition, no date) and are not mentioned at all in his 'Middling Exposition of Special Insight'.

Here I am mainly using Jam-ȳang-shay-b̄a's exposition because (1) it synthesizes D̄zong-ka-b̄a's various presentations, while using the *Essence of the Good Explanations* when the interpretation differs (see n.424), (2) it treats the topics at great length and detail, and (3) it is fairly late, being around 1700, and thus has the advantage of having earlier presentations at hand.

Part Five, chapter two is mainly drawn from *GM*, 224b.5-

6a.4 and a section just preceding it on consequences as noted below. Buddhapālita's commentary on I.1 of Nāgārjuna's *Treatise* is P5242, Vol. 95 75.1.3-2.2, the entire text of which is translated on pp.460-1.

347 In explaining Chandrakīrti's interpretation of Buddhapālita, Jam-ȳang-shay-b̄a (*GM*, 225b.2) gives as the reason of the first consequence, 'because of already existing from the time of its causes' but later (*GM*, 257b.5) declares, in self-contradiction, that such an interpretation is unacceptable. He says that Buddhapālita's phrase 'things which already exist in their own entities' (*svātmanā vidyamānānāṃ padārthānāṃ* [Poussin, 14.2], *dngos po bdag gi bdag nyid du yod pa rnams la*) cannot be explained as 'things which exist at the time of their causes' because the passage must indicate a correct other-approved syllogism proving that it is senseless for a sprout, for instance, to be produced again through the reason that it [already] exists in its own entity. This is based on Chandrakīrti's statement that the phrase 'existing in their own entities' holds the reason.

The principle at work is that even though an other-approved syllogism uses tenets asserted by the other party, its members also must be established in general, whereby it is unsuitable to have as the reason of such an other-approved syllogism 'because [things] exist at the time of their causes' since things simply do not exist at the time of their causes. Thus, for the sake of consistency I have used 'because of already existing in its own entity' or 'because of already existing in their own entities' throughout in accordance with Jam-ȳang-shay-b̄a's own later interpretation.

348 This section on consequences and syllogisms is mainly drawn from Kensur Lekden's contextualization of the controversy between the three Mādhyamika masters.

349 Geshe Gedün Lodrö.

350 *GM*, 222b.1-3a.1. The explanations are taken from Geshe Gedün Lodrö's oral teachings.

351 *GM*, 232b.4. See pp.474-5.

352 *GT*, ca 1a.2.

353 This and the next sentence are drawn from *GT*, ca 62a.5.

354 For the definitions of Svātantrika and Prāsaṅgika and so forth, see Sopa's and Hopkins' *Practice and Theory of Tibetan Buddhism* (London: Rider and Co., 1976), Part Two, chapters seven and eight.

355 Part Five, chapter three is drawn (except as cited in n.372) from *GM*, 226a.4-31a.6 (see n.346).
356 *GM*, 261b.2.
357 P5242, Vol. 95 75.1.3.
358 P5242, Vol. 95 75.2.2.
359 P5242, Vol. 95 75.1.3-2.2.
360 See n.374.
361 Bhāvaviveka's text is P5253, Vol. 95 155.4.7-7.5.2. In Bhāvaviveka's text, 155.4.7, read *'di la* for *'di las* in accordance with Avalokitavrata (Vol. 96 190.2.5) and *GM*, 262a.6.
362 For discussion of the translation of the third fault see n.375.
363 The Tibetan (Vol. 95 155.5.1) lists three points—'things are produced from other, production is fruitful, and production has an end' (*dngos po rnams gzhan las skye ba 'gyur ba dang skye ba 'bras bu dang bcas pa nyid du 'gyur ba dang skye ba thug pa yod par 'gyur ba'i phyir*)—rather than tieing them together, as the Sanskrit does, into the opposite of the original full statement (*parasmādutpannā bhāvā janmasāphalyāt janmanirodhāchcheti* [Poussin, 15.1-2]). The Tibetan seems to accord more with Avalokitavrata's serial lay-out of the three (see pp.465-6), but the mere re-framing of the syllogism in its opposite form leaves more room for the interpretation that Bhāvaviveka's complaint is not with Buddhapālita's asserting that production is fruitful but with his holding that the reasoning refuting ultimately existent production implies something in its place, thus making it an affirming negation rather than a non-affirming negation as it should be. For, as Jam-ȳang-shay-b̄a (*GM*, 262a.6-b.4) says, the three points show that a Mādhyamika tenet, according to Bhāvaviveka, has been contradicted; the three points themselves are the tenet that is contradicted.

'...because production has an end (*janmanirodhāt, skye ba thug pa yod par 'gyur ba'i phyir*)' more literally would be 'because of the cessation of production'. The rendering into Tibetan bothers Poussin (p.15 n.4), but it seems that the translators wanted to avoid *skye ba dgag pa* which might be misinterpreted as 'production is refuted' and thus used *thug pa*, since *thug med* means 'endless' as in an infinite regress and hence *thug pa* means that it has an end, is finite, or is not repetitive.
364 Avalokitavrata's commentary is P5259 Vol. 96 190.2.5-1.2.4.
365 See n.361.

366 Avalokitavrata is referring to the *Akutobhayā* which he clearly accepts as authored by Nāgārjuna. Ḏzong-ka-ḇa and his followers disagree; see p.360 and n.414.

367 The Sanskrit is taken from Chandrakīrti's *Clear Words* (see n.374).

368 The text (Vol. 96 190.5.3) mistakenly repeats the last two sentences.

369 Vol. 96 191.2.1: read *skye ba* for *skye bas.*

370 53.9 (Varanasi edition, 1973).

371 *GM*, 262a.6-b.4.

372 This and the next paragraph are drawn from *GM* 271b.4-273a.3.

373 Kensur Lekden.

374 Part Five, chapter four is drawn from *GM*, 231a.6-43a.2 (see n.346). The entire text of Chandrakīrti's defense of Buddhapālita's refutation of producton from self and criticism of Bhāvaviveka's system, as found in his *Clear Words*, is cited in sections throughout this and the next chapter (P5260, Vol. 98 4.4.2-7.3.2; Buddhist Sanskrit Texts No. 10 5.14-21.23; Poussin, 14.1-36.2). J.W. De Jong's splendid 'Textcritical Notes on the Prasannapadā', *Indo-Iranian Journal* 20 (1978), pp.25-59, has been used throughout. With each citation, the references to Poussin's edition of the *Clear Words* in Bibliotheca Buddhica IV and the Tibetan translation in the Tibetan Publishing House gSung rab gces btus dpar khang edition of 1968 (10.11-25.16) are given in the text in parentheses. Stcherbatsky's very free translation is in his *The Conception of Buddhist Nirvana*, pp.98-125.

Here in Chandrakīrti's citation of Buddhapālita the second fallacy reads *atiprasaṅgadoṣhāchcha*, 'and because of the fault of great absurdity' which is rendered in Tibetan (Vol. 98 4.4.3) as *dang shin tu thal bar 'gyur ba'i phyir*, 'and because it would be very absurd'. The Tibetan of Buddhapālita's text (P5242, Vol. 95 75.1.6), however, is slightly different due, most likely, to a looser translation spelling out the actual absurdity, *dang skye ba thug pa med par 'gyur ba'i phyir*, 'and because production would be endless'. Since the latter is more to the point and is also the reading in Bhāvaviveka's text (P5253, Vol. 95 155.4.7) and Avalokitavrata's commentary on Bhāvaviveka (P5259, Vol. 96 190.3.1) as well as Ḏzong-ka-ḇa's commentary on the *Treatise* (Varanasi 1973 edition, 52.4) I have used it throughout.

375 With respect to the third fault *prasaṅgavākyatvāchcha*, this is translated in the Peking edition of Bhāvaviveka's text (Vol. 95 155.5.1, translation by Jñānagarbha and Lui-gyel-tsen [*gLu'i-rgyal-mtshan*]) as:

glags yod pa'i tshig yin pa'i phyir te

but in the Peking edition of the *Clear Words* (Vol. 98 4.4.4, and in the Shes rig par khang edition, 10.17, these being the same translation by Mahāsumati and Pa-tsap-nyi-ma-drak [*Pa-tshab-nyi-ma-grags*]) as:

thal bar 'gyur ba'i tshig yin pa'i phyir

and in Avalokitavrata's commentary on Bhāvaviveka (P5259, Vol. 96 190.3.8) as:

glags yod pa'i tshig yin pa'i yang phyir te

Only in the last one is the final *cha* of the Sanskrit represented by *yang*, allowing it to be interpreted as a third reason for the unsuitability of Buddhapālita's refutation. In his commentary on the *Treatise* D̄zong-ka-b̄a (Varanasi 1973 edition, 52.12) points out the discrepancy in translation, indicating that he favors *glags yod pa'i tshig yin pa'i yang phyir te* as it is in the edition of Bhāvaviveka he had before him and in Avalokitavrata in the sense of meaning, '[Buddhapālita's interpretation] is also unsuitable because of having words that afford an opportunity [to an opponent to expose contradiction within his own system]'. D̄zong-ka-b̄a identifies that this is the interpretation of Avalokitavrata, and it indeed is as can be seen in translation in the next citation. (The Tibetan of that, in Vol. 96 190.4.7 is: *gnas rtan buddha pa li tas bshad pa de ni rgol ba gzhan gyi klan ka'i glags yog pa'i tshig yin pa'i phyir yang rigs pa ma yin no// yang zhes bya ba'i sgra ni gtan tshigs dang dpe ma brjod pa'i phyir dang gzhan gyis smras pa'i nyes pa ma bsal ba'i phyir rigs pa ma yin par 'ba' zhig tu ma zad gyi/ de ni glags yod pa'i tshig yin pa'i phyir yang rigs pa ma yin no zhes bya bar sbyar ro*).

In this interpretation *prasaṅgavākyatvāchcha* has the sense of 'because of being a statement that is *susceptible* to [absurd] consequences' in the sense of affording an opportunity to an opponent to find holes in one's argument, rather than just meaning 'because of being a statement of [absurd] consequences'. Thus, this is not a description of Buddhapālita's commentary as containing consequences but an indication that it is susceptible to the absurd consequence of contradicting a basic Mādhyamika tenet. The remainder of the passage then spells out what that inner contradiction is. In this interpretation the phrase is taken as a third reason, not as a reason beginning the next sentence. This is also Jam-ȳang-shay-b̄a's opinion (*GM*, 264b.2-6), based on Avalokitavrata (see p464-5).

376 See n.347.

377 P5229, Vol. 95 15.1.1.

378 Until the next note, the material is drawn from *GM*, 273b.1-2.

379 This quote, as well as the next four, and the general argument are taken from D̄zong-ka-b̄a's *Great Exposition of the Stages of the Path*, P6001, Vol. 152 156.2.2ff.

380 The source here is the author's own reading in these texts.

381 This and the next paragraph are drawn from *Ann*, dbu 59a.7ff.

382 This is found in D̄zong-ka-b̄a's *Essence of the Good Explanations*, cited here from *GM*, 233b.4.

383 *GM*, 233b.2, citing D̄zong-ka-b̄a's *Essence of the Good Explanations*.

384 The Sanskrit is Buddhist Sanskrit Texts No. 10 5.16-6.5 and Poussin 15.3-16.10.

385 Poussin's Sanskrit (15.4) reads '... is enquiring in the following way about the purpose in production of the existent ...', but Dr. Vaidya (5.17) drops *vidyamānasya punarutpattau prayojanaṃ* in accordance with the Tibetan.

386 In accordance with J.W. De Jong's 'Textcritical Notes on the Prasannapadā' (p.29, n.15.5) *svata iti hetutvena tad eva chotpadyata iti* should read *svata iti vidyamānaṃ hetutvena bravīṣhi tad eva chotpadyata iti*, which, as he says, is confirmed by the Tibetan.

About this, Jam-ȳang-shay-b̄a (*GM*, 265a.4-6) says, '*Yod pa rgyu nyid* indicates that with respect to all that involve production their existence acts as a cause, and *de nyid skye'o* indicates that all that involve production are produced from their respective existence.' In that, read *rang gi yod pas* for *rang gi yod pa'i* and *yod pa de las* for *yod pa de* in accordance with the Ngawang Gelek edition, 480.5 and 480.6. He cites this passage to show that the Sāṃkhyas '... assert that a sprout exists from the time of its causes and that it is produced from that existence.'

I have translated the first part of this sentence in accordance with his interpretation, but not the second part since the Sanskrit *tad eva chotpadyata iti* does not seem to warrant 'from that', instead meaning 'and just that is produced'.

387 See notes 500 and 501 with respect to the quotations from Āryadeva and Nāgārjuna.

388 The brackets in the second stanza of the *Refutation of Objections* are from the *Four Interwoven Commentaries on (D̄zong-ka-b̄a's) 'Great Exposition of the Stages of the Path'* (New Delhi: Chos-'phel-legs-ldan, 1972) 477.5-8.2.

389 *GM*, 234a.1.

390 *GM*, 229a.6.

391 This sentence is from a work on the Opposite of the Consequences (*thal bzlog*) by Gom-day Nam-ka-gyel-tsen (*sGom-sde Nam-mkha'-rgyal-mtshan*, 1532-92), Mādhyamika Text Series, Vol. 4 (New Delhi: Lha-mkhar Yoṅs-'dzin Bstan-pa-rgyal-mtshan, 1973), 602.5. The two previous sentences are deductions from his commentary. He lists five reasons that the Sāṃkhyas use for proving production from self, all of which lack their intended force according to the Buddhist.

392 *Ann*, dbu 59b.2.

393 Chandrakīrti also sees another correct other-approved syllogism in Buddhapālita's statements: The subjects, objects other than the person, are not produced from self because of existing in their own entities, as in the case of the person. See *GM*, 240b.6.

394 Or, according to the Sanskrit, 'and [thus] due to being established [for the Sāṃkhyas] here it is held as the example'; the Tibetan does not translate *upadānaṃ* (Poussin, 21.10).

395 De Jong (n.21.13) corrects the Sanskrit to *'numānabādhācodanāyām*, which would be 'damage', not 'contradiction', but I have stayed with 'contradiction' *'gal ba* simply because it is easier to follow in translation.

396 With respect to why cloth, or woolen cloth as the word means in Tibetan, is frequently used as the second example after a pot, it strikes me that it is merely because of the similarity in sound between the two words in Sanskrit, *ghaṭa* and *paṭa*.

397 *GM*, 240a.1 and 240b.5-1a.3.

398 Jam-ȳang-shay-b̄a (*GM*, 240b.6) seems to take 'example' as referring to an example of another syllogism, whereas it might

refer (see Poussin, p.22, n.3) to the example in this syllogism (the person) which does not have the fault of indefiniteness in the sense of being overly vast by including everything and thus incurring the fault that when the example is realized, the main thesis would also be realized. However, the latter interpretation does not appear to fit Chandrakīrti's context. Chandrakīrti seems to be concerned that the subject of the main syllogism, not the subject of the example, include all phenomena that are produced. This is probably why Jam-ȳang-shay-b̄a, for the most part, interprets the subject as 'things such as a non-manifest pot and so forth' instead of just as 'things'. In the second syllogism, Chandrakīrti is providing another all inclusive subject; thus it seems that the matter does not revolve around the example (which in the first syllogism is a pot already in its manifest form).

399 Dr. Vaidya (Buddhist Sanskrit Texts 10 p.7, n.4) objects to Poussin's (see p.23, n.1) editing the text from *atha vākyāni* to *arthavākhyāni* in accordance with the Tibetan *don gyi ngag 'di dag*, but the usage of this same term on 7.22 suggests that Poussin could be right.

400 This and the next paragraph are my summary.

401 The remainder of the chapter is drawn from *GM*, 241b.2-3a.2.

402 The Sanskrit (Poussin, 23.4) reads, 'And, due to that, there is no contradiction with a tenet.'

403 From *Gom-day*, 617.6.

404 *Gom-day*, 618.4.

405 *GM*, 242a.5.

406 The bracketed additions in this and the next two sentences are from *Gom-day*, 619.2ff.

407 D̄zong-ka-b̄a's *Ocean of Reasoning*, 55.17.

408 *GM*,. 242b.4.

409 The identification of what is being refuted in these three cases is from *Gom-day*, 621.1ff. The bracketed additions in the first citation are from D̄zong-ka-b̄a's commentary, 136.7, Varanasi 1973 edition.

410 *GM* (242b.5) reads *gzugs ni gzugs ni rgyu med par/ thal bar 'gyur* but should read *gzugs na gzugs ni*, which then would accord more with the Sanskrit (Poussin, 24.10) *rupaṃ prasajyate/ ahetukaṃ* and with D̄zong-ka-b̄a's commentary (129.1, Varanasi 1973 edition) than the Peking (Vol. 98 5.5.3) *gzugs na gzugs kyi rgyu med par/ thal bar 'gyur*. The bracketed additions in the first

citation are from Dzong-ka-ba's commentary, 128.19, Varanasi 1973 edition. Dzong-ka-ba (129.8) says that this implies its opposite meaning. That the other two do so is my speculation.

411 The glosses are from Dzong-ka-ba's commentary, 443.8, Varanasi 1973 edition.

412 The source for the material up to the citation from Chandrakīrti is Dzong-ka-ba's *Ocean of Reasoning*, 56.8-16 (Varanasi 1973 edition).

413 De Jong ('Textcritical Notes' p.30, n.25.3), following Yamaguchi, says that both the first question and the response are spoken by Bhāvaviveka; however, Gom-day Nam-ka-gyel-tsen (621.3-3.2) divides it as I have, though he does not specify the disputants. It fits the pattern of the section better to have a question being put to the hypothetical Bhāvaviveka, his responding, and then being cut off based on his response.

414 As Gom-day, (623.1) points out, it is significant that Chandrakīrti does not mention the *Akutobhayā* as an auto-commentary of Nāgārjuna, adding credence to the argument that it is not his.

415 Part Five, chapter five is drawn mainly from *GM*, 243a.2-57b.4.

416 The Tibetan reads 'are *definite as* not being produced from self' (*bdag las skye ba med par nges te*), but this is not represented in the Sanskrit (see next note). The reason could also be translated as 'because of presently existing' since *vidyamāna* is the present middle participle; however, later (Poussin, 33.4) Chandrakīrti cites the reason as *sattvād*, suggesting that the particular form makes little difference, this perhaps being why it was translated into Tibetan merely as *yod pa'i phyir* instead of *da lta bar yod pa'i phyir*.

417 The Tibetan of the example *shes pa yod pa nyid bzhin* must be a mere translation of the Sanskrit *chaitanya* and not an extension of it to include the reason ('existing'). In any case, the reference is to the *puruṣha*, the person, or pure spirit, pure consciousness. Bhāvaviveka's syllogism in full is: *na paramārthata ādhyātmikānyāyatanāni svata utpannāni vidyamānatvāt chaitanyavad-iti, don dam par nang gi skye mched rnams bdag las skye ba med par nges te yod pa'i phyir na shes pa yod pa nyid bzhin no zhes.*

418 Dzong-ka-ba's *Essence of the Good Explanations*, 117.4 in the Varanasi 1973 edition.

419 For a slightly different citation of this, see p.648; also see n.637. The Tibetan has 'is not produced causelessly' at the end.

Poussin (p.26, n.3) draws our attention to Shāntideva's *Engaging in the Bodhisattva Deeds*, IX.142, and his *Compendium of Learnings* 219.10.

420 Poussin identifies this as 210.3-5. Chandrakīrti cites it again in commentary at the end of chapters two and twenty-one. Poussin calls our attention to Shāntideva's *Compendium of Learnings*, 238.10, 239.4.

421 Since in Ge-luk-b̄a the nature of phenomena is permanent, here 'permanent' is interpreted, as usual, as the extreme of inherent existence.

421a Stcherbatsky (p.113) translates this clause extremely freely, adding in considerable commentary as if Chandrakīrti says such in his text: 'Indeed (Bhāvaviveka) himself being a Mādhyamika does not admit the transcendental reality of separate mental phenomena and at the same time he composes a syllogism about this very non-existing thing.' The last clause is *total* speculation stemming from Stcherbatsky's assumption that Chandrakīrti does not accept the existence of anything.

422 Following De Jong's correction ('Textcritical Notes' p.31, n.28.1) of *vastusatām* to *dravyasatām*.

423 Most of Chandrakīrti's refutation of Bhāvaviveka with respect to Commonly Appearing Subjects is included in D̄zong-ka-b̄a's *Great Exposition of the Stages of the Path* and has been translated by Alex Wayman in *Calming the Mind and Discerning the Real* (New York: Columbia, 1978), pp.309-35. About the first example, a Buddhist's proof for a Vaisheṣhika that sound is impermanent, Wayman (p.309) says, '... in regard to (the proposition) "Sound is not eternal" (maintained by the Buddhist on the side of the Vaiśeṣika)...', thereby suggesting that the Buddhist is proving that sound is impermanent on behalf of a Vaisheṣhika to someone else. Wayman is clearly drawing from a mis-reading of *bye brag pa'i ngor* in the *Four Interwoven Commentaries on (D̄zong-ka-b̄a's) 'Great Exposition of the Stages of the Path'*, 525.5. Though *ngo* means 'side' or 'face', here with the *ra* ending it means, not 'on the side' but 'to the side' and thus, in English, '*to* a Vaisheṣhika'.

That the *conventions (vyavahāra, tha snyad)* of inference and object inferred would be non-existent if the subject, predicate, and so forth were qualified with the particular assertions of one school simply means that we could not speak of inferring anything if the terms were so qualified since the process of inference would get bogged down in merely considering the subject, etc., for the two parties could not come to agreement.

With respect to the second example, a Vaisheṣhika's proving to someone else that sound is impermanent, Jam-ȳang-shay-b̄a (*GM*, 346a.5) identifies the other party as a Nirgrantha (*gCer bu pa*), accepted as another name for Jaina. Stcherbatsky *(The Conception of Buddhist Nirvāṇa*, p.115) identifies the opponent here as a Mīmāṃsaka; he inserts the identification into the text as if Chandrakīrti so specified it, but he did not do so. Gom-day, 633.2, identifies the other party as a Dīpaka (*gSal byed p̄a*) as does the *Four Interwoven Commentaries on (D̄zong-ka-b̄a's) 'Great Exposition of the Stages of the Path'*, 526.4, which says that Dīpaka is a sub-division of Sāṃkhya. Wayman (p.310) goes along with Stcherbatsky. In any case, the assertion of the Vaisheṣhika's opponent is that sound is pre-existent in a non-manifest state and is made manifest by conditions, something which the Vaisheṣhika himself cannot accept.

424 *Gom-day*, 634.4.1, and *Four Interwoven Commentaries*, 530.1. The predicate of what Bhāvaviveka is proving is an absence or negation of production (ultimately) with respect to the subject, eyes and so forth; in this sense, Chandrakīrti says, '... when it is just the case that a negation of production (*utpādapratiṣhedha, skye ba bkag pa*) is asserted (*abhipreta, 'dod pa*) as the predicate of the probandum (*sādhyadharma, bsgrub bya'i chos*)...' Wayman (pp.311-12) misconstrues the sentence to read, 'At the very time that he denies in this phase (of proof) an arising (in the absolute sense) and believes in a feature to be proved (the *sādhya-dharma*)...' The Sanskrit double nominative *utpāda-pratiṣhedho* and *sādhyadharmo* is rendered into Tibetan in a very clear way as an objective nominative *skye ba bkag pa* and an adverbial accusative *bsgrub bya'i chos su*; the particle *su* means 'as' and can in no way be construed as 'and'. Thus, Chandrakīrti is giving the context of his following remarks—that of ultimate analysis, such as in this case when a negation of production is being asserted as, or taken as, the predicate of what one is proving. Many Tibetan scholars take this as showing that Chandrakīrti is speaking only about occasions of debating about the final mode of subsistence of phenomena and that

his remarks about no commonly appearing subjects should not be extended to times when debating about conventional phenomena such as impermanence, since the question of whether the consciousness certifying the subject and so forth is valid with respect to the mode of subsistence is relevant only when one is debating about that mode of subsistence.

Jam-ȳang-shay-b̄a's text (*GM*, 247b.1) mis-reads *de'i tshe de kho nar (tadā tad eva)* instead of *de'i tshe kho nar (tadaiva)* as the Peking edition (Vol. 98 6.3.3) does and which is confirmed by the Sanskrit (Poussin, 30.1). He strains to include *de kho nar* somewhere in the meaning of the sentence; disregarding syntax, he puts it with the first clause, reading it as referring to a reasoning consciousness in the face of which production is refuted. Following this reading, the passage would be:

> ... at this time [of proving that eyes and so forth are without truly established production] when it is just the case that a negation of production in suchness [that is to say, in the perspective of a reasoning consciousness] is asserted as the predicate of the probandum ...

D̄zong-ka-b̄a's *Great Exposition of the Stages of the Path (Lam rim chen mo)* has the same mis-reading (Dharmsala: Shes rig par khang, 448b.3, and the *Four Interwoven Commentaries*, 530.3) but with a different interpretation. There, *de kho nar* is taken in a more syntactically appropriate way as going not with the 'when' clause but with what follows. With this placement the passage reads:

> That is not so, because at this time [of proving that eyes and so forth are without truly established production] when it is just the case that a negation of production is asserted as the predicate of the probandum, this one [Bhāvaviveka] himself just asserts that the entity of the subject [an eye]—the basis of that [predicate, non-production from self]—which is found by a mere erroneous [consciousness] has degenerated from [being established] in suchness [that is to say, is not established ultimately since it is found by a mistaken consciousness]. Erroneous and non-erroneous [consciousnesses] are different.

In this interpretation, (according to the *Four Interwoven*

Commentaries, 530.5-31.2) once Bhāvaviveka asserts that eyes and so forth are not ultimately established and are not ultimates, it is established that they are falsities. Also, since it would be very contradictory for a consciousness of reality which is devoid of dualistic appearance to take such falsities as its objects in the perspective of its perceiving suchness, they must be objects found by erroneous consciousnesses and objects in relation to which a consciousness comes to be considered a mistaken consciousness. However, the Mādhyamika is debating with a Proponent of True Existence who asserts that valid sense consciousnesses are non-mistaken with respect to visible forms and so forth. Therefore, it would be very contradictory for that one object to be that in relation to which a sense consciousness becomes mistaken as in the Mādhyamika system and that in relation to which it becomes non-mistaken [read *tshad ma ma 'khrul ba'i yul* for *tshad ma 'khrul pa'i yul*, 531.2] as in the system of a Proponent of True Existence. Due to this, there is no subject commonly established for both the Mādhyamika and the Proponent of True Existence. For, an erroneous, mistaken consciousness which is polluted by ignorance and a non-erroneous, non-mistaken consciousness of a Superior's meditative equipoise perceiving suchness are different, that is, are mutually exclusive in terms of how they engage their objects, the one dualistically and the other non-dualistically (according to Kensur Yeshe Thupten).

In this interpretation the last sentence—'Erroneous and non-erroneous [consciousnesses] are different'—refers to the possible consciousnesses that could certify the existence of objects that are established by way of their own character, both being rejected. That which is erroneous—a consciousness to which a non-inherently existent object appears to be inherently existent—cannot certify an inherently existent object because that is the very thing with respect to which it is mistaken. That which is non-erroneous, a consciousness of meditative equipoise that does not involve such mistaken appearance, also cannot certify the existence of a conventionality such as eyes and so forth (the subject of our syllogism about non-ultimate production) because conventionalities do not appear to it, even in the case of a Buddha, in terms of its mode of perceiving emptiness non-dualistically since conventionalities can only be perceived in a dualistic mode. Also, in this interpretation the 'degeneration' or non-establishment is taken as referring to Bhāvaviveka's having to assert that eyes and so forth are not established ultimately, that is to say, not established by way of their own character because of being found or certified as existing by erroneous consciousnesses, this in turn being because even he holds that they are not found by a consciousness of meditative equipoise.

D̄zong-ka-b̄a's *Essence of the Good Explanations*, written later in his life than the *Great Exposition of the Stages of the Path*, offers another interpretation of this passage. That text says at the point of explaining Chandrakīrti's response to 'Bhāvaviveka's' proposal that the subject and so forth are established because only generalities are used (191.8-192.10, Varanasi edition).

> Bhāvaviveka himself asserts that the entities of the subjects—eyes and so forth—are not found by mere erroneous [consciousnesses], and [Chandrakīrti] refutes him through demonstrating the reasoning that the erroneous and the non-erroneous are different, a dichotomy, etc. The meaning of [Chandrakīrti's] statements is this: Mere eyes and so forth devoid of qualification of the two truths are not positable as the subjects in the proof that eyes and so forth are not produced from self because [according to Bhāvaviveka] the valid cognizers comprehending those subjects are consciousnesses that are non-mistaken with respect to the nature [inherent existence] of eyes and so forth but false appearances—in which erroneous objects of knowledge appear to exist by way of their own character whereas they do not—do not exist among objects found by non-erroneous consciousnesses that are not mistaken with respect to the nature.
>
> With respect to [Buddhapālita's] asserting the earlier reason [—that according to Bhāvaviveka the valid cognizers comprehending those subjects are consciousnesses that are non-mistaken with respect to the nature or inherent existence of eyes and so forth—] in a system [such as that of Bhāvaviveka] which asserts that whatever exists exists by way of its own entity, if [a consciousness] is mistaken relative to the appearance of the object's being

> established by way of its own character, it cannot be posited as finding [that is, realizing] its object of comprehension. Therefore, whether a valid cognizer is conceptual or non-conceptual, it must be non-mistaken about that with respect to which it is valid, its referent object or appearing object [respectively]. In that case, it must be valid about an entity or nature which is the object's own mode of subsistence and which is not just nominally designated conventionally, and he also asserts this. It is contradictory for whatever is an object found by such a valid cognizer to be an erroneous object of knowledge; thereby, the latter reason [—that false appearances, in which erroneous objects of knowledge appear to exist by way of their own character whereas they do not, do not exist among objects found by non-erroneous consciousnesses that are not mistaken with respect to the nature—] is established. Likewise, it is also contradictory for whatever is an object found by a mistaken consciousness to be a non-erroneous object of knowledge. Therefore, [Bhāvaviveka] cannot dispel the fallacy of the non-establishment of the subject.

In this interpretation, Bhāvaviveka is said to assert, not that eyes and so forth are not established *in suchness* because of being found by mistaken consciousnesses, but that these are not found by mistaken consciousnesses because they must be certified by consciousnesses that are not mistaken with respect to the inherent existence of those objects. However, the former is seen as being forced on him because of his assertions whereas the latter is presented as his actual assertion; thus, the change in Dzong-ka-ba's interpretation does not represent an about-face in terms of delineating Bhāvaviveka's tenets and instead is a different reading of the text. (Also, in this interpretation the last sentence—'Erroneous and non-erroneous are different'—refers not to consciousnesses but to objects of knowledge.)

About the change in interpretation, Dzong-ka-ba himself says in his *Essence of the Good Explanations* (195.20-196.2):

> Although the two—[my] explanation [of this passage] elsewhere [in the *Great Exposition of the Stages of the*

Path] in terms of [Bhāvaviveka's] having asserted that the basal subjects degenerate from [or are not] established as [their own] suchness and this mode [of interpretation]—do not agree, it is not that [my two interpretations] disagree with respect to [the passage's setting forth] the tenet of refuting autonomy.

It is my guess that since in his *Essence of the Good Explanations* D̄zong-ka-b̄a does not use 'in suchness' (*de kho na*:, the mis-reading in *de'i tshe kho nar*) in any way at all, he came to understand it as a mis-reading and, due to this, changed his reading of the text, ingeniously making it mean the same thing, albeit by a very different route. It seems to me that Jam-ȳang-shay-b̄a makes the mistake of trying to keep 'in suchness' (*de kho nar*) when explaining D̄zong-ka-b̄a's new interpretation in his *Essence of the Good Explanations* and thus goes through the verbal gymnastics of moving it, against all sense of syntax, into the previous clause.

In D̄zong-ka-b̄a's *Ocean of Reasoning, Explanation of (Nāgārjuna's) 'Treatise on the Middle Way'* (52.2-7.13), Varanasi 1973 edition), written after his *Essence of the Good Explanations* he refers his readers to the discussion in his '*Essence of the Good Explanations* and so forth' for the topic of Commonly Appearing Subjects, suggesting a preference for the interpretation there over that in the 'Great Exposition of Special Insight'; thus, it may be that in the end he did not hold that these two radically different interpretations are both correct. In any case, Jam-ȳang-shay-b̄a uses the interpretation in D̄zong-ka-b̄a's *Essence of the Good Explanations* for this passage, and hence the interpretation used here in my translation and commentary is the same.

425 *GM*, 249b.2.

426 For this, see D̄zong-ka-b̄a's *Essence of the Good Explanations*, 193.13 (Varanasi: Pleasure of Elegant Sayings edition, 1973).

427 This was cited earlier, p.475. See n.388.

428 For this, see the *Four Interwoven Commentaries on (D̄zong-ka-b̄a's) 'Great Exposition of the Stages of the Path'*, 578.5. The summations following are the author's.

428a Wayman (p.312) translates the last line of this citation as, 'You have no answer to this.' However, the *Four Interwoven*

Commentaries (533.4) make it clear that the reference is to 'Bhāvaviveka's' earlier answer: *khyed kyis lan btab pa 'di ni don dang mthun pa'i lan ma yin pa nyid do* 'The answer which you have given is just not an answer concordant with the fact.' Bhāvaviveka's earlier answer (see p.507) was that just generalities are to be used as subject, predicate, and so forth without being qualified by the particular assertions of the two schools. Chandrakīrti's refutation of this is built around his perception that a tenet unacceptable to a Mādhyamika is automatically attached to the subject and so forth—inherent existence—because schools that propound inherent existence hold that the consciousness certifying the subject perforce *must* certify the subject's inherent existence.

429 Jam-ȳang-shay-b̄a (*GM*, 250a.2) seems to make this conclusion since he does not specify 'Buddhists' here as referring to non-Prāsaṅgikas.

430 *Gom-day*, 633.1, *sangs rgyas pa 'og mas*. A note by Dra-di-ge-shay Rin-chen-don-drup (*Bra-sti-dge-bshes Rin-chen-don-grub*) in the *Four Interwoven Commentaries on (D̄zong-ka-b̄a's) 'Great Exposition of the Stages of the Path'* (546.6) identifies the Buddhists here as Svātantrikas and below.

431 Geshe Gedün Lodrö and Kensur Yeshe Thupten reported this. Wayman (p.316) translates the first clause of the second sentence in the following citation as, 'For in that instance (of example) there is no intention to state a difference between the sound universal and the impermanence universal.' However, the reference here is not to a *difference between* two things but to mere sound and mere impermanence *which are not asserted as qualified (avivakṣhitavisheṣha, khyad par brjod par mi 'dod pa)* with the particular tenets of the two schools. The *Four Interwoven Commentaries* (545.6-6.3) says: *dpe'i skabs der ni sangs rgyas pas bye brag pa la sgra mi rtag par sgrub pa dang bye brag pas gsal byed pa la de ltar sgrub pa'i skabs su rim pa ltar 'byung 'gyur dang nam mkha'i yon tan gnyis dang byas pa dang sngar yod rkyen gyis gsal bar byas pa gnyis te so so'i 'dod pas khyad par ma byas par rang gi mtshan nyid kyis grub pa tsam gyi sgra'i spyi tsam zhig dang phyis 'byung gi rgyu la ltos pa dang ma ltos pa gang gis kyang khyad par du ma byas pa'i sgrub bya'i chos rang gi mtshan nyid kyis grub pa'i mi rtag pa'am 'jig pa nyid kyi spyi tsam zhig la tshad mar song ba de bkod nas so so'i 'dod pa'i khyad*

par de dag sbyar nas brjod par mi 'dod par gnyis ka'i lugs la mthun snang du grub pa zhig brjod par 'dod na ni rgol ba de gnyis ka'i lugs la yang yod pa yin... 'On that occasion of the example when the Buddhist is proving to a Vaisheṣhika that sound is impermanent and a Vaisheṣhika is proving the same to a Dīpaka, a mere generality of sound which is just established by way of its own character but is not qualified by their individual assertions —respectively, being a derivative of the elements and being a quality of space or being a product and being something previously existent which is manifested by conditions—and a mere generality of impermanence or disintegratedness (the predicate of the probandum) which is established by way of its own character but which is not qualified by either depending or not depending on later causes are stated within the context that these have been certified by valid cognition. If, not wishing to express [a subject and predicate] within affixing those qualifications of their individual assertions, they wish to express [a subject and predicate that are] established as commonly appearing in both of their systems, there is such in the systems of both disputants.' As D̄zong-ka-b̄a (*Four Interwoven Commentaries*, 546.6ff) makes clear, 'sound not qualified by being a derivative of the elements or a quality of space' refers to sound's not being so qualified *for the minds* of the two disputants. In other words, the two disputants can speak of sound without putting in the qualifications of their systems even though the Buddhist holds that there is no sound that is not a derivative of the elements and the Vaisheṣhika holds that there is no sound which is not a quality of space. Though the Buddhist holds that sound is necessarily a derivative of the elements and the Vaisheṣhika holds that sound necessarily possesses those attributes (*khyad par dang ldan pa*), it is not necessary that sound be qualified for their minds (*blo la khyad par du byas pa*) by being a derivative of the elements or a quality of space. Conceptuality is able to isolate such generalities. Chandrakīrti is saying that even if in Bhāvaviveka's example such generalities are possible, there is no possibility of such when proving emptiness since the subject must be certified by valid cognition and a non-Mādhyamika feels that this certification also certifies the inherent existence of the subject.

The commentary, as given above, tacks 'established by way

of its own character' onto the generalities, restricting the range of the example to non-Prāsaṅgikas; however, not all scholars hold that this restriction should be made, for even in the Prāsaṅgika system generalities of sound and impermanence are possible even when debating with non-Prāsaṅgikas since the issue of their being established by way of their own character is not pertinent.

432 This and the next paragraph supply background drawn from Kensur Lekden's oral teachings.

433 The *Four Interwoven Commentaries on (Dzong-ka-ba's) 'Great Exposition of the Stages of the Path'*, 566.2-7.1.

434 Gom-day Nam-ka-gyel-tsen ends his commentary at this point.

435 The bracketed material in this sentence is from the *Four Interwoven Commentaries on (Dzong-ka-ba's) 'Great Exposition of the Stages of the Path'*, 561.4ff.

436 The bracketed material in I.7 is from Dzong-ka-ba's *Ocean of Reasoning*, 77.3ff (Varanasi 1973 edition).

437 The bracketed material in this sentence is from the *Four Interwoven Commentaries on (Dzong-ka-ba's) 'Great Exposition of the Stages of the Path'*, 562.5.

438 This and the next sentence are teachings frequently emphasized by Kensur Lekden.

439 The *Four Interwoven Commentaries on (Dzong-ka-ba's) 'Great Exposition of the Stages of the Path'*, 569.5, identifies this term as meaning 'something substantially established which is established by way of its own character' *(rang gi mtshan nyid kyis grub pa'i rdzas grub)*.

440 Reading *ghaṭasya* in accordance with De Jong ('Textcritical Notes' p.31, n.31.14).

441 Following the Tibetan *gzhan gyis*; the Sanskrit is *pare* which Stcherbatsky (p.119, n.7) prefers as *paraiḥ* but De Jong (p.31, n.31.14) decides should be left as it is.

442 The meaning of this is conjectured from discussion with Kensur Yeshe Thupten, who pointed to a statement in Dignāga's *Compendium of Valid Cognition* (P5700, Vol. 130 3.1.3, I.4ab): 'Because [the sense powers] are the uncommon cause [of their respective consciousness], that [consciousness] is designated [with the term 'sense direct perceiver' (*pratyakṣha, dbang po'i mngon sum*)] by way of the sense powers.' (*asādhāraṇa-hetutvād akṣhais tad vyapadishyate, thun mong ma yin rgyu yi phyir/ de'i*

tha snyad dbang pos byed [the Peking mis-reads *de yis tha snyad; de yi* would also be suitable; this reading follows Hattori cited below]. For the Sanskrit and M. Hattori's translation and analysis see his *Dignāga, On Perception* [Cambridge: Harvard, 1968], p.26 and pp.86-7 n.1.30 and n.1.32). Kensur Yeshe Thupten and Hattori also point out that there is a similar statement in Vasubandhu's *Treasury of Knowledge*, I.45: 'Since due to their changing [that is, becoming duller or clearer, the respective consciousnesses] change [becoming duller or clearer], the bases are the eye [sense power] and so forth. Therefore, because of being the uncommon [cause], the consciousnesses are called by way of them [that is, a consciousness of visible forms is called an eye consciousness, not a form consciousness].' (*tad-vikāra-vikārtivād āshrayāsh chakṣhur-ādayaḥ/ ato 'sādhāraṇatvāch cha vijñānaṃ tair niruchyate*, [Hattori, p.76 n.1.11]; *de dag gyur pas 'gyur nyid phyir/ rten ni mig la sogs pa yin/ de phyir thun mong ma yin phyir/ de dag gis ni rnam shes bstan* [148.16, Varanasi 1978 edition].) Thus, a non-Mādhyamika is arguing that since the sense powers are themselves causes, they must be ultimately produced.

Stcherbatsky (p.120) translates the passage as:

> *Thesis:* Internal facts, i.e., mental phenomena really arise, i.e., they have a real existence.
> *Reason:* Because they produce purposive actions directed towards the same objects as our thoughts have been directed to.
> *Major premise:* Whatsoever is efficient is real.

His translation, though a bit strained, is getting at the same point.

443 In the Tibetan Cultural Printing Press edition (22.19), read *shes rab kyi mig* for *shes rab kyis mig* in accordance with the Peking (Vol. 98 6.5.5). It seems to me that the Tibetan would be better rendered as: *dngos po rnams kyi yang dag pa ji lta ba bzhin nyid mthong ba'i rnal 'byor pa mnyam par bzhag pa'i shes rab kyi mig gis skye ba dang 'gro ba la sogs pa dag don dam par yod par bsgrub na ni.*

444 In the Tibetan Cultural Printing Press edition (23.4) read *sgrub par byed pa la yang* for *sgrub par byed pa la yod pa* in accordance with the Peking (Vol. 98 6.5.7). Stcherbatsky (p.121) takes

Bhāvaviveka's refutation of going as a refutation of time; though there is a similarity between space and time, this refutation at least explicitly is concerned with motion, being concerned with the second chapter of Nāgārjuna's *Treatise*, the 'Analysis of Going and Coming'.

445 De Jong (p.31, n.33.1) corrects the Sanskrit *rūpavat* to *svarūpavat* in accordance with Bhāvaviveka's *Heart of the Middle Way*, III.39ab; thus, the Tibetan would be better translated as *rang gzugs bzhin*, 'like its form', meaning the form that the eye sees.

446 Bhāvaviveka's *Heart of the Middle Way*, III.27ab; see De Jong, p.32, n.33.2.

447 *GM*, 253.5: read *'di yang* for *'di la yang* in accordance with Vol. 98 7.1.2. Here, Chandrakīrti (Poussin, 33.4) gives the reason of Bhāvaviveka's syllogism as *sattvāt*, not *vidyamānatvāt* as he did earlier (26.1); the Tibetan is *yod pa'i phyir* throughout.

Stcherbatsky's interpretation (p.123) of the objection is quite fanciful. As this passage is not cited in the *Four Interwoven Commentaries on (D̄zong-ka-b̄a's) 'Great Exposition of the Stages of the Path'*, or in *GM*, or in *Gom-day* whose commentary has ended, the interpretation of the objection as coming from Bhāvaviveka is mine. It makes sense since Chandrakīrti argued earlier for the all-inclusiveness of Buddhapālita's syllogism (see n.398).

448 D̄zong-ka-b̄a's *Great Exposition of the Stages of the Path*, P6001, Vol. 152 160.4.3.

449 Missing in the Tibetan. The Sanskrit (Poussin, 34.5) has *asmadanumānānām*. The *Four Interwoven Commentaries on (D̄zong-ka-b̄a's) 'Great Exposition of the Stages of the Path'*, 572.4, by glossing this as referring to the inferences appearing in Chandrakīrti's *Clear Words* and so forth, interprets the statement as referring not to all syllogistic reasoning in general but to those refuting production from self such as those drawn from Buddhapālita's text. This preserves other-renowned inferences or syllogisms as a means also for positively communicating one's own tenets. The interpretation seems forced; one is drawn into wondering why, if Chandrakīrti meant to be so specific, he did not bother to be this specific.

Later in the same text (573.4), the same passage is glossed this way: '. . . but we [Prāsaṅgikas] do not use autonomous inferences because inferences [used by us Prāsaṅgikas] have the fruit [or purpose] of only refuting the [wrong] theses of other [parties].' In this version, the added commentary is not aimed at preserving the positive use of syllogisms; however, one could merely say that 'inferences' means not all but some inferences stated by Prāsaṅgikas. In any case, the Gel-luk-b̄a position is clear: other-renowned inferences are used for both positive and negative purposes.

450 Poussin (34.6) changes *parash chakṣhuḥ* to *paraṃ chakṣhuḥ* recognizing (see n.5) that the Tibetan (*gzhan*) does not confirm the change, preferring that it read *gzhan la*; however, Dr. Vaidya leaves the manuscript as is, and the *Four Interwoven Commentaries on (D̄zong-ka-b̄a's) 'Great Exposition of the Stages of the Path'*, 573.5, follows the same reading, identifying the term as referring to other parties who assert that the eye sees.

451 *GM*, 255b.1, read *nyid du yang khas* for *nyid du khas* in accordance with the Peking, Vol. 98 7.1.7. The bracketed material in this and the next section is from the *Four Interwoven Commentaries on (D̄zong-ka-b̄a's) 'Great Exposition of the Stages of the Path'*, 573.6-4.2.

452 The bracketed material is from the *Four Interwoven Commentaries on (D̄zong-ka-b̄a's) 'Great Exposition of the Stages of the Path'*, 574.4.

453 Missing in the Tibetan. The Sanskrit (Poussin, 34.11) has *asmadanumānair*.

454 In *GM*, 254a.6, read *gang las* for *gang la* in accordance with Vol. 98 7.2.2.

455 The *Four Interwoven Commentaries on (D̄zong-ka-b̄a's) 'Great Exposition of the Stages of the Path'*, 578.5.

456 The bracketed material is from the *Four Interwoven Commentaries on (D̄zong-ka-b̄a's) 'Great Exposition of the Stages of the Path'*, 591.1ff.

457 The *Four Interwoven Commentaries on (D̄zong-ka-b̄a's) 'Great Exposition of the Stages of the Path'*, 592.2. With respect to 'who do not know suchness' the Sanskrit (Poussin, 36.1) is merely *tadanabhijña* 'who do not know that [or those, which could refer to "the definitions"]' whereas the Tibetan reads *de kho na mi shes pa'i* 'who do not know suchness'. The *Four Interwoven Commentaries* (592.3) takes it even further: *chos kyi de kho na nyid ma shes pa'i* 'who do not know the suchness of phenomena'. I have followed the Tibetan as it presumably

reflects the reading of *tad* as meaning *tattva* (see Poussin, p.36, n.3) by the translators.

458 The rest of the chapter presents the author's reflections on these topics. This first sentence refers to Āryadeva's famous statement in his *Four Hundred* (the *Four Interwoven Commentaries*, 590.2):

> Just as a barbarian cannot be
> Approached with another language,
> So the world cannot be approached
> Except with the worldly.

459 D̄zong-ka-b̄a, *Great Exposition of the Stages of the Path*, P6001, Vol. 152 142.3.6.

460 Kensur Lekden frequently mentioned this as an apparent contradiction; it is from Chandrakīrti's *Commentary on (Āryadeva's) 'Four Hundred'*.

461 Kensur Lekden.

462 Part Five, chapter six is mainly a paraphrase of *J̄ang*, 291.9-299.8, supplemented with information from the N̄yingma Lama Khetsun Sangpo, who in 1972 was working on his own compilation of biographies of Tibetan yogis at the Library of Tibetan Works and Archives, Dharmsala. The identification of the orders of particular scholars and yogis is his, as are the dates with an asterisk. The chapter is not intended as a definitive history of the spread of Buddhism to and development in Tibet, but as a presentation illustrating both the dominance of Prāsaṅgika and the active inter-play between the orders.

463 This paragraph is mostly drawn from the oral teachings of Khetsun Sangpo.

464 Snellgrove and Richardson give the date as 779 in *A Cultural History of Tibet* (New York: Praeger, 1968), p.277.

465 This was reported by Khetsun Sangpo.

466 D̄zong-ka-b̄a, *Middling Exposition*, P6002, Vol. 152 184.2.5.

467 Khetsun Sangpo.

468 Khetsun Sangpo.

469 Khetsun Sangpo.

470 Tibetan Buddhism is usually viewed as having four principal orders, but Khetsun Sangpo follows a system of eight.

471 Part Five, chapter seven is mainly drawn from extended conversations with Kensur Lekden, Geshe Gedün Lodrö, and Geshe

Lhundup Sopa; the chapter attempts to put the Ge-luk-b̄a teachings on valid establishment in context. The next sentence was repeatedly emphasized by Kensur Lekden.

472 *Ann*, dbu 9b.5ff.

473 *Ann*, dbu 9a.7ff.

474 This and the next paragraph are mainly drawn from the oral teachings of Geshe Gedün Lodrö.

475 D̄zong-ka-b̄a, *Illumination of the Thought, Extensive Explanation of (Chandrakīrti's) 'Supplement to (Nāgārjuna's) "Treatise on the Middle Way"'*, P6143, Vol. 154 67.5.2ff. The next paragraph is from Geshe Gedün Lodrö.

476 *Clear Words*, P5260, Vol. 98 53.3.7ff.

477 This and the next paragraph are mainly drawn from the oral teachings of Kensur Lekden.

478 See Tenzin Gyatso's *The Buddhism of Tibet and the Key to the Middle Way* (New York: Harper and Row, 1975), p.74.

479 *GM*, 106a.3ff.

480 Geshe Lhundup Sopa.

481 This paragraph is mostly from Kensur Lekden.

482 *Ornament to Nāgārjuna's Thought, Eloquence Containing the Essence of the Profundities of the Middle Way* (Kalimpong: Mani Printing Works), 14a.6ff. The biographical material comes from his contemporaries, Geshe Wangyal, Kensur Lekden, and Geshe Gelden.

483 This was reported by the inner Mongolian scholar Geshe Gelden.

484 *Presentation of the Lack of Being One or Many*, Collected Works, Vol. 1 (New Delhi: Lama Guru Deva, 1971), 425.1ff.

485 Part Five, chapter eight is drawn from the sources indicated in the subsequent notes in an attempt to contrast the Ge-luk-b̄a interpretation with other prevalent views on the import of Prāsaṅgika-Mādhyamika. The quote here is taken from the Shes rig par khang edition, 435b.3-5, with the answer being from 440a.3-b.1.

486 (New Delhi: Lama Guru Deva, 1972), 18b.3-4.

487 Sopa and Hopkins, *Practice and Theory of Tibetan Buddhism* (London: Rider and Co., 1976), p.137.

488 IBID, p.134-5.

489 See Tenzin Gyatso's *The Buddhism of Tibet and The Key to the Middle Way* (New York: Harper and Row, 1975), pp.55-6.

490 336.4-35b.2.

491 *Jang*, 419.17-420.9.

492 Śata-Piṭaka Series, Volume 28 pp.45-6.

493 *Svarasvati* has not been edited to *Sarasvati* because the *sva* spelling occurs consistently in many Tibetan texts and accords more with the Tibetan translation of the name as *dbyangs*, 'melody' or 'intonation'. Kensur Lekden mentioned that Svarasvati and Mañjughoṣha are special deities for authors, the former assisting with perfect speech and the latter with discriminative wisdom.

494 P6142, Vol. 153 208.5.5 The Peking Edition reads *mtshan 'dzin* instead of *mthar 'dzin*.

D̄zong-ka-b̄a's *Essence of the Good Explanations (Legs bshad snying po)* is the ultimate of his works dealing with comparative schools of tenets. Structured around the topic of the interpretable and the definitive in the Mahāyāna schools, the text is primarily concerned with delineating what the final mode of being of phenomena is according to those schools, on the basis of which the division into what requires interpretation and what does not is made. Thus, the hermeneutical theory of the Chittamātra, Yogāchāra-Svātantrika, Sautrāntika-Svātantrika, and Prāsaṅgika schools is ontologically based, that is, their theories of interpretation of both scripture and objects revolve around what ultimate reality is in contrast to how Buddha spoke to certain trainees in accordance with their interests, dispositions, and capabilities.

As Jam-ȳang-shay-b̄a says at the beginning of his commentary on the *Essence of the Good Explanations* (Buxa edition, 3a.2), D̄zong-ka-b̄a is presenting the essence of all the good explanations (*legs bshad thams cad kyi snying po*), and thus the title, at least according to him, does not indicate that D̄zong-ka-b̄a is saying that his own text has an essence of good explanation or eloquence but that he is presenting the essence of the marvelous explanations on the subject of the interpretable and the definitive from Indian treatises. The title could be translated as *Essence of Eloquence* or *Essence of the Eloquent* as long as eloquence was understood as referring to the Indian scholars' discriminative presentation of the subject matter and not to euphony of expression as in beautiful poetic composition or to D̄zong-ka-b̄a's own presentation. Undoubtedly, D̄zong-ka-b̄a's composition comes to be eloquent by way of containing the eloquence of the Indian scholars, but this does not appear to be the intention of his title.

Jam-ȳang-shay-b̄a would find support in the last two lines of this quote for his position that Buddhapālita is the founder of the Prāsaṅgika system, but those who say that Chandrakīrti is the founder would also find support from the statement just above it that Chandrakīrti 'opened the chariot way' for Prāsaṅgika through clearly differentiating this system from others. I find Jam-ȳang-shay-b̄a's position to be insupportable in the face of (1) his own statement that even though Saraha preceded Nāgārjuna in holding the Mādhyamika view and even though Vimuktisena preceded Shāntarakṣhita in holding the Yogāchāra-Svātantrika view (*GT*, ca 10a.5-11a.4), those two are not posited as the founders of, respectively, the Mādhyamika system and the Yogāchāra-Mādhyamika system because they did not clearly set off those schools in contradistinction to other systems and (2) his admission that Buddhapālita did not do that for Prāsaṅgika (*GT*, ca 9a.5-10a.1) whereas Chandrakīrti did (see p.584). J̄ang-ḡya (288.last line) goes so far as to say that Jam-ȳang-shay-b̄a actually did not hold that Buddhapālita founded Prāsaṅgika for the above reasons. However, the monastic college that uses Jam-ȳang-shay-b̄a's texts, Go-mang, currently holds that Buddhapālita was the founder and that this is Jam-ȳang-shay-b̄a's view.

495 The four types of Superiors (*Āryan*) are Hearer, Solitary Realizer, Bodhisattva, and Buddha Superiors. *Āryan* (*'Phags pa*) is translated as 'Superiors' because, according to Kensur Lekden, these are beings who have risen above the level of common beings (*pṛthagjana, so sor skye bo*) through cognizing emptiness directly on the path of seeing.

Shrāvaka (*Nyan thos*) is translated as 'Hearers' because (*GM*, 16a.3-5) they *hear* (*nyan*) the doctrine, practice it, and then *cause others to hear* (*thos par byed pa*) that they have actualized their goal (see Hopkins' *Compassion in Tibetan Buddhism* [London: Hutchinson, 1980], pp.102-3). This etymology is built around active and causative uses of the verbal root for hearing, *shru*; one hears and then causes others to hear, in this case not what one has heard but what one has achieved after putting into practice the doctrines one has heard by announcing that 'I have done what was to be done; I will not know another life,' etc. The translation of the term as 'disciples' loses this etymological meaning which appears to be important in the tradition as is evidenced by Chandrakīrti's citing it in his *Supplement* (Tibetan Publishing House edition, 3.11) and Dzong-ka-ba's including and expanding on Chandrakīrti in his commentary (*Compassion*, P.102).

Chandrakīrti (*Comm*, 3.14, cited by Dzong-ka-ba in *Compassion*, p.103) gives a second etymology of *Shrāvaka* as Hearer-Proclaimer (*GM*, 16a.5ff) based on the *White Lotus of Excellent Doctrine Sutra* (*Saddharmapuṇḍarīka*, IV.53 [P781, Vol. 30 23.3.2; *Buddhist Sanskrit Texts*, No. 6, p.82] which says:

O Protector, today we have become hearer-proclaimers
(*shrāvakabhuta*).
We will thoroughly proclaim the excellent enlightenment
And will set forth the terms of enlightenment.
Thus we [will be] like formidable Hearer-Proclaimers
(*Shrāvaka*).

Jam-yang-shay-ba (*GM*, 16a.6), expanding on Dzong-ka-ba's explanation (*Compassion*, p.103), interprets this as meaning that Shrāvakas are so called because upon *hearing* (*thos nas*) about the supreme fruit of Buddhahood or about its path from a Buddha they *proclaim* (*sgrogs pa*) it to others without practicing it themselves. He says (*GM*, 17b.4) that at this point in the *Lotus Sutra* Bodhisattvas are saying that they are fit to be derided because, like Hearers, they are proclaiming the fruit of the Mahāyāna or the profound path proceeding to that state without practicing it themselves. The context of the sutra, however, appears to be slightly different as can be seen in Leon Hurvitz's very readable translation in the *Scripture of the Lotus Blossom of the Fine Dharma* (New York: Columbia, 1976, p.98). The Buddha has told the story of the 'prodigal son' (see Whalen Lai's fine article 'The Buddhist "Prodigal Son": A Story of Misperceptions', *Journal of the International Association of Buddhist Studies*, Vol. 4 No. 2, pp.91-8), and the former Hearer, Mahākāshyapa, is re-telling the story, relating it to how he and other Hearers formerly proclaimed the Bodhisattva path but did not practice it:

The Buddha's sons,
Hearing the Dharma from us
And day and night taking thought,
Engaged in cultivated practice. (p.95)

Also:

> So we, though we preached
> The jewel cache of the Buddhadharma,
> Had no hope for it
> In the same way. (p.96)

Also:

> Although we, for the sake of
> The Buddha's sons,
> Preached the Bodhisattvadharma,
> Wherewith the Buddha Path was to be sought,
> Yet, with respect to this Dharma,
> We never had any hopes. (p.97)

Mahākāshyapa then explains that due to having heard that they have the lot of the Mahāyāna and thereupon attained the Mahāyāna path they, like the son in the parable who was gradually led to recognize that he is the son of a wealthy king, have gained something extraordinary which they always had in the sense that they had been preaching it but had no hope to practice it. As Hurvitz translates the stanza in question:

> We now
> Are truly voice-hearers,
> Taking the voice of the Buddha Path
> And causing all to hear it.

Thus, Jam-ȳang-shay-b̄a is certainly right in saying that the *Lotus Sutra* is indicating a dual etymology of *Shrāvaka* as those who *hear* about the highest enlightenment of the Mahāyāna and then *cause others to hear* about it (causative in Sanskrit, *sgrogs* in Tibetan) without practicing it themselves. However, it seems that the specific context here in this stanza is that the now Bodhisattva Mahākāshyapa is saying that he and others are now formidable hearer-proclaimers in that unlike their earlier state as Hearer-Proclaimers who heard and proclaimed the Mahāyāna teaching without practicing it, they have put it to practice, have attained its fruit, and will proclaim it to others. Thus, at this particular point Mahākāshyapa does not seem to be saying that 'we Bodhisattvas are fit to be derided' as Jam-ȳang-shay-b̄a says. This is confirmed in the commentary on the *Lotus Sutra* by Pṛthivibandhu (*Sa'i rtsa lags*), in which in reference to this stanza he says (*The Nyingma Edition of the sDe-dge bKa'-'gyur and bsTan-'gyur*, Dharma Publishing, 1981, Text 4017, Vol. 76 663.6), 'This indicates that, having attained the great fruit, they are fit to help others who are set as Hearer Superiors.' Mahākāshyapa is rejoicing in their new situation.

How the context is interpreted affects the translation of the last line of IV.53, *steno vayaṃ shrāvaka bhīṣhmakalpāḥ, de bas bdag cag nyan thos mi zad 'dra* (*GM*, 16b.2) or *de bas bdag cag sgogs pa mi bzad 'dra* (P781, Vol. 30 23.3.2), 'Thus we [will be] like formidable Hearer-Proclaimers.' The term 'formidable' (*bhīṣhma, mi zad* or *mi bzad*) is missing in Hurvitz's translation from the Chinese. Louis de la Vallee Poussin (*Museon*, ns V.11, 1910 [Vol. 29], p.253) renders the line, 'aussi serons-nous comme d'irrestibles Çrāvakas.' In *Compassion in Tibetan Buddhism* (p.103), I translated it as, 'Thus we are like intractable Hearers,' assuming that Jam-ȳang-shay-b̄a was taking the term in a negative way. '*Irresistible*', like 'formidable', suggests the *might* and *power* (*bhīṣhma*) of their proclamation now that they are proclaiming the Mahāyāna doctrine on the basis of actual attainment, whereas 'intractable' is a reference to the *awful* or *frightful* (*bhīṣhma*) state that they were in when they just caused others to hear about the Mahāyāna but did not practice it themselves. In either case, there is a play on the contrast with their former state. The translation as 'formidable', however, seems to fit the context better.

Based on this etymology of *shrāvaka* as hearing of the highest enlightenment and proclaiming it without practicing it, Hurvitz (p.116) explains that '...by *auditor* is *meant* (italics his) one who lacks knowledge of Emptiness.' However, as D̄zong-ka-b̄a (*Compassion*, pp.150-60) shows, this is not the position of Chandrakīrti and other Prāsaṅgikas; according to him, in Prāsaṅgika the subtlest emptiness must be cognized even to be liberated from cyclic existence and thus Hearers and Solitary Realizers do so. In D̄zong-ka-b̄a's interpretation of Prāsaṅgika, the path that Hearers hear about and proclaim without practicing would be great compassion, the altruistic intention to become enlightened, and meditation on emptiness using a myriad of reasonings rather than just a few. However, with regard to Chittamātra, D̄zong-ka-b̄a and his followers hold that

Hearers and Solitary Realizers do not cognize the subtlest emptiness (see Sopa and Hopkins' *Practice and Theory of Tibetan Buddhism*, pp.117-18), in which case what Hearers hear about and proclaim without practicing is the emptiness of a difference of entity between subject and object, as well as the paths of great compassion and so forth. The Chittamātrin interpretation, therefore, accords with Hurvitz's presentation.

Though this second etymology of hearing and proclaiming without practicing is pejorative, the former is not, as it is frequently reported in sutra itself that upon achieving their goal Hearers report to others the fact that they have completed their path with statements such as, 'I have done what was to be done; I will not know another birth' (*Compassion*, p.102). Thus, given the importance that Chandrakīrti, D̄zong-ka-b̄a, and so forth give to the term itself, this non-pejorative etymology can serve as a basis for a literal translation as 'Hearers'.

Jam-ȳang-shay-b̄a (*GM*, 16b.2) views the two etymologies as built from different roots, but in both cases the Sanskrit seems merely to be a play between the active and the causative uses of *shru*. In the case of the *Lotus Sutra* the causative *saṃshrāvayiṣh-yāmatha* (future causative first person plural) was translated into Tibetan as *sgrogs* rather than as *thos par byed pa* leading to the tradition that there are two etymologies of *shrāvaka*, one as *nyan thos* and another as *thos sgrogs*, whereas it seems that the two are variations of the one play on the active and the causative. In the first etymology the Hearers proclaim or cause others to hear that they have actualized their goal whereas in the second they proclaim or cause others to hear the doctrine that they have heard. Jam-ȳang-shay- b̄a (*GM*, 16b.2) says that the *Lotus Sutra* etymology is built from the verbal root for 'proclaiming the heard' (*thos pa sgrogs pa'i bying*), but he does not cite the actual Sanskrit. However, in accordance with his etymology of the *ka* of *madhyamaka* as from the verbal root for proclaiming, *kai* (meaning 'to sound' according to Apte) following an explanation by Bhāvaviveka (*GM*, 4b.3), we can surmise that he is taking the *ka* of *shrāvaka* as built from the verbal root for proclaiming and 'the heard' as *shruta* from *shru*. However, though there are two etymologies of *shrāvaka*, they are built not around different verbal roots but around the single root *shru* treated in active and passive modes with different interpretations both of what is heard (the Hīnayāna or

Mahāyāna doctrine) and what is proclaimed (one's own attainment of the Hīnayāna enlightenment or the Mahāyāna doctrine one has heard but not practiced).

Pratyekabuddha is translated as 'Solitary Realizer' because of the explanation (*Compassion*, pp.103-4) that *pratyekabuddhas* are not Buddhas but are called *buddha* because of having *realization* of suchness. 'Solitary' indicates that in their last lifetime they practice alone without depending on a teacher in that lifetime.

The terms *Bodhisattva* and *Buddha* are left untranslated as they are sufficiently familiar in English.

496 P5260, Vol. 98 4.5.3, commenting on I.1. The Sanskrit is Buddhist Sanskrit Texts, Vol. 10, 5.24; Poussin, 16.2. The brackets are from *GM*, 232b.6.

Prasannapadā is translated as *Clear Words* though it would be just as suitable as *The Lucidly Worded*, or *The Clear Worded* as Stcherbatsky does in his *The Conception of Buddhist Nirvana* (rpt Delhi: Motilal Banarsidass, 1978), or *Lucid Exposition of the Middle Way* as Mervyn Sprung does in his condensation of the text (London: Routledge & Kegan Paul, 1979). It strikes me that Chandrakīrti gave his commentary on Nāgārjuna's *Treatise on the Middle Way* (*Madhyamakashāstra*) this title in contrast to Bhāvaviveka's commentary, *Lamp for (Nāgārjuna's) 'Wisdom'* (*Prajñāpradīpa*) which, due to its brevity and lack of elaboration, is often difficult to fathom and thus unclear. As an example of such difficulty, see Bhāvaviveka's refutation of Buddhapālita's interpretation of the refutation of production from self on p.461. Also, in the *Clear Words* Chandrakīrti gives a very clear picture of the movement of the refutations by citing the qualm that each step answers, such as in his brilliant commentary on chapter two.

Stcherbatsky, in his *The Conception of Buddhist Nirvana*, however, indicates that at least for him Chandrakīrti's text is not clear and that the title seems ironic (p.75 n.1): 'Candrakīrti has given to his commentary the title of 'The Clearworded' (prasanna-padā) probably not without some dose of irony, since, as Prof. Wassilieff attests, its extreme dialectical subtlety, especially in the first chapter, is equalled by no other work in the whole domain of Northern Buddhist literature.' In the same vein, Mervyn Sprung (p.xii) says about the first chapter, in defense of his abridgements of the text, '. . . [the abridgements] are, without exception I believe, concerned with Candrakīrti's controversy with Bhāvaviveka, his rival commentator within the Mādhyamika school, or with his support of Buddhapālita, a commentator he attempts to follow, or else with traditional arguments of the Sāṃkhya school having to do with causation. These controversies are important, obviously. Yet to place them with all their meticulous, Indian love of syllogistic detail, in what is otherwise a finely targeted introduction to the entire *Prasannapadā*, however natural they were to Candrakīrti's contemporaries, is to make access to the work for contemporary readers difficult and discouraging.' It is interesting to note that in the Ge-luk-b̄a scholastic centers of learning this very controversy between the three Mādhyamika masters is used as the means for gaining access to Mādhyamika, as it is the first major topic of debate in the Middle Way class of ge-s̄hay studies at the point of the sixth chapter of Chandrakīrti's *Supplement to (Nāgārjuna's) 'Treatise on the Middle Way'*. Chandrakīrti's *Clear Words* forms the basis of the study with commentaries such as that by Jam-ȳang-shay-b̄a used to unravel its meaning; it is because of the clarity which I found in using Jam-ȳang-shay-b̄a's commentary that this controversy could be included in Part Five. Thus, I am not making any claims that Chandrakīrti's words in that section were clear to me on their own; still, I think that from his own point of view that section, like the rest of his text, was a good deal clearer than Bhāvaviveka's.

With respect to this citation, the Buddhist Sanskrit Texts edition by Dr. P.L. Vaidya reads *mādhyamikasya sataḥ* which, despite his saying (p.5 n.5) that it is not rendered in the Tibetan, is rendered in the Tibetan by *dbu ma pa yin na ni* (Vol. 98 4.5.3). Poussin's edition (Bibliotheca Buddhica IV, 16.2) reads *mādhyamikasya svataḥ* which he finds to be missing in the Tibetan (see n.3); however, the Tibetan suggests that *sataḥ* is correct.

Stcherbatsky (p.100) seems to follow the Tibetan, loosely translating the passage as, 'But according to the Mādhyamika method of dialectics an independent argument is never needed. This method consists in producing a contrathesis and then balancing two conflicting views without admitting either of them.' Sprung (p.37) follows Poussin's mis-reading, 'It is meaningless for a Mādhyamika, because he cannot accept his opponent's premises, to propound a self-contained argument (*svatantra-anumāna*) from his own point of view (*svataḥ*).' Nga-w̄ang-b̄el-den (*Ann*, dbu 58a.7) interprets the passage differently, 'Here "autonomous inference" is a syllogism [literally, application of a sign] which is established from its own side. "Position" is a word for probandum or thesis. "Another" means [a thesis which is] other than not established from its own side. Therefore, the meaning of this passage is: It is not admissible [for one who is a Mādhyamika] to assert the statement of syllogisms which are established from their own side because [Mādhyamikas] do not assert probanda or theses which are established from their own side.' Thus, for Nga-w̄ang-b̄el-den the question is not about asserting something from one's own point of view or merely playing off others' assertions but about asserting syllogisms and theses that inherently exist.

Jam-ȳang-shay-b̄a's interpretation (*GM*, 232b.5-33a.3) is slightly more detailed, 'It follows that it is unsuitable for anyone who is a Mādhyamika refuting all extremes as in the *King of Meditative Stabilizations Sutra* to use autonomous inferences, that is to say, syllogisms in which the three modes [of the presence of the reason in the subject, the pervasion, and counter-pervasion] are established from their own side because [Mādhyamikas] do not have assertions of other positions from among the four extremes and so forth. That [Mādhyamikas] do not have assertions of other positions from among the four extremes and so forth follows because (1) [Mādhyamikas] do not have positions asserting any extremes—the extreme of existence which is inherent existence, the extreme of non-existence which is utter non-existence, the extreme of both existence and non-existence which is inherent existence and inherent disintegration, or the extreme of a truly established emptiness or middle that abandons the two extremes of existence and non-existence and (2) the honorable Superior [Nāgārjuna] says that he has no thesis contradicting the Mādhyamika system.' The format of such interpretation is clear: every instance where Prāsaṅgikas seem to say that they have no theses is shown, by context, to mean that they do not have *certain* theses, not theses in general.

As is evidenced by Stcherbatsky's and Sprung's translations, they are inserting a good deal of interpretation into the text in an admitted attempt to make it clearer. I prefer more literal translation, resorting frequently to bracketed additions, to accomplish similar goals but to try to keep the original text more available. All translation is interpretation, but it seems appropriate, in the face of radically different interpretations, to make the original text as identifiable as possible.

497 According to Jam-ȳang-shay-b̄a (*GT*, ca 61a.3), the Sanskrit original is *svairī*. As mentioned earlier, *siddha* (*grub pa*) and *sat* (*yod pa*) are often used interchangeably, and thus *svabhāva-siddha* is translated here as 'existing inherently' rather than as 'established inherently' merely because it is a little easier to understand in English.

It needs to be borne in mind that Bhāvaviveka did not call himself a Svātantrika. The term appears to have been coined in Tibet, perhaps by visiting Indian scholars or Tibetans themselves, based on Chandrakīrti's saying that it is not suitable for Mādhyamikas to use *svatantra-anumāna*, autonomous inferences (with the word 'inference' here not referring to a *consciousness* realizing a hidden or obscure object of knowledge in dependence on a correct reason but to the *syllogistic statement* itself). Jam-ȳang-shay-b̄a here equates *svatantra* with terms meaning existing under the object's own power, and thus the term has been translated as 'autonomous'. However, most Western scholars and many non-Ge-luk-b̄a Tibetan scholars have taken the term just to mean a syllogistic statement that the stater himself supports and thus is in his own continuum (*rang rgyud*). This interpretation is rejected by Ge-luk-b̄a writers because then Prāsaṅgikas would absurdly be Svātantrikas since, at least in the Ge-luk-b̄a interpretation, Prāsaṅgikas themselves do use syllogistic reasoning.

Still, it seems to me that the term *svatantra* (*-prayoga*) might refer to the type of syllogism that *must on all occasions* be stated in order to generate in another party a consciousness realizing a thesis. In other words, the very insistence on the statement *on all occasions* of a syllogism that oneself supports indicates that one believes in commonly appearing subjects, predicates, reasons, examples, and so forth and thus implies that these inherently exist since the basic appearance to sense perception, for instance, is not being challenged. This meets back to the assertion that the object of negation in the view of selflessness, according to Bhāvaviveka, does not appear to sense consciousnesses but according to Chandrakīrti does. Through interpreting the term *svatantra* in this way, it is not necessary immediately to equate it with 'existing under the object's own power' or 'inherently existent'; rather, one should see inherent existence as an implication of the *insistence* that a syllogism that oneself supports in one's own continuum be stated. To me, it seems that Chandrakīrti, in his long critique of Bhāvaviveka, is surmising that Bhāvaviveka's insistence on finding a syllogism in Buddhapālita's refutation of production from self stems from the latter's feeling that there are commonly appearing subjects and so forth, and thus his syllogisms are bound by the context of such insistence and all that it implies—commonly appearing subjects and, thus, inherent existence.

In this way, the equation of 'autonomy' with 'inherent existence' is not just on the basis of a flimsy reference to Amarasinha's lexicon (*Jang*, 325.10; *GM*, 229a.6; *GT*, ca 61a.3, *rang rgyud rang dbang bdag dbang* 'Autonomy, own-power, [and] self-power [have the same meaning].'), nor does one have to squeeze Bhāvaviveka's calling for a *rang dbang du rjes su dpag pa* (a self-powered or autonomous inference) in his commentary on the beginning of chapter thirteen of the *Treatise* as if this directly indicates that Bhāvaviveka himself asserts that 'autonomous' means 'inherently existent' (*GT*, ca 61a.7 and *Jang*, 325.12: *da ni sun 'byin pa'i lan btab pa dang rang dbang du rjes su dpag pa'i mthus 'du byed rnams rnam pa las ngo bo nyid med pa nyid bstan pa'i don gyi dbang gis rab tu byed pa bcu gsum pa btsams so* '[Nāgārjuna] composed the thirteenth chapter in order to teach the non-entityness of compositional phenomena through the force of giving answers to [others'] refutations and self-powered [or autonomous] inferences.')

In short, Bhāvaviveka never openly said that *svatantra*, autonomy, equals *svabhāva-siddhi*, inherent existence. Rather, it seems that in such a context he is saying that it is not sufficient merely to refute another's position negatively—one *must* positively set forth one's own position. The implications of this, as explained above, are that Bhāvaviveka accepts a quality of objects that appears in direct perception which Chandrakīrti refutes. The significance of Chandrakīrti's identifying a subtler object of negation and Bhāvaviveka's confusing the existence of an object with its inherent existence is perhaps more accessible when the route of the immediate equation of *svatantra* and *svabhāva-siddhi* is not taken.

498 Brackets are from *Ann*, dbu 58b.1.

499 To speak of a 'thesis which is a position' might seem redundant since position (*pakṣha, phyogs*) and thesis (*pratijñā, dam bca'*) are often synonymous. However, according to Kensur Lekden, a position of one of the extremes is non-existent because it is an extreme, whereas an assertion or thesis of an extreme position does exist.

500 P5246, Vol. 95 140.2.4, XVI.25. For Chandrakīrti's commentary see P5266, Vol. 98, 279.2ff. This is quoted by Chandrakīrti in his *Clear Words* following the last quote, P5260, Vol. 98 4.5.4 (the Buddhist Text Series Sanskrit is No. 10, 5.25; Poussin, 16.4).

According to D̄zong-ka-b̄a (*Ann*, dbu 58b.2-59b.6), Chandrakīrti cites this passage in his *Clear Words* as a source showing that it is unsuitable for a Mādhyamika to assert autonomous theses because existence in the four alternatives is refuted in Mādhyamika texts. Also, D̄zong-ka-b̄a points out that in his commentary on the *Four Hundred* Chandrakīrti says that this passage indicates that censure cannot be expressed, even over a long period of time, to a *proponent* of emptiness; thus, this passage certainly does not indicate that Mādhyamikas have no assertions at all by way of suggesting that they do not even assert emptiness. Also, Chandrakīrti cites the same passage in his own *Commentary on the 'Supplement'* upon saying, 'This propounding of dualism is just unreasonable for proponents of imputed existence (**prajñaptivādin, btags par smra ba*); therefore, Mādhyamikas cannot be defeated in any way through refutations and answers dependent on duality.' As D̄zong-ka-b̄a says, '[This passage] is cited [by Chandrakīrti] as a source showing that those who assert imputed existence which negates substantial existence in the sense of [the object's] being established by way of its own entity cannot be refuted by Proponents of True Existence (**bhāvavādin, dngos po yod par smra ba*) who assert that [phenomena] are established by way of their own entities and by the Proponents of No Things (**abhāvavādin, dngos po med par smra ba*) who assert a negation of all capacity to perform functions in things such as forms. Therefore, it is not suitable as a source [showing that Mādhyamikas] have no system.'

Based on Dzong-ka-ba, Nga-wang-bel-den goes on to identify the four alternatives here as inherent existence, utter non-existence, both, and a truly established category that is neither. The fourth alternative is specified as 'truly established' since a category that is composed of neither of the positions, that is, that objects are neither inherently established nor utterly non-existent is affirmed since objects do indeed exist conventionally.

Nga-wang-bel-den cites a passage from Dzong-ka-ba's 'Great Exposition of Special Insight' in the *Great Exposition of the Stages of the Path* that gives a slightly different version of the four and sets forth the basic Ge-luk-ba perspective on the four alternatives. With respect to the first alternative, he indicates that things which are established by way of their own entities are refuted whether these are asserted to be conventional or ultimate truths, whereas things that are able to perform functions are not refuted conventionally (though indeed ultimately). With respect to the second alternative, he says that non-things (*abhāva, dngos med*), that is to say, uncaused phenomena, are refuted if they are asserted to be established by way of their own entities (and not if they are only asserted to exist conventionally). Likewise, a combination of the two and a truly established position that is neither are refuted. Dzong-ka-ba concludes, 'All refutations of the four alternatives should be understood in this way. If the four alternatives were refuted without affixing such qualification, when [the first two alternatives, that is, that something is] an existent thing (*dngos po yod pa*) and a non-thing (*dngos po med pa*) are refuted and then both are refuted saying "not both", it would directly contradict one's own assertion to make the refutation, "not not both". If you [stupidly] insist that despite this there is no fault, [I can only say,] "We do not debate with the insane."'

In the earlier version, the four alternatives were:

1 inherent existence
2 utter non-existence
3 both
4 a truly established category that is neither.

Here the four are:

1 inherently existent thing

2 inherently existent non-thing (that is, inherently existent uncaused phenomenon)
3 both
4 a truly established category that is neither an inherently existent thing nor an inherently existent non-thing.

In the first way, one would be considering whether something like a chair is inherently existent, utterly non-existent, both, or some inherently truly established possibility that is neither inherently existent nor utterly non-existent, such as that the chair is inherently established as conventionally existent. In the second way, one considers whether the chair is an inherently existent thing, an inherently existent non-thing, both an inherently existent thing and an inherently existent non-thing, or neither an inherently existent thing nor an inherently existent non-thing within being inherently existent. In both cases, the alternatives must be carefully qualified so that conventional existence is not ruled out. The four alternatives, therefore, are all-inclusive only in the sense of including all possibilities of inherently existent phenomena—when these are refuted, it can be decided that phenomena do not inherently exist. They do not include all possibilities whatsoever. If one does not agree that such qualification is needed upon being shown the self-contradictions that are entailed without it, one is considered to be beyond the pale of sensible discourse; as D̄zong-ka-b̄a says, 'We do not debate with the insane.'

Nga-w̄ang-b̄el-den identifies another interpretation of the four alternatives by D̄zong-ka-b̄a's student Kay-drup in his *Opening the Eyes of the Fortunate*; there it is considered whether a chair, for instance, is a truly established existent, a truly established non-existent, a truly established category that is both of those, or a truly established category that is neither. This version is the most symmetrical in that all four alternatives are considered as being qualified by true establishment or inherent existence.

In this tradition of interpretation it is necessary to qualify the first position as 'inherent existence' or 'true existence' because it would be absurd to deny first that something exists and then that the same thing does not exist, for the two are a dichotomy, excluding any third possibility. (The reason why a third possibility of being both existent and non-existent is included is to take account of philosophical systems that posit such and probably also to create a sense of the fullness of the refutation in the meditator no matter how absurd the positions are.) Thus, although it is denied that phenomena are inherently existent, utterly non-existent, both existent and non-existent, or some fourth possibility that is neither existent nor non-existent, phenomena are existent, that is to say, conventionally existent. All possibilities of existence are not denied, only existence that would be able to bear analysis by a reasoning consciousness, and a reasoning consciousness analyzing the ultimate cannot refute conventional existence as that is beyond its province.

A result of this qualification is that there seems to be a lack of symmetry in the four positions; the fourth position, as given above in the first two interpretations, is not simply a denial of a combination of the first two. Although a third position which is a combination of inherent existence and utter non-existence (or inherently existent thing and inherently existent non-thing) is suitable to be refuted, a fourth position which is a mere denial of them is not, for phenomena are neither inherently existent nor utterly non-existent since they are conventionally existent. (Phenomena also are neither inherently existent things nor inherently existent non-things because they are conventionally existent things or non-things.) Once the fourth position is qualified as something inherently existent that is neither of those, it is not a mere denial of a combination of the first two positions.

Through qualifying what is negated, the Ge-luk-b̄a interpreters maintain the commonsense notion that one cannot say that something does not exist and then claim that it also is not non-existent. In this system of interpretation the refutation of four alternatives is not used to lift the mind to a different, non-conceptual level through shock (or perhaps confusion) but to penetrate the nature of phenomena through a reasoned, conceptual process of refutation. When the negation of inherent existence is understood, one's understanding is non-conceptual in the sense of not wandering among many conceptions but remaining on one. Then, through combining that realization with the force of calm abiding, the ability to remain one-pointedly on emptiness is greatly enhanced, but still one needs to alternate stabilizing and analytical meditation on emptiness in order to induce special insight, which in turn is deepened over the path of preparation, resulting in a totally non-conceptual realization of emptiness on the path of seeing.

Thus, even though it is sometimes disappointing to encounter the Ge-luk-b̄as' conceptual qualifications of scriptural passages that seem to lift one beyond conceptuality, it should not be thought that somehow their systemization is intended to intellectualize the profound to a stultifying degree. Rather, they are seeking to put the intellect in its place, using it in a very profound way in a process leading to direct perception.

In this endeavor, Nga-w̄ang-b̄el-den's *Annotations* are invaluable, as they reveal the systematic background of Jam-ȳang-shay-b̄a's citations which, without this contextualization, sometimes even seem to be proving the opposite of what he intends. Until one understands that he intends his text as lecture notes for a teacher competent in D̄zong-ka-b̄a's system, many of his citations are baffling. Undoubtedly, Nga-w̄ang-b̄el-den saw this need and provided the contextualization.

501 P5228, Vol. 95 15.1.1, stanza 29. This is quoted in the *Clear Words* immediately following the last quote, P5260, Vol. 98 4.5.4; Buddhist Text Series No. 10, 6.1; Poussin, 5.7. See K. Bhattacharya's *The Dialectical Method of Nāgārjuna* (Delhi: Motilal, 1978), p.23. The brackets are from *Ann*, dbu 59a.6. For contextualization of this quote see pp.471-3.

With respect to the definition of a Prāsaṅgika given just below, it might be helpful to identify possible English translations for names of the schools of tenets:

> Vaibhāṣhika: Great Exposition School (so called because they follow the text called *The Great Exposition* [*Mahāvibhāṣha*])
> Sautrāntika: Sutra School (so called perhaps because of their emphasis on sutra rather than on *The Great Exposition*)
> Chittamātra: Mind Only School (so called because they propound that all phenomena are of the nature of the mind)
> Mādhyamika: Middle Way School (so called because of propounding a middle that is devoid of the extremes of true existence and utter non-existence).

With respect to the major sub-divisions, there are:

the Sutra School Following Scripture (identified mainly as followers of Vasubandhu),
the Sutra School Following Reasoning (identified as followers of Dignāga and Dharmakīrti),
the Mind Only School Following Scripture (these being the followers of Asaṅga),
the Mind Only School Following Reasoning (these being the Mind Only followers of Dignāga and Dharmakīrti),
the Autonomous Middle Way School (*Svātantrika-Mādhyamika*),
the Consequential Middle Way School (*Prāsaṅgika-Mādhyamika*).

As school names, the English is quite palatable, but to refer to persons it is a bit more cumbersome though still manageable:

Vaibhāṣhika: Proponent of the Great Exposition
Sautrāntika: Proponent of Sutra
  Proponent of Sutra Following Scripture
  Proponent of Sutra Following Reasoning
Chittamātrin: Proponent of Mind-Only
  Proponent of Mind-Only Following Scripture
  Proponent of Mind-Only Following Reasoning
Mādhyamika: Proponent of the Middle Way
  Autonomist, Middle Way Autonomist
  Consequentialist, Middle Way Consequentialist.

I feel that it is important gradually to get beyond the use of Sanskrit terms whenever possible in order to lift Buddhist studies out of the arcane. There is no need to translate persons' names, except perhaps in texts such as certain sutras where some names have great meaning, but the translation of technical terminology can be very helpful. With respect to this, I stand directly opposed to the style of the great French Buddhologist, Louis de La Vallee Poussin, though I do not criticize him for not trying to do what I am. Scholars have different tastes and perceive different needs, and the field is wide enough to accommodate many different approaches. In other words, I disagree entirely with those who call for only one style of translation.

502 As Nga-wang-bel-den says (*Ann*, dbu 59b.2), 'Since consequences must be stated on all [occasions of] generating inferences in

others, they are of greater extent [or usage], but since other-approved syllogisms do not have to be stated for certain disputants of sharp faculties, they are described as being of less extent.'

The translation of the rest of this sentence and the next is doubtful, for, more literally, Jam-ȳang-shay-b̄a seems to be saying, '. . . but they are not at all mutually exclusive. For, most statements of other-approved [syllogisms] also appear to be consequences.' The reason for preferring the other, more loose translation is that consequences and other-approved syllogisms are indeed mutually exclusive, that is, whatever is the one is not the other. His point, rather, seems to be that an other-approved syllogism *can be seen* as a consequence merely by switching the format. Or he may be saying that both other-approved syllogisms and consequences are capable of generating an inferential consciousness and thus in this sense are not mutually exclusive.

His example is a reference to Buddhapālita's refutation of the Sāṃkhya view of production from causes that are of the same entity as the effect (see Part Five, chapters 2-5).

503 P5260, Vol. 98 10.3.1; Buddhist Text Series No. 10, 18.24; Poussin, 54.11. This is quoted in *GM*, 282a.2 and in D̄zong-ka-b̄a's *Illumination*, P6143, Vol. 154 37.5.3 and 38.3.2. The second quote almost immediately follows the first one.

Since causes are not produced in dependence upon their own effects, the meaning of 'mere conditionality' is not limited to just the usual sense of *pratyaya*, condition assisting in production of an object, but refers to the condition or situation that allows the positing of an object, whether that be its own basis of designation or that in relation to which it is posited. A seed is designated in dependence upon its basis of designation, the two halves of the seed, as well as in dependence upon its presumed effect, a sprout. That appearances are posited from the viewpoint of such conditionality 'when there is no analysis and no investigation' does not mean that conventionalities are beyond the sphere of analysis in the sense of the usual worldly investigation of an object to make sure it is there. In other words, conventional phenomena are not just figments of the imagination or even beyond the sphere of logical reasoning in the sense of undergoing investigation by reasoned analysis, for this is how a permanent self and so forth are refuted. Rather, conventionalities cannot withstand ultimate analysis, analysis into their mode of being, such as investigation into whether the object is one with its basis of designation or a different entity from its basis of designation.

504 P5431, Vol. 103 246.5.2. The Peking edition wrongly reads *stong pa gnyis* instead of *stong pa nyid*. The brackets are from *Ann*, dbu 59b.4-7, which confirms the latter reading as does *J̄ang*, 409.10. Nga-w̄ang-b̄el-den says that since Buddha's teaching that all phenomena are selfless cannot be defeated by any opponent, his teaching was proclaimed like the great roar of a lion (whose roar no other animal dares to answer).

The Tibetan scholars with whom I have worked have identified Shūra (*dPa' bo*) as Ashvaghoṣha. For references to controversy about this, see D.S. Ruegg's *The Literature of the Madhyamaka School of Philosophy in India* (Wiesbaden: Otto Harrasowitz, 1981), 119-21.

Jam-ȳang-shay-b̄a uses this passage from Shūra's *Cultivation of the Ultimate Mind of Enlightenment* to show that it is admissible to call Prāsaṅgikas Non-Abiding Mādhyamikas and Thoroughly Non-Abiding Mādhyamikas. Since Shūra's mere mention that the middle way does not abide in any of the extremes does not establish that he used these terms as names for the school, Jam-ȳang-shay-b̄a seems to be saying that these are suitable names for Prāsaṅgika just because Prāsaṅgikas set forth a middle way that does not abide in any of the extremes. However, in that case it would be suitable to call Chittamātrins Thoroughly Non-Abiding Mādhyamikas as they also claim to propound a middle way that does not abide in the extremes. In other words, Jam-ȳang-shay-b̄a's evidence is scant.

His position is an attempt to clarify a point made in passing by D̄zong-ka-b̄a in the latter's *Great* and *Middling Expositions of the Stages of the Path*. D̄zong-ka-b̄a says that earlier Tibetans mistakenly used the term 'Those Who Hold That Illusion is Established by a Reasoning Consciousness' (*sgyu ma rigs grub*) for Svātantrikas and the term 'Thoroughly Non-Abiding Mādhyamikas' (*rab tu mi gnas pa'i dbu ma pa*) for Prāsaṅgikas' (*Middling*, 144a.2 in an unmarked edition of 263 folios). Here, Jam-ȳang-shay-b̄a is trying to show that D̄zong-ka-b̄a's objection was not to the terms themselves but to the meaning assigned these by earlier Tibetans. J̄ang-ḡya (290.6-12) agrees, citing this as the opinion of the great scholar and adept Nor-sang-gya-tso (*Nor-bzang-rgya-mtsho*) and identifying him as using this quote from Ashvaghoṣha for his source. However, other scholars such as Nga-w̄ang-b̄el-den hold that D̄zong-ka-b̄a was refuting both the meaning and the usage of the terms themselves.

Nga-w̄ang-b̄el-den (*Ann*, dbu 59b.7-62a.1) gives a fascinating rendition of the controversy and Sha-m̄ar Gen-dun-d̄en-dzin-gya-tso (*Zhwa-dmar dGe-bdun-bstan-'dzin-rgya-mtsho*, 1852-1910) an even better one in his *Lamp Illuminating the Profound Thought, Set Forth to Purify Forgetfulness of the Difficult Points of (D̄zong-ka-b̄a's) 'Great Exposition of Special Insight' (lHag mthong chen mo'i dka' gnad rnams brjed byang du bkod pa dgongs zab snang ba'i sgron me*, [Delhi: Mongolian Lama Guru Deva, 1972], 19.4-27.5). The extended attention that they give to the topic is typical of the frequent emphasis on points made only in passing in D̄zong-ka-b̄a's writing. These become fascinating areas in which scholars try to apply the founder's principles of interpretation to specific problems, thereby coming to know those principles better through putting them to creative use. A result is that in literature purporting to be presenting D̄zong-ka-b̄a's established views, scholars such as Jam-ȳang-shay-b̄a slip in what is clearly their own opinion on difficult issues as if it were not a matter of controversy. This tradition is maintained even in oral teaching nowadays by some Ge-luk-b̄a scholars, who will sometimes present a controversial position as if it is the only position on a topic. I have learned over the years to presume controversy based on the fervor and amount of repetition of such topics. I do not mean this as a general indictment, as these same scholars have displayed a remarkable ability on other occasions to present many views on an issue. Rather, the tendency to stone-wall probably comes from their long training in debate, and the resorting to such on certain occasions may simply depend on their mood. I try to get around the situation by presenting positions and asking questions in a way that does not polarize the issue.

505 In this paragraph Jam-ȳang-shay-b̄a paraphrases D̄zong-ka-b̄a's *Essence of the Good Explanations*, P6142, Vol. 153 185.4.4.

The word *phyi mo* (*mātṛkā*) has the sense of a root text or model. Nāgārjuna, in his *Precious Garland* (stanza 394), uses the term to refer to the model of an alphabet that a teacher would first use in instructing his students. Although the term also means 'grandmother', the translation of it as 'grandmother' in this context seems a bit inappropriate.

506 A student of Chandrakīrti, as identified in prayers of supplications.

507 P6142, Vol. 153 185.4.6ff. The quotation was lengthened by including the second clause.

508 Nga-w̄ang-b̄el-den (*Ann*, dbu 59.6) points out that D̄zong-ka-b̄a's *Quintessential Instructions on the King of Tantras, the Glorious Guhyasamāja, Lamp Thoroughly Illuminating the Five Stages* (P6167, Vol. 158 179.3.7) says that it appears that Nāgārjuna, having completed the beginning of the second chapter of *The Five Stages* (*Pañchakrama*, P2667), had Shākyamitra complete the chapter.

As above, it is my practice to translate the titles of texts in order to indicate the contents of the text; this, of course, does not imply that the text has been translated. Major translations are indicated in the Bibliography.

509 A commentarial tradition, reported by Geshe Gedün Lodrö, says that the second is Jñānagarbha although it also could be the second Bhāvaviveka, known as the lesser (*chung ba*) who is the author of the *Madhyamakaratnapradīpa* (P5254) which is not to be confused with the *Prajñāpradīpa* (P5253) by the greater Bhāvaviveka, the founder of the Svātantrika system (see *J̄ang*, 283.11). Jñānagarbha is the more likely referent here because his works are widely cited whereas the lesser Bhāvaviveka's are not.

510 P5431, Vol. 103 246.4.8. Kensur Lekden pointed out that the general teaching is that phenomena are like illusions in that just as the latter appear to be real but are not, so phenomena appear to exist objectively but do not and that phenomena are *like* illusions and not just illusions because they can perform functions whereas illusions cannot.

With respect to this particular quote, D̄ak-tsang himself (204.1, Thimphu edition) says that this passage '. . . indicates that due to [holding that] illusions and so forth are established [Svātantrikas] do not perceive the inexpressible Mañjushrī.' Jam-ȳang-shay-b̄a seems to be saying that for him this passage does not refute Svātantrika at all. He also (*GT*, ca 77a.1-4) argues against D̄ak-tsang for holding that in Haribhadra's system '. . . an ultimate reasoning consciousness of meditative equipoise establishes [that phenomena are] like illusions and goes on to say that all real conventionalities are established by reasoning (*rigs grub*), meaning reasoning in general and not a consciousness of meditative equipoise. Jam-ȳang-shay-b̄a thereby suggests that it is suitable to call Svātantrikas *sgyu ma rigs grub*, 'Those Holding That Illusory[-Like Phenomena] Are Established By Reasoning' as long as one understands that it is not a consciousness of meditative equipoise that establishes phenomena as like illusions; however, since Prāsaṅgikas also hold that conventionalities are established by valid cognition, it is unclear why this is a particularly good name for Svātantrikas, except perhaps that such is *emphasized* in their literature.

511 Nga-w̄ang-b̄el-den (*Ann*, dbu 59b.7ff) seems to make the absurd conclusion that Jam-ȳang-shay-b̄a agrees with D̄ak-tsang that this passage does directly refute the Svātantrikas. In that case, Jam-ȳang-shay-b̄a would be contradicting his own pronouncement that Ashvaghoṣha is a non-partisan Prāsaṅgika. The annotator may have missed the meaning of the hypothetical 'if' in Jam-ȳang-shay-b̄a's refutation of D̄ak-tsang.

Showing great independence and intellectual honesty, Nga-w̄ang-b̄el-den often disagrees with Jam-ȳang-shay-b̄a, presenting a carefully framed argument in great detail. In the Go-mang College which uses Jam-ȳang-shay-b̄a's works as their basic textbooks, Nga-w̄ang-b̄el-den's *Annotations* are sometimes described as 'not their own system' (*rang lugs ma yin*) and denigrated as 'annotations [that point out only] mis-printings' (*yig nor mchan 'grel*). For me, they are a necessary key to Jam-ȳang-shay-b̄a's work through providing contextualization and giving an example of rigorous, nonpartisan application of scholarly principles. On this point, however, I do not think that the evidence merits his criticism of Jam-ȳang-shay-b̄a.

In any case, it is abundantly clear that in Ge-luk-b̄a works (except for D̄zong-ka-b̄a's *Golden Rosary*, an early work which presents the view that even in meditative equipoise phenomena which are qualified by emptiness appear, this being dismissed as not D̄zong-ka-b̄a's final position) a reasoning consciousness does not establish conventionalities as like illusions but only establishes emptiness and that this holds true for both Mādhyamika systems. When one rises from meditative equipoise on emptiness, a wisdom consciousness subsequent to meditative equipoise realizes illusory-like phenomena through the continued force of the earlier realization of emptiness and the appearance of conventional phenomena.

512 P6142, Vol. 153 185.4.6ff; the quote has been lengthened by including the first clause. Shākyamitra, Nāgabodhi, and Ashvaghoṣha were students of Nāgārjuna according respectively to *Ann*, dbu 59b.6, Obermiller's *History of Buddhism by Bu-ston*, Vol. 2, p.132, and *Tu-gen*, 15.16.

D̄zong-ka-b̄a's statement that their books on Mādhyamika were not translated into Tibetan is challenged by a hypothetical objector. Jam-ȳang-shay-b̄a somewhat apologetically explains that D̄zong-ka-b̄a means that their *philosophical* treatises on the Mādhyamika *view* were not translated into Tibetan, and Nga-w̄ang-b̄el-den (*Ann*, dbu 62a.1-3) explains that although the text '. . . is a Mādhyamika treatise, it is not a text on the view from among the division into view, meditation, and behavior.' We are to understand that Ashvaghoṣha's *Cultivation of the Ultimate Mind of Enlightenment* is a short *meditation* manual on emptiness according to the Mādhyamika system but not a philosophical treatise. Geshe Gedün Lodrö explained that this is similar to Nāgārjuna's Collections of Praises (*sTod tshogs*), his many praises of the mind vajra and so forth, not being included among his Collections of Reasonings (*Rigs tshogs*) even though they present emptiness by way of limitless forms of reasoning. The premise is that D̄zong-ka-b̄a's reading was so vast and his writing so free of internal contradictions that he neither could have missed nor could have forgotten about Ashvagoṣha's text.

513 Kensur Lekden reported that there were still more of Ashvagoṣha's books in Tibetan than D̄zong-ka-b̄a knew because the S̄a-ḡya-b̄as kept some translations of Ashvaghoṣha secret. Nga-w̄ang-b̄el-den (*Ann*, dbu, 62a.1ff) points out that some scholars say that the author of this book had the same name as Shūra but was not the Shūra, i.e., Ashvaghoṣha, who was contemporaneous with Nāgārjuna. However, J̄ang-ḡya (409.13) dismisses the idea as a proofless thesis and says that the great scholars all consider the book to be reliably his.

For a discussion of works on practice ascribed to Ashvaghoṣha, Shūra, and so forth see D.S. Ruegg's *The Literature of the Madhyamaka School of Philosophy in India* (Wiesbaden: Otto Harrassowitz, 1981), pp.119-21.

514 The seventeen are six mother and eleven son sutras. According to Kensur Lekden, mother sutras are so called because they contain discussion of all eight 'clear realizations' (*abhisamaya, mngon rtogs*) which are the subject matter of Maitreya's *Ornament for Clear Realization*. According to D̄zong-ka-b̄a's *Golden Rosary* (P6150, Vol. 154 200.3.6ff) the six are the *One Hundred Thousand, Twenty-Five Thousand, Eighteen Thousand, Ten Thousand, Eight Thousand*, and *Condensed Perfection of Wisdom Sutras*, and the eleven are the *Seven Hundred, Five Hundred, Three Hundred, Fifty Stanza, One Hundred and Fifty Means, Twenty-Five Doors, Questions of Suvikrāntavikrami, Kaushika, One Letter, Several Words*, and *Heart of Wisdom* Perfection of Wisdom Sutras. D̄zong-ka-b̄a's opinion is stated by Kay-drup who says (p.46), 'Our own system says that the mother and son sutras are not limited to seventeen because there are many more than that.' Thus, Jam-ȳang-shay-b̄a's usage of the formula of seventeen shows that in his opinion D̄zong-ka-b̄a still approved of the designation, though not of a strict determination, as seventeen.

515 No one who can identify these has been found to date.

516 P5260, Vol. 98 92.2.1, Colophon, stanza 10a. For the Sanskrit see J.W. de Jong's very helpful article on this Colophon, missing in Poussin's edition of Chandrakīrti's *Clear Words*, 'La Madhyamakaśāstrastuti de Candrakīrti' in *Oriens Extremus*, Jahrg. 9, 1962, pp.47-56 (reprinted in *J.W. De Jong Buddhist Studies*, pp.541-50 [Rep. of China: Asian Humanities Press, 1979]). This and the next stanza are cited, in pieces, over the next few pages; together, they read:

> 10 Having seen the *Compendium of Sutra*, the *Precious Garland of Advice [for the King]*, the Praises, and with hard work over a very long time the stanzas propounded in the *Treatise*, the *Sixty Stanzas of Reasoning*, the *Finely Woven*, the *Seventy Stanzas on Emptiness*, and the *Refutation of Objections*,
>
> 11 And having seen the *[Four] Hundred* and so forth [by Āryadeva, etc.] and likewise many profound sutras as well as the commentary done by Buddhapālita, I have gathered

> together the good explanations of Bhāvaviveka [and those of these masters] which were transmitted from one to another [and the texts of Shūra, Jñānagarbha, etc.] as well as what I received from [Nāgārjuna's own] analysis [of the meaning of his words] and have expounded this in order to please those of great intelligence.

The bracketed material in stanza 11 is from *GT*, ca 42a.3. Those who do not say that Chandrakīrti was an actual student of Nāgārjuna would not accept Jam-ȳang-shay-b̄a's interpretation that Chandrakīrti is speaking of analysis gained from Nāgārjuna himself. Instead, they would say that it refers to Chandrakīrti's own analysis. If Chandrakīrti is an actual student of Nāgārjuna, it seems strange that he speaks of Nāgārjuna's teaching for a long time, his students' teaching for a long time, and then (in stanza 7) Nāgārjuna's teaching degenerating over a long time to the point where Chandrakīrti needed to compose his texts.

De Jong (p.549 of *Buddhist Studies*) takes *śataka* as being a sutra ('Et aprés avoir lu également ces nombreux sūtra profonds tels que le Śataka . . . '), but Jam-ȳang-shay-b̄a's reading (*GT*, ca 42a.2) as Āryadeva's *Four Hundred* is more plausible especially considering the *dang* in the Tibetan: *rgya pa la sogs de dag dang ni de bzhin* . . . .

517 P5260, Vol. 98 92.2.2.

518 P5260, Vol. 98 92.2.3.

519 This Tibetan translation of the title as *dbU ma lag pa'i tshad* refers to a unit of measure from the elbow to the finger-tips, a cubit, because, as was pointed out by Lati Rinb̄ochay, the text has twenty-four 'feet' (*pāda*) and a cubit has twenty-four finger-widths. Another Tibetan version of the title (*Cha shas kyi yan lag*) means 'members which are parts', this tying in with the presentation of the non-ultimate nature of phenomena through analyzing their parts. The first version (P5248) has twenty-four 'feet', whereas the second (P5244) has twenty-eight.

520 P5260, Vol. 98 92.2.3. Brackets are from *GT*, ca 42a.3. See n.516.

521 D̄ak-tsang asserts that one could first attain Buddhahood through the Perfection Vehicle and then enter the Tantra Vehicle, finally to become an unsurpassed Buddha of the Tantra Vehicle. Though the Ge-luk-b̄as agree that in order to

attain the final achievement one must enter the Tantra Vehicle, they say that the Buddhahood explained in sutra is that explained in tantra (see Ḏzong-ka-ḇa's explanation in *Tantra in Tibet*, pp.139-42). They add that practice only of the Sutra Vehicle yields only the tenth Bodhisattva ground, not Buddhahood, for which one must practice tantra, specifically Highest Yoga Tantra. The point of difference between Ḏak-tsang and Jam-ȳang-shay-ḇa is whether the Buddhahoods described in both vehicles are the same. As a proof that they are, Jam-ȳang-shay-ḇa (*GT*, ca 58a.1ff) points to the fact that the sutras themselves speak of a Buddha as having no inhalation and exhalation and that the winds (*prāṇa, rlung*) which are overcome through the Tantra Vehicle cannot exist without breath.

522 Ḏzong-ka-ḇa quotes this in his *Middling Exposition of the Stages of the Path* (73b.4 in the 1968 Shes rig par khang edition).

523 Colophon, stanza 6. P5260, Vol. 98 92.1.3. For Obermiller's translation of this passage, see his *History of Buddhism by Buston*, II, p.135. Saraha is identified as Rāhulabhadra in Tārānātha's *History of Buddhism in India* (Varanasi: 1964), p.67. For the Sanskrit, see n.516.

524 P5260, Vol. 98 92.1.6; Colophon, 7.

525 See n.244.

526 According to Geshe Lhundup Sopa, the three vows of Bodhisattvas are not actually separate vows but modes of the Bodhisattva vow. They are the ethics of restraining bad deeds, the ethics which are the composite of virtuous practices, and the ethics of aiding the aims of sentient beings.

527 According to Kensur Lekden, this does not mean that there are bad parts in Atīsha's works; rather, Atīsha tends to follow the Yogāchāra-Svātantrika-Mādhyamikas with respect to the path, their description being renowned as the general Mahāyāna explanation.

528 P5260, Vol. 98 7.5.7ff; Poussin, 40.7-2.8. This is partially quoted by Ḏzong-ka-ḇa in his *Ocean of Reasoning, Explanation of (Nāgārjuna's) 'Treatise on the Middle Way'* (P6153, Vol. 156 64.2.3).

Interpretation is not limited to scripture as it also applies to objects. The interpretation or hermeneutic of scripture is called *rjod byed drang nges*, literally, 'the interpretable and the definitive with respect to means of expression', and the hermeneutic of objects is called *brjod bya'i drang nges*, literally, 'the interpretable and the definitive with respect to objects of expression'. 'Objects of expression' means objects such as tables, chairs, bodies, emptinesses, and so forth whch are the objects or referents of words (means of expression) such as 'table', 'chair', 'body', 'emptiness', and so forth. (From this it is clear that referential language is not the object of negation by Mādhyamika reasoning.)

In Mādhyamika the division of scriptures into the two categories of the interpretable and definitive is made based on the school's estimation of what final reality is, what the school's interpretation of emptiness is. It is a task of interpretation to determine why Buddha taught the non-definitive in terms of the need, or existential situation, of the listener. Thus, the hermeneutic is ontologically based within being inextricably involved with consideration of the levels of trainees.

With respect to the two classes of objects, emptinesses are definitive in that they are the final mode of subsistence of objects whereas conventional phenomena are in need of interpretation to determine their final mode of subsistence. Thus, a basic task of all beings is to interpret appearances—to recognize that what is appearing is not the final mode of being of those objects and to seek that final nature, not to obliterate the appearance of the object but to know its inner nature and thereby be better able to respond with respect to it.

529 The term *bhagavan* was translated into Tibetan most frequently as *bcom ldan 'das*, the first two syllables meaning 'possessing conquest' and the last syllable meaning 'supramundane' (*'jig rten las 'das pa*), having been added (according to Kensur Lekden and so forth) to distinguish the Buddhist *bhagavan* from the non-Buddhist. The term is also recognized as meaning *skal ldan*, Fortunate One (or Blessed One as it is usually translated) because of possessing six fortunes. However, since the dominant translation into Tibetan is *bcom ldan 'das*, I am translating it into English with 'Supramundane Victor'.

530 Missing in the Tibetan.

531 The plaintain tree. I assume this to be referring to the trunk of the tree which, much like an onion, has no core. However, Kensur Yeshe Thupten of L̄o-s̄el-l̄ing College takes it as referring to

the fact that such trees bear fruit only once and are useless thereafter.

Poussin (p.41, n.8) says that these lines are cited in the Saṃyuttanikāya III.142.

532 Translation follows the Tibetan.

533 P5224, Vol. 95 3.1.3, I.1. This is quoted in brief by Chandrakīrti (P5260, Vol. 98 8.1.7; Poussin, 42.9).

534 The following three quotes are from the *Treatise on the Middle Way* (XIII.1, XI.1, and XV.7). They are cited by Chandrakīrti in his *Clear Words* (P5260, Vol. 98 8.1.8ff; Poussin, 42.10).

535 The bracketed additions in this stanza are from D̄zong-ka-b̄a's *Ocean of Reasoning, Explanation of (Nāgārjuna's) 'Treatise on the Middle Way'*, 232.2ff, Varanasi 1973 edition.

536 P5263, Vol. 98 43.5.7; Poussin, 270.3.

537 P842, Vol. 34 64.3.6ff. This citation and that in *J̄ang* (313.17ff) agree, but they differ from that in the *Clear Words* (P5260, Vol. 98 8.2.2; Poussin, 43.4). The Peking edition of it is a combination of both.

538 P842, Vol. 34 64.4.2; see previous note. Brackets are from *J̄ang*, 315.17. J̄ang-ḡya (316.1) points out that the long list of synonyms of self refers also to the instruments and objects related to the agent, the person. Geshe Gedün Lodrö said that though the addition of 'inherently existent' in brackets to 'owner' is appropriate, it is not necessary because the word 'self' carries with it the force of inherent existence. He added that this still does not mean that all instances of the word 'self' mean either 'inherent existence' or 'inherently existent person', since it often refers to a nominally existent person. Even a Buddha is a person, self, and I, but he speaks of his 'self' based on a valid consciousness which perceives a nominally existent self. His words are not based on a false view of a self as existing inherently in its basis of imputation.

539 Nga-w̄ang-b̄el-den (*Ann*, dbu 62a.3) finds this paragraph inexplicable; however, Geshe Gedün Lodrö explained it as if without problem. His commentary with the original underlined is: *dgongs gzhi gnas lugs kyi don ni bstan tshul de las gzhan du 'dren pa la dpe yod kyang (cing) de dag dgos pa'i sgo nas drang don du 'grel tshul te drang don gyi mdo sde phal cher la de ltar dgos*

shing brjod bya'i sgo nas drang don du 'grel tshul ni btags don btsal na mi rnyed pa sogs kyi rigs pas gnod . . .

In any case, a passage is said to require interpretation due to having three factors:

a basis in Buddha's thought (*dgongs gzhi*): this is not Buddha's intention or purpose in teaching, for example, a mind-basis-of-all but the ontological basis in his own thought, which in this case is emptiness

a purpose (*dgos pa*): the pedagogical intention, such as providing a means for the connection of actions and effects for those who temporarily are unable to understand such within the context of mere nominal existence

damage to the literal teaching (*dngos la gnod byed*): contradiction of that teaching by reasoning and scripture. Even in the case of literally acceptable teachings such as those of the five aggregates, if one took such to be the final mode of subsistence of the phenomena discussed, this would be contradicted by the reasonings proving emptiness and scriptures on emptiness.

Jam-ȳang-shay-b̄a is working around this format with the addition of examples that contradict the explicit teaching.

540 *J̄ang*, 317.4.

541 P795, Vol. 31 281.1.5, VII.5. This is quoted in the *Clear Words* (P5260, Vol. 98 8.2.8; Poussin, 44.1).

542 P763, Vol. 27 238.5.6, chapter 25; Buddhist Sanskrit Texts No. 1, 286.10. Translation follows the Tibetan. The Peking edition reads *rdul bral*.

543 Here *svabhāva-asiddha* is interpreted as meaning *svalakṣhaṇa-asiddha* because the Chittamātrins assert that imaginary phenomena are *svabhāvasiddha* but not *svalakṣhaṇasiddha* according to *Gön*, 46.7 and 48.8. Thus, 'inherently' in the next sentence means 'by way of the object's own character'.

544 P160, Vol. 6 166.2.2.

545 P5262, Vol. 98 103.3.3, VI.95cd; Poussin's translation is *Muséon*, n.s. v.12, p.250. See *GM*, 459a.6ff, and Jay-d̄zun Chö-ḡyi-gyel-tsen's *Par-chin*, 149.6 (Indian edition, no pub. data). The penetrating debates of the monastic courtyards are a cause

of critical scholarship and a key to Jam-ȳang-shay-b̄a's style. As is the case here, he often introduces a topic, such as the four or five sutras requiring interpretation, not with a general presentation but with a rejection of an 'incorrect' interpretation of a minor point. He reports that some say that the number of passages which Chandrakīrti said were to be interpreted are just four. Jam-ȳang-shay-b̄a corrects this, pointing out that Chandrakīrti is referring to four *types* of passages because these four teachings were framed in many, many different ways. As sources for these four Chandrakīrti refers only to the *Sutra Unravelling the Thought*, but Jam-ȳang-shay-b̄a includes other sutras of similar type, the *Descent into Laṅkā Sutra*, the *Sutra on the Heavily Adorned*, etc., without specifying that these are included by implication.

Without a word of explanation, Jam-ȳang-shay-b̄a includes a fifth type of passage among those which require interpretation, the teaching of a Tathāgata essence (*Tathāgatagarbha*) as in the *Tathāgata Essence Sutra*. In *GM* (459a.6ff), however, he defends the number five, saying that Chandrakīrti was not necessarily referring only to sutras accepted as literal by the Chittamātrins. Still, Nga-w̄ang-b̄el-den (*Ann*, dbu 63a.5ff) disagrees, citing D̄zong-ka-b̄a who indicates that the passages referred to by Chandrakīrti are all taken literally by the Chittamātrins, and thus there are only four since they do not take the teaching of a permanent Tathāgata essence literally.

About the translation of *Madhyamakāvatāra* as *Supplement to (Nāgārjuna's) 'Treatise on the Middle Way'*, see pp.399-405. Kensur Lekden was adamant about taking *avatāra* (*'jug pa*) as 'add on' (*snon pa*) rather than 'introduce'. He based this on statements by D̄zong-ka-b̄a and Jam-ȳang-shay-b̄a that Chandrakīrti was 'filling in gaps' (*kha skong ba*); however, the matter is not easily settled since the evidence seems to go both ways. Let us first cite D̄zong-ka-b̄a's explanation in my *Compassion in Tibetan Buddhism* (pp.97-9), removing the bias of the translation by adding in 'introduce' at every occurrence of 'supplement':

> *Question:* How does Chandrakīrti's text supplement/introduce Nāgārjuna's *Treatise on the Middle Way*?
> *Answer:* One person [Jaya-ānanda] says that in Nāgārjuna's

> *Treatise* conventional and ultimate natures are not taught extensively, but that Chandrakīrti teaches these two extensively here and in this way supplements/introduces Nāgārjuna's *Treatise*.
>
> This is not a good explanation because the forms of reasoning ascertaining suchness are far more extensive in Nāgārjuna's *Treatise on the Middle Way* than in Chandrakīrti's *Supplement/Introduction*. Our own system on this is that Chandrakīrti supplements/introduces Nāgārjuna's *Treatise* in two ways, from the viewpoints of the profound and of the vast.... Therefore, one way in which this book supplements/introduces the *Treatise* is through good determination of the meaning of the *Treatise* from the viewpoint of these two purposes [distinguishing the suchness of the *Treatise* from the interpretations by Svātantrikas and by Chittamātrins].
>
> It also supplements/introduces the *Treatise* from the viewpoint of the vast.... Thus, [Chandrakīrti thought that] it would be very good to fill in the gaps in the paths explained in the *Treatise on the Middle Way*.... the second way that this text supplements/introduces Nāgārjuna's *Treatise on the Middle Way* is in supplementing/introducing the paths of the *Treatise* from the viewpoint of the vast.

There is no question that Chandrakīrti's text serves to introduce Nāgārjuna's *Treatise*; the question is whether this is the meaning of his title. Jaya-ānanda, author of the only extant Indian commentary on this text, sees the mode of its being an *avatāra* as more extensive teaching. At first impression it might seem unsuitable for an introduction to be longer than what it introduces, but given the complexity of Nāgārjuna's text, it makes sense that the introduction be longer than the text. What 'extensive' means, however, becomes an issue; D̄zong-ka-b̄a refutes Jaya-ānanda on the grounds that the *Treatise*, though shorter, is more extensive than Chandrakīrti's text in terms of presenting emptiness from many, many viewpoints. It would seem however, that Jaya-ānanda was thinking of 'extensive' as meaning 'longer' and that he needed correction on just that point. Given that either an introduction or a supplement could be more extensive than the actual text—either in the sense of length or complexity—we need another avenue of examination.

Tibetan scholars who hold that *'jug pa* means 'introduction' assert that the agent, the *'jug pa po*, is the trainee and the means, Chandrakīrti's text. They mean not that the introducer is the student reading the text but that the *enterer* is the student, this being by means of Chandrakīrti's text, and that the entered (*'jug bya*) is Nāgārjuna's *Treatise*. Within the Ge-luk-b̄a tradition of the large monastic colleges, there is no question that what is entered or added onto is Nāgārjuna's *Treatise*, but the question of the agent is by no means easy. On one side are these points:

1 Despite much discussion about the 'special trainees of the *Madhyamakāvatāra*' (*'jug pa'i ched du bya ba'i gdul bya*) there is no mention of this topic in connection with the title. One would think that if the agent, the enterer, were the student reading the text, a discussion of who this student is would ensue here, but it does not.

2 There are several statements by both Jaya-ānanda and Jam-ȳang-shay-b̄a in which the enterer/supplementer can only be interpreted as Chandrakīrti or his text. Jaya-ānanda says:

   bstan bcos 'di de la 'jug par 'gyur ba'o (*GM*, 6a.3) and *bstan bcos 'di de la 'jug pa'o*' (*GM*, 6b.3), 'This treatise [by Chandrakīrti] supplements/introduces that [one by Nāgārjuna].'

   Since *bstan bcos 'di* is in the nominative and not the instrumental case, there is no way to read the sentence as meaning 'a trainee enters that [text by Nāgārjuna] through this treatise [by Chandrakīrti].'

3 D̄zong-ka-b̄a does not refute Jaya-ānanda on this point, and he would if he disagreed, given his frequent refutations of him and the importance of the point.

On the other side is a remark by D̄zong-ka-b̄a: *GM*, 11a.2, *de'i phyir gzhung 'di la rten nas dgos pa de gnyis kyi sgo nas rtsa she'i don legs par nges pa ni gzhung 'dis dbu ma la 'jug pa'i tshul gcig go*. This was given above as: 'Therefore, one way in which this book supplements/introduces the *Treatise* is through good determination of the meaning of the *Treatise* from the viewpoint of these two purposes [distinguishing the suchness of the

Treatise from the interpretations by Svātantrikas and by Chittamātrins].' However, it could also be translated as: 'Therefore, one way in which [a trainee] enters the *Treatise* through this book is to determine the meaning ... ' Furthermore, Jam-ȳang-shay-b̄a (*GM*, 10b.5) calls such ascertainment the 'measure of having entered [or having been introduced to] Nāgārjuna's *Treatise* by way of this [book by Chandrakīrti]' (*nges pa de 'di'i sgo nas rtsa shes la zhugs pa'i tshad yin*). There is no way that this last statement can be construed as not referring to a person, a trainee, and thus the enterer here is clearly the trainee.

As there is undeniable evidence on both sides, we can conclude that the term *avatāra* in this title has both meanings—as a supplement filling in holes and as a means of entry. I find the former to be predominant in the scholastic literature and thus have chosen 'Supplement', within admitting that the text certainly serves to introduce Nāgārjuna's text and that even the title is sometimes taken as referring to a trainee's being introduced to the *Treatise.*

546 The fifth chapter is one, but the other was not located.

547 P6143, Vol. 154 74.5.2.

548 *Ann*, dbu 62a.4ff. This differs some from the citation by Ratnākarashānti in his *Commentary on (Nāgārjuna's) 'Compendium of Sutra'*, P5331, Vol. 102 151.4.8ff.

549 P774, Vol. 29 10.4.5, chap. 7. Brackets are from the sutra itself, just preceding the quote.

550 Brackets are from *Ann*, dbu 62a.6.

551 P731, Vol. 18 198.1.8, chapter 14. The same passage also occurs in the *Eighteen Thousand Stanza* (P732, Vol. 19 297.1.6, chapter 22) and is quoted in Nāgārjuna's *Compendium of Sutra* (P5330, Vol. 102 101.4.2). Brackets accord with the Chittamātra interpretation. The Chittamātrins would also interpret the quote as: 'Those Hearers who strictly abide in the right [that is, in the Hearer path of seeing, mostly] do not have the power to generate the aspiration to unsurpassed, complete, perfect enlightenment.' For the fuller quote see p.606.

552 P744, Vol. 29 10.4.7, chapter 7.

553 P744, Vol. 29 10.4.8, chapter 7. The bracketed material is from *Ann*, dbu 62a.8. With respect to the translation of *arhat* or *arhan* (*dgra bcom pa*) as 'Foe Destroyer', I do this to accord with the usual Tibetan translation of the term and to assist in capturing the

flavor of an oral tradition that frequently refers to this etymology. Arhats have overcome the foe which is the afflictions (*klesha, nyon mongs*), the chief of which is ignorance, the conception (according to the Prāsaṅgika system) that persons and phenomena are established by way of their own character.

The Tibetan translators were also aware of the etymology of *arhat* as 'worthy one' as they translated the name of the 'founder' of the Jaina system, Arhat, as *mchod 'od* 'Worthy of Worship' (see *GT*, ka 62a.3). Also, they were aware of Chandrakīrti's gloss of the term as 'Worthy One' in his *Clear Words: sadevamānuṣhāsurāl lokāt pūnārhatvād arhannityuchyate* (Poussin, 486.5), *lha dang mi dang lha ma yin du bcas pa'i 'jig rten gyis mchod par 'os pas dgra bcom pa zhes brjod la* (409.20, Tibetan Cultural Printing Press edition; also, P5260, Vol. 98 75.2.2), 'Because of being worthy of worship by the world of gods, humans, and demi-gods, they are called Arhats.' Thus, we are not dealing with an ignorant misconception of a term, but a considered preference in the face of alternative etymologies—'Foe Destroyer' requiring a not unusual *i* infix to make *ari-han*. Unfortunately, one word in English cannot convey both meanings; thus, I have gone with what clearly has become the predominant meaning in Tibet. (For an excellent discussion of the two etymologies of Arhat in Buddhism and Jainism, see L.M. Joshi's 'Facets of Jaina Religiousness in a Comparative Light', L.D. Series 85, [Ahmedabad: L.D. Institute of Indology, May 1981], pp.53-8.)

It has been objected that 'Foe Destroyer' is offensively militaristic and that in communicating Buddhism to the West we need to choose terms more suited to our culture. However, we speak of the 'war on poverty', the 'war on smallpox', and so forth. Also, as a translator, one's job is to communicate another culture on its own terms as well as one can, after which readers can pick and choose what is appropriate in their situation.

A more serious objection is to the basic concept of treating one's own afflictive attitudes and emotions in an anthropomorphic way as if they were other people. (Shāntideva prescribes such in his *Engaging in the Bodhisattva Deeds* when he addresses his own afflictions as if they were someone else.) The objection is that using such a bifurcating technique rules out watching the luminous and knowing nature (*gsal rig gi rang bzhin*) of a diseased state of mind as a means of causing it to disappear, this requiring intimate closeness with one's own afflictions. However, treating one's own afflictions as foes seems concordant even with this technique in that it introduces the possibility of not identifying with those afflictions and thus the possibility of their disappearance.

A suggested substitute translation is 'saint'; however, one would not want to limit the *main* use of the word 'saint' to Hīnayāna. 'Saint' seems more appropriate for *ārya* 'Superior'.

Translation equivalents are by no means easy to come by; accessibility is very important, but rich meaning after becoming accustomed to terms is also important. Still, I do not deny that 'Foe Destroyer' is, at first, awkward.

554 P5330, Vol. 102 101.2.3ff. *White Lotus of the Excellent Doctrine Sutra*, P781, Vol. 30 10.1.5, chapter 2. Nāgārjuna has abridged it considerably but fairly. Bracketed material is from Ratnākarashānti (P5331, Vol. 102 150.2.8ff). See Hurvitz's translation in the *Scripture of the Lotus Blossom of the Fine Dharma*, pp.30-1.

555 Chapters 2, 3, etc. according to E. Obermiller's 'The Doctrine of the Prajñā-pāramitā as exposed in the Abhisamayālaṃkāra of Maitreya', *Acta Orientalia* (Lugduni Batavorum: E.J. Brill, 1932), p.30.

556 P5330, Vol. 102 101.3.8ff. The sutra is the *Satyakasatyakī-parivarta* which is not listed in the Peking catalogue but which is mentioned in Haribhadra's *Abhisamaya-ālokā* according to Obermiller, IBID, note on p.30. The next two bracketed additions are from Ratnākarashānti (P5331, Vol. 102 151.2.7ff).

557 The translation of *dharmadhātu* as 'element of qualities' is based on a note by Nga-wang-bel-den (*Ann*, dbu 8b.8): *khyod la dmigs nas sgom pas 'phags chos kyi rgyu byed pas chos dbyings zhes bya la* 'It is called the element of qualities (*dharmadhātu, chos dbyings*) because meditation within observing it acts as a cause of the qualities (*dharma, chos*) of Superiors (*Ārya, 'Phags pa*).' Emptiness, being uncaused, is not itself a cause (element), but meditation on it causes the development of marvelous qualities; thus, emptiness comes to be *called* a cause, an element producing those qualities.

558 P5330, Vol. 102 101.3.8ff. The original is P731, Vol. 18 198.1.7ff, chapter 14, and P732, Vol. 19 297.1.6. For Conze's

translation, see p.205 of *The Large Sutra*, Part II (College Printing and Typing Co., 1964). Brackets accord with the Prāsaṅgika interpretation. For Gyel-tsap's commentary, see 145a.1 of the Indian folio edition of his *Ornament for the Essence*.

559 Source for this and the next set of brackets is *Ann*, dbu 62a.5.

560 P5330, Vol. 102 101.4.4ff. *Questions of King Dhāraṇīshvara Sutra*, P814, Vol. 32 300.5.4ff. Nāgārjuna's version is considerably abridged. First brackets are from Ratnākarashānti (P5331, Vol. 102 151.3.1).

561 Ratnākarashānti, P5331, Vol. 102 151.4.6.

562 P5330, Vol. 102 101.5.6. *Irreversible Wheel Sutra*, P906, Vol. 36 105.3.2ff. Nāgārjuna's abridgement is very slight.

563 The five ruinations are decrease of lifespan, degeneration of views, degeneration of the afflictions, degeneration of beings (for example, more difficult to tame), and degenerate era, according to Das's *Tibetan-English Dictionary*, p.501.

564 P5330, Vol. 102 102.1.2. For the first part of the original see P760.48, Vol. 24 255.5.3 or 255.5.6 or 255.5.8 or 256.1.3. The second part is 258.1.4. The abridgement is considerable. See the translation by A. Wayman and H. Wayman, *The Lion's Roar of Queen Śrīmālā* (New York: Columbia, 1974), pp.81-92.

565 P760.48, Vol. 24 255.5.1ff. See *The Lion's Roar* (op. cit.), pp.80ff.

566 P5330, Vol. 102 102.1.3ff. *Descent into Laṅkā Sutra*, P775, Vol. 29 50.2.4ff. Brackets are from Jñānashrībhadra's *Commentary on the 'Descent into Laṇka'*, P5519, Vol. 107 130.3.2, and Ratnākarashānti, P5331, Vol. 102 152.1.6. Suzuki's translation is p.116.

567 P775, Vol. 29 37.3.8 and 50.3.2. Suzuki's translation is p.58 and p.116 (210). For commentary on the second citation, see Jñānashrībhadra, P5519, Vol. 107 130.5.8ff.

568 This quote was not found in the sutra.

569 P5262, Vol. 98 103.3.3, VI.95cd.

570 P5263, Vol. 98 136.1.1ff, commenting on VI.95cd; Poussin's translation is *Muséon*, n.s. v.12, p.250.

571 P774, Vol. 29 8.2.2, chapter 5.

572 P775, Vol. 29 34.3.5, chapter 2. Suzuki's translation is p.44 (123).

573 P775, Vol. 29 39.5.2, chapter 2. See Jñānashrībhadra, P5519, Vol. 107 112.3.7. Suzuki's translation is p.68.

574 P761.31, Vol. 25 263.3.8, chapter 6. This is quoted in the *Commentary on the 'Supplement'*, P5263, Vol. 98 134.1.5, and in D̄zong-ka-b̄a's *Essence*, P6142, Vol. 153 196.2.6 as well as in his *Illumination*, P6143, Vol. 154 71.5.8.

575 P5262, Vol. 98 103.1.8, VI.84; Poussin's translation is *Muséon*, n.s. v.12, p.239. Brackets are from his own commentary (P5263, Vol. 98 134.1.2).

576 P775, Vol. 29 40.2.6, chapter 2; Suzuki's translation is p.70 (139). See Jñānashrībhadra (P5519, Vol. 107 114.1.6) and Jñānavajra (P5520, Vol. 107 247.2.4). This is quoted in *Commentary on the 'Supplement'* (P5263, Vol. 98 134.2.3).

577 *Ann*, dbu 65a.8, which is based on *Commentary on the 'Supplement'* (P5263, Vol. 98 134.3.8).

578 P761.31, Vol. 25 263.5.6.

579 P775, Vol. 29 53.4.2, chapter 3; Suzuki's translation is p.133 (33). See Jñānashrībhadra, P5519, Vol. 107 138.1.8. The bracketed material is from *Ann*, dngos 104a.8ff.

580 P5225, Vol. 95 11.5.3. The 'basis in Buddha's thought' (*dgongs gzhi*) is not Buddha's intention or purpose in teaching mind-only but the basis in fact that he was working from. According to the Prāsaṅgika system, external objects exist; therefore, the teaching of mind-only meaning no external objects is not founded itself in fact. But on what fact is it founded—what was the basis in Buddha's thought? According to Nga-w̄ang-b̄el-den (*Ann*, dbu 65b.6-6a.2), it was founded on the fact that phenomena are designated by way of their aspect or image (*rnam pa*) being posited in the consciousness observing them, and in this sense the elements and so forth are said in Nāgārjuna's *Sixty Stanzas of Reasoning* to be included in consciousness, for they are only posited by consciousness. With this as the ontological basis in his own thought, Buddha taught that all phenomena are mind-only, intending to communicate that there are no external objects to those temporarily unable to realize this deeper fact. Hence, the thought of the speaker (*gsung ba po'i dgongs pa*) and the thought of what he said (*gsung rab kyi dgongs pa*) differ, as he was not, at that time, communicating his own deeper understanding.

A point to be gleaned from this type of explanation (as found in D̄zong-ka-b̄a's *Essence of the Good Explanations*) is that according to this school of thought Buddha spoke from a basis of specific understanding; his skill in means wrought changes in what he said according to his audience, but it is not that there was no basis in his own thought. Thus, his word needs to be interpreted in terms of both the needs of the listener and his own grounding in actual fact. When the existential need of the trainee was at odds with the ontological fact, his teaching is subject to refutation by scripture and reasoning. Thus, the interpretation of scripture revolves around the triad mentioned above—the basis in Buddha's thought (or the ontological fact), the purpose (or existential need of the trainee), and damage to the explicit teaching (or refutation by valid sources of knowledge).

581 P2665, Vol. 61 285.5.6. Ḡön-chok-d̄en-b̄ay-drön-may (*Explanation*, 6a.5) says, 'This book is called *Essay on the Mind of Enlightenment* because it explains the meaning of a stanza on the mind of enlightenment spoken by Vairochana in the second chapter of the *Guhyasamāja*.'

582 P5658, Vol. 129 181.2.2, stanzas 394-6. Brackets are from *Ann*, stod 26a.5ff. This is quoted in Chandrakīrti's *Clear Words* in commentary on XVIII.6; Poussin, p.359.

583 P5262, Vol. 19 103.3.2, VI.94; Poussin's translation is *Muséon*, n.s. v.12, p.249.

584 P775, Vol. 29 39.5.5ff, chapter 2. Suzuki's translation is p.68. This is quoted in *Commentary on the 'Supplement'* (P5263, Vol. 98 136.1.4ff). Brackets are from Jñānavajra (P5520, Vol. 107 246.4.4).

585 P5262, Vol. 98 102.2.6, VI.43; Poussin's translation is *Muséon*, n.s. v.11, p.322. Commentary is P5263, Vol. 98 127.2.4ff. See D̄zong-ka-b̄a, P6143, Vol. 154 55.5.8. This quote has its own history of disputation because in the Ge-luk-b̄a interpretation of the Prāsaṅgika system the self and the aggregates are asserted to exist conventionally whereas the basis-of-all does not exist in any way whatsoever and yet the three are treated similarly here without seeming to give the self and the aggregates any status which the basis-of-all does not have.

586 P778, Vol. 29 152.2.1.

587 P5263, Vol. 98 127.1.8ff, commenting on VI.42; Poussin's translation is *Muséon*, n.s. v.11, p.321. See D̄zong-ka-b̄a, P6143, Vol. 154 55.5.1ff.

588 P5262, Vol. 98 103.3.4ff, VI.97; Poussin's translation is *Muséon*, n.s. v.12, p.253. Brackets are from *Commentary on the*

'Supplement' (P.5263, Vol. 98 136.3.8ff, and *Ann* (dbu 66b.4ff).

589 P731, Vol. 19 189.2.1. This is quoted in Dzong-ka-ba's *Essence* (P6142, Vol. 153 203.5.8).

590 P5263, Vol. 98 136.4.7ff, commenting on VI.97; Poussin's translation is *Muséon*, n.s. v.12, p.255. This is quoted in Dzong-ka-ba's *Illumination* (P6143, Vol. 154 76.3.6ff) and *Essence* (P6142, Vol. 153 204.5.3ff). See *Ann*, dbu 66b.6ff, and *GM*, 464a.2ff. Brackets are from Dzong-ka-ba's *Illumination*.

591 *Treatise*, XV.2cd.

592 P731, Vol. 19 190.2.8ff. Brackets are mostly from *GM*, 462a.4ff. This is discussed in Dzong-ka-ba's *Essence of the Good Explanations*, P6142, Vol. 153 203.4.6. In *GM* (461b.5-2b.3), Jam-yang-shay-ba identifies the qualm behind Dzong-ka-ba's consideration of this quote as someone's thinking that it is unsuitable to identify the three natures taught in the *Sutra Unravelling the Thought* as requiring interpretation because (1) this chapter of the *Twenty-Five Thousand Stanza Perfection of Wisdom Sutra* presents the three natures and (2) these are asserted by Ratnākarashānti in accordance with the Chittamātrin presentation. In response, Jam-yang-shay-ba explains that this chapter presents the three natures in a different way from the *Sutra Unravelling the Thought* and that Ratnākarashānti is not to be followed here. This is because the *Twenty-Five Thousand Stanza Perfection of Wisdom Sutra* speaks of *all* phenomena as not existing ultimately and only existing conventionally whereas the Chittamātrins say that other-powered phenomena and thoroughly established phenomena ultimately exist whereas imaginary or imputational phenomena do not.

Though it might seem that the *Twenty-Five Thousand Stanza Perfection of Wisdom Sutra* makes a differentiation of status among phenomena like that of the *Sutra Unravelling the Thought* when it says that imagined forms (imaginaries) do not substantially exist whereas imputed forms (other-powered phenomena) do, 'imagined forms' here refer to the ultimate existence imagined of forms which does not exist at all and 'imputed forms' refer to forms themselves which exist conventionally and thus it can be understood that 'substantial existence' here just means existence, not ultimate existence. Ratnākarashānti is faulted for not having taken the context of the sutra into proper account.

Therefore, since the necessarily correct presentation of the three natures in the *Twenty-Five Thousand Stanza Perfection of Wisdom Sutra* is different from that in the *Sutra Unravelling the Thought*, the latter is suitable to require interpretation.

593   P731, Vol. 19 190.1.2ff. This is quoted in D̄zong-ka-b̄a's *Essence*, P6142, Vol. 153 204.3.8, from which the bracketed material is taken.

594   P6142, Vol. 153 205.1.7.

595   *GM*, 461b.1.

596   See n.574.

597   D̄zong-ka-b̄a (*Illumination*, P6143, Vol. 154 56.2.7) identifies the quote as the *Mahāyāna-abhidharmasūtra* which is cited in Asaṅga's *Compendium of the Mahāyāna* as a source for the mind-basis-of-all and in Asaṅga's commentary on Maitreya's *Sublime Continuum of the Great Vehicle* as a source for the Buddha nature. See E. Lamotte, *Mélanges Chinois et Bouddhiques*, troisième volume (1934-5), p.171 n.3.

598   *GM*, 461b.4.

599   P5658, Vol. 129 175.2.6, stanza 99. Brackets are from *Ann*, dbu 67a.1. D̄zong-ka-b̄a quotes this in his *Illumination*, (P6143, Vol. 154 33.1.7).

600   P5246, Vol. 95 136.2.1, VIII.3. Brackets are from Chandrakīrti's commentary (P5266, Vol. 98 229.5.3). D̄zong-ka-b̄a quotes this in his *Illumination* (P6143, Vol. 154 32.4.2). Gyel-tsap quotes this and the next citation in his commentary on the *Precious Garland* (edition of 78 folios in library of H.H. Dalai Lama), 20b.6-21a.2.

601   P5266, Vol. 98 229.5.3, commenting on VIII.3.

602   P760.16, Vol. 23 198.3.8ff, chapter 26. Chandrakīrti briefly cites it in his *Commentary on the 'Supplement'* (P5263, Vol. 98 145.2.4ff), commenting on VI.138-9. Shāntideva cites it in his *Compendium of Learnings*, chapter 14, as does Prajñākaramati in his *Commentary on the Difficult Points of (Shāntideva's) 'Engaging in the Bodhisattva Deeds'*, IX.88.

603   According to Geshe Gedün Lodrö, nails actually are not considered to be conjoined with consciousness.

604   The term 'Bare Mountains' has been untraceable to date. See *Kosha* iii.141 for the mountains. For *kīṭādri*, see *Kosha* iii.147.

605   P5658, Vol. 129 175.2.6, stanza 80. D̄zong-ka-b̄a quotes it in his *Illumination* (P6143, Vol. 154 32.5.1). Jam-ȳang-shay-b̄a's commentary is based on Gyel-tsap's (21b.1-3).

606 As Kensur Lekden emphasized, the terms are only *hypothetical* synonyms because synonyms are existent by definition, and no member of this list exists.

607 P5246, Vol. 95 139.2.7, XIV.23. Brackets are from Chandrakīrti's commentary (P5266, Vol. 98 270.3.6).

608 P5266, Vol. 98 270.3.6, commenting on XIV.23.

609 P5272, Vol. 99 260.4.5, IX.140. See *GM*, 200a.5ff.

610 P5242, Vol. 95 112.1.7ff.; chap. 18.

611 P5260, Vol. 98 56.1.6, commenting on XVIII.7; Poussin, 368.4.

612 '... or reliant on causes and conditions' (*hetupratyayān prāpya*, more literally, 'meeting to causes and conditions') is missing in the Tibetan. The translation of the last sentence follows the Tibetan.

613 P760.43, Vol. 24 194.1.2ff. Brackets are from *Ann*, dngos 77a.7ff and dbu 68b.5ff. There is a similar quote in the *Clear Words* (Poussin, 358.10).

614 P5224, Vol. 95 6.3.7, XV.10.

615 *Ann*, dbu 69a.1.

616 P5262, Vol. 98 103.1.8, VI.83; Poussin's translation is *Muséon*, n.s. v.12, p.238. Chandrakīrti's own commentary is P5263, Vol. 98 133.5.2. Brackets are from *Ann*, dbu 69a.4ff. The second quote is P5262, Vol. 98 104.5.6, VI.159d; Poussin's translation is *Muséon*, n.s. v.12, p.321. Chandrakīrti's commentary is P5263, Vol. 98 147.3.8. The third quote is P5262, Vol. 98 101.5.5, VI.24a; Poussin's translation is *Muséon*, n.s. v.11, p.300. Chandrakīrti's commentary is P5263, Vol. 98 123.3.4.

617 P5266, Vol. 98 103.4.4, chapter 12. This is quoted in D̄zong-ka-b̄a's *Ocean of Reasoning, Explanation of (Nāgārjuna's) 'Treatise on the Middle Way'*, P6153, Vol. 156 66.1.4.

618 Chapters 10 and 22.

619 P5262, Vol. 98 103.4.4, VI.104ab; Poussin's translation is *Muséon*, n.s. v.12, p.267. Chandrakīrti's commentary is P5263, Vol. 98 138.5.4. Kensur Lekden said that this reasoning is called the 'diamond slivers' (*rdo rje gzegs ma*) because each of the four reasons is capable of overcoming a conception of inherent existence just as a piece of diamond has the hardness and so forth of a diamond. Thus, *gzegs ma* (*kaṇā*) means 'piece'; hence 'sliver' should not be thought of as a weak, thin piece but a fragment. According to Apte, the Sanskrit term also means 'facet'; this would seem to be most appropriate when speaking of

diamonds (and more appropriate to the meaning since each of the four reasons alone actually is not capable of refuting inherent existence); however, none of my Tibetan sources, oral or written, has explained it this way. The oral traditions that I have contacted are by no means always accurate; nevertheless, when put together, the various oral strains are quite full and no Tibetan scholar to date has given this interpretation (one said that *gzegs ma* refers to the points of a vajra).

620 P5343, Vol. 103 21.3.6.

621 *GM*, 225b.3.

622 P5242, Vol. 95 75.1.6ff, commenting on I.1. Brackets are from *GM*, 225a.6ff.

623 P5262, Vol. 98 101.3.4, VI.8c-13; Poussin's translation is *Muséon*, n.s. v.11, pp.280-4. Brackets are mostly from Chandrakīrti's own commentary, P5263, Vol. 98 120.3.4ff.

624 *Treatise*, P5224, Vol. 95 8.1.1, XX.19cd and XX.20cd. These are quoted in Chandrakīrti's *Commentary on the 'Supplement'* commenting on VI.14ab.

625 P5262, Vol. 98 101.4.2, VI.14; Poussin's translation is *Muséon*, n.s. v.11, pp.286-7.

626 *Ann*, dbu 71a.8.

627 *Ann*, dbu 71b.2.

628 P5224, Vol. 95 3.1.5, I.5. Brackets are from *Clear Words*, P5260, Vol. 98 14.1.6, commenting on I.5. Chandrakīrti's other interpretation takes *parabhāva* as meaning production from other, but the meaning is roughly the same.

629 P5262, Vol. 98 101.4.3ff, VI.15-19; Poussin's translation is *Muséon*, n.s. v.11, pp.288-93. Brackets are mostly from Chandrakīrti's commentry, P5263, Vol. 98 121.4.3ff, and D̄zong-ka-b̄a's *Illumination*, P6143, Vol. 154 38.3.7ff.

630 This might also be *kesara*; 'Rottieria intcotira; Mimusops Elengi, Mesua Ferrara' according to Poussin (*Muséon*, v.11, 289 n.4). He (IBID, n.5) identifies *kiṃshuka* as 'Butea Frondosa'.

631 *Ann*, dbu 71b.2.

632 P876, Vol. 34 304.3.5. This is cited in Chandrakīrti's *Commentary on the 'Supplement'*, P5263, Vol. 98 122.3.7.

633 Source for the brackets is Chandrakīrti's *Commentary on the 'Supplement'*, P5263, Vol. 98 122.4.2.

634 P5262, Vol. 98 101.5.1, VI.20; Poussin's translation is *Muséon*,

n.s. v.11, p.295. Brackets are mostly from his own commentary, P5263, Vol. 98 122.4.5.

635 P6143, Vol. 154 37.4.1ff. I have disregarded *snga phyi* in the second sentence.

636 *GT*, ca 37b.4ff.

637 P876, Vol. 34 304.2.8 and 305.4.6, with some variation in the reading. See p.502 for a citation of this by Chandrakīrti with a slightly different reading.

638 P5260, Vol. 98 6.1.8, commenting on I.1; Poussin, 27.4. For the context of the quote, see p.503.

639 P5262, Vol. 98 102.1.5, VI.32d. His commentary is P5263, Vol. 98 24.5.8.

640 P5262, Vol. 98 103.3.5, VI.98ab; Poussin's translation is *Muséon*, n.s. v.12, p.256 (misnumbered as 95ab). His commentary is P5263, Vol. 98 136.5.5.

641 See p.150 for a different rendition of this.

642 Artocarpus Lacucha.

642a P5262, Vol. 98 103.3.6, VI.99; Poussin's translation is *Muséon*, n.s. v.12, p.239. His own commentary is P5263, Vol. 98 137.2.8.

643 P5227, Vol. 95 13.1.7.

644 P5231, Vol. 95 52.5.6ff.

645 P5262, Vol. 98 101.5.2, VI.21; Poussin's translation is *Muséon*, n.s. v.11, p.296.

646 P5263, Vol. 98 122.5.2ff. See pp.152-4 for Chandrakīrti's commentary.

647 P5343, Vol. 103 21.3.5.

648 The instrumental *bshad pas* is not an actual one according to Geshe Gedün Lodrö.

649 This is a paraphrase of Kamalashīla's *Illumination of the Middle Way*, P5287, Vol. 101 76.4.2.

650 The *Satyadvayavibhaṅga* is not included in the Peking Tripiṭaka. Brackets, except where noted, are from *Ann*, dbu 73b.3ff.

651 *Ann*, dbu 128b.7.

652 P5260, Vol. 98 3.3.7, commenting on the salutation; Poussin, 6.3-.5. See p.668.

653 P5260, Vol. 98 13.3.7, commenting on I.3; Poussin, 74.3. For Dignāga's presentation of this, see M. Hattori's *Dignaga, On Perception* (Cambridge: Harvard, 1968), p.76 n.1.11 and p.87 n.1.33.

654 P5266, Vol. 98 259.1.5ff, chapter 13. Brackets are from *Ann*, dbu 74b.4. See n.653.

655 P5272, Vol. 99 248.5.3ff, V.15. Brackets are from Gyel-tsap's commentary, 43b. of a Gan-den edition.

656 Relics such as teeth and bone are made into powder, molded, and stamped with a holy image. These are called *sachchha*, or *sāchchha*, perhaps from *sach* meaning 'to be devoted'.

657 P5272, Vol. 99 248.5.4, V.16. This is quoted in D̄zong-ka-b̄a's *Middling Exposition of the Stages of the Path*, 79b.5 (Dharmsala: Shes rig par khang, 1968).

658 P5272, Vol. 99 248.1.2, IV.21ab.

659 P5287, Vol. 101 76.4.2.

660 P5287, Vol. 101 76.5.2.

661 'The effects are plural because the causes are plural.' Actually, the inference is based on the cause and not the effect; however, according to Geshe Gedün Lodrö it is the Buddhist logician's custom to refer even to these as effect-signs.

662 P5224, Vol. 95 9.3.5, XXIV.19. Brackets are from *Ann*, dbu 74a.8.

663 P5246, Vol. 95 136.4.3, IX.2 and IX.5. Brackets are from Chandrakīrti's commentary, P5266, Vol. 98 236.3.3. This is quoted in Chandrakīrti's *Clear Words*, P5260, Vol. 98 78.2.6; Poussin, 505.

664 This is quoted in Chandrakīrti's *Clear Words*, P5260, Vol. 98 78.2.7; Poussin, 505. He also quotes it in his commentary to the *Four Hundred*, P5266, Vol. 98 236.5.2.

665 P5260, Vol. 98 78.2.8, commenting on XXIV.19; Poussin, 505.14.

666 P5224, Vol. 95 9.3.4, XXIV.18. Brackets are from D̄zong-ka-b̄a's commentary, P6153, Vol. 156 148.3.2ff and 148.5.1ff.

667 P5260, Vol. 98 78.2.3, commenting on XXIV.18; Poussin, 504.13.

668 *Ann*, dbu 75a.8.

669 Brackets are from *Ann*, dbu 75a.7.

670 P6016, Vol. 153 37.3.5.

671 P5265, Vol. 98 171.5.1ff.

672 See P5591, Vol. 115 176.2.3ff, and P5593, Vol. 116 175.2.3ff.

673 This is often called a gerund, not like the English declinable noun but the Sanskritic indeclinable continuative indicating often the anterior of two actions.

674 P5767, Vol. 140 5.1.3 *Alaṃkhalvoḥ pratiṣhedhe ktvā vā*. See *Pā*, III.iv.18-20. Hereon, the Sanskrit is taken from the *Cāndravyākaraṇaṃ* (Jodhapura, 1967). Usually the continuative affix is affixed to the former of verbs in a temporal series; 'After *meṅ*' indicates an exception.

675 P5775, Vol. 140 45.3.8.

676 P5767, Vol. 140 13.4.7. *Anañsamāse ktvāḥ lyap*. See *Pā*, VII.i.37.

677 P5775, Vol. 140 45.5.4.

678 P5767, Vol. 140 11.5.7. *Hrasvasya atiṅi piti tuk*. See *Pā*, VI.i.71.

679 P5775, Vol. 140 43.3.8.

680 P5767, Vol. 140 12.1.4. *Akaḥ aki dīrghah*. See *Pā*, VI.i.101.

681 P5767, Vol. 140 6.2.5. *Arthamātre prathamā*. See *Pā*, II.iii.46.

682 P5767, Vol. 140 6.1.2. *Supaḥ asaṃkhyad luk*. See *Pā*, II.iv.82.

683 P5767, Vol. 140 4.3.6. *Ghañ kārake cha*. See *Pā*, III.iii.16, 18, 19.

684 P5775, Vol. 140 45.1.3.

685 P5767, Vol. 140 6.2.5. *Arthamātre prathamā*. See *Pā*, II.iii.46.

686 P5767, Vol. 140 15.5.6. *Sasajuṣhaḥ raḥ*. See *Pā*, VIII.ii.66.

687 P5767, Vol. 140 12.1.6. *Hashi cha ataḥ roḥ*. See *Pā*, VI.i.113, 114.

688 P5767, Vol. 140 16.1.7. *Virāme visarjanīyaḥ*. See *Pā*, VIII.iii.15. The citing here is doubtful because the Tibetan quoted and the Peking translation do not, for the first time, agree.

689 P5260, Vol. 98 3.2.8ff; Poussin, 5.1-4. See the notes in Poussin (p.5ff) throughout.

690 In the Peking catalogue five books are listed as being translated by Sthiramati (*bLo-rtan*).

691 P5260, Vol. 98 3.3.3ff; Poussin, 5.7-8.

692 See *Pā*, IV.iv.98.

693 P5253, Vol. 95 154.1.8.

694 Avalokitavrata, *Commentary on (Bhāvaviveka's) 'Lamp for (Nāgārjuna's) "Wisdom"'*, P5259, Vol. 96 169.5.8ff.

695 Stcherbatsky (p.90) identifies these others as Hīnayānists.

696 This is a paraphrase of *Kalāpa's Aphorisms*; see n.679.

697 *Ann*, dbu 75b.8.

698 *Rice Seedling Sutra*, P876, Vol. 34 303.3.4. Here the word *dharma* (Tib. *chos*) equals *tathatā* (Tib. *de kho na nyid*)

according to Dzong-ka-ba's *Illumination* (P6143, Vol. 154 147.1.3).

699 The Sanskrit has *rūpāṇi*, whereas the version given here follows Jam-yang-shay-ba's transliteration into Tibetan letters (see p.668).

700 P5260, Vol. 98 3.3.5ff; Poussin, 6.1-7.5.

701 The Sanskrit has only 'eye', not 'eye and forms' in this sentence.

702 Putting *cha* between the two words rather than after the second is irregular but still barely possible; thus, I have left it there. The original reads *chakṣhurcha*.

703 P5253, Vol. 95 154.1.6ff. There are minor differences between the Tibetan translations of Bhāvaviveka's own passage and Chandrakīrti's citation of it but none of substance.

The Tibetan translators adopted a code for handling this three-part discussion of the formation of *pratītyasamutpāda*:

prati = *rten cing*
i or *itya* = *'brel bar*
samutpāda = *'byung ba*

Their over-riding concern was with having a three-part translation equivalent that, when together, makes sense in Tibetan. As a result, the individual equivalents often make no sense when associated with these various interpretations.

Some Tibetan scholars claim that *rten cing* and *'brel bar* have different meanings; however, since Chandrakīrti says that *prati* (*rten cing*), which itself means *prāpti* (*phrad pa*), modifies the meaning of *itya* (*'brel ba*) into meaning *prāpti* (*phrad pa*), the two words come to have just one meaning, and thus it seems that the two were separated out in Tibetan merely in order to convey, albeit not very well, this discussion of the meaning of the individual parts. Perhaps a better alternative would have been to transliterate the individual parts into Tibetan rather than attempt a translation.

In Chandrakīrti's interpretation, *pratītya* has just one meaning as a continuative meaning 'having depended' which in Tibetan is *rten nas* as in the commonly used *rten nas 'byung ba* or *rten 'byung*. Strictly speaking, therefore, in Prāsaṅgika *rten nas 'byung ba* or *rten 'byung* is the most appropriate general term, with *rten cing 'brel bar 'byung ba* suitable only as a code equivalent for the three-part discussion. *rten 'brel* is a common usage that is neither.

704 P5260, Vol. 98 3.4.6ff; Poussin, 8.1-3.

705 The Tibetan mis-reads *rten cing 'brel bar 'byung ba* where it should read *rten cing 'brel bar* in accordance with the Sanskrit *pratītya.*

706 P5260, Vol. 98 3.4.7ff; Poussin, 8.3-9.

707 For Chandrakīrti *prati* alone means *prāpti* (meeting, *phrad pa*) as does *pratītya.* In its continuative form *prāpti* (*phrad pa*) is *prāpya* (*phrad nas*).

708 Though the Tibetan here is *phrad pa*, 'meeting', I have rendered it to accord with Nāgārjuna's *prāpya*, 'having met'. The alternation in the use of forms is due to Chandrakīrti's and Jam-ȳang-shay-b̄a's using the general term outside of this particular usage for the more specific term within this usage as a continuative.

The significance of Chandrakīrti's citation is lost in the Tibetan translation *de dang de brten gang 'byung ba/ rang gi ngo bor de ma skyes* which, nevertheless, is an excellent translation in general in that it conveys the meaning. However, to convey the point here it should read *de dang de phrad gang 'byung ba/ rang gi ngo bor de ma skyes.* (The second line could have been rendered as *de ni rang bzhin gyis ma skyes.*) By using *brten* for *prāpya* instead of *phrad* the purpose of Chandrakīrti's stunning citation is lost in the Tibetan.

The text is P5225, Vol. 95 11.4.1.

709 P5260, Vol. 98 3.5.2ff; Poussin, 8.10-9.6. The Tibetan reading is followed in the first two paragraphs of the translation.

710 Brackets are from Avalokitavrata (P5259, Vol. 96 170.1.6). He identifies the two interpretations as 'arising upon depending on and meeting these and those [causes and conditions]' and 'the arising of those which possess individual disintegration' (*de dang de la brten cing phrad nas 'byung ba'i zhes bya ba dang/ so so'i 'jig pa dang ldan pa rnams kyi* [text has *kyis*] *'byung ba zhes bya ba'i don de gnyi ga med pa'i phyir te*).

711 P5225, Vol. 95 11.4.1.

712 P5253, Vol. 95 154.2.1.

713 *Rice Seedling Sutra*, P876, Vol. 34 303.3.8.

714 P5260, Vol. 98 3.5.7ff; Poussin, 9.7-10.2. Literally: 'That system which is presented as "What then? The meaning..." is also incorrect.'

715 Poussin calls attention to *Pā*, II.i.44.

716 P5225, Vol. 95 11.4.1.

717 P5658, Vol. 129 174.4.7, stanza 48ab. The Peking edition has: *'di yod pas na 'di byung dper/ ring po yod pas thung ngu bzhin.*

718 *Ann*, dbu 77b.3 (which is actually 76b.3 due to misplacement in printing).

719 P5260, Vol. 98 4.1.1ff; Poussin, 10.3-9.

720 P5593, Vol. 116 175.2.3.

721 P5246, Vol. 95 139.2.7, XIV.23. Brackets are from Chandrakīrti's commentary (P5266, Vol. 98 270.3.6).

722 P5225, Vol. 95 11.4.1. Chandrakīrti's commentary is P5265, Vol. 98 177.1.3.

723 P5266, Vol. 98 270.3.3, which is commentary preceding XIV.23. Here in the terms *dngos po med par smra ba* and *dngos por smra ba* (in Sanskrit most likely *abhāvavādin* and *bhāvavādin*) the term *dngos po* (*bhāva*) has two different meanings in D̄zong-ka-b̄a's mode of interpretation. In the first it means 'things', i.e., those which are able to perform a function, or even more widely 'phenomena', whereas in the latter it means 'inherent existence'. Thus, conceptual sense is made out of Chandrakīrti's saying that he is neither a proponent of *abhāva* or of *bhāva*. Instead of such statements being taken as a direct call away from conceptuality to another level of consciousness beyond the opposites of *abhāva* and *bhāva*, their different sense is explicated such that we are left not with paradox but with a tidy explanation of two extremes and a middle free from them.

In Ge-luk-b̄a, there is a decided movement away from only smashing two conceptual poles against each other and thereby forcing movement to another level of consciousness in the resulting conceptual hiatus. Rather, a complete conceptual map is laid out with the moves neatly delineated. Still, in order to follow the map, one must undergo the battering and smashing of misbegotten conceptuality, gain the appropriate conceptual realization and then, through becoming accustomed to it, eventually arrive at non-conceptual realization. It would be a mistake to assume that Ge-luk-b̄as are somehow satisfied with a mere verbal lay-out of intricate philosophy. There is a basic recognition that we are controlled by our ideas, and thus re-formation of ideas in a harrowing process of analytical meditation—involving one's feelings in the most intimate sense—is of central importance.

724 P5682, Vol. 129 237.5.7.

725 Mahāmati, *Clear Words, Extensive Explanation of (Nāgārjuna's) 'Friendly Letter'*, P5690, Vol. 129 270.4.3 and 270.4.8.

726 P6016, Vol. 153 38.1.1.

727 *GT* ca 26b.1ff and 43a.2ff. For a discussion of 'able to set itself up' see *Ann*, dbu 10a.5ff. Also see *Ḏak*, 71b.5ff (215.5 in the Thim-phu edition). In chapter eleven of *GT* Jam-ȳang-shay-b̄a cites many scriptures that refer to valid cognition, correct perception, truths, and so forth and concludes that to be validly certified does not necessarily mean to be able to set itself up or to be inherently existent. In D̄ak-tsang's system just the opposite holds: If something is validly certified, it must be self-instituting. Thus, since nothing is able to set itself up in the Prāsaṅgika system, there can be no valid certification of the existence of objects for D̄ak-tsang.

Valid certification for D̄ak-tsang and for D̄zong-ka-b̄a are different; the former sees it as implying self-institution, whereas the latter views it, in Prāsaṅgika, as implying non-self-institution. For D̄zong-ka-b̄a the valid certification of an object is itself a sign that the object does not inherently exist. The process of certification itself cannot bear analysis such as whether, when a consciousness certifies the existence of an object, the object is already certified, is being certified, or is yet to be certified. If the object is already certified, then it perforce is not what is undergoing present certification. If it is yet to be certified, how can it be said that it is being certified? If a certifier certifies what is presently being certified, then two activites are required, one for the designation of the consciousness as the certifier and another for the designation of the object as what is being certified. Also, when a certifier begins to certify an object, what is it acting on? Something already certified? Something being certified? Something yet to be certified? Valid certification of objects cannot bear such analysis; thus, valid certification even conventionally does not inherently exist.

D̄ak-tsang approaches the problem from a different angle; he probably thought that if it were affirmed that objects are validly certified, then students would think that objects as they appear to them would be true, and the knot of cyclic existence would be tied even tighter. Both D̄zong-ka-b̄a and D̄ak-tsang agree that objects do not exist the way they appear, that our assent to these appearances binds us in cyclic existence, and that to free ourselves from cyclic existence we must discover the true nature of these objects. Their means are different.

728 P5709, Vol. 130 88.3.4, chapter 3.

729 Brackets in the root text are from *Ann*, dbu 129a.2.

730 *GM*, 464b.2ff.

731 This is quoted in Chandrakīrti's *Commentary on the 'Supplement'*, P5263, Vol. 98 142.4.8, commenting on VI.126. It is also quoted in Dzong-ka-ba's *Illumination*, P6143, Vol. 154 84.3.7.

732 P5262, Vol. 98 104.1.7, VI.124b; Poussin's translation is *Muséon*, n.s. v.12, p.289. The second quote is P5262, Vol. 98 104.2.6, VI.132cd; *Muséon*, n.s. v.12, p.301.

733 P5263, Vol. 98 141.2.7, commenting on VI.120; v.12, p.283. Brackets are from Dzong-ka-ba's *Illumination*, P6143, Vol. 154 82.2.8.

734 P5242, Vol. 95 111.1.2, commenting on XVIII.2ab.

735 P5263, Vol. 98 141.2.3, commenting on VI.120; v.12, p.282.

736 P5262, Vol. 98 100.2.5, I.3ab; v.8, p.258.

737 P5263, Vol. 98 109.3.5, commenting on I.3; v.8, p.258. Brackets are from Dzong-ka-ba's *Illumination*, Vol. 154 6.5.1.

738 P6153, Vol. 156 65.5.8ff.

739 A point of controversy among the Ge-luk-bas is just what is an illustration (*mtshan gzhi*) of the 'mine'. Jam-yang-shay-ba says that it does not refer to the things which are considered to be mine, such as eyes and ears, but to the person who considers things to be possessions. 'Mine' is a person, but not a second person separate from I because the two are the same entity and different conceptual isolates or opposites of the negatives. 'Mine' cannot be the eyes, ears, tongue, and so forth, because these are the bases of the designation 'mine', and in the Prāsaṅgika system the basis of a designation is not the phenomenon designated. As Kensur Lekden said, if one watches carefully when the thought 'my' or 'mine' appears, this 'my' often appears more on the subject's side than on the object's. He said that as a form of I it is more extensive and active than I.

Still, Jam-yang-shay-ba's annotator, Nga-wang-bel-den, disagrees (*Ann*, dbu 78b.3-80b.5) saying that the eyes, ears, and so forth which are included within one's own continuum are illustrations of mine but not the objects observed by the false view of mine. For Jam-ȳang-shay-b̄a also, the objects of observation of the false view of mine are not the eyes, ears, and so forth but mine itself, which for him is a person, and that person is wrongly conceived to exist inherently.

The problem is largely one of terminology. Since the view of the transitory collection (*satkāyadṛṣhṭi, 'jig tshogs la lta ba*) as inherently existent I and mine refers only to a conception of a self of persons, then even 'mine' would seem to refer only to the person involved in ownership, the 'my'. It makes some sense in English to say that my own ear is not an illustration of 'my', as 'my' is that which makes things into mine, but it is difficult to say that my own ear is not an illustration of 'mine', is not mine, just because it is not what makes such things into mine. Jam-ȳang-shay-b̄a tries to make this distinction in Tibetan by saying that an ear included in one's own continuum is not an illustration of mine (*bdag gi ba'i mtshan gzhi*), is not mine (*bdag gi ba*), but is an illustration of something that is owned (*bdag gi yin rgyu'i mtshan gzhi*) and thus something that is owned (*bdag gi yin rgyu*). According to Nga-w̄ang-b̄el-den, however, 'mine' can refer to phenomena considered to be possessions and included within the continuum of a person, but those phenomena do not have to be the object of observation of a false view of mine—the object of observation perhaps being the I that owns them.

According to Geshe Lhundup Sopa, Jay-d̄zun Chö-ḡyi-gyel-tsen, the textbook author of the Jay (*Byes*) College of S̄e-ra Monastery, avoids the problem by dividing phenomena into not just two categories, persons and other phenomena, but also a third, mine. Here in the false view of mine, 'mine' is not the person and not the eyes, etc., but just the mine itself, technically called the isolate of mine (*nga yi ba'i rang ldog*), or opposite from non-one-with-mine, which means *just* mine and not its illustrations, not the things that are mine. The object of observation of the false view of mine is this mine, but the false view of mine is nevertheless a conception of a self of persons since it is conceiving the I involved in mine to be inherently existent. In this way, my own ear is an illustration of mine, and thus is mine, but is not an object of observation of the false view of mine as this is only the isolate of mine.

In any case, the Ge-luk-b̄a scholars agree that the conception of eyes, ears, and so forth included in one's own continuum as inherently existent is a conception of the inherent existence of phenomena, not of persons, and that in the false view of mine the mine is something different from the person that is conceived to exist inherently in the false view of I. The controversy over what this is draws one into noticing the I as owner.

740 P6153, Vol. 156 66.1.2.

741 Kay-drup's *Opening the Eyes of the Fortunate* (blockprint in the possession of Geshe Wangyal), 105a.6ff.

742 P5260, Vol. 98 53.5.8, commenting on XVIII.2cd; Poussin, 347.13.

743 See n.741.

744 See *GM*, 471a.3ff, for almost the same presentation. Jam-ȳang-shay-b̄a attributes this position to D̄ak-tsang in both *GT* and *GM*, but in neither does he give a source to show that D̄ak-tsang actually asserts this position. The absence of citation often means that D̄ak-tsang does not explicitly assert such but that he is 'forced' to do so as a consequence of other assertions. As Geshe Gedün Lodrö said, it is necessary to determine, when Jam-ȳang-shay-b̄a cites a 'contradiction' in D̄ak-tsang's writings, whether it is an explicit contradiction or whether D̄ak-tsang is being forced into a particular assertion by logical pressure (*rigs pas phul ba*). As the ascription of fantastic positions explicitly unfounded in D̄ak-tsang's writings is a conscious literary device, it does not constitute inaccurate reporting of D̄ak-tsang's positions but does indeed make reading Jam-ȳang-shay-b̄a's text difficult.

My guess on this one is that it stems from a criticism by D̄ak-tsang (see *GT*, ca 47a.8-8b.2) of D̄zong-ka-b̄a for claiming that reasoning refuting artificial misconceptions does not refute the innate. In reply Jam-ȳang-shay-b̄a first explains that D̄zong-ka-b̄a should be understood as saying that 'although one refuted objects imputed by systems of tenets *that do not involve the mode of apprehension by innate [misconceptions]*, this would not damage innate [misconceptions] and although one refuted objects imputed *merely and only* by systems of tenets, this would not harm innate [misconceptions].' This means that refuting that the I, for instance, does not depend on causes and does not change does not refute the innate misconception of the inherent existence of the I, as the conception that the I is independent and immutable does not constitute the innate conception that the I inherently exists or exists in its own right. Rather, refuting such can be a branch of refuting the innate conception of inherent existence when it is understood that if things did inherently exist, they could not depend on causes and could not change.

Having clarified Dzong-ka-ba's meaning, Jam-yang-shay-ba proceeds to accuse Dak-tsang of therefore holding that all forms of artificial misconceptions (such as that the person is permanent, unitary, and under its own power) and all forms of innate misconceptions are exactly the same and that, thereby, refuting the grossest of the gross would mean one had refuted them all—a position Dak-tsang obviously does not assert. Perhaps, it is within this absurd 'extension' of Dak-tsang's views that Jam-yang-shay-ba here claims that Dak-tsang holds that the person and the aggregates always appear as one.

Through studying the points Jam-yang-shay-ba displays in framing his refutation, one learns, not so much about Dak-tsang's views, but a great deal about Jam-yang-shay-ba's own views. This type of polemic is a frequently used technique for conveying information basic to one's own system and needs to be milked for that. If one thinks that it is merely polemic to put down an opponent, a great source of subtle distinctions will be lost. After holding one's nose for a while, the points—devoid of the polemic—become fascinating.

The opinion being forced on Dak-tsang here is that it is wrong to refute the existence of a person different from the aggregates first and then refute a self of phenomena, the reason behind this patently absurd view being that a consciousness innately misconceiving the person always views the person as one with the aggregates. Thus, for 'Dak-tsang' the very refutation of the inherent existence of the I constitutes a refutation of the inherent existence of mind, body, and so forth which are phenomena other than the person.

The refutation of this position provides an opportunity to discuss the extremely subtle and intricate topic of the appearance of an inherently existent I and its relation to the appearance of mind and body. Jam-yang-shay-ba's response revolves around considering an innate consciousness apprehending I (*ngar 'dzin lhan skyes*) in two ways: valid and invalid. He first points out that there are valid conceptions of 'my mind', 'my body', and so forth in which I and mind or body are different and then points out there is a coarse innate misconception of I in which the I and the aggregates are viewed as like a master and subjects, the assumption being that if the I and the aggregates did not appear to be different such could not be misconceived.

745 P5262, Vol. 98 104.1.7, VI.124b. Brackets are from *Ann*, dbu 83a.6.

746 *GM*, 471b.4. Although when the stomach is sick, persons say, 'I am sick,' they do not innately say, 'I am my stomach.' Jam-ȳang-shay-b̄a is making the point that even though the appearance of the I is inseparably mixed with that of the mental and physical aggregates like water in milk, when we conceive the I to exist inherently, we do not conceive it to be either one with or different from the aggregates.

747 P5262, Vol. 98 101.2.3, IV.2d; Poussin's translation is *Muséon*, n.s. v.8, p.311. Brackets are from D̄zong-ka-b̄a's *Illumination of the Thought*, P6143, Vol. 154 27.1.1. *Rang du lta ba dang 'brel* is taken as meaning that what is destroyed is that which is related to the view of self, not relation with the view of self as Poussin takes it ('est détruite toute relation avec l'idée de soi'). The view of self is the subtle misconception of the person as being inherently existent; that which is related with it or is produced in dependence upon it is the coarse view of the person as being self-sufficient. Thus, Chandrakīrti is interpreted as saying that on the fourth ground the Bodhisattva overcomes the corresponding level of the innate coarse misconception of the self in which the I and the aggregates are conceived to be like master and subjects. If the I and the aggregates did not appear differently, such a conception could not take place, in which case Chandrakīrti would absurdly be wrong to say that on the fourth ground the respective level of that affliction is overcome. See *Compassion in Tibetan Buddhism*, p.226.

748 P5263, Vol. 98 118.3.2, end of chapter 4. The sutra is P761.31, Vol. 25 258.2.4. The sutra speaks of the fourth ground Bodhisattva's overcoming what is interpreted as this coarser view of self described in n.747.

749 P5262, Vol. 98 104.1.7, VI.124b; Poussin's translation is *Muséon*, n.s. v.12, p.289. His commentary is Vol. 98 142.3.4. Brackets are from *Ann*, dbu 83a.6.

750 Brackets are from *GM*, 471b.2.

751 P5262, Vol. 98 104.1.8, VI.125; Poussin's translation is

Muséon, n.s. v.12, p.290. Brackets in the citation are from Ḏzong-ka-ḇa's *Illumination of the Thought*, P6143, Vol. 154 84.2.5.

752 Jam-ȳang-shay-ḇa (*GM*, 481a.1) identifies this as Ḏzong-ka-ḇa and his spiritual sons (Gyel-tsap and Kay-drup). In colloquial Tibetan *hrang hrang* is used to depict someone who is alone, someone standing on his own. *Phob phob* seems to mean forthright or concrete, the very sound suggesting the seemingly hard surface of a bubble.

753 *GM*, 481a.2ff. For this same refutation, see *GM*, 481a.1-b.5.

754 Jam-ȳang-shay-ḇa seems to be saying that the appearance of the aggregates is the appearance of the I; however, his *Great Exposition of the Middle Way* (481b.2) words the same point differently: 'It [absurdly] follows that when an embodied self appears to an innate [consciousness] it does not have to appear by way of the appearance of the aggregates' (*lhan skyes la lus can gyi bdag snang ba na phung po'i snang ba'i sgo nas snang mi dgos par thal*). He is clearly holding the opposite of this absurd consequence, i.e., that when the I appears, it appears *by way of* the appearance of the aggregates; this does not mean that the appearance of the aggregates *is* the appearance of the I. Thus, in this reading he is saying only that the I appears together with the aggregates and dependent upon the appearance of the aggregates. This seems the more credible reading since it is clear that he is holding that they appear together but that the I, within that context, appears to be standing by itself and concrete.

When he says that the I and the aggregates appear inseparably, it does not mean that one could not identify the appearance of the I within this conglomerate appearance; it merely means that they appear together and that the I appears by way of the aggregates' appearing.

In accordance with the passage cited above, the passage here might read better as *nga'i gdags gzhi phung po'i rnam pa shar ba'i sgo nas nga'i rnam pa shar ba ma yin pa'i phyir* ('because [according to you] the appearance of the aspect of I is not by way of the appearance of the aspect of the aggregates which are the basis of imputation of "I"').

755 See n.749.

756 P5224, Vol. 95 7.2.8, XVIII.1cd.

757 P5260, Vol. 98 53.3.1ff, commenting on XVIII.1cd; Poussin, 343.8; Buddhist Sanskrit Texts No. 10 146.20ff.

758 'Suitability as form' (*rūpaṇa, gzugs su rung ba*) is rendered by J.W. De Jong in his *Cinq Chapitres De La Prasannapadā* (Paris: Libraire Orientaliste Paul Geuthner, 1949, 4) as 'le pouvoir d'être brisé', 'capable of being broken'. The latter is how Ajitamitra interprets the term in his commentary on the *Precious Garland* (P5659, Vol. 129 notation lost). Therefore, it appears that the translators into Tibetan were aware of both meanings and chose 'suitability as form' here. Lati Rinbochay said that 'capable of being broken' is not appropriate as a definition of form at least in those schools which assert partless particles as these cannot be broken down either physically or mentally. Perhaps this is the reason why the translation as 'that which is suitable as form', meaning whatever one points to when asked what form is, was preferred. Still, Geshe Gedün Lodrö said that partless particles could not be further reduced without disappearing; thus, if we take their physical disappearance as their susceptibility to being broken, this interpretation of *rūpaṇa* as that which is susceptible to being broken would be an appropriate definition of form.

'That which is suitable as form' (*gzugs su rung ba*) appears to be almost a non-definition since it repeats the very term being defined, form; however, it does illustrate the notion that reasoning meets back to common experience in that with form we are at a level of common experience with little else to come up with as a definition other than saying that it is what we point to when we identify form.

759 Blockprint in the possession of Trijang Labrang, 88a.2ff.

760 P6153, Vol. 156 110.3.3, commenting on XI.3.

761 Blockprint in the possession of Trijang Labrang, 89a.6.

762 P5263, Vol. 98 146.1.1, commenting on VI.144; Poussin's translation is *Muséon*, n.s. v.12, p.312.

763 See Chandrakīrti's *Commentary on the 'Supplement'*, P5263, Vol. 98 146.1.3ff, commenting on VI.144; v.12, p.312.

764 *Clear Words*, P5260, Vol. 98 54.5.6ff, commenting on XVIII.5; Poussin 355.5.

765 This is quoted in Chandrakīrti's *Clear Words*, P5260, Vol. 98 54.5.7, commenting on XVIII.5 immediately after the last quote; Poussin, 355.7.

766 *Ann*, dbu 84b.6.

767 *Ann*, dbu 84b.5.

768 Jam-ȳang-shay-b̄a now states the syllogisms establishing the emptiness of a person, citing the two subjects which Nāgārjuna used, the self (translated here as 'person') and the Tathāgata, as in chapters eighteen and twenty-two of the *Treatise*. In this context 'self' is the nominally existent person and not 'self' in the sense of inherent existence, and the Tathāgata is merely an example of a person, albeit the most exalted person. The implicit point is that if even the most exalted person lacks inherent existence, then, of course, ordinary persons lack it.

In this context the term 'Tathāgata' refers to a fully developed Buddha, not to the 'potentiality' for Buddhahood which exists in all sentient beings. The emptiness of the mind is the Tathāgata nature or Buddha lineage, which itself is empty of inherent existence and applies to all persons; however, here the referent of 'Tathāgata' is just the person of a Buddha. Thus, 'Tathāgata and self', the dual subjects in Jam-ȳang-shay-b̄a's syllogisms refuting a self of persons, are not synonyms because there are many selves that are not Tathāgatas. Jam-ȳang-shay-b̄a is merely using the dual subject as a convenient means to establish that not only are persons empty of inherent existence but also, among persons, even a Tathāgata lacks it.

769 Chandrakīrti uses this metaphor in his *Clear Words* P5260, Vol. 98 35.4.3, commenting on X.14; Poussin, 212-13.

770 P5224, Vol. 95 8.3.3, XXII.1. Brackets are from *Ann*, dbu 85a.1ff.

771 P5658, Vol. 129 175.2.8, stanza 82. Brackets are from *Ann*, dbu 85a.2ff.

772 *Ann* (dbu 85a.3) says, 'The self is not inexpressible as either one with or other than the aggregates.' This is the assertion that the self and the aggregates are not mingled like fire and fuel.

773 P5242, Vol. 95 120.4.1, commenting on XXII.1.

774 P5260, Vol. 98 53.1.8, commenting on XVIII.1; Poussin, 341.8.

775 The Buddhist Sanskrit Texts edition of the Sanskrit (145.22) emends the text to read, 'due to the consequence of the fault of manyness'. However, the Tibetan accords with Poussin's Bibliotheca Buddhica edition (p.341) and allows for fallacies other than manyness.

776 *Supplement*, P5262, Vol. 98 104.2.1ff, VI.127-8; Poussin's translation is *Muséon*, n.s. v.12, pp.292-4. Brackets are from his

own commentary, P5263, Vol. 98 142.5.5ff, and Dzong-ka-ba's *Illumination*, P6143, Vol. 154 84.5.4ff.

777 P5242, Vol. 95 120.4.2, commenting on XXII.1. Brackets are from *Ann*, dbu 86b.8.

778 P5260, Vol. 98 55.3.1ff, commenting on XVIII.1; Poussin, 343.8.

779 P5242, Vol. 95 120.4.4ff, commenting on XXII.1.

780 P5263, Vol. 98 145.4.6ff, commenting on VI.142; Poussin's translation is *Muséon*, n.s. v.12, p.310. Brackets are from *Illumination*, P6143, Vol. 154 89.1.3ff.

781 P5242, Vol. 95 120.4.5, commenting on XXII.1.

782 P5262, Vol. 98 104.3.7ff, VI.143; Poussin's translation is *Muséon*, n.s. v.12, pp.310-11. Brackets are from Dzong-ka-ba's *Illumination*, P6143, Vol. 154 89.1.7ff.

783 P5263, Vol. 98 145.5.2ff, commenting on VI.143; Poussin's translation is *Muséon*, n.s. v.12, p.311.

784 P5260, Vol. 98 66.5.4, commenting on XXII.1; Poussin, 435.3. In the eighteenth chapter of the *Treatise* Nāgārjuna presents the reasoning which refutes an inherent existence of persons in abbreviated form. There just two positions are refuted: a self is shown to be inherently neither the same as nor different from the aggregates. In the twenty-second chapter on the Tathāgata, the five-cornered reasoning is presented.

785 P5658, Vol. 129 175.2.7, stanza 81 (for stanza 80 see p.631), and 175.2.8, stanza 83. Brackets in the first quote are from *Ann*, dbu 67b.4-8; in the second, from *Ann*, dbu 87a.5ff. (In my translation of the *Precious Garland*, published as Volume 2 of the Wisdom of Tibet Series, I used the Sanskrit edition as well as Ajitamitra's commentary though I cited neither—*mea culpa*.)

The four elements conventionally exist in mutual dependence; the one cannot exist without the others. However, one of them is not the others because then it would have the character of the others whereby the character of the elements would become confused. They also do not inherently depend on each other, because then they would be inherently existent others, capable of standing alone whereas they are not. They also cannot subsist without the others. This is the fourfold analysis (dependence being considered two ways) which establishes that the elements do not inherently exist, that is, are not established as their own reality.

786 The term *dngos smra ba* (*bhāvavādin*) usually refers to those schools which assert true existence (*bden grub*), these being Vaibhāṣhika, Sautrāntika, and Chittamātra, and thus has been translated as 'Proponents of True Existence' or 'Proponents of Truly Existent Things'. However, here the term includes the Svātantrikas, who although they do not propound true existence do assert inherent existence (*svabhāvasiddhi, rang bzhin gyis grub pa*). That they propound inherent existence is indicated by the fact that they assert the self *to be* a consciousness, for instance. In other words, when the object designated as 'person' is sought, something is found—a consciousness. (See also n.723.)

787 P5262, Vol. 98 104.4.6, VI.151; Poussin's translation is *Muséon*, n.s. v.12, p.316. Brackets are from D̄zong-ka-b̄a's *Illumination*, P6143, Vol. 154 90.2.4ff. Chandrakīrti's own commentary is P5263, Vol. 98 146.4.1ff.

788 P5262, Vol. 98 105.1.3ff, VI.166-7; Poussin's translation ends with VI.165. Brackets are from his own commentary, P5263, Vol. 98 148.5.1ff, and D̄zong-ka-b̄a's *Illumination*, P6143, Vol. 154 93.1.4ff.

789 D̄zong-ka-b̄a (*GM*, 477a.1) identifies *chags pa* (*rakta*) in this context as referring to the mind or person that is desirous of an object—that which is made impassioned by passion, i.e., the impassioned.

790 'Illustration' (*mtshan gzhi*) most likely is *lakṣhya* in Sanskrit, which is translated into Tibetan both as *mtshon bya* 'definiendum' and *mtshan gzhi* 'illustration', the latter being a basis in which the definition illustrates the definiendum. It seems to make no difference here whether the term is translated as 'illustration' or 'definiendum'. I prefer the latter for broader symmetry but have deferred to the Tibetan translation and used 'illustration'.

791 *D̄ak*, 80b.1-4 (239.5-40.3 in the Thim-phu edition): '[D̄zong-ka-b̄a's] explanation that among our own schools only the Vatsīputrīyas propound a substantially existent self and [his] assertion that there are Mādhyamikas and Chittamātrins such as Bhāvaviveka and so forth who propound the mental consciousness as an illustration of the self are contradictory. Therefore, our own schools, except for the Vatsīputrīyas, disagree about the basis of the designation which is imputed as the self or

person—all five aggregates, the mental consciousness, the basis-of-all, its continuum, and so forth—but they all only assert the object designated, the actual person, as either a substantially existent or imputedly existent non-associated compositional factor. There is no one who asserts that there is a common locus of form or consciousness and person . . . '

According to Jam-ȳang-shay-b̄a (for the corresponding presentation in *GM* see 474a.2-6a.4), D̄ak-tsang is saying that the Vatsīputrīyas assert that the five aggregates are the basis of the designation 'person' whereas Bhāvaviveka only asserts that the mental consciousness is such. Jam-ȳang-shay-b̄a refutes the suggestion that for Bhāvaviveka the collection of the body and the senses are not the basis of designating 'I' with a quote from the *Blaze of Reasoning* (P5256, Vol. 96 36.4.5) which says the opposite, 'Thus, [the self] is imputed to the collection of the body and the senses.'

Jam-ȳang-shay-b̄a's basic point is that if for Bhāvaviveka the mental consciousness is just the basis of the designation 'I' and not the I, then there would be no difference between Bhāvaviveka and Chandrakīrti with respect to the nature of the conventionally existent I. He is showing that Bhāvaviveka asserts that the mental consciousness *is* the I and, thereby, that he asserts that persons (and other phenomena) exist from their own side or are established by way of their own character since when they are sought, something that is them is found. Jam-ȳang-shay-b̄a (*GM*, 475b.5-6) clearly makes this point: 'It [absurdly] follows that those [scholars, Bhāvaviveka and so forth,] do not assert that the self is established from its own side because [according to you] they do not assert that, when sought, it is found.' In other words, whoever asserts that when an object is sought analytically it is found thereby asserts inherent existence.

It is central to the Ge-luk-b̄a presentation of the four schools of tenets that only Prāsaṅgika asserts an emptiness of inherent existence and thus that all other schools assert that when an object is sought one can come up with something that is it. This is based on comments by Chandrakīrti such as that analyzing the object designated is not suitable in the context of positing conventionally existent phenomena (*GM*, 275b.6) in which he is seen to be refuting the other schools. It becomes incumbent then to discover what each school asserts the self and so forth to be, and thereby what may have been at most a minor topic in those schools becomes major in the Ge-luk-b̄a presentation of tenets. Whereas it would have been unthinkable in Indian Buddhism to compile and correlate (at least in print) the assertions of the various Buddhist schools on the identification of the person, in the Ge-luk-b̄a texts this is found in books of tenets under the topic of 'object-possessors' (*yul can*) which is sub-divided into the three topics of expressional terms (*rjod byed kyi sgra*), consciousness (*shes pa*), and persons (*gang zag*). In the latter section (see *Practice and Theory of Tibetan Buddhism*, pp.78, 101, 115, 125, and 136) we learn that:

1 in Vaibhāṣhika, all five aggregates are the person for some Saṃmitīyas and the mind alone for the Avantakas,
2 in Sautrāntika, the continuum of the mental and physical aggregates is the person for the Sautrāntikas Following Scripture and the mental consciousness, for the Sautrāntikas Following Reasoning,
3 in Chittamātra, the mind-basis-of-all is the person for the Chittamātrins Following Scripture and the mental consciousness, for the Chittamātrins Following Reasoning,
4 in Mādhyamika, a subtle neutral form of the mental consciousness is the person for the Svātantrikas whereas the mere I that is imputed in dependence upon its basis of imputation, the aggregates, is the person for the Prāsaṅgikas.

In the lower schools, the person is designated to the mental consciousness and so forth, meaning that the mental consciousness, for instance, *is* the person, whereas in Prāsaṅgika the person is designated *in dependence upon* the mental consciousness and so forth and thus is not those phenomena.

Just this point is the pivot of Ge-luk-b̄a commentary, the brilliant discovery of D̄zong-ka-b̄a's analysis, the over-riding organizing principle of their philosophical presentations, their dazzling insight into the Indian Buddhist schools, the core of their practice of emptiness, the grindstone for reducing other interpretations to unintelligible powder, the insight that makes the presentation of moral behavior in the four systems feasible, the foundation for making sense out of the controversies between the Indian schools, the cause impelling the drawing of nearly incredible distinctions about the person, the magnifying glass for discovering hidden assertions of what the person is, and the foundation for recognition that even in Buddhism with selflessness as the core doctrine there are selves, there are persons, there are agents, there is a basis for moral retribution, there is someone to achieve nirvana, there are other sentient beings not just on a baseless level of pre-wisdom ignorance but validly established. It is a magnificent stroke.

It is necessary to search thoroughly among the teachings of each school in order to find its views on the existent self because most of their attention is paid to the non-existent self, be it self-sufficiency, true establishment, inherent existence, etc. In his *Blaze of Reasoning* Bhāvaviveka says that to prove to him that the mental consciousness is the self would be a case of proving what he already accepted. Bhāvaviveka also says that since the mental consciousness takes rebirth, it is called the self. Jam-ȳang-shay-b̄a takes the latter to mean that for Bhāvaviveka the mental consciousness *is* the self, not just its basis of designation, since Bhāvaviveka says that it is unnecessary to prove to him that the mental consciousness is the person. Also, Bhāvaviveka says that the senses and the body are the basis of the designation 'self'. Thus, (*GM*, 475a.4) for him there are two types of selves, a temporary one such as a human merely designated to the aggregates and a continual one which is a subtle type of mental consciousness that has travelled ceaselessly in all types of lives and therefore (according to Kensur Lekden) exists even during deep sleep, fainting, and meditative absorption in cessation. Still, Bhāvaviveka is not teaching that yogis should engage in a particular type of practice in order to identify this ever-present consciousness as the self; the mental consciousness which he considers to be the person is subtle, and neither he nor anyone else puts forth practices aimed centrally at realizing or making manifest this subtle form of consciousness.

According to Kensur Lekden, Jam-ȳang-shay-b̄a told his own students that if a hypothetical Bhāvaviveka asked a Prāsaṅgika why the mental consciousness could not be the self, the Prāsaṅgika would have difficulty replying. For the mental consciousness travels from life to life right through to the attainment of Buddhahood, and even the Prāsaṅgikas say that 'mind-only' sometimes literally means that the mind is the main creator.

However, the Prāsaṅgikas say that the reasoning that the selves would bc as many as the many moments of the mental consciousness opposes asserting that the mental consciousness *is* the person. The person and the mental consciousness are related as object imputed and basis of imputation; therefore, the I is not the mental consciousness.

In a similar vein, D̄zong-ka-b̄a and Jam-ȳang-shay-b̄a say that the Chittamātrins following Asaṅga assert the mind-basis-of-all (a subtle consciousness much like Bhāvaviveka's subtle type of mental consciousness), which is substantially existent, as the person and thus as the substantially existent person (*dravyasat-pudgala, rdzas yod kyi gang zag*). Like Bhāvaviveka, Asaṅga says that the person itself imputedly exists, but, in this interpretation, that which is the person substantially exists. (The main difference between Asaṅga's mind-basis-of-all and Bhāvaviveka's subtle mental consciousness is that the former is the repository of the seeds which produce the appearance of external objects whereas the latter does not have this function because for Bhāvaviveka there are external objects.) Still, it is difficult to find any passage in Chittamātrin literature which proclaims that the mind-basis-of-all is a substantially existent self. Also, the *Sutra Unravelling the Thought* (*J̄ang*, 206.10) is often quoted to show that the mind-basis-of-all should not be conceived as a self: 'I do not teach this [mind-basis-of-all] to children because they would take it as a self.' Jam-ȳang-shay-b̄a's commentary is that Buddha is referring to conception of the mind-basis-of-all as a self-sufficient substantially existent person (*rang rkya thub pa'i rdzas yod kyi gang zag*). Although the mind-basis-of-all is substantially existent and thus capable of being apprehended self-sufficiently (*rang rkya 'dzin thub pa'i rdzas yod*), it is not a self-sufficient person like a controller.

D̄ak-tsang, however, argues that there is no Buddhist school which says that a mind *is* the person. D̄ak-tsang accuses D̄zong-ka-b̄a of committing the absurdity of saying on the one hand that the Chittamātrins do not accept that the self is substantially existent in the sense of being self-sufficient and saying on the other hand that they accept that the mind-basis-of-all is substantially existent and is the self. The Ge-luk-b̄a answer is that for the Chittamātrins the person itself is not substantially existent, but the consciousness which is the illustration of the person is substantially existent. Technically (*GM*, 476.2), the illustration-isolate of the person (*gang zag gi gzhi ldog*) substantially exists, but the self-isolate of the person (*gang zag gi rang ldog*) does not. As J̄ang-ḡya (*J̄ang*, 190.7) says, '... the Proponents of True Existence and below [that is, non-Buddhists] assert that there must be something self-sufficiently substantially existent as the basis of designation of imputedly existent things ...' It is only the Prāsaṅgikas who do not require this.

The gist is that the Chittamātrins do not accept the existence of the self as it is usually conceived, but do accept the substantial existence of a consciousness which performs all the functions of rebirth and thus is a self. In practice, the Chittamātrins present a Hīnayāna path which concentrates on the non-existence of a substantially existent self and a Mahāyāna one which centers around the non-difference of entity between subject and object; there are no special reasonings aimed at discovering the mind-basis-of-all as the actual self.

Have these distinctions between self-isolate, illustration-isolate, and so forth made it impossible to reflect on the insubstantiality of the person according to the lower systems? How could one meditate on the self-isolate of the person and not the illustration-isolate (the thing that is the person)? Is it possible to zero in on the person devoid of everything that is it, recognize that we have been conceiving it to exist substantially, and realize that it does not? Is the 'self-isolate of the person' so abstract that it reduces a most profound and emotionally trying meditation to mere superficial intellectual verbiage? Or is there something inside us, quite familiar, that corresponds to this term and the identification of which is aided by such hair-splitting distinctions?

The pressing question is: Why not say that the lower schools present a path to realization of the non-inherent existence of the person but are not able to extend this realization to other phenomena? One would have to say that they are blocked from making the extension that everything lacks inherent existence by views that it would be an extreme of nihilism to go so far and thus hold that the person does not inherently exist but its basis of designation must. After all, realizing that the Atlantic Ocean is deep does not mean that you realize that the Pacific Ocean is deep!

I believe that the answer to this revolves around what realization of emptiness means. As Āryadeva says, the viewer (or person realizing the emptiness) of one thing is capable of realizing the emptiness of all things. As the Dalai Lama said in lectures on D̄zong-ka-b̄a's *Middling Exposition of the Stages of the Path* in 1972, if you want to test your supposed realization of the emptiness of the person, switch to another object such as your head and see if the same realization of emptiness applies to it. He said that if it does not, you have realized something more coarse. Thus, even though, when a yogi realizes that whatever is not findable in the seven ways is not inherently existent, he does not at that time realize the absence of inherent existence of all phenomena, superimpositions contrary to such realization are removed. Therefore, a person capable of realizing the emptiness of inherent existence of the person is capable of realizing the absence of inherent existence of any phenomenon as long as the functioning of that first consciousness has not diminished. Also, because the person is imputed in dependence upon the aggregates, there would be no way to realize the emptiness of inherent existence of the object imputed (the person) without removing the superimposition that the bases of its designation (the mental and physical aggregates) inherently exist. Hence, there is no way to say that the lower schools realize the emptiness of inherent existence with respect to the person but not with respect to other phenomena, in which case what they realize must be coarser. Since the meaning of inherent existence implies that the object can be found under analysis, those schools must be holding that objects, even the self, can be found under analysis. Even though they make a distinction between imputed and substantially existent objects, the former must, in the end, have the latter as their basis of designation. Hence, even the self or person has a substantially existent phenomenon as its basis of designation, and since the person is findable under analysis, that substantially existent phenomenon must *be* the person. What they refute is that the person, in isolation, substantially exists.

792 P5256, Vol. 96 36.4.5. *J̄ang*, 431.1, has *brjod pa* for *dran pa*.

793 See previous note. In *GM* (475b.1-3) Jam-ȳang-shay-b̄a says that this passage posits consciousness as the self that continuously takes rebirth and indicates (1) that the mere collection of

the body and senses is the self and (2) that the five aggregates—the body and so forth—are the basis of designation of the self, just as, for example, (1) the mere collection of the parts of a chariot is the chariot and (2) its parts are the basis of designation. Here, he words it slightly differently, indicating that the collection is the basis of designation and thus is the phenomenon designated.

794 P5256, Vol. 96 36.4.6. Throughout this series of consequences Jam-ȳang-shay-b̄a is operating based on D̄ak-tsang's actual assertions, drawing them out so as to contrast their full import with D̄zong-ka-b̄a's teachings. This is not a case of pinning a fancied extension of an assertion on D̄ak-tsang and then drawing absurd contradictions, as sometimes is the case.

795 Brackets in the root text are from *Ann*, dbu 129a.6.

796 *GT*, ca 40a.5ff.

797 It is not that D̄ak-tsang manifestly asserts that in the Prāsaṅgika system there are autonomous syllogisms. Quite the contrary, he asserts (*D̄ak*, 76a.4, Thim-phu edition 227.4) that it is contradictory to say that there are no autonomous proof statements and still hold that there is inference. Jam-ȳang-shay-b̄a feels that D̄ak-tsang must hold that there are proofs, whereby, due to his own assertion, he is forced to assert that there are even autonomous syllogisms in Prāsaṅgika. It is over-play that, for me, falls flat.

798 Prāsaṅgikas do not accept that the subject, reason, example, and so forth, of a syllogism appear similarly to a Mādhyamika and a non-Mādhyamika. For the Prāsaṅgikas, a valid cognizer which seems to an opponent to establish the subject, etc., is non-existent in the way that the opponent asserts it because a non-Mādhyamika views a valid cognizer as certifying that the object is inherently existent, but for a Prāsaṅgika nothing inherently exists. In this way, there can be no common establishment.

However, when Prāsaṅgikas debate among themselves, the subject, etc., are accepted as appearing similarly to both parties in the sense that both assert that the subject and so forth are certified by valid cognizers that are not valid with respect to the inherent existence of the object. As mentioned earlier (p.511-12), there is no way to have commonly appearing subjects with respect to proving emptiness even when Prāsaṅgikas debate among themselves, because if they can understand that the subject and so forth are established by a valid cognizer that is not valid with respect to the inherent existence of the object, they have come to be able to distinguish between existence and inherent existence and this can only be done upon having realized emptiness. In that case, there is no need to prove emptiness to such a person. As D̄zong-ka-b̄a's *Essence of the Good Explanations* (194.17 Varanasi 1973 edition) says:

> If the subject is posited as established by a conceptual or non-conceptual mistaken consciousness which is such that [the object] does not exist in accordance with how it appears to be established by way of its own character, then the meaning of the absence of inherent existence—the probandum—has already been established. Therefore, how could [such a person] be suitable as another party for whom that would have to be proved?

Thus, Jam-ȳang-shay-b̄a appears to contradict D̄zong-ka-b̄a here when he speaks of commonly appearing subjects within the context of two Prāsaṅgikas' examining emptiness. However, in the *Four Interwoven Commentaries* (536.5-7.2) he indicates that a Proponent of True Existence who has discarded his assertion of inherent existence and become a full-fledged second party about to realize the absence of inherent existence simultaneously has become someone for whom dependent-arising is a reason having the three modes of presence in the subject, pervasion, and counter-pervasion. Thus, that person has ascertained with valid cognition that whatever is a dependent-arising is necessarily without inherent existence and is about to realize the particular subject, such as I, as not existing inherently. Jam-ȳang-shay-b̄a is saying that at that point the other party has become a Prāsaṅgika due to realizing that whatever is a dependent-arising is without inherent existence but has not realized emptiness, though just about to. It is only in such a hair-splitting situation, however, that he can speak of commonly appearing subjects within the context of two Prāsaṅgikas' examining emptiness.

799 The source for this appendix is mainly the oral teachings of Kensur Lekden. The teaching is standard to that part of the study of the *Collected Topics of Valid Cognition* (*bsDus grva*)

called 'Awareness and Knowledge' (*bLo rig*). See Lati Rinbochay's and Elizabeth Napper's *Mind in Tibetan Buddhism*, (London: Rider and Co., 1980), for a full discussion.

800 See n.174 for the sources for this appendix.

801 *Ann*, dngos 16b.

802 Paul Demiéville, 'L'origine des sectes bouddhiques d'après Paramārtha', *Mélanges Chinois et Bouddhiques*, premier volume (1931-2), p.19.

803 *GT*, kha 6b.

804 Anton Schiefner, *Geschichte Des Buddhismus in Indien* (St. Petersburg, 1869), p.206 of text and p.270 of translation.

805 *GT*, kha 7a.

806 Schiefner (see n.804), p.271 of translation.

807 *Blaze of Reasoning*, P5256, Vol. 96 68.4.3.

808 *GT*, kha 6b.5.

809 Bimala C. Law, trans., 'The Chronicle of the Island of Ceylon, or the Dīpavaṃsa', *The Ceylon Historical Journal*, Vol. VII (1957-8), pp.162-4. Wilhelm Geiger, trans., *The Mahāvaṃsa, or the Great Chronicle of Ceylon* (London: Pāli Text Society, 1934), pp.26-7. For an excellent discussion of the eighteen schools and the different interpretations of their origins see André Bareau's *Les Sectes Bouddhiques du Petit Véhicule* (Saïgon: École Française D'extreme-Orient, 1955).

810 The main source for this appendix is Pur-bu-j̄ok's (*Phur-bu-lcog Byams-pa-rgya-mtsho*, 1825-1901) *Presentation of Collected Topics of Prime Cognition, Revealing the Meaning of the Texts on Prime Cognition, Magical Key to the Path of Reasoning (Tshad ma'i gzhung don 'byed pa'i bsdus grva'i rnam bzhag rigs lam 'phrul gyi lde mig)*, specifically the section on The Greater Path of Reasoning (*Rigs lam che ba*) [modern blockprint, no publication data], 23a.6-36a.4. Only material concordant with Prāsaṅgika has been used. D̄zong-ka-b̄a makes a similar presentation in his *Essence of the Good Explanations*, 239.1-41.17, Varanasi 1973 edition.

811 *GM* 238b.6ff. The material in this appendix is taken from the oral teachings of Geshe Gedün Lodrö.

Tibetan Text
for Part Six

Sa-gya Paṇḍiṭa Jam-yang-gun-ga-gyel-tsen

Tibetan Text

REMARKS

As mentioned on pp.691-3, the basis for this critical edition of Jam-ȳang-shay-b̄a's text is a hand-written copy made at the Go-mang College of the Dre-b̄ung Monastic University in Mundgod, N. Kanara, Karnataka State, India, in 1970. It was first compared with three other editions of the same basic edition (see pp.691-3), and the many source quotes from Indian Buddhist texts were compared with the Peking edition (Suzuki Research Foundation, Tokyo-Kyoto, 1956) of the canon. Nga-w̄ang-b̄el-den's *Annotations*, which identify and correct many mis-printings, were used throughout. The shortened quotations were restored to full length, mainly using the Peking edition; these are indicated by a broken underline and brackets in the text. The restorations comprise approximately one third of the final text.

Fortunately, the D̄ra-s̄hi-kyil edition, which is better in many respects than the other basic edition (see pp.691-3), was subsequently published with minor corrections by Ngawang Gelek Demo (The Collected Works of 'Jam-dbyaṅs-bźad-pa, Vol. 14, New Delhi, beginning in 1972), allowing comparison with it. The result is the first corrected edition of these pages of Jam-ȳang-shay-b̄a's text with all quotes restored to full length, making this an anthology of Prāsaṅgika literature.

The numbers beneath lines in the text refer to the emendations and variant readings given in notes following the text. The Tibetan letters in parentheses under a line indicate a note in Nga-w̄ang-b̄el-den's

Annotations (see Bibliography). All poetry is given with a separate line for each 'foot' beginning from the margin, except for Jam-ȳang-shay-b̄a's root text which is also indented. The bracketed material without underline was added for the sake of clarification.

With respect to the root text of the *Great Exposition of Tenets* (written in 1689), there are four versions in the Collected Works:

1 Volume 1, 750-802, with brief annotations which are presumably by Jam-ȳang-shay-b̄a himself but perhaps are notes taken by a student; the section corresponding to that given here is found on 789.1-92.4.
2 Volume 3, 807-52, with brief annotations that differ from the former in many places, perhaps taken down by another student but done in the same style; the section corresponding to that given here is found on 840.5-44.1.
3 Volume 14, 1-31, with no annotations; the section corresponding to that given here is found on 22.4-4.6.
4 Volume 14, scattered throughout 33-1091, this being Jam-ȳang-shay-b̄a's own lengthy commentary in which he cites the entire root text. (Differences among these four editions are miniscule with respect to the portion of the root text relevant here.)

More helpful than these two very brief sets of annotations are the word commentary to the root given at the end of each chapter in Nga-w̄ang-b̄el-den's *Annotations* (the corresponding section being *Ann* dbu 176b.8-29.6) and L̄o-sang-ḡön-chok's (*bLo-bzang-dkon-mchog*) *White Crystal Mirror, Word Commentary on the Root Text of (Jam-ȳang-shay-b̄a's) 'Tenets' (Grub mtha' rtsa ba'i tshig ṭik shal dkar me long)* found in *Three Commentaries on the Grub mtha' rtsa ba gdon lna'i sgra dbyaṅs of 'Jam-dbyaṅs-bźad-pa'i-rdo-rje Nag-dbaṅ-brtson-'grus* (Delhi: Chophel Legden, 1978), the corresponding section being 216.2-42.3. (In the *Three Commentaries* the first commentary is L̄o-sang-ḡön-chok's text; the second is the elaboration of contents extracted from Jam-ȳang-shay-b̄a's own commentary; and the third is Nga-w̄ang-b̄el-den's *Annotations*.)

The text of Jam-ȳang-shay-b̄a's commentary, the *Great Exposition of Tenets*, corresponding to that part of the twelfth chapter translated here was written out after the initial editing by Lobsang Dorje in Madison, Wisconsin, in September, 1971. Alterations were subsequently made upon comparison with the Ngawang Gelek D̄ra-s̄hi-kyil edition, finishing in 1983.

༄༅། །འཇམ་དབྱངས་བཞད་པས་མཛད་པའི་
གྲུབ་མཐའི་རྣམ་བཤད་རང་གཞན་གྲུབ་མཐའ་ཀུན
དང་ཟབ་དོན་མཆོག་ཏུ་གསལ་བ་ཀུན་བཟང་ཞིང་
གི་ཉི་མ་ལུང་རིགས་རྒྱ་མཚོ་སྐྱེ་དགུའི་རེ་བ་ཀུན
སྐོང་ཞེས་བྱ་བ་ལས་ལེའུ་བཅུ་གཉིས་པ་དཔལ
1 ལྡན་ཐལ་འགྱུར་བའི་སྐབས་ཀྱི་འགྲེལ་པ་བཞུགས་སོ།།

ས་བཅད།

ཐལ་འགྱུར་བའི་ལུགས་འཆད་པ་ 1.1

I. མཚན་ཉིད་སྒྲ་བཤད་དང་བཅས་པ་ 2.12

II. མིང་གི་རྣམ་གྲངས་ 5.2

III. དབྱེ་བ་ 6.5

IV. གང་ལ་བརྟེན་པའི་གཞུང་ 8.6

V. དེའི་གྲངས་ངེས་ 14.15

VI. གྲུབ་མཐའ་བཤད་པ་ 57.11

A. གཞི་ 57.11

1. དགག་བྱའི་ཁྱད་པར་ 57.12

a. དགག་བྱའི་ཚད་ 57.15

b. དེའི་འཐད་པ་ 70.14

2. འགོག་བྱེད་རིགས་པའི་ཁྱད་པར་ 75.15

a. མདོར་བསྟན་པ་ 76.1

b. རྒྱས་པར་བཤད་པ་ 77.13

(1) ཆོས་བདག་འགོག་པའི་རིགས་པ་ 77.13

(a) རྡོ་རྗེ་གཟེགས་མ་ 77.15

1' རྟགས་དགོད་པ་ 78.4

2' རྟགས་ཚུལ་སྒྲུབ་པ་ 79.12

a' བདག་ལས་སྐྱེ་བ་མེད་པ་ 79.12

b' གཞན་ལས་སྐྱེ་བ་མེད་པ་ 83.8

1" དངོས་ 83.8

2" འཁྲུལ་པ་སྤངས་པ་ 88.8

c' གཉིས་ཀ་ལས་སྐྱེ་བ་མེད་པ་ 90.1

d' རྒྱུ་མེད་ལས་སྐྱེ་བ་མེད་པ་ 90.10

(b) མཐའ་བཞི་དང་ཡོད་མེད་སྐྱེ་འགོག་
ཚིག་ཙར་བཤད་པ་ 91.15

(c) མུ་བཞི་སྐྱེ་འགོག་ 94.12

1' དངོས་ 94.12

2' འཁྲུལ་སྤོང་ 97.11

(d) ཆོས་ཀུན་གདན་ལ་འབེབས་བྱེད་རྟེན་འབྲེལ་གྱི་རིགས་པ་ 101.13

1' དངོས་ 101.13

a' འཐད་པ་བཞག་ 106.1

1" རྟེན་འབྱུང་གི་སྒྲ་སྦྱོར་ལུགས་ 106.2

2" རྟེན་འབྱུང་གི་སྒྲ་བཤད་པ་ 108.15

b' འཁྲུལ་པ་དགག་ 110.10

1" འགྲེལ་བྱེད་གཞན་གྱི་ལུགས་དགག་པ་ 110.11

a" འདོད་པ་བརྗོད་པ་ 110.12

b" དེ་དགག་པ་ 113.2

2" ལེགས་ལྡན་གྱི་ལུགས་དགག་པ་ 115.12

a" ལེགས་ལྡན་ཀྱིས་གཞན་བཀག་རྒྱུལ་མི་འཐད་པ་ 115.12

b" རང་ལུགས་ཀྱི་སྒྲ་དོན་མི་ཚོང་བའི་སྐྱོན་ 120.14

2' འཁྲུལ་སྤོང་ 127.4

(2) གང་ཟག་གི་བདག་འགོག་པའི་རིགས་པ་ 128.1

(a) དངོས་ 128.2

(b) འཁྲུལ་སྤོང་ 154.3

1

༄༅། །ན་མ་སྨྲ་རསྭ་ཧེ་ཏྭེ་ཙ་ཀྲ་ཏུ་མཉྫུ་གྷོ་ཥཱ[2]་ཡ་ཏེ། འདིར་རྗེ་བླ་མ་ཙོང་ཁ་པ་ཆེན་པོས།

འཛམ་གླིང་མཁས་པའི་རྒྱན་གྱུར་འདི་རྣམས་ཀྱི།།
ལེགས་བཤད་ཀུན་ལ་སྙིང་ནས་གུས་མོད་ཀྱང་།།
འཁོར་འདས་རྟེན་འབྱུང་མི་སླུའི་གནད་ཚོགས་ཀྱིས།།
མཐར་འཛིན་དམིགས་གཏད་ཐམས་ཅད་འཇིག་བྱེད་པ།།
ཟླ་བ་ལས་འོངས་ལེགས་བཤད་འོད་དཀར་གྱིས།།
བློ་མིག་ཀུནྡའི་ཚལ་རབ་ཕྱེ་བའི་ཚེ།།
སངས་རྒྱས་བསྐྱངས[3]་ཀྱིས་བསྟན་པའི་ལམ་མཐོང་ནས།།
ཀླུ་སྒྲུབ་ལུགས་བཟང་གཙོ་བོར་མི་འཛིན་སུ།།

ཞེས་གསུངས་པ་ལྟར། གཞུང་ལུགས་དང་གྲུབ་པའི་མཐའོ[4] ཚིག་གི་ཡང་རྩེ་དུས་གསུམ་གྱི་འཕགས་པ་ཐམས་ཅད་དང་རྒྱལ་བ་ཐམས་ཅད་ཀྱིས་བགྲོད་ཅིང་བགྲོད་ལ་བགྲོད་པར་འགྱུར་བའི་ཕ་རོལ་ཏུ་ཕྱིན་པའི་གཞུང་ལམ་རྒྱལ་བ་སྲས་བཅས་འཕགས་པ་ཐམས་ཅད་སྐྱེད་པའི་ཡུམ་ཆེན་མོ…

2

ཟླ་དང་བྲལ་བ། མཚུངས་པ་མེད་པ། བགྲོད་པའི་ལམ་གྱི་དམ་པ་གཅིག་པུར་གྱུར་པ། སངས་རྒྱས་བྱང་འཕགས་ཐམས་ཅད་ཀྱིས་ལུས་དང་ལོངས་སྤྱོད་སོགས་ལ་མི་བལྟ་བར་འབད་བརྩོལ་སྒོམ་སེམས་གཞན་ལ་དཀའ་སྤྱོད་འབྱེད་པའི་བདུད་རྩི་བླ་ན་མེད་པ་མཐའ་དང་ཆ་ཐར་འཛིན་ཕྲ་རགས་ཐམས་ཅད་སེལ་བའི་ཟབ་མོ་དབུ་མའི་ལམ་ཀླུ་སྒྲུབ་ཀྱི་དགོངས་པ་མཐར་ཐུག་སངས་རྒྱས་བསྐྱངས་ཀྱིས་ཐལ་འགྱུར་དུ་སྤྲོལ་བཏོད་ཟླ་བའི་ཞབས་ཀྱིས་ཤིང་རྟའི་ལམ་ཆེན་པོར་མཛད་པ་དབུ་མ་ཐལ་འགྱུར་བའི་ལུགས་འཆད་པ་ལ[5]… མཚན་ཉིད་སྔོན་བཤད་དང་བཅས་པ་དང་། མིང་གི་རྣམ་གྲངས་དང་། དབྱེ་བ་དང་། གང་ལ་བརྟེན་པའི་གཞུང་དང་། དེའི་ངང་ངེས་དང་། གྲུབ་མཐའ་བཤད་པ་དྲུག་ལས། དང་པོ་ནི།

རང་རྒྱུད་མི་བཞེད་ཕྱིར་ནོལ་ཁས་བླངས་ལ།།
འགལ་བརྗོད་ཐལ་འགྱུར་གཙོ་ཕྱིར་ཐལ་འགྱུར་བ།།

ཞེས་སྨྲས་ཏེ། ཚིག(ཀ)་གསལ་ལས། དབུ་མ་པ་ཡིན་ན་ནི་རང

3

གི་རྒྱུད་ཀྱི་རྗེས་སུ་དཔག་པ་བྱ་བར་རིགས་པ་ཡང་མིན་ཏེ། ཕྱོགས་གཞན་ཁས་བླངས་པ་མེད་པའི་ཕྱིར་རོ། ཞེས་གསུངས་པ་ལྟར་རང་དབང་དུ་གྲུབ་པ་དང་རང་བཞིན་གྱིས་གྲུབ་པ་དང་རང་རྒྱུད་དོན་གཅིག དེ་ལྟ་བུའི་ཚུལ་གསུམ་པའི་རྟགས་སྦྱོར་ནི་རང་རྒྱུད་ཀྱི་རྗེས་དཔག་ཡིན་པས་དེ(ཁ)་འདྲ་ཁས་བླངས་ན་སྐྱེ་བ་ཡང་རང་གིས་གྲུབ་པས། དཔྱེད་པན་མཐའ་བཞི་སོགས་གང་རུང་གི་ཕྱོགས་དང་། དེ་བཞི་གང་རུང་གི་ཕྱོགས་ཀྱི་དམ་བཅའ་དགོས་ན་དེ་ཡང་མི་རུང་སྟེ། དེ་དག་བསལ་བའི་དབུ་མའི་དོན་འཛིན་དགོས་པའི་ཕྱིར་ཏེ། འཕགས་པ་ལྷས།

ཡོད་དང་མེད་དང་ཡོད་མེད་ཅེས།།
གང་ལ་ཕྱོགས་ནི་ཡོད་མིན་པ།།
དེ་ལ་ཡུན་ནི་རིང་པོ་ནའང་།།
ཀླན་ཀ་བརྗོད་པར་ནུས་མ་ཡིན།།

ཞེས་དང་། རྩོད(ག)་ཟློག་ལས།

གལ་ཏེ་ངས་དམ་བཅས་འགའ་ཡོད།།

4

དེས་ན་དལ་སྐྱོན་དེ་ཡོད།།
ངལ་དུབ་བཅའ་མེད་པས་ན།།
ངའི་སྐྱོན་མེད་ཕོན་ཡིན།།
ཞེས་གསུངས་པས་རང་རྒྱུད་ཐ་སྙད་དུ་མི་བཞེད་ལ། དེ་ལྟ་ན་འང་ཕྱིར་རྒོལ་ལ་བདེན་མེད་རྟོགས་པའི་ལྟ་བ་སྐྱེད་བྱེད་ཤེས་ན་ཡོད་དེ། ཕྱི་རོལ་གྱི་…མཐའ་བཞི་གང་དུ་ཁས་བླངས་པ་དེ་ལ་འགལ་བརྗོད་ཀྱི་ཐལ་འགྱུར་ཡང་དག་བཀོད་དོན་འཕེན་པ་དང་མི་འཕེན་པ་སོགས་ཐལ་འགྱུར་ཅི་རིགས་ཀྱིས་འགལ་བ་…བརྗོད་ནས་འགོག་པ་འོག་ཏུ་འཆད་འགྱུར་ལྟར་གཙོ་བོར་འགོད་པའི་དབུ་མ་པ་དེ་དབུ་མ་ཐལ་འགྱུར་བའི་མཚན་ཉིད་དང་ཐ་སྙད་ཡང་དེས་སོང་ངོ། (ཇ) འདིར་ཐལ་འགྱུར་དང་གཞན་གྲགས་བཀོད་པ་གཉིས་ལ་ཁྱབ་ཆེ་ཆུང་ཡོད་ཀྱང་ཤིན་ཏུ་མི་འགལ་ཏེ། གཞན་གྲགས་བཀོད་པ་ཕལ་ཆེར་ཐལ་འགྱུར་དུ་ཡང་སྣང་བའི་ཕྱིར་རོ། དཔེར་ན་དངོས་པོ་བདག་གི་བདག་ཉིད་དུ་ཡོད་པ་ནི་ཡང་སྐྱེ་བ་ལ

5

དགོས་པ་མེད་དོ། མངོན་གསལ་ལ་གྱི་བུམ་པ་བཞིན་ཞེས་པ་ལྟ་བུའོ།། །།གཉིས་པ་ནི།

ཐལ་འགྱུར་སྣང་ཙམ་མི་གནས་དབུ་མར་གྲགས།།

ཅེས་སྨྲས་ཏེ། གཞན་ལ་ལྟ་བ་སྐྱེད་བྱེད་ཐལ་འགྱུར་གཙོ་བོར་བཞེད་པས་ཐལ་འགྱུར་བ་དང་། ཚིག་གསལ་ལས། རྐྱེན་འདི་པ་ཙམ་གྱིས་ཀུན་རྫོབ་གྲུབ་པར་ཁས་ལེན་གྱི་ཕྱོགས་བཞི་ཁས་བླངས་པའི་སྒོ་ནས་ནི་མིན་ཏེ། ཞེས་དང་། རྐྱེན་(ཟ) ཉིད་འདི་པ་ཙམ་ཞིག་ཁས་བླངས་ན་འདི་རྒྱུ་དང་འབྲས་བུ་གཉིས་ཕན་ཚུན་ལྟོས་པའི་ཕྱིར། ངོ་བོ་ཉིད་ཀྱིས་གྲུབ་པ་ཡོད་པ་མིན་པས་ཞེས་པ་ལྟར་མ་བརྟགས་མ་དཔྱད་པར་རྐྱེན་གྱིས་སྣང་བ་འདི་ཙམ་ཁས་ལེན་པའི་དབུ་མ་པ་དང་། དཔའ་བོའི་དོན་(ཚ) དམ་བྱང་ཆུབ་སེམས་སྒོམ་ལས།

བདག་མེད་སེང་གེའི་སྒྲ་ཆེན་བསྒྲགས།།
སྟོང་པ་ཉིད་སོགས་རྣམ་གྲངས་སྒོ།།
སྒྱུ་མ་འདྲ་སོགས་དཔེ་མཐའ་ཡས།།

6

རིགས་པ་སྣ་ཚོགས་ཐབས་ཚུལ་གྱིས།།
མི་གནས་དབུ་མ་ཉེ་བར་མཚོན།།

ཞེས་པ་ལྟར་རྟག་ཆད་ཀྱི་མཐའ་གང་ལ་འང་མི་གནས་པས་ན་མི་གནས་དབུ་མ་པ་དང་རབ་ཏུ་མི་གནས་དབུ་མ་པ་ཞེས་བྱའོ།། །།གསུམ་པ་ནི།

དབྱེ་བ་ཕྱི་མོ་ཕྱོགས་འཛིན་མི་འཛིན་གསུམ།།

ཞེས་སྨྲས་ཏེ། དེ་ལ་དབྱེན་འཕགས་པ་ཡབ་སྲས་ནི་ཐལ་རང་གི་ཤིང་རྟའི་སྲོལ་བྱེད་གཉིས་སོགས་ཐམས་ཅད་ཀྱིས[6] ཁྱད་མེད་དུ་མཛད་པས་བོད་སྔ་མ་རྣམས་ཀྱིས་ཡབ་སྲས་གཉིས་ལ་གཞུང་ཕྱི་མོའི་དབུ་མ་པ་ཞེས་བརྗོད་དང་མཐུན་ལ། ཕྱོགས་འཛིན་པས་རང་རྒྱུད་བསྐྱངས། ཟླ་བའི་ཞབས། ཞི་བ་ལྷ་རྣམས་དང་། ཕྱོགས་མི་འཛིན་ཀྱང་ལྟ་བ་འདི་འཛིན་པ་ནི། ལེགས་བཤད་སྙིང་པོ་ལས། དེ་ཡང་སློབ་དཔོན་དཔའ་བོ་དང་ཀླུའི་བྱང་ཆུབ་ལ་སོགས་པ་མཁས་པའི་དབང་པོ་མང་པོ་ཡོད་མོད་ཀྱང་[7] ཁྲིད་དག་

7

གེས་བཀྲལ་བའི་དབུ་མའི་བསྟན་བཅོས་འགྱུར་བ་མི་སྣང་བས།] ཞེས་པ་ལྟར་ཤཱནྟི་བ་ཤེས་གཉེན་དང༌། ཀླུ་བྱང་དང་རིགས་པའི་ཁུ་བྱུག་སོགས་འཛོག་སྟེ། ཤཱནྟི་བ་(ཛ)ཤེས་གཉེན་གྱིས་རིམ་ལྔའི་ཡང་གཉིས་པའི་སྒྲད་བརྩམས་པར་མཛད་པའི[8]་དོན་ལ་ལྟ་བ་འདིར་གསལ། ཀླུ་བྱང་གི་ལས་མཐའ་རྣམ…[9]འབྱེད་སོགས་ལ་དཔག་གནའང་དེ་ལྟར་དང༌། དཔའ་བོའི་ཀྵ་བ་འདིར་ཤིན་ཏུ་གསལ་ཀྱང་སྐབ་ཚང་པས་ཕྱི་མོར་འདོད་པ་དང་རང་རྒྱུད་དངོས་སུ་བཀག་པར་འདོད་པ་འགལ་ལ་སངས་རྒྱས་བསྐྱངས་དང་ཀླུ་བྱང་སོགས་ཀྱིས་ཤེས་བྱེད་བྲངས་པ་མི་སྣང་ལ། ལེགས་ལྡན་གཉིས་དང་ཟླ་བ་ཕྱིན་ཆད་ནས་དྲངས་ཡང་དེ་ཙམ་གྱིས་ཕྱི་མོར་མི་འགྲུབ་ལ། (ཉ)དཔའ་བོས། སྒྱུ་མ་འང་སྒྱུ་མ་ཙམ་མིན་ཏེ། སོགས་ཀྱིས་རང་རྒྱུད་བཀག་ན་ཕྱོགས་འཛིན་པའི་དབུ་མ་ཐལ་འགྱུར་བར་མངོན་ནོ། འོ་ན། གཞུང་འདི་དཔའ་བོའི་ཡིན་ན། ལེགས་བཤད་སྙིང་པོ་ལས། ཇེ་ཡང་སློབ་དཔོན་དཔའ་བོ་དང་ཀླུའི་བྱང་ཆུབ

8

ལ་སོགས་པ་མཁས་པའི་དབང་པོ་མང་པོ་ཡོད་མོད་ཀྱང་།] འདི་ཀ་གིས་བཀྲལ་བའི་དབུ་མའི་བསྟན་བཅོས་འགྱུར་བ་མི་སྣང་བས། ཞེས་གསུངས་པ་དང་མི་འགལ་ལམ་ཞེ་ན། (ཏ)འདི་སློམ་ཡིག་ཡིན་པས་དོན་དབུ་མ་བསྟན་ཀྱང་བསྟོད་ཚོགས་དང་རིགས་ཚོགས་སོ་སོར་བཤད་པ་བཞིན་མཛད་པས་སོ།། ||བཞི་པ་ནི།

གཞུང་ནི་ཟབ་མདོ་རིགས་ཚོགས་བཞི་བརྒྱ་པ།།
སྤྱོད་འཇུག་མདོ་བཏུས་གཉིས་དང་ལམ་སྒྲོན་སོགས།།

ཞེས་སྨྲས་ཏེ། མཚན་ཉིད་མེད་པའི་ཆོས་འཁོར་ཤེར་ཕྱོགས་ཡུམ་སྲས་བཅུ་བདུན་དང༌། བློ་གྲོས་མི་ཟད་པ། ཏིང་འཛིན་རྒྱལ་པོ། ཆོས་ཡང་དག་པར་སྡུད་པ། ཀླུའི་རྒྱལ་པོ་མ་དྲོས་པས་ཞུས་པ། རྒྱ་མཚོས་ཞུས་པ་དང༌། དཀོན་མཆོག་འབྱུང་གནས་དང༌། འཇམ་དཔལ་ལ[10 རྣམ]་རོལ་དང༌། དཀོན་བརྩེགས་ཀྱི་ལེའུ་དང་པོ་སྡོམ་པ་གསུམ་བསྟན་པ་དང༌། གཞན…ཡང་འོད་སྲུངས་ལེའུ། བྱང་ཆུབ་སེམས་དཔའི་སྡེ་སྣོད

9

གསང་བ་བསམ་གྱིས་མི་ཁྱབ་པ་སོགས་འཕགས་པ་ཡབ་སྲས་ཀྱི་ངེས་དོན་ཤེས་བྱེད་དུ་དྲངས་པ་རྣམས་ཟབ་དོན་སྟོན་པའི་མདོར་བྱ་ལ། མདོ་སྡེ་ས་བཅུ་པ་དང༌། སངས་རྒྱས་ཐམས་ཅད་ཀྱི་ཡོན་ཏན་དང་ཡེ་ཤེས་ཡུལ་ལ་འཇུག་པ་དང༌། བློ་གྲོས་རྒྱ་མཚོས་ཞུས་པ་དང༌། ཏིང་འཛིན་བཞིའི་མདོ་བཞི་དང༌། ཕལ་ཆེན་དང༌། གཟུངས་རྒྱལ་གྱི་མདོ། རྒྱན་སྟུག་སོགས་ནི་ཟབ་རྒྱས་གཉིས་ཅར་སྟོན་པའི་མདོ་ཡིན་ལ། དགོངས་འགྲེལ་ཟ་བོ་ཆེ་དང༌། སྙིང་པོའི་མདོ་དང་དེ་མཐུན་དགོངས་འགྲེལ་འཁོར་ལོ་ཐ་མའི་མདོ་རྣམས་དྲང་དོན…ཡིན་ཀྱང་ཕྱིན་དྲུག་སོགས་དེ་ལ་བརྟེན་ལ། དགོངས་འགྲེལ་གྱི་བསྟན་བཅོས་གང་ལ་བརྟེན་ན་མཐའ་གཅིག་ཏུ་ཚད་མར་མཛད་པའི་གཞུང༌། ཚིག་གསལ་ལས།

མདོ་སྡེ་ཀུན་ལས་བཏུས་དང་གཏམ་བྱ་རིན་ཆེན…[11]ཕྲེང་དང་།
ཡང་དག་བསྟོད་པ་དང་།།

ཞེས་མདོ་ཀུན་བཏུས་དང་གཏམ་བྱའི་རིམ་པ་དབུ་མ་རིན

10

ཆེན་ཕྲེང་བ་དང་དོན་དམ་ལ་བརྩམ་པའི་ཡང་དག་པའི་བསྟོད་པ་ལ་[12]ཆོས་དབྱིངས་བསྟོད་པ་དང་། འཇིག་རྟེན་ལས་འདས་པར་བསྟོད་པ་ཡང་ཡང་བཀོད་ལ། གཞན་ཡང་། སྐུ་གསུམ་ལ་བསྟོད་པ་དང་། དཔེ་མེད་པར་བསྟོད་པ་དང་། བསྟོད་པ་···ལས་འདས་པར་བསྟོད་པ་དང་། བསམ་མི་ཁྱབ་ཀྱི་བསྟོད་པ། སེམས་ཀྱི་རྡོ་རྗེ་ལ་བསྟོད་པ་སོགས་བཤད་ལ། ཡང་དེ་ཉིད་ལས།

འབད་པས་ཞིན་ཏུ་ཡུན་རིང་འཕགས་པའི་བསྟན་བཅོས་···
ལས་བསྟན་ཚིག་ ་ལེའུར་བྱས་དེ་དང་།།
[13]རིགས་པ་དྲུག་ཅུ་ཞེས་བྱ་རྣམ་པར་འཐག་བཅས་སྟོང་ཉིད་
བདུན་ཅུ་པ་དེ་དང་།།
གང་ཡང་རྩོད་པ་རྣམ་པར་བཟློག་པ་བཀོད་པ་དེ་དག་ཀྱང་ནི་
མཐོང་གྱུར་ཅིང་།།

ཞེས་དབུ་མ་རྩ་བ་དང་རིགས་པ་དྲུག་ཅུ་པ་དང་རྣམ་པར་···འཐག་བཅས་ནི་ཞིབ་མོ་རྣམ་འཐག་དང་སྟོང་ཉིད་བདུན་

11

ཅུ་པ་དང་རྩོད་བཟློག་སྟེ་རིགས་ཚོགས་ལྔ་དང་། ཡང་དེ་ཉིད་ལས།

བརྒྱ་པ་ལ་སོགས་དེ་དག་དང་ནི་དེ་བཞིན་མདོ་སྡེ་ཟབ་མོ་···
རྣམ་མང་དང་།།

ཞེས་འཕགས་པ་ཀླུའི་བཞི་བརྒྱ་པ་དང་སོགས་སྨྲས་···འཕགས་པ་ཀླུའི་དབུ་མ་ལ་ག་པའི་ཚད་དང་འཁྲུལ་བཟློག་དང་། གཞན་ཡང་བྱང་ཆུབ་ཀྱི་[14]ཚོགས་སོགས་ཀྱི་གཞུང་འགའ་རེ་དང་མདོ་སྡེ་ཟབ་མོ་ཕྱར་སྦྱོས་པ་མདོ་བཏུས་དང་སློབ་དཔོན་འདིས་ཤེས་བྱེད་དུ་དྲངས་པ་རྣམས་ཡིན་ཅིང་སངས་རྒྱས་བསྐྱངས་ཀྱི་···འགྲེལ་པ་ཡན་ཆད་གཅིག་ཏུ་[15]ཚད་མར་མཛད་ཅིང་། ཡང་དེ་ཉིད་ལས།

སངས་རྒྱས་བསྐྱངས་ཀྱིས་མཛད་པའི་འགྲེལ་པ་མཐོང་
ནས་ལེགས་ལྡན་འབྱེད་ཀྱི་ལེགས་བཤད་གང་།།
གཅིག་ནས་གཅིག་ཏུ་བརྒྱུད་ལས་འོངས་དང་བདག་གིས་
རྣམ་པར་ཕྱེ་ལས་རྙེད་པ་གང་།།

12

དེ་དག་བསྒོམ་སྐྱེ་བློ་ཆེན་ལྡན་རྣམས་མགུ་བར་བྱ་ཕྱིར་ཡང་
དག་བསྟན་པ་ཡིན།།

ཞེས་ལེགས་ལྡན་སོགས་ཀྱིས་བཤད་པ་ཡང་དག་གཅིག་ནས་གཅིག་ཏུ་བརྒྱུད་པ་རྣམས་ལ་བརྟེན་དགོས་ཀྱི་མདོ་དང་དགོངས་འགྲེལ་མེད་པར་སངས་འཕགས་རྒྱུད་ཀྱི་སློམ་ཐང་སྐོར་དགུ་སོགས་ཀྱི་བློ་བཟོས་རྒྱལ་བའི་བསྟན་པར་རྩ་འཛིན་པར་མི་བྱ། རྗེ་བོ་རིན་པོ་ཆེ་དང་སྟོན་པ་རིན་པོ་ཆེས་རྗེ་བོ་པ་སློང་ཁམས་ཆེ་མི་ནུད་ལས་འབྲས་འདི་ཟབ་གསུང་བདང་། སྟོན་པ་སངས་རྒྱས་ཀྱིས་ཀུན་དགའ་[16]བོ་ལ་དེ་ཕྱིར་ནན་ཆེར་གཏད་ལུགས་རྣམས་བསམས་ནས་རང་གཞན་ཕུང་ལ་མི་གཏོང་བར་ཀུན་ལ་ཐལ་མོ་སྦྱར་འཚལ། ཡང་དེ་ཉིད་ལས།

ཀླུ་སྒྲུབ་ཟླ་གྲགས་འཇོན་ནི་བཟང་པོའི་ཞལ་སྔ་དང་བཅས་
ཕྱིས་ཀྱང་གསུང་རྗེས་སུ།།
འབྲངས་པས་དེ་ཡི་ཚུལ་ལུགས་དུས་ནི་ཡུན་རིང་ཞིག་

ཏུ་གསལ་བར་འཆད་པར་མཛད།།
དེ་ཡི་སློབ་མ་བསྟན་བཅོས་དེ་ལ་རྣམ་པར་འབྱེད་པས་རྣམ་
རིས་བློ་ལྡན་པ།།
རྣམས་ཀྱིས་ཀྱང་ནི་སྔ་རྟེགས་མ་ལུས་ཕམ་བྱས་ཐུབ···
མཆོག་བསྟན་པ་ཡུན་རིང་བཞད།།

ཅེས་པས་སློབ་དཔོན་འཕགས་པས་ཡུན་རིང་དུ་བཞད་[17]རྒྱལ་དང་། དེའི་སློབ་མ་རྣམས་ཀྱིས་ཀྱང་སློབ་དཔོན་གཞུང་གི་རྣམ་བཤད་མང་པོ་བྱས་རྒྱལ་དང་། སྔ་རྟེགས་ཆེར་བཙད་ལུགས་བཤད་པས་དེ་དག་གི་བཤད་རྒྱུན་ལའང་སློབ་དཔོན་འདེས་བསྟན་པར་མཛད་ཀྱང་གཞུང་ཕལ་ཆེ་བ་དེ་དུས་ནས་མེད་པར་བཤད་ཅིང་། སློབ་དཔོན་ཟླ་བས་དབྱིག་གཉེན་···ཕྱོགས་སྐྱང་སོགས་ཀྱི་མཆན་སློས་ནས་བཀག་ཀྱང་ཟླ་བར་སུས་ཀྱང་མཆན་[18]སློས་ནས་བཀག་པ་མེད། ས་བཅུའི་སེམས་དཔར་གྲགས་པ་སློབ་དཔོན་འདིའི་འགྲེལ་ཆེན་བཞི་སོགས་དང་རྒྱལ་སྲས་ཞི་བ་ལྷའི་[19]སྤྱོད་འཇུག་དང་བསླབ་

བཏུས་ནི་སྤྱིར་དཔྱད་འཇོག་གི་སྒོམ་དང་བཤེས་གཉེན་བསྟེན་པ་ནས་བཟུམས་ཏེ་རྒྱལ་སྲས་ཀྱི་སྡོམ་པ་གསུམ་དང་ཟབ་དོན་སྒོམ་ཚུལ་སོགས་དང་ཉན་བཤད་སོགས་རྒྱས་པས་འདི་གཉིས་གཅིག་ཏུ་ཚད་ཐུབ་དང་། ལམ་སྒྲོན་དང་སོགས་སྒྱས་དབུ་མའི་མན་ངག་དང་། བདེན་གཉིས་དང་། དབུ་མའི་མན་ངག་གི་འགྲེལ་པ་རྣམས་ཚད་ཐུབ་བྱ་ལ། སྤྱོད་འཇུག་འགྲེལ་ཆེན་དང་ལམ་སྒྲོན་རང་འགྲེལ་སོགས་ཀྱི་ཡང་···ལེགས་ཆ་ལེན་ཅིང་། རྒྱུད་བླ་མ་རྩ་འགྲེལ་ཚད་ཐུབ་དང་མངོན་རྟོགས་རྒྱན་དང་འཕགས་སེང་གི་ཡང་ལམ་སོགས་ཐལ་རང་ཐུན་མོང་བ་གང་བས་ལ་ལེན་ལ་ཐུན་མོང་མིན་པར་བསེ་སྐད་མེད་པར་བྱ་ཚུལ་རྗེ་བདག་ཉིད་ཆེན་པོ་ཡབ་སྲས་གསུམ་གྱི་ལེགས་བཤད་ལ་ཚད་མར་བྱས་ནས་ལུང་མ་བྲིས་ཀྱང་དོན་དེ་ཁོ་ན་ལྟར་བཤད་པར་བྱ་སྟེ། འཁྲུལ་པ་[20]བྲལ་ཞིང་རིགས་ལམ་བྱེ་བས་གསལ་པོར་མཛད་པའི་ཕྱིར་རོ།།

༎ལྟ་བ་དེའི་དྲང་ངེས་ཀྱི་ཁྱད་པར་ནི།

བདེན་པ་གཉིས་རྟོན་མདོ་རིམ་དྲང་ངེས་ཏེ།།
གཞན་དུ་དྲང་དགོས་གནས་ཚུལ་དེར་ངེས་ཕྱིར།།
སྒྲས་ཟིན་འདང་མི་རུང་དྲང་དང་སྒྲས་ཟིན་དོན།།
[21]གྲུབ་ཀྱང་གནས་ལུགས་མིན་པས་དྲང་ཚུལ་གཉིས།།
ཚིག་མཐའ་དྲང་དོན་བཞག་པ་ངེས་དོན་མདོ།།
ལང་ཀ་ཤེགས་དགོངས་འགྲེལ་རྒྱན་སྟུག་མདོ་ཚོན་ལྟས།།
བྱེད་པོ་གཞན་མེད་སྟོང་ཉིད་ལ་དགོངས་ནས།།
སེམས་ཙམ་ཕྱི་དོན་མེད་དང་སྙིང་པོ་རྟག།
ཀུན་གཞི་ཡོད་དང་གཞན་དབང་ཡོད་ངེས་གྲུབ་བདེན།།
མཐར་ཐུག་ཐེག་གསུམ་རྟོན་ལྡ་དྲང་དོན་བསྒྲུབ།།

ཅེས་སྨྲས་ཏེ། སློབ་དཔོན་འཕགས་པས་དབུ་མ་རི་བསྟན་བཅོས་བརྩམས་ཏེ་དྲང་ངེས་ཕྱེ་བ་ལ་དགོས་པ་དུ་མ་ཡོད་དེ། བདེན་གཉིས་ལ་མི་རྨོངས་པ་དང་དེའི་དགོས་···པ་ཤེས་པ་དང་། ཡང་དྲང་དོན་དང་ངེས་དོན་གང་ཡིན་སྙམ་པའི་[22]གཉིས་ཐེ་ཚོམ་དང་དྲང་དོན་ལ་གནས་ལུགས་ངེས་དོན་དུ···

16

འཛིན་པའི་ལོག་ཤེས་བསལ་བའི་ཆེད་དུ་ཡིན་པའི་ཕྱིར་ཏེ།
ཚིག་གསལ་ལས། སློབ་དཔོན་གྱིས་དྲང་བ་དང་ངེས་པའི་
དོན་གྱི་མདོ་སྡེའི་རྣམ་པར་དབྱེ་བ་བསྟན་པའི་ཕྱིར་དབུ་མའི་
བསྟན་བཅོས་འདི་མཛད་པ་ཡིན་ནོ། ཞེས་པ་ནས། [དེ་ལ་
རྟེན་ཅིང་འབྲེལ་བར་འབྱུང་བའི་སྐྱེ་བ་ལ་སོགས་པ་དགག་པ་བསྟན་
པ་གང་ཡིན་པ་དེ་དག་ནི་མ་རིག་པའི་རབ་རིབ་དང་བྲལ་བ་དག་གི་
ཡེ་ཤེས་ཟག་པ་མེད་པའི་ཡུལ་གྱི་རང་བཞིན་ལ་བལྟོས་ནས
···ནི་མ་ཡིན་ནོ། འོན་ཅེ་ཞེ་ན། མ་རིག་པའི་རབ་རིབ་ཀྱིས་བློ་
གྲོས་ཀྱི་མིག་ཉམས་པར་གྱུར་པ་དག་གི་ཤེས་པའི་ཡུལ་ལ་
བལྟོས་ནས་ཡིན་ནོ། དེ་ཁོ་ན་གཟིགས་པ་ལ་བལྟོས་ནས་ནི་
བཅོམ་ལྡན་འདས་ཀྱིས་དགེ་སློང་དག་འདི་ནི་བདེན་པ་དམ་
པ་སྟེ། འདི་ལྟ་སྟེ། བསླུ་བ་མེད་པའི་ཆོས་ཅན་མྱ་ངན་ལས་
འདས་པའོ། འདུ་བྱེད་ཐམས་ཅད་ནི་རྫུན་པ་བསླུ་བའི་ཆོས་
ཅན་ནོ་ཞེས་བྱ་བ་ལ་སོགས་པ་གསུངས་སོ། དེ་བཞིན་དུ་འདི་
ན་དེ་བཞིན་ཉིད་དམ་ཕྱིན་ཅི་མ་ལོག་པའི་དེ་བཞིན་ཉིད་ནི་མེད་

17

ཏེ། འདི་དག་ནི་བསླུ་བར་བྱེད་པའི་ཆོས་ཅན་ནོ། ཅི་དག་ནི་རྫུན་པ
སྒྱུ་མ་བྱིས་པ་འཕྲིད་པའོ་ཞེས་གསུངས་སོ། །དེ་བཞིན་དུ།
གཟུགས་ནི་དབུ་བ་རྡོས་པ་འདྲ།།
ཚོར་བ་ཆུ་ཡི་ཆུ་བུར་བཞིན།།
འདུ་ཤེས་སྨིག་རྒྱུ་ལྟ་བུ་སྟེ།།
འདུ་བྱེད་ཆུ་ཤིང་སྡོང་པོ་འདྲ།།
རྣམ་ཤེས་སྒྱུ་མ་ལྟ་བུ་ཞེས།།
ཉི་མའི་གཉེན་གྱིས་བཀའ་སྩལ་ཏོ།།
ཞེས་བྱ་བ་དང་། དེ་བཞིན་དུ་དགེ་སློང་བརྩོན་འགྲུས་བརྩམས
པ་དྲན་པ་དང་ཤེས་བཞིན་དང་ལྡན་པ་ཉིན་དང་མཚན་དུ་ཆོས
ལ་སོ་སོར་རྟོག་པར་བྱེད་པ་ན། འདུ་བྱེད་ཐམས་ཅད་ནི་ཉེ་
བར་ཞི་བའི་གོ་འཕང་ཞི་བ། ཆོས་རྣམས་བདག་མེད་པ་
ཉིད་རྟོགས་པར་འགྱུར་རོ། །ཞེས་བྱ་བ་ལ་སོགས་པ···
གསུངས་སོ། །དེ་ལྟ་བུར་བསྟན་པའི་དགོངས་པ་མི་ཤེས་
པས། འདིར་]དེ་ཁོ་ནའི་དོན་ཅན་གྱི་བསྟན་པ་ནི་གང་ཞིག་

18

ཡིན། དགོངས་པ་ཅན་ནི་གང་ཞིག་ཡིན་སྙམ་དུ་ཐེ་ཚོམ་དུ་འགྱུར་
བ་དང་། གང་ཞིག་བློ་ཞན་པ་ཉིད་ཀྱིས་དྲང་བའི་དོན་བསྟན་པ
ལ་ངེས་པའི་དོན་དུ་རྟོག[23]·· པ་དེ་གཉིས་ཀའི་ཐེ་ཚོམ་དང་
ལོག་པའི་ཤེས་པ་དགག་རིགས་པ་དང་ལུང་གཉིས་ཀའི···
སྒོ་ནས་བསལ་བར་བྱ་བའི་ཕྱིར་སློབ་དཔོན་གྱིས་འདི·····
བརྩམས་སོ། །ཞེས་སོ། དྲང་ངེས་འབྱེད་བྱེད་ཡོད་དེ།
རྟོན་པ་བཞིས་འབྱེད་པའི་ཕྱིར་དང་། རྩ་ཤེས་ལས།
བདག་ལས་མ་ཡིན་གཞན་ལས་མིན།།
[གཉིས་ལས་མ་ཡིན་རྒྱུ་མེད་མིན།།
དངོས་པོ་གང་དག་གང་ན་ཡང་།།
སྐྱེ་བ་ནམ་ཡང་ཡོད་མ་ཡིན།།]
སོགས་རིགས་པ་དང་།
བཅོམ་ལྡན་འདས་ཀྱིས་ཆོས་གང་ཞིག།
སླུ་བ་དེ་ནི་རྫུན་ཞེས་གསུངས།།
[འདུ་བྱེད་ཐམས་ཅད་བསླུ་བའི་ཆོས།།

རྗེས་ན་དེ་དག་བརྗོད་པ་ཡིན།།
སྔོན་མཐའ་འམ་ཐོན་ནམ་ཞེས་ཞུས་ཚེ།།
ཐུབ་པ་ཆེན་པོས་མིན་ཞེས་གསུངས།།
འཁོར་བ་ཐོག་མ་མཐའ་མེད་དེ།།
དེ་ལ་སྔོན་མེད་ཕྱི་མ་མེད།།
བཅོམ་ལྡན་དངོས་དང་དངོས་མེད་པ།།
མཁྱེན་པས་ཀཱ་ཏྱཱ་ཡ་ན་ཡི།།
གདམས་ངག་ལས་ནི་ཡོད་པ་དང་།།
མེད་པ་གཉི་གའང་དགག་པ་མཛད།།

ཞེས་སོགས་དུ་མས་ལུང་བཀོད་ནས་ཕྱེ་བའི་ཕྱིར། དྲང་ངེས་ཀྱི་ཁྱད་པར་བརྗོད་བྱའི་སྒོས་བཞག་སྟེ། དོན་དམ་གཙོ་བོར་སྟོན་པ་ངེས་དོན་གྱི་དང་། ཀུན་རྫོབ་གཙོ་བོར་སྟོན་པའི་མདོ་དྲང་དོན་དུ་བཤད་པའི་ཕྱིར་ཏེ། བློ་གྲོས་མི་ཟད་པའི་མདོ་ལས། ངེས་པའི་དོན་གྱི་མདོ་སྡེ་ནི་གང་ཡིན། དྲང་བའི་དོན་གྱི་མདོ་སྡེ་ནི་གང་ཞེ་ན། མདོ་སྡེ་གང་དག་ཀུན་རྫོབ་བསྒྲུབ་

པ་བསྟན་པ་དེ་དྲང་བའི་དོན་ཅེས་བྱའོ། །མདོ་སྡེ་གང་དག་དོན་དམ་པ་སྒྲུབ་པ་བསྟན་པ་དེ་དག་ནི་ངེས་པའི་དོན་ཅེས་བྱའོ། ཞེས་སོ། །དེའི་ཀུན་རྫོབ་སྒྲུབ་ལུགས་དང་དོན་དམ་པ་སྒྲུབ་ལུགས་ཇི་ལྟ་བུ་ཞེ་ན་ཡོད་དེ། རིམ་བཞིན་དུ་ཚིག་དང་ཡི་གེ་སྣ་ཚོགས་ཀྱི་བྱ་བྱེད་སྣ་ཚོགས་ཅི་རིགས་སྟོན་པ་དང་། དམིགས་མེད་དང་བློ་འདས་སོགས་བརྟག་དཀའ་བའི་རྟོགས་དཀའ་བའི···ཆོས་བསྟན་པ་དེ་ཡིན་པའི་ཕྱིར་ཏེ། མདོ་དེ་ཉིད་ལས། མདོ་སྡེ་གང་དག་ཚིག་དང་ཡི་གེ་སྣ་ཚོགས་པས་བསྟན་པ་དེ་དག་ནི་དྲང་བའི་དོན་ཅེས་བྱའོ། །མདོ་སྡེ་གང་དག་ཟབ་མོ་ལྟ་དཀའ་བ་རྟོགས་པར་དཀའ་བ་བསྟན་པ་དེ་དག་ནི་ངེས་པའི་དོན་ཅེས་བྱའོ། །མདོ་སྡེ་གང་དག་བདག་དང་སེམས་ཅན་དང་སྲོག་དང་གསོ་བ་དང་སྐྱེས་བུ་དང་གང་ཟག་དང་ཤེད་ལས་སྐྱེས་དང་ཤེད་བུ་དང་བྱེད་པ་པོ་ཚོར་བ་པོ་སྐད་སྣ་ཚོགས་ཀྱི་བཤད་པར་བྱ་བ་བདག་པོ་མེད་པ་ལ་བདག་པོ་ལྟ་བུར་བསྟན་པ་དེ་དག་ནི་དྲང་བའི་དོན་ཅེས་བྱའོ། །མདོ་སྡེ་གང་དག་དངོས་པོ་

སྟོང་པ་ཉིད་དང་མཚན་མ་མེད་དང་སྨོན་པ་མེད་པ་དང་མངོན་པར་འདུ་བྱེད་མེད་པ་དང་། མ་སྐྱེས་པ་དང་སེམས་ཅན་མེད་པ་དང་སྲོག་མེད་པ་དང་གང་ཟག་མེད་པ་དང་བདག་པོ་མེད་པ་རྣམ་པར་ཐར་པའི་སྒོ་སྟོན་པ་དེ་དག་ནི་ངེས་པའི་དོན་ཅེས་བྱ་སྟེ། འདི་ནི་ངེས་པའི་དོན་གྱི་མདོ་སྡེ་ལ་རྟོན་གྱི་དྲང་བའི་དོན་གྱི་མདོ་སྡེ་ལ་མི་རྟོན་པ་ཞེས་བྱའོ། །ཞེས་སོ། །འཁོར་ལོ་དང་པོ་དང་དགོངས་འགྲེལ་ལྟ་བུ་ཀུན་རྫོབ་སྟོན་པ་ཆོས་ཅན། དྲང་བའི་དོན་ཅན་ཡིན་ཏེ། དངོས་བསྟན[24]་དོན་དེ་ལས···གཞན་དུ་དྲང་ནས་གནས་ལུགས་ཚོལ་དགོས་པའི་ཕྱིར། ཏིང་འཛིན་རྒྱལ་པོ་དང་འབུམ་སོགས་ཆོས་ཅན། ངེས་པའི་དོན་ཅན་ཡིན་ཏེ། ཆོས་ཀྱི[25]་གནས་ལུགས་ཐོད་ཀྱི་དངོས···བསྟན་གྱི་དོན་དེར་ངེས་པའི་ཕྱིར་ཏེ། གནས་ལུགས་དེ་ལས[26]གཞན(ཐ)དུ་འདྲེན་པ་ལ་དཔེ་ཡོད་ཀྱང་དེ་དགོས་པའི་སྒོ་ནས་དྲང་ཚུལ་ཏེ་དྲང་དོན་ཕལ་ཆེར་ལ་དགོས་ཤིང་བརྗོད་བྱའི་དྲང་ཚུལ་མི་སྲིད་པ་སོགས་རིགས་པས་གནོད། འདུས་

22

རྒྱུས་ཐམས་ཅད་རྫུན་པར་[27]གསུངས་པ་བདེན་པ་གཅིག་ཏུ་གསུངས[27]པ་སོགས་ལུང་གིས་གནོད་ཅིང་། སྒྱུ་མ་སོགས་དཔེ་དགུ་མདང་བཅས་ན་མི་རྙེད་པ་སོགས་ཀྱི་རིགས་པ་དང་། ཟབ་མོ་སྤྲོས་མེད་སྟོན་པའི་ལུང་དུ་མས་གནས་ལུགས་ཀྱི་དོན་དེར་ངེས་པའི་ཕྱིར་ཏེ། འདིར་དྲང་དོན་གྱི་དྲང་ཚུལ་ལ་གཞུགཔ་ལྡེམ་དགོངས་ཀླུ་བུའི་གདུལ་བྱ་ར་དྲང་ཚུལ་མ་ཡིན···པས་བརྗོད་བྱའི་སྒོ་ནས། ཕ་དང་མ་ནི་བསད་བྱ་ཞིང་། ཀླུ་བུའི་སྐྲས་ཟིན་མདོ་དེའི་བརྗོད་བྱ་ཙམ་དུ་ཡང་མི་རུང་བའི་དྲང་ཚུལ་དང་། ལས་དཀར་ནག་ལས་བདེ་སྡུག་འབྱུང་བར་སྟོནཔ་སྒྲ་ཇི་བཞིན་ཡིན་ཀྱང་ལས་དཀར་ནག་ལས་འབྲས་བུ་བདེ་སྡུག་འབྱུང་བ་ནི་ལས་དེ་གཉིས་ཀྱི་གནས་ལུགས་ཡིན་པར་འདོད་པ་ལ་ལས་གཉིས་ཀྱི་གནས་ལུགས་དེར་མི་རུང་གི་དེ་ལས་གཞན་དུ་བདག་མེད་དུ་དྲང་དགོས་པ་ཀླུ་བུའི་སྒྲ་ཇི་བཞིན་པ་ཡིན་མིན་གྱི་དྲང་ཚུལ་བརྟགས་ན་གཉིས་ཡོད་པའི་ཕྱིར་ཏེ། ཏིང་འཛིན་རྒྱལ་པོ་ལས།

23

སྟོང་པ་བདེ་བར་གཤེགས་པས་བསྟན་པ་ལྟར།།
ངེས་དོན་མདོ་སྡེ་དག་གིས་བྱེ་བྲག་ཤེས།།
གང་ལས་སེམས་ཅན་གང་ཟག་སྐྱེས་བུ་བསྟན།།
ཆོས་དེ་ཐམས་ཅད་དྲང་བའི་དོན་དུ་སྟོན།།
ཞེས་སོ། །ངེས་ན་འཁོར་ལོ་གསུམ་གྱི་ཁྱད་པར་ཡང་།
ཟབ་ཞི་སྤྲོས་བྲལ་འོད་གསལ་འདུས་མ་བྱས།།
[ཁྱད་ཅི་ཆོས་ནི་བདག་གིས་ཐོབ་པར་གྱུར།།
བདག་གིས་བསྟན་ཀྱང་གཞན་གྱིས་མི་ཤེས་ཏེ།།
མི་སྨྲར་ནགས་འདབ་གནས་པར་བྱ་བ་སྙམ།།]

སོགས་དང་། རྗེ་ཞེས་ལས་དམན་མདོ་བཀོད་པའི་མདོ་དོན་དམ་དངོས་སུ་སྟོན་པ་རྣམས་འཁོར་ལོ་དང་པོ་ཡིན་ཀྱང་དྲང་དོན་མིན་པར་བཤད་པས། འཁོར་ལོ་གསུམ་སོ་སོ་ལ···དགོངས་འགྲེལ་གྱི་འཁོར་ལོ་དང་པོ་སོགས་ཀྱིས་མ་ཁྱབ་པ། དགོངས་འགྲེལ་གྱི་འཁོར་ལོ་གསུམ་གྱི་འཁོར་ལོ་དང་པོ་བདེན་བཞི་སོགས་རང་མཚན་གྱིས་ཡོད་པར་བཤད

24

པ་དང་། འཁོར་ལོ་ཐམས་[28] ཀུན་བརྟགས་རང་བཞིན་མེད་པ་དང་གཞན་དབང་[29]ཡོངས་གྲུབ་རང་བཞིན་གྱིས་ཡོད་པར་དོན་དམ་པར་ཡོད་ཚུལ་བཤད་པའི་མདོ་གཉིས་དྲང་དོན་དང་། བར་པའི་ཤེར་སྙིང་ལྟ་བུར་ཡང་། རང་བཞིན་གྱིས་སྟོང་པར་ལྟར། གསུངས་པས་ངེས་དོན་གྱི་མདོ་ཡིན་ལ། ཚུལ་འདི་དགོངས་འགྲེལ་དང་མི་མཐུན་ཀྱང་དགོངས་པ་མི་འགལ་ཏེ། གདུལ་བྱའི་ཁྱད་པར་སོ་སོ་ལ་དེ་ལྟར་འཆད་ཀྱང་དགོངས་པ་མི་འགལ་བའི་ཕྱིར་ཏེ། དཔེར་ན་ཉན་ཐོས་ལ་སྔོན་ཏེ། སྲོག་གཅོད་ནམ་ཡང་མི་གནང་ལ། ཐེག་ཆེན་གྱི་ཁྱད་པར་འགའ་ཞིག་ལ་དགོས་དབང་གིས་གནང་བ་གསུངས་པ་པོ་གཅིག་གི་ལུགས་ཡིན་ཀྱང་མི་འགལ་བ་བཞིན་ནོ། འོན་སྐབས་འདིར་དྲང་དོན་དུ་འགྲེལ་རྒྱུ་ལ། དགོངས་གཞི་དགོས་པ་དངོས་ལ་གནོད་བྱེད་ཇི་ལྟ་བུ་སྙམ་ན། ལ་ལན་ནི།

རྣམ་པ་དེ་ལྟའི་མདོ་སྡེ་གཞན་ཡང་ནི།།
དྲང་དོན་ཉིད་དུ་ལུང་འདིས་གསལ་བར་བྱེད།།

25

ཅེས་པའི་དྲང་དོན་དུ་འགྲེལ་རྒྱུ་ལ་སེམས་ཙམ་པའི་མཚན་ཉིད་གསུམ་སྟོན་པའི་དགོངས་འགྲེལ་དང་ཀུན་གཞི་སྟོན་པའི་དགོངས་འགྲེལ་ལེའུ་གཉིས་དང་། འགྲེལ་པའི་སོགས་སྒྲས་ཕྱི་དོན་མེད་པར་སྟོན་པའི་བྱམས་ཞུས་དང་། མཐར་ཐུག་ཐེག་པ་གསུམ་དུ་སྟོན་པའི་དགོངས་འགྲེལ་གྱི་ལུང་བཞིན་དེས་ཟེར་བ་སོགས་ཡོད་དོ། །དེ་མི་འཐད་དེ། རྣམ་བཤད་ལས། ལུགས་འདིས་སྔར་བཤད་པའི་དོན་ཚན་བཞི་ཀ་དྲང་དོན་དུ་འགྲེལ་གྱི་[ཞེས་]…གསུངས་པ། བརྗོད་དོན་སྟོན་བསྟུས་ཏེ་རང་འགྲེལ་གྱི…དངོས་སུ་སྨོས་པ་གསུམ་དང་མདོ་ཀུན་འདུས་ཀྱི་མཐར…ཐུག་ཐེག་གསུམ་སྟོན་པ་བརྗོད་དོན་སྨོས་གཅིག་ཏུ་བྱས་ནས་བཞེར་གཙོ་བོར་བཤད་ཀྱི། བརྗོད་བྱེད་ཚད་དང་དབྱེ་བའི་སྨོས་ཕྱིན་ཞིན་ཏུ་མང་པོ་ཡོད་པའི་ཕྱིར། དཔེར་ན་མཐར་ཐུག་ཐེག་པ་གསུམ་དུ་སྟོན་ཚུལ་ལྷ(ད)་ཏུ་རའི་མདོ་དང་དགོངས་འགྲེལ་[ལས་]དེ་ལ་དགོངས་ནས་ཐེག་པ་གཅིག་ཏུ་བསྟན་ཏེ། སེམས་ཅན་གྱི་ཁམས་ན། ཞེས་པ་ནས། [སེམས་

26

ཅན་རང་བཞིན་གྱིས་དབང་པོ་རྟུལ་པོ་རྣམས་དང་། དབང་པོ་འབྲིང་རྣམས་དང་། དབང་པོ་རྣོན་པོ་རྣམས་ཀྱི་]སེམས་ཅན་གྱི་རིགས་སྣ་ཚོགས་དག་ཀྱང་མེད་པ་མ་ཡིན་ནོ། །ལྷ་བུ་དང་། རིགས་(ན)་བདེན་གྲུབ་སོ་སོར་དམིགས་པ་དང་། ཤེར་མདོ་ལས། [གང་དག་ཡང་དག་པ་ཉིད་དུ་ངེས་པར་ཞུགས་པ་དེ་དག་ནི་བླ་ན་མེད་པ…ཡང་དག་པར་རྫོགས་པའི་བྱང་ཆུབ་ཏུ་སེམས་བསྐྱེད་པའི་མཐུ་མེད་དོ། དེ་ཅིའི་ཕྱིར་ཞེ་ན་]དེ་དག་འཁོར་བའི་རྒྱུན་གྱི་མཚམས་བཅད་པའི་ཕྱིར་རྟ་བུ་དགྲ་བཅོམ་པ་སླར་འཕོས་ནས་མི་སྐྱེ་བ་དང་། དགོངས…འགྲེལ་ལས། ཞི་བ་བགྲོད་པ་གཅིག་པུ་པ་ནི་[ཞེས་པ་]ནས་[སངས་རྒྱས་ཐམས་ཅད་བརྩོན་པ་དང་ལྡན་པར་གྱུར་ཀྱང་བྱང་ཆུབ་ཀྱི་སྙིང་པོ་ལ་བཞག་སྟེ་བླ་ན་མེད་པ་ཡང…དག་པར་རྫོགས་པའི་]བྱང་ཆུབ་ཏུ་སེམས་བསྐྱེད་པའི་མཐུ་མེད་དོ། །སོགས་དང་། འཇིགས་(པ)་ལྷ་སངས་རྒྱས་ཀྱི་གདུང་ཆད་པ་ལྟ་བུ་དེ་དག་གིས་ཅི་ཙམ་བསྒོམས་ཀྱང་

27

སྙིང་རྗེ་དང་ལྷག་བསམ་མི་སྐྱེ་བར་བཤད་པའི་ལུང་དུ་མ་དང་སྟོན་ཚུལ་དུ་མ་ཡོད་པའི་ཕྱིར་དང་། དེ་དག་རེ་རེ་ནས་དྲང་དོན་དུ་འགྲེལ་བྱེད་ལུང་སོ་སོ་བ་མདོ་ཀུན་བཏུས་ལས་བཤད་པ་རྣམས་འདིར་མ་དྲང་པ་ཙམ་ཡིན་པའི་ཕྱིར་ཏེ། མདོ་ཀུན…བཏུས་ལས། ཐེག་པ་གཅིག་ལ་མོས་པའི་སེམས་ཅན་དེ་དག་ནི་ཤིན་ཏུ་སྙེད་པར་དཀའ་སྟེ། ཐེག་པ་གཅིག་ཏུ་ཟད་པ་ནི་མདོ་སྡེ་དུ་མ་ལས་གསུངས་པའི་ཕྱིར་དང་། འཕགས་པའི་དམ་པའི་ཆོས་པདྨ་དཀར་པོ་ལས། ད(ཡ)་ཡང་ཐེག་པ…གཅིག་ལས་བརྩམས་ཏེ། སེམས་ཅན་རྣམས་ལ་ཆོས…འཆད་པ་[འདི་ལྟ་སྟེ། སངས་རྒྱས་ཀྱི་ཐེག་པ་ཐམས་ཅད་མཁྱེན་པ་ཉིད་ཀྱི་མཐར་ཐུག་པ་སྟེ། ཐེག་པ་གཉིས་སམ…གསུམ་ཞེས་བྱ་བ་དག་ཀྱང་མེད་དོ། །ཕྱོགས་བཅུའི་འཇིག་རྟེན་ཐམས་ཅད་ན་ཡང་ཆོས་ཉིད་ནི་འདི་འོ། དེ་ཅིའི་ཕྱིར་ཞེ་ན། ཕྱོགས་བཅུའི་འཇིག་རྟེན་གྱི་ཁམས་ཐམས་ཅད་དུ་གང་འདས་པའི་དུས་ན…བྱུང་བའི་དེ་བཞིན་གཤེགས་པ་དེ…

28

དག་ཐམས་ཅད་ཀྱང་ཐེག་པ་གཅིག་ལས་བརྩམས་ནས། སེམས་ཅན་རྣམས་ལ་ཆོས་བསྟན་ཏེ། གང་འདི་སངས་རྒྱས་ཀྱི་ཐེག་པའོ། །གང་མ་འོངས་པའི་དུས་ན་འབྱུང་བའི་དེ་བཞིན་གཤེགས་པ་དེ་དག་ཀྱང་། སངས་རྒྱས་ཀྱི་ཐེག་པ་གཅིག་པུ་ལ་བརྩམས་ནས། སེམས་ཅན་རྣམས་ལ་ཆོས་སྟོན་པར་འགྱུར་རོ། །གང་ད་ལྟར་བྱུང་བའི་དུས་ན་ཕྱོགས་བཅུའི་···འཇིག་རྟེན་གྱི་ཁམས་ཐམས་ཅད་ཀྱི་དེ་བཞིན་གཤེགས་པ་དེ་དག་ཐམས་ཅད་ཀྱང་སངས་རྒྱས་ཀྱི་ཐེག་པ་གཅིག་པུ་ལ་བརྩམས་ནས། སེམས་ཅན་རྣམས་ལ་ཆོས་སྟོན་ཏོ། །རྣམ་གྲངས་འདིས་ཀྱང་འདི་ལྟར་རིག་པར་བྱ་སྟེ། ཕྱོགས་བཅུའི་འཇིག་རྟེན་གྱི་ཁམས་གང་ན་ཡང་ཐེག་པ་གཉིས་སུ་བཏགས་པ་ཡང་མེད་ན། གསུམ་ལྟ་ཅི་སྨོས་ཞེས་གསུངས་སོ།]·····སོགས་ཀྱིས་དུས་གསུམ་གྱི་སངས་རྒྱས་ཐམས་ཅད་དང་ད···ལྟར་གྱི་ཕྱོགས་བཅུའི་སངས་རྒྱས་ཐམས་ཅད་ཐེག་གཅིག་སྟོན་པར་བཤད་པ་དང་། མདོ་འདིར་ཤཱ་རིའི་བུ་སོགས་ཉ

29

མེད་དུ་ལུང་ཡང་བསྟན་ལ། བདེན་པ་པོའི་ལེའུ་ལས།[31] འཇམ་དཔལ་ཐེག་པ་གཅིག་གིས་ངེས་པར་འབྱུང་བའི་ཕྱིར། [སངས་རྒྱས་ཀྱི་ཞིང་དེ་ནི་ཐེག་པ་ཆེན་པོའི་སྙིང་པོ་དང་ལྡན་པ་ཡིན་ནོ། །ང་ལ་ཉན་ཐོས་དང་། རང་སངས་རྒྱས་ཀྱི་ཐེག་པ་རྣམ་པར་དགོད་པ་མེད་དོ། །དེ་ཅིའི་ཕྱིར་ཞེ་ན། དེ་བཞིན་གཤེགས་པ་ལ་འདུ་ཤེས་སྣ་ཚོགས་མེད་པའི་ཕྱིར་ཏེ། འཇམ་དཔལ་ཀུལ་(བ)་ཏེ་དེ་བཞིན་གཤེགས་པས་ལ་ལ་དག་ནི་ཐེག་པ་ཆེན་པོའོ། །ལ་ལ་དག་ནི་རང་སངས་རྒྱས་ཀྱི་ཐེག་པ། ལ་ལ་དག་ནི་ཉན་ཐོས་ཀྱི་ཐེག་པ་བཤད་པར་གྱུར་ན་དེ་ནི་དེ་བཞིན་གཤེགས་པའི་སེམས་ཡོངས་སུ་མ་དག་པར་འགྱུར་ཏེ། མངོན་པར་ཞེན་པའི་སྐྱོན་དུ་ཡང་འགྱུར། སྙིང་རྗེ་ཆེན་པོ་ཉི་ཚེ་བར་ཡང་འགྱུར། ང་ཆོས་ལ་སློབ་དཔོན་དཔེ་མཁྱུད་བྱས་པར་ཡང་འགྱུར་རོ། །འཇམ་དཔལ་ངས་སེམས་ཅན་རྣམས་ལ་ཆོས་གང་དང་གང་བསྟན་པ་དེ་དག་ཐམས་ཅད་ནི་འདི་ལྟ་སྟེ། ཐམས་ཅད་མཁྱེན་པའི་ཡེ་ཤེས་ཐོབ་པར་བྱ་བའི་ཕྱིར་བྱང་ཆུབ་ལ་གཞོལ་བ། ཐེག་

30

པ་ཆེན་པོ་ལ་འབབ་པའི་ཐམས་ཅད་མཁྱེན་པ་ཉིད་བསྒྲུབ་པ། ཡུལ་གཅིག་ཏུ་ཡང་དག་པར་ཕྱིན་པར་བྱེད་པ་སྟེ། དེ་བས་ན་ང་ལ་ཐེག་པ་རྣམ་པར་དགོད་པ་མེད་དོ། །འཇམ་དཔལ་ལ···ཐེག་པ་རྣམ་པར་དགོད་པ་ཞེས་བྱ་བ་འདི་ནི། དེ་བཞིན་གཤེགས་པ་རྣམ་པར་དགོད་པར་མཛད་པའོ། །དེ་ནི་གང་ཟག་རྣམ···པར་དགོད་པར··········མཛད་པའོ། །ཚོགས་ཆུང་ངུ་དང་། ཚོགས་ཚད་མེད་པ་རྣམ་པར་དགོད་པར་མཛད་པ་སྟེ། ཆོས་ཀྱི་དབྱིངས་ཐ་དད་པ་མེད་པའི་ཕྱིར་འདི་ལ་ཐེག་པ་ཐ་དད་པ་མེད་དེ། དེ་ནི་ཀུན་རྫོབ་ཏུ་འཇུག་པ་བསྟན་པ་འཇུག་པའ···སྒོ་ཙམ་དུ་བརྗོད་པའོ། །གང་དོན་དམ་པར་ཐེག་པ་གཅིག་པ་ནི་གཉིས་པ་མ་ཡིན་]སོགས་ཀྱིས་ཐེག་པ་ཐ་དད་པ····བསྟན་ན་འདུ་ཤེས་པ་ཐ་དད་པ་སོགས་དང་། དཔེ་འཁྱུད་ཀྱི་སྒྲོན་ཡོད་ལ་ཐེག་པ་ཆེན་པོ་ལ་གཞོལ་བ་འབབ་པ་ཤ་སྟག་ཏུ་བཤད་པ་དྲང་། ཤེར་མདོ་ལས། ལྷའི་བུ་གང་དག་[བླ་ན་མེད་པ་ཡང་དག་པར་རྫོགས་པའི་བྱང་ཆུབ་ཏུ་སེམས་

31

མ་བསྐྱེད་པ་དེ་དག་གིས། བླ་ན་མེད་པ་ཡང་དག་པར་རྫོགས་པའི་བྱང་ཆུབ་ཏུ་སེམས་བསྐྱེད་པར་བྱའོ། །གང་དག་ཡང་དག་པ་ཉིད་དུ་ངེས་པར་ཞུགས་པ་དེ་དག་ནི་བྱང་ཆུབ་ཏུ་སེམས་བསྐྱེད་པའི་མཐུ་མེད་དོ། །དེ་ཅིའི་ཕྱིར་ཞེ་ན། དེ་དག་འཁོར་བའི་རྒྱུན་གྱི་མཚམས་བཅད་པའི་ཕྱིར་རོ། །དེ་དག་གལ་ཏེ་བླ་ན་མེད་པ་ཡང་དག་པར་བྱང་ཆུབ་ཏུ་སེམས་བསྐྱེད་ན་ནི། ང་ཡང་རྗེས་སུ་ཡི་རང་ཞིང་། ང་དེ་དག་གི་དགེ་བའི་རྩ་བ་ལ་བར་(མ)ཆད་མི་བྱེད་དེ། ཁྱད་པར་དུ་འཕགས་པ་ནས་ཀྱང་ཤིན་ཏུ་ཁྱད་པར་དུ་འཕགས་པའི་ཆོས་རྣམས་ལ་ལྷག་པར···དམིགས་པར་བྱའོ།] ཅེས་སོགས་ཀྱིས་དགྲ་བཅོམ་པས་ 32 ཀྱང་སེམས་བསྐྱེད་ན་ཡིད་རང་ལ་བར་ཆད་མི་བྱ་ཞིང་ཤིན་ཏུ་ཁྱད་པར་དུ་འཕགས་པའི་ཆོས་ལ་དམིགས་པར་བྱ་ཞེས་དགྲ་བཅོམ་ལ་ཡང་སེམས་བསྐྱེད་སྐྱེ་བ་དངོས་སུ་བསྟན་ནས་ལུང་གསུམ་པོ་དྲང་དོན་དུ་བཤད། གཟུངས་རྒྱལ་གྱིས··(ཚ)ཞུས་པ་ལས། སངས་རྒྱས་བཅོམ་ལྡན་འདས་རྣམས་

32

ནི་[གནམ་སྣ་ཚོགས་ཀྱི་ཚེད་དུ་འབྱུང་བ་མ་ཡིན་ཏེ་ཆོས་ཀྱི་དབྱིངས་རོ་གཅིག་པ་སྒྲིབ་པ་མེད་པ། སེམས་ཅན་ཐམས་ཅད་ལ་གོ་སྐབས་འབྱེད་པ་མངོན་པར་རྫོགས་པར་སངས་རྒྱས་ནས། སེམས···ཅན་རྣམས་ཁོང་དུ་ཆུད་པར་བྱ་བའི་ཕྱིར། འདི་ལྟ་སྟེ། ཕྱིར་མི··ལྡོག་པའི་འཁོར་ལོ་རབ་ཏུ་བསྐོར་རོ། རིགས་ཀྱི་བུ་འདི་ལྟ་སྟེ་དཔེར་ན། ནོར་བུ་མཁན་གྱིས་ནོར་བུའི་རིགས་ལས་སྦྱང་བ་མ་བྱས···(ཚ)བའི་ནོར་བུ་རིན་པོ་ཆེ་བླངས་ནས། བུལ་ཏོག་གི་ཆུ་རྣོན་པོས···བཀྲུས་ཏེ། སྣ་ནག་པོའི་ཁ་བས་ཕྱི་དོར་བྱ་བས་ཕྱི་དོར་བྱས་ཀྱང་དེ་ཙམ་གྱིས་བརྩོན་འགྲུས་རྒྱུན་མི་གཅོད་དེ། དེའི་འོག་ཏུ་དངུལ་ཆུ་རྣོན་པོ་དང་བཙས་པས་བཀྲུས་ཏེ། ཤིང་དང་སྐུམ་བུས་ཕྱི་དོར་བྱ་བས་ཕྱི་དོར་བྱེད་དོ། །དེ་ཙམ་གྱིས་ཀྱང་བརྩོན་འགྲུས་རྒྱུན་མི་གཅོད་དོ། །དེའི་འོག་ཏུ་ཡང་སྨན་ཆེན་པོའི་ཁུ་བས་བཀྲུས་ཏེ། རས་ཕྲ་མོས་ཕྱི་དོར་བྱས་པས་ཕྱི་དོར་བྱེད་དོ། །ཕྱི་དོར་བྱས་ཏེ་ནོར་བུ་འཆིང་བུའི་རིགས་དང་བྲལ་ནས་ནི་བཻཌཱུརྱ་ཞེས་བྱའོ། །དེ་བཞིན་དུ་དེ་བཞིན་གཤེགས་པས་ཡོངས་སུ་མ་དག་པའི་སེམས་

33

ཅན་གྱི་ཁམས་རིག་ནས་མི་རྟག་པ་དང་། སྡུག་བསྔལ་བ་དང་། བདག་མེད་པ་དང་། མི་སྡུག་པ་ཡིད་འབྱུང་བར་འགྱུར་བའི···གཏམ་གྱིས་འཁོར་བ་ལ་མངོན་པར་དགའ་བའི་སེམས་ཅན་རྣམས་ཡིད་འབྱུང་བར་བྱེད། འཕགས་པ་ཆོས་འདུལ་བ་ལ་འཇུག་པར་བྱེད་དོ། །དེ་ཙམ་གྱིས་དེ་བཞིན་གཤེགས་པ་བརྩོན་འགྲུས་རྒྱུན་མི་གཅོད་དེ། དེའི་འོག་ཏུ་སྟོང་པ་ཉིད་དང་། མཚན་མ་མེད་པ་དང་། སྨོན་པ་མེད་པའི་གཏམ་གྱིས་དེ་བཞིན་གཤེགས་པའི་གཏམ་གྱི་ཚུལ་ཁོང་དུ་ཆུད་པར་བྱེད་དོ། །དེ་ཙམ་གྱིས···ཀྱང་དེ་བཞིན་གཤེགས་པ་བརྩོན་འགྲུས་རྒྱུན་མི་གཅོད་དེ། དེའི་འོག་ཏུ་ཕྱིར་མི་ལྡོག་པའི་འཁོར་ལོའི་གཏམ་དང་། འཁོར་གསུམ་ཡོངས་སུ་དག་པའི་གཏམ་གྱིས། སེམས་ཅན་དེ་དག་དེ་བཞིན་གཤེགས་པའི་ཡུལ་ལ་འཇུད་དོ། །སེམས་ཅན་རྒྱུད་དང་རང་བཞིན་སྣ་ཚོགས་པ་དེ་དག་མཉམ་དུ་ཞུགས་ནས། དེ་བཞིན་གཤེགས་པའི་ཆོས་ཉིད་ཁོང་དུ་ཆུད་པས། སྦྱིན་གནས་བླ་ན་མེད་པ་རྣམས་ཞེས་བྱའོ།] སོགས་ཀྱིས་ནོར་བུ་བཀྲུ

34

བ་གསུམ་གྱི་དཔེས་དགྲ་བཅོམ་པའི་ཡང་སྲིད་པའི་དྲི་མ་བཀྲུས་ནས་སངས་རྒྱས་སུ་འགོད་པར་བཤད་པས་ཉན་ཐོས་དགྲ…བཅོམ་པ་ལ་ཐེག་པ་མཐར་ཐུག་མེད་པ་དང་སངས་རྒྱས་པའི་ནུས་པ་མེད་པ་དྲང་དོན་དུ་བཤད། ཕྱིར་མི་ལྡོག་པའི་འཁོར་ལོའི་(ཛ)མདོ་ལས། འཇམ་དཔལ་གཞོན་ནུར་གྱུར་པས་གསོལ་པ་[སངས་རྒྱས་བཅོམ་ལྡན་འདས་རྣམས་ཀྱིས་ཆོས་བསྟན་པ་ཇི་ཙམ་ཞིག་མཐུན་བཀའ་སྩལ་བ། སངས་རྒྱས་བཅོམ…ལྡན་འདས་རྣམས་ཀྱིས་ཆོས་བསྟན་པ་ནི་ཕྱིར་མི་ལྡོག་པའི་ཆོས་ཀྱི་འཁོར་ལོར་མཐུན་ནོ། །གསོལ་པ། བཅོམ་ལྡན་འདས་ཇི་ལྟར་བཅོམ་ལྡན་འདས་ཐེག་པ་གསུམ་ལ་བརྩམས་ཏེ། དེ་ལྟར་ཆོས་སྟོན། བཀའ་སྩལ་པ། རིགས་ཀྱི་བུ་སེམས་ཅན་དེ་དག་ནི་དམན་པ་ལ་མོས་པ་དག་སྟེ། དེ་དག་ཐེག་པ་གཅིག་ལ་མི…འཇུག་པས་ན། ཐབས་མཁས་པས་དེ་དག་དེ་ལྟར་ནི་བར་ཁྲིད་དེ་རིགས་ཀྱི་བུ། སངས་རྒྱས་བཅོམ་ལྡན་འདས་རྣམས་ནི་ཐབས་མཁས་པ་ཆེན་པོ་དང་ལྡན་པའོ། །བཅོམ་ལྡན་འདས

35

དེ་ནི་སྙིགས་མ་ལྔའི་དུས་ན་བྱུང་སྟེ། དེ་དག་ནི་ཐེག་པ་གཅིག་ལ་མ་མོས་པ་དག་གོ] སོགས་ཀྱིས་ཐེག་པ་གཅིག་ལ་མི་འཇུག[33]པ་ཁ་དྲང་བའི་ཕྱིར་དུ་ཐེག་པ་གསུམ་བསྟན་པ་བཤད་པ་དང་། དཔལ་ཕྲེང་སེང་གེའི་ང་རོའི་མདོ་ལས། ཡོངས་སུ་མྱ་ངན(ཕྲ)ལས་འདས་པ་ཞེས་[བྱ་བ་ནི། དེ་བཞིན་གཤེགས་པ་རྣམས་ཀྱི་ཐབས་སོ། །ཐེག་པ་གསུམ་པོ་ཐམས་ཅད་ཀྱང་ཐེག་པ་གཅིག་པོའི…གྲངས་སུ་འགྲོ་སྟེ། ཐེག་པ་གཅིག་ཁོང་དུ་ཆུད་པས་བླ་ན་མེད་པ་ཡང་དག་པར་རྫོགས་པའི་བྱང་ཆུབ་ཁོང་དུ་ཆུད་དོ།] སོགས་ཀྱིས་མྱང་འདས་མཐར་ཐུག་སངས་རྒྱས་མིན་པ་ལ…མེད་པར་བཤད་པ་དྲངས་ཡ་ཕྱོགས་གཅིག་སྟེ་མདོ་འདི་དག་དྲང་བའི་ཕྱིར་དང་། སྡོད(ཞི)འདིར་སྔར་ལྟར་དགྲ་བཅོམ་འཆི…འཕོ་དང་སྐྱེ་རྒྱུད་བཤད་པས་དགྲ་བཅོམ་པ་སླར་མི་སྐྱེ་བ་དྲང་དོན་དུ་སྟོན་པ། [འཕགས་པ་ལང་ཀར་གཤེགས་པའི་མདོ་ལས་ཀྱང་། ཉན་ཐོས་དང་། རང་སངས་རྒྱས་རྣམས་བག་ཆགས…ཀྱི…ཉེས་པ་དང་། ཏིང་ངེ་འཛིན་གྱི…མྱོས་པ་མེད་པར་གྱུར

36

ནས། ཟག་པ་མེད་པའི་དབྱིངས་ནས་སླར་སད་དེ། ཡང་འཇིག་རྟེན་གྱི་དང་། འཇིག་རྟེན་ལས་འདས་པ་ཟག་པ་མེད་པའི…དབྱིངས་སུ་གསོགས་པའི་ཚོགས་རྣམས་ཡོངས་སུ་བཀང་ནས། ཆོས་ཀྱི་སྐུ་བསམ་གྱིས་མི་ཁྱབ་པ་ལ་དབང་བྱེད་པར་རབ་ཏུ་ཐོབ་པར་འགྱུར་རོ། །ཞེས་གསུངས་སོ།] ལང་གཤེགས་ལས། ཏིང་ངེ་འཛིན་གྱི་བདེ་བ་ལ་གནས་པ་ཐོབ་ནས་ཉན་ཐོས་རྣམས་ཀྱང་རྒྱལ་བའི་སྐུའི་སྐུ་ཉིད་རབ་ཏུ་འཐོབ་པར་འགྱུར་རོ། །ཞེས་དང་།

ཏིང་ངེ་འཛིན་གྱི…ལུས་ཐོབ་ནས།།[34]
[བསྐལ་པའི་བར་དུ་དེ་མི་སད།།
ཇི་ལྟར་སྨྱོས་བུ་ར་རོ་བ།།
ཆང་དང་བྲལ་ནས་སད་འགྱུར་བཞིན།།
དེ་ན་དེ་དག་ང་ཡི་ཡང་།།
ཆོས་ཀྱི་སྐུ་ནི་ཐོབ་པར་འགྱུར།།]

སོགས་ཀྱིས་ཀྱང་དགྲ་བཅོམ་པ་སླར་སྐྱེ་རྒྱུ་ལ་དང་། སངས

37

རྒྱས་ཀྱིས་བསྐུལ་ནས་ཐེག་ཆེན་གྱི་ལམ་སྒྲུབ་ཚུལ་སོགས་
མདོ་མང་ཡང་མཐར་ཐུག[35]ཐེག་པ་གཅིག་ཏུ་སྟོན་པ་ཞེས་གྲགས་
གཅིག་ཅེས་པ་ལྟ་བུ་ཡིན་ལ། དེར་མ་ཟད་གཞན་ཡང་རིགས་
སོ་སོ་བདེན་པར་ཡོད་པ་དྲང་དོན་དུ་སྟོན་པའི་མདོ་ཏིང་འཛིན་
རྒྱལ་པོ་ལས།
བདེ་གཤེགས་སྙིང་པོས་འགྲོ་བ་ཡོངས་ལ་དང་།།
འདི་ན་སྐལ་མེད་སེམས་ཅན་འགའ་ཡང་མེད།།
ལྟ་བུ་དང་། བདེ་གཤེགས་སྙིང་པོའི་མདོ་དང་རྒྱུད་བླ་མས་...
སེམས་ཅན་ཐམས་ཅད་ལ་སངས་རྒྱས་ཀྱི་རིགས་ཡོད་པར་
བཤད་པ་རྣམས་.......... ཀྱང་ཐེག་པ་གཅིག་སྟོན་པར་བསྡུས་
ཙམ་མོ། །དེས་ན་...འཇུག་པ་ལས།
རྣམ་པ་དེ་ལྟའི་མདོ་སྡེ་གཞན་ཡང་ནི།།
(ཐ)
དྲང་དོན་ཉིད་དུ་ལུང་འདིས་གསལ་བར་བྱེད།།
ཅེས་པའི་རང་འགྲེལ་ལས། རྣམ་པ་དེ་ལྟ་བུའི་མདོ་སྡེ་གང་
ཞེ་ན། ཇི་སྐད་དུ་དགོངས་འགྲེལ་བའི་མདོ་ལས། བརྟགས་[36]

38

པ་དང་གཞན་གྱི་དབང་དང་། ཡོངས་སུ་གྲུབ་པ་ཞེས་གསུངས་
པའི་རང་བཞིན་གསུམ་བསྟན་པ་ལས་བཏགས་པ་མེད་པ་ཉིད་དང་
གཞན་གྱི་དབང་ཡོད་པ་ཉིད་དང་། དེ་བཞིན་དུ།
ལེན་པའི་རྣམ་པར་ཤེས་པ་ཟབ་ཅིང་ཕྲ།།
ས་བོན་ཐམས་ཅད་ཆུ་བོའི་རྒྱུན་བཞིན་འབབ།།
བདག་ཏུ་རྟོགས་པར་གྱུར་ན་མི་རུང་ཞེས།།
འདི་ནི་བྱིས་པ་རྣམས་ལ་ངས་མ་བསྟན།།
ཞེས་བྱ་བ་ལ་སོགས་པ་སྟེ། འདི།
ཇི་ལྟར་ནད་པ་ན་བ་ལ།།
སྨན་པས་སྨན་རྣམས་གཏོང་བ་ལྟར།།
སངས་རྒྱས་དེ་བཞིན་སེམས་ཅན་ལ།།
སེམས་ཙམ་དུ་ཡང་རབ་ཏུ་གསུང་།།
ཞེས་གསུངས་པའི་ལུང་འདིས་དྲང་བའི་དོན་ཉིད་དུ་གསལ་
བར་བྱེད་དོ། །ཞེས་གསུངས་པ་ལྟར། སྨན་པས་ནད་པ་དང་
འཚམ་པའི་སྨན་སོ་སོར་གཏོང་བ་ལྟར་སངས་རྒྱས་ཀྱིས་

39

ཀྱང་། གདུལ་བྱ་ལ་སེམས་ཙམ་སོགས་སྟོན་གསུངས་པ་དང་།
སེམས་ཅན་གྱི་བསམ་པའི་དབང་ཙམ་གྱིས་བསྟན་པ་ཐམས་
ཅད་དྲང་དོན་དང་། དེ་ལྟར་བཟུང་ན་འཁྲུལ་པ་སྨིག་རྒྱུ་ལ་ཆུར་
འཛིན་ལྟ་བུར་འགྲོ་བས་ཚིག་ལ་མི་ཆགས་པར་ངེས་དོན་...
བཙལ་དགོས་པར་བཤད་པ་ལང་གཤེགས་ལས། མདོ་སྡེ་
ནི་སེམས་ཅན་གྱི་བསམ་པ་བཞིན་བསྟན་པ་དོན་འཁྲུལ་པ་
ཡིན་ཏེ། དེ་ཁོ་ནའི་གཏམ་མིན་ནོ། །དཔེར་ན་སྨིག་རྒྱུ་ནི་ཆུ་...
མེད་པས་ཆུར་ཞེན་པའི་རི་དྭགས་སླུ་བ་བཞིན་དུ་བསྟན་...
པའི་ཆོས་ཀྱང་བྱིས་པ་མགུ་བར་བྱེད་ཀྱི་འཕགས་པའི་ཡེ་
ཤེས་རྣམ་པར་དགོད་པའི་གཏམ་མིན་ནོ། །དེས་ན་ཁྱོད་...
ཀྱིས་དོན་གྱི་རྗེས་སུ་འབྲང་བར་བྱ་ཡི་བརྗོད་པ་ལ་ཆགས་པར་
མི་བྱའོ། ཞེས་གསུངས་པ་ལ་འདིས་དྲང་དོན་ཐམས་ཅད་
བཤད་མོད། སོ་སོར་བཤད་ན་སྐབས་འདིར་སེམས་ཙམ་
དང་ཕྱི་དོན་མེད་པ་དང་། དེ་བཞིན་གཤེགས་པའི་སྙིང་པོའི་
མདོ་ལས་སེམས་ཅན་ཐམས་ཅད་ཀྱི་རྒྱུད་ལ་སྙིང་པོ་རྟག་...

40

བརྟན་མཚན་དཔེ་ཅན་བཤད་པ་དང་། ཀུན་གཞི་བཤད་པ་དང་།
[གཞན་དབང་ཡོངས་གྲུབ་བདེན་གྲུབ་ཏུ་བཤད་པ་དང་།] མཐར་
[37] ཐུག་ཐེག་གསུམ་སྟོན་པའི་མདོ་ལྟ་བུ་དོན་དུ་འཆད་དེ། ལང་
གཤེགས་ལས་ནད་པའི་དཔེས་སེམས་ཙམ་བསྟན་པར་....
བཤད་པ་དེས་དགོངས་འགྲེལ་བྱམས་ཞུས་ལས་སེམས་..
ཙམ་དུ་བཤད་པ་དྲང་དོན་དུ་བཤད་ལ། (ཀི) ས་བཅུ་པ་ལས། ཁམས་
གསུམ་པོ་འདི་ནི་སེམས་ཙམ་མོ། །ཞེས་པ་མུ་སྟེགས་ཀྱི་བྱེད་
པོ་མེད་པར་སེམས་ཙམ་ཞིག་གཙོ་བོར་བྱེད་པ་པོ་ལེགས
[38] ལྡན་ལྟར་བཤད་དེ། འཇུག་པ་ལས།

མངོན་གྱུར་མངོན་ཕྱོགས་བྱང་ཆུབ་སེམས་དཔའ་ཡིས།།
སྲིད་གསུམ་རྣམ་ཤེས་ཙམ་དུ་གང་རྟོགས་པ།།
རྟག་བདག་བྱེད་པོ་བཀག་པ་རྟོགས་ཕྱིར་དེས།། [39]
བྱེད་པ་པོ་ནི་སེམས་ཙམ་ཡིན་པར་རྟོགས།།

ཞེས་ས་བཅུ་པ་རང་ལས་བཤད་ལ། དེར་མ་ཟད་ལང་གཤེགས
ལས་ཀྱང་།

41

གང་ཟག་རྒྱུན་དང་ཕུང་པོ་དང་།།
དེ་བཞིན་རྐྱེན་དང་རྡུལ་དག་དང་།།
གཙོ་བོ་དབང་ཕྱུག་བྱེད་པོ་རྣམས།།
སེམས་ཙམ་དུ་ནི་ངས་བཤད་དོ།།

ཞེས་ཆོས་འདི་པ་ཡིན་ཀྱང་གང་ཟག་རྫས་ཡོད་དང་། རྒྱུན་...
དང་ཕུང་པོ་གང་ཟག་ཏུ་འདོད་པ་བྱེད་པོ་དང་རྐྱེན་རྫས་ཡོད་...
བྱེད་པོ་དང་། བྱེ་བྲག་པ་རྡུལ་ཕྲ་རབ་འཇིག་རྟེན་བྱེད་པོ་དང་།
གྲངས་ཅན་གཙོ་བོ་དང་། དབང་ཕྱུག་པ་དབང་ཕྱུག་བྱེད་པོར
སྨྲ་བ་བསལ་ཏེ། སེམས་ཙམ་ཞིག་བྱེད་པོར་གསུངས་པའི
ཕྱིར་དང་། (ཡི) སེམས་ལས་གཟུགས་མེད་ན་འདུ་བྱེད་ཀྱི་རྐྱེན...
གྱིས་རྣམ་ཤེས་[ཅིའི་ཕྱིར་] [40] གསུངས་ཤིང་མིང་གཟུགས་སོགས་ཀྱང་ [41]
བཀར་སྐྱལ་ཡང་མི་འགྱུར་ལ་སེམས་ཀྱིས་འཇིག་རྟེན་སྣ་ཚོགས
བྱས་པར་བཤད་པས། སེམས་གཙོ་བོར་མིན་པའི་བྱེད་པོ
བཀག་པར་ཞེས་སོ། །འོ་ན་ལང་གཤེགས་ལས།

ཕྱི་རོལ་སྣང་བ་ཡོད་མིན་ཏེ།།

42

སེམས་ནི་སྣ་ཚོགས་རྣམས་སུ་སྣང་།། [42]
ལུས་དང་ལོངས་སྤྱོད་གནས་འདྲ་བ།།
སེམས་ཙམ་དུ་ནི་ངས་བཤད་དོ།།

ཞེས་པ་འང་དེ་ལྟར་བཤད་དམ་སྙམ་ན་མིན་ཏེ། འདིར་ཕྱི་རོལ་
མེད་པ་སེམས་ཙམ་ཞེས་བཤད་ཅིང་ལུས་ལོངས་སྤྱོད་གནས་
སུ་སྣང་བ་ཡང་སེམས་ཀྱི་ངོ་བོར་བཤད་པ་དང་དགོངས་འགྲེལ་
སོགས་ཀྱིས་དེ་ལྟར་བཤད་པ་གདུལ་བྱ་གཟུགས་སོགས་ལ་
ཆགས་པ་བཟློག་པའི་ཆེད་དུ་དགོངས་གཞི་རིགས་པ་དྲུག་ཏུ་ (ཟ)
པ་ལྟར་སེམས་ཀྱི་རྣམ་པས་བཞག་ཙམ་ལ་དགོངས་པར་མངོན་
པས་དེ་ལྟར་བཤད་ལ་ལེགས་ལྡན་དང་སློབ་དཔོན་འདི་གཉིས་..
ཀའི་སེམས་ཙམ་བཀག་པ་འཕགས་པའི་དགོངས་པ་ཡིན་
ཏེ། (ས) བྱང་ཆུབ་སེམས་འགྲེལ་ལས།

འདི་དག་ཐམས་ཅད་སེམས་ཙམ་ཞེས།།
ཐུབ་པ་ཡིས་ནི་གང་གསུངས་པ།།
བྱིས་རྣམས་སྐྲག་པ་སྤང་དོན་ཏེ།།

43

དེ་ཉིད་བཞིན་ཉིད་མ་ཡིན༎
ཞེས་དང་། རིན་ཆེན་ཕྲེང་བ[43]་ལས་ཀྱང་།
བརྡའ་སྤྲོད་པ་དག་ཇི་ལྟ་བུར༎
ཡི་གེའི་ཕྱི་མོ་ཀློག་འཇུག་ལྟར༎
དེ་བཞིན་སངས་རྒྱས་གདུལ་བྱ་ལ༎
ཇི་ཙམ་བཟོད་པའི་ཆོས་སྟོན་ཏོ༎
ནས།
[ཁ་ཅིག་ལ་ནི་སྡིག་པ་ལས༎
རྣམ་པར་བཟློག་ཕྱིར་ཆོས་སྟོན་ཏེ༎
ཁ་ཅིག་བསོད་ནམས་འགྲུབ་བྱའི་ཕྱིར༎]
ཁ་ཅིག་ལ་ནི་གཉིས་བརྟེན[44]་པ༎
ཁ་ཅིག་ལ་ནི་གཉིས་མི་བརྟེན[44]༎
ཟབ་མོ་སྐྲག་འཇིགས་ཅན་འཇིགས་པ༎
སྟོང་ཉིད་སྙིང་རྗེའི་སྙིང་པོ་ཅན༎
བྱང་ཆུབ་སྒྲུབ་པ་ཁ་ཅིག་ལའོ༎

44

ཞེས་གསུངས་པས། འཇུག་པར།
མདོ་སྡེ་གང་ལས་ཕྱི་རོལ་སྣང་ཡོད་མིན༎
སེམས་ནི་སྣ་ཚོགས་སྣང་ངོ་ཞེས་གསུངས་པ༎
གཟུགས་ལ་ཤིན་ཏུ་ཆགས་གང་དེ་དག་ལ༎
གཟུགས་བཟློག་པ་སྟེ་དེ་ཡང་དྲང་དོན་ཉིད༎

ཅེས་སོ། །དེ་བཞིན་དུ་ལང་(ཀ)ཀར་གཤེགས་པ་ལས། བཅོམ་ལྡན་འདས་ཀྱིས[45]་མདོ་བརྗོད་པ་ལས[46]་དེ་བཞིན་གཤེགས་པའི་སྙིང་པོ······གསུངས[47]་པ་དེ་བཅོམ་ལྡན་འདས་ཀྱིས[48]་རང་བཞིན་གྱིས་འོད······གསལ་བ་རྣམ་པར[49]་དག་པས་ཐོག་མ་ནས་རྣམ་པར་དག་པ··ཉིད་མཚན་སུམ་ཅུ་རྩ་གཉིས་དང་ལྡན་པ། སེམས་ཅན་ཐམས་ཅད་ཀྱི་ལུས་ཀྱི་ནང་ན་མཆིས་པར་བརྗོད་དེ། ཞེས་པ་ནས། (བཅོམ་ལྡན་འདས་ཀྱིས་རིན་པོ་ཆེ་རིན་ཐང་ཆེན་པོ་གོས་དྲི་མ་ཅན་གྱིས་ཡོངས་སུ་དཀྲིས་པ་ལྟར་ཕུང་པོ་དང་། ཁམས་དང་། སྐྱེ་མཆེད་ཀྱི་གོས་ཀྱིས་ཡོངས་སུ་དཀྲིས་པ། འདོད་ཆགས་དང་། ཞེ་སྡང་དང་། གཏི་མུག་གིས་ཟིལ་གྱིས་ནོན་པ། ཡོངས་

45

སུ་རྟོག་པའི་དྲི་མས་དྲི་མ་ཅན་དུ་གྱུར་པ། རྟག་པ་དང་། བརྟན་པ་ཐེར་ཟུག་པར་ནི་བརྗོད་ན། བཅོམ་ལྡན་འདས་དེ་བཞིན་གཤེགས་པའི་སྙིང་པོར་སྨྲ་བ་འདི་མུ་སྟེགས་བྱེད་ཀྱི་བདག་ཏུ་སྨྲ་བ་དང་ཇི་ལྟར་མི་འདྲ་བ་ལགས། བཅོམ་ལྡན་འདས་མུ་སྟེགས་བྱེད་རྣམས་ཀྱང་རྟག་པ་དང་། བྱེད་པ་པོ་མ་ཡིན་པ། ཡོན་ཏན་མེད་པ། ཁྱབ་པ་མི་འཇིག་པའོ་ཞེས་བདག་ཏུ་སྨྲ་བ་སྟོན་པར་བགྱིད་དོ། །བཅོམ་ལྡན་འདས་ཀྱིས་བཀའ་སྩལ་པ། བློ་གྲོས་ཆེན་པོ་ངའི་དེ་བཞིན་གཤེགས་པའི་སྙིང་པོ་བསྟན་པ་ནི་མུ་སྟེགས་ཅན་གྱི་བདག་ཏུ་སྨྲ་བ་དང་མཚུངས་པ་མ་ཡིན་ཏེ། བློ་གྲོས་ཆེན་པོ་དེ་བཞིན་གཤེགས་པ་དགྲ་བཅོམ་པ་ཡང་དག་པར་རྫོགས་པའི་སངས་རྒྱས་རྣམས་ནི་སྟོང་པ་ཉིད་དང་། ཡང་དག་པའི་མཐའ་དང་། མྱ་ངན་ལས་འདས་པ་དང་། མ་སྐྱེས་པ་དང་། མཚན་མ་མེད་པ་དང་། སྨོན་པ་མེད་པ་ལ་སོགས་པའི་ཚིག་གི་དོན་རྣམས་ལ། དེ་བཞིན་གཤེགས་པའི་སྙིང་པོར་བསྟན་པར་བྱས་ནས། བྱིས་པ་རྣམས་བདག་མེད་པས་འཇིགས

46

པར་འགྱུར་བའི་གནས་རྣམ་པར་སྤང་བའི་དོན་དུ་དེ་བཞིན་གཤེགས་
པའི་སྙིང་པོའི་སྒོ་བསྟན་པས་རྣམ་པར་མི་རྟོག་པའི་གནས་སྣང་བ་
མེད་པའི་སྤྱོད་ཡུལ་སྟོན་ཏེ། འདི་ལ་བློ་གྲོས་ཆེན་པོ་མ་འོངས་
པ་དང་། ད་ལྟར་བྱུང་བའི་བྱང་ཆུབ་སེམས་དཔའ་སེམས་དཔའ་
ཆེན་པོ་རྣམས་ཀྱིས་བདག་ཏུ་མངོན་པར་ཞེན་པར་མི་བྱའོ། །བློ་
གྲོས་ཆེན་པོ་དཔེར་ན་རྫ་མཁན་ནི་འཇིམ་པའི་རྡུལ་གྱི་ཕུང་པོ་
གཅིག་ལས་ལག་པ་དང་། བཟོ་དང་། ལག་རྡུང་དང་། ཆུ་
དང་སྲད་བུ་དང་། ནན་ཏན་ལྡན་པ་ལས་སྣོད་རྣམ་པ་སྣ་ཚོགས་
བྱེད་དོ། །བློ་གྲོས་ཆེན་པོ་དེ་བཞིན་གཤེགས་པ་རྣམས་ཀྱང་ཆོས་
ལ་བདག་མེད་པ་རྣམ་པར་རྟོག་པའི་མཚན་ཉིད་ཐམས་ཅད་
རྣམ་པར་ལོག་པ་དེ་ཉིད་ཤེས་རབ་དང་། ཐབས་ལ་མཁས་པ་
དང་ལྡན་པ་རྣམ་པ་སྣ་ཚོགས་ཀྱིས་དེ་བཞིན་གཤེགས་པའི་སྙིང་
པོར་བསྟན་པའམ། བདག་མེད་པར་བསྟན་པས་ཀྱང་རུང་སྟེ།
རྫ་མཁན་བཞིན་དུ་ཚིག་དང་། ཡི་གེའི་རྣམ་གྲངས་]རྣམ་པ་
སྣ་ཚོགས་ཀྱིས་[50] སྟོན་ཏོ། །ཞེས་པས་སྙིང་པོའི་མདོ་ལས་

47

མཚན་དཔེས་བརྒྱན་པའི་སྐུ་རྟག་པ་སྐྱོབས་སོགས་དང་ལྡན་པ
སེམས་ཅན་ཐམས་ཅད་ཀྱི་རྒྱུད་ལ་ཡོད་པར་བཤད་པ་ལ་དགོངས
གཞི་དགོས་པ་དང་། དངོས་ལ་གནོད་བྱེད་གསུམ་གྱིས་སྔར་ལྟར
དྲང་དོན་དུ་བཤད་ལ་འདི་དང་ཀུན་གཞི་ཡོད་པར་བཤད་པ……
གཉིས་དགོངས་གཞི་སྟོང་ཉིད་ལ་དགོངས་དངོས་ལ་གནོད
བྱེད་སྒྲས་ཟིན་ལྟར་ན་མུ་སྟེགས་པ་ལྟར་འགྱུར[51]་བས་གནོད
པས་དྲང་དོན་དུ་རིགས་པ་གཅིག་གིས་འགྲུབ་སྟེ། འདུག་པར།
ཀུན་གཞི་ཡོད་ཅིང་གང་ཟག་ཉིད་ཡོད་ལ།།
[ཕུང་པོ་འདི་དག་འབའ་ཞིག་ཉིད་ཡོད་ཅེས།།
བསྟན་པ་འདི་ནི་དེ་ལྟར་ཆེས་ཟབ་དོན།།
རིག་པར་མི་འགྱུར་གང་ཡིན་དེ་ལ་འོ།།]
སོགས་དང་། རྒྱན་སྟུག་བཀོད་པ་ལས།
ས་རྣམས་སྣ་ཚོགས་ཀུན་གཞི་སྟེ།།
བདེ་གཤེགས་སྙིང་པོ་དགེ་བའང་དེ།།
སྙིང་པོ་དེ་ལ་ཀུན་གཞིའི་སྒྲས།།

48

དེ་བཞིན་གཤེགས་རྣམས་སྟོན་པར་མཛད།།
སྙིང་པོ་ཀུན་གཞིར་བསྒྲགས་པ་ཡང་།།
བློ་ཞན་རྣམས་ཀྱིས་མི་ཤེས་སོ།།
ཞེས་སེམས་ཅན་ཐམས་ཅད་ཀྱི་སེམས་བདེན་སྟོང་(ས)་རང་བཞིན་
གནས་རིགས་དང་བདེ་གཤེགས་སྙིང་པོ་དང་སངས་རྒྱས་ཀྱི་
རིགས་ཞེས་བྱ་བ་དེ་དངོས་པོ་ཐམས་ཅད་ཀྱི་རང་བཞིན་དུ་རྗེས་
སུ་ཞུགས་པས་ཀུན་གཞི་དང་འདྲེས་རྣམ་པར་ཤེས་པ་དང་
འདེར་རྣམ་པར་ཏེ་བྱེ་བྲག་མ་ཕྱེད་པར་དུ་ཤེས་པས་ན་རྣམ་
ཤེས་ཞེས་བཤད་པ་གཉིས་ལས་ཕྱི་མའི་དབང་དུ་བྱས་ནས་
རྣམ་ཤེས་ཞེས་བསྒྲགས་པའི་ཕྱིར་ཏེ། འདུག་འགྲེལ་ལས།
དངོས་པོ་ཐམས་ཅད་ཀྱི[52]་རང་བཞིན་གྱིས་རྗེས་སུ་ཞུགས་པའི་
ཕྱིར། སྟོང་ཉིད་ཁོ་ན་ཀུན་གཞི་རྣམ་པར་ཤེས་པའི་སྒྲས……
བསྟན་པར[53]་རིག་པར་བྱའོ། །ཞེས་སོ། །འདུག་པར། (ཀ)
དེ་ལྟར་ལུང་གི་ལོ་རྒྱུས་ཤེས་བྱས་ཏེ།།
མདོ་གང་དེ་ཉིད་མ་ཡིན་བཤད་དོན་ཅན།།

[དྲང་དོན་གསུངས་པའང་རྟོགས་ནས་དྲང་བྱ་ཞིང་།།
སྟོང་ཉིད་དོན་ཅན་ངེས་དོན་ཤེས་པར་གྱིས།།]
ཞེས་སོགས་ཀྱིས་སེམས་ཙམ་པའི་མཚན་ཉིད་དང་པོ་གཉིས
ཀྱི་ཡོད་མེད་ཀྱི་ཁྱད་པར་སྟོན་པའི་དགོངས་འགྲེལ་དྲང་དོན
དུ་བཤད་དེ། དངོས་པོ་བདེན་གྲུབ་སོགས་སྟོན་པ་དྲང་དོན
ཡིན་པར་བློ་གྲོས་མི་ཟད་པ་སོགས་ཀྱིས་བཤད་པའི་ཕྱིར་དང་།
མཚན་ཉིད་གསུམ་ལ་ཡོད་མེད་ཀྱི་ཁྱད་པར་ཤེར་ཕྱིན་བྱམས
(ཡུམ)
ཞུས་ལྟར་གཟུགས་ནས་རྣམ་མཁྱེན་གྱི་བར་དོན་དམ་པར
མེད་ལ། འཇིག་རྟེན་གྱི་བརྡའ་དང་ཐ་སྙད་ཙམ་དུ་ཡོད་པའི···
ཕྱིར་ཏེ། ཉི་ཁྲིའི་བྱམས་ཞུས་ལས་གཟུགས་སོགས་ཇི་ལྟར
མཆིས་ཞུས་པའི་ལན་དུ། འཇིག་རྟེན་གྱི་བརྡའ་དང་ཐ་སྙད
དུ་ཡོད་ཀྱི་དོན་དམ་པར་ནི་མ་ཡིན་ནོ། །ཞེས་རྣམ་མཁྱེན་གྱི
བར་ལ་དེ་ལྟར་གསུངས་པའི་ཕྱིར་དང་། དེས་ན་འདུག་འགྲེལ
ལས། ཚིགས་ཙམ་ཞིག་ནི་བརྗོད་པར་བྱ་སྟེ། དཔེར་ན
སྦྲུལ་ནི་[ཐག་པ་བརྟགས་པ་རྟེན་ཅིང་འབྲེལ་བར་འབྱུང

བ་ལ་བཏགས་པ་ཡིན་ཏེ། དེ་དེ་ལ་ཡོད་པ་མ་ཡིན་པའི་ཕྱིར་རོ།
དེ་སྦྲུལ་དངོས་ལ་ནི་ཡོངས་སུ་གྲུབ་པ་ཡིན་ཏེ། དེ་ཀུན་ཏུ་མ·····
བཏགས་པའི་ཕྱིར་རོ། །དེ་བཞིན་དུ་རང་བཞིན་ཡང་གཞན་གྱི
དབང་བྱས་པ་ཅན་ལ་ནི་ཀུན་ཏུ་བཏགས་པ་ཡིན་ཏེ།
རང་བཞིན་དག་ནི་བཅོས་མིན་དང་།།
གཞན་ལ་བལྟོས་པ་མེད་པ་ཡིན།།
ཞེས་འབྱུང་བས་ངོ་བོ་ཉིད་ནི་བྱས་པ་ཅན་མ་ཡིན་ནོ། །བཟུང
བཞིན་པའི་རྟེན་ཅིང་འབྲེལ་བར་འབྱུང་བ་བྱས་པ་ཅན·····
གཟུགས་བརྙན་དང་འདྲ་བ་ལ་བཏགས་པ་གང་ཡིན་པ་དེ
ནི་སངས་རྒྱས་ཀྱི་སྤྱོད་ཡུལ་ལ་ནི་དངོས་ཡིན་ཏེ། ཀུན་ཏུ་མ
བཏགས་པའི་ཕྱིར་ཏེ། དངོས་པོ་བྱས་པ་ཅན་ལ་མ་རིག་པར
རང་བཞིན་འབའ་ཞིག་མངོན་སུམ་དུ་མཛད་པས་དེ་ཉིད···
ཐུགས་སུ་ཆུད་པའི་ཕྱིར་སངས་རྒྱས་ཞེས་བརྗོད་དོ། །དེའི
ཕྱིར་དེ་ལྟར་བཏགས་པ་དང་གཞན་གྱི་དབང་དང་ཡོངས
སུ་གྲུབ་པ་ཞེས་བྱ་བ་ངོ་བོ་ཉིད་གསུམ་རྣམ་པར་བཞག

པ་རྟོགས་པར་བྱས་ནས་མདོའི་དགོངས་པ་རྣམ་པར་བཤད་པར
བྱའོ། །གཟུང་བ་དང་འཛིན་པ་གཉིས་ནི་གཞན་གྱི་དབང་ལས
མ་གཏོགས་པར་དངོས་པོ་མེད་པའི་ཕྱིར་ན། གཞན་གྱི་དབང
ལ་དེ་གཉིས་ཀུན་ཏུ་བཏགས་པ་ཉིད་བསམ་པར་བྱ་སྟེ།]
ཞེས་སོགས་ཀྱི་ཚིག་དོན་ཅུང་གསལ་བྱས་ན། ཀུན་བཏགས
ཚུལ་ནི་རང་བཞིན་གནས་ལུགས་ནི་གཞན་དབང་ལ་སྣང་བ
[སྣར་][54] མེད་བཞིན་དུ་སྒྲོ་བཏགས་ནས་སྣང་བ་ཡིན་ཏེ། གཞན
དབང་རང་གི་སྡོད་ལུགས་སུ་མེད་བཞིན་དུ་ཡོད་པར་སྣང
བ་སྒྲོ་བཏགས་པའི་ཀུན་བཏགས་ཡིན་པའི་ཕྱིར་ཏེ། དཔེར
ན་སྦྲུལ་དེ་ཐག་པ་ལ་མེད་བཞིན་དུ་ཐག་པ་སྦྲུལ་འཛིན་གྱི
སྒྲོ་བཏགས་པ་ལྟ་བུ་ཡིན་པའི་ཕྱིར་ཏེ། གཞན་དབང་འདི
རང་བཞིན་བཅོས་མིན་སོགས་ཀྱི་དོན་མ་ཚང་བའི་ཕྱིར།
བཟུང་བཞིན་པ་འཇམ་མཐོང་བཞིན་པའི་གཞན་དབང་སྣང
ཚུལ་གནས་ཚུལ་མི་མཐུན་པའི་གཟུགས་བརྙན་ལྟ་བུའི
རང་བཞིན་གཤིས་ལུགས་ནི་སངས་རྒྱས་ཀྱི་གཟིགས

52

པ་ལྟར་ཡོངས་གྲུབ་དངོས་ཡིན་ཏེ། དེ་ལ་མེད་བཞིན་དུ་ཡོད་པར་སྒྲོ་མ་བཏགས་པར་གཟིགས་པའི་ཕྱིར། དཔེར་ན་སྤྲུལ་དེ་སྤྲུལ་དངོས་ལ་སྒྲོ་མ་བཏགས་པར་བཟུང་བའི་དོན་ཡོངས་སུ་གྲུབ་པ་བཞིན་ཡིན་པའི་ཕྱིར། འདིས་ཡོངས་གྲུབ་ཀྱི་མཚན་ཉིད་དང་སྒྲ་བཤད་གྲུབ་ཅིང་། གཞན་དབང་ནི་ཀུན་བཏགས་ཀྱི་སྒྲོ་འདོགས་གཞི་དང་། ཡོངས་གྲུབ་ཀྱི་སྟོང་གཞིར་བཤད་དོ།[55] གལ་ཏེ་བྱམས་ཞུས་ལས། བྱམས་པ་ཀུན་བཏགས་པའི་···· གཟུགས་དེ་ནི་རྫས་སུ་མེད་པར་བལྟ་བར་བྱའོ། །རྣམ་པར་བཏགས་པའི་གཟུགས་གང་ཡིན་པ་དེ་ནི་རྣམ་པར་རྟོག་པ་··· རྫས་སུ་ཡོད་པའི་ཕྱིར། རྫས་སུ་ཡོད་པར་བལྟ་བར་བྱ་སྟེ་རང་དབང་འབྱུང་བའི་ཕྱིར་ནི་མ་ཡིན་ནོ། ཞེས་གསུངས་པ་·· ཇི་ལྟར་ཞེ་ན། འདིའི་རྫས་སུ་ཡོད་པ་ནི་ཡོད་ཙམ་ཡིན་ཏེ། དེ་ལས··· གཞན་འདུས་བྱས་ཀྱི་རྫས་དང་རྫས་ཡོད་ཀྱི་རྫས་དང་རང་བཞིན་གྲུབ་པའམ་བདེན་གྲུབ་ཀྱི་རྫས་གང་ཡང་མ་ཡིན་པར་མདོ་ལས་ཤེས་པའི་ཕྱིར་ཏེ། མདོ་དེ་ཉིད་ལས།

53

འདུ་བྱེད་ཀྱི་མཚན་མའི། ཞེས་སོགས་ནས། [དངོས་པོ་དེ་དང་དེ་དག་ལ་གཟུགས་སོ་ཞེས་མིང་དང་འདུ་ཤེས་དང་ཐ་སྙད་དུ་བྱ་བ་ལ་བརྟེན་ནས། གཟུགས་ཀྱི་ངོ་བོ་ཉིད་དུ་ཡོངས་སུ་བཏགས་པ་གང་ཡིན་པ་འདི་ནི་ཡོངས་སུ་བཏགས་པའི་གཟུགས་སོ།····· བྱམས་པ་འདུ་བྱེད་ཀྱི་མཚན་མའི་དངོས་པོ་དེ་དང་དེ་དག་ལ་ཚོར་བ་དང་། འདུ་ཤེས་དང་། འདུ་བྱེད་དང་། རྣམ་པར་ཤེས་པ་ནས་སངས་རྒྱས་ཀྱི་ཆོས་སོ་ཞེས་བྱ་བའི་བར་དུ་མིང་དང་འདུ་ཤེས་དང་། གདགས་པ་དང་། ཐ་སྙད་དུ་བྱ་བ་ལ་བརྟེན་··· ནས། ཚོར་བའི་ངོ་བོ་ཉིད་དང་། འདུ་ཤེས་དང་། འདུ་བྱེད་དང་། རྣམ་པར་ཤེས་པ་ནས་སངས་རྒྱས་ཀྱི་ཆོས་ཀྱི་ངོ་བོ་ཉིད་དུ····· ཡོངས་སུ་བརྟགས་པ་གང་ཡིན་པ་འདི་དག་ནི། ཡོངས་སུ··· བརྟགས་པའི་ཚོར་བ་དང་། འདུ་ཤེས་དང་། འདུ་བྱེད་དང་། རྣམ་པར་ཤེས་པ་ནས། སངས་རྒྱས་ཀྱི་ཆོས་ཀྱི་བར་དུ་འདི··· དག་ནི་ཡོངས་སུ་བཏགས་པའི་སངས་རྒྱས་ཀྱི་ཆོས་སོ། འདུ་བྱེད་ཀྱི་མཚན་མའི་དངོས་པོ་དེ་དང་དེ་དག་ལ་རྣམ་པར

54

རྟོག་པའི་ཆོས་ཉིད་ཙམ་དུ་གནས་པའི་རྣམ་པར་རྟོག་པ་ལ་བརྟེན་ནས། མངོན་པར་སྦྱ་བ་གང་ལ་འདི་ནི་མིང་དང་། འདུ་ཤེས་དང་། གདགས་པ་དང་། ཐ་སྙད་ཀྱི་གཟུགས་སོ། ཚོར་བ་དང་། འདུ་ཤེས་དང་། འདུ་བྱེད་དང་། རྣམ་པར་ཤེས་པ་ནས་སངས་རྒྱས་ཀྱི་ཆོས་ཀྱི་བར་དུའོ། །ཞེས་བྱ་བ་གང་ཡིན་པ་འདི་ནི་རྣམ་པར་བརྟགས་པའི་གཟུགས་སོ། །འདི་ནི་རྣམ་པར་བརྟགས་པའི་ཚོར་བ་རྣམ་པར་བརྟགས་པའི་འདུ་ཤེས་རྣམ་པར་བརྟགས་པའི་འདུ་བྱེད། རྣམ་པར་བརྟགས་པའི་རྣམ་པར་ཤེས་པ་ནས། རྣམ་པར་བརྟགས་པའི་སངས་རྒྱས་ཀྱི་ཆོས་ཀྱི་བར་དུའོ། །དེ་བཞིན་གཤེགས་པ་རྣམས་བྱུང་ཡང་རུང་། དེ་བཞིན་གཤེགས་པ་རྣམས་མ་བྱུང་ཡང་རུང་། ཆོས་ཉིད་དང་། ཆོས་ཀྱི་གནས་ཉིད་ཀྱི་དབྱིངས་འདི་དག་ནི་གནས་པ་ཉིད་དེ། བརྟགས་པའི་གཟུགས་གང་ཡིན་པ་དེས། རྣམ་པར་བརྟགས་པའི་གཟུགས་དེ་རྟག་ཅིང་རྟག་པའི་དུས་བརྟན་ཞིང་བརྟན་པའི་དུས་སུ་ངོ་བོ་ཉིད་མེད་ཅིང་ཆོས་བདག་མེད་

པ་དང་། དེ་བཞིན་ཉིད་དང་། ཡང་དག་པའི་མཐའ་གང་ཡིན་པ་འདི་ནི་ཆོས་ཉིད་ཀྱི་གཟུགས་སོ། །འདི་ནི་ཆོས་ཉིད་ཀྱི་··· ཚོར་བ་དང་། འདུ་ཤེས་དང་། འདུ་བྱེད་དང་། རྣམ་པར་ཤེས་པ་ནས། འདི་དག་ནི་ཆོས་ཉིད་ཀྱི་སངས་རྒྱས་ཀྱི་ཆོས་སོ··· ཞེས་བྱ་བའི་བར་དུའོ། །དེ་སྐད་ཅེས་བཀའ་སྩལ་པ་དང་། བཅོམ་ལྡན་འདས་ལ་བྱང་ཆུབ་སེམས་དཔའ་བྱམས་པས་འདི་སྐད་གསོལ་ཏོ། །བཅོམ་ལྡན་འདས་གཟུགས་འདི་གསུམ་ལས་གཟུགས་གང་རྫས་མ་མཆིས་པར་བལྟ་བར་བགྱི། གང་རྫས་མཆིས་པ་ལགས། གང་རྫས་མཆིས་པ་ཡང་མ་ལགས། རྫས་མ་མཆིས་པ་ཡང་མ་ལགས་ལ། དོན་དམ་པས་རབ་ཏུ་ཕྱེ་བ་ལགས། བཅོམ་ལྡན་འདས་ཚོར་བ་འདི་གསུམ་དང་། འདུ་ཤེས་འདི་གསུམ་དང་། འདུ་བྱེད་འདི་གསུམ་དང་། རྣམ་པར་ཤེས་པ་འདི་གསུམ་ནས། སངས་རྒྱས་ཀྱི་ཆོས་འདི་གསུམ་གྱི་བར་དུ་སངས་རྒྱས་ཀྱི་ཆོས་གང་རྫས་མ་མཆིས་པར་བལྟ་བར་བགྱི། གང་རྫས་མཆིས་པར་བལྟ་བར་བགྱི། གང་རྫས་མ་མཆིས་པ་ཡང་མ་

ལགས། རྫས་མཆིས་པ་ཡང་མ་ལགས་པར་བལྟ་བར་བགྱི་ཞིང་དོན་དམ་པས་རབ་ཏུ་ཕྱེ་བ་ལགས། དེ་སྐད་ཅེས་གསོལ་པ་དང་། བཅོམ་ལྡན་འདས་ཀྱིས་བྱང་ཆུབ་སེམས་དཔའ་བྱམས་པ་ལ་བཀའ་སྩལ་པ། བྱམས་པ་ཡོངས་སུ་བརྟགས་པའི་གཟུགས་གང་ཡིན་པ་དེ་ནི་རྫས་མེད་པར་བལྟའོ། རྣམ་པར་བརྟགས་པའི་གཟུགས་གང་ཡིན་པ་དེ་ནི་རྣམ་པར་རྟོག་པ་རྫས་ཡོད་པའི་ཕྱིར་རྫས་ཡོད་པར་ལྟའི་རང་དབང་དུ་འདུག་པ་ནི་མ་ཡིན་ནོ།] གང་ཆོས་ཉིད་ཀྱི་གཟུགས་དེ་ནི་རྫས་སུ་མེད་པ་འང་མིན་རྫས་སུ་ཡོད་པ་འང་མ་ཡིན་ཞིང་། དོན་དམ་པས་རབ་ཏུ་ཕྱེ་བར་བལྟ་བར་བྱའོ། །ཞེས་དང་། ལེགས་བཤད་སྙིང་པོ་ལས། དེའི་ཕྱིར་བྱམས་ཞུས་ལས་རྫས་སུ་ཡོད་མེད་གསུངས་པའི་རྫས་ནི་གཞུང་གཞན་ནས་རྫས་བཏགས་གཉིས་བཤད་[56] པའི་རྫས་ཀྱང་མིན་ལ། དབུ་མ་པས་རང་གི་མཚན་ཉིད་ཀྱིས་གྲུབ་པ་ལ་རྫས་སུ་བཤད་པ་ཡང་མིན་པས་ཡོད་པ་ཙམ་མོ། །ཞེས་གསུངས་སོ། །དེས་ན་ས་བཅུ་པ་ལས།

ཁམས་གསུམ་པོ་འདི་ནི་སེམས་ཙམ་མོ།།
ཞེས་དང་།
ཐོག་མ་མེད་པའི་དུས་ཀྱི་ཁམས།།
[ཆོས་རྣམས་ཀུན་གྱི་གནས་ཡིན་ཏེ།།
དེ་ཡོད་པས་ན་འགྲོ་ཀུན་དང་།།
མྱ་ངན་འདས་པའང་ཐོབ་པ་ཡིན།།]

ཞེས་སོགས་ཀྱི་དོན་སྒྲ་ཇི་བཞིན་པར་སྨྲས་འདིར་ཁས་ལེན་པས་སེམས་ཙམ་པས་སྒྲ་ཇི་བཞིན་པའམ་ངེས་དོན་དུ་ཁས་ལེན་པ་ཐམས་ཅད་འདི་པས་སྒྲ་ཇི་བཞིན་མིན་པས་ཁྱབ་པ་དང་། བཟློག་ནས་ཁྱབ་པ་གང་ཡང་འདོད་པར་མི་བྱའོ།། ||

ཐུག་པ་སྒྲུབ་མཐའ་ལ། གཞི་ལམ་འབྲས་བུའི་རྣམ་བཞག་གསུམ་ལས། དང་པོ་ལ་དགག་བྱའི་དང་། འགོག་བྱེད··· རིགས་པའི་དང་། གཞི་བདེན་གཉིས་ཀྱི་དང་། ཐུན་མོང་མ་ཡིན་པའི་དང་། དེ་དག་ངེས་བྱེད་ཚད་མའི་ཁྱད་པར་འཕྲུལ་སྤྱོད་དང་བཅས་པ་ལྔ་ལས། དང་པོ་ལ། དགག་བྱའི་ཚད་

58

དང་། དེའི་འཆད་པ་གཉིས་ལས། དང་པོ་ནི།

འཁོར་འདས་སྣང་གྲགས་ཇི་སྙེད་ཀུན།།
མ་བརྟགས་ལྷན་སྐྱེས་འཛིན་རྟེན་ཙ་སྙད་དུ།།
འཛོག་ཕྱིར་རྟོག་པས་བཏགས་པ་མིན་ཡུལ་སྟོང་ནས།།
གྲུབ་དང་རྫས་ཡོད་རང་མཚན་རང་ངོས་གྲུབ།། 57
བདེན་གྲུབ་ངོ་བོས་གྲུབ་སོགས་དགག་བྱར་གཅིག།

ཅེས་སྨྲས་ཏེ། འཁོར་བ་ཀུན་ཉོན་ཕྱོགས་དང་བྱང་འདས་རྣམ་བྱང་ཕྱོགས་ཀྱི་གཟུགས་སོགས་ཆོས་སྣང་ཞིང་ཡིད་ལ་རྣམ་པ་ཤར་བ་ནི་ཡིད་ལ་གྲགས་པའི་ཇི(ཀ)ལྟ་བ་དང་ཇི་སྙེད་པས་བསྡུས་པ་ཀུན། བདེན་གྲུབ་ཏུ་འཛིན་པས་སྒྲོ་མི་འདོགས་པའི་འཛིན་རྟེན་པའི་ལྷན་སྐྱེས་བཏགས་དོན་མི་དཔྱོད་པའི་ངོ་བོར་འཛིན… 58 དགོས་པའི་ཕྱིར། ཇི་ལྟ་ཇི་སྙེད་ཐམས་ཅད་སྒྲ་རྟོག་གིས… པར་བཏགས་ཙམ་ཡིན་ཏེ། དེ་དག་མིང་གིས་པར་བཏགས་ 58 ཙམ་མ་གཏོགས་ཆ་རེ་རེ་དང་ཚོགས་ཙམ་དང་དངོས་པོ… རྣམས་ཀྱི་རྒྱུན་སོགས་གང་ཡང་ཆོས་དེ་མིན་པའི་ཕྱིར་ཏེ།

59

དཔེར་ན་སྨན་རབ་རིབ་ལ་ཚག་ཁྲ་འཁྱིལ་བ་ལ་སྦྲུལ་རྟོག་པས་བཏགས་པ་དང་། རྒྱང་རིང་བ་ནས་ཐོ་ཡོར་ལ་མིར་བློ་བཏགས་ཙམ་བཞིན་ནོ། །རིན་ཆེན་ཕྲེང་བ་ལས།

གཟུགས་ཀྱི་དངོས་པོ་མིང་ཙམ་ཕྱིར།།
(ཁ) ནམ་མཁའ་ཡང་ནི་མིང་ཙམ་མོ།།
འབྱུང་མེད་གཟུགས་ལྟ་ག་ལ་ཡོད།།
དེ་ཕྱིར་མིང་ཙམ་ཉིད་ཀྱང་མེད།།

ཅེས་དང་། བཞི་བརྒྱ་པ་ལས།

རྟོག་པ་མེད་པར་འདོད་ཆགས་ལ།། 59
སོགས་ལ་ཡོད་ཉིད་ཡོད་མིན་ན།།
ཡང་དག་དོན་དང་རྟོག་པ་ཞེས།།
བློ་དང་ལྡན་པ་སུ་ཞིག་འཛིན།།

ཞེས་དང་། དེའི་འགྲེལ་པར། རྟོག་པ་ཡོད་པ་ཁོ་ནས… ཡོད་པ་ཉིད་དང་། རྟོག་པ་མེད་པར་ཡོད་པ་ཉིད་མེད་པ་དེ་དག་ནི་གོར་མ་ཆགས་པར་ཐག་པ་བཛོགས་པ་ལ་བཏགས་

60

པའི་སྦྲུལ་ལྟར་རང་གི་ངོ་བོས་མ་གྲུབ་པར་ངེས་སོ། །ཞེས་དང་། ཡབ་སྲས་འཇལ་བ་ལས། རྒྱལ་པོ་ཆེན་པོ་སྐྱེས་བུ་གང་ཟག་ནི་ཁམས་(ག)དྲུག་པ་རེག་པའི་སྐྱེ་མཆེད་དྲུག་པ། ཡིད་ཀྱི་ཉེ་བར་སྤྱོད་པ་བཅོ་བརྒྱད་པའོ། །ཞེས་པ་ནས། སྐྱེས་བུ་འདི་ནི་ཁམས་དྲུག་པ་ཞེས་གང་སྨྲས་པ་དེ་ཅི་ལས་བརྟེན་ཏེ་སྨྲས་ཤེ་ན་རྒྱལ་པོ་ཆེན་པོ་ཁམས་དྲུག་ནི་འདི་དག་གོ །དྲུག་གང་ཞེ་ན། འདི་ལྟ་སྟེ། སའི་ཁམས་དང་། ཆུའི་ཁམས་དང་། མེའི་ཁམས་དང་། རླུང་གི་ཁམས་དང་། ནམ་མཁའི…ཁམས་དང་། རྣམ་པར་ཤེས་པའི་ཁམས་སོ། །རྒྱལ་པོ་ཆེན་པོ་དེ་དག་ནི་ཁམས་དྲུག་སྟེ། སྐྱེས་བུ་འདི་ནི་ཁམས་དྲུག་པའོ། ཞེས་ངས་སྨྲས་པ་དེ་ནི་དེ་ལ་བརྟེན་ཏེ་སྨྲས་སོ། །སྐྱེས་བུ་དེ་ནི་རེག་པའི་སྐྱེ་མཆེད་དྲུག་པའོ། །ཞེས་གང་སྨྲས་པ་དེ་ཅི་ལས་བརྟེན་ཏེ་སྨྲས་ཤེ་ན། རྒྱལ་པོ་ཆེན་པོ་རེག་པའི་སྐྱེ་མཆེད་དྲུག་ནི་འདི་དག་སྟེ། དྲུག་གང་ཞེ་ན། གཟུགས་རྣམས་ལ་བལྟ་བའི་ཕྱིར་མིག་རེག་པའི་སྐྱེ་མཆེད་དང་། སྒྲ་རྣམས་ལ་ཉན་པའི··

61

ཕྱིར་རྣ་བ་རིག་པའི་སྐྱེ་མཆེད་དང་། དྲི་རྣམས་ལ་སྣོམ་པའི་ཕྱིར
སྣ་རིག་པའི་སྐྱེ་མཆེད་དོ། །རོ་རྣམས་ལ་མྱང་བའི་ཕྱིར་ལྕེ་རིག
པའི་སྐྱེ་མཆེད་དང་། རེག་བྱ་རྣམས་ལ་རེག་པའི་ཕྱིར་ལུས·····
རིག་པའི་སྐྱེ་མཆེད་དང་། ཆོས་རྣམས་རྣམ་པར་ཤེས་པའི
ཕྱིར་ཡིད་རིག་པའི་སྐྱེ་མཆེད་དོ། །རྒྱལ་པོ་ཆེན་པོ་དེ་དག་ནི···
རིག་པའི་སྐྱེ་མཆེད་དྲུག་སྟེ། སྐྱེས་བུ་འདི་ནི་རིག་པའི་སྐྱེ་མཆེད
དྲུག་པའོ་ཞེས་གང་ངས་སྨྲས་པ་དེ་ནི་དེ་ལ་བརྟེན་ཏེ་སྨྲས་སོ།
རྒྱལ་པོ་ཆེན་པོ་སྐྱེས་བུ་འདི་ནི་ཡིད་ཀྱི་ཉེ་བར་སྤྱོད་པ་བཅོ···
བརྒྱད་པའོ་ཞེས་བ་ང་སྨྲས་པ་དེ་ཅི་ལས་བརྟེན་ཏེ་སྨྲས་ཤེ་ན།
རྒྱལ་པོ་ཆེན་པོ་ཡིད་ཀྱི་ཉེ་བར་སྤྱོད་པ་བཅོ་བརྒྱད་ནི་འདི་དག
ཡིན་ཏེ། བཅོ་བརྒྱད་གང་ཞེ་ན། འདི་ལ་མིས་མིག་གིས་གཟུགས
མཐོང་ན། ཡིད་བདེ་བ་དང་ཡིད་མི་བདེ་བ་དང་། བཏང་སྙོམས
སུ་འགྱུར་བར་གཟུགས་ལ་ཉེ་བར་སྤྱོད་དོ། །རྣ་བས་སྒྲ་ཐོས
ན་ཡིད་མི་བདེ་བ་དང་བཏང་སྙོམས་སུ་འགྱུར་བར་སྒྲ་ལ་ཉེ
བར་སྤྱོད་དོ། །སྣས་དྲི་ཚོར་ན་ཡིད་བདེ་བ་དང་། ཡིད་མི་བདེ

62

བ་དང་བཏང་སྙོམས་སུ་འགྱུར་བར་དྲི་ལ་ཉེ་བར་སྤྱོད་དོ། །ལྕེས
རོ་མྱོང་ན་ཡིད་བདེ་བ་དང་། ཡིད་མི་བདེ་བ་དང་བཏང་སྙོམས
སུ་འགྱུར་བར་རོ་ལ་ཉེ་བར་སྤྱོད་དོ། །ལུས་ཀྱིས་རེག་བྱ་ལ···
རེག་ན་ཡིད་བདེ་བ་དང་། ཡིད་མི་བདེ་བ་དང་། བཏང་སྙོམས
སུ་འགྱུར་བར་རེག་བྱ་ལ་ཉེ་བར་སྤྱོད་དོ། །ཡིད་ཀྱིས་ཆོས···
རིག་ན་ཡིད་བདེ་བ་དང་ཡིད་མི་བདེ་བ་དང་། བཏང་སྙོམས
སུ་འགྱུར་བར་ཆོས་ལ་ཉེ་བར་སྤྱོད་དོ། །རྒྱལ་པོ་ཆེན་པོ་དེ
ལ་གང་དག་ཡིད་བདེ་བར་ཉེ་བར་སྤྱོད་པ་དྲུག་དང་། གང
དག་ཡིད་མི་བདེ་བར་ཉེ་བར་སྤྱོད་པ་དྲུག་དང་། གང་དག···
བཏང་སྙོམས་སུ་འགྱུར་བར་ཉེ་བར་སྤྱོད་པ་དྲུག་པོ། དེ་དག
གཅིག་ཏུ་བསྡུས་ན། ཡིད་ཀྱི་ཉེ་བར་སྤྱོད་པ་བཅོ་བརྒྱད་དུ···
འགྱུར་རོ། །རྒྱལ་པོ་ཆེན་པོ་བཅོ་བརྒྱད་པོ་དེ་དག་ནི་ཡིད
ཀྱི་ཉེ་བར་སྤྱོད་པ་སྟེ། རྒྱལ་པོ་ཆེན་པོ་སྤྱོད་པ་འདི་ནི་ཡིད་ཀྱི
ཉེ་བར་སྤྱོད་པ་བཅོ་བརྒྱད་པའོ། །ཞེས་གང་ངས་སྨྲས་པ
དེ་ནི་དེ་ལ་བརྟེན་ཏེ་སྨྲས་སོ། །རྒྱལ་པོ་ཆེན་པོ་དེ་ལ་སའི····

63

ཁམས་ནི་རྣམ་པ་གཉིས་ཏེ། ནང་གི་ཡང་ཡོད། ཕྱི་རོལ་གྱི་ཡང
ཡོད་དོ། རྒྱལ་པོ་ཆེན་པོ་ནང་གི་སའི་ཁམས་གང་ཞེ་ན། གང
ཅི་ཡང་རུང་སྟེ། ལུས་འདི་ལ་ནང་གི་ཁོང་ན་སྲ་བ་དང་།·····
མཁྲང་བའི་རྣམ་པ་དང་ཉེ་བར་གྱུར་པ་དང་ཟིན་པའོ། །དེ···
ཡང་གང་ཞེ་ན་འདི་ལྟ་སྟེ་སྐྲ་དང་ཁ་སྤུ་དང་། སེན་མོ་དང་། སོ
དང་། རྡུལ་དང་དྲི་མ་དང་། པགས་པ་དང་། ཤ་དང་། རྩ་དང་།
རྒྱུ་རྒྱུས་དང་། རུས་པ་དང་། རྐང་དང་། སྙིང་དང་། མཆིན
པ་དང་། གློ་བ་དང་། མཁལ་མ་དང་། མཚེར་བ་དང་།
མཆིན་དྲི་དང་། རྒྱུ་མ་དང་། གཉེ་མ་དང་། ལྷད་པ་དང་། སྤུལ
མོངས་དང་། ཕྱི་ས་དང་། གཞང་དང་། ལྒང་པ་དང་། ལྒང
རྒྱུས་དང་། གཞན་ཡང་གང་ལུས་འདི་ལ་ནང་གི་ཁོང་ན་སྲ
བ་དང་། མཁྲང་བའི་རྣམ་པ་དང་། ཉེ་བར་གྱུར་པ་དང་། ཟིན
པ་འདི་ནི་ནང་གི་སའི་ཁམས་ཞེས་བྱའོ། །རྒྱལ་པོ་ཆེན་པོ
ཕྱི་རོལ་གྱི་སའི་ཁམས་གང་ཞེ་ན། གང་ཅི་ཡང་རུང་སྟེ་ཕྱི
རོལ་གྱི་སྲ་བ་དང་མཁྲང་བའི་རྣམ་པ་དང་ཉེ་བར་མ་གྱུར

64

པ་དང་། མ་ཟིན་པ་འདི་ནི་ཕྱི་རོལ་གྱི་སའི་ཁམས་ཤེས་བྱའོ། །རྒྱལ་པོ་ཆེན་པོ་དེ་ལ་ནང་གི་སའི་ཁམས་འབྱུང་བའི་ཚེ་གང་ནས་ཀྱང་མི་འོང་འགགས་པའི་ཚེ་ཡང་གང་དུ་ཡང་སོགས་པར་མི་འགྲོའོ། རྒྱལ་པོ་བུད་མེད་ནང་དུ་བདག་ནི་བུད་མེད་དོ་ཞེས་རྟོག་ཅིང་དེ་ནང་དུ་བུད་མེད་ཅེས་བརྟགས་ནས། ཕྱི་རོལ་ཏུ་སྐྱེས་པ་ལ་སྐྱེས་པ་ཞེས་རྟོག་གོ །དེ་ཕྱི་རོལ་དུ་སྐྱེས་པ་ལ་སྐྱེས་པ་ཞེས་བརྟགས་ནས་ཆགས་པར་གྱུར་ཏེ། ཕྱི་རོལ་གྱི་སྐྱེས་པ་དང་ཕྲད་པར་འདོད་དོ། སྐྱེས་པ་དེ་ཡང་ནང་དུ་བདག་སྐྱེས་པའོ་ཞེས་རྟོག་སྟེ། ནང་དུ་བདག་ནི་སྐྱེས་པ་ཞེས་བརྟགས་ནས། ཕྱི་རོལ་ཏུ་བུད་མེད་ལ་བུད་མེད་ཅེས་རྟོག་གོ །ཕྱི་རོལ་དུ་བུད་མེད་ལ་བུད་མེད་ཅེས་བརྟགས་ནས་ཆགས་པར་འགྱུར་ཏེ། ཕྱི་རོལ་གྱི་བུད་མེད་དང་ཕྲད་པར་འདོད་དོ། །ཕྲད་པར་འདོད་པས་ཕྲད་པར་འགྱུར་རོ། །ཕྲད་པའི་རྐྱེན་གྱིས་མེར་མེར་པོ་སྐྱེ་བར་འགྱུར་བའི་དུས་དེ་ཡོད་དོ། །རྒྱལ་པོ་ཆེན་པོ་གང་ལ་ཀུན་ཏུ་བརྟགས་པ་དང་། གང་ཀུན་ཏུ་རྟོག་པ་དེ་གཉིས་ཀ་ཡང་མེད་

65

དོ། །བུད་མེད་ལ་ནི་བུད་མེད་མེད་དོ། །སྐྱེས་པ་ལ་ནི་སྐྱེས་པ་མེད་དོ། །དེ་ལྟར་མེད་ཅིང་ཡང་དག་པ་མ་ཡིན་པ་ཀུན་ཏུ་རྟོག་པ་སྐྱེས་ཏེ། ཀུན་ཏུ་རྟོག་པ་དེ་ཡང་ངོ་བོ་ཉིད་ཀྱིས་མེད་དོ། །ཀུན་ཏུ་རྟོག་པ་ཇི་ལྟ་བ་བཞིན་དུ་འཕྲད་པ་དང་མེར་མེར་པོ་ཡང་ངོ་བོ་ཉིད་ཀྱིས་མེད་དོ། །གང་ངོ་བོ་ཉིད་ཀྱིས་མེད་པ་དེ་ཇི་ལྟར་སྲ་བ་སྐྱེད་པར་འགྱུར། རྒྱལ་པོ་ཆེན་པོ་དེ་ལྟར་ཀུན་ཏུ་རྟོག་པ་ཤེས་པར་བྱས་ནས་སྲ་བ་ཉིད་རྟོགས་པར་བྱ་སྟེ། ཅི་ནས་སྲ་བ་ནི་སྐྱེ་བའི་ཚེ། གང་ནས་ཀྱང་མི་འོང་བར་ཤེས་པར་བྱའོ། །རྒྱལ་པོ་ཆེན་པོ་འདི་ད་ལྟར་གང་ལུས་འདི་དུར་ཁྲོད་ཀྱི་མཐར་འགྱུར་བའི་དུས་དེ་ཡོད་དེ། དེའི་སྲ་བ་དེ་འཇིག་ཅིང་འགག་པར་འགྱུར་བའི་ཚེ། ཤར་ཕྱོགས་སུ་མི་འགྲོའོ། །ལྷོ་ཕྱོགས་དང་། ནུབ་ཕྱོགས་དང་། བྱང་ཕྱོགས་དང་། སྟེང་དང་འོག་དང་ཕྱོགས་མཚམས་རྣམས་སུ་ཡང་མི་འགྲོ་སྟེ། རྒྱལ་པོ་ཆེན་པོ་ནང་གི་སའི་ཁམས་ནི་དེ་ལྟར་བལྟའོ། །རྒྱལ་པོ་ཆེན་པོ་འཇིག་རྟེན་གནས་པ་འདི་ནམ་མཁར་གྱུར་པ་ལ་ཚོངས་པའི་

66

གཞལ་མེད་ཁང་རིན་པོ་ཆེ་སྣ་བདུན་གྱི་རྒྱུ་ལས་གྲུབ་པ་གནས་པའི་དུས་དེ་ཡོད་དེ། རྒྱལ་པོ་དེའི་སྲ་བ་དེ་འབྱུང་བའི་ཚེ་གང་ནས་ཀྱང་མི་འོང་ངོ་། །གཞན་འཕྲུལ་དབང་བྱེད་ཀྱི་ལྷ་རྣམས་ཀྱི་གཞལ་མེད་ཁང་རིན་པོ་ཆེ་སྣ་བདུན་གྱི་རྒྱུ་ལས་གྲུབ་པ་འབྱུང་ཡང་། རྒྱལ་པོ་ཆེན་པོ་དེའི་སྲ་བ་དེ་འབྱུང་བའི་ཚེ་གང་ནས་ཀྱང་མི་འོང་ངོ་། འཁོར་ཡུག་དང་འཁོར་ཡུག་ཆེན་པོའི་རི་རབ་རྡོ་རྗེའི་རྒྱུ་ལས་གྲུབ་པ་སྲ་ཞིང་བརྟན་ལ་ཧྲུན་སྟུག་པ་རྣམས་གནས་པར་གྱུར་ཀྱང་། དེ་དག་གི་སྲ་བ་དེ་འབྱུང་བའི་ཚེ། གང་ནས་ཀྱང་མི་འོང་ངོ་། །རིའི་རྒྱལ་པོ་རི་རབ་དང་། གཉའ་ཤིང་འཛིན་དག་དང་། མུ་ཁྱུད་འཛིན་དག་དང་། གཤོལ་མདའ་འཛིན་དག་དང་། རྡོ་རྗེ་འཛིན་དག་དང་། སེང་ལྡེང་ཅན་དག་དང་། རྣམ་པར་འདུད་དག་དང་། རི་ཏ་ན་དག་དང་། བལྟན་སྡུག་དག་དང་། བལྟན་སྡུག་ཆེན་པོ་དག་དང་། ཤིར་སྡི་དག་དང་། ཡོས་ཀྱི་དང་ལྡན་དག་དང་། གདངས་རི་དག་དང་། དེ་མ་ཡིན་པའི་རི་ནག་པོ་དག་གནས་པ་དང་། ཐམས་ཅད

67

དང་ལྡན་པའི་སྟོང་གསུམ་གྱི་སྟོང་ཆེན་པོའི་འཇིག་རྟེན་གྱི་ཁམས
གནས་པ་དང༌། ཛམས་སུ་དཔག་ཚད་བརྒྱད་ཁྲི་བཞི་སྟོང་ཡོད་ལ།
རྒྱར་དཔག་ཚད་དྲུག་ཁྲི་ཡོད་པའི་ས་ཆེན་པོ་གནས་པར་གྱུར་ཀྱང༌
རྒྱལ་པོ་ཆེན་པོ་སྲ་བ་དེ་འབྱུང་བའི་ཚེ་གང་ནས་ཀྱང་མི་འོང་ངོ།
རྒྱལ་པོ་ཆེན་པོ་འཇིག་རྟེན་འདི་འཇིག་པར་འགྱུར་བའི་ཚེ། ས
ཆེན་པོ་འདི་མེས་ཚིག་པའམ། ཆུས་བཤིག་པའམ། རླུང་གིས
གཏོར་བར་འགྱུར་བའི་དུས་དེ་ཡོད་དེ། དེ་མེས་ཚིག་ནས་ནི་ཐ
བ་ཡང་མི་མངོན། ཐལ་བའི་ལྷག་མ་ཡང་མི་མངོན་པར་འགྱུར
རོ། །འདི་ལྟ་སྟེ་དཔེར་ན། ནམ་མཁའ་ལ་མར་རམ། འབྲུ…
མར་གྱི་མེས་བསྲེགས་ན་དུ་བ་འང་མི་མངོན་ཞིང༌། ཐལ…
བའི་ལྷག་མ་ཡང་མི་མངོན་པར་འགྱུར་རོ། །དེ་བཞིན་དུ་སྟོང
གསུམ་གྱི་སྟོང་ཆེན་པོའི་འཇིག་རྟེན་གྱི་ཁམས་འདི་མེས…
ཚིག་པའི་ཚེ། དུ་བ་ཡང་མི་མངོན་ཞིང༌། ཐལ་བའི་ལྷག་མ་ཡང
མི་མངོན་པར་འགྱུར་རོ། །ཆུས་བཤིག་པའི་ཚེ་ཡང་ལྷག
མ་ཙེ་ཡང་མི་མངོན་པར་འགྱུར་ཏེ། འདི་ལྟ་སྟེ་དཔེར་ན།

68

ལན་ཚྭ་ཆུའི་ནང་དུ་ཞུ་བ་ནི་ལྷག་མ་ཅུང་ཟད་ཀྱང་མི་མངོན་པར
འགྱུར་རོ། །དེ་བཞིན་དུ་སྟོང་གསུམ་གྱི་སྟོང་ཆེན་པོའི་འཇིག
རྟེན་གྱི་ཁམས་འདི་ཡང་ཆུས་བཤིག་པའི་ཚེ་ལྷག་མ་ཅུང…
ཟད་ཀྱང་མི་མངོན་པར་འགྱུར་རོ། །རླུང་གིས་གཏོར་བའི
ཚེ་འང་ལྷག་མ་ཅུང་ཟད་ཀྱང་མི་མངོན་པར་འགྱུར་ཏེ། འདི་ལྟ
སྟེ་དཔེར་ན་རྣམ་པར་འཐོར་རླུང་གིས་བདས་པའི་ཚེ་ཕྱེ་ཞུ་ནི
ལྷག་མ་ཅུང་ཟད་ཀྱང་མི་མངོན་པར་འགྱུར་རོ། །དེ་བཞིན་དུ
སྟོང་གསུམ་གྱི་སྟོང་ཆེན་པོའི་འཇིག་རྟེན་གྱི་ཁམས་འདི་ཡང
རླུང་གིས་གཏོར་བའི་ཚེ་ལྷག་མ་ཅུང་ཟད་ཀྱང་མི་མངོན་པར
འགྱུར་རོ། །རྒྱལ་པོ་ཆེན་པོ་དེ་ལྟར་སའི་ཁམས་དེ་འབྱུང་བ
ཡང་སྟོང༌། སའི་ཁམས་འཇིག་པ་དང་འབྱུང་བ་ཡང་ངོ་བོ་ཉིད
ཀྱིས་སྟོང་ངོ༌། །རྒྱལ་པོ་ཆེན་པོ་]སའི་ཁམས་ནི་ཐ་སྙད་ཙམ
མ་གཏོགས་པར་སའི་ཁམས་ཉིད་དུ་མི་དམིགས་ཏེ། ཐ
སྙད་དེ་ཡང་ཡུལ་མེད་མ་ཡིན། སྐྱེས་པ་མ་ཡིན་གྱི། རྒྱལ་པོ
དེ་ལྟར་དེ་ཡང་དག་པ་ཇི་ལྟ་བ་བཞིན་དུ་ཤེས་རབ་ཀྱིས…[60]

69

རྟོགས་ཤིག །ཅེས་དང༌། དེ་བཞིན་དུ་ཁམས་རེ་རེ་ནས་གསུངས[61]
པའི་ཕྱིར་དང༌། མདོ་དེའི་དོན་ནི་མི་དམིགས་ཏེ་ཡན་ཆད་ཀྱིས
མིང་གིས་བཏགས་ཙམ་ལས་མེད་པར་བཤད། ཐ་སྙད་དེ་ཡང
ཡུལ་མེད་མིན་སྐྱེས་པ་མིན་ཞེས་པས་གདགས་གཞི་ཐ་སྙད[62]
པ་དེ་ཡང་བཏགས་ཆོས་ཡུལ་མེད་དང་སྐྱེས་པ་མིན་པར་བཤད
པའི་ཕྱིར། དེའི་དོན་བསྡུས་ནས་རིན་ཆེན་ཕྲེང་བ་ལས།
སྐྱེས་བུ་ས་མིན་ཆུ་མ་ཡིན།།
མེ་མིན་རླུང་མིན་ནམ་མཁའ་མིན།།
རྣམ་ཤེས་མ་ཡིན་ཀུན་མིན་ན།།
དེ་ལས་གཞན་ན་སྐྱེས་བུ་གང༌།།
ཞེས་གསུངས་ཏེ། རྣམ་ཤེས་མ་ཡིན་ཞེས་པ་ཡན་ཆད་ཀྱིས
གདགས་གཞི་རེ་རེ་མ་ཡིན་པར་བཤད། ཀུན་མིན་ཞེས་པས
གདགས་གཞི་ཚོགས་པ་ཡང་མ་ཡིན་པར་བཤད། དེ་ལས
གཞན་ན་ཞེས་པས་གདགས་གཞི་ལ་མ་ལྟོས་པའི་ཡང
མེད་པར་བཤད་པའི་ཕྱིར། དེས་ན་རང་རྒྱུད་པ་སོགས…

70

སྣར་[63]མ་ཡིན་པར་ ཤེར་མདོ་སྣར་བྱུང་འདས་དང་སྟོང་ཉིད་ཀྱང་མེད་དང་རྟོག་པས་[64]ཕར་བཞག་ཙམ་མ་གཏོགས་གདགས་ཡུལ་གྱི་སྙིང་ནས་ཡོད་པ་དང་། རྫས་ཡོད་དང་རྫོགས་ཐུབ་ཏུ་གྲུབ་པ་གཉིས་རྟེན་འབྲེལ་གྱི་བཟློག་ཟླ་དང་། རང་མཚན་གྱིས་[65]གྲུབ་པ་དང་རང་ངོས་ནས་གྲུབ་པ་དང་རང་དབང་གིས་གྲུབ་པ་དང་བདེན་པར་གྲུབ་པ་དང་ངོ་བོ་ཉིད་ཀྱིས་གྲུབ་པ་རྣམས་མིང་མི་གཅིག་པ་མ་གཏོགས་དོན་འདྲ་བར་རྟགས་ཀྱི་དགག་བྱར་དོན་གཅིག་པར་བྱ་སྟེ།[66] བཞི་བརྒྱ་པ་ལས།

འདི་ཀུན་རང་དབང་མེད་པ་སྟེ།།
དེས་ན་བདག་ནི་ཡོད་མ་ཡིན།།

ཞེས་དང་། (ཆ)འགྲེལ་པ་ལས། འདི་ན་གང་རང་གི་ངོ་བོ་དང་རང་བཞིན་དང་རང་དབང་དང་གཞན་ལ་རག་མ་ལས་པ་ཉིད་ཡིན་པ་དེ་ལ་ནི། རང་ལས་[67]གྲུབ་པས་རྟེན་ཅིང་འབྲེལ་པར་འབྱུང་བ་ཡོད་པ་མིན་ནོ། །ཞེས་སོ།། །།གཉིས་པ་ནི།

71

རང་ངོས་མེད་དང་མིང་རྟོག་ཕར་བཏགས་འདེར།།
བྱ་བྱེད་ཀུན་འཇོག་མཐའ་བྲལ་དབུ་མ་སྟེ།།
འདི་ལས་རིགས་ལྡན་གང་ཞིག་ཐག་ཆོད་མཐར།།

ཞེས་སྨྲས་[68]པ་ལ། དེ་ལྟར་དགག་བྱ་ཕྲ་མོ་ནས་ངོས་ཟིན་དགོས་ཏེ། དེ་ངོས་མ་ཟིན་ན་དེ་བཀག་པའི་དངོས་མེད་རྣལ་མ་མི་རྟོགས་པའི་ཕྱིར་ཏེ། སྤྱོད་འཇུག་ལས།

བརྟགས་པའི་དངོས་ལ་མ་རེག་པར།།
དེ་ཡི་[69]དངོས་མེད་འཛིན་མ་ཡིན།།

ཞེས་གསུངས་པའི་ཕྱིར་དང་། དཔེར་ན་སྐྱེ་བ་ཐ་ཕྱི་རང་བཞིན་མེད་པའི་རྣམ་པ་ངོས་མ་ཟིན་པར་སྐྱེ་བ་ཐ་ཕྱི་མི་སྣང་བའི་སྟོང་ཁང་པ་ཙམ་གྱིས་སྟོང་ཉིད་མི་རྟོགས་པར་སངས་རྒྱས་བསྐྱངས་དང་ཟླ་བའི་ཞབས་ཏུ་མས་བཞེད་པའི་ཕྱིར་ཏེ། བུདྡྷ་པཱ་ལི་ཏ་ལས། [སྨྲས་པ། གང་འཇིག་རྟེན་འདི་མེད་དོ། །འཇིག་རྟེན་ཕ་རོལ་མེད་དོ། །སེམས་ཅན་བརྫུས་ཏེ་སྐྱེ་བ་མེད་དོ། །ཞེས་བྱ་བ་ལ་སོགས་པར་ལྟ་བ་དེ་དང་། གང་དངོས་པོ་ཐམས་ཅད

72

མ་སྐྱེས་པ་དང་མ་འགགས་པ་ཞེས་བྱ་བར་ལྟ་བ་དེ་གཉིས་ལ་ཁྱད་པར་ཅི་ཡོད། བཤད་པ། དེ་གཉིས་ལ་ཁྱད་པར་ཤིན་ཏུ་ཆེ་ན། ཁྱོད་ནི་སྟོང་པ་ཉིད་ཀྱི་དོན་རྣམ་པར་མི་ཤེས་ནས་དེ་གཉིས་འདྲའོ་སྙམ་དུ་སེམས་སོ། །འདི་ལ་(E)སོ་སོར་མ་བརྟགས་པར་བཏང་སྙོམས་བྱེད་པ་གང་ཡིན་པ་དང་། སོ་སོར་བརྟགས་ནས་བཏང་སྙོམས་བྱེད་པ་གང་ཡིན་པ་དེ་གཉིས་བཏང་སྙོམས་བྱེད་པར་ནི་འདྲ་མོད་ཀྱི་སོ་སོར་མ་བརྟགས་པར་བཏང་སྙོམས་བྱེད་པ་ནི་མ་རིག་པའི་ཀུན་ཏུ་སྦྱོར་བ་དང་ལྡན་པར་བསྟན་ལ། བཏང་སྙོམས་བྱེད་པ་ཅིག་ཤོས་ནི་སངས་རྒྱས་བཅོམ་ལྡན་འདས་རྣམས་ཀྱིས་ཀུན་ཏུ་བསྟེན་པ་ཡིན་པས།] དེ་གཉིས་ལ་ཁྱད་པར་ཤིན་ཏུ་ཆེ་བ་[70]དེ་བཞིན་དུ་འདི་ལ་ཡང་འཇིག་རྟེན་འདི་མེད་དོ་ཞེས་བྱ་བ་ལ་སོགས་པ་དེ་ལྟར་མཐོང་བ་ནི་མ་རིག་པས་ཀུན་ཏུ་སྐོངས་པའི་སེམས་དང་ལྡན་པ་ཡིན་གྱི། དངོས་པོ་ཐམས་ཅད་ངོ་བོ་ཉིད་སྟོང་པའི་ཕྱིར་མ་སྐྱེས་པ་དང་མ་འགགས་པར་མཐོང་བ་གཅིག་ཤོས་ནི་ཤེས་པ་སྔོན་དུ་བཏང་བ་ཡིན་པས་དེ····

73

གཉིས་ལ་ཁྱད་པར་ཤིན[70]་ཏུ་ཆེའོ། །ཞེས་དང་། ཚིག་གསལ་ལས། འདིར་ཁ་ཅིག་དབུ་མ་པ་ནི་མེད་པ་བ་དང་ ཁྱད་པར་མེད་པ་ཡིན་ཏེ། ཞེས་པ་ནས། [གང་གི་ཕྱིར་དགེ་བ་དང་མི་དགེ་བའི་ལས་དང་། བྱེད་པ་པོ་དང་། འབྲས་བུ་དང་། འཇིག་རྟེན་... ཐམས་ཅད་རང་བཞིན་གྱིས་སྟོང་པར་སྨྲ་བ་ཡིན་ལ། མེད་པ་... དག་ཀྱང་དེ་དག་མེད་དོ་ཞེས་སྨྲ་བར་བྱེད་པ་ཡིན་པ་དེའི་ཕྱིར། དབུ་མ་པ་ནི་མེད་པ་པ་དང་ཁྱད་པར་མེད་དོ་ཞེས་བྱ་བར་བྱེད་དོ།] དེ་ལྟར་ནི་མ་ཡིན་ཏེ། དབུ་མ་པ་དག་ནི་རྟེན་ཅིང་འབྲེལ་པར་... འབྱུང་བ་སྨྲ་བ་ཡིན་ལ། རྟེན་ཅིང་འབྲེལ་པར་འབྱུང་བའི་ཕྱིར་འཇིག་རྟེན་འདི་དང་འཇིག་རྟེན་ཕ་རོལ་ལ་སོགས་པ་ཐམས་ཅད་རང་བཞིན་མེད་པར་སྨྲ་བར་བྱེད་དོ། །མེད་པ་བ་དག་གིས་ནི་དེ་ལྟར་རྟེན་ཅིང་འབྲེལ་པར་འབྱུང་བ་ཡིན་པའི་ཕྱིར། རང་བཞིན་གྱི་སྟོང་ཉིད་ཀྱི་སྒོ་ནས་འཇིག་རྟེན་ཕ་རོལ་ལ་སོགས་པ་དངོས་པོ་མེད་པར་རྟོགས་པ་མ་ཡིན་ཏེ། ཞེས་གསུངས་སོ། །དེའི་ཕྱིར་དགག་བྱ་ཕྲ་མོ་... རང་ངོས་ནས་གྲུབ་པ་རྡུལ་ཙམ་མེད་པ་བཀག་ཀྱང་མིང་ཙམ་དང་

74

རྟོག[71]་པས་ཕར་བཏགས་ཙམ་འདིར་འཁོར་འདས་ཀྱི་བྱ་བྱེད་ཀུན་འཐད་ཤེས་པ་དེ་རང་བཞིན་གྲུབ་པ་སོགས་ཀྱི་ཡོད་མཐའ་དང་རྟག་མཐར་མི་གནས་ལ་ཐ་སྙད་དུ་མིང་ཙམ་ལ་ཐམས་ཅད་རུང་བ་ཆད་མཐའ་དང་མེད་མཐར་མི་གནས་པའི་དབུ་མ་...ཡིན་ཏེ། འོད་སྲུང་གི་ལེའུ་ལས། ཡོད་ཅེས་བྱ་བ་ནི་མཐའ་གཅིག་གོ། མེད་ཅེས་བྱ་བ་དེ་ནི་མཐའ་གཉིས་སོ། །དེ་གཉིས་ཀྱི་དབུས་གང་ཡིན་པ་དེ་ནི། དཔྱད(ཀ)་དུ་མེད་པ་བསྟན[72]་དུ་མེད་པ། རྟེན་མ་ཡིན་པ། སྣང་བ་མེད་པ། རྣམ་པར་རིག་པ་མེད་པ་གནས་མེད་པ་སྟེ། འོད་སྲུང་འདི་ནི་དབུ་མའི་ལམ་ཆོས་རྣམས་ལ་སོ་སོར་... རྟོག་པ་ཞེས་བྱའོ། །ཞེས་དང་། རྩ་ཤེས་ལས་ཀྱང་།

[ཡོད་ཅེས་བྱ་བ་རྟག་པར་འཛིན།།
མེད་ཅེས་བྱ་བ་ཆད་པར་ལྟ།།
དེ་ཕྱིར་ཡོད་དང་མེད་པ་ལ།།
མཁས་པས་གནས་པར་མི་བྱའོ།།]

དེ་ལྟར་གསུངས་པའི་ཕྱིར་དང་། རང་བཞིན་ཕྱིར་ནས་མེད་

75

མཐའ་ཡང་སེལ་ལ་བཏགས་ཙམ་གྱིས[73]་ཡོད་མཐའ་ཡང་སེལ་བས་ན་རང་རྒྱུད་པ་ལྟར་འདི་ལས་དགག་བྱ་རགས་པ་དང་འོད་ཁ་ཅིག་ལྟར་མེད་བཏགས་ཙམ་ལའང་འཇིག་རྟེན་པའི་བདེན་... རྫུན་ཁས་མི་ལེན་པར་སྨྲ་མའི་རྟ་དང་རྟ་གཉིས་ལ་སྣང་བ་ལྟར་གྲུབ་མ་གྲུབ་[འདྲ][74]ཀྱང་ཡོད་མེད་ཀྱི་བདེན་རྫུན་མ་བྱས་ན། ཟླ་བས།

[གལ་ཏེ་ཁྱོད་ལ་འཇིག་རྟེན་མི་གནོད་ན།།
འཇིག་རྟེན་ཉིད་བལྟོས་འདི་ནི་དགག་པར་གྱིས།།]
ཁྱོད་དང་འཇིག་རྟེན་འདི[75]་...ནི་རྩོད་ཀྱིས་དང་།།
[ཕྱི་ནས་སྟོབས་ལྡན་བདག་གིས་བརྟེན་པར་བྱ།།]

ཞེས་དང་།

འཇིག་རྟེན་གྲགས་པའི་ཀུན་རྫོབ་མ་བརྟག་ཅིག།

ཅེས་དང་།

མཐོང་བ་[illegible] འདྲ་རྣམ་པ་གཉིས་འདོད་དེ།།

སོགས་དང་འགལ་ཞིང་མཐར་འཛིན་ལས་མི་འདའ་བར་ཤེས་ནས་ངོར་དགོས་སོ།། །།གཉིས་པ་འགོག་བྱེད་རིགས་པ་ལ།

༧༦

བསྟན་བཤད་གཉིས་ལས། དང་པོ་ནི། རང་རྒྱུད་པ་མན་ཆད་དང་བོད་ཀྱི་ཐལ་འགྱུར་བ་ཁ་ཅིག་ལྟར་བདག་མེད་གཉིས་ལ་ཕྲ····རགས་དགག་བྱ་མི་འདྲ་བར་བྱས་ནས་རིགས་པ་སོ་སོས་གཏན་ལ་འབེབས་སམ་ཞེ་ན། དགག་བྱ་དང་། བདག་མེད་གཉིས་ལ་ཕྲ་རགས་མེད་ཀྱང་གཏན་ལ་འབེབས་པའི་རིགས་པ་སོ་སོར་བསྟན་པའི་ཕྱིར།

གང་ཟག་ཆོས་སྟེང་བདག་གཉིས་དེར་མེད་གཉིས།།
བདག་མེད་གཉིས་བཞེད་ཆོས་བདག་རྡོ་རྗེ་ཡི།།
གཟེགས་མ་ལ་སོགས་བཞིས་འགོག་གང་ཟག་བདག།
[76] ཟླ་བདུན་གྱིས་འགོག་གཉིས་ཀའང་རྟེན་འབྲེལ་གྱིས།།

ཞེས་སྨྲས་ཏེ། དེ་ཡང་བརྒྱ་པའི་འགྲེལ་པ་ལས། དེ་ལ་བདག་ཅེས་བྱ་བ་ནི་གང་ཞིག་དངོས་པོ་རྣམས་ཀྱི་གཞན་[77 (ཏ)] ལ་རག····མ་ལས་པའི་ངོ་བོ་རང་བཞིན་ཏེ། དེ་མེད་པ་ནི····བདག་མེད་པའོ། །དེ་ནི་ཆོས་དང་གང་ཟག་གི་དབྱེ་བས····གཉིས་སུ་རྟོགས་ཏེ། ཆོས་ཀྱི་བདག་མེད་པ་དང་གང་ཟག་

༧༧

གི་བདག་མེད་པ་ཞེས་བྱའོ། །གསུངས་པ་ལྟར་སྨྲ་རྟོག་སོགས་གཞན་ལ་མ་ལྟོས་པ་དང་། རག་མ་ལས་པ་དགག་བྱའི་བདག་དང་དེ་གཞི་གང་ཟག་གི་དང་ཆོས་ཀྱི་སྟེང་དུ་མེད་པ་གཉིས···ནི་རིམ་པ་བཞིན་གང་ཟག་གི་བདག་མེད་དང་ཆོས་ཀྱི་བདག་མེད་ལ་འཇོག་སྟེ་སློབ་དཔོན་སངས་རྒྱས་བསྐྱངས་ཀྱི་[78] དགོངས་པ་ཡིན་ལ། རྡོ་རྗེ་གཟེགས་མ་སོགས་རིགས་པ་བཞིས····ཆོས་བདག་འགོག་ཅིང་། མདོ་དང་རྩ་ཤེས་ནས་རྣམ་ལྔར་བཙལ་བའི་རིགས་པ་དང་། འཇུག་པས་དེའི་སྟེང་དུ་ཚོགས་ཙམ་གདགས་[79] གཞིར་བཤད་པ་ལ་བརྟེན་ནས་ཚོགས་ཙམ་དང་དབྱིབས་བདག་ཏུ་འདོད་པ་འགོག་པ་གཉིས་ཏེ་རྣམ་བདུན་དུ་བཙལ་བའི་རིགས་པས་གང་ཟག་གི་བདག་འགོག་ལ། གཅིག་ཏུ་[80]བྲལ་དང་རྟེན་འབྲེལ་གྱི་རྟགས་ཀྱིས་བདག་གཉིས་ཀ་འགོག་སྟེ་བཤད···པར་འགྱུར།། །།གཉིས་པ་ལ། ཆོས་བདག་འགོག་པའི་དང་། གང་ཟག་གི་བདག་འགོག་པའི་རིགས་པ་འཁྲུལ་སྤོང་དང་བཅས་པ་གཉིས། དང་པོ་ལ། རྡོ་རྗེ་གཟེགས་མ་དང་།

༧༨

མཐའ་བཞི་སྐྱེ་འགོག་དང་ཡོད་མེད་སྐྱེ་འགོག་གི་དང་། རྒྱུ་བཞི་སྐྱེ་འགོག་འཁྲུལ་སྤོང་དང་བཅས་པ་དང་། ཆོས་ཀུན་གཏན་ལ་འབེབས་བྱེད་རྟེན་འབྲེལ་གྱི་རིགས་པ་འཁྲུལ་སྤོང་དང་བཅས་པ་བཞི། དང་པོ་ལ། རྟགས་དགོད་པ་དང་རྩོད་སྤོང་བ་གཉིས། དང་པོ་ནི། འགོད་ཚུལ་ཐོག་མར་ཐལ་འགྱུར་གྱིས་བདེན་ཞེན་གྱི་ལོག་རྟོག་གི་རྩེ་མ་བཅོམ་པར་སྒྲུབ་ངག་མི་བྱེད་པ་མདོ····སེམས་དབུ་མ་པ་གསུམ་མཐུན་ཀྱང་འདིར་བཤད་སྐབས····དབང་དུ་བྱས་ནས།

བདག་དང་གཞན་དང་གཉིས་དང་རྒྱུ་མེད་ལས།།
སྐྱེ་བ་མིན་ཕྱིར་རང་བཞིན་སྐྱེ་བ་མེད།།

ཅེས་སྨྲས་ཏེ། སྐྱེ་ལྡན་(སྐྱེ)གྱི་དངོས་པོ་རྣམས་ཆོས་ཅན། རང་བཞིན་གྱིས་སྐྱེ་བ་མེད་དེ། བདག་དང་གཞན་དང་བདག···[81] གཞན་གཉིས་ཀ་དང་རྒྱུ་མེད་ལས་ཀྱང་སྐྱེ་བ་མེད་པའི་ཕྱིར་ཏེ། དཔེར་ན་མེ་ལོང་གི་གཟུགས་བརྙན་བཞིན། འཇུག་པ་ལས།

གང་གི་ཕྱིར་ན་བདག་དང་གཞན་དང་གཉིས་ཀ་ལས་སྐྱེ་དང༌།།
རྒྱུ་ལ···མ་ལྟོས་ཡོད་པ་མིན་པས་དངོས་རྣམས་རང་བཞིན་བྲལ།།
ཞེས་དང༌། ལམ་སྒྲོན་ལས།
དངོས་པོ་རང་ལས་མི་སྐྱེ་ཞིང༌།།
གཞན་དང་གཉིས་ཀ་ལས་ཀྱང་མིན།།
རྒྱུ་མེད་ལས་མིན་དེ་ཡི་[82]ཕྱིར།།
ངོ་བོ་ཉིད་ཀྱིས་རང་བཞིན་མེད།།

ཅེས་སོ། །བདེན་པར་སྐྱེ་བ་མཐའ་བཞི་གང་རུང་དུ་སྐྱེ་དགོས་ཤིང་དེ་བཞི་གང་ལས་ཀྱང་མ་སྐྱེས་པ་ལ་བདེན་པའི་སྐྱེ་བ་ཁེ···འོང་བས་ཁྱབ་པ་རིགས་པས་གྲུབ་པར་མ་ཟད་བདེན་སྐྱེ་ཁས་ལེན་མཁན་རྣམས་ཀྱིས་ཀྱང་འདོད་ཕྱིར་སྒྲུབ་མི་དགོས་སོ།། ||

གཉིས་པ་རྟགས་ཚུལ་སྒྲུབ་པ་ལ་བཞི་ལས། དང་པོ་ནི།

བདག་ལས་སྐྱེ་ན་དོན་མེད་ཐུག་[83]མེད་འགྱུར།།
གང་དེ་དེ་ཇེ་ན་རྒྱུ་འབྲས་རྟག་མཐོང་འགྱུར།།
འཇིག་རྟེན་མཐོང་འགལ་བྱ་བྱེད་ཀུན་གཅིག་འགྱུར།།

ཞེས་པ་ནི། གྲངས་(ང)ཅན་ན་རེ། མྱུ་གུ་རང་གི་བདག་ཉིད་དམ་རང་གི་ས་བོན་གྱི་དུས་ན་ཡོད་ལ་ས་བོན་དང་མྱུ་[84]གུ་གཉིས་ཀྱི་རང་བཞིན་ཆ་མེད་པའི་གཅིག་པུ་ཡིན་ཁྱབ་མཉམ་ཡོད་པས་རྒྱུ···འབྲས་མི་འཆོལ་བ་དང་སྐྱེ་བ་འཐད་ཀྱི་དེ་ལྟར་རྒྱུ་དུས་ན་ཅི···ཡང་མེད་ན་མེད་པ་མི་སྐྱེ་སྟེ། སྐྱེ་ན་རི་བོང་རྭ་ཡང་སྐྱེ་བར་འགྱུར། ཞེས་ཟེར། ཕྱིར་མེད་པ་མི་སྐྱེ་བས་ཡོད་པ་ཅིག་སྐྱེ་ལ། དེ་ཡང་རང་སྐྱེ་བའི་སྔ་རོལ་དུ་མེད་པ་གཅིག་ཡོད་པའི···བདག་ཉིད་ཐོབ་པའི་ཕྱིར་སྐྱེ་བར་སྨྲ་(ཉ)དོ་སྟེ་པ་ཡན་ཆད་མཐུན་གྲངས་ཅན་ལྟར་བདག་ཉིད་ལས་སྐྱེ་བ་དང་སླར་ཡང་སྐྱེ་བ་སྐྱུས་ཀྱང···མི་འདོད་པས་སྐྱེ་(ཕ)ལྡན་གྱི་དངོས་པོ་ཆོས་ཅན། སླར་ཡང་སྐྱེ་བ་དོན་མེད་པར་ཐལ། རང་གི་བདག་ཉིད་ཐོབ་ཟིན་པའི་ཕྱིར། མ་ཁྱབ་ན། དེ་ཆོས་ཅན། སྐྱེ་བ་ཐུག་མེད་དུ་ཐལ། ཡོད་ཟིན་སླར་ཡང་སྐྱེ་བ་དོན་ཡོད་པའི་ཕྱིར། འདི་ལ་འང་གྲངས་ཅན་གྱིས་[85]མ་ཁྱབ་ཟེར་ཡང་ལན་[86]མི་ཐེབས་ཏེ། སྔར་མེད་པ་གསར་སྐྱེ་མི་འདོད་པའི་ཕྱིར་དང༌། རང་ཉིད་རང་ཉིད་ལས་[87]སྐྱེ་བ་ལ···

ཡོན་ཏན་འགའ་ཡང་མེད་པར་ཐལ། རང་གི་བདག་ཉིད་སྔར་ནས་ཐོབ་ཟིན་པའི་ཕྱིར་དང༌། ཡང་(ཕ)ན་ས་བོན་སྔོ་བོ་འབའ་ཞིག་རྟག་མེད་དུ་བརྒྱུད་པ་དང༌། ཡང་ན་མྱུ་གུ་སྔོན་པོ་འབའ་ཞིག་བརྒྱུད་ནས་སྐྱེ་བ་རྟག་པ་མེད་པ་(ར)[88]ཐལ་ལོ། །སྐྱེས་ཟིན་སླར་ཡང་སྐྱེ་བའི···ཕྱིར་དང༌། རྒྱུ་ས་བོན་སྐྱེ་བོ་ལྟ་བུ་ཞིག་ནམ་མེད་ཀྱང་འབྲས་བུ་མྱུ་གུ་(བ)[89]མཐོང་བའི་ཕྱིར། ས་རྒྱུག་གཅིག་ཅར་འཇིག་རྟེན་ཀྱིས་ཀྱང་ཁས་མི་ལེན་ཞིང༌། མཐོང་བ་དང་ཡང་འགལ་བར་འགྱུར་ལ། རྒྱུ་འབྲས་ཀྱི་བྱ་བྱེད་གཅིག་ཏུ་ཐལ། རང་ཉིད་ཀྱིས་རང་ཉིད་སྐྱེད་པའི་ཕྱིར་ཏེ། སངས་རྒྱས་བསྐྱངས་ཀྱིས། དངོས་པོ་རྣམས་བདག་ལས་སྐྱེ་བ་མེད་དེ། དེ་དག་གི་[90]སྐྱེ་བ་དོན···མེད་པ་ཉིད་དུ་འགྱུར་བའི་ཕྱིར་དང༌། ཤིན་ཏུ་ཐལ་བར་འགྱུར་བའི་ཕྱིར་ཏེ། དངོས་པོ་བདག་གི་བདག་ཉིད་དུ་ཡོད་པ་ལ་ནི་ཡང་སྐྱེ་བ་ལ་དགོས་པ་མེད་དོ། །ཇི་སྟེ་ཡོད་ཀྱང་སྐྱེ་ན་ནམ་ཡང་མི་སྐྱེ་བར་མི་འགྱུར་རོ། ཞེས་དང༌། འཇུག་པར།

དེ་(སྒ)[91]ནི་དེ་ལས་བྱུང་ན་ཡོན་ཏན་འགའ་ཡང་ཡོད་མ་ཡིན།།

82

ནས།
[སྐྱེས་པར་གྱུར་པ་སླར་ཡང་སྐྱེ་བ་རིགས་པའང་མ་ཡིན་ཉིད།།
སྐྱེས་ཟིན་སླར་ཡང་སྐྱེ་བར་ཡོངས་སུ་རྟོག་པར་འགྱུར་ན་ནི།།
མྱུ་གུ་ལ་སོགས་རྣམས་ཀྱི་སྐྱེ་བ་འདིར་རྙེད་མི་འགྱུར་ཞིང་།།
ས་བོན་སྲིད་མཐར་ཐུག་པར་རབ་ཏུ་སྐྱེ་བ་ཉིད་དུ་འགྱུར།།
ཇི་ལྟར་དེ་ཉིད་ཀྱིས་དེ་རྣམ་པར་འཇིག་པར་བྱེད་པར་འགྱུར།།
བྱེད་རྒྱུས་བོན་གྱི་ལས་ཐ་དད་མྱུ་གུའི་དབྱིབས་དང་ནི།།
ཁ་དོག་རོ་ནུས་སྨིན་པའི་ཚ་དང་ཚོད་ལ་མེད་པར་འགྱུར།།
གལ་ཏེ་སྔར་གྱི་བདག་གི་དངོས་པོ་བསལ་ནས་དེ་ལས་གཞན།།
ངོ་བོར་འགྱུར་ན་དེ་ཚེ་དེ་ཡི་དེ་ཉིད་ཇི་ལྟར་འགྱུར།།
གལ་ཏེ་ཁྱོད་ཀྱིས་བོན་མྱུ་གུ་འདིར་གཞན་མ་ཡིན་ན།།
ས་བོན་བཞིན་དུ་མྱུ་གུ་ཞེས་བྱ་དེ་བཟུང་མེད་པ་འམ།།
ཡང་ན་དེ་དག་གཅིག་པས་ཇི་ལྟར་མྱུ་གུ་འདི་བཞིན་དུ།།
དེ་ཡང་བཟུང་དུ..........ཡོད་འགྱུར་དེ་ཕྱིར་འདི་ནི་ཁས་མི་བླངས།།
གང་ཕྱིར་རྒྱུ་ཞིག་ན་ཡང་དེ་ཡི་འབྲས་བུ་མཐོང་བའི་ཕྱིར།།

83

དེ་དག་གཅིག་པ་ཡིན་ཞེས་འཇིག་རྟེན་གྱིས་ཀྱང་ཁས་མི་ལེན།།
དེ་ཕྱིར་དངོས་པོ་བདག་ལས་འབྱུང་ཞེས་རབ་ཏུ་བརྟགས་པ་འདི།།
དེ་ཉིད་དང་ནི་འཇིག་རྟེན་དུ་ཡང་རིགས་པ་མ་ཡིན་ནོ།།
བདག་ལས་སྐྱེ་བར་འདོད་ན་བསྐྱེད་པར་བྱ་དང་སྐྱེད་བྱེད་དང་།།
ལས་དང་བྱེད་པ་པོ་ཡང་གཅིག་ཉིད་འགྱུར་ན་དེ་དག་ནི།།
གཅིག་ཉིད་མ་ཡིན་པས་ན་བདག་ལས་སྐྱེ་བར་ཁས་བླང་བར།།]
བྱ་མིན་ཉེས་ཆེར་བཤད་པའི་ཉེས་པར་ཐལ་བར་འགྱུར་ཕྱིར་རོ།།
ཞེས་སོ།། །།གཉིས་པ་ལ[92] དངོས་དང་། འཇུག་པ···
སྤངས་པ་གཉིས། དང་པོ་ནི།
གཞན་ལས་སྐྱེ་ན་མེ་ལས་མུན་འབྱུང་ཞིང་།།
རྒྱུ་དང་རྒྱུ་མིན་ཀུན་ལས་ཀུན་འབྱུང་འགྱུར།།
གཞན་ཕྱིར་རྒྱུད[93] གཅིག་མི་རུང་གྲོ་ནས་བཞིན།།
དུས་མཉམ་དེ་མེད་གཞན་ལས[94] གཞན་སྐྱེ་ཙེ།།
ཞེས་བྱ་བ་ལ། གཞན་ལས་སྐྱེ་ན་ལུང་རིགས་དུ་མ་དང་འགལ་ཏེ། རིགས་པ་ནི། མེ་ལྕེ་(ཙ) ལས་ཀྱང་མུན་པ་འཐུག་པོ་འབྱུང་བར

84

ཐལ། རང་མཚན་གྱིས་གཞན་ལས་གཞན་འབྱུང་བའི་ཕྱིར་དང་། འཕགས་པས་ཀྱང་།
རྒྱུ་དང་འབྲས་བུ[95] གཞན་ཉིད་དུ།།
ནམ་ཡང་འཐད་པར་མི་འགྱུར་རོ།།
རྒྱུ་དང་འབྲས་བུ་གཞན་ཉིད་ན།།
རྒྱུ་དང་རྒྱུ་མིན་མཚུངས་པར་འགྱུར།།
ཞེས་གསུངས་པ་ལྟར་རྒྱུ་དང་རྒྱུ་མིན་ལས་ཐམས་ཅད་འབྱུང་བར་ཐལ། རྒྱུ་འབྲས་རང་མཚན་གྱིས་གཞན་ཡིན་པའི···
ཕྱིར་ཏེ། འཇུག་པར།
གཞན་ལ་བརྟེན་ནས་[གལ་ཏེ་གཞན་ཞིག་འབྱུང་བར་འགྱུར་ན་ནི།།
འོ་ན་མེ་ལྕེ་ལས་ཀྱང་མུན་པ་འཐུག་པོ་འབྱུང་འགྱུར་ཞིང་།།
ཐམས་ཅད་ལས་ཀྱང་ཐམས་ཅད་སྐྱེ་བར་འགྱུར་ཏེ་གང་གི་ཕྱིར།།
སྐྱེད་པར་བྱེད་པ་མ་ཡིན་མ་ལུས་ལ་ཡང་གཞན་ཉིད་མཚུངས།།]
སོགས་སོ། ཡང་ཁོ་ན་རེ། ཐལ་བ་དེའི་སྐྱོན་མི་ཡོང་སྟེ། འདིར་གང་ཞིག་འབྲས་བུ་ལ་ཕན་པར་བྱ་བ་དེ་ཉིད་དེའི་འབྲས་བུ[96]···

༨༥

ཡིན་ལ། རྒྱུ་ཉེར་ལེན་དང་འབྲས་བུ་ནི་ས་བོན་དེའི་རྒྱུད་གཅིག་ཏུ་གཏོགས་པའམ་རྒྱུན་ཅིག་པ་ཅིག་དགོས་ཀྱི་རྒྱུན་ཐ་དད་པ་ལ་ཉེར་ལེན་སོགས་མི་རུང་བ། དཔེར་ན་ནས་ཀྱི་ས་བོན་དང་རྒྱུན་ཅིག…པའི་ནས་ཕྱུག་གི་རྒྱུ་ཡིན་ཀྱང་[97] ཀེང་ཤུའི་མིན་པ་ལྟར་རོ། ཞེ་ན། ཉེར་ལེན་ནས་ཀྱི་ས་བོན་དང་འབྲས་བུ་ནས་ཕྱུག་ཚོས་ཅན། རྒྱུད་ཅིག་མིན་པར་ཐལ། ཕན་ཚུན་རང་མཚན་གྱིས…[98] གཞན་ཡིན་པའི་ཕྱིར། དཔེར་ན་བྱམས་པ་དང་ཉེར་སྦས་བཞིན་དང་གྲོ་ནས་བཞིན། ཐུ(ཚ)རྒྱུག་རང་མཚན་གྱིས་གཞན་མ་ཡིན་པར་ཐལ། དུས་མཉམ་དུ་མེད་པའི་ཕྱིར་དང་། ཉེ་འདྲའི་གཞན་ལ་སྐྱེ་འགག་གི་བྱ་བ་སོགས་ཀྱང་མི་འཐད་པའི་ཕྱིར་ཏེ། འཕགས་པས།

དངོས་པོ་རྣམས་ཀྱི་རང་བཞིན་ནི།།
རྐྱེན་ལ་སོགས་པ་ཡོད་མ་ཡིན།།
བདག་གི་[99] དངོས་པོ་ཡོད་མིན་ན།།
གཞན་དངོས་ཡོད་པར་ག་ལ་འགྱུར།།

༨༦

ཞེས་དང་། འཇུག་པར།

[རབ་ཏུ་བྱ་བར་ནུས་པ་དེ་ཕྱིར་འབྲས་བུར་དེས་བརྗོད་ཅིང་།།
གང་ཞིག་དེ་བསྐྱེད་ནུས་པ་དེ་ནི་གཞན་ནའང་རྒྱུ་ཡིན་ལ།།
རྒྱུད་གཅིག་གཏོགས་དང་སྐྱེད་པར་བྱེད་ལས་སྐྱེ་བ་དེ་ཡི་ཕྱིར།།
ས་ལུའི་མྱུ་གུ་ནས་ལ…སོགས་ལས་དེ་ལྟ་མིན་ཞེ་ན།།]
ཇི་ལྟར་ནས་དང་གེ་སར་དང་ནི་ཀིང་ཤུ་ཀ་ལ་སོགས།།
ས་ལུའི་མྱུ་གུའི་སྐྱེད་པར་བྱེད་པར་འདོད་མིན་ནུས་ལྡན་མིན།།
རྒྱུད་གཅིག་ཁོངས་སུ་གཏོགས་མིན་འདྲ་བ་མ་ཡིན་ཉིད་དེ་བཞིན།།
ས་ལུའི་ས་བོན་ཡང་ནི་དེ་ཡི་མིན་ཏེ་གཞན་ཉིད་ཕྱིར།།
མྱུ་གུ་ས་བོན་དང་ནི་དུས་མཉམ་ཡོད་པ་མ་ཡིན་ཏེ།།
གཞན་ཉིད་མེད་པར་ས་བོན་གཞན་པ་ཉིད་དུ་ག་ལ་འགྱུར།།
དེས་ན་མྱུ་གུ་ས་བོན་ལས་སྐྱེ་འགྲུབ་པར་འགྱུར་མིན་པས།།
གཞན་ལས་སྐྱེ་བ་ཡིན་ཞེས་བྱ་བའི་ཕྱོགས་འདི་བཏང་བར་བྱོས།།
ཇི་ལྟར་སྲང་གི་མདའ་གཉིས་མཐོ་བ་དང་ནི་དམའ་བ་དག། (ཇ)
དུས་མཉམ་མ་ཡིན་པར་ནི་མིན་པར་མཐོང་བ་དེ་བཞིན་དུ།།

༨༧

བསྐྱེད་པར་བྱ་དང་སྐྱེད་བྱེད་དག་གི་སྐྱེ་འགག་འགྱུར་ཞེ་ན།།
གལ་ཏེ་གཅིག་ཚེ་ཡིན་ན་འདི་ དུས་གཅིག་མེད་དེ་ཡོད་མིན།།
གལ་ཏེ་སྐྱེ་བཞིན་པ་དེ་སྐྱེལ་ཕྱོགས་པས་ཡོད་མིན་ཞིང་།།
འགག་བཞིན་པ་ནི་ཡོད་ཀྱང་འཇིག་ལ་ཕྱོགས་པར་འདོད་འགྱུར་བ།།
དེ་ཚེ་འདི་ནི་ཇི་ལྟ་བུར་ན་སྲང་དང་མཚུངས་པ་ཡིན།།
སྐྱེ་བ་འདི་ནི་བྱེད་པོ་མེད་པར་]རིགས་པའི་དངོས་འདང་མིན།།

ཞེས་སོ། །འདི་ལ་དབུ་མ་རང་རྒྱུད་པ་དག་ན་རེ། བདེན་གྲུབ་ཀྱི…གཞན་དང་སྐྱེ་འགག་བྱ་བ་གཅིག་ཅར་མེད་པ་བདེན་མོད། མ…བརྟགས་པར་རང་ངོས་ནས་ས་[100] བོན་འགག་པའི་བྱ་བ་དང་མྱུ་གུ་སྐྱེ་བའི་བྱ་བ་ཅིག་ཅར་ཡོད་པ་ཤཱ་ལུ་ལྗང་པའི་མདོའི་དགོངས་པ་མིན་ནམ། ཞེ་ན། དེ་ལ་ཡང་སྔར་ལྟར་གནོད་པ་འབབ་ལ། མདོའི་དགོངས་པ་ཐ་སྙད་དུ་ཡིན་གྱི…[101] རང་ངོས་ནས་མ་ཡིན་ནོ། །གལ་ཏེ་མིག་(མི)དང་གཟུགས་སོགས་དང་ཚོར་བ……ལྷན་ཅིག་པ་ཚོན་ལ་བརྟེན་ནས་མིག་གི་རྣམ་ཤེས་སྐྱེ་བས་གཞན་སྐྱེ་ཙམ་གྲུབ་བོ། ཞེ་ན། མིག་གི་རྣམ་ཤེས་ཆོས་ཅན། རང་གི་སྐྱེད་བྱེད…

༨༨

གཟུགས་དང་མིག་དང་ཚོར་སོགས་དུས་མཉམ་ཅིག་ཏུ་གྲུབ་པ་
གཞན་ལས་མི་སྐྱེ་བར་ཐལ། ཚོད་དེ་དག་དང་དུས་མཉམ་པར་
གཞན་དུ་གྲུབ་ཟིན་པའི་ཕྱིར་ཏེ། འཇུག་པར།
[ཀ་ལ་ཏེ།]མིག་གི་བློ་ལ་[རང་གི་སྐྱེད་བྱེད་དུས་གཅིག་པ།།
མིག་ལ་སོགས་དང་ལྷན་ཅིག་འབྱུང་བ་འདུ་ཤེས་ལ་སོགས་ལས།།
གཞན་ཉིད་ཡོད་ན་ཡོད་ལ་འབྱུང་བས་དགོས་པ་ཅི་ཞིག་ཡོད།།
ཅི་སྟེ་དེ་མེད་ཅེ་ན་འདི་ལ་ཉེས་པ་བཤད་ཟིན་ཏོ།།]
སོགས་སོ།། །།གཉིས་པ་ནི།

ལྷ་སྦྱིན་གཞན་འགོག་ཐོག་ཕུང་གཅིག་སོགས་འཁྲུལ།།
མཐའ་བཞི་མི་འདོད་གཞན་སྐྱེ་འཇིག་རྟེན་དུའང་།།
མེད་པར་བཤད་ཕྱིར་འདིར་འདོད་སྨོན་པའི་གར།།

ཞེས་པ་ནི། རྣམ་བཤད་(ཞི)དགོངས་པ་རབ་གསལ་ལྟར་བོད་ཁ་
ཅིག་ཙམ་[102]ལྷ་སྦྱིན་གཞན་འགོག་པ་དང་། ལ་ལ་ལྷ་སྦྱིན་ཐོག་ཕུང་
གཅིག་ཏུ་འཕུལ་[103]བར་འདོད་པ་སོགས་འཁྲུལ་པར་རྟོགས་
སླ་ལ། རྟག་ཚང་པས་ལྷར་ལྟར་སྐབས་འདིར་ཡང་གཞན་…

༨༩

སྐྱེ་འདོད་པ་ནི་སྨོན་པའི་ཆ་བྱ་གར་བྱེད་པའི་མགོ་བོ་བཅད་ནས་
མཇུག་མར་བཏགས་ནས་གར་བྱེད་འདོད་པའི་རང་བཞིན་ནོ་
ན་ཡིན་ཏེ། སཱ་ལུ་ལྗང་པ་ལས།[104] ས་བོན་གྱི་རྒྱུ་[105]ལས་ལྡང་བའི་
མྱུ་གུ་དེ་ཡང་སྐྱེ་བ་ན། བདག་གིས་མ་བྱས། གཞན་གྱིས་མ་
བྱས། གཉིས་ཀས་མ་བྱས། དབང་ཕྱུག་གིས་མ་བྱས། དུས་
ཀྱིས་མ་བསྒྱུར། ཕྲ་རབ་ལས་མ་བྱུང་། ངོ་བོ་ཉིད་ལས་མ་བྱུང་།
རྒྱུ་མེད་པ་ལས་མ་སྐྱེས། ཞེས་དྲངས་པ་དང་། ཚིག་གསལ་
ལས། འཇིག་རྟེན་པས་ནི་བདག་དང་གཞན་ལས་ཞེས་
གསུངས་པའི་དེ་ལྟ་བུ་ལ་སོགས་པའི་རྣམ་པར་དཔྱོད་པའི་…
འཇུག་པ་མེད་པར་བྱས་ནས་རྒྱུ་ལས་འབྲས་བུ་འབྱུང་ཞེས་
བྱ་བ་འདི་ཙམ་ཞིག་རྟོགས་པ་ཡིན་ནོ། །སློབ་དཔོན་ཡང་དེ་
ལྟར་རྣམ་པར་བཞག་པ་མཛད་པ་ཡིན་ཏེ། ཞེས་དང་། …
འཇུག་པར།
གཞན་ལས་སྐྱེ་བ་འཇིག་རྟེན་ལས་ཀྱང་མེད།།
ཅེས་པའི་ལུགས་དེ་ཚོད་བྱང་འཆད་འདོད་པས་སོ།། ॥

༩༠

གསུམ་པ་ནི།

བདག་གཞན་རེ་རེའི་མིན་ཕྱིར་གཉིས་སྐྱེའང་ཁེགས།།

ཞེས་བྱ་བ་ནི། དབང་ཕྱུག་རྒྱུར་སྨྲ་བའི་གྲངས་ཅན་དང་གཅེར་
བུ་པ་གཉིས་ཀས་བུམ་སོགས་བདག་གཞན་གཉིས་སྐྱེད་ཕྱར་[106]
ལྟར་འདོད་པས་དེ་མི་འཐད་དེ། དེའི་བདག་སྐྱེ་ལ་ཕྱར་གྱི…
གནོད་བྱེད་དང་། གཞན་སྐྱེ་བའི་ཆ་ཕྱར་གྱི་གཞན་སྐྱེ་འགོག
པའི་རིགས་པས་གནོད་པའི་ཕྱིར་ཏེ། འཇུག་པར།
གཉིས་ལས་སྐྱེ་བ་རིགས་པའི་ངོ་བོ་མ་ཡིན་གང་གི་ཕྱིར།།
བཤད་ཟིན་ཉེས་པ་དེ་དག་ཐོག་ཏུ་འབབ་པ་ཡིན་ཕྱིར་རོ།།
ཞེས་སོ།། །།བཞི་པ་ནི།

རྒྱུ་མེད་སྐྱེ་ན་འབད་པ་དོན་མེད་ཅིང་།།
མཐོང་དང་འགལ་ལ་ཀུན་ལས་ཀུན་སྐྱེ་འགྱུར།།

ཞེས་པ་ནི། གནས་སྐབས་དང་མཐར་ཐུག་གི་འབྲས་བུ…[107]
འབྱུང་བའི་ཆེད་དུ་ས་བོན་འདེབས་པ་དང་གཙོ་སྲེག་བྱེད
པ་དང་ནོ་ཚོང་སོགས་བྱེད་པ་དོན་མེད་པར་ཐལ། རྒྱུ…

91

མེད་ཀྱང་འབྲས་བུ་འབྱུང་བའི་ཕྱིར་དང་། བྱ་རོག་ལ་རྨ་བྱིའི··· མདོངས་དང་ཏ་ལ་ཏྲ་དང་ཤིང་པ་ནས་རང་གི་ཤིང་ཏོག་གི་ རྒྱུ་མིན་པ་དེ་བཞིན་དུ། ནིམ་པ་དང་ཨ་མྲ་ལ་སོགས་པ་འབྲས་ བུ་ཅན་གྱི་ཤིང་རྣམས་ཀྱང་རང་གི་འབྲས་བུ་ཤིང་ཏོག་གི་རྒྱུ་མ་ཡིན་ [108] པར་ཐལ་བ་དང་། ཨ་མྲ་དང་ལ་ཀུ་ཙ་ལ་སོགས་པ་སྨིན་པ་དུས་ ལ་མི་ལྟོས་པར་ཐལ་བ་སོགས་འགྱུར་ཏེ། རྒྱུ་མེད་ལས་སྐྱེ་བའི་ ཕྱིར། འདོད་ནའང་མི་རིགས་ཏེ། དེ་འདྲ་འཇིག་རྟེན་གྱི་མཐོང་ བ་དང་འགལ་བར་མ་ཟད། རྒྱུ་མེད་ལས་སྐྱེ་བའང་འཇིག་རྟེན་ [109] གྱི་མཐོང་བ་དང་ཆེས་འགལ་བ་སོགས་ཀྱིས་གནོད་བྱེད་དུ་མ་ འབྱུང་བའི་ཕྱིར་ཏེ། འཇུག་པར།

[གལ་ཏེ།] རྒྱུ་མེད་ཁོ་ནར་སྐྱེ་བར་ལྟ་ཞིག་འགྱུར་ན་ནི།།
དེ་ཚེ་མཐའ་དག་རྟག་ཏུ་ཐམས་ཅད་ལས་ཀྱང་སྐྱེ་འགྱུར་ཞིང་།།
འབྲས་འབྱུང་ཆེད་དུ་འཇིག་རྟེན་འདི་ཡིས་ས་བོན་ལ་སོགས་ནི།། [110]
བརྒྱ་ཕྲག་དག་གིས་ཉོ་ནས་སྡུད་པར་བྱེད་པར་ཡང་མི་འགྱུར།།

ཞེས་སོ། །འདི་ངག་ཐར་བཀག་ཟིན་ཏོ།། ། །གཉིས་པ····

92

མཐའ་བཞི་དང་ཡོད་མེད་སྐྱེ་འགོག་ཚིག་ཙམ་བཤད་པ་ནི།

གཞན་ལས་སྐྱེ་ན་ཡོད་མེད་གཉིས་མིན་བྱང་།། [111]
ཡོད་ལ་ཅི་དགོས་མེད་ལ་བྱ་བྱེད་བྲལ།།
གཉིས་ཡིན་དེས་བསལ་གཉིས་བྲལ་ལ་དེས་ཅི།།

ཞེས་པ་ནི། (ཟ) དངོས་པོ་གང་ཡང་རང་བཞིན་གྱིས་སྐྱེ་འགག··· [112] གནས་གསུམ་དང་གཞན་སྐྱེ་བ་གང་ཡང་མེད་དེ། ཡོད་མེད་ དང་གཉིས་དང་གཉིས་མིན་གང་ལའང་མི་སྐྱེ་བའི་ཕྱིར། ཁྱབ་ པ་ཐར་ཐར་དང་རྟགས་ཚུལ་བཞི་ལས་ཡོད་པའི་བདག་ཉིད··· ཐོབ་ཟིན་སླར་མི་སྐྱེ་སྟེ། བདག་སྐྱེ་བའི་གནོད་པ་རྣམས་འབྱུང་ བའི་ཕྱིར། གཏན་མེད་མི་སྐྱེ་སྟེ། དེ་ལ་བྱ་བ་མི་འཐད་པའི་ ཕྱིར། གཉིས་ཡིན་མི་སྐྱེ་སྟེ། ཡོད་མེད་གཉིས་འགལ་བས་ [113] གཅིག་ལ་མི་འདུ་བའི་ཕྱིར། ཡོད་མེད་གཉིས་ཀ་རེ་རེ་ནས་ མིན་པའང་མི་སྐྱེ་སྟེ། དེ་མི་སྲིད་པའི་ཕྱིར་ཏེ། སྟོང་ཉིད་བདུན་ ཅུ་པ་ལས།

ཡོད་པ་ཡོད་ཕྱིར་སྐྱེ་མ་ཡིན།།

93

མེད་པ་མེད་པའི་ཕྱིར་མ་ཡིན།།
ཆོས་མི···མཐུན་ཕྱིར་ཡོད་མེད་མིན།།
སྐྱེ་བ་མེད་ཕྱིར་གནས་འགག་མེད།།

ཅེས་དང་། དེའི་རང་འགྲེལ་ལས། དངོས་པོ་ཡོད་པའི་ཕྱིར། ནས། [རྒྱུ་ལས་སྐྱེ་བར་མི་འགྱུར་ཏེ། ཡོད་པ་ནི་ཡོད་བཞིན་པ་ཞེས་ བཤད་པས་སོ། །མེད་པ་ནི་མེད་པའི་ཕྱིར་རྒྱུ་ལས་སྐྱེ་བ་མེད་དོ། ཡོད་མེད་ནི་མི་འདྲ་བའི་ཕྱིར་སྐྱེ་བ་མ་ཡིན་ཏེ་ཕན་ཚུན་འགལ་ལོ། འདི་ལྟར་ཡོད་པ་དང་མེད་པ···དག་ནི་ཕན་ཚུན་འགལ་བའི་ཆོས་ ཅན་ཡིན་པས་ཆོས་མི་མཐུན་པའི་ཕྱིར་ཡོད་པ་ཡང་ཡིན་མེད་པ་ ཡང་ཡིན་པ་ག་ལ་སྐྱེ།] སྐྱེ་བ་མེད་པའི་ཕྱིར་གནས་པ་དང་ འགག་པ་ཡང་མེད་དོ། ཞེས་དང་། འཇུག་པར།

[སྐྱེད་པར་བྱེད་པ་བསྐྱེད་བྱ་གཞན་བསྐྱེད་པ་དེ་རྒྱུ་ཡིན་ན།།
ཡོད་པའམ་འོན་ཏེ་མེད་དང་གཉི་ག་གཉིས་བྲལ་ཞིག་བསྐྱེད་བྱང་།།]
ཡོད་ན་སྐྱེད་བྱེད་ཅི་དགོས་མེད་ལའང་དེས་ནི་ཅི་ཞིག་བྱ།།
གཉིས་ཉིད་ལ་དེས་ཅི་བྱ་གཉིས་དང་བྲལ་ལའང་དེས་ཅི་བྱ།།

94

ཞེས་དང་། འགྲེལ་པར་རྟགས་སོ་སོ་ནས་སྤྲུལ་བ། ལམ་…
སྒྲོན་ལས།

ཡོད་པ་སྐྱེ་བ་རིགས་མིན་ཏེ།།
མེད་པའང་ནམ་མཁའི་མེ་ཏོག་བཞིན།།
ཉེས་པ་གཉིས་ཀ་ཐལ་འགྱུར་ཕྱིར།།
གཉིས་ཀ་དག་ཀྱང་འབྱུང་བ་མིན།།

ཞེས་སོ། །འཇུག་པས་གཞན་སྐྱེ་སྤྱིར་ལ་འཕགས་པ་དང་ཇོ་ [114]
བོས་ཕྱིར་བཤད་པས་སྐྱེ་བ་གཅིག་པུར་མ་ཟད་གནས་འགག
སེལ་བྱེད་ཡང་ཡིན། དེ་ཡང་ཡོད་པ་ཕྱོན་དང་།མེད་པ་ཕྱོན་དང་།གཉིས་
ཀ་དང་།གཉིས་མིན་ཞེས་མུ་སྟེ་རྒྱུ་ཡོད་པས་མུ་བཞི་སྐྱེ་འགོག
ཡང་བྱས་ཚོག་པས་མཐའ་བཞིའི་འགོག་པ་དང་འགལ་བར་མ
སེམས་ཤིག། །གསུམ་པ་མུ་བཞི་དེ་ལ་དངོས་དང་འབྲེལ་…
ཕྱོང་གཉིས། དང་པོ་ནི། རང་ཕྱི་དངོས་སྨྲ་རྣམས་ཀྱིས་བདེན
པར་མི་སྐྱེ་བ་མི་རུང་སྟེ། རྒྱུ་ས་བོན་གཅིག་ལས་འབྲས་བུ་
དུ་མ་དང་གཅིག་སྐྱེ་བའང་ཡོད་ལ། རྒྱུ་རྐྱེན་དུ་མས་ཀྱང་འབྲས

95

བུ་དུ་མ་དང་གཅིག་སྐྱེ་བར་བཤད་ཅིང་། མཐོང་བས་སོ། ཞེས་དབུ་མ་
སྣང་བར་བཀོད་པ་ལྟར་འདོད་པའི་ལུགས་དེ་དགག་པའི་…
ཕྱིར།

དངོས་པོ་བདེན་པར་རྒྱུ་ཡིས་བསྐྱེད་མིན་ཏེ།།
གཅིག་གིས་གཅིག་མིན་དུ་མས་གཅིག་མི་སྐྱེད།།
གཅིག་གིས་དུ་མིན་དུ་མས་དུ་མའང་མིན།།

ཞེས་པ་ནི། དངོས་པོ་རྣམས་ཆོས་ཅན། རྒྱུ་ཡིས་དོན་དམ་པར་མི་སྐྱེད་དེ།
དོན་དམ་པར་རྒྱུ་གཅིག་གིས་འབྲས་བུ་ [115] གཅིག་མིན། དོན་དམ་
པར་རྒྱུ་དུ་མས་ཀྱང་འབྲས་བུ་དུ་མ་མིན། དོན་དམ་པར་རྒྱུ་གཅིག
གིས་ཀྱང་འབྲས་བུ་དུ་མ་མིན་ལ། དོན་དམ་པར་རྒྱུ་དུ་མས་
ཀྱང་འབྲས་བུ་གཅིག་སྐྱེད་པ་མ་ཡིན་པའི་ཕྱིར་ དཔེར་ན་མིག
ཤེས་གཅིག་ལ་རྒྱུ་དུ་མའི་ [116] ལག་རྗེས་ཡོད་ན་དོན་དམ་པར་རྒྱུ་
གཅིག་གིས་སྐྱེད་པར་མི་འགྱུར་ལ། རྒྱུ་དུ་མ་ལྟར་ལག་རྗེས་ཀྱི [117]
འབྲས་བུ་ཡང་རྣམ་ཤེས་དུ་མ་རུ་ཐལ་བར་འགྱུར་བ་སོགས
ཀྱི་རིགས་པ་མཁས་པའི་ཡིད་འཕྲོག་པ་དག་ཡོད་པའི་ཕྱིར་ཏེ།

96

(ཞ)བདེན་གཉིས་ལས།

དུ་མས་དངོས་པོ་གཅིག་མི་བྱེད།།
དུ་མས་དུ་མ་བྱེད་མ་ཡིན།།
གཅིག་གིས་དུ་མའི་དངོས་མི་བྱེད།།
གཅིག་གིས་གཅིག་བྱེད་པ་ཡང་མིན།།

ཞེས་དང་།དེ་ཉིད་ལས། [118]

(ཡ)འབྲས་བུ་ཟ་དད་མ་ཡིན་ཡང་།།
བྱེ་བྲག་རྣམས་ནི་ཟ་དད་དང་།།
གཞན་མིན་ཕྱེད་འདོད་དེ་བས་ན།།
ཀྱི་ཆེ་དབང་ཕྱུག་གིས་བྱས་སམ།། [119]

ཞེས་དང་།

(ར)ཅིག་ལ་ཅིག་ཆར་སྐྱེ་བ་དང་།།
མི་སྐྱེ་དེ་བཞིན་སྐྱེད་བྱེད་དང་།།
སྐྱེད་བྱེད་མ་ཡིན་ཡང་དག་པར།།
ཅི་ཡི་ཕྱིར་ན་མི་འགལ་སྨོས།།

༩༧

སོགས་དང་།

ཀྱཻ(ཀྱེ)་ཧོ་བྱེ་བྲག་ཅན་རྣམས་ལས།།
ཕྱེ་བར་འདོད་ན་རེ་རེ་ནི།།
ཕྱེད་པར་བྱེད་པ་མ་ཡིན་འགྱུར།།
ཡིན་ནའང་འབྲས་བུ་རྒྱུ་མེད་འགྱུར།།

ཞེས་དང་།

ཀྱཻ(ཀྱེ)་ཧོ་ཁྱེད་ནི་ཅན་རྣམས་ལས།།
འབྲས་བུ་ཕྱེ་བར་འདོད་ན་ནི།།
ཐ་དད་ཐ་དད་མ་ཡིན་པ།།
ལྟ་མ་བཞིན་དུ་རྒྱུ་མེད་ཐལ།།

སོགས་སོ།། །།གཉིས་པ་ནི།

གཅིག་གིས་གཅིག་སྐྱེད་སྒྲུབ་ཕྱིར་གཞན་ཟུང་ཕྱིར།།
འདིར་ནི་དགག་བྱའི་ཁྱད་པར་མི་སྦྱོར་འཁྲུལ།།

ཞེས་སྨྲས་ཏེ། འདི་ལ་ཡང་སྔག་ཚང་པ་ན་རེ། རྒྱུ་གཅིག་གིས་འབྲས་བུ་གཅིག་སྐྱེད་པ་སོགས་རྒྱུ་བཞི་མེད་པས་དོན་དམ་

༩༨

དང་རང་བཞིན་སོགས་ཀྱི་དགག་བྱའི་ཁྱད་པར་མི་སྦྱོར་ཟེར་བ་མི་འཐད་དེ། རྒྱུ་མིག་དབང་སྐད་ཅིག་མ་གཅིག་གིས་འབྲས་བུ…མིག་གི་རྣམ་ཤེས་སྐད་ཅིག་མ་གཅིག་བསྐྱེད་པར་བཞེད་པའི་ཕྱིར་དང་། ཚིག(ས)་གསལ་ལ་ལས། མིག་དང་གཟུགས་ལ་བརྟེན་ནས་ཞེས་དོན་གྱི་ཁྱད་པར་དངོས་སུ་ཞལ་གྱིས་བཞེས་ཤིང་མིག་གི[120] དབང་པོ་གཅིག་གི་རྒྱུ་ཅན་གྱི་རྣམ་པར་ཤེས་པ་གཅིག་ཀྱང་སྐྱེ་བར་བཞེད་པ་ན་བརྟེན་ནས་ཞེས་ཟ་བའི[121]་སྒྲ་ལ་བློས་པའི་དོན་ཉིད་ཡོད་པར་ག་ལ་འགྱུར་ཞེས་རྟེན་འབྲེལ་སྐབས་དང་། མངོན[122]་སུམ་གྱི[123]་སྒྲ་དོན་སྐབས་སུ་ཡང་། དེ་ཉིད་ལས། བློས་པའི་དོན་མེད་པའི་ཕྱིར། དབང་པོའི་སྐད་ཅིག་གཅིག་གི་རྟེན་ཅན་ཤིག…[124] གི་རྣམ་པར་ཤེས་པ་གཅིག་མངོན་སུམ་ཉིད་དུ་ཡང་མི་འགྱུར་ལ།[125] ཞེས་དང་། བཞི་བརྒྱ་པའི་འགྲེལ་པ་ལས་ཀྱང་། འོ་ན་རྣམ(ཅ)་པར་ཤེས་པའི་སྐད་ཅིག་མ་གཅིག་ཇི་ལྟར་མངོན་སུམ་ཉིད་ཡིན། དེ་ནི་དབང་པོ་དང་དབང་པོ་ལ་བརྟེན་ནས་འདུག་པ་མ་ཡིན་ཏེ། ཐུན་མོང་མ་ཡིན་པའི་ཕྱིར་དང་། དབང་པོ་དང་རྣམ་པར་ཤེས

༩༩

པའི་སྐད་ཅིག་དག་སྐྱེས་མ་ཐག་ཏུ་འཇིག་པ་ཉིད་ཀྱི་ཕྱིར། ཞེས་གསུངས་ལ་མངོན་པ་ཀུན་བཏུས་ལྟར་ལས་གཅིག་གིས་ལུས་དུ་མ་དང་ལས་དུ་མས་ལུས་གཅིག་དང་ལས་དུ་མས་ལུས་དུ་མ་དང་ལས་གཅིག་གིས་ལུས་གཅིག་འཕེན་པར་བཤད་པ་མདོ་དག་ནས་སོ་སོར་གསུངས་པ་བཏུས་པ་ཡིན་ཅིང་། སྐབས་འདིར་ཡང་བཞེད་དེ། སྤྱོད་འཇུག་ལས།

སེམས་གསལ་ལ་གཅིག་བསྐྱེད་འབྲས་བུ་གང་།།
ཚོངས་ལ་སོགས་པ་ཡིན་པ་ལྟར།།
ལུས་ངག་བཅས་པའི་འབྲས་བུ་ཡང་།།
སྤྱོད་པ་ཞན་པས་དེ་ལྟར་མིན།།

[126] ཞེས་དང་། ཐར་དྭངས་པ་ལྟར་སངས་རྒྱས་ཁྱང་སེམས་ལ་དང་པ་སྐད་ཅིག་མ་(རྡོ)[127]་རེའི་འབྲས་བུ་དཔག་མེད་དང་རིང་སྤེལ་ཉིང་པོ་ཅན་གྱི་ས་རྐྱ་གཅིག་བྱས་ནའང་དེའི་རྡུལ་གྱི་གྲངས་དང་མཉམ་པའི་འཁོར་སྒྱུར་དུ་སྐྱེ་བར་བཤད་པ་སོགས་དང་། རྟེན་ནམ་སེམས་ཞན་པས་དགེ་སོགས་ཡུན་རིང་སྤྱད…པས་ཀྱང་

100

འབྲས་བུ་ཆུང་བ་ཡང་། སྤྱོད་འཇུག་ལས།
བསྐལ་བརྗོད་དང་ནི་དཀའ་ཐུབ་ཀུན།།
ཡུན་རིང་དུས་སུ་སྤྱད་བྱས་ཀྱང་།།
སེམས་གཞན་གཡེང་བས་བྱས་པ་ནི།།
དེ་ཉིད་རིག་⋯པས་དོན་མེད་གསུངས།།
ཞེས་དང་། གསུང་རབས་ཚུལ་མདོ་ལས། དགེ་སློང་དག་འདོད་པ་ལ⋯སེམས་གཡེང་བའི་དཀའ་ཐུབ་དང་ཁ་ཏོན་ལ⋯སོགས་པ་ནི་འབྲས་བུ་མེད་པར་འགྱུར་རོ། །ཞེས་དང་།
སྤྱོད་འཇུག་ལས།
སྣད་ཅིག་གཅིག་བྱས་སྡིག་པས་ཀྱང་།།
བསྐལ་པར་མནར་མེད་གནས་འགྱུར་ན།།
ཞེས་པ་ལྷ་བུའི་ཐུང་བའི་མཚའ་དུ་མ་དང་སྐྱེས་པའི་རབས་དག་ལས་ཞེས་པར་བྱལ་མདོ་བཀུས་སོགས་ལྷ་ཞིང་དོན་བརྟུས་ན། དབུ་མ་སྣང་བ་ལས། གཅིག་ལས་དུ་མ་སྐྱེ་བ་དང་། དུ་མ་ལས་གཅིག་སྐྱེ་བ་ཞེས་བྱ་བ་མཐོང་བ་མ་ཡིན་ནམ། དེའི་

101

ཕྱིར་འདི་ཇི་ལྟར་ཐད་བར་ནུས་ཤེ་ན། [128] འདི་ནི་ཐུང་བ་མ་ཡིན་ཏེ། ཁོ་བོ་ཅག་ཀྱང་འདི་མ་མཐོང་ངོ་། ཞེས་ནི་མི་སྨྲ་བོ། །ཞེས་དོན་དམ་པར་མི་ཐུང་བ་དང་མངོན་སུམ་མ་མཐོང་བ་མིན།⋯ཞེས་བཤད་པ་དང་། ཡང་དེ་ཉིད་ལས། སློབ་དཔོན་གྱིས་ཀྱང་ཀུན་རྫོབ་ཏུ་རྒྱུ་དང་འབྲས་བུའི་ངོ་བོར་འདུག་པ་ལ⋯ཐ་སྙད་དུ་གཅིག་ལས་དུ་མ་སྐྱེ་བ་དང་། དུ་མ་ལས་གཅིག་སྐྱེ་བ་ཇི་ལྟར་གྲགས་པ་བཞིན་མཐོང་བའི་ཕྱིར་དང་། མིག་(སྨ) ལ་སོགས་པ་ཡང་རྗེས་སུ་འགྲོ་བ་དང་ལྡོག་པའི་སྒོ་ནས་མིག་གི་རྣམ་པར་ཤེས་པ་ལ་སོགས་པའི་རྒྱུ་ཉིད་རྟོགས་ནས⋯བྱེས་པའི་སྐྱེ་བོ་གཟུང་བའི་ཕྱིར། འབྲས་བུའི་གཏན⋯ཚིགས་བསྟན་པར་བྱ་བའི་ཚེ། རྒྱུ་དང་ནུ་དང་པར་འགྱུར་བར་སྨྲས་ཀྱི། དོན་དམ་པར་ནི་མ་ཡིན་པར་རིག⋯པར་བྱ་སྟེ།
ཞེས་སོ།། ||བཞི་པ་རྟེན་འབྲེལ་ལ། དངོས་དང་འབྲེལ་ཐོང་གཉིས། དང་པོ་ནི།
རྟེན་འབྱུང་མིན་པའི་ཆོས་ནི་འདིར་མེད་ལ།། [129]

102

རྟེན་འབྱུང་ཕྱད་སྟོས་བརྟེན་ནས་གྲུབ་ཚམ་ཕྱིར།། [130]
ཆོས་ཀུན་ཚོགས་ཐུབ་རང་ངོས་གྲུབ་རྣམས་མེན།།
ཟབ་རྒྱས་མཐའ་གཉིས་སེལ་འདི་རིགས་པའི་རྒྱལ།།
ཞེས་སྨྲས་ཏེ། འདིར་དངོས་སྨྲ་བ་ལྟར་མ་ཡིན་པར་རྟེན་འབྱུང་མིན་པའི་ཆོས་མི་འདོད་དེ། ཡོད་ན་སྟོས་གྲུབ་དང་རང་བཞིན་མེད་པ་གཉིས་ཀ་ཡིན་དགོས་པའི་ཕྱིར་ཏེ། དབུ་མ་ལས། (ས) [131]
གང་ཕྱིར་རྟེན་འབྱུང་མ་ཡིན་པའི།།
ཆོས་འགའ་ཡོད་པ་མ་ཡིན་པ།།
དེ་ཕྱིར་སྟོང་པ་མ་ཡིན་པའི།།
ཆོས་འགའ་ཡོད་པ་མ་ཡིན་ནོ།།
ཞེས་དང་། བརྒྱ་པ་ལས་ཀྱང་།
གང་ཞིག་གང་ནནམ་གྱི་ཚེ་འང་།།
མ་བརྟེན་པར་ནི་ཡོད་མེད་ཉིད།།
[རྟེན་ནམ་ཡང་འགའ་ཞིག་ཏུ།།
རྟག་པ་འགའ་ཡང་ཡོད་མ་ཡིན།།

103

ནམ་མཁའ་ལ་སོགས་རྟག་གོ་ཞེས།།

སོ་སོའི་སྐྱེ་བོ་···དག་གིས་རྟོགས།།

མཁས་པ་རྣམས་ཀྱིས་དེ་དག་ལ།།

འཇིག་རྟེན་པས་ཀྱང་དོན་མ་མཐོང་།།]

སོགས་དང་། མདོ་ལས་ཀྱང་།

[མཁས་པས་རྟེན་འབྱུང་ཆོས་རྣམས་རྟོགས་འགྱུར་ཏེ།།

མཐར་ལྟ་བ་ལ་བརྟེན་པར་ཡང་མི་བྱེད།།

རྒྱུ་དང་བཅས་ཤིང་རྐྱེན་བཅས་ཆོས་ཤེས་ཀྱི།།]

རྒྱུ་མེད་རྐྱེན་མེད་ཆོས་ཉིད་ཡོད་མ་ཡིན།།

ཞེས་དང་། ཚིག་གསལ་ལས། དེ་ལྟར་རྟེན་ཅིང་འབྲེལ་བར་འབྱུང་བ་མ་ཡིན་པའི་ཆོས་འགའ་ཡང་ཡོད་པ་མ་ཡིན་ལ། རྟེན་ཅིང་འབྲེལ་པར་འབྱུང་བ་ཡང་སྟོང་པ་ཡིན་པ་དེའི་ཕྱིར། སྟོང་པ་མ་ཡིན་པའི་ཆོས་ཡོད་པ་མ་ཡིན་ནོ། །ཞེས་དང་། དབུ་མ་ལས།

རྟེན་ཅིང་འབྲེལ་པར་འབྱུང་བ་གང་།།

104

དེ་ནི་སྟོང་པ་ཉིད་དུ་བཤད།།

དེ་ནི་རྟེན་ནས་གདགས་པ་སྟེ།།

དེ་ཉིད་དབུ་མའི་ལམ་ཡིན་ནོ།།

ཞེས་དང་། ཚིག་གསལ་ལས། ཡོད་པ་དང་མེད་པའི་མཐའ་གཉིས་དང་བྲལ་བའི་ཕྱིར། རང་བཞིན་གྱིས་མ་སྐྱེས་པའི་མཚན་ཉིད་ཅན་གྱི[132] སྟོང་ཉིད་དེ་ཉིད་དབུ་མའི་ལམ་སྟེ་དབུ···མའི་ཕྱུལ་ཞེས་བྱའོ། །དེའི་ཕྱིར་ནེ་ལྟར་ན་སྟོང་ཉིད་དང་བརྟེན་ནས་གདགས་པ་དང་དབུ་མའི་ལམ་ཞེས་བྱ་བ་འདི་དག་ནི···རྟེན་ཅིང་འབྲེལ་པར་འབྱུང་བ་ཉིད་ཀྱི་མིང་གི་བྱེ་བྲག་ཡིན་ནོ། །ཞེས་གསུངས་སོ། །རྟེན་འབྱུང་གི་སྒྲ་དོན་ལ་བརྟར···ཕྲོད་པ་དག་གིས་བརྟེན་པ་དང་ཕྲད་པ་རྒྱུ་དང་འབྲས་བུ་ཡིན་ན་རྒྱུ་རྟེན་ནས་སྒྲུབ་པས་འབྱུང་བ་ཞེས་པ་མི་འཐད་པར་འགྱུར་ལ་རྒྱུ་རྟེན་ན་ཡོད་པར་མི་འདོད་པ་དང་འགལ་ཞེས་རྟེན་འབྱུང་གི་སྒྲ་དོན་གང་ཡང་མི་འདོད་དངོས་སྨྲ་རྣམས་ཀྱིས་རྟེན་འབྱུང་ལ་བདེན་གྲུབ་དང་འདུས་བྱས་ཀྱིས·····[133]

105

ཁྱབ་པས་རྟེན་འབྱུང་གིས[134] བདག་མེད་སྒྲུབ་པ་འགལ་ཁྱབ་ཏུ་འདོད་དེ། རྟེན་འབྲེལ་བསྟོད་པ་ལས།

[135] འགྲལ་བ་དང་ནི་མ་གྲུབ་པར།།

མཐོང་བ་འདི་ཡིས་ཁྱོད་ཀྱི་ལུགས།།

ཇི་ལྟར་ཁོང་དུ་ཆུད་པར་ནུས།།

ཞེས་དང་། རིགས་པ་དྲུག་ཅུ་པ[136]འི་འགྲེལ་པ་ལས། འདིར་སྨྲས་པ། ཁྱོད་ཀྱི་ཚིག་གི་ཚུལ་འདི་ནི་ཐོན་མེད་པ་ཞིག་གོ། རྟེན་ཅིང་འབྲེལ་པར་འབྱུང་བ་གསུངས་པ་ཉིད[137]་ནི་སྐྱེ་བ་དང་འགག་པ་མེད་པར་སྟོན་པར་བྱེད་པ་མི་རུང་སྟེ། ཁྱོད་ཀྱིས་དུ་སྐྱེས་སོ་ཞེས་སྨྲས་པས་ནི་ཁྱོད་ཀྱིས་དུ་མ་སྐྱེས་སོ་ཞེས་སྨྲས་པར་འགྱུར་བ་མ་ཡིན་པ་དེ་བཞིན་དུ་འདི་ཡང་མི་རིགས་པ་ཉིད་དོ། །ཞེས་སོ། །ཇེས་པར་མཛོད་འགྲེལ་འགྲེལ···བཤད་དང་རྟེན་འབྲེལ་མདོ་འགྲེལ་འགྲེལ་བཤད་སོགས་སུ་བལྟ་ལ། སྨྲ་སྒྲུབ་ལུགས་ཡང་མི་འདྲ་བས་ཕྱོན་གྱི་ལོ་ཆེན་རྣམས་ཀྱི་ཕྱག་རྗེས་དང་ཀ་ཆེན་བསྒྲིགས་ནས་ཚིག་གསལ་

ཀྱི་དགོངས་པ་ཅུང་ཟད་བཤད་ན་འཆད་པ་བཞག །འགྲེལ་པ་དགག་པ་གཉིས། དང་པོ་ནི། ཆེན་འབྱུང་གི་"ཟླ་ཟླུ་བ་བཤད་···· གཉིས་ལས། དང་པོ་ནི། པྲ་ཛྙཱ་ཏྲ་ས་མུ་ཏྲ་དཿ ཞེས་པ་སྒྲུབ་ན། མི་ཏ་འགྲོ་བ་ལའོ། །ཞེས་འགྲོ་བའི་ཕྱིར་མི་ཏ་བཞག ཏ་རྗེས་འབྲེལ་ཡིན་པས་ཕྱིས། མི་བཞག་དེའི་སྔོན་དུ་པྲ་ཀེ་བཞག །དེ་ལ་སུ་ཕྱིན་མི་ཟད་པ་ལས་སུ་འཛེག། [138] ཙཀྲའི····[139] ལེ་ཙ་དང་པོའི་སྐད་པ་གསུམ་པ་ལས། ཨ་ལ་ཀྱ་དང་ཁ་ལུ་[140] དག་ལ་སོ་སོར་སྦྱོད་པ་ལ་ཀྲྀ་ཏུང་ངོ། [141] །མེད་ལས་སོ། [142] །ཕྱིད་པ་པོ་གཅིག་པ་དག་ལ་ཐ་མ་ལས་སོ། ཞེས་དང་། ཀ་ལྔ་པའི་ཀྲྀ་ཏ་[143] ལེ་ཙ་དྲུག་པར། ཨ་ལ་ཀྱ་ཁ་ལུ་དག་ལ་དགག་པ་ལ་ཀྲྀ་[144] ཡང་ནའོ། །མེད་ལས་སོ། [145] །ཕྱིད་པོ་གཅིག་དག་གི་ཐ་མའི་དུས་ལའོ། །ཞེས་པས་ཀྲྀ་[146] ཕྱིན། ཙཀྲའི་ལེ་ཙ་ལྔ་པའི་བཞི་ལས། ནཱ་[147] མ་ཡིན་པའི་བསྐྱུ་བ་ལ་ཀྲྀའི་ཕྱིད་རོ། ཞེས་པའི་ཀྲྀ་ཕྱིད་ཏུ་བསྒྱུར། ཀ་ལྔ་པའི་[148]··· ཀྲྀད་དྲུག་པ་ནར···· ཀྲྀ་ཡ་ཕུ་ཕྱིད་ཀྱང་། ཆིག་གསལ་ལ་ཙཀྲ་པ་དང་མཐུན་ནོ།····

ཀྱུ་ཊཱ་ཀྱི་ལྟ་དབྱངས་དོན་དང་། ཕཱ་ཡིག་ཏུ་ཀཱ་[149] ཨཱ་ག་མ་སྐྱེར་བའི་རྟགས་དོན་ཡིན་པས་ཕྱིས་ལ། ཡ་བཞག་ཙ་ལས། རྩང་ངུའི་ཀྱིང་མ་ཡིན་པ་ལ། པིཏ་ལ་ཏུ་ཀཱོ། [149] །ཞེས་པས་ཤི་དང་ཡའི་བར་དུ་ཏུ་ཀཱ་ཕྱིན། ཀཱ་རྟགས་དོན། སུ་བརྗོད་དོན་གཉིས་ཕྱིས་ཏ་བཞག་ཀ་ལྔ་པའི་དང་པོར་ཕྱིངས་ཀྱི་མཐར་ཕཱ···· རྗེས་སུ་འབྲེལ་པ་ལ་ཏའོ་ཞེས་པས་ཤི་རྗེས་སུ་ཏ་སྐྱེར། གསལ་ཕྱིད་དབྱངས་མེད་ཕ་རོལ་ཀྱི་ཡི་གེར་བྲངས་པས་ཙྪ་བུ། ཙ་བ་ལས་ཨ་ཀཱའི་[150] ཨ་ཀཱ་ལ་རིང་ངོ། ཕྲ་ཏི་དང་མི་སྦྱར་རེང་པོར་ཐལ། པྲ་ཏྲི་ཙྪ་བུ་སྟེ་མིང་ཡིན། དེ་ལ་ཙ་བའི་[151] གཉིས་[152] པའི་དང་པོར། དོན་ཙམ་ལ་དང་པོའོ། ཞེས་པའི···· རྣམ་དབྱེ་དང་པོའི་གཅིག་ཚིག····སུ་ཕྱིན། ཀ་སྔར་ན་སི་དང་། ཙ་བའི་གཉིས་པའི་[153] དང་པོར་སུ་ཕྲའི་[154] གྲངས་མེད་ལ་དབྱེའོ་ཞེས་དང་། ཀ་ལས་མི་ཟད་པ་ལས་ཀྱང··· ངོ་། ཞེས་སུ་[155] ཕྱིས་པས་པྲ་ཏི་ཙྪ་བུ་སྟེ། ཕྲད་པ་དང་སྔོས་པ་དང་རྟེན་གསུམ་ལ་འཇུག་སྟེ། འདིར་སྐབས་སུ་གང

བབས་ཀྱིས་འཆད་ཀྱི་གཅིག་ཁོ་ནར་མི་དགོས། ཡང་པ་ཏུ་[156] འགྲོ་བ་ལའོས། པ་ཏུ་[156] བཞག་དེའི་སྔོན་དུ་ཉེར་བསྒྱུར་ཨུ་ཏ་དང་། དེའི་སྔོན་དུ་ས་མ་བཞག་དེ་གཉིས་ལ་སུ་ཕྱིན་དབྱེ་བ་སྦྱར་དང་"འདྲ། ཙ་བའི་དང་པོའི་གསུམ་པར། སྨྲྀ་[157] ཕྱིད་པ་ལ་ཡང་ངོ།···· ཞེས་དང་ཀྲྀཏ་ལྷ་པར་པ་[158] ཏུ། ཙུ་ཏུ། བི་ཤུ། སྦྱི་ཤུ། ཀྱུ་རྟ···· རྣམས་ཀྱི་སྨྲྀ་ཏོ། ཞེས་པས་ཕྱིས་པ་ཏ་[159] ཀྱི་མཐར་སྨྲྀ་ཕྱིན། སྭཱ་རྗེས་འབྲེལ་ཏྲ་འཕེལ་བའི་དོན་ཀྱི་རྗེས་འབྲེལ་གཉིས་ཕྱིས་ཨུ་ཏྲ་ཞག་ཕྱིངས་ཀྱི་དང་པོ་འཕེལ་བ་བྱས་རིམ་བཞིན······ ཀུའི་སྦྱོག་གི་[160] [161] མཚམས་སྦྱར་ནས། ས་མུ་ཏྲ་དཱ་སྒྲུབ། དེ་ལ་ཙ་བ་ལས། དོན་ཙམ་ལ་དང་པོའོ་ཞེས་[162] སུ་ཕྱིན་སུ་ཕྱིས། ས་ས་[163] དྲུ་ཏྲའི་ཏུའོས། [164] སུ་[165] རྣ་ཏུ་བྱས་ཨུ་ནི་ཙ་བ་ལས། ཤ་ཤུ་[166] ལ་ཡང་ཨ་སུ་ལས་ཏུའི་རོ། །ཞེས་པའི་སུ་[167] རྟགས་དོན་ཡིན་པས་ཕྱིས། ཙ་བ་ལས། རེ་[168] བའི་རྗེས་པ་ལ་རྣམ་པར་བཅད་པའོ་ཞེས་པས་ར་རྣམ་བཅད་བྱས་[169] པས། ས་མུ་ཏྲ་དཿ སྒྲུབ་སྟེ་འབྱུང་བ་དང་སྒྲུབ་པ་དང་ཡོད་པ་ལ་སྐབས་འདིར་བཤད་དོ། །གཉིས

109

པ་ནི་དེ་ལྟར་ན་དངོས་པོ་རྣམས་ཀྱི་འབྱུང་བ་རྒྱུ་ལ་ལྟོས་པ་ནི་རྟེན་ཅིང་འབྲེལ་འབྱུང་གི་དོན་ཡིན་ཏེ། ཕྲ་ཏྱེ་ནི་ཕྲད་པར་སྒྱུར་བྱེད་ཀྱི་དོན་དང་། ཨི་ཏི་ནི་ཨི་ཎ་འགྲོ་བའི་བྱིངས་ཡིན་ཀྲཏ་ད……[170] ཨུཏྤ་ཀྱི་མཐའ་ཅན་ཕྲ་ཏྱཱ་ཡ་ཞེས་པ་ཞེར་བསྒྱུར་གྱིས་བསྒྱུར་བས་ཕྲ་ཏྱཱ་ཡ་ནི་ཕྲད་པ་དང་ལྟོས་པ་ལ་འཇུག་ཅིང་། ས་མུཏ་གོང་ན་ཡོད་པའི་ལྟ་ད་ཡང་འབྱུང་ བ་ལ་ འཇུག་ཅིང་སྐབས་[171] གཞན་དུ་ཡོད་པ་དང་གྲུབ་པ་ལ་འང་བཤད་པའི་ཕྱིར་ཏེ།……ཚིག་གསལ་ལས། (༣) དེ་ལ་ཕྲ་ཏྱེ་ནི་ཕྲད་པའི་དོན་ཏོ། ཨི་ཏི་ནི་འགྲོ་བའི་དོན་ཏོ། ཨུཏྤ་ཀྱི་མཐའ་ཅན་ཕྲ་ཏྱཱ་ཡའི་སྒྲ་ནི་ཕྲད་པ་སྟེ། ལྟོས་པ་ལ་འཇུག་ཅེས་པ་ནས། ཕ་ཡིན་ཏེ། སྐད་ཀྱི་བྱིངས་ནི་ཉེ་བར་བསྒྱུར་བས་ཡོངས་སུ་བསྒྱུར་བའི་ཕྱིར་རོ།།

ཉེ་བར་བསྒྱུར་བའི་དབང་གིས་ནི།།
སྐད་བྱིངས་དོན་ནི་ཡོངས་བསྒྱུར་ཏེ།།
གངྒཱའི་ཆུ་ནི་མངར་མོད་ཀྱི།།

110

རྒྱ་མཚོ་ཆུ་ཡིས་ཟེ་བཞིན་ནོ།།

ཞེས་བཤད་དོ།] ས་མུཏ་གོང་ན་ཡོད་པའི་ལྟ་ད་ནི་འབྱུང་བའི་[172] དོན་ཅན་ཡིན་པས་ས་མུཏྤ་དའི་སྒྲ་ནི་འབྱུང་བ་ལ་འཇུག་གོ། དེའི་ཕྱིར་དངོས་པོ་རྣམས་ཀྱི་[173] འབྱུང་བ་རྒྱུ་དང་རྐྱེན་ལ་ལྟོས་པ་ནི་རྟེན་ཅིང་འབྲེལ་པར་འབྱུང་བའི་དོན་ཏོ།[174] ཞེས་སོ།[175] དེ་ལྟར་བཤད་པ་ཏཱིཀ་བྱེད་མང་པོས་ཨུཏྤ་ཀྱི་སྐད་དོད་ཡིན་སྙམ་པ་དང་ཕྲ་ཏི་དང་ཨི་ཏི་ཞེས་ཚིར་བཀགས་པ་མཐོང་ལ། ལོ་ཆེན་བློ་བརྟན་གྱིས་སྒྲ་སྦྱོར་ཡང་མི་གསལ་ལ། འདི་དག་མ་གོ་ན་ཚིག……[176] གསལ་གྱི་ཕྱོད་[177] ཆ་མི་གོ་བར་མཐོང་ནས་འཁྲུལ་ཟླ་ཞུང་གསལ་རེ་སྨྲས་སོ། གཉིས་པ་ལ……འགྲེལ་བྱེད་གཞན་གྱི་ལུགས་དགག །ལེགས་ལྡན་གྱི་ལུགས་དགག་པའོ། །དང་པོ་ལ་འདོད་པ་བརྗོད་པ་དང་དེ་དགག་པ་གཉིས། དང་པོ་ནི། སློབ་ཀྱི་དུས་[178] ཀྱི་སངས་རྒྱས་བསྐྱངས་དང་ལེགས་ལྡན་ལས་གཞན་པའི་རྩ་ཤེས་ཊཱིཀ་བྱེད་ལ་ལ་དག་ན་རེ། ཕྲ་ཏི་སྒྲ་སོ་སོ་བའམ་དེ་དེ་

111

ལ་བུའི་ཟློས་དོན་དང་། ཨི་ཏི་སྟེ་ཨི་ཏ་ནི་འགྲོ་བ་སྟེ་ཆས་པ་དང་འཇིག་པའི་དོན་དང་། བྱིངས་དེ་ལ་ཡ་རྐྱེན་བྱིན་པའི་ཨི་ཏྱ་ནི་[179] འགྲོ་བར་རུང་བ་ཡིན་ལ་ཨི་ཏྱ་དེ་ཕན་གྱི་ཚིད་པར་ཏྱ་སྒྲ……ནས་སོ་སོ་སོ་སོར་འགྲོ་ཞིང་འཇིག་པ་དང་ལྡན་པ་རྣམས་ཀྱི་འབྱུང་བ་ནི་ཞེས་བཤད་དེ། ཚིག་གསལ་ལས། གཞན་དག་ནི་ཕྲ་ཏི་ནི་ཟློས་པའི་དོན་ཏོ། །ནས། [ཨི་ཏི་ནི་འགྲོ་བའི་སྟེ་ཆས་པ་དང་འཇིག་པའོ། །ཨི་ཏྱ་ནི་འགྲོ་བར་རུང་བ……དག་གོ་ཞེས་དེ་ལྟར་ཨི་ཏྱའི་སྒྲ་དེ་ལ་ཕན་པའི་མཐའ་ཅན་དུ་བྱེ་བྲག་ཏུ་བཤད་ནས། སོ་སོ་སོ་སོར་འགྲོ་ཞིང་འཇིག་པ་དང་ལྡན་པ་རྣམས་ཀྱི་འབྱུང་བ་ནི་རྟེན་ཅིང་འབྲེལ་པར་འབྱུང་བའོ་ཞེས]] བརྗོད་པར་བྱེད་དོ། ཞེས་དང་། ཤེས་རབ་སྒྲོན་མེ་ལས། གཞན་དག་ན་རེ། སོ་སོ་འཇིག་པ་དང་[180] [ལྡན་པ་རྣམས་ཀྱི་འབྱུང་བ་ནི་རྟེན་ཅིང་འབྲེལ་པར་འབྱུང་བའོ་ཞེའོ།]སོགས་དང་། དེའི་འགྲེལ་བཤད་ལས། གཞན་དག་ན་རེ་ཞེས་བྱ་བ་ནི་དབུ་མ་པའི་གྲུབ་པའི་མཐའ་སྨྲ་བ་[གཞན་དག་ན་རེའོ །སོ་

112

སོར་འཛིན་པ་དང་ལྡན་པ་རྣམས་ཀྱི་འབྱུང་བ་ཞེས་བྱ་བ་ནི་རྒྱུ་དང་རྐྱེན་སོ་སོར་ངེས་པ་སྐད་ཅིག་སོ་སོ་རེ་རེ་ལ་འཛིན་པ་དང་ལྡན་པའི་འབྲས་བུ་རྣམས་ཀྱི་ཚོགས་ཤིང་འབྱུང་བ་སྟེ། ཕྱད་ནས་འབྱུང་བ་ཞེས་བྱ་བའི་ཚིག་གོ །རྟེན་ཅིང་འབྲེལ་པར་འབྱུང་བའོ་ཞེས་བྱ་བས་ནི་ཚིག་གི་དོན་ཟླ་མའི་མཇུག་བསྡུ་བ་བསྟན་ཏེ། རྒྱུ་དང་རྐྱེན་སོ་སོར་ངེས་པ་སྐད་ཅིག་སོ་སོ་རེ་རེ་ལ་འཛིན་པ་དང་ལྡན་པའི་འབྲས་བུ་རྣམས་ཀྱི་ཚོགས་ཤིང་འབྱུང་བ་གང་ཡིན་པ་དེ་ནི་རྟེན་ཅིང་འབྲེལ་པར་འབྱུང་བའོ་ཞེས་བྱ་བར་སྦྱོར་ཏོ…ཞེའོ་ཞེས་བྱ་བ་ནི། འགྲེལ་པ་བྱེད་པ་རང་ཉིད་མ་ཡིན་པ་དབུ་མ་པའི་གྲུབ་པའི་མཐའ་སྨྲ་བ་གཞན་དག་དེ་སྐད་ཟེར་རོ…ཞེས་བྱ་བའི་ཚིག་གོ] སོགས་སོ། འདི་ལྟར་སྨྲ་སྨྲབ་ན་འགྲོ་བའི་བྱེད་ཀྱི་ཀྲའི་ཀྲ་ཕྱེས་ཀྲི[181]ཏྭཱ་ཡིན། ཡོངས་རྫོགས…ཕྱེས་པས[182]་བྱེད་ཀྱི་མཐར་ལྱཔ[183]་རྗེས་འབྲེལ་ལ[184]་ཀྲ[185]་རོས་པ…འགྲོ་བའི་དོན་གྱིས་ཀྲ[185]་ཡིན་པས[186]་དེར་ལེགས་ཕན་པ་ལ་ཡང་ཡ་ཞེས་པས་དེ་ཕན་གྱི་རྐྱེན་ཡ་ཡིན་སོ་ཡིན་ནས་ལྱ་ཏེ

113

དང་སྦྱར་བས་ལྱ་ཀྲི་ཏྭཿཕྱུག་མ་འདྲ་ལ་རྣམ་དབྱེ་ཕྱེས་པར…འདོད་པ་ལའང་དགག་པ་མཛད་དོ། །གཉིས་པ་ནི་དེའི…(ཏ) བློས་དང་། མི་རུ་དེ་ཕན་མཐའ་ཅན་གཉིས་མི་འཆད་དེ།…བློས་བ་ཤད་དེ་སྐྱེ་རྩམ་ལ་འཆད་ཀྱང་ཚེ་ཐག་ལ་མ་ཁྱབ་པའི་ཕྱིར། སྒུས་རྟེན་ཅིང་འབྲེལ་འབྱུང་མཐོང་བ་ངེས་ཞེས་སྦྱོར་བཏང་ནས་མང་པོ་བློས་སྨྲ་ཡང་འཆད་ལ། སྒུས་རྟེན་འབྲེལ་མཐོང་བ་སོགས་ལ་ཚིག་སྤྱད་སྦྱང་བས་ཚིག་སྤྱད་ཀྱི་རྣམ་དབྱེ་ཕྱི་བ་འཆད་ཀྱང་ཕྱེ་བྲག་ཏུ་མིག་དང་གཟུགས་ལ་བརྟེན་ནས་མིག་གི་རྣམ་ཤེས་འབྱུང་ཞེས་པ་ལྟ་བུ་ཕྱེ་བྲག་གཅིག་ལ…བློས་པ་མི་རུང་ཞིང་། དེ་ལ་ཚིག་སྤྱད[187]……མེད་པའི་ཕྱིར། ཚིག་སྤྱད[187]……མི་རུང་སྟེ། མིག་དང་གཟུགས་ལ་ཞེས་པའི་དང་གི་སྐད་དོད་ཙ་དང་གཟུགས་ལ་ཞེས་པའི་ཨསྨ་མ་ཕྱེས་པའི་ཕྱིར་དང་། [188]བརྟེན་ནས་དང་མིག་གི་བར་དུ…རྣམ་དབྱེ་མ་མཐོང་བའི་ཕྱིར་ཏེ།[189]ཡུཀྟ་ཀྱི་མཐའ་ཅན་མི་ཟད་པར་རིགས་པའི་ཕྱིར་ཏེ། ཚིག……གསལ་ལས་དེ་དག

114

[190]གི་ལྟར་ན་དགེ་སློང་དག །ཅེས་པ་ནས། [ཇི་ལ་རྟེན་ཅིང…འབྲེལ་པར་འབྱུང་བ་བསྟན་པར་བྱ་ཡི། སྒུས་རྟེན་ཅིང་འབྲེལ་པར་འབྱུང་བ་མཐོང་བ་ངེས་ཆོས་མཐོང་ངོ་ཞེས་བྱ་བ་དེ་ལྟ་བུ་ལ་སོགས་པའི་ཡུལ་ལ་ནི་བློས་པའི་དོན་སྲིད་པའི་ཕྱིར་དང་། ཚིག་བསྡུ་བ་ཡོད་པའི་ཕྱིར་ཕྱེ་བྲག་ཏུ་བཤད་པ་ལེགས་པར…འགྱུར་ན། མིག་དང་གཟུགས་ལ་བརྟེན་ནས་མིག་གི་རྣམ་པར་ཤེས་པ་འབྱུང་ངོ་ཞེས་བྱ་བ་དེ་ལྟ་བུ་ལ་སོགས་པའི་ཡུལ་འདིར་ནི་མིག་དང་གཟུགས་ལ་བརྟེན་ནས་ཞེས་དོན་གྱི་ཁྱད་པར་དངོས་སུ་ཞལ་གྱིས་བཞེས་ཤིང་། མིག་གི་དབང་པོ་གཅིག་གི་རྒྱུ་ཅན་གྱི་རྣམ་པར་ཤེས་པ་གཅིག་ཀྱང་སྐྱེ་བར་བཞེད་པ་ན་བརྟེན་ནས་ཞེས་བྱ་བའི་སྒྲ་ལ་བློས་པའི་དོན་ཉིད་ཡོད་པར་ག…ལ་འགྱུར། ཕྱད་པའི་དོན་ནི་ཕྱད་ནས་འབྱུང་བ་ནི་རྟེན་ཅིང་འབྲེལ་པར་འབྱུང་བའོ་ཞེས་དོན་གྱི་ཁྱད་པར་ཞལ་གྱིས་མ་བཞེས་པའི་རྟེན་ཅིང་འབྲེལ་པར་འབྱུང་བའི་སྒྲ་ལ་ཡང་ཡོད་པ་ཡིན་ལ། དོན་གྱི་ཁྱད་པར་ཞལ་གྱིས་བཞེས་པ་ལ་ཡང…

115

ཡོད་པ་ཡིན་ཏེ། མིག་དང་གཟུགས་ལ་བརྟེན་ནས་མིག་དང···
གཟུགས་ཐུད་ཙེད་མིག་དང་གཟུགས་ལ་བལྟོས་ནས་ཞེས···
བཤད་པའི་ཕྱིར་རོ། །མི་ཏྲའི་སྐྱ་དེ་ལ་ཕན་པའི་མཐའ་ཅན
ཡིན་ན་ནི་མིག་དང་གཟུགས་ལ་བརྟེན་ནས་མིག་གི་རྣམ་པར
ཤེས་པ་འབྱུང་ངོ་། །ཞེས་བྱ་བ་འདིར་ཕྱི་ཏྲའི་སྐྱ་ནི་ཟད་པ་
མ་ཡིན་པའི་ཕྱིར་དང་། ཚིག་བསྡུ་བ་ཡོད་པ་མ་ཡིན་པའི་ཕྱིར
རྣམ་པར་དབྱེ་བ་ཚོས་པར་འགྱུར་བ་ཡིན་དང་། མིག་དང···
གཟུགས་ལ་བརྟེན་པ་རྣམ་པར་ཤེས་པ་ཞེས་བྱ་བར་འདོན
པར་འགྱུར་བ་ཞིག་ན། འདི་ནི་དེ་ལྟ་བུ་ཡང་མ་ཡིན་པས།]
ལྷུཏྲ་ཀྱི་མཐའ་ཅན་མི་ཟད་པ་ཁོ་ནར་ཆེ་བག་ཏུ་བཤད་པར···
ཁས་བླང་པར་བྱའོ། །ཞེས་སོ། །དོན་ནི་ཙཀྵུརྦིཛྙཱ་ནཾ་པ
ཏྲི་ཏྱ་ཙཀྵུ་ཞེས་འབྱུང་བའི་ཕྱིར། ཞེས་པའོ། གཉིས་པ
ནི་ལེགས་ལྡན་གྱིས་གཞན་བཀག་རྒྱལ་ཡང་མི་འཐད་ལ།
རང་གི་ལུགས་ཀྱི་ཡང་སྒྲ་དོན་མ་ཚད་བའི་སྐྱོན་གཉིས་ཡོད
དེ། ལེགས་རབ་སྐྱོན་མེ་ལས། རྟེན་ཅིང་འབྲེལ་པར་འབྱུང་

116

བ་ཞེས་བྱ་བ་ལ་ཁ་ཅིག་ན་རེ། རྟེན་ཅིང་ཞེས་བྱ···བའི་ཚིག
གི་ཐུད་ནི་ཐྲོས་པའི་དོན་ཅན་ཡིན་པའི་ཕྱིར་དང་། འབྲེལ་
པར་ཞེས་བྱ་བ་ནི་ཕྲད་པའི་དོན་ཡིན་པའི་ཕྱིར་དང་། འབྱུང་
བ་ཞེས་བྱ་བའི་སྒྲ་ནི་སྐྱེ་བའི་དོན་ཡིན་པའི་ཕྱིར་རྟེན་ཅིང་འབྲེལ་
པར་འབྱུང་བ་སྟེ། དེ་དང་དེ་ལ་རྟེན་ཅིང་ཕྲད་ནས་འབྱུང་བའོ་
ཞེའོ། ཞེས་སངས་རྒྱས་བསྐྱངས་ཀྱི་ལུགས་བརྗོད་ལ་སྦྱར···
ལྟར་ཡང་བརྗོད་དོ། །དེ་ལྟར་བཤད་པ་དེ་ནི་སློབ་དཔོན་ལེགས་
ལྡན་ཕྱོགས་སྔ་བརྗོད་པ་ལ་མི་མཁས་སོ། །ཕྱི་མ་དུ་བྲི···
བས་བཞེད་དེ། སངས་རྒྱས་བསྐྱངས་ཀྱི་དགོངས་པ་ལེགས་ལྡན
གྱིས་བརྗོད་པ་ལྟར་མ་ཡིན་པར་རྟེན་ཅིང་འབྲེལ་པར་ཏེ་པྲ
ཏྱ་ཡ་ནི་ཕྲད་པའི་དོན་དུ་བཤད་པས་ན་རྟེན་ཅིང་གི་སྐད་དོད་པྲ
ཏི་བློས་པའི་དོན་དུ་མིན་ལ། འབྲེལ་པར་ཏེ་ཨི་ཏྱ་ཡང་ཕྲད
པའི་དོན་མ་ཡིན་པའི་ཕྱིར་ཏེ་ཚིག···གསལ་ལས། གཞན
གྱི་བཤད་པ་རྗེས་སུ་བརྗོད་ནས་ཞེས་པ་ནས། [སྐུན་འཇིན་པར
བྱེད་པ་དེ་ནི། རེ་ཞིག་གཞན་གྱི་ཕྱོགས་རྗེས་སུ་བརྗོད་པ···

117

ལ་མི་མཁས་པ་ཉིད་དོ་སྙམ་མོ། །ཅིའི་ཕྱིར་ཞེ་ན། གང་ཞིག
རྟེན་ཅིང་འབྲེལ་པར······[191] ཀྱི་སྒྲ་ཕྲད་པའི་དོན་ཅན་དུ་འཆད
པ་དེས་ནི་རྟེན་ཅིང་ཞེས་བྱ་བ་ཐྲོས་པའི་དོན་དུ་མ་ཡིན་ཞིང···
འབྲེལ་པར་ཞེས་བྱ་བ] ཕྲད་པའི་དོན་དུ་ཡང་མིན་ནོ།[192] །ཞེས
སོ། །འོན་ཅི་ཞེ་ན་སངས་རྒྱས་བསྐྱངས་ནི་རྟེན་ཅིང་ཕྲ་ཏི་ཏེ་ནི
ཕྲད་པའི་དོན་ཅན་དང་། འབྲེལ་བར་ཨི་ཏྱ་ནི་འགྲོ་བའི་དོན
ཡིན་ལ།[193] སོ་སོ་ལ་དེ་ལྟར་དོན་ཐ་དད་ཡིན་ཀྱང་དེ་གཉིས་ཚོགས
པ་ན་གངྒཱའི[194]་ཆུ་མངར་བ་དེ་ལ་ན་ཚའི་ཆུ་དང་ཕྲད་པས་ལན
ཚའི་ཆུར་འགྱུར་བ་བཞིན་དུ་ཉེར་བསྒྱུར་གྱི་དབང་གིས···
ཚིག་འོག་མའི་དོན་འགྱུར་ནས། ཚིག་གཉིས་ལས་དོན་ཕྲད
པ་གཅིག་པུ་སྟོན་པའི་ཕྱིར། ཕྲད་ནས་འབྱུང་བ་རྟེན་འབྱུང
གི་དོན་ཡིན་ལ། རྟེན་ཅིང་འབྲེལ་འབྱུང་གི་སྒྲ་དངོས་པོ་ཐམས
ཅད་ལ་སྦྱོར་ཚེ་ཏུ་པྲ་ཏཱི་ཏྱ་ས་མུཏྤཱ་དཿཞེས་བརྗོད་པ་ན་རྒྱུ
རྐྱེན་གྱི་ཚོགས་པ་དེ་དང་དེ་ཕྲད་ནས་འབྱུང་བ་བློས་པ་དང···
འབྲེལ་བར་བྱེད་ལ། ཆེ་བག་ཏུ་མིག་དང་གཟུགས་ལ······

118

བརྟེན་ནས་ཞེས་པ་ནྲ་ཏུ་ལ་བློས་པར་སངས་རྒྱས་བསྐྱངས་མི་བཞེད་པའི་ཕྱིར་ཏེ། ཚིག···གསལ་ལས། འོ་ན་ཅི་ཞེ་ན། རྟེན་ཅིང་ནི། ཞེས་པ་ནས། [ཕྲད་པའི་དོན་ཡིན་ཞིང་། འབྲེལ་བར་འགྲོ་བའི་དོན་ཡིན་ལ། ཚོགས་པ་རྟེན་ཅིང་འབྲེལ་པའི་སྒྲ་ནི···ཕྲད་པ་ཉིད་ཡིན་པར་འཆད་པར་བྱེད་དོ། །དེས་ན་དེ་ནི་ཕྲད་ནས་འབྱུང་བ་ནི་རྟེན་ཅིང་འབྲེལ་པར་འབྱུང་བའོ་ཞེས་དེ་ལྟར་བཤད་པར་སྒྱུར་པའི་རྟེན་ཅིང་འབྲེལ་པར་འབྱུང་བའི་སྒྲས···གལ་ཏེ་དངོས་པོ་སྲིད་ཚད་མ་ལུས་པ་འཛིན་པར་བརྗོད་པར··འདོད་པ་དེའི་ཚེ་ནི། རྒྱུ་དང་རྐྱེན་གྱི་ཚོགས་པ་དེ་དང་དེ་ཕྲད་ནས་འབྱུང་བ་ནི་རྟེན་ཅིང་འབྲེལ་པར་འབྱུང་བའོ་ཞེས་བློས་པ་དང་འབྲེལ་བར་བྱེད་ལ། འོན་ཏེ་བྱེ་བྲག་འཛིན་པ་དེའི་ཚེ་ནི་མིག་དང་གཟུགས་ལ་བརྟེན་ནས་ཞེས་བློས་པ་དང···འབྲེལ་བ་མ་ཡིན་ནོ། །དེ་ལྟར་ན་རེ་ཞིག་སློབ་དཔོན་ནི···རྗེས་སུ་བརྗོད་པ་ལ།] མི་མཁས་སོ། །ཞེས་སོ། །དེར་མ···ཟད་གཞན་ལུགས་བཀག་ཚུལ་ཡང་མི་འཐད་དེ། རིགས་

119

པ་མེད་པར་མི་འཐད་ཅེས་པའི་དམ་བཅའ་ཙམ་དུ་ཟད་པའི་ཕྱིར་དང་། འོན་ཀྱང་རྣམ་ཤེས་གཟུགས་ཅན་མ་ཡིན་པའི་ཕྱིར། མིག་དང་གཟུགས་ལ་ཕྲད་པ་མེད་དེ། ཕྲད་པ་ནི་གཟུགས་ཅན་ཁོ་ན་ལ་ཡོད་པའི་ཕྱིར། ཞེ་ནའང་། མི་འཐད་དེ། མདོ་ལས། དགེ་སློང་འདི་ནི་འབྲས་བུ་ཐོབ་པ་ཡིན་ནོ། ཞེས་དགེ་སློང་དང···འབྲས་བུ་བཞི་ཕྲད་པ་ཁས་བླང་པའི་ཕྱིར་ལ། ཕྲད་ནས་ཞེས་པ་ཉོས་ནས་ཞེས་པའི་རྣམ་གྲངས་ཡིན་པའི་ཕྱིར་དང་། རྟེན་ཅིང་འབྲེལ་པའི་སྒྲ་དོན་ནི་འཕགས་པས།

དེ་དང་དེ་བརྟེན་གང་འབྱུང་བ།།
རང་གི་ངོ་བོར་དེ་མ་སྐྱེས།།

ཞེས་ཕྲད་པའི་དོན་དུ་ཁས་བླངས་པའི་ཕྱིར་ཏེ། ཚིག་གསལ་ལས། དེ་ཡང་མི་རུང་སྟེ་མིག་དང་། ཞེས་པ་ནས། [གཟུགས་ལ་བརྟེན་ནས་མིག་གི་རྣམ་པར་ཤེས་པ་འབྱུང་ཞེས་གསུངས་པ་འདི་ལ་དོན་གཉིས་ག་མེད་པའི་ཕྱིར་རོ་ཞེས་སུན་འབྱིན་སྨྲས་པ་གང་ཡིན་པ་དེ་ཡང་མི་འཐད་དོ། །ཅིའི···

120

ཕྱིར་ཞེ་ན། ཇི་ལྟར་མེད་ཅེས་བྱ་བའི་རིགས་པ་མ་བཀོད་པས། དམ་བཅའ་བ་ཙམ་ཡིན་པའི་ཕྱིར་རོ། །འོན་ཏེ་རྣམ(ཤ)་པར་ཤེས་པ་ནི་གཟུགས་ཅན་མ་ཡིན་པའི་ཕྱིར་མིག་དང་ཕྲད་པ་ཡོད་པ་མ་ཡིན་ཏེ། གཟུགས་ཅན་རྣམས་ཁོ་ན་ལ་དེ་དང་ཕྲད་པ་མཐོང་བའི་ཕྱིར་རོ། སྨྲས་པའི་བསམ་པ་འདི་ཡིན་ན་ནི། དེ་ཡང་མི་རིགས་ཏེ། དགེ་སློང་འདི་ནི་འབྲས་བུ་ཐོབ་པ་ཡིན་ནོ···ཞེས་བྱ་བ་འདིར་ཕྲད་པ་ཁས་བླངས་པའི་ཕྱིར་དང་། ཕྲད་ནས་ཞེས་བྱ་བའི་སྒྲ་ཡང་བསྙོས་ནས་ཞེས་བྱ་བའི་སྒྲའི་རྣམ་གྲངས་ཡིན་པའི་ཕྱིར་དང་། རྟེན་ཅིང་འབྲེལ་བར་ཞེས་བྱ་བའི་སྒྲ་ནི།

དེ་དང་དེ་བརྟེན་གང་འབྱུང་བ།།
རང་གི་དངོས་པོར་དེ་མ་སྐྱེས།།

ཞེས་སློབ་དཔོན་ཀླུ་སྒྲུབ་ཀྱིས་ཀྱང་ཕྲད་ནས་ཞེས་བྱ་བའི་དོན་ཉིད་དུ་ཞལ་གྱིས་བཞེས་པའི་ཕྱིར་རོ། །དེས་ན་] སྤྱོན་ཡང་མི་འཐད་དོ་ཞེས་གཞན་དག་ཟེར་རོ། །ཞེས་སོ། །གཉིས་པ་ལེགས་ལྡན་ རང་ལུགས་ཀྱི་བཤད་ཚུལ་དེ་ཡང་མི་འཐད

121

དེ། ཞེ་བྲག་ཏུ་འཆད་པར་བཞེད་ཀྱང་རྟེན་ཅིང་འབྲེལ་པར་དང་། འབྱུང་བའི་སྒྲ་དོན་གྱི་ཁྱད་པར་སོ་སོར་མ་བརྗོད་ཅིང་འདི་ཡོད་པས་འདི་འབྱུང་ལ་འདི་སྐྱེས་པའི་ཕྱིར་འདི་སྐྱེ་བ་སྟེ··· ཞེས་བྱ་བ་རྐྱེན་འདི་དང་ལྡན་པ་ཉིད་ཀྱི་དོན་ནི་རྟེན་ཅིང་འབྲེལ་པར་འབྱུང་བའི་དོན་ཏེ་ཞེས་པ་ཙམ་ལས་མ་བཤད་པའི···ཕྱིར་ཏེ། ཚིག···གསལ་ལས། གང་ཡང་འོན་གང་ཡིན···ཞེ་ན། འདི་ཡོད་པས་ཞེས་པ་ནས་[འདི་འབྱུང་ལ། འདི་སྐྱེས···པའི་ཕྱིར་འདི་སྐྱེ་བ་སྟེ་ཞེས་བྱ་བ་རྐྱེན་འདི་དང་ལྡན་པ་ཉིད···ཀྱི་དོན་ནི་རྟེན་ཅིང་འབྲེལ་པར་འབྱུང་བའི་དོན་ཏོ་ཞེས་རང···གི་ལུགས་རྣམ་པར་བཞག་པ་དེ་ཡང་འཐད་པ་མ་ཡིན་ཏེ། རྟེན་ཅིང་འབྲེལ་པར་ཞེས་བྱ་བ་དང་འབྱུང་བ་ཞེས་བྱ་བའི་སྒྲ་གཉིས་རེ་རེ་ལ་དོན་གྱི་ཁྱད་པར་མ་བརྗོད་པའི་ཕྱིར་ལ། དེ།] ཞེ་བྲག་ཏུ་བཤད་པ་ཡང་བརྗོད་པར་འདོད་པའི་ཕྱིར[196] རོ། [ཞེས་སོ།][197] གཞལ་(ང།)[198] ཏེ་དགོན་པའི་ཤིག་ལེ་ཞེས་བྱ་བ་དང་ལ་སོགས་པས་ཐུ་མའི་གསུང་རྒྱུན་ནས་སྐམ་སྐྱེས་པ་བཏྲར···

122

མཚོ་སྐྱེས་དང་། ལངས་པའི་མ་ཏི[199]་ལ་སར་ཞལ། ཞེས་པ···ལྟར་རྟེན་ཅིང་འབྲེལ་པར་འབྱུང་བའི་སྒྲ་ནི་བཤད་པའི་རྒྱུ་མཚན་ཅན་མ་ཡིན་པར་གཏིང་ཚུགས་པ་སྟེ་འདུག་པའི་སྒྲར་ཁས་བླངས་ནས་བཤད་ཅེ་ན། དེ་ཡང་མི་འཐད་དེ་རྟེན་ཅིང་འབྲེལ་པར་དང་འབྱུང་བའི་དོན། སློབ་དཔོན་འཕགས་པས།

དེ་དང་དེ་བརྟེན་གང་འབྱུང་བ།།
རང་གི་ངོ་བོར་དེ་མ་སྐྱེས།།[200]

ཞེས་པའི་དེ་དང་དེ་བརྟེན་དང་། འབྱུང་བ་ཞེས་པ་རྣམས···ཀྱི···སྒྲ་དེའི་ཡན་ལག་སོ་སོར་ཕྱེ་ནས་གསུངས་པའི···ཕྱིར་དང་། ཅི་སྟེ་ཚོད་རིན་ཆེན་ཕྲེང་བ་ལས།

འདི་ཡོད་ན་ནི་འདི་འབྱུང་སྟེ།།
ཐུང་ངུ་ཡོད་ན་རིང་པོ་བཞིན།།

ཞེས་པ་ལྟར་བཤད་འདོད་ན་ཡང་ཕྲད་པའི་སྒྲར[201]་བཤད་དགོས་པའི་ཕྱིར་གཞན་སུན་འབྱིན་པ་ལ་ཡང་དེར་འགྱུར་རོ།།······

123

ཚིག··· གསལ་ལས། ཅི་སྟེ་དགོན་པའི་ཤིག་ལེ་ཞེས་བྱ་བ། ཞེས་པ་ནས། [ལ་སོགས་པ་ལྟར་རྟེན་ཅིང་འབྲེལ་པར་འབྱུང་བའི་སྒྲ་ནི་གཏིང་ཚུགས་པའི་སྒྲར་ཁས་བླངས་ནས་དེ་སྐད་དུ་བརྗོད་དོ་ཞེ་ན། དེ་ཡང་མི་འཐད་དེ། རྟེན་ཅིང་འབྲེལ་པར···འབྱུང་བའི་སྒྲ་ནི་སློབ་དཔོན་གྱིས།

དེ་དང་དེ་བརྟེན་གང་འབྱུང་བ།།
རང་གི་དངོས་པོར་དེ་མ་སྐྱེས།།

ཞེས་ཡན་ལག་གི་དོན་དང་རྗེས་སུ་འབྲེལ་པ་ཉིད་དུ་ཞལ་གྱིས་བཞེས་པའི་ཕྱིར་རོ། །ཅི་སྟེ་འདི་ཡོད་ན་ནི་འདི་འབྱུང་སྟེ། ཐུང་ངུ་ཡོད་ན་རིང་པོ་བཞིན། ཞེས་བྱ་བས་འཆད་པར་བྱེད་པས་ནི་ཐུང་ངུ་དང་ཕྲད་ཅིང་ཐུང་ངུ་བརྟེན་ཏེ། ཐུང་ངུ··ལ་བལྟོས་ནས་རིང་པོར་འགྱུར་རོ་ཞེས་དེ་ཉིད་ཁས་བླངས་པར་འགྱུར་རོ།] དེའི་ཕྱིར་གང་ཞིག་སུན་འབྱིན་པ་དེ་ཉིད་ཁས་ལེན་པར་རིགས་པ་མིན་ནོ། །ཞེས་སོ། །དེས་ན་བརྟེན་ནས་འབྱུང་བའི་དོན་ནི་རང་གི་རྒྱུ་རྐྱེན་ལ་ལྟོས་ནས་འབྱུང་

124

བ་འདུས་བྱས་ཀྱི་རྟེན་འབྲེལ་གྱི་དོན་དང་། རང་གི་ཆ་ཤས་སམ་གདགས་གཞིའམ་ཡན་ལག་ལ་ལྟད་པའམ་ལྟོས་ནས་གྲུབ་པ་རྟེན་ཅིང་འབྲེལ་བར་འབྱུང་བའི་དོན་ཡིན་ཏེ། འབྱུང་བའི་སྐད་དོད་ས་མུཏ྄་པཱ་དའི་རྟེན་འབྲེལ་མདོ་འགྲེལ་ལས་ས་མྲ་འདུ་བ་དང་། ཚོགས་པ་སོགས་དང་། རྒྱལ་སྲས་མ་ལས་ལྟད་ཡོད་པ་ལ···ལྟད་པ་སོགས་ཀྱིས་[202] གྲུབ་པའི་ཕྱིར་དང་། ལྟད(ཀ)་ལྟོས་བཏེན་ནས་གྲུབ་ཙམ་[203] ཡིན་པའི་ཕྱིར། ཆོས་ཐམས་ཅད་ཚོགས་ཟུབ་བམ་རང་དབང་གིས་གྲུབ་པ་མེད་དེ། བརྒྱ་པ་ལས།[204]

ཀུང(ཁ)་ལ་བརྟེན་ནས་འབྱུང་ཡོད་པ།།
དེ་ནི་རང་དབང་མི་འགྱུར་རོ།།
འདི་ཀུན་རང་དབང་མེད་པ་སྟེ།།
དེས་ན་བདག་ནི་ཡོད་མ་ཡིན།།

ཞེས་དང་། འཕགས་པས་ཀྱང་།

དེ་དང་དེ་བརྟེན་གང་འབྱུང་བ།།
རང་གི་ངོ་བོར་དེ་མ་སྐྱེས།།

125

ཞེས་དང་། བརྒྱ་པའི་འགྲེལ་པ་ལས། བྱུང(ག)་ནི་དངོས་པོ་མེད་པར་སྒྲུབ་མ་ཡིན་ཏེ། རྟེན་ཅིང་འབྲེལ་པར་འབྱུང་བ་སྒྲུབ་པའི་ཕྱིར་རོ། །ཅི་ཁྱོད་དངོས་པོར་སྨྲ་བ་ཞིག་གམ། ཞེ་ན། མི་ན་ཏེ་རྟེན་ཅིང་འབྲེལ་པར་འབྱུང་བ་སྨྲ་བ་ཡིན་པའི་ཕྱིར་རོ། །ཁྱོད་ཅི་སྨྲ་བ་ཞིག་ཅེ་ན། རྟེན་ཅིང་འབྲེལ་པར་འབྱུང་བ···སྨྲ་བའོ། ཡང་རྟེན་ཅིང་འབྲེལ་པར་འབྱུང་བའི་དོན་གང་ཞིག་ཅེ་ན། རང་བཞིན་མེད་པའི་དོན་ཏེ། རང་བཞིན་གྱིས་མ་སྐྱེས་པའི་དོན་དང་། སྒྱུ་མ་དང་། སྨིག་རྒྱུ་དང་། གཟུགས་བརྙན་དང་། དྲི་ཟའི་གྲོང་ཁྱེར་དང་···སྤྲུལ་པ་དང་རྨི་ལམ་དང་མཚུངས་པའི་རང་བཞིན་གྱི་འབྲས་[205] བུ་འབྱུང་བའི་དོན་དང་སྟོང་ཉིད་བདག་མེད་པའི་དོན་ནོ། །ཞེས་གསུངས་པ་ལྟ་བུ་དང་། འདི་ལ་ཟབ་པ་རང་བཞིན་མེད་དེ་ཞེས་པའི་སྒྲུབ་ཆོས་དང་། རྒྱ་ཆེ་བ་རྟེན་འབྱུང་གི་གཏན་ཚིགས་ལ་ཚད་ཚུལ་སོགས་རྒྱས་པར་རིགས་པ་དྲུག་ཅུ་པ་རྩ་འགྲེལ་སྟོང་ཉིད་[206] བདུན་ཅུ་པ་རང་འགྲེལ་དང་རིན་ཆེན་ཕྲེང་བ་དང་དེའི་དར་ཊཱི་ཀ་སོགས་སུ་བཙལ་ལ། བཤེས་སྤྲིང་ལས།

126

རྟེན(ང)་ཅིང་འབྲེལ་པར་འབྱུང་འདི་རྒྱལ་བ་ཡི།།
གསུངས་ཀྱི་མཛོད་ཀྱི་གཅེས་པ་ཟབ་མོ་སྟེ།།
གང་གིས་འདི་ནི་ཡང་དག་མཐོང་བ་དེས།།
སངས་རྒྱས་དེ་ཉིད་རིག་པ[207]···ནམ་མཆོག་མཐོང་།།

ཞེས་དང་། བློ་གྲོས་ཆེན་པོས་དེའི་འགྲེལ་པ་ལས། རྟེན་ཅིང···འབྲེལ་པར་འབྱུང་བ་འདི་ནི་དེ་བཞིན་གཤེགས་པའི་གསུང་གི་གཅེས་པར་གྱུར་པ་ཡིན་ཏེ། འདི་ལྟར་གང་གིས་འདི་ལེགས་པར······ཤེས་པ་དེ། དེ་བཞིན་གཤེགས་པའི་བསྟན་པ་ཡང་དག་པར་རྟོགས་པ་ཡིན་ནོ། །ཟབ་མོ་སྟེ་ཞེས་བྱ་བ་ནི་ཟབ་མོ་ཉིད་ཀོ་ན་སྟོན་པ་བྱེད་པ་ཡིན་ནོ། །ཞེས་དང་། ཡང་ན་གང་གིས་འདི་ནི་ཡང་དག་མཐོང་ཞེས་བྱ་བ་ལ་སོགས་པས་ནི་རྒྱལ་བའི་གསུང་གི་མཛོད་ཀྱི་གཅེས་པ་ཉིད་སྟོན་པར་བྱེད་དོ། །ཟབ་པ་ཉིད་ནི་རང་གིས་མ་ཤེས། གཞན་གྱིས་མ་ཤེས་སོགས་ལྟར་མཐའ་གཉིས་སུ་འཛིན་པ་མཐའ་དག་སེལ་བ་འདི་རིགས་པའི་རྒྱལ་པོ་ཡིན་ཏེ། རྗེ་བླ་མས།

སྟོན་པའི་ནང་ན་རྟེན་འབྲེལ་སྟོན་པ་དང་།།
ཤེས་རབ་ནང་ན་རྟེན་འབྲེལ་ཤེས་པ་གཉིས།།
འཇིག་རྟེན་དག་ན་རྒྱལ་བའི་དབང་པོ་བཞིན།།

ཞེས་སོ། །གཉིས་པ་ནི།

དེའི་ཕྱིར་དོན་དམ་ཚུགས་ཐུབ་ནམ་མཁའ་ཟ།།
སུས་ཀྱང་ཚད་གྲུབ་ཚུགས་ཐུབ་དོན་མ་ཟུས།།

ཞེས་པ་ནི། སྟག་ལོས་སྔར་ལྟར་དོན་དམ་ཚུགས་ཐུབ་དང་ཚད་གྲུབ་གསུམ་དོན་གཅིག་འདོད་པ་ནི་འཕགས་པ་ཡབ···སྲས་གསུམ་གྱིས་རྟེན་འབྱུང་ལ་རང་དབང་བ་མི་ཡོད་པར་ 208 བཤད་པ་དེའི་ཕྱིར། དོན་དམ་ཚུགས་ཐུབ་འདོད་པ་ནི་ནམ་མཁའ་ཟ་བར་འདོད་པ་ཡིན་ལ། རྣམ་འགྲེལ་ལས་ཀྱང་།

གཞལ་བྱ་གཉིས་ཕྱིར་ཚད་མ་གཉིས།།

ཞེས་སྤྱི་མཚན་ཡང་ཚད་གྲུབ་ཏུ་བྱེ་མདོ་སོགས་འདོད་པས་ན་སུས་ཀྱང་ཚད···གྲུབ་ཀྱི་དོན་ལ་རང་གི་ཚུགས་ཐུབ་དགོས་པར་འདོད་པ་གཅིག་ཀྱང་མེད་པས་བསྟན་པར་རྨ་མི་འབྱིན་པར་

མཛོད་ཅིག། ༎གཉིས་པ་གང་ཟག་གི་བདག་འགོག་པའི་དེ་ 209 ལ། དངོས་དང་། འཁྲུལ་སྤོང་གཉིས། དང་པོ་ནི།

རང་དབང་བདག་མེད་ཕུང་མིན་དེ་གཞན་མིན།། 210
ཕུང་པོའི་རྟེན་མིན་ཕུང་པོར་བརྟེན་པའང་མིན།། 211
ཕུང་དང་མི་ལྡན་དབྱིབས་མིན་ཚོགས་མིན་ཕྱིར།།
ཤིང་རྟ་བཞིན་དུ་ཆོས་རྣམས་ཀུན་ལ་སྦྱར།།

ཞེས་སྨྲས་ཏེ། འདིར་ང་དང་ང(མི)ཡི་བ་གཉིས་དང་འཇིག་ལྟ་གཉིས་དང་ངར་འཛིན་པ་དང་། ང་ཡི་འཛིན་པའི་ཞེན་སྣང···པའི་ཡིད་མངོན་ཚད་མ་གཉིས་དང་གདགས་གཞི་གདགས་ཆོས་སོགས་ལ་ལོག་རྟོག་མང་བ་གཞན(ཅི)དུ་རྒྱས་པར་བཀག་པས་ན་འདིར་དཀའ་གནས་མཚོན་ཙམ་བསྟན་ན། མདོ···ལས། དགེ་སློང་དག་དགེ་སྦྱོང་དམ་བྲམ་ཟེ་གང་སུ་དག···ཅིག་བདག་གོ་སྙམ་དུ་ཡང་དག་པར་རྗེས་སུ་ལྟ་བ་དེ་དག་ནི་ཉེ་བར་ལེན་པའི་ཕུང་པོ་ལྔ་པོ་འདི་དག་ཁོ་ན་ལ་ཡང་དག་པར···རྗེས་སུ་ལྟའོ། ཞེས་དང་། རྩ་བར།

ཕུང་པོ་མ་གཏོགས་དེ་འཛིན་མ་གྲུབ་ཕྱིར།།

ཞེས་དང་།

དེ་ནི་ཕུང་ལས་གཞན་བདག་འགོག་པ་སྟེ།།
[གཟུགས་བདག་མིན་སོགས་མདོ་གཞན་གསུངས་ཕྱིར་རོ།།]

ཞེས་སོགས་དང་། རང་འགྲེལ་ལས། དེའི་དམིགས་པ་ནི···བདག་ཁོ་ན་ཡིན་ཏེ། ངར་འཛིན་པ་བདག་གི་ཡུལ་ཅན་ཡིན་པའི་ཕྱིར་རོ་ཞེས་འཇིག་ཚང་དུ་མ་ཚོགས་པའི་ཕུང་པོ་ལ་བརྟེན་ནས 212 ངར་སྣང་བ་དང་བདག་དང་སེམས་ཅན་དང་ལྷ་སོགས་སུ་སྣང་བ་ནི་ང་དང་བདག་དང་སེམས་ཅན་དང་ལྷ་སོགས་ཡིན་ལ། ཡང་བུདྡྷ་པཱ་ལི་ཏ་ལས། འདི་ལྟར་བདག་ཅེས་བྱ་བའི་གང་ཡིན་པ་དེ་བདག་གི་ཞེས་གསུང་ན། ཞེས་གསུངས་པ་ལྟར་བདག་གི་དངོས་པོ་ཡིན་རྒྱུའི་མིག་སོགས་བདག་གི་ཡིན་པས་ཁྱད་པར་དུ་བྱས་པའི་བདག་གིར་འཛིན་པ་པོ་དེ་བདག་གི་བ་དང་ 213 ང་ཡི་བ་དང་སེམས་ཅན་གྱི་ང་ཡི་བ་དང་ལྷའི་ང་ཡི་བ་སོགས་སུ 214 བཞག་ཅིང་དེ་གཉིས་ལ་དམིགས་ནས་ངར་བདེན་པར་བཟུང་

130

བའི་ལྟ་བ་དང་། ང་ཡིར་བདེན་པར་བཟུང་བའི་ལྟ་བ་དེ་གཉིས་འཇིག་ལྟ་དང་མ་རིག་པ་གཉིས་ཀ་ཡིན་ཏེ། འཇུག་འགྲེལ་ལས། དེ་ལ་འཇིག་ཚོགས་[215]ལ་ལྟ་བ་ནི་ང་དང་ང་ཡི་སྙམ་པ་དེ་ལྟ་བུའི་རྣམ་པར······ཞུགས་པ་ཤེས་རབ་ཉོན་མོངས་ཅན་ནོ་ཞེས་འཇིག་ལྟར་དངོས་སུ་གསུངས་པ་དང་། འཇུག་པ་ལས།

དང་པོར་ང་ཞེས་བདག་ལ་ཞེན་གྱུར་ཅིང་།།
བདག་གི་འདི[216]་ཞེས་དངོས་ལ་[ཆགས་བསྐྱེད་པ།།]

ཞེས་དང་། རང་འགྲེལ་ལས། [འཇིག་རྟེན་འདི་ནི་བདག་གིར···མངོན་པར་ཞེན་པའི་ཐ་སྙད་ཉིད་དུ་]ངར་འཛིན་པས། ནས། [ཡོད་པ་མ་ཡིན་པའི་བདག་ཡོད་དོ་སྙམ་དུ་ཉེ་བར་བརྟགས་ནས་འདི་ཉིད་དུ་བདེན་པར་མངོན་པར་ཞེན་ཞིང་།] འདི་ནི་བདག་གིའོ·····སྙམ་དུ་ངར་འཛིན་པའི་ཡུལ་ལས་གཞན་པའི་དངོས་པོ་[འི····རྣམ་པ་མ་ལུས་པ་ལ་མངོན་པར་ཞེན་པ་ཡིན་ནོ།] ཞེས་དང་། ཞིབ་པར་རྣམ་བཤད་རིགས་པའི་རྒྱ་མཚོ་ལས། ངའོ་སྙམ་པ་སྐྱེ་བའི་གཞི་ང་ལ་དམིགས་ནས་རྣམ་པ་རང་གི་མཚན་ཉིད་ཀྱིས་གྲུབ[217]་

131

པར་འཛིན་པ་ནི་ངར་འཛིན་གྱི་འཇིག་ལྟ་ལྷན་སྐྱེས་དང་གང་ཟག་གི་བདག་ཏུ་རྨོངས་པ་གཉིས་ཀའོ། །ང་ཡི་བ་ལ་དམིགས་ནས་རྣམ་པ་རང་གི་མཚན་ཉིད་ཀྱིས་གྲུབ་པར་འཛིན་པ་ནི་ང་ཡིར་འཛིན་པའི་འཇིག་ལྟ[218]་ལྷན་སྐྱེས་དང་གང་ཟག་གི[219]་བདག་གི་བ··ལ་རྨོངས་པའི་མ་རིག་པ་གཉིས་ཀའོ། །ཞེས་སོ། །དེ་ལྟར་ན་ཡང་གང་ཟག་དེ་རྒྱུད་དུ་མར་མི་འགྱུར་བ་ནི་ངོ་བོ་གཅིག་ལ···རྟོག་ངོར་ལྡོག་པས་ཕྱེ་ཙམ་ཡིན་པས་སྐྱོན་མེད་དེ། དཔེར་ན་[220](ཚ)འཕགས་པ་ཀུན་དགའ་བོའི་རྒྱུད་ཀྱི་ང་དང་དགེ་སློང་དང་མི་དང་རྒྱུན་ཞུགས་དང་ལྔ་བཅུ་པ་དང་རྒྱལ་རིགས་ཡིན་པ་རྣམས···དོན་ཐ་དད་ཀྱང་རྒྱུད་གཅིག་པ་བཞིན་ནོ། །དེས་ན་དེའི་རྒྱུད་ཀྱི་ངར་འཛིན་ཡང་དུ་མ་ཤེས་དགོས་ལ། ཕུང་པོ་ལ་ངར་སྣང་བ་དང་ཕུང་པོ་ལ་བརྟེན་ནས་ངར་སྣང་བ་ང་ཡིན་ཀྱང་། ཕུང་པོ་ང་མ་ཡིན་པར་མཐད་ཕུང་པོ་ངར་སྣང་བ་ཡང་ང་མིན་ཏེ། ང་རང་ངོས་ནས་གྲུབ་པར་སྣང་བ་ངའི་དོན་མ་ཡིན་པའི···ཕྱིར་དང་། མིག་རྣ་སོགས་ང་ཡི་བའི་གདགས་གཞི་དང་།

132

ང་ཡི་ཡིན་རྒྱུའི་མཚན་གཞི་ཡིན་ཀྱང་ང་ཡི་བ[221]་མིན་ཏེ། དེ་དག་ང··ཡི་ཙན་དང་ང་ཡིར་ཆེད་པ་པོ་མིན་པའི་ཕྱིར་དང་། དེ་དག་རང་མཚན་དུ་འཛིན་པ་ཆོས་ཀྱི་བདག་འཛིན་ཡིན་ལ། དེ་དག་ལ···བརྟེན་ནས་ང་ཡིར་སྣང་བ་དེ་རང་བཞིན་གྲུབ་པར་འཛིན་པ་ང་ཡིར་འཛིན་པ་ཡིན་པའི་ཕྱིར་ཏེ། རྣམ་བཤད་རིགས་པའི་རྒྱ་མཚོ་ལས། ང་ཡི་བའི་གཞི་མིག་རྣ་སོགས་ལ་དམིགས་ནས་དེ་ལྟར་འཛིན་པ་ཆོས་ཀྱི[222]་བདག་འཛིན་ཡིན[223]་པས་ང་ཡི་བ་ལ་དམིགས་ཞེས་པ་ནི་དེ་དག་ལ་དམིགས་པ་མིན་ནོ། །ཞེས་དང་། སྐལ[224]་བཟང་མིག་འབྱེད་ལས། རང་རྒྱུད་ཀྱིས་བསྡུས་པའི་མིག་རྣ་སོགས་ནི་ང་ཡི་བའི་མཚན་གཞི་དང་གང་ཟག་དང་ཆོས་གཉིས་སུ་ཕྱེ་བའི་ཡ་གྱལ་གྱི་ཆོས་ཀྱི་མཚན་གཞི་གཉིས་ཀ་ཡིན་ལ། ཞེས་གསུངས་པས་ནི་བདག་གི་ཡིན་རྒྱུའི་མཚན་གཞི···སོགས་བཤད་ལ། ཚིག·····གསལ་ལས་ཀྱང་། བདག་ལ་ཕན་པ་ནི་བདག་གི་སྟེ། བདག་གི་བའི་ཕུང་པོ་ལྔ་ཞེས་བྱ་བའི་དོན་ཏོ་ཞེས་པས་ཀྱང་བདག་གི་བའི་གཞི་བསྟན་ལ། སྐལ[224]་བཟང་

མིག་འཛིན་ལས། [རང་རྒྱུད་ཀྱིས་བསྡུས་པའི་མིག་རྣ་སོགས་ནི་ང་ཡི་བའི་མཚན་གཞི་དང་གང་ཟག་དང་ཆོས་གཉིས་སུ་ཕྱེ་... བའི་ཡ་ཀྱལ་ཀྱི་] ཆོས་ཀྱི་མཚན་གཞི་གཉིས་ཀ་ཡིན་ལ། དེ་དག་བློ་ལྡན་སྐྱེས་ལ་ཡུལ་གྱི་རང་ངོས་ནས་གྲུབ་པའི་ང་ཡི་བར་སྣང་བའམ་དེ་དག་བློ་ལྡན་སྐྱེས་ལ་ང་ཡི་བར་སྣང་ཞིང་། དེ་འདྲའི་ང་ཡི་བ་ལ་དམིགས་ནས་རང་གི་མཚན་ཉིད་ཀྱིས་གྲུབ་པར་ཞེན་པ་ནི་ངའི་ཡིད་ལ་འཛིན་པ་ལྷན་སྐྱེས་ཡིན། ཞེས་གསུངས་པས་ང་ཡིར་[225] འཛིན་པའི་འཇིག་ལྟ་སྐྱེ་ཡུལ་གཞིར་[226] བཞག་ཅིང་། སངས་རྒྱས་ལ་ང་ཡི་བ་སྣང་བ་ན་གདགས་གཞི་ལ་བཏགས་ཙམ་དུ་སྣང་གི་གདགས་གཞི་གདགས་ཆོས་སུ་མི་སྣང་བ་དང་འཕགས་པ་འོག་མ་ལ་གཉིས་ཚོགས་སྣང་བ་སོགས་ཞེས་པར་བྱ། ཡང་སྙིག་ཆེད་བ་སོགས་ན་རེ། བདག་འཛིན་དཔྱོད་ཚུལ་ཕུང་པོ་[227] དང་ཟ་དད་པའི་བདག་ངོས་འཛིན་འགོག་ཅིང་། དེ་རྗེས་སུ་ཕུང་པོ་བདེན་གྲུབ་འགོག་པ་མི་འཐད་དེ། ལྷན་སྐྱེས་ལ་བདག་ཕུང་གཅིག་ཏུ་སྣང་བའི་ཕྱིར་ཏེ། རྩ་བར།

ཕུང་པོ་མ་གཏོགས་དེ་འཛིན་མ་གྲུབ་ཕྱིར།།
(ཇ)
ཞེར་ནས་ལྟ་ཁྲིད་དག་ལ་ཟུར་ཟ་བར། རང་ཕྱོགས་ཀྱི་ཏོག་གེ་བ་[228] ཁ་ཅིག་ཡང་སྨྲའོ། འདི་དག་གཡག་ཞར་གྱི་རྫོ་ལྟར་ཕྱོགས་མཐོང་[229] རེའི་ངན་སྐད་ཡིན་ཏེ། འོ་ན་བློ་ལྡན་སྐྱེས་ལ་ཡང་ངའི་ལུས་ངའི་སེམས་ཞེས་ཟ་དད་དུ་འཛིན་པ་མེད་པ་ཐལ་བ་དང་། བདག་ཕུང་རྗེ་ཁོལ་ལྟར་འཛིན་པའི་ལྷན་སྐྱེས་མེད་པར་ཐལ་བ། དེ་འདོད་ན། རྩ་བར།

རང་དུ་ལྟ་བ་དང་འབྲེལ་ཡོངས་སུ་ཟད།།
(ཐ)
ཅེས་གསུངས་པ་མི་འཐད་པར་ཐལ་བ། དེའི་ཐད་ཀྱིས་བཏུའི་ས་བཞི་[230] པའི་མདོ་མི་འཐད་པ་ཐལ་བ་སོགས་མང་ལ། རྩ་བར།

ཕུང་པོ་མ་གཏོགས་དེ་འཛིན་མ་གྲུབ་ཕྱིར།།

ཞེས་པས་ཕུང་པོ་དང་མཚན་ཉིད་མི་མཐུན་པའི་བདག་དང་ཕུང་པོ་ལ་མ་ལྟོས་པའི་རྟག་བདག་བཀག་ཀྱང་། བདག་ཕུང་ཟ་དད་ཙམ་མ་བཀག་པའི་ཁྱད་པར་མི་འཐད་པར་ཐལ། དམ་བཅའ་དེའི་ཕྱིར། འཁོར་གསུམ། འདོད་ན། བདག་ཕུང་ཡོད་ལ་ཟ་དད་བཀག་པས་གཅིག་ཏུ་ཐལ་བ་དང་། རྩ་བར།

[ཀུང་དག་དུད་འགྲོར་བསྐལ་མང་བརྒྱལ... སྒྲུར་པ།།]
(ཞ)
དེས་ཀྱང་མ་སྐྱེས... རྟག་འདི་མ་མཐོང་ལ།།
[231]
ངར་འཛིན་དེ་དག་ལ་ཡང་འཇུག་མཐོང་སྟེ།།
དེས་ན་ཕུང་པོ་ལས་གཞན་བདག་འགའ་མེད།།

ཅེས་གསལ་བར་གསུང་བ་མི་འཐད་པར་ཐལ་ལོ། །ཡང་དེ་ལྟར་སྦྲ་བཞིན་དུ་མིའི་རྒྱུད་ཀྱི་ངའི་སྣང་ཚུལ་ང་རྒྱང་རྒྱང་བ་དང་... ཡོབ་ཡོབ་པ་ལྟ་བུ་ཕུང་པོ་དང་དབྱེར་མེད་དུ་འཆར་བར་གསུང་བ་ལའང་ཡོ་ན་རེ། ང་སྣང་ཚུལ་དེ་འདྲ་གཏན་ནས་མི་འཐད་པར་ཐལ། ང་ལྟན་མིན་འདུ་བྱེད་ཡིན་པའི་ཕྱིར་དང་། ལྟ་ན་མིན་འདུ་བྱེད་དེ་འདྲ་མི་འཆར་བའི་ཕྱིར་སོགས་ཟེར། འོ་ན། ང་འཆར་ཚུལ་མེད་པར་ཐལ། ངའི་གདགས་གཞི་ཕུང་པོའི་རྣམ་པར་ཤར་བ་ངའི་རྣམ་པ་ཤར་བ་མ་ཡིན་པའི་ཕྱིར་དང་། འཁོར་གསུམ། ང་འཆར་ན་ལྟོས་མེད་ཀྱི་ང་གཅིག་འཆར་བར་ཐལ། ཕུང་པོའི་རྣམ་པ་ཤར་བ་ལ་མ་ལྟོས་པར་ང་གཅིག་འཆར་བ་དགོས་པའི་ཕྱིར། འཁོར་གསུམ། ལྷན་སྐྱེས་ལ་སྣང་བ་ན་གདགས་གཞི་ཕུང་པོ་མི་སྣང་བར་བཏགས་ཆོས་ང་[232] གཟུགས་དང་ཤེས་པ་མིན་ཙམ་གྱི་སྣང་བ་འཆར་བར་ཐལ་ལོ། །དམ་བཅའ

136

འཆད་པའི་ཕྱིར། འདོད་ན།
ཕུང་པོ་མ་གཏོགས་དེ་འཛིན་མ་གྲུབ་ཕྱིར།།
དང་ཡང་འགལ་བར་མ་ཟད། ཉན་སྤྱེས་ལ་ངའི་གདགས་གཞི་གདགས་ཆོས་ཞོ་ཆུ་འདྲེས་པ་བཞིན་དབྱེར་མེད་པར་འདྲེས་པའི་ཕུང་པོའི་དོན་ནས་ངའི་སྣང་ཚུལ་འཆར་བའི་ཕྱིར་ཏེ། དེའི་ཚེ་གདགས་གཞི་ཕུང་པོ་དང་གདགས་ཆོས་ངའི… སྣང་ཚུལ་འདྲེས་པའི་སྒོ་ནས་སྣང་དགོས་ཀྱི་ཕུང་པོ་ལས་ཟུར་དུ་ཤར་ན་བདག་ལ་ཕུང་པོའི་མཚན་ཉིད་སྐྱེ་འཇིག་དང་དཔེར་སོགས་དང་ཚོར་བ་པོ་འདུ…ཤེས་པོ་ལས… [233] སོགས་འདུ་བྱེད་པ་པོ་དང་རྣམ་པར་ཤེས་པ་པོ་སོགས་མི་སྣང་བར་འགྱུར་བའི་ཕྱིར་ཏེ། རྩ་ཤེས་ལས།
(ཟ) གལ་ཏེ་ཕུང་པོ་རྣམས་ལས་གཞན།།
ཕུང་པོའི་མཚན་ཉིད་མེད་པར་འགྱུར།།
ཞེས་དང་། ཚིག…གསལ་ལས། གལ་ཏེ་བདག་ཕུང་པོ་ལས་ཐ་དད་ན་དེ་ཕུང་པོ་མིན་པའི་མཚན་ཉིད་ཅན

137

དུ་འགྱུར་ཏེ། ཕུང་པོ་ལྔ་ནི་གཟུགས་སུ་རུང་བ་དང་ཉམས་སུ་མྱོང་བ་དང་། མཚན་མར་འཛིན་པ་དང་། མངོན་པར་[234] འདུ་བྱེད་པ་དང་། ཡུལ་སོ་སོར་རྣམ་པར་རིག་པ་ཡིན་ན། [235] [བདག་ནི་གཟུགས་ལས་རྣམ་པར་ཞེས་པ་བཞིན་དུ་ཕུང་པོ་དག་ལས་ཐ་དད་པར་འདོད་པ་ན་མཚན་ཉིད་ཐ་དད་པར་གྲུབ་པར་འགྱུར་ལ། མཚན་ཉིད་ཐ་དད་པར་གྲུབ་པ་ནི་གཟུགས་ལས་སེམས་ལྟར་བཟུང་བར་འགྱུར་ན། འཛིན་པ་ཡང་མ་ཡིན་ནོ། དེའི་ཕྱིར་ཕུང་པོ་ལས་ཐ་དད་པ་ཡང་ཡོད་པ་མ་ཡིན་ནོ།] སོགས་དང་། བུདྡྷ་པཱ་ལི་ཏ་ལས་ཀྱང་དེ་ལྟར་བཤད་ལ་རྟ་དཀར་པོ་དང་བ་གླང་ཁྲ་བོ་སོགས་མི་འཆད་པར་ཡང་འགྱུར་བའི་ཕྱིར་དང་། མཁན་ཆེན་རྒྱལ་བའི་དབང་པོའི་འཇམ་དཔལ་ཞལ་ལུང་ལས། (འ) [རེས་ལུས་ཀྱི་སྟེང་དུ་ཡོད་པ་འདུག། རེས་སེམས་ཀྱི་སྟེང་དུ་ཡོད་པ་འདུག། རེས

138

ཕུར་གཞན་རྣམས་སོ་སོའི་སྟེང་དུ་ཡོད་པ་འདུ་བསོགས།] འཆར་ཚུལ་སྣ་ཚོགས་པ་ཞིག་བྱུང་བའི་མཐར་ལུས་སེམས་གཉིས་པོ་འདི་ཆུ་དང་འོ་མ་འདྲེས་པ་ལྟ་བུ་[236] དབྱེར་མི་ཕྱེད་པ་ཞིག་གི་སྟེང་ནས་ང་[ད་ངའི་ངོས་ནས་ཡོད་པའི་རང་བཞིན་གྱིས་གྲུབ་པའི་རྟོགས་སེ་བ་གཏོད་མ་ནས་གྲུབ་པ་ཞིག་ངོས་འཛིན་འོང་བས་དེ་ནི་གནད་དང་པོ་དགག་བྱ་ངོས་པ་ཡིན་པས་འདི་ལ་སྒོང་བ་གཏིང་མ་ཕྱིན་གྱི་བར་དུ་དཔྱད་དོ།། དེ་ལྟར་རྒྱུད་ལ་སྦྱངས་པ་ནས་ངར་འཛིན་ལྷན་སྐྱེས་ཀྱིས་བཟུང་བའི] ང་དེ་དང་རང་གི་ཕུང་པོ་ལྔ་པོ་རྣམས་རྒྱ་ལ… རྒྱ་བཞག་པ་ལྟ་བུའི་ཚུལ་གྱིས་[རྟོགས་ཐབ་ཏུ་གྲུབ་པར་ངོས་བཟུང་བ་དེ་ངེས་པ་ཡིན]ཞེས་སོ།།

139

འདི་ནི་ཀླུ་སྒྲུབ་ཡབ་སྲས་ཀྱི···[237] གཞུང་དོན་སྟོང་ཐོག་ནས་བཤད་པ་སྔོན་མེད་པའི་ལེགས་བཤད་གཅིག་སྣང་ངོ་། །དེས་ན་ལྷས་བྱིན་ལྟ་བུའི་གང་ཟག་དེའི་བློས་ངའོ་སྙམ་ཡུལ་ལ་རྒྱུད་ཙམ་དང་མེད་ཀྱང་རྒྱུད་གཅིག་པའི་ལྷ་མི་དུད་འགྲོ་སོགས་སུ་མ་ཡོད་དེ། དེའི་རྒྱུད་ཀྱི་ང་དང་སེམས་ནི་ཚེ་ཐོག་མ་མེད་པ་ནས་ཞུགས་ལ་སྐྱེ་འགག་བྱེད་ཀྱང་མི་ལྡོག་ལ་ལྷ་དུད་འགྲོ་སོགས་ཀྱི་གནས་སྐབས་ལུས་འདོར་ལེན་ཀྱིས་གྲུབ་པ་དང་ལྡོག་པ་སོགས་ཀྱི་ཞིབ་ཆ་ཤེས་དགོས་པའི་ཕྱིར་དང་། ལྷ་མི་སོགས་ལུས་རྟེན་གྱིས་འབྱེད་པས་ལུས་ཀྱི་སྟེང་ན་ཡོད་པ་འདྲ་བ་དང་ང་ཙམ་སངས་རྒྱས་བར་དུ་འགྲོ་བ་སེམས་ལ་ལྟོས་པས་ང་སེམས་སྟེང་ན་ཡོད་པ་ལྟ་བུ···རྣམས་ལྟ་བ་ཕྱུ་ཚག་ཆོད་པ་གཅིག་བྱེད་ན་རྩ་ཤེས་དང་དེའི་ཊཱིཀ་ཆེན་ལྟར་ལེགས་པར་དཔྱད་དགོས་པའི་ཕྱིར་ཏེ། རྣམ་བཤད་རིགས་པའི་རྒྱ་མཚོ་ལས། དེས་ན་ངའོ་སྙམ་དུ་ཐ་སྙད་འདོགས···མཁན་གྱི་མི་དང་ཐ་སྙད་གདགས་པའི་གཞི་བདག་གཉིས···ཁྱབ་མཉམ་དུ་མི་བཟུང་བར་མི་དེ་བདག་དེའི་ཆ་གཅིག་ཡིན

140

པར་ཤེས་པར་བྱོས་ཤིག །ཅེས་དང་། [ཕྱིས་བྱིན་གྱི་དུས་སུ་ཕྱིའི་བདག་སོ་སོར་མ་ཕྱེ་བར་ངའོ་སྙམ་དུ་འཛིན་པའི་དམིགས་པའི་གཞིར་གྱུར་པའི་བདག་ནི་ཐོག་མ་མེད་པ་ནས་ཞུགས་པའི་ང་ཙམ་ཡིན་པས། ལྷ་ལ་སོགས་པའི་ལུས་བླངས་དུས་ཀྱི] འགྲོ་བ་སོ་སོའི་བདག་རྣམས་ནི་སྔ་མའི་བྱེ་བྲག་རེ་འོ། །ཞེས་དང་། རྒྱལ་བའི་དབང་པོའི་གསུང་དེ་ཉིད་ལས། རེས་ལུས་ཀྱི་སྟེང་ན་ཡོད་པ་འདྲ་བ་རེས་སེམས་ཀྱི་སྟེང་ན་ཡོད་པ་འདྲ་བ། ཞེས་གསུངས་པའི་ཕྱིར་དང་། རང་འགྲེལ་ལས། ཀླུའི་སྐྱེར་ཕྱུད་ཞེ[238]་ཕ་མ་གཏོགས་པར་ནི་འགའ་ལ་ཡང་བདག་ཏུ་མངོན་པར་ཞེན་པ་མེད་པས་འཇིག་ཚོགས་ལ་ལྟ་བའི་རྣམ་པ་ཞུ་བ་མི་སྐྱེད་དོ། །ཞེས་གསུངས་པ་ལྟར་འཇིག་ལྟ་ཀུན་བཏགས་ནི་ཕྱུ་རིའི་རྩེ་མོ་ནི་ཕྱུ་དང་མཚུན་པར་ཡོད་པ་དེ་འཛོམས་བྱེད་ཀྱི་གཉེན་པོར། ཟླ་བས་མདོ་དྲངས་པ་ལས། གཟུགས་བདག་མ་ཡིན། བདག་གཟུགས་དང་ལྡན་པ་མིན། གཟུགས་ལ་བདག་མེད་པ་བདག་ལ་གཟུགས་མེད་དེ་བཞིན་དུ་བདག་རྣམ་པར

141

ཤེས་པ་མ་ཡིན། བདག་རྣམ་པར་ཤེས་པ་དང་ལྡན་པ་མ་ཡིན། རྣམ་པར་ཤེས་པ་ལ་བདག་མེད།[239] [བདག་ལ་རྣམ་པར་ཤེས་པ་མེད།] ཅེས་པའི་བར་གསུང་པའི་དོན་དེ་རྟགས་སམ་རྒྱུ་མཚན་དུ་བཀོད་ནས། ཡང་མདོ་ལས། ཆོས་ཐམས་ཅད་བདག་མེད་པའོ། ཞེས་གསུངས་པའི་ཕྲ་བའི་བདག་མེད་ཆོས་ཐམས་ཅད་ངོ་བོ་ཉིད་མེད་པར་སྒྲུབ་པས་ན། རྗེ་རིན་པོ་ཆེས་ཀུན་བརྟགས་འགོག་པ་ལྷན་སྐྱེས་འགོག་པའི···ཡན་ལག་ཡིན་གསུངས་པའི་དོན་དེ་འདྲ་དང་ཆོས་ཀྱི་བདག་མེད་ལ་མཐའ་བཀག་པ་རྟགས་སུ་བྱས་པ་སྟེ། མདོ་དེ་དག་གི་དོན་གྲིལ་ན་དེ་བཞིན་གཤེགས་པ་དང་བདག་ཆོས་ཅན། རང་དབང་དམ་ངོ་བོ་ཉིད་ཀྱིས་མེད་དེ། ཁྱོད་གདགས་གཞི་ཕུང་པོ་ཡིན་པ་འམ་དེ་དང་གཅིག་ཡང་མིན་ལ། ཁྱོད་ལ་དེ་མ···གཏོགས་པའི་གཞན་པ་འམ་དེ(ར)་དང་ངོ་བོ་ཐ་དད་དུ་གནས་པ་ཡང་མིན། ཁྱོད་ཕུང་པོའི་རྟེན་འཁར་གཞོང[240]་དང་ཕུང་པོ་ཀྱི་ཤུག··· ལྟར་ངོ་བོ་ཉིད་ཀྱིས་རྟེན་དུ་ཡང་མེད། ཁྱོད···

142

ཕུང་པོ་ལ་ངོ་བོ་ཉིད་[241]ཀྱིས་དེ་ལྟར་བར་[242]བརྟེན་པ་ཡང་མ་ཡིན། ཕུང་པོ་
དང་ངོ་བོ་ཉིད་ཀྱིས་ལྷས་སྦྱིན་རྣ་བ་དང་ལྡན་པ་ལྟ་བུའི་ངོ་བོ་གཅིག
ཉིད་དང་ལྷས་སྦྱིན་ནོར་དང་ལྡན་པ་ལྟར་ངོ་བོ་ཐ་དད་པའི་བདེན
པ་ཡང་མེད་པའི་ཕྱིར་ཏེ། རྩ་ཤེས་ལས།
ཕུང་(ལ)མིན་ཕུང་པོ་ལས་གཞན་མིན།།
དེ་ལ་ཕུང་མེད་དེར་དེ་མིན།།
དེ་བཞིན་གཤེགས་པ་ཕུང་ལྡན་མིན།།
ཞེས་རྟགས་དང་།
དེ་བཞིན་གཤེགས་པ་གང་ཞིག་ཡིན།།
ཞེས་པས་སྒྲུབ་བྱེད་བསྟན་ཅིང་། རིན་ཆེན་ཕྲེང་བ་ལས་ཀྱང་།
ཕུང་(ཕྱི)བདག་མ་ཡིན་དེར་དེ་མིན།།
དེ་ལ་དེ་མིན་དེ་མེད་མིན།།
ཕུང་པོ་མེ་ཤིང་ལྟར་འདྲེས་མིན།།
དེའི་ཕྱིར
ཞེས་པས······རྟགས་བསྟན་ལ་འདྲེས་པ་ནི་སྔར་དགག་བྱའི་སྐབས

143

ལྟར་ཏེ་ངོ་བོ་གཅིག་ལྡན་གྱི་དོན་ཡིན་ལ།
བདག་ནི་དེ་ལྟར་ཡོད།།
ཅེས་པས་སྒྲུབ་བྱེད་བསྟན་ཅིང་། རྟགས་སོ་སོ་ནས་སྒྲུབ་ཚུལ་ཡང་
དེ་(སྨྲ)གཉིས་ཕུང་པོ་དང་གཅིག་ན་མི་རྟག་པར་ཐལ་བ་དང་། དུ་མར་
ཐལ་བ་དང་། བདག་ཁས་བླངས་པ་མེད་པར་ཐལ་བ་དང་། སྐྱེ་བ་
དྲན་པ་མི་འཐད་པར་ཐལ་བ་སྟེ།[243] བུདྡྷ་པཱ་ལི་ཏ་ལས། རེ་ཞིག་ཕུང་
པོ་རྣམས་ཉིད་དེ་བཞིན་གཤེགས་པ་མིན་ཏེ། ཅིའི་ཕྱིར་ཞེ་ན།
ཕུང་པོ་རྣམས་འབྱུང་བ་དང་འཇིག་པའི་ཆོས་ཅན་ཡིན་པའི་
ཕྱིར་དེ་བཞིན་གཤེགས་པ་མི་རྟག་པ་ཉིད་དུ་ཐལ་བའི་ཕྱིར་དང་།
ཉེ་བར་ལེན་པ་པོ་དང་ཉེ་བར་ལེན་པ་དག་གཅིག་པ་ཉིད་དུ་
མི་འཐད་པའི་ཕྱིར་རོ། །ཞེས་དང་། ཚིག······གསལ་ལས།
དེ་ལ་གལ་ཏེ་ཕུང་པོ་བདག་ཡིན་ནོ་ཞེས་རྟོག་ན་[244] [ཏེ།] དེས་
ན་སྐྱེ་དང་འཇིག་པ་ཅན་ཏེ། བདག་སྐྱེ་བ་དང་འཇིག་པ་ཅན་དུ···
འགྱུར་ཏེ། ཕུང་པོ་རྣམས་སྐྱེ་བ་དང་འཇིག་པ་ལ་བརྟེན་པའི་
ཕྱིར་རོ། །བདག་ནི་དེ་ལྟར་འདོད་པ་ཡང་མ་ཡིན་ཏེ། ཉེས་

144

པ་དུ་མར་ཐལ་བར་འགྱུར་བའི་ཕྱིར་རོ། འདི་ལྟར།
མ་བྱུང་བ་ལས་བྱུང་མིན་ཏེ།།
འདི་ལ་སྐྱོན་དུ་ཐལ་བར་འགྱུར།།
བདག་ནི་བྱས་པར་འགྱུར་བ་དང་།།
འབྱུང་བ་རྒྱུ་མེད་ཅན་དུ་འགྱུར།།
ཞེས་བྱ་བ་དང་། དེ་བཞིན་དུ།
ཉེ་བར་ལེན་ཉིད་བདག་མ་ཡིན།།
དེ་འབྱུང་བ་དང་འཇིག་པ་ཡིན།།
ཉེ་བར་བླང་པ་ཇི་ལྟ་བུར།།
ཉེ་བར་ལེན་པོ་ཡིན་པར་འགྱུར།།
ཞེས་འཆད་པར་འགྱུར་རོ། །གཞན་ཡང་ཕྱོགས་འདི་ནི།
གལ་ཏེ་ཕུང་པོ་བདག་ན་དེ་ཕྱིར་དེ།།
མང་བས་བདག་དེ་དག་ཀྱང་མང་པོར་འགྱུར།།
བདག་ནི་རྫས་སུ་འགྱུར་ཞིང་དེར་ལྟ་བ།།
རྫས་ལ་འཇུག་པས་ཕྱིན་ཅི་ལོག་མི་འགྱུར།།

145

རྒྱུ་དང་འདས་ཚེ་ངེས་པར་བདག་ཆད་འགྱུར།།
རྒྱུ་དང་འདས་སྔོན་སྐད་ཅིག་... དག་ལ་ནི།།
སྐྱེ་འཇིག་བྱེད་པོ་མེད་པས་འབྲས་མེད་ཉིད།།
གཞན་གྱིས་བསགས་པ་གཞན་གྱིས་ཟ་བར་འགྱུར།།] 245

སོགས་སོ། །དེ(སྐྱེ)་གཉིས་ཕུང་པོ་དང་ངོ་བོ་ཐ་དད་ན་ཕུང་པོ་མ་ཡིན་པར་ཐལ་བ། ཚོར་བ་པོ་སོགས་མ་ཡིན་པར་ཐལ་བ་དང་། རྟག་པར་ཐལ་བ་དང་། ཕུང་པོ་ལས་ཟུར་དུ་བཟུང་དུ་ཡོད་པར་ཐལ་བ་དང་། བདག་ཡོད་པ་...མེད་པར་ཐལ་བ་དང་། ཁ་ཅེད་མེད་པར་ཐལ་བ་སོགས་སྟེ། བུདྡྷ་པཱ་ལི་ཏ་ལས། ཕུང་པོ་རྣམས་ལས་དེ་བཞིན་གཤེགས་པ་གཞན་པ་ཕུང་པོ་མེད་པའི་ཆོས་ལོགས་ན་ཡང་མེད་དེ། ཅིའི་ཕྱིར་ཞེ་ན། ཕུང་པོ་མི་རྟག་པ་རྣམས་ལས་ཆོས་མི་མཐུན་པའི་ཕྱིར། རྟག་པ་ཉིད་དུ་ཐལ་བར་འགྱུར་བའི་ཕྱིར་དང་། གཞན་ཉིད་ཡིན་ན་གཟུང་དུ་ཡོད་པར་ཐལ་བར་འགྱུར་བའི་ཕྱིར་ [ཏེ། གཟུང་དུ་ཡང་མེད་པས་དེའི་ཕྱིར་ཕུང་པོ·····

146

རྣམས་ལས་དེ་བཞིན་གཤེགས་པ་གཞན་ཡང་མ་ཡིན་ནོ།] སོགས་དང་། ཚིག་···གསལ་ལས། གལ་ཏེ་བདག་ཕུང་པོ་ལས་ཐ་དད་ན། [དེ་ཕུང་པོ་མ་ཡིན་པའི་མཚན་ཉིད་ཅན་དུ་འགྱུར་ཏེ། ཕུང་པོ་ལྔ་ནི་གཟུགས་སུ་རུང་བ་དང་། ཉམས་སུ་མྱོང་བ་དང་། མཚན་མོར་འཛིན་པ་དང་། མངོན་པར་འདུ་བྱེད་པ་དང་། ཡུལ་སོ་སོར་རྣམ་པར་རིག་པའི་མཚན་ཉིད་ཅན་ཡིན་ན། བདག་ནི་གཟུགས་ལས་རྣམ་པར་ཤེས་པ་བཞིན་དུ་ཕུང་པོ་དག་ལས་ཐ་དད་པར་འདོད་པ་ན་མཚན་ཉིད་ཐ་དད་པར་གྲུབ་པར་འགྱུར་ལ། མཚན་ཉིད་ཐ་དད་པར་གྲུབ་པ་ནི་གཟུགས་ལས་སེམས་ལྟར་བཟུང་བར་འགྱུར་ན། འཛིན་པ་ཡང་མ་ཡིན་ནོ། དེའི་ཕྱིར་ཕུང་པོ་ལས་ཐ་དད་པ་ཡང་ཡོད་པ་མ་ཡིན་ནོ།] སོགས་སོ། (ཀ)བདག་དང་དེ་བཞིན་གཤེགས་པ་གཉིས་ངོ་བོ་ཉིད་ཀྱིས་ཕུང་པོའི་རྟེན་བྱེད་པ་དང་། དེ་གཉིས་ངོ་བོ་ཉིད་ཀྱིས་ཕུང་པོ་ལ་བརྟེན་ན་ཡང་ཕུང་པོ་ལས་ཐ་དད་པའི་སྐྱོན་དེ་དག 246 འོང་སྟེ། བུདྡྷ་པཱ་ལི་ཏ་ལས། དེ་བཞིན་གཤེགས་པ་ལ

147

ཕུང་པོ་རྣམས་གདངས་ལ་ཤིང་ལྗོན་པའི་ནགས་ཚལ་བཞིན་དུ་མེད་དེ། ཅིའི་ཕྱིར་ཞེ་ན། རྟེན་དང་བརྟེན་པ་གཞན་ཡིན་···པའི་ཕྱིར་རྟག་པ་ཉིད་དུ་ཐལ་བར་འགྱུར་རོ། །ཕུང་པོ་རྣམས་ལ་ཡང་དེ་བཞིན་གཤེགས་པ་ཤིང་ལྗོན་པའི་ནགས་ཚལ་ན་སེང་གེ་བཞིན་དུ་མེད་དེ། ཅིའི་ཕྱིར་ཞེ་ན། སྐྱོན་བརྟན་མ་ཐག་པ་ཉིད་དུ་འགྱུར་རོ། །ཞེས་དང་། འཇུག་འགྲེལ་ལས་ཀྱང་། གཞན་ཉིད་ཡོད་ན་རྟེན་དང་བརྟེན་པའི་དངོས་པོར···རིགས་པར་འགྱུར་ཏེ། [དཔེར་ན་འཁར་གཞོང་ན་ཞོ་ཡོད་དོ་ཞེས་ 247 བྱ་བ་ལྟ་བུ་འོ། འཁར་གཞོང་དང་ཞོ་གཉིས་ནི་འཇིག་རྟེན་ན་གཞན་ཉིད་ཡིན་པ་ན་རྟེན་དང་བརྟེན་པའི་དངོས་པོར་མཐོང་ངོ་། །ཕུང་པོ་རྣམས་ནི་དེ་ལྟར་བདག་ལས་ཐ་དད་པ་མ་ཡིན་ལ་བདག་ཀྱང་ཕུང་པོ་རྣམས་ལས་ཐ་དད་པ་མ་ཡིན་པས་དེ་གཉིས་ལ་རྟེན་དང་བརྟེན་པའི་དངོས་པོ་ཡོད་པ་མ་ཡིན་ནོ།] སོགས་སོ། །དེ(ཀ)་གཉིས་ཕུང་པོ་དང་ངོ་བོ་ཉིད་ཀྱིས་ངོ་བོ་ཐ་དད་དང་ཐ་མི་དད་ 248 ཀྱི་ལྡན་ཚུལ་གཉིས་ཀྱང་མེད་དེ། ངོ་བོ་ཉིད་ཀྱིས་ཐ་མི་དད་པ

148

འདྲེས་པའམ་སྙིང་པོ་ལྟར་ལྡན་ན་ཕུང་པོ་དང་གཅིག་པའི་སྐྱོན་མི་རྟག་པར་ཐལ་བ་སོགས་འོང་། ངོ་བོ་ཉིད་ཀྱིས་ཐ་དད་པའི་ལྡན་ཚུལ་ལྟར་ན་བདག་ཕུང་ཐ་དད་པའི་སྐྱོན་དེ་དག་འཇུག་པའི་ཕྱིར་ཏེ། བུདྡྷ་པཱ་ལི་ཏ་ལས། དེ་བཞིན་གཤེགས་པ་ཕུང་པོ་རྣམས་དང་། ཤིང་ལྡན་པ་སྙིང་པོ་དང་ལྡན་པ་བཞིན་དུ་ལྡན་པ་མ་ཡིན་ཏེ། ཅིའི་ཕྱིར་ཞེ་ན། ཕུང་པོ་རྣམས་ལས་གཞན་མ་ཡིན་པའི་ཕྱིར། མི་རྟག་པ་ཉིད་ཀྱི་སྐྱོན་དུ་འགྱུར་བའི་ཕྱིར་རོ།

ཞེས་དང་། འཇུག་པར།

བདག་ནི་གཟུགས་ལྡན་མི་འདོད་གང་ཕྱིར་བདག
[ཡོད་མིན་དེ་ཕྱིར་ལྡན་དོན་སྦྱོར་བ་མེད།།
གཞན་ན་གནག་ལྡན་གཞན་མིན་གཟུགས་ལྡན་ན།།
བདག་ནི་གཟུགས་ལས་དེ་ཉིད་གཞན་ཉིད་མེད།།]

ཅེས་སོགས་དང་འཇུག་འགྲེལ་ལས། ལྡན་པའི་རྒྱུན་ཡང་ལྷས་སྦྱིན་གཟུགས་དང་ལྡན་ནོ། ཞེས་བྱ་བ་དེ་ནི་ཐ་མི་དད་པ་ཉིད་ལ་དམིགས་ལ། བ་ལང་དང་ལྡན་ནོ། ཞེས་བྱ་བ་ནི་ཐ་དད་པ་ཡིན་

149

ན། [དེ་ཉིད་དང་གཞན་ཉིད་དེ་དག་ནི་གཟུགས་དང་བདག་ལ་ཡོད་པ་མ་ཡིན་པས་བདག་གཟུགས་དང་ལྡན་ནོ་ཞེས་བྱ་བ་འདི་ཡང་མི་སྲིད་དོ།] སོགས་སོ། དེས་ན་འདི་དག་བསྡུས་ན་གཅིག་ཏུ… བྲལ་དུ་འདུ་ཡང་འཇིག་ལྟའི་འཛུག་ཚུལ་ལ་ལྟོས་ནས་བཀག་པར་ཆེག… གསལ་ལས་བཤད་ཅིང་། ཆོས་ཐམས་ཅད་ལ་རིགས་པ་དེས་བདག་མེད་སྒྲུབ་རྒྱུབ་ནི། ཕུང་ཁམས་སྐྱེ་མཆེད་གང་ལ… ཡང་གདགས་གཞི་དང་གདགས་ཆོས་དཔྱད་ན་རྣམ་པ་ལྔར་མེད་པས་ཀུན་བཏགས་ཀྱི…ཞེན་ཡུལ་འགོག་བྱེད་རྟགས་སུ་བྱས་ནས་ལྷན་སྐྱེས་ཀྱིས་གདགས་གཞིའི་ངོས་ནས་བཏགས་ཆོས་ཡོད་པར་འཛིན་པ་འགོག་པའི་ཕྱིར་ཏེ། རིན་ཆེན་ཕྲེང་བ་ལས།

249

སྐྱེས་བུ་ཁམས་དྲུག་འདུས་པའི་ཕྱིར།། (སྐྱེ)
ཡང་དག་མ་ཡིན་ཇི་ལྟ་བར།།
དེ་བཞིན་ཁམས་ནི་རེ་རེ་ཡང་།།

250

འདུས་ཕྱིར་ཡང་དག་ཉིད་དུ་མིན།།

ཞེས་དང་།

150

འབྱུང་གསུམ་ས་མིན་འདི་ལ་མིན།།
དེ་ལ་འདི་མིན་དེ་མེད་མིན།།
རེ་རེ་འང་དེ་བཞིན་དེ་ཡི་ཕྱིར།།

251

འབྱུང་བ་རྣམས་ཀྱང་བདག་བཞིན་རྫུན།།

ཞེས་སོ། ཡང་རང་སྡེ་དངོས་སྨྲ་དང་རང་རྒྱུད་པ་ཁ་ཅིག་སྐྱེ་བ… སྔ་ཕྱི་ལེན་མཁན་གྱི་བདག་སེམས་ལ་དངོས་སུ་འཛོག་ཅིང་། ཀླུ་དང་མི་ནི་ལས་ཀྱིས་ཕུང་པོའི་བཀོད་པ་ཁྱད་པར་བ་ཞིག་གིས་འཛོག་པའི་ཕྱིར་ཕུང་(ག)པོའི་བཀོད་པ་ཁྱད་པར་བ་དེའདག་ཏུ་སྨྲ་སྟེ། དེ་འགོག་པའི་ཕྱིར་དུ་ཚོགས་ཙམ་བདག་མིན་པ་དང་། དབྱིབས་བདག་མིན་པའི་རྟགས་ཟུར་གཉིས་བསྟན་ཏེ། འཇུག་པར།

(ང) ཤིང་རྟ་རང་ཡན་ལག་ལས་གཞན་འདོད་མིན།།
གཞན་མིན་མ་ཡིན་དེ་ལྡན་ཡང་མིན་ཞིང་།།
ཡན་ལག་ལ་མིན་ཡན་ལག་དག་དེར་མིན།།
འདུས་པ་ཙམ་མིན་དབྱིབས་མིན་ཇི་བཞིན་ནོ།།

ཞེས་སོ། རྣམ་བདུན་གྱིས་དཔྱད་པ་འདི་ཡང་གཟུགས་སོགས···
ཐམས་ཅད་བདེན་མེད་དུ་གཏན་ལ་འབེབས་པའི་རིགས་པའི་
མཆོག་ཡིན་ཏེ། འཇུག་པར།
བུམ་པ་སྣམ་བུ་རེ་ལྡེ་དམག་དང་ནགས་ཚལ་ཕྲེང་བ་ལྗོན་ཤིང་དང༌།།
ཁང་ཁྱིམ་ཤིང་རྟ་ཕྱན་དང་འགྲོན་གནས་ལ་སོགས་དངོས་རྣམས་གང་དག་དང༌།།
དེ་བཞིན་གང་དག་སྐྱེ་བོས་སྒྱུ་འདེས་བརྗོད་པ་དེ་རྣམས་རྟོགས་བྱ་སྟེ།།
གང་ཕྱིར་ཐུབ་དབང་དེ་ནི་འཇིག་རྟེན་ལྷན་ཅིག་རྩོད་མི་མཛད་ཕྱིར་རོ།།
ཡན་ལག་ཡོན་ཏན་འདོད་ཆགས་མཚན་ཉིད་དང་ནི་བུད་ཤིང་ལ་སོགས་དང༌།།
ཡོན་ཏན་ཅན་ཡན་ལག་ཅན་ཆགས་དང་མཚན་གཞི་མེ་ལ་སོགས་དོན་དག།
དེ་རྣམས་ཤིང་རྟའི་རྣམ་དཔྱད་བྱས་པས་རྣམ་བདུན་ཡོད་པ་མ་ཡིན་ཞིང༌།།
དེ་ལས་གཞན་དུ་རྒྱུར་པར་འཇིག་རྟེན་གྲགས་པའི་སྒོ་ནས་ཡོད་པ་ཡིན།།
སོགས་སོ། །འདི་ལ་འང་ཕྱག་ལོ་ན་རེ། མང་བཀུར་བ་སོགས
གྱིས་ཕུང་པོ་ལྔ་བདག་གི་གདགས་གཞི་དང་ལེགས་ལྡན་སོགས
གྱིས་སེམས་ཁོ་ན་གདགས་གཞིར་འདོད་ཀྱི་སེམས་བདག་ཏུ
འདོད་མཁན་གྱི་རང་སྡེ་མི་ཡོད་ཟེར་བ་ཡང་ལེགས་ལྡན་གྱི···

གཞུང་དང་ཟླ་བའི་གཞུང་གང་ལའང་དཔེ་སྒྲོགས་ཙམ་ཡང་མ་བྱུས
པར་ཁ་ཚོན་གཅོད་པར་དཔའ་བས་རང་གི་སྨོངས་པའི་ནང་གྲོལ
ཕྱིར་བསྟན་པ་ཡིན་ཏེ། འོ་ན་གཞན་སྡེས་ལེགས་ལྡན་ལ་ཡིད་ཀྱི
རྣམ་ཤེས་བདག་ཡིན་པར་སྒྲུབ་ན་གྲུབ་པ་ལ་སྒྲུབ་པ་མ་ཡིན་པར
ཐལ་བ་དང༌། ལུས་དང་དབང་པོའི་ཚོགས་བདག་གི་གདགས
གཞིར་མི་འདོད་པར་ཐལ། ལེགས་ལྡན་གྱིས་ཡིད་ཀྱི་རྣམ་ཤེས
བདག་ཏུ་མི་འདོད་ཅིང༌། ཕུང་པོ་ལྔའི་ནང་ནས་དེ་ཁོ་ན་གདགས
གཞིར་བྱེད་པའི་ཕྱིར། འཁོར་གསུམ། ཐལ་བ་གཉིས་ལ་འདོད
ན། རྟོག···[252] གེ་འབར་བ་ལས། གྲུབ་པ་སྒྲུབ་པ་ཉིད་ཀྱང་ཡིན་ཏེ།
འདི་ལྟར་ཁོ་བོ་ཅག་ཀྱང་ཐ་སྙད་དུ་རྣམ་པར་ཤེས་པ་ལ་བདག
གི་སྒྲ་དངོས་སུ་འདོགས་ཏེ། འདི་ལྟར་རྣམ་པར་ཤེས་པ་ནི་ཡང
སྲིད་པ་ལེན་པའི་ཕྱིར་བདག་ཡིན་ནོ། །ཞེས་པའི་གྲུབ་པ་ལ
སྒྲུབ་པར་བཤད་པ་མི་འཐད་པར་ཐལ་བ་དང༌། རྣམ་པར་ཤེས
པ་ལ་བདག་གི་སྒྲ་དངོས་སུ་འདོགས་ཞེས་བདག་སྒྲ་རྣམ་ཤེས
ལ་དངོས་མེད་དུ་འཇུག་པར་བཤད་པ་དང༌། ཡང་སྲིད་ལེན

པའི་རྟགས་ཀྱིས་རྣམ་ཤེས་བདག་ཡིན་པར་སྒྲུབ་པ་གཉིས་ཀྱང···
མི་འཐད་པར་ཐལ་བ་དང༌། ཡང་རྟོག[252]་གེ་འབར་བ་ལས། འདི
ལྟར་རྣམ་པར་ཤེས་པ་སྲིད་པ་ལེན་པའི་ཕྱིར་བདག་ཡིན་ནོ།
ཞེས···ལུས་དང་དབང་པོའི་ཚོགས···[253] དག་ལ་ནི་བར་འདོགས
པའི་ཕྱིར། ཞེས་ལུས་དང་དབང་པོའི་ཚོགས་(པ་)[254] བདག་གི་གདགས
གཞིར་བཤད་པ་དང༌། དེའི་ཤེས་བྱེད་དུ། ཇི་སྐད་དུ།
དཔེར་ན་ཡན་ལག་ཚོགས་རྣམས་ལ།།
ཤིང་རྟ་ཞེས་ནི་ངན་པ་ལྟར།།
དེ་བཞིན་ཕུང་པོ་རྣམས་བརྟེན་ནས།།
ཀུན་རྫོབ་ཏུ་ནི་སེམས་ཅན་བརྗོད།།
ཅེས་ཕུང་པོ་གདགས་གཞིར་སྟོན་པ་དྲངས་པ་མི་འཐད་པར་ཐལ
བ་དང༌། ཟླ་བས་ཀྱང་མདོ་འདི་དྲངས་ནས། ཕུང་པོ་གདགས
གཞི་ཡིན་པ་བཀག་པར་ཐལ་དང༌། ཟླ་བས་སེམས་དང་ཕུང་པོ
གདགས་གཞིར་མི་བཞེད་པར་ཐལ་བ་དང༌། ལེགས་ལྡན་དང
ཟླ་བ་གཉིས་ལ་རང་མཚན་གྱིས་གྲུབ་པ་འདོད་མི་འདོད་ཀྱི···

ཁྱད་པར་མེད་པར་ཐལ། གདགས་གཞི་ལ་གདགས་ཆོས་མི་འཛོག་པར་འདུ་བའི་ཕྱིར་སོགས་འཁོར་གསུམ་གྱི་[255] ཕུང་པོ་ཡོད་དོ།། ། གཉིས་པ་ནི།

སྐབས་འགར་ཚུལ་གསུམ་མཚན་སྣང་ཚད་གྲུབ་དང་།།
རྟགས་ཙམ་བཞེད་ཀྱང་རང་དབང་ཚད་མིན་ཕྱིར།།
རང་རྒྱུད་མི་འདོད་ལུགས་འདིར་རང་རྒྱུད་འཁྲུལ།།

ཞེས་སྨྲས་ཏེ། སྟག་ཚང་པས་རང་རྒྱུད་ཐ་སྙད་དུ་འདོད་ཟེར་བ་ནི་གཞན་གྲགས་ཀྱི་[256] རྟགས་དང་རང་རྒྱུད་གཅིག་པར་འཁྲུལ་པ་ཆེ་ཤོས་ཕྱར་ལྟར་ཡིན་ཏེ། ཐལ་འགྱུར་བ་ནང་པན་ཚུན་ཟབ་དོན་ལ་བཀལ་བརྟགས་བྱེད་པའི་སྐབས་འགར་གོལ་བ་གཉིས་ལ་ཚུལ་གསུམ་མཚན་སྣང་སྤྱི་མ་ལྟ་བུའི་ཚད་གྲུབ་དང་ཆོས་ཅན་དང་། རྟགས་མཚན་སྣང་བ་སྤྱི་མ་ལྟ་བུ་གྲུབ་ཀྱང་རང་དབང་གྲུབ་པའི་ཚུལ་གསུམ་ཚད་གྲུབ་མ་ཡིན་པའི་ཕྱིར་དང་། དེ་ཐ་སྙད་དུ་ཡང་མི་བཞེད་དེ་ཐ་སྙད་དུ་རང་བཞིན་གྱིས་གྲུབ་པ་མེད་པར་འདོད་པའི་ཕྱིར་རོ།། ||

Emendations

The sources for the emendations are given in abbreviated form (for full entries of texts see the Bibliography):

Ann dbu: the Mādhyamika section of Nga-w̄ang-b̄el-den's *Annotations* to Jam-ȳang-shay-b̄a's *Great Exposition of Tenets*
ed: the editor
GL: Geshe Gedün Lodrö, a Go-mang scholar at the University of Hamburg until his untimely death in 1979
GM: Jam-ȳang-shay-b̄a's *Great Exposition of the Middle Way*
J̄ang: J̄ang-ḡya's *Presentation of Tenets*
NG: Ngawang Gelek Demo's publication of The Collected Works of 'Jam-dbyaṅs-bźad-pa, Vol. 14, New Delhi, beginning in 1972
Vol.: Volume in the Tibetan Tripiṭaka Research Foundation publication of the Peking edition of the canon
An asterisk indicates that an emended reading is also suitable.

	Page & Line	*Was*	*Emended to*	*Source*
1	i.5	skongs	skong	*NG* 33.1
2	1.1	ṣhayā	ṣhāya	ed
3	1.9, 77.5, 81.9, 110.14, 116.6, 116.9, 117.5	skyangs	bskyangs	*NG* 894.3, etc.
4	1.11	(*NG* 894.4 reads: mtha' yod do cog)		

	Page & Line	*Was*	*Emended to*	*Source*
5	2.9	las	la	*NG* 895.1
6	6.8	kyi	kyis	*J̄ang* 285.14
7	6.14	las sogs	la sogs	*NG* 897.3
8	7.4	(*NG* 897.4 reads: rim pa gnyis pa'i)		
9	7.5	gis	gi	ed
10	8.13	dpal rol	dpal rnam rol	*NG* 898.3
11	9.13	'phreng ba dang	phreng dang	*GT* ca 42a.5; *Ann* dbu 13b.4
12	10.1	'phreng	phreng	IBID
13	10.9	las gtan tshigs	las bstan tshig	*NG* 899.3
14	11.6	legs	lag	Vol. 95 Contents
15	11.10	kyis	kyi	*NG* 899.6
16	12.9	kyi	kyis	*NG* 900.3
17	13.6	ces pa'i	ces pas	*NG* 900.5
18	13.12	kyis	kyi	ed
19	13.14	de'i	'di'i	*NG* 901.1
20	14.13	dris	bris	*NG* 901.5
21	15.3	(*NG* 901.6 reads: zin mi)		
22	15.14	don gang	don gnyis gang	*NG* 902.2
23	18.3	rtogs pa	rtog pa	*NG* 902.4
24	21.8	stan	bstan	*NG* 904.1
25	21.11	chos kyis	chos kyi	*NG* 904.2
26	21.12	stan	bstan	*NG* 904.2
27	22.1 (twice)	gsung	gsungs	*NG* 904.3
28	24.1	mas rang	mas kun btags rang	*NG* 905.3
29	24.2	yang	dbang	*NG* 905.3
30	26.15	kyis gdung bshad	kyi gdung chad	*Ann* dbu 62a.8
31	29.1	so so'i	po'i	*NG* 907.3
32	31.10	kyi	kyis	*NG* 907.4
33	35.2	kyi	kyis	ed
34	36.9	gyis*	gyi	Vol. 29 50.3.2
35	37.2	thugs	thug	*NG* 908.4
36	37.15	btag	brtag	*NG* 909.1
37	40.2	(bracketed addition)		GL
38	40.8	byed pa	byed po	*NG* 910.3
39	40.12	rtog	rtogs	Vol. 98 103.1.8

	Page & Line	*Was*	*Emended to*	*Source*
40	41.11		[ci'i phyir]	*Ann* dbu 65b.3
41	41.11	gzugs kyi bkal bar	gzugs sogs kyang bkar stsal bar	*NG* 911.1
42	42.1	su yang	su snang	*NG* 911.2; Vol. 29 53.4.2
43	43.2	'phreng	phreng	see 9.13
44	43.11, 43.12	rten	brten	Vol. 129 181.2.3
45	44.7	kyi	kyis	*NG* 912.2; Vol. 98 131.1.4; Vol. 29 39.5.5
46	44.7	pa'i	pa las	Vol. 98 136.1.4, 5; Vol. 29 39.5.6
47	44.8	gsung	gsungs	IBID; *NG* 912.2
48	44.8	'das kyi	'das kyis	Vol. 98 136.1.4, 5; Vol. 29 39.5.6
49	44.9	ba de rnam	ba rnam	IBID
50	46.15	kyi	kyis	Vol. 98 136.2.7; Vol. 29 40.2.1
51	47.6	(*NG* 912.5 reads: 'gyur bas drang)		
52	48.11	(*NG* 913.2 reads: rang bzhin du; Vol. 98 127.1.8 reads: rang bzhin rjes)		
53	48.13	rigs	rig	*NG* 913.3; Vol. 98 127.2.1; *GM* 458b.1
54	51.7		[ltar]	*GM* 464a.3
55	52.6	bshad de	bshad do	*NG* 914.4
56	56.12	rdzas gnyis	rdzas btags gnyis	Vol. 153 205.1.8
57	58.5	dngos	ngos	*NG* 915.6; *Ann* dbu 127b.7
58	58.11, 58.13	brtags	btags	*NG* 916.2; see 59.2, 59.3, etc.
59	59.9	rtogs	rtog	*NG* 916.4; Vol. 95 136.2.1; see 59.13, 59.14
60	68.15	kyi	kyis	*NG* 917.1; Vol. 23 199.3.4
61	69.1	gsung	gsungs	*NG* 917.1

	Page & Line	*Was*	*Emended to*	*Source*
62	69.4	(*NG* 917.2 reads: zhes pa'i)		
63	70.1	ltar sher	lta ma yin par sher	*NG* 917.4
64	70.2	rtogs	rtog	*NG* 917.5
65	70.5	gyi	gyis	*NG* 917.5
66	70.8	byas te	bya ste	*NG* 917.6
67	70.13	las ma grub	las grub	Vol. 98 270.3.7
68	71.4	(*NG* 918.2 reads: smos pa)		
69	71.8	de'i*	de yi	Vol. 99 260.4.5
70	72.11, 73.1	par che	par shin tu che	Vol. 95 112.2.3, 112.2.4
71	74.1	rtogs	rtog	*NG* 919.2
72	74.7	(*NG* 919.4 mis-reads: bsten)		
73	75.1	gyi	gyis	ed
74	75.5		['dra]	GL
75	75.8	(Vol. 98 103.1.8 reads 'dir)		
76	76.9	gzigs	gzegs	*NG* 920.3; see 77.6
77	76.12	kyis	kyi	Vol. 98 256.1.8
78	77.5	kyis	kyi	*NG* 920.6
79	77.8	gdag	gdags	*NG* 921.1
80	77.11	tu	du	*NG* 921.2
81	78.12	gyi	gyis	*NG* 921.5; *Ann* dbu 128a.4
82	79.6	de'i*	de yi	*NG* 922.1; Vol. 103 21.3.6
83	79.13	thugs	thug	*NG* 922.2; see 80.12
84	80.2	rgyu	myu gu	ed (context)
85	80.14	gyi	gyis	*NG* 922.6
86	80.14	len	lan	*NG* 922.6
87	80.15	nyid la	nyid las	ed
88	81.4	med pa	med par	*NG* 923.1
89	81.6	gu ma mthong	gu mthong	*NG* 923.2; *Ann* dbu 70b.4
90	81.10	gis	gi	*NG* 923.3; Vol. 95 75.1.6
91	81.15	nyid*	ni	Vol. 98 93.4.7, 101.3.4

	Page & Line	*Was*	*Emended to*	*Source*
92	83.8	las	la	*NG* 923.5
93	83.12	rgyu	rgyud	*NG* 923.5; see 85.6
94	83.13	la	las	*NG* 923.6; *Ann* dbu 127a.8
95	84.3	bus	bu	*NG* 924.1, Vol. 95 8.1.1
96	84.15	(*NG* 924.2 reads: byed pa)		
97	85.4	keng	king	Vol. 98 121.5.4
98	85.6	gyi	gyis	*NG* 924.4; see 85.8
99	85.14	gis	gi	Vol. 95 3.1.6
100	87.9	na	nas	*NG* 924.6
101	87.12	gyis	gyi	*NG* 925.1
102	88.13	gi	gis	*NG* 925.4
103	88.14	(*NG* 925.4 mis-reads: 'khrul)		
104	89.3	sa	sā	Vol. 34 p.7 Contents
105	89.3	gyis	gyi	*NG* 925.5
106	90.4	skyer	skyed	*NG* 926.3
107	90.13	thugs	thug	*NG* 926.5
108	91.4	gyis	gyi	*NG* 926.6
109	91.8	la	las	*NG* 927.1
110	91.13	yi	yis	*NG* 927.2; Vol. 98 137.3.5
111	92.2	grangs	grang	*NG* 927.3; *Ann* dbu 128b.4
112	92.5	gyi	gyis	*NG* 927.4
113	92.11	ba'i	bas	ed
114	94.7	skyes	skye	Go-mang scribe
115	95.8	gi	gis	*NG* 929.1
116	95.12	mas	ma'i	ed
117	95.13	kyis	kyi	ed
118	96.6	de'i rang 'grel	de nyid	ed (still from root text)
119	96.10	skye	kye	*Ann* dbu.73b.4
120	98.5	mig gis	mig gi	Vol. 98 3.3.7
121	98.7	ba la	ba'i sgra la	Vol. 98 3.3.8

	Page & Line	Was	Emended to	Source
122	98.8	gnyis	nyid	*NG* 930.3; Vol. 98 3.3.8
123	98.9	gyis	gyi	*NG* 930.3
124	98.10	gcig gis	gcig gi	ed
125	98.11	gis	gi	*NG* 930.4; Vol. 98 13.3.8
126	99.10	(*NG* 931.2 mis-reads: zhan pa'i)		
127	99.12	re'i	re re'i	*NG* 931.2
128	101.1	zhe	she	*NG* 931.4; Vol. 101 76.4.3
129	101.15	na	la	*NG* 932.3
130	102.1	rten	brten	*NG* 932.4
131	102.6	dbu ma snying po las	dbu ma las	*Ann* dbu 74a.7
132	104.6	gyis	gyi	Vol. 98 78.2.3
133	104.15	kyi	kyis	*NG* 933.4
134	105.1	gi	gis	ed
135	105.2	du	tu	*NG* 933.5
136	105.6	pa las	pa'i 'grel pa las	*NG* 933.6
137	105.8	(*NG* 933.6 reads: pa 'di ni)		
138	106.6	'jigs	'jig	*NG* 934.3
139	106.6, 106.12, 106.15	tsantra'i	tsandra'i	Vol. 140 p.1 Contents
140	(pp.106-14: In the Ngawang Gelek edition the virāma is used under the final consonant in *tuk, nany, yap, lyap, ghany, pad, samut, k, s, as,* and *t*. However, it is not used with *kṛt, alam, l, pit, ruj, vish, spṛsh, uch, gh, p, am, mut, sam*, or *sup* for no explicable reason; thus, it has been added to these.)			
141	106.8	ktva	ktvā	Vol. 140 45.2.8
142	106.8	ming	meng	Vol. 140 45.2.8
143	106.10, 106.14, 108.5	krit	kṛt	Vol. 140 46.2.1 etc.
144	106.11	kta	ktvā	Vol. 140 45.3.8
145	106.11	ming	meng	Vol. 140 45.3.8
146	106.12, 106.13, 106.14, 106.15	ktva	ktvā	ed

	Page & Line	*Was*	*Emended to*	*Source*
147	106.13	na nya	nany	*NG* 934.5; Vol. 140 13.4.7
148	106.14	ka la pa ltar	ka lā pa'i	*NG* 934.5
149	107.1, 107.3	tu ka	tuk	*NG* 934.6; see 107.4
150	107.8	a ka ni a ka la rings pos	ak'i ak la ring ngo	Vol. 140 12.1.4
151	107.9, 107.12, 108.4	rtsa ba'i	tsa ba'i	*NG* 935.2 and .4; 'Chandrapa', i.e., Chandragomin
152	107.10	bzhi	bnyis	ed (location of source)
153	107.12	pa'i por	pa'i dang por	*NG* 935.2
154	107.12	sus	sup'i	*NG* 935.2; Vol. 140 6.1.2
155	107.14	(*NG* 935.3 reads: si)		
156	108.1, 108.2	pa da	pad	*NG* 935.3
157	108.4	gha nya	ghany	*NG* 935.4; Vol. 140 4.3.6
158	108.5	pad du dza bi sha u ca	pad rudz vish spṛsh uts	*NG* 935.4; Vol. 140 45.1.3
159	108.6	bying sad	byings pad	*NG* 935.4
160	108.8	phyis a	phyis gh'i srog gi a	*NG* 935.5
161	108.8	kyis	kyi	*NG* 935.5
162	108.10	po 'os*	po'o zhes	Vol. 140 6.2.5; ed for zhes
163	108.10	(*NG* 935.5 mis-reads: s sa dzu)		
164	108.11	tu'o	ru 'os	*NG* 935.6; Vol. 140 15.5.6 misreads rung go, but Sanskrit is obvious
165	108.11	sa'i tu	s ni ru	ed; *NG* 935.6 reads: s (with virāma) sa ru

	Page & Line	Was	Emended to	Source
166	108.11	ha sha la'ng	hash la yang	ed; *NG* 935.6: ha sha l'ng; Vol. 140 12.1.6: has la yang
167	108.12	pa'i rtags	pa'i u rtags	*NG* 935.6
168	108.13	(*NG* 935.6 reads:	re pha'i)	
169	108.14	(*NG* 935.6 reads:	byas/ sa)	
170	109.3	da	de	*NG* 936.2
171	109.6	'byung 'jug	'byung ba la 'jug	*NG* 936.2
172	110.2	mud	mut	*NG* 936.3
173	110.4	kyis	kyi	*NG* 936.4; Vol. 98 3.3.3
174	110.5	no	to	*NG* 936.4; Vol. 98 3.3.3
175	110.5	(*NG* 936.4 reads:	zhes gsungs so)	
176	110.9, 111.5, 113.15, 116.13, 118.2, 119.11, 123.1, 132.13, 136.14, 143.11, 146.2, 149.5	tshigs	tshig	*NG* 936.5, etc.; Vol. 98 Contents
177	110.9	stong	stod	*NG* 936.5
178	110.13	kyis	kyi	*NG* 936.6
179	111.2	'jigs	'jig	Vol. 98 3.3.4
180	111.12	'jigs	'jig	*NG* 937.2; Vol. 96 169.5.8
181	112.12	kvis	kvip	ed
182	112.13	kas	pas	ed
183	112.13	pa	p	ed; *NG* 937.3 reads: ba
184	112.13	'grel	'brel	*NG* 937.3; see 106.5
185	112.13, 112.14	ta	t	ed
186	112.14	kas	pas	ed
187	113.10, 113.11	tshigs sdus	tshig sdud	see 113.7
188	113.13	rten	brten	see 113.8
189	113.14	te kyi	te lyap ki	*NG* 938.1; see 115.10

	Page & Line	Was	Emended to	Source
190	114.1	gis	gi	*NG* 938.1; Vol. 98 3.3.5
191	117.2	par 'byung ba'i	par gyi	See n.705
192	117.4	du min	du yang min	*NG* 938.6; Vol. 98 3.4.7
193	117.6	'brel par	'brel bar	*NG* 938.6
194	117.8	ganga'i	gangā'i	*NG* 938.1; Vol. 98 3.3.2
195	119.6	khas mi blang	khas blang	see 120.7
196	121.13	pa rjod	pa yang brjod	*NG* 940.3; Vol. 98 4.1.1
197	121.14		[zhes so]	ed. (end of quote)
198	121.14	*NG* 940.3 reads: ci ste yang)		
199	122.1	mi lha	ma he	*NG* 940.4; *Ann* dbu 76b.1 (which is misnumbered as 77b.1)
200	122.8	gis	gi	*NG* 940.5; Vol. 95 11.4.1
201	122.14	sgra	sgrar	*NG* 940.6
202	124.6	kyi	kyis	*NG* 941.3
203	124.7	tsam ma yin	tsam yin	ed (context)
204	124.8	pa'i 'grel pa las	pa las	ed (not the comm., but the basic text)
205	125.9	gyis	gyi	Vol. 98 270.3.5
206	125.13	tsangs	tshang	*NG* 942.2
207	126.4	rigs pas	rig pa	Vol. 129 237.5.7; *NG* 942.3 reads: rig pas
208	127.9	(*NG* 943.2 reads: ma yin par)		
209	128.1	(*NG* 943.4 reads: pa 'di la)		
210	128.3	bzhin	gzhan	*NG* 943.4; *Ann* dbu 129a.3
211	128.4	rten	brten	*Ann* dbu 129a.3
212	129.7	rten	brten	*NG* 944.2
213	129.13	gis	gi	*NG* 944.4; see 129.14

	Page & Line	Was	Emended to	Source
214	129.14	sogs bzhag	sogs su bzhag	*NG* 944.4
215	130.3	'jigs	'jig	*NG* 944.5; Vol. 98 141.2.3
216	130.7	gis	gi	Vol. 98 109.3.4
217	130.15	kyi	kyis	*NG* 945.1; Vol. 156 65.5.8
218	131.3	kyi	kyis	*NG* 945.2; Vol. 156 66.1.1
219	131.4	zag gis	zag gi	*NG* 945.2; Vol. 156 66.1.1
220	131.7	rtogs	rtog	*NG* 945.3
221	132.1	(*NG* 945.5 reads: nga yir)		
222	132.7	kyis	kyi	*NG* 946.1; Vol. 156 66.1.2
223	132.7	(*NG* 946.1 mis-reads: pa'i)		
224	132.9, 132.15	bskal	skal	*NG* 946.1, .3
225	133.7	ngar 'dzin lhan	nga yi bar 'dzin pa lhan	See n.741
226	133.7	gsung	gsungs	*NG* 946.4
227	133.12	spyod	dpyod	*GM* 241a.3
228	134.2	rtogs	rtog	*NG* 947.1
229	134.3	rtsa	rtsva	*NG* 947.1
230	134.8	gsum	bzhi	ed (location of source)
231	135.2	bdag	rtag	*NG* 947.4; Vol. 98 104.1.8
232	135.14	chos dang gzugs	chos nga gzugs	*GM* 481a.5
233	136.9	'dus	'du	GL
234	137.2	mtshan mor	mtshan mar	*NG* 948.6
235	137.3	'dud	'du	*NG* 948.6; Vol. 98 53.3.2
236	138.3	(*NG* 949.1 reads: po 'o chu 'dres pa bzhin)		
237	139.1	kyis	kyi	ed (possessive)
238	140.9	phung ma	phung po ma	*NG* 950.1
239	141.2	med ces	med [bdag la rnam par shes pa med] ces	ed (parallelism)

	Page & Line	*Was*	*Emended to*	*Source*
240	141.14	mkhar	'khar	Vol. 98 145.4.7; *Ann* dbu 87a.1
241	142.1	nyid med pas de	nyid kyis de	*Ann* dbu 84b.8
242	142.1	rten	brten	ed
243	143.6	thal ste	thal ba ste	*NG* 951.4
244	143.12	rtogs	rtog	*NG* 951.6; Vol. 98 53.1.8
245	145.5	(add in also inside the bracket with broken underline: zhes bya ba la sogs pa dbu ma la 'jug pa las rgyas par rnam par dpyad pa byas pa las khong du chud par bya ste/ 'dir ni spros pa rgyas par mi brtsam mo//de ltar re zhig phung po bdag ma yin no//)		
246	146.14	la	las	ed
247	147.8	rig	rigs	*NG* 952.6; Vol. 98 145.4.7
248	147.14	kyi	kyis	ed (see 147.15)
249	149.10	'phreng	phreng	*NG* 953.6
250	149.13	l'ang	yang	*Ann* dbu 67b.7; Vol. 129 175.2.7 reads: l'ang
251	150.3	min pa'i	de yi	*Ann* dbu 87a.7; Vol. 129 175.3.1
252	152.9, 153.2	rtogs	rtog	*NG* 955.2, .4; Vol. 96 p.1 Contents
253	153.4	tshogs bdag	tshogs dag	Vol. 96 36.4.6; *GM* 475a.6
254	153.5	tshogs bdag gis	tshogs pa bdag gi	*NG* 955.5
255	154.2	gyis	gyi	*NG* 956.2
256	154.8	kyis	kyi	*NG* 956.3

List of Charts

1 Modes of Existence 39
2 Faults of Meditative Stabilization and their Antidotes 72
3 States and Factors in Achieving Calm Abiding 81
4 Path of Seeing 97
5 Innate Afflictions Forsaken on the Path of Meditation in Terms of the Three Realms and Nine Levels 105
6 Eight Levels of Approaching and Abiding 107
7 Divisions of the Selfless 213
8 Divisions of Existents 215
9 Divisions of Permanent Phenomena 217
10 Divisions of Things 220
11 Divisions of Forms 221
12 Divisions of Visible Forms 223
13 Divisions of Colors 224
14 Divisions of Shapes 226
15 Divisions of Sounds 227
16 Divisions of Odors 228
17 Divisions of Tastes 228
18 Divisions of Tangible Objects 229
19 Divisions of Forms for the Mental Consciousness 233
20 Divisions of Consciousness 235
21 Divisions of Minds 237
22 Divisions of Mental Factors 238
23 Divisions of Omnipresent Mental Factors 239

24 Divisions of Determining Mental Factors 246
25 Divisions of Virtuous Mental Factors 248
26 Divisions of Root Afflictions 256
27 Divisions of Afflicted Views 259
28 Divisions of Secondary Afflictions 262
29 Divisions of Changeable Mental Factors 267
30 Divisions of Non-Associated Compositional Factors 268
31 Divisions of Non-Person Non-Associated Compositional Factors 270
32 The Five Aggregates 271
33 The Eighteen Constituents 273
34 The Twelve Sources 274
35 Buddha's Explicit Teaching in the 'Rice Seedling Sutra' of One Round of a Twelve-Membered Dependent-Arising 279
36 Principal Objects of Meditation 298
37 Self 299
38 Obstructions 300
39 Selflessness 301
40 Divisions of Vaibhāṣhika into Eighteen Schools 340
41 Types of Awareness 702
42 A Version of Buddha's Implicit Teaching According to Asaṅga (two lives, one unit) 708
43 A Version of Buddha's Implicit Teaching According to Asaṅga (three lives, one unit) 709
44 A Version of Buddha's Implicit Teaching According to Asaṅga (two lives, two units) 710
45 A Version of Buddha's Implicit Teaching According to Asaṅga (three lives, two units) 711
46 Bhāvaviveka's First Rendition of the Eighteen Vaibhāṣhika Schools 714
47 Bhāvaviveka's Second Rendition of the Eighteen Vaibhāṣhika Schools 715
48 Vasumitra's Rendition of the Eighteen Vaibhāṣhika Schools 716
49 Vinītadeva's Rendition of the Eighteen Vaibhāṣhika Schools 717
50 Padmasaṃbhava's Rendition of the Eighteen Vaibhāṣhika Schools 718
51 The Rendition of the Eighteen Vaibhāṣhika Schools according to the 'Dīpavaṃsa' and 'Mahāvaṃsa' 719

D̄zong-ka-b̄a

Index

Abhayākara, 388
Abhidharmakosha, see Treasury of Higher Knowledge
Abhidharmakoshabhāṣhya, see Explanation of the 'Treasury of Knowledge'
Abhidharmakoshaṭīkā, see Commentary on (Vasubandhu's) 'Treasury of Knowledge'
Abhidharmasamuchchaya, see Compendium of Knowledge
Abhisamayālaṃkāra, see Ornament for Clear Realization
Abhyagirikas, 717, 718
Able to establish itself (*tshugs thub tu grub pa*), 36, 172-3, 676
Absolute Truth, unsuitability as a translation term, 419-20
Absorption of cessation, 207, 269, 270
Achintyastava, see Praise of the Inconceivable
Action, complete path of, 276
Action Tantra, 112
Activities of mind, eighteen, 627, 628
'Advice to Kātyāyana', 598
Affirming negatives, 133, 459, 467-8, Appendix 4 pp.723-5
Affixing a qualification to the object of negation, 135-6, 144-8, 159-60, 501-4, 655, 658
Affixing the qualification 'ultimately' in Svātantrika, 500-5
Afflicted mind, 384-5
Afflicted view, 256, 258-61, Chart 27 p.259
Afflictions, *see* Root afflictions *and* Secondary afflictions
Afflictive obstructions, 297ff, 342-3, *see also* Obstructions to liberation
Aggregates, five, 201, 271-2,

Aggregates *(cont.)*
Chart 32 p.271, 278, 285
Aishvaras, 239, 318, 613
Akṣhayamatinirdesha, see Teaching of Akṣhayamati Sutra
Akutobhayā, 360, n.366 p.818, n.414 p.823
Ālayavijñāna, see Mind-basis-of-all
Ālayavijñāna, etymology, 617
Analysis, 267-8
need for and purpose of, 30-4, 188, 200, 409-10, 529, 555-6, 560
Analytical cessations, 217, 218, 344, 390, n.191 p.806
Analytical meditation, 83, 89-90, 91ff, 113-15, 557-8
Anavatapatanāgarājaparipṛchchhā, see Questions of the King of Nāgas, Anavatapta, Sutra
Anger, 256-7, 261, 263
Annotations for (Jam-yang-shay-ba's) 'Great Exposition of Tenets', 12-13, 565-6, 578, n.500 p.854
Antidotes to faults in meditation, eight, 71-80, Chart 2 p.72, 245, 253
Aparashailas, 714, 715, 716, 717, 718
Appearance of inherent existence, 44-5, 450, 683-5, *see also* Object of negation in Prāsaṅgika
Appearing but not ascertained, 702-4
Appearing object, 511, 701
Appearing object of thought, 346-8, 701
Arhan, explanation of etymology and translation as Foe Destroyer, n.553 pp.871-3, *see also* Foe Destroyer
Arhat, teacher of the Forders, 320, n.553 p.872
Artificial afflictions, *see* Misconceptions of inherent existence, artificial
Artificial false views of an inherently existent person, 177
Āryadeva, 167, 359, 431, 537, 570, 572, 587, 591, 676
citation of texts by, 30, 33, 291, 555, 585, 627, 632, 660, 674, n.458 p.837
Aryavimuktisena, 594
Asaṅga, 236, 359ff, 363, 366, 372, 383, 384, 593, 656, 707-11
Ascertainment of pervasion, 47-8, 53-4, 57, 62, 63, 65, 146-7, 179
Ashoka, 358
Aṣhṭasāhasrikāprajñāpāramitā, see Eight Thousand Stanza Perfection of Wisdom Sutra
Ashvaghoṣha, 363, 432, 570, 572, 586, 587-8, n.504 p.857, n.512-3 p.861
Aspiration, 245-6
Atīsha, 154, 432, 534-5, 571, 572, 592, 593, 640, 653, n.527 p.864
Attachment, 275, 280-81ff
Attention, *see* Intention
Autonomous inferences, 452, 456, 480, 523-4, 584-5, n.496 pp.847-9, n.497 pp.848-50
Autonomous reason, 697

Autonomous syllogisms, 431-2, 456, 470-1, 473-4, 475-80, 489, 504, 521-2, 564, 697
Avaivartachakra, see Irreversible Wheel Sutra
Avalokitavrata, 165-6, 318, 324, 358, 360, 361, 363, 426, 462, 571, 572, 666, 667, n.366 p.818
Avantakas, 714, 717, 718
Awareness to which the object appears but is not ascertained, *see* Appearing but not ascertained
Awarenesses, types of, Appendix 1 pp.701-5
Āyatana, see Sources

Ba-kay-gay (*Ba-khe-gad, Khe-gad-'khor-lo-grags*), 536
B̄a-tsap-nyi-ma-drak-b̄a (*Pa-tshab-nyi-ma-grags-pa*), 535
Bahushrutīyas, 340, 714, 716, 717, 718, 719
Bases of contact, six, 627-8
Basis in Buddha's thought, purpose, and refutation of the explicit meaning, 602, 616, n.539 pp.866-7, n.580 pp.875-6
Basis-of-all, *see* Mind-basis-of-all
Beings of the three capacities, 32, 251
B̄el-den-chö-jay (*dPal-ldan-chos-rje*), 565, *see also* Nga-w̄ang-b̄el-den
Belief, 246
Belligerence, 261, 262, 263
Bhadrayānīyas, 340, 714, 715, 716, 719
Bhairava, 538
Bhāva, 220, *see also* Things
  different meanings of, 391-2, 438, n.723 p.886, n.786 p.897
Bhāvaviveka, 320, 321, 339, 358, 360-3, 378, 399, 431, 441, 449, 450, 455-68, 469-98 passim, 499-530 passim, 570, 571, 572, 574, 575, 587-8, 591, 592, 612, 614, 694-6, 713-17, n.497 pp.848-50, n.791 pp.897-902
  citation of texts by, 30-31, 461, 463, 666, 668-9, 695-6
  criticism of Buddhapālita, 441, 455-68, 470, 476, 480, 490
  founder of Svātantrika, 361-3
  interpretation of dependent-arising, 165-6, 666-73
  other names of, 360
Bhikṣhuvarṣhāgrapṛchchhāsūtra, 718
Blaze of Reasoning (Tarkajvālā), 320, 321, 571, 575, 695-6, 713, 714, 715
Bodhibhadra, 321
Bodhichittavivaraṇa, see Essay on the Mind of Enlightenment
Bodhidharma, 536, 537
Bodhimārgapradīpapañjikā, see Commentary on the Difficult Points of 'Lamp for the Path to Enlightenment'
Bodhisattva, 22, 98-109, 111-12, 128, 296ff, 342-3, 379, 417, 426
Bodhisattva grounds, 98-109, 111-15, 302, 345, 404
Bodhisattva Section Sutra, 589

Bodhisattvacharyāvatāra, see Engaging in the Bodhisattva Deeds
Bodhisattvacharyāvatārabhāshya, see Explanation of (Shāntideva's) 'Engaging in the Bodhisattva Deeds'
Bodhisattvapiṭaka, see Bodhisattva Section Sutra
Bön, 318
Bowl of fluid, example of mind only, 372, 376-7
Brahman, 186-7
Brāhmaṇas, 318, 564
Brahmāparipṛchchhā, see Questions of Brahmā Sutra
Bu-dön (*Bu-ston*), 435, 535
Buddha, 22, 237, 288, 342, 379-80, 392-3, 407, 417, 423, 529, 542, 572, 604, *see also* Shākyamuni Buddha
Buddha Bodies, 117-23, 285, *see also* individual listings for Form Body, Truth Body, Nature Body, Emanation Body, Complete Enjoyment Body, *and* Wisdom Body
Buddha lineage, 617, *see also* Buddha nature *and* Tathāgata essence
Buddha nature, 357, 381-3, 396-7, 535, 617
Buddha's acceptance of what the world accepts, 502, 526-30
Buddhadeva, 343
Buddhaguhya, 532
Buddhahood, 109, 115, 117-23, 237, 382, 404, 543, n.521 pp.863-4
Buddhapālita, 29, 165, 359-60, 363, 449, 455-68, 469-98 passim, 570, 572, 587, 588, 633, 637, 668- 70, 676, 685
  citation of text by, 455, 460, 558, 633, 641, 678, 689, 690, 691, 692
  founder of Prāsaṅgika, 359-60, 363, 431-2, 584, 587, n.494 p.840
  refutation of Sāṃkhya, 441-3, 455-63, 469-71, 474, 476-7, 481-9
Buddhapālita's Commentary on (Nāgārjuna's) 'Treatise on the Middle Way', 455, 459, 460-1, 558, 570, 591, 633, 641, 678, 689, 690, 691, 692
Buddhapālitamūlamadhyamakavṛtti, see Buddhapālita's Commentary on (Nāgārjuna's) 'Treatise on the Middle Way'
Buddhāvataṃsaka Sutra, 590
Buddhāvataṃsakanāmamahāvaipulya, see Buddhāvataṃsaka Sutra
Buddhist and non-Buddhist, differentiating, 188, 319-20, 335
Buddhist, definition of, 335-6
Buddhist proponent of tenets, definition of, 336-7

Calm abiding, 67-90, 91, 93, 112-14, 247, 404, 557-8
  etymology, 67
  nine states in developing, 80-6, Chart 3 p.81, 253
  objects of, 69-71, 88-9
  prerequisites, 68-9
Cataracts example, 509-10
Cause and effect, non-simultaneity of in Chittamātra, 367-8

Cause and effect (*cont.*)
simultaneity of in Vaibhāṣhika, 139, 339
Certification of objects by valid cognition, 508-11, 518, 527-8, 539-47, 574, n.727 p.887, *see also* Valid establishment of phenomena
Ceylonese Chronicles, 718, 719
Chaitikas, 340, 714, 715, 716, 719
Chandragomin, 569, 572
Chandragomin's [Sanskrit] Grammar, 569, 662-4
Chandrakīrti, 11, 13, 29, 131, 136, 154, 169, 178, 186, 193, 195, 320, 360-2, 363, 399, 403-5, 411, 420, 422, 449, 497, 538, 541, 542, 569, 571, 572-4, 587, 592-3, 633, 637, 653, 675, 682, 687, 696, 729, n.516 p.863
citation of texts by, 30, 152-3, 170, 182, 184, 192, 200, 469, 472-3, 474-5, 477-8, 480-81, 483-6, 488, 489, 492, 493, 496, 497, 500, 502-3, 504, 505, 507, 508-10, 512-14, 517-8, 519-20, 521, 523-4, 525, 526, 541, 554, 556, 558, 586, 590, 591, 592, 596-7, 602, 610, 612, 614, 616, 617, 618, 627, 632, 634, 636, 637, 640, 641, 644, 645-7, 648, 649, 650, 652, 655-6, 660-2, 664-5, 666, 667-8, 669, 670, 671, 672, 673, 674, 678-9, 680-1, 682, 683, 684, 686, 689-93, 694, n.244 p.808, n.516 pp.862-3
defense of Buddhapālita, 441, 469-98
differentiation of the interpretable and the definitive, 425, 596-7, 602-4, 610-11
etymology of *saṃvṛtisatya*, 417-8
interpretation of mind-only, 377-8, 614
interpretation of *pratītyasamutpāda*, 164-7, 662-74
opening the way of/founding Prāsaṅgika, 360-2, 431-2, 584, 587, n.494 p.840
presentation of the sevenfold reasoning, 44, 48, 178-93, 687-96
refutation of Bhāvaviveka, 499-530, n.497 p.849
Chāndravyākaraṇa, see Chandragomin's [Sanskrit] Grammar
Changeable mental factors, 238, 266-8, Chart 29 p.267
Chapter of the True One Sutra, 571, 605
Chapter Showing the Three Vows Sutra, 589
Chariot example, 179-83, 694
Chārvākas, 319, 327-33, *see also* Hedonists
other names for, 327
Chatuḥshataka, see Four Hundred
Chatuḥshatakaṭīkā, see Commentary on (Āryadeva's) 'Four Hundred'
Chittamātra, 38, 39, 128-9, 135, 139, 172, 181, 231, 234, 336,

Chittamātra (*cont.*)
344, 359, 361, 365-97, 404, 434, 436, 533, 565, 602, 622-3, 639, 641, n.501 pp.854-5
differentiation of the interpretable and the definitive, 424, 426-7, 601, 611-12, 615, 623
identification of selflessness, 38-9, 128-9, 296-301, 366, 368-70, 385
interpretation of dependent-arising, 38, 167
simultaneity of object and subject, 367-8
Chittamātrins Following Asaṅga, *see* Chittamātrins Following Scripture
Chittamātrins Following Reasoning, 344, 366, 385, 396, n.501 p.855
Chittamātrins Following Scripture, 366, 383-7, 392, 393-4, 603, 611-12, n.501 p.855, n.791 p.901
Chittavajrastava, see Praise of the Mind Vajra
Clairvoyances, five, 208, 255
Classification of the Ends of Actions, 588
Clear Words, 136, 360, 426, 473, 569, 590, 593, 662, 663, 665, 693, n.496 pp.845-8, n.516 pp.862-3
citation of, 469-70, 474-5, 477-8, 480-1, 483-6, 488, 489, 492, 493, 496, 497, 500, 502-3, 504, 505, 507, 508-9, 509-10, 512-4, 517-8, 519-21, 525-6, 525, 526,
Clear Words (*cont.*)
541, 584, 586, 590, 591-2, 593, 596-7, 634, 648, 655-6, 660, 661, 664-5, 666, 667-8, 669, 670, 671, 672, 673, 680-1, 684, 689-90, 690-91
reason for translation thus, n.496 pp.845-6
Cloud of Jewels Sutra, 31
Coarse selflessness of the person, 296-304, 341
Cognitions, four, 371-2
Cognizing consciousness, 701, *see also* Valid cognizer
Collections of Praises, 588, 590, n.512 p.861
Collections of Reasonings, 15, 588, 591, 782-3, n.512 p.861
Colors, 223-5, Chart 13 p.224, 232, 233
Commentary on (Āryadeva's) 'Four Hundred', 192, 570, 593, 627, 632, 637, 656, 674-5
Commentary on (Atīsha's) 'Quintessential Instructions on the Middle Way', 593
Commentary on (Bhāvaviveka's) 'Lamp for (Nāgārjuna's) "Wisdom"', 462-6, 571, 666
Commentary on (Dignāga's) 'Compendium of Valid Cognition', 571, 676
Commentary on (Nāgārjuna's) 'Friendly Letter', 570, 675
Commentary on (Nāgārjuna's) 'Seventy Stanzas on Emptiness', 593, 652, 675
Commentary on (Nāgārjuna's) Sixty Stanzas of Reasoning', 200, 571, 593, 661-2, 675

Commentary on the Difficult Points of (Atīsha's) 'Lamp for the Path to Enlightenment', 593
Commentary on the 'Supplement to (Nāgārjuna's) 'Treatise on the Middle Way'', 152-3, 182, 472-3, 569, 602, 603, 604, 610, 617, 618-9, 678, 679, 682, 686, 691, 692-3
Commentary on the 'Sutra on Dependent-Arising', 662, 674
Commentary on (Udbhaṭasiddhasvāmin's) 'Exalted Praise', 320
Commentary on (Vasubandhu's) 'Treasury of Knowledge', 662
Commonly appearing subject, 450-1, 452, 505-15, 522, 529, 697, n.346 pp.814-5, n.424 pp.825-30, n.798 pp.904-5
Compassion, three types, 404
Compendium of Doctrine Sutra, 571, 589
Compendium of Knowledge, 236, 656
Compendium of Learnings, 589, 593, 657
Compendium of Sutra, 569, 572, 589, 590, 591, 603, 604-9, 657
Compendium of Valid Cognition, 344, 366, n.442 p.833
Compendium on Reality, 575
Concealment, 262, 263
Concentrations, Four, 104ff, 206, 207, 241, 353-4
Conception of a (bad) view as supreme, 259, 260, 289
Conception of (bad) ethics and modes of conduct as supreme, 259, 260, 289
Conception of inherent existence, 177-8, 288, 450, 680, *see also* Misconceptions of inherent existence, artificial and innate
Conception that phenomena exist naturally as bases of engagement of names, 300, 369-72, 389
Conceptual consciousnesses, 346-9, 701, 704, 722
Conceptuality, use and purpose of, n.500, pp.853-4, *see also* Analysis, uses and purpose of *and* Inferential realization of emptiness
Conditionality, 432-5, 586, 672, n.503 pp.856-7
Conscientiousness, 248, 252-3
Consciousness, 201, 235-68, Chart 20 p.235, 271, 272ff, 275, 278
Consciousnesses, eight in Chittamātra, 366-7, 384-7
Consequences (*prasaṅga*), 134-5, 360, 431-2, 441-9, 451, 452, 470-1, 479-81, 482, 489, 490-1, 493, 494-7, 529-30, 584-6, 640, 730, 733
  and syllogisms, use of as a means of distinguishing the Mādhyamika schools, 360, 452-3, 497, 733, n.497 p.848
  five types, 445-9, 493
Constituents (*dhātu*), 222, 223, 273-4, Chart 33 p.273
  six, 627ff

Contact, 201-2, 244-5, 275, 280, 386
Contradictory consequences, 446-8, 470, 479, 585, 640
Contrition, 267
Conventional truths, *see* Truths, conventional
Conventional valid cognizer, 419, *see also* Valid establishment of phenomena *and* Valid cognizer
Conventionalities, status of, 435,635-6
Conventionally existent production, 459-61
Conventionally existent self, nature of, 189, 315, 380, 385-6, 679
Correct assumption, 701-4
Council of Rājagṛha, 713
Creator in Buddhism, 612-13
Cultivation of the Ultimate Mind of Enlightenment, 570, 586, 588, n.512 p.861
Cyclic existence and nirvana, non-difference of, 219, 415

D̄ak-tsang (*sTag-tshang*), 15, 147, 172-3, 343, 411-12, 539-40, 563, 573, 576-7, 588, 592, 648, 655, 676, 681, 683, 694-5, 697, n.521 pp.663-4, n.727 p.887
Dalai Lama, 14-15, n.791 p.903
Dashabhūmika, see Sutra on the Ten Grounds
de Jong, J.W., n.374 p.818, n.516 pp.862-3, n.758 p.894
Debate, purpose and function as a learning device, 576-8
Deceit, 262, 263-4
Definitive and interpretable, differentiating, 422-8, 595-623
Definitive sutras, 422-8, 595-601
Deity yoga, 113, 115
D̄en-dar-hla-ram-b̄a (*bsTan-dar-lha-ram-pa*), 545
Dependence, meaning of in Prāsaṅgika, 37, 432-5
Dependent-arising, 37, 161-73, 432-5, 445-6, 634, 655-6, 659-76
- applicability to non-products, 167-8, 432-3, 659-61
- formation of the Sanskrit term, 163, 564, 662-7, n.703 pp.884-5
- meaning of the term, 37, 163-8, 433, 655-6, 659, 663, 664-74, n.703 pp.884-5
- reasoning of, 53-5, 161-2, 168-71, 445-6, 637, 659-62, 675
- twelve links of, 203, 275-83, Chart 35 p.279, 287, 423, Appendix 2 pp.707-11

Dependent-designation, 169
Dependent imputation, 472, *see also* Imputation of objects by thought
Descent into Laṅkā Sutra, 162, 358, 383, 570, 595, 602, 609, 610-14, 615-6
Desire, 255-6
Desire Realm, 104ff, 236, 277, 353-4
Destruction of the world, 630
Determining mental factors, 238, 245-8, Chart 24 p.246

Devasharma, 360, 361, 462
Dhāraṇīshvararājaparipṛchchhā, *see Questions of King Dhāraṇīshvara Sutra*
Dharmadhātu, explanation of etymology and translation equivalent, n.557 p.873, *see also* Element of qualities
Dharmadhātustotra, see Praise of the Element of Qualities
Dharmaguptakas, 340, 714, 715, 716, 717, 718, 719
Dharmakīrti (the logician), 31, 296, 344, 366, 374, 396, 449, 556, 571, 572, 676, 730
Dharmakīrti (not the logician), 532, 533
Dharmapāla, 343, 362
Dharmasaṃgīti, see Compendium of Doctrine Sutra
Dharmottara, 344
Dharmottaras, 340, 714, 715, 716
Dharmottarīyas, 719
Dhātu, see Constituents
Dialectician Nihilists, 41, 328-30, 436
Diamond slivers, 57-9, 61, 129, 131-50, 151, 169, 637, 639-40ff, n.500 pp.851-4, n.619 pp.879-80, *see also* Refutation of the four extreme types of production
Dichotomies, 412
Dignāga, 344, 362, 366, 449, 525, 592, 730, n.442 p.833
Dīpakas, 294, n.423 p.825
Dīpavaṃsa, 719
Direct cognition of emptiness, nature of, 96-105, 128, 133, 187, 188-9, 193-4, 237-8, 290,
Direct cognition of emptiness (*cont.*) 349, 380, 407, 408-10, 415, 416, 422, 510, 552, 704-5
Direct perceiver (*pratyakṣha*), Chandrakīrti's explanation of the term, 656
Direct valid cognizer, 702-5
Discipline, 532
Discrimination, 241-3, 271, 272, 278-9, 386-7
Discrimination of the Two Truths, 155, 570, 654-5
Dissimulation, 262, 264
Distraction, 262, 266
Doors of liberation, three, 207-8
Doors of retention, four, 208
Dor-jay-day-b̄a (*rDo-rje-bzlas-pa*), 538
Doubt, 196, 248, 256, 258, 702-4
D̄ra-s̄hi-kyil (*bKra-shis-'khyil*), 567, 568-9
Dream objects and consciousnesses, 234
Dre-b̄ung Monastery, 12, 13, 563-4
Dro (*Bro, 'Bro Shes-rab-grags*), 536
Drok-mi Shākya-ye-s̄hay (*'Brok-mi Shākya-ye-shes*), 536
Drom-d̄ön (*'Brom-ston*), 534, 592
Dualistic appearance, removal of, 66, 93, 94-6, 118, 416
D̄zong-ka-b̄a, 11, 135-6, 144-8, 182, 186, 194-5, 315, 318, 324, 361, 405, 409, 415, 466, 473, 495, 513, 517, 528, 534, 536, 539-43, 549-551, 567, 570, 571, 572, 573-5, 588, 594,

Dzong-ka-ba (*cont.*)
648, 686, 687, n.346 pp.814-15, n424 p.830, n.494 p.839
citation of texts by, 31-2, 33, 525, 549-50, 558, 583, 587, 588, 603, 622, 661, 675-6, 679, 680, n.424 pp.828-30

Earth constituent, 628-31
Effort, 73, 81, 85, 245, 248, 251-2, 289
Eight levels of Approaching and Abiding, 106-8, Chart 6 p.107, 403, 670
Eight Thousand Stanza Perfection of Wisdom Sutra, 29
Ekavyāvahārika, 340, 341, 714, 716, 719
Element of qualities, 606, 607, n.557 p.873
Elements, 203, 229-30, 232, n.785 p.896
definitions of the four, 230
Emanation Body, 118, 119, 121-3
Embarrassment, 248, 250
Emptiness, 9-11, 17, 29, 33, 35-6, 38-40, 119-20, 162, 196, 199-201, 214, 216, 217, 218-19, 254, 288-9, 292-3, 302, 349, 387, 391, 396-7, 402, 406-11, 415, 418, 420, 433, 722, 725-6, *see also* Direct cognition of emptiness, nature of, *and* Meditation on emptiness
and dependent-arising, synonymity, 170, 219, 415
Emptiness (*cont.*)
compatibility with conventionalities, 38-40, 192-3, 401-5, 438-9, 523, 575, 634-5
Emptiness as a non-inherently existent phenomenon, 33-4, 171-3, 391-2, 406-7, 410, 433, 631
Emptiness of existing naturally as a basis of a name, 369-72, 389-90
Emptiness of other, 35-6, 326, 415-6, 535
Emptiness of self, 415
Emptiness of the mind as the Buddha nature, 381-3, 396-7, 616-7, 623
Emptiness that is the non-existence of subject and object as different entities, 297ff, 367-74, 388-9
Emptinesses, eighteen, 204-5
Engaging in the Bodhisattva Deeds, 358, 570, 589, 593, 633, 657,
Enjoyment Body, 118, 119, 121-2, 345, 395
Entwinements, three, 103
Equanimity, 72, 79, 248, 253
Equipoise of cessation, 207, 386, 387, *see also* Absorption of cessation
Essay on the Mind of Enlightenment, 359, 388, 415, 472, 571, 614, n.581 p.876
Essence of the Good Explanations, 570, 583, 587, 588, 622, n.346 p.815, n.424 pp.828-30, n.494 p.839

Establishment of the Reasoning and Logic Refuting Error, 591
Evolutes of the elements, 229, 230-31, 232
Example of illusion from sutra, 597
Examples of illusoriness, seven, 132
Examples supporting mind-only, 372-3, 376
Excitement, 72, 74-80, 83-6, 113-14, 253, 262, 265
Exclusion (*apoha*), 347-8, *see also* Negative phenomena
Existence able to establish itself, 36, 37, 172-3
Existence as [its own] reality, 36, 39
Existence as [its own] suchness, 36, 39
Existence from the object's side, 36, 39
Existence from the side of the basis of designation, 36, 37
Existence in the manner of covering its basis of designation, 36
Existence in the object that receives designation, 36
Existence right in the basis of designation, 36
Existence through its own entityness, 36
Existence through its own power, 36, 37, 156, 175, 584
Existent, synonyms of, 214-15, 721-2
Exorcism, 537
Explanation of (Chandrakīrti's) 'Supplement', 571, *see also Illumination of the Thought*
Explanation of (Maitreya's) 'Treatise on the Sublime Continuum of the Great Vehicle', 594
Explanation of (Nāgārjuna's) 'Treatise on the Middle Way', 570
Explanation of (Shāntideva's) 'Engaging in the Bodhisattva Deeds', 593
Explanation of the Conventional and the Ultimate in the Four Systems of Tenets, 551
Explanation of the 'Treasury of Knowledge', 662
Explanation of (Vasubandhu's) 'Commentary on the "Sutra on Dependent-Arising"', 662
Extensive Sport Sutra, 502, 571, 600-1
External objects, different schools' assertions on their existence or non-existence, 362
  non-existence of in Chittamātra, 367-8, 611, 613, 623
Extreme views, 318-9
Extremes, falling to, 11, 40, 195, 402, 451-2
Eye consciousness, three causes of production, 156ff, 222-3, 647, 654-5

Faith, 72-3, 245, 248-50, 265
'Father and mother are to be killed', 423, 600, 602

Faults in meditation, five, 71-80, Chart 2 p.72
Fearlessnesses, four, 210-11
Feeling, 203, 239-41, 271, 272, 278-9, 280, 386-7
Fifth Dalai Lama, 43, 45, 571, 572, 573, 685, 686
Final vehicle, one, 366, 396-7, 604-10
Final vehicles, three, 366, 392-6, 596, 602, 603-4, 609, 611
Findability under analysis, 173, 406, *see also* Unfindability of objects under analysis
Finely Woven, 591
Five Collections of Reasonings, 356
Five-cornered set of reasonings, 129, *see also* Fivefold reasoning
Five Stages, 587
Five Treatises on the Levels, 359, 366
Fivefold reasoning, 129, 176-8, 637, 687-93
Foe Destroyer, 106-8, 206, 212, 239, 288, 296, 329, 341-2, 344, 393, 417, 603, 604, 606-7, 608, 610
  etymology and reason for translating the term thus, n.553 pp.871-73
Forbearances, eight, 96-8
Forders, (*Tīrthika*), 186, 320-1, 347, 615-6
Forgetfulness, 262, 266
Form Body, 113, 117-18
Form Realm, 87, 104ff, 236, 277, 353-4
Formation of the universe, 353-5, 375
Former and future lives, existence of 40-1, 160, 282, 328-33
Formless Absorptions, Four, 104ff, 187, 207
Formless Realm, 104ff, 236, 277, 278
Forms, 220-35, Chart 11 p.221, 271, 272ff, 278ff, n.758 p.894
Forms for the mental consciousness, 232-4, Chart 19 p.233
Four alternatives, n.500 pp.851-54, *see also* Refutation of the four alternative types of production *and* Diamond slivers
Four extremes, *see* Refutation of the four extreme types of production *and* Diamond slivers
Four Hundred, 291, 555, 570, 585, 588, 591, 627, 632, 660, 674, n.458 p.837
Four Interwoven Commentaries on (D̄zong-ka-b̄a's) 'Great Exposition of the Stages of the Path', n.423 p.825, n.431 pp.831-32
Friendly Letter, 571, 675
Fundamental Tantra of Mañjushrī, 358
Fundamental Treatise on the Middle Way Called 'Wisdom', *see Treatise on the Middle Way*

Ḡa-dam-b̄a (*bKa'-gdams-pa*), 534, 538
Ḡa-gyu-b̄a (*bKa'-brgyud-pa*), 15, 534, 537, 538

Gam-b̄o-b̄a (*sGam-po-pa*), 537
Gan-den Monastery, 566
Ge-luk-b̄a (*dGe-lugs-pa*), 11-13, 15-17, 188, 344, 378, 383, 388, 399, 405, 406, 409-10, 415, 416, 492, 534, 538, 549, 567, 574, 576, n.500 pp.851-54, n.511 p.860, n.723 p.886, n.791 pp.898-903
  education, 399, 405, 534, 538, 572, n.346 pp.814-5
  presentation of valid establishment, 409-10, 539-47
Gen-dün-chö-pel (*dGe-'dun-chos-'phel*), 544, 547
Gen-jak-tang-d̄a, (*Gan-jag-thang-ta*), 533
Generic image, 347-9
Ghanavyūha, see Sutra on the Heavily Adorned
Go-mang, 12, 13, 563-4, 567, 576, n.494 p.840, n.511 p.860
Gö-rin-b̄o-chay Kuk-b̄a-hlay-d̄zay (*'Gos-rin-po-che Khug-pa-lhas-btsas*), 536
Gokulikas, 340, 715, 719
Gom-day Nam-ka-gyel-tsen (*sGom sde Nam-mkha'-rgyal-mtshan*), 513, n.346 p.814, n.414 p.823
Ḡön-chok-d̄en-b̄ay-drön-may (*dKon-mchog-bstan-pa'i-sgron-me*), 287, 291
Ḡön-chok-jik-may-w̄ang-b̄o (*dKon-mchog-'jigs-med-dbang-po*), 12, 552
Grammar, Chandragomin's, 569, 662-4
Grammarians, 164-5, 661
Grasping, 275, 280-81ff
Great Cloud Sutra, 358
Great Drum Sutra, 357, 358, 590
'Great Exposition of Special Insight', 545, n.346 p.815
Great Exposition of Tenets, 11-14, 17, 343, 563-77
Great Exposition of the Concentrations and Formless Absorptions, 553-8
Great Exposition of the Middle Way, 13, 17, 445, 564
Great Exposition of the Stages of the Path, 525, 534, 545, 549-50, 554, n.346 p.815
Guhyakas, 318, 564
Guhyasamāja Tantra, 362
Gung-tang (*Gung-thang*), *see* Ḡön-chok-d̄en-b̄ay-drön-may
Guṇamati, 360, 462, 662
Guṇashrī, 360, 462
Gyel-tsap (*rGyal-tshab*), 324, 594, 675

Haimavatas, 339, 340, 714, 715, 716, 717, 718
Haribhadra, 594
Harmfulness, 262, 264
Harmonies with enlightenment, thirty-seven, 205-6
Hastavālaprakaraṇakārikā, see Length of a Forearm
Haughtiness, 262, 264
Heap of Jewels Sutra, 589
Hearers (*Shrāvaka*), 98, 99, 106-8, 114, 128, 195, 288, 296ff, 342, 366, 378-9, 392-3, 394-5, 427, 601, 603-4, 605, 606, 609
  etymology of the term, 394, n.495; pp.840-45

Heart of the Middle Way, 358, 575
Heart of Wisdom Sutra, 413, 423, 424, 571, 601
Heart Sutra, *see Heart of Wisdom Sutra*
Heavily Adorned, *see Sutra on the Heavily Adorned*
Hedonists (*Chārvāka*), 293, 294, 319, 327-33, 564
Hermeneutics, Buddhist, 422-8, n.494 p.839, n.528 pp.864-5
Hetuvādins, 714, 716
Highest Pure Land, 121, 395
Highest Yoga Tantra, 11, 75, 112, 113-15, 200, 380
Hīnayāna, 98, 106-9, 335-51, 358, 359, 378-9, 393, 395, 426, 427, 601
Hīnayānists, differentiated by tenet and path, 342, 346, 379-80
Hla-to-to-ri-ñyan-d̄zen (*Lha-tho-tho-ri-gnyan-bstan*), 531
Ho-s̄hang Mahāyāna (*Hva-shang*), 410, 533, 555
Hurvitz, Leon, n.495 pp.841-44

Identifying the object of negation, 44-6, 53, 54, 57, 62, 63, 64-5, 189, 243, 685
Ignorance, 256, 257-8, 275, 276-8, 416-7, 420, 678
Illumination of the Middle Way, 412, 426, 570, 653, 657-8
Illumination of the Thought, Extensive Explanation of (Chandrakīrti's) 'Supplement to (Nāgārjuna's) "Treatise on the Middle Way"', 405, 571, 603, 648
Illusory body, 115
Illusory objects, 193
Imaginary natures, 388-92, 601, 610, 611, 618-20
Immeasurables, four, 206
Impermanence in Vaibhāṣhika and Sautrāntika, 350
Imputation of objects by thought, 37-8, 167, 192, 385-6, 437-8, 542, 626-7ff, 635-6
Imputed existence, 338, 344
Imputedly existent person, 303-4, 308-9
Individual analytical cessation, n.191 p806, *see also* Analytical cessations
Indrabhuti, 361
Indrabodhi, 533
Indriya, 222, *see also* Sense powers
Inference, 450, 701-4
  way in which it is mistaken, 348-9, 701
Inference for oneself, 526
Inference renowned to oneself, 524
Inferential realization of emptiness, 47-8, 66, 113, 133, 134, 193, 195, 237-8, 286, 407, 408, 450-1, 552
Inferential valid cognizer, 702-4
Inherent existence, 9-10, 36, 38, 39-40, 55, 65, 133-4, 150, 154, 175, 199, 361, 391, 437, 584, 636-7, 697, n.791 p.903
Innate afflictions, *see* Misconceptions of inherent existence, innate
Innate false view of an inherently existent person, 177, 679

Innate intellect in Prāsaṅgika, 201, 527-8, 530, 682-4
Innate misconceptions of inherent existence, *see* Misconceptions of inherent existence, innate
Innate sense of I, 44-5, 303-4, 684-5, n.744 p.891
Intensity of clarity, 74
Intention, 243-4, 386
Intermediate state, 278
Interpretable and definitive, differentiating, 422-8, 595-623, n.528 pp.864-5
Interpretable sutras, 422-8, 595-623
Introduction to the Two Truths, 593
Introspection, 72, 76, 80, 83, 377
Investigation, 267-8
Investigations, four, 371
Irreversible Wheel Sutra, 571, 608
Īshvara, 149, 239, 322, 325, 326-7
Isolates, 347-9, 368, 390, 413-5

Jainas, 149, 295, 296, 318, 320, 506, 507, 565, 649
Jam-ȳang-shay-b̄a (*'Jam-dbyangs-bzhad-pa*), 11-13, 16-17, 33, 43, 135, 155, 195, 199, 232, 318, 320, 343, 360, 362, 374, 403-4, 406-13, 421, 431, 445, 461, 467, 477, 487, 490, 492, 494, 500, 552, 563-78, 713, 715, 717, 718, 729, n.298 p.811, n.494 p.840
refutation of D̄ak-tsang, 147, 171-3, 343, 411-12, 563,
Jam-ȳang-shay-b̄a (*cont.*) 573, 576-7, 588, 592, 648, 655, 676, 681, 683, 694-5, 697
Jang-d̄zay College, 566
J̄ang-ḡya (*lCang-skya*), 17, 155, 191, 193, 320, 374, 533, 545, 558, 563, n.494 p.840
Jay-d̄zun Chö-ḡyi-gyel-tsen (*rJe-btsun Chos-kyi-rgyal-mtshan*), 566, n.298 p811, n.739 p.889
Jaya-ānanda, n.545 pp.868-71
Jealousy, 262, 263
Jetavanīyas, 717, 718
Jewel Mine Sutra, 589
Jinba, Geshe, 14
Jīva, 46, 187
Jñānagarbha, 155, 570, 572, 588, 591, 654-5
J̄ö (*gCod*), 537, 538
Jo-nang-b̄a (*Jo-nang-pa*), 36, 415-6, 535
Jor-druk (*sByor-drug*), 538

Kālachakra Tantra, 535, 538, 554, n.249 p.809
Kalāpa, 570, 572
Kalāpa's Aphorisms, 570, 662-4
Kalāpasūtra, *see Kalāpa's Aphorisms*
Kamalashīla, 412, 426, 533, 570, 572, 653, 657-8
Kanakamuni Buddha, 355
Kanakavarman (*gSer-gyi-go-cha*), 535
Kapila, 320, 321, 322, 323
Kāpilas, 318, 321, 564
Karma, 22, 160, 239-40, 244, 276-8, 375

Karma (*cont.*)
creation of the environment by, 375
Karmāntavibhaṅga, see Classification of the Ends of Actions
Kāshyapa Buddha, 355
Kāshyapa Chapter Sutra, 571, 589, 635
Kāshyapaparivarta, see Kāshyapa Chapter Sutra
Kāshyapīyas, 340, 714, 715, 716, 717, 718, 719
Kay-drup (*mKhas-grub*), 43, 45, 318, 362, 546, 571, 572, 594, 680, 681
Kāyatrayastotra, see Praise of the Three Bodies
Kensur Lekden, 12-14, 415, 563, 566, 567, 569, 577, 578
Khetsun Sangpo, 15, n.249 p.809
King of Meditative Stabilizations Sutra, 31, 408, 471, 554, 555, 570, 589, 599, 600, 610
Kliṣhṭamanas, see Afflicted mind
Knowledge, 248
Knowledges, eight, 96-8
Krakuchchhanda Buddha, 354
Kukkulikas, 716
Kurukullas, 714, 717, 718

Lalitavistara, see Extensive Sport Sutra
Lamp for (Nāgārjuna's) 'Wisdom', 426, 461, 462, 463, 570, 666, 668-9, 672
Lamp for the Path to Enlightenment, 534, 571, 589, 593, 640, 653
L̄ang-dar-ma (*gLang-dar-ma*), 534
Laṅkāvatārasūtra, see Descent into Lankā Sutra
Laxity, 72, 74-5, 76-8, 83-6, 113, 253
Laziness, 71-2, 245, 262, 265
Lectures on the Stages of the Path, 67, 277
Length of a Forearm, 591, n.519 p.863
Lethargy, 75, 88, 262, 265
Liberation, 29, 30-31
Liberations, eight, 207
Life faculty, 269, 270
Limitation of possibilities, 47, 65, 133-4, 640
Lineages, five, 394
Ling Rinbochay, 43, 45
Lion's Roar of Shrīmālādevī Sutra, 357, 571, 609
Literal and non-literal, differentiating, 423ff, 600, 612
L̄o-den-s̄hay-rap (*bLo-ldan-shes-rab*), *see* Ngog, the translator
L̄o-s̄el-l̄ing College, 566
Lodrö, Geshe Gedün, 14, 576, 578
Lokachakṣhu, 328
Lokātītastava, see Praise of the Supramundane
Lokesh Chandra, 566
Lokottaravādins, 714, 716, 717, 718
L̄ong-chen-rap-jam (*kLong-chen-rab-'byams*), 15

Ma-j̄i-lap-drön (*Ma-cig-lab-sgron*), 537

Madhyamakahṛdaya, see Heart of the Middle Way
Madhyamakashāstra, see Treatise on the Middle Way
Madhyamakāvatāra, see Supplement to (Nāgārjuna's) 'Treatise on the Middle Way'
Madhyamakāvatārabhāṣhya, see Commentary on the 'Supplement to (Nāgārjuna's) "Treatise on the Middle Way"'
Madhyamakopadesha, see Quintessential Instructions on the Middle Way
Madhyamakopadeshavṛtti, see Commentary on (Atīsha's) 'Quintessential Instructions on the Middle Way'
Mādhyamika, 11, 13, 16, 135-6, 139, 167, 173, 336, 356, 358, 388, 399-428, 451-3, 565, 572, 574, 639, 641, n.501 pp.854-5, *see also* Prāsaṅgika-Mādhyamika *and* Svātantrika-Mādhyamika
  as proponents of dependent-arising, 167-71, 634
  compatibility of emptiness and conventional phenomena, 38-40, 192-3, 401-5, 438-9, 523, 575, 634-5
  definition of, 451
  differentiated from Nihilists, 40-41, 543, 633-4
  having no theses, discussion, 471-3, 492-3, 549-51, n.496 p.847
  in Tibet, 13, 531-8, 572
  interpretations refuted by Dzong-ka-ba, 16, 135-6, 144-8, 200-1, 471-4, 549-59, 574, 727, n.500 p.850
  mode of abiding in the middle way, 40, 162, 169, 436-9, 451-2, 634-5
  modern interpretations, 16, 492-3, 549ff
  study of in Ge-luk-ba, 13, 404-5, 563-7, 572-8
  view, 193, 523
'Mādhyamikas using what is renowned in the world', 435
Magician's illusion, example of, 372, 417, 436-7
Mahābherīhārakaparivarta, see Great Drum Sutra
Mahāgirikas, 340
Mahāmati, 570, 572, 675
Mahāmegha, see Great Cloud Sutra
Mahāmūdra, 538
Mahāsaṃghikas, 339, 340, 713, 714, 715, 716, 717, 718, 719
Mahāshāsakas, 340, 341, 714
Mahāvaṃsa, 719
Mahāvihārins, 717, 718
Mahāyāna, 31, 108-9, 329, 336, 344, 345-6, 349-50, 378-80, 393, 395-6, 426, 427, 601, 605
  history of, 353-64
Mahāyāna Sutra of Knowledge, 623
Mahāyānābhidharma, see Mahāyāna Sutra of Knowledge

Mahāyānasūtrālaṃkāra, see Ornament for the Mahāyāna Sutras
Mahāyānist, differentiation of by path and tenet, 342, 346, 379
Mahāyānottaratantrashāstra, see Sublime Continuum of the Great Vehicle
Mahāyānottaratantrashāstra-vyākhyā, see Explanation of (Maitreya's) 'Treatise on the Sublime Continuum of the Great Vehicle'
Mahīshāsakas, 715, 716, 717, 718, 719
Maitreya, 357, 358, 359, 362, 403, 572, 593, 594, 610
Maitreya Buddha, 355
Maitripāda, 537
Mandala, 22
Mañjushrī, 361
Mañjushrīmūlatantra, see Fundamental Tantra of Mañjushrī
Mañjushrīvikrīḍita, see Sport of Mañjushrī Sutra
Manual of Instructions on the View, 43, 45
Mar-b̄a, 536, 537
Materials for a History of Tibetan Literature, 566-7
Matter, Prāsaṅgika assertion on the existence of, 231-2
Meaning-generalities, 347-9, 551
Meditating Nihilists, 41, 328, 330
Meditation on emptiness, correct form of, 30-4, 38-40,
Meditation on emptiness (*cont.*) 51, 66, 88-90, 92ff, 468, 724, *see also* Direct cognition of emptiness *and* Inferential cognition of emptiness
five stages in, 43ff, 66, 67ff, 80, 88, 91, 96ff, 112, 114
incorrect views of, 30-31, 33-4, 200-1, 409, 552-8
Meditative stabilization, 245, 247, 289, *see also* Calm abiding
Meditative stabilizations, four, 208
Meeting of Father and Son Sutra, 405, 410, 412, 571, 627
Mental engagement, 245, 387
Mental engagements, four, 80-6, Chart 3 p.81, 92
Mental factors, 235, 238-68, Chart 22 p.238, 272
'Mere I', 185, 189, 308, 315, 386, 387, 686
Mi-gyö-dor-jay (*Mi-bskyod-rdo-rje*), 15
Mi-la-re-b̄a (*Mi-la-res-pa*), 537, 538
Middle way, 11, 40, 162, 168, 193, 195, 435-7, 439, 451, 632, 634-5
how different systems claim to occupy it, 436-7
Mīmāṃsakas, 318, 564
'Mind apprehending the sign', 733
Mind as creator or main agent in Buddhism, 374-6, 612-13, 623
Mind-basis-of-all, 359, 366,

Mind-basis-of-all (*cont.*)
382-8, 396, 595, 602, 611, 612, 616-7, 623, n.791 p.901
Mind of clear light, 114-15
Mind-only, 363, 365, 367-81, 595, 611-14, 623, *see also* Chittamātra
Mindfulness, 72-3, 76, 79-80, 83, 247, 289
Minds (*chitta*), 235-8, Chart 21 p.237, 272
'Mine', 193-4, 678-81, n.739 pp.888-90
Mirror-like wisdom, 384
Misconception of a self separate from the aggregates, 681-7
Misconceptions of inherent existence, artificial, 96-9, 114, 177, 687, n.744 pp.890-92
Misconceptions of inherent existence, innate, 40, 96, 99-109, Chart 5 p.105, 114, 177, 679, 682, 687, n.744 pp.890-92
Miserliness, 262, 263
Mode of appearance of I according to Jam-ȳang-shay-b̄a, 683-7, n.754 p.893
Model Mādhyamikas, 359, 431, 587-8, n.505 p.858
Mongolia, 364
Mother sutras, 589, n.514 p.862
Motivation, 32, 111-12, 117, 251, 282-3, 335-6, 379, 530
Mūlasarvāstivādins, 718
Mūlasthaviras, 340
Muruntakas, 714
Myrabola, see Sutra on the Myrabolan Fruit
Nāgabodhi, 69, 363, 432, 587-8
Nāgārjuna, 11, 29, 30, 32, 128, 131-2, 154, 166, 168, 177-8, 388, 399-405, 431, 438, 455, 459, 467, 481, 489, 494-6, 497, 500, 501, 502-3, 531, 538, 558-9, 569, 570, 571, 572-4, 587-8, 590, 592, 596, 603, 604, 614, 637, 653, 657, 675, 676, n.298 p.811
biography, 356-9, 363
citation of texts by, 30, 100-103, 153, 154, 162, 165, 168, 178, 199, 388, 438, 460, 471, 472, 475, 494, 495, 496, 502-3, 510, 518, 522, 585, 597-8, 604-9, 614, 619, 626, 631, 635, 644, 645, 652, 660, 670-1, 672, 673, 674, 675, 684, 688, 689, 693
differentiation of the interpretable and the definitive, 425-6, 596-8, 603
meaning of his statement that Mādhyamikas have no theses, 471-3, 475, 492-3, 549-51, n.496 p.847
on the meaning of *pratītyasamutpāda*, 166, 670, 672
on the two truths, 400-403, 415
Naiyāyikas, 294, 318, 339, 565
Name and form (*nāmarūpa*), 275, 278, 279ff
Naming, process of, 347-8
Nāropa, 537
Natural existence, 9, 36, 39, 175, 182

Natural lineage, 617
Natural nirvana, 218-9
Nature Body, 118, 119-20, 382
Natures, three, 388-92, 601, 602, 610, 617-20
Negative phenomena, 347-8, 410, Appendix 4 pp.721-7, *see also* Non-affirming negatives *and* Affirming negatives
Never Returner, 106-7, 212
Nga-wang-bel-den (*Ngag-dbang-dpal-ldan*), 12-13, 135, 551, 565-6, 569, 578, n.500 pp.851-54, n.511 p.860
Ngog, the translator (*rNgog-lo-tstsha-ba, bLo-ldan-shes-rab*), 406-11, 535
Nihilists, 40, 41, 149, 318, 327-33, 633-4
Nikāyabhedavibhaṅgavyākhyāna, 713
Nirgranthas, 318, 565, 649
Nirupamastava, see Peerless Praise
Nirvana, 22, 31, 94, 218, 288, 337, 495, 496, 596, 631
  with remainder, 342, 395
  without remainder, 342, 393, 394-5, 603, 606
Nirvana Sutra, 381
Nominal existence, 40, 133, 182, 185, 192, 194, 315, 380, 547
Nominal imputation, 626, 631
Nominal production, 133, 159-60, 459-61, 467-8
Nominally existent self, 678
Non-Abiding Mādhyamikas, 435-6, 586-7, n.504 pp.857-8
Non-affirming negatives, 133, 214, 217, 349, 374, 410, 458-9, 467-8, 496, Appendix 4 pp.723, 725-7
Non-afflictive obstructions, 342-3
Non-analytical cessations, 217, 218, 285, 344, 390
Non-associated compositional factors, 268-71, Chart 30 p.268
Non-attachment, 248, 250-1, 253
Non-Buddhist systems, 317-33
Non-cognizing consciousness, 702
Non-conscientiousness, 262, 264, 265-6
Non-deceived consciousness in Prāsaṅgika, 510, 511
Non-defective sense consciousness, 436-7, 449-50, 452
Non-dualism, four types, 416
Non-embarrassment, 262, 264-5
Non-existents, 214
Non-faith, 262, 265
Non-finding of the self, 192, *see also* Unfindability of objects
Non-harmfulness, 248, 253
Non-hatred, 248, 250-1, 253
Non-ignorance, 248, 250-1, 253
Non-introspection, 262, 266
Non-mistaken consciousness in Prāsaṅgika, 510, 511
Non-Partisan Mādhyamikas, 587-8
Non-Partisan Prāsaṅgikas, 432
Non-person non-associated compositional factors, 269-71, Chart 31 p.270

Non-revelatory forms, 234, 289
Non-shame, 262, 264
Non-valid consciousness, 702
Non-virtues, 255, *see also* Root and Secondary afflictions *and* Virtuous mental factors
Nor-sang-gya-tso (*Nor-bzang-rgya-mtsho*), n.504 p.858
Not unable, 87
N̄yen (*gNyan, gNyan Dar-ma-grags*), 536
N̄ying-ma, 15, 532, 534, 538

Object of negation in Chittamātra, 128-9, 296-301, 367-74
Object of negation in Prāsaṅgika, 35-40, 66, 127-9, 189, 200-1, 297-304, 549-60, 625-38, *see also* Identifying the object of negation
  appearing to sense consciousnesses, 167, 449-50, 452, 509-11, 515-6, 529, 552
  synonyms, 36-9, 584, 626, 632
Object of negation in the four schools, Charts 37 and 38 pp.299-300, 341-2, 385-6, 436
Object of negation not appearing to the sense consciousnesses in Svātantrika, 450, 516, n.497 pp.848-9
Object of observation of the view of self, 177-8, 678-9
Object of the mode of apprehension, 701
Objective existence, 9, 36, 175, 194, 419, 445-6
Objects of meditation in the four schools, Chart 36 p.298
Obstructions to liberation, 104-9, 114, 119, 195, 210, 297, Chart 38 p.300, 302
Obstructions to liberation and omniscience in the four schools, Chart 38 p.300
Obstructions to omniscience, 103-4, 108-9, 111, 115, 117-18, 119, 210, 297, Chart 38 p.300, 302, 345, 416
Ocean of Reasoning, Explanation of (Nāgārjuna's) 'Treatise on the Middle Way', 466-7, 679, 680, 686, n.346 p.815, n.424 p.830
Odors, 226, Chart 16 p.228, 232, 273, 274
Omnipresent mental factors, 238-45, Chart 23 p.239, 278, 386-7
Omniscience, 10, 29, 118-23, 302, 331, 407
Once Returner, 106-7, 212
One Hundred Thousand Stanza Perfection of Wisdom Sutra, 356, 599
Only Appearance Mādhyamikas, 432-5, 586
Only-designated, 38, *see also* Only-imputed
Only-imputed, 38, 385-6, 626, *see also* Only-designated
Opening the Eyes of the Fortunate, Treatise Brilliantly Clarifying the Profound Emptiness, 546, 571, 680, 681, n.500 p.852

Opposite of the Consequences, (*thal bzlog*), 492, n.346 p.814-6
Opposites of the negatives, *see* Isolates
Ornament for Clear Realization, 362, 403, 594
Ornament for the Mahāyāna Sutras, 358
Ornament of the Wisdom Engaging the Sphere of All Buddhas Sutra, 357
Other-approved inference, 478-9, 481-2, 485, 486-8, 489
Other-approved reason, 478
Other-approved syllogism, 478-9, 481-2, 521-6, 525, 586, n.347 p.816
Other-emptiness, 35-6, 326, 415-6, 535
Other-powered natures, 388-92, 595, 601, 610, 611, 618-20
Other-renowned inferences, n.449 pp.835-6, *see also* Other-approved inferences
Other-renowned reason, 697, *see also* Other-approved reason
Other-renowned syllogism, 524-5, *see also* Other-approved syllogism

Pa-bong-ka (*Pha-bong-kha*), 67, 69, 79, 277
Pa-dam-b̄a-s̄ang-gyay (*Pha-dam-pa-sangs-rgyas*), 536
Padmasaṃbhava, 363, 532, 533, 718
Pak-mo-drup-dor-jay-gyel-b̄o (*Phag-mo-grub-rdo-rje-gyal-po*) 538
Paṇ-chen S̄ö-nam-drak-b̄a (*Pan-chen bSod-nams-grags-pa*), 566, n.298 p.811
Pañchakrama, see Five Stages, 587
Paramārtha, 713
Paramārthabodhichittabhāvanākramavarṇasaṃgraha, see Cultivation of the Ultimate Mind of Enlightenment
Paramārthasatya, see Truths, ultimate
Paratantra, see Other-powered natures
Parikalpita, see Imaginary natures
Parinirvāṇa, 609, *see also* Nirvana
Parinishpanna, see Thoroughly established natures
Particles, partless, 39, 337-8, 346
  Chittamātra refutation of, 373
Partisan Prāsaṅgikas, 432, 587-8
Partless particles, *see* Particles, partless
Patañjali, 322
Path, eightfold, 206
Path of accumulation, 94, 111, 205, 206, 379
Path of meditation, 96, 99-109, Chart 5 p.105, 111, 296, 407
Path of no more learning, 108
Path of preparation, 93-6, 98, 111, 206, 302-3, 380
Path of release, 96-8, 105ff, 119
Path of seeing, 96-9, Chart 4 p.97, 106, 107, 111, 114, 296

Path structure in Prāsaṅgika, 93-109, 111-15, 195, 297-304, 378-80
Path structure in Vaibhāṣhika, 342-3, 392-3
Paths of manifestation, three, 207
Peerless Praise, 590
Perfection of Wisdom Sutras, 11, 29, 33, 173, 201, 220, 356, 423-4, 427, 570, 574, 589, 606, 607, 631, n.298 p.811
Performance Tantra, 112
Permanence, meaning of, 216, 382
Permanent phenomena, 215-19, Chart 9 p.217, 285, 344, 347, 349, 390, 432-3
Person, 268, 282, *see also* Self
  identification of in the different schools, Chart 37 p.299, 385-6, 693-4, 695, n.791 pp.897-903
Perverse view, 259, 260-1, 289
Phaṭ, technique for forceful removal of laxity, 77
Phenomena, 214-5, 433
  as the basis for the division into positive and negative phenomena, 721-3
  as the basis for the division into the two truths, 405-15
  of the afflicted class, fifty-three, 201-3, 275, 434
  of the pure class, fifty-five, 201, 204-12, 434
Phonetic system, 19-22
Pitāputrasamāgama, see Meeting of Father and Son Sutra
Pliancy, 86-7, 88, 93, 245, 248, 252
Positive phenomena, 721-2
Powers, six, 80-6, Chart 3 p.81
Powers, ten, 208-10, 255
Praise of Dependent-Arising, 571, 661, 675-6
Praise of the Element of Qualities, 590
Praise of the Inconceivable, 590
Praise of the Mind Vajra, 590
Praise of the Supramundane, 472, 590
Praise of the Three Bodies, 590
Praise of What Surpasses Praise, 590
Praises of Reality, 590
Prajñāhṛdaya, see Heart of Wisdom
Prajñāmokṣha, 593
Prajñāpradīpa, see Lamp for (Nāgārjuna's) 'Wisdom'
Prajñāpradīpaṭīkā, see Commentary on (Bhāvaviveka's) 'Lamp for (Nāgārjuna's) "Wisdom"'
Prajñapti-mātra, see Only-designated *and* Only-imputed
Prajñaptivādins, 340, 714, 716, 717, 718, 719
Prajñāvarman, 320
Pramāṇa, etymology, 701, *see also* Valid cognizer
Pramāṇasamuchchaya, see Compendium of Valid Cognition
Pramāṇavārttika, see Commentary on (Dignāga's) 'Compendium of Valid Cognition'

Prāsaṅgika-Mādhyamika, 9, 11, 36-41, 98, 104, 128-9, 134-5, 144-8, 155, 159-60, 164, 167, 172-3, 182-3, 195, 231, 234, 290, 297ff, 309, 337, 359-61, 367, 385-6, 396-7, 405, 419, 421, 431-9, 441, 445, 449-53, 455, 514-5, 526-30, 539ff, 549ff, 565, 583, 704, 733, n.504 pp.857-8
acceptance of what the world accepts, 435, 439, 526, 528, 635-6
accord with the conventions of the world, 435, 502, 526-30
appearance of the object of negation to the sense consciousnesses, 44-5, 167, 449-50, 452, 509-11, 514-6, 529, 552
appelation of the name in Tibet, 497, 530, 586
commentarial sources, 569-73, 588-9, 590-94
definition of, 452, 584-6
differentiated from Nihilists, 40-41, 543, 633-4
differentiation of the interpretable and the definitive, 422-8, 595-623, n.528 pp.864-5
divisions of, 359-63, 431-2, 441, 455, 587-8, n.501 pp.854-5
etymology of, 452-3, 584-6
in Tibet, 11-15, 531-8
interpretation of dependent-arising, 163-9, 432-5, 663, *see also* Dependent-arising
interpretation of mind-only, 374-8, 611-14
interpretation of the three natures, 391-2, 617-20
mode of abiding in the middle way, 40, 436-9, 162, 169, 451-2, 634-5
object of negation, 35-40, 66, 127-9, 189, 200-1, 297-304, 549-60, 584, 625-38
path structure, 93-109, 111-15, 195, 297-304, 378-80
presentation of conventional phenomena, 539-47, 549ff, 574-5, *see also* Valid establishment of phenomena
refutation of a mind-basis-of-all, 387-8
refutation of Sāṃkhya, 137-40, 441-5, 455-8ff, 469-71, 474, 476, 479-94, 499-526, 641-3
sutra sources, 569-73, 588-90
synonyms of, 432, 435-6, 586-7, n.504 pp.857-8
use of consequences, 134-5, 360, 431-2, 443-5, 449-51, 452, 489, 494-7, 529, 585-6, 733
Prasannapadā, see Clear Words
Pratītyasamutpāda, see Dependent-arising
Pratītyasamutpādādivibhaṅga-nirdesha, see Commentary on the 'Sutra on Dependent-Arising'
Pratyakṣha, Chandrakīrti's explanation of the term, 656
Pratyekabuddha, etymology, n.495 p.845, *see also* Solitary Realizers

Precious Garland of Advice for the King, 15, 30, 100-3, 357, 388, 569, 590, 614, 626, 631, 673, 675, 688, 693
Precious Treasury of the Supreme Vehicle, 15
Preparations for concentrations, 87
Presentation of conventionalities in Prāsaṅgika, 539-47, 549ff, 574-5
Presentation of Tenets, 17, 563
Presentation of Tenets, Roar of the Five-Faced [Lion] Eradicating Error, Precious Lamp Illuminating the Good Path to Omniscience, see Root text, Jam-ȳang-shay-b̄a's
Presentation of the Lack of Being One or Many, 545-7
Pride, 256, 257
Principal, of Sāṃkhya, 321-6, 504, 613
Production, non-refutation of nominal production, 145, 159-60, 162, 183-4, 433
Production, refutation of, 131, 133-4, 150, 161-2, 183-5, *see also* Refutation of the four extreme types of production *and* Refutation of the four alternatives of production
Production that is asserted, 142, 144-5, 148, 185, 501-2, 641
Proof statement, five membered, 483, 489, Appendix 5 pp.729-33
Proof statement, two-membered, Appendix 5 pp.730-3
Prophecy about Buddhism in Tibet, 33
Proponents of True Existence, n.786 p.897
Pudgalavādins, 385
Pure lands, 375-6, 395
Purpose of the Prāsaṅgika refutations, 526-30, 539
Pūrvashailas, 714, 715, 716, 717, 718

Qualifying the object of negation, 424
Questions of Brahmā Sutra, 31
Questions of King Dhāraṇīshvara Sutra, 359, 571, 590, 607
Questions of Sāgaramati Sutra, 161, 590
Questions of the King of Nāgas, Anavatapta, Sutra, 161, 162, 589
Questions of the King of Nāgas, Sāgara, Sutra, 571, 589, 660
Quintessential Instructions on the Middle Way, 593

Ra (*Rva, Rva rDo-rje-grags*), 536
Rāhulabhadra, 592
Rājagirikas, 715
Rājaputra Yashomitra, 662, 674
Ratnākara, see Jewel Mine Sutra
Ratnakūṭa, see Heap of Jewels Sutra
Ratnamegha, see Cloud of Jewels Sutra
Ratnāvalī, see Precious Garland
Real and unreal conventionalities, 421, 635-6

Realization of subtle selflessness, need for, 30-1
Reasoned analysis, object found by, 406, 410, 411
Reasoning, 10, 31-2, 115, 129, 551-3, *see also* Analysis
Reasoning establishing the lack of being one or many, 61, 64-5, 638
Reasoning of dependent-arising, 52-5, 61, 129, 161-73, 637, 639, 659-62ff, 675
Reasonings refuting a self of persons, 677-97, *see also* Fivefold reasonings *and* Sevenfold reasonings
Reasonings refuting a self of phenomena, 693, 694, *see also* Diamond slivers, Refutation of production of the four extreme types of production, Refutation of production of the four alternative types, *and* Reasoning of dependent-arising
Reasonings refuting inherent existence, 636-7, 639, 693, *see also* specific reasonings as cross-listed above
Referent object, 701
Refuge, 335-6
Refutation of a self of persons in Prāsaṅgika, 677-97, *see also* Fivefold reasoning *and* Sevenfold reasoning
Refutation of a self of phenomena in Prāsaṅgika, 693, 694, *see also* Diamond slivers, Refutation of the four extreme types of production,
Refutation of a self of phenomena (*cont.*)
Refutation of production of the four alternative types, *and* Reasoning of dependent-arising
Refutation of causeless production, 149-50, 649-50
Refutation of inherently existent mine, 193-4
Refutation of Objections, 471, 472, 473, 475, 497, 510, 550, 551, 571, 585, 591
Refutation of production from both self and other, 148-9, 649
Refutation of production from other, 135-6, 140-8, 154, 433, 460, 643-8, 653
Refutation of production from self, 136-40, 144-8, 441-3, 455-64, 470-1, 474-94, 499-505ff, 640-3
Refutation of production from self, other, etc., *see* Diamond slivers
Refutation of the four alternative types of production, 61, 63-4, 129, 151, 155-60, 639, 653-8
Refutation of the four extreme types of production, 61-3, 129, 151-4, 433, 458-61ff, 467-8, 490, 500, 639, 651-3, *see also* Diamond slivers
Refutation of the Sāṃkhya assertion of production from self, 137-40, 441-3, 455-8ff, 469-71, 474, 476, 479-94, 499-526, 641-3

Reliances, four, 425, 597
Ren-da-wa (*Red-mda'-ba*), 536
Resentment, 262, 263
Retentions, 208
Rice Seedling Sutra, 143, 279, 501, 502, 570, 646, 648
Rik-b̄ay-ku-juk (*Rigs-pa'i-khu-byug*), 432, 587
Rin-chen-sang-b̄o (*Rin-chen-bzang-po*), 531-2, 534
Robinson, Richard, 13, 25
Root afflictions, 238, 255-61, Chart 26 p.256, 287
Root of cyclic existence, 368, 417
Root text, Jam-ȳang-shay-b̄a's, citation of, 565, 584, 586, 587, 588-9, 595-6, 625-6, 632, 637, 640, 640-1, 643-4, 647-8, 649, 651, 654, 655, 659, 676, 677, 697
Rope-snake example, 37, 437-8, 619-20, 626, 627
Ruinations, five, 33, 608, n.563 p.874

S̄a-ḡya (*Sa-skya*), 15, 147, 343, 534, 535, 536, 538, 573
S̄a-ḡya Paṇḍiṭa Jam-ȳang-ḡün-ga-gyel-tsen, 536
Sacred Word of Mañjushrī, 43, 571, 685, 686
Saddharmapuṇḍarīka, see White Lotus of the Excellent Doctrine Sutra
Sāgaramatiparipṛchchhāsūtra, see Questions of Sāgaramati Sutra
Sāgaranāgarājaparipṛchchhā, see Questions of the King of Nāgas, Sāgara, Sutra
S̄am-yay (*bSam-yas*), 532, 533
Samādhirāja, see King of Meditative Stabilizations Sutra
Samayabhedoparachanachakre Nikāyabhedopadeshanasaṃgraha, 717
Saṃdhinirmochana, see Sutra Unravelling the Thought
Samenesses of phenomena, ten, 131-2
Saṃghabhadra, 343
Sāṃkhya, 35, 239, 294, 295, 318, 320-27, 339, 411, 415, 436, 471, 564, 613, 649
  refutation of their assertion of production from self, 137-40, 441-3, 455-8ff, 469-71, 474, 476, 479-94, 499-526, 641-3
Saṃkrāntivādins, 340, 714, 716, 719
Saṃmitīyas, 340, 341, 694, 714, 715, 716, 717, 719
Saṃvṛtisatya, see Truths, conventional
Saṇṇagarikas, 340, 715, 716, 717, 719
Saraha, 356, 358, 361, 592
Sarvabuddhaviṣhayāvatāra-jñānālaṃkāra, see Ornament of the Wisdom Engaging the Sphere of All Buddhas Sutra
Sarvāstivāda, 339, 340, 532
Sarvāstivādins, 339, 340, 714, 715, 716, 717, 718, 719
Satyadvayāvatāra, see Introduction to the Two Truths
Satyadvayavibhaṅga, see Discrimination of the Two Truths
Satyakaparivarta, see Chapter of the True One Sutra
Sautrāntika, 98, 135, 139, 167,

Sautrāntika (*cont.*)
172, 181, 234, 336, 343-51, 367, 369, 370, 392, 393, 434, 436, 551, 565, 639, 641, 676, 709, 716, 719, n.501 pp.854-5
definition, 351
etymology, 343, n.501 p.854
object of negation, 296-303, 345
Sautrāntika Following Reasoning, 39, 296, 344, 346-51, 366, 385, 551, n.501 pp.854-5
Sautrāntika Following Scripture, 344-6, 350, 351, 385, n.501 pp.854-5
Sautrāntika-Svātantrika-Mādhyamika, 296ff, 361, 362,367, 378, 385, 450
refutation of mind-only, 361, 363, 378
Scale example with regard to production, 143, 646-7
Scattering, 75, 83, 265
Sciences, four, 211
S̄e-ra Jay College, 566
Seals, four, 319, 336-7, 345-6
Secondary afflictions, 238, 261-6, Chart 28 p.262, 287
Self, 175, 186-9, 268, 307-15, 636-7, *see also* Selflessness
hypothetical synonyms in Prāsaṅgika, 36-7, 38, Chart 1 p.39, 584, 626, 632
in the four schools, Chart 37 p.299, 385-6, 693-4, 695, n.791 pp.897-903
permanent, single, and independent, 299-302, 341, 385
Self (*cont.*)
substantially existent, 303-4 307-15, 341-2, 385, *see also* self-sufficient person
synonyms, 175, 315
that is negated in Prāsaṅgika, 175, 189, 297-304, 307-15, 385-6, 636-7
Self-approved inference, 478, 481-2
Self-approved reason, 478
Self-consciousness, 350-1, 373-4, 377
Self-emptiness, 35-6
Self-sufficient person, 296-304, 341-2, 384-5
Selfless, 213-14, Chart 7 p.213
Selflessness
in the four schools, 296-302, Chart 39 p.301
of phenomena, 61-5, 127-9, 176, 177-8, 194, 196, Chart 39 p.301, 345, 636-7, 693, 694
of phenomena in Chittamātra, 128-9, 297-301, 367-74, 388-90
of the body, 54-5, 57-9, 176
of the person, 44-66, 127-9, 175-92, 196, 293, 296-304, 307-15, 341-2, 636-7
that is a lack of being a self-sufficient person, 293, 296-304, 341-2
Selflessnesses, two, 636-7, *see also* Selflessness of persons *and* Selflessness of phenomena
Selves, two, 636-7, *see also* Self
Sense consciousnesses, mistakenness in Prāsaṅgika, 449-50, 452, 509-11, 514-6, 529, 552

Sense consciousnesses, non-mistakenness in Svātantrika, 449-50, 452, 508-9, 514-6
Sense perception in Prāsaṅgika, 417, 449-50, 452
Sense powers (*indriya*), 202, 221-3, 232, 273-4, 279-80
S̄er-gi-go-cha, *see* Kanakavarman
S̄er-līng-b̄a, *see* Suvarṇadvīpa
Seven Treatises of Higher Knowledge, 344
Seven Treatises on Valid Cognition, 344, 366
Seven-cornered set of reasonings, 129, *see also* Sevenfold reasoning
Sevenfold reasoning, 44, 48-51, 54, 55, 61, 66, 169, 170, 176-92, 637-8, 677, 687-97, *see also* Fivefold reasoning
Seventy Stanzas on Emptiness, 570, 591, 652
Shaivas, 318, 565
Shākya clan, etymology, 355
Shākyamitra, 363, 432, 587
Shākyamuni Buddha, 342, 355, 358, 392-3, 403
Shākyaprabha, 718
Shālistamba, see Rice Seedling Sutra
Shamatha, see Calm abiding
Shame, 248, 250
S̄hang-b̄a Ḡa-gyu (*Shang-pa bKa'-rgyud*), 538
Shāntarakṣhita, 362-3, 532-3, 575
Shāntideva, 31, 358, 422, 432, 570, 587, 593, 633, 657
Shapes, 223, 225-6, Chart 14 p.226, 232, 233
Shar-dzay College, 566
Shāriputra, 605
Shātavāhana, 357
Shi-jay (*Zhi-byed*), 536, 537, 538
Shikṣhāsamuchchayakārikā, see Compendium of Learnings
Shrāvaka, discussion of etymology and reasons for translation, n.495 pp.840-45, *see also* Hearers
Shrīmālādevīsiṃhanāda, see Lion's Roar of Shrīmālādevī Sutra
Shūnyatāsaptati, see Seventy Stanzas on Emptiness
Shūnyatāsaptativṛtti, see Commentary on (Nāgārjuna's) 'Seventy Stanzas on Emptiness'
Shūra, 432, 586, 587-8, 591, n.504 p.857, *see also* Ashvaghoṣha
Siddhārthikas, 715
Similarities, five, 236
Similarly appearing subject, *see* Commonly appearing subject
Sixty Stanzas of Reasoning, 165, 199, 388, 472, 570, 591, 614, 670-71, 672, 674, 675
Skhalitapramathanayuktihetusiddhi, see Establishment of the Reasoning and Logic Refuting Error
Sleep, 266, 267
Snake-rope example, *see* Rope-snake example
Solitary Realizers, 98, 99, 106-8, 128, 195, 212, 288, 296ff, 342, 378-9, 392-3, 427, 605, 609, n.495 p.845

Son sutras, 589, n.514 p.862
Sōng-dzen-gam-bo (*Srong-bstan-sgam-po*), 531
Song on the Practice of the View, 545
Sopa, Geshe Lhundup, 12
Sounds, 226, Chart 15 p.227, 232, 273, 274
Sources, (*āyatana*), twelve, 222, 223, 273, 274, Chart 34 p.274, 278-9ff
Space, 217, 233-4, 285, 337, 344, 390
Space-like meditative equipoise, 66, 95
Special insight, 67, 70, 88, 89, 91-109, 112-14, 247, 404, 534, 557-8
  definition, 92
Spite, 262, 263
Sport of Mañjushrī Sutra, 589
Spread of Buddhism to Tibet, 531-8
Sprung, Mervyn, n.496 pp.845-8
Stabilization, 247
Stabilizing meditation, 89-90, 91ff, 113-15, 557-8
Stage of completion, 113-15, 200
Stage of generation, 113-14, 380, 409
Stages of Meditation (Bhāvanākrama), 533
States arisen from hearing, thinking, and meditating, 93
Stcherbatsky, Theodore, n.374 p.818, n.421a p.824, n.423 p.825, n.496 p.845-8
Sthavira-chaitikas, 340
Sthaviras, 340, 713, 714, 715, 716, 717, 718, 719
Sthaviravādins, 719
Sthiramati, 360, 462, 665
Stream Enterer, 98, 106-7, 212
Stutyatītastava, see Praise of What Surpasses Praise
Sublime Continuum of the Great Vehicle, 357, 359, 572, 593, 610
Substantial establishment, 338
Substantial existence, 338, 344
Substantially existent, 36, 37, 303, 620-2, 632
Suchness, 217, 218-19
Sudden enlightenment, 537
Suffering, three types, 286-7
Sugar-Cane-One, etymology, 355
Sugata essence, 617, *see also* Buddha nature *and* Tathāgata essence
Suhṛllekha, see Friendly Letter
Suhṛllekhaṭīkā, see Commentary on (Nāgārjuna's) 'Friendly Letter'
Superiors, 98, 289-90, 378-80, n.494 p.840
Supplement to (Nāgārjuna's) 'Treatise on the Middle Way', 13, 131, 320, 399, 400, 403-5, 528, 538, 569, 572, 610, 637, 653
  citation of, 30, 153, 169, 170, 184, 554, 556, 558, 602, 610, 612, 614, 616, 617, 636, 640, 641, 644, 645-7, 648, 649, 650, 652, 678, 679, 681, 682, 683, 689-90, 692, 694
  meaning and translation of title, n.545 pp.868-71

Sutra, 22
meaning of the term, 423
Sutra citations, unidentified, 596-7, 657, 670, 678, 687, 696
Sutra example of illusoriness, 597
Sutra examples supporting mind-only, 372-3, 376
Sutra on the Heavily Adorned, 571, 590, 595, 616-7
Sutra on the Myrabolan Fruit, 603, 607
Sutra on the Ten Grounds, 131, 378, 570, 589, 612, 613, 623, 682
Sutra Showing the Inconceivable Secrets of the Tathāgatas, 589
Sutra Showing the Realm of the Inconceivable Qualities and Wisdom of the Tathāgatas, 589
Sutra Unravelling the Thought, 359, 415, 416, 424, 426-7, 570, 590, 595, 599, 600, 601-2, 603, 604, 607, 610, 612, 613, 618, 619
Sūtrasamuchchaya, see Compendium of Sutra
Sūtravādins, 715
Suvarṇadvīpa (*gSer-gling-pa*), 535
Suvarṣhakas, 714, 716
Svabhāva, different meanings of the term, 391-2, 438, *see also Bhāva*
Svātantrika-Mādhyamika, 135, 155, 167, 181, 361-4, 404 431-2, 434, 436, 441, 445-6, 450-3, 455, 636, 646, 693,
Svātantrika-Mādhyamika (*cont.*) 695-6, n497 pp.848-50, n.501 pp.854-5, n.510 pp.859-60
definition of, 452
differentiation of the interpretable and the definitive, 424
non-mistakenness of sense consciousnesses, 449-50, 452, 508-9, 514-6
object of negation, 39, 128-9, 296-303, 361-3, 436-7, 450, 574, 631, 635, 636, 847-8
use of syllogisms, 135, 361, 431, 450-2, n.497 pp.848-50
Syllogisms (*prayoga*), 134-5, 360, 361, 431-2, 444-5, 449-51, 489, 491, 494, 497, 529, 731
implied, 444-5

Tāmrashātīyas, 340, 715, 717, 718
Tang-s̄ak-b̄a (*Thang-sags-pa*), 411
Tangible objects, 229-31, Chart 18 p.229, 232, 273, 274,
Tantra, 9, 11, 22, 71, 109, 111-15, 117, 188, 200, 247, 319, 409, 451, 532
Tāranātha, 713, 717
Tarkajvālā, see Blaze of Reasoning
Tastes, 228-9, Chart 17 p.228, 232, 273, 274
Tathāgata essence, 357, 381, 610, 611, 612, 615-7, 623, *see also* Buddha nature
Tathāgata Essence Sutra, 357, 359, 381, 590, 610, 611, 616

Tathāgata L̄u-rik-gyel-b̄o, 356
Tathāgatāchintyaguhyanirdesha, see Sutra Showing the Inconceivable Secrets of the Tathāgatas
Tathāgatagarbhasūtra, see Tathāgata Essence Sutra
Tathāgataguṇajñānāchintya-viṣhayāvatāranirdesha, see Sutra Showing the Realm of the Inconceivable Qualities and Wisdom of the Tathāgatas
Tattvasaṃgraha, see Compendium on Reality
Teaching of Akṣhayamati Sutra, 425, 570, 589, 598-9, 618
Theravāda, 315
Things, 219-20ff, Chart 10 p.220, 271ff
Thoroughly established natures, 388-92, 410, 596, 601, 610, 611, 618-20
Thoroughly Non-Abiding Mādhyamikas, 435-6, 534, n.504 pp.857-8
Those Who Hold That Illusion is Established by a Reasoning Consciousness, n.504 pp.857-8, n.510 pp.859-60
Thought, *see* Conceptual consciousnesses
Three modes of a correct sign, 449, 450, 452, 697, 730-3
Three natures, *see* Natures, three
Thu-mi-sam-bho-ta, 531
Tīrthika, see Forders
Transliteration system, 19-22
Treasury of Knowledge, 236, 344, n.442 p.834
Treasury of Tenets, 15
Treatise Called 'The Finely Woven', see Finely Woven
Treatise of Four Hundred Stanzas, see Four Hundred
Treatise on the Middle Way, 32, 128, 131, 178, 356, 399-405, 455, 459, 460, 467, 472, 489, 494-6, 500, 501, 538, 558-9, 569, 572, 574, 591, 596, 597, 637, 686, n.298 p.811
  citation of, 153, 154, 162, 168, 178, 400-404, 438, 460, 472, 494, 495, 496, 502-3, 518, 522, 597-8, 619, 635, 644, 645, 660, 684, 688, 689
  eight Indian commentaries on, 360, 462
  explanation of the title, 399-400
Treatise on the Sublime Continuum of the Great Vehicle, see Sublime Continuum of the Great Vehicle
Tri-s̄ong-day-d̄zen (*khri-srong-lde-btsan*), 532, 533
Trisambaranirdeshaparivarta, see Chapter Showing the Three Vows Sutra
Trisvabhāva, see Natures, three
True cessations, 97, 218, 255, 288-9, 294-5, 382, 412
True establishment, 36, 39
True existence, 36, 39
True origins, 97, 287-8, 293-4, 412
True paths, 97, 286, 289, 290, 295-6, 382, 412

True sufferings, 97, 285-7, 288, 292-3, 412
Truth Body, 117-19, 382
Truths, conventional, 338, 349, 400-3, 405-21, 422
  etymology, 416-8
Truths-for-a-concealer, 405-21, *see also* Truths, conventional
  etymology, 416-8, 421
Truths, four noble, 96-8, 206, 285-304, 412
  etymology, 289-90
  meditation on, 292-6
  order, 290-1
  sixteen attributes of, 292-6
Truths, two, 172, 285, 290, 338, 346, 349, 400-3
  as taught by Nāgārjuna, 400-3, 415, 596
  basis of the division, 405-12, 418-9, 420
  in Chittamātra, 390
  in Mādhyamika, 400-3, 405-21
  in Sautrāntika, 346-50
  sameness of entity, 413-15
Truths, ultimate, 338, 346, 400-3, 405-21, 422-4
  etymology, 416
  reason for translating thus, 419-20
Tu-gen, 385
Turnings of the wheel of doctrine, three, 426-7, 595
Twenty false views of a real self, 176-8, 687
Twenty-five Thousand Stanza Perfection of Wisdom Sutra, 603, 618, 620-1
Two compendiums, 359
Two disseminations of Buddhism in Tibet, 531-2, 534
Two truths, *see* Truths, two

Ultimate analysis, 144-5, 148, 185
  ability to bear, 406, 410, 435
Ultimate existence, 36, 39, 156
Ultimate truths, *see* Truths, ultimate
Understanding All Tenets, 15, 563
Unfindability of objects, 144, 136, 170, 173, 192, 195, 380, 437-8, 631, n.727 p.887
Uninterrupted path, 96-8, 104ff, 117ff, 288
Unmoving actions, 277, 288
Unravelling the Thought, see Sutra Unravelling the Thought
Unreal and real conventionalities, 421
Unshared attributes of Buddhas, eighteen, 211
Unwanted consequences, 441, 493
Uttaratantra, see Sublime Continuum of the Great Vehicle
Uttarīyas, 714

Vaibhāṣhika, 39, 98, 135, 139, 167, 172, 181, 219, 234, 269, 290, 296ff, 303, 315, 329, 336, 337-43, 344, 350, 367, 392, 434, 436, 565, 676, n.501 pp.854-5
  definition, 351

Vaibhāṣhika (*cont.*)
eighteen subschools, 339-41, 343, Appendix 3 pp.713-19
etymology of the name, 337, n.501 p.854
Kashmiri, 337-8, 385
object of negation, 296-303, 315, 341-3
simultaneity of cause and effect, 139, 339
Vaidakas, 294
Vaidalyasūtranāma, *see Finely Woven*
vaidurya, sutra description of, 607
Vairochana, 533
Vaisheṣhika, 141, 294, 318, 337, 339, 447, 506, 507, 565, 613, n.423 pp.824-5
Vaiṣhṇavas, 318, 564
Vajra, 22
Valid cognizer, 511, 518, 701-5
Valid establishment of phenomena, 136, 148, 172-3, 194-5, 409-10, 418-9, 420, 518, 539-47, 574-5, 676, 697, n.727 p.887, *see also* Certification of objects by valid cognition
Vasubandhu, 236, 344, 359, 362, 525, 592, 662, 674, n.442 p.834
Vasumitra, 343, 716, 718
Vātsīputrīya, 339, 340, 714, 715, 716, 717, 718, 719
Vedānta, 46, 186-7
Vedāntins, 318, 564
Vedas, 320, 321
Vibhajyavādins, 340, 714, 715 717, 718
View holding to an extreme, 259, 260, 289
View of the transitory collection, 103, 257, 258-9, 260, 280, 289, 308, 315, 677-9, 686-7, 693, n.739 p.889
Views of annihilation, 318, 319, 320
Views of permanence, 318-9, 320
Vigrahavyavārtanī, see Refutation of Objections
Vimalamitra, 532
Vimuktisena, 362
Vinītadeva, 717, 718
Virtues, 254-5, *see also* Virtuous mental factors
Virtuous mental factors, 238, 248-55, Chart 25 p.248
Visheṣhastavaṭīkā, see Commentary on (Udbhaṭasiddhasvāmin's) 'Exalted Praise'
Visible forms, 223-6, Chart 12 p.223, 232, 273, 274
Vyākaraṇas, 318, 564, *see also* Grammarians

Wangyal, Geshe, 12
Wayman, Alex, n.423 pp.824-5, n.430a p.830, n.431 p.831
Wheel of doctrine, three turnings of, 426-7, 595, 599, 601
White Lotus of the Excellent Doctrine Sutra, 571, 604-5, n.494 pp.841-44
Wisdom Body, 118, 119, 120, 382
Wisdom of sameness, 385

World, destruction of, 630
Worldly assertion of causation, 501-2, 503
Wrong consciousness, 702-4
Wrong livelihood, 263-4, 289
Wylie, Turrell, 19

Yar-lung-drang-druk (*Yar-klung-grang-'brug*), 532
Yashomitra, 662, 674
Ye-shay-day (*Ye-shes-sde*), 533-4
Ye-shay-gyel-tsen (*Ye-shes-rgyal-mtshan*), 115
Yoga Tantra, 112
Yogāchāra-Svātantrika-Mādhyamika, 234, 297ff, 362-4, 367, 378, 385, 388
Yogāchārins, 365-6, *see also* Chittamātra
Yogi, 22
Yu-mo-ba (*Yu-mo-pa*), 535
Yuktiṣhaṣhṭrikā, see Sixty Stanzas of Reasoning
Yuktiṣhaṣhṭikāvṛtti, see Commentary on (Nāgārjuna's) 'Sixty Stanzas of Reasoning'

Dedication

May whatever merit there is in writing this book bring freedom and happiness to all sentient beings.